Professional School Counseling:
A Handbook of Theories, Programs, & Practices

SECOND EDITION

Edited by Bradley T. Erford

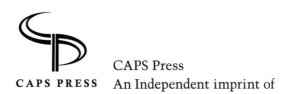

CAPS Press
An Independent imprint of

pro·ed
An International Publisher

8700 Shoal Creek Boulevard
Austin, Texas 78757-6897
800/897-3202   Fax 800/397-7633
www.proedinc.com

© 2010, 2004 by PRO-ED, Inc.
8700 Shoal Creek Boulevard
Austin, Texas 78757-6897
800/897-3202   Fax 800/397-7633
www.proedinc.com

Library of Congress Cataloging-in-Publication Data

Professional school counseling: a handbook of theories, programs &
practices / edited by Bradley T. Erford.—2nd ed.
      p.   cm.
   ISBN 978-1-4164-0435-4
   1. Educational counseling—United States—Handbooks, manuals, etc.
I.   Erford, Bradley T.
LB1027.5.P6593 2009
371.4—dc22

                                                      2008051958

This book was developed and produced by CAPS Press, formerly
associated with ERIC/CASS, and creator of many titles for the
counseling, assessment, and educational fields. In 2004,
CAPS Press became an independent imprint of PRO-ED, Inc.

Art Director: Vicki DePountis
Designer: Vicki DePountis
This book is designed in Trump Mediaeval and Scala Sans.

Printed in the United States of America

1 2 3 4 5 6 7 8 9 10   18 17 16 15 14 13 12 11 10 09

CONTENTS

SECTION 5: ASSESSMENT IN SCHOOL COUNSELING

SECTION 7: SPECIAL ISSUES AND POPULATIONS IN SCHOOL COUNSELING

FOREWORD

Almost daily, professional school counselors and counselor educators encounter situations that call for authoritative information on a variety of topics. Typically, they must seek information from multiple sources, often of variable quality and applicability. The task is often time-consuming, and the results can be less than what is needed or expected. This handbook was developed to address this problem by providing a single source that will meet most of the professional school counselor's information needs.

A review of the table of contents will reveal the exceptional breadth and comprehensiveness of this publication. In fact, it is so broad, and the articles are so authoritatively written, that it would suffice as an excellent source and resource for all of the many topics covered in an accredited school counselor education program. For the practicing counselor, it will provide a highly useful resource for the myriad questions a counselor must respond to in a typical day.

Whatever your position, be it counselor, counselor educator, administrator, or interested citizen, this handbook provides an excellent means to update your knowledge about the school counseling profession.

Dr. Bradley Erford is a highly respected leader in counseling, and, as such, he was able to assemble a body of writers of exceptional counseling expertise and writing skill. It is a book that provides a quick (but authoritative) study, and it does so in an interesting and nonpedantic fashion. Unlike some large and impressive-appearing tomes, which are used only once, this book will "hook" the reader, and he or she will want to refer to it again and again. We predict that almost everyone involved or interested in professional school counseling will want to have his or her own copy of this handbook. Why not begin now and reap the benefits of having the all-encompassing resource you've always needed and wanted?

Garry R. Walz and Jeanne C. Bleuer

The first edition of the Handbook was published in 2004. Who would have thought so much about school counseling would have changed in just 4 or 5 years? A dynamic wave of change has swept over school counseling programs all across the country. Since 2003, the American School Counseling Association (ASCA) published the *National Model for School Counseling Programs* (ASCA; 2003, 2005), which led to several important changes in how school counselors implement their school counseling programs. The model emphasizes four themes (i.e., leadership, advocacy, collaboration, and systemic change) that are infused throughout four elements, which help structure program formation and implementation: foundation, delivery system, management system, and accountability.

This second edition of the Handbook integrates and expands upon the changes brought about by the ASCA national model. Revisions to each chapter reflect the influence of the model as appropriate. Several new chapters have been added to give further substance and clarification to implementation of the model, including chapters in the new section on Leadership and the Professional School Counselor in the "ASCA National Model," "Professional Advocacy," "Advocacy in Action: The Voice of the Student," and "The Professional School Counselor and Leadership." An additional welcome addition to this book is the chapter "Sage Perspectives on School Counseling," which features the perspectives of four long-time observers and shapers of the school counseling profession: Stan Baker, Norm Gysbers, Pat Henderson, and Ed Herr. They provide historical perspectives and highpoints from the past 50 years and glimpses into future challenges.

Several other educational initiatives and societal dilemma have either stemmed from or occurred simultaneously with the model. First, school reform has created a data-driven focus to programmatic changes; that is, data is used to define and demonstrate problems *before* strategies and innovations are implemented to address the problems. In the past, perceptions-based or subjective sources of information were used. Thus a new chapter, "Data-Driven School Counseling Approaches," was added. Second, more attention is being given to the training of school counselors, particularly during school-based practica and internships. To help school-based practitioners orient to the different, albeit exciting, role of intern supervisor, the chapter titled "Supervising School Counselor Interns" was added. Third, several clinical problems have received increased prominence in the schools over the past few years. The chapter on Habit Disorders was revised to include self-mutilation, as cutting among adolescents has become far too common in our schools. Also, the redefining of the autism spectrum to include children with high-functioning conditions has led to professional school counselors providing more frequent social interventions and academic advocacy to students within this clinical subpopulation. Finally, a number of chapters focusing on a school counselor's work with special populations of students and special topics in schools were added, including "Counseling Children of Poverty," "Counseling Multiracial Students," "Emotional Safety in the Classroom," and "The Special Needs of Boys."

The section structure of the second edition of the Handbook also underwent a bit of modification as the order of several sections was changed to establish their prominence earlier in the book. The new order is as follows:

Section 1: The Foundations of School Counseling
Section 2: Leadership and the Professional School Counselor
Section 3: Comprehensive School Counseling Programs
Section 4: Techniques and Approaches to Counseling in Schools
Section 5: Assessment in School Counseling
Section 6: Clinical Issues in School Counseling
Section 7: Special Issues and Populations in School Counseling

In adition, the chapter references are now available on an accompanying CD-ROM. The list of sources used in this edition can be searched by author, title, or keyword.

As society and schools continue to change, a dynamic relationship with school counseling will continue to evolve. To school counseling professionals who use this book to retool and update skills, I hope the excitement of these transitions help you to provide even better services to your students and school community. To students who are entering the field for the first time, I hope this book provides you with a strong foundation of the current state of school counseling but also gives you some perspective as to how the profession evolved to its current state and some insights into where you will take the field in the future. You could not have chosen a more challenging and gratifying career...Enjoy!

Bradley T. Erford
Professor, School Counseling Program
School of Education, Loyola University
July 2008

ACKNOWLEDGMENTS

Projects such as this are the work of many individuals. I am especially thankful for the efforts of two outstanding graduate assistants who contributed substantially to the organization and flow of this effort: Megan P. Earl and Lacey L. Wallace, two of the most dedicated and capable professional school counselors I have had the privilege to instruct.

This effort is dedicated to The One—the Giver of energy, passion, and understanding—who makes life worth living and endeavors worth pursuing and accomplishing; the Teacher of love and forgiveness.

THE FOUNDATIONS OF SCHOOL COUNSELING

PROFESSIONAL SCHOOL COUNSELING: INTEGRATING THEORY AND PRACTICE INTO A DATA-DRIVEN, OUTCOMES-BASED APPROACH

Bradley T. Erford and Kristi McCaskill

Preview

The introduction of the ASCA national model (ASCA; 2005) by the American School Counselor Association (ASCA) and data-driven school counseling practices have dramatically changed how professional school counselors have operated in contemporary practice over the past 10 years. The focus of this transformed role is to build on the broad-based theoretical and practical counseling skills that have become the core of a professional school counselor's training and to expand into a more data-driven, systemic orientation to meet the needs of all students. The systemic, data-driven approach highlights comprehensive services, social advocacy, and accountability dimensions to remove barriers to student performance and promote a system of equity and access for all students.

Society in general and school systems in particular continue to change. As a result, the school counseling profession necessarily undergoes a continuous evolution, but the changes during the past 10 years are the most dramatic since those that followed the National Defense Education Act of 1959 (Herr & Erford, 2007). This current evolution involves both the traditional roles and functions of professional school counselors as well as the comprehensive school counseling programs that professional school counselors strive to implement—a program that serves the academic, career, and personal–social needs of every student. The task of meeting the developmental needs of all students is ominous:

- Substance Abuse and Mental Health Services Administration (SAMHSA; 2006) indicated that 5.5 million youths ages 12 to 17 years (21.8%) received counseling or some other form of treatment for emotional or behavior problems in the previous year. Adolescent females were more likely than adolescent males (23.6% vs. 20%) to seek mental health treatment.
- Up to 50% of students with significant emotional impairments drop out of school (U.S. Department of Education, 2001).
- Nine percent of adolescents (2.2 million) had at least one major depressive episode during the previous year, but only 40.3% sought treatment (SAMHSA; 2005).
- For 15- to 24-year-olds and children ages 10 to 14 years, suicide is the third leading cause of death, claiming nearly 30,000 deaths annually (S. Rep. No. 107-216, 2003).
- Between 3% and 5% of children have attention-deficit/hyperactivity disorder (ADHD), or approximately 2 million children in the United States (National Institute of Mental Health, 2006).

- Approximately 6.5 million children received special education services in 2002, up from 4.7 million in 1992 (U.S. Department of Education, 2002).

Society and governments turn to schools for help in meeting the needs of students. Unfortunately, the ratio of professional school counselor to student is only 1:488 (ASCA; 2005) and has remained near that level throughout much of the past 2 decades—substantially higher than the 1:250 recommended by ASCA—with no real hope of dramatic improvement in the near future.

Given that the problems continue to mount and service availability remains stagnant, what is the solution? While the answer is in no way simple, the transformed role of the contemporary professional school counselor requires that counselors became agents of social change, school reform, and accountability as well as experts in the traditional theory and practice of individual and small-group counseling (Erford, House, & Martin, 2007). This shift from an individual, student-centered focus to a systemic intervention focus stems from the realization that, while essential in some cases, "fixing" students one at a time is akin to sticking one's finger in a dike:

> A look to the left and right will often show other professionals using their fingers to plug a hole. By joining with other professional counselors . . . and speaking with a united voice in advocating for the needs of students, they are seeking solutions not only for the students they are working to help, but for all students—those that colleagues are seeking to serve, and those that will seek help in the future. (Erford et al., 2007, p. 14)

THE ASCA NATIONAL STANDARDS AND ASCA NATIONAL MODEL

Over the years, many have deliberated, evaluated, and argued over the role and professional identity of professional school counselors. Some assert that school counselors are teachers who educate students on how to behave and make better life decisions. Others maintain that school counselors should focus their attention solely on those students who are at risk and underserved by traditional classroom interventions. Neither of these views accurately reflects the precise knowledge and skills of professional school counselors, and these views confuse important decision makers, including administrators and politicians. Sadly, even some practicing school counselors fail to challenge these misconceptions. Schmidt (2003) succinctly connected the importance of professional identity and the future of school counseling:

> The future of school counseling as a profession depends on the ability of counselors to become an integral part of the school setting while maintaining their unique role and contribution to student welfare and development. To accomplish this goal, effective counselors identify their role, select appropriate functions; plan programs of services for students, parents, and teachers; strengthen their professional development; and evaluate their effectiveness in schools. (Schmidt, 2003, p. 25)

The ASCA national model (2005) provides a structure for the development of a comprehensive counseling program that permits professional school counselors to draw on their specialized skills to meet the needs of all students. The purpose is to promote academic success and to encourage the implementation of proactive strategies designed to meet the needs of students through the various stages of development. Furthermore, this model incorporates student competencies and measurable performance indicators. Perhaps the most notable distinction is the *encouragement* to transform the role of professional school counselors into effective leaders and advocates of change. Knowledgeable about the challenges and systematic hurdles, professional school counselors may be in the best position to effect changes and limit factors restricting student success (ASCA; 2005).

TRANSFORMING THE PROFESSIONAL SCHOOL COUNSELOR'S ROLE: FIVE GUIDING REALIZATIONS

Herr and Erford (2007) discussed five realizations that can spawn changes in the ways professional school counselors approach program implementation and service delivery:

1. *Professional school counselors receive extensive training in consultation, collaboration, and team or relationship building.* Professional school counselors can use these skills to reach beyond the counseling office, think systemically, and build partnerships with other educators, mental health resources, community organizations, parents, and others to provide needed services to *all* students, but especially those who have been marginalized or oppressed.

2. *Professional school counselors cannot do it all!* The "lone ranger" approach of a single, autonomous professional school counselor "hanging out a shingle" and providing the equivalent of "private practice services" to a select few will perpetuate the "finger in the dike" phenomenon. Thinking systemically and building partnerships with valuable internal and external resources will help far more students in the short and long term.

3. *Comprehensive developmental school counseling programs are efficient and effective.* Face it: If a professional school counselor does not implement a comprehensive developmental school counseling program, none will exist in that school! Professional school counselors who spend most of their time engaged in a single activity (e.g., individual counseling, paperwork, classroom guidance) are not implementing a comprehensive program.

4. *All professional school counselors have strengths and weaknesses; thus, each provides services of varying quality to varying clientele.* The key here is to know one's proficiencies and use these strengths to benefit all students while developing strategies and partnerships with other resource providers to cover the other areas of a comprehensive program.

5. *Many students are not getting what they need from our educational and mental health systems.* Professional school counselors need to become skilled social advocates and develop effective referral procedures through partnerships with community organizations. The training of professional school counselors is broad by design so that one can serve in the "triage role," allowing the professional school counselor to prioritize the allocation of services in the most efficient manner. This often means that

professional school counselors can best serve the greatest number of students by making referral arrangements for the neediest students or those most able to afford services available in the community, thus freeing the professional school counselor to focus on the students for whom the counselor is the last (and perhaps only) hope for effective treatment.

Erford et al. (2007) explained the complex interplay of the services provided by a professional school counselor through the metaphor of various-sized nets:

> A comprehensive developmental school counseling program with its focus on large-group guidance and prevention-based programs is the first and highest net attempting to catch students and keep them on track developmentally. But as fate would have it, some students' needs are more serious and not necessarily developmental in nature, thus requiring intervention services. The next level of netting attempting to catch students in need may be group counseling with students or consultation or collaboration with parents and teachers. While many students are put back on track through effective implementation of these services, some require additional interventions (nets) that are more individualized. Individual counseling, or referral to qualified mental health professionals when lack of time or skill requires it, serves as that next level of nets. However, even after individualized services, some students will still present with unmet needs. These students are the ones who in the past have been described as "falling through the cracks" and require a more systemic service delivery approach. This is where school–community agency partnering and social and academic advocacy come in. These systemic interventions (nets) are essential to ensure that the needs of all children in our society are addressed. (Erford et al., 2007, pp. 10–11)

TEN CURRENT AND EMERGING ROLES AND PRACTICES OF THE PROFESSIONAL SCHOOL COUNSELOR

The realizations described in the previous section give rise to potential changes in how professional school counselors function. Herr and Erford (2007) proposed 10 roles or functions that should be adopted to varying degrees by professional school counselors. Some of these roles and functions are traditional; some are less so, but are of equal importance:

1. Professional
2. Developmental classroom guidance specialist
3. Career-development and educational-planning specialist
4. School and community agency consultation or collaboration specialist
5. Provider of individual and group counseling services
6. Safe schools, violence-prevention, at-risk specialist
7. Agent of diversity and multicultural sensitivity
8. Advocate for students with special needs
9. Advocate for academic and social justice
10. School reform and accountability expert

While there are those who will argue about which of these 10 roles and functions is most important, each is an essential component of a comprehensive program designed to meet the needs of *all* students. Please note, however, that all subsequent components flow from the first one: "Professional school counselors use effective techniques and practices implemented through legal, ethical, and professional means. Belonging to a profession requires one to adhere to the highest standards of that profession . . . [because] how one behaves, good or bad, reflects on all" (Herr & Erford, 2007, p. 14). All professional school counselors should belong to local, state, and national counseling organizations so that the profession can speak as one voice. Advocacy is sometimes accomplished most effectively with one's pocketbook—paying your membership dues could be one of the best advocacy actions of your career and for the future of your profession!

OUTCOMES-ORIENTED, DATA-DRIVEN ACCOUNTABLE SCHOOL COUNSELING PROGRAMS

One cannot overemphasize the importance of accountability and data-driven or outcomes-oriented decision making in the implementation and continuous improvement of any comprehensive developmental school counseling program. A number of comprehensive reviews have been conducted, which have resulted in moderate to strong support for the effectiveness of school counseling services (Borders & Drury, 1992; Sexton, Whiston, Bleuer, & Walz, 1997; Whiston, 2007; Whiston & Sexton, 1998). Other chapters in this book address these studies more directly. Likewise, data-driven approaches to identifying needs and "closing the gap" between high-achieving and low-achieving students describe how students develop as a result of the school counseling program. In particular, ASCA's national model challenges professional school counselors to determine how counseling programs facilitate student development.

The model (ASCA; 2005, p. 59) incorporates three different intervals:

Short-term:	Data collected at the completion of the program that provide information regarding student progress
	Example: Students participating in a counseling group to reduce aggression are able to identify other behavioral responses and coping strategies
Intermediate:	Data used to indicate students' progress toward a goal over an extended time
	Example: Teachers report that students display a lower rate of classroom outbursts; conduct grades improve during the next grading period
Long-term:	Data that reflect the effectiveness of a particular intervention or activity
	Example: Suspension rates decline for group participants

Over time, the collection of data provides professional school counselors with the information needed to review the effectiveness of school counseling programs and, if necessary, adjust to meet the changing needs of the student population.

The critical issue remains, however, that outcomes research in the school counseling field lags behind that of other counseling specialties, and what the research indicates as effective or not effective is frequently not known by the average practitioner in the field. The uneven application of an outcomes-driven approach by school-based practitioners presents one of the greatest challenges to a profession that strives to meet the academic, career, and personal–social needs of every student. School counseling professionals must strive to (a) conduct more outcomes research to determine which services and strategies are effective and which are not; and (b) disseminate this information to school-based practitioners, supervisors, and counselor educators so that practitioners' theoretical orientation and practice can be driven by an understanding of what is and is not effective. In many ways, the purpose of this book is to provide a resource that is not just accessible and understandable to the practicing professional school counselor or counselor-in-training but that is also informed by outcomes research, thereby providing a wealth of information for practitioners regarding what is and is not effective in our work with students.

THE FUTURE OF SCHOOL COUNSELING

The school counseling profession has been shaped by numerous events and initiatives, including *Sputnik* and the National Defense Education Act. Wrenn's (1962) *The Counselor in a Changing World*, ASCA's *National Standards for School Counseling Programs* (Campbell & Dahir, 1997), The Education Trust's (1999) "Transforming School Counseling Initiative," and *The ASCA National Model: A Framework for School Counseling Programs* (ASCA; 2005). Throughout the last century, the profession has evolved to meet changing societal and school-system demands.

For some time now, doomsayers have predicted the demise of the school counseling profession. Well, the reports of our demise are premature! Perhaps Herr and Erford (2007) said it best:

> The historical roots that have spawned the need for counselors in schools and future issues that remain to be fully resolved at the beginning of the 21st century suggest that the role of the professional counselor is not a rigid and static set of functions. Rather, it is in a constant state of transformation in response to the changing demands on American schools and the factors and influences that affect the growth and development of America's children and youth. Across the one hundred years or so that comprise the history of school counseling in the United States, the questions and issues have changed. However, there is no longer the question of whether professional school counseling will survive or whether it is relevant to the mission of the school. The questions today are how to make its contribution more explicit, how to distribute its effects more evenly across school and student groups, and how to deploy these precious professional resources in the most efficient and effective manner. These are the

challenges that the future professional school counselor will face. (Herr & Erford, 2007, p. 36)

Undoubtedly, the school counseling profession will continue to evolve and thrive so long as professional school counselors strive to meet the academic, career, and personal–social needs of all students.

SUMMARY/CONCLUSION

The school counseling profession has a rich history of evolving in new and necessary directions to address societal, systemic, and student needs. The current phase of evolution, or transformation, must be driven by data and outcomes research that identifies effective practices. In addition to the traditional emphasis on theoretical counseling orientations and practices, the contemporary professional school counselor must emphasize accountability, social advocacy, and systemic interventions, all within the umbrella of a comprehensive developmental school counseling program that removes barriers to student success and addresses the academic, career, and personal–social needs of *all* students.

(Note: See the CD-ROM for a list of references.)

CHAPTER 2

THE HISTORY OF SCHOOL COUNSELING

Mei Tang and Bradley T. Erford

Preview

Reviewing the history of a profession generally serves two purposes. One is to understand how our profession came into being and how it reached its current status. The other is to look for a direction for the future. This chapter will focus on the first goal, to explore the roots and developmental stages of school counseling as a profession, providing context for several of the chapters that follow, which address the later purpose. As Herr and Erford (2007) argued, counseling in schools did not arise in a vacuum; it is necessary to review the development of school counseling in the historical context: "The historical moment must be right for the ingredients of change to take root and begin to flourish" (Herr & Erford, 2007, p. 18). This chapter will chronicle school counseling developmental periods through four dimensions: historical context, external forces or significant events that have had momentous impact on the growth and direction of the school counseling profession, theoretical frameworks that have influenced professional school counselors' work, and roles and functions professional school counselors have performed.

EMERGING YEARS (1900–1915)

HISTORICAL CONTEXT

At the beginning of the 20th century, American society went through vast changes as a result of the Industrial Revolution. The Industrial Revolution resulted in a concentration of the work force, a demand for skilled workers, uncertainty in the labor market, and, consequently, a growth in secondary school enrollment and a challenge to the classical education that was not preparing skilled workers (Dixon, 1987). The other societal and contextual factors for these changes during the early 1900s included urbanization, a large influx of immigration, the abuses of child labor, city ghettos, and neglect of individual rights and integrity (Herr, 2002; Minkoff & Terres, 1985; Schmidt, 2004).

Brewer (1942) identified four important economic and social conditions (i.e., division of labor, technological innovations, vocational education, and modern democracy) that influenced the rise of educational reform and vocational guidance, while Traxler and North (1966) pointed to "philanthropy or humanitarianism, religion, mental hygiene, social change, and the movement to know pupils as individuals" (p. 6). These changes forced schools to address the needs of students and respond to the social, economic, and educational problems. Bookish learning and impractical instruction were criticized for failing to prepare students adequately to avail themselves of the growing opportunities as they entered into the work force. At the same time, because the labor division was so differentiated and comprehensive, family and friends could no longer provide essential information and assistance for occupational choice (Herr & Erford, 2007). Therefore, it became necessary for schools to provide vocational guidance for these youngsters. *Vocational guidance,* as the root for school counseling, has been well documented in the literature (Baker, 2000; Gysbers, 2001; Herr & Erford 2007; Minkoff & Terres, 1985; Schmidt, 2004) as a response to the effects of industrial growth in the late 19th and beginning of the 20th century: "Vocational guidance was not only viewed as assisting the development of individuals, but also seen as a means for achieving social goals" (Dixon, 1987, p. 112).

EXTERNAL FORCES AND SIGNIFICANT EVENTS

The pioneering work of early practitioners created a foundation for vocational guidance and career education that is still useful today. Important figures emerged: George Merrill developed the first systematic vocational guidance program in San Francisco in 1895; Eli W. Weaver authored *Choosing a Career* and organized guidance services for New York City; Frank Goodwin developed a system-wide guidance program for Cincinnati, Ohio; Meyer Bloomfield and Anna Reed established a guidance program with a focus on employability of students and the ethics and practice of business; Jesse B. Davis and Frank Parsons were acknowledged in the literature for their significant ground-breaking work in incorporating vocational guidance programs into school systems (Gysbers & Henderson, 2001; Herr & Erford 2007).

From 1889 to 1907, Jesse B. Davis was a school administrator and counselor in Detroit and was greatly concerned with students' vocational and social needs. When he became the principal of the high school in Grand Rapids, Michigan, in 1907, Davis introduced the first guidance course as a part of the school's English curriculum—for the first time making guidance an accepted part of the school program (Beale, 1986).

Frank Parsons, known as the "father of guidance," founded the Vocation Bureau of Boston in 1908 and authored *Choosing a Vocation,* a major text in the field, in 1909. Parsons was concerned about the transition from school to the world of work and society's failure to develop resources and services for human growth and development (Schmidt, 2004). His work at the bureau aimed to help young students make appropriate choices for a vocation by using a scientific approach (Gysbers & Henderson, 2005). Parsons also designed training programs to help young men become vocational counselors. His work was instrumental in creating the first counselor certification program in Boston and was eventually adopted by Harvard University as the first college-based counselor education program (Miller, 1968). His book "laid out the principles and methods of implementing vocational guidance, collecting and publishing occupational information, conducting a group study of occupations, carrying on individual counseling, and processing individual assessment" (Herr & Erford, 2007, p. 18), which also set the tone for the trait-and-factor approach that later became a major school of career development theories.

In 1913, the National Vocational Guidance Association (NVGA) was founded in Grand Rapids, Michigan. This organization was one of the founding divisions of the American Personnel and Guidance Association (APGA) in 1952 (later renamed the American Association for Counseling Development [AACD], and now called the American Counseling Association [ACA]). NVGA was also the original publisher for two current important journals: *Career Development Quarterly* and *Journal of Counseling and Development* (Schmidt, 2004). The significance of NVGA is its instrumental role in the unification and identification of what has become the counseling profession and, particularly, the school counseling profession.

THEORETICAL FRAMEWORK

Parsons (1909) articulated the principles and methods of providing vocational guidance in the most influential theoretical work of that time and for many decades to come. He specified three essential factors in choosing an appropriate vocation: clear self-understanding of one's aptitudes, abilities, interests, resources, limitations and other qualities; understanding of the requirements and conditions, pros and cons, compensation, opportunities, and prospects of different jobs; and understanding of the relationship between the two groups of factors. The goal of the early guidance movement was to prepare students for the world of work.

ROLES AND FUNCTIONS

In the early 1900s, there were no job titles such as *professional school counselor* or *guidance counselor*. The implementation of guidance was accomplished by appointed teachers who provided guidance and counseling without relief from their regular teaching loads or additional pay (Gysbers & Henderson, 2001). These teachers were given a list of activities relating to vocational guidance but no organized structure in which to work.

FORMATIVE YEARS (1915–1930S)

HISTORICAL CONTEXT

In the years following the early vocational guidance movement in the 1900s, there was a continual emphasis on vocational guidance within education; however, educational reform and concerns about the dignity and rights of children emerged (Gysbers & Henderson, 2001; Herr & Erford, 2007). The National Education Association supported guidance activities for education but not for vocation or employment, believing that vocational guidance was irrelevant to the needs of college-bound students (Minkoff & Terres, 1985). In the 1920s and 1930s, the school counseling focus was shifted from job-oriented counseling to personal counseling and academic advisement. A number of movements (e.g., mental hygiene, measurement, developmental studies of children, introduction of cumulative records, progressive education) influenced the changing purpose of vocational guidance (Gysbers, 2001). A broader focus including issues of personality and human development beyond vocational guidance started to emerge.

During this period, World War I and the Great Depression were two major events that affected the development of the school counseling profession. World War I affected the development and growth of testing. During the Great Depression, many young people were out of school or work and needed guidance to address livelihood needs.

EXTERNAL FORCES AND SIGNIFICANT EVENTS

The mental hygiene movement, which reformed mental health services, was influenced by Clifford Beers, a former patient with a mental illness, and his book, *A Mind That Found Itself*. Published in 1908, this book was instrumental in reforming the treatment of patients with mental illness. The mental hygiene movement contributed to the acceptance and understanding of mental illness by society (Dixon, 1987). It also brought rising attention to students' personality and maladjustment issues (Herr & Erford, 2007). As a result, a clinical model of guidance and personal counseling began to dominate practice.

Psychological testing and measurement, another contributing force for counseling development, experienced a tremendous growth during this time. During World War I, the U.S. military began to use group training and testing procedures to screen and classify draftees (Schmidt, 2004). This classification provided impetus for further development of aptitude and interest measurement for the subsequent decades. The testing movement served to provide a conceptual strength and methodology to guidance.

Progressive education in the schools, introduced by John Dewey, emphasized the school's roles in guiding students' personal, social, and moral development (Nugent, 1994). Guidance activities were incorporated into the school curriculum to help students develop skills for living (Schmidt, 2004). While progressive education was criticized for not attending to the fundamentals of education, the most significant influence of progressive education was supporting the establishment of the guidance counselors.

Several other significant events followed. In 1926, New York became the first state to require certification for guidance workers. In 1938, a Guidance and Personnel branch was created in the U.S. Division of Vocational Education. Finally, in 1939, the first edition of the *Dictionary of Occupational Titles* was published by the U.S. Department of Labor, providing a reference for job descriptions and related job titles (Beale, 1986; Herr & Erford, 2007).

THEORETICAL FRAMEWORKS

Guidance was less concerned with social and industrial issues than with personal and educational issues during this period, yet there were no major theories or models of school counseling (Herr & Erford, 2007). The rapid development of measurement and subsequent availability of numerous tests saw an increased use of the trait-and-factor approach. Williamson (1939) developed a directive, or counselor-centered approach, which stated that counselors should enlighten students through exposition. In this direct approach, counselors were expected to collect data, synthesize data, and deliver the results with the purpose of motivating students.

Burnham, referred to as the "father of elementary school guidance" (Stone & Bradley, 1994), authored *Great Teachers and Mental Health* (1926), which advocated for the necessity of guidance in elementary schools. He emphasized the critical role of classroom teachers in the mental health of children and the importance of developmental and preventive guidance programs.

ROLES AND FUNCTIONS

The work of the pupil personnel, the organizational framework of the time, focused on bringing the pupils of the community to the educational environment and enabled them to maximize their desired development (Myers, 1935). Personnel involved in pupil personnel work included attendance officers, visiting teachers, school nurses, school physicians, and vocational counselors. Herr and Erford (2007) summarized the roles and functions of professional school counselors in the 1920s to 1940s as

- helping students gain more personalized educational experience (to counteract the insensitive education system);
- helping students sort through educational positions and create a unified course of instruction to discover the student's talents and locate the resources to develop these talents; and
- coordinating the student personnel services to provide integrated support rather than compartmentalized assistance.

Professional Identity and Growth (1940s–1950s)

HISTORICAL CONTEXT

The onset and end of World War II increased government involvement in the counseling profession. During the war, many psychologists and counselors were needed to help screen and train military and industrial specialists. After the war, many veterans needed services to readjust to civilian life. One particular governmental influence was the George-Barden Act of 1946, which provided funds to develop and support guidance and counseling activities in schools:

> For the first time in history, school counselors and state and local supervisors received resources, leadership, and financial support from the government. This action fueled the start of a period of rapid growth for guidance and counseling services in schools. (Schmidt, 2004, p. 12)

The problems in school counseling (such as limited preparation of professional school counselors, lack of advocacy for professional school counselors, no systematic professional organization, and little legislative support for school counseling) began to change (Herr & Erford, 2007). Renewed hope also came from the emergence of person-centered counseling, developed by Carl Rogers, and the first national school counselor organization.

EXTERNAL FORCES AND SIGNIFICANT EVENTS

Carl Rogers published his monumental books, *Counseling and Psychotherapy: Newer Concepts in Practice* (1942) and *Client-Centered Therapy: Its Current Practice, Implications, and Theory* (1951). Most importantly, Rogerian influences emphasized a growth-oriented counseling relationship as opposed to an informational and problem-solving approach (Dixon, 1987; Schmidt, 2004).

In 1948, the *Occupational Outlook Handbook* was first published. In 1949, Robert Mathewson published *Guidance Policy and Practice*, a pioneering work on planning and implementing developmental guidance programs in schools (Beale, 1986). In 1952, professional school counselors formed their own professional organization, the American School Counselor Association (ASCA). The impetus for the new organization stemmed from school counselors' belief that the National Vocational Guidance Association no longer served the needs of school counseling adequately, given that the professional school counselor's role and responsibilities extended beyond merely vocational guidance (Minkoff & Terres, 1985). ASCA became the fifth division in APGA (now the American Counseling Association [ACA]) in 1953. As professional school counselors became more recognized in schools across the country, ASCA reinforced the unique role professional school counselors performed and provided a forum for communication among professional school counselors (Herr, 1979).

THEORETICAL FRAMEWORKS

Rogers (1942, 1951) developed one of the most widely used counseling frameworks in history. He encouraged counselors to attend to the person in the process, and his ideas transformed counseling from medical and problem-solving models to a personal-growth model. This theoretical approach fit naturally with the gradually emerging theme since the 1920s—individual counseling that focused on the personal and emotional needs of students.

The pupil personnel work structure continued to dominate guidance and counseling in schools (Gysbers, 2001). Counseling services were a subset of services in the educational system to be delivered by professional school counselors. The clinical model of guidance made individual counseling emerge as the central part of guidance. The nature and scope of counseling services expanded, compared to earlier decades, but there was still no unified, systematic, standard framework for what professional school counselors did. As a result, counseling services depended to a large extent on the mandates of local school districts.

ROLES AND FUNCTIONS

Professional school counselors started to provide more than just vocational and personal counseling. Their responsibilities included orientation, individual appraisal, information, placement, follow-up, individual and group guidance, and consultation with parents and teachers (Schmidt, 2004).

BOOMING YEARS (LATE 1950S, 1960S, & 1970S)

HISTORICAL CONTEXT

The late 1950s through the 1960s produced legislation initiatives that served to define school counseling's importance throughout the second half of the 20th century. The 1960s saw the expansion of school counseling across the nation. More training programs for professional school counselors were developed, and professional school counselors were hired. It is interesting that the school counseling movement occurred primarily as a result of the Cold War. After World War II, the United States and Soviet Union became world superpowers, representing two very different ideological frameworks. When the Soviet Union launched *Sputnik* in 1957, the first man-made earth satellite, the United States was alarmed. A serious concern arose as to whether the United States had the scientific and technological capability to compete with the Soviet Union in space programs and eventually win the Cold War. A series of initiatives in the late 1950s and throughout the 1960s increased the competitive ability of the United States (Herr & Erford, 2007). As a result of federal funding and legislative support, school counseling positions expanded to unprecedented levels, as did the quantity and quality of professional school counselor training programs.

EXTERNAL FORCES AND SIGNIFICANT EVENTS

The passage of the National Defense Education Act (NDEA) in 1958 was one of several legislative initiatives to counteract the perceived threat of the Soviet Union. The NDEA provided funding to enhance school counseling programs in public schools, aiming to identify and encourage talented students to enter science and engineering careers. The funding also benefited new and existing counselor education programs, as the need for training professional school counselors was enormous. Most important for the school counseling profession, the counselor training programs became more systematic and integrated, state certification requirements were established, and many more students were served (Herr & Erford, 2007).

In 1964, the NDEA Title V-A was passed to extend guidance and counseling for all students, including those in elementary schools and various types of postsecondary schools (Herr, 1979). Despite this addition, elementary school counseling was not yet readily accepted within school systems or by the public. In the mid-1960s, several national studies, investigating the functions and roles of elementary school counselors, gave visibility, clarity, and direction to elementary school counseling, resulting in more counselors becoming employed in that setting (Schmidt, 2004).

In 1966, the U.S. Department of Education established the Educational Resources Information Center (ERIC) to provide for education the same systematic acquisition and dissemination of relevant, quality information that had already been established for the physical sciences. A key feature of the ERIC system was its decentralization, in which individual clearinghouses had the responsibility of ensuring that the ERIC database included the important literature and met the information needs of its designated scope-area constituents. Fourteen clearinghouses were established, with scope areas that included math and science, reading, early childhood education, and others. A proposal by Dr. Garry R. Walz at the University of Michigan led to the establishment of an ERIC Clearinghouse on Counseling and Personnel Services. This assured that all relevant counseling journals and publications—and particularly the school counseling literature—were processed for input into the national database.

At the same time, numerous pieces of legislation were being passed to address social issues such as unemployment, poverty, and civil rights. In response to the Elementary and Secondary Education Act of 1965 and the Vocational Education Amendments of 1968, school counseling services incorporated attention to school dropouts, the economically and academically disadvantaged, and students with disabilities. The myriad legislation enacted in the 1960s also created vocational guidance, career education, and other career-related projects, emphasizing the role of professional school counselors in preparing students for transition from school to work (Herr, 2002; Herr & Erford, 2007; Minkoff & Terres, 1985).

In the 1970s, two important pieces of legislation had significant impacts on professional school counselors. The first was the Education for All Handicapped Children Act of 1975, which involved professional school counselors in program planning, counseling, consulting, and curriculum monitoring for exceptional children (Schmidt, 2004). The other was the Family Educational Rights and Privacy Act of 1974 (known as the Buckley Amendment), which limited access to a student's records.

Other significant events during this period included the emergence of two important and widely read publications. In 1959, *The American High School Today*, authored by James Conant, inspired the idea that all students should have access to counseling and advocated for one full-time professional school counselor for 250 to 300 students (Baker, 2000; Herr, 2002; Herr & Erford, 2007). This student-to-counselor ratio is still widely espoused today but is not fully implemented in most states. Also, C. Gilbert Wrenn (1962) wrote *The Counselor in a Changing World*, in which he strongly stressed the importance of building a developmental elementary and secondary school counseling program rather than a crisis-oriented remedial program.

THEORETICAL FRAMEWORKS

Even though there was still no unified and systematic school counseling theory per se, the 1960s saw the rise of several counseling and career development theories (Brown & Srebalus, 1996; Nugent, 1994). Many counseling theories (e.g., Ellis' rational emotive therapy, Glasser's reality therapy, behavioral counseling introduced by Wolf and Krumboltz, Super's career development theory, Holland's theory of occupational types) familiar to contemporary counselors across practice settings were developed in this period. Other influential approaches to school counseling included Keat's (1974) multimodal counseling approach, which promoted examining and treating the student across several dimensions rather than on the presenting problem alone, and Egan's (1975) concept of stages in the counseling process, which provided professional school counselors a road map for how to counsel.

ROLES AND FUNCTIONS

One of the primary goals of increasing the number of professional school counselors was to identify and encourage talented students to pursue science and engineering careers. In addition to the coordination role, which assisted students in achieving educational and vocational goals, professional school counselors continued to provide individual counseling to students, albeit generally in reaction to events or circumstances. Baker (2001), in reviewing his professional school counselor job in the 1960s, stated that

> there was not enough time for proactive guidance programming. [Time was spent] scheduling all students over the summer (without pay) and making sched-

ule adjustments in the fall—all by hand, lunch-room monitoring, student council advising, junior and senior proms, senior-class awards day, and graduation.
(Baker, 2001, p. 76)

Nonetheless, the literature during and following the 1960s emphasized broader
programmatic roles and functions for professional school counselors. Preferred services
included developing comprehensive guidance programs to incorporate into the school
curriculum, individual and group counseling, student assessment, and consultation
with parents and teachers (Schmidt, 2004). Much of this focus on services stemmed
from efforts by the National Association of Guidance Supervisors and Counselor Trainers, which, in 1959, began a 5-year project to construct educational standards for preparing high school counselors.

CHALLENGE AND OPPORTUNITY (LATE 1970S–PRESENT)

HISTORICAL CONTEXT

The years after the boom (between the late 1970s and 1990s) observed several significant events in the United States and the world. In U.S. society, these decades observed
the movements of civil rights, women's liberation, school desegregation, a sharp rise
in drug abuse, an AIDS epidemic, and the end of the Cold War. Problems of inner-city
schools, high dropout rates, diversity of student populations (in terms of racial or ethnic,
cultural and socioeconomic backgrounds), readiness to learn, violence in schools and
homes, teenage pregnancy, peer pressure, and limited resources have presented enormous challenges to school counseling professionals and educators in general (Baker,
2000; Rye & Sparks, 1999).

In the 1970s, a decade of enrollment decline in schools along with a depressed
economy forced local school districts to reduce the numbers of professional school
counselors (Baker, 2000, 2001). The fact that professional school counselors are often
the victims of budget cuts in school systems has caused the profession to focus on two
pertinent issues: role clarification and accountability. The debate about the definition
and direction of roles, functions, and responsibilities of professional school counselors
has centered on the training, capabilities, and certification of professional school counselors compared to counseling in other settings (Aubrey, 1977; Paisley & McMahon,
2001; Schmidt, 2004). The focus on accountability has provided evidence of the effectiveness of school counseling services (Baker, 2001). The last 2 decades in the 20th century observed the second immigrant influx—different from the first, because a majority
of the immigrants were from Asian and Hispanic cultural backgrounds. The diverse
school-age population, particularly in urban settings, presented new challenges for professional school counselors.

EXTERNAL FORCES AND SIGNIFICANT EVENTS

The Career Education Incentive Act of 1978 and the Carl Perkins Vocational Education Act of 1984 steered the development of career education programs in schools. The
School to Work Opportunities Act of 1994 "has endeavored to create new models of

collaboration between schools, transition mechanisms designed to facilitate the successful movement of students between school and employment, and employers" (Herr, 2002, p. 228).

By 1970, all states had professional school counselor certification (Stone & Bradley, 1994). The department of education in each state regulates the requirements of training and experiences for school counseling certification. In 1982, The National Board of Certified Counselors (NBCC) was developed to certify counselors across the states (Stone, 1985). NBCC provided a consistent credentialing process across the country and offers a National Certified School Counselor (NCSC) credential.

Beginning in the 1980s, the comparison between students in the American education system and those in other developed countries alarmed educational professionals, politicians, and the public. In 1983, the National Commission on Excellence issued the publication *A Nation at Risk* to advocate for more rigorous standards for high school graduation (Herr, 2002). As the 21st century approached, ASCA called for professional school counselors to take action to help students be academically competitive and productive citizens.

Throughout the 1980s and early 1990s, federal funds for school counseling programs were provided primarily through the Carl D. Perkins Vocational Education Act of 1984 and the Carl D. Perkins Vocational and Applied Technology Act of 1990 (Herr & Erford, 2007). The Elementary School Counseling Demonstration Act of 1995 provided federal grants to local school districts to make counseling services available to all students. Counselor preparation programs began to collaborate with K–12 schools to provide assistance to students in school settings. According to Herr and Erford (2007), this act provided the impetus for orienting school counseling to include more than just career guidance.

During the 1970s to the present, the ERIC database grew to be the most used education database in the world, eventually containing over 1 million documents. In 1993, Dr. Garry Walz and Dr. Jeanne Bleuer moved the ERIC Clearinghouse on Counseling and Personnel Services (ERIC/CAPS) from the University of Michigan to the University of North Carolina at Greensboro. At that time, the name was changed to the ERIC Clearinghouse on Counseling and Student Services (ERIC/CASS). Although the U.S. Department of Education abolished the decentralized structure of ERIC and closed the 16 ERIC clearinghouses in December of 2003, during its 38 years of existence, ERIC/CAPS (CASS) acquired and processed over 25,000 counseling-related documents, indexed and abstracted over 50 journals, and published over 250 books and 200 ERIC Digests. In addition, the clearinghouse conducted 25 heavily attended national workshops devoted to cutting-edge topics that were relevant to school counseling (e.g., assessment and testing, use of computers and technology in guidance programs, life or career development, and leading and managing comprehensive school counseling programs).

Although the ERIC/CASS Clearinghouse has closed, Drs. Walz and Bleuer have established a new organization, Counseling Outfitters, to continue and, in fact, expand many of the services and products that had been offered by the Clearinghouse. This book is an example of the new line of resources produced by CAPS Press, the publishing division of Counseling Outfitters.

Near the beginning of the third millennium, school reform and accountability movements lead a group of forward-thinking, nationally focused school counselors and counselor educators to professionalize and standardize the approach to school counseling. ASCA published the *National Standards for School Counseling Programs* in 1997 (Campbell & Dahir, 1997) and later the *Vision Into Action: Implementing the National Standards for School Counseling Programs* (Dahir, Shelton, & Valiga, 1998). The standards were aimed at providing guidelines and a framework for professional school counselors to develop and implement comprehensive developmental counseling programs for all students in the personal–social, academic, and career-development areas. It emphasized the importance of assessment of students' needs and evidence-based research to make the school counseling program accountable. But still, an agreed-upon framework or model for school counseling had yet to emerge.

THEORETICAL FRAMEWORKS

The concept of comprehensive developmental school counseling programs, rather than a professional school counselor providing an ancillary set of services, has evolved since the 1970s and has become an adopted guideline by ASCA for all professional school counselors to follow. Gysbers and Henderson's (1988) innovative work provided a conceptual and practical guide for the profession to develop and manage a school guidance program: "The emergence of developmental guidance and counseling in the 1970s and 1980s provided a central organizing structure for counselors and counselor educators to reframe their work" (Sink, 2001, p. 157).

But a true turning point in history of school counseling occurred between 1997 and 2003, when ASCA published two important documents: ASCA's *National Standards for School Counseling Programs* in 1997 (Campbell & Dahir, 1997) and *The ASCA National Model: A Framework for School Counseling Programs* in 2003 (ASCA; 2003, 2005). These two publications provided a framework for professional school counselors to turn to for defining their job responsibilities. As a result, the school counseling profession has a unified voice in communicating with other school personnel and the public about what professional school counselors do—develop and manage comprehensive and developmental school counseling programs that help all students with academic, personal–social, and career development.

Recently, a particular counseling approach has gained popularity in the school counseling profession—brief, solution-focused counseling (Davis & Osborn, 2000; Sklare, 2005). The reason for this approach's appeal to professional school counselors lies in the promise of efficiently solving the problem in a short time frame. Traditional approaches may be effective, but professional school counselors simply do not have time for long-term therapy.

ROLES AND FUNCTIONS

Despite the debate about the roles and functions of professional school counselors (Schmidt, 2004), in the past 3 decades, professional school counselors have performed duties widely perceived as *traditional* (i.e., academic advising, vocational planning, personal–individual counseling, reactive or crisis-oriented counseling, participating in Individualized Education Programs [IEPs], test administration and scoring, and scheduling). At the same time, professional school counselors were torn between providing direct services or working as social change agents to provide a better school environment for students (Whiston, 2001). It was recommended that professional school counselors need to function as counselor, consultant, facilitator, coordinator, change agent, a team player and leader to successfully develop and implement a comprehensive developmental school counseling program (Baker, 2000; Erford, 2007; Paisley & McMahon, 2001; Schmidt, 2004). Professional school counselors are also expected to be culturally responsive counselors and to advocate for student needs in the culturally diverse school and community settings (Lee, 2001).

Summary/Conclusion

School counseling was rooted in vocational guidance at the beginning of the 20th century as a response to the needs of students in transition from an agricultural to an industrial economy. In almost to a century, the direction of school counseling was often shaped by social reform, school reform, and the national welfare (see the timeline provided in Table 2.1). The school counseling profession has evolved from "a peripheral, ancillary role in schools to a more central one" (Herr, 2002, p. 230). School counselors need to provide the comprehensive, preventive, systematic, culturally appropriate and accountable programs to serve all the students.

TABLE 2.1

TIMELINE OF SIGNIFICANT EVENTS IN SCHOOL COUNSELING HISTORY

Timeline	Significant Event and Impact
Emerging Years (1900–1915)	
Late 19th century and early 1900s	Industrialization, urbanization, influx of immigrants, classification of labor; demand for skilled work force and need for employment guidance
1908	Frank Parsons founded the Vocational Bureau of the Civic Services in Boston; pioneer work in schools to help students
	Jesse Davis introduced the first guidance course as part of the English curriculum in Detroit, making guidance accepted as part of the school curriculum
	Clifford Beers authored *A Mind That Found Itself*; brought the treatment of mental patients to public attention
1909	Parsons' book *Choosing a Vocation* published 1 year after his death; laid out principles and methods of providing vocational guidance
1913	Founding meeting of National Vocational Guidance Association in Grand Rapids, Michigan; first professional counseling organization —later became a founding division of ACA
Formative Years (1915–1930s)	
1920	Mental hygiene, measurement movement, progressive education
1926	Burnham published *Great Teachers and Mental Health;* first to advocate for elementary school counseling
1926	New York requires certification for guidance workers
1938	A Guidance and Personnel Branch was created in the Vocational Education division in the U.S. Office of Education
1939	First edition of *Dictionary of Occupational Titles* (DOT) was published
Professional Years (1940s–1950s)	
1942	Carl Rogers published *Counseling and Psychotherapy*
1948	*The Occupational Outlook Handbook* was first published
1952	American School Counseling Association (ASCA) was founded
1953	ASCA became the fifth division in the American Personnel and Guidance Association
1958	National Defense Education Act was passed, expanding the training and hiring of school counselors
1959	James Conant published the *America n High School Today*, suggesting 1:250 to 1:300 school counselor-to-student ratio

(continues)

TABLE 2.1. *(continued)*

Timeline	Significant Event and Impact
Booming Years (1960s–1970s)	
1962	Wrenn published *The Counselor in a Changing World;* influential guide for the school profession in the years to follow
1964	NDEA Title A—legislation to extend counseling to elementary schools
1966	The U.S. Department of Education established the ERIC Clearinghouse on Counseling and Personnel Services (ERIC/CAPS) at the University of Michigan
1976	Career Education Incentive Act; infusion of career education in schools
Challenge and Opportunity Years (Late 1970s–Present)	
1988	Gysbers and Henderson published *Developing and Managing your School Guidance Program*
1993	ERIC/CAPS moved to the University of North Carolina and became ERIC/CASS (Counseling and Student Services)
1994	School to Work Act was passed, reinforcing career guidance and counseling
1995	Elementary School Counseling Demonstration Act provided $20 million to assist schools in making counseling services available
1997	ASCA publishes the *National Standards for School Counseling Programs;* aims at providing benchmark for school counseling programs to promote student competency
2003	ASCA publishes *The ASCA National Model: A Framework for School Counseling Programs*
2005	Second edition of the ASCA national model published

(Note: See the CD-ROM for a list of references.)

CHAPTER 3

CURRENT AND FUTURE PERSPECTIVES
ON SCHOOL COUNSELING

Joyce A. DeVoss

Preview

Since the turn of the 21st century, professional school counselors in the United States have made significant progress in addressing numerous challenges to their profession, including clarifying role definition; integrating programming; defining delivery systems; deciding on generalist versus specialist roles; attaining reasonable student-to-counselor ratios; accepting leadership, advocacy, and public-relations roles; developing technological competencies; developing data-driven school counseling programs; and obtaining optimal professional development. Professional school counselors in the United States have developed a systematic approach to creating and managing school counseling programs that includes using data to demonstrate how they make a difference for their students. In this chapter I address current and future challenges for professional school counselors as educational programs become influenced by social changes and socioeconomic pressures and as the profession of school counseling advocates for needed social changes.

School counseling's origins go back more than 100 years. Its development was influenced by a variety of forces, including the industrial revolution's exploitation of children, population immigration and migration, the educational reform movement at the turn of the 20th century, the evolution of counseling theory, and the national agenda. At the turn of the 21st century, educational reform once again became a primary source of influence on the evolution of the profession. In the recent atmosphere of school reform and accountability, professional school counselors have been called upon to act as assertive advocates for students and the profession of school counseling.

Several authors have identified and discussed current and future challenges for professional school counselors (Baker & Gerler, 2004; Gysbers, 2001; Herr & Erford, 2007; Paisley & Borders, 1995; Paisley & McMahon, 2001; Sandhu, 2001; Sears & Granello, 2002). In addition, in February 2002, in Greensboro, North Carolina, a group of approximately 300 counselors, counselor educators, central office personnel, and state-level personnel attended a national conference titled Leading and Managing Comprehensive School Guidance Programs and listed 10 critical issues in school counseling (American School Counselor Association [ASCA]; 2002b). These key challenges and issues facing professional school counselors are addressed within this chapter and are organized by the following topics: school counselor role definition, school counselor preparation, school counseling programming, school counseling program delivery system, generalist versus specialist, reasonable student-to-counselor ratios, leadership or advocacy or public relations, technological competencies, and professional development.

PROFESSIONAL SCHOOL COUNSELOR ROLE DEFINITION

Defining the professional school counselor's role has been challenge for the school counseling profession—one that has caused considerable difficulty in daily practice, limiting credibility for the profession. Perceptions of professional school counselor roles vary widely, even within the same school district. Some professional school counselors reported experiencing a lack of administrative support, confusing expectations, and lack of respect (ASCA; 2002a; Hurst & Eggert, 2006). Sears and Granello (2002) noted that professional school counselors struggled with role definition. Paisley and Borders (1995) stated that professional school counselors experienced a lack of control over day-to-day duties and sometimes had to deal with competing expectations from principals and counseling directors.

Based on results of a Missouri statewide study, which surveyed professional school counselors and administrators about the level of implementation of comprehensive guidance programs during the 2004–2005 school year, Lapan, Gysbers, Cook, Bragg, and Robbins (2006) concluded that implementation is especially a concern in high school, where counselors continue to be inundated with clerical tasks. They noted that non-guidance tasks hurt program implementation. Baker (2000) stated that "school counseling, long viewed by some as an ancillary service in the schools, remains unclearly defined both within and outside the profession" (p. v). Baker and Gerler (2004) offered the following advice: "The next generation of school counselors will have to be more active than their predecessors if the counselor role challenge is to be resolved" (p. 307). It is important for the role of the professional school counselor to be clear, with some uniformity, yet broad-ranged and not so demanding as to limit effectiveness.

In the early stages of the National Transformation of School Counseling Initiative, House and Martin (1998) outlined the new vision of the school counselor role and compared it to the traditional role of professional school counselor. The new vision professional school counselor is expected to be a proactive leader who is committed to quality education and equity of access to higher education for all students. The professional school counselor is envisioned as an assertive advocate and social activist on behalf of students, parents, schools, and the school counseling profession. The Education Trust (1999) defined school counseling as "a profession that focuses on the relations and interactions between students and their school environment with the expressed purpose of reducing the effect of environmental and institutional barriers that impede student academic success" (The Education Trust, 1999, p. 1).

> The school–community collaboration model (Adelman & Taylor, 2002) also emphasized the school counselor's roles as advocate, collaborator, catalyst, and facilitator of social reform while working to remove barriers to student learning. This approach outlined six objectives for focusing the integration of school and community resources on addressing learning barriers:
>
> - Effectiveness in the classroom
> - Support families in transitions, and increase family support of student learning
> - Crisis prevention and intervention services

- Comprehensive social, emotional, and physical health services for families
- Meaningful partnerships with community organization

The ASCA national model (ASCA; 2005) listed and described the roles of professional school counselors as designers, coordinators, implementers, managers, and evaluators of their school counseling programs. Quality graduate training programs provide school counselor trainees with an understanding of, as well as practical experience with, the new vision roles described by the ASCA national model and other current professional school counseling initiatives.

PROFESSIONAL SCHOOL COUNSELOR PREPARATION

To effectively carry out the mission of schools and to function optimally as part of school leadership teams, professional school counselor trainees must receive adequate training. Potential professional school counselors have choices from diverse training programs. With some basic knowledge about program accreditation, national trends, and professional standards, they should be able to locate quality graduate programs that meet the national standards of the Council for the Accreditation of Counseling and Related Educational Programs (CACREP; 2008) as well as incorporate The Education Trust's vision of professional school counselors, the school–community collaboration model (Adelman & Taylor, 2002), and the ASCA national model (ASCA; 2005) for school counseling programs. Many state departments of education are adopting CACREP standards as minimum standards for certification or licensure (Baker & Gerler, 2004; Sears & Granello, 2002).

Even with CACREP standards, there has been little consistency across school counseling training programs. In 1992, although 195 graduate programs in 72 institutions were CACREP accredited (Kandor & Bobby, 1992), the curriculum varied considerably from one graduate school counseling program to another. CACREP (2008) standards for master's-level school counseling programs require a minimum of 48 semester hours of graduate study, including the following eight areas:

- Professional identity
- Social and cultural diversity
- Human growth and development
- Career development
- Helping relationships
- Group work
- Assessment and research
- Program evaluation

In addition, CACREP specifies that professional school counselor trainees must successfully complete a 100-hour practicum and a 600-hour internship in school settings. These are considered minimal standards for counselor preparation.

ASCA (2000) developed a list of professional school counselor competencies that fall into three domains: knowledge competencies, skill competencies, and professional competencies. Some examples of the *knowledge competencies* are human development theories and concepts, career decision-making theories and techniques, and program development models. Some of the *skill competencies* include diagnosing student needs, career and educational counseling and planning, and conducting in-service training for staff. *Professional competencies* include conducting a self-evaluation to determine strengths and areas needing improvement, advocating for appropriate state and national legislation, and adopting a set of professional ethics to guide practice. It is in the best interest of prospective professional school counselors to seek graduate preparation programs that, in addition to being CACREP accredited, have been continuously updated and aligned with national standards and the Transformation of School Counseling Initiative. This is one way to help ensure that new school counselors will be well prepared as they enter the workforce.

In addition to the professional school counselor competencies, ASCA (2000) identified a list of personal attributes of successful professional school counselors, including (a) a genuine interest in the welfare of others; (b) openness to learning; (c) willingness to take risks; (d) a strong sense of self-worth, caring, and warmth; and (e) a keen sense of humor. Some of these characteristics can be acquired during the course of training; others are inherent to the trainee.

School Counseling Programming

Hart and Jacobi (1992) identified six problems with school counseling programs. In a 2002 presentation at The Education Trust Summer Academy, in Chicago, Kuranz reminded participants of those six problems: lack of basic philosophy, poor integration, insufficient student access, inadequate services for some students, lack of counselor accountability, and failure to use other resources.

BASIC PHILOSOPHY

Kuranz (2002) noted, with a sense of urgency for the continued existence of the profession, that, in Iowa, elementary-level professional school counselor positions were threatened because their focus was not clearly tied to academic achievement. As recently as 2005, in a large district in Tucson, Arizona, professional school counselor positions narrowly escaped elimination for budgetary purposes after stakeholders presented evidence of the strong connection between school guidance and the academic mission of schools. If school counseling programs in K–12 settings are going to survive, it is imperative that they be systematically planned and focused on academic results instead of the traditional focus on services offered.

The basic philosophy and mission of a school counseling program should be tied directly to the school's mission. Examples of desired results might include improved national and state test results, improved graduation rates, improved attendance, decreased behavioral referrals, decreased dropout rates, increased enrollment in postsecondary education programs, and increased enrollment of poor and minority students in high-level math and advanced placement courses.

INTEGRATED, LONGITUDINAL DEVELOPMENTAL COUNSELING

Integration of school counseling goals, objectives, and activities is a key characteristic of an effective school counseling program. An effectively integrated program needs to be truly longitudinal (Herr & Cramer, 1996) and should span from elementary school through secondary school. Sandhu (2001) stressed that, starting with elementary school, counseling programs need to emphasize the interconnections among cognitive, physical, and social development of children. Gysbers (2001) is a leading advocate of "fully implemented comprehensive guidance and counseling programs" (p. 103) for all U.S. schools. Gysbers and Henderson (2006) described in detail the steps in designing a comprehensive guidance program for a school building or district. The process involves concretely describing the content, organizational framework, time allotted, and resources needed. It is a time-intensive process but is well worth the investment for the program.

For maximum effectiveness and relevance to all students, Sandhu (2001) recommended that school counseling programs be proactive and positive in approach. It is reasonable that these programs be comprehensive and well integrated into the mission of the school. Gysbers and Henderson (2006) reported that comprehensive guidance programs are becoming a reality in school districts across the United States. These programs are staffed by professional school counselors concerned with serving all students instead of focusing only on high- and low-achieving students and providing less than adequate services to all others.

STUDENT ACCESSIBILITY AND SERVICES FOR ALL STUDENTS

ASCA has developed national standards for school counseling programs (Campbell & Dahir, 1997) that are the essential elements of an effective school counseling program at any level of K–12 education. They address program content and expected knowledge, attitudes, and skill competencies for all students in schools with comprehensive school counseling programs. Three content areas include academic, career, and personal–social development. Under each of these headings are three standards, which describe the outcomes for students of an effective school counseling program. For example, under the career development domain, Standard B states that "students will employ strategies to achieve future career success and satisfaction" (Campbell & Dahir, 1997, p. 92). The trifold developmental focus, including career development, should start in elementary school and continue through 12th grade (Sandhu, 2001).

Gysbers and Henderson (2006) described in detail how to adapt a school counseling program model to meet the specific needs of a school district or a school building and to balance the use of the professional school counselor's time, according to predetermined priorities. The use of established steering and school–community advisory committees is recommended throughout the decision-making process. This collaborative approach ensures that the school counseling program adopted by the decision makers will adequately address the systemic needs of the district or school.

The ASCA national model creates a common vision for professional school counselors. This model includes four major components: foundation, delivery system, management system, and accountability. The model integrates an emphasis on advocacy, leadership, and systemic change in keeping with the themes of the school counseling reform movement. It provides professional school counselors with a framework for the development of school counseling programs while allowing flexibility for responsiveness to local community needs. Professional school counselors can achieve recognition for their school counseling program by meeting the criteria for and having their program reviewed by a designated ASCA review committee. The recognition is known as a Recognized ASCA Model Program (RAMP).

School counseling programs are faced with responsibility for guidance of all students. This means that counselors in the 21st century must be prepared to provide appropriate school counseling services to students and families of diverse cultural and ethnic backgrounds, learning disabilities, sexual orientations, emotional and physical disabilities, and religious beliefs and practices (Sandhu, 2001). It also means that professional school counselors need to meet the challenge to become assertive advocates for all students, especially disadvantaged and minority students, in the important work of closing the achievement gap between these students and their peers. Gysbers (2001) contended that professional school counselors can reach all students by using comprehensive school counseling programs with planned guidance activities in the classrooms. He cited research indicating that comprehensive guidance programs do benefit students academically, in career development and in school climate.

Traditionally, stage models of development have been the foundation for school counseling programs. Some question the adequacy of these models for this purpose (Green & Keys, 2001; Sears & Granello, 2002). The models may not sufficiently take into account issues of diversity and other contextual factors important to consider when developing a comprehensive developmental school counseling program.

Green and Keys (2001) recommended using a development in context paradigm in school counseling program designs. This model takes into consideration contextual factors such as culture, values, and living environment that impact student development. Professional school counselors operating from this model facilitate student awareness of self in context, an awareness of the multiple contexts impacting the student's life.

Although the profession emphasizes the role of school counselors in the delivery of comprehensive guidance programs, there are many obstacles (Sandhu, 2001). Although the comprehensive guidance approach is preplanned, proactive, and comprehensive in nature, in practice the professional school counselor must constantly strive to achieve and maintain balance in the school counseling program. Despite the best planning efforts, there continues to be many demands on the professional school counselor's time and effort.

Sears and Granello (2002) noted that professional school counselors get pulled in different directions as they attempt to conform to the national reform agenda. For better or worse, professional school counselors respond to more school-based crises and intervene on behalf of both greater numbers of students and students who are more intensely emotionally disturbed or troubled. Baker (2000) acknowledged many demands to which counselors in schools are expected to respond. The ASCA national model (ASCA; 2005) and national standards (Campbell & Dahir, 1997) as well as the national, state, and local school counseling organizations are resources that are available to help professional school counselors meet the challenges of setting and assertively maintaining priorities for their comprehensive, developmental school counseling programs.

ACCOUNTABILITY

Baker and Gerler (2004) explained the difference between the terms *evaluation* and *accountability:* "Evaluation is the act of gathering information about one's services; accountability is the act of reporting the results of the evaluation" (p. 322). They described basic professional school counselor accountability competencies, such as how to do a needs assessment and how to assess consumer satisfaction and cost effectiveness.

Accountability is expected of all educators, including professional school counselors, and data from schools are readily available for professional school counselors to use in evaluating the impact of school counseling programs. Professional school counselors have made progress and will be expected to access and disaggregate data for developing data-driven school counseling programs. When professional school counselors report the outcomes of their interventions on achievement data, other educators begin to understand the connection between counseling programs and the mission of schools.

In 1970, in the midst of economically hard times, Arbuckle (as cited in Baker, 2000) wrote an article titled "Does the School Really Need Counselors?" which challenged the profession to become more accountable. In response, some individuals developed models of accountability; others reiterated the need for accountability; and some state legislation mandated accountability of school counseling programs and professional school counselors. Yet many professional school counselors resisted instituting evaluation measures. Since that time, the pressure for accountability has mounted to an all-time high.

In the face of current educational reform and No Child Left Behind legislation that mandates educational accountability, professional school counselors can no longer afford to resist. With the economic stresses and decreased educational funding following the terrorist attack of September 11, 2001, some school districts are again asking Arbuckle's question. Professional school counselors are challenged to advocate for their survival. Advocacy via the use of data that indicate the impact of school counseling programs on achievement can be powerful and gives the profession credibility.

At the 2006 ASCA conference in Chicago, representatives from the Wake County Public School System and EDSTAR staff of Raleigh, North Carolina (Johnson, Lambright, Sparks, Stiff, & Taft, 2006), presented a useful guide, including 13 ways to prepare your school or district to implement the ASCA national model.

OTHER RESOURCES AND THE NEED FOR COLLABORATION

Considering the challenge for professional school counselors to meet the needs of all children, success in serving students may best be achieved through a team effort. Because typical school student-to-counselor ratios are far in excess of the ideal of somewhere between 200:1 and 300:1 (Baker & Gerler, 2004), professional school counselors cannot adequately meet those needs on their own. An ASCA (2002a) study reported that in 1999–2000, the national average student-to-counselor ratio was 490:1. This data lend support to professional school counselor efforts to collaborate with others in delivering services to students.

Paisley and McMahon (2001) believed that professional school counselors must foster collaborative relationships with other school personnel, parents, professionals, and other community members to combine efforts and meet student needs. By doing so, professional school counselors enlarge the pool of talent and resources available to the school community. In one example, teachers effectively delivered guidance curriculum in the classroom. (Although involvement of others besides professional school counselors in the counseling program can be beneficial to students, ethical and professional practice requirements [ASCA; 1994, 2004] dictate that counseling-related activities performed by noncredentialed personnel be supervised and coordinated by credentialed professional school counselors.)

SCHOOL COUNSELING PROGRAM DELIVERY SYSTEM

The ASCA national model outlined the delivery system for school counseling programs. Professional school counselors must be competent in the following areas to meet basic practice standards of the profession: implementing developmental guidance curriculum, providing individual planning, offering responsive services to meet immediate needs, and performing systems-support administration and management activities.

Currently, there is considerable consensus in the field of school counseling that the resources of the professional school counselor can best be used with a proactive developmental approach (Gysbers & Henderson, 2006; Sandhu, 2001). The professional school counselor is looked upon to coordinate the design, planning, and implementation of the school counseling program with care and flexibility to adequately meet the needs of students, parents, teachers, administrators, and other school community stakeholders.

GENERALIST VERSUS SPECIALIST

Professional school counselors must decide on the extent to which they are generalists or specialists. This decision may be made best according to the needs of the school district or individual school and may be influenced based on the degree to which teams are used. If the school building has a counseling department, the professional school counselors may be expected to be part of the departmental team. In the new vision role (House & Martin, 1998), the professional school counselor is likely to be a member or leader of one or more school leadership team (e.g., staff development planning, suicide prevention, crisis response).

Such teams can operate in a variety of ways: In some settings, the most efficient teamwork occurs when members are specialists who continuously hone specific knowledge bases and related skills. In the case of a counseling department team, the counselors might divide the departmental responsibilities based on the specialties of its members. In other settings, professional school counselor team members might work optimally as generalists and provide an array of services to preassigned caseloads of students. And in yet other environments, a department may operate most efficiently with a mixture of some specialists and some generalists.

When a school building has only one professional school counselor assigned, that counselor is most likely to function as a generalist. This is frequently the case for elementary school counselors. These professional school counselors can become isolated if they are not proactive in assuring involvement on leadership teams and in other collaborative relationships.

REASONABLE STUDENT-TO-COUNSELOR RATIOS

Reasonable student-to-counselor ratios are essential for professional school counselors to become adequately familiar with students and their needs. Because of the amount of variation in type and intensity of the needs in student populations and in the expectations of professional school counselors, it is difficult and unrealistic to determine a standard student-to-counselor ratio to fit all settings.

In general, however, caseloads of 300 or fewer are seen as optimal (Baker & Gerler, 2004). According to Shaw (as cited in Baker & Gerler, 2004), these ratios are determined primarily by financial conditions and secondarily by the perceived value of the school counseling program. Gysbers and Henderson (2006) offered a formula that calculates approximate student-to-counselor ratios in an optimal school counseling program. The ratio varies, depending on the prearranged counseling program activities for the school and, therefore, the professional school counselor's availability to provide the program activities.

LEADERSHIP, ADVOCACY, PUBLIC RELATIONS

Professional school counselors must successfully articulate to policy makers, media, and the public their essential contributions to the mission of their schools. To effectively educate the community about the important role of school counseling, professional school counselors must actively promote the profession and its mission. Baker and Gerler (2004) suggested that social activism is the approach needed to accomplish recognition of the preferred identity for professional school counselors. The Education Trust (n.d.) outlined "the new vision" role of the professional school counselor as leader, advocate, collaborator, and consultant:

> The profession fosters conditions that ensure educational equity, access, and academic success for all students, K–12. . . . The trained school counselor must be an assertive advocate creating opportunities for all students. . . . The school counselor serves as a leader as well as an effective team member working with teachers, administrators and other school personnel to make sure that each student succeeds. The school counselor as consultant empowers families to act on behalf of their children . . . as well as access available resources. (The Education Trust, n.d., ¶ 2)

With a clearer definition of school counseling and the roles of professional school counselors, the local and national community can have a better understanding of key contributions made by professional school counselors in achieving educational equity for all children. Baker (2000) believed that professional school counselors and their supporters needed to join national professional organizations like the American School Counselor Association (ASCA), Association for Counselor Education and Supervision (ACES), and American Counseling Association (ACA), and the regional or state affiliates of these organizations in order to initiate grassroots efforts to achieve dramatic educational change on a national level. He expressed concern that less than half of all professional school counselors are members of any professional organization.

TECHNOLOGICAL COMPETENCE

Professional school counselors are expected to be competent in the use of technology (Sandhu, 2001). ACES's Technology Interest Network (1999) established 12 technological competencies for counselors that should be included in counselor education. These competencies, which are expected to need updating every 3 years, are summarized here.

Counselors need to be able to do the following:

- Use productivity software to develop Web pages, group presentations, letters, and reports
- Use audiovisual equipment such as video recorders, audio recorders, projection equipment, videoconferencing equipment, and playback units
- Use computerized statistical packages
- Use computerized testing, diagnostic, and career decision-making programs with clients
- Use e-mail
- Help clients search for various types of counseling-related information via the Internet, including information about careers, employment opportunities, educational and training opportunities, financial assistance or scholarships, treatment procedures, and social and personal information
- Subscribe to, participate in, and sign off of counseling-related Listservs
- Access and use counseling-related CD-ROM databases
- Know strengths and weaknesses of counseling services provided via the Internet
- Know the legal and ethical codes that relate to counseling services via the Internet
- Use the Internet for finding and using continuing education opportunities in their profession
- Evaluate the quality of Internet information[1]

Sabella and Tyler (as cited in Sandhu, 2001) provided a detailed description and discussion of each of these competencies. Current technology skills are necessary tools or supporting effective school counseling services.

PROFESSIONAL DEVELOPMENT

Due to the rapidly changing educational environment, professional development is a priority for counselors, and they can and should use available professional development

---

[1] Adapted from *ACES Technology Competencies 2007, 1991*, by Association for Counselor Education and Supervision, 2007. Retrieved June 8, 2008, from the ACES Web site (http://files .changemywebsite.com/774116/doc/ACES_Technology_Competencies_2007.pdf). Adapted with permission.

opportunities to stay current in the profession and to maintain their professional identity. Furthermore, professional school counselors can view professional development as an opportunity to network and exchange innovative ideas in the profession. Hatch and Bowers (2002) strongly urged counselors to become actively involved in professional development and reminded them of state requirements to maintain certification.

Professional school counselors are encouraged to become members of at least one professional organization. Fewer than half of professional school counselors take advantage of such a membership. The benefits may include subscriptions to the publications of the organization, liability insurance, notices of professional development or networking opportunities as well as discounts on conferences and professional publications. These organizations offer potential leadership roles for professional school counselors along with the opportunity to make a difference at a systemic level. ASCA is the national school counselor professional organization, and each state also has a state school counselor association.

SUMMARY/CONCLUSION

School counseling in the United States has evolved for more than a century of rapid social, political, and economic change. The profession has been affected by myriad influences, including social reform efforts, immigration, economic changes, national defense issues, and the advancement of psychological and developmental theory. The impact of its meandering evolutionary process left the school counseling profession with numerous challenges at the end of the 20th century, including (a) clarifying role definition; (b) identifying and obtaining optimal preparation; (c) integrating programming; (d) clearly defining program delivery systems; (e) deciding on a generalist versus specialist role; (f) attaining reasonable student-to-counselor ratios; (g) accepting leadership, advocacy, and public relations roles; (h) developing technological competencies; and (i) participating in relevant professional development.

The role of the professional school counselor in the 21st century remains fluid and constantly changing in response to the changing demands of our schools and our local and national communities. However, as the profession continued the transformation process that was begun at the end of the last century, it has sought to become an active participant in the educational reform movement, unlike its limited (if any) role in past reform movements. Aided by the ASCA national model, The Education Trust's Transforming School Counseling Initiative (1999), and the school-community collaboration model (Adelman & Taylor, 2002), professional school counselors have begun to address the challenges and issues discussed in this chapter. They are encouraged to continue this important work. Through strong professional organizations, professional school counselors have learned to speak as advocates with one voice toward ensuring that all students have equal access to quality education and that, in reality, no child is left behind.

(Note: See the CD-ROM for a list of references.)

CHAPTER 4

OUTCOMES RESEARCH
ON SCHOOL COUNSELING

Bradley T. Erford and Lacey L. Wallace

Preview

A continuing trend in mental health and education is a push for evidence-based practice and accountability. Professional school counselors have limited outcome research available for practice, which presents both a challenge and an opportunity. We offer a summary of current outcome research in school counseling as well as implications and recommendations for practicing professional school counselors.

The school counseling profession has seen a great deal of reform in the last decade. Comprehensive school counseling programs (Gysbers & Henderson, 2005) have helped to organize and professionalize the services that professional school counselors provide, while the American School Counselor Association's (ASCA) national standards have prescribed types of student outcomes school counseling programs should produce (Dahir, 2001). More recently, the "Transforming School Counseling Initiative" has suggested a stronger focus on academic achievement and increased leadership and advocacy roles (Sears, 1999). The emergence of the ASCA national model (ASCA; 2005) builds on these previous efforts and consolidates a comprehensive system of advocacy, collaboration, systemic change, and leadership towards the ASCA national standards. *Accountability*, a familiar word to all school personnel, is a core part of the new ASCA national model. The accountability theme endorses program evaluation, appropriate performance evaluation, and results reports. Within the recommended results reports, effectiveness data for immediate, intermediate, and long-range results serve as tools for advocacy for students and school counseling programs.

In addition to school counseling, research and professional trends in psychotherapy and education have also focused more attention on effectiveness and results. Using rigorous scientific methodology, empirically validated treatments (interventions proven to be effective) are promoted for psychotherapy and, at times, are the only accepted treatments for managed care. At the same time, the field of education is focused on accountability. While the process or means of determining academic accountability has been debated, the demand for results is inescapable. Many teachers and schools are now measured by student performance on state mandated standardized achievement tests. In fact, in many states, funding and teacher incentives are tied to the outcomes on student tests.

As teachers and schools are measured by client or student outcomes, so are professional school counselors. In 1993, Fairchild found that 67% of professional school counselors were involved in some type of accountability effort. They must increasingly describe their contributions to student achievement and validate their time spent with students. This push for counseling science or school accountability requires professional

---

Patrick Akos authored a previous version of this chapter in the first edition of this book.

school counselors to measure and determine the effectiveness or outcomes of interventions. Along with the responsibility for accountability comes an ethical duty of making informed decisions about interventions (Lambert, 1991). Professional responsibility and the direction of education and counseling reform beg an important yet difficult question: What school counseling services or interventions work to create desired student outcomes? We provide a brief summary of the outcome research, put the findings in perspective, and suggest several implications for professional school counselors.

Major Findings in School Counseling Outcome Research

In general, research has demonstrated that psychotherapy with children and adolescents is effective (Kazdin, 1993). Although school counseling has less empirical evidence to support practice, as compared to other types of counseling, several meta-analytic reviews of the outcomes research in school counseling have suggested moderate to positive results (Baker, Swisher, Nadenichek, & Popowicz, 1984; Nearpass, 1990; Prout & DeMartino, 1986; Prout & Prout, 1998; Sprinthall, 1981). Qualitative reviews of school counseling have generally shown positive affects (Borders & Drury, 1992; Whiston & Sexton, 1998), specifically for low-achieving students (Wilson, 1986), elementary school students (Gerler, 1985), and middle school students (St. Clair, 1989).

Reviews of school counseling can also be made quantitatively through meta-analyses, a technique that allows empirical studies to be examined across a quantitative index that provides meaning (Erford, 2007). This quantitative index is known as the *effect size* (ES). Cohen (1988) specified an effect size of 0 to signify no effect from the treatment, an effect size of .20 signifying a small effect, an effect size of .50 to signify a medium effect, and an effect size of .80 or higher to signify a large effect from the treatment. The calculation of the Pearson r is another way of expressing effect sizes in correlational research (Erford, 2007). In this case, an effect size of $r = .10$ is small, .30 is medium, and .50 is large. Among the many formulas for effect size estimates, these are the two principal statistics found in the literature. Effect sizes for empirical studies testing differences between treatment and control conditions are interpreted as the number of standard deviations a given treatment mean score lies above or below the mean score of the control group. Meta-analysis has been employed in counseling and educational research because of its meaningful, generalizable characteristics, allowing summarization of results across a number of studies at once (Ioannidis, Cappelleri, & Lau, 1998; Shadish, 1996; Sharpe, 1997; Sohn, 1997). Research reviews are particularly helpful in evaluating the multitude of duties performed by professional school counselors (Whiston, 2007). Considering the content areas in the ASCA national model, evidence exists to show that professional school counselors have been effective in promoting career, personal–social, and academic development in students.

CAREER DEVELOPMENT

Career development, it seems, has the greatest amount of outcome or effectiveness evidence. Two meta-analytic reviews concluded that career counseling interventions had large effect sizes of .85 and .82 (Oliver & Spokane, 1988; Spokane & Oliver, 1983), respectively. Both meta-analyses (Whiston & Sexton, 1998) and narrative reviews (Palmer

& Cochran, 1988) have supported the effectiveness of career interventions, especially through individual planning. Individual student planning involves professional school counselors coordinating continuous systemic activities to aid students in deciding on personal goals and evolving plans for the future (ASCA; 2005). The overall weighted effect size for 10 studies that addressed individual planning, with the majority of the studies involving high school students, was statistically significant (ES = .27).

Two meta-analyses conducted by Oliver and Spokane (1988) and Whiston, Sexton, and Lasoff (1998) indicated the most effective methods of delivering career counseling services were through individual career counseling or classroom guidance. Programs that employed computer-based career guidance programs or career sources from the Internet lacked the guidance of a professional school counselor and were not as effective (Whiston, Brecheisen, & Stephens, 2003). However, students did gain from the use of these computerized guidance programs when a counselor integrated other activities into the program.

Students also benefited from parent consultation about career development. Kush and Cochran (1993) and Palmer and Cochran (1988) found that adolescents' career development was positively affected by teaching parents methods for helping their children in their chosen career path. There is evidence that both parents and students would like more emphasis on career guidance and development activities (Scruggs, Wasielewski, & Ash, 1999).

Gysbers (1988) described various benefits of classroom guidance in outcomes related to developing career goals, college attendance, and career-planning skills. The outcome research also revealed that career services have been useful to a variety of students, including ethnic minorities, the academically gifted, and students with disabilities (Sexton, Whiston, Bleuer, & Walz, 1997).

In addition to the mode of career counseling interventions, students' age was also a factor contributing to career counseling success (Sexton et al., 1997). Oliver and Spokane (1988) concluded that career counseling was effective for college students but even more effective for junior high and high school students. For middle school and junior high students, the effect size for individual planning activities was 1.01, which indicates the importance and effectiveness of individual planning activities for those students in middle or junior high school (Whiston, Eder, Rahardja, & Tai, 2005). In general, professional school counselors can be assured that career development activities are effective (Whiston, 2007).

PERSONAL–SOCIAL DEVELOPMENT

In terms of personal–social development, group counseling was found to be effective in helping elementary students adjust to family difficulties (Whiston & Sexton, 1998). Social skills training also helped many students. Borders and Drury (1992) suggested that attitudes and behavior toward the students' school improved among students who had undergone counseling services. They also found that small-group counseling helped improve students' attendance, classroom behaviors, self-esteem, self-concept, and attitudes towards themselves and others.

Additional studies showed classroom guidance activities were effective in improving school behavior, attitudes toward school, attendance, and coping skills (Bundy &

Boser, 1987; Gerler & Anderson, 1986; Myrick, Merhill, & Swanson, 1986). Students who have access to school counseling programs reported greater feelings of fitting in and safety in their schools (Lapan, Gysbers, & Sun, 1997). These outcomes for personal–social development were found to generalize across widely varying groups of students (e.g., across age, race).

ACADEMIC DEVELOPMENT

Guidance activities promoted self-esteem and exhibited trends of positive influence on academic achievement (Whiston & Sexton, 1998; Wilson, 1986). Borders and Drury (1992) suggested that students who received counseling services also had improved academic performance, although this qualitative review had methodological limitations.

A causal comparative study was conducted by Sink and Stroh (2003) to determine if the implementation of a comprehensive developmental guidance program produced higher achievement scores in students. The results were inconclusive, although it was clear that elementary students who were enrolled in the same school for 3 years or longer performed better academically, whether or not the school counseling program was fully implemented.

Another study conducted by Gerler and Herndon (1993) also focused on student academic achievement. After a 10-session guidance curriculum was implemented, students were more aware of how to succeed in school. A replication of this study by Lee (1993) used the same guidance curriculum but split the participants into treatment and control groups. Students who participated in the 10-session guidance curriculum performed significantly higher on posttest math scores than did students who did not participate in the guidance curriculum.

CHARACTERISTICS OF EFFECTIVE SCHOOL COUNSELING

Research suggested that a variety of factors affect school counseling outcomes. Lambert (1986) found that common factors were evident across counseling approaches that were responsible for about 30% of client improvement. Students' characteristics can affect outcomes; for example, outcomes vary depending on level of education (elementary, middle, high) (Nearpass, 1990; Prout & DeMartino, 1986; Prout & Prout, 1998), although it was clear that the least amount of research exists for middle school counseling (St. Clair, 1989; Whiston & Sexton, 1998). Programs that required students to participate in counseling services often were less successful than programs that allowed students to volunteer participation (Wilson, 1986). In addition, while some research suggested that student factors like gender, age, socioeconomic status, parental marital status, academic variables, and referral status (self vs. other) affect outcomes, other research suggested that a variety of demographic and school factors were unrelated to counseling outcomes (Hagborg, 1993).

Students of all ages showed improvements as a result of the implementation of a school counseling program. However, certain age levels were differentially affected. Whiston et al. (2005) found an effect size of .25 for elementary students who were exposed to a school counseling intervention, .39 for middle school students, and .34 for high school students. Prout and DeMartino (1986) suggested that older students benefited more from school counseling interventions than did younger students. Even older high school students, such as 11th and 12th graders, were impacted more by the interventions than were 9th- and 10th-grade high school students. Prout and DeMartino conducted another study in 1998 which, in contrast, concluded that elementary school students achieved the greatest gains. Elementary students showed improved affective, behavioral, and interpersonal development as a result of school counseling programs (Gerler, 1985).

The least amount of research regarding effective school counseling has been conducted on middle school students (St. Clair, 1989; Whiston & Sexton, 1998), but the results are consistent with other age groups. In one study, behavior management, daily progress reports, and self-relaxation techniques were found to be beneficial to middle school students who were exposed to a school counseling program (St. Clair, 1989).

Ethnicity was not a significant factor in successful counseling; however, student–counselor ethnic similarity was shown to affect dropout rates (Sexton et al., 1997). Therefore, if outcome is measured by dropout rate, ethnic similarity may be important.

Certain professional characteristics also had an impact on counseling outcome. Qualitative reviews found no relationship between training or experience and outcomes of counseling (Auerbach & Johnson, 1977; Beutler, Crago, & Arizmendi, 1986; Christenson & Jacobson, 1993), while some meta-analytic reviews provided mixed results (Sexton et al., 1997). One meta-analytic study found no relationship between experience and client outcome but did find higher rates of success for counselors who had been professionally trained, regardless of experience (Stein & Lambert, 1995).

Therapeutic skills have not always increased with the length of training or experience (Beutler, Machado, & Neufeldt, 1994; Dobson, 1989). Treatment manuals have been integrated into professional practice to enhance standardization of treatment and equalize counselor skill (Erford, 2007). Treatment manuals use a research-based, standardized treatment approach and have been shown to enhance treatment outcome. However, Robinson, Berman, and Neimeyer (1990) determined that the use of treatment manuals was no more effective than counseling without treatment manuals.

Personal characteristics of the counselor, such as self-confidence and adjustment level, were significantly related to outcome (Lambert & Bergin, 1983; Sexton & Whiston, 1991). For professional counselors undergoing therapy, there was only a slight relationship with their clients' treatment outcomes (Sexton et al., 1997). However, reasons for professional counselors seeking therapy in these studies may have led to extraneous error; that is, it was not clear whether the counselors in the studies sought counseling for therapeutic and personal insight or because of personal problems.

The therapeutic alliance also may have some effect on counseling outcomes. The American Psychological Association Division 29 Psychotherapy Task Force (Steering Committee, 2002) identified seven therapeutic alliance characteristics that appeared to enhance effectiveness. These included positive regard, genuineness, self-disclosure, repairing alliance breaks, quality of interpretations, management of countertransference by the counselor, and feedback.

Additionally, counselors in highly effective school counseling programs spent more than 70% of their time in direct services, such as individual and group counseling, rather than other unrelated, clerical activities (Wiggins & Moody, 1987). The school counseling programs that were rated as below average were not organized, and these professional school counselors were not as knowledgeable about conducting needs assessments and applying the results to their counseling programs.

CLASSROOM GUIDANCE

Classroom guidance is designed to address all students in a developmentally appropriate manner. Guidance curriculum activities form the core of the school counseling program. According to Whiston (2007), students who attended a school in which a guidance curriculum was implemented scored about one third of a standard deviation above those who did not receive classroom guidance activities. Middle school students benefited the most from classroom guidance activities, with an effect size of .41. High school students were not far behind, with an effect size of .39, while elementary students yielded an effect size of .29.

Some research found that classroom guidance activities can be successfully combined into an academic curriculum with middle and high school students (Hughey, Lapan, & Gysbers, 1993). Collaboration between classroom teachers and professional school counselors to implement a combined language arts and career guidance unit was successful in giving students the opportunity to develop academic proficiency and explore career topics. While some outcome studies have found positive outcomes for classroom guidance, the research is very limited (Whiston, 2007).

GROUP COUNSELING

Research shows that certain methods of interventions were more frequently researched or had more positive outcomes than other methods of intervention. Although it is not conclusive, it seems that outcome research has examined and supported group counseling as much or more as it has individual counseling. Wilson (1986) concluded that group counseling was more effective than individual counseling in improving academic achievement for low-achieving students. One study addressing failing elementary students concluded that 83% of the students placed in small-group counseling experienced improvement in grades (Boutwell & Myrick, 1992). Social skills training and discipline problems were most effectively treated through group counseling (Whiston & Sexton, 1998). Students showed short- and long-term positive effects after participating in parental divorce groups (Omizo & Omizo, 1988; Pedro-Carroll & Alpert-Gillis, 1997; Pedro-Carroll, Sutton, & Wyman, 1999).

Cognitive-behavioral group counseling has effectively increased high school students' self-esteem and academic self-concept (Bauer, Sapp, & Johnson, 2000; Nelson & Dykeman, 1996; Shechtman, 1993). Racial attitudes of elementary school students also were positively influenced through small-group counseling sessions (Reeder, Douzenis, & Bergin, 1997). Other group counseling studies (a) demonstrated improved self-concept among children of alcoholics, (b) reduced at-risk behaviors among adolescent girls, and (c) reduced aggressive and hostile behavior among elementary students involved in a social skills training group (Riddle, Bergin, & Douzenis, 1997; Whiston & Sexton, 1998; Zinck & Littrell, 2000). Confirmation of the effectiveness of group counseling was largely provided for younger students; the effects on older students need to be studied further (Whiston, 2007).

INDIVIDUAL COUNSELING

In some instances, individual counseling was found to be more effective than group counseling with school-aged students (Nearpass, 1990). Also, counselors who primarily used individual counseling were more effective than counselors who used primarily classroom guidance in achieving positive student outcomes, although methodological problems existed within the study (Wiggins & Wiggins, 1992).

For example, an individual dropout prevention program, comprised of tutoring and counseling, significantly improved school success, confidence, and classroom behavior in at-risk students (Edmonson & White, 1998). Individual counseling did not have to be long term to be effective. Brief individual counseling can be just as effective as long-term counseling. For example, three approaches to brief counseling that address emotional adjustment of high school students were implemented by Littrell, Malia, and Vanderwood (1995). Participants in any of the three conditions reduced worries and were motivated to move closer to their goals.

Behavioral approaches in individual counseling were most effective when addressing aggressive behavior (Wilson, Lipsey, & Derzon, 2003), and Lavoritano and Segal (1992) found that misbehavior decreased as individual counseling progressed.

PEER MEDIATION

Popularity of conflict resolution programs has increased during recent years. During the early 1990s, peer mediation programs increased in schools by about 40% (Sheperd, 1994). Whiston et al. (2005) discovered that peer mediation interventions had an effect size of .39, but Wilson et al. (2003) found that peer mediation programs had little influence on aggressive behavior. Questions about leadership roles and training for these programs have also risen (Lewis & Lewis, 1996). Gerber and Terry-Day (1999) disputed the amount of empirical evidence to support the popularity of peer mediation programs. More research is necessary before any conclusions can be made about the effectiveness of peer mediation programs.

CONSULTATION OR COLLABORATION

Professional school counselors consult with teachers, parents, and other educators, and by collaborating with these stakeholders, they can implement systemic and programmatic changes in schools and communities to prevent students from dropping out of school. Growing empirical evidence suggests that consultation was effective as a method of resolving problems (Murphy, 1999; Zins, 1993). Elementary school students' behaviors were affected by consultation between teachers and counselors (Gerler, 1985). Borders and Drury (1992) found that consultation was effective for both elementary and middle school students, and, as a result of a counselor's consultation workshop, more students were referred to counseling (Otwell & Mullis, 1997).

Skillful demonstrations by professional school counselors determined the effectiveness of consultation. Gresham and Kendell (1987) concluded that problem identification was the most important factor within the consultation process. If counselors directly trained consultees in problem solving, communication, and intervention techniques, consultation between counselors, parents, and teachers were more successful (Zins, 1993). When counselors modeled the problem-solving process for their consultees, consultation was also more effective. Furthermore, investigation of typical activities let by professional school counselors (e.g., peer mediation, family education, consultation) produced mixed findings, and conclusions were difficult to draw because of the variations in professional school counselor involvement and functioning.

Outcome Research in Perspective

Research on school counseling is based on probabilities, rather than assurances of effectiveness or prescriptive directions (Martin & Hoshmand, 1995), and most of the research is correlational, which does not suggest causality (Gelso, 1979). So, although research is available to support school counseling effectiveness, the research is neither vast nor methodologically strong.

In a comprehensive review of published school counseling literature from 1988 to 1995, Whiston and Sexton (1998) found no consistent type of outcome targeted, no consistent measure or instrument used, and most research focused on responsive services rather than on preventative or developmental activities. With only 22% of the studies incorporating experimental design and the majority focused on remediation, research has not consistently shown the effectiveness of school counseling services nor focused on the preventative or proactive nature of helping (Sexton et al., 1997). Whiston and Sexton's (1998) review suggested no clear trend in the research favoring one method over another (individual, group, classroom). Disturbingly, the review also suggested that the many flaws with the existing research limit confidence in results (e.g., lack of experimental design, convenience samples, nonstandard outcome measures). Even the psychotherapy literature was often based on laboratory research (Sexton, 1999). In fact, most of the research on children and adolescents was conducted in clinical or research settings (Kazdin, 1993).

Additionally, it is a challenge for practicing professional school counselors to keep up with outcome research articles as they appear in journals (Sexton, 1996). Often, results are difficult to decipher, and it is a challenge to find results pertinent to practice (Whiston, 2007). Furthermore, choosing interventions from a list often inhibits innovation, dehumanizes students, and puts too much attention on technique (Waehler, Kalodner, Wampold, & Lichtenberg, 2000). This approach of matching treatment or intervention to remedial need dismisses many influences important to professional school counselors, including diversity, career counseling, psychoeducational and developmental concerns, and prevention or proactive programs. Additionally, the counselor must have the knowledge and ability to assess presenting concerns and appropriately apply these treatments (Sexton, 1999).

IMPLICATIONS FOR PROFESSIONAL SCHOOL COUNSELORS

BE AN ACTIVE CONSUMER OF OUTCOME RESEARCH IN SCHOOL COUNSELING

Although reports of evidence-based interventions for professional school counselors are not conclusive, it is important to be an astute consumer and incorporate research into practice. Research has shown that some practices are more effective than others, and some client problems are helped most by specific counseling models (Sexton, 1999). Professional school counselors must examine a diverse set of published research in a variety of journals and read each study with caution. Therefore, professional school counselors must examine effectiveness research as one step in the decision-making process to determine an appropriate intervention.

KEEP GROUNDED IN CORE CONDITIONS OF EFFECTIVE HELPING

In reality, the great majority of what works will be determined by efforts related to, but distinct from, determining an appropriate intervention. Research has suggested that the specific psychological technique accounts for only 15% of the outcome (Lambert, 1991). Lambert suggested that 30% of the outcome in counseling is related to common factors evident in therapy, regardless of type of theory or intervention. These common factors include (a) the supportive value of a collaborative counseling relationship; (b) the value of learning (through affective experiencing, corrective emotional experiences, or skills acquisition); and (c) action (through behavior change, successful experiences, behavioral regulation, and mastery) (Sexton, 1999).

Professional school counselors improve the outcome of helping when they work with these common factors. For example, counselors often see challenging students who are referred by teachers or parents. Many counselors scour the research literature for a solution that uses the newest technique, but they often fail first to focus on and establish a collaborative counseling relationship. Research suggests that the type of counseling relationship that is established would dictate the student's value of learning from the counselor and the action taken. Historically, demographic factors, professional identity, and even experience have been thought to influence the effectiveness of the counselor; however, current evidence suggests that, when all things are equal, these three factors are unrelated to the counseling outcome (Sexton, 1999). Instead, counselors' skill level (competence), cognitive complexity (ability to think diversely and complexly about cases), and an ability to relate and relationally match with the clients are important to outcomes (Sexton, 1999).

Lambert (1991) further suggested that 15% of the counseling outcome depends on client expectations. Students view professional school counselors with varying levels of expectation for change. Again, students who are referred by others often have limited desires or expectations for change. Client expectations are shaped by the student's experience, background, and relationship with counselors, and professional school counselors are again challenged to create expectations for change when determining what works (much like how solution-focused counseling builds with the miracle question). Beyond the relationship and client expectations, various factors outside of the counseling dynamics influence outcomes.

In terms of counseling or therapy in general, Lambert (1991) proposed that 40% of outcomes in therapy are attributed to factors outside of the counseling relationship. For professional school counselors, two influential aspects include (a) the systems involved in student's lives and (b) the context or culture of the school and the student. An element that is perhaps unique to the professional school counselor's role (as compared to other types of counselors or therapists) is that professional school counselors often have access to and can influence many of the factors outside of the counseling session. In an ecological framework, this element is where a variety of helping services (e.g., consultation, collaboration, coordination, leadership, advocacy, parent education) may be influential to outcomes in school counseling.

CONSIDER MULTIPLE SYSTEMS, CULTURE, AND SCHOOL CONTEXT

Most of the published school counseling outcome studies examine a specific school or district sample, so it is important for professional school counselors to consider how to apply the research to their individual context and students. Schools are stratified context issues including, but not limited to, structural factors (e.g., urban or rural, public or private, academic grouping, disability services); instructional factors (e.g., teacher expectations, qualifications, behavioral management); and relational factors (e.g., peer rejection, peer influence, school or class social dynamics) (Farmer & Farmer, 1999). All of these factors influence the outcomes of a professional school counselor's efforts to help students. For example, the way a professional school counselor helps a student who has a learning disability and exhibits behavioral problems may be differentially effective, depending on whether the student is mainstreamed in the regular classroom or is in a self-contained classroom. In the same way, school climate may dictate the effectiveness of a peer helping program.

The multiple systems in a student's life can reinforce or inhibit professional school counselor practice. Students do not live in a laboratory, nor do they operate only in one type of school. Although scientific research on professional school counselor intervention does not always account for multiple influences inside and outside of the school, professional school counselors can use their understanding of the school context.

Consideration of the developmental forces in children and adolescents is essential to both the school context and the student culture. Students experience a great deal of developmental change that is independent of the professional school counselor intervention. For example, the participants' developmental level will greatly influence a professional school counselor's group intervention to promote healthy body image. Whereas a mixed gender group of elementary school students may focus on generalized self-esteem, a gender-specific middle school group may focus on the messages of popular culture to women and girls. Although both of these groups would be described as a group intervention for personal–social development, the outcomes will be greatly influenced by the developmental stages and needs of the students.

Even when multiple systems and contexts are considered in determining interventions that work, professional school counselors have a responsibility to serve all students in the school. Most of the research about effectiveness or best practices is centered on helping students who demonstrate problems. An effective professional school counselor, when selecting what works, should also consider the effectiveness of pro-active activities targeted toward normal or optimal development.

IMPLEMENT ACTION RESEARCH ON YOUR OWN DEVELOPMENTAL, PREVENTATIVE, AND PROACTIVE INTERVENTIONS

Where school counseling research leaves off, professional school counselors can re-search their own programs. Relevant, simple research designs may not immediately prove useful to the field of school counseling as a whole, but a wealth of information can be maintained by practicing professional school counselors about what works in their own schools. Systematically piecing together smaller studies can show effective school counseling services (Myrick, 1984).

One particularly useful research design includes *action research*. Action research is varied but is used for immediate local needs and applications rather than generaliza-tion of results (Allen, 1992). For example, a middle school counselor may choose to un-derstand what interventions help English as a second language (ESL) students feel con-nected and perform well academically in school. Determining a research design (e.g., comparison study), treatment or interventions (e.g., group vs. classroom guidance), data collection (e.g., connectedness measure, grades, test scores), and data analysis (e.g., *t* test between groups) may allow the professional school counselor to make an informed choice about providing services to ESL students. Collaborative designs with others (i.e., professional school counselor educators, educational or psychology professionals inside and outside of the school) also hold great promise. Many school–university partnerships produce fruitful research and provide both professional school counselors and univer-sity faculty a means for professional development.

Summary/Conclusion

Several authors (Allen, 1992; Deck, Cecil, & Cobia, 1990) have suggested that profes-sional school counselors have little interest in the research or science of school counsel-ing, or they see it as beyond their responsibility. Although reforms and national models are useful, professional school counselors cannot establish or maintain an important role in the school without science to validate their presence. At the extreme, several states and districts may have already cut school counseling positions because they are viewed as ancillary services.

"The outcome-based knowledge is currently not, and may never be, refined to the point that it will dictate specific treatments for an individual client" (Sexton, 1996, p. 598). There is no study that dictates how professional school counselors can best help students. Determining what works needs to be contextualized within the student, professional school counselor, school, family, and community framework. Selecting what works is also highly dependent on student needs. Making choices on what works will involve a combination of knowledge and use of current research, a commitment to actively researching what works, and continuing to be an inner-critic to choice of interventions.

(Note: See the CD-ROM for a list of references.)

CHAPTER 5

CODES OF ETHICS AND ETHICAL AND LEGAL CONSIDERATIONS FOR STUDENTS, PARENTS, AND PROFESSIONAL SCHOOL COUNSELORS

Lynn E. Linde and Carolyn Stone

Preview

One of the hardest challenges facing all counselors today, and particularly professional school counselors, is how to determine the best and most appropriate way of working with students who present myriad complex problems. While federal and state laws apply in some situations, many of the issues with which counselors deal fall into a gray zone: There is no clear guideline for handling the situation. Fortunately, the American Counseling Association (ACA; 2005), the American School Counselor Association (ASCA; 2004), and the National Board for Certified Counselors (NBCC; 2005) have developed codes of ethics that provide guidelines for ethical behavior. Each section of these codes applies to different situations that counselors face. We also discuss the rights and responsibilities of minors and their parents and the implications of these rights on the professional school counselor's work. Ethical codes, federal statutes, state laws, and court cases that involve student and parental rights are examined. Furthermore, we address complications that professional school counselors encounter as they work to protect students' rights while remaining aware that their obligations extend beyond the minor student to the student's parents.

Whenever supervisors for school counseling programs or professional counselor associations survey members regarding topics for professional development, ethics and legal issues always rank at or near the top of the list. Schools and school systems are no longer immune from the litigious society in which they operate. Parents are fast to complain and hire lawyers when they feel that their rights have been violated or when they question the way in which the school or a staff member has handled a situation. Professional school counselors often feel overwhelmed by the variety of problems that students present each day, and they struggle to find the best legal or ethical way to work with students and strive continually to balance the needs of the students with the needs of the school or family.

The legal and ethical complexities of working with minors in schools require that professional school counselors remain vigilant about the rights and responsibilities of minors and their parents and the implications of these rights on the counselor's work. A school's legal and ethical landscape is complicated, because a professional school counselor's obligation extends beyond the minor student to the parents, who have considerable rights. Private and agency counselors who work with minors usually do so because parents seek their help. Students are sent to school for academics, so the dynamics are quite different when they show up at the professional school counselor's door through a teacher's suggestion or self-referral. A professional school counselor's multiplicity of responsibility to parents, students, administrators, teachers, and others in a setting designed to deliver academic instruction complicates the legal and ethical world of school counseling (Alexander & Alexander, 2005; Imber & Van Geel, 2004; Linde, 2007; Remley & Herlihy, 2005; Stone, 2004).

The very nature and function of school (i.e., to provide a free and appropriate quality education) creates immediate conflict when a student seeks a professional school counselor's help for emotional or social needs. When a student approaches a professional school counselor without his or her parent's knowledge or consent, immediate tension arises between the student's right to privacy and the parents' right to be the guiding voice in their child's life. Generally, the younger the child, the more rights are vested in the parents. The conflict between a parent's right to be informed about what is happening in the child's personal life and the child's need and right to privacy is a decided challenge for professional school counselors who are charged with protecting the rights of both students and parents (Alexander & Alexander, 2005; Imber & Van Geel, 2004; Linde, 2007; Remley & Herlihy, 2005; Stone, 2004).

We examine some of the ethical codes, federal statutes, laws, and court cases that involve student and parental rights and this chapter should be augmented by texts that address the legal rights of students and parents and the ethical behavior of professional school counselors. (See Remley and Herlihy, 2005, and Alexander and Alexander, 2005, among others, for a more thorough review of legal and ethical issues.) Professional school counselors are encouraged to attend legal and ethical workshops and university courses to increase their comfort level and competence in student and parental rights. Consulting with other professionals and seeking guidance is paramount when addressing issues of student and parental rights.

Some, but not all, situations are clearly defined by federal or state law or by local policy. Local boards of education are hesitant to pass policies or procedures for controversial issues, and it is likely if they *did* create such policies, they might significantly limit the ability of professional school counselors to operate without informing parents about everything. Fortunately, the professional associations for counselors have developed codes of ethics and standards that provide a framework for professional conduct. To understand the applicability of the codes of ethics to professional school counselors, it is helpful to understand something about the organizations that create the codes.

PROFESSIONAL COUNSELING ASSOCIATIONS

The American Counseling Association is the professional association for all counselors. The mission of the association is to promote public confidence and trust in the counseling profession. Organizationally, ACA is a partnership of associations representing professional counselors who enhance human development. It is composed of 19 divisions that represent specific work settings or interest areas within the field of counseling, and 56 state or affiliate branches that are divided into four regions representing major geographical areas. Through its activities and entities, ACA influences all aspects of professional counseling. These areas include the credentialing of counselors and the accreditation of counselor education programs, developing and promulgating ethical standards, offering professional development, offering professional resources and services, and influencing public policy and legislation.

ACA has 15 active standing committees that address much of the professional business of the association. One of those committees, the Ethics Committee, is responsible for updating the association's ethical standards and investigating and adjudicating ethical complaints. Counselors must sign a statement agreeing to abide by the Code of Ethics when they join ACA. Additional information about ethics, ethical issues, and professional behavior is available through a number of services and resources offered by the association. ACA and its entities offer a variety of training and professional development opportunities, some of which are offered at state, regional, and national conferences; others are workshops and learning institutes, which are offered throughout the year.

The journals published by ACA and its divisions provide current research, professional practices, and other information valuable to the practicing counselor. Articles and information about professional behavior is frequently covered in these sources. ACA's monthly newsletter, *Counseling Today*, includes valuable information about general counseling topics as well as covering special topical issues. ACA publishes many books about counseling that cover current trends and topics in the field and which are frequently used as texts in counseling courses. One example is the sixth edition of the *ACA Ethical Standards Casebook*, by Herlihy and Corey (2006). This is a valuable resource for all professional counselors and is an excellent addition to the 2005 ACA Code of Ethics. ACA staff is available for consultation on a variety of issues, including legal and ethical questions. In summary, ACA touches all counselors' lives, from the training they receive, the requirements they must achieve to be credentialed, the way in which they conduct themselves across all counseling specialty areas, and the professional development in which they engage. More information about the American Counseling Association is available on their Web site (http://www.counseling.org).

The American School Counselor Association (ASCA) became a division of ACA in 1953. During the past decade, it has become a more autonomous organization, but it still remains a division. ASCA supports professional school counselors' focus on the academic, personal–social, and career development of all students. According to ASCA (2004), its members assist in the growth and development of each student and "uses his/her highly specialized skills to protect the interests of the counselee within the structure of the school setting" (p. 1). ASCA focuses its efforts on professional development, publications and other resources, research, and advocacy for school counseling.

The structure of ASCA is similar to that of ACA. ASCA has a number of committees, one of which is the Ethics Committee, which is responsible for the development of the Ethical Standards for School Counselors, the code of ethics for professional school counselors that will be discussed in the next section. ASCA sponsors a national conference and offers a number of professional development activities for professional school counselors. One of the topics covered at some of these events concerns ethics and professional behavior. More information about the American School Counselor Association is available on their Web site (http://www.schoolcounselor.org).

The National Board for Certified Counselors (NBCC) began as a corporate partner of ACA and is now an autonomous organization. While the link between ACA and NBCC remains strong, it was necessary to separate the certifying entity from ACA to eliminate any potential conflicts of interest. Headquartered in Greensboro, North Carolina, NBCC is the only national credentialing organization for professional counselors. All other licenses and certifications for counselors are obtained through state agencies and local organizations. NBCC has established the National Certified Counselor (NCC) credential and several specialty-area certifications. Counselors must pass the National Counselor Exam (NCE) as part of the process to become nationally certified. Many states use the NCE as the exam required for professional counselor licensure or certification; in some states, counselors may be eligible for certification by the state board of education if they are an NCC. The NBCC has also developed a code of ethics that must be followed by counselors who hold this certification. More information about this association and certification is available on their Web site (http://www.nbcc.org).

Purposes of Ethical Standards

Both laws and ethical standards are based on generally accepted societal norms, beliefs, and customs (Fischer & Sorenson, 1996). However, laws are more prescriptive and carry penalties for noncompliance. Laws "dictate the *minimal* standards of behavior that society will tolerate, whereas ethics represent the *ideal* standards expected by the profession" (Remley & Herlihy, 2005, p. 3). Ethical standards are usually developed by professional associations to guide the behavior of their specific group of professionals. Ethical standards are usually divided into two types: mandatory ethics and aspirational ethics. A counselor who adheres to mandatory ethics is following the "musts" of the profession. Counselors who practice aspirational ethics follow the "oughts" of the profession; they must adhere to the highest standards and think about the impact of their actions. Herlihy and Corey (2006) suggested that for a counselor to practice aspirational ethics, the counselor must understand the underlying intent and principles of the ethical standards.

The ACA's (2005) Code of Ethics is based on five general moral principles (Herlihy & Corey, 2006) that guide counselors' behavior. *Autonomy* refers to the clients' ability to choose and make decisions about their behavior and choices for themselves. *Nonmalfeasance* means to do no harm. Counselors always need to ensure that they operate in ways that neither result in harm nor potentially result in harm. *Beneficence* means to always promote that which serves the growth and good of their clients. *Justice* refers to fairness in counselors' relationships and includes fair treatment and consideration of clients. The last principle is *fidelity*, which refers to honesty in the counselor–client relationship, honoring one's commitment to the client, and establishing an accepting relationship.

Within ACA and its divisions, there are multiple codes of ethics. ACA (2005) has the Code of Ethics to which members must adhere. Several divisions, specifically the American School Counselor Association, the American Rehabilitation Counseling Association (ARCA), The American Mental Health Counselors Association (AMHCA), The National Career Development Association (NCDA), and the International Association for Marriage and Family Counseling (IAMFC) have their own codes. The Association for Specialists in Group Work (ASGW) has developed Best Practice Guidelines to supplement ACA's Code of Ethics. These codes of ethics parallel the ACA Code of Ethics but speak more directly to practice within the specialty area. For example, ASCA's (2004) Code of Ethics discusses what ethical behavior consists of in a school setting, and the ASGW (2007) Best Practice Guidelines address ethical behavior when conducting groups.

Many counselors belong to multiple organizations, some of which have their own code of ethics. Professional counselors may also hold credentials from organizations or state credentialing boards that either have their own code of ethics or require that a particular code of ethics be followed. It is sometimes confusing and difficult to discern which code takes precedence. While all professional counselors need to make that decision for themselves, there are two general guiding principles: First, in what type of setting is the professional counselor practicing, and is there a designated code that applies or that is required for that setting? Second, what is the professional counselor position in that setting? In reality, all codes of ethics are very similar, are based on the same general principles, and serve the same general functions.

All codes of ethics concern behaving in an appropriate and professional manner; always functioning in the best interests of the client or student; and always practicing within the scope of one's education, training and experience. Counselors who behave ethically should not be concerned about multiple codes of ethics. Codes of ethics serve another important function: They protect and educate the public about the standards of behavior they should expect from counselors.

ACA's 2005 Code of Ethics

The ACA 2005 Code of Ethics delineates the responsibilities of professional counselors toward clients, colleagues, workplaces, and themselves by describing the ideal standards for counselors' behavior. All ACA members are required to abide by the 2005 Code of Ethics. Any violation of ethical behavior will result in action taken against the member. The ACA cannot take much action against professional counselors who are not members; however, as these are the standards of the profession, all professional counselors are held to them, regardless of their professional association membership status. Failure to be familiar with, use, or comprehend the 2005 Code of Ethics is not a legally valid excuse for unethical or inappropriate behavior. In the absence of any law or written policy or procedure, courts will use the 2005 Code of Ethics as the standard for all professional counselors.

ACA states that the 2005 Code of Ethics serves five main purposes:

1) The *Code* enabled the association to clarify to current and future members, and to those served by members, the nature of the ethical responsibilities held in common by its members; 2) The *Code* helps support the mission of the association; 3) The *Code* established the principles that define ethical behavior and best practices of association members; 4) The *Code* serves as an ethical guide designed to assist members in constructing a professional course of action that best serves those utilizing counseling services and best promotes the values of the counseling profession; and 5) The *Code* serves as the basis for processing of

ethical complaints and inquiries initiated against members of the association. (ACA; 2005, p. 4)

The 2005 Code of Ethics addresses the responsibilities of professional counselors toward their clients, workplace and colleagues, and themselves. It is divided into eight areas:

- *Section A: The Counseling Relationship* covers all areas related to the nature of the relationship with the clients. It includes the subtopics of client welfare, client rights, clients served by others, personal needs and values, beneficial and harmful relationships with clients, sexual intimacies with clients or their family members, multiple clients, group work, fees and bartering, termination and referral, end-of-life issues, and use of technology in counseling. The Ethical Standards for Internet Online Counseling, which were adopted by ACA in 1999, were incorporated into this section as part of the 2005 revision process. In general, counselors must always put the best interests of their clients first and ensure that clients understand the extent and limitations of counseling.
- *Section B: Confidentiality, Privileged Communication, and Privacy* covers all areas related to the confidentiality rights of the client or clients and discusses the limits to confidentiality. It includes the subtopics of right to privacy, groups and families, minor or incompetent clients, records, research and training, and consultation. This section now also addresses the confidentiality rights of deceased clients and discusses the issues of confidentiality when counseling families.
- *Section C: Professional Responsibility* covers counselors' responsibilities toward their clients, themselves, other professionals, and the public. It includes the subtopics of standards of knowledge, professional competence, advertising and soliciting clients, credentials, public responsibility, and responsibility to other professionals. This section also addresses counselor impairment and the transfer of records and clients in the event of the death of a counselor and discusses the counselor's responsibility to use a scientific basis for treatment.
- *Section D: Relationships With Other Professionals* covers work setting issues and includes the subtopics of relationships with employers and employees, consultation, fees for referrals, and subcontractor arrangements and issues related to interdisciplinary treatment teams and the way in which they should function.
- *Section E: Evaluation, Assessment, and Interpretation* covers standards related to the assessment of clients, the counselor's skills, and appropriateness of assessment. It includes the subtopics of general appraisal issues, competence to use and interpret tests, informed consent for appraisal, releasing information, proper diagnosis of mental disorders, test selection, conditions of test administration, diversity in testing, test scoring and interpretation, test security, obsolete tests and outdated test results, test construction, and forensic evaluations.
- *Section F: Supervision, Training, and Teaching* covers issues related to training counselors and counselor education programs. It covers the subtopics of counselor educators and trainers, counselor education and training programs, and students and supervisees.

- *Section G: Research and Publication* covers issues related to the ethical treatment of participants and ethical research procedures. Subtopics include research responsibilities, informed consent, reporting results, and publication.
- *Section H: Resolving Ethical Issues* covers the procedure professional counselors should follow when they suspect another counselor of unethical behavior. Subtopics include knowledge of standards, suspected violations, and cooperation with the ethics committee.

The 2005 ACA Code of Ethics reflects some significant changes from the 1995 Code. The Standards of Practice, which were part of the 1995 Code of Ethics, have been incorporated into the current code. Each of the eight sections is now prefaced by an introduction to that section which sets the tone for the section. Additionally, multicultural and diversity issues are infused into the code as opposed to a stand-alone section. The 2005 Code addressed end-of-life issues, the increased use of technology in counseling, and added a glossary of terms. More information is available about the 2005 Code of Ethics and other ethics resources on the ACA Web site (http://www.counseling.org/Resources/CodeofEthics/TP/Home/CT2.aspx).

ASCA ETHICAL STANDARDS FOR SCHOOL COUNSELORS

The American School Counselor Association has developed a parallel set of ethical standards that specifically address professional school counseling. The ASCA (2004) Code of Ethics and Standards of Practice for professional school counselors is an attempt by the profession to standardize professional practice for the purpose of protecting students, parents, and the professional school counselor. ASCA's ethical standards are a guide to help meet the needs of individual situations, but they are rarely appropriate for rote application, because it is the context of the dilemma that determines appropriate action.

It is only the professional school counselor, in consultation with other professionals, who can determine how to apply an ASCA ethical code to further the best interest of the student: "Codes are not intended to be a blueprint that removes the need for judgment and ethical reasoning" (Welfel & Lipsitz, 1983, p. 6). A summary of each of the eight sections follows.

- *Section A: Responsibilities to Students* covers the professional school counselor's responsibilities to treat each student as a unique individual; maintain confidentiality as appropriate in the relationship; develop counseling plans; make appropriate referrals; use appropriate evaluation and assessment techniques, information, and technology; and ensure the welfare of students in peer helper programs.

    Confidentiality for students is an area that is tough to negotiate while protecting both student and parental rights. Confidentiality is a cornerstone of individual counseling and facilitates a trusting relationship between students and professional school counselors. The ASCA code promotes the philosophy that professional school counselors have a primary obligation and loyalty to students. However, confidentiality is far from absolute for minors in a school setting. Parental rights must also be considered in any value-laden work, such as individual counseling, that a professional school counselor does with a student. Parents are continually vested by our courts with legal rights to be the guiding voice in their children's lives (Bellotti v. Baird, 1979; H. L. v. Matheson, 1982).

- *Section B: Responsibilities to Parents* covers parents' rights and responsibilities regarding the professional school counselor's behavior and confidentiality.
- *Section C: Responsibilities to Colleagues and Professional Associates* covers relationships with other professionals, including sharing information.
- *Section D: Responsibilities to the School and Community* covers the professional school counselor's responsibility to identify any situations in the work that may be adverse for students, work only in settings for which he or she is qualified, assist with developing programs to meet students' needs, and work with outside groups and agencies.
- *Section E: Professional Competence* covers the professional school counselors' responsibility for maintaining their professional growth and multicultural skills and monitoring their effectiveness.
- *Section F: Responsibilities to the Profession* covers ethical behavior and involvement with professional associations.
- *Section G: Maintenance of Standards* covers the process for dealing with concerns about potential ethical violations.
- *Section H: Resources* lists a number of resources for professional school counselors to increase their knowledge and information.

Codes give professional school counselors guidance in their ethical responsibility to students and parents, but they do not propose or attempt to provide complete answers. Ethics are situational and have to be considered in the context of institutional and community standards, school-board policy, and the circumstances surrounding each ethical dilemma. It is ultimately the responsibility of the professional school counselor to determine the appropriate response for individual students who put their trust in the security of the counseling relationship (Stone, 2004).

Professional school counselors frequently ask what should be done when laws and ethical standards appear to be in conflict. Both laws and ethics are based on the same standards generally accepted by society, but laws are written into statute and therefore carry sanctions for failure to follow them. Usually, the most significant penalty an association can impose on a professional counselor is to revoke membership. Both laws and ethical standards are created to protect the public or society by outlining behavioral expectations for the practitioners. When laws and ethical standards conflict with each other, the professional counselor must attempt to resolve the issue. Because penalties are associated with lawbreaking, professional school counselors will generally choose the legal course of action, provided it does not harm the client. Ethical standards recognize that laws, policies, and procedures must be followed and recommend that professional school counselors advocate changes to any requirements that are not in the best interests of their clients.

STUDENTS' RIGHTS AND RESPONSIBILITIES

The legal status of minors is complicated. Salo and Shumate (1993) discussed the difficulties of working with minor students in schools and pointed out the inconsistencies in juvenile and tort law:

Minors generally cannot be bound by their contracts, but they can be held liable for intentional and negligent injuries inflicted on others. Once minors reach teenage years and display increasing capacity for rational decision making, both the common law and statutory law recognize this capacity by providing more legal autonomy for minors in carefully prescribed areas. (pp. 73–74)

Minors are emancipated or free from parental or guardian control when they reach the age of 18 years, enter the military, marry, or are declared emancipated by the Circuit Court. Emancipated minors do not enjoy all the rights of the age of majority (e.g., they cannot buy, sell, or consume alcohol until they reach the age of 21). These inconsistencies affect the professional school counselors' ability to rely on clearly stated principles of legal policy (Stone, 2004).

Students' rights and responsibilities are far reaching and differ by states (consult your state's statutes). In most states, however, there are similar student responsibilities while they are on school grounds or under school supervision. Students must avoid unlawful activity, including sexual behavior, using profanity, drinking alcohol, gambling, using dangerous drugs or tobacco, or causing damage or injury to persons or property. Infractions may result in suspension, expulsion, or financial restitution. Students and their parents or guardians are liable for damages they cause to persons or property of the school district and for all property, such as books, that have been lent to them and not returned (Lee County Comprehensive Strategy, 2004).

What happens when a student gets involved in the Juvenile Justice System (JJS)? The JJS is devoted to a number of legal entities, such as the Juvenile Division of the Circuit Court and the State Attorney's Office, that are designed to address issues for youth younger than 18 years of age. Juvenile Court is a special branch of the Circuit Court whose judges hear cases in which minors are believed to have violated the law (delinquency) or when they need help because of family or personal problems (dependency).

When a student becomes part of the JSS, the State Attorney decides if his or her case will be handled judicially or nonjudicially, which means the case may be dismissed, go to Juvenile Arbitration, or be referred to a diversionary program. If the State Attorney decides to handle the case judicially, it may be transferred to Adult Court, or it may be referred to Juvenile Court for an adjudicatory hearing (a non-jury trial). If, at the adjudicatory hearing, a minor is found not guilty, then he or she will be released. If the minor is found delinquent or if adjudication is withheld, the case will be disposed of in one of three ways: commitment, community control, or other alternative judicial services. Commitment includes direct release and postplacement services such as aftercare, postcommitment community control, or furlough. Community control includes probation. Alternative juvenile services include work restitution, community service, or judicial warnings. Minors are released from the JJS when they have successfully completed their commitment, community control, or alternative services (Santa Rosa County Public Schools, 2000).

An area of student and parental rights that has far-reaching ramifications for professional school counselors involves the value-laden areas of abortion and sexual activity, which often involve a family's religious beliefs, values about sexual conduct, and parental rights to be the guiding voice in their children's lives. Professional school counselors need to be advocates and sources of strength for students who come to them for help in dealing with areas such as sexual activity and abortion, but principles of law and school board policy must be considered.

Currently, there are 42 states that have laws on the books that require varying degrees of parental involvement before their child can obtain an abortion (Planned Parenthood, 2004). Laws that determine the right of parents to be involved in their children's abortion decision affect how professional school counselors must behave when a student confides in them that they are pregnant and considering abortion. Generally speaking, unless there is a school-district policy that forbids discussing abortion, contraceptives, and so forth, professional school counselors, in the course of fulfilling their job responsibilities, may assist students with value-laden issues such as abortion if they are competent to give such advice and if they proceed in a professional manner.

Under what circumstances might a counselor be held liable for giving abortion advice? In Arnold v. Board of Education of Escambia County (1989), Jane and John, two high school students, filed suit along with their parents against the School District of Escambia County, Alabama, alleging that the professional school counselor, Kay Rose, and the assistant principal, Melvin Powell, coerced and assisted Jane in getting an abortion (Arnold v. Board of Education of Escambia County, 1989; Zirkel, 2001). During the process of discovery, the trial court concluded that the students were not deprived of their free will, had chosen to obtain an abortion, had chosen not to tell their parents, and that there was no coercion on the part of school officials (Arnold v. Board of Education of Escambia County, 1989; Zirkel, 2001). However, the outcome of the trial would likely have been very different if the courts had found that Rose and Powell had coerced this student to have an abortion. Professional school counselors must always consider that their responsibilities extend beyond the student to parents and guardians and take great care in value-laden issues such as abortion counseling. Fischer and Sorenson (1996) stated the following:

> If an immature, emotionally fragile young girl procures an abortion with the help of a counselor, under circumstances where reasonably competent counselors would have notified the parents or would have advised against the abortion, liability for psychological or physical suffering may follow. The specific facts and circumstances must always be considered. (p. 60)

Students who give birth and decide to abandon the baby can do so anonymously in some states. For example, in Florida, parents can abandon a baby at a hospital or fire station within 3 days of its birth. The courts assume that the abandonment means the mother is consenting to terminate parental rights (Florida Statute 188, 2000.213).

PARENTS' RIGHTS AND RESPONSIBILITIES

The Family Educational Rights and Privacy Act (FERPA) of 1974 (often referred to as the "Buckley Amendment") is the federal law that protects the privacy of all student records in all PreK–12 schools that accept funding from programs administered by the U.S. Department of Education. FERPA defines education records as being all information collected by a school for attendance, achievement, group and individual testing, assessment, behavior, and school activities for all students. Personal notes and some confidential information such as reports of child abuse and neglect are not considered part of the educational record. FERPA governs the disclosure of information from edu-cation records, gives parents the right to talk to teachers and school administrators about their children, see their children's education records, and decide if their child will participate in a questionnaire, survey, or examination regarding a parent's personal beliefs, sex practices, family life, or religion. FERPA allows parents to request that in-formation that they believe to be inaccurate or misleading be purged from their child's educational record. Under FERPA, only persons with a "legitimate educational inter-est" can access a student's record. Some personally identifiable information, referred to as *directory information,* is considered public information and can be released without signed, informed consent by the parent.

The major exception to the confidentiality of student records involves law enforce-ment issues; the school must comply with a judicial order or legally executed subpoena. Additionally, in the case of an emergency, relevant information can be released without the parent's consent, such as in a medical emergency. In situations in which a referral has been made to Social Services or another agency charged with protecting the child, sufficient information can be released to support the allegation. For example, in the case of a neglect referral the school could release to the appropriate agency attendance and other information that they used in the development of the referral.

The No Child Left Behind Act of 2001 (NCLB) enacted several significant changes to FERPA. Specifically, it now requires that discipline records are part of the educa-tional record and are transferred along with the rest of the record as requested. Schools must

> facilitate the transfer of disciplinary records, with respect to a suspension or expulsion, by local education agencies to any private or public elementary school or secondary school for any student who is enrolled or seeks, intends, or is in-structed to enroll, on a full- or part-time basis, in the school. (20 U.S.C. §7165)

Schools are also allowed to share appropriate discipline information with those teach-ers and officials in a school who have a legitimate educational interest in the behavior of the child. NCLB also amended the Protection of Pupil Rights Amendment (PPRA); it increased the areas protected when surveys are administered to students and added restrictions to the administration of certain physical examinations, excluding vision, hearing, and scoliosis screenings.

The rights of consent transfer to students upon their 18th birthday or to students under the age of 18 when they enter a postsecondary program. However, for students still in secondary schools when they turn 18 years, the law does not limit the rights of the parents to continue to be able to access their child's records. Noncustodial par-ents have the same rights under FERPA as custodial parents, unless a court order has limited the rights of one or both parents. Other family members, such as step-parents and grandparents are not recognized as having any rights under FERPA unless they are granted such rights by the courts. More information about FERPA is available on the U.S. Department of Education Family Policy Compliance Office Web site (http://www .ed.gov/policy/gen/guid/fpco/index.html).

A second major law that has implications for records is the Health Insurance Porta-bility and Accountability Act (HIPAA) of 1996. The passage of HIPAA required the U.S.

Department of Health and Human Services (HHS) to adopt national standards for the privacy of individually identifiable health information. The law also outlined patients' rights and established criteria for access to health records. The law further required the adoption of national standards for electronic health-care transactions. The Privacy Rule, which became effective in 2001, functions for health records much the same way FERPA functions for education records. It gives patients the right to inspect and request corrections to their health records, affords some control over the disclosure of their records, and provides a complaint process. It also requires that health-care providers give patients a privacy notice and obtain a signed acknowledgement of this notice.

School systems are required to operate under the guidelines of FERPA, so school records are exempt from HIPAA regulations. However, schools often receive records from outside providers that are covered by HIPAA, so it is helpful to have a basic understanding of this law. School systems are continuing to work with their departments of health and other entities regarding HIPAA's impact on records that schools receive from agencies, organizations, and providers governed by this law. Examples of records governed by HIPAA include outside evaluations, medical and mental health records from agencies or private providers, and other information for students receiving services from non–school-system personnel. These records are often sent to the school to be used in the appropriate placement or determination of student services, particularly special education services. Once they are received, they generally become part of the educational record and are governed by FERPA, unless the parent or provider of the record indicates that the information should not be redisclosed.

The mandates of both HIPAA and FERPA are consistent with ethical standards and therefore should not prove to be a barrier to sound professional practice. Informed consent, limits to access to, disclosure and redisclosure of records, review and appeals processes, and the confidentiality of records are all part of ethical standards and should direct the practice of professional school counselors (Linde, 2007).

MINOR CONSENT LAWS

All states have a minor consent law that allows certain minors to seek treatment for specific conditions involving substance abuse, mental health, and some reproductive health areas. These laws are based on the federal regulation 42 U.S.C §§ 290dd-3; 42 C.F.R. Part 2, which addresses the confidentiality of patient records for drug and alcohol abuse assessment, referral, diagnosis, and treatment. The law further prohibits the release of these records to anyone without the client's informed consent and includes clients under the age of 18 years, even if they are in school and living with parents or guardians.

As states have incorporated this federal law into their statutes, they have taken different approaches to deciding to whom this law applies and for which conditions or issues. The statutes suggest that the patient must be old enough to understand the problem, the treatment options available, and the possible consequences of each option. Some states may have no age limits and maintain that a minor has the same capacity as an adult to consent to certain services. Other states have designated a specific age at which the minor may consent to mental health treatment, reproductive or substance abuse services, or treatment for sexually transmitted diseases (STDs) and HIV/AIDS. Information about your state's requirements can be found on the Alan Guttmacher Web site (http://www.guttmacher.org).

There is tremendous variability across districts regarding what is permissible under the law. Medical personnel, including the school nurse, are covered, but it is questionable whether a professional school counselor or school psychologist is covered. It is critical that counselors and other student services personnel become familiar with the minor consent law in the state in which they work and their local school systems policies to ensure compliance (Linde, 2007).

EDUCATORS' RIGHTS AND RESPONSIBILITIES REGARDING STUDENTS AND PARENTS

Educators have a responsibility to provide students with an environment conducive to learning in which sexual harassment is not allowed. The U.S. Supreme Court, in Davis v. Monroe County Board of Education (1999), in combination with Title IX of the Education Amendments of 1972, established that public schools may be forced to pay damages for failing to address student-on-student sexual harassment. Sexual harassment can no longer be ignored or given cursory attention by school districts. The Davis case demands advocacy against known sexual harassment. According to the Supreme Court, liability may be imposed when the school district is deliberately indifferent to sexual harassment of which the recipient has actual knowledge (Biskupic, 1999). The harassment must be severe, pervasive, and deprive the victim of access to an equal educational opportunity.

Most states have statutes giving educators the right to conduct searches of students on public school property, school buses, and at school events based on reasonable suspicion of criminal activity. School officials can question students without informing them of their constitutional rights; the constitutional rights of minors are not equated with that of adults in most states. For example, school officials can establish dress codes and grooming requirements as part of the student code of conduct.

APPLICATION OF STUDENT AND PARENTAL RIGHTS THROUGH CASE STUDIES

The following cases are presented to highlight additional legal and ethical principles in an effort to raise awareness, reduce risk, and transfer the principles of these cases to other situations.

RIGHTS FOR NON-CUSTODIAL PARENTS I: WORKING THROUGH A CASE STUDY

> A student's mother, who is incarcerated, requested copies of her son's education records. Are you legally required to provide her with education records?

Non-custodial parental rights are often misunderstood. FERPA makes it clear that both parents have equal access to education records. Even incarcerated parents, parents who have refused to pay child support, and abusive parents have rights to education records under FERPA unless there is a court order expressly forbidding a parent to have education records.

Rights for Non-Custodial Parents II: Working Through A Case Study

Sharon, a 9-year-old student, occasionally seeks your help with relationship issues with her mother, the custodial parent. Sharon's parents are divorced and generally at war over everything, including how to raise Sharon and her sister. Sharon describes her mother as being very strict. A teacher expressed concern that Sharon's grades have been plummeting and that she seems distracted and withdrawn, a marked contrast to how Sharon usually behaves. After meeting with Sharon, you believe you need to involve her parents. Sharon begs you to call her father instead of her mother. You believe Sharon's mother will be upset that you contacted Sharon's father instead of her. Can you consult Sharon's father without seeking permission or notifying her mother, the custodial parent?

Professional school counselors can find guidance in the court case Page v. Rotterdam-Mohonasen Central School District (1981). John Page had visitation rights for his son, Eric, but repeated requests to the school district to provide him with education records went unheeded. Mikado Page, Eric's mother, sent a statement to the school (at what was believed to be the school's request) explaining that she has legal custody of Eric and that she did not want John Page to have Eric's education records, participate in teacher–parent conferences, or in any way engage in the education of Eric. The court found that John Page was not trying to alter custodial rights but simply to participate in his son's educational progress. The court found that school districts have a duty to act in the best educational interest of the children committed to their care, which means providing educational information to both parents (Alexander & Alexander, 2005; Fischer & Sorenson, 1996; Page v. Rotterdam-Mohanasen Central School District, 1981).

Parents, whether or not they have legal custody, do not have to give up their rights to be involved in their children's education or psychological care. Consulting with your building-level supervisor or your district-level supervisor of guidance can help answer the legal rights of non-custodial parents and also shed light on what is in Sharon's best interest and the best interest of the family.

Students Right to a Public Education and the Right to Privacy: Working Through a Case Study

A preschool student with autism and physical disabilities entered your school. You accidentally acquire information that this 4-year-old child is HIV positive. The principal has warned you that you are not to reveal the child's HIV positive status to the teacher. This 4-year-old is not potty trained and is a biter. It is inconceivable to you that this information is being withheld from the teacher. You are seriously considering dropping some hints to the teacher, such as, "This school year, you need to be especially careful to use your rubber gloves when cleaning up after your students." Is there an ethical dilemma here? Is there a legal dilemma here?

The Family Educational Rights and Privacy Act (1974) bestows on parents the privacy rights of their minor children regarding education records. Professional school counselors can find guidance in FERPA if their state does not have a statute addressing the privacy rights of children who are HIV positive in schools. FERPA gives parents the authority to release records to third persons; therefore, it follows that parents can decide who in the school will know that their child is HIV positive or has AIDS. Most states have statutes protecting the privacy rights of people who are HIV positive to protect them against the fear and prejudice directed toward them (Stone, 2004). Schools need protective safeguards in place to keep sensitive information from being acquired accidentally.

Additional guidance can be found in Martinez v. School Board (1988), in which a Federal Court of Appeals ruled that a 7-year-old boy who had AIDS could not be excluded from his Trainable Mentally Disabled class. The court would not exclude the student from school in the face of theoretical possibilities. The court ruled that the overwhelming medical evidence is that AIDS is not transmitted in schools through casual contact, and therefore the court would not exclude a student from a free appropriate public education (Martinez v. School Board, 1988). The Individuals with Disabilities Education Improvement Act (IDEIA) of 2004 and Section 504 of the Rehabilitation Act of 1973 guarantee this student a free education in the least restrictive environment. Supported by legislation and recommended by the Centers for Disease Control, students who are HIV positive should be afforded a free, appropriate public education.

For most school-aged children who are infected, the benefits of an unrestricted setting would outweigh the risks of their acquiring potentially harmful infections in the setting and the apparent nonexistent risk of transmission (in this case, of HIV). The children should be allowed to attend school and after-school day care and be placed in a foster home in an unrestricted setting (Centers for Disease Control, 2002).

Runaway Children: Working Through a Case Study

You have been counseling Whitney for several months. You believe Whitney's parents emotionally abuse her, and you have twice reported this suspicion to the Department of Children and Family Services. Emotional abuse has never been established. You recognize how hard it is to determine emotional abuse, and you believe that Whitney will never find relief from authorities. You believe that at 15 years of age, Whitney's best course of action is to flee the abuse. You have never suggested to Whitney that she leave home, but she has brought it up several times, and you do not encourage or discourage this course of action. You have listened and asked questions about her plans. Whitney finally leaves home, and you learn from her friend that she is safe with friends. Whitney's parents call the school, inquiring if school officials would ask Whitney's friends, teachers, and counselor if they had any information about her whereabouts. When asked, you remain quiet. Have you acted illegally?

In most states, it is unlawful to aid a runaway who is unmarried or a minor. If anyone who is not authorized by the Department of Juvenile Justice or the Department of Children and Family Services knows that a child has left home without parental consent or knows that the child is being provided shelter and does not report this to law enforcement authorities, then that person is guilty of a first-degree misdemeanor in most states (Children and Families in Need Services Act, 2000; Delinquency; Interstate Compact on Juveniles Act, 2000).

Summary/Conclusion

One of the most important sources of information for professional school counselors to use in their practice to ensure appropriate behavior is the code of ethics from professional associations. ACA, ASCA, and NBCC have all developed codes of ethics that cover counselors' responsibilities to themselves, their clients, or students, colleagues, other staff in their workplace, and communities in which they work. The ASCA codes dictate that professional school counselors have a primary obligation and loyalty to students, but they also state that parents need to be involved, because parents are continually vested by our courts with legal rights to guide their children (Bellotti v. Baird, 1979; H. L. v. Matheson, 1982). Community standards, a counselor's own personal values, school board policy, the school setting, and state and federal statutes all contribute to the complex nature of working with minors in schools.

The rights and responsibilities of students and their parents have considerable implications for all educators, but in many ways they are even more complicated for professional school counselors because their work involves the personal–social arena. The multiplicity of responsibility to parents, students, administrators, teachers, and others in a setting designed to deliver academic instruction requires a vigilance to not only protect the rights of students but also consider parents and others who have rights to influence students.

Professional school counselors must be constant consumers of legal and ethical information by seeking the counsel of colleagues, administrators, supervisors, school attorneys, and Title IX officers. Such supervision and advice make the legal and ethical world of professional school counselors less daunting. Counselors must become familiar with the specifics of which code they deem most appropriate for them and implement its standards in their practice. When professional school counselors behave ethically, they ensure quality services to their students and limit the possibility of getting into legal difficulty. The final decision regarding one's conduct and course of action always resides with the counselor.

(Note: See the CD-ROM for a list of references.)

CHAPTER 6

CERTIFICATION, LICENSURE, AND ACCREDITATION IN SCHOOL COUNSELING

Brent M. Snow and C. Marie Jackson

Preview

In this chapter we will attempt to clarify the confusion and differential requirements that are related to certification, licensure, and accreditation in the field of school counseling. A brief history of credentialing, state certification in school counseling, national certification in counseling, licensure in professional counseling, and national accreditation of graduate programs in school counseling will be discussed.

School counseling, along with other specialty fields in education, historically has required practitioners to meet certain requirements to work with children in public schools. In addition to teachers, administrators, and other specialists, stakeholders in school counseling have developed standards in every state, requiring a credential to work in the schools as a professional counselor. In addition to state certification in school counseling, professional school counselors with appropriate training and education are eligible for licensure as professional counselors in most states and also for national certification in counseling.

Many counselors-in-training—those just graduating from master's degree programs and those contemplating a career in school counseling—are confused about the whole issue of credentialing, including licensure and certification. Bloom and Clawson (1992) indicated that "credentialing is probably the most complicated issue for most new professional counselors" (p. 4). Most experienced counselors and counselor educators would agree with this statement, based upon many years of answering questions on these topics.

Because of the lack of standardization of terminology and differential requirements between states and credentialing bodies, we will attempt to clarify this confusion. In addition to a brief history of credentialing, we will address state certification in school counseling, licensure in professional counseling, national certification in counseling, and accreditation of graduate programs in counseling.

WHY ALL THE CONFUSION WITH THIS CREDENTIALING STUFF?

Until the 1970s, there was very little, if any, confusion about credentials in the field of counseling. That is because until that time there were basically only two creden-

The authors wish to acknowledge the contributions of Dr. Sally Murphy to this chapter. Dr. Murphy authored the chapter "Professional Training and Regulation to School Counseling," which was published in the first edition of this handbook.

tials that affected counselors: state certification in school counseling (administered by a state department of education or similar body) and licensure as a psychologist (administered by a state licensure board). State certification in school counseling controlled who could be a professional school counselor in a public school, and psychologist licensure controlled who could practice psychology (e.g., counseling, psychotherapy), either independently or in private practice. As a result, if a professional was not interested in working in a school or private practice, credentials were not an issue. State and private agencies and other employers of counselors simply developed their own requirements for hiring counselors. At that time, counselors with doctoral degrees were routinely licensed as psychologists (Snow, 1982). Although school counseling was not particularly affected, Snow (1981) indicated that

> there has been considerable dialogue in recent years alluding to difficulties between psychologists and counselors regarding who should or should not be licensed (as psychologists) and who can do what to whom. The problem seemed to magnify in the early 1970s as state psychology licensing boards became more restrictive in just who they were willing to identify as psychologists. (p. 80)

With licensure as a psychologist (led by the American Psychology Association) becoming more restrictive, *counselors* (led by the American Personnel and Guidance Association, now called the American Counseling Association [ACA]) began to advocate for separate licensing laws that governed private, independent practice. In 1976, Virginia became the first state to enact a separate licensure law that allowed counselors to engage in private practice, and, today, most states license counselors as *professional counselors*. A the same time, other specialties that were represented by professional associations, such as the American Association for Marriage and Family Therapy, began to push for separate licensure as well. Many states now separately license psychologists, professional counselors, marriage and family therapists, and social workers, thus adding to the confusion surrounding licensure relative to private practice in the helping professions.

STATE CERTIFICATION IN SCHOOL COUNSELING

According to Gladding (2000), certification is a professional, statutory, or nonstatutory process by which an agency or association grants recognition to an individual for having met certain predetermined professional qualifications. State certification for professional school counselors is a statutory process and is a requirement in all states, according to Randolph and Masker (as cited in Schmidt, 1999). The procedures and requirements for obtaining certification vary from state to state, but they all require a minimum of some graduate education for initial certification in school counseling. Even the training program requirements outlined by state agencies vary across states, with some state education agencies reviewing and approving university programs. A few states continue to require teaching experience prior to certification. Previous teaching experience as prerequisite is a long-debated issue in the field of school counseling, even though research does not indicate a link between teaching experience and successful counseling practice (Baker, 1994). Counselor educators (i.e., professors who train counselors at colleges and universities) agree that master's degree–level counselors-in-training do not need prior teaching experience to be successful professional school counselors (Smith, 2001).

According to Paisley and Hubbard (1989), a majority of states allow employees to become certified before they complete all requirements, and some states offer provisional certification, allowing counselors-in-training to be placed in professional school counselor positions prior to finishing degree requirements. Provisional certifications often have a limited time frame during which degree requirements must be completed and full certification earned. An overview of state certification requirements in school counseling can be summarized as follows (ACA; 2000): All states require graduate education in guidance and counseling; 12 states require supplemental graduate education in addition to counseling; 28 states require completion of a school-based practicum or internship; 21 states require previous teaching or related experience; 23 states use standardized examinations as part of the certification process; and 35 states require a criminal background check. In a more recent update, 44 states and the District of Columbia require a master's degree in school counseling. The remaining 6 states require a bachelor's degree in education, with a minimum of 30 hours in graduate-level work in school counseling (American School Counselor Association [ASCA], 2002b).

Once a counselor receives certification, he or she must keep it in effect by acquiring the appropriate continuing education that each state agency requires. Counselors must also apply for renewal, usually every 5 to 8 years. Additional coursework can serve as continuing education for recertification purposes. According to Clawson (as cited in Wittmer, 2000), credentialing professional school counselors protects the counselor as well as the general public. State certification allows the professional school counselor to practice as a school counselor and, theoretically, prohibits those without appropriate credentials from legitimately being employed in those positions (although Clawson reported that exceptions are common practice). Clawson also suggested that credentialing protects the professional school counselor in the case of salary equity questions and adds to the potential for a clearly defined counselor role. State school counseling certification is meant to ensure the public (e.g., parents, teachers, students, community members) that counselors who are hired in these positions have had the minimum training required, no character defects, and other necessary qualifications to provide the designated services to students.

NATIONAL CERTIFICATION IN SCHOOL COUNSELING

Unlike state certification, which is mandatory for professional school counselors, national certification is a voluntary professional credential and is not required for the counselor to practice in the schools, in other agencies, or in independent private practice. Rather, it indicates that a professional school counselor meets national standards developed by counselors, for counselors (rather than by legislators or education departments). While it does not or cannot substitute for state credentials, it is an avenue for identifying counselors who meet rigorous national standards.

Presently, the two national organizations that certify professional school counselors are the National Board for Certified Counselors (NBCC) and the National Board for

Professional Teaching Standards (NBPTS; see additional information for certification requirements in Table 6.1). Of these two, the oldest, largest, and best known is NBCC, which was created in the early 1980s. This credentialing body certifies *general* counselors who, when certified, are referred to as a National Certified Counselor (NCC). Additionally, the organization also credentials three counseling specialties, referred to as a National Certified School Counselor (NCSC), Certified Clinical Mental Health Counselor (CCMHC), and Master Addictions Counselor (MAC). There are over 32,000 NCCs, about 1,100 NCSCs, 1,400 CCMHCs, and 700 MACs. Requirements (NBCC, 2002) for becoming a nationally certified or general counselor include a combination of education (at least a master's degree), supervised experience, and passing an examination known as the National Counselor Examination (NCE) for licensure and certification. There are several options that allow for combinations of education and experience, including benefits associated with graduating from a program accredited by the Council for Accreditation of Counseling and Related Educational Programs (CACREP). Requirements for obtaining the NCSC credential from NBCC include completing a graduate degree in counseling, with 48 semester or 72 quarter hours of coursework covering eight content areas and including two academic terms of field experience (e.g., practicum, internship); 3 years of post–master's degree supervised experience as a professional school counselor; and passing the National Certified School Counselor Examination. Recently, it has become possible for applicants to take the school counseling examination only and obtain both the general (NCC) and school counseling certification (NCSC) (Clawson, Henderson, Schweiger, & Collins, 2004).

In recent years, the National Board for Professional Teaching Standards (NBPTS) has developed a strong presence in certifying teachers at the national level. One of the major thrusts pushing this movement is the willingness of states and school systems to financially reward teachers who gain such national recognition through certification. Financial incentives for teachers becoming nationally certified exist in many states and have resulted in a large number of teachers becoming nationally certified, with a trend suggesting many more to follow. Professional school counselors have obviously desired to be included in these financial incentives programs.

In 2002, the National Board for Professional Teaching Standards adopted 11 standards of accomplished practice for professional school counselors that serve as the basis for certification. The resulting credential is referred to as the Early Childhood through Young Adulthood/School Counseling (ECYA/School Counseling) certificate. Recently developed eligibility requirements include a baccalaureate degree, 3 years of school counseling experience, and state certification or licensure in school counseling. After meeting these requirements, an additional assessment process involves presenting a portfolio with work samples, videotapes, and other evidence demonstrating effectiveness in meeting the 11 standards. The assessment also includes a *test*, which demonstrates the counselor's knowledge in human growth and development, school counseling programs, diverse populations, theories, data and change, and collaboration.

There were early attempts to unify certification between NBCC and NBPTS and create one national credential and process. While many had hoped that the NBPTS would adopt the requirements already existing in the NBCC and the NCSC credential, this never occurred, leaving these two national certification bodies competing with

TABLE 6.1
ADDITIONAL INFORMATION

State School Counselor Certification Requirements

The American School Counselor Association Web site contains State Certification and Continuing Education requirements within the section on Career Roles.

www.schoolcounselor.org

1-800/306-4722

State Professional Counselor Licensure Requirements

The American Counseling Association Web site contains information on licensure and certification.

www.counseling.org

1-800/347-6647

National Board for Certified Counselors (NBCC) Requirements

The National Board for Certification Web site provides information about the various certifications available through NBCC.

www.nbcc.org

336/547-0607

National Board for Professional Teaching Standards (NBPTS) Requirements

The NBPTS Web site provides information about various teacher certifications available and also includes information about the certification of school counselors.

www.nbpts.org

703/465-2700

each other. It remains to be seen which credential, or if both credentials, stand the test of time in influencing national recognition in school counseling.

LICENSING IN PROFESSIONAL COUNSELING

All but five states currently license professional counselors (ACA; 2002). Terminology varies, but the most common titles for those licensed are *professional counselor, professional mental health counselor, clinical professional counselor,* or *clinical mental health counselor* (ACA; 1997). Licensure laws are passed by state legislatures and, generally, regulate the title and practice of counseling. Essentially, licensure laws govern the independent, private practice of professional counselors. Counselors who work in government agencies and schools are generally exempted from compliance with licensure laws. The ACA has developed model legislation for states to use in developing counseling licensure laws, and many have followed these guidelines. Some states, of course, have not done so, resulting in licensure laws with varying requirements to become licensed and differing definitions of counseling practice. The model law includes the following definitions in the scope of practice of professional counselors (ACA; 1995):

The practice of professional counseling includes but is not limited to: individual, group, and marriage and family counseling and psychotherapy; assessment; crisis intervention; diagnosis and treatment of persons with mental and emotional disorders; guidance and consulting to facilitate normal growth and development, including educational and career development; utilization of functional assessment and counseling for persons requesting assistance in adjustment to a disability or handicapping condition; consulting; research; and referral. Assessment shall mean selecting, administering, scoring, and interpreting psychological and educational instruments designed to assess an individual's attitudes, abilities, achievements, interests, personal characteristics, disabilities, and mental, emotional, and behavioral disorders and the use of methods and techniques for understanding human behavior in relation to coping with, adapting to, or changing life situations. (p. 3)

Most states require a master's degree, supervised experience, and the passing of an examination—most often the NCE, which is developed by the NBCC. All states exempt professional school counselors from the requirement of becoming a licensed professional counselor to practice counseling. Many professional school counselors, however, qualify and are eligible for state licensure, if they desire it. Professional school counselors who have private, independent practices outside of their employment in the schools must be licensed in those states with licensure laws.

ACCREDITATION OF GRADUATE PROGRAMS IN COUNSELING

Accreditation is a system for recognizing universities and colleges as well as professional programs affiliated with those higher education institutions for a level of quality performance and integrity based on review and comparison with a set of standards (CACREP; 2002). In the field of counseling, there are two major accrediting bodies: the Council of Accreditation for Counseling and Related Educational Programs (CACREP) and the Council on Rehabilitation Education (CORE). These are noncompeting organizations; they accredit different specialties in the field. The American Psychological Association also accredits counseling psychology programs at the doctoral level, but only if they are considered a *psychology* program rather than a *counseling* program. CORE serves as the primary accrediting organization for university programs that prepare rehabilitation counselors.

Since 1981, CACREP has been the primary professional counseling accreditation organization (CACREP; 2002). Accreditation of counseling programs continues to grow, as does the associated influence, recognition, and prestige. For example, the Georgia Board of Regents, the umbrella administrative organization of state colleges and universities, has mandated that all university school counseling programs in the Georgia system be accredited by CACREP. While this is unusual, it does suggest the growing importance for university counselor education programs to pursue accreditation by CACREP. Program accreditation provides the foundation for graduate-level school counseling programs to achieve and maintain a high level of quality and integrity based on rigorous national standards. In addition to school counseling programs, CACREP also accredits master's-degree programs in career counseling; college counseling; community counseling; gerontological counseling; marital, couple, and family counseling or therapy; mental health counseling; and student affairs as well as doctoral programs in counselor education and supervision.

CACREP standards require entry-level (generally at the master's-degree level) counselor education programs to have a minimum of 2 full academic years of graduate study to include a minimum of 48 semester or 72 quarter hours of credit. Standards stipulate eight academic common-core areas: professional identity, social and cultural diversity, human growth and development, career development, helping relationships, group work, assessment, research and program evaluation, and specialized studies in school counseling. These additional specialty standards in school counseling include preparation in the foundations of school counseling in areas such as ethical and legal issues, as are addressed in the American Counseling Association and the American School Counselor Association's codes of ethics. Additional areas of preparation are focused on the contextual dimension of school counseling, the knowledge and skill requirements for professional school counselors, and clinical instruction. This *practical* instruction is an important element, and the standards require students to obtain a supervised practicum (a minimum of 100 clock hours) and a 600-hour internship in a school setting, under the site supervision of a qualified professional school counselor.

As of January 2006, there were 200 institutions of higher education that had CACREP accredited programs (totaling 497 specialized programs). Of these programs, about 175 were school counseling programs. As there are well over 300 school counselor education programs in the United States (Hollis & Dodson, 2000), many, if not most, school counselor education programs do not offer a CACREP accredited program. Even so, many of these nonaccredited programs are aligned with CACREP's core curriulum requirements. However, these programs may significantly differ from the quality curriculum required in a program accredited by CACREP.

Cutting-edge school counselor education programs also align themselves with ASCA's national model (ASCA; 2005), the national standards incorporated within the model, and with the essential elements and focus of the transforming school counseling movement initiated by The Education Trust. These standards and elements are briefly discussed in the next section.

Transforming School Counseling Initiative

Counselor educators, professional school counselors, and other education experts recently began to examine the role of the professional school counselor in the school reform movement (Bemak, 2000; Burnham & Jackson, 2000; House & Hayes, 2002). The educational reform for professional school counselors not only examines the role of the counselor within the school community but also addresses the training of preservice school counselors based on professional standards and regulations as well as current research and practice. A more comprehensive discussion of this reform is covered in other chapters, but it is important to understand the integral role it has in the training of professional school counselors.

Although CACREP provided the guidelines for core curriculum requirements within a school counselor education program, these core areas only begin to address the training needs of the professional school counselor for the 21st century. Funded by the DeWitt-Wallace Reader's Digest Fund, The Education Trust, and six universities (University of West Georgia, University of North Florida, California State University–Northridge, Indiana State University, Ohio State University, and the University of Georgia) have played a significant role in the research, dialogue, and training to improve school counseling by focusing particularly on the graduate-level preparation of professional school counselors (Perusse & Goodnough, 2001). This focus has helped define a new role for professional school counselors and has become known as the Transforming School Counseling Initiative (TSCI). There was some initial concern that this initiative diminished the counseling role of the professional school counselor, but the position of the professional school counselor in this respect has been clarified: The mental health component remains, but the goal is not to be a counselor in private practice who works in the school. Brent Snow, from the University of West Georgia, has stated the goal this way: "The school counselor is the mental health expert in the school. The school counselor is not the mental health counselor practicing in the school" (The Education Trust, 2000, p. 13).

The Education Trust's new vision for professional school counselors "describes school counseling as a profession that focuses on educational equity, access, and academic success, with a concentration on interventions that will close the achievement gap between poor and minority children and their more advantaged peers" (Perusse & Goodnough, 2001, p. 100). It highlights five domains intrinsic to the role of the professional school counselor: (1) leadership, (2) advocacy, (3) teaming and collaboration, (4) counseling and coordination, and (5) assessment and the use of data. These are closely aligned with the ASCA (2005) national model themes.

The Education Trust (2003) delineated eight essential elements for school counselor education change: (1) criteria for selection and recruitment of candidates for counselor preparation programs; (2) curricular content, structure, and sequence of courses; (3) methods of instruction, field experiences, and practices; (4) induction process into the profession; (5) working relationships with community partners; (6) professional development for counselor educators; (7) university or school district partnerships; and (8) university or state department of education partnerships. Prospective graduate students in counseling should weigh these program components against their professional goals as they consider what counselor education program best fits their needs.

The Education Trust challenges school counselor education programs to expand beyond the basic training to include specific counseling skills that are necessary to transform the role of the school counselor. In addition to its focus on leadership and advocacy skills, The Education Trust promotes specific training in multicultural counseling and cross-cultural communication skills to better serve increasingly diverse school communities.

The Education Trust also stresses the need for pre-service counseling students to have training in the use of technology used for monitoring student progress and student career planning and in acquiring and accessing data needed to inform decision making with individual students. The use of quantitative data and qualitative data is critical if professional school counselors are to effect changes within schools.

ASCA National Model

ASCA, the primary association for professional school counselors, provides the structure and standards for school counselors and school counseling programs (ASCA; 2002a) and describes the role of the professional school counselor. The structure for school-based counseling programs, which should be part of the counselor education curricula, is found in the second edition of *The ASCA National Model: A Framework for School Counseling Programs* (ASCA; 2005). The national model presents an organized approach to program foundation, delivery, management, and accountability, which are the four major elements for school counseling programs. This model also incorporates four overarching school counselor role description themes of leadership, advocacy, collaboration and teaming, and systemic change. These four themes were drawn from The Education Trust, and ASCA worked with those in the Transforming School Counseling Initiative to infuse these themes throughout the model, as they represent the importance of professional school counselors' skills that lead to systemic change and academic achievement.

ASCA's model incorporates the ASCA national standards (Campbell & Dahir, 1997), which are categorized as academic development, career development, and personal–social development. The model reflects current education reform initiatives including the No Child Left Behind Act of 2001 legislation and builds upon its philosophy of "one vision and one voice" (ASCA; 2002a). Thus, ASCA provides all school counselor educators with a professional, organized, and consistent framework for developing, managing, and delivering school counseling programs. By integrating ASCA's national model within a quality school counselor education program, preservice school counselors graduate with the skills and knowledge necessary to work with diverse school communities and student populations.

Summary/Conclusion

With a brief background and understanding of credentialing and accreditation in the field of counseling, professional school counselors in practice as well as aspiring school counselors can better assess the value of the various certifications and licenses. In this chapter we provided information to help sort out licenses, certifications, and program accreditation in the field of school counseling. All professional school counselors must become state certified in order to practice in the schools. To practice outside of the school in an agency or private practice, most states require an additional license as a professional counselor. Achieving national board certification identifies the professional school counselor as having achieved professional standards and qualifications at the highest level. Graduating from a nationally accredited program in school counseling, such as those approved by CACREP, adds an element of distinction to one's degree and can be a benefit when seeking national certifications. Clearly, professional school counselors can add to their professionalism and credibility through the credentialing process, and this process can be facilitated by graduating from a CACREP accredited program.

(Note: See the CD-ROM for a list of references.)

CHAPTER 7

MULTICULTURAL COUNSELING COMPETENCE IN SCHOOL COUNSELING

Cheryl Moore-Thomas

Preview

The rapidly changing demographics of the nation's student population demand that professional school counselors work effectively with all students. Multicultural counseling competence, therefore, is imperative. This chapter explores key definitions and elements of multicultural counseling competence for the professional school counselor. General strategies and considerations regarding the role of the multiculturally competent professional school counselor are identified. The chapter concludes with sample counseling interventions appropriate for the elementary, middle, and high school levels.

Public and private school enrollments have increased 19% since 1989 (National Center for Education Statistics [NCES], 2005). This record enrollment, totaling over 54 million in 2002, is expected to increase another 3% by 2014. In addition, closer examination of these demographics indicates substantial increases in the minority student population. In 2004, public school minority enrollment was approximately 42% of the total K–12 enrollment. This represented a gain of 20 percentage points in minority enrollment over the last 30 years (NCES; 2005). Projections indicate that by 2020, most school-age children attending public schools will come from minority (non-White) cultures (P. Campbell, 1994).

These changing demographics demand that professional school counselors be able to work effectively with students from various cultures (Constantine, 2001; Lee, 2001). The American School Counselor Association (ASCA) position statement on multicultural counseling calls on professional school counselors to "take action to ensure students of culturally diverse backgrounds have access to services and opportunities that promote maximum academic, personal/social and career development" (ASCA; 2004, p. 1). Professional school counselors must understand diversity in order to be effective (Herring, 1997), and, therefore, multicultural counseling competence, is of great consequence.

DEFINITIONS

Multicultural counseling is "a helping process that places the emphases for counseling theory and practice equally on the cultural impressions of both the counselor and the client" (Lee & Richardson, 1991, p. 3). More simply, multicultural counseling is the facilitation of human development through the understanding and appreciation of cultural diversity (ASCA; 2004). Multicultural counseling demands that professional school counselors work with students within appropriate cultural contexts. To do this, professional school counselors must fully consider the language, values, beliefs, social class, level of acculturation, race, and ethnicity of their students and only use counseling interventions and techniques that are consistent with those cultural values.

Although the ramifications of multicultural counseling may initially appear overwhelming, it should not be reduced to an *add-on*, or a list of stereotyped preferences. Multicultural counseling is a process (Spindler & Spindler, 1994; Sue, Ivey, & Pedersen, 1996). For the professional school counselor, the multicultural counseling process involves a shift in paradigm, which leads to true acceptance of and respect for the student in relation to self, others, and the environment.

Within discussions of multicultural counseling the terms *culture, race,* and *ethnicity* are often used interchangeably, but they have important distinctions. *Culture* is the set of "values, beliefs, expectations, worldviews, symbols, and appropriate behaviors of a group that provide its members with norms, plans, and rules for social living" (Gladding, 2001, p. 34). As the definition suggests, culture is complex, multidimensional, and integrated. Professional school counselors might recognize several cultures and subcultures within their student population, and, although this adds to the complexity of the construct, understanding and appreciating culture and its multidimensionality gives professional school counselors valuable insights to their students' sense of self, language, communication patterns, dress, values, beliefs, use of time and space, relationships with family and significant others, food, play, work, and use of knowledge (Whitefield, McGrath & Coleman, 1992).

Race, often referenced in conjunction with culture, is a separate construct that has little if any relevance to the understanding of culture. Race is an anthropological concept based on the classification of physiological characteristics (Gladding, 2001). There exists, however, a strong argument that race is a political and socioeconomic construct, which is correlated with artificially categorical differences in physical appearance (Brace, 1995; Yee, Fairchild, Weizmann, & Wyatt, 1993). Understanding this concept enables the professional school counselor to more appropriately address students' concerns that, on the surface, appear to involve race but, on closer examination, also involve issues that are political, psychological, social, or economic. Furthermore, this consideration will enable professional school counselors to examine the effects of students' *racial identity development* (see Benedetto & Olisky, 2001; Bradley & Kiselica, 1998; Helms, 1995; Karl Kwan, 2001; Tatum, 1997), a race-related adjustment process rooted in sociopolitical and cultural constructs and on academic, career, and personal–social development.

Ethnicity refers to the "group classification in which members believe they share a common origin and a unique social and cultural heritage such as language or religious belief" (Gladding, 2001, p. 45). Ethnicity describes a shared social and cultural heritage that is often passed from generation to generation. Ethnic classifications may help to shape students' sense of identity, appropriate behavior, and opportunity (Blum, 1998). Ethnic classifications include African American, Asian American, European American, Hispanic American, and Native American. In an attempt to be inclusive, institutions such as educational systems have adopted the use of many categories of ethnicity. This growth in awareness and sensitivity is to be commended. In the midst of the growing and ever-changing terminology, the professional school counselor must remember that sensitivity to students' needs is paramount. When it is necessary for the professional school counselor to identify ethnicity, it is essential for him or her to use the term most preferred by the student and the student's family. It is equally important not to rely on any single term to define students. For example, some students of Latin American descent may find the term *Hispanic* offensive, as it refers to a Spanish influence, which many found oppressive.

Diversity simply means "differences." The professional school counselor appreciates and understands diversity in the areas of race, ethnicity, gender, age, exceptionality, language, sexual orientation, spiritual identity, and socioeconomic status. The professional school counselor works to ensure that students of diverse backgrounds have access to needed services and opportunities (ASCA; 2004).

Role of the Multiculturally Competent Professional School Counselor

The professional school counselor uses the helping processes of counseling, consulting, and coordinating to assist students, parents, teachers, and administrators (C. Campbell & Dahir, 1997). These processes must become manifest in comprehensive developmental counseling programs that are appropriate for students of culturally diverse backgrounds. When designing such a counseling program, professional school counselors should consider using the following:

- Strategies that increase sensitivity and awareness of the school population to cultural diversity, culturally diverse persons and populations, and enhance the school and community climate
- Consultation skills that identify factors in attitudes and policies that hinder the learning process of culturally diverse students
- Approaches that ensure that all students' rights are respected and all students' needs are met
- Counseling interventions that maximize students' potential (ASCA; 2004)

Additionally, the professional school counselor must continually work toward multicultural counseling competence by engaging in the following:

- Increasing awareness of one's own culture and the culture of others through articles, books, conversations, activities, reflection, and experiences
- Becoming aware of and working to eliminate personal and school-wide barriers to effective multicultural counseling
- Refraining from using a "cookbook"—a stereotypical approach to counseling students from specific racial or cultural groups
- Demonstrating mastery of a variety of individual and group counseling approaches and techniques that, when evaluated based on the students' needs, prove appropriate for individual culturally and ethnically diverse students
- Understanding reluctance and resistance to counseling that may be attributed to cultural factors (Baruth & Manning, 2000)

- Increasing abilities to eliminate hostilities and satisfactorily resolve conflicts involving diversity, race, ethnicity, beliefs, or worldview (Baruth & Manning, 2000; Stone, 2003)
- Respecting the indigenous support and healing systems of all students
- Understanding possible stressors for students of diverse cultures (e.g., issues of acculturation, identity development, self-esteem, worldview, values, marginalization, social isolation, prejudice, oppression, racism, opportunity, discrimination; see Arredondo, 1999)
- Understanding the specific ways race, ethnicity, and culture might affect students' counseling decisions and academic, career, personal–social development
- Assuming multiple helping roles, based on the needs of students (e.g., advisor, advocate, facilitator of indigenous support systems, facilitator of indigenous healing systems, consultant, change agent; Atkinson, Thompson, & Grant, 1993)
- Providing student resources that are reflective of a diverse population
- Promoting school-wide programs and staff development opportunities that are inclusive of the school community and reflective of a diverse population

Tools such as the *Multicultural Counseling Checklist* (Holcomb-McCoy, 2004) and the *Multicultural Counseling Guidelines for Working With Children and Adolescents* (Liu & Clay, 2002) can be used to further guide professional school counselors' multicultural counseling development and training.

MULTICULTURAL COUNSELING COMPETENCE IN PRACTICE

The sample lessons in Tables 7.1, 7.2, and 7.3 illustrate the use of many of the multicultural counseling strategies listed in the previous section. The samples integrate strategies in multiculturally competent school counseling interventions that are appropriate for the elementary, middle, and high school levels. These samples, aligned with the *ASCA National Model: A Framework for School Counseling Programs*, Personal–Social Domain, Standard A (ASCA; 2005), demonstrate just a few of the many effective ways professional school counselors may work with students from diverse cultural and racial backgrounds.

TABLE 7.1

ELEMENTARY-LEVEL LESSONS

Domain: Personal–Social

Standard A: Students will acquire the knowledge, attitudes, and interpersonal skills to help them understand and respect self and others.

Competency: Acquire self-knowledge.

Indicator: Identify and recognize changing family roles.

Objective: After participating in the developmental guidance lesson on families in the community, 80% of the students will be able to identify two ways that families differ.

Materials: One "Families Worksheet" for each student (See Figure 7.1).

TABLE 7.2

MIDDLE-SCHOOL-LEVEL LESSONS

Domain: Personal–Social

Standard A: Students will acquire the knowledge, attitudes, and interpersonal skills to help them understand and respect self and others.

Competency: Acquire self-knowledge.

Indicator: Develop positive attitudes toward self as a unique and worthy person.

Objective: After participating in the counseling group on self-esteem, 90% of the participants will complete the "Self-Esteem Questionnaire" (see Figure 7.2), reporting positive characteristics and statements about themselves.

Materials: One "Self-Esteem Questionnaire" for each student (See Figure 7.2); popular magazines and books that are designed for young female audiences

TABLE 7.3

HIGH-SCHOOL-LEVEL LESSONS

Domain: Personal–Social

Standard A: Students will acquire the knowledge, attitudes, and interpersonal skills to help them understand and respect self and others.

Competency: Acquire self-knowledge.

Indicator: Identify and discuss changing personal and social roles.

Objective: After completing the junior counseling session, 80% of the students will be able to identify two implications of their impending role change from high school student to high school graduate.

Activity: Primary Grade-Level Developmental Guidance Lesson Conducted in Classroom Settings

The professional school counselor collaborates with teachers to introduce various family structures and family roles to primary students. The professional school counselor ensures that ethnically and racially diverse families are represented through visual and audiovisual materials. Students discuss characteristics of families (members, customs, practices, etc.). The professional school counselor ensures that students understand that families are different in membership, member roles, and practices and introduces the term *diverse*. Students complete the "Families Worksheet" (see Figure 7.1) and are given an opportunity to share their worksheets. In closing, the professional school counselor emphasizes the value of all families not being the same.

Evaluation: The professional school counselor collects and evaluates the students' worksheets. If 80% of the students completed the worksheet identifying at least two ways families are different (specific, appropriate responses to worksheet questions 3 and 4), the goal was met.

FAMILIES WORKSHEET

Name: _____

Directions: Draw a picture of your family in the box, and then complete the sentences that follow. You may use the word bank at the bottom of the page.

MY FAMILY

Families are _____.

All families are not the _____.

My family _____, but some families _____.

Some families_____, but my family _____

_____.

It is good that families are different!

That means each family is _____.

Word Bank: Diverse   Unique   Special   Same

FIGURE 7.1. Example of a families worksheet.

Activity: Girls Counseling Group on Self-Esteem

Session 1. The professional school counselor discusses the purpose of the group. The group then works to establish ground rules. The members interview and introduce each other to the entire group. The group concludes with a discussion of member similarities to create universality, while noting differences to promote acceptance and tolerance.

Session 2. Participants review the ground rules and what occurred in the first session. Students use a go-around technique to respond to the following: "I feel good about myself when . . . ." The professional school counselor links commonalities and similarities to create universality, while noting differences to promote acceptance and tolerance.

Session 3. Students summarize the previous session. The professional school counselor facilitates the group's processing of factors that get in the way of positive self-esteem. Media images are considered, and, specifically, the messages given to girls of diverse racial, cultural, and ethnic backgrounds are explored. Multiethnic magazines, video clips, and books should be provided as resources. Responses and feelings in reference to those images are processed.

Session 4. The group members summarize content and feelings explored in the third session. The professional school counselor works with the students to process strategies that can be used to combat factors and emotions that hinder positive self-esteem development. Group members should be encouraged to share, but not to advise. The professional school counselor models acceptance and appreciation of each member's participation. Attention is given to the diverse ways and the context within which the group's participants foster self-esteem development. Issues of self in relation to self, others, and the environment are explored.

Session 5. Students use a go-around technique to respond to the following: "Share one thing you learned about yourself and others in the group. Share one thing you value about yourself and others in the group." The professional school counselor summarizes the group's sharing and learning. Appreciation of diversity and other emergent diversity themes are emphasized.

Session 6. Members conclude the group experience by responding to the following prompt: "I feel good about myself when . . . ." The professional school counselor links commonalities and similarities to create universality while noting differences to promote acceptance and tolerance. Group members are encouraged to share and celebrate positive changes in each other's responses. Growth in depth and quality of the responses is noted. Group members complete the "Self-Esteem Questionnaire" (see Figure 7.2) to culminate the group experience. The professional school counselor collects the questionnaires for review and evaluation. The questionnaires are returned to group members in individual follow-up and feedback sessions.

Activity: Individual counseling sessions with high school juniors.

The professional school counselor conducts an individual counseling session with each junior. In addition to discussing senior-year course selections and graduation requirements, the counselor engages the student in a consideration of changing roles, expectations, and feelings. The professional school counselor's knowledge of cultural and racial identity development and other issues of diversity allows conceptualization of the student's needs and responses that is appropriate, culturally sensitive, and facilitates the beginning of the successful transition from the role of high school student to graduate. The professional school counselor uses multiculturally competent counsel-

---

SELF-ESTEEM QUESTIONNAIRE

Name _____ Date _____

Directions: Complete each of the following sentences.

I feel good that I _____.

My best quality is _____.

Group members appreciate that I _____

_____.

I am proud that I _____.

When I don't feel good about myself, I know that I can _____

_____.

FIGURE 7.2. Example of a self-esteem questionnaire.

ing skills (e.g., individual counseling approaches that incorporate racial and cultural identity development factors as well as consideration of possible student stressors like social isolation, marginalization, and discrimination) to help the student identify effective strategies for effectively addressing any noted expectations, feelings, and implications within the appropriate cultural context. Specifically, the professional school counselor asks each student to identify at least two implications of the role change from high school student to graduate. An action plan is discussed and implemented as appropriate.

Evaluation: If 80% of the students were able to identify two implications of their impending role change from high school student to prospective graduate, the objective was met.

SUMMARY/CONCLUSION

Student populations are undoubtedly becoming more diverse. As the professional school counselor looks toward the future, professional integrity and competence must include the ability to effectively meet the needs of all students. The rapid growth of diversity in public and private school populations may make the task of meeting all students' needs appear, at times, quite awesome. However awesome they may be, the professional school counselor must certainly meet the challenge: The professional school counselor's commitment to students' uniqueness and maximum development of potential demands no less.

(Note: See the CD-ROM for a list of references.)

CHAPTER 8

PROFESSIONAL ADVOCACY: MELDING THE ASCA NATIONAL MODEL AND MARKETING STRATEGY

Laurie A. Carlson and Teresa I. Yohon

Preview

In this chapter we introduce and support the concept of professional advocacy for professional school counselors. Professional advocacy is essential to the continued strength of the school counseling profession, and professional school counselors themselves play a critical role (Meyers & Sweeney, 2004). The main sections of this chapter include "The ASCA National Model, a professional mandate"; "Public Awareness and the Professional School Counselor"; "From the Marketing Field to Professional School Counselors"; and "Advocacy Beyond Marketing."

The evolution of the school counseling profession has lead to confusion and debate regarding the definition of professional school counseling, and for too long the professional school counselor's role has been defined by individuals outside of the profession (Lambie & Williamson, 2004; Monteiro-Leitner, Asner-Self, Milde, Leitner, & Skelton, 2006; Paisley & Borders, 1995; Paisley & McMahon, 2001). These factors emphasize the critical need for professional school counselors to use effective leadership skills as they advocate for themselves and their profession (Dollarhide, 2003).

Professional school counselors often struggle when they try to help others learn about the school counselor's role within the school community (Sabella, 2003); therefore, professional school counselors "need to learn leadership and advocacy skills as well as skills needed to promote change in already established systems" (Sears & Haag-Granello, 2002, p. 169). Certainly, particular dispositions, knowledge, and skills are required for effective advocacy (Trusty & Brown, 2005). Formally training professional school counselors in the skills of professional advocacy, including public and political policy awareness and development, could fill the apparent gaps in such knowledge (Anderson, 2002; Carlson, 2002; Tysl, 1997). In this chapter, we outline the mandate for professional advocacy that was put forth by the ASCA national model (ASCA; 2005), review strategies related to public awareness campaigns and program promotion, introduce concepts and effective marketing strategies as a complementary approach to professional advocacy, and identify resources available to professional school counselors.

THE ASCA NATIONAL MODEL: A PROFESSIONAL MANDATE FOR ADVOCACY

The ASCA national model emphasizes accountability, collaboration, leadership, and systemic change (ASCA; 2005; Trusty & Brown, 2005). These qualities are particularly directed toward advocacy for students and, ultimately, for the profession. *Accountability* is about the results of a school counseling program's implementation. This accountability first begins with systematic documentation of the program's impact upon student success (ASCA; 2005; Erford, House, & Martin, 2007; Whiston, 2007). Collecting documentation is not enough; one must then share such documentation with stakeholders: "By sharing results, school counselors can begin to advocate for their profession and educate the community about the value of school counseling" (Conrad, 2006, p. 44). A strong collaborative relationship between the professional school counselor, administrators, teachers, and the larger community is necessary to reach the level of results sharing that is required to effectively advocate for one's program and profession.

Schools can characteristically be closed systems, difficult to permeate; young professional school counselors need to be trained in the skills required for infusing change. Identifying and including community values into the school counseling program is a critical task that is related to infusing this change and establishing school counseling programs into existing systems. Rye and Sparks (1999) offered many helpful strategies to professional school counselors who desire to weave a school counseling program into an existing school system. Strong and insightful program planning uses the ASCA national model guidelines (ASCA; 2005) to represent best practice, while core values from the community provide both a marketable program and an accepting market.

PUBLIC AWARENESS AND THE PROFESSIONAL SCHOOL COUNSELOR

Gysbers and Henderson (2005) included marketing as an essential component of effective, comprehensive guidance program implementation. Professional school counselors must rely on strong public awareness strategies to effectively market school counseling programs. Public awareness can be achieved through accountability, professional service, professionalism, publicity, student activities and events, and visual displays within the school (VanZandt & Hayslip, 2001). Promoting public awareness of school counseling programs and policies is a foundational component of professional advocacy:

> Both external and internal publics are important in the ongoing dialogue about the role and function of professional school counselors. Part of the professional school counselor's essential role in schools is to ensure that professional school counselors are defined and affirmed as supporting the academic, career, and interpersonal success of all learners in a school. . . . A strong internal and external public relations effort is essential to ensure that professional school counselors are seen as central to the school's mission of educating all students effectively. (Bailey, Getch, & Chen-Hayes, 2007, p. 115)

More will be offered concerning internal and external audiences in the marketing section of this chapter. VanZandt and Hayslip (2001) offered professional school counselors the following suggestions for promoting public awareness:

- Submit an annual report to the school board, demonstrating how well you have addressed the goals of your comprehensive plan.
- Meet regularly with building administrators. Serve on the advisory committee of a local community service organization.

- Be an advisor for a school club.
- Present a workshop at a state counseling conference.
- Be a model of mental and physical wellness.
- Regularly send out a school counseling program newsletter.
- Share program activities through the local cable TV station.
- Celebrate National School Counseling Week (always the first full week of February).
- Develop a Step-Up Day for students who will be entering or leaving the school the following year.
- Develop attractive bulletin boards that focus on the themes from the guidance curriculum.
- Wear lapel pins with counseling messages on them.

There are many stand-alone resources available for professional school counselors who are looking for ideas concerning public awareness. One resource is the American Counseling Association's (ACA; n.d.) *Public Awareness Ideas and Strategies for Professional Counselors*, and a sample public relations activity is provided in Table 8.1. Information regarding this material can be found on ACA's Web site (http://www.counseling .org). ASCA also offers the *School Counselor's Resource Kit* from their Web site (http://www.schoolcounselor.org).

FROM THE MARKETING FIELD TO PROFESSIONAL SCHOOL COUNSELORS

The key to successful marketing is developing consumer satisfaction by meeting the needs and wants of the customer. A marketing mix, consisting of pricing, product, distribution, and promotion, is developed for marketing tangible products. These marketing-mix components are also important for services such as professional school counseling, but since counseling services are intangible, additional marketing-mix components (i.e., people, physical environment, and process) must also be considered.

In professional school counseling, satisfaction for the student and the educational community depends on the interplay between the student and the counselor with the support of the school, businesses, and community agencies. In other words, the student participates in and affects the outcome of the service. Because of this interplay, there is variability in the success of counseling experiences. Additionally, the need for counseling varies, depending on the time of year and special needs (i.e., school violence, death in student body or faculty). This variability means that the marketing mix developed by professional school counselors must pay special attention to the consumers, the process of counseling, and physical evidence of successful counseling experiences (Zeithaml & Bitner, 1996).

THE MARKETING "MIX" AND REACHING YOUR AUDIENCES

The important marketing-mix components for professional school counseling centers on counseling program elements (i.e., guidance and counseling services, program management, and student advocacy projects); the availability of these components; the qual-

SENDING OUT A NEWS RELEASE

Sending news releases to local media is a basic, cost-effective public awareness tool that you should use when you want to announce special events, including speaking engagements, a new service or program, a promotion, election to office in an organization, or receipt of awards or other honors.

When considering news releases for publication, editors expect them to meet 3 basic criteria: your news must be of local significance, it must be timely, and it must be accurate, truthful, and complete.

The nature of your announcement will also determine to which editor you should send your news release. Review the primary newspapers, both daily and weekly, as well as any other local news and feature publications in your community for regular columns and departments, such as health, education, family living, religion, community calendar, special events, people, etc. to identify the appropriate individuals to whom you should direct your release.

If you are announcing an event, send your release at least ten days in advance of the event to daily news outlets; for weekly outlets, send the release at least three weeks in advance.

When writing a news release, follow these guidelines.

FORMAT

- Prepare the news release on the business letterhead of your organization, school or other institution, or private practice.
- Type your release double-spaced, with one-inch margins on all sides. Use only one side of the paper (yes, this is wasteful, but one-sided releases are what editors prefer).
- In the upper left-hand corner, type "FOR IMMEDIATE RELEASE."
- Include the date you are sending the release, either directly below "FOR IMMEDIATE RELEASE" or at the end of the release.
- On the next line, type "CONTACT:" and include your name, address, and telephone numbers (day and evening when possible).
- Leave approximately ten spaces before you type and center the headline. This gives the editor ample space to write instructions or comments.
- Whenever possible, limit the length of the release to one page.
- If you need additional pages, type and center – MORE– at the bottom of the first page. On subsequent pages, retype part of the headline in the top left corner and identify page numbers in the top right corner, using this notation: ADD ONE, ADD TWO, etc.
- Do not carry over paragraphs from one page to the next. Also avoid splitting a sentence between two pages.
- If you use multiple pages, do not staple them together.
- Use bullet points whenever you can. Leave plenty of white space; this makes your release easier to read.
- To signify the end of the release, type and center three hash marks: ###.

(continues)

FIGURE 8.1. Sample public relations activity: Sending out a news release. *Note.* From *Public Awareness Ideas and Strategies for Professional School Counselors* by American School Counseling Association. Available online from www.counseling.org/resources. Reprinted with permission from the American School Counseling Association.

CONTENT

- In general, a news release should mimic a regular news story: written in the third person and setting out factual information in an objective way.
- Your headline should be no more than one clause that succinctly states the essence of the release and who it is about, such as "AREA SCHOOL COUNSELORS TO SPONSOR COMMUNITY AWARENESS EVENT."
- The first paragraph (or lead) should be a concise statement of the most important facts: who, what, when, where, and why. It should be one or two sentences at most.
- Insert additional details and supporting information in the succeeding paragraphs with the most important points mentioned first.
- Write the release so it may be cut at the end of any paragraph. Editors cut from the bottom to fit the space available.
- Keep your paragraphs short.
- While not required, incorporating quotes from yourself or others sometimes adds color to the release. They can also be used to emphasize the importance of the event or activity or to editorialize on the subject matter.
- Don't assume that the editor has background knowledge needed to understand the context of the event/activity, and its importance. Include in the release all information that is needed by people from all educational levels and backgrounds to fully understand what you are announcing. And never use jargon.

STYLE

Press release writing has a style of its own. Two of the best reference books for style and form are *The Associated Press Stylebook*, and *The Elements of Style* (William Strunk, Jr., and E. B. White). Here are some highlights from these two texts:

- Write in a way that comes naturally. Do not use excessively flamboyant words. Write clearly and concisely.
- Write primarily with nouns and verbs. Persons, places and things in action bring writing to life. Adjectives and adverbs should be used sparingly and placed carefully. You're writing editorial copy, not advertising copy.
- Do not overstate. Exaggeration puts the reader instantly on guard. Everything you write will be suspect because the reporter or editor has lost confidence in your judgment.
- Avoid the use of qualifiers. Rather, very, little, pretty—these are nuisance words that only clutter your story.
- Do not use unnecessary adverbs after a quote. The statement itself should disclose the speaker's manner or condition without adverbs like "happily" or "enthusiastically" being added. The word "said" after a quote is sufficient.
- Beware of redundancies. Don't say "10 a.m. this morning."
- Do not use "th" or "st" following numbers. Use January 1, not January 1st.
- When in doubt, look it up. Your release will be received more positively if your grammar, spelling, and style are correct.
- Revise and rewrite. Write it, read it, edit it.

FIGURE 8.1. *Continued.*

SAMPLE NEWS RELEASE

FOR IMMEDIATE RELEASE

DATE:

CONTACT: Your name and phone number.

AMERICAN COUNSELING ASSOCIATION MEMBERS TAKE ON CAPITOL HILL DURING ANNUAL "DAY ON THE HILL"

The American Counseling Association brought 67 attendees from 25 states and the District of Columbia to Washington for an intensive legislative training at the annual ACA Legislative Institute.

Each attendee at the Legislative Institute paid a visit to their respective congressional offices to lobby for the needs of the counseling profession. "Our hope is that people who attend the Legislative Institute will not only help us out on the federal issues that we're working on, but also get involved on their own at state level," said ACA Director of Public Policy and Legislation Scott Barstow.

Sessions at the Legislative Institute taught participants the basics of the policymaking process, the differences between state and federal advocacy, and how to conduct a lobbying visit. The institute also covered lobbying on issues specific to different areas of counseling, including school counselors, rehabilitation counselors, and mental health counselors.

(name), a counselor with the _____ County Mental Health Division was surprised by what he learned. "One of the most important issues for me was to have my Member of Congress ask, "what is a professional counselor, and what is the difference between a clinical counselor and a school counselor? Often, a school counselor is the only counselor someone may have known in their past.

Founded in 1952, the American Counseling Association is the world's largest nonprofit organization for professional counselors. Dedicated to promoting public confidence and trust in the counseling profession, the American Counseling Association serves more than 55,000 members in the United States and 50 other countries.

FIGURE 8.1. *Continued.*

ity of the professional school counseling personnel and other help agencies; and the school counseling process. These professional school counseling marketing-mix components should be *promoted* to audiences that use or support the professional school counseling program.

Professional school counselors need to focus marketing and promotional activities to reach three distinct audiences: internal marketing (e.g., marketing between counselors and faculty, administrators, and staff); external marketing (e.g., marketing between the counseling program and the community); and client marketing (e.g., marketing between the counseling program and students). Internal marketing is crucial to a successful school counseling program. In fact, the promotion of the school counseling program to administrators, teachers, and staff, including secretaries, janitors, or security personnel, should be done before external or client marketing. Internal marketing ensures that people who come in contact with students are aware of the help available through the counseling program.

External marketing is directed toward people outside the school. Parents, business people, and community agencies such as child protection and health agencies are among the targets of external marketing. These groups support the school counseling program by sharing knowledge about the program to students and families who may use their services and through extended services that are not being provided internally through the school counseling program. External marketing is part of external advocacy, a topic covered later in this chapter.

Client marketing makes certain that students, the end user of school counseling services, are familiar with available counseling services and know that professional school counselors possess the skills and attitudes that make students feel *safe* in using the counseling service. Typical client marketing activities include brochures about services that are offered, information workshops, bulletin boards about the counseling services, and classroom visitations.

Counseling *quality* involves the technical and functional quality of the individual counseling experience and the overall professional counseling program. The *technical* quality is concerned with whether or not the counseling process helps students. The *functional* quality relates to the degree to which professional school counselors within the program showed concern, were nonjudgmental, and inspired more successful student behavior. A needs assessment is an essential tool for listening to all audiences and developing a well-rounded program that matches the needs of the local community. These audiences also should evaluate the counseling program based on the goals and mission of the school counseling program. Evaluation should include quantitative data (such as the number of students served or a documented decrease in negative behavior) and qualitative data (that may include student narratives via focus groups or case studies). Evidence collected about the counseling program's effectiveness should be shared with the counseling program's audiences and is part of internal advocacy, as outlined later in this chapter.

MARKETING PLAN FOR A PROFESSIONAL SCHOOLCOUNSELING PROGRAM

A professional school counseling program's marketing plan focuses on the program's audiences and the messages these audiences need to hear. These messages may include (a) goals and objectives of the counseling program, (b) research or evaluation information about the program, (c) available services, (d) new programs, (e) local student advocacy programs, and (f) state and national school counseling initiatives. A professional school counseling program marketing plan should be developed every year.

Program goals and audiences change, and the marketing plan should therefore be updated as well. To develop a marketing plan, the professional school counselor must first identify the audiences. Second, the counselor should decide what message to send to each audience. To help determine the message, it is useful for the professional school counselor to ask questions such as, "What does a parent, an administrator, or businessperson need to know about the school counseling program?" After determining what information is important to each audience, the counselor must determine what action is desired from the audience upon hearing the message. Actions include students coming to the counseling office, business leaders supporting a career development workshop, or internal support for a crisis management team. The final task is to determine how to most effectively deliver the message to the audience. A school counseling program can provide workshops, develop a Web site describing services and providing online career information, or host a parent night. A marketing plan worksheet is provided in Table 8.1.

Advocacy Beyond Marketing

Marketing and public awareness are merely the beginning. Advocacy goes beyond public relations and marketing in that it seeks to influence, not merely inform (Lenhardt & Young, 2001). Professional school counselors have a long and rich history in advocacy, especially advocacy surrounding student and social issues (Borders, 2002; Gysbers, 2001). But professional school counselors need to go beyond advocating for students and take an active role in advocating for their profession (Lenhardt & Young, 2001; Meyers & Sweeney, 2004; Meyers, Sweeney, & White, 2002; O'Bryant, 1992; Paisley & McMahon, 2001; Sears & Haag-Granello, 2002; Trusty & Brown, 2005). The American School Counselor Association provides an example of advocacy materials through its publication *Public Relations and Advocacy: Promoting the Role of the School Counselor* (ASCA; 2003).

Internal Advocacy

Internal advocacy measures are those that are essentially local in scope. Lenhardt and Young (2001) outlined the following internal advocacy strategies:

- Provide accountability for your program
- Conduct research on the efficiency of school counseling
- Establish a networking system with influential community members
- Complete an annual needs assessment
- Market your program
- Join your school's site-based management team
- Join outside community organizations
- Keep abreast of legislative issues

As was indicated previously, program accountability begins with strong program planning that is based on meaningful goals and objectives that are developed from an understanding of professional and community core values and identified needs. Sample needs assessment instruments can be found in the needs assessment chapter of this book and in several school counseling texts, including Erford (2007), Rye and Sparks (1999), and Wittmer (2000). From the basis of strong program planning, appropriate and meaningful program evaluation can be carried out. It is important for school counseling programs to institute both formative and summative evaluation. Many leaders in the field have devoted much effort to advancing the skills of program evaluation. For some guidelines on program evaluation, see Erford (2007), Gysbers and Henderson (2005), Rye

TABLE 8.1
MARKETING PLAN DEVELOPMENT WORKSHEET

	Internal Audiences			External Audiences		Students
	Administration	Teachers	Staff	Business/Community	Help Agencies	
Summer *Overall Goal:* Program information	*Message:* Changes in counseling program, staff, etc., which enhance student support	*Message:* Changes in counseling program, staff, etc., which enhance student support	*Message:* Changes in counseling program, staff, etc., which enhance student support	*Message:* School counseling program's goals and objectives; how business and whole community can participate in the program	*Message:* School counseling program's goals and objectives	*Message:* School counseling program's goals and objectives; staff list; available support services
	How delivered: E-mail	*How delivered:* E-mail; updated Web-site info	*How delivered:* E-mail; updated Web site	*How delivered:* Brochures; scheduled future presentations	*How delivered:* Brochures; scheduled future presentations or meetings with staff	*How delivered:* Brochures; Bulletin boards; class presentations, etc.
	Action to be taken: Feedback on e-mail	*Action to be taken:* Use of new services and staff in the school year	*Action to be taken:* Student referrals to counseling center	*Action to be taken:* Business and community leaders involved in school counseling program as mentors, job interview coaches, etc.	*Action to be taken:* List of agencies that will provide support services to students and school staff	*Action to be taken:* Students use counseling services more frequently
August *Overall Goal:* Develop community resources and increase knowledge on bullying	*Message:* Bullying resources available for student and staff use	*Message:* Bullying resources available for student and staff use	*Message:* Bullying resources available for student and staff use	*Message:* You are a valuable resource for students; ways to support students' career development	*Message:* You are a valuable partner in student counseling support	*Message:* School counseling program's goals and objectives; staff list; available support services
	How delivered: E-mail	*How delivered:* E-mail; workshops; updated Web site	*How delivered:* E-mail	*How delivered:* Presentations; brochures; personal contacts	*How delivered:* Presentations	*How delivered:* Brochures; bulletin boards; class presentations, etc.
	Action to be taken: Use information when teachers have problems with bullying in their classrooms	*Action to be taken:* Recognize students who are being bullied; help students themselves or refer them to the counseling office	*Action to be taken:* Recognize students who are being bullied; refer them to the counseling office	*Action to be taken:* Businesses provide job shadowing experiences and career information to students	*Action to be taken:* Become part of a "advocate agency" list with specific contact people where students can be referred	*Action to be taken:* Students use counseling services more frequently

and Sparks (1999), Stone and Dahir (2007), VanZandt and Hayslip (2001), and the ASCA national model (ASCA; 2005). Program evaluation and program accountability are related but not synonymous. Program accountability requires that evaluation results and other similar information, such as research findings, be shared with the stakeholders in the school district. Modes of dissemination of information include, but are not limited to, district newsletters, local newspapers, community service bulletins, and public forums.

For too long, professional school counselors have ascribed to the notion that research is just for counselor educators and other academicians. Practice-based research is essential not only for individual program accountability but also for the advancement of professional practice. The Center for School Counseling Outcome Research at the University of Massachusetts in Amherst (http://www.umass.edu/schoolcounseling) provides a wealth of information about research issues in school counseling and is a shining example of what collaborative outcome research can accomplish. It is imperative that professional school counselors understand that the parameters surrounding research are extensive. Research designs can range from descriptive to experimental, qualitative to quantitative, and single case study to large samples. A single intervention with one student can be carefully documented and analyzed to provide meaningful practice-based research. It is also important to regularly read the professional literature. Not only does the literature provide insight and new strategies for practice, it also gives the professional school counselor a guide for research sought after in professional publications.

Data-driven professional school counseling programs provide a wide scope of information for external, internal, and client audiences (ASCA; 2005). Data types include process, perception, and results data (ASCA; 2005; Stone & Dahir, 2007). Within these broad categories, data may be related to student achievement (e.g., grade point average, standardized test scores); student choices (e.g., attendance numbers, student behavior, course enrollments); program resources (e.g., counselor–student ratio, percentage of time spent with students, resource availability); counseling services (e.g., individual and group counseling, consultation, referrals, crisis response); and guidance activities (e.g., academic, career, and citizenship support). Examples of data-driven student advocacy programs, particularly advocacy programs emphasizing student achievement, can be found from the Portland Oregon public schools (http://159.191.14.139/.docs/pg/10840). One example of a comprehensive counseling program data collection format is Indiana's School Counseling Portfolio (http://www.doe.in.us/octe/goldstar/docs/PortfolioGuidelines-REVISED2004-FINAL-10-23-04.doc).

Establishing a strong community network and joining outside community organizations are closely related. Professional school counselors cannot passively expect the community to know and understand the school counseling profession. They must demonstrate their skills through active leadership, not only in school-based collaborative programs but also in community-based programs (Dollarhide, 2003; Green & Keys, 2001; Paisley & McMahon, 2001). There are many organizations that can benefit from the expertise of professional school counselors, and that can offer a valuable connection to community leaders. Examples of such organizations include child protection teams; corrections advisory boards; early childhood programs; service organizations, such as Jaycees; and community arts councils. Some of the internal advocacy strategies discussed in this section are closely related to those in the next section, and, at times, advocacy strategies straddle the line between internal and external advocacy.

EXTERNAL ADVOCACY

External advocacy strategies are typically more regional or national in scope. According to Lenhardt and Young (2001), external advocacy strategies include (a) membership in professional organizations; (b) state and national credentials; (c) organization of a guidance task force or advisory committee; (d) regular meetings with local businesses and service agencies; (e) repeated contact with legislators; (f) applications for local, state, and federal grants; and (g) appointment of legislative liaisons within professional organizations.

Many professional school counselors are exposed to professional organizations during their training programs. The image of the counseling profession rests on the shoulders of both professional organizations and individual counselors themselves (Van-Zandt & Hayslip, 2001). Active membership in professional organizations can provide professional school counselors with an opportunity to demonstrate a dedication to the profession, and it is set forth as a standard of practice in the ASCA ethical guidelines (ASCA; 2004). Networking and connection with other professional school counselors is the most direct benefit of membership. This professional connection manifests through not only meetings and conferences but also through newsletters, journals, and other print materials. Local and state organizations typically provide extensive opportunities for networking, and regional and national organizations have the fiscal and staffing resources to provide valuable support resources. Professional school counselors who are tempted to seek membership in only local or state school counseling associations should seriously consider the benefit of joining not only ACA and ASCA but also other related professional organizations.

The National Career Development Association (NCDA) and the Association for Counselor Education and Supervision (ACES) have both done much to support school counseling (Paisley & Borders, 1995). Because so much of what professional school counselors do is related to career planning and the life skills gained throughout a student's development, NCDA is an extremely valuable resource. The most readily available resources from NCDA can be found on the organization's Web site (http://www.ncda. org), on which the organization offers material for professional school counselors at the elementary, middle, and senior high school levels. The support emerging from ACES tends to be more indirect: ACES is committed to addressing training and supervision issues for professional school counselors.

Perhaps one of the greatest influences on the profession is the Council for the Accreditation of Counseling and Related Educational Programs (CACREP). Many professional counselors are familiar with the work of CACREP; however, most are unaware that the council was first formulated by ACES to govern the training of professional school counselors in particular (Wittmer, 2000). Accreditation is a voluntary process that training programs dedicate themselves to for various reasons, including a demonstration of commitment to professionalism.

Just as accreditation is a programmatic commitment to professionalism, seeking certification is the individual professional's commitment to professionalism. The National Board for Certified Counselors (NBCC) offers not only the Nationally Certified Counselor (NCC) credential, but also the Nationally Certified School Counselor (NCSC) credential. Information regarding the acquisition of the NCSC credential can be found on the Internet (http:// www.nbcc.org/cert/ncsc.htm).

In October of 2002, the National Board for Professional Teaching Standards (NBPTS) developed national standards for the certification of professional school counselors. General information regarding the pursuit of certification from the NTBS board can be found online (http://www.nbpts.org/standards/nbcert.cfm) as well as specific information regarding the school counselor certification (http://www.nbpts.org/candidates/guide/whichcert/27SchoolCounseling.html). The pursuit of national certification is a strong statement by professional school counselors regarding their dedication to professionalism, regardless of which certification they achieve, and this dedication is an important component of effective professional advocacy.

Unfortunately, sometimes a lack of financial resources can hinder both the marketing and the outreach of school counseling programs as well as the involvement of professional school counselors in the leadership of professional organizations—hence the importance of grant writing. Regrettably, many professional school counselors are not exposed to training related to specific skills that are necessary for successful grant writing. Grants usually come from two places: national or state agencies and foundations. National or state grants usually require extensive writing, often 20 to 25 pages of narrative plus various appendixes. Foundations tend to require a brief project statement and a budget, usually about five pages in length. Whether the grant proposal is sent to an agency or foundation, five key strategies should be followed when writing the proposal:

1. *Follow the grant's writing directions exactly.* This includes number of pages, font size, and table format. The narrative should be organized in the exact sections indicated in the grant's Request for Proposal. Using the exact section titles allows grant reviewers to find needed information quickly and increases the chances of maximum points in each section.

2. *Review past grants that have been funded by the agency or foundation.* Understanding prior funding history increases one's understanding of what types of projects the agency funds and how the proposed project is unique from past-funded projects.

3. *Clearly state the problem the grant proposal is designed to solve.* In most cases, the problem needs to be stated in both local and national contexts. The local context provides the reason for the grant request, while the national perspective provides a funding rationale if the grant activity presents a model that can be applied to a more universal problem.

4. *Understand who the grant readers will be.* Grant readers have their own "lenses" and interpretations of the grant guidelines and what important problems can be solved via grant monies. Call the grant program director or foundation liaison to clarify what types of projects are most likely to be funded and from where grant readers will be solicited.

5. *Write measurable outcomes for the grant project, and then write the evaluation plan to measure these outcomes.* Evaluation plans are hard to write, so think about evaluation throughout the grant writing process.

These are just a few basic strategies for professional school counselors to consider when writing successful grant proposals. It is also wise to seek the counsel of other professionals who have a history of success. Grants are often linked in one way or another to public policy and legislation, and this enforces the fact that informed political involvement is a key to effective professional advocacy.

PUBLIC POLICY AND LEGISLATION

Public policy and legislative action are critical elements of professional advocacy. Professional school counselors need to help shape education through active involvement and leadership regarding local, state, and national policy that leads to stronger legislative support of guidance and counseling programming (Anderson 2002; Gysbers, 2001; Lenhardt & Young, 2001; Roberts, 1996). The school counseling profession has a long-standing and essential relationship with legislative action. From the National Defense Education Act of 1958 and the Elementary and Secondary Education Act of 1965, to the Elementary School Counseling Demonstration Act of 1995, federal legislation has significantly influenced the creation and definition of the school counseling profession (Paisley & Borders, 1995). Beyond federal legislation, state licensing laws and mandates have further defined and influenced the profession of school counseling. It is imperative that professional school counselors individually take responsibility for understanding and influencing legislation at all levels.

Writing to a state or United States legislator is an important tool in political advocacy. In writing a letter or sending e-mail to legislators, keep the communication brief—ideally, only one page in length. Discuss only one bill or issue per correspondence. The correspondence should include the following:

- An introduction of yourself or the organization on whose behalf you are writing.
- A straightforward introduction to the issue, such as support of a bill.
- The bill number, if available.
- A concise explanation of why you support or oppose a particular bill or issue (bullet points are very effective).
- How the bill or issue will affect your local situation.
- Specific facts or an example to illustrate your point.
- Contact information for follow-up, if the legislator desires. E-mail is just as effective as a letter and may be received more promptly by a legislator, since posted letters undergo a more stringent review before going to the legislator.

Both ACA and ASCA offer professional school counselors valuable resources related to legislation and political advocacy. Professional school counselors have access to the public policy page of ACA's Web site (http://www.counseling.org/public), on which professionals will find links to the ACA Legislative Action Center, Washington Update Archives, Library of Congress Legislative Information, and other important links. Through ACA's links for public policy (http://www.counseling.org/public/links.htm), one can find links to such legislative sources as the ARCA/Alliance Legislative Page; the White House; the U.S. Senate; the House of Representatives; Thomas (a searchable database concerning the U.S. Congress and the legislative process where one can search bills by topic, bill number, or title); and a link to help send a message to Congress. The ACA Legislative Action Center and these Web-based resources are extraordinarily valuable to professional counselors committed to making a difference through public policy.

In addition to ACA's resources, ASCA offers comprehensive resources for public policy and legislative issues in school counseling. The professional school counselor will find a link titled "Legislative Affairs" on the ASCA Web site (http://www.school-counselor.org/content) that will provide members with an opportunity to sign up for legislative updates that are delivered electronically through e-mail and links similar to those offered by the ACA site.

SUMMARY/CONCLUSION

The topics and specific strategies presented in this chapter provide a foundation and starting point for professional school counselors as they embark on the critical road to professional advocacy. The future of school counseling rests squarely on the shoulders of professional school counselors who possess the skills and passion to advance the profession through effective marketing, thoughtful program planning, program delivery that enlists the cooperation of numerous stakeholders, leadership at multiple levels, program enhancement through successful grant writing, and legislative involvement.

(Note: See the CD-ROM for a list of references.)

LEADERSHIP AND THE PROFESSIONAL SCHOOL COUNSELOR

CHAPTER 9

THE PROFESSIONAL SCHOOL COUNSELOR AND LEADERSHIP

Joyce A. DeVoss

Preview

Effective professional school counselors accept leadership, advocacy, and public relations roles, all of which require specific leadership skills that can be learned. Professional school counselors understand that leadership is a key component of their professional identity, and it is through leadership behavior that school counselors contribute to systemic change for the benefit of all students. Counselor preparation programs have begun to incorporate leadership skills training and development into their curricula (DeVoss & Andrews, 2006; Murphy, 2004). Experienced professional school counselors who have found their educational and professional training lacking in leadership have sought specific training through district, state, and national professional development opportunities. A systematic approach to leadership development, which is described in this chapter, includes becoming familiar with leadership theories and models and completing leadership assessment and incorporation of feedback, mentoring, and learning into a leadership improvement plan and into the school counselor's professional practice.

THE CALL FOR PROFESSIONAL SCHOOL COUNSELOR LEADERSHIP

A review of the 13 ASCA school counselor performance standards described in the ASCA national model (ASCA; 2005) clarified the expectation that professional school counselors act as educational leaders. Professional school counselors are expected to plan, organize, coordinate, and manage the guidance program for their schools. In addition, they are expected to perform educational leadership activities such as establishing and convening a guidance advisory council on a regular basis, collecting and analyzing data to drive the guidance program, and conducting an annual program audit. They are looked upon as student advocates, educational planners and reformers, team members and collaborators as well as systems change agents. They are members and chairs of school and district committees.

Davis (2005) stated that "the students, their families and the community are the recipients of the benefits of school counselors with strong leadership skills" (p. 220). Without a minimum of basic leadership-skills training, professional school counselors lack the essential tools that are needed to adequately perform their jobs. Murray (2004) noted that burnout and attrition is high in the school counseling profession and in a review of literature found that inadequate job preparation is a crucial variable. Development of school counselor leadership, advocacy, and public relations skills has the potential to benefit the helper and prevent burnout as well as meet the needs of students.

There has been some debate over the question of whether leaders are born or developed. Some who are involved in the debate use a very narrow definition of leadership that includes aspects of dominance and having overt influence over others, and see these as inherited human traits. Others believe that we all have leadership capabilities that need to be developed and strengthened. From this perspective, effective leadership is a result of the use of the best leadership practices in our environment. Good leadership starts from within, through understanding one's own style of leadership. In addition to this understanding, good leaders continue to learn about leadership and to develop their leadership skills.

EDUCATIONAL LEADERSHIP THEORIES HIGHLIGHTED

Professional school counselors who develop an awareness of some of the contemporary theories and models of leadership that have influenced the field of education position themselves to confidently take their places on school leadership teams. Such a foundation is necessary to share a common understanding and language of leadership with other educational leaders. In addition, knowledge and understanding of theories and models of leadership are useful when a professional school counselor articulates his or her own leadership approach. Some of the currently popular leadership models described in this chapter include the Situational Model, of Hersey and Blanchard; the Transformational Model, of Bennis and Deming; the Moral Model, of Sergiovanni; the Learning Organization Model, of Senge; the Servant Leadership Model, of Covey; and the Empowerment Models of Bennis, and Kouzes and Posner.

SITUATIONAL LEADERSHIP (HERSHEY AND BLANCHARD)

The situational leadership model was developed in the late 1960s (Hersey & Blanchard, 1969). Hersey and Blanchard developed a model that was focused on adapting one's approach to situational demands. Such a model requires that the leader determine the readiness level, which involves both ability and the willingness (Hersey, 1984) of people being addressed. Two dimensions of leadership behavior described in this model include *task behavior* and *relationship behavior*. When using a task behavior style, the leader explains the task, how to do it, and when to do it. When using a relationship approach, the leader supports and facilitates the process of task completion.

TRANSFORMATIONAL LEADERSHIP (DEMING AND BENNIS)

Transformational leadership was developed by W. Edwards Deming (1993) and Warren Bennis (1994). It is an approach that views the leader as change agent who has vision and is inspirational. The leader is responsible for relationship building and involving others in leadership. Deming's Total Quality Management approach emphasized 14 points, which focused on process, including teaching and learning, attention to classroom climate, curriculum, and relationship within the school environment (see Table 9.1). Ensuring quality in these areas in the educational setting leads to high-quality outcomes.

Deming believed that his 14 principles must be applied as a whole. However, legislation such as the No Child Left Behind Act of 2001 makes adoption of this model as a whole by American schools unfeasible. In spite of this, many of Deming's ideas continue to be applied by educational leaders who share a similar philosophy.

Bennis (1994) conceptualized leadership as full expression of oneself. He emphasized ideas, relationships, and adventure—ideas for change; relationships for harmonious and open interactions and empowerment as well as inclusion of all; and adventure for risk, curiosity, and challenge. Leaders are effective when they express themselves well, know their strengths and weaknesses, and manage them well. They know what they want, how to communicate, how to achieve goals, and how to garner support of others. After interviewing 28 leaders, Bennis (1994) concluded that leaders are made, and they continue to grow and learn to develop their voice across their life span. They take charge of their lives and their lifestyles. The process of becoming a leader is a transformational process in which there are unlimited opportunities and challenges along the way (Bennis, 1994).

Four basic leadership ingredients of Bennis's approach include (a) a guiding vision of what the leader wants to do professionally and personally; (b) a passion for life and course of action; (c) integrity including self-knowledge, candor, and maturity; and (d) curiosity and daring. The leader learns to innovate through active and imaginative anticipation, listening to others, participation in shaping events, and self-direction. Leaders learn to lead by listening to one's inner voice (Bennis, 1994) and leading. Transformational leadership is a lifelong developmental process of becoming fully oneself, a concept similar to that of self-actualization, as described by Maslow (1968) and Carl Rogers (1980).

TABLE 9.1

THE 14 POINTS OF DEMING'S TOTAL QUALITY MANAGEMENT

1. Create constancy of purpose for the improvement of product and service.
2. Adopt the new philosophy.
3. Cease dependence on mass inspection.
4. End the practice of awarding business on price tag alone.
5. Constantly improve the system of production and service.
6. Institute training.
7. Institute leadership.
8. Drive out fear.
9. Break down barriers between staff areas.
10. Eliminate slogans, exhortations, and targets for the workforce.
11. Eliminate numerical quotas.
12. Remove barriers to pride of workmanship.
13. Institute a vigorous education and retraining program.
14. Take action to accomplish the transformation.

MORAL LEADERSHIP (SERGIOVANNI)

Sergiovanni (1992), the leading crafter of moral leadership, described this model as one that connects the interactions of the heart, head, and hand. The connection starts with the heart, then the head, and then the hand. The *heart* consists of what one values and believes. The *head* includes one's mental picture of how the world works. The *hand* represents one's decisions, actions, and behaviors. Leadership in this model is a form of behavior and a form of stewardship. Sergiovanni emphasized building a sense of community in schools in which teachers, principals, and counselors are stewards and servant leaders with shared values and a sense of empowerment regarding their duties in the learning community. The focus in the learning community is sharing a common vision instead of having one leader to follow.

Sergiovanni's (1992, 2001) concept of moral leadership includes emotions, group membership, meaning, morality, intuition, and obligation. Like Bennis, Sergiovanni (1992, 2001) maintained that moral leaders strive to do "the right things" rather than "do things right" (Sergiovanni, 1992, p. 4) He described the virtuous school as one in which the educational leaders believe that every student can learn and the learning community seeks to serve the whole student. Parents, teachers, the community, and school are viewed as partners in the virtuous school.

LEARNING ORGANIZATION LEADERSHIP (SENGE)

Senge (1990) described five disciplines that overcome organizational learning disabilities in his Learning Organization model. Leaders in a learning organization emphasize continuous feedback to foster learning for improvement of the organization as a whole. The first discipline is *personal mastery*, which includes personal growth, learning, and personal vision. The second discipline is *mental models*, which includes one's internal images of how the world works. The third discipline is *a shared vision*, a connection to learning and work that people share in their hearts. The fourth discipline is *team learning*, learning in which a group functions as a whole and synergizes efforts. The fifth discipline is *systems thinking*, an approach to thinking in which the four other disciplines are integrated into the big picture and their interrelationships are considered. Members of learning organizations recognize that, through their connection to their organizations, they affect the world.

SERVANT LEADERSHIP (COVEY)

Two significant contributors to the servant leadership model were Thomas J. Sergiovanni (1992), previously mentioned as the lead author of the moral leadership model, and Stephen Covey (1991), who wrote about principle-centered leadership. Many of Sergiovanni's relevant concepts were addressed in the Moral Leadership section, so this section will focus on Covey's contributions to the servant leadership model.

Covey offered a framework for leadership that focused on relationships, including both personal and professional relationships. The servant leader strives for balance among family, personal, and professional life through effective relationships. Servant leadership is developed from within. It is practiced on four levels: personal, interpersonal, managerial, and organizational.

Servant leaders learn continually. They care about the needs of others. They are service oriented and have a positive outlook and positive energy. They believe in other people. They are willing to take some risks. They believe in synergy, that the whole is more than the sum of parts. They exercise for self-renewal and lead balanced lives. They create environments in which others thrive and are empowered to develop as leaders.

Covey recommended that leaders develop a clear mission statement and described steps for developing a personal and organizational mission statement. Such statements help leaders to gain and maintain awareness of their destinations and to stay focused on the activities designed to get them there. Effective school counseling programs have clear mission statements guiding them. Professional school counselors can apply the idea of a mission statement to their personal as well as professional lives. Some have separate professional and personal mission statements; others have one broad mission that covers all aspects of their lives.

Covey (1991) recommended developing a personal mission statement through a reflective process, in which one examines one's roles and the contributions for which one would like to be remembered in each role. He suggested considering the characteristics, values, and principles represented in the contributions. The mission statement should be inspiring and empowering. It should represent the person's higher purpose and alignment with his or her vision and values. Figure 9.1 provides instructions for development of a personal or professional mission statement. A written mission statement represents a personal commitment to oneself to live by one's values and principles to achieve a higher purpose.

EMPOWERMENT LEADERSHIP (BENNIS, KOUZES, AND POSNER)

Research by Kouzes and Posner (1995) and Bennis (1994) found that effective leaders accept input from others, share power with others, and motivate others toward success. These are empowering behaviors. Bennis made contributions to both transformational leadership and empowerment leadership theories. Some of his concepts were addressed in an earlier section in this chapter, so the focus here will be on the leadership challenge model of Kouzes and Posner (1995). This model recognizes the human need for respect and acknowledgement. It includes five practices and 10 commitments that came out of more than 10 years of study of personal best cases of leadership in accomplishing extraordinary things.

The first of the five practices is *challenging the process,* with the associated two commitments of searching out challenges and taking risks. The second practice is *inspiring a shared vision,* associated with the commitments of envisioning an uplifting future and enlisting others in common vision. The third practice is *enabling others to act,* with the commitments of fostering collaboration and strengthening people by giving power and support. The fourth practice is *modeling the way,* with the commitments of setting the example and promoting small victories for progress. The fifth practice is *encouraging the heart,* with associated commitments of recognizing individual contributions and celebrating team accomplishments.

Kouzes and Posner's leadership challenge model addresses the potential for leadership development in everyone. A leadership assessment instrument called the *Leadership Practices Inventory* is associated with this model and will be described in the next section. The leadership challenge process includes assessment, review, and analysis of results; development of action plans; and ongoing behavioral changes to improve leadership effectiveness.

LEADERSHIP ASSESSMENT

Assessment provides the professional school counselor educational leader with feedback from self and others about his or her leadership characteristics and skills. Feedback is useful in evaluating which areas of leadership capabilities need to be developed and strengthened, thus directing leadership development and improvement. Many leadership assessment instruments are self-assessment devices. It is useful to incorporate

Instructions: Follow the steps below to develop a personal or professional mission statement. Write the resulting statement on a large sheet of paper and post prominently.

1. In the first column, list the roles you fill.
2. In the second column, list your contributions for each role.
3. In the third column, list the values, characteristics, and principles reflected in your contributions for each role.
4. Review all columns and summarize in a concise mission statement that you will be able to commit to memory.
5. Post your mission statement in a prominent place where you can review it regularly.

YOUR ROLES	YOUR CONTRIBUTIONS	YOUR VALUES, CHARACTERISTICS, AND PRINCIPLES

Mission statement: _____

FIGURE 9.1. Worksheet for development of a mission statement.

with the results of such devices some feedback of others who have observed the professional school counselor in leadership behaviors. This will give a more balanced and objective leadership assessment. Four leadership assessment tools appropriate for professional school counselors will be described in this section. Many other leadership assessment tools are easily accessible to the professional school counselor.

MYERS-BRIGGS TYPE INDICATOR

The *Myers-Briggs Type Indicator* (MBTI; Myers, McCaulley, Quenk, & Hammer, 2003) helps people to better understand their thinking, behavior, and emotions and identify their strengths and weaknesses as information processors and decision makers. Based on Carl Jung's Jungian Analytical Psychology theory, the MBTI is a self-report questionnaire of 16 personality types. It assesses psychological type on four dimensions: extraversion–introversion, sensing–intuiting, thinking–feeling and judging–perceiving.

Each dimension is represented by a letter (i.e., I = Introversion, E = Extraversion, N = Intuition, S = Sensing, T = Thinking, F = Feeling, P = Perceiving, J = Judging), and the person who completes the MBTI assessment is assigned four letters based on their preferences on the assessment items. The four letters represent the person's personality type (e.g., INTJ, ESTP, ENFP, INSJ). Each of the types has a corresponding type description (e.g., "ISTJs judge the information they take in logically, analytically, and impersonally. They approach things from a practical point of view"; Brownsword, 1990, p. 18). The original purpose of the MBTI was to assist people in career choice. Now it is widely used as a tool for team building and leadership development. It is offered by some university and community college testing centers.

TRUE COLORS SELF-ASSESSMENT SYSTEM

True Colors was developed by Don Lowry (1990). This assessment is based on four psychological types and has a foundation in Carl Jung's theory of personality, the work of Katharine Briggs and Isabel Myers in developing the MBTI, and Keirsey's research on temperament and development of the *Keirsey Temperament Sorter*. The True Colors Assessment assigns a color to each of the four different personality types, reflecting differences in how people of different types think and behave. Each of the personality types and defining characteristics is briefly described in the following list:

Green—analytical, reflective, ingenious, seeks knowledge

Blue—creative, thoughtful, compassionate, inspiring

Gold—organized, traditional, responsible, trustworthy

Orange—playful, fun loving, optimistic, energetic, bold

Two components of the assessment include character cards and a word sort. An additional assessment is available online and consists of multiple-choice responses to 24 questions. The character cards have characters on them demonstrating behaviors associated with each of the four colors. The respondent must choose the color card with the character who behaves most like them. In the word sort, respondents must give weighted scores to groups of words to indicate which words are most like them (4) to which words are least like them (1). The totals from each column correspond to a color. The highest score indicates the person's dominant color, the next highest is the second color in dominance, and so forth. The true colors multiple-choice assessment can be taken online through the True Colors Web site (http://www.mytruecolors.com) and paying a fee. Respondents receive a 20-page report, summarizing the results of this assessment.

LEADERSHIP PRACTICES INVENTORY

The *Leadership Practices Inventory* (LPI) is based on Kouzes and Posner's (1995, 2001) research on leadership, with more than 4,000 cases and 200,000 surveys. The LPI has two versions: one is for self-assessment and the other is for one or more observers to complete. The inventory consists of 30 items that assess the use of the five practices and 10 commitments of the leadership challenge model of leadership development. The items are rated on a 10-point scale, according to the degree to which the leader being assessed uses the skills listed on the questionnaire. This instrument has been found to have high reliability and good validity. The results of the inventory are likely to be a good predictor of leadership behavior. The LPI is available online through (http://www.pfeiffer.com) and can be taken online or purchased as a paper-and-pencil version.

LEADERS AS RELATIONSHIP BUILDERS

Dubrin (2004) identifies seven relationship-oriented attitudes and behaviors that help to get people working together smoothly. Professional school counselors are likely to find a number of their leadership strengths among these attitudes and behaviors. They are listed and described here:

Aligning and mobilizing people—getting people to work together smoothly.

Concert building—building a work group into a well-functioning, ongoing system.

Creating inspiration—triggering powerful emotional experiences in others by building enthusiasm, stimulating thinking, enabling leadership in others, recognizing others' contributions, and developing people's talents. Being visible and accessible reinforces inspiration.

Satisfying higher level needs—learning what is important to others and facilitating opportunities for getting those needs met.

Giving emotional support and encouragement—accomplished by expressing appreciation of others and through the sharing of leadership and decision-making opportunities.

Promoting principles and values—advocating for good causes uplifts and motivates others to care about and act in the interest of the common good.

Being a servant leader—being committed to service and helping others achieve their goals.

On the Relationship-Oriented Attitudes and Behaviors assessment form provided in Table 9.2, rate yourself on a scale of 1 to 5, where 1 = *very weak* and 5 = *very strong* on these seven attitudes and behaviors, as described by Dubrin (2004).

When reviewing your scores, consider the leadership relationship dimensions you scored at 4 or 5 as strengths, and those you scored at 1 or 2 as areas that need improve-

TABLE 9.2

RELATIONSHIP-ORIENTED ATTITUDES AND BEHAVIORS

	Very Weak ⟵⟶ Very Strong				
Aligning and mobilizing people	1	2	3	4	5
Concert building	1	2	3	4	5
Creating inspiration	1	2	3	4	5
Satisfying higher level needs	1	2	3	4	5
Giving emotional support and encouragement	1	2	3	4	5
Promoting principles and values	1	2	3	4	5
Being a servant leader	1	2	3	4	5

ment. Make note of your strengths and areas for improvement on the lines that follow each item. Consider the areas listed for improvement when you review and revise your leadership improvement plan.

LEADERSHIP IMPROVEMENT PLAN

Once a professional school counselor becomes familiar with leadership theory and concepts and completes a self-assessment using the instruments previously described or other leadership assessment tools, the professional school counselor can use the results to identify strengths and areas for improvement. From this list, the professional school counselor can choose items to address on a leadership improvement plan, formulate objectives for improvement, and identify specific strategies for improvement. Methods for monitoring progress need to be built into the plan so that the professional school counselor has some way available to obtain ongoing feedback on how well the plan is working and whether adjustments in the strategies need to occur. A sample leadership improvement plan is provided in Figure 9.2. It can be duplicated for more than one behavior or skill for improvement.

The leadership improvement plan should be discussed with a mentor and incorporate the mentor's suggestions. In seeking a mentor, it is helpful to make a list of what is needed from the relationship and what qualities are valued in a mentor. Discuss with a potential mentor what is needed in the mentoring relationship and to consider together the time commitment involved. The school counselor leader should meet regularly with mentors to update them on progress and to discuss possible adjustments to the plan, as necessary.

Journaling is a common approach for reflection on one's progress in leadership skill or behavior improvement. The professional school counselor can document examples of opportunities to practice leadership skills and note how well the opportunity was used. The journal can be used to document feedback from trusted colleagues. The journal provides the professional school counselor with a record of progress to review in meetings with a mentor.

Summary/Conclusion

Bennis (1994) emphasized that leaders learn to lead by leading. Professional school counselors need to develop their own leadership styles and practice acquired leadership skills on a continuous basis. Ongoing mentoring for professional school counselors can be instrumental to growth as a leader when it is related to specifically identified goals and objectives to which there is commitment indicated on the leadership improvement plan. The professional school counselor who is flexible and adaptive can learn to integrate newly acquired leadership knowledge and skills into their unique perspective as an educational leader. This chapter provided both an overview of professional school counseling leadership and various resources for developing a leadership improvement plan to guide the professional school counselor in realizing his or her full potential as an educational leader.

(Note: See the CD-ROM for a list of references.)

Professional School Counselor Leadership Improvement Plan

Behavior or skill to improve

_____

Objectives

1. _____
2. _____
3. _____

Mentors

_____

_____

Strategies to Achieve Objectives

1. _____
   _____
2. _____
   _____
3. _____
   _____

Strategies to Monitor Progress

1. _____
   _____
2. _____
   _____
3. _____
   _____

Figure 9.2. Sample of a leadership improvement plan.

CHAPTER 10

SAGE PERSPECTIVES ON SCHOOL COUNSELING

Stanley Baker, Norman C. Gysbers, Patricia Henderson, and Edwin L. Herr

Preview

In this chapter, we present perspectives on the current status and future of the school counseling profession, provided by four sages. Each has contributed mightily to the extant school counseling literature, has authored textbooks in the field, and has been particularly influential within the profession.

THE FUTURE OF SCHOOL COUNSELING: TESTING THE NATIONAL MODEL

Stanley B. Baker

THE CURRENT STATE OF SCHOOL COUNSELING

One of the several challenges facing anyone who is trying to speculate about the future of school counseling, or any profession, is being able to make accurate estimations about the state of that profession at the time futuristic speculations are being made. So, what is the current state of the school counseling profession? My opinions are restricted by access to school counseling programs in central North Carolina and the professional literature and popular media with which I am familiar.

Central North Carolina. In my area of North Carolina, school counseling has different faces. We have a county school district that has adopted the ASCA national model (American School Counselor Association [ASCA], 2003), identifies schools that are Recognized ASCA Model Programs (RAMPs), hires only professional school counselors that are licensed by the state, and has several persons in its ranks who are, or who have been, actively engaged in state and national professional school counseling leadership positions. On the other hand, there are also school districts in which school counseling is a set of traditional services, including numerous administrative functions, that have high student-to-counselor ratios and who are forced to hire professional school counselors with temporary licenses. Therefore, where I am located, the state of school counseling is uneven. Yet, it is clear to me that in both of these differing situations there is much we can do as advocates for our profession and for those whom we serve.

The professional literature. Dissatisfaction with the state of school counseling has produced numerous publications stating its shortcomings and advocating how those shortcomings might be addressed. The list of recognized school counseling's shortcomings includes the following:

- Being perceived as an ancillary service rather than an integral program in the school

- Not being perceived as an important contributor to the academic development of students
- Being perceived as primarily engaged in providing individual counseling services to a small group of at-risk students (aka, clients)
- Failing to sufficiently establish proactive large-group comprehensive school counseling curriculums that are designed to enhance student academic, career, and personal–social development
- Failing to provide leadership and enhance collaboration in the schools and communities
- Not being sufficiently accountable to a variety of stakeholders

Summing up and looking ahead. These circumstances and criticisms indicate that the school counseling profession has clear challenges facing it in the 21st century, and it appears as if everyone who is invested in the profession has roles to play in moving the profession forward. Addressing these challenges seems daunting indeed, yet I think there is hope on the horizon.

Progress requires grassroots support, and I believe that the best vehicle for achieving that grassroots support is the *The ASCA National Model: A Framework for School Counseling Programs* (ASCA; 2003). The national model (a) has articulate spokespersons; (b) is founded on constructive and achievable goals; (c) is supported by national, regional, and state professional organizations; (d) has been presented comprehensively in the professional literature; and (e) has potential for addressing the aforementioned criticisms.

PROJECTING INTO THE FUTURE

Several important features of the national model support this belief in its potential (Baker & Gerler, 2008):

- It attempts to define the role of professional school counselors.
- There is a comprehensive emphasis on meeting the developmental needs of students across academic, career, and personal–social domains.
- The standards-based focus emphasizes the importance of professional school counselors being accountable for setting and achieving goals and objectives and having a positive influence on students.
- The national model has a historical connection to the existing knowledge base in counseling and education and was developed in cooperation with individuals who for decades have been important contributors to the profession's development.
- Although there seems to be a greater emphasis on proactive prevention and large-group guidance-related curricular programming than on responsive services and individual and small-group counseling in the national model, it still has the elements of a balanced program within the framework.
- Important concepts such as leadership, advocacy, and collaboration are emphasized.
- There is an emphasis on working within school systems for constructive change.
- There is advocacy of a system for managing and delivering services within school counseling programs.

- There is some empirical evidence that professional school counselors throughout the United States support the model
- ASCA has a system in place for promoting and recognizing implementation of the national model.
- ASCA is establishing a National School Counseling Research Center.

While I believe that the national model has great potential for enhancing the school counseling profession, it remains imperfect in nature. For example, school counseling competencies have yet to be defined within the national model, and, although advocacy is one of the principles stated within the national model, it does not appear to directly address multicultural competence, an appreciation for diversity, and advocacy for social justice.

I recommend viewing the national model as analogous to a theory. Let it be developed and tested. Use the findings to modify the national model and enhance the school counseling profession. Make the findings readily available to professional school counselors and counselor educators, and encourage adoptions and adaptations concurrently with evaluations and accountability.

I am not certain what will remain and what will change in the current national model (ASCA; 2005). Yet, I look forward to being a witness and a participant in the process of promoting, testing, and developing this effort to enhance the school counseling profession.

COMPREHENSIVE GUIDANCE AND COUNSELING PROGRAMS: A RICH HISTORY AND A BRIGHT AND PROMISING FUTURE

Norman C. Gysbers and Patricia Henderson

As the guidance and counseling movement (then called *vocational guidance*) began to unfold in the United States at the turn of the 20th century, teachers, often part time or with no release time, were appointed as counselors and given a list of duties to perform. By the 1920s, the guidance and counseling movement had spread across the country. Educational guidance became a priority along with vocational guidance. During the late 1920s and early 1930s, efforts were made to identify what the activities of guidance and counseling should be, to establish "the standard setup" for guidance and counseling. During this same period of time, personal–social guidance and counseling emerged, as did the services model under the banner of pupil personnel work. Thus, by the 1930s, the three aspects of guidance and counseling (i.e., vocational, educational, and personal–social) and the services model combined with the position of *counselor* had been established. With the aid of federal legislation in the 1940s and 1950s, guidance and counseling in the schools continued to expand and became a part of overall education in the United States.

In the 1960s and 1970s, owing to concerns about the efficacy of the position-services model of guidance and counseling, the program model began to emerge. While not a new concept, the program model has become, during the 1980s, 1990s, and the early years of the 21st century, the major way of organizing and managing guidance and counseling in the schools. The position-services model has been transformed and incorporated into a developmental, comprehensive program.

A comprehensive guidance and counseling program, as described by Gysbers and Henderson (2006), consists of four elements: (a) content; (b) organizational framework; (c) resources; and (d) development, management, and accountability. The *content* element identifies competencies considered important by schools districts for students to master as a result of their participation in the district's comprehensive guidance and counseling program. The *organizational* framework contains three structural components (i.e., definition, rational assumptions); four program components (i.e., guidance curriculum, individual student planning, responsive services, system support); along with an example of the suggested distribution of a school counselor's time by grade levels across the four program components. The *resource* element consists of the human, financial, and political resources required to fully implement the program. Finally, the *development, management, and accountability* element describes the process of putting a program into place, managing it, and evaluating and enhancing it.

A BRIGHT AND PROMISING FUTURE

Given that professional consensus has been reached concerning the organizational framework for guidance and counseling in the schools, what does the future hold? We believe that the future is bright and promising. We envision fully implemented comprehensive guidance and counseling programs in every school and district in the United States, serving all students and their parents, staffed by active, involved professional school counselors as the 21st century continues to unfold. We believe that when guidance and counseling is conceptualized, organized, and implemented as a program, it places school counselors in the center of education. As a result, guidance and counseling becomes an integral and transformative program, not a marginal and supplemental position and service.

The vision we see for guidance and counseling in the 21st century cannot become a reality, however, without full professional attention to a number of challenges. While much has been accomplished, more work remains to be done to fully realize our bright and promising future. What are some of these challenges? They include the need for full program implementation; diversity-sensitive and responsive school counselors; attention to local, state, and national policies; local, state, and national leadership; and accountability.

Full program implementation. Even though substantial strides have been made in implementing comprehensive guidance and counseling programs in school districts across the country, implementation gaps remain. The difficulty in achieving fully implemented comprehensive guidance and counseling programs is often due to the weight of tradition, resistance to change, and the burden of non-guidance and counseling tasks. To close the implementation gap, we must overcome tradition, reckon with change, and focus on time-on-task through calendaring (Gysbers, 2005).

Diversity sensitive and responsive school counselors. The American School Counselor Association's *Ethical Standards for School Counselors* (2004) states that

> each person has the right to be respected, be treated with dignity and have access
> to a comprehensive school counseling program that advocates for and affirms
> all students from diverse populations regardless of ethnic/racial status, age,

economic status, special needs, English as a second language or other language group, immigration status, sexual orientation, gender, gender identity/expression, family type, religious/spiritual identity and appearance. (Preamble)

Diversity in all of its aspects will continue to increase in our society. Schools in particular will face increasing diversity in their student populations. As a result professional school counselors must be diversity sensitive and responsive. Their pre- and in-service diversity training must be expanded and extended to incorporate the latest in diversity knowledge, skills, and attitudes.

Local, state, and national policy. We believe policy formulation has been overlooked in the work of comprehensive guidance and counseling program development and implementation. While some progress has been made, it is time to turn full professional attention to policy formulation for guidance and counseling at local, state, and national levels. For example, school-board policies and state and national laws that endorse and support school counselors working in comprehensive guidance and counseling programs must be a national priority for professionals at all levels.

Local, state, and national leadership. The position-services model of guidance and counseling tended to fragment guidance and counseling activities and isolate practitioners from one another. The program approach, however, requires building and district coordination and collaboration as well as state leadership. All out efforts must now be made to identify and train guidance leaders at the building, district, and state levels. We believe that ASCA, working closely with the Association for Counselor Education and Supervision (ACES), is in a strong position to develop training standards for leaders and establish and support a leadership academy for future leaders. ASCA already provides leadership training for its state and local leaders. The Association now needs to go the next step and create and operate a National Leadership Academy. The purpose of the Academy would be to train local building and district guidance and counseling leaders as well as state directors and/or supervisors of guidance and counseling.

Accountability. Accountability in guidance and counseling has a long history, beginning at almost the same time that guidance and counseling were emerging in the schools (Gysbers, 2004). Over the decades, many studies have been conducted on the impact of guidance and counseling activities, services, and programs. These kinds of studies must continue. In addition, there is a need to train professional school counselors to regularly evaluate their work. Technology has caught up with the need for evaluation, making it possible for all professional school counselors to show how their work makes a difference in the lives of students. At lease one state, the state of Missouri, is "taking major steps to harness the power of technology and comprehensive school counseling programs to provide all school counselors with the knowledge, skills, and attitudes to conduct results-based evaluation as a regular part of their work" (Gysbers, Lapan, & Stanley, 2006, p. 36). This kind of effort must be done in every state.

In addition to the work that is being done to enable all professional school counselors to conduct results evaluation, substantial national efforts are required to improve results evaluation procedures and methods and the corresponding use of technology. What is needed is a national alliance of counselor educators and others with results evaluation expertise to join with the personnel in existing centers and the National Office of Research at the American School Counselor Association to expand and extend the frontiers of current results evaluation knowledge and skills.

Perspectives on the Future of School Counseling

Edwin L. Herr

Predicting the future is always difficult. The multitude of contextual and internal factors that can affect the results about which predictions are made can divert or interrupt a process and throw predictions askew. In particular, school counseling is a process, the shape and content of which is affected by many variables: state and national mandates; legislation; guidelines; demographics of a particular school at a particular point in time; priorities of the school administrator; the resources allocated; and perceptions of students, teachers, and parents among many other possible factors.

In essence, school counseling programs or services do not exist in a vacuum. What they are in a particular school depends upon the interaction of school counseling with the previously identified factors as well as the critical needs that are unique to a particular school or school district. Thus, school counseling is vulnerable to many forces that can alter its course and its particular emphases on student needs for academic, career, and personal counseling, mentoring, nurturance, and development.

Having stated the caveats about making predictions related to the future of the profession of school counseling, let me now turn to some predictions that seem to be inevitable aspects of that future.

School counseling, as a program or a process, does not stand alone. Like other forms of counseling, it is typically a subsystem in an institution for which counseling is not the major purpose. Therefore, strategic or program planning in school counseling must first be oriented or aligned with the mission of the organization, the particular school or school district, in which counseling services are deployed. Such planning must connect its purposes or processes to those that the school emphasizes.

In its evolution during the 20th century, school counseling, like schools per se, has been the object of many expectations: the prevention of child abuse, including bullying; early identification and treatment of children at risk of social, academic, or economic failure; preparing secondary school students with the knowledge and skills necessary for effective decision making, related to the choice of college or a workplace; assisting in the inclusion and support of minority students in the total school experience—academic and extra-curricular; working with children who have returned to school after periods of drug dependence to help them avoid relapse. Some of these expectations have arisen from federal legislation that identifies national goals to which school counseling is expected to contribute (e.g., The No Child Left Behind Act of 2001). In this sense, school counseling has been and will continue to be seen as a sociopolitical instrument of importance to achieving selected national or state goals for education. In other cases, these expectations for school counseling are seen as crucial to the needs of a particular school's climate and demographic or championed by parents on behalf of particular student populations. In either case, without constant planning and priority setting within a particular school, school counseling can be without the control of its focus and its use of resources.

Varying expectations of school counseling, from whatever sector they come, will continue to be present in different schools. Certainly, in many schools, they will dominate what professional school counselors do. They are legitimate issues, but the question for the future is, should they be the province of school counseling or should they be addressed by others in the school or, indeed, in the community? In any case, they need to be part of the planning, priority-setting, and, ultimately, the accountability of professional school counselors.

As part of its evolution toward the increased professionalization of the school counseling profession, the American School Counselor Association has developed *National Standards for School Counseling Programs* (Campbell & Dahir, 1997). These standards speak of the purpose of a counseling program in a school setting as promoting and enhancing the learning process and facilitating student development in three areas: academic development, career development, and personal–social development. These standards are intended to be used by schools and school systems to "develop quality and effective school counseling programs" (Campbell & Dahir, 1997, p. 6) that are designed to foster effective school counseling programs for all students, not just subpopulations of students in crisis. Thus, the fundamental goals of school counseling, according to these standards, is to "implement strategies and activities to support and maximize each student's ability to learn" (p. 6), acquire "the skills, attitudes, and knowledge that enable students to make a successful transition from school to work" (p. 6), and to help students acquire the skills, attitudes, and knowledge which provide a "foundation for personal and social growth as students progress through school and into adulthood" (p. 6).

These national standards for school counseling emphasize the need for sequential and developmental counseling activities for all students as they obtain the competencies identified in the three domains (i.e., academic, career, and personal–social) and as primary responsibilities of professional school counselors in fostering such processes and results.

The need for sequential, developmental, comprehensive programs of school counseling has been emphasized in theory, if not in practice, since the 1970s and 1980s. Now that an agreed-upon set of national standards for school counseling is available under the auspices of the professional organization for professional school counselors, it is likely that the content and practices espoused by these standards will grow in usage in more schools throughout the 21st century. The language of these standards will be used to establish a core role for school counseling and a basis for their accountability, although it is not likely that the range of expectations for professional school counselors to work with students in various types of crisis (e.g., physically and sexually abused, chemically dependent, early school learners, estranged from families, engaged in violent or abusive behavior) will suddenly end. Rather, the future is likely to see new models by which technology will increase its use to reduce the time expenditure that professional school counselors must now commit to non-counseling activities and to the management of school counseling programs. Further, and more likely in the future, is the active and systematic use of community mental health practitioners to provide counseling to students who are experiencing major behavioral crises. Such practitioners will likely be contracted by schools to augment professional school counselors in dealing with student needs that go beyond those identified in the national standards.

The underlying issue for the future is that school counseling has different types of relevance for different schools with different demographics and behavioral profiles. Urban, rural, suburban schools, schools dealing with large proportions of children from different cultural traditions, students from bilingual or immigrant families each may have different needs and expectations for school counseling, even though the content of the national standards may be important to most of these students. Such differences among schools will continue to raise future issues about how professional school counselors should be organized to deal with children who have normal developmental issues and those who are in crisis, and how to deliver the content and activity of the national standards and also deal effectively with attitudinal and behavioral problems that inhibit their academic learning and their interpersonal growth.

What seems clear is that school counseling in the future must be more than a loose collection of services that are reactive and remedial, and that do not touch the needs for student decision-making, readiness to learn, and the acquisition of skills, knowledge, and attitudes that are required in a world in rapid change (e.g. personal flexibility, adaptability to change, and the ability to take responsibility for one's academic, career, and personal–social life).

It would appear that to achieve such goals will continue to require excellent and focused preparation for professional school counselors. The current and future contributions to counselor education programs by the Council for the Accreditation of Counseling and Related Educational Programs (CACREP) and the reinforcement of these standards by the National Board for Certified Counselors and by state licensure statutes will continue to be major factors in the growing professional expertise of professional school counselors. But not all counselor education programs are CACREP accredited, provide the same levels of comprehensive preparation for professional school counselors, teach them about the national standards, or how to cope with the organization of school counseling programs to address the many expectations that will affect their practice. As a result, greater standardization of the preparation of professional school counselors will be needed. Beyond these continuing concerns, counselor preparation programs will increasingly need to encourage professional school counselors to be aware of and creative in the use of their resources, technologies, best practices, group work, paraprofessionals, and community mental health practitioners. To be able to do so effectively will require more attention to the need for leadership and management of school counseling programs by persons trained in school counseling who can negotiate with administrators, advocate for the importance of school counseling, participate in strategic planning, and be attentive to accountability processes.

(Note: See the CD-ROM for a list of references.)

CHAPTER 11

ADVOCACY IN ACTION: THE VOICE
OF THE STUDENT

James R. Cheek and Reese M. House

Let us think of education as the means of developing our greatest abilities, because in each of us there is a private hope and dream which, fulfilled, can be translated into benefit for everyone and greater strength for our nation.

—*John F. Kennedy*

Professional school counselors have an opportunity to make these words of President John F. Kennedy a reality. The overwhelming conclusion of data that has been gathered from various sources and populations proves that all students' abilities and dreams are not being encouraged, supported or fulfilled—the achievement gap among demographic lines alone give witness to the fact that schools are not accomplishing the goals of the educational system. Many professional school counselors may question, *I am just the "guidance" counselor—why does this matter to me?* In his final column as head of the National Center for Transforming School Counseling, Dr. Reese House (2005) stated that

> school counselors are perfectly placed to be key players in school reform. This comes from a firm belief that school counselors are the eyes, ears and heartbeat of the school. They are in a position to see more, hear more and know more than any other staff member in schools. This allows school counselors to be leaders in the school and advocates for all students. We have a moral and ethical obligation to students to eliminate inequities and provide access for all students. We must take on the mantle of leadership and advocate for all students. (p. 1)

Historically, advocacy was thought to be one of the key distinguishing elements between social workers and counselors (Sosin & Caulum, 1983). However, the keeping of such strict and discrete activities between those in the helping fields has become obsolete. The demanding nature of society and schools requires that professional school counselors adopt and assimilate a much-needed and vital role as advocate for all students—in social, emotional, and academic arenas.

The term *advocacy* has been used in mental health, social, and medical literature since the early 1700s (Brooks & Weikel, 1996). As with many different terminologies, the term *advocacy* has swung in and out of favor, often with various meanings and concepts attached. Over the past several decades, this concept has become increasingly vital to the daily work of mental health and social service workers (Bemak & Chung, 2005).

Dworkin and Dworkin (1971) framed the centuries-old concept of advocacy into an action-based call for all counselors to become leaders in social change rather than observers of the process. House and Martin (1998) further clarified advocacy as the belief that each person's actions, whether implemented individually or as part of a group, can lead toward improving conditions for the benefit of all people, especially the disenfranchised and disengaged. Further, advocacy must be an intentional effort that directly addresses proactive change to all levels of the learning environment, including policies, practices, and procedures, whether existing or proposed (Ezelle, 2001).

The process of integrating this systemic approach into the school counseling professional has been slow and somewhat tedious. Nonetheless, recent reform efforts, empirical evidence on educational gaps, and the passage of the No Child Left Behind Act of 2001 (U.S. Department of Education, 2002) have created an opportunity for professional school counselors to effectively demonstrate and implement advocacy for all stakeholders in their school. In fact, the opportunity and necessity for professional school counselors to redefine their role is vital.

As individuals and a profession as a whole, professional school counselors must demonstrate their ability to lead, advocate, and create change in the system that will provide greater benefit for all students. Today, consequences are dire for schools as budgetary considerations and high-stakes accountability standards are driving the future of education and all who are involved. If professional school counselors are not a strong and visible part of the solutions and reform of current educational dilemmas and inadequacies, their positions will be replaced with different staff and interventions to meet these new standards (Bailey, Getch, & Chen-Hayes, 2007).

Opportunities have opened recently for advocacy in counseling to move from an awareness of the need for advocacy to a level of knowledge about the tenets involved to its current position—an action-oriented skill that can be implemented, measured, and reported. The American Counseling Association recently adopted a set of advocacy competencies (Lewis, Arnold, House, & Toporek, 2006) that explicitly state that "advocacy-oriented counselors recognize the impact of social, political, economic and cultural factors on human development" (p. 1). Further, the advocacy competencies challenge counselors to adopt an advocacy orientation that identifies the strengths and resources of their consumers and to not only act on behalf of their stakeholders but to teach self-advocacy as they act in collaboration toward advocacy. The ASCA national model (American School Counselor Association [ASCA], 2005) included a skill-based framework for programmatic transformation and the implementation of advocacy for all stakeholders. In fact, when professional school counselors renovate their programs based on advocacy in combination with specifically stated competencies and expected outcomes, they are able to create a climate of supportive holistic development, based on strengths and competencies. The adoption of this responsibility as ally and change agent places counselors in an educational leadership role working to create systemic change that ultimately benefits students, schools, and society (Bailey et al., 2007; Dollarhide & Lemberger, 2006).

The process of implementing systemic change and advocacy is not easy, especially in schools where the role of counselors has always been nebulous, if not altogether focused on non-counseling-related tasks. Professional school counselors must take a stand for advocacy based on their training in human relationships and the ethical standards to which the profession adheres. "All students can learn" has long been used throughout educational arenas as a necessary battle cry for widespread school reform.

However well-intentioned the motto may be, it is very limiting in that all students DO learn—they either learn that they can succeed or they learn to fail. If the school system fails to provide students with qualified teachers and a rigorous curriculum, students often learn that school is not working for them. Indeed, students learn an identity that they internalize and put into action. It is in this setting that professional school counselors must undertake the role of advocate. Each and every student, regardless of identity, deserves and needs a voice. If professional school counselors do not assume the role of an advocate, they are in fact maintaining the status quo of social and academic inequity and continuing the system of injustice that is becoming evident to the general public (Bemak & Chung, 2005). Simply stated, the professional school counselor is, in fact and in practice, the voice of the student.

Following is a logical progression of action steps that can lead to the creation and development of an advocacy-based systemic school counseling program:

Step 1: Survey the Data!

The first step in initiating advocacy plans for schools is to start at the end. In other words, what do the data indicate? High-stakes testing and other accountability measures provide a rich source of information for the professional school counselor to use. Data such as test scores, discipline referrals, student self-report surveys, and attendance rates can supply professional school counselors with a huge variety of quantitative information about the school, faculty, the surrounding community, and, most important, students.

Data can provide objective and candid insights about the students, school, and community. Upon analysis, evidence of inequitable access issues may arise, thus leading to systemic issues that will require revision. Data provide a direction for programmatic planning and implementation as well as an accountability tool for the evaluation of those programs.

Most administrators and faculty understand the performance gaps and are rigorously expected to bring their schools in line with district, state, and federal standards. Previously, professional school counselors have not been part of the conversations regarding data and have not been included as part of the intervention and reformation process (Bemak, 2000; Taylor & Adelman, 1996). By using data, professional school counselors can specifically and behaviorally state quantifiable goals and objectives that can be implemented as part of the school counseling program. Through this process, school counselors become an important voice in the leadership and direction of the school.

Step 2: Define What You Do

Professional school counselors must provide a clear and concise definition of their role and function to students, teachers, administrators, and the community in general. The vague and undeveloped definition of school counseling in the past has created the breach for individual administrators and school districts to define each counselor and campus according to their own perceived need, which often changes from year to year and student to student. In fact, Bernstein (1995) accurately described the dilemma:

When schools fail to clearly define the counselor's role, school administrators, parents with special interests, teachers, or others may feel their agenda ought to be the school counseling program's priority. The results often lead to confusion and criticisms when they are disappointed.

The adoption of a clear definition of school counseling, preferably at the district level, will fashion the expectations of professional school counselors in a consistent and ultimately more productive outlook. In order to be effective, a clear program definition should identify its consumers, summarize the active components, articulate the competencies involved and emphasize the essential nature of the program to the overall educational environment (Ripley, Erford, Dahir & Eschbach, 2003; Wittmer, 2000). The Education Trust (2002) defined school counseling as a "profession that focuses on the relations and interactions between students and their environment with the expressed purpose of reducing the effect of environmental and institutional barriers that impede student success" (p. 2). This definition summarizes not only the definition of school counseling but leads to the next major step in pushing the progress of professional school counselors as advocates.

Step 3: Create an Active Mission Statement

Next, professional school counselors need to design and develop a school counseling mission statement that represents the school and community. Although many school counseling departments (and most schools) have a mission statement, it is often produced and then placed in a dusty binder on a shelf to be thrown away years later. A true mission statement captures not only the focus and target of the services delivered but also concentrates on the underlying philosophies and foundations of the school. If the counseling program does not have a mission statement, counselors must formulate one that echoes and demonstrates how professional school counselors are going to support and elevate the overall aim of the school. Once a mission statement is in place, then professional school counselors need to post it, publish it, share it with stakeholders, and, most important, own the mission personally and professionally to the point that it truly represents the daily tasks of the professionals who implement it. Used in this manner, the active mission statement will drive a program that will be aligned with the goals and mission of the school.

Step 4: Clearly Define Your Role as Advocate

As professional school counselors review the data and the mission of the school, information will be provided that supports their role as advocate or the *voice of the student*. As stated by Bemak and Chung (2005, p. 197), "it is not easy to move from being a well-liked and friendly school counselor to being an advocate." Within the spectrum of relationship building, professional school counselors can educate and reform administrative expectations to view professional school counselors as the students' advocate. The evolution of the counselor's role as an ally will not always be received as it is intended, and certain resistance and resentment is bound to occur with faculty, staff, and administrators. However, by using data to demonstrate the effectiveness of creating a safe environment for learning and achievement, professional school counselors can start to create an atmosphere of understanding. For example, within the present era of reform and high-stakes accountability, school administrators are held to extreme standards regarding the academic, fiscal, and security status of their campuses. When professional school counselors can directly tie their role of advocate into the accomplishment of administrators' objectives and goals, they are more likely to receive support for transforming the overall counseling program of their schools.

One of the means of educating others and integrating this role into the vernacular of the school is to actively state and act as the students' voice. For example, when attending a meeting to discuss a discipline problem, professional school counselors can articulate at the beginning of the meeting that they are there to represent the student's perceptions and views, as an ally. Again, this may be seen as oppositional to the process, but if school counselors are not the student's spokesperson in these meetings, who will be?

Meetings and situations such as this are the instruments that allow the qualitative stories behind the quantitative data to be told. In many situations, counselors know the story behind the quantitative statistics that can assist in decisions and interventions for students. The key lies in the delivery of the information and the relationships that are cultivated on the campus.

To be ultimately successful, schools must move away from an "Us vs. Them" conceptualization and into an "Us for Them" undertaking. With the training and educational background required, professional school counselors are the ideal professional to assist all members of the educational team to move towards this paradigm shift. At times, it may be necessary for professional school counselors to revisit and remind their colleagues of Maslow's Hierarchy of Needs (Maslow, 1987); especially acknowledging that the lower level (more fundamental needs) must be met before there can be a successful implementation of higher levels of thinking and achieving. By reminding professional educators of the developmental needs of their students, more effective interventions can be put in place to meet students where their individual needs are demonstrated. As developmental and relationship experts on the campus, professional school counselors should view their role as advocate in terms of *academic case management*, as they give perspective and professional guidance toward student development and achievement.

Step 5: Set Your Goals!

The goals of the school counseling program will define how the academic case management of each student is delivered. The ASCA national model (2005) delineated three major areas of development: academic, personal–social, and career development. Outcome measures for each student on the counselor's caseload can be articulated by the specified competencies in each of these three major developmental areas. By using a nationally standardized model, professional school counselors add to the validity and integrity of their programmatic goals and interventions.

It is no longer necessary for professional school counselors to design and develop their own comprehensive and developmental program. We recommend that self-advocacy, capacity, and resiliency building activities should be incorporated into the counseling program. The Search Institute's (1997) 40 Developmental Assets offers research-based strategies and competencies that assist students in developing the resilient and strength-based behaviors that assist them in their development into healthy and productive adults. These user-friendly materials are readily available and incorporate many of the interventions needed to boost student achievement, regardless of their racial–ethnicity or social identity (Scales & Roehlkepartain, 2003; Sesma & Roehlkepartain, 2003). Professional school counselors can integrate the assets and strengths of the student with information and education on being a self-advocate. By helping students to learn how to advocate for themselves by requesting meetings, writing letters, role-playing, and participating in other activities, professional school counselors are building on the resiliency of the students themselves.

As an advocate, professional school counselors must strive to remove barriers and promote high achievement on all levels by spotlighting the resiliency and capacities of its consumers. Professional school counselors are in the unique position to change the focus to what is right and competent about each student and situation rather than perpetrating the view that students are somehow broken and must be fixed. By discussing and monitoring students' strengths and concerns in all levels of academic, personal–social, and career development in combination with the self-advocacy efforts of the students, a relationship of trust and competency is cultivated that ultimately raises the achievement for all stakeholders through a renewed sense of personal, emotional, and physical safety and resiliency, thus creating a stable base of success for future growth.

Step 6: State How You Will Get There!

Usually, the modes of service delivery are the most recognized and comfortable area for professional school counselors to navigate. Through the modalities of the school guidance curriculum, individual student planning, responsive services, and system support, professional school counselors can ensure that all students in their care are achieving to their fullest potential. It is essential that professional school counselors evaluate their knowledge and skills in each area and seek out professional development opportunities to increase their knowledge and skills when needed. The service-delivery modalities are the vehicles that allow data-driven objectives to be delivered to the consumers, including students, teachers, parents, or the community.

It is imperative that counselors analyze and systematically plan the delivery of their comprehensive programs based on the needs of the population, not based on their own comfort level. Communities, schools, and students change and evolve over time. The topics and objectives that were relevant for one group may not meet the needs of another. Professional school counselors working as advocates are proactive and responsive to the actual needs as they are revealed through data.

As high stakes and accountability become more prevalent and demanding, time factors and extra duties make effective academic case management more difficult. Teachers and administrators are less flexible in permitting time during the school day to be devoted to the implementation of the counseling program. Therefore, counselors are often more stressed and stretched than ever. Professional school counselors must overcome this frustration and integrate their program into the school plan.

There are several strategies for integrating counseling advocacy efforts throughout the school day. Most academic programs and subject areas have curriculum maps or pacing guides that direct the flow and dispersion of the various subject areas. Based on the needs of the school, counselors can also create a curricular map of the needed services for the school. As part of the leadership team of the school (a critical necessity), professional school counselors can design and integrate school counseling programmatic pacing guides demonstrating how the counseling curriculum is directly tied into the subject matter or themes that are being taught throughout the year. In this manner, the school counselor's implementation of services becomes both inter- and intracurricular.

For example, upon review of the discipline data, it is clear that fighting and conflict are increasing in the school. By working with the various academic teams, professional school counselors are able to instruct teachers and students alike in conflict resolution and transformation strategies. Then, as each subject-matter teacher addresses their specific topic, these skills are reinforced and discussed. A language arts teacher might discuss which character in a piece of literature experienced conflict and how the students could propose a better or different way to solve that conflict. A social studies instructor might have students role-play conflict mediation between two warring nations as part of a history lesson.

Another possibility for integrating through the curriculum is the creation of teacher-led activities that use counseling topics as part of testing practice. For example, counselors can create small worksheets from which students read a passage regarding a historical figure that demonstrated advocacy and conflict resolution skills, and then answer the questions that are formatted in a context similar to the standardized testing modes.

By connecting the delivery of needed information in a format that ties into the academic curriculum, professional school counselors can gain more access to students, even vicariously, as well as create an impact on a school-wide basis. As barriers and time constraints are positioned against the delivery of effective academic case management, professional school counselors can think of their data-driven competencies in terms of a *virus*; by attaching it to each curricular area's content, a *positive contamination* occurs that will standardize and stabilize the entire climate of the school. Once students start hearing and experiencing interventions that are relevant to their daily struggles and life issues, they will start forming and maintaining positive attachments to the safe atmosphere that is being created. If students feel safe with significant adults who are allies, their achievement will increase (Scales & Roehlkepartain, 2003) and further provide supporting data for counselor involvement.

Step 7: Positively Contaminate Your School With the Advocacy "Virus"!

As success grows, professional school counselors can bring other allies from the school and community into the advancement for advocacy and achievement of all. There is far too much needed by today's students and families for one person to create the change alone, although professional school counselors must be integrally involved in starting the process. As supportive evidence and data grow, more stakeholders will join in the paradigm shift. At that point, creating collaborative efforts to build relationships and teaming in order to complete tasks can successfully shift from a focus on specific individuals to a positive support of systemic change (National Center for Transforming School Counseling, 2003).

SUMMARY/CONCLUSION

Change is a process, and not always an easy one. It takes time, is messy, and is somewhat scary. When the process becomes difficult, professional school counselors must reach into their own resiliency, integrity, and passion to recharge and regain perspective on the far-reaching positive contributions that they are creating. Pat Martin (2005), a professional school counselor, summed up the new face of professional school counselors as advocates:

> We must get out of the business of 'fixing kids'. . . . Instead of standing at the bottom of the waterfall, and catching kids as they slip off, we need to go to the top of the waterfall and figure out what the kids are slipping on.

As society and the world in general have changed tremendously, the field of school counseling has been forced to transform and sprint forward to meet the changing needs of its consumers. It is an exciting time to be involved in the school counseling profession. Being an advocate is a never-ending process, not a product. There has never been a more opportune time for professional school counselors to demonstrate their value and impact on the entire educational community, and, as delineated by John F. Kennedy, ultimately provide a significant benefit and greater strength for our nation.

(Note: See the CD-ROM for a list of references.)

CHAPTER 12

THE PROFESSIONAL SCHOOL COUNSELOR'S ROLE IN RAISING STUDENT ACHIEVEMENT

Teesue H. Fields and Peggy LaTurno Hines

Preview

The Education Reform Movement of the 1990s continues to have a tremendous impact upon schools in the 21st century. Through the No Child Left Behind Act of 2001, schools are now held accountable for the academic achievement level of all students. The professional school counselor brings important knowledge and skills to a school's improvement process. We discuss how the professional school counselor can contribute to a school's effort to raise student achievement.

K–12 education in the new millennium has focused upon improving the academic achievement of every student. The U.S. Congress and numerous state legislatures have enacted legislation to hold schools accountable for raising the academic achievement level of all students (Indiana Department of Education, 1999; U.S. Department of Education, 2001). The belief that schools are responsible for teaching all students to reach rigorous academic standards is now the norm by which schools are evaluated (Haycock, 2002; Hines & Fields, 2004; Reynolds & Hines, 2001b; Tucker & Codding, 1998).

This emphasis on high academic achievement for all students should put professional school counselors at the center of the business of education. Professional school counselors focus on the academic, career and personal–social development of all students and are trained to help students who are having difficulty in those areas. However, education reform models omit professional school counselors from the planning process for achieving educational excellence. For example, professional school counselors are never mentioned in the U.S. Department of Education's publication, *School-Based Reform: Lessons From a National Study* (Quellmalz, Shield, & Knapp, 1995). When professional school counselors are mentioned in reform models, it is only to include their position on an advisory committee (U.S. Department of Education, 1998). Professional school counselors are seen as peripheral at best, and unnecessary at worst, in the effort to raise student achievement (House & Martin, 1998).

Professional school counselors are the eyes and ears of the school (House, 2002). They know the issues and concerns of students, parents, faculty, administration, and the community. In addition, professional school counselors possess knowledge and skill sets that are unique within the school environment. While both professional school counselors and administrators are trained in leadership and research skills, professional school counselors are the only educators skilled in counseling, group facilitation, collaboration and consultation, and advocacy (Hines & Fields, 2004). The uniqueness of the position, coupled with the knowledge and skills, place professional school counselors in a position to contribute significantly to the school's mission of raising student achievement (Fields & Hines, 2000).

The second edition of *The ASCA National Model: A Framework for School Counseling Programs* (American School Counselor Association [ASCA], 2005) stresses the importance of the school counseling program's contribution to student achievement. Professional school counselors play a critical role in efforts to raise student achievement through the implementation of system-centered and student-centered activities. *System-centered* activities are designed to influence adult behavior or the educational environment. From a system-centered standpoint, professional school counselors join with building administrators to help facilitate school improvement efforts. A critical system-centered professional school counselor activity is facilitating the creation of interventions designed to remove barriers impeding academic achievement. Additional system-centered activities include using data to spur change, task group facilitation, advocacy, collaboration, and conducting research.

Student-centered interventions are activities created to directly affect students. From a student-centered perspective, professional school counselors work to align their counseling program priorities with the school's student-achievement goals through the design of a continuum of interventions that help students master the school guidance standards and indicators that will help students be successful in school. Student-centered activities include developmental guidance lessons and small-group and individual counseling.

In this chapter, we describe how professional school counselors can use their skills and knowledge to contribute significantly to the academic mission of the school. It will examine system-centered and student-centered ways in which professional school counselors can influence student achievement. Examples will be provided through the lens of South Middle School (SMS), a fictional middle school (Grades 6–8), with a student body consisting of 25% African American students, 3% Asian American students, 45% European American students, and 27% Hispanic American students. Forty percent of SMS students receive free or reduced-price lunch. At SMS, there are three professional school counselors who loop with their 6 through 8 grade levels. Thus, they work with the same students for 3 years, and over 3 years will work closely with all of the teacher teams in the building. The professional school counselors are in a unique position to understand all of the strengths and weaknesses of both the staff and the students at SMS as well as the South City community. They are well versed in the educational and community resources available for students and their families.

SYSTEM-CENTERED ACTIVITIES

Professional school counselors understand the process of systemic change and are familiar with education reform models. They know that to raise student achievement the focus must not be solely on helping students gain the knowledge and skills needed to help them achieve. They must also help adults create and implement effective strategies that encourage student achievement. Through the activities of collaboration and teaming, school data analysis, group facilitation, advocacy, and research, professional school counselors can effectively join with building administrators in facilitating the school improvement process.

COLLABORATION AND TEAMING

The creation of an effective school improvement plan requires a tremendous amount of collaboration and teaming. It is important for the school to involve faculty, parents, students, and community stakeholders (Reynolds & Hines, 2001b). Professional school counselors know how to form effective task groups and can use their teaming and collaboration skills to bring teachers, parents, and community members together. Professional school counselors are skilled at using a wide variety of resources and are natural liaisons between the school and community. Professional school counselors can be an invaluable resource for involving the broader community in efforts to raise academic achievement. Collaboration will also be necessary during the strategy implementation process. The counselor can help the various constituent groups stay involved in program and strategy implementation and ensure that all groups have an opportunity for continued input. The following is an example:

> SMS is beginning a school improvement process. The principal and professional school counselors work together to create a school improvement team (SIT), consisting of faculty, parents, and community representatives. The principal and professional school counselors collaborate on meeting agendas and take turns facilitating various portions of the meetings. At the same time, they meet with the grade-level instructional teams in the building. They actively collaborate to engage the entire faculty in the school improvement effort.

SCHOOL DATA ANALYSIS

Data-driven decision making is a critical element in successful school improvement efforts (Green, 2001). Professional school counselors are skilled in the collection, analysis, and presentation of student achievement and related data. Their skills can help facilitate the school improvement team's examination of data, such as standardized test scores, grades, teacher assessments, and student management data. They also understand the importance of disaggregating data by variables such as gender, ethnicity, and socioeconomic status to discover underlying access and equity issues that influence student achievement. Data analysis is used to drive interventions, programs, and activities that are designed to raise student achievement:

> The SMS counselors may facilitate an in-depth examination of SMS student achievement and related data. The first thing the school improvement team does is look at the standardized test scores, grade reports, and school management data for the current year and for the previous 2 years. This gives the SIT team an overall report on their student outcomes. All the data are disaggregated by gender, ethnicity, and socioeconomic status so the improvement team can look at gross outcomes as well as the outcomes for subgroups of students. The SMS team discovers that, at all grade levels, female students are well below average in

math scores. Girls are also underrepresented in pre-algebra and algebra classes. In addition, there is a higher math failure rate for Hispanic girls. The SMS school improvement team shares this information with the entire faculty, who decide to create a goal to improve the math scores of females in general and Hispanic females in particular.

GROUP FACILITATION

Small-task groups perform much of the work in raising student achievement (Murphy & Lick, 1998). Although a school administrator often leads the school improvement team, other staff members will lead many of the subgroups and strategy teams. Professional school counselors are logical leaders for these groups due to their task group leadership skills (Fields & Hines, 2000). They understand the stages of group development, the importance of group process, and group-facilitation skills. Professional school counselors expect groups to move through the typical stages of forming, storming, norming, performing, and adjourning (Tuckman, 1965). Professional school counselors help the group move through these stages in a healthy way so that the group task gets accomplished and the group does not get stuck in any stage.

During early meetings, professional school counselors help the members understand themselves in relation to the task and work to establish a sense of trust, thus enabling the group to proceed more smoothly (Coyne, 1989). As experienced group leaders, professional school counselors recognize that a certain amount of disagreement among members is to be expected (Gladding, 2003) and that their job is to normalize this stage and help members use the energy to seek better solutions to the task at hand. As the group works to finalize its report and agree on strategies, it is important that conflicts among various viewpoints be resolved. The steps are essentially the same as in conflict resolution, but the leader's issues revolve around the task rather than personal conflicts. Professional school counselors help members examine various perspectives (e.g., whether or not to require a teacher recommendation for algebra enrollment) and then develop strategies that both sides can accept:

> Jacinda Brown, the seventh-grade SMS professional school counselor is the facilitator of a math curriculum task group. One of the members of the group is Mr. Pi, an experienced math teacher. The group's task is to examine the problem of the low math achievement by female students. The committee is discussing the idea of removing lower level math options for all students as a way of raising the rigor of math. Mr. Pi is adamant that math content not be watered down. He is concerned that any effort to include underprepared students will affect his ability to teach math in a way that will prepare his students for high school math classes. He believes that not all students can learn math and, therefore, lower level math courses are needed. The other group members have heard Mr. Pi repeat this opinion over the years, and they are frustrated with his lack of willingness to try new strategies to reach these students. Ms. Brown carefully facilitates the meeting, making sure that the group hears Mr. Pi. She helps the group begin to brainstorm various strategies, making sure that Mr. Pi's concerns are taken

into consideration. Ms. Brown models respect for the opinions of all members and facilitates the resolution of disagreements into the creation of strategies that the group can support.

ADVOCACY

Many forces influence student achievement. These include school policies, teacher quality, attendance and discipline procedures, parent and community involvement, instruction and assessment methods, expectations, and guidance standards (Haycock, 2002; Reynolds & Hines, 2001b). Professional school counselors advocate for programs and experiences that are needed to lower barriers to learning. They point out inequities and policies that discriminate, and they use their advocacy skills to gain support with parents and community stakeholders (House & Martin, 1998). Professional school counselors are in a prime position to raise probing questions, be a voice for the students most often left behind, and mobilize allies outside the schools:

> At SMS, the eighth-grade counselor, Michael Justice, has noticed that a large number of Latina students have limited English proficiency. He is also aware that math is not considered an important skill for girls to learn in many Hispanic American homes. Mr. Justice approaches the math curriculum committee with his concerns about the influence of limited English proficiency on the Latina student math achievement levels and actively works to find strategies to address this barrier. He also teams with a Hispanic English teacher. They meet with leaders of the local Hispanic community and provide information about the skills needed by Latinas to be successful in the workforce. They collaborate with the leaders to set up tutoring centers in area churches that will work with Hispanic students.

ACTION RESEARCH

Professional school counselors are trained action researchers. Schools expend many resources on strategies to improve student achievement. It is imperative that the outcomes of these strategies be studied in order to examine their effectiveness. Professional school counselors can help the school plan, collect, and analyze data on school improvement efforts:

> As the SMS task groups develop strategies, the professional school counselors collaborate with the groups to develop an evaluation plan. The plan includes the collection of baseline data. The professional school counselors continue to work with the groups through the implementation phase, supporting needed professional development, and working with any resistance.

STUDENT-CENTERED ACTIVITIES

Professional school counselors are perhaps more familiar with student-centered activities than with system-centered activities. Student-centered programs and activities are often based on a student needs assessment (Gysbers & Henderson, 2005). However, when professional school counselors are focused on raising student achievement, student-centered activities are designed from a counseling program that is aligned with the academic goals of the school. Student-centered activities affect student knowledge, skills, and behavior. They contribute to the academic goals of the school by helping all students master those guidance standards that will support goal attainment. In order to ensure that every student masters the standards, it is important that a continuum of interventions be created. Thus, student-centered activities include aligning the school counseling program with the school's academic goals, creating developmental guidance classroom lessons, conducting small-group counseling sessions, and counseling individual students.

ALIGNING THE SCHOOL COUNSELING PROGRAM WITH THE SCHOOL'S ACADEMIC GOALS

The ASCA national model (ASCA; 2005) emphasizes the importance of aligning the school counseling program with the academic goals of the school. To do this, professional school counselors work with their faculty and advisory council to ensure that the standards with the greatest potential to help students reach the school's academic goals receive the greatest attention (Reynolds & Hines, 2001a). Once the standards are prioritized, the professional school counselor then designs a continuum of interventions designed to make certain that every student masters those standards. While additional interventions are created on a responsive services basis for those students with individual personal–social problems, it is important to note that the focus of student-centered interventions is on contributing to the school's academic goals and, thus, follows a top-down rather than bottom-up plan:

> SMS's sixth-grade team has set a goal to raise math scores on the state standardized test. Ashlyn Glenn is the sixth-grade professional school counselor. She works with the faculty and the school counseling program community council to prioritize the student guidance standards and indicators by answering the question, *Which of our school counseling program standards and indicators do you believe are the most important for our sixth-grade students to master to help them raise their math achievement level?* Ms. Glenn designs the year's guidance curriculum, based upon the established priorities. She then works with the faculty to map how the curriculum will be delivered.

CLASSROOM GUIDANCE

Once the school's counseling program standards are prioritized based on the school's academic goals, the professional school counselor designs the classroom guidance curriculum, which may be delivered in many ways. Professional school counselors may come into classrooms, faculty may teach the standards through the regular curriculum or by adapting the curriculum to fit the guidance standards, and appropriate community members may deliver the curriculum (ASCA; 2005; Reynolds & Hines, 2001a, 2001b):

> Ashlyn Glenn, the sixth-grade SMS professional school counselor, goes into each sixth grade classroom the first 2 weeks of school and conducts lessons on study

skills, time management, and asking for help (ASCA Standard A; Campbell & Dahir, 1997). Each teacher follows up on these lessons by giving each student a planner and helping them map out assignments for the first grading period. The teachers also give tips for studying their particular subject and use many study aids for students during the first grading period. Each teacher also uses strategies to encourage students to ask for help, particularly students who are having difficulty. Thus, all students in sixth grade are getting the same study skills instruction. Because SMS has decided to focus on math achievement, the sixth-grade counselor and the math teacher present some extra lessons on how to study math and how to deal with math anxiety. These supplemental lessons deal with the specific academic goals of the school to improve math skills.

SMALL-GROUP COUNSELING

Professional school counselors often conduct small groups, which may be based on a general needs assessment or may be in response to specific problems (Smead, 1995), such as a number of students who have experienced loss of a loved one. While this is one way to establish a small-group program, professional school counselors offering a continuum of services aligned with the school's academic goals will use small-group counseling as a follow-up to classroom guidance for those students who experience difficulty in mastering the guidance standard. Using this model, professional school counselors are able to use group counseling to work on difficulties that prevent students from mastering the school counseling program standards.

The small group is an ideal way to work with these types of problems because a level of trust can be established in a small group that is difficult to achieve in the classroom. Professional school counselors can use group counseling leadership skills to establish trust among group members, help the members set individual goals, and provide opportunity for the members to practice new skills (such as asking for help) in the group. Counselors also use basic group work skills in drawing out, connecting, and cutting off to help all members of the group benefit from participation. If personal issues surface in the small group, professional school counselors use evaluation skills to determine the seriousness of such issues and make referrals for individual counseling or other resources as needed:

> After the classroom guidance classes on study skills and the additional lessons on math study skills at SMS, there is still a group of girls who teachers identify as being very anxious about learning math. Ms. Glenn, the sixth-grade counselor, invites the girls to join a group that will focus on individual ways to deal with math anxiety.

INDIVIDUAL COUNSELING

Professional school counselors know that some students need individual counseling to work on issues that are negatively influencing their academic achievement or mastery of the school counseling program standards. Assuming that the system barriers have been removed and that adequate support is now available, it is more likely that each student has an idiosyncratic problem. Individual counseling provides an opportunity for more in-depth help with these issues. This type of counseling is usually short term in nature (ASCA; 2005). Professional school counselors are familiar with community resources and refer students and families appropriately:

> At SMS, even with the systemic changes, classroom guidance lessons, and small-group time, there are still several eighth-grade Hispanic girls who are not achieving well in math. At this point, the eighth-grade counselor, Michael Justice, sees each girl individually to further analyze the issues. Marisa is a bright Hispanic student who is still making Cs and Ds in pre-algebra, even though she participates in the new group tutoring and homework sessions and has access to an individual tutor. When Mr. Justice talks with Marisa, he discovers that the family has been under a lot of stress because a family member has a chronic illness. Marisa has had difficulty concentrating on her schoolwork and, since math is her most difficult subject, the lack of concentration shows up in pre-algebra the most. Mr. Justice works with Marisa to devise solutions that will relieve some of her anxiety about the family situation while still giving math some of her energy. They go to the math teacher together and explain the situation. All three agree that if there has been a crisis with the sick family member, Marisa can ask to have a test postponed or have an extra day for homework. Just knowing that this is a possibility relieves a lot of Marisa's stress, and her grades start to improve almost immediately.

Summary/Conclusion

Raising the academic achievement level of all students is the primary goal for K–12 schools. While typically left out of school reform, professional school counselors bring important knowledge and skills to the school improvement process and are valuable and essential resources in raising the academic achievement of all students. Professional school counselors need to be actively engaged in both system-centered and student-centered activities. System-centered activities place professional school counselors in positions that facilitate the school improvement process and advocate for programs, policies, and environments that promote academic growth. Student-centered activities create a school counseling program that is aligned with the academic goals of the school and provide a continuum of strategies designed to help every student master guidance standards that promote learning. The activities of professional school counselors are beneficial to all students and staff as the education community seeks to achieve higher levels of performance.

(Note: See the CD-ROM for a list of references.)

CHAPTER 13

ORGANIZATION DEVELOPMENT IN SCHOOLS

Joyce A. DeVoss

Preview

Organization development in schools is an ongoing effort to create and maintain a model, structure, and environment that produce the highest possible effectiveness in promoting student success. This chapter describes organization development in schools and reviews some models for K–12 school reform and their potential benefits and limitations. Professional school counselors in the 21st century use the ASCA National Model (American School Counselor Association [ASCA], 2005) for school counseling programs as a guide to their proactive participation in organizational development for school improvement. Professional school counselors align their programs with the mission of schools for the benefit of all students.

School districts across the country are trying to improve instruction. The extent to which reform efforts affect individual schools or whole districts varies, as do the methods that are used, including new curricula, extensive professional development programs, and comprehensive school reform. The federal government created the Comprehensive School Reform Demonstration Act in 1998 (CSRD), earmarking $145 million for incentives to schools that were using one or more comprehensive improvement plans or developing their own. The CSRD interventions that were used are departures from current practice, requiring all members of school communities to learn new knowledge, skills, and practices. Often, these interventions require organizational changes and incorporate collective learning. The more ambitious and unconventional the interventions, the more learning is necessary; the more comprehensive the approach, the greater the need for organization development.

In the last decade of the 20th century, the school counseling profession began adopting comprehensive school guidance programs that required school organizational changes and promoted collective learning and a focus on fostering the academic and life success of all students. Comprehensive guidance programs are integrated into school curriculum and incorporate a prevention component. The movement toward adopting statewide comprehensive guidance programs positioned school counselors to become active participants and leaders in school reform.

Comprehensive school reform focuses on reorganizing and revitalizing entire schools rather than implementing isolated reforms. It is a systemic approach to school reform that uses well-researched models for change that is supported by expert trainers and facilitators. Most comprehensive school reform models include high academic standards, relevant professional development, and community involvement. Schools undergoing reform typically engage in some degree of organization development, "an ongoing effort to create and maintain a model, structure, and environment that produce the highest possible effectiveness" (Coll, 1994, p. 47). Successful organization development in schools is ongoing, organization wide, and supported by school stakeholders, with the overall goal being to improve student academic achievement. Professional school counselors support this overall goal.

The professional development component of organization development is critical to comprehensive school reform. Hixson and Tinzmann (1990) identified three challenges for professional development in 21st century schools: (a) meeting the needs of diversity in the student population; (b) adopting appropriate goals for schooling; and (c) implementing organizational structures to promote shared responsibility, collaboration, and a community of continual learning. In light of these challenges, Hixson and Tinzmann (1990) identified new priorities for professional development: a focus on systemic change, or change in the *culture* of the school; continuing focus of change at the school level and focus of professional development on developing *learning communities*; learning that is continuous for students, teachers, counselors, and administrators; and responsibility that falls on all educational staff to continue their professional development. These priorities for professional development concepts are consistent with the values of the profession of school counseling.

Models for K–12 School Improvement

In the past, numerous new school reform models have been developed and evaluated. As members or potential members of school improvement leadership teams, professional school counselors would be wise to develop a familiarity with some of the current school reform models. This section reviews a few of the many models available to schools and their approaches to organization development.

North Central Regional Educational Laboratory

Hassel, Raack, Burkhardt, Chapko, and Blaser (2000) developed a guide for the North Central Regional Educational Laboratory (NCREL) school reform model with the following components:

- Strategizing through goal and standard setting
- Building support from stakeholders
- Facilitating informed choice, with each school developing their own strategy to meet their school's needs
- Forging a new compact with schools, whereby they receive greater authority for reform strategies along with accountability for results
- Building capacity for strengthening teaching, learning, and leadership

Each component has related action steps, examples of which for the first component of *strategizing through goal and standard setting* are as follows:

1. Identifying the district's key priorities
2. Determining how comprehensive school reform supports the district's mission, vision, and goals
3. Identifying the district's assets
4. Determining method and schedule of implementation
5. Identifying financial resources for comprehensive school reform efforts
6. Determining evaluation strategies

School counseling programs are currently customized to support district and school missions, visions, goals, and, most important, their students.

This guide was developed to help districts make comprehensive school reform an integral part of strategies for improving student achievement. When identifying the district's assets, the school reform leadership team should carefully consider the type of leadership needed and the composition of the leadership team, the school–media relationship, the dedication level of school personnel, the level of support of constituents and local businesses, the commitment level of teachers and staff, available funding through grants and other sources, potential partnerships, and opportunities for collaboration. Professional school counselors should actively advocate for representation on school leadership teams. They are key relationship and partnership builders for schools.

VISION-BASED LEADERSHIP AND THE LEARNING SCHOOL

Wallace, Engel, and Mooney (1997) stressed vision-based leadership as critical to school success. They proposed a model of a learning school in which everyone is a learner. Their model demonstrated how theory and research can influence educational vision by incorporating concepts from Senge's (1990) learning organization in the role of leadership in the learning school. For Senge, dialogue is critical among all levels of the organization. Furthermore, he incorporated the disciplinary elements of personal mastery, mental models, shared vision, team learning, and systems thinking in his vision of the learning organization.

Sergiovanni (as cited in Brandt, 1992) contributed the moral dimension of leadership in the learning community that complements Senge's (1990) concept of a learning organization. He stated that discussion about attitudes and values inform the role of the leader. Sergiovanni also proposed the idea of shared leadership, with emphasis on the content of education. His moral basis for educational leadership stems from the leader's perceived obligations and duties implied from shared values, ideas, and ideals. The model for the learning school includes integration of elements of a shared vision, authentic teaching and learning, a supportive school organization, and the use of assessment.

Wallace et al. (1997) explained how to achieve shared governance and how leaders can engage others to achieve a shared vision. They discussed how to engage the broader community in the learning community model, borrowing their underlying message from the Bible: "Where there is no vision, people perish" (Proverbs 29:18). Wallace et al. believed that the sharing of a mission should be systemic, and that the values, sentiments, and beliefs of communities connect people in a common cause. Communities give us norms to structure what we do and give us reason why we do what we do. Professional school counselors in the 21st century are key players in the learning community. They promote the development of the whole student. They need to accept a place on leadership teams for organizational development to reform schools.

NEW DESIGNS FOR LEARNING

New Designs for the learning process (Copa, 1999) is one in which staff, students, community, and a team of school designers work together to discover new ways to design a school's learning experiences and environment. Goals include

- representing the leading edge of a new breed of schools;
- operating the school as a learning community;
- drawing more attention to learning versus teaching;
- more closely aligning learner expectations with learning process organization and environment;
- promising the idea of a common set of learner outcomes for all;
- relating learner expectations to challenges and opportunities in work, family, community, and personal life;
- providing a positive special school character with more focus, coherence, and spirit to learning; and
- wanting schools that do not cost more to build or operate.

Some of the key learning elements in this model include context, expectations, process, partnerships, staff development, celebration, and accountability. At the inception of the comprehensive school reform process, the formal school leadership carefully chooses a team devoted to the design of the school's learning process and environment. Design group members come from inside and outside the school. The professional school counselor should advocate to be part of the leadership team. Team members are expected to think comprehensively and long term. The model seeks to reawaken learners' potential as well as that of staff and community and fosters a special spirit that gives meaning to all dimensions of learning. This model gives students multiple pathways to learn, thereby leveling the playing field for all learners.

The learning community's attention to learning organization concepts influences organization of time, learners, staff, process, decision-making technology, and settings. Emphasis is given to the learning staff and staff development focused on current and future needs. Consideration is also given to who can best provide staff training. Design group members act as role models for others, relying on more than one way of doing things, bringing the rest of the learning community along with reform efforts, and thinking comprehensively and long term.

THE COALITION OF ESSENTIAL SCHOOLS

Theodore R. Sizer founded the Coalition of Essential Schools (CES), a comprehensive school change project, while at Brown University in 1984. CES was influenced by the Model Schools Project movement sponsored by the National Association of Secondary School Principals between 1969 and 1974. CES initially focused on high schools, and then expanded to lower grades. CES reform came from the grassroots, including the local community, and maintains that no two good schools are the same.

CES reform principles highlight school climate and a set of organizational principles to govern behavior and beliefs of member schools and the national organization. CES stresses the importance of documenting change, valuing local wisdom, and responding flexibly to local contexts. CES values collaboration and changes to school structures to accommodate CES principles. Advocated school changes include a view of students as workers, smaller class sizes, personalization, professional sharing among teachers, and collaborative conceptions of curriculum, instruction, and assessment.

Professional school counselors are trained in relationship building that can lead to collaboration and coordination of services in an effort to bring about the types of changes proposed by the CES model.

SUCCESS FOR ALL, AND ROOTS AND WINGS

Success for All (SFA) is a comprehensive school-wide reform model developed by Robert Slavin and colleagues at Johns Hopkins University (Lockwood, 1998) for elementary schools that are focused on reading and students at risk of academic failure. The program stresses that reform efforts must deal with instruction, curriculum, and school organization in order to be successful over time and not regress to the old system. SFA believes that all children must read at grade level by third grade. They use tutors to ensure that students do not fall behind. Furthermore, they administer assessments at 8-week intervals to regularly monitor progress. This model has the advantage of also being available in Spanish.

Roots and Wings (Slavin & Madden, 2000; Slavin, Madden, & Wasik, 1996) is a comprehensive school reform model that incorporates all elements of Success for All. It also includes MathWings, based on the National Council of Teachers of Mathematics standards, and WorldLab, which uses simulations and group-learning projects for social studies and science. Schools implementing Roots and Wings generally do so over a 3-year period, starting with the SFA components in the first year, MathWings in the second year, and WorldLab in the third year.

SFA, and Roots and Wings are structured models that provide complete sets of student materials, teacher's manuals, and other support. Furthermore, Roots and Wings uses a Family Support Team in each school, made up of concerned school personnel who are focused on attendance, school-based intervention, parental involvement, and connections with community service providers. Elementary schools are where professional school counselors devote the most time to delivery of school guidance services to students and can offer strong support of this type of school reform effort.

THE PAIDEIA PROGRAM

The Paideia Program (Lockwood, 1998) was based on the writings and ideas of American educator and philosopher Mortimer Adler, now supported by the National Paideia Center (NPC), founded in 1988 and housed at University of North Carolina at Chapel Hill. It provides training and technical assistance in Paideia methods, researches the results of the methods, and acts as a clearinghouse for schools establishing the Paideia program.

The basic belief of this model is that a democratic society needs to provide excellent education to all students. The program provides a rigorous liberal arts education in K–12 that fosters critical thinking and the necessary skills for full participation in a democratic society. It employs cooperative learning and collaborative seminars and views teachers as facilitators. As with other school reform programs, the Paideia Program could be strengthened with a comprehensive school guidance program, based on the ASCA national model and customized to support the program's goals.

COMER SCHOOL DEVELOPMENT PROGRAM

The Comer Process is a school-wide intervention approach developed by Dr. James P. Comer, a professor of child psychiatry at Yale University. This approach maintains that healthy child development is key to academic and life success. Child development is described as occurring along six developmental pathways: physical, cognitive, psychological, language, social, and ethical. These pathways are the framework for which decisions are made to benefit children in Comer School Development Programs. This approach has demonstrated effectiveness in increasing academic achievement, improving behavior and attendance, and improving students' self-concepts. Professional school counselors are trained to take child developmental issues into consideration as they make decisions to choose appropriate interventions for their students. Furthermore, their mission aligns with the school mission to improve student success, as demonstrated by indicators monitored by the Comer Process, as well as other indicators of student success.

The Comer Process emphasizes the need for a team approach and the development of a school culture that is characterized by respectful problem solving, consensus building, and collaboration. These are processes for which professional school counselors are well prepared. They have much to offer to enhance the success of this and other school-wide intervention approaches.

There are many other promising whole-school reform programs, including School-wide Projects and eight designs representing diverse approaches within the New American Schools programs. Information on these programs can be found in the ERIC Digest titled *Whole School Reform* (McChesney, 1998) and in other educational publications such as the *Phi Delta Kappan*. A familiarity with current school reform programs can benefit professional school counselors as they contribute to the development of school reform and organizational development efforts and align their school counseling programs with these initiatives.

LIMITATIONS OF SCHOOL REFORM EFFORTS

Cohen and Loewenberg Ball (2001) reported that the history of instructional intervention is one of very limited success. They noted that interventions tend to be surface level, do not last long, are affected by rapid staff turnover, and subject to poorly integrated accumulation of past interventions. They offer three plausible explanations for these observations. First, while no intervention can be totally comprehensive, most have been only partial. Second, many interventions provide principles and directions but leave a lot of specifics to be filled in by teachers and schools. Finally, those who initiate the interventions rarely provide the training needed for school personnel, parents, and students. These observations and explanations offer support for whole-school, systemic approaches to school reform. They offer support for comprehensive school guidance programs based on the ASCA national model that are whole-school, systemic approaches to meeting the needs of all students.

Schwartz (2001) reported that school efforts to close the achievement gap between ethnic and racial minorities and White students have generally been unsuccessful. However, recently developed knowledge-based strategies for school improvement promote optimism. Rose (2001) also contended that policy makers need to listen to the public and improve the public schools that currently exist, to provide all children with education in safe buildings conducive to quality education. However, it may be difficult for policy makers to remain focused on the public school with the charter school and voucher systems on their agenda.

Goertz (2001) observed that while state and federal policies gave strong signals about goals of standards-based reform, they offered limited direction as to its substance. This has led to teacher and district complaints about standards that are too general, leaving the task of developing appropriate curriculum and instruction to teachers. Teachers do not have the time to develop new curriculum to fit under the new standards. Simply setting goals for standards-based reform is not enough to guarantee adequate success in America's schools. Policy makers must consider the benefits of providing more specific standards while allowing enough flexibility in local school improvement efforts.

In past school reform movements, schools were often focused on as the primary unit of change, frequently overlooking the role of the school district. Under these circumstances, states intervene directly in low performing school operations, ignoring district responsibilities for school performance. With the focus on school instead of district accountability, the consequences for individual schools can be more serious than in the past and can include substantial bonuses or school closure and reconstitution. Under the No Child Left Behind Act of 2001, the emphasis is shifting back to school-district accountability.

Hatch (2002) identified a paradox in improvement programs. Hatch emphasized that schools are frequently faced with the task of putting more than one improvement program in place at one time. Hatch observed that this can create too much demand on the school's resources, teachers, and administrators. School personnel in this predicament often experience high levels of frustration and anger. Schools often face competing and even conflicting demands from a variety of sources. Hatch recommended that, in order to embrace improvement programs that were likely to be successful, school leaders needed to select appropriate programs based on sufficient knowledge, plan for adequate resources to be devoted to the chosen programs, and figure out how to integrate school improvement interventions into the school. Professional school counselors have a roadmap in the ASCA national model to develop and manage comprehensive school guidance programs that integrate other school reform and organizational development efforts.

THE ROLE OF THE PROFESSIONAL SCHOOL COUNSELOR IN SCHOOL IMPROVEMENT AND ORGANIZATION DEVELOPMENT

Historically, professional school counselors have been left out of school improvement and organizational development efforts. In the last decade, however, counselors have begun to participate in comprehensive school reform. They have begun to serve on the school leadership teams. In that leadership role, professional school counselors have assured that comprehensive school guidance programming with the trifold focus on academic, career, and personal–social student needs is integrated into the school improve-ment plan. Additionally, because of their personal connections and knowledge of the school community, professional school counselors help foster support for comprehensive school reform from teachers and parents, identify some of the district's key resources, and help craft homegrown comprehensive school reform models (Hassel et al., 2000). Counselors have begun to effectively help implement action steps and promote school-wide support for the comprehensive school reform. ASCA's (2005) national model for school counseling programs emphasizes a direct connection between the comprehen-sive school counseling program and the mission of the school. In addition, the model stresses an organizational framework, accountability systems, and positions counselors to integrate school counseling programs with comprehensive school reform.

Johnson noted that with increasing decentralization of power in school districts, educators have begun to use data not only to assess student performance but also to make changes at a systems level, "to help them make better choices and uncover better ways of serving students and the community" (Johnson, 1997, p. 1). Educators, includ-ing professional school counselors, can create databases used to make program changes, to share with other educators, and to adjust teaching styles based on what is learned. These databases hold keys to identifying target areas for school change at a systems level. Johnson suggested making better use of existing data on attendance, grades, referrals, re-tentions, and standardized test results to make comparisons with other, similar schools.

Schools can begin to make better use of the existing data by first analyzing what the data can reveal as to patterns not previously seen and opportunities for continuous data-driven improvement. The data can be broken down (i.e., disaggregated) by such categories as gender, race, and socioeconomic status. Other data can be collected, such as test results and numbers of books read. Professional school counselors and teachers, individually and collaboratively, are in an excellent position to do small-scale relevant research, called *action research*, to help make informed decisions regarding their work, based on the findings.

By virtue of their unique training and expertise, professional school counselors are excellent resources for providing staff development and facilitation of teams. Such functions are generally important in comprehensive school reform and organization de-velopment activities. Professional school counselors' knowledge of systems theory and group dynamics are necessary qualifications for roles as trainers and facilitators.

While professional school counselors have historically been left out of the school reform movement, the profession has recently proactively emphasized the importance of aligning the school counseling program with the mission of the school and school reform efforts. Emphasis has been placed on the role of the professional school coun-selor as leader, collaborator, change agent, and advocate for quality education for all students. The potential contributions of professional school counselors to school leader-ship teams, comprehensive school reform, and organizational development are numer-ous. School leaders can reap benefits for their schools by using the previously untapped resource of professional school counselors as they plan for school reform and organiza-tion development.

Lapan, Gysbers, Cook, Stanley, and Robbins (2006) believe that it is the critical mission of professional school counselors to fully implement the ASCA national model for all students. The researchers also recommended that professional school counselors communicate with administrators, parents, school board members, and elected officials about their work and the benefits provided to all students. For school districts interested in further development of professional school counselors as resources for leadership teams for school improvement and organizational development, The Education Trust offers specific workshops to professional school counselors and administrators that focus on transforming the work of professional school counselors. The goal is to develop professional school counselors who aggressively support quality education for all students, creating a school climate where access and support for rigorous preparation is expected.

The trainers are a cadre of Metlife Fellows who were trained in February 2002 to become workshop presenters and consultants to school systems. The workshops for the school districts address four themes: working as members of the school leadership team, teaming and collaboration to increase access and equity for all students, serving as advocates for success of all students, and designing and delivery of data-driven counseling programs. To set up training for a school district, contact Peggy Hines, National Center for Transforming School Counseling Director, at The Education Trust (phines@ edtrust.org).

SUMMARY/CONCLUSION

In this chapter I defined and described organization development in the context of school reform efforts, provided a brief examination of some models of school improvement, looked at the limitations of reform attempts, and explored the potential for increasing professional school counselors' involvement in school improvement efforts and organization development in schools. The valuable contributions professional school counselors can make to school reform were identified and described.

Successful school improvement takes an investment of resources such as personnel, time, effort, and money, which need to be allocated where they will make the most difference in quality of education and academic results. Professional school counselors are beginning to be tapped as a viable resource for school leadership teams. A familiarity with current school reform programs and the No Child Left Behind requirements is important to professional school counselors as they participate in school reform and organizational development efforts and align their school counseling programs with reform initiatives and legislation. ASCA and The Education Trust support professional school counselors as leaders, advocates, and collaborators in school improvement. Professional school counselors contribute a valuable knowledge base and skills to team efforts in comprehensive school reform and organizational development. They are encouraged to continue to work on fully implementing their comprehensive school guidance programs based on the ASCA national model.

(Note: See the CD-ROM for a list of references.)

CHAPTER 14

ASSESSING AND CHANGING SCHOOL CULTURE

Mei Tang and Barbara L. Carlozzi

Preview

School culture is important for professional school counselors because the mission and goals of education cannot be fulfilled if the context in the school setting does not support high academic achievement and personal growth and development. Professional school counselors, with their special training, are capable of taking a leadership role in making the school culture more accommodating for teacher and staff development, and students' growth and learning. In this chapter, we will discuss the importance of assessing and changing school culture and suggest strategies professional school counselors can implement to improve the school climate for quality education.

DEFINITION OF SCHOOL CULTURE (STRUCTURE, TEACHER, STUDENT PROCESS, AND PRODUCT)

The definition of *school culture* is varied because different people have different understandings of what constitutes *culture*. In the literature, a similar concept, *school climate*, is often used as well. The study of school culture was derived from anthropology and organizational cultural studies, with an intention to improve the school environment by understanding various dimensions of school life. In this sense, school culture is a multifaceted concept that makes a difference in the effectiveness of schooling (Maehr & Midgley, 1996). Each school has distinguishable characteristics and a kind of social psychological life of its own. These characteristics might be the shared set of organizing principles (Erickson, 1991), beliefs, and values (Cunningham & Cresso, 1993), or accustomed ways of thinking and acting (Sarason, 1995). A school culture is "a system of ordinary, taken-for-granted meanings and symbols with both implicit and explicit content (e.g., norms, values, beliefs, assumptions) that is, deliberately and nondeliberately, learned and shared among members" (Erickson, 1987, p. 1).

From an organizational perspective, school culture includes three levels (Schein, as cited in Shaw & Reyes, 1992): (a) observable behaviors (i.e., visible but often not decipherable, such as artifacts); (b) shared values (i.e., may or may not be visible, requiring greater awareness; members' sense what ought to be); and (c) organizational assumptions about reality (i.e., invisible and preconscious, such as teachers' orientations and outlooks). The nature of school personnel's shared norms, values, beliefs, and assumptions defines the content of a school's culture (Leithwood, 2002).

School culture is shaped by its members, including teachers, staff, students, parents, and the community (Cunningham & Cresso, 1993). Schools are not separable from social context, and therefore the development of school culture is embedded in the school organization, policies, resources, ethos, school district and state policies, local communities, educational professional environment, occupational systems, and societal cultures (Talbert & McLaughlin, 1999).

IMPORTANCE OF SCHOOL CULTURE

The most significant factors in shaping minds are the cultural settings where learning takes place, the activities participants engage in, and discussion among participants (Wells & Claxton, 2002). School culture has been found to affect teacher and staff development and empowerment (Hamilton & Richardson, 1995; Short & Rinehart, 1993), teacher collaboration (Andringa & Fustin, 1991), students' academic and social behavior and performance (McEvoy & Welker, 2000), students' aspiration (Plucker, 1998), and professional school counselors' self-efficacy and outcome expectancy (Sutton & Fall, 1995). Caring school environments profoundly impact a students' understanding of self and others, positive emotions and interactions, the ability to act responsibly, to appreciate a variety of relationships, and to link empathy to moral behavior (Cooper, 2004). School culture is equally important for reform and improvement in schools, because success is not possible if there is no supportive environment or climate to nourish the change.

Maehr and Midgley (1996) argued that the school's cultures directly relate to the purpose of schooling (i.e., motivation and learning). One of the functions of education in the United States is to prepare its citizens to participate in a democratic society. At a minimum, young people should leave school with the knowledge and skills they need to be employable, and they must have the knowledge and motivation to intelligently contribute to a democratic system of government. As noted by Beane (1998), this requires a balance between self-interest and concern for the welfare of others. Of course, many of us expect far more than the minimum from our schools, believing that schools should also cultivate the full potential of each individual; a love of learning; a respect for human dignity, equity, justice, caring, and diversity; and the desire and creativity to create a better world than the one he or she was born into.

Common to differing beliefs about the function of education is the belief that we must prepare students for employment and we must instill in them a desire for the common good. Students' investment in learning, the effort they put forth, whether they feel a sense of belonging, and concern for others in their school community and beyond is related to what schools stress and reward. Schools that emphasize ability and achievement (outcomes) versus task approach and growth (process) are likely to produce students whose aspirations relate more to self-interest and predetermined goals than to concern for others and a desire to improve the world.

Of course, the school environment is not the single determinant of young people's development. The perceived family environment has a significant impact on students' academic achievement. Responsive parenting contributes to an individual's ability to care about others (Staub, 2005). However, even children who grow up without responsive parents or who encounter other high-risk factors can still become happy, caring, successful adults (Staub, 2005; Werner, 1989; Wolin & Wolin, 1993). Staub (2005) called this "altruism born of suffering" (p. 60). It is related to what others have called *resil-*

iency (Werner, 1989; Wolin & Wolin, 1993). These resilient adults often have developed or experienced one or more of the following characteristics or conditions:

- Easygoing temperaments
- Social competence
- The ability to reason, problem-solve, or think critically
- A close bond with at least one caregiver
- Interest, support, and positive connection to one or more adults
- Autonomy, self-efficacy or initiative, a sense of purpose and future
- Morality
- The ability to reframe pain through humor, creativity, or altruism (Staub, 2005; Werner, 1989; Wolin & Wolin, 1993)

According to Marchant, Paulson, and Rothlisberg (2001), school context (teacher responsiveness, school responsiveness, and a supportive social environment) and family context (parental values) have been found to be significantly related to students' motivation, school competence, and academic achievement. Similarly, a school environment promoting academic achievement also promotes higher aspirations of students (Plucker, 1998). The conditions for the positive school environment included having positive relationships with adults, valuing a positive outlook in life, and respecting diversity.

After all, how members in the schools perceive and feel about their interaction with the environment matters. It is the culture that makes the difference in teacher, student, and staff lives in schools. "Greatness does not grow out of a focus on structure and process, but is found in the culture of the organization and the spirit and purposefulness of the lives of people who belong to that organization" (Cunningham & Cresso, 1993, p. 25).

CHARACTERISTICS OF EFFECTIVE SCHOOLS

Research indicates that effective schools are characterized by a culture that focuses on collaboration among all shareholders, open communication, and continuous improvement (Cunningham & Cresso, 1993; Johnson, Snyder, Anderson, & Johnson, 1997; Smith & Scott, 1990). Specifically, the characteristics presented in Table 14.1 are considered to define and sustain educational excellence. Schools that foster altruism must facilitate students' empathic orientation toward others, since empathy has been strongly related to altruism (Cooper, 2004; Fry, 1976; Oswald, 1996).

UNFAVORABLE FACTORS FOR EFFECTIVE SCHOOLS

DeWit et al. (2000) found that low teacher and classmate support, student conflict, unfair school rules and disciplinary practice, and low student autonomy in decision making were associated with low attachment to learning, behavior problems, attendance, and substance abuse. A similar finding by Plucker (1998) also showed that the lack of support for curiosity, respect for independent thinkers, and care from adults tended to lower students' aspirations for learning.

Staub (2005) identified the following factors as detrimental to the development of *altruism*:

- Excessive control, blaming, or scapegoating
- Abuse, neglect, rejection, hostility, or excessive physical punishment
- barriers to connection with others
- a lack of guidance or permissiveness

Cooper's (2004) research noted the following impediments to *empathic* environments:

- Unempathic teachers who were aloof, snobby, overbearing, overly authoritarian, or unable or unwilling to relate individually to students
- An overfilled curriculum that left teachers feeling pressure for student achievement
- Overlarge class sizes in which teachers were unable to know and interact individually with students
- Not enough time to tailor instruction to individuals or small groups or for teachers to interact with parents, school personnel, or personnel in community agencies
- Management policies and leaders who failed to demonstrate concern for the needs of individuals and groups
- Highly competitive environments
- Environments that had a high proportion of needy individuals, whether the needs were for social, emotional, physical, or academic support
- School environments with inadequate space, resources, or equipment

ASSESSING SCHOOL CULTURE

"The secret for successful change in a school is to identify an existing school culture and reshape it" (Bulach, 2001, p. 8). Before implementing change, it is necessary to understand what is happening in the school and to have a complete picture of the practice and perceptions of all shareholders. It is important to know what works and what does not work. Otherwise, the change loses its direction.

The other purposes of assessing school culture include providing baseline data for future evaluation, having a need for accountability (Milstein, 1993), identifying positive features and areas for improvement, and providing necessary information for strategic planning. It is important to note that assessment is an integral part of restructuring the school for better results and is not cause for anxiety.

METHODS OF ASSESSING SCHOOL CULTURE

The concept of school culture is complex and multifaceted, and no single source or method of assessment can answer all questions. A variety of information as well as multiple ways of collecting the information should be used to obtain a comprehensive understanding of the numerous aspects of school culture. Because *culture* is a product as well as a process, the strategies for assessing school culture should incorporate process into the assessment plan.

TABLE 14.1
CHARACTERISTICS OF EFFECTIVE SCHOOLS

Key members work together to develop a collective vision of what school should be like, focusing on a vision, not deficiencies

Foster individual identities of group members and build a collegial relationship among members

Trust, support, and mutual understanding of each other within the organization

Access to quality information for all members

Open and fluid communication

Promoting lifelong professional development and personal growth

Empowerment of individuals to take risks and make a difference

Collaboration between administrators, teachers, parents, community partners, and students to make a decision

Face-to-face involvement of appropriate stakeholders

Shared values, interests, and vision of an ideal school

Strategic planning by groups within the organization

Continuous incremental and systematic improvement

Valuing students' growth and improvement rather than mere achievement

Every student is important and has equal rights to adequate opportunities

Accountability and constant feedback on results

Sustainable changes

Where to look for data. Handbooks, mission statements, announcements, newsletters, school calendars, yearbooks, and annual reports are sources of information for understanding the symbolic aspects of school environment (Wren, 1999). School rules, ceremonies, rituals and routines can also provide valuable information about school culture, as can the school policies regarding behaviors and performance (e.g., how students' conduct is rewarded or disciplined in nonacademic and academic domains).

Other sources of data come from the subjective measures of members of the school setting, whose perceptions and observations of the school operation are essential because they construct the *culture*. Members may include, but are not limited to, teachers, administrators, staff, paraprofessionals, students, parents, community partners, custodians, bus drivers, and volunteers. Interactive data are composed of information about interaction among members and practices in various school settings (e.g., interactions among administrators, staff, and teachers in meetings; teacher and student interactions in classrooms; how school personnel interact with parents; how students interact with each other in classrooms, on playgrounds, and on the bus).

How to gather the data. Data-collection methods vary depending on the data needed and the assessment's purpose. The advantages of formal measurement and standardized instruments are the reliability and validity associated with them, but the disadvantages are the costs and amount of time consumed. The following suggestions are easy-to-use and low-cost ways of collecting data:

- Design a chart to collect pertinent information from records and documents about the nature, frequency, intensity, and scope of the event.
- Interview members within the organization regarding their perceptions and insights about the schools or about aspects of school life. The interview should lead to an ecological profile, which would provide valid information about the assets and resources as well as barriers for a change in the school system.
- Develop a questionnaire to solicit participants' input about different aspects of school culture. The content and format of the questionnaire need to be consistent with the purpose of the inquiry as well as the target participants. For instance, the questionnaire about resource allocation might mean different things to teachers and students.
- Go to classrooms, faculty meetings, and student-oriented activities to make an observation as a participant or as an observer. Use field notes and audio or video to document the observation.
- Use informal, cost-effective index card methods (Bulach, 2001) to understand teachers' and students' expectations about the school environment and the leadership styles of administrators. Also use this method to collect information on how a particular change is perceived by the stakeholders in the school. Writing responses to one question on one index card makes it easier and less labor intensive to analyze.
- Collaborate with an outside consultant who is an expert in assessing organizational culture. Outside, objective sources can provide available insights, especially because stakeholders may have limited or biased views of their own contexts.

Table 14.2 provides an informal school culture assessment grid that is helpful in assessing school culture.

STANDARDIZED INSTRUMENTS

The most popular instrument for measuring school climate and environment is the *Charles F. Kettering Ltd. (CFK) School Climate Profile* (Johnson & Johnson, 1995). The *CFK School Climate Profile* has four sections—General Climate Factors, Program Determinants, Process Determinants, and Material Determinants—and a total of 120 questions. The section of General Climate Factors is most frequently used in research and has eight subscales: Respect, Trust, High Morale, Opportunity for Input, Continuous Academic and Social Growth, Cohesiveness, School Renewal, and Caring. Several studies (Dixon & Johnson, 1991; Johnson & Johnson, 1992a, 1995) found the scale to be valid for the intended purpose, but factor analysis revealed the presence of some empirical dimensions or subscales that might not correspond with the original design. *What works* and *what doesn't work* seem to be the two new structures underlying the subscales. Table 14.3 includes other measures used for assessing school climate and environment.

TABLE 14.2
School Culture Assessment Grid

Area	What Is Now (To what extent has the school attained goals in the *What Should Be* list?)	What Should Be	Strategies to Change (What can be done to change the school culture in this area?)
Vision/Mission		Every student is important and deserves quality education. The school promotes lifelong professional development and personal growth. All members of the school and community are involved in the education process. The reward system is fair and focuses on improvement and growth rather than on mere academic achievement.	
Communication		There are open channels for everyone to voice his or her opinion. There is a system in which all shareholders can exchange information and ideas. All members have equal access to information. The school's mission and policies are clearly communicated to all shareholders via multiple methods.	
Relationships		There is a trust and mutual understanding of each other within the organization. Administrators support teachers' work and vice versa. Teachers and students have a trusting relationship.	
Shared Values		Members within the organization share the values, interests, and vision of an ideal school. Strategic planning is shared by all members. All members believe in the mission of the school.	
Collaboration		Administrators, teachers, parents, community partners, and students collaborate to make all decisions. All shareholders collaborate on strategic planning.	
Structure		The organization is accountable for its mission. Organizational structures are effectively designed and aimed at achieving excellence. Every member within the organization is accountable for his or her responsibility.	
Physical Environment		The school building is clean and safe. The school environment is inviting and friendly for students and parents. The classroom has basic facilities for learning.	

TABLE 14.3

OTHER ASSESSMENT INSTRUMENTS FOR ASSESSING SCHOOL CLIMATE AND
ENVIRONMENT

Litwin and Stringer Climate Questionnaire (1968): 50 items assessing eight dimensions (structure, responsibility, reward, risk, support, standards, conflict, and identity).

Halpin's and Croft's *Organizational Climate Description Questionnaire* (Halpin, 1966): 64 items measuring the degree of satisfaction with teacher–principal interaction.

Likert Profile of a School Questionnaire (Likert & Likert, 1972): 100 items measuring goal commitment, decision-making processes, and team cooperation.

High School Characteristics Index (Stern & Richman, 1964): 300 items assessing teachers' perceptions of climate and students' attitudes and feelings about their school's environment, curriculum, staff, student activities, and interests.

Brookover Elementary School Social Climate Questionnaire (Brookover, 1978): 115 items assessing relative contribution of composition and climate variables (pertaining to teacher, students, and principal) to differences in school achievement (Johnson & Johnson, 1992a).

Quality of School Life Scale (Epstein & McPartland, 1976; Johnson & Johnson, 1992b): 27 items measuring students' general reaction to school, levels of students' interests in school work, and nature of student–teacher relationships.

School Administrator Assessment Survey (Braskamp & Maehr, 1985): 19 scales assessing school administrators' perception of the culture of the school district and their perceptions of job opportunities, individual improvement, and personal development, and the culture or climate of the work setting.

STRATEGIES TO CHANGE SCHOOL CULTURE

"Culture building requires that school leaders give attention to the informal, subtle and symbolic aspects of school life which shape the beliefs and actions of each employee within the system" (Cunningham & Cresso, 1993, p. 25). Discussions about school culture is often found in the educational administration literature; principals are not the only ones who can take the leadership role. In fact, professional school counselors can and should take leadership roles to transform the culture of schools (Littrell & Peterson, 2001). Professional school counselors also possess the skills to bridge the school administration rules and the purposes of schooling for students (Kaplan, 1995).

Professional school counselors are in the position to help the school community develop a shared mission and goal, and they are in a good position to emphasize the importance of a caring, responsive environment. Many of the constraints to empathic environments are especially relevant to professional school counselors' training. Professional school counselors understand how to demonstrate empathy and how to respond to insensitive communication. They understand the qualities and processes of groups that can be either supportive or destructive of community harmony. Professional school counselors are also knowledgeable about discipline and management issues. They understand the strengths and limitations of differing management systems and how the developmental needs of students must be considered when designing a management system. Professional school counselors know about some of the curricular programs that promote empathy. Some of these programs (e.g., literature programs that develop empathy) need not be additional to an already overfilled curriculum. Finally, professional school counselors are trained to facilitate positive, constructive group interaction. These skills are essential for working with parents, students, teachers, administrators, and community members to systematically address factors that contribute to or detract from caring school environments. By interacting with every member in the school system, they are in a unique position to be change agents for school culture (Kaplan & Geoffroy, 1990). Their leadership skills can help them develop teams of invested individuals to work on issues such as promoting a quality environment and addressing problems of time, teacher–pupil ratio, and rigid or inflexible curricula.

Other factors also impact school culture: treating each student with dignity and as an individual who can learn and be successful in school; changing the thinking from "own students in an isolated classroom" to "our students in teams and families" (Burrello & Reitzug, 1993, p. 672); making opportunities for students to identify meaning and relevance in their school experiences and future lives (Kaplan & Geoffroy, 1990); promoting teacher and student ownership and investment in their own growth; developing open and effective communication skills; solving the problems with a solution rather than focusing on victims; and presenting meaningful and interesting lessons and units of study (Ediger, 1997).

As noted by Erford (2003), professional school counselors alone cannot assume responsibility for positive school environments and academic achievement. They can, however, function as team facilitators, advocates, and collaborators with families, community members, and school personnel. As team facilitators, professional school counselors can help family–school teams, mental health teams, and action teams by using group process skills to foster productive outcomes and positive relationships. The day-to-day lives of school counselors are full of stories of victimization, stories that provide a window to the inner life of students and place professional school counselors in a unique position to advocate for those who cannot or will not advocate for themselves. Understanding the causes or reasons behind undesirable behavior enhances both problem solving and compassion for those we find difficult to deal with. Finally, as collaborators, school counselors facilitate networking between people and organizations. This role is a natural outgrowth of the multifaceted job of the professional school counselor, which permits interaction with a wide variety of people. Additionally, the communication skills of professional school counselors encourage open and respectful communication between people (see Bryan, 2005, for a more complete explanation of the roles of advocate, facilitator, and collaborator).

Professional school counselors are in a unique position to promote a positive school culture. Their knowledge, skills, and interactions with a wide variety of people have great potential to facilitate changes in school culture (Bryan, 2005; Kaplan & Geoffroy, 1990). The following activities summarize what professional school counselors can do to promote school culture change:

- Identify the need for change by coordinating assessment and evaluation of school culture.

- Advocate for changes to address the unmet needs of students, teachers, and other members of the school community. In a professional manner, share the personal stories of those whose voice is neglected, misunderstood, or silenced. Every player needs to be healthy and happy to make the system work.
- Collaborate with members of the school community to develop clearly defined and fair school policies and rules for discipline and performance. Encourage management systems that support a cooperative, caring school culture.
- Provide in-service training for members of the school community to promote empathy for one another and help them interact more effectively.
- Coordinate with every member in the school system to find meaning in common experiences and a sense of belonging and community.
- Take the initiative in facilitating proactive teams to develop strategic plans for continuous improvement. Encourage open dialogue and promote respect for the unique contributions of each team member. Facilitate member involvement in school reform and improvement.
- Facilitate networking and member involvement in school reform and improvement.
- Make changes incremental, systematic, and sustainable.

SUMMARY/CONCLUSION

School culture explicitly or implicitly tells the individuals within the school system what is important, expected, and valued. School culture defines a school, so it is essential for professional school counselors to be cognizant of the various dimensions of school culture and facilitate the necessary changes to provide a healthy, safe, and supportive environment for learning and growth. Professional school counselors should take the leadership role in constructing a school environment with a sense of belonging, in which every member feels safe, valued, cared for, and respected; a context where individuals experience personal and professional development and growth and where every member finds meaning and purpose.

(Note: See the CD-ROM for a list of references.)

CHAPTER 15

Supervising School Counseling Interns

Sally Murphy and Carol J. Kaffenberger

Preview

*Providing quality supervision for school counseling interns is both a leadership re-
sponsibility and a challenge for professional school counselors in the field. We present
specific requirements of supervision while offering a unique supervision format specifically developed within the framework of ASCA's national model.*

Quality Supervision of School Counseling Interns

A critical leadership responsibility of professional school counselors that leads to the
training of exemplary professional school counselors for the 21st century is the quality supervision of school counseling interns. As gatekeepers of the profession, on-site
school counseling supervisors assume the role of mentor, teacher, counselor, evaluator,
consultant, facilitator, and administrator (Bernard, 1979; Bernard & Goodyear, 2004)
as they work with school counseling students during their field experiences. On-site
supervisors provide focused support for school counseling interns who aspire to become
professional school counselors (Roberts & Morotti, 2001).

We present a supervision format for professional school counselors who have vol-
unteered to be on-site supervisors for student counselors participating in practicum and
internship field experiences. We outline the prerequisites needed to become a site supervisor and describe a supervision model (Murphy & Kaffenberger, 2007) that was developed and structured within the four components of ASCA's national model (American
School Counselor Association [ASCA], 2005a).

PREREQUISITES FOR THE SUPERVISORY ROLE

School districts and individual school counselors must know the requirements to become on-site supervisors. These prerequisites are outlined in the Council for Accreditation of Counseling and Related Educational Programs' (CACREP; 2008) *Standards for
School Counseling Programs: Clinical Instruction.*

A site supervisor must possess the following minimum requirements to become
an on-site school counselor supervisor:

- Minimum of a master's degree in counseling or a related profession with equivalent qualifications including appropriate certifications and/or licenses.
- Minimum of 2 years pertinent professional experience in the program area in
  which the student is completing clinical instruction.
- Knowledge of the program's expectations, requirements, and evaluation procedures
  for students (CACREP; 2008, Section III).

DEFINITION OF SUPERVISION

What is supervision? It is a method of conveying the "skills, knowledge, and attitudes of a particular profession to the next generation of that profession" (Bernard & Goodyear, 2004, p. 6). Consistent supervision ensures that the student counselor's counseling skills will improve over time. The on-site supervisor should offer constructive and timely feedback, allowing for the mutual sharing of ideas and challenging assumptions. Supervision creates a context in which learning occurs, so on-site supervisors must create a safe environment in which respect, honesty, trustworthiness, and responsiveness are evident (Baltimore & Crutchfield, 2003). Effective supervision relies on the strength of the professional relationship between the supervisor and the school counseling student.

Understanding the meaning of supervision and perceiving the importance of the relationship component in supervision are the beginning of the supervision process. The next step is implementing a model of supervision. This is critical for an organized, intentional, and grounded approach to training school counseling interns.

SUPERVISION MODEL

Although much has been written about various supervision models (e.g., Bernard & Goodyear, 2004; Roberts & Morotti, 2001; Spruill & Benshoff, 1996; Studer, 2005), the use of the *discrimination model* (Bernard, 1979; Bernard & Goodyear, 2004; Luke & Bernard, 2006) is ideal for professional school counselors to use as on-site supervisors. The discrimination model provides categories of options, or discriminations supervisors use when training school counseling interns during their clinical field experiences. Supervisor roles include teacher, counselor, and consultant and the on-site supervisor focus is on the areas of intervention, conceptualization, personalization, and professional behaviors and standards (Bernard & Goodyear, 2004; Lanning, 1986; Luke & Bernard, 2006).

Other variables in supervision. Other variables also influence the supervision used and the supervisor–supervisee relationship. Benshoff (2003) stressed the importance of recognizing that process variables (supervision stages and the student school counseling intern's development) may affect the supervision process. He also highlighted the constant variables (i.e., gender, age, race, ethnicity, and personality characteristics) that are evident in supervision. Cultural beliefs held by the on-site supervisor and the school counseling intern that pertain to diversity issues affect all aspects of supervision and counseling (Helms & Cook, 1999). It is critical that the on-site supervisor and the school counseling intern discuss their diversity perspectives to foster professional growth (Aponte & Wohl, 2000). The fundamental question the supervisor must ask is, "Is the school counseling intern a culturally competent counselor?"

In the following section, we describe how to use ASCA's national model (ASCA; 2005a) as the basis for supervision (Murphy & Kaffenberger, 2007). We also include an explanation of the supervision roles and areas of focus: key components of the discrimination model (Bernard, 1979).

INTRODUCTION TO SUPERVISION WITHIN ASCA'S NATIONAL MODEL

ASCA is the national organization for professional school counselors. It is critical that professional school counselors adhere to ASCA's standards, position statements, and program framework to have uniform quality programs, policies, and procedures (ASCA; 2005b). ASCA has developed a second edition of the ASCA national mode (ASCA; 2005a), a structure to further assist professional school counselors. Professional school counselors assume the responsibility and the challenge of simultaneously managing their school counseling programs per ASCA's national model and authenticating that school counseling interns are trained in the correct method of the implementation of these programs. Relying on their professional organization's direction for effecting change within their school communities, professional school counselors who assume the responsibility of being a supervisor to perspective new counselors are also providing a role model for leadership.

The beauty of the ASCA national model is that it immediately makes sense to practicing school counselors and provides a framework for organizing what they already do. It is also an ideal basis on which to structure the supervision of school counseling interns. The four components of the national model—foundation, delivery systems, management systems, and accountability—provide opportunities for the site supervisor to structure the internship experience and ensure that the school counseling interns are exposed to all aspects of the counseling program (Murphy & Kaffenberger, 2007).

Foundation. The supervision of school counseling interns starts within the foundation component. On-site supervisors explain their own belief systems the school counseling interns (e.g., "I believe change occurs when..."). By talking about their academic qualifications and experiences, supervisors help ensure that interns value the supervision from and experienced on-site supervisor. On-site supervisors also share how the counseling program's mission statement connects with the school's mission statement. This critical discussion lays the groundwork for the intern to more fully understand the connection of the school counseling program to the school's overall mission and goals.

Delivery system. On-site supervisors use the delivery system component to help the intern focus on school guidance curriculum, individual planning, and system support. Supervisors ask interns to develop and implement guidance units. Interns should also participate in parent education activities, group counseling, the special education process, crisis response, and/or individual counseling.

Conducting supervision meetings. Embedded within the delivery system component, within system support, are the underlying elements of clinical supervision. Weekly supervision meetings between the school counseling intern and the on-site supervisor are critical to the overall growth of the intern's field experience (see Figure 15.1 for a checklist of supervision activities). The weekly supervision time (scheduled for 1 hour a week, either in a 60-minute block or two 30-minute blocks) is an essential professional growth experience for the student counselor (ACA; 2005). Formal supervision meetings enrich the field experience and pull everything together for the student counselor–supervisee.

During weekly supervision meetings, the on-site supervisor focuses on the school counseling intern's areas of strength and areas for growth (it is critical for the intern to be open to hearing about areas of strength and growth for progress to occur). It is more than a question of semantics when the supervisor addresses the intern's *area for growth* instead of calling it an *area of weakness*. It frames the suggestions in a positive light and sets the stage for the intern to more readily hear and implement feedback. An example of highlighting one of the intern's strengths might be, "Your ability to establish a genuine rapport with the students was evident when you worked with . . . ." Likewise, the on-site supervisor might need to point out that the school counseling intern needs to talk less and do more listening. By focusing on this as an area for growth (instead of a weakness), the intern is immediately positioned for success.

Another important aspect of the weekly supervision meetings is when intern and supervisor both review the intern's log of hours to ensure that a variety of experiences are incorporated into the field experience over the semester. The supervisor and intern also use supervision time to complete short- and long-term planning for the school counseling program.

Supervision roles and focus areas. To determine what role will be prominent at any time during supervision, it is helpful to consider the purpose of the role (see Table 15.1). Supervisors, as teachers, determine what is critical for the school counseling intern to learn during the clinical field experience. They give information, instruction,

---

ON-SITE SUPERVISION CHECKLIST

Weekly supervision meetings are required: One 60-minute block or two 30-minute blocks.

School Counseling Intern's Name: _____.

Date: _____.

Time: _____.

SUPERVISION ACTIVITIES: IN PROGRESS (IP) OR COMPLETED (C)

PHASES OF INTERNSHIP

IP C

☐ ☐ Orientation and shadowing
☐ ☐ Cocounseling and coteaching (guidance lessons)
☐ ☐ Independence
☐ ☐ Closure

REFLECTIVE PRACTICE

IP C

☐ ☐ Emphasize intern's areas of *strength* (be specific)
☐ ☐ Address intern's areas for *growth* (be specific)
☐ ☐ Encourage intern's questions and exchange of ideas
☐ ☐ Review counseling (case) interventions and conceptualizations
☐ ☐ Review the log of hours to ensure a balance of activities over time
☐ ☐ Discuss short-term planning
☐ ☐ Discuss long-term planning
☐ ☐ Address supervisor's concerns about intern's issues (e.g., promptness, appearance, resistance, ethical issues, professional behavior)

FIGURE 15.1. On-site supervision checklist.

ASCA NATIONAL MODEL

Has the intern been exposed to aspects of the school's counseling program that align with the model?

IP   C

❑   ❑   Foundation (e.g., counseling program's mission statement)

❑   ❑   Delivery
- School guidance curriculum
  - Classroom instruction, group activities, parent workshops and instruction
- Individual student planning
- Responsive services
  - Individual and small-group counseling, crisis counseling
  - Referrals, peer facilitation, parent education, special education (attends local screen, reviews 504, develops referral lists, reviews school crisis intervention plan)
- System support
  - Professional development, consultation, collaboration, teaming

❑   ❑   Management
- Use of time, use of data, advisory council, monitoring student progress

❑   ❑   Accountability (e.g., program evaluation)

OBSERVATIONS AND INTERACTIONS

Has the intern been observed in these situations?	Has the intern participated in meetings?
IP C	IP C
❑ ❑ Guidance lesson	❑ ❑ Faculty
❑ ❑ Small-group counseling	❑ ❑ Guidance
❑ ❑ Individual counseling	❑ ❑ Team meetings
❑ ❑ Parent conference	❑ ❑ Teacher/Administration interaction

UNIVERSITY SUPPORT (e.g., site visits, e-mails, phone contact, hardcopy correspondence)

IP   C

❑   ❑   Communication with the University Supervisor: Initiated by me (M) or University (U)

FIGURE 15.1. *Continued.*

and guidance to the intern, and it is in this role that supervisors must also evaluate the intern by giving regular verbal and written feedback about the intern's strengths and areas for growth.

When on-site supervisors are engaged in the counselor role, they help school counseling interns focus on their inter- and intrapersonal interactions. This supervisory role is especially important when helping school counseling interns conduct a self-evaluation.

In the function as a *consultant*, the third role used in the discrimination model, the on-site supervisor acknowledges the collegial relationship with the school counseling intern. The intern is encouraged to offer suggestions for treatment of the client and to make suggestions for programmatic changes. The supervisor and the intern have a mutually respectful relationship, in which both benefit.

In addition to the three roles of supervision, supervisors have four focus areas that they address to assess their intern's skills. When focusing on intervention, on-site supervisors help school counseling interns improve the type of clinical interventions used during a counseling session (e.g., *Does the school counseling intern have the correct counseling skills and techniques to address the client's issues?*).

On-site supervisors focus on conceptualization when they want to determine how well school counseling interns understand what is happening in the counseling session (e.g., *Is the school counseling intern able to articulate the correct areas to be addressed? Can the school counseling intern communicate the appropriate interventions that would best help the client in his or her particular situation?*).

Personalization addresses the personal counseling style that school counseling interns implement when they work with clients while maintaining a professional approach (e.g., *Does the school counseling intern understand boundary issues and the importance of avoiding counter-transference responses? Does the school counseling intern know the importance of limiting or avoiding self-discourse statements?*).

Supervisors' focus on their interns' professional behaviors and standards is constant throughout the entire clinical field experience. This concentration highlights the need for school counseling interns to develop ethical behavior and demonstrate appropriate professional demeanor and attire (e.g., *Does the school counseling intern exhibit, on a consistent basis, through verbal and nonverbal behavior, the professional standards commensurate with the role of the professional school counselor? Does the school counseling intern model leadership, advocacy, collaboration, and systemic change? Does the school counseling intern consistently wear suitable professional attire?*).

The supervisor addresses these focus areas by alternately using the discrimination model's three roles (Bernard, 1979): teacher, counselor, or consultant. While one role may be primary, all three roles may come into play during a supervision session.

It takes skill, training, practice, and learning to think like a supervisor (Benshoff, 2003) and to effectively supervise school counseling interns, which is especially important when addressing the school counseling intern's resistance, avoidance, or conflict (Nelson & Friedlander, 2001). It is important that on-site supervisors understand that these behaviors are normal reactions for some beginning student counselors. It is helpful to describe and interpret the resistance, offering specific feedback to the student counselor in order to clarify or restate the behavior. On-site supervisors are encouraged to use positive framing (Masters, 1992) when describing the school counseling intern's resistant behavior (e.g., "We've been focusing on your need to become more assertive with several of the teachers. I see this as a challenge for you, not a problem."). Using role-play scenarios helps the supervisor and the intern identify the cause of resistant behaviors. Supervisors can audiotape the supervision sessions so the school counseling intern can review the session. The supervision training stresses the importance of involving the university supervisor in any relevant concerns. On-site supervisors fully understand that they are not alone in the supervision of school counseling interns. A collaborative partnership must exist between the university supervisor and the on-site school counseling supervisor.

TABLE 15.1
SUPERVISION ROLES AND AREAS OF FOCUS: RESPONSIBILITIES AND EXAMPLES

Roles	Responsibilities	Examples
Teacher and Evaluator	Provide information about the counseling internship, including an explanation of the supervision and evaluation components.	Does the school counseling intern have the knowledge and information about the role of the school counselor in a school setting?
	Determine what to include in the field experience.	Does the intern understand the rights and responsibilities of an intern to the school community's stakeholders?
	Demonstrate specific techniques.	
	Instruct intern about specific school or district policies and procedures.	Does the intern understand the components involved in his or her supervision and evaluation?
	Use specific, behavioral, observable, and constructive feedback.	
Counselor	Addresses the intern's areas of strength and areas for growth regarding the intern's specific counseling skills and interventions.	Does the school counseling intern have the correct counseling skills and techniques to address clients' issues?
	Addresses issues concerning the intern's inter- and intrapersonal interactions.	Is the school counseling intern able to conduct a self-evaluation of inter- and intrapersonal interactions?
Consultant	Exchange ideas about interventions, goals, and program plans.	Does the school counseling intern have opportunities to exchange ideas and make suggestions about interventions, goals, and program plans?

Focus	Responsibilities	Example
Intervention	Help intern develop clinical interventions to be used in counseling.	Does the school counseling intern have the correct counseling skills and techniques to address the client's issues?
	Underscore the importance of using a multicultural counseling approach.	Is the intern culturally competent?
Conceptualization	Help intern understand what is going on in the counseling session: What are the central issues and factors that are in play?	Does the school counseling intern accurately understand the client's issues?
		Can the intern communicative the appropriate interventions that would best help the client in his or her particular situation?

(continues)

TABLE 15.1 (*continued*)

Personalization	While maintaining a professional approach, address the personal counseling style that school counseling interns implement when working with clients .	Does the school counseling intern understand boundary issues and the importance of avoiding counter-transference responses?
		Does the intern know the importance of limiting or avoiding self-discourse statements?
Professional Behaviors and Standards of School Counseling	Address ethical behaviors and standards commensurate with the role of the professional school counselor.	Does the school counseling intern model leadership, advocacy, collaboration, systemic change, and multiculturalism?
	Address appropriate professional demeanor and attire.	Does the intern accept feedback, constructive criticism, and suggestions in an open and positive manner?
		Does the intern consistently wear suitable professional attire?
		Is the intern prompt?

Ethical and legal issues in clinical supervision are the final, and perhaps the most important, components in the delivery section. The American Counseling Association (ACA; 2005) delineates ethical guidelines for counselor supervisors that include competence to supervise; boundaries of the supervisory relationship; confidentiality, accountability and liability; and evaluation.

ACA also provides direction for legal issues. The on-site supervisor must understand the meaning of *direct liability*—that is, the on-site supervisor is legally responsible for all of the school counseling intern's actions at the school site. The impact of this issue underscores the need for quality supervision and supervision training.

Several years ago, toward the end of a supervision workshop, Dr. James Benshoff summarized the essence of an exemplary supervisor with this statement: "Supervision is the question asked, rather than the answer given" (Benshoff, 2003). A good supervisor knows that the more the supervisee is engaged in the process, the more the supervisee will benefit and grow. Benshoff emphasized the importance of how directional a supervisor's questions can be for the school counseling intern. It is through quality and intentional supervision that school counseling interns learn how to conduct themselves that is consistent with their professional standards, critically analyze their own efforts, and mature from the constructive feedback of their on-site supervisors.

Management system. Supervision within the third component in the ASCA national model focuses on management agreements, planning, an advisory council, and use of data for systemic change. While many on-site supervisors plan their yearly school counseling programs around the school calendar, most are unfamiliar with management agreements, use of data, and advisory councils. On-site supervisors should discuss these issues with their school counseling interns. The management system component provides an excellent opportunity to ask them to think about how they communicate with administrators about their program goals, how their programs connect to the mission of the school, and how they collaborate with stakeholders.

Accountability. This fourth, and last component of the ASCA national model is one that many on-site supervisors are least familiar. While they understand that schools are in an era of accountability, collecting and disaggregating data have not been part of their counselor role. Accountability is described in terms of the three purposes of using data: to monitor student progress, to assess counseling programs, and to demonstrate counselor effectiveness. Each school counseling intern should conduct data collection for the site (i.e., in collaboration with the on-site supervisor, choose an aspect of the site's school counseling program to evaluate). One example would be for the school counseling intern to conduct a needs assessment to determine what new programs or services are needed at the school. Other examples of projects include an evaluation of a career-day program, a needs assessment concerning staff diversity training, and the effectiveness of an 8-week counseling group. Once the purpose of the project is agreed upon, the school counseling intern develops the instruments needed to collect the information, gains approval from administration, gathers the data, analyzes the data (perhaps using Excel charts to organize the findings), makes recommendations based on the data, and prepares the documents for a presentation to the on-site supervisor or others at the school. The process of using data to understand school-counseling-related educational issues is new to many on-site supervisors, but they are quick to see the power of data.

UNIVERSITY SUPPORT FOR ON-SITE SUPERVISORS

Are you alone in the supervision process? Absolutely not. The university supervisor should be available to the on-site supervisor throughout the entire field experience. There should be an initial meeting at the site with the school counseling intern, the on-site supervisor, and the university supervisor. At that meeting, the university supervisor should provide a written manual or handbook (e.g., Murphy, 2005) that includes a description of the program and course requirements, a contract that describes the field experience expectations and responsibilities, an evaluation instrument, and other pertinent documents needed by the school counseling intern, the on-site supervisor, or the university supervisor. Additional visits and communication via phone and e-mail should continue throughout the field experience. At a minimum, there should be a midsemester contact, to ensure that the school counseling intern is making progress and meeting all program and site requirements. The last contact should be at the end of the field experience. Even though the on-site supervisor will complete a final evaluation of the school counseling intern, the university supervisor should see if there are additional issues to be discussed. The university supervisor should be readily available at all times during the semester, to provide support to the on-site supervisor and school counseling intern.

Summary/Conclusion

Providing quality supervision to school counseling interns is critical to their future success as professional school counselors. Most on-site supervisors assume the responsibilities of supervising a counseling student without previous supervision training. The best way to assure that on-site supervisors are prepared, and that school counseling interns are receiving the highest quality of supervision that is consistent with the guidelines provided by professional counseling organizations, is for universities to conduct ongoing supervision training with all site supervisors. As school counseling programs and counselor education programs adopt the ASCA national model (ASCA; 2005a) as the framework for their school counseling programs, it is essential that the ASCA national model be infused into the supervision of school counseling interns (Murphy & Kaffenberger, in press).

(Note: See the CD-ROM for a list of references.)

COMPREHENSIVE SCHOOL
COUNSELING PROGRAMS

CHAPTER 16

THE STANDARDS-BASED EDUCATIONAL REFORM MOVEMENT

Patricia Jo McDivitt

Preview

In this chapter, I summarize what assessment professionals and counselors need to know about the standards-based educational reform movement, including its ties to assessments used in the current classroom. The reform movement challenged and continues to challenge educators and others in the educational community to "demonstrate a core belief of public education in American—that all children can learn at high levels, given the time, tools, teaching, and encouragement to do so" (Lachat, 2004, p. 6).

A Brief History of the U. S. Educational Standards Movement

Historically, the K–12 educational system in the United States has best been described as a system with two separate tracks: The first track provided an organizational structure designed to help the majority of students build mastery of a core set of basic foundation skills, and the second track was designed to provide additional advanced skills instruction to a subset of students who were bound for postsecondary education, including college.

The standards-based educational reform movement that began in the 1980s eliminated the two-tiered system. The guiding principles of the reform movement included requiring all students, teachers, administrators, and others in the educational community to meet high academic expectations.

The standards-based educational reform movement actually began in response to the publication, *A Nation at Risk* (National Commission on Excellence in Education, 1983). This report took the position that schools in the United States were not adequately preparing students for the future. According to Keifer (2001), the report suggested that the United States was fundamentally threatened by the strength of the economies of other nations. If schools in the United States did not begin to do a better job of preparing students for the workforce, life in the United States would change dramatically. Basically, the report contended that world-class standards were needed in schools to bolster the U.S. economy, and assessment activities were put at the top of the list for pushing or pulling educational reform (Keifer, 2001).

A Nation at Risk did have its critics, but the report alarmed many state and federal policy makers at the time, and many considered its message to be tied directly to the economic future of the country. As a result, in 1986, the nation's governors, acting collectively through the National Governors Association (1986), developed and issued a report titled *Time for Results*. Among other things, this report called for greater accountability in the nation's public schools (Kean, 2004). In 1989, during President George H. W. Bush's administration, a national education summit was held, and the results led to the call for the creation of a broad set of National Education Goals, which were developed and released in 1990. At the same time, The National Education Goals Panel, a federal commission, was created by Congress. The purpose of the National Education Goals Panel was to track national and state efforts to reach a broad set of National Education Goals by the year 2000 (Kean, 2004).

President Bush's (1992) education proposal, *America 2000*, further defined voluntary national academic curriculum standards for what students should know and be able to do in various content areas, including reading and mathematics. *America 2000* also introduced the concept of national assessment, including the use of assessments designed to measure a prescribed set of rigorous academic content curriculum standards.

The *America 2000* proposal did not become law. However, under President Clinton's administration, a similar proposal was presented, *Goals 2000*, which was signed into law as the Goals 2000: Educate America Act of 1994. Goals 2000 called for federal incentives for states to create new systems of accountability by developing their own world-class rigorous academic content curriculum standards. It also called for the development of assessments designed to measure those state-specific standards. As a result of Goals 2000, states began the process of developing their own academic curriculum content standards for what students should know and be able to do, and by the end of the 1990s, almost every state had established a set of standards.

Goals 2000 also called for voluntary national testing of reading and mathematics at certain grades. Voluntary national testing did not take place; however, large-scale testing did remain a key component of the standards-based educational reform movement as Goals 2000 was substantially strengthened by the No Child Left Behind legislation. In 2001, President George W. Bush signed into law the No Child Left Behind Act of 2001 (NCLB), which served to significantly strengthen the federal government's role in both elementary and secondary education and included a plan for educational reform that placed a key focus upon accountability and the use of high-stakes assessment results to help raise the academic achievement of all students. Basically, the overarching goal of NCLB was to have every student achieve academic proficiency in reading, mathematics, and science by 2014.

As an integral component of the standards-based educational reform movement, and in order to comply with NCLB, every state has now developed an accountability system, including high-stakes testing of all students in Grades 3 through 8 and one grade of high school every year in reading and mathematics. Beginning in 2008, the testing of science in one elementary, middle, and high school grade has also taken place. As a result, the development of rigorous academic content standards is the core of a federally mandated accountability system that is directly aimed at improving the quality of teaching and learning in schools. The belief at the federal level is that U.S. education will significantly change for the better if high standards are set and assessments are used to hold districts, schools, and teachers accountable for student learning (Lachat, 2004).

The standards-based educational reform movement, with its resulting legislation, has challenged and continues to challenge educators to no longer accept low expectations for students. By creating stronger connections between what and how students learn in school and how they will be expected to perform in adult life, the standards-based educational reform movement demanded and continues to demand instructional approaches that develop students' reasoning and problem-solving skills. This new vision of teaching and learning has required educators and the public to understand that high academic curriculum content standards are as important in K–12 education as they are in other professions. Academic curriculum content standards serve to define what is essential for successful performance, and standards encourage students to strive to be the best they can be (Lachat, 2004).

The Foundation of the Standards-Based Educational Reform Movement: Content and Performance Standards

The standards-based educational reform movement is based on several important principles:

1. Educators can clearly define what students should know or be able to do at a given grade level (academic curriculum content standards).
2. Academic curriculum content standards can be taught.
3. Students can demonstrate various levels of proficiency in achieving the standards (performance standards), which involves a valid, reliable, and fair assessment of student performance.

Key terms for understanding the standards-based educational reform movement follow.

ACADEMIC CURRICULUM CONTENT STANDARDS

The academic curriculum content standards are the overarching goals that describe in the broadest terms what all students should know and be able to do as a result of the prekindergarten through Grade 12 program. Content standards define the focus of curriculum and instruction within and across content areas, and they describe what teachers are expected to teach and what students are expected to learn. "They represent the curricular priorities of the state or district, and they serve as starting points for curriculum improvement because they describe what is important for all students to learn in the various subject areas" (Lachat, 2004, p. 3). In other words, academic curriculum content standards are the clearly stated long-term learning targets for students. Here is an example of an academic curriculum content standard for reading: *Using a variety of strategies, students read, comprehend, and respond to a wide range of reading materials.*

BENCHMARKS OR GRADE-LEVEL EXPECTATIONS

The standards-based educational reform movement includes a series of benchmarks or grade-level expectations that let teachers, parents, professional school counselors, administrators, or other assessment professionals know if students are on the right track. Basically, benchmarks or grade-level expectations are used to measure a student's progress toward meeting the academic curriculum content standards. They are more specific statements of what all students should know and be able to do at a specified time in their schooling. They are subcomponents of content standards that identify the expected understandings and skills for a content standard at different grade levels. Here is an example of a benchmark or grade-level expectation for reading: *Students will identify story elements (e.g., setting, plot, character, theme) and literary devices, such as figurative language, within a selection.*

PERFORMANCE STANDARD

Whereas curriculum content standards outline what students should know and be able to do as a result of instruction in the common core of knowledge and skill areas, *performance standards* indicate the degree to which the academic curriculum content standards have been attained. They describe how good is *good enough*, and they provide the basis for judging student achievement, including what it takes to succeed. The nature of excellence is clearly defined, and performance standards are set. Assessment results or score reports are provided to parents, teachers, or other assessment professionals using the performance-standards-referenced descriptions of student learning. Students can determine where they are, and teachers can tell parents how their children are progressing toward proficiency or building toward mastery of the defined academic curriculum content standards.

PERFORMANCE-LEVEL DESCRIPTORS

Performance standards are aligned with states' academic curriculum content standards, and they clearly differentiate what students' mastery of the academic curriculum content standards looks like at various stages of learning. Performance standards are clearly measurable and accessible to all students. To meet NCLB requirements, *performance* standards include at least two levels of achievement (proficient and advanced) that describe mastery of the learning targets in a state's content standards. A third level of achievement (basic) is required to provide information about students' progression toward the mastery of the *content* standards.

Each performance standard, representing different levels of performance or achievement, is described using performance-level descriptors. In the standards-based educational reform movement, the performance-level descriptors are statements (e.g., below basic, basic, proficient, advanced) that describe the knowledge and skills that are expected at different performance levels with respect to the academic curriculum content standards. They are written to provide guidelines or descriptions of the competencies as to what should constitute the different levels of performance. The descriptors form the foundation for determining what and how much students are expected to know and be able to do in a given content (i.e., reading, mathematics, science) domain. The performance standards (scores) are typically standardized with performance-level descriptors in place. An example of performance-level descriptors for Grade 3 reading is provided in Table 16.1.

SETTING STANDARDS

In the standards-based educational reform movement and with high-stakes testing, once the performance-level descriptors are written and in place, the actual standards for passing or failing are typically set by a group of educators (standard-setting committee) during a standard-setting process. The members of the standard-setting committee usually consist of educators who have knowledge of what students should know and be able to do at a given grade level and content area to which the performance levels or standards are being set. The committee members are trained to internalize the performance-level descriptors (e.g., basic, proficient, advanced) to understand what skills or knowledge is typical of a given content domain. They are then asked to consider a student who might minimally meet each category of requirements (e.g., basic, proficient, advanced) and to judge how this student might respond to a given set of questions on the test.

Agreeing on the various levels of performance or the score for each level of performance is difficult for standard-setting committee members, but regardless of which of the many models or methods are used, the setting of performance standards is generally an iterative process in which committee members receive feedback data including other members' ratings; empirical data on how students performed on the test questions; and impact data, or what percentage of students in a particular group would be classified in each category based on the proposed cutoff scores (D. Harris, 2004).

Regardless of the standard-setting model or method used, human judgment is involved, and different underlying assumptions associated with different standard-setting methods may result in very different standards being set. As a result, the final recommendations from the standard-setting committee are typically further reviewed by a panel of experts and policy makers, and the final decision as to what the various cut

TABLE 16.1

EXAMPLE OF READING PERFORMANCE-LEVEL DESCRIPTORS FOR GRADE 3

Advanced	The student performing at this level typically uses context clues and structural elements to determine meaning of unfamiliar words and phrases; identifies statements in text to support a conclusion; identifies accurate restatements and summaries of text; states main idea of text; and describes all of the story elements in a variety of stories.
Proficient	The student performing at this level typically uses knowledge of phonics to decode unfamiliar words; uses text features and visual cues to obtain information from text; locates information directly stated in the text and identifies key details; identifies main idea or central concept in various types of text; describes some of the story elements in a variety of stories; makes simple connections between texts; and locates details in texts to illustrate relevant connections between texts.
Below Proficient	The student performing at this level typically uses knowledge of phonics to recognize the sounds of letters and letter combinations, including beginning consonant and vowel blends in words; identifies the main idea in a simple story; and identifies one or two story elements in fiction.

scores at the performance levels will be is usually set by another entity, such as a board of education for a given state (Yen & Henderson, 2002).

THE ROLE OF ASSESSMENT

Assessments most commonly used in the K–12 classrooms have their roots in the standards-based educational reform movement, with the majority of these assessments designed to measure higher expectations of what students should know and be able to do. These assessments, often referred to as *high-stakes assessments*, are tied to accountability systems wherein the results have consequences for students or others in the educational community.

The two major types of high-stakes tests that are used in states' accountability systems are the norm-referenced achievement test and the criterion-referenced or standards-based assessment. Historically, the main purpose of administering a norm-referenced achievement test was to receive information that allowed teachers, professional school counselors, and other assessment professionals to compare performance of students in order to determine relative strengths and weaknesses based upon a set of academic foundation skills (McDivitt, 2004). Most norm-referenced achievement tests used today, however, have been augmented with new questions designed specifically to cover the academic curriculum content standards within a given subject or grade.

The criterion-referenced test or standards-based assessment, on the other hand, is used to determine what students can do and what they know rather than how they compare to others. When used in statewide high-stakes testing programs, they are designed to measure how well a student has learned a particular body of knowledge without regard to how well other students at the same age or grade level have learned it. As an integral component of the standards-based educational reform movement, they typically measure students' mastery of the learning targets as defined by a set of specific academic curriculum content standards.

Regardless of which type of assessment is used, norm-referenced or criterion-referenced assessment, both must be content valid in terms of measuring what students should know and be able to do as defined by the standards. Alignment, therefore, is a major focus for assessments used as the key component of the standards-based educational reform movement.

ALIGNMENT

In current high-stakes accountability assessments, determining alignment usually involves subject-area teachers, curriculum experts, and other educators who are familiar with the state's content standards or learning targets and benchmarks or grade-level expectations for a given grade level and content area. These educators are asked to use their professional judgment to determine whether or not the test questions do, in fact, measure the designated content standards or learning targets, as adopted by the state in which the test is being administered. As a result, they pay careful attention to the educational significance of the test questions to ensure that the test will mirror sound instructional practices. In addition, every question will have a purpose, and this purpose will be clearly defined in the question specifications. Webb (2002) described this alignment as the degree to which grade-level expectations and assessments are in agreement and serve in conjunction with one another to guide the system toward students learning what they are expected to know and be able to do.

ALIGNMENT PROCESS

Aligning test questions to curriculum content standards is complex and involves many layers. Alignment not only involves determining whether a test question is measuring what it is intended to measure, but it also involves determining the complexity or depth of knowledge that is required by the question and the designated curriculum content standard. Perhaps the best known model for assessment and curriculum alignment is based upon Norman Webb's work involving the analysis of depth of knowledge. According to Webb (2002), depth of knowledge consistency between curriculum content standards and test questions on an assessment are aligned if what students elicit is as cognitively demanding as what is stated in the content area grade-level expectations for the content standards or learning targets.

As an integral part of the alignment process, therefore, subject-area teachers, curriculum experts, and other educators must carefully analyze each test question and academic curriculum content standard for depth of knowledge. Webb's alignment model (2002) involves four levels of depth of knowledge, as summarized in Table 16.2.

As the standards-based reform movement has charged forward, however, its reliance on large-scale assessment has provoked criticism. Many educators have felt there has been a tendency to "rush to test," outpacing a balanced approach to education reform in which the introduction of large-scale standardized testing is meant to improve education and instruction, not distract from it. This desired use encourages teachers and educators to redesign the curriculum, to establish teacher preparation programs, and to create intervention and remediation programs that reflect clearly defined content standards. These activities are not high stakes because they are not used to make

TABLE 16.2

DEPTH OF KNOWLEDGE

Recall	Answering the test question requires *recall*—remembering a fact, information, or procedure.
Basic Application of Skill or Concept	Answering a test question requires using information, conceptual knowledge, and procedures. In addition, answering the question usually involves two or more steps.
Strategic Thinking	Answering a question involves strategic thinking, which requires reasoning and developing a plan that has a sequence of steps. Therefore, the test question is usually complex, with more than one possible answer. The question usually takes 10 minutes to answer.
Extended Thinking	Extended thinking questions or tasks require an investigation, and students must have time to think and process multiple conditions for the given problem or task. Each investigation usually requires more than 10 minutes.

individual student decisions. For state testing proponents, the key drivers are content standards (W. G. Harris, 2004).

SUMMARY/CONCLUSION

The goals of the standards-based reform movement, which involve setting high standards for all students, are valid; however, the success of the reform movement relies heavily upon whether the education reforms prove helpful to student populations that have been denied access to a challenging, high-quality education. This will depend largely on whether students gain access to the essential instruction, resources, and conditions that support learning and achievement. According to Lachat (2004), education standards and accountability mandates will not improve student learning unless they are accompanied by policies and practices that directly address inequities in conditions for learning.

(Note: See the CD-ROM for a list of references.)

CHAPTER 17

THE ASCA NATIONAL STANDARDS:
THE FOUNDATION OF THE ASCA NATIONAL MODEL

Carol A. Dahir and Lawrence E. Tyson

Preview

In this chapter, we describe the history and impact of the American School Counselor Association (ASCA) Sharing the Vision: The National Standards for School Counseling Programs *(Campbell & Dahir, 1997). The standards and its accompanying competencies were created to provide direction to help every student acquire attitudes, knowledge, and skills (competencies) in academic, career, and personal–social development. The standards have been incorporated as the foundation for the* ASCA National Model: A Framework for School Counseling Programs *(ASCA; 2003).*

Professional school counselors face the enormous challenge of preparing students to meet the expectations of high academic standards and to become well-educated and contributing members of a complex and changing society. The school improvement agenda of the 1990s directed the development of national standards across the academic content areas to improve educational practice and pedagogy. However, this movement largely ignored the contributions of school counseling to student achievement and development. The development of the national standards for school counseling programs (Campbell & Dahir, 1997) positioned professional school counselors to play an increasingly important role in contemporary school improvement. The standards and accompanying competencies were developed to provide direction to help every student acquire attitudes, knowledge, and skills in the areas of academic, career, and personal–social development. The foundation of ASCA's national model (2003) is based on the national standards and emphasizes the importance of having a mission, a vision, and a proactive belief system that ensures that every student will benefit from the school counseling program.

THE MOMENTUM FOR CHANGE

Concerned about the absence of references to school counseling contributions to the Goals 2000 statute (U.S. Department of Education, 1994), ASCA, the national professional association representing professional school counselors, determined it was important to develop national standards for school counseling programs. The ASCA leaders anticipated the development of national standards for school counseling programs would

- create a framework for a national model for school counseling programs;
- establish school counseling as an integral component of the academic mission of the educational system;

- encourage equitable access to a school counseling services for all students, provided by a credentialed professional school counselor;
- identify the knowledge and skills all students should acquire as a result of the
  school counseling program; and
- ensure that school counseling programs are comprehensive in design and delivered
  in a systematic fashion for all students.

The National Education Goals Panel (1994) described program content standards as specifying what students should know and be able to do. The ASCA Governing Board adopted the definition of the National Goals Panel and determined that the development of school counseling content standards would define what students should know and be able to do as a result of participating in a school counseling program (Campbell & Dahir, 1997). As a result of a national survey and extensive field reviews, nine national standards, three in each of the areas of academic, career, and personal–social development, became the foundation for the content of school counseling programs (Campbell & Dahir, 1997).

With accountability driving school reform, there was a critical need to inform stakeholders of the relationship of school counseling programs to student learning and achievement (Dahir, Sheldon, & Valiga, 1998). The national standards for school counseling programs (Campbell & Dahir, 1997) offered professional school counselors, administrators, teachers, and counselor educators a common language to promote student success through involvement or participation in school counseling programs. The concept of standards was readily understood by colleagues who were involved in school improvement and the implementation of standards across other disciplines. Standards-based school counseling programs also have characteristics similar to other educational programs, including a scope and sequence, student outcomes or competencies, activities and processes to assist students in achieving these outcomes, professionally credentialed personnel, materials and resources, and accountability methods.

The national standards for school counseling programs (Campbell & Dahir, 1997) help to facilitate student development in three broad content areas: (a) academic, (b) career, and (c) personal–social development. There are three standards for each of the domains, which provide guidance and direction for individual schools to develop quality and effective school counseling programs (see Table 17.1).

The national standards promote academic and personal–social development as the foundation for every student's future career success. The integration of academic, career, and personal–social development assists students to acquire the attitudes, knowledge, and skills for success in school and success in life (see Figure 17.1).

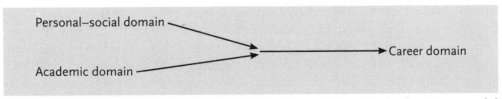

Figure 17.1. Merging of student academic and personal–social domains leading to successful career and life choices.

TABLE 17.1

NATIONAL STANDARDS FOR SCHOOL COUNSELING PROGRAMS

Domain		Standard
Academic	A	Students will acquire the attitudes, knowledge and skills contributing to effective learning in school and across the lifespan.
	B	Students will complete school with the academic preparation essential to choose from a wide range of substantial postsecondary options, including college.
	C	Students will understand the relationship of academics to the world of work and to life at home and in the community.
Career	A	Students will acquire the skills to investigate the world of work in relation to knowledge of self and to make informed career decisions.
	B	Students will employ strategies to achieve future career goals with success and satisfaction.
	C	Students will understand the relationship between personal qualities, education, training, and the world of work.
Personal–Social	A	Students will acquire the knowledge, attitudes, and interpersonal skills to help them understand and respect self and others.
	B	Students will make decisions, set goals, and take necessary action to achieve goals.
	C	Students will understand safety and survival skills.

Note. Adapted from *Sharing the Vision: The National Standards for School Counseling Programs,* by C. Campbell and C. Dahir, 1997, Alexandria, VA: American School Counselor Association. Adapted with permission.

Each of the nine standards is associated with a list of student competencies that defines the specific attitudes, knowledge, and skills that students should obtain or be able to demonstrate as a result of participating in a school counseling program. Student competencies support the goals of the national standards, guide the development of strategies and activities, and are the basis for assessing student growth and development. The 122 ASCA student competencies are arranged in the three domain areas and provide direction to achieving the nine standards.

The standards provide professional school counselors with a significant resource to help restructure and improve their counseling programs and help ensure that all students have access to high-quality, comprehensive school counseling programs (Perusse, Goodnough, & Noel, 2001). A school counseling program that is based on national standards provides all the necessary elements for students to achieve success in school. This programmatic approach helps professional school counselors to continuously assess their students' needs, identify the barriers and obstacles that may be hindering student success, and advocate programmatic efforts to eliminate these barriers (Herr, 2001).

The ASCA leadership envisioned that the publication and dissemination of the standards would motivate the school counseling community to identify and implement goals for students that were deemed important by the school environment, clarify the relationship of school counseling to the educational system, and address the contributions of school counseling to student success in school (Campbell & Dahir, 1997). Because the purpose of a school counseling program is to promote and enhance the learning process, standards-based school counseling supports all students in achieving success in school and developing into contributing members of society.

According to Schmidt and Ciechalski (2001), the national standards promoted student learning and development while also defining the major components of a comprehensive school counseling program, including the traditional components of counseling (individual and small group), consultation, coordination, case management, guidance curriculum, program evaluation and development, and program delivery. Additionally, professional school counselors were encouraged to shift from the delivery of a menu of student services to the design and implementation of a structured and programmatic approach of school counseling that addresses the needs of all students (Gysbers & Henderson, 2000). Professional school counselors had to shift from a role-and-position focus to a comprehensive-program focus to affect student achievement and school success through school counseling programs (Dahir, 2001).

THE NATIONAL STANDARDS AND COMPREHENSIVE SCHOOL COUNSELING: A HISTORICAL PERSPECTIVE

For the last 30 years, professional school counselors have applied and integrated different paradigms and approaches (Gysbers & Moore, 1974; C. D. Johnson & Johnson, 1982; Myrick, 1997). For example, developmental school counseling (Myrick, 1997) addressed the needs of students that are consistent with the expected stages of growth and learning. The comprehensive developmental model (Gysbers & Henderson, 2000) provided a system for delivering and organizing the school counseling program, while the results-based approach (C. D. Johnson & Johnson, 2002) offered a methodology for demonstrating outcomes and impact. The national standards complement these established approaches and were not meant as a substitute for a comprehensive, developmental, and results-based program. Rather, the standards provide the content for the school counseling program. The national standards define *what* students should know and be able to do as a result of participating in school counseling programs. A comprehensive, developmental, and results-based program provides direction for *what* and *how* services are delivered. The national standards and the student competencies are not "guidance curriculum" but make up every aspect of professional school counselors' work with students. These approaches independently and collectively complement each other.

THE COMPREHENSIVE MODEL

The comprehensive model is a systemic process for the development, implementation, and evaluation of a school counseling program. The characteristics are similar to other programs in education such as student outcomes or competencies, activities to achieve the desired outcomes, professional personnel, materials, resources, and a delivery system. The national standards are delivered by using each of the four components of the comprehensive model: (a) individual student planning, (b) responsive services, (c) system support, and (d) the school counseling (guidance) curriculum. The comprehensive model identifies competencies for students and uses varying strategies to deliver the content of the program to every student (National Consortium for State Guidance Leadership, 2000). The competencies delivered at the building or district level emphasize early intervention, prevention, and responsive services. The national standards and the competencies selected by the school or district guide the development of the program content for student growth and achievement in the academic, career, and personal–social domains and are an integral part of individual planning, guidance curriculum, responsive services, and system support. Most important, the comprehensive process links school counseling to the total educational process and involves all school personnel (Stanciak, 1995).

DEVELOPMENTAL APPROACH

Because children do not develop linearly, according to a timetable, it is essential to focus on students' developmental growth progression in pre-K through Grade 12. Therefore, developmental school counseling

> is for all students, has an organized and planned curriculum, is sequential and flexible, is an integrated part of the total educational process, involves all school personnel, helps students learn more effectively and efficiently, and includes counselors who provide specialized counseling services and interventions. (Myrick, 1997, p. 48)

Myrick's (1997) developmental approach emphasized programs for all students; the importance of using an integrated approach involving all school personnel in the delivery of "guidance activities"; and a guidance curriculum that is sequential, age appropriate, planned, and organized. Thus, the school counseling program must include age-appropriate and sequential learning experiences to deliver the national standards and competencies to every student.

RESULTS-BASED APPROACH

Results-based guidance is also a competency-based approach. Developed by Johnson and Johnson in the 1980s, it emphasized a total-pupil-services approach, with the student as the primary client (C. D. Johnson & Johnson, 1991, 2002). This approach also emphasized the importance of students acquiring competencies to become successful in school and in the transitions from school to postsecondary education or to employment. At the center of the results-based approach is accountability to the student and to the building administrator (S. Johnson, Johnson, & Downs, 2006). As a result, management agreements between the principal and counselor are a means of measuring accomplishments.

According to Herr (2001), the national standards are congruent with results-based approaches (C. D. Johnson & Johnson, 1982, 2001, 2002) and to the organization and effects of school-based counseling programs. Today's professional school counselors are challenged to demonstrate the effectiveness of their programs and must collect data supporting and linking the school counseling program to students' academic success (ASCA; 2003). Standards-based and comprehensive school counseling programs are also data driven. The use of data to effect change within the school system ensures that every student receives and benefits from the program. Professional school counselors should demonstrate that activities implemented as part of the school counseling program were developed from a careful analysis of student needs, achievement, and related data. To create a data-driven school counseling program, professional school counselors must look at a variety of data from several perspectives (ASCA; 2003; Stone & Dahir, 2006), including achievement data; standards and competency-related data; disaggregated data; program evaluation data; process, perception, and results data; as well as data over time (ASCA; 2003).

The school counseling program must be organized as an integral and essential part of the broader school mission (Gysbers & Henderson, 2000). The evolution of comprehensive and developmental school counseling and guidance clearly support the imminent need for school counseling programs to be aligned with and tied to the mission of schools (Gysbers, 2001, 2005). As a result, school counseling programs promote educational excellence through individual excellence; provide prevention and intervention programs and experiences; create a collaborative model that integrates the expertise of professional school counselors, other pupil services personnel, business, and community into the total program; and is current with the needs and expectations of the education agenda and societal issues (Dahir, 2001; Gysbers & Henderson, 2000; Myrick, 1997). Random acts of guidance are no longer acceptable in 21st-century schools (Bilzing, 1996).

THE NATIONAL STANDARDS: THE FOUNDATION OF THE ASCA NATIONAL MODEL

The national standards and competencies became the foundation for ASCA's national model (2003) and oriented the school counseling program in the direction of an organized, planned, sequential school guidance curriculum for every student. Implementation required an organizational framework and accountability systems to determine how well students met the standards or achieved intended outcomes. The competencies delivered at the building or district level emphasize early intervention, prevention, and responsive services.

The foundation quadrant of the ASCA national model asked school counselors to develop a mission statement that connects school counseling to the school building or district's mission (Hatch & Bowers, 2002). Embedded in every mission statement are the standards and competencies that support student achievement, success in school, and school improvement. School counselors also engaged stakeholders in a collaborative school-wide effort that looked at data to identify student needs as the *foundation* for the comprehensive school counseling program (Stone & Dahir, 2004).

The ASCA national model is grounded in the delivery methods that are also the basis for comprehensive, developmental, and results-based models. The standards are delivered through individual student planning, responsive services, the school counseling (guidance) curriculum, and system support.

INDIVIDUAL STUDENT PLANNING

Individual planning provides opportunities for students to plan, monitor, and evaluate their progress and learn to take ownership and assume responsibility for their academic and affective learning and development. Students' activities might include goal setting; career planning; understanding, interpreting, and applying assessment information in a meaningful way to academic planning; postsecondary planning; and course selection. Individual planning should also include parental involvement and provide multiple opportunities to personalize the educational experience. Through the individual planning process, students can set academic, career, or behavioral goals and develop a pathway to realize their dreams. Individual planning documents the achievement of specific competencies that will ultimately support every student's attainment of the national standards. The use of data can present a picture of the struggles and achievements of both individual students and groups of students.

RESPONSIVE SERVICES

The tradition of training professional school counselors, both preservice and in-service, predominantly focused on interventions for mental health problems. Until recently, many school personnel believed this was the primary orientation for counselors in schools. In a comprehensive school counseling model, responsive services are much broader than interventions that are essential for at-risk students. All students are at risk at some time in their school careers. Responsive services consist of individual and group counseling, consultation, referral to community agencies, and crisis intervention and management. The impetus for response and intervention is often dominated by presenting student issues, school building and faculty concerns, parental trepidations, and community matters. Data paint a clear picture of a school and its students, thereby depicting a vivid representation of the successes and failures in school buildings and systems.

Responsive services that are data based, can address issues such as peer pressure, resolving conflict, family relationships, personal identity issues, substance abuse, motivation, and achievement concerns. Responsive services can be delivered in a direct (e.g., individual counseling, group counseling) or indirect (e.g., consultation, outside referral) manner and show the achievement of growth and development in academic, career, and personal–social development.

SCHOOL COUNSELING (GUIDANCE) CURRICULUM

Professional school counselors provide developmental and sequential information, knowledge, and skills about academic, career, and personal–social development that are frequently delivered through large-group meetings which offer opportunities to provide guidance to the largest number of students in a school. Usually, professional school counselors first work with students in large groups, when appropriate, because it is the most efficient use of time. Professional school counselors and teachers in classrooms or advisory groups deliver the guidance and counseling curriculum to students through the use of organized activities. The activities and lessons give attention to particular developmental issues or areas of concern in the school building or district.

Professional school counselors regularly partner with teachers and other members of the school community to deliver the school counseling curriculum. This collaborative effort is intended to assure that each student achieves specific competencies that will ultimately support attainment of the national standards.

SYSTEM SUPPORT

System support is often misconstrued as "non-counseling" assignments in schools, such as hall monitoring, class coverage, or bus duty. In actuality, system support is intended to provide ongoing support to the school environment and to organize, deliver, manage, and evaluate the comprehensive school counseling program. Most of the services are considered indirect; that is, they are not delivered directly to students. The coordination of services involves planning and connecting activities and services to the national standards and the goals of the counseling program in the school. For example, hosting an advisory committee helps to inform the direction of the program and provides a sounding board for discussion about what is working, what needs to change, and how the comprehensive school counseling program can better support student success. System support also provides professional school counselors with opportunities to facilitate discussions about school improvement, examine data that may be affecting the success of students, and assisting with the professional development and in-service activities for the faculty.

Effective professional school counselors possess the attitudes, knowledge and skills to effectively provide both the direct and indirect components of a comprehensive school counseling program. Direct services, which usually target students, typically include individual counseling, small-group counseling, and classroom guidance. Indirect services include the management of resources, consultation, collaboration and teaming, advocacy, and the coordination of services and are essential to affect systemic change and support the "new vision" of school counseling (Ripley, Erford, Dahir, & Eshbach, 2003). In all instances, student growth and development is monitored by the achievement of competencies, which ultimately result in the attainment of the nine national standards. As a result, professional school counselors can clearly connect their work to the purpose of school and contribute to student success and achievement.

COLLABORATING FOR SYSTEMIC CHANGE

Most professional school counselors agree their skills, time, and energy should be focused on balancing direct and indirect services to students. School counseling programs and the primary methods of delivery are determined by the extent of the need for student academic, career, and personal–social development. The counselor is in a key position to identify the issues that affect student learning and achievement by becoming involved at the core of school planning, developing programs, and affecting the school climate. This cannot be accomplished unilaterally. The professional school counselor

implementing a national standards-based school counseling program uses a collaborative model as a springboard for success.

Professional school counselors do not work alone; all educators play a role in creating an environment that promotes the achievement of identified student goals and
outcomes. The counselor facilitates communication and establishes linkages for the
benefit of students, with teaching staff, administration, families, student service personnel, agencies, businesses, and other members of the community. Student success in
school depends upon the cooperation and support of the entire faculty, staff, and student
services personnel.

Combining specialized services and competencies helps students learn more effectively and efficiently, and provides opportunities for professional school counselors
to assess the impact of these efforts (ASCA; 1994). Professional school counselors coordinate the objectives, strategies, and activities of a comprehensive school counseling
program to meet the academic, career, and personal–social needs of all students (ASCA;
1997). Once the school counseling program has an organization and structure like the
other disciplines in school, it is no longer perceived as ancillary but rather as an integral
component directly linked to student achievement and school success. When guidance
and counseling is conceptualized, organized and implemented as a program, it places
professional school counselors at the center of education, making it possible for them to
be active and involved (Gysbers, 2001).

Knowledge and skills that students acquire in the areas of academic, career and
personal–social development must surpass what are perceived to be predominantly
"counseling related" services. Program delivery consists of the many ways professional
school counselors provide services to students, including individual and group counseling, large- and small-group guidance, consultation, management of resources, and
through the coordination of services. The professional school counselor uses a variety
of strategies, activities, delivery methods, and resources to facilitate student growth
and development. In order to accomplish this, the professional school counselor must
possess a solid knowledge base and be able to serve as an advocate for students, provide
direct and indirect services, and ascribe to the belief that all children can learn and
achieve through their actions.

THE MOTIVATION AND MOMENTUM FOR MOVING FORWARD

There is consensus among school counseling professionals that the widespread use of
the national standards offers consistency in the description of school counseling programs, the content of the program, and how the comprehensive program should be delivered. More than 45 state departments of education or state school counselor associations have promoted the implementation of comprehensive school counseling program
models (Sink & MacDonald, 1998) and all of the newly revised or designed state models
have incorporated the national standards as the content for school counseling state
models (Dahir, 1998). Most important, collaborative efforts between state departments
of education and school counselor associations have increased with a significant number of newly published models and several in the development stage that will affect the
way programs are designed and delivered in schools across the United States.

Counselor education programs have integrated the teaching of the national standards as part of the graduate curriculum. The results of a national survey (Perusse et al., 2001) reported approximately 69% of counselor education programs were using the national standards for school counseling programs (Campbell & Dahir, 1997) to some degree within the curriculum to train the next generation of professional school counselors.

Renewal and Opportunity for School Counseling

The national standards movement presented the opportunity to establish the role of school counseling programs in the American educational system. The national standards for school counseling programs helped to eliminate the confusion among the public and within the profession about understanding what school counseling programs accomplish and how school counseling programs benefit students. The most recent school improvement agenda, No Child Left Behind Act of 2001, intended to close the achievement gap between disadvantaged students and other groups of students. This has presented yet another opportunity for professional school counselors and school counseling programs to vocalize strategies and create meaningful conversations among professional school counselors, school administrators, teachers, parents, and representatives of business and community about expectations for students' academic success and the role of counseling programs in supporting and enhancing student learning (Dahir et al., 1998). As powerful allies in school improvement, professional school counselors can document and demonstrate their contribution to student growth and learning, thus supporting the national goals to improve results for every student. By taking a position on important educational issues, professional school counselors advocate for change and continuous improvement (Clark & Stone, 2000).

National standards-based comprehensive school counseling programs, linked directly to the mission of the school, promote and enhance the learning process (Campbell & Dahir, 1997). The emphasis is on making the school counseling program an integral part of the total school program (Clark & Stone, 2000). Professional school counselors can no longer rely on their reputations and good intentions as dedicated helpers—they must be accountable for their efforts (L. S. Johnson, 2000). As part of an educational team, professional school counselors must accept the challenge of preparing students to meet the expectations of higher academic standards and to become productive and contributing members of society. Counselors have been asked to demonstrate positive school outcomes that support the mission of the school (Paisley & McMahon, 2001). Increased accountability practices can meaningfully change the substance and perception of school counseling in the context of today's reform agenda (L. S. Johnson, 2000).

Summary/Conclusion

The national standards have established a baseline to monitor student progress in the areas of academic, career, and personal–social development as part of a comprehensive school counseling program. By shifting the focus from the position or the role of the professional school counselor to implementing a comprehensive program, the work of the school counselor is measured by the impact of the school counseling program on student achievement and school success. School counseling programs must be of benefit and delivered to every student.

ASCA's national standards (Campbell & Dahir, 1997) and national model (ASCA; 2003) affect not only the profession of school counseling but also the training of professional school counselors. Pre-service programs must reevaluate the focus and content of their training process in order to train professional school counselors for the 21st century. The emphasis placed on counselor education programs to adhere to the CACREP accreditation standards has standardized and strengthened training programs. ASCA's national standards and the national model have strengthened school counseling from pre-service programs to practice across the country.

ASCA has advocated that professional school counselors establish their identity, and clearly articulate and define the role school counseling programs play in promoting student achievement and educational success. Professional school counselors are challenged to demonstrate accountability, document effectiveness, and promote school counseling's contributions to the educational agenda. School counseling programs that are defined by statements of what students should know and be able to do are seen as accountable, viable, and visible in the eyes of school stakeholders. Comprehensive, developmental, results-based, national standards-based school counseling programs have established a presence and continue to define our future.

(Note: See the CD-ROM for a list of references.)

THE ASCA NATIONAL MODEL: A FRAMEWORK FOR SCHOOL COUNSELING PROGRAMS: ONE VISION, ONE VOICE FOR THE PROFESSION

Trish Hatch

Preview

In this chapter, I discuss the history behind the need for "one vision, one voice" within the profession of school counseling and introduce The ASCA National Model: A Framework for School Counseling Programs *(American School Counselor Association [ASCA], 2003). I also review the development of the model, the original criteria agreed upon by summit members, its first public draft release, the final release, and the impact of the document thus far. Finally, I review a summary version of each component within the model and offer suggestions for the profession's next steps.*

The American School Counselor Association created the ASCA national model (ASCA; 2003) to connect school counseling with current educational reform movements that emphasize student achievement and success. The ASCA national model provides an organizational framework that is designed to assist professional school counselors to develop or redesign their programs to meet the current educational needs of students. By using the model to align the school counseling program with the school's mission and school improvement plans, professional school counselors partner as leaders in systemic change, ensure equity and access to a rigorous education, and promote academic, career, and personal–social development for *every* student.

As we head further into the 21st century, professional school counselors continue to define new directions for the profession. Historically, school counselors have lacked legitimization, have been professionally marginalized, and, in many states, remain expendable by definition, because there is no education code that requires their services or programs within schools. ASCA's (2003) release of the ASCA national model was intended to provide one vision, one voice for the profession, in hopes of addressing this professional need. But before looking to the school counseling profession's future, it is crucial to understand its past.

OUR PAST

At the turn of the 20th century, school counselors did not exist. Instead, teachers used a few minutes of their time to offer vocational guidance to students who were preparing for work in a democratic society. The current school mission is not altogether different than that of the 1900s. Today, in a world enriched by diversity and technology, professional school counselors' chief mission is still supporting the academic achievement of all students so they are prepared for life beyond school. However, professional school counselors no longer work in isolation; instead, they align with other educational professionals, which is integral to the total educational program for student success. This evolution from teachers sparing minutes a day to trained professionals implementing a comprehensive school counseling program did not take place without professional scholars and counselors having the vision, knowledge, and determination to move forward (Gysbers, 2001).

Professional school counselors began as vocational counselors in 1908, and the profession has evolved to incorporate the domains of academic, career, and personal–social development (Campbell & Dahir, 1997; Miller, 1961). During this evolution, differing philosophical perspectives developed between and among academic counselors, career counselors, and personal–social or mental health counselors regarding their role and function, purpose, and focus. Lacking clear role definition as a profession, school counseling became a house divided by controversy between those who focused on vocational guidance (which later became *educational guidance*) and those who attended to the personal–social foundational needs of students in education (Aubrey, 1991).

While procedures were similar, methods were varied. Counseling could be either directive or nondirective—two somewhat opposing methods of delivery. In directive counseling, the focus on intellectual interpretation was counselor directed, while nondirective counseling was client centered and focused on the release of feelings and the achievement of insight. The first approach was delivered by the counselor; the latter was discovered by the student. Most vocational counselors were directive, whereas social workers, mental hygienists, and child-guidance clinicians were nondirective (Warters, 1946). In the 1960s, the directive approach to counseling was encouraged by the National Defense Education Act of 1958. Professional school counselors in U.S. schools identified and herded the best and the brightest students toward math and science majors in college, in an effort to win the Space Race with the Soviet Union. Meanwhile, Carl Rogers (1951) was training counselors in a nondirective, more passive approach.

Counselors who trained in programs rooted in psychological and clinical paradigms differed greatly from those who were rooted in educational paradigms. Postsecondary training programs contained conflicting and varied theoretical perspectives between and within their programs and, consequently, professional school counselors' training and perspectives about their role and function varied substantially. Not unlike today, professionals within school counseling debated whether counselors are mental health workers within schools or educators with a mental health perspective.

The counseling and guidance movement was also characterized by a proliferation of competing methodologies that focused more attention on the technique of counselors and the process of counseling and less on the content and objectives of the program. This alteration in counseling methodology led to changes in the substance and the priority that guidance programs were given (Aubrey, 1991). "The focus was on a position (counselor) and a process (counseling), not on a program (guidance)" (Gysbers & Henderson, 1997, p. 1). Consequently, guidance became an ancillary support service and not a program integral to the total educational program of student success. The result was that professional school counselors were (and in some cases still are) more likely to be saddled with administrative tasks and clerical duties (Roeber, Walz, & Smith, 1968).

In the 1970s and 1980s, several attempts were made to unify the profession. Emerging from this movement were several theoretical models of comprehensive programs, many of which were based on the expansion of the career guidance model. Norman Gysbers and Patricia Henderson wrote textbooks and developed and trained districts and states in comprehensive guidance programs models (Gysbers & Henderson, 1997; Henderson & Gysbers, 1998); C. D. "Curly" Johnson and Sharon Johnson (1991, 1997) focused their counselor training on designing results-based school counseling programs; and Robert Myrick (2003) wrote his textbook on planned developmental guidance programs. In addition, the ERIC Clearinghouse on Counseling and Student Services published several books and conducted four national conferences that offered training in the development and implementation of comprehensive school guidance programs. Despite the tremendous impact of these forward thinkers, the legitimization of the school counseling program within schools remained quite tenuous.

For decades, the school counseling profession attempted to respond to the question, *What do counselors do?* However, that question only confused those within and outside the profession because of the various models in which counselors were trained or loyal to. In addition to listing myriad counseling-related duties (e.g., guidance lessons, group counseling, academic planning, individual counseling, consultation, collaboration), professional school counselors complained about "doing" a variety of quasi-administrative and non-counseling duties. Just as preservice training varied for professional school counselors, so too did administrative expectations for school counselors, based on administrative preservice training (or lack of it) with regard to school counseling programs (Olson, 1979).

These changes and varying models confused professional school counselors as well as school administrators, teachers, and parents.

> When schools fail to clearly define the counselor's role . . . school administrators, parents with special interests, teachers or others may feel their agenda ought to be the school counseling program's priority. The results often lead to confusion and criticisms when they are disappointed. (Cunnan & Maddy-Berstein, 1998, slide 4)

MORE RECENT CHALLENGES

In 1992, Phyllis Hart and Marilyn Jacobi wrote *From Gatekeeper to Advocate: Transforming the Role of the School Counselor*, in which they discussed the six problems in school counseling programs, summarized here:

1. *Lack of basic philosophy.* Few professional school counselors are guided by a well-developed philosophy or belief system, one that drives the entire program and the behaviors of the counselors within the program. Rather, they tend to work independently and are often reactive.

2. *Poor integration.* School counseling remains an ancillary rather than a core component of K–12 education. Professional school counselors must connect with other stakeholders in the school system as an integral partner in the total educational program.

3. *Insufficient student access.* Student-to-counselor ratios are high, and many students do not have the opportunity to meet with their professional school counselors. High ratios are only part of the problem, however. Another is that some counselors still insist on focusing on individual counseling rather than ensuring that every student receives school counseling services through a school-wide guidance curriculum.

4. *Inadequate guidance for some students.* Economically disadvantaged students and students of color are often denied the opportunity to enroll in rigorous academic coursework at the same level that is often afforded to other students.

5. *Lack of counselor accountability.* There is no common understanding about what constitutes accountability and in what way counselors are to be held accountable for the results of their program.

6. *Failure to use other resources.* Professional school counselors cannot deliver the entire counseling program; rather, they are encouraged to better use school and community resources to create networks, garner referrals, and meet a variety of students' needs.

MORE RECENT TRENDS

Recent trends in education include the reform and accountability movement, standards-based education, high-stakes testing, achievement-gap issues of equity and access, an increase in legislation supporting student retention, the funding of new programs through block grants, the use of technology and data to drive decisions and effect change, school safety issues, and the movement from an educational culture of entitlement to one of performance. No longer can educators focus on how hard they work or how well meaning they are; they must answer their stakeholders' question: *How are students different as a result of your program?*

Current trends in the school counseling field have included the development of the ASCA national standards, which contain the student content standards used to design competencies for students in the areas of academic, career, and personal–social development (Campbell & Dahir, 1997). In 1997, ASCA published *Sharing the Vision: The National Standards for School Counseling Programs* (Campbell & Dahir, 1997) as a conscious effort to participate in the national reform agenda through the development of national standards. This landmark document for the profession, endorsed by national educational and professional organizations, contains student standards for school counseling programs in the areas of academic, career, and personal–social development.

VISION INTO ACTION: IMPLEMENTING THE NATIONAL STANDARDS FOR SCHOOL COUNSELING PROGRAMS

Dahir, Sheldon, and Valiga (1998) provided professional school counselors tools for selecting student competencies and suggestions for infusing the competencies into the school counseling program. ASCA's national standards have been widely used in designing standards for students in school counseling programs. Other trends include the Transforming School Counseling Initiative (The Education Trust, 2003; Martin & House, 1998), which redefines the role of professional school counselors as integral to ensuring equity and access to a rigorous education for every student, particularly students of color and those of a lower socioeconomic status. In addition, state departments, school districts, and professional school counselors have developed state and local models, and an increase in legislative activity promoting school counseling for students has emerged. Nonetheless, the following questions remained unanswered by many professional school counselors nationwide:

- What is the purpose of your school counseling program?
- What are the program's desired outcomes?
- What is being done to achieve these results?
- What evidence is there that the objectives have been met?
- Is the program making a difference?

ONE VISION, ONE VOICE

To address these professional concerns, ASCA's governing board, at its March 2001 meeting, agreed to develop a national program model. The standards provided content for the foundation of a program; however, board members agreed that the next logical step would be the development of a framework to maximize the full potential of the standards documents. This new document would reflect current education reform movements, including the No Child Left Behind Act of 2001, which mandates that all federally funded programs be accountable for and directly connected to student learning and student improvement. Furthermore, ASCA decided to hold a national summit to create an ASCA national model to bring the leaders in the field together and create One Vision, One Voice for all professional school counselors. ASCA moved forward to develop the model to address the historical concerns and current challenges and to assist practicing school counselors in planning for the future of their programs and the profession through one common lens.

MODEL DEVELOPMENT

From the first stages of development, ASCA called upon the expertise of national leaders and practicing school counselors. The first ASCA Summit for School Counseling was held June 1 through June 3, 2001, in Tucson, Arizona. The purpose of the summit was to discuss the future of school counseling programs and to develop a framework for a national model. The following professionals participated in the summit:

Dr. Judy Bowers, ASCA Supervisor/Postsecondary Vice President and Guidance Coordinator, Tucson Unified School District, Arizona

Dr. Trish Hatch, ASCA Supervisor/Postsecondary Vice President Elect and Coordinator of Student Services, Moreno Valley School District, California

Pam Gabbard, ASCA President Elect and counselor at Ballard County Elementary, Barlow, Kentucky

Dr. Norm Gysbers, counselor educator, University of Missouri, Columbia

Dr. Peggy Hines, counselor educator, Indiana University, Bloomington

Dr. C. D. "Curly" Johnson, consultant, San Juan Capistrano, California

Dawn Kay, Utah State Department of Education

Mark Kuranz, ASCA President and counselor at Case High School, Racine Wisconsin

Dr. Stan Maliszewski, counselor educator, University of Arizona, Tucson

Pat Martin, program director, The Education Trust (currently with College Board)

Susan Mellegard, counselor educator, Arizona State Department, Phoenix

Dr. Robert Myrick, counselor educator, University of Florida, Gainesville

Dr. Pat Schwallie-Giddis, counselor educator, George Washington University, Washington, DC

Richard Wong, ASCA Executive Director, Alexandria, Virginia

(Also invited but unable to attend were Carol Dahir and Carolyn Sheldon)

CRITERIA FOR THE DEVELOPMENT OF THE MODEL

For 2½ days, summit participants brainstormed, collaborated, and finally achieved consensus on how the model would be structured. Summit participants agreed to develop a model that would consist of three levels of program implementation: foundation, delivery and management, and accountability. There would be four or five components in each of the three levels. The ASCA national standards would be the foundation upon which the building blocks of the program curriculum would be built.

As a basis for a national model, participants incorporated theories and concepts from programs designed by Dr. Norman Gysbers, Dr. C. D. "Curly" Johnson, Dr. Robert Myrick, The Education Trust, and the ASCA national standards. The document would be written by Trish Hatch and Judy Bowers and would incorporate samples of their work with professional school counselors in the Moreno Valley Unified School District in California, and the Tucson Unified School District in Arizona, respectively. State and school counselor association documents of comprehensive programs would also be reviewed and used in the development of the document.

In developing the national model, participants agreed on the following assumptions and criteria:

- ASCA's national standards are a framework or foundation for the development of a school counseling program. (Many states also have standards that align with the ASCA standards.)
- A distinction must be made among the school counseling standards for every student, school counseling standards for the program, and school counseling standards for the professional school counselor.
- A school counseling program must provide a framework that allows flexibility for states and school districts to create a program based on the districts' individual needs and accountability.
- A school counseling program must be integral to students' academic achievement, particularly in facilitating improvement in academic achievement, and must help set higher standards for student achievement.
- A school counseling program must be data driven (disaggregated) and results based and should not focus only on methods and techniques.

- School counseling programs should be developed and implemented district wide, not just at individual schools.
- Successful development and implementation of a school counseling program relies on school–community collaboration.
- A school counseling program should provide intentional guidance to specifically address the needs of every student, particularly students of culturally diverse, low socioeconomic status, and other underserved or underperforming populations.
- A school counseling program empowers professional school counselors and teaches them how to work with administrators to reassign non-guidance activities such as master scheduling or testing.
- The design of a school counseling program model must include accountability tools for measuring results.
- To facilitate the adoption of a school counseling program model by school districts, ASCA will identify and disseminate best practices for designing, developing, coordinating, implementing, evaluating, and enhancing the program.
- A school counseling program must include plans for the effective use of a counselor's time within the delivery system.
- A school counseling program should be preventive in design and developmental in nature.
- Professional school counselors will play leadership roles in defining and carrying out a school counseling program.
- Licensed or credentialed professional school counselors must implement a school counseling program.
- In a school counseling program, professional school counselors work as change agents within the educational system to advocate for students' needs and students' results.
- Professional school counselors must use data to advocate for students and a school counseling program.
- A school counseling program should demonstrate evidence of the use of technology to implement the program; to advocate for the program; and to collect, analyze, and interpret data.
- In a school counseling program, professional school counselors must strive for continued improvement and use results to continually improve the program for students.

A preliminary graphic (see Figure 18.1) that included the content of the four major components of the model (foundation, delivery system, management system, and accountability system) was developed and approved by the summit participants. The themes of advocacy, leadership, collaboration, and systemic change were woven throughout the model.

WRITING THE MODEL

Throughout following months, Judy Bowers and Trish Hatch wrote the first draft. They researched dozens of state department and state association school counseling documents. Reading, sorting, and sifting through thousands of pages was a daunting task and responsibility. Each document was dissected in light of its possible contribution to the overall, agreed-upon framework. The responsibility to effectively represent the requirements of the summit group and to address each component was taken very seriously. Working with ASCA's graphic artist, several versions of the graphic were reviewed, until the final version was agreed upon.

In November 2001, the first rough draft was reviewed by Summit I members and test-driven by professional school counselors in Tucson, Arizona, and at the Moreno Valley School Counselors Academy in California. Counselors and administrators were trained in the model, reviewed the manuscript, and provided valuable feedback. The authors made revisions and submitted a new draft in May 2002 at Summit II, which was held in Washington, DC. Following final revisions, the final draft was released nationwide to professional school counselors.

PUBLIC RELEASE OF THE FIRST DRAFT

The first public draft was unveiled during ASCA's national school counselor conference, in Miami, in June 2002. Keynote conference speakers, leaders in the school counseling field who attended the initial model development summit meeting, included Norman Gysbers, Clarence "Curly" Johnson, and Robert Myrick. Several conference sessions were devoted to providing an overview of the model. An intensive, 3-hour workshop conducted by Judy Bowers and Trish Hatch (the draft authors) drew more than 200 participants. The focus of the workshop was on how professional school counselors could implement the model in their own districts.

ASCA provided an online version of the model and solicited national public comment for the 4-month period following the conference. The document received overwhelmingly positive responses. Professional school counselors and counselor educators nationwide provided praise, helpful and constructive criticism, and made suggestions for improvement. The authors analyzed the feedback and provided a revised version to the Summit III participants in November 2002. After a final Christmas vacation rewrite, the authors submitted their gift[1] (a final version) to ASCA for an initial printing to coincide with National School Counselors Week in February 2003.

THE ASCA NATIONAL MODEL

The ASCA National Model: A Framework for School Counseling Programs (ASCA; 2003) is written to reflect a comprehensive approach to program foundation, delivery, management, and accountability. It provides a framework for the program components, the professional school counselor's role in implementation, and the underlying philosophies of leadership, advocacy, and systemic change. The model provides the mechanism with which professional school counselors and school counseling teams will design, coordinate, implement, manage, and evaluate their programs for students' success.

With the national model, professional school counselors switch their emphasis from service-centered for some of the students to program-centered for every student.

---

[1] Trish Hatch, PhD, and Judy Bowers, co-authors of the *ASCA National Model: A Framework for School Counseling Programs*, were paid no royalties for their work. They wrote the document as a gift to the profession. ASCA recommended the citing as (ASCA; 2003) to promote "One Vision, One Voice" within the profession.

FIGURE 18.1. Preliminary graphic for the ASCA national model.

The model not only answers the question, *What do professional school counselors do?* but it also requires a response to the question, *How are students* different *as a result of what we do?* School counseling programs based on the national model are designed to ensure that *every* student receives the benefits of the program. Historically, many professional school counselors spent 80% of their time responding to the needs of 20% of their students (i.e., high achieving or high risk). The ASCA national model recommends that 80% of the professional school counselor's time be spent in direct service to all students so that *every* student receives the program benefits.

The ASCA national model incorporates school counseling content standards and competencies for every student, which serve as the foundation for the program and focus the direction for an organized, planned, sequential, and flexible school counseling curriculum. The model uses disaggregated data to drive program and activity development, thus enabling professional school counselors to design interventions to meet the needs of all students and to close the gap between specific groups of students and their peers. The model emphasizes an organizational framework and accountability system to determine how well students have met the standards or have achieved intended outcomes. The school counseling program reduces confusion, aligns goals and objectives with the school's mission, and ultimately leads to student achievement, as is demonstrated by results data.

The ASCA national model serves as a template for the development of a school counseling program; it is not meant for exact replication. Because attention to local demographic needs and political conditions is necessary for effective school counseling program development, the ASCA national model is meant to integrate with and adapt to the school's current program. There is no one "ideal program" that can or should be used as a cookie-cutter approach throughout the nation. Rather, ASCA's goal is to provide professional school counselors with a document that will institutionalize the framework of a comprehensive school counseling program.

Leadership skills are critical to the successful implementation of new or remodeled programs at the school, district, and state levels. Professional school counselors are change agents, collaborators, and advocates. As professional school counselors become proficient in retrieving and analyzing school data to improve student success, they ensure educational equity for every student. Using strong communication, consultation, and political skills, professional school counselors collaborate with other professionals in the school building to influence systemic change and advocate for every student.

Learning from the past is critical to developing a new school counseling program. The ASCA national model provides a program audit which, when completed by the school counseling team, assists them in analyzing their current program so that areas of improvement can be identified. Looking at recent and current achievement and achievement-related data in the school will illuminate performance trends. This analysis is imperative because professional school counselors can use this data to recognize if program changes are needed—and they must be prepared to make needed changes, no matter how comfortable the status quo or how difficult or uncomfortable the change may be.

ELEMENTS OF THE ASCA NATIONAL MODEL FOR SCHOOL COUNSELING PROGRAMS

The following sections describe the various elements outlined in the ASCA national model, including the Foundation, Delivery System, Management System, and Accountability components.

FOUNDATION

Beliefs and Philosophy—The philosophy is a set of principles (usually a set of "we agree" statements) that guide the development, implementation, and evaluation of the program. Ideally, all stakeholders involved in managing and implementing the program will reach consensus on each belief or guiding principle contained in the philosophy.

Mission—A mission statement describes the purpose of the program and provides the vision of what is desired for every student. Ideally, the school counseling program mission statement aligns with and is a subset of the school and district's mission.

ASCA National Standards and Competencies—The ASCA national standards and student competencies are the foundation for the school counseling program. Student competencies define the content for the knowledge, attitudes, or skills that students should obtain or demonstrate as a result of participating in a school counseling program. They are developed and organized into content areas of academic, career, and personal–social development.

DELIVERY SYSTEM

Guidance Curriculum—The guidance curriculum component consists of structured developmental lessons designed to assist students in achieving the competencies. Guidance curriculum is driven by standards and is provided systematically through classroom and group activities in K–12 classrooms. The purpose of the guidance curriculum is to provide every student with the appropriate knowledge and skills for their developmental level.

Individual Planning With Students—The individual planning component consists of professional school counselors coordinating ongoing systemic activities designed to assist the individual student in establishing personal goals and developing future plans.

Responsive Services—The responsive services component consists of activities designed to meet the immediate need of students. Professional school counselors respond by providing counseling, consultation, referral, peer mediation, or information.

Systems Support—The systems support component consists of the administration and management activities that establish, maintain, and enhance the total guidance program.

MANAGEMENT SYSTEM

Management Agreements—Professional school counselor or administrator agreements ensure effective implementation of the delivery system to meet students' needs. These agreements, which address how the school counseling program is organized and what will be accomplished, should be negotiated with and approved by designated administrators at the beginning of each school year.

Advisory Council—An advisory council is a group of people appointed to review guidance program results and to make recommendations. The group representatives are students, parents, teachers, counselors, administration, and community members.

Use of Data—The use of data to effect change within the school system is integral to ensuring that every student receive the benefits of the school counseling program. Professional school counselors use process, perception, and results data to determine areas of need, analyze the effects of their program, and improve the program.

Student Monitoring—Monitoring students' progress by monitoring student achievement data, achievement-related data, and standards and competency-related data ensures that each student receives what he or she needs to achieve success in school. Collection, analysis, and interpretation of student achievement data may be systemic by district, or it may be specific to school site, grade, class, or individual.

Closing the Gap—Closing-the-gap (intentional guidance) activities are data driven. Student needs surface when disaggregated data are analyzed to address attendance, behavior, and achievement gaps. Discrepancies between the desired results and the results being achieved are defined as the *gap*. These may be addressed by counseling with students or by working within educational systems to create equitable policies and procedures for all students.

Action Plans—There are two types of action plans: *guidance curriculum* and *closing the gap*. Guidance curriculum action plans are standards driven and include a scope and sequence for the content of guidance instruction *every* student receives. Guidance curriculum action plans include the following components:

- The domain, standard, and competency that is addressed.
- The description of the actual activity.
- Curriculum or materials to be used.
- The time in which the activity is to be completed.
- The person(s) responsible for the delivery.
- The means of evaluating student success (i.e., process, perception, and results data).
- The expected result for student(s).
- The implications.

Closing the gap (intentional guidance) action plans are data driven and designed to address the specific data-driven needs of underperforming students in the areas of attendance, behavior, or achievement. Closing the gap (intentional guidance) action plans include all of the components of guidance curriculum, but they also provide the specific data that drive the decision to address the attendance, behavior, or achievement gap.

Use of Time—ASCA's national model recommends that professional school counselors spend 80% of their time in direct service (contact) with students and provides a guide for professional school counselors and administrators to determine the amount of time their program can devote to each of the four components of the delivery system. Resources are limited, and therefore professional school counselors' time must be protected and their duties must be limited to program delivery and direct counseling services. Non-school counseling activities should be reassigned whenever possible.

Use of Calendars—Once professional school counselors determine the amount of time that is necessary in each area of the delivery system, they can publish a master and weekly calendar that will assist them in keeping students, parents, teachers, and administrators informed. Calendars assist counselors in planning the program and ensuring the implementation of a standards-based guidance curriculum.

ACCOUNTABILITY

Results Reports—Results reports (which include process, perception, and results data) ensure that programs are carried out, analyzed for effectiveness, and modified and improved as needed. Sharing these reports with stakeholders serves as advocacy for the students and the program. Immediate, intermediate, and long-range results are collected and analyzed for program improvement.

School Counselor Performance Evaluation—The professional school counselor's performance evaluation contains basic standards of practice that are expected of school counselors implementing a school counseling program. These performance standards serve as both a basis for counselor evaluation and as a means for counselor self-evaluation.

Program Audit or Evaluation—The program audit provides evidence of the program's alignment with the ASCA national model. Completing the program's audit provides initial direction for program development, provides direction for program improvement, and, when completed annually, assesses the program's progress towards full implementation of the ASCA national model.

IMPLEMENTATION

As the school counseling department implements a program, it must engage administrators early in the process, because administrators will be partners in program design and development. School boards, staff, and stakeholders must all be informed and involved in the exciting process of the program's transformation and improvement. The school counseling program belongs to the entire school, and, as such, it is everyone's responsibility to ensure that each student receives the benefit of a school counseling program that is based and aligned with standards, driven by data, measures results, and shares successes.

WHAT'S NEXT?

The ASCA national model has become the standard of training in counselor education programs on a national level, and professional school counselors and school districts throughout the United States have aligned or transformed their programs according to the recommendations put forth in the model. Dozens of proposals for the annual ASCA national conference include references to the impact of the ASCA national model on school counseling programs. ASCA also honors schools or districts that meet certain criteria for transforming or aligning their programs and proclaiming them a RAMP (Recognized ASCA Model Program) school or district.[2] In addition, the National Board for Professional Teaching Standards (NBPTS) incorporated the concepts of the model into their standards for the new NBPTS school counseling certification.

POSSIBLE CHANGES?

To date, the authors have received very few suggestions for changes or improvements to the ASCA national model. Rather, we have been truly overwhelmed by the appreciation that counselors and administrators have shown us for our work, and we are very grateful. However, there is always room for improvement and additional clarification. When providing training on the model, I find that professional school counselors appreciate the types of in-depth discussions that data counselors can collect and that they might use this data to determine not only which services to offer but to measure the results of their program and to provide suggestions for program improvement. After carefully reviewing the differences between process, perception, and results data, professional school counselors are strongly encouraged to start slowly, select carefully what they will measure, and measure only *one thing* first. Professional school counselors are reminded that "You can't measure everything; you'll lose your mind; and we can't have that because we need you!"

Undoubtedly, more support will be needed in this area, and projects are in the works to more clearly demonstrate how counselors can use data to affect not only program but also systems change. In January 2004, ASCA devoted its entire *School Counselor* magazine to the "Use of Data" issue. One article, "When It's Time to Change," tells the story of professional school counselors who use data to affect a systems change to promote equity and access to a rigorous education (Hatch, Holland, & Meyers, 2004). They successfully challenged a curriculum guide with gate-keeping prerequisites for higher level math courses.

---

[2] For more information, contact ASCA at www.schoolcounselor.org

For some, more clarification is needed between the two types of action plans: guidance curriculum and closing the gap. It helps to remember that the action plan for guidance curriculum is *standards driven* and is designed for every student. The action plan for closing the gap is *data driven* and is designed for students who are identified (when querying the data) as needing more help.

More clarification may also be needed to help professional school counselors better understand the relationship between the ASCA national model and The Education Trust's *The Met Life: Transforming School Counseling Initiative.*[3] The concepts of advocacy, leadership, systemic change, and collaboration are infused throughout both; however, professional school counselors remain confused about which training to receive ASCA's national model or Met Life's initiative. A quick response would be that the ASCA national model is the actual functional organizational system for the school counseling program in place at each site, and Met Life training provides the skills necessary to implement this system in support of every student. They are, therefore, interdependent, intertwined, and interrelated. Professional school counselors who believe strongly in equity, access, and social justice issues are able to use the structure of the ASCA national model along with the skills gained in the Met Life training to become leaders and advocates for systems change that benefits every student.

Summary/Conclusion

Writing *The ASCA National Model: A Framework for School Counseling Programs* (ASCA; 2003) has been the highlight of my professional career (so far). The opportunity to collaborate with those involved and to be entrusted (along with Judy Bowers) with the challenge to synthesize their work with ours into a single document was an amazing gift. I have learned much and grown incredibly, both personally and professionally, during this most humbling experience, and I now move forward to continue working with passionate advocates in the field to promote and preserve the profession of school counseling for the benefit of every student.

The future of school counseling is tenuous. After 100 years of marginalization and efforts to operationally legitimize a profession, only time will tell if the ASCA national model will move the profession closer to accomplishing this vital and daunting task. Research supporting the efficacy of model school counseling programs is vital. A recent National Summit on School Counseling Research was held to begin these conversations. In addition, the National Panel for Evidenced-Based School Counseling Practices is working to design the parameters for research in the field of school counseling by reviewing the research base, determining which practices are evidence based, and identifying areas in which additional research is needed. The goal is to improve the available research within the profession to validate evidenced-based programs and practices. Citing evidenced-based practices is necessary not only for program improvement but also to advocate at the local, state, and national levels for legislation to support and promote school counseling programs.

(Note: See the CD-ROM for a list of references.)

---

[3] For more information on The Education Trust's *The Met Life: Transforming School Counseling Initiative,* go to www.edtrust.org

CHAPTER 19

DATA-DRIVEN SCHOOL COUNSELING

Carolyn B. Stone and Carol A. Dahir

Preview

In this chapter, we emphasize the powerful influence and impact that using data has on both school counseling practice and programs. In this age of accountability, school counselors must not be left behind. Data-driven school counseling demonstrates the powerful contributions of school counselors to the school success agenda, to successful outcomes for students, and, most important, to the goals of school improvement.

Without data, you don't know where you are, you don't know where you are going, and you don't know if you ever got there.

—Jim Macgregor, High School Counselor, Kissemmee, Florida (Stone & Dahir, 2006)

Jim MacGregor has been using data to give advantage to students for over 2 decades. Jim MacGregor, steward of equity and access, persevered until all students in his high school were supported with access to algebra and safety nets to ensure their success. Jim's extraordinary personal–social consciousness skills guided him to understand and apply the tenets of equity and access in a sophisticated way. Instead of just opening the door for students to access higher level academics, Jim supported students to be successful once they entered the inner sanctum of rigorous course work. Jim not only advocated for his students to have greater opportunities, he raised their aspirations by implementing a career awareness program for every student in the school to help them see the interrelationship between postsecondary education and their future economic opportunities. Jim's strategies were numerous, and some of the more effective ones included (a) changing the systemic approach to course enrollment patterns to support more students to access higher level academics; (b) using data and anecdotal information about student success in higher level academics to change attitudes and beliefs; (c) using disaggregated test results so that teachers had better information about student weaknesses; (d) implementing large- and small-group sessions on motivation and problem solving and implementing 4-year plans using software that easily tracked every student from ninth grade so that course selections were in writing and matched students' aspirations; and (e) establishing a mentoring program (Stone & Dahir, 2007).

When Jim moved to a school system in Florida, he brought his passion for equity and advocacy with him. Four years ago, when Jim arrived at his new high school, only 129 advanced placement (AP) exams were administered. The number of low socioeconomic students represented in AP courses was minimal. In 2006, after receiving intentional, focused efforts in a school with a 56% free and reduced-price lunch population, the opportunities for these low socioeconomic students increased dramatically. Forty-seven percent of the students in AP were of low socioeconomic status, and 740 exams were given. Jim's story is but one example of thousands of professional school counselors who are now using data to inform their practice, to the advantage of students. Data-driven school counseling improves students' opportunities for brighter futures and affects the achievement gap while demonstrating the value that professional school counselors add to improving student achievement.

Data inform and challenge one's thinking to determine the need for systemic change, confirm progress, and reveal shortcomings in student performance. Closely examining critical data elements in the areas of attendance, socioeconomic impact on class enrollment, graduation and postsecondary planning rates, and standardized testing results not only identifies the needs of students but also the school- and system-wide issues that affect success. By using data, professional school counselors can present a picture of the current situation of student needs and examine the practices that can lead to higher levels of success.

Disaggregating data by variables such as ethnicity, gender, socioeconomic status, or teacher assignment is important in the analysis of student performance. The disaggregation of data makes it possible to determine how policy and practices affect issues of equity. It is now possible to more closely examine which groups of students are successful and which are meeting failure. Using data enables professional school counselors to work closely with building administrators and faculty to close the achievement and opportunity gaps. Professional school counselors who focus their efforts on moving data in a positive direction demonstrate a strong commitment to sharing the responsibility and accountability for student outcomes.

In this chapter, organized around seven themes, we will address the powerful way that data can inform your comprehensive school counseling program:

1. A Data-Driven Program Initiates a Powerful Comprehensive Program
2. A Data-Driven Program Focuses Our Efforts
3. A Data-Driven Program Affects Student Achievement
4. A Data-Driven Program Supports School, System, and National Improvement Goals
5. A Data-Driven Program Shares Accountability
6. A Data-Driven Program Helps Identify Effective Strategies and Stakeholders
7. A Data-Driven Program Identifies and Rectifies Issues That Stratify Student Opportunities

A Data-Driven Program Initiates a Powerful Comprehensive Program

A comprehensive school counseling program can be developed in a step-by-step manner, beginning with the foundations, including a mission statement and advisory council, and eventually proceeding to data evaluation. However, for some professional school counselors, developing a comprehensive program can be overwhelming or too complicated. Another way counselors can develop a school counseling program is to start with the data. Without data, a comprehensive school counseling program will result in loosely held together components that may be unrelated. Data can be instrumental in evaluating a comprehensive school program, but data can also be the first step in initiating a comprehensive school counseling program (Stone, 2007). The process of developing a comprehensive program begins with a piece of critical data that can be positively affected. To demonstrate this, let us work through an example using discipline referrals as the critical data element.

BEGINNING WITH DATA

Discipline referrals were identified by the school on the school improvement plan as an area in need of attention. The professional school counselor, along with other educators, disaggregated the discipline referrals to achieve a better understanding of the problem. The disaggregated data revealed that discipline referrals occurred in every grade level, but they were concentrated in the fourth and fifth grades, especially during lunch, and mostly on Mondays. Rather than separately gathering all the pieces of a comprehensive program to address this issue, the professional school counselor could start with the data element *discipline referrals* and the knowledge gained by looking at the disaggregated data and start to put into place components that are needed, such as responsive services, individual student planning, and system support to move the critical piece of data. In this way, the task of beginning to develop a comprehensive program is bite sized, doable, and generates a good start toward a comprehensive school counseling program. Professional school counselors can become paralyzed by the thought of having all of the pieces for a comprehensive program in place, but everyone can think about what specific interventions in the following areas might be needed for a reduction in discipline referrals.

Foundation. This component connects the professional school counselor's work to the school's mission by supporting a safer, more respectful school climate and by focusing efforts on reducing the discipline referrals. The foundation also facilitates student development in three broad domains—academic, career, and personal–social development—to promote and enhance the learning process. Using focused strategies to reduce discipline referrals allows work in all three domains.

ASCA national standards and competencies. These define the knowledge, attitudes, or skills students should obtain or demonstrate as a result of participating in a school counseling program. Developing in students the skills, attitudes, and knowledge to discontinue or to avoid discipline problems meets the competencies of the ASCA national standards (American School Counselor Association [ASCA]; 2006).

Guidance curriculum. The guidance curriculum can be developed as the professional school counselor starts to address a focused need. For example, as the professional school counselor works to reduce discipline referrals, he or she may deliver classroom guidance lessons in areas such as bully-proofing the school. The guidance curriculum is designed to assist students in achieving the knowledge and skills that are appropriate for the students' developmental level (ASCA; 2006).

Individual planning with students. The professional school counselor will work in an intentional way to help students understand the interrelationship between school and their future. This is one way the individual planning component assists individual students in establishing personal goals, developing future plans, and making better choices in school that do not include office visits for misbehavior.

Responsive services. With discipline issues as the data-driven focus, the professional school counselor will develop and focus responsive services to meet the immediate needs of students. These needs require counseling, consultation, referral, peer mediation, or information (ASCA; 2003, 2005).

Use of data. A comprehensive school counseling program is data driven. The use of data to affect change within the school system is integral to ensuring that every student receives the benefits of the school counseling program. Professional school counselors must show that each activity implemented as part of the program was developed from a careful analysis of students' needs, achievement, and related data (ASCA; 2006).

Student monitoring. By disaggregating the data, the professional school counselor is able to understand who the multiple discipline offenders are and the types of offenses. This helps the professional school counselor to monitor students' progress in order to ensure that each student receives what is needed to achieve success in school. Areas to be monitored can include student achievement data, achievement-related data, and standards and competency-related data. Collection, analysis, and interpretation of student achievement data may be systemic by district or be specific to a school site, grade, class, or individual (Stone & Dahir, 2007).

Action plans. By joining with other stakeholders, the professional school counselor can develop an action plan to achieve the desired result (Stone, 2007).

A DATA-DRIVEN PROGRAM FOCUSES OUR EFFORTS

When professional school counselors focus their efforts on the mission of school improvement, they widen educational opportunities for every student and positively affect student achievement by

- raising student aspirations;
- helping students acquire resiliency and coping skills for school and life success;
- managing and accessing resources for student support;
- collaborating with faculty to share the responsibility for student progress;
- engaging students in educational and career planning that present students with a wide variety of quality postsecondary opportunities; and
- working intentionally toward closing the gap in student performance.

Professional school counselors who embrace a leadership mindset also act on their beliefs and advocate for the removal of institutional and environmental barriers that impede success in school. As advocates advancing a social justice agenda, professional school counselors purposely promote equitable access to quality education for all students. Counselor behaviors begin with a commitment to a programmatic approach that is systemic in impact; grounded in social justice; driven by advocacy and equity; aligned with the state, system, and building mission; and collaboratively developed and delivered.

Social advocacy implies questioning the status quo and challenging the rules and regulations that decrease opportunities for the underrepresented (Osbourne et al., 1998). "Research has helped school people realize not only that equity is a moral obligation of schools, but that student learning and achievement are highly related to equitable practices" (Shakeshaft, 1990, p. 213). The American free public school system is a mechanism that should guarantee an open society in which students from all segments of society and from all social classes have an equal chance to develop their talents and achieve success.

Professional school counselors can collect and analyze student data to inform and guide the development of a comprehensive school counseling program based upon school-wide issues. Critical data elements can usually be found on the school's district or building report card. School systems routinely collect and store academic and demographic data in a retrievable form, and professional school counselors have ready access to data in areas that contribute to achievement such as course enrollment patterns and attendance. For example, if a counselor learns that the ninth-grade retention rate is 40%, this is information that can be used to inform and influence this area as an identified need for attention and strategies.

Data help professional school counselors identify the institutional or environmental barriers that may be adversely influencing the data elements and impeding student achievement. Professional school counselors can initially determine which elements to tackle first and which elements the school counseling program can move in a positive direction. A quick look at data alone does not tell the whole story. It is important to disaggregate the critical data elements on which you are focusing in a variety of ways to ensure that the system addresses access and equity issues. When the school-based data is disaggregated by ethnicity, gender, race, socioeconomic status, or teacher assignment, it is possible to identify institutional and environmental barriers impeding student success. Disaggregated data also identifies specific groups of students that professional school counselors can target to ensure that no one is barred from any opportunity (Stone & Turba, 1999).

A DATA-DRIVEN PROGRAM AFFECTS STUDENT ACHIEVEMENT

The American School Counselor Association's (ASCA) national standards for school counseling programs (Dahir, Sheldon, & Valiga, 1998) and the national model (ASCA; 2003, 2005) emphasize the importance of professional school counselors delivering accountable school counseling programs that carefully consider local demographic needs and the political climate of the community. The four main components of the model follow:

The *foundation* of the program requires the implementation of the belief and mission that every student will benefit form the school counseling program.

The *delivery system* defines the implementation process and the components of the comprehensive model (i.e., guidance curriculum, individual planning with students, responsive services, and system support).

The *management system* presents the organizational processes and tools needed to deliver a comprehensive school counseling program, including agreements of responsibility, use of data, action plans for guidance curriculum and closing the gap, and time and task analysis.

The *accountability system* helps professional school counselors demonstrate the effectiveness of their work in measurable terms, such as impact over time, performance evaluation, and a program audit.

The national model (ASCA; 2003, 2005) speaks to the importance of having an accountability system and an organizational framework that documents and demonstrates how students are different as a result of the school counseling program. A commitment to accountability shifts public perception from questions such as *What do professional school counselors really do?* to demonstrating that professional school counselors are key players in the academic success story for students and partners in student achievement.

When counselors work with data, they are contributing to each of these critical elements and to bringing attention to student progress and results. Professional school counselors can positively affect student achievement by

- working with students to increase their desire to access rigorous academic work;
- motivating students and raising aspirations;
- managing and accessing resources to help students succeed;
- ensuring every student had an educational and career plan;
- encouraging students to achieve good attendance; and
- presenting students with a wide array of postsecondary opportunities.

Professional school counselors who address improving student results will contribute to raising the achievement level for every student. By examining their practice and looking carefully at their way of working, professional school counselors can articulate and communicate how their contributions positively affect student achievement and thus share accountability for school improvement with other members of the faculty. Partnership with education professionals demonstrates a willingness to improve results and to help to close the achievement gap that exists among students of color and students of poverty. Measurable success resulting from a concerted effort on the part of professional school counselors to expand educational opportunities can be documented by an increased number of students completing school with the academic preparation, career awareness, and the personal–social growth that is essential when choosing from a wide range of substantial postsecondary options, including college (The Education Trust, 1997). Aligning the purpose of the school counseling program with the school improvement plan presents professional school counselors as champions and collaborators who encourage high aspirations and create opportunities for students to realize their dreams.

The school counseling program, aligned with the educational enterprise, is data driven, proactive, and preventive in focus and assists students in acquiring and applying lifelong learning skills. Professional school counselors can advocate for the academic success for every student while delivering the content of the school counseling program in a comprehensive and accountable manner.

A DATA-DRIVEN PROGRAM SUPPORTS SCHOOL, SYSTEM, AND NATIONAL IMPROVEMENT GOALS

The No Child Left Behind Act of 2001 (NCLB) is a clear imperative for professional school counselors to accept the responsibility to support academic achievement, share the pressures of school accountability, and demonstrate advocacy for every student to experience success. Traditionally, professional school counselors were not held to the same accountability standards as other educators. They were rarely included in conversations about contributions that affect the critical data elements that are publicly displayed on school report cards. In a climate of school improvement, it has become increasingly important for professional school counselors to play a proactive role in identifying and responding to the issues, policies, and practices that stratify student opportunity and inhibit access to equitable educational opportunities.

Accountability, as defined in NCLB, offers an opportunity for professional school counselors to significantly affect school improvement through targeted interventions that affect important school-based data. Professional school counselors are in a unique position to review data in schools and can identify the gaps that exist in student success. Professional school counselors, using their leadership and advocacy skills, ensure that appropriate resources and programs are in place to offer each student equitable access to challenging curriculum and all options to access postsecondary opportunities. Professional school counselors can influence the school climate to ensure that high standards are the norm in a safe and respectful environment. Professional school counselors, working together with the principal, can bring to the faculty's attention the importance of creating safe and drug-free communities.

At the district and building level, stakeholders may no longer be asking *What do counselors do?* but rather *How did the conflict resolution program reduce bullying incidents?* and *Have the chronic offenders who are frequently suspended benefited from weekly group counseling?* Professional school counselors have always supported a student's personal and emotional needs and helped students acquire coping and resiliency skills to stay focused and succeed academically. The greater opportunity is to demonstrate how the conflict resolution program contributed to improved school climate, reduced discipline, or improved attendance—all of which contribute to academic success. When a professional school counselor delivers targeted interventions in collaboration with classroom teachers for seven chronic offenders who were frequently suspended, and the suspension rate is reduced, the work of the professional school counselor contributes to the goals of school improvement. When monthly conflict resolution lessons are delivered in collaboration with the seventh-grade teacher teams and a documented reduction in fighting is noted, the data show the contribution to school climate and school improvement.

Professional school counselors are at risk of being viewed as ancillary in the climate of high property tax assessments that support school funding and high stakes testing that is the current barometer of adequate yearly progress. School counseling programs have been perceived to be a fiscally irresponsible and an ineffective use of resources by some policy makers, school boards, and school-system leaders who are held accountable for increasing student achievement (Whiston, 2002). Professional school counselor accountability is a commitment to affecting the key data elements that publicly demonstrate a school's success and the achievement of its students.

The No Child Left Behind Act of 2001 challenges the beliefs and attitudes of every educator to support all students to achieve high standards. Professional school counselors who purposely promote equitable access to quality education for all students and use data to advance a social justice agenda are key contributors to advancing the national, state, and system goals to improve our schools and close the opportunity gap.

A DATA-DRIVEN PROGRAM SHARES ACCOUNTABILITY

Professional school counselors have traditionally offered time-on-task data (Gysbers & Henderson, 2000) or a numerical summary of the types of activities they have delivered as a means of assessing and evaluating the impact of a school counseling program. Merely presenting the numbers of students seen individually, in groups, or in classrooms is no longer enough; time and task analysis does not show any relationship to affecting student achievement—rather, it is perceived as a defense mechanism to document productivity by those who are most concerned with the accountability measures that are necessary to improve student achievement. Sharing accountability for school improvement requires professional school counselors—as it does all educators—to systematically collect, analyze, and use critical data elements to understand, contribute to, and eliminate the achievement gap. When the school counseling program is aligned with the educational enterprise, it is data informed, proactive and preventive in focus, it assists students in acquiring and applying lifelong learning skills, and is delivered in a comprehensive and accountable manner (Stone & Dahir, 2007). Professional school counselor accountability involves collaboration with all education professionals to ensure that every student has the opportunity and access to a quality education.

Accountability offers the opportunity for professional school counselors to demonstrate how they can effectively identify and rectify issues that impede student achievement, contribute to each of these critical data elements, and bring attention to student progress and results. Sharing accountability for student success has become a driving force for transforming and reframing the work of school counselors (ASCA; 2003, 2005; Gysbers & Henderson, 2000; Lapan, 2001; Stone & Dahir, 2004).

A DATA-DRIVEN PROGRAM HELPS IDENTIFY EFFECTIVE STRATEGIES AND STAKEHOLDERS

Professional school counselors, as managers of resources, join existing groups of stakeholders (such as the school improvement team) or use their leadership skills to bring other stakeholders and resources together to create and implement an action plan. Professional school counselors identify stakeholders to become part of a team to address the movement of the critical data elements. Counselors should include all concerned members of the internal and external school community, secure their commitment, and determine who will bring them together. If possible, an existing school action committee can be used. Accountability for professional school counselors involves teaming and collaborating with other stakeholders and avoiding tackling issues in isolation, which can be accomplished by

- identifying the additional stakeholders from the internal and external school community,
- securing their commitment,

- working with the school leadership team to facilitate this process, and
- involving any existing committees to address the concerns around the critical data elements.

Strategies are developed by the counselor individually and in collaboration with others that will change systems as well as affect individual students and targeted groups of students. *Impacting systems* means (a) replicating successful programs and interventions; (b) identifying barriers that adversely stratify students' opportunities to be successful learners; and (c) developing strategies to

- change policies, practices, and procedures;
- strengthen curriculum offerings;
- maximize the instructional program;
- enhance the school and classroom culture and climate;
- provide student academic support systems (e.g., safety nets);
- influence course enrollment patterns to widen access to rigorous academics;
- involve parents and other critical stakeholders (internal and external to the school);
- raise aspirations in students, parents, teachers, the community; and
- change attitudes and beliefs about students and their abilities to learn.

Publicizing to critical stakeholders the results of an effective school counseling program is a vital step in the accountability model, and it is important to success because stakeholders will have a deeper understanding about the contributions of the school counseling program to student achievement. Professional school counselors will thus be seen as partners in school improvement and will have demonstrated a willingness to be accountable for changing critical data elements. Because of these efforts, professional school counselors are viewed as essential to the mission of the school.

At Ribault High School, in Jacksonville, Florida, using and monitoring data has focused professional school counselor efforts, and, in collaboration with all stakeholders in the middle feeder school and high school, they shared responsibility for improving postsecondary admissions. Using and monitoring data clearly demonstrated the intentional focus of the school counseling program on improving the postsecondary admission rate. In 2006, fifty-three percent of the graduating class went on to enroll in college—a huge leap from the less that 15% who even applied to college just 5 years prior. This collaborative effort made the change happen, and the professional school counselors' commitment as key players in school improvement was well established and acknowledged. As the strategies delivered in K–12 positively moved this data forward, the measurable results showed how the school counseling program can work to increase the postsecondary admission rate through a system-wide, focused effort.

A DATA-DRIVEN PROGRAM IDENTIFIES AND RECTIFIES ISSUES THAT STRATIFY STUDENT OPPORTUNITIES

Accountability shows that all educators, especially professional school counselors, intentionally and purposely act to close the achievement gap. If administrators, faculty, and all stakeholders truly believe that all children can learn and achieve, then professional school counselors, by their beliefs and behaviors, demonstrate their willingness to work side by side with colleagues. Professional school counselors form partnerships with principals and key stakeholders to embrace accountability and promote systemic change with the expressed purpose of furthering the academic success of every student (Stone & Clark, 2001). With an accountable, data-driven school counseling program, professional school counselors are seen as powerful partners and collaborators in school improvement and essential to fulfilling the mission of every school. Accepting the challenge of accountability propels professional school counselors to accept the responsibility of removing barriers to learning and achievement and raise the level of expectations for students for whom little is expected.

Professional school counselors who work within an accountability framework can challenge the pervasive belief that socioeconomic status and color determine a young person's ability to learn. By acting as agents of school and community change, professional school counselors can create a climate in which access and support for quality and rigor is the norm. In doing so, underserved and underrepresented students have a chance at acquiring the education skills necessary to fully participate in the 21st-century economy.

Summary/Conclusion

Closing the gap in student performance is central to affecting systemic change. The use of demographic and performance data makes it possible for counselors to determine how policies and practices are effecting issues of equity. Student achievement data can be collected and analyzed systematically to inform and guide the development and construction of a school counseling program, based upon school-wide issues. Professional school counselors can initiate, develop, and coordinate prevention and intervention systems that are designed to improve the learning success for every student who is experiencing difficulty with challenging academic coursework. Viewing the world of schools through a data-driven perspective helps professional school counselors to act on their belief system and assume a leadership role in identifying and rectifying issues that affect every student's ability to achieve at expected levels.

(Note: See the CD-ROM for a list of references.)

COMPREHENSIVE DEVELOPMENTAL SCHOOL COUNSELING PROGRAMS

Cheryl Moore-Thomas

Preview

School counseling is an ever-transforming field (Eschenauer & Chen-Hayes, 2005; McCurdy, 2003; Paisley, 2001; Paisley & Peace, 1995). Amidst the change in the field, comprehensive developmental school counseling programs have remained central to the work of professional school counselors (Green & Keys, 2001; Gysbers, 2001). In this chapter, I discuss components of comprehensive developmental school counseling programs, including mission, developmental approaches, diversity, student competencies, delivery systems, resources, and program evaluation.

Most professional school counselors are familiar with the phrase "comprehensive developmental school counseling program." Few, however, are able to clearly define it (Borders & Drury, 1992). This is understandable, given the variability and flexibility that exist in effective comprehensive developmental programs. In spite of this variability, effective programs do share some characteristics.

Gysbers and Henderson (2005) and Gysbers (2001) suggested that true comprehensive developmental school counseling programs complement the existing academic programs and are well integrated into a curriculum that supports the mission of the school and district. They also provide a full range of services, including counseling, referral, consultation, information, and assessment, which are implemented through a variety of delivery systems. Inherent in the provision of a full range of counseling services is the understanding that professional school counselors are pivotal to but not the sole service providers of a school counseling program. Comprehensive developmental school counseling services are most effectively offered through a team approach. Professional school counselors work in consultation and collaboration with guidance advisory committees; school staff (including teachers, resource teachers, principals, school psychologists and social workers, pupil personnel workers, nurses, secretaries, building services workers, and instructional assistants); parents, grandparents, and guardians; and community stakeholders (Gysbers & Henderson, 2005; House & Martin, 1998; Ripley, Erford, Dahir, & Eschbach, 2003).

School counseling programs are *developmental* in that they provide regular, systematic opportunities for students to achieve competencies that are focused on their growth and development (Gysbers & Henderson, 2005). Effective school counseling programs result from planned, sequential, flexible curricula that complement the academic curriculum and emphasize the life skills and experiences that all students need to become successful in school and adulthood (Myrick, 1997). Further definition of comprehensive developmental school counseling was offered by Borders and Drury (1992), who suggested that comprehensive developmental school counseling programs are proactive, preventative, and aimed at helping all students acquire the knowledge, skills, self-awareness, and attitudes necessary for normal development. In order to determine if comprehensive developmental school counseling programs are in fact meeting these aims, student progress, program results, and other relevant data are collected, analyzed, and effectively used to make warranted program adjustments. Although it is important to understand what comprehensive developmental school counseling programs are doing, it is more important to understand the results of school counseling programs. The "so what" question, answered by results and perception data, is extremely significant for the viability of school counseling programs (American School Counselor Association [ASCA], 2005a); professional school counselors collaborate with others to answer this important question.

In summary, comprehensive developmental school counseling programs

- embody the school mission and philosophy;
- offer students proactive opportunities to learn the skills, knowledge, and attitudes that are necessary for healthy development;
- provide a full range of school counseling services, implemented through varied delivery systems;
- complement other school programs;
- involve advisory committees, school staff, parents, guardians, and community members;
- monitor and support student progress;
- collect and analyze process and results data; and
- evaluate and adjust program elements as warranted.

The ASCA National Model: A Framework for School Counseling Programs (ASCA; 2005a) provides a specific structure for comprehensive developmental school counseling programs. Because it is focused on the national education mission for improved student achievement, this data-driven model ensures access to appropriately rigorous education through the delivery of a systematic knowledge- and skill-based program for students in K–12 (ASCA; 2005b). In this chapter I discuss the major components of comprehensive developmental school counseling programs and the ASCA national model in more depth.

Program Mission

School counseling programs are an integral component of the education environment. They are not isolated, stand-alone services or activities. All elements of the school counseling program are meant to support the educational mission of schools in ways that appreciate and facilitate students' development and academic achievement. To ensure that this occurs, professional school counselors work collaboratively with community stakeholders to create clear, concise, student-focused school counseling program mission statements that parallel the local school, district, and national vision of quality education while describing the distinctive purpose, vision, and contributions of school counseling (ASCA; 2005a). Relevant mission statements ground comprehensive developmental school counseling programs and affect and focus program planning, implementation, evaluation, and funding. Extraordinary leadership, advocacy and courage are therefore required to create a bold and timely vision of school counseling programs that provide appropriate service and opportunities for all students (Ripley et al., 2003). The following example of school counseling program mission statements highlight a student focus and appropriate, rigorous education for all.

The mission of the Lakeside Elementary School Counseling Program is to enable all students to maximize their potential by providing guidance and counseling in the areas of academic, career, and personal–social development that recognizes and respects individual uniqueness and personal worth.

The mission of the Edgemere Middle School Counseling Program is to help students become successful learners, responsible citizens, and full participants in a diverse and changing world.

The school counseling program at Hillsdale High School is designed to empower all learners, regardless of individual differences, to lead responsible and fulfilling lives in the present and to make promising and productive linkages to the future.

DEVELOPMENTAL APPROACH

The research and theoretical base for school counseling programs is largely found in the theory and practice of human development (Green & Keys, 2001). Basically, developmental theory deals with the manner in which individuals change over time (Thomas, 1996). The specific stages, characteristics, and contextual considerations of change are described in a variety of human development theories including, but not limited to, psychosocial development, cognitive development, ethnic identity development, moral development, spiritual development, and self-concept development. Gysbers and Henderson (2005) suggested that a human development approach has specific applicability to school counseling. Their conceptualization of life career development is depicted as "self-development over the lifespan through the integration of roles, settings, and events in a person's life" (p. 49).

Well-planned and well-executed school counseling programs help students gain the knowledge, skills, and attitudes that are necessary for the mastery of normal developmental tasks (Sears & Granello, 2002). Research suggested that students functioning at high levels of development are better able to handle the tasks of living and learning (Borders & Drury, 1992; Paisley & Peace, 1995). These data appear to strongly support developmental school counseling programs. It is prudent, therefore, that professional school counselors and other school counseling program stakeholders appreciate, understand and use the principles of human development theory. On a practical level, this process involves the identification and selection of age-appropriate tasks and challenges, which are sequentially organized within a school counseling program at each grade level.

DEVELOPMENTAL APPROACH AND ISSUES OF DIVERSITY

Professional school counselors must make certain that the foundational developmental theories of the comprehensive school counseling program are appropriate for *all* students. Professional school counselors ensure that school counseling programs meet the needs of students of all racial, ethnic, and socioeconomic backgrounds and that they serve all students, regardless of achievement level, gender, sexual orientation, family structure, language, or any other aspect of diversity (ASCA; 2004; Green & Keys, 2001; Gysbers, 2001; House & Martin, 1998; Sears & Granello, 2002). This task is challenging due to the rapidly increasing diversity in schools. Approximately 42% of the K–12 population is minority or non-White (National Center for Education Statistics, 2004). Population projections indicate that by 2020 more than 50% of school-age children attending public schools will come from minority cultures (Campbell, 1994). The relevance, effectiveness, and ethical standing of comprehensive developmental school counseling programs are therefore dependent upon the critical alignment of culturally relevant developmental approaches and counseling services. The American School Counselor Association (2004) called on professional school counselors to "take action to ensure students of culturally diverse backgrounds have access to appropriate services and opportunities that promote maximum academic, personal/social and career development" (p. 1); however, there are data which suggest all students, especially those of color and those from low socioeconomic statuses, are not receiving adequate services (Lapan, Gysbers, & Sun, 1997). Developmental principles cannot be blindly applied. Effective school counseling programs are built on developmental models that are applied and interpreted in the cultural context of students and their communities (Green & Keys, 2001). To ensure that pertinent diversity aspects are appropriately reflected in the comprehensive developmental school counseling program, professional school counselors and other stakeholders should engage in professional development opportunities related to diversity, consult and collaborate with experts in cultural competence, and use tools like the *Multicultural Competence Checklist* (Holcomb-McCoy, 2004) for self-assessment.

Program Benefits

One of the most valuable benefits of a comprehensive developmental school counseling program is that it provides professional school counselors with a rationale and framework for providing service to students (Lapan, Gysbers, & Petroski, 2001). Furthermore, comprehensive developmental programs move the work of professional school counselors from random, ancillary guidance activities that benefit a few students to focused, mission- and data-driven school counseling services and programs that benefit all students. The systemic, continuous nature of comprehensive developmental school counseling programs decreases the likelihood that needy students will go unserved or underserved while increasing the likelihood that all students will benefit from the developmental and preventative nature of school counseling programs (Paisley & Peace, 1995). Clearly, students are the greatest benefactors of comprehensive developmental guidance programs, but the benefits to the entire school community cannot be overlooked. Comprehensive developmental school counseling programs benefit teachers and other educators, parents, and community stakeholders through the implementation of proactive, collaborative programs that provide continuous data regarding student development and performance in a variety of domains, including areas of academic achievement.

Program Competencies

An important initial step in developing a comprehensive developmental school counseling program is identifying student competencies. *Competencies* are the skills or abilities students are expected to acquire as a result of participating in the comprehensive developmental school counseling program. In determining and selecting appropriate competencies for a specific school population, professional school counselors should consult school district goals, needs assessment data, outcome data, professional research literature, and professional organizations' position statements (Gysbers, 2001). Table 20.1 provides a brief listing of current curricular terminology and definitions. *The ASCA National Model: A Framework for School Counseling Programs* (ASCA; 2005a) proposes student competencies grouped by the academic, career, and personal–social domains and provides accompanying standards. These resources assist professional school counselors in selecting the complement of competencies that best meets the needs of the students at each developmental level in a particular school community.

Selected student competencies must be further defined by outcomes and indicators, which assist the professional school counselor and other stakeholders in assessing student success. Careful consideration and articulation of "what success will look like" (e.g., evidence of the achievement of the competencies) goes a long way to support school counseling program accountability.

Selection of an appropriate competency, outcome, and indicator is demonstrated in the following example:

> The professional school counselor of a large urban elementary school, in consultation with the school counseling advisory committee, reviewed 2 years of school and district data which seemed to suggest that the local suspension rate increases significantly at the fourth-grade level. Qualitative data revealed that the suspensions were primarily due to student fights and verbal conflicts. These data were troubling, given the school and district's mission of success for all students. The professional school counselor, administrator, and school leadership team decided to address this concern through various school programs, including the comprehensive developmental school counseling program. Knowing that a critical step in developing a comprehensive developmental school counseling program is to select competencies that are aligned with institutional goals and data, and undergirded by sound culturally appropriate developmental principles, the professional school counselor used ASCA national model (ASCA; 2005a) as a blueprint. The counselor incorporated the standards as part of the school counseling plan for the upcoming academic year and highlighted a framework (provided in Table 20.2) for beginning to address the school's troubling suspension rate.

PROGRAM DELIVERY SYSTEM

Comprehensive developmental school counseling programs are delivered to students through many processes—some of which provide direct service to students; others, indirect. Guidance curriculum, a *direct* process, consists of classroom lessons, interdisciplinary curricula, and school-wide activities (Borders & Drury, 1992; Gysbers, 2001). Individual student planning, another direct service, involves small-group and individual student appraisal and advisement regarding issues such as test results, career awareness, and course selection. Responsive counseling, the most frequently used delivery system, involves a host of counseling services and activities, including individual and

TABLE 20.1

TERMINOLOGY

Term	Definition
Competency:	Skill or ability
Domain:	Developmental area
Goal:	Broad statement of desired student achievement that embodies the mission and purpose of the institution or program
Indicator:	Specification or delineation of a student outcome
Objective:	Measurable evidence of students' skills, knowledge, or attitudes
Standard:	Statement of what students should know or be able to do, indicating a level or standard of expected performance

group counseling, consultation, crisis counseling, and referral. ASCA suggested that professional school counselors spend 80% of their time in direct service to students through the delivery of a comprehensive developmental school counseling program (ASCA; 2005b).

System-support activities are *indirect* services that maintain and enhance the comprehensive developmental school counseling program. They are defined by the delivery of school counseling services through training and professional development, community outreach, advisory boards and councils, and program and total school management.

The professional school counselor and other stakeholders must select the most appropriate delivery process for each aspect of the comprehensive developmental school counseling program. Student needs determine the most appropriate delivery processes. For example, a group of ninth-grade students in one community may be served best by small-group counseling services that focus on body image and self-esteem, while the developmental needs, regarding the same topic, of a different ninth-grade community may most appropriately be met through an interdisciplinary classroom lesson that is developed and implemented by the professional school counselor and health education teacher.

Program delivery systems clearly suggest that professional school counselors are central to the comprehensive developmental school counseling program, but they are not the entire school counseling program. The success of each delivery system is dependent on the support of the entire school community.

PROGRAM RESOURCES

Human and financial resources undergird comprehensive developmental school counseling programs. Human resources for counseling programs include the leadership and service of the professional school counselor working in collaboration with students, teachers, administrators, other school staff, advisory committees, parents, and community members (Gysbers & Henderson, 2005). Each has a role and responsibility regarding the development and implementation of effective counseling programs.

TABLE 20.2

FRAMEWORK FOR ADDRESSING SUSPENSION RATES THROUGH A COMPREHENSIVE
DEVELOPMENTAL SCHOOL COUNSELING PROGRAM

Program Component	Content
School Goal:	Academic success for all students
Domain:	Personal–social
Standard:	Students will make decisions, set goals, and take necessary action to achieve goals (ASCA; 2005a)
Competency:	Self-knowledge application
Indicators:	Students will use a decision-making and problem-solving model Students will understand consequences of decisions and choices Students will know how to apply conflict resolution skills (ASCA; 2005a)
Objectives:	1. After participating in the school-wide classroom guidance unit on conflict resolution skills, 80% of the school's third-grade students will be able to apply conflict resolutions skills to a given hypothetical situation with 100% accuracy. 2. Eighty percent of the targeted fourth-grade students, after having participated in small-group counseling on conflict resolution, will be able to identify the three steps of the problem-solving model.

Financial resources include district and local dollars and in-kind services provided for school counseling programs. Budget restraints sometimes prohibit school counseling programs from receiving optimal levels of financial support. This demands that all individuals who are responsible for counseling programs engage in creative problem solving to meet the financial needs of programs. This problem solving could lead to advocacy and lobbying for full funding of school counseling and other educational programs; partnerships with community businesses; or the facilitation of school, community, and student-led fund-raising activities.

PROGRAM EVALUATION

Evaluation of comprehensive school counseling programs is an important, multifaceted process (Gysbers & Henderson, 2005; Lapan, 2001). Terenzini (1989) suggested that program evaluation be framed by two questions:

- Does the school have a written, comprehensive program that is fully implemented and aligned with district, state, and national standards?
- Does the educational program in fact produce the intended outcomes?

Practical guidelines for conducting program evaluations are important and discussed in depth elsewhere (ASCA; 2005a; Atkinson, Furlong, & Janoff, 1979; Erford, 2007; Krumboltz, 1974; also, see Chapter 25). It is practical and highly desirable to connect program concerns to only one or two well-articulated questions to focus and manage evaluation. It may also work to ensure that the specific program component under evaluation is being fully and appropriately examined.

The school counseling program evaluation process is systematic, ongoing, and cyclical (Lapan, 2001). It starts small and builds upon what the data suggest works. Successful methods and delivery processes are determined and replicated so that over time, necessary program refinements work to build a comprehensive developmental school counseling program that fully supports the school's mission and simultaneously meets the needs of all learners.

Effective evaluation always begins with the school's mission. The mission provides the basis from which meaningful, institution-specific assessment questions arise. These assessment questions lead to the determination of what evidence must be collected. Evidence can provide crucial information about program evaluation and program results.

Evidence can be derived from standardized or informal measures, student performances, or student products. Once evidence has been gathered, it must be interpreted. Conclusions can then be drawn regarding the counseling program's value, strengths, weaknesses, and outcomes, and program improvements can be made. As assessment information is used to prompt programmatic changes, goal setting and the posing of new questions begin again. Meaningful, thorough program evaluation provides professional school counselors with opportunities to collaborate with counselor educators, educational accountability experts, consultants, and other program evaluation experts. Collaboration, assessment questioning, data gathering and interpretation, and results reporting can be conducted in clear and practical ways that benefit students and the entire school community.

Important work regarding broad questions of comprehensive developmental school counseling program accountability has been conducted in studies on academic achievement (Sink & Stroh, 2003), student satisfaction (Lapan et al., 2001), and student preparation for the future (Lapan et al., 1997). Initial results data seem to suggest that comprehensive developmental school counseling programs are making a positive difference in students' lives. This line of inquiry must continue, however, with carefully designed studies of what students know and can do as a result of comprehensive developmental school counseling programs (Brown & Trusty, 2005).

SUMMARY/CONCLUSION

Comprehensive developmental school counseling programs are vital to the work of today's professional school counselors. Rooted in developmental theory, comprehensive programs use well-selected student competencies, delivery systems, resources, and assessment processes to assist students in acquiring the culturally appropriate knowledge, skills and attitudes needed for healthy development. As professional school counselors, administrators, teachers, parents, and others work together to design and implement comprehensive developmental school counseling programs, continual systematic movement is made toward the healthy development of all students.

(Note: See the CD-ROM for a list of references.)

CHAPTER 21

NEEDS ASSESSMENTS:
THE KEY TO SUCCESSFUL AND MEANINGFUL
SCHOOL COUNSELING PROGRAMS

Jan R. Bartlett

Preview

Needs assessments empower professional school counselors through data. By gathering the input of the school's stakeholders, professional school counselors gain the information necessary to create programs that truly reflect the unique needs of their community. In this chapter, I discuss the steps necessary to gain support and cooperation from coworkers, administration, community, and the school board to build a strong foundation for conducting a needs assessment.

*E*xciting, fun, engaging, enlightening, meaningful, and *essential* are, one hopes, words associated with your school counseling program. Can the majority of the students, parents, and teachers in your district and school speak knowledgeably about your program? Does your program make a difference in the life of every child? Our community schools, whether rural, urban, or suburban, need to have school counseling programs built on information that is collected and evaluated on a regular basis. By bringing together feedback from students, teachers, parents, school-board members, administrators, and community leaders, professional school counselors can develop a program that truly reflects the unique needs of each school community. *Assessment* and *observable outcomes* are key words that are frequently heard in the education field. Increasingly, actions and decisions in our society are guided by findings from collected information, which in turn drive movement and choices; therefore, these decisions are based on research. Developing an effective, successful, and meaningful school counseling program is no different. By assessing the specific needs of the community, the professional school counselor gathers significant information that emerges from data, enabling the school counseling program to determine a purposeful path of action. This data, aligned with the ASCA national standards (Campbell & Dahir, 1997) and national model (American School Counselor Association [ASCA], 2005) for school counseling programs, can create a powerful tool for positive change in the school. A comprehensive and developmental school counseling program is based on research and built with the combined efforts of the professional school counselor and stakeholders of the school and community. Needs assessments are about empowering professional school counselors through data.

Approaches to needs assessment vary, and there are many surveys available for use in schools. The purpose of the survey may be remedial, preventative, or both. Needs assessments may be purchased commercially, borrowed, or adapted from an existing source; a school district may also decide to create a needs assessment for their own use (Gladding, 2000). Surveys are included in many books that address school counseling program development, and many texts in the school counseling field either include sample needs assessments or address needs assessments in varying detail, including Baker (2000), Cobia and Henderson (2003), Erford (2007), Gladding (2000), Greenberg (2003), Schmidt (2003), and VanZandt and Hayslip (2001). For a book devoted entirely to the process of developing, administering, and evaluating a needs assessment, Rye and Sparks (1999) is an excellent resource. It provides sample needs assessments for all school levels, an example of results, and a plan developed from the sample data provided.

NEEDS ASSESSMENT DESIGN

Some needs assessment designs promote a comprehensive approach, in which all the elements of goals and topics that might realistically be components of a comprehensive school counseling program are addressed. This approach may be most suitable for school districts that are establishing a baseline and implementing their initial assessment, with no previously collected data. Other designs consider assessing certain topics or concerns explicitly, so they are targeting issues; this would be helpful when a district or school is updating or altering a program based on an existing needs assessment (Erford, 2007). In all, seven methods have been determined for assessing the needs for a school: surveys (questionnaires and inventories), analysis of records, personal interviews, visits to classrooms, contracting an outside consultant, counseling statistics, and systematic evaluation of the existing school counseling program (Stone & Bradley, 1994). Collecting information using any of these sources is extremely valuable; however, in this chapter I focus on the most frequently used tool for needs assessments—the survey. I will also discuss factors that are critical to the successful implementation and use of the needs assessment.

Here are some additional ideas that will boost your enthusiasm for this endeavor. Whether you select an existing survey or develop your own, developmental variables and patterns might help you collect valuable information for your survey. For example, a study of needs assessments conducted with students from kindergarten to ninth grade recommended a shift in guidance topics, with an individual and family focus during early elementary years to larger social context issues as students matured (Drefs, 2003). Social context issues might include drug and alcohol use, sexual activity, disease risks and education about HIV/AIDS and hepatitis C, and Internet safety. Topics could also be a call to social and civic responsibility, which might address poverty, social justice topics, energy and sustainability, global warming, and other global or local concerns to engage students in debate and discussion. The self-reported needs of students in the previously mentioned study helped to identify these developmental shifts in the entire school population. Tracking these shifts may prove to be useful for decisions regarding curriculum, resources, community opportunities for mentoring, and the creation of group opportunities.

Another study stressed the need for appropriate school services for homeless children (e.g., children who might be residing in shelters within your district); many of these children had experiences in counseling and reported them positively (Nabors et al., 2004). Examine your survey and consider the viewpoint and perspective of the homeless parent or child to ensure that it is sensitive and relevant. Another key point is that the needs assessment may provide valuable information regarding the varying needs of multicultural and diverse populations within schools and district (Carter & Spera, 1992).

GETTING STARTED: BUILD A STRONG FOUNDATION

"A school system is no more stable than its base of community support" (Rye & Sparks, 1999, p. 1). The same sentiment may be extended to a school counseling program and its needs assessment efforts. Aim for the highest and most wide-ranging level of support. First, gain the support of the entire counseling staff, either in your building or district (if you succeed in capturing their attention and commitment, the chances for strong involvement and overall success are strengthened). If it is not possible to do a district-wide assessment, then shifting the focus to a specific school may be the best place to start.

Second, after gaining the support of professional school counselors, attempt to gain endorsement and backing of both the administration and the school board by developing a formal proposal to gain the endorsement for the needs assessment. Not only should the school board and administration be included in the process, but they must also be made aware of the school counseling program's efforts to improve services. Once the proposal is completed, the next step is to request the endorsement of the plan by the school board at a regular meeting. This lends an air of legitimacy to the process, which will hopefully result in supportive principals and central office administrators.

Once the needs assessment data has been collected, evaluated, and implemented regarding plans for program development, then the school board should also endorse the final plan. This allows for some sense of permanence and stability for the school counseling program. If, for instance, changes occur within an administration, then less disruption to the school counseling program might occur.

Accountability for the school counseling program is another key reason for involving the administration and the school board at the very beginning of the needs assessment process. Data from a needs assessment can be used effectively in establishing priorities for program development (Erford, 2007). Because of the No Child Left Behind Act of 2001, it is critical that professional school counselors think of their program in terms of accountability. Purposeful programming, based on data collected from the needs assessment, which is tied to the personal–social, career, and academic standards and competencies from the national standards developed by Campbell and Dahir (1997), indicate and demonstrate the link to a research base. It is essential that the programming be regularly evaluated to demonstrate measurable outcomes and that this information be presented and shared with the staff, administration, school board, and community. Press releases or articles written by professional school counselors or other committee members regarding the goals and objectives for the needs assessment can further expand support, endorsement, and involvement from students, parents, and the community. Also, the membership and involvement of the advisory board or committee working in conjunction with professional school counselors throughout the entire process should be highlighted.

CONTENT OF PROPOSAL

The proposal should include at least the following components, accompanied with specific and detailed information:

1. Address the broad aim and purpose for the needs assessment. Discuss general goals for the school counseling program. Topics might include creating the highest quality program; continued improvement for the program; identifying and addressing changes in the student body and community (Rye & Sparks, 1999); determining the priorities for services from the stake holders; and matching services with school and community needs.

2. Address who will be involved in the process. Introduce the advisory board or committee, and discuss the membership of this group. The advisory board is composed of representatives of the stakeholders in the school district: administrators, teachers, staff, students, school board members, parents, and a community representative. This is a good time to discuss the organizational needs of the advisory board. A large school district may need a district-wide steering committee as well.

3. How will the needs assessment be organized? Address in broad terms the responsibilities of the various members, including training, setting goals, conducting needs assessment, planning strategies, and evaluation. Include details for implementing the evaluation data and plans for ongoing revisions.

4. Provide a detailed timeline for the completion of the needs assessment's planning stage. Emphasize that each planning cycle leads to an evaluation of the data, which is the basis for redirection and fine-tuning of the existing program (Rye & Sparks, 1999).

5. Estimate how long it will take. Include in the proposal a prediction for when a document will be available for the school board to review and a date for when the plan will be completed.

Include a statement regarding the perceived impact of the resulting plan. Remember to stress the importance and benefits of the planning process; do not only emphasize the outcomes.

ADVISORY COMMITTEE

The advisory committee, sometimes called the "group advisory team" or "advisory board," is composed of representatives of the stakeholders in the school—individuals in the school and community who are committed to the success of the school and students. It is wise to identify a list of potential individuals including students, teachers, administrators, parents, and community leaders (e.g., ministers, business leaders, mental health professionals, law enforcement officers, government officials; Rye & Sparks, 1999).

The professional school counselors might organize this group or the school board might appoint it. Alternatively, the group could be selected and organized and then appointed by the school board. Along with the professional school counselors, the committee will be involved in planning, implementing, and evaluating the counseling program. Once the group or committee has been identified, essential communication between the members will be necessary to move the needs assessment forward. This work may be time-consuming, but it will provide a solid foundation for future activities and discussion.

Each community is unique, and the services that are needed from the school counseling program will vary. Because of variables such as the size of the school, socioeconomic status of the community, cultural diversity, concentration of learning problems found in the school, educational backgrounds of parents, community's attitude toward the school and education, and leadership of the school and district (Schmidt, 2003), it is essential and advisable that the community be reflected in the advisory committee as closely as possible.

BUILDING A PROGRAM BASE

By bringing together elements of a school and community to design the comprehensive program, the energies are channeled toward a common goal rather than competing or fragmenting the efforts of the needs assessment (Rye & Sparks, 1999). A comprehensive school counseling program is not the sole domain or responsibility of the professional school counselor. It includes many people to expand the base of support (Schmidt, 2003).

Instead of a discussion on the roles and function of professional school counselors, Rye and Sparks (1999) presented fundamental beliefs of a comprehensive school counseling program:

1. Governing values are the foundation of all human endeavors.
2. Education is the top priority for ensuring a positive future for all.
3. Comprehensive counseling programs are essential elements of any quality educational process for students.
4. Quality counseling programs must be developed from explicitly stated value bases and have both administrative and community support.
5. Comprehensive services must be systematically planned, implemented, and evaluated over an extended period of time.
6. Program planning is most effective when it is centered in an informed team of school and community representatives.
7. Effective counseling programs are specifically designed to meet identified needs in the school and community populations.
8. Programs of excellence offer services that build self-understanding and a variety of skills in a pattern of increasing levels of difficulty as students move from grade to grade. (Rye & Sparks, 1999, p. 4)

A decision should be made about whether to look at existing models for school counseling programs or to start fresh. One may consult VanZandt and Hayslip (2001) as a resource that includes information on several models: the Missouri model, the multidimensional model, and the national model. The professional school counselor should make a basic presentation of the national standards for school counseling programs (Campbell & Dahir, 1997) and ASCA national model (ASCA; 2005) to committee members. The national standards provide detailed student competencies for each of the core domains of personal–social, career, and academic success.

Core values. The committee might begin by discussing the group's understanding of core values. Chances for success are further enriched by exploring the committee members' values for the school's counseling program. Failure to determine a shared set of values coupled with the lack of a process to resolve value differences can lead to divisiveness within the committee (Rye & Sparks, 1999). The stated and expressed values from the committee should also be reflected within the larger community and within the cultural context surrounding the school; this is essential to attain and retain credibility.

To explore the respective values held by committee members, examine and discuss mission statements for the school, school counseling program, parent–teacher groups, businesses, and any other existing documents. This can help to provide a starting point for processing and clarifying individual values. Are there key words that are prominent in the documents? Is there a common ground? Within the profession there is still some question as to whether there is consensus on core values, but in a school district, the professional school counselors should articulate their own values and link them to those of the community (Rye & Sparks, 1999). Is there a common theme that runs through the community committee members? Work in small groups around general questions, and then chart the key points on large paper to be shared and organize the discussion. Possible starter questions may include, *What elements do members see as essential in a happy and successful student? What are the core values members want to see delivered through a school counseling program?*

Values to vision. Once the group's values have been clarified, the next step is to connect them to a shared vision for the future. Possible questions for exploring the vision for the program might include, *How are students different because of the school counseling program? When students move on from this school to another level or graduate, what skills do we want them to have? What will be the attributes of this student?* One helpful activity might be to ask committee members to close their eyes for a few minutes and reflect on what an exemplary school counseling program would look like and how it would affect students. Then let the group members spend a few moments writing notes based on their reflections. Encourage the members to share their ideas in small groups, where ideas can be documented and then shared with the larger group. Develop a vision or a mission statement for the school counseling program based on what emerges from the group. It should be a vision that all can agree on and support enthusiastically. In larger communities and communities with diverse students in the school district (e.g., cultural, religious, ethnic, racial, socioeconomic status), the professional school counselor might consider conducting focus groups to gather additional information to ensure all voices are included in the vision.

THE NEEDS ASSESSMENT

A needs assessment helps the school counselor determine stakeholders' needs and develop or refine program goals and objectives. Considerations for developing a needs assessment include (a) developing a timeline, (b) populations to be assessed, and (c) the instrument used.

DEVELOP A TIMELINE

Rye and Sparks (1999) stated the time commitment for an in depth and thorough needs assessment process will be 5 to 6 years, with the first year devoted to the following:

1. Preparing and organizing the advisory team into a working group.
2. Reviewing and refining the beliefs, vision, and mission of the counseling program.
3. Conducting a needs assessment among students, parents, and school personnel.
4. Identifying high-priority needs.
5. Writing objectives.
6. Helping the counseling staff develop activities to address identified needs. (Rye & Sparks, 1999, p. 34)

The next 4 years would involve the implementation, monitoring, evaluation, and revision of the plan that was initially developed. In the 5th year, another needs assessment could be conducted and a new plan developed and written, based on emergent needs.

Within the same time frame is another exciting possibility. An approach using a continuous cycle of assessing program needs, which could be tied to the national standards (Campbell & Dahir, 1997), could allow an assessment of each of the three areas of academic, career, and personal–social to occur on specific years in a 6-year cycle (Moore-Thomas & Erford, 2003). A possible cycle involves a focus in years 1 and 2 on assessment of academic needs, years 3 and 4 on the needs for career development and educational planning, and years 5 and 6 on personal–social issues. Once a program is clearly established, adjustments might be made in a 3-year improvement cycle (Erford, 2007). If drastic changes occur within the community, either because of shifts in demographics or some type of national, state, or local crisis of political or natural causes, it may be necessary to respond and adjust in a time frame other than the one planned.

POPULATIONS TO BE ASSESSED

All stakeholders in the community will have valuable information and opinions to share regarding the direction for the school counseling program. The groups commonly asked to participate in the needs assessment are students, parents, administrators, and teachers. Critical issues are frequently determined and discovered when surveying these groups (Schmidt, 2003). Information from community organizations and local business leaders can be helpful, but it may be difficult to obtain a large enough response sample. Therefore it may be prudent to gather this data through personal interviews and contacts (Erford, 2007). Additional information may be gleaned from school volunteers, the school nurse, school psychologist, social worker, and professional organizations. Input from these sources can assist in understanding expectations for the services to be provided (Schmidt, 2003) and supplement other feedback.

Because the return rate is essential for accurate and meaningful needs assessment results, students should fill out their survey while at school, perhaps at the end of a class period. It is important to share with the students their significant role in the survey. Stress that their opinion and insights are valued and that honest responses are sought. Teachers and staff generally respond well, especially if the administration is vocally supportive. The challenge is for a high return rate from parents. A "captured audience" can maximize the return rate, so consider gatherings at faculty meetings, class, or parent meetings for distributing and collecting surveys (Erford, 2007).

Brainstorm ideas with committee members to garner high enthusiasm and participation rates. Free food is always a draw. Consider enlisting the community, students, and faculty in a spaghetti dinner or fish fry. The ticket in could be a completed parent survey; the community could donate food, and students and school personnel could cook and serve. Send the surveys home with students ahead of time and have plenty of extra copies at the door. This gathering would provide a wonderful opportunity for building connections with parents. It would also be a forum for sharing information on a host of issues at the school and enlisting parent support. Student groups could be asked to participate to encourage further parent involvement.

THE INSTRUMENT

As stated earlier, there are many sample surveys available. The survey can address the same content area, even for elementary students with minor adjustments. The questions should not use education- and counseling-specific vocabulary (Cobia & Henderson, 2003). Some surveys use a Likert-type scale that rates the severity or importance of the issue or concern from 1 to 5 or 1 to 7, using *never* at one end of the spectrum and *always* at the other extreme. Other approaches include answers of *yes, no,* and *sometimes.* Other surveys have boxes to be checked for *rarely, sometimes, frequently, most of the time,* and *almost always.* There are many variations, and the committee may decide either to alter an existing survey to accommodate perceived needs or create their own. The content for the needs assessment should be topical, such as questions related to social skills, changes within families, substance abuse, or college application procedures (Erford, 2007). The format for the survey may use questions or statements; for example, *How important is it that "jokes" regarding sexual orientation be eliminated from the school community?* or *Students need to be more tolerant of people whose views, appearances, or actions differ from their own.* The committee may also decide to provide a space for collecting qualitative data with an open question (e.g., "Is there anything else you would like to share with the committee?"). This will allow for information to emerge that may have otherwise been missed or overlooked.

The Plan and Evaluation

Once the data have been collected and evaluated, the highest priority needs may be determined and used to establish program goals (Rye & Sparks, 1999). The committee will need to weigh and rank results from the surveyed data and groups. The students' highest priority may be different from that of the parents. The needs assessment may lead the committee to ask further questions in focus groups and individual interviews to clarify the data. Gathering additional information may be critical to goal setting and sorting the priorities. In the first year after the needs assessment, the school counseling program may elect to focus efforts on the top three to five priorities that emerged. These goals should be concentrated on for at least a year before adding additional goals. An exemplary school counseling program evolves over a number of years, not in 1 year. Remember to seek the school boards' endorsement after the needs assessment is completed and goals and objectives have been determined.

Summary/Conclusion

After joining and merging the voices from students, teachers, parents, school-board members, administrators, community leaders, and professional school counselors the emerging school counseling program will reflect the unique needs of the community. In turn, by focusing on prevention and developmental goals for students, professional school counselors do more than repair wounds and mend fences; they create healthy school climates and enhance human relationships (Schmidt, 2003). Administering a needs assessment is a time-consuming, tedious, and necessary adventure that binds together the school's stakeholders with the professional school counselors in a noble and worthwhile cause: the creation of a meaningful and successful program that makes a real difference in the lives of students, families, and the community.

(Note: See the CD-ROM for a list of references.)

CHAPTER 22

HOW TO WRITE LEARNING OBJECTIVES

Bradley T. Erford

Preview

The information in this chapter will help professional school counselors develop measurable learning objectives to guide the activities that comprise developmental guidance programs and individual and group counseling activities. Special emphasis is given to aligning objectives with programmatic standards, competencies, and assessment strategies so that evidence can be generated to document that program standards and student learning outcomes are being met.

It has been said that "if you don't know where you're going, you can't get there" (Saphier & Gower, 1997, p. 397). In addition, it does not matter in which direction you go. Obviously, such an approach is disastrous in the educational setting, because effective instruction is supposed to change behaviors, thoughts, and feelings in a desirable direction (Mager, 1997). Yet for years, some professional school counselors have entered the classroom to provide developmental guidance activities with wonderfully entertaining materials, interesting activities, or professionally produced videos but no clear understanding or statement of what changes in student thoughts, feelings, and behaviors were to be accomplished.

The same was true for individual and small-group work. Professional school counselors have often viewed the provision of these services as ends in themselves rather than as means to an end (Erford, 2007). Thus, students of divorce participated in a group or individual counseling experience because these were ways to provide services, but little thought was given to what the students were supposed to get out of these services (i.e., the outcomes). Often, these outcomes simply went unstated, but, in many instances, there was no guiding plan to move students in a positive developmental or therapeutic direction.

This lack of direction was in part due to the lack of an agreed-upon domain of knowledge or of behaviors specific to school counseling programs (Herr & Erford, 2007). Other academic disciplines (e.g., math, social studies, science) have well-defined and agreed-upon domains of knowledge that result, for example, in first-grade teachers across the country teaching basically very similar content and skills. While variations in curriculum no doubt occur—particularly as students get into middle school and high school—all academic disciplines plan for learning to occur in a systematic, sequential, and developmental manner. Until recently, this domain of knowledge and planfulness has been missing in many school counseling programs.

The ASCA national standards (Campbell & Dahir, 1997) was a positive step toward conceptualizing and establishing a school counseling domain of knowledge. They also provided competencies associated with each standard to further explain what was to be accomplished. In Chapters 20 and 23 of this book, the curriculum development sequence is identified as follows: standards, competencies and outcomes, objectives, activities, and assessment. Whether one uses the ASCA national standards or state or local standards or goals, good curriculum development starts with standards or goals to ensure that the broad domain of knowledge is identified. Competencies (sometimes analogous to the term *outcomes*) capture in broad terms the actions, skills, or abilities students must develop. Objectives help to further define and explain competencies and must be stated in specific, measurable terms to identify what will be accomplished as a result of the student's participation in the planned activities. Lessons or activities are then developed to provide the knowledge or experiences that allow students to accomplish the objectives. Finally, the objectives are assessed to determine the extent to which student learning, skills, and abilities developed during the lessons. If the objective is stated correctly, the professional school counselor will be able to assess whether the objective has actually been met.

THE OBJECTIVE OF THE OBJECTIVE

Mager (1997, p. 3) defined an objective as a "collection of words and/or pictures and diagrams intended to let others know what you intend for your students to achieve." In curriculum development, one first must determine where one wants students to end up (the objective) before creating the means to move them there (lessons and activities) and finally evaluating whether they have arrived (assessment). Thus, objectives are focused on outcomes rather than process, are measurable and specific rather than broad or general, and are student focused rather than teacher focused.

THE PURPOSE OF A LEARNING OBJECTIVE

Learning objectives serve several purposes (Mager, 1997). First, objectives help professional school counselors to develop activities and select procedures, resources, and materials. A plumber does not select a tool until he or she knows what needs to be accomplished. Likewise, a professional school counselor should not select a favored or entertaining activity and make it "fit" into the curriculum. Second, learning objectives help to obtain consistent results. Objectives serve as road maps leading to a reliable and consistent outcome. Finally, learning objectives make instruction more efficient. When a professional school counselor selects appropriate learning objectives, it is assumed that those objectives serve to structure the available time. If activities do not support a learning objective then the activity becomes nonessential. This is not to say that students will not learn important lessons from nonessential activities, just that what they learn might lie outside of the domain of knowledge that should be mastered.

TYPES OF "TEACHER THINKING"

According to Mager (1997), there are five basic types of objectives, and each is linked to a specific purpose that an instructor may have. A *coverage objective* merely involves a description of what will be covered in a lesson (e.g., students will learn to resolve conflict). An *activity objective* designates the actual activities that students will engage in (e.g., students will read pages 54–59). An *involvement objective* specifies what students will "get into" (e.g., students will react to a poem on the virtues of problem solving as opposed to aggression when resolving conflict). *Thinking skills objectives* focus on the thought processes that must be developed in order to achieve mastery objectives (e.g., students will develop the ability to think critically about the causes and solutions to conflict). *Mastery objectives* state in specific, measurable terms what a student will be able to do after a lesson (e.g., after observing four role-plays of students in conflict, 90% of students will be able to list at least three nonviolent ways to resolve a conflict). Most educators tend to think in terms of the first four types of objectives. However, mastery objectives are essential to the curriculum because they relate to outcomes that result in student change and development, thereby subsuming all the other types of objectives.

QUALITIES OF MEASURABLE LEARNING OBJECTIVES

High-quality learning objectives effectively communicate what is to be accomplished in specific terms (Mager, 1997). As such, some words commonly used in nonspecific learning objectives (e.g., *to know, to understand, to appreciate, to internalize, to believe, to enjoy*) leave one wondering how to demonstrate that the student has accomplished what he or she set out to do. Therefore, words that lead to more specific interpretations and which can be demonstrated through student performance should be used (e.g., *to write, to compare/contrast, to solve, to construct, to identify, to build*).

TEACHING THE ELUSIVE INTANGIBLES

Historically, many professional school counselors have resisted the accountability movement—some out of frustration of trying to describe the complex developmental change processes that students must undergo to become productive citizens; others, particularly recalcitrant professional school counselors, take the position that the changes one seeks to make in students are too complex or intangible to measure. After all, how does one measure motivation, self-esteem, and success? This view of school counseling program outcomes as intangible and immeasurable is counterproductive at best and self-extinctive at worst.

Think about it: How long would a math curriculum (or math teacher) survive if the students subjected to it did not improve their math skills? Likewise, now that a domain of knowledge and behavior (standards and competencies) has been established for school counseling programs, how long will school counseling programs (or professional school counselors) survive if the students subjected to it do not improve their academic, career, and personal–social development? The issue is no longer *can* we measure student performance in these three domains but rather how *will* we measure it? The *how* is made possible through writing specific learning objectives.

"If you are teaching things that cannot be evaluated, you are in the awkward position of being unable to demonstrate that you are teaching anything at all" (Mager, 1997, p. 113). This is a classic dilemma: If one is teaching something that is intangible, it cannot be evaluated; if it cannot be evaluated, one cannot determine that it has been mastered; and if it cannot be mastered, why would one teach it? What value could it possibly have within a curriculum?

The answer to this dilemma, of course, is to teach what can be mastered and write the learning objective in a way that mastery can be determined. At a basic level, this is the difference between process and outcomes. *Process* has to do with the instructional methodology (e.g., exploring, debating), which is the means and not the end. The *outcome* is the end. The outcome involves the actual learning result that can be demonstrated through assessment of the learning objective. The bottom line is that if one is willing to decide (intuitively) that a student is performing satisfactorily on some intangible process, then with a little more effort, one can understand, describe, and develop criteria to assess the basis for that satisfaction.

THE ABCDs OF A WELL-WRITTEN LEARNING OBJECTIVE

A well-written learning objective focuses the lesson on specific student outcomes and accomplishments. While experts generally agree on the essential components of a learning objective, they do not always agree on the components that lead to a determination of mastery. Because the emphasis of this chapter is on helping professional school counselors develop mastery objectives, an integrated approach is used (Goodnough, Perusse, & Erford, 2007; Kellough & Roberts, 1998; Mager, 1997; Saphier & Gower, 1997). Here is an ABCD model for writing learning objectives:

Audience
Behavior
Conditions
Description of the expected performance criterion

AUDIENCE

The first essential component of a well-written learning objective involves the audience for whom the objective is intended. Because the primary recipient of an individual or group counseling session or large-group developmental guidance lesson is the student, almost all applicable objectives will be targeted at the student audience. Thus, many learning objectives begin with phrases such as, "Students will . . . ." or "Students will be able to . . . ." Less frequently used audiences may include teachers, parents, or an entire class or group of students.

BEHAVIOR

The second essential component addresses the behavior that the student is expected to engage in to be able to think, solve, or do. "These behaviors are typically descriptive verbs that address the . . . outcome around which the lesson is structured" (Goodnough et al., 2007, p. 157). Here are some examples of objectives using these descriptive verbs: *Students will be able to recognize cooperative group behaviors* or *Students will be able to identify five methods that would help them cope with loss and subsequent grief.* The behavioral component of a learning objective deals with cognitive, affective, or behavioral outcomes.

CONDITIONS

This component describes the conditions under which the behavior is supposed to occur (Mager, 1997). It is essential to identify *when* or *how* the behavior will be measured. Typical conditions are tests, worksheets, observations, role-plays, or after engaging in some structured activity. Here are some examples of the conditions component: *After completing a worksheet listing 10 scenarios of cooperative group behaviors, students will be able to recognize cooperative group behaviors*, or *After reading an article on loss, students will be able to identify five methods that would help them cope with loss and subsequent grief.* Mager (1997) suggested that conditions address three main questions: "What will the learner be expected to use when performing . . . not be allowed to use . . . . What will be the real-world conditions under which the performance will be expected to occur" (p. 87).

DESCRIPTION OF THE EXPECTED PERFORMANCE CRITERION

The final component of a well-written learning objective, and the one that is most often left out, is a *description of the criterion for expected performance.* Generally, this criterion takes the form of the amount of a task the student must perform successfully (e.g., 90% correct on a test) or the percentage of students that successfully display the behavior under the given conditions (e.g., 80% of students). The criterion sets the level of acceptable performance, the level that students are challenged to surpass. Thus, examples of completed objectives using the ABCD model include, *After completing a worksheet listing 10 scenarios of cooperative group behaviors, 75% of fifth-grade students will be able to recognize one cooperative group behavior in each scenario*, or *After reading an article on loss, 80% of students will be able to identify five methods that would help them cope with loss and subsequent grief.*

The criterion for mastery is an essential part of a learning objective, because, without it, the expectation is for perfection. While it is praiseworthy to strive for perfection, student motivation, preparation, test-taking skills, work habits, instructional strategies, and myriad other potential problems often interfere with performance and lead to some degree of nonmastery.

If one sets the criterion too high, then the objective is not met. If objectives are not met, then no evidence exists that competencies (or outcomes) have been met. If competencies have not been met, this means that the standards (or goals) have gone unmet. In this case, the professional school counselor has no proof that the school counseling program has had any desirable impact—at all! Thus, it is essential to set a reasonable criterion for each objective so that students are challenged and at the same time accurate accountability measurement occurs. The criterion can be qualified to include the number of times a student must perform, the length of time of a performance, an accuracy ratio (percentage of time), the percentage of students who can perform the task, and the quality of the task (generally scored according to some rubric of quality indicators).

Mager (1997) underscored the importance of the behavioral criterion by pointing out that a criterion provides a standard against which the success of the instruction or intervention can be tested, tells students when they have met or exceeded expectations, and provides a basis for concluding that students can do what an instructor sought to accomplish.

AVOIDING THE PITFALLS

The preceding sections focused on what professional school counselors should do to write effective learning objectives, but Mager (1997) pointed out a number of important characteristics of ineffective objectives that should be avoided. First, avoid terms that indicate a *false performance*, or no real performance at all. For example, how would one determine whether a thorough understanding of peer mediation ever existed? Second, one should avoid *false givens* (conditions) (e.g., "Given adequate practice in time management . . . ."). Third, avoid *gibberish* (e.g., "Demonstrate a comprehensive understanding of . . . ."). Finally, avoid identifying *instructor performance*—what the professional school counselor or teacher is supposed to accomplish (e.g., "The professional school counselor will help students to . . . ."). The emphasis is always on the stakeholder who is to demonstrate mastery. Avoiding the pitfalls will help the professional school counselor construct concise learning objectives that will demonstrate mastery performance and effective school counseling services.

SUMMARY/CONCLUSION

A well-written learning objective is an essential starting point for demonstrating the effectiveness of a comprehensive developmental school counseling program. The ABCD model (**A**udience, **B**ehavior, **C**onditions, and **D**escription of expected performance criterion) has all the components necessary to craft a well-written mastery-level learning objective. Objectives written in this way provide a built-in process for accountability of school counseling programs, particularly when used to structure and guide individual and group counseling sessions and classroom guidance.

(Note: See the CD-ROM for a list of references.)

CHAPTER 23

DESIGNING DEVELOPMENTAL
GUIDANCE LESSONS

Ann Vernon

Preview

In this chapter, I address practical considerations to help professional school counselors effectively deliver the developmental and preventive component of a comprehensive school counseling program. Specific topics include how to develop grade-level objectives, how to write and adapt lessons using a guidance lesson-plan format, and how to determine the scope and sequence of lessons. Sample lessons are provided as well as a discussion about implementing the school counseling curriculum and the role that teachers and professional school counselors should assume.

In the early years of the school counseling profession, guidance was considered an ancillary support service, conceptualized as a position rather than a program (Gysbers & Henderson, 2005). Narrow in scope, the focus was on providing selected services for problem students (Thompson, 2002). However, schools must now be more responsive to the increasing complexity and diversity of our society as well as to changes in personal and social values and social structures. Gysbers (2001) noted that "these changes are creating complex challenges for students as they anticipate the future" (p. 96). Increasing violence, substance abuse, teenage suicide, sexual experimentation, and a rapidly changing work force, among other factors, have a significant impact on student development (Gysbers & Henderson, 2000). Poverty, child abuse, homelessness, and lack of access to postsecondary education add to the mix (Ripley, Erford, Dahir, & Eschbach, 2003). According to Gysbers and Henderson (2001), guidance services must be reconceptualized to better address these challenges as well as those brought about by technology and an increasing societal complexity that affects life roles (Gysbers & Henderson, 2005).

A significant aspect of the reconceptualization of guidance services has been the gradual evolution from a smorgasbord-of-services approach to a comprehensive program. Paisley and Borders (1995) noted that school counseling programs should be comprehensive and developmental, emphasizing primary prevention and healthy development for all students. Green and Keys (2001) concurred, pointing out that "a developmental orientation has become a highly desired, core characteristic of school counseling programs" (p. 85). Sink (2005) also stressed the developmental emphasis, stating that professional school counselors should implement programs that are proactive, prevention oriented, and accountable.

In support of the comprehensive program focus, and in an effort to better prepare students to deal with factors that affect their development, the American School Counselor Association (ASCA) assumed a key leadership role in developing national standards for a comprehensive approach to program delivery, management, and accountability (Hatch & Bowers, 2002). The national model for school counseling programs (Dahir, 2001) is designed to promote and enhance the learning process by facilitating student development in three domains: academic, career, and personal–social. This model "incorporates school counseling standards and competencies for every student, which serve as the foundation for the program and focus the direction for an organized, planned, sequential and flexible counseling curriculum" (Hatch & Bowers, 2002, p. 15).

As professional school counselors transform their programs to reflect the beliefs and practices of a comprehensive developmental program, it becomes increasingly important that they know how to design, develop, and deliver the developmental and preventive component that forms the core of the comprehensive program. Through the guidance lessons that are integral to this component, students are taught developmentally appropriate personal–social, academic, and career development concepts to increase their knowledge and skills and to help ensure healthy development. As Goodnough, Perusse, and Erford (2003) noted, professional school counselors have a unique opportunity to help students master these developmental changes through a sequential K–12 curriculum.

The purpose of the information in this chapter is to describe the process of identifying grade-level competencies and how to develop guidance lessons that address specific competencies. A guidance lesson plan format is described, along with information about scope and sequence of lessons and developmental considerations. In addition, the role of the professional school counselor and teacher in implementing guidance lessons as part of the developmental and preventative component of a comprehensive program will be discussed.

DESIGNING THE DEVELOPMENTAL CURRICULUM

Incorporating developmental principles into a comprehensive curriculum is a daunting yet critical task for professional school counselors at all levels. In designing this curriculum, professional school counselors need to assume a leadership role in developing the scope and sequence of the program, in accordance with developmental considerations. The national standards for school counseling programs (Dahir, 2001), which are based on extensive research and field reviews, provide professional school counselors with the attitudes, knowledge, and skills that students should acquire in the areas of personal–social, academic, and career development and include examples of three broad standards in each of these domains that can serve as a basis for the curriculum. The ASCA standards also identify competencies, which were developed as a result of extensive research with professional counselors at all levels (Ripley et al., 2003). These are very general, however, and professional school counselors will need to develop more specific grade-level competencies for each of the standards in each domain so that distinct concepts can be presented at each grade level.

In designing these competencies, it is important to consider the developmental tasks students must accomplish in Grades K–12 and identify specific competencies accordingly. For example, an appropriate interpersonal relationship competency for kindergartners would be to learn to share and cooperate, whereas an appropriate interpersonal relationship competency for eighth graders would be to learn effective ways to deal with peer pressure, and understanding how to deal with dating relationships would be an appropriate interpersonal relationship competency for 11th graders. It is important to consult sources such as Vernon and Clemente (2005) or other child development texts for information about developmental tasks.

In writing the competencies, professional school counselors should be very specific and avoid words like *to understand* or *to appreciate*, because they are harder to measure. In this era of accountability, words such as *identify, differentiate,* or *describe* allow practitioners to develop ways to measure what students have learned. It is also easier to design a lesson that addresses the competencies when they are concrete and specific.

It is necessary to determine the number of competencies per grade level, which is usually based on the number of lessons you intend to deliver throughout the course of a year. Assuming that there will be 30 to 36 lessons (one per week), you would take the three standards (personal–social, academic, career development), decide if you want to give equal emphasis to them (12 competencies per standard) or weigh one more heavily than the others, and then identify specific grade-level competencies accordingly. To illustrate, the ASCA standards (Dahir, Sheldon, & Valiga, 1998, p. 16) for personal–social development include the following:

Standard A—Students will acquire the attitudes, knowledge, and interpersonal skills to help them understand and respect self and others.

Standard B—Students will make decisions, set goals, and take necessary action to achieve goals.

Standard C—Students will understand safety and survival skills.

There are 21 competencies in Standard A, divided into two categories: acquire self-knowledge and acquire interpersonal skills. There are also 12 competencies in Standard B and 11 in Standard C. Professional school counselors should study these competencies to determine if they want to use them as a basis for developing their own grade-level competencies, if there are others that should be added, or if there are some that would fit better under one standard than another. For example, "learning to cope with peer pressure," which is listed under personal–social development Standard C (*understand safety and survival skills*) could also be included under Standard A (*acquire the attitudes, knowledge and interpersonal skills to help them understand and respect self and others*). Likewise, "demonstrate a respect and appreciation for individual and cultural differences," which is included under Standard B (*students will make decisions, set goals, and take necessary action to achieve goals*) is perhaps better suited for Standard A, since it relates to respecting self and others. As professional school counselors study the competencies, they may also see areas that are not addressed and should be included. This is the process of *personalizing* the curriculum for individual school districts. Also, remember that while the general focus of a comprehensive program is on development, there may also be some situation-specific areas that need to be added to the curriculum to address needs in a particular school district. For example, if students live in a high poverty area, the professional school counselor would want to reword the competency that reads "recognize, accept, and appreciate ethnic and cultural diversity" (Dahir et al., 1998, p. 16) to also include sensitivity to socioeconomic diversity.

After studying the ASCA competencies, you may decide to modify them, not use them at all and write your own, or use them as they are. If you use them verbatim and also incorporate the 43 career development competencies and the 34 academic development competencies, you would have a total of 121 competencies to separate into grade-level categories. This would roughly be the equivalent of 10 competencies for each Grade 1 through 12, or 9 competencies for Grades K–12. Therefore, if you intend to have a year-long curriculum, which would be approximately 30 to 36 weeks, you would either need to have multiple lessons for each competency or add competencies.

GRADE-LEVEL COMPETENCIES

To illustrate this process, the following section is part of the personal–social domain, with examples of grade-level competencies. The ASCA Standard A under personal–social development has been rewritten as follows: *Students will acquire the attitudes, knowledge, and skills to help them understand and respect self and others and identify and effectively express feelings.* This standard as reworded includes self-development, emotional development, and social development. Instead of using the ASCA competencies, the following uses specific grade-level competencies or objectives from *The Passport Program: A Journey Through Social, Emotional, Cognitive, and Self-Development* (Vernon, 1998a; 1998b; 1998c). Due to space limitations, Table 23.1 lists only three competencies per grade level, but there are at least six per grade level (with corresponding lessons) in these curriculums. Also due to space restrictions, the self-development competencies will be identified only for Grades 1 through 5, emotional development competencies only for Grades 6 through 8, and social development competencies only for Grades 9 through 12, even though there are competencies for each grade in each of these areas. The intent here is to give the reader an idea of the scope and sequence when developing grade-level competencies. Had there been space to reproduce all the objectives, the reader would be able to see the developmental progression from grade level to grade level as well as recognize that most of the ASCA competencies are represented in the more specific grade-level competencies of *The Passport Program*.

When developing a total comprehensive curriculum, a similar process would include grade-level competencies for decision making (ASCA personal–social Standard B) and safety and survival skills (ASCA personal–social Standard C), as well as competencies for the career and academic development standards.

DEVELOPMENTAL GUIDANCE LESSONS

After developing the grade-level competencies for personal–social, academic, and career development, the next step is identifying the objectives and activities to achieve the competency. Again, this may seem like a monumental task, but in reality the field is replete with emotional education curricula, career development programs, games, workbooks, and bibliotherapy resources. The problem lies in selecting programs or materials that correspond to the specific competencies and that have been proven effective. One way to address this problem is to write your own lessons. See Vernon's Passport Programs (Vernon 1998a, 1998b, 1998c) for examples of lesson plans.

TABLE 23.1

SELECTED COMPETENCIES FROM *THE PASSPORT PROGRAM*

Self-Development—Grade 1

Students will:

Learn that everyone has strengths and weaknesses.

Develop an attitude of self-acceptance.

Identify ways in which they are growing and changing.

Self-Development—Grade 2

Develop awareness of abilities and attributes.

Learn to accept oneself with these abilities and attributes.

Recognize that strengths and limitations are part of one's self-definition and to not put themselves down because of limitations.

Self-Development—Grade 3

Learn that how one acts does not determine self-worth.

Learn that nobody is perfect and to accept themselves as less than perfect.

Identify characteristics of self, including strengths and weaknesses.

Self-Development—Grade 4

Learn that making mistakes does not make one a bad person.

Learn that others' approval is not required to be worthwhile.

Identify individual preferences, characteristics, and abilities.

Self-Development—Grade 5

Identify specific characteristics that are like or unlike oneself.

Identify feelings associated with varying rates of development.

Differentiate between making mistakes and being a total failure.

Emotional Development—Grade 6

Learn that feelings can change.

Learn specific ways to feel happier.

Understand the connection between feelings and behaviors.

Emotional Development—Grade 7

Identify what experiences trigger anger and how to effectively control and/or express anger.

Identify ways to increase positive feelings.

Identify strategies for dealing with intense negative emotions.

Emotional Development—Grade 8

Learn effective ways to deal with the ups and downs associated with puberty.

Learn how thinking affects feeling and how to change feelings by changing thoughts.

Learn how to distinguish between healthy and unhealthy ways to relieve emotional pain.

Social Development—Grade 9

Develop skills for dealing with interpersonal relationship problems.

Examine the positive and negative aspects of peer pressure.

Identify ways to resist peer pressure.

TABLE 23.1. *(continued)*

Social Development—Grade 10

Learn how to stop the negative cycle of rumors, gossip, and assumptions that affect relationships.

Identify feelings and issues involved in the termination of a romantic relationship.

Identify effective ways to deal with the breakup of a relationship.

Social Development—Grade 11

Learn to distinguish between healthy and unhealthy dependence in relationships.

Learn what one can and cannot control in relationships with others.

Learn to distinguish between healthy and unhealthy ways to deal with relationship issues.

Social Development—Grade 12

Identify effective strategies for dealing with parent–teen relationships.

Identify ways to deal with competition in relationships.

Identify feelings and issues involved in intimate relationships.

Note. Adapted from *The Passport Program: A Journey Through Emotional, Social, Cognitive, And Self–Development* (Grades 1–5); *The Passport Program: A Journey Through Emotional, Social, Cognitive, and Self–Development* (Grades 6–8); and *The Passport Program: A Journey Through Emotional, Social, Cognitive, and Self–Development* (Grades 9–12), by A. Vernon, 1998, Champaign, IL: Research Press. Copyright 1998 by Research Press. Adapted with permission.

LESSON PLAN FORMAT

The first step in writing a guidance lesson would be to specify the grade level, the standard (personal–social, academic, or career development), the grade-level competency or competencies (usually no more than two per lesson), and the lesson objective(s) (also usually no more than two per lesson). The next step is to create a short (15–20 minutes, depending on the amount of time allotted) stimulus activity that addresses each competency. The stimulus activity might include, for example, bibliotherapy, role-play activities, simulations, games, worksheets, or music and art activities. Professional school counselors can create their own activities or find activities from commercial sources that match their competencies. In selecting activities from commercial sources, it will often be necessary to adapt the activity so that it directly addresses the specific competency. In other words, if the competency is *Students will identify various degrees of anger*, it would not be appropriate to have a general lesson on feelings, because the lesson should specifically relate to anger. Likewise, if the competency is *Students will identify five tease tolerance strategies*, the lesson should directly address one's tolerance for teasing and not a more general lesson on getting along with others.

After the activity has been written or selected from commercial resources, the next step is to identify two types of discussion questions to help process the lesson. Although the stimulus activity is an important way to introduce the concepts, the discussion is equally important, because it helps students clarify and reinforce what they learned. This part often gets slighted because the activity takes up too much time, so it is critical to allow at least 15 minutes of the allotted lesson time for discussion. The discussion questions developed for this lesson prototype include content questions and personalization questions. Content questions pertain to the content of the activity (e.g., what happened in the story they read, what occurred during the role play, what their responses were on the worksheet they completed). For example, if they had just played a group decision-making game, content questions might be, "How did your group arrive at the decision?" "What was the most challenging part of this decision-making process?" "What was the easiest part of this decision-making process?" Personalization questions help students personalize the information and apply it to their own lives. For instance, if they read a story about a boy who was teased, personalization questions might be, "Have you ever been teased? If so, how did you feel and how did you handle it?" "What does it say about you if you are teased? What can you do next time you are teased?"

The final step in the lesson plan format is the assessment component. This might take the form of a short quiz about the content of the lesson, a homework assignment in which students are asked to apply what they learned and report back in the form of a short report, or having students develop a short skit to convey what they learned from the lesson.

To further illustrate the lesson plan format and the examples of content and personalization questions, a lesson for eighth graders is presented in Figure 23.1. Developmentally, many adolescents experience discouragement, ambivalence, depression, shame, and confusion that often seem unbearable. Many lack the ability to deal constructively with their feelings and adopt unhealthy ways to relieve their pain. A lesson of this nature helps them learn more effective coping strategies.

Using the lesson plan format shown in Figure 23.1 provides professional school counselors and teachers with a framework that helps organize the lesson and assure greater accountability, because the content and personalization questions relate specifically to the identified competency.

IMPLEMENTING THE COUNSELING CURRICULUM

Although the phrase "for all students" is rooted deep within the philosophy of a comprehensive program and has generally been a characteristic of elementary counseling programs since their conception, this concept necessitates a role change for professional school counselors, particularly at the high school level, where functions have been more traditional. Numerous authors (Gysbers, 2001; Gysbers & Henderson, 2000; Paisley & McMahon, 2001; Ripley et al., 2003; Sink, 2005; Tollerud & Nejedlo, 2004) support this change because it has the potential to impact so many students and assist them with the mastery of developmental tasks. Tollerud and Nejedlo (2004) stressed that "prevention can be integrated into individual and small group counseling, but for children and adolescents, its primary infusion comes through the counseling and guidance curriculum offered in the classroom" (p. 394).

As professional school counselors transition into the classroom, it is important to remember that classroom developmental guidance needs to be a team effort. Professional school counselors may teach or team teach the lessons as well as serve as a resource person to the teacher who assumes the leadership role in the delivery process (Gysbers & Henderson, 2005). As specified in the underlying principles of a comprehen-

PAIN RELIEVERS

Competency: To distinguish between healthy and unhealthy ways to relieve emotional pain.

Objective: After completing a tag-board poster, all groups of students will be able to identify at least two healthy and unhealthy ways to deal with a painful emotion.

Materials: A chalkboard and the following for each group of four students: magazines, scissors, glue, a large sheet of tag board, and markers.

Procedure/Activities:

1. Introduce the activity by having students quickly brainstorm examples of painful emotions. As they identify examples, write them on the board. Next, discuss the difference between healthy and unhealthy ways of dealing with painful emotions. For example, anger can be a painful emotion. An unhealthy way to deal with anger would be to get drunk. A healthy way to deal with it would be to talk it out.

2. Divide students into groups of four, and distribute the materials. Instruct them to make two columns on the bottom half of the tag-board poster and to label one side Healthy Ways to Deal With Painful Emotions and the other side Unhealthy Ways to Deal With Painful Emotions. Ask each group to list two or more painful emotions at the top of the poster, then have them look through the magazines for pictures representing at least two healthy and two unhealthy ways to deal with these emotions. If they cannot find appropriate pictures, have them draw pictures or symbols. In either case, students should use words to represent their suggestions.

3. After the posters have been completed, have the small groups share them with the total group.

4. Discuss the content and personalization questions.

Discussion Content Questions:

1. Which are harder to identify: healthy or unhealthy ways to deal with painful emotions?

2. In general, were the small groups in agreement with each other? Were there some ideas that one group labeled unhealthy that you might have considered healthy, or vice versa? (Ask students to share examples and remember that what students identify as healthy and unhealthy may vary depending on culture.)

3. What makes the unhealthy methods unhealthy? Do you really think they help relieve pain in the long term? Why or why not?

Personalization Questions:

1. Are your "pain relievers" generally healthy or unhealthy? How do you feel about that?

2. If you have tried unhealthy methods in the past, how has this affected your life? If you had it to do over, what might you do differently, if anything?

3. Did you learn anything from this lesson that will be helpful to you in dealing with painful emotions? (Invite sharing.)

Assessment: The instructor should collect the tag-board posters to verify that each group of students could list at least two healthy and two unhealthy ways to deal with a painful emotion. If all groups are able to do so, the objective for the session has been met.

FIGURE 23.1. Example of a lesson plan format for eighth graders. *Note.* Adapted from *The Passport Program: A Journey Through Emotional, Social, Cognitive, And Self-Development (Grades 6–8)* (pp. 203–204), by A. Vernon, 1998, Champaign, IL: Research Press.

sive program, this team approach is imperative because the professional school counselor is *not* the counseling program. Although the intent of a comprehensive program that emphasizes prevention is to reduce the focus on crisis and remedial intervention, it is naïve to assume that we can eliminate all problems through prevention. Because professional school counselors, not teachers, are the ones who are trained to do crisis and remedial intervention, they must continue to assume this role—but it is also unreasonable to think that they can do this on top of all the prevention. For this reason, training teachers to take an active role in delivering developmental classroom guidance lessons is crucial.

According to Tollerud and Nejedlo (2004), professional school counselors can train teachers in the types of lessons as well as the process. They can model the teaching of personal–social, academic, and career guidance lessons that ultimately enhance development. In addition, professional school counselors can assist teachers in identifying ways to incorporate personal–social, academic, and career development objectives into their specific subject matter.

Tollerud and Nejedlo (2004) outlined several key principles of a counseling curriculum: that they help students cope with normal developmental issues and problems; that they consider the nature of human development, including the general stages and tasks of normal development; and that they not only encompass a remedial and crisis approach but a preventative focus as well. Gysbers and Henderson (2001) and Sink (2005) also stressed that the human development perspective is the foundation for the program and the basis for identifying the competencies that students need to master. Sharing these principles with teachers and administrators will help clarify misconceptions they may have about a guidance curriculum.

Summary/Conclusion

The purpose of this chapter was to give professional school counselors suggestions for promoting healthy development in all students by implementing, in conjunction with teachers, the core component of a comprehensive developmental program: the guidance curriculum. Use of the ASCA standards and broad competencies as a basis for developing specific grade-level competencies was described to help professional school counselors move to the next level: identifying or writing developmentally appropriate guidance activities to achieve the competencies. The lesson plan is a viable format for teachers and professional school counselors to use, and readers are encouraged to use a structure that emphasizes knowledge and skill acquisition and also helps students personalize the information to their own situations for optimal learning.

(Note: See the CD-ROM for a list of references.)

CHAPTER 24

SETTING UP AND MANAGING A CLASSROOM

Carlen Henington and R. Anthony Doggett

Preview

The information in this chapter will provide the professional school counselor with recommendations for school personnel to get the school year off to a good start and to maintain an efficient and effective classroom environment throughout the year. This chapter includes (a) information about effective physical arrangement of the classroom; (b) procedures to establish and teach classroom rules and procedures; and (c) use of effective behavior management strategies including differential reinforcement, group contingencies, token economies, behavior contracts, overcorrection, time-out, and response-cost procedures. To address recent accountability and response to intervention mandates, we will also offer suggestions for how professional school counselors could make recommendations for tracking children's behavior prior to and during implementation of classroom management strategies (i.e., responsiveness to intervention). To maximize the recommendations presented in this chapter, we advise that professional school counselors assist teachers in developing a comprehensive plan for their classroom at the very beginning of the school year, prior to student attendance. However, the information within this chapter can be implemented with minor modifications at any time during the school year. As such, professional school counselors may want to consult this chapter throughout the academic year as they receive student or classroom referrals.

At the end of the first month of school, Mr. Jones, a new teacher, approached Mrs. Williams, the professional school counselor. He stated that he did not believe he was cut out to be a teacher. Mrs. Williams wondered, "What had gone wrong?" On his first day of school, Mr. Jones had told her that he was looking forward to having his own classroom, meeting the children, and making a difference in their lives. He was finally a teacher! However, he is concerned about the focus on high-stakes testing and the accountability for students' progress as mandated by the No Child Left Behind Act. Mr. Jones stated he had recently been informed of several students who had been identified as at-risk, based on grade retention and knew they were struggling to meet the demands of classroom instruction. As she spoke with Mr. Jones, Mrs. Williams discovered that, like many new teachers, he was having difficulty keeping his students on task. He had spent so much of the day trying to redirect them that he was not able to get through the material he had prepared for the class. He also was concerned about his need to attend and present information at problem-solving meetings for those at-risk students. He asked, "Mrs. Williams, do you have any suggestions?"

This scenario is common in schools across the United States. The professional school counselor may be asked to design a learning environment for students (e.g., a social-skills class for students experiencing peer-relation difficulties) to assist a new teacher in getting the new school year off to a good start or assist in the school-level meetings for at-risk students (e.g., teacher or student support meetings). Professional school counselors also need to assist in the development of behavior plans and tracking behavior change in response to required documentation for referrals for assessment. At other times, the professional school counselor might be asked to make a presentation to more seasoned teachers, so that they are more likely to have a smooth running classroom during the school year and understand recent changes in school procedures to address behavior and academic concerns for the students in their school.

Recommendations for classroom management start before the first day of class and continue through the school year. This chapter will include suggestions for

- physical classroom structure;
- rules, schedules, and procedures;
- managing transitions;
- enhancing and maintaining student motivation; and
- tracking the effectiveness of the procedures through data collection.

Although there are other areas that foster a proficient classroom environment, professional school counselors are frequently asked to address these five areas. A recent trend in classroom management is to consider practices in classroom management in a tier process (Brown-Chidsey & Steege, 2005). This tier process is often referred to as the response to intervention (RTI) model. Although the complete description of the model is beyond the scope of this chapter, the professional school counselor will need a basic understanding of the model. This chapter will therefore begin with a brief overview of the tier model and then will focus on suggestions that the professional school counselor may provide the classroom teacher to address the five previously identified areas. It is important to note that the concepts apply equally to professional school counselors when conducting developmental classroom guidance.

RESPONSE TO INTERVENTION

The RTI model is founded upon the work of special educators (e.g., Deno's cascade model of special education service delivery; Deno, 1970) and a number of mandated regular education initiatives (Brown-Chidsey & Steege, 2005). RTI is believed to address the evidence-based practice requirements for both the No Child Left Behind Act (NCLB) of 2001 and the 2004 reauthorization of the Individuals with Disabilities Education Improvement Act (IDEIA; National Association of State Directors of Special Education, 2005). This model is a data-based problem-solving model that, most commonly, uses a three-tiered approach to intervention in regular education classrooms. At each tier, school personnel must rely upon information (i.e., empirically collected data) to make the decision to move to the next tier. The professional school counselor should read Brown-Chidsey and Steege (2005) for complete information and how-to tips and tools for implementation of the complete RTI model.

Tier 1 is considered to be "good classroom teaching" in the general education curriculum for all students. In this tier, students' needs are anticipated and accommodated by teachers, perhaps with some assistance from the professional school counselor, within a typical classroom environment. The assumption is that students receive adequate education from well-trained teachers in adequately resourced classrooms and includes the use of the good classroom management procedures described in this chapter.

Tier 2 is directed toward students with a need for more intensive and specific instruction in the school environment. This need may be academic or behavioral in nature. For example, a student who is falling behind in his or her class work as a result of noncompletion of homework may be the focus of Tier 2 assistance. The professional school counselor may suggest to the teacher that the student be provided additional instruction in a small group following the presentation of new material and also assist the teacher in the design of a motivation strategy to increase homework completion. Thus, Tier 2 involves supplemental instruction and broad-based intervention provided to the student in the classroom setting. Typically, about 10% to 20% of students in a classroom might receive Tier 2 interventions.

Tier 3 is the provision of more comprehensive and intensive intervention for the individual who does not respond to the Tier 2 interventions and is at risk for significant school failure. Approximately 3% to 5% of students in a classroom may receive Tier 3 interventions. For example, the Tier 2 student is provided small-group instruction and is awarded with stickers for each homework assignment that is turned in. At the end of 9 to 12 weeks, the teacher and professional school counselor determine—based on information collected by the teacher—that the student is not responding adequately to finely tuned interventions. Thus, despite many weeks of appropriate intervention, the student continues to fail. At this point, the student would be referred for Tier 3 intervention. This intervention would be designed by a specially selected group of education personnel (e.g., the school principal, professional school counselor, school psychologist, a curriculum specialist, the classroom teacher). This team is often referred to as a student or teacher assistance team (i.e., SAT or TAT, respectively) or student or teacher support team (i.e., SST or TST, respectively). This team then would complete a series of activities: (a) assess the student's situation (e.g., classroom environment, academic performance, behavioral referrals, attendance record); examine detailed records of the past interventions (e.g., progress tracking sheets and integrity records for the interventions); (b) make recommendation for intensive, one-on-one interventions to address the academic and/or behavior concerns identified in the first step; (c) regularly monitor the student's response to the intervention and the integrity with which the intervention is implemented; and (d) make suggested changes to the intervention, if needed. Should the child not respond to this high-intensity, resource-rich intervention, he or she would then be referred for evaluation for eligibility for special education services.

It is important to note that the transition between each of the tiers is reliant upon appropriate documentation of the student's response to the instruction and intervention implemented at each tier. This documentation includes the exact nature of the intervention, the integrity with which it was implemented, and regular monitoring of academic progress (or changes in behavior if appropriate). Thus, each of the following sections might need to be included as documentation as the child moves through the tier process.

PHYSICAL CLASSROOM STRUCTURE

Organization of a classroom requires planning in a number of areas. The well-prepared professional school counselor will begin preparation tasks long before the first day of school, including gathering information about the students who will be in the classroom. This foreknowledge allows the counselor to anticipate many situations that may cause difficulty later (e.g., behavior referrals, academic progress, previously implemented special accommodations).

CLASSROOM ARRANGEMENT

Researchers have long established that the physical arrangement of a classroom has a direct effect on student behavior (Rathvon, 1999). For example, students with attention-deficit/hyperactivity disorder may respond to preferential seating, in which they are placed near the front of the classroom, away from windows, air conditioners, and other distracting stimuli, and close to the teacher. When careful consideration is made of these situations, a distractible student has been found to be more productive and less disruptive in the classroom.

Paine, Radicchi, Rosellini, Detchman, and Darch (1983) listed a number of reasons to consider room arrangement, including management of noise level and disruptions during activities, facilitation of quality student interactions and deterring inappropriate interactions, effective use of available space, and enhancement of academic productivity. Because large structures such as blackboards and bulletin boards are already in place, furniture placement is usually the primary arrangement consideration in a classroom.

Before you consider seating arrangements, however, determine what activities will occur within the classroom (e.g., independent seatwork, small-group and free-time activities). Other space may be required for storage, a quiet time area (e.g., a student retreat), time-out or penalty area, the teacher's desk, computer area, and announcement board. Colvin (2002) provided recommendations and considerations for these and other classroom activities and requirements. Table 24.1 provides information that will assist the professional school counselor and teacher to plan for each of these typical classroom requirements.

STUDENT SEATING

Once the classroom functions and requirements have been considered and arrangements have been made for them, it is time to consider student desk arrangement. Strategies for student seating have evolved over the years, with evidence that a wide variety of arrangements are effective.

There are numerous suggestions for seating to facilitate classroom management and student learning. Initially, the teacher should assign seats to the students. However, as the year continues, the teacher may allow the students to participate in seat selection as well as desk arrangements. Some variations to the traditional straight-row layout include semicircular and cluster arrangements or a combination of these. To increase opportunity for development of new friendships, place students next to someone they have not sat next to in the past. The seating arrangement might also depend on the unit being taught in a particular subject. Students become aware of this and anticipate the new arrangement as each unit is finished. The teacher can use student selection as a motivator for doing well on the unit exam (this will be discussed further in the chapter).

Classroom arrangement can be an important tool in facilitating student learning, student cooperation, and enjoyment of the classroom. Be sure to consider the functions and activities that will occur in the class. Avoid placing obstacles to traffic flow in high-traffic areas. Make sure all students can see the instructional area and the teacher can see all areas of the classroom when engaged in a variety of tasks and activities. Be sure to have frequently used supplies and materials well organized and arranged for easy access.

CLASSROOM RULES AND PROCEDURES

Determining the classroom schedule and teaching students the rules and procedures at the beginning of the school year are extremely important and necessary. Often, preferred teachers are those who imposed structure (i.e., expectations for classroom behavior) and enforce class rules, procedures, and routines. For those students with special needs (e.g., those with developmental delays, mental deficiencies, behavior disorders, learning difficulties), this structure is key in the learning environment. Enforcement of rules and procedures can make the difference between optimal functioning and academic failure and behavior difficulties.

RULES

Much attention in the education literature has been paid to the importance of rules in the management of a classroom. Rules must be taught by teachers and learned by students, and the professional school counselor should remind teachers to include the school rules in their plan and to take time to teach students rules on the first day of class. The most effective classroom managers understand that well-established, effective educational practice must be applied to teaching classroom rules. Any teaching process requires several steps, and it may require the first 2 weeks of the new school year for the students to master all the rules. Colvin (2002) stated that the appropriate behavior of students is dependent upon instruction of the rules and the teacher's expectation for adherence to them.

Rules communicate to students what the teacher expects them to do and not to do in the school environment. A general recommendation is that teachers determine general rules to be implemented, but students should be allowed to participate in the development of the wording for the class rules. This enhances students' sense of "ownership" in the rules and is likely to increase adherence to the rules. Teachers and students should develop about five proactive classroom rules (e.g., *Use inside voices; Treat others with respect*). Furthermore, rules can address both social and academic behaviors. Other examples include, *Keep your eyes on the teacher while he or she is teaching; Raise your hand to speak or request permission; Keep hands, feet, and objects to self; Use appropriate language; Walk in the classroom; Turn assignments in on time;* and *Place your homework in the homework tray.* Rules should be placed in a prominent

TABLE 24.1
CONSIDERATIONS FOR CLASSROOM SPACE ARRANGEMENT

Task/Function	Considerations	Recommendations
Independent work	Requires minimal distractions	Individual seating, room to spread out, avoid high traffic areas
Small-group work	Requires student attention to teacher and other group members	Consider a circle, semicircle, or similar configuration; be sure teacher is able to monitor the entire room
Free time area	Usually used when children finish work before other students	Restrict to an area away from the main classroom to minimize distraction; implement specific rules of use for this area
Storage	Requires easy access without disrupting the class	Keep neat and organized; locate in low-traffic area; be sure cabinet does not obstruct view of teacher or students
Quiet area	Often used for students who require a place to retreat when overwhelmed or stressed; is often used at the student's request rather than the teacher's	Place in an isolated area of the classroom to discourage other students from interacting with the child using this area
Time-out area	Used as a consequence for unacceptable behavior	Area requires a desk in a corner or other out-of-the-way place, but where the teacher can closely monitor the child (there may be more than one time-out area)
Teacher's desk	Requires confidentiality and security of contents	Place out of high-traffic area, but in a location where the teacher can supervise and monitor all students at the same time; avoid an obstructed view
Bulletin board	Has multiple purposes including posting rules and announcements such as news events and special projects	Keep up-to-date, attractive, and uncluttered
Computer area	May also serve as a free-time area; chairs and table need to be adequate to allow work space and student collaboration.	Place out of high-traffic area but also in a location that can be easily monitored and supervised by the teacher; provide a storage area or shelf for necessary computer hardware (e.g., headphones)

location in the room and referred to several times throughout the day when praising students and disciplining them. An often-forgotten midyear routine is to reteach the class rules (or even revamp them) following the winter holiday break.

PROCEDURES

A plethora of interruptions and breaks are imposed on the school day. Instruction in the routines and procedures at the beginning of the school year serve three goals: (a) increase time for learning, (b) facilitate access to learning, and (c) foster self-management skills in students. The achievement of these goals is likely to establish and maintain a healthy learning environment, with few behavior problems or other unplanned disruptions to distract the teacher and students.

Teachers allocate a specific amount of time for learning; however, time spent actively learning (engaged time or time on task) is frequently less than allocated time. Additionally, time on task varies considerably from student to student. An important goal is to have all allocated time spent in learning engagement and to have each student engaged for a similar amount of time. An important consideration is that, although students may be on task, they may not be succeeding at the learning task. When students are truly learning and understanding, the time can be termed academic learning time. Researchers have found that of the over 1,000 hours in a school year mandated by most states, only 300 to 400 hours are spent in academic learning time (Weinstein & Mignano, 1997).

Researchers have shown that when students work directly with the teacher they have higher rates of engaged time, whereas students who work on their own are engaged in the task for about half the time (Frick, 1990). Thus, when independent seatwork is assigned, the teacher should carefully monitor the students to increase time on task. Two of the most common losses of time during independent seatwork are a lack of understanding by the student about what to do next and a lack of necessary materials at hand. Therefore, a teacher who is aware of everything that is happening in the classroom (i.e., has "with-it-ness") is more likely to be able to assist students. Several additional teacher skills include the ability to supervise several activities at once, keep several students involved in activities, and keep the instruction and students (as a group) moving through assigned tasks at an appropriate pace. One method to accomplish these tasks is to have prescribed procedures that students understand and can implement with minimal supervision. This fosters students' self-management of their own learning activities.

PROCEDURES AND RULES

The effective classroom manager communicates to students how activities will be accomplished and expectations for behavior in the classroom. It is important to distinguish between classroom procedures and classroom rules. Effective classroom managers develop clear and simple expectations for classroom behavior that are understood by all the students. According to Weinstein and Mignano (1997), a typical day in a classroom might have the following activities:

1. Administrative routines (e.g., attendance taken)
2. Student movement (e.g., changing classes, going to lunch)
3. Housekeeping (e.g., putting away instructional materials)
4. Routines for completing lessons (e.g., collecting assignments)

5.   Student–teacher interactions (e.g., asking for help)
6.   Student–student interactions (e.g., socializing)

Having clear rules and expectations for these six activities will facilitate effective classroom management. Although some of these activities will have their own rules and procedures, a few general rules will often clarify expectations for appropriate behavior, and procedures for one activity will generalize to other activities. When teaching the procedures to students, be sure to use specific and concrete procedures, model, rehearse, and provide corrective feedback to the students on how well they follow the procedures. Continue to review the procedures for several weeks at the beginning of the school year and again following any major breaks in the school year (winter holidays, fall and spring breaks). It is acceptable to add new procedures as needed, but be sure to follow the same teaching principles.

The following are general guidelines for the development and implementation of procedures:

1. Determine procedures for housekeeping activities before the first day of class. Teach the procedures to the students, and reward compliance during the first several weeks of school. Make sure there is a place for everything and that time is allocated to accomplish housekeeping tasks.

2. Decide how students are to enter and leave the classroom. Teach this procedure to students on the first day. Expect compliance every time students enter or leave the class whether they are in a group or by themselves. When students fail to comply, have them come back to enter or leave correctly.

3. Establish a signal to alert the students. There may be more than one signal that students learn (e.g., one each for instructional time, recess, walking in the hall).

4. Be sure all students understand the procedures for participation in class. Will the student raise a hand for assistance or to answer questions? How will students know that a choral response is required? What are the procedures for using the different areas of the room?

5. Teach students the procedure for assignment completion. Where will assignments be posted, where are they to be turned in, and how will the student know how they did on an assignment?

Now that students understand the procedures for engagement in classroom activities, it is time to develop classroom rules. Researchers have found that having students involved in the development of rules increases their motivation to adhere to the rules. Generally, classroom rules address student-to-student interactions (e.g., *Hands and feet to self*) and personal property (e.g., *Ask before borrowing*). Other rules address teacher expectations for student preparation (e.g., *Bring all needed materials to class*). Finally, rules may be intended to facilitate adherence to more general school rules (e.g., dress codes, forbidden items and activities). When teaching rules, effective classroom managers provide examples and nonexamples of the rule to facilitate student understanding. Additionally, it is important for students to understand that they will be held accountable for their behavior in following rules and that rules will have consequences.

CONSEQUENCES FOR RULE VIOLATIONS

Generally, it is best to implement a consequence for misbehavior. Alberto and Troutman (1995) outlined the following hierarchy:

1. *Level I*—Differential reinforcement (e.g., reinforcing behavior that is incompatible with problem behavior).
2. *Level II*—Extinction (e.g., withdrawing reinforcement for undesired behavior).
3. *Level III*—Removal of desirable stimuli (e.g., time-out procedures, response-cost procedures, staying in from recess).
4. *Level I*— Presentation of aversive stimuli (e.g., corporal punishment, spanking). This is the least desirable form of consequence to use for problem behavior and should be avoided if at all possible.

MANAGING TRANSITIONS

Anytime a change in activity occurs, it is likely that loss of learning time will also occur. The average classroom makes 8 to 10 transitions per day—the equivalent of a full day each week spent in transitions (Rathvon, 1999). Effective classroom managers limit the number of transitions in a day, and making these transitions smooth will likely result in less lost teaching time. Furthermore, disruptive behavior is more likely to occur during transition times. Similar to teaching procedures, the effective classroom manager uses direct instruction of the procedures for transitions and provides guided practice (rehearsal with feedback) to teach students expected behavior. One effective method to decrease time spent in transition is to use a beat-the-clock game. Another effective method includes peer or self-monitoring with rewards for following procedures and making quick changes between activities. Table 24.2 includes additional tips for handling misbehavior in the classroom.

METHODS FOR MOTIVATING STUDENTS AND ADDRESSING BEHAVIORS

Difficult to manage behavior is often the result of low student motivation. As a first line of intervention, at any of the tiers in the intervention process, the professional school counselor may assist the teacher in developing strategies to increase student motivation and increase the likelihood that a student will engage in appropriate behaviors. Should these interventions prove to be ineffective and the student engages in undesired behaviors, the goal would be to decrease the likelihood of the undesired or problematic behaviors while still increasing the appropriate behavior. The following sections provide a basic overview of a number of strategies to address behaviors in the classroom. The first section will assist in development of strategies to increase desired behavior, and the second section will outline strategies to decrease undesired behavior.

REINFORCEMENT-BASED PROCEDURES

One of the most difficult tasks in classroom management is to facilitate and maintain student motivation. However, if students are motivated to do well in the classroom and to follow procedures and rules, the teacher is likely to find that effective classroom management is relatively easy to facilitate. Several methods are available for the teacher to increase students' motivation to follow rules and procedures and engage in academic activities. These include differential reinforcement, the Premack principle, group contingencies, token economies, behavior contracts and charts, time-out, and overcorrection procedures.

Differential reinforcement. One of the most influential management strategies readily available to the teacher throughout the day is the social attention provided to students. Unfortunately, teacher attention can be used to reinforce both appropriate and problem behavior, so the teacher has to be cognizant of the behaviors for which he or she provides attention. Differential reinforcement is a procedure whereby the teacher actively ignores or "extinguishes" the display of problem behavior, and actively provides social attention for the display of appropriate behavior (Alberto & Troutman, 1995). Social attention used in this manner has been labeled *time-in* or *catching them being good* (Christophersen, 1983) and *strategic attention* (Hembree-Kigin & McNeil, 1995). Generally, teachers are encouraged to use differential reinforcement to teach students to follow rules and display appropriate behaviors in the classroom.

Hembree-Kigin and McNeil (1995) identified four types of social attention teachers use to reinforce rule-following and the performance of appropriate behavior: descriptions, reflections, imitations, and praise. *Descriptions* describe the student's actions that are desirable and conducive to active learning and acknowledge the performance of behavior without directly providing praise statements. For example, the teacher may say, "Timmy, I see that you are looking at the board" while teaching from the front of the room, or "Sally, I see that you have completed five math problems" shortly after handing out a math worksheet.

TABLE 24.2

TIPS FOR HANDLING MISBEHAVIOR IN THE CLASSROOM USING CLASSROOM RULES

1. Always implement a consequence for a broken rule, and select an appropriate consequence for the infraction.

2. State the rule and the consequence but nothing else (this prevents arguing and deal making).

3. Avoid making an example out of the student in front of peers (this avoids making the student or the teacher feel like they need to win).

4. Avoid asking questions to which you already know the answer (e.g., "What are you supposed to be doing right now?").

5. Control your anger and try to remember that most rule infractions are not personally directed toward you, the teacher.

6. Always consider that the preferred outcome is for the student to learn to avoid the infraction in the future.

7. Seek assistance and work with other school professionals in a team format to avoid burnout.

Reflections demonstrate to the student that the teacher is attentive and listening while, at the same time, increasing communication between the teacher and students. For example, after the student has said "Mrs. Jones, look I made a perfect grade on the spelling test," the teacher may say, "Yes, Sarah, I do see that you made a 100 on your spelling test."

Imitations increase the teacher's involvement with students, improve sharing and turn-taking skills, and increase other students' imitation of appropriate behavior. For example, during an art project a teacher may say, "I'm going to draw a tree in my picture like Josie drew in her picture."

Finally, *praise statements* increase desired behaviors, improve the relationship between the teacher and child, and increase the child's self-esteem. Praise statements can be global and general or very specific. Examples of global praise statements include "great," "good job," or "way to go"; whereas, specific praise statements include "Thank you, Timmy, for sitting quietly," or "Sarah has drawn a beautiful tree." Teachers can also provide praise to students through physical means. For example, teachers can increase desirable behaviors by providing hugs, pats on the head or shoulder, high fives, or other appropriate forms of physical interaction.

Teacher attention should be contingent upon appropriate behavior and provided frequently and enthusiastically. Social attention follows the *if–then* rule: Behaviors that the teacher wants to see repeated should be followed by some positive form of teacher attention. Conversely, most minor problem behaviors should receive no attention or very minimal attention. Appropriate behaviors should receive frequent reinforcement. Teachers should provide attention early and often. In fact, researchers have encouraged teachers to follow a minimum 3:1 ratio of attention for appropriate behavior versus attention for problem behavior (Sprick & Howard, 1995). Finally, teacher attention should be provided enthusiastically. Teachers should strive to provide attention with expression in their voice and a varied tone as opposed to using a flat, monotone voice. Most students enjoy receiving attention from teachers; however, use of unconvincing or canned statements or praise can quickly erode the effectiveness of adult attention.

Premack principle. As discussed previously, appropriately scheduled activities and transitions can effectively prevent the display of many problematic behaviors in the classroom. However, the schedule of activities can also be used to motivate the students. For example, teachers can use *grandma's rule*, or the Premack principle (Premack, 1959), to shape the occurrence of appropriate student behavior. The Premack principle involves having the students perform a less preferred activity before being allowed to engage in a more preferred activity. In a sense, this principle is similar to the mealtime rule used by many grandmothers over the generations, who have told children that they must eat their vegetables before being allowed to eat dessert. As such, teachers should schedule more demanding or difficult classes or materials before more socially rewarding activities such as recess, break times, group story times, or individual free time.

This principle also could be incorporated into the scheduled change seating arrangements in the classroom in the manner previously described in the chapter. For example, the teacher could establish the expectation in the classroom that successful completion of a unit would lead to preferred seating arrangements that are decided collectively by the students. Additionally, with a little scheduling creativity, teachers could intersperse preferred and nonpreferred activities or classes throughout the day both to prevent problem behaviors and reinforce the occurrence of appropriate behaviors.

Group contingency systems. Another classroom management strategy that has proven successful in management of student behavior and improvement in academic performance involves the use of group contingencies. Litow and Pumroy (1975) identified three group contingency systems. The first system, *dependent group-oriented contingency*, uses reinforcement for the entire class contingent on the performance of a selected student or a particular group of students. For example, if Mark and Sally can improve their vocabulary quiz grade by 10% above their scores on the last quiz, then the whole class will get extra free time after lunch.

The second system, *interdependent group-oriented contingency*, provides each member access to reinforcement contingent (or interdependent) upon some group level of performance. For example, if the class average is 80% or higher on the math quiz today, then the students will have extra free time this afternoon.

The third system, *independent group-oriented contingency*, uses reinforcement for each student contingent on their individual performance independent of the group performance or the performance of their peers (e.g., whoever turned their homework in this morning can now go to recess). It is important to note that independent group-oriented contingency is generally the preferred system to use in a classroom to avoid undue pressure on the children's social interaction. It would be easy to imagine the hurt feelings that might arise from denial of a reward to the entire class, based on the actions of just one child.

One example of an interdependent group-oriented contingency system that has been used with great success in classrooms is the *Good Behavior Game* (GBG), originally presented by Barrish, Saunders, and Wolf (1969). In the GBG, the class is divided into two or more teams. Team names are posted on the board beside a list of target behaviors or classroom rules that have been operationally defined (specifically, described with observable and quantifiable behaviors) and discussed with the class. The classroom teacher places a mark under the team name any time a member of the team violates one of the rules. At the end of a predetermined period (academic period, morning, afternoon, end of day), the team or teams scoring below a predetermined criterion wins the game and receives a reward. Although originally developed to increase the performance of prosocial behaviors, replication studies have also found the GBG to effectively increase the performance of academic behaviors. An attractive aspect of the GBG is its flexibility; rewards (e.g., extra free time, special jobs, extra recess, special badges, other special privileges) and targeted behavior (e.g., academic performance, compliance with classroom rules and procedures) may be varied. Furthermore, the delivery of rewards may range from several times daily to once per week. For a more thorough review of the GBG, consult the review by Tingstrom (2002).

Token economy systems. Originally used in residential settings to improve hygiene, social skills, and work skills of individuals with developmental disabilities (Ayllon & Azrin, 1968), the token economy has also proved to be a beneficial addition to group-contingency and other classroom management systems in school settings. A token economy is a reinforcement system in which conditioned reinforcers called tokens are delivered to students contingent upon the display of appropriate behavior. The tokens are then exchanged for backup reinforcers at a later period in the day.

Token economies can be very effective interventions for managing student behavior in the classroom. However, poor planning in the initial stages of development of the program can often lead to failure of the intervention (Moore, Tingstrom, Doggett, & Carlyon, 2001). As such, Miltenberger (2001) effectively discussed several important issues that the professional school counselor should consider when suggesting the implementation of a token economy in a school setting. First, the professional school counselor and classroom teacher should clearly and concretely define the desired behaviors. These behaviors may include academic skills, social skills, vocational skills, self-help skills, or general compliance with classroom rules.

Second, school personnel should identify developmentally appropriate items for use as tokens. Tokens must be tangible objects that can be delivered immediately upon the display of appropriate behavior. Common examples include poker chips, coins, play money, stamps, stickers, stars, check marks on or hole-punches in cards, or puzzle pieces that can be used to complete an entire puzzle.

Third, the professional school counselor and teacher should collaborate to identify effective backup reinforcers. Development of the backup reinforcers should be one of the most important considerations of the system, as the tokens obtain their reinforcement value from the backup reinforcers. In other words, if the students do not view the backup reinforcers as valuable, they will not be motivated to engage in appropriate behavior or to exert effort to earn tokens throughout the day. Identification of such reinforcers does not have to be difficult, as most students are often motivated by activity reinforcers (e.g., free time, computer time, movie time, special jobs) that can easily be incorporated into the regular classroom routine. Other reinforcers could also be incorporated into the system (e.g., snacks, pencils, erasers, movie rentals, restaurant coupons) to provide variety and to avoid satiation by the students.

Fourth, an appropriate schedule of reinforcement must be decided upon. Initially, the classroom teacher should deliver tokens to the students frequently and liberally throughout each period to shape up the display of appropriate behavior. As teachers observe improvement, they can move from a continuous schedule of reinforcement to a more intermittent schedule to maintain improvement in student behavior.

Fifth, the professional school counselor should help the teacher establish the token exchange rate. School personnel should determine how many tokens students might potentially earn in a day and then set the exchange rate based on this criterion. Smaller items (e.g., pencils, erasers) will typically cost less, whereas larger items (e.g., 15 minutes of individual computer time) will require the exchange of more tokens.

Sixth, an appropriate time and place for the exchange of tokens must be decided before the program is implemented. Many teachers have created a school store or treasure chest from which students could purchase backup reinforcers at set periods during the day (e.g., morning or afternoon break).

Seventh, the professional school counselor assists the teacher with decisions of whether the display of undesirable behaviors will compete with the performance of appropriate behaviors in such a manner that a response-cost component is warranted.

Response cost is defined as the withdrawal of specific amounts of a reinforcer contingent upon the display of problem behavior (Alberto & Troutman, 1995). As such, response cost is often viewed as a system of leveling fines for the display of inappropriate behavior, similar to the tickets motorists receive for speeding or parking in a protected parking space. To maximize all parts of the system, the token economy should be implemented for a few weeks before the response-cost component is added to ensure that the tokens are truly functioning as conditioned reinforcers. The undesirable behaviors should then be clearly defined, and appropriate fine levels should be established. As with the delivery of tokens, fines should be delivered contingent upon the display of problem behavior. It is extremely important to remember that, for the entire system to function effectively, the students must earn tokens more frequently than they experience fines.

Overall, school personnel need to examine some practical considerations when implementing a token economy system. For example, the portability and ease of delivery of the actual token should be considered. Additionally, storage of the tokens and the potential of theft must be evaluated. Bartering or trading among students should also be eliminated when setting up a token economy. Finally, the delivery of tokens should always be paired or associated with teacher praise, as the system will eventually need to be phased out to allow student behavior to be maintained by natural reinforcers, such as teacher praise and attention.

Behavior contracts and charts. Up to this point, this chapter has focused primarily on the motivation of students through reinforcement procedures to the entire group of students in the classroom. However, seasoned professional school counselors and classroom teachers know that some students need individual reinforcement systems to assist in managing behavior. One such system involves the use of behavior contracts or charts. Specifically, a behavior contract is a written document that specifies a particular target behavior for a student and the consequences that will be delivered contingent upon the occurrence or nonoccurrence of the behavior at the end of a predetermined period (Miltenberger, 2001). Generally, these contracts are written in paragraph form, with signature lines at the end of the document. In contrast, behavior charts often specify several behaviors that are evaluated at preset periods during the school day, leading to corrective and reinforcing feedback reliably provided throughout the day and at the end of each day. Generally, these charts are developed as a table with the desired behaviors listed in rows and the evaluation periods grouped in columns next to the behaviors. One example of an empirically based behavior chart is the school–home note developed by Kelley (1990). Examples of each form are presented in Figures 24.1 and 24.2, respectively.

Regardless of which contract system is used, Miltenberger (2001) identified several important steps that must be considered. First, the target behaviors must be clearly defined in proactive terms. In other words, the form should list the behaviors *to be performed* as opposed to specifying behaviors to be eliminated. Second, all parties must agree on a measurement system for monitoring the behaviors. This can be completed through the evaluation of permanent products (e.g., completion of a worksheet) or through direct observation and documentation of the performance of the behavior (e.g., *Stayed in seat throughout the reading period*). Third, the specific times for the performance of the behavior should be clearly stated. Fourth, a reinforcement or punishment contingency must be stated on the form. As with most motivational systems, the use of positive reinforcement is most desirable with behavioral contracting; however, a response-cost component similar to that explained in the token economy section could be used with this system as well. Finally, the behavior contract or chart should identify all parties responsible for providing the contingency or reinforcement or punishment; doing so will increase the integrity with which the system is implemented.

Readers who are interested in further learning about contingency contracting and implementing individual management systems should refer to Jenson, Rhode, and Reavis (1994); Kelley (1990); Miltenberger (2001); and Rhode, Jenson, and Reavis (1992).

PUNISHMENT-BASED PROCEDURES

Other methods used to manage student behavior involve the use of punishment procedures. By strict definition, punishment is a procedure whereby the presentation or removal of a stimulus or event *decreases* the likelihood that a particular behavior will be performed in the future. Two forms of punishment have been identified. Positive punishment refers to *the presentation of an aversive stimulus* following the occurrence of a behavior that leads to a decrease in the likelihood that the behavior will be performed in the future. Negative punishment refers to the *removal of a preferred stimulus* following the occurrence of a behavior that leads to a decrease in the probability that the behavior will occur at a later time.

Positive punishment procedures. Overcorrection is an example of a positive punishment procedure. Originally developed by Foxx and Azrin (1972, 1973) for use with individuals in institutional settings, overcorrection requires a student to engage in a predetermined behavior for an extended period of time contingent upon each occurrence of the problem behavior. Two forms of overcorrection have been identified: positive practice and restitution.

In positive practice, the student is required to engage in the correct form of the appropriate behavior for a specified period of time (e.g., 5–15 minutes) or a specified number of times (e.g., 3 times). For example, a group of students may enter the classroom too loudly. The teacher could have the students go back into the hall and quietly enter the classroom three times. This repetition would provide positive practice of the appropriate behavior. This intervention has application for academic behavior as well. Skinner and colleagues (Skinner, Belfiore, & Pierce, 1992; Skinner, McLaughlin, & Logan, 1997; Skinner, Shapiro, Turco, & Cole, 1992; Skinner, Turco, & Beatty, 1989; Smith, Dittmer, & Skinner, 2002) have used positive practice as an effective component of the cover, copy, and compare academic intervention to increase accuracy rates for students. In this intervention, the student is required to perform an academic task (e.g., take a spelling test). Upon completion of the test, the student compares her words to a list containing the correct spelling of the words. Upon comparison, the student identifies two words that are misspelled. The student is then required to rewrite the misspelled words three times each, which provides for positive practice of the correct spelling of each word. As is illustrated with this example, the goal is to decrease the behavior (i.e., misspelled words) rather than to be punitive toward the student.

Restitution requires students to not only correct the environmental effects of the problem behavior but also to restore the environment to a better condition than before the behavior occurred. For example, two boys were found writing on a wall in a bathroom stall at school. After consultation with the professional school counselor, the teacher decided to have the boys clean not only the wall on which they wrote words but the other walls in the stall as well.

Negative punishment procedure. Negative punishment procedures involve the removal of a stimulus or event in order to reduce the probability of the occurrence of problem behavior. One such procedure has already been discussed in the token economy and behavioral contracting sections and involves the use of response-cost procedures. Another example of a negative punishment procedure involves the use of time-out. Specifically, time-out is a shortened version of the term "time-out from positive reinforcement," has been labeled as a Level III management procedure, and is preferable to the use of aversive procedures (Level IV; Alberto & Troutman, 1995). With the exception of response-cost and overcorrection/restitution procedures, most of this section has focused on reinforcement procedures for motivating students primarily because such procedures must be in place before a punishment procedure such as time-out is used. In other words, the classroom teacher should be discouraged from using time-out until a "time-in" rich environment has been created through the use of differential attention, Premack principle, group-oriented reinforcement techniques, and behavioral contracting. Furthermore, these more positive procedures are often sufficient to improve a student's behavior to desired levels.

Alberto and Troutman (1995) defined three time-out procedures: seclusionary, nonseclusionary, and exclusionary. In *nonseclusionary time-out*, the teacher denies access to reinforcement; however, the student is not removed from the actual instructional setting (e.g., "Timothy, please place your head on your desk for talking out."). In *exclusionary time-out*, the teacher removes the student from the classroom or activity area (e.g., "Sam, please stand quietly in the hall for pushing Sarah."). In *seclusionary time-out*, the teacher removes the student to a time-out room for a period of time.

BEHAVIOR CONTRACT FOR HOMEWORK

I, _____, agree to complete my homework assignments in _____ with at least _____% accuracy each night from _____ to _____.
For meeting the criterion on _____ out of _____ days, I can earn _____ to be delivered on _____ (when) by _____ (person).

_____   _____
Student Signature   Date

_____   _____
Teacher Signature   Date

FIGURE 24.1. Sample behavior contract for homework.

Student Procedures

1. Carry the note to school every day.
2. Have the teacher rate your behavior at the end of each period.
3. Carry the note home each day to be reviewed by your parents.

Classroom Procedures

1. Student behavior is evaluated at the *end* of each period.
2. Record a "1" if the behavior was displayed.
3. Record a "0" if the behavior was not displayed.
4. Provide social praise for behavior that was displayed.
5. Provide a brief explanation and encouragement for behavior that was not displayed.
6. The last teacher of the day should check to see if minimum points were achieved.
7. Consequences at school should be administered based on number of points earned.
8. The note should be sent home at the end of each day to be reviewed by the parent.

Home Procedures

1. Review the note with your child.
2. Provide praise for behavior that was displayed.
3. Provide the appropriate reward if the criterion was met.
4. Remove the appropriate privileges for lost notes, changed notes, etc.

Name: _____

Date: _____

Behaviors:	Reading	Spelling	Centers	Lunch	Math	Recess
1. Follows directions 1st time given						
2. Keeps hands and feet to self						
3. Uses appropriate language						
Total Points						
Teacher Initials						

FIGURE 24.2. Sample school–home note.

Of the three time-out procedures described, nonseclusionary and exclusionary time-out procedures are easier to implement by teachers and are generally favored over the use of seclusionary time-out. In fact, Erford (1999) presented procedures for a particularly effective version of exclusionary time-out—the contingency-delay model. The professional school counselor should be sure to remind the teacher that time-out is a concept that involves the removal of all forms of reinforcement (e.g., social attention, food, favorite activities) and is not simply a location, such as a chair, corner of the room, or spot on the floor. It is generally suggested that the teacher have a predetermined location for time-out. However, it must be remembered that if the student still receives access to reinforcement in the form of teacher- or peer-provided stares, comments, smiles, or other types of attention, the time-out procedure may become ineffective. Time-out does not have to last long. In fact, releasing the child after a few seconds of quiet behavior can be effective. In most situations, a child should not stay in time-out for longer than 5 minutes after he or she has calmed down and sat quietly in the time-out location. Finally and most important, the professional school counselor should remind the teacher to socially reinforce the child for displaying appropriate behavior as quickly as possible after leaving time-out; doing so will help generate the contrast between receiving reinforcement for appropriate behavior and the loss of reinforcement (i.e., time-out) for problematic behavior. For more assistance with the implementation of time-out in school settings, the professional school counselor is referred to Sterling and Watson (1999).

SUMMARY/CONCLUSION

With increasing demands placed upon school personnel for the accountability of student progress, it is important for the professional school counselor and teachers to establish a strong working relationship to provide a secure, well-managed learning environment for students. A number of activities and procedures have been discussed within this chapter: Use of a tiered model to address teacher concerns, design of a classroom to set up the teacher for success, and use of well-established management procedures to maintain appropriate behavior in the classroom.

According to Alberto and Troutman (1995), those teachers who are most likely to motivate students and to be remembered as special have personal characteristics such as a sense of humor, warmth and caring manifested as sensitivity and an interest in the personal well-being of the students. One avenue to accomplish this style as a teacher is to have an effectively managed classroom through the use of well-developed rules, effective instructions, well-managed transitions, proper scheduling, differential attention, group-oriented contingencies, behavioral contracting, response cost, and time-out procedures.

(Note: See the CD-ROM for a list of references.)

CHAPTER 25

PROGRAM ACCOUNTABILITY

Bradley T. Erford, Cheryl Moore-Thomas, and Lacey L. Wallace

Preview

The information in this chapter gives professional school counselors the basic tools that are needed to design and conduct effective outcomes assessments and program evaluations to determine and document the quality of comprehensive developmental school counseling programs.

The increasing push for school reform and educational accountability was driven by the 1983 report, *A Nation at Risk* (Angelo & Cross, 1993; Finn & Kanstroom, 2001) and the No Child Left Behind Act of 2001. The increasing concern regarding quality education across the nation makes outcomes assessment and program evaluation more important than ever. Until recently, however, professional school counselors have provided little evidence that school counseling interventions were achieving intended results; thus, school counseling programs and services lacked substantive accountability.

Historically, the response to this criticism was that school counseling services are so complex that evaluating such services and results is difficult, if not impossible (Erford, 2007). Others noted that school personnel are so busy meeting the needs of students that they shift time that should be spent in evaluation to instruction and programming. Whatever the reason, the lack of accountability threatens the success of students and the future of school counseling programs. Educators are bound by professional and ethical obligations to ensure that educational programs are of high quality and effective in meeting student needs. Without accountability, the determination of program quality will always be suspect.

The six purposes of evaluation suggested by Stone and Bradley (1994) are to

- measure the effectiveness of the total program and its activities;
- collect data that will help determine what program modifications are needed;
- determine the level of program acceptance and support from stakeholders;
- obtain information that can be used to inform the public;
- collect data that add to staff evaluation; and
- analyze the program budget and compare expenditures to future program needs.

Outcomes assessment and program accountability allow for the documentation and determination of the worth of a school counseling program and are part of a program of continuous quality improvement (Erford, 2007). Table 25.1 provides definitions of important terms associated with outcomes assessment and program evaluation (Erford & Moore-Thomas, 2003).

The Assessment Loop

Two key elements of a comprehensive developmental guidance program, as described by Gysbers and Henderson (2005), are program evaluation (process or audit) and results (outcomes) evaluation. *Program evaluation* is the process of systematically determining whether the components have been fully implemented. The process of program evaluation is similar to the concept of content validity. Content validity is a systematic examination of a test's content. In the context of school counseling program evaluation, an important guiding question emerges: Is there a preexisting, comprehensive written program that is fully implemented and aligned with district, state, and/or national standards? Simply put, program evaluation involves determining whether written documentation exists and whether implementation of the written program is indeed occurring. Schools and school systems should have well-developed standards/goals, competencies/outcomes, objectives, and curriculum lessons that guide the implementation of a comprehensive developmental guidance program. School-based programs rely on this curricular information to implement consistent and effective developmental services. Unfortunately, this form of program evaluation, while important, only indicates the existence and adherence to a planned program. It does not indicate the results or outcomes of the implemented program.

Outcomes evaluation, on the other hand, answers the question, *Does the program produce the intended outcomes?* (Terenzini, 1989). In order to ensure focused and manageable assessment, it is most practical to connect program concerns to only a few clearly defined questions (Atkinson, Furlong, & Janoff, 1979; Fairchild, 1986; Krumboltz, 1974).

A great deal of confusion exists regarding the purpose of program evaluation and outcomes assessments. Assessment of a school counseling program should not focus on the professional school counselor and is not an assault on the school counselor's freedom. Erford (2007) indicated that program assessment is cyclical and systematic, a way of answering important questions about a program, and a means to a better education for all students through continuous quality improvement.

TABLE 25.1

ASSESSMENT TERMINOLOGY

Evaluation is the measurement of worth and indicates that a judgment will be made regarding the effectiveness of a program.

Evidence is qualitative or quantitative data that help make judgments or decisions.

Formative evaluation is evaluative feedback that occurs during the implementation of a program and allows for midcourse corrections to occur.

Summative evaluation is feedback collected at a specified endpoint in an evaluation process.

A *stakeholder* is anyone involved or interested in or potentially benefiting from a program. Students, parents, teachers, professional school counselors, administrators, community leaders, college faculty, and local employers, among others, are potential educational stakeholders.

Note. From "Program Evaluation and Outcomes Assessment," by B. T. Erford and C. Moore-Thomas, 2003, in J. Wall and G. Walz (Eds.), *Measuring Up,* pp. 517–523. Austin, TX: PRO-ED. Reprinted with permission.

Because the assessment process is cyclical and systematic, program evaluation and outcomes assessment processes should start small and build upon successes. Effective methods for individual programs can then be determined and replicated so that, over time, necessary program refinements can be implemented, resulting in a comprehensive developmental school counseling program that meets a school's mission. The assessment loop presented in Figure 25.1 helps to visually conceptualize program evaluation and the ways in which outcome studies can be used to improve educational programs. Assessment is often viewed as a component that concludes a process. However, it should be an integrated part of a continuous process to improve the program. The school's mission drives the program content and therefore drives the assessment process. "A school's mission should be evident in its structure, decision-making processes, interpersonal interactions, programmatic regularities, and behavioral regularities [and] provides the basis from which meaningful, institution-specific assessment questions will arise" (Erford & Moore-Thomas, 2003, p. 519). These questions lead to the determination of the kinds of evidence that must be collected. Evidence provides crucial information about program evaluation and results (outcomes).

Evidence can come from numerous and varied sources, including portfolios, external judges or examiners, observations, local tests, purchased tests, student self-assessments, surveys, interviews, focus groups, standardized or informal measures, student performances, or student products. A great deal of evidence is routinely collected in schools. After evidence is collected, interpretation ensues so that conclusions may be reached about the program's value, strengths, weaknesses, and outcomes. As a final step before the process cycles again, interpretations and conclusions are used to adjust to or change program components as needed. Once the changes have been made, new questions can be posed and the cycle begins anew, representing a continuous process of quality improvement.

RESULTS EVALUATION

"Questions of worth and effectiveness are derived from a confluence of values, needs, goals, and mission, and these questions lead to the determination of what evidence must be collected" (Erford, 2007, p. 250). The system for how the evidence is collected warrants further discussion, because how one designs evaluation studies will determine the validity of the findings. At least two primary methods for documenting program effectiveness may be useful to professional school counselors: aggregation and outcomes evaluation.

AGGREGATION

Aggregation involves a process of combining many small pieces of evidence to document that components of a larger program are indeed effective. A comprehensive developmental school counseling program curriculum is based upon some hierarchical system, usually involving standards (or goals), competencies (or outcomes), and objectives. Figure 25.2 provides a simple hierarchical structure demonstrating this typical system. At the most basic level, demonstrating effectiveness through aggregation depends upon well-written learning objectives.

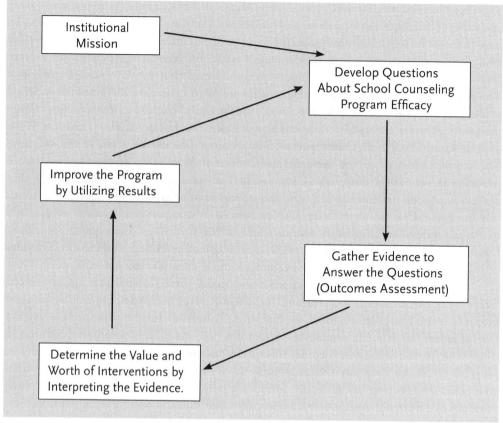

FIGURE 25.1. Assessment loop.

If a learning objective is written in measurable terms with an appropriate expected performance criterion, it can be determined that the objective has been met. Demonstrating that an objective has been met provides evidence that a competency has been met. Furthermore, when evidence is provided that competencies (or outcomes) have been met, then evidence is also provided that a standard (or goal) has been met. It all starts with measurable learning objectives (see Chapter 22).

Using Figure 25.2, consider an example in which learning objectives O_1–O_6 were met, while learning objectives O_7–O_9 were not. In such a scenario it is easy to determine that evidence exists that standard 1 (S_1) was met, because objectives 1–4 (O_1–O_4) were met. The first two objectives (O_1 and O_2) were met, providing evidence that the first competency (C_1) was met. The second two objectives (O_3 and O_4) were met, providing evidence that the second competency (C_2) was met. Because both competencies (C_1 and C_2) were met, sufficient evidence exists that the first standard (S_1) was met.

Now consider the scenario for Standard 2, in which the first two objectives (O_5 and O_6) were met, thus providing evidence that the first competency (C_3) was met. The final three objectives (O_7, O_8, and O_9) were not met, thus failing to provide evidence that the final competency (C_4) was met. Because only one of the two competencies (C_3

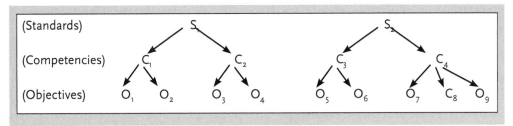

FIGURE 25.2. Hierarchical structure of a typical curriculum development system.

but not C_4) was met, sufficient evidence does not exist that the second standard (S_2) was met. From this demonstration of the aggregation process, it is easy to conclude that the determination of school counseling program effectiveness begins with learning objectives written in measurable terms, but it also relies heavily on setting a challenging, yet attainable, performance criterion (the "D" component of a learning objective, discussed in Chapter 22).

CONDUCTING OUTCOME STUDIES

Outcome studies are generally empirical in nature and involve exercising some control over the conditions under which the evidence is collected (e.g., research design). Campbell and Stanley (1963) wrote the classic work on this topic and provide a helpful summary of research designs that professional school counselors can use to show the effectiveness of interventions. Campbell and Stanley conceptualized research designs as preexperimental, true experimental, and quasi-experimental. Commonly used research designs are presented in Table 25.2.

In general, true experimental designs are characterized by a randomization of participants that controls for all known sources of internal invalidity. This gives true experimental designs the advantage of allowing causative conclusions to be drawn about the effectiveness of the intervention. For example, if a professional school counselor wanted to know the effectiveness of a group counseling experience for students from changing families, she may choose a pretest–posttest control group design (Design B from Table 25.2), randomly assigning the participants to two or more groups and administering an outcome measure (i.e., a measure of behaviors, thoughts, and feelings that the group counseling intervention was meant to change) to the treatment and control groups before and after treatment. The data can then be analyzed to determine if the participants that received the group counseling intervention changed significantly on the outcome measure (O) as compared to the control group. Of course, if the treatment was effective, the control group should be given the chance to participate in the group counseling intervention.

This example of a group counseling intervention for students from changing families can also be applied to all of the other designs listed in Table 25.2, randomizing, observing, and intervening, as specified. Whenever possible, professional school counselors should collect evidence using a true experimental design; such evidence is conclusive. On the other hand, preexperimental and quasi-experimental designs, while

TABLE 25.2

COMMON RESEARCH DESIGNS

True Experimental Designs								
A. Posttest-Only Control Group Design					R	T	O	
					R		O	
B. Pretest–Posttest Control Group Design					R	O	T	O
					R	O		O
Quasi-Experimental Designs								
C. Time Series	O	O	O	T	O	O	O	
D. Nonequivalent Control Group Design					O	T	O	
					O		O	
E. Separate-Sample Pretest–Posttest Design					R	O	T	O
					R			
Preexperimental Designs								
F. One-Group Pretest–Posttest Design					O	T	O	
G. One-Shot Case Study						T	O	
H. Static-Group Comparison						T	O	
							O	

Note. R = randomization of participants; O = observation (i.e., data-collection procedure); T = treatment (counseling or learning intervention).

helpful, lead to speculative results that can be questioned and explained through alternative means.

EXAMPLES OF PROGRAM EVALUATION

CASE STUDY

A case study was conducted by a professional school counselor to determine if middle school students had improved study skills as a result of the counseling program unit. One group of students was exposed to the 4-week classroom guidance unit, while a comparison group of students did not participate in the study skills unit. The professional school counselor's goal was for all students involved in the treatment group to improve their study skills and learning. This improvement of learning served as the school counselor's competency. To decide if the competency had been met, the professional school counselor must make sure that the objectives under the competency had been met. The school counselor developed objectives to serve as goals for the study skills unit—such as, 80% of students will apply cooperative study skills necessary for academic success by successfully completing a written task with a partner during the group activity, 80% of students will use knowledge of learning styles to achieve a grade of *B* on a social studies test, and 80% of students will become a self-directed and independent learner by completing a homework assignment on their own during the group activity. Students were expected to meet these objectives at the end of the unit to determine whether the academic standard had been met.

After the second session, the professional school counselor collected the activity in which students were required to work with a partner and complete a worksheet by applying necessary study skills. If students scored above 85%, they had met the objective. Once all of the worksheets were corrected, the counselor determined that 80% of students had appropriately applied their study skills; therefore, the objective had been met.

In between sessions, the teacher observed the students take a social studies test. In preparing for the test, the students were to choose and use a specific type of learning style technique introduced in previous sessions. The teacher determined whether students were using their knowledge of a learning style to positively influence their school performance. If 80% of students achieved a grade of *B* or better, the counselor verified that the objective had been met.

Lastly, students individually completed a homework assignment during the group session by using skills they had learned throughout the group meetings. By observing and correcting the homework assignment, the professional school counselor confirmed that 80% of the students had completed the assignment independently, which met the third objective.

By meeting all three objectives, one may conclude that the students also met the competency of improving learning among students. In order for the competency to have been met, all three of the objectives must be met. If, for some reason, one of the objectives is not met, the professional school counselor may conclude the competency was only partially met.

PROGRAM AUDIT

A program audit was conducted by a professional school counselor at the end of the school year to determine if the comprehensive developmental school counseling program was fully implemented. The program audit provided by the American School Counselor Association (ASCA; 2005) was used as a comprehensive guide. Although each facet of the comprehensive audit was evaluated, Table 25.3 provides a brief summary of only the guidance curriculum components. After examining the program audit, the professional school counselor determined the strengths and weaknesses of the program and created goals for the following school year to address full implementation of curriculum evaluation components that were "in progress" or "completed" but not fully implemented.

OUTCOME EVALUATION

A professional school counselor conducted an outcomes evaluation to determine how high school students were different as a result of small-group counseling addressing depression. The professional school counselor set up a nonequivalent control group design, a quasi-experimental design, which did not control for participant randomization. Students were self-referred to participate in the depression group. After 20 were selected, they were split in half and placed into either the control group ($n = 10$) or the treatment group ($n = 10$).

Before treatment began, each participant completed the 30-item *Reynolds Adolescent Depression Scale–Second Edition* (RADS-2; Reynolds, 2001) in order for the professional school counselor to determine each student's pretreatment severity of depression. The average severity of depression for both the treatment and control groups were moderate. After the treatment group had experienced group counseling for 6 weeks and the control group had undergone study skills group training for 6 weeks (the placebo condition), the RADS-2 was administered again. Students who had participated in the treatment group reported an average of mild levels of depression. In contrast, the control group again reported moderate levels of depression on the posttest. Data were statistically analyzed using SPSS, and results indicated significant differences occurred. Thus, the professional school counselor concluded that the group counseling intervention was successful in decreasing levels of depression among high school students (although the quasi-experimental design did not allow for specific causative inference).

REPORTING ASSESSMENT RESULTS

It is an excellent and essential practice to report assessment findings to administrators, teachers, staff members, parents, students and other appropriate stakeholders. The school counseling program advisory committee and professional school counselor should write and be involved in every step of the reporting process. Generally, a comprehensive report is helpful for program analysis and decision making, while a one- or two-page executive summary should be released to system administrators and the general school community. As general guidelines for report writing, Heppner, Kivlighan, and Wampold (1992) suggested, "(1) be informative, (2) be forthright, (3) do not overstate or exaggerate, (4) be logical and organized, (5) have some style, (6) write and rewrite, and (7) when all else fails, just write!" (p. 376). Perhaps the final guideline was offered in jest,

TABLE 25.3

PROGRAM AUDIT OF THE GUIDANCE CURRICULUM COMPONENTS OF A COMPREHENSIVE DEVELOPMENTAL SCHOOL COUNSELING PROGRAM

5.1. Guidance curriculum for all three domains has been written and adopted based on local site needs (Implemented)

5.2. All students receive, in a systemic way, the content to acquire knowledge, attitudes and skills to enhance their academic, career, and personal–social development (Completed, but not fully implemented)

5.3. Content is measurable (pre–post tests, product creation, or other methods) (In progress)

5.4. Materials, equipment, and facilities are available to support the program delivery (Implemented)

5.5. Effectiveness of curriculum is evaluated annually (In progress)

5.6. The school counseling curriculum has been presented to and accepted by administration, counselors, and the school counseling advisory council (Implemented)

but it is important to note that results must be documented, discussed, and reported for accountability to occur.

SUMMARY/CONCLUSION

Program accountability is one of the most important responsibilities of the professional school counselor. It is essential to understand that assessment is a cyclical process that results in continuous quality improvement. Aggregation and outcomes evaluation are strategies for providing documented evidence that the school counseling program is effectively meeting the needs of students and supporting the school's mission.

(Note: See the CD-ROM for a list of references.)

CHAPTER 26

CAREER DEVELOPMENT INTERVENTIONS
IN THE SCHOOLS

Spencer G. Niles, Jerry Trusty, and Brian Hutchison

Preview

In this chapter, we provide an overview of developmentally appropriate career inter-
ventions for students in Grades K–12. The National Standards for School Counseling Programs *(Campbell & Dahir, 1997) provided a general starting point for con-*
structing career interventions. Additionally, the U.S. Department of Education
Office of Vocational and Adult Education (OVAE) contracted with DTI Associates,
Inc., A Haverstick Company, to develop very specific National Career Development
Guidelines (NCDG) to help counselors identify developmentally appropriate career
development goals and interventions across the life span (Kobylarz, Crow, & Ettinger
2004). The NCDG guidelines are used as a framework for discussing career interven-
tions across educational levels. A primary theme in this chapter is that career devel-
opment interventions must help students prepare for the tasks they will encounter as
adults. Moreover, career development interventions must help students connect cur-
rent school activities with their futures. This connection is key to increasing school in-
volvement and school success.

The National Standards for School Counseling Programs (Campbell & Dahir, 1997)
identified career development as an essential element in effective school counseling programs. Specifically, the standards stipulated that, with regard to career development, students will complete the following:

> Standard A . . . acquire the skills to investigate the world of work in relation to
> knowledge of self and to make informed decisions . . . Standard B . . . employ
> strategies to achieve future career success and satisfaction . . . [and] . . . Standard
> C ... understand the relationship among personal qualities, education and train-
> ing, and the world of work. (Campbell & Dahir, 1997, p. 16)

These standards make sense, because school experiences prepare students for subsequent life experiences and work is a central life-role for most adults. However, school-
based career development interventions have a mixed record of success. In the past,
career development programs have not been created systematically, and little attention
has been devoted to devising comprehensive career interventions from early childhood
through secondary school. Too often, career development programs at one level (e.g.,
middle school) are not coordinated with programs at another level (e.g., high school). In
the 1980s, Gysbers and Moore (1981) introduced the comprehensive guidance program,
a way of organizing guidance activities and services in schools, including competency
expectations organized by grade level, that the American School Counselor Association

(ASCA) has used to develop the ASCA national model (ASCA; 2005). This model includes career guidance competencies, activities, and services as part of the comprehensive guidance program (Gysbers, 2005).

Professional school counselors often do not evaluate the efficacy of career-related interventions, thereby limiting opportunities for improving services and demonstrating the importance of career interventions to school administrators, parents, teachers, students, and other stakeholders in the educational enterprise. Awareness of the need for intervention efficacy evaluation has been heightened since the enactment of the No Child Left Behind Act of 2001 (NCLB). NCLB supports four key principles: (a) strong accountability for increased student performance; (b) more freedom at the state and community level; (c) the use of evidence-based education methods; and (d) giving parents more choice in their students' education. As a result of NCLB, a new culture of accountability and evidence-based education has evolved (Dahir & Stone, 2003), giving professional school counselors an opportunity to share the burden of improving schools and student academic performance as well as tying career interventions into the overarching goals of NCLB and comprehensive guidance programs.

Many of these challenges confronting professional school counselors emanate from individuals who fail to see the value of career interventions. Those questioning the usefulness of career development interventions assume that career-related activities take students away from time spent focusing on core academic subjects. They assume (incorrectly) that career interventions do not connect to academic subjects. Additionally, some career development critics assume that career development programs pressure students to pursue work immediately after high school rather than pursue a college education. Many people who are unfamiliar with how careers develop do not understand why career development interventions are important at the elementary, middle, and high school levels. Those arguing against career interventions for elementary school students often view career decisions as events that occur at particular points during the course of secondary school education (e.g., when students must select a curriculum of study when they leave high school). These perspectives lack an appreciation of the developmental context from which a readiness for career decision-making emerges. Thus, to confront these challenges effectively, many professional school counselors must provide career interventions differently. More specifically, career interventions must be systematic, coordinated, comprehensive, and developmentally appropriate.

SYSTEMATIC AND COORDINATED PLANNING FOR CAREER DEVELOPMENT PROGRAMS IN THE SCHOOLS

Walz and Benjamin (1984) provided important recommendations that professional school counselors can use to address the challenges confronting them as they design career development programs. These recommendations are also useful for creating systematic, coordinated, and developmentally appropriate career development intervention programs. Specifically, Walz and Benjamin recommended the following when implementing career programs in the schools:

- Involve a team of knowledgeable professionals, parents, and representatives from the community in all phases of program planning.

- Use developmentally appropriate interventions.
- Be sure that the program goals and objectives are clearly communicated to all involved in the program.
- Make sure the program is based on student needs.
- Have an evaluation component to determine the degree to which the program goals and objectives have been achieved.
- Make sure that those involved in program delivery are highly competent.

An implicit theme in these recommendations is that program planners need to be sensitive to the political climate in which they operate. For example, in some locations, not clearly connecting career development interventions to student academic achievement will significantly decrease the chances of program success. Also, not adequately communicating successful program outcomes to educational stakeholders (e.g., school-board members, parents, administrators, teachers) will result in the program resources being vulnerable to funding cuts. If school personnel view the program as an additional burden to their already heavy workloads, then there is little chance that the program will succeed. Thus, the "marketing" of the program to all stakeholders becomes an important aspect of program development and implementation. Clearly defined behavioral objectives that address the specific needs of students will be useful in marketing the program and providing outcome data that demonstrate program benefits. Lapan (2001) provided six fundamental questions professional school counselors can ask to define their essential work and communicate its importance to constituents:

1. How can counselor roles, duties, functions, and interventions be transformed to be of greater benefit and impact for all students?
2. How can counselor time on task be redistributed to maximize benefits for all students?
3. How can a program be tailored to better meet the needs of each school?
4. How can the program become central to the overriding mission of each school?
5. How can better partnerships between school personnel, parents, and business and community leaders be established?
6. How can counselors better advocate for their programs with local, state, and national policymakers?

Another theme implicit in these recommendations for planning career development programs is the importance of taking a team approach to service delivery. One person cannot accomplish all the goals and objectives of an effective career development program. Thus, program personnel need to be clear about their roles and responsibilities. Inevitably, there will be some overlap in the functions performed by program personnel. For example, professional school counselors may, at times, provide classroom instruction and teachers may, at times, perform more career counseling-related functions. Although there is no one prescription for how the roles and responsibilities should be defined, it is logical that professional school counselors take the lead role in developing and implementing career development intervention programs. Professional school counselors are often the only professionals in the school system with specific training in career development. Therefore, professional school counselors possess the knowledge of career development theory and practice that is necessary for formulating appropriate career development program interventions. Moreover, the processes typically used in program delivery relate to counselors' primary areas of expertise. These processes include counseling, assessment, career information services, placement services, consultation procedures, and referrals.

Developing a systematic and coordinated career development program from early childhood through Grade 12 (EC–12) requires understanding the developmental tasks confronting students as they progress through school. Understanding the career development tasks confronting students at all levels of schooling prepares school personnel to work collaboratively in program design and implementation. A comprehensive understanding of the career development process also sets the stage for developing program interventions that are sequential and cohesive. Thus, the following sections of this chapter focus on career development tasks, goals, and interventions for elementary, middle or junior high school, and high school students, respectively.

CONSTRUCTING DEVELOPMENTALLY APPROPRIATE CAREER INTERVENTIONS

NATIONAL CAREER DEVELOPMENT GUIDELINES

Although the ASCA standards for career development provide general guidelines for career competencies students need to develop, the U.S. Department of Education Office of Vocational and Adult Education contracted with DTI Associates, Inc., A Haverstick Company, to develop very specific National Career Development Guidelines (NCDG; America's Career Development Network, n.d.). The NCDG guidelines are used as a framework for discussing career interventions across educational levels to help professional school counselors identify developmentally appropriate career goals and interventions across the life span. The framework is organized into three domains, each with goals that define broad areas of career development competency. Indicators of mastery are highlighted under each goal. These indicators are presented in three learning stages (Knowledge Acquisition, Application, and Reflection) based upon Bloom's Taxonomy (Bloom, 1956). It is important to note that these learning stages are not associated with an individual's age or grade level but instead are a developmental sequence (Kobylarz et al., 2004). The specific career development domains and goals are identified as follows:

1. Personal–Social Development Domain
   - Develop understanding of self to build and maintain a positive self-concept.
   - Develop positive interpersonal skills including respect for diversity.
   - Integrate growth and change into your career development.
   - Balance personal, leisure, community, learner, family, and work roles.

2. Educational Achievement and Lifelong Learning Domain
   - Attain educational achievement and performance levels needed to reach your personal and career goals.
   - Participate in ongoing, lifelong learning experiences to enhance your ability to function effectively in a diverse and changing economy.

3. Career Management Domain

- Create and manage a career plan that meets your career goals.
- Use a process of decision making as one component of career development.
- Use accurate, current, and unbiased career information during career planning and management.
- Master academic, occupational, and general employability skills in order to obtain, create, maintain or advance your employment.
- Integrate changing employment trends, societal needs, and economic conditions into your career plans.

CAREER DEVELOPMENT INTERVENTIONS IN THE ELEMENTARY SCHOOL

Magnuson and Starr (2000, p. 100) offered the following thoughts to guide professional school counselors as they plan career development interventions at the elementary school level:

1. Become a constant observer of children:
   - Notice how children approach tasks.
   - Notice the activities in which children choose to participate.
   - Observe and encourage the child's initiative-taking.
   - Notice the thematic patterns emerging in each child's activities.
2. Consider the processing of an activity as important as the activity itself:
   - To help children develop a sense of industry rather than inferiority, focus feedback on the specifics of children's efforts.
   - Accompany career awareness and career exploration activities with opportunities for students to express their beliefs about themselves in relation to various occupations. (p. 100)

Personal–social development. Because self-awareness provides the foundation for processing career information, career development interventions in the primary grades can focus on helping students develop more sophisticated self-knowledge. For example, in Grades EC–1, students can increase their self-knowledge by describing themselves through drawings, writing sentences describing the things they like and the things that are important to them, and bringing some of their favorite things to school to show to their classmates. Sharing their self-descriptions with others helps students to clarify their self-concepts. Each of these activities can also emphasize the importance of appreciating the similarities and differences that exist among students in the classroom. Activities that encourage students to focus on clarifying their global self-concepts can be emphasized and can be easily infused into the curriculum during the first years of school.

Educational achievement and lifelong learning. Activities that help students learn more about themselves can be supplemented with activities that focus on educational and occupational exploration as students progress through the primary and intermediate grades. For example, in the primary grades, students can identify the occupations of their family members (e.g., parents, grandparents, aunts, uncles) as well as the level and type of education each family member has attained. As students share this information, the relationship between education and work can be stressed (e.g., some jobs require a college education, others may require a different type of training, such as trade school or an apprenticeship). Differences in family members' occupations can be discussed as strengths (e.g., it takes people working in a wide variety of occupations to make our society function effectively). To counteract occupational stereotyping, men and women working in gender nontraditional occupations can be invited to school to discuss their work.

Students in Grades K–1 can begin the process of learning about work by focusing on occupations with which they have the most immediate relationship (e.g., occupations of family members, occupations in the school setting, occupations in their neighborhoods and of neighbors). Then, elementary school students can gradually learn about occupations that are more remote (e.g., occupations in the community, occupations in the state, occupations in the nation, occupations throughout the world) as they progress from Grades 2–5. Using a proximity–distance scheme to guide students in the acquisition of occupational information helps students understand the relevance of work in their lives and the ways in which various workers contribute to society. At each level of proximity, the relationship between work and the educational requirements for performing specific occupations can be highlighted. Students can also discuss what is required to perform occupations successfully. Job-content skills (the specific skill requirements for each occupation), functional skills (the skills that are transferable across occupations), and self-management skills (e.g., being reliable, getting along with one's coworkers, being trustworthy, completing assignments on time) can be integrated into these discussions as well.

Career management. Activities to help students learn about the career planning and decision-making process could include the following:

- Having students read biographies and then discuss the important career decisions people made in the biographies they read. Students can be encouraged to consider what constitutes a *good* rather than *bad* career decision as they discuss the biographies they read.
- Students can use a timeline to chart important events that have influenced the life decisions made by the people they read about.
- Encouraging students to read stories about people working in nontraditional occupations can contribute to counteracting the effects of occupational sex stereotyping.
- Discussions of the ways in which culture, gender, and social class may have influenced the career development of the person in the biography.

PARENTAL INVOLVEMENT

Parents have substantial influence over the career development of their children, and these influences are strong through elementary school, middle school, high school, and into adulthood (Trusty, 1998, 1999). Young (1994) suggested that the influence parents exert on the career development process is most effective when it is planned, intentional, and goal oriented. However, many parents possess minimal knowledge regarding career-development theory and how environmental factors influence the career-development process of children. Thus, it is important that professional school counselors help parents learn ways to contribute positively to the career development of their children. Professional school counselors can begin by providing parents with information about the career-development process. Professional school counselors can also explain to parents how the environment impacts options that children are willing to consider (e.g., the influence of occupational stereotyping within the media and gender role stereotyping can be discussed with parents). Finally, professional school counselors can help parents identify specific strategies they can use to facilitate career development in their children. Herr, Cramer, and Niles (2004) identified eight ways parents can help children advance in their careers. These strategies included the following:

- Parents can encourage children to analyze important self-characteristics (e.g., interests, capacities, values).
- When parents are familiar with specific work requirements for jobs, they can communicate these to their children.
- Parents can discuss the importance of work values in work behavior.
- Parents can explain the relationship between work, pay, and the economic condition of the family.
- Parents can connect children with informational resources (e.g., other workers, books, films) for acquiring accurate career information.
- Parents can be careful to avoid stereotyping occupational alternatives and workers.
- Parents can provide children with opportunities for work in the home and community.
- Parents can provide children with opportunities to learn and practice decision making skills. (Herr et al., 2004, p. 349)

Several studies have supported the positive effects of parents' involvement on their children's career development, and parental involvement has been quantified in various ways (e.g., parents' school-based involvement, involvement in school policy making, help with homework). The type of parental involvement that appears to have the strongest positive effects on children's educational and career development is parents' home-based involvement (Trusty, 1999). Home-based involvement is the degree to which parents communicate positively with their children and support children in their educational and career development. Home-based parental involvement does not appear to be domain specific; that is, through factor analysis using a national sample, Trusty, Watts, and Erdman (1997) found one home-based involvement factor spanning areas of education, vocation, and leisure.

From research on parents and parental involvement (Trusty, 1998, 1999; Trusty, Watts, & Crawford, 1996; Trusty et al., 1997), there are five main reasons that professional school counselors should focus on parents helping their children with their career development:

- There is generally no *generation gap* between parents and children in the area of career development.
- Children and adolescents want parents' help, and parents want to help their children.
- Work with parents promotes positive communication within the family.
- Contact between professional school counselors and parents enhances parents' perceptions of professional school counselors and schools as resources for their children.

- Parents serve as continual resources for their children, whereas professional school counselors' efforts are temporal.

Professional school counselors' helping parents become aware of their own attitudes toward work and occupations, exposing students to work opportunities in the home and community, and providing support to students as they engage in career decision-making tasks are all ways to help students cope effectively with the career-development process and lay a solid foundation for coping with the career-development tasks of middle or junior high school.

CAREER DEVELOPMENT INTERVENTIONS IN MIDDLE AND JUNIOR HIGH SCHOOL

Thematic consideration of middle and junior high school–level career development goals reveals the importance of students acquiring the necessary knowledge, skills, and understanding to advance in their career development. Based on their literature review of school-based career intervention research, Hughes and Karp (2004) suggested that a greater investment be made in middle school career guidance and academic counseling interventions, because this is potentially the most effective school population for such activities.

Sink (2005) offered the following recommendations for middle school counselors wishing to foster academic development and learning when implementing interventions:

- Lessons and activities should be designed to advance student cognition and metacognition.
- Encourage healthy student psychosocial development.
- Partner with teachers to develop and implement lessons and interventions.
- Augment the work of teachers by focusing interventions on enhancing academic skills and student motivation to learn.

Personal–social development. It is also important at this developmental level that career interventions continue to stimulate curiosity in students. Students who are curious about their emerging self-concepts (e.g., their avocational and vocational interests, skills, and values) are more likely to engage in exploratory behavior to acquire the information they need for self-concept clarification. Helping students identify and connect with role models can also facilitate a sense of internal control and future time perspective which can, in turn, lead to *planful* behaviors and the development of effective problem-solving skills (Super, 1990).

Providing career assessment activities (as described in Chapter 50) are essential to helping students expand their self-knowledge in a systematic fashion. Interest and aptitude assessment are particularly useful at this developmental level. In selecting career assessments, it is important that the reading level, language, and normative samples are appropriate for the school population with which the assessments will be used. Interest inventory results can foster more systematic thinking about the activities in which students enjoy participating. Aptitude tests can also help students acquire accurate estimates of their abilities. Interest and aptitude assessments are often administered to students during the middle or junior high school grades. Combining interest inventory with aptitude test results provides a useful foundation for the exploration process.

Educational achievement and lifelong learning. Students will find it useful to explore occupational areas for which they have high interest and high aptitude. When the results of an interest inventory suggest that a student has no area of above-average or high interest, it may be that the student will need exposure to activities across several interest areas to determine if these areas hold any interest for the student. Thus, a key to assessments, especially interest inventories, being useful is that students must have the experiential base to draw upon to respond to assessment items. Students with limited exposure to a variety of activities will be forced to guess at appropriate responses to questions requiring them to identify their likes and dislikes.

When school systems have a systematic career development intervention program in place for all grades, then it is safer to assume that middle and junior high school students have been exposed to activities that have fostered their self- and career exploration. When no such programs exist, then professional school counselors must be especially cognizant of the possibility that many students will need more remedial career development interventions prior to being administered career assessments.

Providing middle school students with exposure to work facilitates the acquisition of knowledge, skills, and awareness related to the career development domains of (a) educational achievement and lifelong learning and (b) career management. Teaching students how families of occupations can be clustered according to factors such as skill requirements, interests, or training helps students organize the world of work and connect their characteristics to occupational options. For example, Holland's classification system uses six personality types (i.e., Realistic, Investigative, Artistic, Social, Enterprising, and Conventional) to organize the world of work (Holland, 1985). *Realistic* occupations include skills trades and technical occupations. *Investigative* occupations include scientific and technical occupations. *Artistic* occupations include creative occupations in the expressive arts. *Social* occupations include the helping professions. *Enterprising* occupations involve managerial and sales occupations. Lastly, *Conventional* occupations include office and clerical occupations. Occupations are classified according to the degree to which the activities of the occupation draw upon the Holland types. The three most dominant types reflected in the occupation are used to classify each occupation.

Clustering systems such as Holland's can be used to guide career exploration by using the types to organize career information resources, career fairs, curricula experiences (e.g., students can be assigned the task of writing an essay about occupations that fall within their dominant Holland type), job-shadowing experiences, participation in extracurricular activities, avocational pursuits, college exploration, and part-time employment experiences. With accurate self-knowledge and systematic educational and career exploration, students develop readiness to engage in career planning.

Career management. Effective career management at the middle school or junior high school level requires students to know how to make decisions, understand the interrelationship of life-roles, know about different occupations and changing male/female roles, and understand the process of career planning. An effective tool for helping middle or junior high school students engage in purposeful planning, exploring, information gathering, decision making, and reality testing related to two prominent life-roles (e.g., student and worker) is an educational and career planning portfolio. Educational and career planning portfolios are typically used to help students chart their academic and career decision making. This charting process can begin in middle or junior high school and continue until the student leaves high school. By making at least annual entries into the portfolio, the student and professional school counselor can track the student's career development progress. They can also make systematic educational and career plans that build upon the student's growing base of self- and occupational knowledge. In essence, the portfolio provides a vehicle for the student and professional school counselor to discuss what the student has done and what the student will do next to advance his or her career development.

To help students focus on the interrelationship of life-roles, and to engage in planning related to their salient life-roles, the educational and career planning portfolio can be expanded to a life-role portfolio by addressing students' readiness for life-roles beyond those of student and worker. Students can be encouraged to plan, explore, and gather information for each of the major roles of life. For example, students who anticipate one day being a parent can plan for this role by considering how parenting interacts with other roles. Students can explore different styles of parenting by interviewing parents about their parenting practices and philosophies. Students can also gather information about the skills required for effective parenting (perhaps by taking a parenting class). Through these activities, students can learn about the factors that are important to consider in making decisions about parenting. Finally, students can reality-test their interest in parenting through participating in childcare activities. Thus, the life-role portfolio serves as a stimulus for meetings between professional school counselors and students that are focused on planning, exploring, information gathering, decision making, and reality testing vis-à-vis the major life-roles. When the portfolio is used over successive years, it also provides developmental documentation of activities and decisions related to major life-roles.

CAREER DEVELOPMENT INTERVENTIONS IN HIGH SCHOOL

As students transition from middle or junior high school, they focus more directly on the task of identifying occupational preferences and clarifying career or lifestyle choices. According to Super (1955, 1957) the tasks of crystallizing, specifying, and implementing tentative career choices occur during early (ages 12–15 years), middle (ages 16–18 years), and late (ages 18–24 years) adolescence and will be useful to students as they move forward and will help to normalize the transition process.

The emphasis on knowledge, skills, and understanding that emerged in the middle or junior high school–level domains is continued in the high school domains. The high school domains, however, challenge students to become more focused on making career plans by translating their self- and career information into career goals. At the high school level, students' level of sophistication in the domains of personal–social development, educational achievement and lifelong learning, and career management is such that there is substantial overlap among them. Interventions tend to involve all three domains; this section discusses them collectively.

Savickas (1999) proposed career development interventions that foster the sort of self-knowledge, educational and occupational exploration, and career planning described in the high school competencies. Specifically, these interventions focus on (a) orienting students' comprehension of careers; (b) developing students' competence at planning and exploring; (c) coaching students to develop effective career management techniques; and (d) guiding students in behavioral rehearsals, to become prepared for coping with job problems.

To orient ninth-grade students to the planning tasks they will encounter as they move through high school, Savickas (1999) recommended using a group guidance format to discuss items on career development inventories such as the *Career Maturity Inventory* (Crites, 1978) or the *Adult Career Concerns Inventory* (ACCI; Super, Thompson, & Lindeman, 1988). Using inventory items to orient students to the tasks they need to address in order to manage their career development effectively helps provide a stimulus for planning and exploring behaviors (Savickas, 1990). For example, the ACCI measures developmental task concern for the career stages of Exploration, Establishment, Maintenance, and Disengagement. Reviewing the career stages and tasks within the ACCI teaches high school students about the general process of career development. Using ACCI items, adolescents can identify those career development tasks they are likely to encounter in the near future. Strategies for coping with current and near future career development tasks can be identified. In this way, high school students' understanding of time perspective or *planfulness* can be enhanced (Savickas, Stilling, & Schwartz, 1984).

Results from interest and abilities measures administered at the end of middle school or at the beginning of high school provide direction as to which of the occupational environments offers the best potential for fruitful exploration. The range of career assessment possibilities that can be used systematically with youth is substantial. To measure interests, professional school counselors can use instruments that provide information related to students' Holland types such as the *Self-Directed Search* (Holland, 1985, 1994) and the *Career Assessment Inventory* (Johansson, 1986). Ability measures include the *Differential Aptitude Test* (Bennett, Seashore, & Wesman, 1992), *The Ability Explorer* (Harrington & Harrington, 1996), and assessments of functional skills from school transcripts or educational and career-planning portfolios. Areas of high interest and ability can be matched to occupational clusters and students can identify specific occupations for in-depth exploration.

Although interest and ability assessment results provide important data pertaining to career choice content (i.e., relating students' abilities and interests to occupational options), these data fail to address whether students have developed readiness for career decision making (Super, 1983). Approaches to career assessment must attend to both content and process variables in order to adequately address the needs of youth (Savickas, 1993). Specifically, interests and abilities can be considered as career-choice content data that must be viewed in light of career-choice process data, such as readiness for career decision making, life-role salience, and values, which can be labeled as moderator variables (Super, Osborne, Walsh, Brown, & Niles, 1992). To be ready to effectively choose and adapt to an occupation, it is important for high school students to "see themselves as coping with certain developmental tasks, at a stage in life at which they are expected, and may expect themselves to make certain decisions and acquire certain competencies" (Super, 1983, p. 559). Students who have not successfully accomplished the career-development tasks presented to them at previous educational levels will need remedial interventions (e.g., additional opportunities for self-concept clarification, training in acquiring occupational information) prior to focusing on career decision making.

From this perspective, addressing career choice readiness (Super, 1974) becomes a necessary precursor to the effective use of ability and interest assessment data. According to Super, career choice readiness involves five dimensions: (a) having a *planful* attitude toward coping with career stages and tasks, (b) gathering information about educational and occupational opportunities, (c) exploring the world of work, (d) knowing how to make good career decisions, and (e) being able to make realistic judgments about potential occupations. These dimensions are important because if an adolescent knows little about the world of work, then interest inventories that use occupational titles or activities may produce misleading scores and poor choices may be made (Super, Savickas, & Super, 1996). Likewise, when adolescents do not engage in appropriate career planning, they often encounter career tasks for which they are not prepared (Herr et al., 2004). Thus, assessing high school students' resources for choosing and adapting to an occupation requires conducting appraisals of career-choice content (e.g., abilities, interests, values) and process (e.g., life-role salience, career-choice readiness) variables. When a student is lacking in any of the five dimensions comprising career-choice readiness, then the professional school counselor should focus interventions to help the student progress in that particular domain prior to focusing on career choice content.

It is important to note that traditional assessment approaches focusing only on career-choice content variables assume that all individuals place a high value on work and that all individuals view work as the prime means of values realization. It can be argued that this is a Western middle-class male view of career development and thus is a culturally encapsulated view of life-role salience. Different patterns of life-role salience exist, and they must be considered in helping high school students clarify and articulate their career goals (Niles & Goodnough, 1996). For example, when salience for the work role is high, youth view work as providing meaningful opportunities for self-expression. In such cases, high school students are often motivated to develop the career maturity necessary (e.g., to be *planful*, to explore opportunities, to gather information) for making good career decisions. When work-role salience is low, however, adolescents often lack motivation and career maturity. In the latter instances, professional school counselors need to begin the career development intervention process by arousing the individual's sense of importance for the worker role (Super, 1990). Disputing irrational beliefs, exposing young people to effective role models and providing mentors are examples of activities that foster career arousal (Krumboltz & Worthington, 1999).

To help students further clarify their life-role self-concepts, professional school counselors can encourage high school students to consider life-role salience questions (e.g., How do I spend my time during the course of a typical week? What changes would I like to make in how I spend my time? How important is each life-role to me? How important is each life-role to my family? What do I like about participating in each life-role? What do I hope to accomplish in each life-role? What does my family expect me to accomplish in each life-role? What life-roles do I think will be important to me in the future? What must I do to become more prepared for the life-roles that will be important to me in the future?). Discussing these questions helps high school students clarify and articulate their life-role self-concepts. Specifically, by discussing these questions during the first years of high school, adolescents can become clearer as to the values they seek to express in each life-role. This information is vital not only for guiding high school students in the selection and pursuit of appropriate educational and occupational options, but also in developing appropriate expectations for values satisfaction within the respective life-roles.

These discussion questions also provide opportunities for exploring the individual's level of acculturation, cultural identity, and worldview. For example, high school students can discuss family expectations and other cultural factors influencing their life-role participation. Finally, discussing these questions helps professional school counselors become aware of potential barriers as well as potential sources of support for students as they move closer to negotiating the school-to-work or school-to-school transition. These discussions also foster the acquisition of the high school–level career development competencies related to understanding the interrelationship of life-roles and understanding the changing nature of male/female roles. This information also helps high school students identify those roles in which they spend most of their time, those that they are emotionally committed to, and those that they expect to be important to them in the future. By clarifying information concerning life-role salience (and the cultural factors influencing role salience), high school students establish the foundation for making accurate self-evaluations and developing career choice readiness.

Clarifying values is an important task in acquiring adequate self-knowledge for effective educational and occupational exploration because values are indications of the qualities people desire and seek, in "the activities in which they engage, in the situations in which they live, and in the objects which they make or acquire" (Super, 1974, p. 4). Because values reflect the individual's goals, they provide a sense of purpose and direction in the career planning process (Super et al., 1996). However, while many agree that values clarification is critical to choosing an occupation, relatively few put forth the effort to examine their values in a systematic way (Harrington & Harrington, 1996). Values card sorts (e.g., *Career Values Card Sort Kit, Non-sexist Vocational Card Sort*) and instruments such as the *Career Orientation Placement and Evaluation Survey* are instruments that are useful in values clarification. Interest inventory results can also be used to identify work-related activities that provide opportunities for values expression.

These interventions represent examples of ways in which high school counselors can help students prepare for a successful school-to-work or school-to-school transition. When professional school counselors at all grade levels work collaboratively to develop systematic career development interventions, there is a greater likelihood that students will be prepared for the career development tasks they will encounter as they move through high school.

Summary/Conclusion

More than ever, systematic career development interventions are needed to help young people advance in their career development. The nature of work is changing dramatically, requiring new skills sets (e.g., transition skills, stress management, the ability to engage in lifelong learning, personal flexibility, computer skills) that suggest that change, rather than constancy, will be the norm. Workers in the 21st century will experience multiple career changes that will bring associated levels of stress that must be managed effectively. It is naïve to expect parents, many of whom are struggling to manage their own careers effectively, to provide children and adolescents with the competencies they need to advance in their careers in the 21st century. In light of the challenges that young people face, all stakeholders—especially professional school counselors, parents, and schools—must work together to support students in their career development. Career development interventions must help students prepare for the tasks they will encounter as adults. Moreover, career development interventions must help students connect current school activities with their futures. This connection is key to increasing school involvement and school success.

In many respects, professional school counselors are the human development specialists in the schools. Educating stakeholders about the developmental process students will experience as they move through school helps students, teachers, administrators, and parents develop the awareness to think proactively about the tasks students will encounter. Thus, infusing the curriculum with developmental concepts helps students acquire the awareness that fosters a *planful* approach to coping with career development tasks.

(Note: See the CD-ROM for a list of references.)

CHAPTER 27

SECONDARY AND POSTSECONDARY EDUCATIONAL PLANNING

Suzanne M. Dugger and John B. Boshoven

Preview

Designed for current and future professional school counselors, this chapter provides an overview of educational planning in comprehensive school counseling programs. Educational planning, as addressed in this chapter, is inextricably tied to the career development process and represents an essential component in a school counseling program. The chapter includes step-by-step information that can be used to guide professional school counselors through the educational planning process used for assisting high school students to plan their secondary coursework; it also addresses the planning process for postsecondary education.

The educational planning component is a key component of any successful school counseling program. Whereas the primary mission of professional counselors in community agencies is to promote mental health, the primary mission of professional school counselors is to promote educational achievement. Ultimately, the hope is that educational achievement will serve as the foundation for students' career development and productivity as citizens. Toward this end, professional school counselors systematically assist students and parents with the process of educational planning. The goal is to assist students in preparing for careers and fulfilling lives with intentionality. Rather than finishing school and assuming a job, career, or life by chance (i.e., whatever option happens to be available and accessible at the time), sound educational planning supports students in exercising choice about their career and life destinations.

Simply put, educational planning can be defined as the process of assisting students and parents in understanding the connection between education and career or life planning, setting goals, making decisions regarding academic course selection and scholastic experiences that will contribute to the achievement of these goals, evaluating progress toward these goals, and modifying educational plans as needed. The purpose of this chapter is to provide an overview of the educational planning process and to offer specific ideas about the integration of educational planning services into an already existing school counseling program. Toward this end, we will address the educational planning process as it pertains both to a high school curriculum and to postsecondary options.

The process of educational planning may be conceptualized as a role of a professional school counselor (Schmidt, 2003) or as a part of the individual planning component of a comprehensive guidance and counseling program (Gysbers & Henderson, 2005). The latter conceptualization suggests that professional school counselors work within a programmatic framework. According to Gysbers and Henderson (2005), this framework involves the provision of responsive services (e.g., individual and small-group counseling); individual planning, which tends to focus on the educational and career planning process; curriculum guidance, in which professional school counselors systematically design and deliver classroom guidance lessons in three broad content areas; and system support (e.g., the managerial aspects of coordinating a program and making fair-share contributions to the school as an organization). Although the individual planning component is perhaps most closely related to educational planning, the curriculum guidance component may also be used for this purpose. Consistent with the national model put forth by the American School Counselor Association (ASCA; 2005), the three content areas targeted by curriculum guidance units are (a) academic development, (b) career development, and (c) personal–social development. Additionally, Myrick (2002) delineated several aspects of educational planning. These were to recognize options that are available for planning; illustrate the need to plan ahead; learn a language of educational planning (common terms); learn the sequence of academic courses; identify academic requirements and electives; develop an educational plan for middle or high school; and register for next year's courses.

In approaching the topic of educational planning, we based the information in this chapter on the following assumptions:

- *All students need assistance with educational planning.* Regardless of whether they are college bound or looking toward a career that does not require additional education, all students need and deserve assistance with the educational planning process.
- *There is value in all work and that one type of career aspiration is neither better nor worse than another.* It logically follows, then, that the quality of an educational plan is to be judged not by the highest level of education to be achieved by a student but rather by the goodness of fit with the student's aspirations. How well an educational plan prepares a student for whatever career and life he or she has chosen is the issue. This second assumption is especially important given that "while only about 30% of new jobs created in the next 10 years will require at least a bachelor's degree, more than 70% of parents seem to believe their child will fill one of these jobs" (Parnell, as cited in Hoyt, 2001, p. 6).
- *Educational planning is necessarily tied to career planning.* Indeed, educational plans should be developed to support a student's career aspirations and interests.

JOURNEYS AND DESTINATIONS

Before developing an educational plan, professional school counselors must work with students and parents to develop an understanding of the student's long-term goals. If the educational plan is likened to a road map, the student's career aspirations and interests may be likened to the destination. Certainly, it is difficult to develop a detailed road map without a sense of the destination. Because students need more guidance than "Go forward," it becomes essential to begin the career exploration and development process early. It is for this reason that ASCA (2005) recommends career development activities as early as elementary school.

Career development experts and professional school counselors are not alone in their perception of the need for educational and career planning. In fact, Libsch and

Freedman-Doan (1995) found that 49% of high school seniors indicated that they would prefer more assistance in choosing their courses, and 54% expressed a preference for more help in developing educational plans. In addition, 61% reported that they would prefer more attention to career planning and job selection.

As professional school counselors work with students and their parents to look ahead to postsecondary options, it is important to address (a) the amount of formal postsecondary education or training a student is willing to attain; (b) the general career pathway (or specific career) in which the student is interested; and (c) the type of education or training that is best suited to prepare the student for his or her chosen career pathway. When the professional school counselor discusses with students and parents the amount of formal postsecondary education or training a student is willing to complete, it is helpful to review a variety of options rather than to erroneously suggest that a 4-year college degree is the only viable route to a successful career (Hoyt, 2001). When discussing career pathways, professional school counselors will do well to use their own state's terminology when labeling the career categories or pathways. Many states, for example, will organize careers into six pathways:

1. Arts and communications
2. Business, management, marketing, and technology
3. Engineering/manufacturing and industrial technology
4. Health sciences
5. Human services
6. Natural resources and agri-sciences (terminology from the Michigan Department of Career Development, 2002).

Because students are generally unable to identify one specific career goal and are better able to identify a cluster of careers in which they are interested and display talent, the use of pathways is becoming the norm in many school counseling programs. Each pathway includes careers that involve a wide range of postsecondary education and training. Some involve 4 or more years of college; others involve on-the-job training, and still others require vocational training. In addressing postsecondary options, therefore, professional school counselors will want to work with students and parents to find the length and type of education most likely to assist the student in reaching his or her goals within a given career pathway.

It is essential that the process of discussing postsecondary options begin early—preferably in middle school—in order to develop such an educational plan. As Sears (1995) stated, "Students and their parents need to understand . . . that committing to an educational plan, accidentally or on purpose, has long-range consequences" (p. 37). For example, the ability of students who eventually want to go to college to do so will depend greatly upon the selection of courses as early as middle school. Without appropriate coursework and achievement in middle school math and English, a high school freshman will be positioned poorly to begin college prep coursework in these subjects. Sears reported on a study conducted by the College Board, which revealed that only half of all high school students who intended to go to college were actually enrolled in courses appropriate for this future plan. These students apparently chose their courses without understanding the implications of their selections on their future educational career. Sears suggested that "many parents are also unaware of the significance of these early decisions" (1995, p. 38).

THE EARLY DECISION-MAKING PROCESS

Clearly, early discussion of career interests and aspirations is inextricably tied to the educational planning process. To assist students and their parents in this early career exploration and educational planning process, professional school counselors will want to proactively guide students and parents through a decision-making process. Ideally, this process will include helping students assess their career-related interests, skills, personality, and values.

With regard to the assessment of interests, professional school counselors may conduct interviews with students on an individual, small-group, or classroom basis; use formal interest inventories; provide informal interest questionnaires; or facilitate the use of computer software programs that include interest assessment components. Standardized interest inventories most commonly used in the K–12 academic setting include the *Self-Directed Search* (SDS; Holland, 1994); the *Strong Interest Inventory and Skills Confidence Inventory* (Betz, Borgen, & Harmon, 2004); and the *Career Occupational Preferences System* (COPS; EdITS, 1995). A number of computer software programs, including DISCOVER (American College Testing Program, 2006); the *Career Explorer Online* (CX Online; Bridges.com, 2006); and *COIN Educational Inventory* (COIN Educational Products, 2007) also include components that assess students' interests.

The assessment of interest, however, is not sufficient for the career development and educational planning process. Certainly, another important dimension involves skills. Whether these skills are conceptualized as aptitudes, achievement, or ability, it is essential that professional school counselors also assist students in considering the relevance of skills to their future. In assessing skills, professional school counselors tend to rely on student self-report during interviews, on academic performance (as evidenced by GPA.), and on standardized test scores. Standardized tests commonly used during the career development and educational planning process include the *Differential Aptitude Test* (DAT; Psychological Corporation, 1992); the *PSAT* (College Board, 2005b); *SAT* (College Board, 2005a); the *PLAN* (American College Testing Program, 2005b); *ACT* (American College Testing Program, 2005a); and the *Armed Services Vocational Aptitude Battery* (ASVAB; U.S. Department of Defense, 2005).

Also important to the early decision-making process is the assessment of students' personality styles as they relate to career planning. This is based, in part, on Holland's contention that a match between an individual's personality style and the "personality" of a given occupation or career leads to increased job satisfaction and success (Brown & Brooks, 1990). However, formal personality testing is rarely conducted by professional school counselors. Instead, professional school counselors tend to use career instruments or informal measures to help students identify career-related personality preferences. For example, the SDS (Holland, 1994) helps describe student personalities by identifying a student's three-letter preference. Otherwise known as the "Holland Code," these three letters identify the student's personality preference from six possible styles: Realistic, Investigative, Artistic, Social, Enterprising, or Conventional. Some professional school counselors also use tests such as the True Colors program (Imai & Berry, 2001; Kalil & Lowery, 1999) to help students conceptualize aspects of their personality. Still others may use the Kiersey Temperament Sorter (Kiersey, 1998) to help students determine the direction of their preference across four domains: extroversion vs. introversion, sensing vs. intuition, thinking vs. feeling, and judging vs. perceiving.

The final aspect of assessment that generally contributes to the early decision-making process involves the exploration of students' education and career-related values. In facilitating this exploration, professional school counselors seek to assist students and their parents in identifying and examining values that should contribute to their educational and career decisions. For example, students may value high salaries; prestige associated with a career, flexibility of scheduling, autonomy, the opportunity to make a difference or contribute to society, adventure, or intellectual stimulation. In helping students identify their values and apply them to the career decision-making and educational planning process, professional school counselors may use formal tests such as the *Minnesota Importance Questionnaire* (Rounds, Henly, Dawis, & Lofquist, 1981), informal checklists, interviews, or value card sorts.

Through the process of helping students understand how their interests, skills, personality, and values relate to their educational and career decisions, professional school counselors facilitate the early career decision-making process. Specifically, professional school counselors assist students and their parents in applying this knowledge to select an initial career pathway and to estimate the amount and type of postsecondary education that is necessary for the student to reach his or her career and life goals.

THE BALANCING ACT

Helping students make career decisions early enough in their academic career to support the educational planning process for high school course selection requires that professional school counselors successfully negotiate two separate balancing acts. First, because this early decision-making process is ideally completed during the middle school or junior high years, professional school counselors must balance the self-report and autonomy of students (young adolescents) with the influence of others. For example, professional school counselors will want to help students balance their own aspirations, however immature, with the wisdom, caring and, perhaps, dominance of their parents. As another example, it is essential that professional school counselors assist students in ferreting out the influence of their peers when making decisions for themselves. Additionally, professional school counselors will want to proactively assist students in limiting the impact of culturally sanctioned sex-role stereotypes when considering various career options (ASCA; 2005; Drummond & Ryan, 1995).

Certainly, the difficulty in achieving this balance and assisting students in deciding how much consideration to give to parental and peer input about their future is considerable during early adolescence, a time in which students' sense of self and their ability to effectively make decisions that have long-term consequences is limited. Indeed, achieving this balance is difficult, even during late adolescence. This balancing act was approached from a constructive developmental perspective by McAuliffe and

Strand (1994) when they applied Kegan's (1992) developmental theory to the academic advising process. Although they focused on advising at the college level, the following point would also appear to have salience for the process of assisting young adolescents with making decisions regarding their future educational and career plans:

> Many forces will seem to conspire to maintain Interpersonalism, such as group-think peers or parents who expect adherence to family and cultural norms. Nevertheless, the advisor, from the constructive developmental perspective, must challenge Interpersonally embedded individuals' expectations that others will supply them with decisions. (McAuliffe & Strand, 1994, p. 27)

The second balancing act necessitates an awareness that decisions made by students during middle and even high school may change over time. Whereas a student in middle school may firmly believe that he or she wants to become a physician and seek a medical degree, this same student may alter plans as a result of experiences with college prep coursework. Similarly, another student may initially plan to seek employment immediately following high school graduation but later express an interest in going to college. As students develop their self-awareness (Schmidt, 2003), accumulate real-life experience with academic coursework, and improve their understanding of career possibilities, their educational and career goals may change. Such changes are commonplace and to be expected. Therefore, professional school counselors must balance the process of helping students make enough of a decision to support educational planning with the importance of also allowing room for students to change their plans.

MATCHMAKING

Keeping these balancing acts in mind, the professional school counselor's next task is to assist students and their parents in creating an educational plan designed to facilitate students' progress toward their postsecondary educational and career goals. Indeed, it is the process of matching educational plans with student goals that constitutes the majority of a professional school counselor's activities within the educational planning domain.

For the majority of students, graduating from high school constitutes a fundamental goal that serves as a foundation for their future plans. In helping students match their educational plans with this goal, professional school counselors typically engage in a myriad of educational planning activities. First, high school counselors educate students about graduation requirements. This process generally begins in the eighth grade and frequently involves collaboration between the high school and middle school or junior high counselors. In helping students understand graduation requirements, it is necessary to teach them about credits (i.e., the curricular requirements necessary for graduation) and the grades needed to achieve credit in any given course. Figure 27.1 provides a sample handout used to explain graduation requirements. Additionally, Sill (1995) suggested that this early orientation should also address "honors requirements, vocational and college prep information, prerequisite information, and other items of interest" (p. 89).

GRADUATION REQUIREMENTS

Credit Rquirements	12 Required Credits
	11 Elective Credits
	23 Total Credits

Common Learnings	3.5 **English**
	1.0 9th Grade English
	1.0 10th Grade English
	0.5 Literature
	0.5 Composition
	0.5 Speech
	2.5 **Mathematics**
	2.5 **Science**
	2.5 **Social Studies**
	1.0 U.S. History
	0.5 Government
	0.5 **Physical Ed**
	0.5 **Health**
	0.5 **Computers Tech**
Electives	11 Elective Credits

FACTORS FOR ADMISSION CONSIDERATION

1. High school diploma from an accredited high school
2. Grades in academic subjects
3. Grade point average
4. Trend of grades
5. ACT and/or SAT scores
6. Extracurricular activities
7. Community service

RECOMMENT COLLEGE PREPERATORY PROGRAM

Course	Number of Credits	Comments
English	4	Writing emphasis
Math	4	Algebra 2 and Geometry
Science	3	Biological and Physical Science
Social Studies	3	US History and Government
Foreign Language	2	

FIGURE 27.1. Sample handout explaining graduation requirements.
Note: From U.S. Government Printing Office.

HIGH SCHOOL CURRICULAR PLANNING

Next, the majority of high schools require the preparation of an Educational Development Plan (EDP) for each student. In addition to ensuring that the EDP includes all graduation requirements, professional school counselors use the EDP process to assist students in selecting curricular options that will best meet their postsecondary educational and career plans. The preparation of an EDP may be accomplished through the individual planning or the guidance curriculum components of a comprehensive guidance and counseling program (Gysbers & Henderson, 2005).

However, many professional school counselors mistakenly believe that the individual planning activities must be accomplished through the use of individual sessions with students. Such a use of time is inefficient, given the high student–counselor ratios across the country, and the process of assisting with individual planning can also be achieved through the use of classroom and small-group meetings (Stanciak, 1995). Professional school counselors who are interested in quantifying time saved and/or the differential impact of providing individual planning services in classroom or small-group settings are referred to the section on impact analysis in Gysbers and Henderson (2005). Professional school counselors using a small-group format may wish to group students according to postsecondary plans in order to maximize their efficiency. For example, they may meet with students planning for vocational postsecondary training in one group, with students planning for community college in another group, and with students hoping for admission to 4-year colleges in yet another.

Regardless of a student's postsecondary plans, and regardless of the format in which a professional school counselor chooses to discuss EDPs, the EDP form itself is a primary tool. Figure 27.2 offers a sample EDP form. This form offers a simple way to assist students in (a) understanding and tracking their progress toward graduation requirements; (b) understanding general university admissions requirements; (c) recording and updating information about educational and career goals; and (d) planning specific coursework for Grades 9 through 12. Within the section General High School Credit Requirements, students are able to check boxes for each half credit earned in a given subject. This allows for a quick visual check on progress toward graduation requirements. Within the section General University Admissions Requirements, professional school counselors should caution students to verify these requirements with the specific colleges they are considering. The section on Career/Educational Goals should serve as a basis for course selection, and it is the professional school counselor's role to assist students in understanding what courses are best suited to the student's goals. Finally, the section reserved for planning specific coursework will need considerable attention. Each grade level has two columns, one for each semester. In assisting students with coursework planning, professional school counselors must be prepared to discuss with students the sequencing of classes, explain the importance of prerequisites, and offer insight regarding the coursework necessary for a variety of postsecondary educational and career plans.

Figures 27.3, 27.4, and 27.5 present sample EDPs that are designed to represent varying postsecondary educational and career plans. Figure 27.3, for example, provides

text continues on p. 286

EDUCATIONAL DEVELOPMENT PLAN

Name _____ Student # _____ Professional School Counselor _____ Grade _____
(last name, first name)

Career/Educational Goals from assessment results.

1. _____
2. _____

Possible Occupations/careers from selected pathway.

1. _____
2. _____
3. _____

Educational/Training Goals
___ High school diploma
___ Career/Technical Center certificate
___ On-the-job training
___ Apprenticeship
___ Trade & technical certification
___ Two-year associate's degree
___ Tech Prep (2+2, 2+4)
___ Four-year bachelor's degree
___ Master's degree
___ Doctoral degree
___ Military
___ Other

General High School Credit Requirements
12 Required Units of Credit
11 Elective Units of Credit
23 Units of Credit Total for Graduation

3-5 English
1.0 9th Grade English
1.0 10th Grade English
.5 Literature
.5 Composition
.5 Oral Communication

2.5 Mathematics

2.5 Science

2.5 Social Studies
1.0 Geography
1.0 U.S. History
.5 American Government

.5 Health

.5 Personal Fitness

General University Admissions

Required:
4.0 English
3.0 Mathematics
3.0 Science
3.0 History/Social Sciences

Recommended:
2.0 Foreign Language
2.0 Fine & Performing Arts
1.0 Computer Literacy

*Athletes Check NCAA Requirements

Grade 9	Grade 10	Grade 11	Grade 12

Alternate

Student Signature _____ Professional School Counselor Signature _____ Parent Signature _____

White - File   Yellow - Return with Parent Signature   Pink - Student

FIGURE 27.2. Educational development plan (EDP).

EDUCATIONAL DEVELOPMENT PLAN

Name ___Hansen, Joanie___ Student # ___000832___ Professional School Counselor ___Phillips___ Grade ___9___
(last name, first name)

Career/Educational Goals from assessment results.
1. 4 years of college plus graduate school
2. 4 years of college plus pharmacology school

Possible Occupations/careers from selected pathway.
1. Veterinarian
2. Pharmacist
3.

Educational/Training Goals
__ High school diploma
__ Career/Technical Center certificate
__ On-the-job training
__ Apprenticeship
__ Trade & technical certification
__ Two-year associate's degree
__ Tech Prep (2+2, 2+4)
__ Four-year bachelor's degree
__ Master's degree
_x_ Doctoral degree
__ Military
__ Other

General High School Credit Requirements
12 Required Units of Credit
11 Elective Units of Credit
23 Units of Credit Total for Graduation

3-5 English
1.0 9th Grade English
1.0 10th Grade English
.5 Literature
.5 Composition
.5 Oral Communication

2.5 Mathematics
2.5 Science
2.0 Foreign Language
1.0 Computer Literacy
2.5 Social Studies
1.0 Geography
1.0 U.S. History
.5 American Government

.5 Health
.5 Personal Fitness

General University Admissions

Required:
4.0 English
3.0 Mathematics
3.0 Science
3.0 History/Social Sciences

Recommended:
2.0 Fine & Performing Arts

*Athletes Check NCAA Requirements

Grade 9		Grade 10		Grade 11		Grade 12	
Acc. English 9	Acc. English 9	Acc. English 10	Acc. English 10	Acc. English 11	Acc. English 11	A P English	A P English
World History	World History	A P U.S. History	A P U.S. History	A P Government	A P Government	Indv. Life Sports	Community Service
Molecular Biology	Molecular Biology	Inorganic Chemistry	Inorganic Chemistry	A P Chemistry	A P Chemistry	A P Biology	A P Biology
Acc. Geometry	Acc. Geometry	Acc. Algebra2	Acc. Algebra 2	Acc. Analysis	Acc. Analysis	A P Calculus	A P Calculus
Physical Education	Information Tech	Health	Zoology	Physics	Physics	A P Physics	A P Physics
Spanish 1	Spanish 1	Spanish 2	Spanish 2	Yearbook	Yearbook	Yearbook	Yearbook
Alternate Chorus	Chorus	Orchestra	Orchestra	Info Tech 2	Journalism	Career Internship	Career Internship

Student Signature _____   Professional School Counselor Signature _____   Parent Signature _____

White - File   Yellow - Return with Parent Signature   Pink - Student

FIGURE 27.3. EDP for a student pursuing an advanced medical degree.

EDUCATIONAL DEVELOPMENT PLAN

Name ___Brady, Mike___   Student # ___000987___   Professional School Counselor ___Phillips___   Grade _9_
(last name, first name)

Career/Educational Goals from assessment results.
1. Associate's Degree
2. Trade & Technical Certification

Possible Occupations/careers from selected pathway.
1. Architectural Assistant
2. Computer Aided Designer
3.

Educational/Training Goals
— High school diploma
— Career/Technical Center certificate
— On-the-job training
— Apprenticeship
— Trade & technical certification
_X_ Two-year associate's degree
— Tech Prep (2+2, 2+4)
— Four-year bachelor's degree
— Master's degree
— Doctoral degree
— Military
— Other

General High School Credit Requirements
12 Required Units of Credit
11 Elective Units of Credit
23 Units of Credit Total for Graduation

3.5 English
1.0 9th Grade English
1.0 10th Grade English
.5 Literature
.5 Composition
.5 Oral Communication

2.5 Mathematics
2.5 Science
2.0 Foreign Language
1.0 Computer Literacy
2.5 Social Studies
1.0 Geography
1.0 U.S. History
.5 American Government

.5 Health
.5 Personal Fitness

General University Admissions

Required:
4.0 English
3.0 Mathematics
3.0 Science
3.0 History/Social Sciences

Recommended:
2.0 Fine & Performing Arts

*Athletes Check NCAA Requirements

Grade 9	Grade 10	Grade 11	Grade 12
English 9	English 10	Composition	Speech
Geography	U.S. History	Government	Psychology
Physical Science	Biology	Inorganic Chemistry	Physics
Algebra 1	Geometry	Algebra 2	Engineering Tech
Spanish 1	Spanish 2	Architectural Tech	Engineering Tech
Manufacturing Tech	Drafting 1	Architectural Tech	Co-Operative Training
Drawing 2	Team Sports	Photography 1	Information Tech
English 9	English 10	Mythology	Research Tech
Geography	U.S. History	Physical Education	Health
Physical Science	Biology	Inorganic Chemistry	Physics
Algebra 1	Geometry	Algebra 2	Engineering Tech
Spanish 1	Spanish 2	Architectural Tech	Engineering Tech
Applied Tech	Drafting 1	Architectural Tech	Co-Operative Training
Alternate Drawing 1	Swimming	Photography 2	Dual Enrollment

Student Signature _____   Professional School Counselor Signature _____   Parent Signature _____

White - File   Yellow - Return with Parent Signature   Pink - Student

FIGURE 27.4. EDP for a student pursuing an associate's degree.

EDUCATIONAL DEVELOPMENT PLAN

Name ___Keaton, Elyse___ Student # ___000452___ Professional School Counselor ___Phillips___ Grade _9_
   (last name, first name)

Career/Educational Goals from assessment results.
1. Employment after high school
2. Trade & Technical Certification

Possible Occupations/careers from selected pathway.
1. Child-Care Worker
2. Work in family business
3.

Educational/Training Goals
- X High school diploma
- __ Career/Technical Center certificate
- __ On-the-job training
- __ Apprenticeship
- __ Trade & technical certification
- __ Two-year associate's degree
- __ Tech Prep (2+2, 2+4)
- __ Four-year bachelor's degree
- __ Master's degree
- __ Doctoral degree
- __ Military
- __ Other

General High School Credit Requirements
- 12 Required Units of Credit
- 11 Elective Units of Credit
- **23 Units of Credit Total for Graduation**

3.5 English
- 1.0 9th Grade English
- 1.0 10th Grade English
- .5 Literature
- .5 Composition
- .5 Oral Communication

2.5 Mathematics

2.5 Science

2.5 Social Studies
- 1.0 Geography
- 1.0 U.S. History
- .5 American Government

- .5 Health
- .5 Personal Fitness

General University Admissions

Required:
- **4.0 English**
- **3.0 Mathematics**
- **3.0 Science**
- **3.0 History/Social Sciences**

Recommended:
- **2.0 Foreign Language**
- **2.0 Fine & Performing Arts**
- **1.0 Computer Literacy**

*Athletes Check NCAA Requirements

Grade 9	Grade 10	Grade 11		Grade 12	
English 9	English 10	Composition	Short Stories	Speech	Research
Geography	U.S. History	Government	Physical Education	Psychology	Sociology
Physical Science	Biology	Hydrology	Information Tech 1	Health	Personal Finance
Algebra 1	Geometry	Cont. Algebra 2	Algebra 2	Marketing	Entrepreneur
Spanish 1	Spanish 2	Choir	Choir	Choir	Choir
Choir	Child Development	Child Care Professional	Child Care Professional	Child Care Cooperative	Child Care Cooperative
Alternate Info Tech 1	Info Tech 2	Photography 1	Photography 2	Community Service	Office Assistant	Family Living	Life Management

Student Signature _____ Professional School Counselor Signature _____ Parent Signature _____

White - File   Yellow - Return with Parent Signature   Pink - Student

FIGURE 27.5. EDP for a student pursuing a career in child care or business.

an EDP for Joanie Hansen, a student intent on pursuing a doctoral degree in veterinary medicine or pharmacology. Figure 27.4 provides an EDP for Mike Brady, a student interested in earning an associate's degree to become an architectural assistant or a computer-aided designer. Figure 27.5 offers an EDP for Elyse Keaton, a student intending to either work in child care or in her family's business immediately following high school graduation. In comparing the three completed example EDPs in Figures 27.3, 27.4, and 27.5, one will note significant differences in course planning. These differences involve both the level of courses planned and the type of courses selected. With regard to the level of courses planned, for example, Joanie's professional school counselor strongly encouraged her to take high-level math classes throughout high school, because she is planning to pursue a doctorate in a medical field. Because Joanie is scheduled to take Accelerated Geometry as a freshman, Joanie will need to have taken prerequisite coursework during middle school. This highlights the importance of early interventions to assist with educational and career planning during middle and even elementary school. In comparison to Joanie's math schedule, both Mike and Elyse have planned to take Algebra I during their freshman year.

The professional school counselor will have worked with these students to assist them in identifying classes related to their postsecondary educational and career plans. Although the majority of classes are selected for the purpose of meeting graduation requirements and of ensuring a well-rounded education for each student, there invariably exists room for electives. The choice of electives, therefore, can and should allow students to explore more deeply their tentative postsecondary plans. As an illustration, Mike Brady has expressed interest in both architecture and computer-aided design. In consultation with his professional school counselor, Mike has therefore chosen courses such as manufacturing technology, drafting, and architectural technology as electives. This can be contrasted with Elyse's choice of child development, child care co-op, marketing, and personal finance. Each of these electives is intended to assist Elyse in exploring possible careers in child care and in business.

TURNING VISION INTO REALITY

Once the initial EDP has been developed, students are equipped with a road map to a set of possible postsecondary destinations. As students begin taking courses in accordance with their EDP, they will have an opportunity to reaffirm or question their initial postsecondary plans. Again, their reaction may be to the level of difficulty associated with the courses or to the topics addressed in their courses. Additionally, because students are developing and maturing, it is also possible that their interests may change, and as a consequence, it is essential that the educational planning process continue well beyond the completion of the EDP. Professional school counselors will need to periodically meet with students to check on the goodness of fit between the students' EDPs and their developing self-awareness and postsecondary interests and plans. As goals change, of course, it will be appropriate to update the EDP to reflect new postsecondary goals and to identify courses appropriate to the new plans. As the vision changes, a new route must be charted in order to assist the students in turning their vision into reality.

CONTINUED CAREER DEVELOPMENT

In addition to responding to changes in student goals that develop as a result of coursework and maturation, professional school counselors also proactively work with students to facilitate continued career development. They may do so in a variety of ways: through curriculum guidance units delivered in classroom settings, through a school-based career development center, through after-school seminars offered to students and their parents, through guest speakers, and through job-shadowing programs. With regard to curriculum guidance units, ASCA (2005) and the National Career Development Association (National Occupational Information Coordinating Committee, 2004) each offered a set of competencies specific to the needs of K–12 students.

School-based career development centers are also common in high schools. Most often, these centers are staffed by a career development specialist or by a professional school counselor. The centers tend to offer a wide variety of career-related resources, including college applications and catalogs, information on scholarships and financial aid, literature about other postsecondary training options, resources about a wide variety of careers, information related to résumé writing and successful interviewing, and employment information.

EDUCATIONAL PLANNING FOR POSTSECONDARY OPTIONS

To guide students and their families through the process of postsecondary educational planning, a wise professional school counselor will begin early rather than waiting for the "senior stampede." Without such systematic planning, professional school counselors will find that, as students near graduation, they and their parents frequently flood into the counseling office, desperate for assistance in finding the right colleges with which to apply, the right training programs to attend, or the right branch of the military in which to serve. Despite even the most careful educational planning process for the EDPs, these students and their parents tend to experience the planning process for postsecondary options as critical to their future. Therefore, specific activities targeting postsecondary educational planning are essential for the high school counselor.

One common method of providing guidance is by offering after-school seminars on topics such as career nights, college nights, and financial aid nights. For each seminar, professional school counselors may serve either as facilitators/coordinators or presenters. Additional topics frequently addressed in after-school or in-school seminars involve military educational and career opportunities, vocational training opportunities, and NCAA requirements for Division I eligibility. Finally, professional school counselors frequently coordinate job-shadowing programs to facilitate student exploration of possible career options. Each of these career development opportunities assists students in testing their initial aspirations and interests against reality.

Another method involves the professional school counselor's library of postsecondary resources. Although such libraries have historically consisted of shelves and shelves of books and college catalogs, technology now allows for Internet-based resources as well. Many school counseling departments now manage a Web site on which students and families can access a wealth of information regarding the postsecondary educational planning process. (For an example of one such Web site, see http://www .communityhigh.org/counseling)

Technological advances have also resulted in significant changes in school-based career centers (Refvem, 2000; Sabella, 2003), as centers now also tend to feature computers equipped with career-related software programs or access to Internet sites relevant to career exploration and planning. Examples of widely used programs include *Career Cruising* (2006), *SIGI*[3] (Valpar International Corporation, 2006), *DISCOVER* (American College Testing Program, 2006) and *CX Online* (Bridges.com, 2006).

Most school counseling departments also periodically publish a newsletter, either in hard copy or electronic format, and this is an outstanding way to heighten student and family awareness of issues related to postsecondary planning. It is useful to include sections in the newsletter dedicated to each grade level and to provide postsecondary planning advice for each grade level in each respective section.

Professional school counselors will want to meet with all juniors to discuss their academic record and their preliminary ideas regarding postsecondary options and to provide them with information regarding college entrance examinations and the college search process. Often, they seek the "perfect" option. To assist students, parents, and even fellow professional school counselors in managing this process, Boshoven (2003) cautioned that there is not necessarily a single perfect college or postsecondary training option.

Adapting Mathews' (2003) metaphor likening the college search to a search for a house, Boshoven (2003) suggested that selecting a postsecondary training option is similar to buying a coat. He specifically challenged the notion that there is a perfect college that is somehow perfect for everyone and suggests that colleges, like coats, are not "one size fits all" (p. 8). In working with students and families, he strives to help them find the best fit for them personally rather than applying to the schools to which everyone else wants to go. To assist them, Boshoven encourages students and parents to consider the factors related to a goodness of fit. As part of finding the best fit, Boshoven identified the additional factors of feel, fashion/flair, fiscal and other factors as they pertain not only to buying a coat but also to selecting a college or other form of postsecondary education.

In Boshoven's (2003) conceptualization, "fit" may refer to a school's size, geographic location, curricular offerings, extracurricular opportunities, political atmosphere, religious affiliation, or presence of a Greek (fraternity, sorority) system. The "feel" dimension is best captured by student comments such as "the first time I visited, it just felt right!" (p. 8). "Fashion/flair" refers to matching the style of a student to the style of the school. This may relate to average incoming grades and standardized test scores or to career options such as astrophysics, culinary schools, building trades or premed. He cautioned that the fashion/flair of a school needs to suit the specific student, not the student's friends or family members.

The "fiscal" factor, of course, is a pragmatic factor often considered paramount by families as they anticipate the expense of postsecondary educational options. Professional school counselors do not need to become privy to the details of a family's financial situation, but it is essential that a discussion occur between the student approaching graduation and parents so that the student understands clearly to what degree parents can and will contribute to the costs of postsecondary education. In addition, professional school counselors should educate students and parents about other elements related to financing college. Financial aid workshops are a popular way of doing so, and these workshops should not only include assistance with the completion of the *Free Application for Federal Student Aid* (FAFSA) but should also include a discussion of other issues. Boshoven (2003) offered the following observations:

- Scholarships are available.
- "Private colleges give more money in aid than public universities" (p. 9).
- "Community colleges are less expensive and can offer a number of scholarships" (p. 9).
- Students can work during summers and during the school year to earn money toward the cost of their education.
- Students may look for jobs in which their employers will assist them with the costs of additional education or training.
- Students may consider loans as an option.
- The military, though costing in time, does offer free education.
- Sometimes you get what you pay for. Before gravitating toward the least expensive option, consider factors such as class size and the percentage of courses taught by professors as opposed to teaching assistants.

DEVELOPING YOUR OWN EXPERTISE AS A PROFESSIONAL SCHOOL COUNSELOR

In order to be effective in helping students find the "best fit" for postsecondary education, it is essential that professional school counselors develop their own expertise in this area. Fortunately, there are a wide variety of print resources available. Figure 27.6 provides an annotated listing of recommended readings. In addition to relying upon print resources, professional school counselors will want to maintain membership in several professional associations that regularly provide support in the area of educational planning. Figure 27.7 provides a partial listing of such organizations.

SUMMARY/CONCLUSION

In this chapter, we provided an overview of the educational planning process and offered specific ideas about the integration of educational planning services into an already existing school counseling program. We emphasized the inextricable link between career development and educational planning and encouraged professional school counselors to incorporate educational planning into their career exploration, development, and planning activities. Toward this end, we recommend helping students explore their interests, skills, values, and personality; facilitating student exploration and selection of career pathways; assisting students with development of an Educational Development Plan (EDP) that is consistent with their preferred career pathway(s); and providing substantial guidance related to postsecondary educational planning. Finally, we emphasized the importance of involving parents and families in the overall process of career development and educational planning.

AUCC Publications. (2006). *Directory of Canadian Universities* (40th ed.). Ottawa, Ontario: Author.

This is a dry but complete listing of programs at Canadian universities.

Antonoff, S. R. (1999). *The College Finder.* New York: Fawcett Books.

This little gem serves students as the book of college trivia, from kosher kitchens to ping pong and debate championships. It is arranged topically and by school.

Antonoff, S. R., & Friedmann, M. A. (2006). *College Match* (9th ed.). Alexandria, VA: Octameron Associates.

This is a 150 page, ultra-practical, step-by-step guide for the college bound student and family.

Asher, D. (2000). *Cool Colleges For The Hyper-Intelligent, Self-Directed, Late Blooming, and Just Plain Different.* Toronto: Ten Speed Press.

This is a nice guide for those "out-of-the-boxers."

Barron's Educational Series. (Ed.). (2006). *Profiles of American Colleges With CD-ROM* (27th ed.). Hauppaugh, NY: Author.

This is an annual compendium that gives general statistics and overviews of colleges and students.

Coburn, K. L., & Treeger, M. L. (1997). *Letting Go: A Parent's Guide to Understanding the College Years.* New York: HarperCollins.

This classic book helps parents and students identify and deal with all the emotional issues of separation and change.

College Bound Sports. (2005). *The High School Athlete's Guide to College Sports: How to Market Yourself to the School of Your Dreams.* Lanham, MD: Taylor Trade.

This is a useful guide for the high school athlete and helps guide them through the complexities of their applications to college.

Dance Magazine. (2005). *Dance Magazine College Guide.* Oakland, CA: Author.

This is a helpful annual guide of programs and contacts for students interested in a career related to dance.

Everett, C. J., & Topaz, M. (1998). *Guide to Performing Arts Programs.* New York: Princeton Review.

For our singers, dancers, and thespians, a guide to assist in finding summer programs and college options.

Fiske, E. B. (2006). *The Fiske Guide to Colleges 2006.* Naperville, IL: Sourcebooks.

This annual guide is written by the former Education Writer for *The New York Times* and is Boshoven's favorite source for looking at great U.S. and Canadian colleges and universities.

Fiske, E. B., & Hammond, B. G. (2001). *Getting Into the Right College* (2nd ed.). Naperville, IL: Sourcebooks.

FIGURE 27.6. Annotated listing of recommended readings for professional school counselors. *Note.* The Octameron Series features 16 handy and inexpensive guides covering various college counseling questions. The complete set is available at a discount at http://www.octameron.com

A beach read, this tome is written in a practical, sensible manner, allowing students to examine themselves and picking types of colleges that may "match" them best.

Fiske, E. B., & Hammond, B. G. (2005). *Fiske What To Do When For College 2005-2006: A Student and Parent's Guide to Deadlines, Planning and the Last Two Years of High School*. Naperville, IL: Sourcebooks.

For those students needing definite structure in accomplishing the tasks needed to accomplish the college application process, this little guide can definitely help.

Franek, R., et al. (2003). *The Best Midwestern Colleges: 150 Great Schools to Consider*. New York: Princeton Review.

A companion to the *Fiske Guide*, these regional books describe the student and academic life of a wider range of selective regional colleges and universities.

Greene, R., (2001). *The Teenager's Guide to School Outside the Box*. Minneapolis, MN: Free Spirit.

Free-spirited students tend to appreciate a book that attempts to engage them in the college process. One student beamed, "You mean there is a college just right for liberal me?"

Hall, C., & Lieber, R. (1996). *Taking Time Off: Inspired Stories of Students Who Enjoyed Successful Breaks From College and How to Plan Your Own*. New York: The Noonday Press.

Not every student is ready to launch off to college. This book offers good rationale and options for spending productive time between high school and college.

Hammond, B. G. (2005). *Discounts and Deals at the Nation's 360 Best Colleges*. New York: St. Martin's Griffin.

College is expensive, and families need our help in aiming them at possible scholarships.

Killpatrick, F., & Killpatrick, J. (2002). *The Winning Edge: The Student-Athlete's Guide To College Sports*. Alexandria, VA: Octameron Associates.

Athletes have double the work in applying to college but also have some definite advantages in admission. The handy guide will help in making sure they've thought of everything.

Kravets, M. B., & Wax, I. F. (2003). *The K & W Guide to Colleges for the Learning Disabled* (7th ed.). New York: Princeton Review.

An essential resource for assisting students who learn differently with the postsecondary educational planning process. Finding appropriate support at college can be the difference between success and failure.

Leider, A. (2005). *Don't Miss Out: The Ambitious Student's Guide to Financial Aid* (30th ed.). Alexandria, VA: Octameron Associates.

There's money out there for students willing to work to find it. Here's a helpful start.

Leider, A. (2000). *I Am Somebody: College Knowledge for At-Risk Students* (9th ed.). Alexandria, VA: Octameron Associates.

A friendly little guide for students wondering if college is appropriate.

(continues)

FIGURE 27.6. *Continued.*

Leider, A. (2005). *The A's & B's of Academic Scholarships* (25th ed.). Alexandria, VA: Octameron Associates.

Merit scholarships are available at many colleges and universities, and this resource provides a helpful and manageable listing of them.

Mathews, J. (2003). *Harvard Schmarvard: Getting Beyond the Ivy League to the College That's Best for You.* New York: Prima.

The education writer for the *Washington Post* restates Loren Pope's points well.

Mayher, B. (1998). *The College Admissions Mystique.* New York: Noonday Press.

This expose reveals Brown's strategies for becoming the "hot" Ivy League college prospect and explores the psychology of college admissions marketing.

Pasisk, P. (1998). *Almost Grown: Launching Your Child From High School to College.* New York: Norton.

This is an outstanding "dealing-with-emotions" book in which the author chronicles her and her son's angst in preparing for the launch to college.

Pintoff, E. (1994). *The Complete Guide to American Film Schools and Cinema and Television Courses.* New York: Penguin Books.

Although dated, this book provides a good description of the various options for artsy, more hands-on learners.

Pope, L. (2006). *Colleges That Change Lives: 40 Schools You Should Know About Even if You're Not A Straight-A-Student* (3rd ed.). New York: Penguin Books.

This should be required reading for all students and families. The author examines the fit of colleges and the mission of state universities and private colleges.

Pope, L. (2007). *Looking Beyond the Ivy League: Finding the College That's Right for You* (2nd ed.). New York: Penguin Books.

Pope's research about colleges and the difference they can make if the right fit is there.

Re, J. M. (2005). *Financial Aid Financer: Expert Answers to College Financing Questions* (17th ed.). Alexandria, VA: Octameron Associates.

Parents get nervous about the costs of college. Here's a handy book to guide them in finding money that may be available to help them .

Ripple, G. G. (2001). *Campus Pursuit: Making the Most of Your Visit and Interview* (9th ed.). Alexandria, VA: Octameron Associates.

This is a helpful guide to help students learn to "kick the tires" and make the most of a campus visit.

Rogers Publishing, Ltd. (2006). *Maclean's Guide to Canadian Universities.* Toronto, Ontario: Author.

Although the rankings are suspect, the program descriptions are valuable.

Rubenstone, S., & Dalby, S. (2002). *College Admissions: A Crash Course for Panicked Parents* (3rd ed.). Lawrenceville, NJ: Thomson Peterson's.

This sensible guide is a terrific reference for families wondering what to do and when to do it.

FIGURE 27.6. *Continued.*

Rugg, F. E. (2006). *Rugg's recommendations on the colleges* (23rd ed.). Fallbrook, CA: Ruggs Recommendations.

This trade publication can help counselors get college lists started for students with particular academic interests.

Seghers, L. (Ed.). (2005). *Peterson's Professional Degree Programs in the Visual & Performing Arts 2006*. Lawrenceville, NJ: Thomson Peterson's.

A specific guide for artists and performers.

Steinberg, J. (2002). *The Gatekeepers: Inside the Admissions Process of a Premier College*. New York: Penguin Books.

Not for the faint of heart, this scary book highlights the subjective world of the admissions office of Wesleyan University.

Suskind, R. (1999). *A Hope in the Unseen: An American Odyssey From the Inner City to the Ivy League*. New York: Broadway Books.

This sensitive book follows a first generation African American student in an Ivy League college.

Thacker, L. (2004). *College Unranked: Affirming Educational Values in College Admissions*. Portland, OR: The Education Conservancy.

This book normalizes student confusion about the college admissions process. In it, seasoned admissions folks put it all into perspective.

The College Board. (2004). *The College Board Index of Majors & Graduate Degrees 2004: All-New Twenty-Sixth Edition*. New York: Author.

What college offers what major? The complete list by subject relates to the college search engine on their Web site.

Wildavsky, B. (2004). *Ultimate Guide to Becoming a Teacher*. Naperville, IL: Sourcebooks.

This is a helpful listing of teacher-preparation programs in colleges and universities.

Yale Daily News. (2006). *The Insider's Guide to the Colleges* (32nd ed.). New York: St. Martin's Griffin.

Students like the gritty social-life reviews, but counselors find the reviews inconsistent and slanted.

FIGURE 27.6. *Continued.*

(Note: See the CD-ROM for a list of references.)

American Counseling Association

5999 Stevenson Ave. Alexandria, VA 22304

800/347-6647

http://www.counseling.org

The American Counseling Association (ACA) is a not-for-profit, professional and educa-tional organization that is dedicated to the growth and enhancement of the counseling profession. Founded in 1952, ACA is the world's largest association, exclusively represent-ing professional counselors in various practice settings. By providing leadership training, publications, continuing education opportunities, and advocacy services to nearly 45,000 members, ACA helps counseling professionals develop their skills and expand their knowl-edge base. ACA has been instrumental in setting professional and ethical standards for the counseling profession. The association has made considerable strides in accredita-tion, licensure, and national certification. It also represents the interests of the profession before Congress and federal agencies, and strives to promote recognition of professional counselors to the public and the media. One of the two general organizations serving pro-fessional school counselors, the national organization sponsors local and state branches that are instrumental in networking and professional development opportunities.

American School Counselor Association

1101 King St., Suite 625

Alexandria, VA 22314

703/683-ASCA or 800/306-4722

http://www.schoolcounselor.org

The American School Counselor Association (ASCA) supports professional school coun-selors' efforts to help students focus on academic, personal–social, and career develop-ment so they achieve success in school and are prepared to lead fulfilling lives as respon-sible members of society. ASCA provides professional development, publications and other resources, research and advocacy to more than 18,000 professional school coun-selors around the globe. The other professional association specializing in serving school counselors, ASCA sponsors local and state branches that are instrumental in networking and professional development opportunities.

National Association for College Admission Counseling

1631 Prince Street

Alexandria, VA 22314-2828

703/836-2222

http://www.nacacnet.org

The National Association for College Admission Counseling (NACAC) is an organization of more than 10,000 professionals from around the world, dedicated to serving students as they make choices about pursuing postsecondary education. NACAC is committed to maintaining high standards that foster ethical and social responsibility among those involved in the transition process, as outlined in the NACAC Statement of Principles of Good Practice (SPGP). NACAC's award-winning publications and other media resources, professional development programs and practical research efforts have all been designed to give counseling and admission professionals the tools they need to improve the coun-seling services they provide to students. NACAC sponsors many college and performing arts fairs nationwide and beyond. The Web site is a valuable resource for counselors, and the E-List helps counselors connect with questions and resources.

FIGURE 27.7. National organizational resources for professional school counselors.

CHAPTER 28

DIRECT BEHAVIORAL CONSULTATION: AN EFFECTIVE METHOD FOR PROMOTING SCHOOL COLLABORATION

T. Steuart Watson, Tonya S. Watson, and Adam D. Weaver

Preview

As specified in the American School Counselor Association (ASCA) guidelines, consultation is one of the major roles of professional school counselors. Direct behavioral consultation (DBC) is one of the most effective types of consultation and will assist in more efficiently helping the large number of students with diverse concerns.

According to the guidelines of the American School Counselor Association (ASCA), primary roles of the professional school counselor include counseling/therapy, consulting, and coordinating services to help students achieve maximum academic potential (Dunn & Baker, 2002; Lum, 2001). Professional school counselors are also required to make referrals to other professionals, serve on interdisciplinary teams, and help ensure school safety (Casey-Cannon, Hayward, & Gowen, 2001). Although ASCA recommends a counselor-to-student ratio of 1:250 (Lum, 2001), actual ratios are typically much higher (Astramovich & Holden, 2002).

Although there are many avenues by which students come to the professional school counselor for services, office referrals are one of the most common. Sugai, Sprague, and Horner (2000), for example, found that the number of daily office referrals increased with the age of students and that almost half of their middle school sample had been referred to the office at least once during the school year. By the time a student is referred from the office to the professional school counselor, the classroom teacher and principal (or another administrator) have spent considerable time addressing the problem. Providing assistance to teachers before they make numerous office referrals would result in less time that teachers and administrators spend "disciplining" or "fixing" the problem and increase the student's amount of academic-engaged time.

Schools are legally mandated to serve the increasing number of students who are identified as having disabilities. It is estimated that approximately 1% to 18% of the school-age population qualified as having a disability (Parrish, 1999; Wood & Baker, 2002). Perhaps more troubling than the percentage of students identified as having disabilities is the upward trajectory over the past 20 years of the numbers of students being diagnosed with some type of educational disability (Snyder & Hoffman, 2001). Students with disabilities are at greater risk of developing academic or behavior problems that are both related and unrelated to their particular disability (Rosenberg, Wilson, Maheady, & Sindelar, 1992). Thus, students with a wide range of disabilities may be referred to the professional school counselor for assistance. In some instances, professional school counselors are in charge of coordinating services for students with disabilities (Wood &

Baker, 2002). A recent survey of elementary school counselors found that being a consultant and problem solver was a frequently perceived expectation by significant others in the educational setting (e.g., teachers, parents, administrators, students) and by counselors themselves when working with children with disabilities (Dunn & Baker, 2002).

In addition to providing the aforementioned services, professional school counselors are often obligated to perform many tasks such as clerical, scheduling, disciplining, or other administrative duties that are not part of their professional association job description (Fitch, Newby, Ballestero, & Marshall, 2001). Studies indicated that typical counselors spend approximately 50% of their time devoted to actual guidance and counseling services (Partin, 1993). However, ASCA explicitly stated that professional school counselors should spend 70% of their time providing direct services to students.

As the school counseling profession calls for counselors to have more skills (Herr, 2002) and to work with an increasing number of students, professional school counselors need an efficient method for interacting with teachers that alleviates a problem before an inordinate amount of teacher and administrator time is spent trying to solve the problem. By consulting (i.e., collaborating) with teachers, professional school counselors can assist teachers in improving their overall behavior management and instructional skills and increase their ability to more effectively deal with classroom problems as they occur.

CONSULTATION IN SCHOOLS

Teachers are faced with a number of challenges in today's classrooms. In addition to meeting the educational needs of their class as a whole, they are often called upon to meet additional and specific academic, behavioral, and emotional needs of students. Many times, however, teacher training programs, in an effort to provide a breadth of training in general educational practices, fail to adequately prepare teachers to meet these additional needs when they arise (Watson, 1994). As a result, there is an increasing need for teachers to collaborate and consult with other professionals including professional school counselors, school psychologists, and school social workers (Dougherty, 2000). Federal and state legislation mandating the inclusion of students with mental, emotional, and physical disabilities have increased interest in consultation and collaboration services as well (Noell & Witt, 1999).

Professional school counselors have long worked with general education teachers to enhance academic and social skills and to prevent special education placement (Gutkin & Curtis, 1999; Noell & Witt, 1999). Generally, the focus has been on academic and behavior challenges (e.g., reading difficulties, inattention, talking out, noncompliance). However, there are many additional areas in which professional school counselors may be asked to assist. These may include mental health concerns (e.g., depression, anxiety) and students adjusting to physical disabilities. In addition, teachers may turn to professional school counselors for assistance in cases when physical or sexual abuse is suspected or when they suspect a student may be involved in unhealthy activities such as substance abuse or promiscuous sex (Lockhart & Keys, 1998).

Referrals such as those listed will generally take one of two tracks. In some cases, it will be determined that the student's needs would best be met through counseling.

In such cases, the professional school counselor provides direct service to the student, either through individual or group counseling, and the teacher shoulders little or no responsibility for intervention. However, in other cases, the determination is made that the student's needs would best be met through a classroom-based intervention. In these cases, the professional school counselor indirectly provides service to the student through consultation or collaboration with that student's teacher.

The primary goal of consulting with teachers is to clarify and resolve the presenting problem (Gutkin & Curtis, 1999; Watson & Sterling-Turner, 2004). When consulting with teachers, it is assumed that there is shared expertise and responsibility for assessment and treatment of the problem. It is important to remember that consultation is an indirect service delivery model in which the consultee (i.e., teacher) is responsible for carrying out the intervention while the consultant (i.e., professional school counselor) provides the expertise and is responsible for the integrity of the process (Gutkin & Curtis, 1999). A secondary yet very important goal of consultation is to improve the functioning of the consultee, whereby the skills taught during the consultation process will be available in future situations (Dougherty, 2000; Gutkin & Curtis, 1999).

Generally, the professional school counselor's response to student referrals has been to assess the situation through interviews with teacher and student, and occasionally to augment this information with direct observation of the student in the classroom setting (Fall, 1995; Myers, Shoffner, & Briggs, 2002; Sandoval, 2002). Individual counseling with the student has traditionally been seen as the most prominent and important means of benefiting the student (Jackson, 2000; Morse & Russell, 1988). In many cases, individual or group counseling may be an appropriate intervention. However, there are times when the best intervention may be for the teacher to change his or her behavior in response to the problem behaviors of the student (Alberto, & Troutman, 1995; Fall, 1995; Gutkin & Curtis, 1999; Tingstrom & Edwards, 1989).

There are a number of concerns associated with the process of consulting with teachers. First, although consultation is conceptualized as a voluntary activity (Zins, Kratochwill, & Elliott, 1993), this may not be the case in every instance. There are occasions when a teacher may be required by an administrator to work with a professional school counselor. In such cases, there may be significant resistance—either overt or covert—on the part of the teacher to engage in the consultation process. Thus, it is important to be skilled not only in problem-solving and consultation but also in overcoming teacher resistance (Butler, Weaver, Doggett, & Watson, 2002).

Second, when the intervention calls for behavior change on the part of the teacher, there is often the belief on the part of consultants that teachers possess the skills that are required to effectively implement interventions (Noell & Witt, 1999; Watson & Robinson, 1996). However, even the most willing teacher will demonstrate poor treatment integrity if he or she lacks the ability or skills to carry out the intervention (Watson, 2004).

Finally, without a clearly defined means and method of data collection, it is extremely difficult to gauge and document progress in treating the problem behavior. Thus, assessment and treatment approaches that rely strictly on verbal interaction between the consultant and the teacher or student often make it difficult to evaluate the success of the intervention. Conversely, the success of the treatment or the need to adjust treatment is more easily evaluated if data have been collected throughout the consultation process (Foster, Watson, Meeks, & Young, 2002). The following sections will outline an empirically supported consultation model and will describe a means of alleviating many of the previously described concerns.

BEHAVIORAL CONSULTATION

Behavioral consultation (BC) is the most popular model of consultation used in schools (Freer & Watson, 1999; Gutkin & Curtis, 1999). In this consultation model, a professional school counselor assists a teacher in changing a student's behavior. The role of the counselor is to teach skills to the teacher that will aid in the problem-solving process (Sterling-Turner, Watson, & Moore, 2002; Sterling-Turner, Watson, Wildmon, Watkins, & Little, 2001; Watson & Robinson, 1996).

The interaction between the professional counselor and teacher is almost completely verbal, as the counselor and the teacher discuss the problem behavior and the counselor verbally describes procedures for an intervention. However, teachers often lack the skills or knowledge to effectively carry out an intervention (Sterling-Turner et al., 2001). Research has shown that when teachers were trained with verbal instructions, they were not able to identify and analyze problems as accurately as teachers who were trained with modeling and rehearsal methods (Watson & Kramer, 1995). Also, if the teacher is not observed for treatment accuracy and consistency, then it is impossible to determine if treatment failure was due to the intervention or the failure to carry out the treatment properly (Gresham, 1989; Watson, 2004). Therefore, the role of the professional school counselor should include a more direct role so that teachers can be appropriately trained to address problem behaviors observed in the classroom (Watson & Robinson, 1996).

DIRECT BEHAVIORAL CONSULTATION

The goals of both traditional and direct behavioral consultation (DBC) include (a) identifying the problem behavior and (b) providing teachers with skills that will help in the current and future cases. The difference in the models is evident in the way that the goals are achieved. In traditional behavioral consultation, the professional school counselor trains the teacher with verbal instructions. In DBC, the professional school counselor models the procedure for the teacher and allows the teacher to rehearse the procedure while receiving positive and corrective feedback (Watson & Robinson, 1996). Findings have indicated that when teachers are trained with the DBC model they are more likely to implement the intervention consistently and accurately than when they are trained with the traditional behavioral consultation model (Sterling-Turner et al., 2001; Sterling-Turner et al., 2002).

DBC includes describing the procedures to the teacher, modeling the procedure with the teacher, and then allowing the teacher to rehearse with the child while receiving corrective and positive feedback (Watson & Robinson, 1996). The four stages used in the DBC model are identical to the stages used in the behavioral consultation model: (1) problem identification, (2) problem analysis, (3) plan implementation, and (4) plan evaluation. The differences between the models occur in the role of the professional school counselor at each stage. For a graphic flowchart description of the direct behavioral consultation process, see Figure 28.1.

PROBLEM IDENTIFICATION

The professional school counselor begins by interviewing the teacher about the child's behavior so that the target behavior can be selected and defined. To assess the accuracy in the description of the behavior by the teacher, the counselor then observes the child in the natural setting. This allows the counselor to compare observation of the child's behavior to that reported by the teacher. The professional school counselor can then confirm or disconfirm the teacher's report of the problem behavior.

Direct observation of the child also allows the professional school counselor to collect reliable baseline data and model for the teacher how to accurately record the child's behavior. The data collected also serves as a means for the counselor to form hypotheses on the function of the behavior and plan a functional assessment for the next stage of the consultation process. (For a variety of forms that are useful for interviewing teachers and conducting direct observations, see Watson & Steege, 2003.)

PROBLEM ANALYSIS

One of the roles of the professional school counselor is to provide a rationale for conducting a functional assessment. This is done by explaining that this procedure aids in the understanding of why the child is engaging in the behavior and in determining the environmental variables or skills that need to be modified to change the child's behavior. The counselor then models the functional assessment procedures with the teacher. Finally, the teacher practices the procedure while receiving feedback from the counselor.

PLAN IMPLEMENTATION

The professional school counselor's role in this stage is to ensure that the treatment is understood and carried out correctly by the teacher. There are two primary reasons for failure by the teacher to implement the intervention in this stage: the teacher lacks the needed skills, or the teacher has the skills needed but fails to implement the intervention. The counselor should make no assumptions about the teacher's ability to implement the intervention. The collaboratively derived treatment should always be modeled for the teacher followed by the opportunity to rehearse while receiving feedback from the counselor. The professional school counselor may then fade his or her role once the teacher has demonstrated competence at carrying out the plan.

PLAN EVALUATION

Because the teacher has been trained in data collection, he or she can now collect data during the treatment process. The role of the professional school counselor is to monitor the teacher's data collection periodically for reliability purposes and to aid in the modification of the intervention as needed.

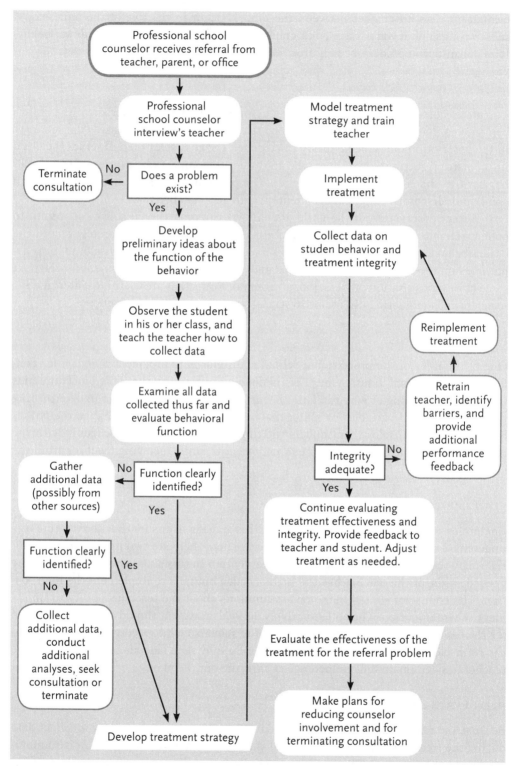

Figure 28.1. A graphic representation of the steps and consultant responsibilities associated with the steps of direct behavioral consultation (DBC).

CASE STUDY USING THE DBC MODEL

Susan, a third-grade teacher, requested that the professional school counselor assist her with Josh, an 8-year-old in her class. During the interview, Susan defined the problem behavior as "aggressive outbursts." The counselor then observed Josh in the classroom and discovered that the aggressive outbursts occurred infrequently when compared to his refusal to complete academic tasks. The counselor explained to the teacher that the problem behavior appeared to be Josh's work refusal, which occurred frequently throughout the day and most always preceded the aggressive outbursts. The teacher agreed that it did create problems for the class when he refused to do his work.

The professional school counselor then designed a recording system to collect baseline data (Foster et al., 2002), explained the recording system to the teacher, and modeled how to accurately record Josh's work refusal behavior. Following the modeling, the teacher began recording the behavior while receiving feedback from the counselor. Based on the baseline data, the professional school counselor and teacher established a treatment goal for the target behavior.

The professional school counselor then explained that the next step was to conduct a direct descriptive functional assessment to better understand why Josh engages in work refusal and what environmental variables could be changed in the classroom to modify his behavior (Watson & Steege, 2003). Based on their direct behavioral observations and structured interviews, the teacher and counselor hypothesized that escape from the task was maintaining Josh's work refusal. Examination of work samples indicated that Josh had the skills to do the tasks that were being presented to him. The counselor explained the findings to the teacher and modeled the intervention that involved escape extinction (not allowing Josh to escape his work contingent upon his refusal to do tasks) and differential reinforcement (allowing Josh brief breaks and access to more highly preferred activities for brief periods of time) when he completed shortened assignments. As he became more proficient at completing assignments without refusing and showing aggressive behavior, the length of the tasks was gradually increased. The teacher then practiced the intervention with Josh while being coached and given feedback by the professional school counselor. Performance feedback, by itself, has been shown in a number of studies to improve treatment integrity and student outcome (Noell et al., 2000; Noell et al., 2005).

The intervention involving extinction and differential reinforcement was sufficiently effective for reducing the frequency of work refusal such that modification of the treatment was not needed. The teacher was also able to use the skills obtained from the consultation process to implement the intervention with other students displaying problem behaviors.

Summary/Conclusion

There is a greater need and demand for school-based collaboration than ever before (Gutkin & Curtis, 1999). Because of the abundance and diversity of needs represented in the educational system, and the increasing role of professional school counselors in meeting those needs, it is critical that professional school counselors have at their disposal not only skills in implementing effective interventions but also the skills necessary to function effectively as collaborators with other school-based personnel. One of the most efficient and effective means of promoting collaboration is through consultation—more specifically, through direct behavioral consultation.

There are a number of potential pitfalls in the consultation process. Specifically, difficulties may arise in the form of consultee resistance and poor treatment integrity and evaluation resulting from skill deficiencies on the part of the consultee in treatment implementation and data collection. The consultant should remain aware and vigilant of these potential difficulties when entering a consultation relationship. The direct behavioral consultation model provides the additional benefit of countering the difficulties listed previously. Although more effort intensive and time intensive at the outset, this model offers the greatest probability of both treatment integrity and likelihood that consultee skills will generalize to other situations (Watkins-Emonet, Watson, & Shriver, 2002).

The advantages of DBC greatly outweigh the initial time requirement. DBC is easy for the professional school counselor to learn and to implement. In addition, the skills of DBC are applicable to the majority of problems across all ages of children. Even though professional school counselors may initially spend slightly more time using DBC with a referral, the time is made up because teachers can apply their skills obtained during DBC to other situations. As a result, teachers become more reliant on their own classroom-management skills and are less dependent on the professional school counselor for daily assistance.

(Note: See the CD-ROM for a list of references.)

CHAPTER 29

CONSULTING IN THE SCHOOLS: THE ROLE OF THE PROFESSIONAL SCHOOL COUNSELOR

Donna M. Gibson

Preview

Consultation with parents and teachers is one of the most important services provided by of the professional school counselor, because it bridges the communication gap among adults that can directly affect the life of a student. This chapter focuses on the consultation process and offers guidelines to professional school counselors conducting parent and teacher consultation conferences.

The role of the professional school counselor is defined often by the three *C*s of school counseling activities: counseling, consulting, and coordination (American School Counselor Association [ASCA], 1999). Even more recently, ASCA (2005) has emphasized the importance of consultation and collaboration services in a comprehensive developmental school program. It is the consulting role of the professional school counselor that is more observable by administrators, parents, and teachers. Thus, it is imperative for professional school counselors to understand the purpose of consulting and how to make these experiences meaningful, especially for parents and teachers.

THE PURPOSE OF CONSULTING

There are several purposes and settings for consulting (Brown, Pryzwansky, & Schulte, 2006; Dinkmeyer, Carlson, & Dinkmeyer, 2005; Kampwirth, 2006). In general, most consultations are conducted to solve a problem (Dougherty, 2005); however, consultation is different from counseling in two important ways. First, the counseling process involves two parties, the counselor and client. In contrast, consultation involves more than two people; generally, the professional school counselor (consultant), teacher or parent (consultee), and student (client). Second, counseling involves dealing with personal problems. In consultation, the process involves work-related or caretaking-related concerns. The teacher (consultee), for example, would be consulting with the professional school counselor (consultant) about the student's (client) behavior in class. The teacher would be consulting with the professional school counselor about alternative behavior management strategies for dealing with the student in the classroom. Therefore, the focus is not on the personal problems of the child as much as the work-related/ caretaking concerns of the teacher. Hence, professional school counselors need to monitor their consultation behaviors to prevent consulting from becoming counseling.

Although the general purpose of consultation may be to solve a problem, professional school counselors need to look at consultation as a systematic process that can be used in a variety of situations. Professional school counselors usually consult with administrators, parents, and teachers. Holding conferences with parents and teachers, however, can provoke the anxiety for all parties involved. To reduce or eliminate this anxiety, the professional school counselor needs to establish the goal for the consultation.

To establish a consultation goal, the professional school counselor needs to assess the expectations of the consultation with the individual he or she is meeting (Hall & Lin, 1994). Goals will vary, based on the theoretical orientation of the professional school counselor to the stage of the consultation process. For example, if the problem is not clear to the individuals in the consultation, then the goal may be to identify and clarify the problem. Follow-up meetings may focus on the goal of evaluating the progress that has been made in working or caring for the student by the consultee.

In establishing consultation goals, the parent or teacher (consultee) needs to be aware of his or her role in this process. In this process, the consultee is a collaborator with the consultant (professional school counselor), working in a partnership with shared responsibilities (Dougherty, 2005). If the professional school counselor is offering information in advisement to help the consultee, the consultee is not obligated to follow that advice. However, the consultee is ultimately responsible for the client. In this case, the parent or teacher is responsible for the welfare of the student.

As the professional school counselor and consultee are working on goals in consultation, they are working on building a relationship with each other (Hall & Lin, 1994). At this point, it is also important to consider the role of culture in this relationship. If necessary, collaborating and arranging for interpreters to be present in consultation meetings will help meet the needs of linguistically diverse families (Lopez, 2000). Professional school counselors should also be able to identify any prejudicial attitudes that affect the consultation process and act to modify them (Holcomb-McCoy, 2004). Additionally, issues related to cultural influence on how to handle emotional issues should be considered. This relationship evolves as consultant and consultee progress through the stages of consultation.

Hall and Lin (1994) outlined four stages of consultation: entry, diagnosis, process, and disengagement. During the *entry* stage, the primary task of the professional school counselor is to assess the situation. The advantage of the professional school counselor is that her or she is physically located at the school and is available to teachers and parents. In this assessment process, the professional school counselor needs to determine if he or she is prepared to handle the situation. If necessary, appropriate referrals can be made at this time.

If the situation is appropriate for the professional school counselor, then he or she can outline expectations to the teacher or parent. This could include meeting to identify their concerns and goals for the client. While many students (clients) are not mature enough to understand and contribute to consultation meetings, it may be appropriate to invite mature students to attend early meetings to provide their perception of the problem. Consultants must use listening skills, such as empathy, genuineness, and respect, to enlist the consultee's help, lessen anxiety, and avoid resistance to the process (Hall & Lin, 1994).

The purpose of the *diagnosis* stage is to define the problem and any relevant factors related to the situation. First, the consultant must gather information about the situation, which could include information about the client's behavior, feelings, aptitude, achievement, or social skills. Second, the consultant and consultee must mutually agree on a definition of the problem. This definition needs to be created in concrete terms so that interventions and evaluations to address the problem can be formulated. Third, goals need to be written in specific terms from the definition. Fourth, interventions need to be designed from the goal statements.

The third stage of the consultation, *process*, is implementation of the consultation plan. Dougherty (2005) outlined four questions the consultant must ask the consultee to complete this stage: (a) What are we going to do? (b) How are we going to do it? (c) When and where are we going to do it? and (d) How well did we do it? To address the first question, the consultant and consultee can review the interventions planned during the diagnosis stage. Part of planning interventions is to address who will carry them out, when it will occur, and how it will occur. Since consultees have the most responsibility for students, consultees direct most interventions. When professional school counselors meet with parents about their children, parents are responsible for carrying out interventions at home. If necessary, the professional school counselor and parent may have to consult with the child's teacher in order to carry out interventions at school. Of course, these interventions should be evaluated for effectiveness as they are carried out and adjusted to meet the consultation goals. The consultation form provided in Appendix 29.A can be copied and used for the planning and implementation of consultation in the schools.

The *disengagement* stage is the ending stage of the consultation process. This stage includes an overall evaluation of the effectiveness of the consultation. This can be a formal or informal process whereby the professional school counselor interviews the consultee about the process or requests that the consultee complete a questionnaire or rating form. It is also during this stage that the consultant and consultee decrease or cease their consulting relationship. In the school, it is not necessary to terminate a relationship, but consultation about a student for a specific problem should decrease.

This systematic consultation process can vary in the amount of time allotted for one problem. It is necessary to understand the process, however, and use the designed activities to help the consultee. In the following sections, the role of the professional school counselor in parent and teacher consultations is explained, and specific recommendations are made to promote effective conferences.

CONSULTING WITH PARENTS

Professional school counselors have several opportunities to consult with parents. Within the realm of a comprehensive developmental counseling program, counseling activities and programs often induce some form of parental consultation. It may be introduced by either the parent or the professional school counselor. In initial meetings with parents, the professional school counselor should minimize the use of technical jargon and attempt to understand any social language or jargon used by parents (Knotek, 2003). Doing this will help to eliminate confusion and build the partnership between the consultant and consultees during the consultation process (Putnam, Handler, Rey, & McCarty, 2005).

Although the majority of professional school counselors do not conduct family counseling within the schools, it is important to understand the functioning of families and family dynamics. Understanding that affecting one family member's behavior will usually have an effect on another family member's behavior, will enable the counselor to convey the importance of intervention, and will allow the interventions to have a better chance of being supported by the family (Mullis & Edwards, 2001). Professional school counselors can gain the support of faculty and staff when they offer an explanation of the effects of family dynamics on student behavior.

Professional school counselors can serve as primary resources for parents who are trying to sort through various issues, such as divorce, grief, disability, and illness (Mullis & Otwell, 1998). Parents look to schools for information about these issues, and professional school counselors can provide information and resources. In addition, parents look to schools for both cognitive and emotional support. Consider the following case example:

> Mr. Hampton, the professional school counselor, had an appointment to meet with Jacob's father. Jacob's grades had dropped significantly over the last 9 weeks, and he was reported by his teacher to be withdrawn in class. When Mr. Turner, Jacob's father, arrived, he appeared upset about the appointment. After Mr. Hampton reviewed the purpose for the meeting, he asked Mr. Turner how things were at home. With some hesitation, Mr. Turner reported that Jacob's mother had moved out of the house. He reported being so preoccupied with his own thoughts and feelings about this change that he assumed Jacob was doing well. After some discussion, Mr. Hampton and Mr. Turner agreed that Jacob may be exhibiting some of these behaviors because of his parent's separation. Mr. Hampton provided some information about the effects of separation and divorce and agreed to see Jacob in counseling. He encouraged Mr. Turner to consult with his wife and possibly seek family counseling.

In this scenario, it took minimal discussion to discover the family dynamics that may have been affecting Jacob's behavior. For the father, this could have been the first opportunity to discuss his separation with his wife and how it has affected his own life. The professional school counselor provided both cognitive and emotional support in this one brief session. However, follow-up consultation will allow the professional school counselor to determine if the simple interventions discussed in the first session have met the desired goal of improved grades and better class participation for Jacob.

Although professional school counselors can be resources for parents, many parents bring anxiety and anger to consultation. This anxiety and anger needs to be evaluated by the professional school counselor to determine the appropriate response to parents. In many cases, anxiety appears as anger or aggression. The majority of parents are worried about their children, and this worry can prevent them from hearing or understanding the purpose of the consultation. Anger can be a natural response for parents who see their children as an extension of themselves and are asking, "What are they saying is wrong with my child (me)?" The following case example illustrates this point:

> Tamara, a 10-year-old girl, was reported by her teacher for bullying a younger girl in the hall at school. After discussing this with her, the professional school counselor decided to contact her parents, as per the school policy on bullying. When Tamara's mother arrived, she immediately voiced her annoyance at the school

for calling her in because she believes her child needs to take up for herself. Allowing the mother to vocalize her objections, the professional school counselor was able to assess that the mother may have issues of feeling like she needs to defend herself. Instead of revealing her insight, the professional school counselor reflected the mother's objections and spent some time in establishing rapport with her. After discussion of the details of the bullying incidences, the mother admitted that she had misinterpreted Tamara's disclosure of these incidences. She reported that she had inadvertently supported Tamara's behavior at home. The professional school counselor and Tamara's mother discussed ways that the mother could discuss bullying behaviors with Tamara at home.

When parents appear to take the student's problem on as their own, they may need to vent their frustration and anger initially in the consultation session. Professional school counselors can help diffuse these feelings by engaging in active listening and not becoming defensive. Often, the professional school counselor can spend an initial consultation session normalizing behavior or helping parents perceive their children's behaviors, emotions, and attitudes as normal (Mullis & Edwards, 2001).

Parents may see their children in a negative way, so professional school counselors may have to reframe their statements to put a positive light on the problem or situation. Reframing can act as another resource for parents, because they may not have been able to see the positiveness of the situation prior to the consultation. It is the encouragement from these reframes that provide parents with the incentive to carry out interventions that will help their children at home and school.

CONSULTING WITH TEACHERS

Similar to consulting with parents, the professional school counselor's schedule offers several opportunities for teachers to consult with the counselor and vice versa. In fact, professional school counselors strongly rely on teachers for referrals of students (Davis & Garrett, 1998). Therefore, one of the first steps in consulting with teachers occurs prior to the actual consultation. The most important step is establishing strong rapport and mutual understanding between counselor and teacher.

In attempts to establish this relationship, professional school counselors need to make their services known to the faculty of the school. In a study of future school administrators, 100 participants ranked consulting with teachers as the fifth most important duty of professional school counselors (Fitch, Newby, Ballestero, & Marshall, 2001). Enlisting the support of the school administrator in publicizing the duties of the professional school counselor may help endorse these activities for the teachers. Additionally, the professional school counselor can introduce him- or herself at faculty meetings, create and distribute a brochure about the role of the professional school counselor, and visit each teacher individually to discuss the professional school counselor's role and any concerns of the teacher (Davis & Garrett, 1998).

Professional school counselors are at an advantage, because they are based in schools. The majority of consultations are usually about students' problem academic or social behaviors in the school, and their teachers usually have a wealth of knowledge about the students and these behaviors. Although the professional school counselor may be initiating the consultation process, the teacher actually began it when initiating a referral about the student. It is useful to remember that teachers may feel similar to parents when consulting with the professional school counselor. The following case example illustrates this:

> Ms. Allen, the professional school counselor, stopped by Ms. Henry's class during her planning period at an appointed time to discuss Michael's behavior. As they discussed Ms. Henry's observations, Ms. Henry became upset and started to cry. Ms. Allen attempted to understand Ms. Henry's observations and began to reflect her feelings. She reflected that Ms. Henry seemed to be frustrated with Michael's behavior and was afraid that she could not help him learn anything. After Ms. Henry calmed down, Ms. Allen suggested that she, as the professional school counselor, observe Michael. After this observation, they would meet again to plan some interventions for him in Ms. Henry's classroom.

In this example, it became clear that Ms. Henry was placing a lot of responsibility for Michael's behavior on herself. This is not uncommon for teachers, especially in current educational systems where accountability is stressed. Many teachers feel that their self-worth is based on teaching students to learn. When those students are not learning, it can affect the self-worth of those teachers. Hence, we saw and heard Ms. Henry's self-worth being affected by her frustration with Michael's behavior.

However, research also indicated that teachers perceive family and student-centered issues to contribute more to the students' problems than the teachers' contributions (Athanasiou, Geil, Hazel, & Copeland, 2002). Considering this, it may be necessary to help teachers gain different perspectives on students' problems. Professional school counselors can offer to provide services to teachers in order to help them gain a different perspective on the situation, such as observation. Classroom observation is a way of gathering data and providing additional information to the parties involved in consultation (Davis & Garrett, 1998). In general, teachers do not take issue with the professional school counselor making observations, because it indicates the counselor's level of commitment to helping the child and the teacher.

In consulting with teachers, professional school counselors need to be mindful of the teacher's schedule when planning meetings. Additionally, professional school counselors should remember that consultation is a partnership that is based on trust and respect. Therefore, teachers should be made to feel trusted and respected as they are asked for their own expertise in creating, implementing, and evaluating interventions that will help students.

THE NUTS AND BOLTS OF PARENT AND TEACHER CONSULTATION

In helping students achieve success in and out of school, professional school counselors have the distinction of bridging the communication gap between family and school. Communication between the professional school counselor and faculty is also effective in planning appropriate services for the needs of students in the school. Table 29.1 provides a list of suggestions for professional school counselors to review as they plan consultations with parents and teachers. Since many consultations take place in a conference format, logistical recommendations are listed.

Summary/Conclusion

Consulting with parents and teachers is an important part of the role of the professional school counselor. As consultant, one can be the catalyst for change in the lives of the families and faculty of students. The change created through consultation can help students become more academically and interpersonally successful.

(Note: See the CD-ROM for a list of references.)

TABLE 29.1

CONSULTATION SUGGESTIONS

Determine the purpose of the consultation meeting and what needs to be discussed and done during the consultation.

Be mindful of parents' or teachers' schedules when planning the consultation meeting. Be flexible in scheduling conferences before or after school hours to meet these needs.

When notifying parents or teachers of a needed meeting, explain the purpose and reason for the meeting. This can decrease the anxiety of all individuals involved in the conference.

Hold conferences in a comfortable atmosphere, with adult-sized chairs and a table, if needed. In meeting with teachers, their classroom may be the most convenient and comfortable.

Greet parents and teachers in a friendly manner. For parents, professional school counselors should introduce themselves immediately and shake the hands of all the individuals attending the meeting. Thank parents and teachers for making the time to meet.

Reexplain the purpose and reason for the meeting. Go straight to the point, and do not use technical or educational jargon when explaining information. Be honest about the school's concerns.

Encourage parents and teachers to provide their perspective of the student's behavior. Use active listening skills, especially when emotions run high. Make sure to have tissues on hand.

Provide positive examples when describing the student's behavior. You want to provide another perspective of the student. However, you are emphasizing the behavior that needs to be addressed, which is often not positive.

Establish a supportive relationship with parents or teachers in conferences. Do not become defensive, and continue active listening in order to collect more information about the student.

Create and maintain equal working relationships by encouraging parents or teachers to cocreate intervention ideas that can be used at home or school. Set-up the plan for implementing and evaluating the interventions.

Provide resources for parents and teachers, such as handouts and books about the specific behavior being exhibited, including a bibliography of references.

Thank parents and teachers again at the end of the meeting for investing time into the student's needs.

Follow up with parents and teachers to review the child's progress, and make needed adjustments to the interventions being implemented.

Document all of your contacts with parents and teachers to review when following up or in future consultations about the student.

Consultation Planning and Intervention Form

Consultant's name: _____

Consultee's name: _____

Client's name: _____

Reason for Consultation: _____
_____
_____

Identification of Issue/Problem: _____
_____
_____

Definition of Problem: _____
_____
_____

Goals and Interventions for Implementation: _____
_____
_____

Implementation Evaluation

Goals	Who Will Implement Goal?	When Will Intervention Begin?	When Will Intervention Be Assessed?

Evaluation of Consultation Process: _____
_____
_____
_____
_____
_____
_____
_____
_____

CHAPTER 30

THE FAMILY RESOURCE CENTER

Patricia L. Barton and Gayle Cicero

Preview

Ideally, counselors work collaboratively with a school counseling leadership team that is composed of administrators, teachers, pupil-services team members, students, parents, and community leaders to develop a Family Resource Center, which is one approach professional school counselors can employ to increase student achievement. The team uses a systematic and results-based 5-phase process to develop an effective center. The ultimate challenge of bringing parents into the center is addressed through continuous evaluation and strategic marketing. A successful Family Resource Center helps professional school counselors to work as change agents to increase opportunities for parents to be involved in their children's education.

"Professional school counselors work collaboratively with parents or guardians, community members and other support services professionals as part of the student support services team to ensure academic success for students" (American School Counselor Association [ASCA], 2005, p. 16). Family Resource Centers provide direct services and combine multiple programs within schools, agencies, and private networks. To be successful, these programs are linked administratively and financially to ensure appropriate and effective service delivery (Waddell, Shannon, & Durr, 2001). Waddell et al. explained that family support initiatives have appeared in many states, and higher GPAs were reported for selected students that participated in Family Resource Initiatives. The ASCA national model (ASCA; 2005) provided an operational structure for school counseling programs that can be applied to the development of the Family Resource Center (see Table 30.1).

TABLE 30.1

THE FAMILY RESOURCE CENTER, ALIGNED WITH ASCA NATIONAL MODEL COMPONENTS

Foundation	Delivery System	Management System	Accountability
What is the purpose of the center?	How will the services be delivered?	What will the calendar and action plan look like?	How will students be affected as a result of the program?
How will the center facilitate student development in the three broad domains (personal–social, academic, and career)?	What student needs will be addressed?	What data will be used to develop the calendar and action plan?	How will results reports be analyzed for program effectiveness and changed or improved as needed?

Research confirms that students with involved parents perform better at school: "They earn higher grades and test scores than their peers, attend school and complete homework more regularly, are better behaved, and are more likely to graduate from high school and attend college" (Shaeffer, 2002, p. 1). The ASCA *National Standards for School Counseling Programs* (Campbell & Dahir, 1997) clearly focus on increasing student achievement and supporting educational equity for all students. Professional school counselors are frequently called upon to develop strategies and programs that will increase academic success for underachieving students. Providing opportunities to engage parents in the educational process directly supports the national standards and national model (ASCA; 2005).

Family Resource Centers may vary greatly in their size and scope; however, all strive to provide access to information, education, and services (Waddell et al., 2001). This one-stop-shopping approach serves as a single point of entry to necessary services for students and their families. Waddell et al. identified five attributes of successful Family Resource Centers:

- Community/neighborhood focus
- Collaboration among stakeholders
- Inclusion of multiple agencies
- Integrated services and case management
- A comprehensive view of children's needs within the context of their school and neighborhood

Epstein, Coates, Salinas, Sanders, and Simon (1997) developed a framework of six major types of parental involvement to help schools develop comprehensive programs of school and family partnerships:

- Parenting
- Communicating
- Volunteering
- Learning at home
- Decision making
- Collaborating with community

Epstein's research formed the foundation for the National PTA's Standards for Family Involvement to guide program development and provide a means for evaluating program quality. All six types of parental involvement are readily incorporated into the scope of a Family Resource Center. Table 30.2 provides a list of potential purposes the family resource center can support (U.S. Department of Education, 1996).

Five Steps for Developing a Family Resource Center

The Family Resource Center is a mechanism for bringing together resources within the community and focusing these resources on results for children and families (Doktor & Poertner, 1996). Services provided in the center tend to focus on families in the school and surrounding neighborhood. Many of these programs are begun and operated through grant funding. Some considerations regarding the establishment of a Family Resource Center are described by the Family Involvement Center (1997).

TABLE 30.2

PURPOSES OF A FAMILY RESOURCE CENTER

Meeting space for parent groups and workshops.

Informal location for individual parent–teacher or parent–principal discussions.

Site for special education team meetings.

Lounge or "waiting room" for parents in school for other business.

Recruiting site for tutors and classroom volunteers.

Central location for information and guidance about higher education opportunities.

Information source for cultural and community services and agencies that help families with educational, health, and social service needs.

Parenting videos and books on a variety of topics, such as discipline, learning disabilities, and child development.

A play area equipped with toys and books.

Educational books and games for parents to use with their children.

Information about current school-based programs and events.

A professional library for school staff.

Telephone service to answer concerns and provide referrals to community resources.

Brochures or flyers from local agencies and service providers.

Meeting space for small groups.

Dahir, Sheldon, and Valiga (1998) identified five steps for the conception, implementation and evaluation of school counseling programs:

- Discussion
- Awareness
- Design
- Implementation
- Evaluation

This 5-phase process structures the development of the Family Resource Center. Many of the practical suggestions woven into the five steps that follow are taken from the Family Involvement Center (1997).

To develop and sustain a viable Family Resource Center, it is important that the development of the center be a systematic, results-based process. The process and procedures for developing the center will emanate from a team committed to making the vision for the center a reality. The school counseling leadership team (Dahir et al., 1998) can provide the synergy needed to create the family resource center. Because the team consists of major stakeholders (i.e., administrators, teachers, pupil personnel team members, students, parents, professional school counselors, and community leaders), it can provide guidance and direction in order to sustain meaningful development.

DISCUSSION

In the *discussion* phase, the members of the team convene to build relationships and gain the perspective of each of the stakeholders. By communicating and synthesizing all points of view with knowledge of the school–community profile, a vision for the center emerges. The vision outlines the ideal expectations and goals for the center. The team will align the goals for the center with the school's strategic plan.

AWARENESS

During the *awareness* phase, data are collected, analyzed, and prioritized. The school–community profile, which is discussed in the first phase, is further developed to include the following: standardized test scores, attendance rate, retention or drop-out rate, free or reduced-price lunch, racial or ethnic data, underachieving subgroups, students with disabilities (percentage and type), mobility rate, discipline statistics, family structure, crime statistics (drug and alcohol, domestic violence, etc.), employment rate and types of employment, educational levels of parents, access to services, and housing. Perception data will also be useful in designing relevant programs to meet the needs of community members.

Although school data is readily available, community information may be gained through census reports, surveys, and interviews. Potential survey or interview questions may include the following:

What specific issues and concerns do you have in raising your children?

What kind of learning experiences would be most helpful to you (brochures, books, videos, audiotapes, lectures, informal group discussions with other parents, etc.)?

What are good/bad times to hold parent events?

How can you help us to have the best center possible (volunteer, speaker, business support, marketing)?

What are the barriers preventing your child from meeting with success in school?

Here are some suggestions for getting the best response to a needs survey: Make the survey easy to complete; consider conducting phone surveys, personal interviews, and online access; bring the survey to local events or meetings, service agencies, businesses, churches, and so forth; and include all members of the leadership team in collecting the information. As community members are contacted, develop a file for future involvement and solicit resource support, such as brochures, information packets, facilitators for parental information and support sessions, surplus furnishings, and help with meeting expenses. In turn, the school-based Family Resource Center can be offered as a comfortable, familiar location for community workers to meet with families.

When the data are collected, the team will summarize and analyze results. By disaggregating the data, the team will identify the needs of specific subpopulations within the school and community to develop an action plan. This procedure will assist the team in linking the goals of the Family Resource Center to achieving the mission.

Measurable results for the center grow out of an understanding of needs. All services provided by the center will focus on identified, measurable results linked to the vision for the center. In alignment with ASCA's national standards, Doktor and Proertner (1996) promoted a focus on results as opposed to services and needs, and contended that as long as needs and services are the focal point of discussion, a results orientation seldom occurs.

PROGRAM DESIGN

During the *program design* phase, the program components are specified. Identify a program, grant, or initiative to drive the efforts of the center to achieve its mission. In addition, the nuts-and-bolts work of securing the ideal location, furnishings, and materials are undertaken. A spare classroom is an ideal location for the center, but other potential sites include a section of the media center, a conference room, a portable classroom, the school foyer, or an alcove. Providing phone and Internet service are valuable assets in the center. An interactive Web page and Web-site manager are critical to providing timely updates in programs and services.

The design phase involves the following components:

- Outcome Setting: What will be accomplished?
- Programming: How will it be accomplished?
- Scheduling: When will activities/services be offered?
- Budgeting: How will financial and time resources be obtained?
- Fixing Accountability: How and when will the outcomes be measured?
- Reviewing and Adjusting: How and when will changes be made?

IMPLEMENTATION

The fourth phase, *implementation,* initiates the program plan and is best accomplished with a phase-in approach. During this phase, the center is open and offering programs and services. Starting with an open house or resource fair will bring people to the center. During the phase-in, consider a short-term plan with several benchmarks toward the long-term goal. Identifying milestones facilitates reporting on the center's systematic development to constituents (e.g., school improvement team, board of education, community associations, local politicians, possible funders).

The work of the Family Resource Center is divided into management and operations. Management encompasses planning, organizing, staffing, training, directing, coordinating, reporting, budgeting, and evaluating; operations refer to the services provided through the family resource center.

Implementation phase considerations include the following:

- What is the scope of assistance the staff can provide (e.g., regular and special education information, school and community sponsored events, referral to school and community services)?
- What level of involvement should staff provide in assisting parents with their problems?
- How will staff ensure that the information parents give is accurate?
- Will a "parent to parent" network be established? If so, how will you obtain permission for the use of parents' names and telephone numbers?
- How and to what degree will telephone conversations and personal meetings be documented?
- How will you ensure confidentiality of parents' disclosures?

Ideally, programs and services will be tailored to specific needs of targeted populations. Possible target groups include parents (whose children have academic challenges, exhibit behavior or self-control difficulties, demonstrate poor interpersonal skills, have a history of excessive absences, receive special education services, etc.), economically disadvantaged families, single parents, transient families, ESL families, stepparents, fathers only, custodial grandparents or relatives, and foster or adoptive parents.

Strategically, marketing programs and services to target groups is essential. A brochure is a simple, inexpensive way to communicate information to the public. Brochures should include the center's name and logo, location, phone number, Web site, e-mail address, mission and/or objectives, hours of operation, services, and an invitation to participate or volunteer. To use the brochure as an effective marketing tool, it may be mailed out to the community, disseminated at open houses and conference times, given as a resource at special education meetings, and displayed at local agencies and businesses.

Another way to market events at the center is through a monthly calendar. The calendar may be attached to the school newsletter, mailed or e-mailed to agencies that work with targeted populations, and posted in local libraries and on the school or school-system's Web site. The calendar should be easy to read and should include a phone number and method of registering for events. Consider having the calendar reflect the logo, color, and design of the brochure.

A resource fair also promotes the center and enables the development of collaborative relationships with community agencies and businesses. Offer services that may attract specific populations. For example, blood pressure screening, flu shots, free consultations with mental health providers, inspirational speakers, entertainment for children, and refreshments may draw peoples' attention. Families, school staff, and community members, including local politicians and board of education members, will find a well-planned resource fair of interest. To advertise the fair, inform local newspapers and television stations.

Finally, designing and maintaining a Web page is an effective marketing strategy. By linking with an existing school-system page, the site will have more hits than a "stand alone" Web page. Also, the center will be viewed as part of the existing whole, as it should be.

EVALUATION

The fifth phase, *evaluating*, is congruent with a results-based approach and guides the center's continued development. Key questions during the evaluation phase include the following:

- Have timelines established during the design phase been met?
- To what extent have short-term goals been met?
- What data were used to measure results?
- To what degree did the center support the school's strategic plan?
- Were desired results achieved?
- Was student achievement improved?
- Was school attendance increased?
- Was student behavior improved?
- Did students and families access needed services?

The process of the center's development is documented in the room use log, phone log, and written evaluations from parents, teachers, and agency personnel. The process and product (results) evaluations are combined to give a complete picture of the center's success. In addition, the evaluation drives future programming and funding.

Developing and operating a family resource center holds many challenges. Initially, the collaboration process will involve turf and communication issues. Counselors' extensive training in the cycle of change and group dynamics is essential to the effective functioning of the school counseling leadership team.

Budget requirements for the operation of a Family Resource Center can be burdensome. Both financial and time resources need to be considered. Though the time element is often overlooked, it is the people to people contact that transforms the Family Resource Center from a physical space to a functioning, service-providing organization. Financial support may be acquired through school-based organizations and fundraisers, community agencies and businesses, or grants. Data collected during the needs assessment and evaluation phases are critical to developing effective time and financial budgets. Getting people into the center to use the resources and services is the ultimate challenge. The emphasis on strategic marketing is necessary to sustain the center.

Professional school counselors must remind themselves that their leadership efforts will improve the academic achievement of students (Barton & Cicero, 2003). In particular, they are in a key position to be change agents in increasing opportunities for parents to be involved and supportive of their child's education.

Summary/Conclusion

A Family Resource Center is a useful tool in breaking down many barriers between home and schools and can create positive outcomes for students. Professional school counselors are positioned to facilitate the development of Family Resource Centers in schools and encourage parental or family involvement in education. The development of a center requires counselors to use their leadership, advocacy, and collaborative skills to ensure student achievement. By using the 5-phase model, the approach becomes collaborative and includes important stakeholders. Careful planning and evaluation ensure the center's sustained presence within the school.

(Note: See the CD-ROM for a list of references.)

CHAPTER 31

CONFLICT RESOLUTION

Nadine E. Garner

Preview

In this chapter, I present an overview of conflict-resolution programs in the schools, research on their effectiveness, and both immediate and long-range strategies for designing a conflict-resolution program. Using a multiple intelligences approach, techniques that professional school counselors can readily integrate into their work with individuals, groups, and guidance experiences are provided.

There is no doubt of the real need for comprehensive conflict-resolution programs in the schools. The Center for Disease Control and Prevention has stated that violence in the United States has reached epidemic proportions and that all students from preschool through 12th grade should be involved in a conflict-resolution program. The summary of the position statement on conflict resolution by the American School Counselor Association declared, "a comprehensive conflict-resolution program promotes a safe school environment that permits optimal personal growth and learning. Through participation in a comprehensive conflict-resolution program, students learn skills that maximize their potential for reaching personal goals and success in school" (ASCA; 2006, ¶ 1).

The ability to effectively and peacefully handle conflict is not necessarily intuitive; rather, it is a learned skill. Johnson and Johnson (1991), echoed these sentiments when, after more than 30 years of research, they stated that "most students simply do not know how to manage their conflicts constructively" (p. 3). They found that students struggled with issues of verbal harassment, verbal arguments, rumors, gossip, and dating or relationship issues.

CONFLICT-RESOLUTION PROGRAMS

Conflict-resolution programs have various names, including Conflict Resolution Education (CRE), Peace Education, Peacemaking, Violence Prevention, or Violence Reduction. Conflict-resolution models have common goals because they seek to create opportunities for students and other members of the school community to (a) recognize that conflict is a natural part of life and that it can be resolved peacefully, (b) develop awareness of their own unique responses to conflict and to understand the diversity with which others respond, (c) learn and practice the principles of conflict resolution and the skills of peaceful problem-solving processes, (d) empower themselves to be individually and cooperatively responsible for resolving conflicts peacefully, and (e) integrate this responsibility in their daily lives.

An authentic conflict-resolution program contains two key elements: (a) the *principles* of conflict resolution (separate the people from the problem; focus on interests, not positions; invent options for mutual gain; use objective criteria as the basis of decision making) and (b) a *problem-solving process* (negotiation, mediation, or consensus decision making; Crawford & Bodine, 1997). (See Chapter 32 in this book.) These two components are common factors in the following four approaches to conflict resolution that are currently used in the schools:

1. *Process curriculum*—A specific time (e.g., separate course, distinct curriculum, daily lesson plan) is dedicated to teaching conflict resolution.
2. *Mediation program*—Adults or students who are trained in conflict-resolution principles and the problem-solving process of mediation act as neutral third-party facilitators to help disputants reach a resolution.
3. *Peaceable classroom*—Conflict resolution is integrated into the core curriculum and classroom management. Peaceable classrooms form the foundation for the peaceable school.
4. *Peaceable school*—All members of the school community (teachers, staff, students, administrators, parents) receive training in conflict resolution (Crawford & Bodine, 1997).

THE PROFESSIONAL SCHOOL COUNSELOR'S ROLE

Nationwide, the number of school-based conflict-resolution programs has skyrocketed from approximately 50 programs in 1984 to more than 6,000 programs involving over 300,000 students in 1995 (Girard & Koch, 1996). These programs have been implemented in the majority of schools, and professional school counselors often take a leading role in the implementation of them. The specialized expertise of professional school counselors places them in a distinct position to facilitate change in the school culture (Hovland, Peterson, & Smaby, 1996).

ASCA (2006) recommended the professional school counselor assume the leading role in the following components of school-wide comprehensive conflict-resolution programs: design, implementation, monitoring, and evaluation. Furthermore, ASCA recommended that professional school counselors include the following elements in such programs:

- Prevention services
- Training
- Education in recognition of early warning signs
- Intervention services
- Crisis response and follow-up
- Community involvement
- Peer mediation programs
- Evaluation of program effectiveness

INDICATIONS FROM THE RESEARCH

Research indicates it may take 1 to 2 years for teachers to feel comfortable integrating the concepts of conflict resolution into classroom activities (Johnson & Johnson, 1991), and other studies show that it may take 3 to 5 years for it to take hold in the larger school environment. As such, it is not uncommon for programs to be disbanded or deemed failures before even given a chance.

Lindsay (1998) suggested that the elements of high-quality conflict-resolution programs include recognition that school programs alone are no panacea, given the influence of families and communities on students. Programs in the schools should be part of a larger strategy that includes addressing conflict resolution in families and in the community. Sandy (2001) reported that conflict-resolution programs can positively affect the school and classroom climate most strongly when there is an involvement of the total school community.

IMMEDIATE AND LONG-RANGE STRATEGIES FOR IMPLEMENTING A CONFLICT-RESOLUTION PROGRAM

Due to the multidimensional nature of conflict-resolution programs, the prospect of implementing a comprehensive conflict-resolution program can appear to be an overwhelming task for professional school counselors. A more manageable approach to developing a comprehensive conflict-resolution program is to plan for its development by using both long-range and immediate strategies.

LONG-RANGE STRATEGIES

"It takes a village." Research indicates that the most successful conflict-resolution programs are ones in which the whole school community is an active participant in the process of training, practice, and evaluation and links with mediation agencies to develop training programs for the school community.

Conflict-resolution committee. Instead of handling such a large task alone, professional school counselors may organize a conflict-resolution committee to plan and implement the long-range conflict-resolution program goals for the school. Membership on this committee builds a foundation of supporters and should include professional school counselors, teachers, students, administrators, parents, and community members. The conflict-resolution program should be seen as a shared opportunity. By involving members from all segments of the school community, the professional school counselor is not viewed as the sole proponent of the conflict-resolution program.

Exploration of available curricula. There are numerous programs available that are designed specifically for elementary, middle, or high school levels. Many programs offer comprehensive curricula complete with lesson plans, training materials, reproducible handouts, transparency masters, videos, instructor's guides, and evaluation tools. Some programs are tailored to specific areas of conflict resolution such as bullying and relational aggression.

IMMEDIATE STRATEGIES

Small changes lead to larger changes. Using Milton Erickson's analogy of a hole in a dam, in which even a small hole may lead to changing the structure of the whole dam (Haley, 1973), look for opportunities to integrate concepts that focus on conflict resolution into your existing work with students. When consulting with teachers, ask them what small steps they would be willing to take now to infuse conflict-resolution concepts into their existing curriculum. In so doing, when it is time to implement a comprehensive curriculum, there will already be a core group of people who are taking proactive steps.

A multiple intelligences approach to conflict resolution. Garner (1996) introduced a training program for counselors to use with students titled *A Multiple Intelligences Approach to Conflict Resolution.* Using Howard Gardner's (1983, 1999) theory of multiple intelligences to draw out students' differing learning styles, the program encourages students to develop an increased awareness of how they use the various intelligences to think about and deal with conflict and conflict resolution. The program teaches students about the multiple intelligences, presents activities that need one or more of the intelligences to be activated in order to complete them, and asks students to reflect on which intelligences and activities are strengths for them. Armstrong (1993), one of the pioneering authors to apply the use of multiple intelligences to educational settings, supported the use of the intelligences as an effective way to teach the most students through a variety of learning pathways. The following section describes the intelligences used in each of the four activities presented in the chapter. (See Table 41.1 in Chapter 41 for a brief description of how each of the intelligences relates to different types of learners). Although Gardner has recently proposed two additional intelligences (naturalist and existential), only the original seven intelligences are addressed in this chapter.

Application to real life. Students are better able to synthesize and retain concepts when they make personal or real-life connections to the material. The four activities presented in this chapter provide opportunities for students to make these important connections.

SAMPLE TECHNIQUES FOR IMMEDIATE INTEGRATION

The following four activities are techniques that professional school counselors can readily integrate into their work with individuals, groups, and guidance experiences and can be adapted to suit elementary, middle, and high school settings.

Activity 1: Applying Glasser's Psychological Need

Intelligences Addressed: Logical–Mathematical, Verbal–Linguistic, Intrapersonal, Interpersonal

Teach students about Glasser's (1984) explanation of psychological needs and their relationship to conflict. Copy and use The Four Psychological Needs table, located in Appendix 31.A, as an overhead or handout. According to Glasser, we are driven by the needs for *belonging/love* (belonging, sharing, and cooperating with others); *power* (achieving, accomplishing, being recognized and respected); *freedom* (making choices in our lives); and *fun* (laughing and playing). In order to be psychologically healthy, we need to find responsible ways to have these needs met. Conflicts arise, among other reasons, when one does not fulfill one or more of these needs. The figure in Appendix 31.A titled "Apply the Four Psychological Needs" provides students the opportunity to respond to scenarios as part of a classroom guidance lesson, based on real-life experiences of students. Students can discuss why they chose their answers and how they can relate the concepts of psychological needs and conflict to their own lives. It also asks them to identify which of the multiple intelligences are used to complete the activities.

Activity 2: Needs Circle

Intelligences Addressed: Visual–Spatial, Intrapersonal, Interpersonal, Verbal–Linguistic

The figure in Appendix 31.A titled "My Needs Circle" can be reproduced as an overhead or handout for immediate use. Begin the activity by having students draw a vertical and horizontal line inside the circle to divide it into four quadrants. Label each quadrant on the outside of the circle with one of Glasser's psychological needs. In each quadrant, students list how they get this particular need filled in their lives and answer the reflective questions below the circle. Students then share with a partner or small group the elements of their needs circle. This activity can be used in individual, group, or classroom guidance experiences to help students identify how they are fulfilling their psychological needs. The needs circle is a helpful illustration for a professional school counselor to see what areas of a student's life are strengths for the student and which areas are a cause for concern and may be potential areas of conflict. This is an especially useful activity for a student who has moved or experienced a recent life change. The student can complete two circles: one before the change and one that represents the present time. This activity may also act as a springboard for discussion with a student who is reticent to disclose personal information verbally or who is better able to organize information and communicate with visual–spatial aids. (I would like to acknowledge Ella Kwisnek, a graduate counselor-in-training at Duquesne University in the late 1990s, for presenting the basic diagram of the Needs Circle).

Activity 3: Draw a Picture of Conflict

Intelligences Addressed: Visual–Spatial, Intrapersonal, Interpersonal

Students draw a picture of what conflict looks like to them. They share the pictures and try to understand others' meaning of conflict. Ask students to discuss which of the multiple intelligences they activated in order to accomplish the activity. Younger students are often better able to synthesize their understanding of conflict by creating pictures first and then explaining them.

Activity 4: Folding Paper Cranes for Peace

Intelligences Addressed: Bodily–Kinesthetic, Verbal–Linguistic, Logical–Mathematical, Visual–Spatial, Interpersonal, Intrapersonal

For more information on this origami activity, visit www.sadako.com. This activity borrows from the true story of Sadako Sasaki, a girl who developed leukemia in 1955 from the effects of radiation caused by the bombing of Hiroshima.

There is an ancient Japanese legend that says that by folding 1,000 paper cranes, your wish will come true. Sadako began folding a thousand cranes while hospitalized, wishing for world peace and personal health, but she died before the project was completed. To this day, people all over the world are still folding cranes and sending them to Hiroshima's Peace Park.

Schools often use this activity to unite the school community with a common theme around peace (Levenson, 2006). One memorable example is from Millersville University, in which the Department of Housing and Residential Programs coordinated a project to enlist the campus in making 3,022 paper cranes, each representing a life lost in the World Trade Center tragedy of September 11, 2001. The cranes were fashioned into large mobiles and displayed in the Multipurpose Room on September 11, 2002, during a Remembrance Ceremony. Since then, the mobiles have been permanently installed on campus. This activity is easily integrated into the curriculum as students learn about history and multicultural issues and need to use math and cooperation skills.

Summary/Conclusion

Conflict-resolution programs encourage the development of useful skills for resolving conflict peacefully that can be applied across the life span. When implemented comprehensively, such programs promote a positive school climate. There are a variety of approaches from which to choose. The most effective program is a comprehensive one that strives to train and support all members of the school community. A conflict-resolution program is not an instant solution—it is a long-term commitment requiring patience, training, support at all levels of the school community, and ongoing evaluation to tailor the program to the needs of the school. The following are resources for further consideration:

American School Counselor Association (www.schoolcounselor.org)

Baker, S. (Ed.). (1996). Conflict resolution: Part I [Special issue]. *The School Counselor,* 43(5).

Baker, S. (Ed.). (1996). Conflict resolution: Part II [Special issue]. *The School Counselor,* 44(1).

Teaching Tolerance (www.Tolerance.org). An organization for educators, parents, and students, focusing on reducing conflict and promoting multicultural awareness. Free materials for educators, such as videos, curricula, and a magazine are available. It was founded by the Southern Poverty Law Center, a nonprofit legal and educational foundation.

(Note: See the CD-ROM for a list of references.)

THE FOUR PSYCHOLOGICAL NEEDS

According to William Glasser, we need to have these four psychological needs fulfilled in order to be psychologically healthy:

1. Belonging/Love
   - Belonging
   - Sharing
   - Cooperating with others

2. Power
   - Achieving
   - Accomplishing
   - Being recognized and respected
   - Being responsible for something/someone
   - Being dependable

3. Freedom
   - Making choices in our lives

4. Fun
   - Laughing
   - Playing
   - Finding Humor

In order to be psychologically healthy, we need to find responsible ways to have these needs met. Conflicts may arise when we do not fulfill one or more of these needs.

Note. Adapted from *Control Theory*, by W. Glasser, 1984, New York: Harper & Row.

APPLY THE FOUR PSYCHOLOGICAL NEEDS: BELONGING, POWER, FREEDOM, FUN

Read each scene. Then write down the psychological need that fits. You may find that there is more than one correct answer.

1. Julio does not feel wanted at home. His parents are divorced and have new families now. He does not feel part of either family. He joins a gang where he feels needed and wanted. What psychological need is he filling? _____

2. Kim likes to be in charge of things. She likes responsibility and needs to have a say in what goes on at school. She runs for class president. What psychological need is she filling? _____

3. Takeda has to baby-sit for her three younger siblings while her mom works. She likes being part of a family and enjoys taking care of the kids, but she gets upset when she can't go to the mall with her friends, because of her responsibilities to her family. What psychological need is she *not* having fulfilled? _____ What psychological need *is* she filling? _____

Briefly describe a conflict that you are experiencing (or have experienced) in your own life:

What psychological need(s) might *not* be filled in this situation?

Describe a positive situation or relationship that you currently have (or have had):

What psychological need(s) were filled in this situation?

Which of the multiple intelligences did you use in order to complete the activities on this page?

Which of these intelligences do you feel are strengths for you?

MY NEEDS CIRCLE

What are some positive ways that you meet your four psychological needs?

What are some possible areas of conflict in your Needs Circle? What changes would you like to make in the way that you meet your needs?

What interesting patterns do you notice about your Needs Circle? (Which areas of the circle are more full/less full? Did you list some things in more than one part of the circle?)

Which of the multiple intelligences did you need to use to complete the Needs Circle activity?

CHAPTER 32

THE EVOLUTION AND APPLICATION OF PEER MEDIATION IN SCHOOLS

Carl J. Sheperis and Tiffany D. Chandler

Preview

Peer mediation is a popular and frequently endorsed conflict-resolution intervention for today's schools. In fact, over 10,000 peer-mediation programs are currently in existence across the United States (Lee & Throckmorton, 2007). Although authors have detailed the fundamental aspects of mediation programs, few have reported the effects those programs have on school climate, discipline referrals, or on the mediators themselves. We provide an overview of the structure of peer-mediation programs and evidence related to the efficacy of mediation as a tool for conflict resolution.

School violence is a topic of concern for many professional school counselors. School shootings, such as those at Columbine High School in Colorado and Pearl High School in Mississippi, have been heralded in the media, placing a focus on shootings or guns at school. However, school violence also includes behaviors such as teasing, bullying, and fighting or arguing at recess or between classes. Although these interpersonal conflicts receive less attention in the media, they represent the majority of conflicts occurring in school settings on a daily basis.

The traditional method of addressing interpersonal conflicts in schools has been "punishment based" (e.g., parent conferences, detentions, suspension, or expulsion; Johnson & Johnson, 1995a). However, there is little evidence to support the efficacy of these methods in reducing interpersonal conflict in schools. Further, researchers usually have concluded that punishments do not resolve interpersonal problems among students or produce the desired result of increased positive behavior. Therefore, education professionals still seek new methods to address aggressive behavior and conflict among and by students. One popular and frequently endorsed potential solution for today's schools is peer mediation (D'Andrea & Daniels, 1996).

Peer mediation is a form of conflict resolution often used in school settings that involves use of a third party—presumably, an impartial person—to assist in resolving a dispute between two or more people (Girard, Rifkin, & Townley, 1985). This voluntary negotiation helps to define and clarify issues and needs, create solutions, and reach mutually satisfactory agreements (Roush & Hall, 1993). Peer mediation is a form of facilitated interpersonal communication that requires the application of problem-solving methods to achieve agreement between or among disputants (Sweeney & Carruthers,

1996). Peer mediation differs from other peer-led programs such as peer counseling or peer helpers, because it involves a well-defined, structured process with distinct roles for each participant (Smith & Daunic, 2002).

School districts within the United States have increasingly adopted peer-mediation programs over the last decade with over 10,000 programs in existence today (Lee & Throckmorton, 2007). Many authors have detailed the fundamental aspects of mediation programs (e.g., Lee & Throckmorton, 2007; Schrumpf, Crawford, & Bodine, 1997; Schrumpf, Crawford, & Usadel, 1991; Smith & Daunic, 2002), but few have reported the effects those programs have on school climate, discipline referrals or on the mediators themselves. We will provide professional school counselors with an overview of the structure of peer-mediation programs and report on evidence related to the efficacy of mediation as a tool for conflict resolution. The authors have given specific attention to several areas, including (a) the evolution of conflict resolution, (b) models of peer mediation, and (c) the efficacy of mediation programs. With regard to the efficacy of programs, this chapter explores the impact of these mediation programs on school climate, mediators, and reduction in number of discipline referrals. The material presented will assist professional school counselors in the selection of mediation programs and provide appropriate rationale for school administration.

Conflict Resolution

Before engaging in a discourse about peer mediation, it is important for professional school counselors to recognize that conflict is a naturally occurring phenomenon. Maurer (1991) defined conflict as "disagreement resulting from incompatible demands between or among two or more parties" (p. 1). Throughout history, conflict has been resolved through a continuum that ranges from the most destructive form, warfare, to instances of cooperative and other constructive resolutions (Sweeney & Carruthers, 1996). In fact, conflict is often associated with negativity when, actually, it can be positive if it provides insight and personal growth as well as social change (Cowan, Palomares, & Schilling, 1992; Deutsch, 1994; Johnson & Johnson, 1991; Lee & Throckmorton, 2007). Every conflict has a consequence and if seen as a process, it will lead to an eventual conclusion. Since conflict is dynamic, change begins the very moment conflict arises and continues until the conflict is resolved. The quality of change due to conflict is dependent upon the skill in which the conflict is managed and resolved (Cowan et al., 1992; Johnson & Johnson, 1991).

Research conducted by DeCecco and Richards (1974) revealed that 90% of conflicts reported by students were either unresolved or resolved in destructive ways. Negotiation of conflicts was almost nonexistent. In order for students to manage their conflicts constructively, there must be a shared understanding of appropriate procedures (Johnson & Johnson, 1991). Constructive conflict management becomes more pressing with the knowledge that conflicts with destructive outcomes among students in the United States are climbing at an alarming rate. Arrest rates for aggravated assault by youth were 70% higher in 1999 as compared to 1983 (U.S. Department of Health and Human Services, 2000). It is also estimated that over 25,000 handguns enter schools daily, and a quarter of all high school seniors have reported threats of violence.

PEER INVOLVEMENT

Myrick and Erney (1985) emphasized that one of the most important conflict-related educational concepts to emerge has been that of students helping students. The modern view on student discipline moves the emphasis away from punitive measures as an outcome of conflict to more self-discipline and student-controlled methods of conflict resolution (i.e., negotiation and mediation). Programs that depend solely on adult decision making fail to teach students appropriate resolution skills to use in the absence of adult supervision (Roush & Hall, 1993). Maxwell (1989) stated that self-regulation can be fostered in students when they are given the opportunity to participate in decisions relating to their own lives.

ELEMENTS OF CONFLICT-RESOLUTION PROGRAMS

The use of conflict-resolution techniques in schools has grown rapidly. For example, the National Association for Mediation in Education (NAME) estimated that the number of school-based conflict-resolution programs has grown from 50 in 1984 to well over 8,500 (Cornell, Loper, Atkinson, & Sheras, 1999). The Responding to Conflict Creatively Program (RCCP), one of the earliest conflict-resolution programs, now operates in approximately 300 schools nationwide. Other programs have increased and expanded similarly. For example, the New Mexico Center for Dispute Resolution has conducted a statewide school-mediation program for 10 years, and its programs currently involve over 30,000 students. Similarly, through the Community Board Program, a majority of San Francisco's schools have peer conflict managers (National Institute for Dispute Resolution, 1993).

Conflict-resolution programs typically include a curriculum designed to provide basic knowledge to students about individual differences, changing win–lose situations to win–win solutions and using negotiation to resolve conflicts effectively (Smith & Daunic, 2002). These programs often focus on social skills such as empathy training, effective communication, and stress and anger management; attitudes about conflict; bias awareness; and negotiation and large-group problems solving (Cowan et al., 1992; Johnson & Johnson, 1991). Teachers or other school professionals help students learn a process for handling interpersonal conflict by focusing on skill development within a general conceptual framework rather than on how to solve an immediate, specific problem (Smith & Daunic, 2002).

Through a variety of learning experiences and focus on student empowerment, conflict-resolution curricula can (a) facilitate the understanding of conflict and its determinants; (b) teach students effective communication, problem solving, and negotiation; (c) provide a foundation for education about peace and nonviolence; and (d) transfer students' responsibility for choosing which strategy to use in response to actual conflict situations (Cowan et al., 1992; Johnson & Johnson, 1991; Smith & Daunic, 2002; Woody, 2001).

PEER MEDIATION AS CONFLICT RESOLUTION

Peer mediation is both the most typical and most recommended form of conflict resolution in today's schools (Johnson & Johnson, 1995a; Lee & Throckmorton, 2007). Typically, there are three stages in the implementation of a school-based peer-mediation program. The introductory stage involves (a) making operational decisions, (b) introducing the program to the school staff, and (c) gaining support for its implementation from a variety of interested parties. This process is followed by the training stage which involves selecting and training the peer mediators. The final operational stage involves (a) operating the program, (b) evaluating its effectiveness, and (c) planning for its future (Lupton-Smith & Carruthers, 1996).

Johnson and Johnson (1995b) claimed that peer-mediation programs can be implemented in either total school or cadre approaches. The cadre approach, which has two models (elective course or student club), involves training a small number of students to serve as peer mediators and is based on the assumption that a few specially trained students can defuse and constructively resolve interpersonal conflicts among students. This type of training usually occurs in an intensive workshop or semester-long course.

Although the approaches and models of peer-mediation implementation maintain theoretical distinctions, they can overlap in practice. For example, some schools have established both club and elective course models simultaneously, while other schools have a total school program that has evolved from a cadre approach (Lee & Throckmorton, 2007; Lupton-Smith & Carruthers, 1996).

CLUB MODEL

The student club model of peer mediation involves selecting students from the entire student body and bringing them together at a time and place outside of their regular curriculum. Training times may occur while school is in session (e.g., club periods, study halls, specific class period) or outside of school hours (e.g., weekends, before/after school, or summer). An advantage to this model is the ability of the coordinator to select mediators from the school population who will represent the total student body, ensuring diverse perspectives and representation among mediators. Some disadvantages to this model include (a) less depth in training, (b) decreased access to support systems as compared to the elective course model, and (c) difficulty with supervision for mediations (Lee & Throckmorton, 2007; Lupton-Smith & Carruthers, 1996).

ELECTIVE COURSE MODEL

Graham and Cline (1989) suggested that an elective course model, dedicated to conflict resolution and specifically peer-mediation training, can be implemented either as a general elective or as a part of a social studies curriculum. This model provides more consistency with regard to training conditions (e.g., training, supervision, debriefing, and further leadership development) and flexibility for scheduling mediations. However, a considerable weakness in this model is that selection of mediators is limited to only those students enrolled in the course. Thus, diversity within the mediator pool is limited by nature of the model. Within this model, the pool of mediators is further limited by restrictions to class size (Lee & Throckmorton, 2007; Lupton-Smith & Carruthers, 1996).

TOTAL SCHOOL MODEL

Johnson and Johnson (1994) have advocated for the total school approach, in which all students are taught the principles and practices of conflict resolution and peer mediation and are encouraged to serve as mediators. This approach can be easily infused into a language arts or social studies curriculum (Lee & Throckmorton, 2007). The total school approach ensures that the entire student body is exposed to conflict-resolution concepts, resulting in a developmental learning opportunity within each student's educational experience. However, this approach requires a considerable amount of time and commitment from the school staff and administration. In addition, this approach may be more applicable in an elementary school format, where teachers retain the same students for most of the school day (Lupton-Smith & Carruthers, 1996).

Although there are several models of mediation, all tend to follow the same general process, where mediators (a) provide a nonthreatening environment in which disputants can tell their side of the story, (b) focus disputants on mutually identified problems and identify any common ground, (c) help disputants develop a list of possible solutions and rationale for each solution, (d) assist disputants to take each other's perspective accurately and fully, and (e) guide disputants to mutually agreed-upon resolutions and formalize each agreement (Johnson & Johnson, 1991; Smith & Daunic, 2002).

EFFICACY OF PEER-MEDIATION PROGRAMS

When examining the literature to determine the effectiveness of peer-mediation programs, two things become apparent. One is that, despite the widespread popularity and use of peer-mediation programs, there is a relatively small amount of literature on the evaluation of such programs (Webster, 1993). What also quickly becomes apparent is the lack of consistency in available research results. This may be due to a number of factors, including (a) methodological shortcomings, (b) the number of different models of peer-mediation programs in existence (i.e., total school model vs. cadre model), and (c) the fact that many programs are used in conjunction with other types of conflict-resolution programs (Carruthers & Sweeney, 1996). It is important to remember that because such programs are in place in schools, they will naturally lack the research safeguards that are in place in the laboratory setting. Thus, it is difficult to control for internal as well as external variables in school-based research.

It is also important to remember that adequate evaluation of mediation programs requires specific parameters and criteria. For instance, a given program may be said to improve the social standing and negotiation abilities of peer mediators and yet have little impact on the number of disputes referred to teachers from the student body. Without standard criteria to gauge the success of such a program, the door is open for disagreement among teachers, parents, and the public at large on whether or not the program has been successful.

One potential causative factor in the lack of available parameters for evaluating mediation programs is the lack of applicability of quantitative evaluation methods. More specifically, the characteristics of mediation programs (e.g., lack of consistency in design and implementation) violate the rules of many statistical analyses. For instance, proponents of mediation may decide that a specific peer-mediation program will be considered successful if it improves the school climate in those schools in which it has been implemented. In such a case, evaluation is difficult because school climate is based on perception. The questions then become *Whose perception? Students? Teachers? Administrators? Parents?* and *How are these perceptions measured?*

Because of the amount of resources necessary to establish and effectively operate a peer-mediation program, it is critical that such expenditures of time and energy be justified on a continual basis. For this reason alone, despite all the difficulties involved in conducting research in school settings, it is crucial that such evaluation does take place. At present, many school officials base their justification on several claims that have been made regarding the efficacy of school peer-mediation programs. Proponents of mediation as an effective method of conflict resolution have claimed that such programs may improve school climate, may improve certain skills and functioning of the mediators, and may reduce the number of disputes reported to teachers (Lam, 1989; Tolson, McDonald, & Moriarty, 1992). Following is a review of the literature related to each.

IMPACT ON SCHOOL CLIMATE

A number of studies on the nature and pervasiveness of school conflict have followed the seminal efforts of DeCecco and Richards (1974). Although there are varied reports on the most common types of school conflict (Johnson, Johnson, & Dudley, 1992; Johnson, Johnson, Dudley, Ward, & Magnuson, 1995), researchers have painted a picture of widespread conflict and daily disputes in the lives of most students. Many researchers and practitioners have thus begun to focus on ways to improve students' skills in dealing with conflict (Johnson, Johnson, & Dudley, 1994). It was hoped that by improving these skills in students, a more positive school climate could be achieved.

Claims of improved school climate are typically based on the perception of a group of people familiar with the school both before and after implementation of the program. The vast majority of studies reviewed included some type of assessment of the attitudes of students, teachers, administrators, or parents toward the program and its impact (e.g., Johnson et al., 1994; Lindsay, 1998; Roush & Hall, 1993). Generally, these attitudes have been very positive, and it is common for teachers and parents to report an improvement in school environment, morale, and safety. Thompson (1996) found that 92% of surveyed teachers reported the belief that a peer-mediation program at a middle school in Georgia had effectively improved school morale. It is also not uncommon for mediators to report an improved attitude toward school and school activities (Araki, 1990). However, because peer-mediation programs reviewed in the literature were often used as a part of larger conflict management programs, it is impossible to state affirmatively that improvements in school climate were due only to the peer-mediation portion of conflict-resolution programs.

IMPACT ON PEER MEDIATORS

A number of studies have looked at changes in the abilities and social status of student mediators following implementation of a peer-mediation program. The reported findings have been quite interesting, though far from consistent. Generally, there have been positive findings in the areas of mediator skills and abilities. Roush and Hall (1993) found that following implementation of a peer-mediation program, teachers reported positive changes in peer mediators in areas of listening and problem-solving skills. Lane-Garon (1998) demonstrated that mediation training may benefit mediators by increasing cognitive and affective perspective taking. Some researchers have suggested that mediation training may have a positive effect on academic performance (Araki, 1990; Johnson & Johnson, 1994).

There is also evidence that the conflict-resolution skills derived from training at school may generalize to other settings (Johnson et al., 1992). Gentry and Beneson (1992) reported that following participation in peer mediation, mediators perceived a decrease in the frequency and intensity of conflicts with their siblings at home. Parents of these mediators also reported a decrease in conflicts between their children. Despite the evidence on generalization, there is less evidence on how well these skills are maintained over time. Studies have shown that mediators retain conflict-resolution skills after training (Johnson et al., 1992), but no studies have demonstrated maintenance over a longer period of time.

In the area of mediator social status, there has been far less agreement. One might expect that there would be some positive changes in how peer mediators are perceived by other students. Looking at students' methods of dealing with conflict and social status apart from any type of mediation program, Bryant (1992) found a correlation between the two variables. Students who were generally regarded more favorably by peers were viewed as more likely to use a calm approach to conflict resolution. Thus, it should not be surprising that most mediators report enjoying being mediators (Humphries, 1999; Schrumpf et al., 1991).

However, many mediators also reported some drawbacks to the experience. Humphries (1999) interviewed peer mediators at an elementary school program. Although every mediator stated that they enjoyed being a peer mediator and a large majority viewed the process as favorable overall, many also reported negative aspects. Problems mentioned included being antagonized by nonpeer mediators and having a negative popularity status. Though it is impossible to empirically establish a causal relationship between participation as a peer mediator and such negative experiences, these reports rightfully raised concerns among professional school counselors. Self-concept is another area that has yet to be fully understood. Roush and Hall (1993) found a significant increase in the self-concept of junior high students enrolled in a conflict-resolution course, but no increase in the self-concept of elementary school peer mediators.

IMPACT ON REDUCTION OF DISCIPLINE REFERRALS

One of the most common findings in research literature on peer mediation is the high percentage of disputants who reach agreement after having their conflict mediated by a peer. Most evaluations (Johnson & Johnson, 1994; Johnson et al., 1992, 1994; Schrumpf et al., 1991) have reported agreement rates of over 80%. Using this factor, among others, as criteria for success, Daunic, Smith, Robinson, Landry, and Miller (2000) and Smith and Daunic (2002) reported positive results in three middle schools. Over the course of several years, over 95% of mediated conflicts resulted in a solution acceptable to both parties. However, in each of the three schools, peer mediation was used in conjunction with a school-wide conflict-resolution program (Pitts et al., 1996), thus it is impossible to measure the effects of peer mediation alone. Lupton-Smith and Curruthers (1996) discussed three peer-mediation programs used in an elementary school, a middle school, and a high school. Although each program was different, the authors reported that each of the three programs resulted in at least 95% of mediated disputes resolved peacefully. However, they cautioned that program evaluation should be based on additional factors beyond the number of disputes peacefully mediated.

In addition, some reports have claimed that peer-mediation programs have helped to reduce the number of discipline events or discipline referrals at school. For example, Thompson (1996), reporting on the effectiveness of one peer-mediation program, found that over the course of 2 years, student suspensions were reduced by 50%. While this claim is one of the most powerful arguments for implementing peer-mediation programs, there is a lack of strong empirical evidence for such claims. Carruthers and Sweeney (1996) noted that reductions in discipline referrals may simply be the result of different classifications for incidents that go to mediation as opposed to incidents that are referred to administration. As evidence, Tolson et al. (1992) reported that a peer-mediation program in a suburban high school showed a significant reduction in the number of discipline referrals for interpersonal problems; however, there was no change in the total number of discipline referrals.

Summary/Conclusion

As more research is produced, a clearer picture regarding the impact of peer mediation on schools, mediators, and disputants will emerge. At present, it appears that peer mediation can be a positive and significant resource for professional school counselors. Although a number of authors have questioned the effectiveness or the use of peer-mediation programs for adolescents (Gerber, 1999; Webster, 1993), others have described successful high school programs (e.g., Lupton-Smith & Carruthers, 1996). The claims related to benefits of peer mediation are numerous, including that peer-mediation programs foster a cooperative and comfortable atmosphere in which students can learn more efficiently and teachers can spend more time teaching. In addition, there is some evidence that students involved in peer-mediation programs develop feelings of empowerment, learn to take responsibility, and develop constructive solutions for interpersonal problems (Maxwell, 1989). Evidence also exists that peer-mediation programs offer potential reductions in violence, vandalism, chronic school absence, and student suspensions in schools (Araki, 1990; Koch, 1988; McCormick, 1988). Finally, some authors have asserted that peer mediation reduces the time teachers spend involved in resolving conflicts in their classrooms, thus focusing more time on student learning (Johnson & Johnson, 1994). Future studies should investigate maintenance of learned skills as well as progress monitoring the effectiveness of peer-mediation programs. Although more research needs to be conducted in order to further substantiate these claims, it appears that peer-mediation programs have an overall positive impact on school systems, mediators, and disputants.

(Note: See the CD-ROM for a list of references.)

TECHNIQUES AND APPROACHES
TO COUNSELING

CHAPTER 33

PROFESSIONAL SCHOOL COUNSELORS
AND REALITY THERAPY

Robert E. Wubbolding

Preview

The WDEP (Wants, Direction or Doing, Evaluation, Plans) system of reality therapy provides a practical, useable system for professional school counselors in their many roles. When implementing this system, counselors help students, clients, staff, and parents to conduct inner self-evaluations of their behaviors. Reality therapy also focuses on the overall atmosphere of the classroom and school building through the use of class meetings that have a clearly defined and readily adaptable format.

Most, but not all, human problems are rooted in dysfunctional, disturbed, or out-of-balance relationships. Effective participant interdependence, on the other hand, facilitates and supports the success of most human endeavors. W. Glasser (2005) described healthy human relationships as the cornerstone of mental health: "You are mentally healthy if you enjoy being with most of the people you know, especially with the important people in your life" (p. 2). The school setting is one of the most important human endeavors in which human relationships provide a foundational and crucial position. When a school faculty "get along well" with each other, the school is a joyful place, and students learn at a higher level (Ludwig & Mentley, 1997). If students believe their teachers care about them, respect their opinions, listen to them, and try to make learning fun, they are more inclined to want to learn and, in turn, get along with each other. Therefore, achieving in school and healthy relationships are interconnected. Wubbolding (2005) stated that "a job successfully performed results in the satisfaction of power (achievement) and sometimes belonging" (p. 43).

The results of using reality therapy, called *lead management* in schools, are not perfect, but a total immersion can result in major improvements for individual students and for the entire organization. Chaddock School, a residential school for court-referred students in Quincy, Illinois, reduced behavioral incidents to an insignificant level in just over 3 years (Wubbolding, 2000). By following the teaching of W. Edwards Deming (1993), institutions and individuals implementing the philosophy of continuous improvement see ongoing progress rather than remaining in a holding pattern emphasizing mere survival. Reality therapy and lead management are effective vehicles for expediting this journey.

Clearly, the professional school counselor's mission in the context of reality therapy is the enhancement of relationships. This does not imply a blind, cultic uniformity of viewpoints, but rather a healthy give and take, based on respect for diverse ways of doing things. A key question professional school counselors ask of students and staff is, "Are our current actions bringing us closer together, or are they distancing us from each other?" One of the appealing aspects of reality therapy is its practicality and usefulness with individuals and groups of students, faculty, and parents as well as its organizational applications.

The acronym WDEP summarizes the professional school counselor's use of reality therapy and helps the user remember the concepts. It serves as a pedagogical tool, providing all staff members with a common language as well as a structure for intervening in their classrooms and in all their human interactions.

The professional school counselor wears many hats and has a variety of overlapping roles: counselor, consultant, parent educator, in-service trainer, personal-growth facilitator, advocate, community leader. The WDEP system of reality therapy applies to each of these roles in that it is based on universal principles that are applicable to virtually every human interaction (Wubbolding, 2006a).

THE WDEP SYSTEM

Grounded in choice theory, the WDEP system assists human beings to satisfy five generic human motivators: (a) survival or self-preservation, (b) love or belonging, (c) power or achievement, (d) freedom or independence, and (e) fun or enjoyment. When people interact with their environment, they build an internal collection of specific wants or pictures that are related to the motivators or needs. In the first step in employing the WDEP system (W–*wants*), a professional school counselor helps students define and clarify their wants, goals, hopes, and dreams related to belonging, power, freedom, and fun. For example, students define what they want from school, parents, teachers, and friends. In consulting with teachers, professional school counselors assist them to define what they want from students and parents as well as to disclose their own expectations (wants) to their students in direct, firm, but nonpunitive ways. When children are obstinate, uncooperative, and resistant, teachers and parents are astounded to see such behaviors diminish or vanish when they ask, "What do you want right now?" or "How hard do you want to work at changing your situation?" Of course, interventions based on this question do not produce a magical, immediate, or total reversal of behavior. Rather, such interventions need to be habitual.

Professional school counselors encourage teachers to teach the five motivators and ask students what they want from themselves, by defining their levels of commitment regarding how hard they want to work at satisfying their needs and get what they want. If professional school counselors and teachers visibly display the levels of commitment for all to see, they can reinforce their teaching at strategic moments (Wubbolding, 2000).

COMMITMENT LEVEL I: "I DON'T WANT TO DO ANYTHING."

This is, in fact, no commitment, but resistant students, parents, and even teachers often manifest little or no commitment to improve. Professional school counselors using the WDEP system see these behaviors not as mere obstacles but as opportunities to raise their skills to a higher level. Oftentimes, the most negative adults become enthusiastic supporters and users of reality therapy in education.

COMMITMENT LEVEL II: "I'LL TRY." "I MIGHT." "I COULD."

This middle level of commitment is more likely to succeed but still retains an escape hatch to failure. "Trying" to study, be patient, or develop better interpersonal relationships is not identical with successful followthrough. Professional school counselors need to encourage everyone to raise his or her level of commitment. "I know you'll try, but will you do it?" School personnel realize that athletic team members describing their commitment as "We will try to win" appears less confident than the team who yells "We're number one" or "We *will* win."

COMMITMENT LEVEL III: "I WILL."

Here, the person expresses a genuine desire to move forward, solve a problem, and take effective action. A school faculty might agree to implement the quality school philosophy (W. Glasser, 1998) and to use the WDEP system to focus on classroom management, absenteeism, raising test scores, or a variety of other objectives.

The levels of commitment provide a language for counselors' own use as well as a system for assisting teachers to elicit a higher level of student motivation. As Wubbolding and Brickell (2005) stated, "The levels of commitment . . . operationalize the proven fact that strong and explicit statements bring about change in behavior" (p. 41).

Consequently, the WDEP system is more than a vague "What do you want?" approach. It can get as intricate and extensive as is necessary for initiating and accomplishing the many tasks involved in school improvement. (See Appendixes 33.A and 33.B at the end of this chapter.)

"What are you doing?" (D) represents a simplified question related to the exploration of four aspects of behavior:

Physiology—"Does anything hurt?"

Feelings—"How do you feel?"

Thinking—"What are you telling yourself about your current situation?"

Actions (the most changeable part of this suitcase of behavior)—"Tell me what's going on now." "What did she say?" "What happened?"

Emphasizing actions in counseling and consultation draws attention to the most easily changed component of the behavioral system. When a person chooses to change his or her actions, the other components are brought along. When a person acts enthusiastic, tagging along behind is a change in feelings. Genuine feelings of enthusiasm are likely to be a consequence of the initial change in actions. Teachers, parents, and others learn that effective change in students' attitudes follow upon a change in students' actions.

Professional school counselors who work with children or adults do not ignore feelings; rather, they listen empathically to the emotional level. They acknowledge feelings, help clients accept their feelings, and discuss them as openly as is reasonable. Yet, as quickly as possible, they encourage clients to discuss the components of human behavior over which they have most control, actions, and secondarily, thinking. They emphasize that behavior is a choice, especially *actions*, the most clearly chosen aspect of behavior. Though no one explicitly chooses anger, shame, rage, guilt, loneliness, or depression, many individuals choose an action that brings pain along with it, as a car brings along a trunk filled with baggage. Thus, a student cursing a teacher in anger and rage chooses the action. An inseparable part of the total behavior is the feeling of rage and accompanying self-talk or inner discourse.

Reality therapy lends itself to a discussion of students' thinking as well as to actions and feelings. Wubbolding (2000) identified several negative or less effective self-talk statements concomitant with less effective actions:

A. "I am powerless and have no choices" accompanies depression.

B. "No one can tell me what to do" accompanies antisocial actions.

C. "Even though what I'm currently doing is not effective, still I will choose it again and again" accompanies repeated self-destructive actions.

Professional school counselors using the WDEP system of reality therapy teach this recent addition to students, faculty, parents, and the public. The final and most important self-talk statement is operationalized in many ways: "If I'm frustrating myself by doing something which is ineffective or harmful in order to improve, I will do more of what has not helped me."

Professional school counselors teach more effective cognitive statements to their various groups of consumers. These include:

A. "I have choices and I choose my behaviors."

B. "I am happy when I live within reasonable boundaries."

C. "If my current behavior is not working for me, I'll choose a different action."

Implementing the "D" (doing) of the WDEP system means that each component of the behavior is discussed with emphasis on the action element. It is as though the action is the handle of the suitcase of human behavior. When someone chooses to grab the handle and lift, the entire suitcase follows.

Self-Evaluation (E) is the cornerstone of the WDEP delivery system and constitutes the major prerequisite for change. No one changes a behavior or makes a better choice until he or she judges that the current course of action is not helpful. Students not studying, wasting time by hanging out, or yielding to harmful impulses do not change a direction until they formulate a want, look searchingly at their choices, and make a firm judgment about the usefulness of their behavior. Working in groups or individually, professional school counselors help students, faculty or parents describe what they want, and connect their actions to their wants by assisting them to courageously evaluate whether their actions are helping or hurting.

Wubbolding (2000) has enumerated 22 kinds of self-evaluation. The following are among the most important questions:

- Is your current behavior bringing you closer or farther away from the people around you?
- Is what you're doing getting you what you want?
- Is what you're doing helping or hurting the people around you?

- Is what you're doing against the law, the rules—written or unwritten?
- Is what you want realistic or attainable?
- Is what you want really and truly good for you in the long run, not merely in the short run?
- Is your current level of commitment high enough?
- Is your plan for improvement an effective plan?

In any role, the professional school counselor facilitates a discussion of current wants and behaviors, an inner self-evaluation of them, and a plan of action (P). Effective plans need not be grandiose. Useful plans are SAMIC plans:

Simple—not complicated

Attainable—realistically doable

Measurable—answers the question, "When will you do it?"

Immediate—performed sooner rather than later

Controlled by the planner—not dependent on someone else's plans

While asking the question "What's your plan?" seems clear and direct, there is an underlying metacommunication present. The person asked this simple question and other questions in the WDEP system gains a sense of hope and a belief in personal responsibility through an implicit awakening: "Change is possible and I can make it happen. I cannot blame others for my plight."

Case Example 1: Jamal

Jamal, age 11, says he "hates school." It is evident to all that he has no friends in school, is a discipline problem for teachers, and has poor grades. The professional school counselor helps Jamal define his wants regarding (a) having more friends and getting along with his teachers (belonging), (b) getting better grades and learning school subject matter (power), and (c) making school more enjoyable (fun). Jamal describes his current behavioral choices as the counselor helps him evaluate them with such questions as, "If you tell off the teacher, will you get what you want from her?" and "If you fight with the other students, will you gain any friends?" If Jamal is amenable to the idea, the professional school counselor helps him make a realistic, doable plan perhaps to act appropriately for 1 hour a day or to attempt to befriend one student. The counselor might tell him, "A journey of a thousand miles is begun with one step." Consequently, this realistic plan is a beginning. If his teachers are learning the WDEP system, they too realize that Jamal will not make an immediate 180° turn. The philosophy underlying this effort is based on the principle that when Jamal fulfills his needs within the school setting, his failure choices will diminish, and he will be on the road of continuous improvement.

Case Example 2: Teacher Group

Seven English teachers in a large high school seek better behavior management skills for their classes. The professional school counselor leads a discussion about the ABC toxic behaviors—behaviors that damage relationships and chill warm friendships. These include (a) arguing, attacking, accusing; (b) bossing, blaming, belittling; and (c) criticizing, coercing, condemning.

Using the WDEP system, the professional school counselor helps the teachers define what they want from the students, what they can settle for, and what they're doing to get what they want. In a nonjudgmental atmosphere, they evaluate whether and to what degree they are succeeding in achieving their goals. The professional school counselor facilitates making plans and provides many resources, such as the *Phi Delta Kappan* article "Choices for Children: Why and How to Let Students Decide," by Alfie Kohn (1993). This article provides a review of studies showing that when students are accorded choices in classrooms, their overall performance improves.

CASE EXAMPLE 3: MIDDLE SCHOOL TEACHERS

Eight middle school teachers seeking ways to prevent problems and increase students' curiosity for learning meet with the professional school counselor to brainstorm solutions and explore the possibility of coordinated action. They have heard about class meetings as a central component of Glasser's quality school (W. Glasser, 2001). They ask the professional school counselor to discuss the mechanics and the benefits of implementing this strategy. The professional school counselor, serving as in-service trainer, teaches about class meetings from the outline provided in the following section.

CLASS MEETINGS

Class meetings provide a structure for discussion of timely and relevant topics and are designed to help students satisfy one or more of the five human needs or motivators. Carleen Glasser (2004) developed resource materials on class meetings for teachers that professional school counselors can also use as they consult with teachers. The teacher helps students gain a sense of belonging, a feeling of inner control (as one student stated, "The teacher respects my opinion"), fun (the reward of learning), and freedom or independence. In general, as Erwin (2006) stated, "holding regular class meetings can develop and maintain a strong sense of community" (p. 13). It should be noted that while the class meeting leader is most often a teacher, a professional school counselor might also volunteer to conduct class meetings. Thus, the following discussion provides the professional school counselor with knowledge that will help him or her in either a direct intervention role or in the role of consultant.

TOPICS

Students begin by discussing intellectual topics, especially if this structure is new to them. Only when they become comfortable with this format should the teacher use the meetings for more emotional topics or problem solving. Consequently, meetings are *not* therapy sessions in which there is confrontation, personal self-disclosure, catharsis, or direct disputation of others' judgments. Selected topics may include value of homework, need for rules, friendship, respect for property (especially computers), quality of work, and effort. Topics related to curriculum may be why one should study math, definitions of old age, the value of knowing history, and various topics related to science.

PROCESS

The teacher plays an unambiguous role as a leader, asking students to express their opinions or to simply "pass" if they do not want to speak aloud. Teachers need to realize that during the class meeting the emphasis is on opinions; therefore, there is no need to correct factual inaccuracies. More direct pedagogy is reserved for the major part of the students' school time outside class meetings. The 3-step process, Define, Personalize, and Challenge, provides a clear, nonthreatening format.

Define. Many teachers find a discussion of *effort* useful. This topic could be repeated occasionally when appropriate (e.g., at the start of the school year, after holidays, during the midwinter letdown). Questions focus on "What is effort?" "How do you know you are making a good effort to do quality work?" "What is quality?" In a science class, a teacher might ask students to define *fire*. In one school, there had been a fire across from the school, making the meeting even more relevant. "What are helpful fires (e.g., the sun) and harmful fires (e.g., a fire in the house)?"

Teacher creativity and ingenuity usually produce many extensions of this component. In another meeting, students defined what old age means to them. Some responded that anyone who is 18 years of age or older is old. Others had grandparents or even great grandparents and saw old age as 70, 80, or older.

Personalize. An effective meeting on *effort* involves questions such as, "What motivates you to put forth extra or high-quality effort?" "If someone were to see you exerting low-, middle-, or high-quality effort, what would they see?" A skilled teacher or professional school counselor demonstrating a class meeting asks such questions as, "Have you ever seen a fire?" "What treasures would you take with you if you had to escape from a fire?" "Do you know what to do if we had to leave this building because of fire?" Questions centering on the meeting about old age could include, "Do you know anyone who is old?" "What do people who are old do for fun?" "How are they the same or different from anyone else?"

Challenge. In this step, teachers push students to reflect on their knowledge, to reevaluate it, and to further develop it. Three types of questions constitute the *challenge* phase of the meeting. Keep in mind the focus is on opinions and questions to which there need not be correct answers.

- *Why?* Students are challenged to examine the basis of their beliefs. Some "Why?" questions are unanswerable, beyond the current intellectual level of students, or require additional thought. "Why do people exert high or low levels of effort?" "Why does fire exist?" "What would we do without fire?" "Why do people grow old?" "If you could drink a potion and live to be 200 years old, would you drink it? Why or why not?" "Would you drink if there were only enough for the members of this class? Why or why not?"

- *What if?* Another challenge question revolves around imaginative thinking: "What if people always make the lowest or highest effort possible?" "How would your life be different if everyone made a high-level effort to be your friend, to play the athletic game to the best of their ability, to provide the best service possible?" "What if you could start or stop a fire just by thinking about it?" "What would life be like if the sun became much hotter or cooler?" "What if there were two suns instead of one sun?" "What if no one would grow old?" "What if all diseases were curable?"
- *What's the difference?* In "What's the difference between . . . ?" questions, students learn to make distinctions in their thinking as a result of class meetings. "What's the difference between low-level effort and high-level effort?" "What's the difference between high-quality and low-quality relationships, toys, bicycles, schoolwork, and so on?" "What's the difference between a helpful fire and a harmful fire?" "Could a helpful fire ever become a harmful one?" In one class, students talked about the dangers of sunburn and how to take precautionary steps to avoid it. "What's the difference between maturity and old age?" Does wisdom always come with age?" "Can a young person be wise and an older person not so wise?" "How could people in this class become wiser?"

GOALS

As a result of stimulating intellectual discussions in which students express a wide range of viewpoints, experiences, and opinions, they learn respect for each other, gain a genuine appreciation of diversity, experience an increase in self-confidence, and develop deeper humanistic values. When students feel a sense of interdependence and connection, they grow in knowledge and their behavior improves. Additionally, they develop an appreciation for ideas and for intellectual discussions. This is especially valuable in an age when many kids' discussions and interactions often consist of demeaning and sarcastic humor.

TYPES OF MEETINGS

Professional school counselors understand the value, purpose, and process of class meetings. They provide demonstrations for teachers and coach teachers to conduct three types of meetings: open-ended, educational/diagnostic, and problem solving.

Open-ended meetings. The previously described meetings on the topics of old age and effort/quality are open ended, opinion centered, "no-correct answers" meetings. Teachers should conduct these meetings until the students and teachers feel comfortable with such discussions and they come to realize that, regardless of their opinions, they will not be criticized or put down.

Educational/diagnostic meetings. Some teachers using educational/diagnostic meetings begin each new study unit with a series of questions related to the topic. In these meetings, teachers conduct an informal verbal assessment of students' prior knowledge of the topic. The meeting centering on *fire* could be such a meeting, though it could also be an open-ended meeting. A history teacher could begin the school year with a meeting built around such questions as *What is history? Do you have your own personal history? Of what value is history? Why do we study history? What if you didn't know anything that happened prior to today?* Science, language, and computer teachers could begin their courses with similar questions. Revisiting these general topics throughout the school year is also useful.

Problem-solving meetings. Teachers wishing to solve problems often initiate class meetings focused on antisocial behavior and irresponsible behavior such as class disruption, respect for adults, drug use, homework, or others. These are the most difficult to conduct because of emotional overtones and the tendency for participants to blame individuals.

One teacher, a union leader in a junior high school who taught difficult classes with hard-to-reach students, told me in October, "I hate to come to this class," when referring to a class of seventh-graders. In April, he related that he looked forward to this same class of seventh-graders. Describing interventions causing this change, he related that he started with open-ended meetings during which students learned to respect various viewpoints. Then they discussed a school policy regarded as unfair (i.e., punishing all students sitting at a table in the cafeteria when only one student acted out). The class agreed to approach the student council, which presented the class consensus to the assistant principal, who agreed to change this ineffective and unfair rule. The teacher related that the students came to believe their judgment was worthy of respect. Their effective choices fulfilled their need for power or achievement in a positive way. They were then less inclined to choose self-defeating actions.

GUIDELINES AND CAUTIONS

The following guidelines are useful for professional school counselors who are either modeling class meetings or teaching other school staff the art of conducting them.

- Make every attempt to sit in a circle. Ideal and desirable, this rearrangement of chairs might be time-consuming, inconvenient, and even impossible. Students should know that "we're having a meeting"—even if adherence to a circled discussion is impractical. Nor should teachers rigidly wed themselves to the large circle structure when variations prove to be useful adjuncts. Some teachers train students to lead the meetings, split the group into two smaller groups, or combine the class meeting with cooperative learning activities (Wubbolding & Brickell, 2001). Buzzwords for teachers to consider are *flexibility, creativity, reevaluation, outcome focused,* and *consultation* with other professional school counselors and teachers. Meetings can be brief; they need not be lengthy. It is better for students to need more time than to be bored.
- Problem-solving meetings should focus on *conditions*, not the behavior of specific students. Emphasizing the negative behavior of specific students can result in criticism, embarrassment, and even humiliation for scapegoated children. Effective meetings emphasize positive outcomes and specific ways to improve the school atmosphere.
- A helpful first meeting for professional school counselors who are demonstrating class meetings or coaching teachers is a "meeting on rules" or a "meeting on meetings." Useful questions include, *What is a rule? What are rules you find helpful?*

What is your favorite rule? What's the difference between a rule, a law, and a suggestion? What if we had no rules? How would this class function without rules? How would society function? What rules do we need for our class meetings? Meetings focusing on the nature of a meeting could emphasize questions such as, *What is a meeting? Do your parents go to meetings? Why do people have meetings? What if no one ever went to a meeting? What do meetings accomplish? What makes for a good meeting?*

- Do not allow meetings to degenerate into gripe sessions. School rules, antisocial behavior, homework, the role of authority, and other topics can easily deteriorate if students and teachers are inexperienced in the art of group meetings. The structured process of *define, personalize, and challenge* combined with the WDEP system provide a viable alternative to such disasters.

- Class meetings enable students to develop appropriate language for expressing their opinions, to appreciate a diversity of worldviews and experiences, to enjoy intellectual conversations, to gain a feeling of respect from other students and teachers, and to engage in behaviors that enhance interpersonal relationships. These characteristics of class meetings are at the core of mental health. As Wubbolding (2006b, p. 6) stated, "Mental health has many implications: helping friends and family, acceptance of people who are different without demeaning criticism, and willingness to contribute to society."

SUMMARY/CONCLUSION

Professional school counselors interface with virtually every person associated with the school—students, faculty, administrators, parents, community members. The WDEP system provides a practical, research-based structure for counseling and consultation as well as content for in-service training. It also enriches the *define, personalize, and challenge* format for problem-solving class meetings. Asking students, "What do you want?" helps them to focus their attention on themselves rather than on everyone else. Asking students, "What are you doing?" narrows the discussion by focusing on the most easily controllable component of human behavior—actions. Self-evaluation is the necessary prelude to any change, and planning means taking responsibility for the future. Professional school counselors adopting the WDEP system of reality therapy have a comprehensive and programmatic basis for school improvement.

(Note: See the CD-ROM for a list of references.)

CYCLE OF MANAGING, SUPERVISING, COUNSELING AND COACHING

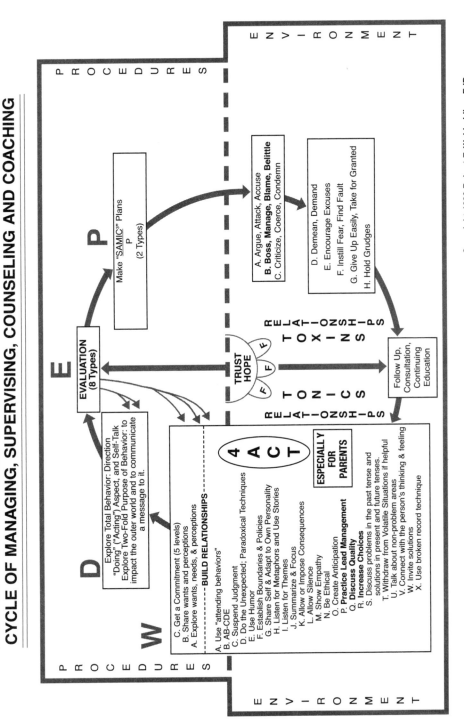

PROCEDURES

ENVIRONMENT

D Explore Total Behavior: Direction
"Doing" ("Acting") Aspect, and Self-Talk
Explore Two-Fold Purpose of Behavior: to
impact the outer world and to communicate
a message to it.

E EVALUATION
(8 Types)

P Make "SAMIC³" Plans
P
(2 Types)

W BUILD RELATIONSHIPS

A. Use "attending behaviors"
B. AB-CDE
C. Suspend Judgment
D. Do the Unexpected; Paradoxical Techniques
E. Use Humor
F. Establish Boundaries & Policies
G. Share Self & Adapt to Own Personality
H. Listen for Metaphors and Use Stories
I. Listen for Themes
J. Summarize & Focus
K. Allow or Impose Consequences
L. Allow Silence
M. Show Empathy
N. Be Ethical
O. Create Anticipation
P. **Practice Lead Management**
Q. **Discuss Quality**
R. **Increase Choices**
S. Discuss problems in the past tense and
solutions in present and future tenses.
T. Withdraw from Volatile Situations if helpful
U. Talk about non-problem areas
V. Connect with the person's thinking & feeling
W. Invite solutions
X. Use broken record technique

A. Explore wants, needs, & perceptions
B. Share wants and perceptions
C. Get a Commitment (5 levels)

4 A C T

ESPECIALLY FOR PARENTS

RELATIONSHIP-BUILDING
FFFF
TRUST
HOPE
RELATIONSHIP-DESTROYING

A. Argue, Attack, Accuse
B. **Boss, Manage, Blame, Belittle**
C. Criticize, Coerce, Condemn

D. Demean, Demand
E. Encourage Excuses
F. Instill Fear, Find Fault
G. Give Up Easily, Take for Granted
H. Hold Grudges

Follow Up,
Consultation,
Continuing
Education

Developed by **Robert E. Wubbolding, EdD**
from the works of William Glasser, MD

Copyright 1986 Robert E. Wubbolding, EdD
15th Revision 2006

SUMMARY DESCRIPTION OF THE
"CYCLE OF MANAGING, SUPERVISING, COUNSELING AND COACHING"

The Cycle is explained in detail in books by Robert E. Wubbolding:
Employee Motivation, 1996: Reality Therapy for the 21st Century, 2000
A Set of Directions for Putting and Keeping Yourself Together, 2001

Introduction:

The Cycle consists of two general concepts: Environment conducive to change and Procedures more explicitly designed to facilitate change. This chart is intended to be a **brief** summary. The ideas are designed to be used with employees, students, clients as well as in other human relationships.

Relationship between Environment & Procedures:

1. As indicated in the chart, the Environment is the foundation upon which the effective use of Procedures is based.

2. Though it is **usually** necessary to establish a safe, friendly Environment before change can occur, the "Cycle" can be entered at any point. Thus, the use of the cycle does **not** occur in lock step fashion.

3. Building a relationship implies establishing and maintaining a professional relationship. Methods for accomplishing this comprise some efforts on the part of the helper that are Environmental and others that are Procedural.

ENVIRONMENT:

Relationship Tonics: a close relationship is built on TRUST and HOPE through friendliness, firmness and fairness.

A. Using Attending Behaviors: Eye contact, posture, effective listening skills.
B. AB = "Always **B**e . . ." Consistent, **C**ourteous & **C**alm, **D**etermined that there is hope for improvement, **E**nthusiastic (Think Positively).
C. Suspend Judgment: View behaviors from a low level of perception, i.e., acceptance is crucial.
D. Do the Unexpected: Use paradoxical techniques as appropriate; Reframing and Prescribing.
E. Use Humor: Help them fulfill need for fun within reasonable boundaries.
F. Establish boundaries: the relationship is professional.

4 A C T

- Affirm feelings
- Accept
- Show affection
- Action consequences
- Conversation (WDEP)
- Time together

G. Share Self: Self-disclosure within limits is helpful; adapt to own personal style.
H. Listen for Metaphors: Use their figures of speech and provide other ones. Use stories.
I. Listen to Themes: Listen for behaviors that have helped, value judgements, etc.
J. Summarize & Focus: Tie together what they say and focus on them rather than on "Real World."
K. Allow or Impose Consequences: Within reason, they should be responsible for their own behavior.
L. Allow Silence: This allows them to think, as well as to take responsibility.
M. Show Empathy: Perceive as does the person being helped.
N. Be Ethical: Study Codes of Ethics and their applications, e.g., how to handle suicide threats or violent tendencies.
O. Create anticipation and communication hope. People should be taught that something good will happen if they are willing to work.
P. **Practice lead management, e.g., democracy in determining rules** .
Q. **Discuss quality.**
R. **Increases choices.**
S. Discuss problems in the past tense, solutions in present and future tenses.
T. Withdraw from volatile situations if helpful.
U. Talk about non-problem areas.
V. Connect with the person's thinking and feeling.
W. Invite solutions.
X. Use broken record technique.

Relationship Toxins:

Argue, **Boss Manage,** or Blame, Criticize or Coerce, Demean, Encourage Excuses, Instill Fear, or Give up easily, Hold Grudges.

Rather, stress what they **can** control, accept them as they are, and keep the confidence that they can develop more effective behaviors. Also, continue to us "WDEP" system without giving up.

Follow Up, Consult, and Continue Education:

Determine a way for them to report back, talk to another professional person when necessary, and maintain ongoing program of professional growth.

PROCEDURES:

W D E P

Build Relationships:

A. Explore **W**ants, Needs & Perceptions: Discuss picture album or quality world, i.e., set goals, fulfilled & unfulfilled pictures, needs, viewpoints and "locus of control."
B. Share Wants & Perceptions: Tell what you want from them and how you view their situations, behaviors, wants, etc. This procedure is secondary to A above.
C. Get a Commitment: Help them solidify their desire to find more effective behaviors.

Explore Total Behavior:

Help them examine the **D**irection of their lives, as well as specifics of how they spend their time. Discuss ineffective & effective self talk. Explore two-fold purpose of behavior: to impact the outer world and to communicate a message to it.

Evaluation – The Cornerstone of Procedures:

Help them evaluate their behavioral direction, specific behaviors as well as wants, perceptions and commitments. Evaluate own behavior through follow-up, consultation and continued education.

Make **P**lans: Help them change direction of their lives.

Effective plans are **S**imple, **A**ttainable, **M**easurable, **I**mmediate, **C**onsistent, **C**ontrolled by the planner, and **C**ommitted to. The helper is **P**ersistent. Plans can be linear or paradoxical.

Note: The "Cycle" describes specific guidelines & skills. Effective implementation requires the artful integration of the guidelines & skills contained under Environment & Procedures in a spontaneous & natural manner geared to the personality of the helper. This requires training, practices & supervision. Also, the word "client" is used for anyone receiving help: student, employee, family member, etc.

For more information contact:

Robert E. Wubbolding, EdD, Director

Center for Reality Therapy
7672 Montgomery Road, #383
Cincinnati, Ohio 45236

(513) 561-1911 • FAX (513) 561-3568
E-mail: wubsrt@fuse.net • www.realitytherapy.com

The Center for Reality Therapy provides counseling, consultation, training and supervision including applications to schools, agencies, hospitals, companies and other institutions. The Center is a provider for many organizations which award continuing education units.

CHAPTER 34

USING COGNITIVE BEHAVIORAL TECHNIQUES

Ann Vernon

Preview

The purpose of this chapter is to provide an overview of cognitive behavioral principles, with specific emphasis on practical applications of cognitive behavior therapies (CBT) and rational emotive behavior therapy (REBT) that professional school counselors can use in working with students in individual and small-group counseling. The focus is on both intervention and how to develop a preventative approach that integrates cognitive principles into classroom guidance lessons. Further applications with parents and teachers are also highlighted.

Rational emotive behavior therapy (REBT), founded by Dr. Albert Ellis, was the first of the cognitive behavior therapies (CBT) and has been in existence since 1955 (Ellis, 1957; Vernon, 2006a, 2006b). After Ellis originated REBT, Beck developed his approach, known as *cognitive therapy* (CT), and Meichenbaum followed with another alternative, *cognitive behavior modification* (CBM), which focused on changing clients' self-verbalizations (Corey, 2001). These three forms of cognitive behavior therapy (CBT) encompass a variety of strategies and procedures, but they "all share the tenet that learning plays a central role in the acquisition and maintenance of behavior, whether adaptive or dysfunctional—and that learning involves the manner in which the individual processes information cognitively" (Finch, Nelson, & Ott, 1993, p. 5).

A fundamental assumption of cognitive behavioral therapies is that emotions and behavior are influenced by cognitions (Mennuti, Freeman, & Christner, 2006; Reinecke, Dattilio, & Freeman, 2003). Because emotional and behavioral problems are influenced by how events are perceived, they can be addressed most effectively through cognitive restructuring—that is, showing people how their irrational beliefs or cognitive distortions upset them and how they can modify this inaccurate thinking using a variety of methods. Cognitive therapies emphasize the present, are time limited, and solution focused (Corey, 2001; Mennuti et al., 2006).

Although REBT and CBT share this common philosophical basis concerning the effect of beliefs on feelings and behaviors, REBT is considered more comprehensive and integrative than most other cognitive therapies because unlike the other CBT therapies, REBT has very strong emotional and behavioral components in addition to the cognitive components. As such, it is considered more multimodal in nature (Ellis & Poppa, 2001).

Cognitive therapies are increasing in popularity and are used extensively throughout the world—not only with adults, but also with children and adolescents (Corey, 2001; Reinecke et al., 2003). Meichenbaum's self-instructional training program (SIT) was originally designed to teach impulsive children to identify verbal self-commands that would help them regulate their own behavior, and Beck's cognitive therapy initially focused on the treatment of depression (Finch et al., 1993).

REBT has a long-standing history of application with children, most notably through The Living School that Ellis established in 1971 to help young people learn rational principles. Since that time, it has been applied to children of all ages for a variety of problems, including school phobia, depression, anger, underachievement, acting out, anxiety, perfectionism and procrastination, as well as typical developmental issues (Bernard, 1991; Ellis & Wilde, 2002; Vernon, 2004).

An integral part of REBT is its strong emphasis on prevention and emotional education. Several programs have been designed to help children and adolescents apply rational thinking skills to promote emotional and behavioral well-being (Bernard, 2001; Knaus, 1974; Vernon, 1998a, 1998b, 1998c, 2006a, 2006b). These programs can be used in classroom and small-group counseling settings to teach rational principles.

The purpose of this chapter is to describe practical applications of CBT and REBT that professional school counselors can use in individual and small-group counseling. Classroom guidance applications that emphasize prevention will also be addressed, as well as how to employ these principles with parents and teachers.

COGNITIVE THEORY: A BRIEF OVERVIEW

"What we feel is what we think" is a simplistic way of describing the philosophic basis of the cognitive behavior therapies. Maladaptive thoughts affect how people perceive activating events and result in distressing emotions. Beck (1988), Burns (1999), Ellis (2001a), and Meichenbaum (1977) all identified overgeneralizing, awfulizing, and musturbating as key dysfunctional beliefs as well as mind reading, focusing on the negative, dichotomous thinking, personalizing, magnification, arbitrary inference, and perfectionizing (Beck, Rush, Shaw, & Emery, 1979; Ellis, 2001b). According to these experts, dysfunctional beliefs have to be challenged or restructured in order for individuals to experience less intense negative emotions, behave in more self-enhancing ways, and think more functionally and rationally.

Cognitive restructuring can be accomplished in a variety of ways, depending on the professional counselor and the specific orientation. Ellis, for example, favors a very active-directive and oftentimes confrontational method of disputing (Ellis, 2001b; Ellis & MacLaren, 1998). However, Ellis acknowledged that the degree to which the professional counselor is active-directive is a choice (Dryden & Ellis, 2001), and practitioners working with children and adolescents would be well advised to be flexible and less directive in addition to employing a wide range of disputing strategies (Vernon, 2002, 2004). Beck used more of a reflective questioning process that helped the clients discover their own misconceptions, while Meichenbaum's self-instructional therapy helped clients gain awareness of their own self-talk (Corey, 2001).

This overview of the basic premises of CBT is simplistic, and the major focus is on practical applications with children and adolescents. Readers are therefore encouraged to engage in further study and training in the theory and practice of these therapies.

EFFECTIVENESS WITH SCHOOL-AGE POPULATIONS

Use of cognitive behavioral therapies with children and adolescents increased rapidly during the 1990s through the present (Reinecke et al., 2003) and are very effective with children and adolescents for the following reasons (Vernon, 2004):

- CBT is easily understood and can be adapted to children of most ages, cultures, and intelligence levels.
- CBT involves short-term problem-solving forms of counseling, which makes them particularly applicable in school settings, where time for counseling is often limited.
- Briefer forms of counseling are especially important for young clients whose sense of time is immediate (i.e., young clients need something to help them now).
- The teachable concepts readily lend themselves to skill acquisition.
- CBT approaches teach behavioral and emotional self-control by helping children understand the connection between thoughts, feelings, and behaviors.
- CBT helps children deal realistically with what they can change in their lives and cope more effectively with what they cannot change.
- The cognitive principles empower children to deal not only with present concerns but also give them tools to use for solving future problems.
- CBT approaches are particularly effective with children in the concrete operational stage of development, because children in this developmental stage have a natural tendency to think dichotomously and lack the ability to reason abstractly. Teaching students to challenge their cognitive distortions helps minimize cognitive deficiencies.

In addition, Mennuti et al. (2006) emphasized that educators are more accepting of CBT because the structure parallels other educational services. It can be readily adapted to provide interventions on a "continuum from prevention to early identification to direct individual service" (Mennuti et al., 2006, p. 7), which is particularly advantageous in school settings.

Cognitive therapies promote skill acquisition by helping children acquire practical coping skills. More important, they teach children how to *think* better. As a result, youngsters do not just *feel better*, they also *get better*, because they correct the faulty thinking that creates and perpetuates problems. For this reason, as well as for those previously mentioned, professional school counselors will see that using cognitive behavioral approaches with children and adolescents is an efficient and effective approach for problem remediation and prevention.

INDIVIDUAL COUNSELING APPLICATIONS

Children and adolescents have to deal with typical developmental problems, and many have to deal with more serious situational problems stemming from dysfunctional family environments, death, illness, or other major issues. Because their sense of time is more immediate and their array of coping skills may be limited, it is critical to employ developmentally appropriate strategies that address the specific problem. Accurate problem assessment is the first phase of this process.

PROBLEM ASSESSMENT

Problem assessment consists of assessing cognitive distortions and irrational beliefs as well as negative feelings and problematic behaviors. Since children (and many adolescents as well) may not be verbally adept and will struggle to label their feelings or articulate their thoughts, professional school counselors have to be creative and use a variety of methods in the assessment process. Inviting younger clients to draw, role-play, or use puppets to describe the problem may be necessary. Likewise, using techniques such as feeling flash cards, unfinished sentences, or feeling games may be good assessment strategies.

After getting a sense of the problem and how the child feels and behaves, it is important to determine the frequency, intensity, and duration of the problem: How long has it been going on, how often does it occur, and how intense is it? It may be helpful to ask clients to fill out a feeling–behaving chart, in which they rate the frequency of the problematic feeling or behavior every hour of the day for a week. This visual record is an excellent way for the student and the young client to better understand the problem. Another effective strategy is to use an *emotional pie* (Merrell, 2001), in which the client draws a circle and divides it into pie-shaped spaces of differing sizes, representing how they felt that week. For example, a small sliver of the pie might be labeled with an *A* for "anger," a larger portion might be identified with a *W* for "worry," and an even larger segment might be a *D* for "depression." This visual not only is an effective assessment technique but it also can be used as a springboard for initiating discussion about how to decrease the negative feelings during the intervention stage.

After establishing what the problem is, how the student feels and behaves, and how intense the problematic emotions and behaviors are, it is time to assess the beliefs. Keep in mind that not all beliefs are dysfunctional or irrational. For example, it is perfectly normal for a 10-year-old student to feel worried about her sick grandmother. One would detect the presence of irrational beliefs by asking her what she is thinking about her grandmother's situation. If she says that all she can think about is that her grandmother will die and that when that happens she wants to die too because she could not stand to live without her grandmother, the professional school counselor would know that this student was *catastrophizing*, since she is certain that her grandmother will die from a not-so-serious illness and that if this happens, *she* cannot go on living. On the other hand, if the student is thinking that her grandmother could possibly die and that if this occurs she would be very sad because she loves her, there is little that is irrational or dysfunctional about her thinking. The same holds true for an adolescent who did not receive the scholarship he thought he would get. He naturally would feel disappointed, but if he were devastated, he would be telling himself that this was the worst thing that could ever happen to him, that it proves he is worthless, and that it will do no good to ever apply for scholarships again, because he will never get one. These cognitive distortions contribute to his extreme emotional reaction.

In assessing irrational and cognitive distortions, the professional school counselor needs to detect musts (e.g., I *must* always do well; others *must* treat me as I deserve to be treated), *catastrophizing* and blowing problems out of proportion (e.g., This is so awful, nothing could be worse), low frustration tolerance (e.g., Things should come easily to me; I shouldn't have to work too hard at anything), dichotomous thinking (e.g., It's either this way or that way), overgeneralizing (e.g., She will always be mean) or personalizing (e.g., It's all my fault she ignored me), and self-downing (e.g., I'm no good if I got a bad grade on an exam).

INDIVIDUAL INTERVENTIONS FOR CHILDREN

As previously noted, cognitive interventions can address a wide array of childhood problems ranging from typical developmental problems such as fighting with friends to more serious situational problems such as coping with the death of a parent. Following is an intervention that helps children understand the cognitive theory concepts.

Don't blow it out of proportion (Vernon, 2007). To help students understand the concept of dichotomous thinking, put a long strip of masking tape on the floor. Use a typical example, such as "I assume I will fail a test." On an index card write "fail the test," and put this card at one end of the masking tape strip. Then, involve students in helping to identify at least 4 or 5 other points along the strip. For example, "getting a super good grade on the test" could be at the other end, "missing only a few questions," could be somewhere in between, and so forth. Process this by pointing out to children that there are more than two ways of looking at most situations. Have them give you examples as they apply this process to personal situations. In addition to employing interventions that help children understand the general cognitive concepts, interventions such as the following can be developed for a variety of typical childhood problems.

Adios anxiety (Vernon, 2002). This is a concrete way to help a young student deal with anxiety. The professional school counselor will need a plastic tablecloth with a large hopscotch board drawn on it. When a student describes things he or she is anxious about, such as taking a test, swimming in the lake, riding in an airplane, or doing something for the first time, indicate that you will be the student's secretary and write down all the thoughts he or she has about one of these anxious events. Next, invite the student to stand on the first square of the hopscotch board and read off something he or she was anxious about. If the student can think of a positive statement that will help to decrease the level of anxiety, he or she can hop to the next square. Read the next item, and ask the student to think of something that would make the student less anxious in that context. If he or she can, have the student hop to the next square. You may have to offer suggestions if the student does not understand the task or concept. For example if a student were anxious about swimming in the lake, the student could tell herself that by wearing a life jacket she will probably be very safe, that she could stay in shallow water, or that she could wear shoes if she were afraid she would get bitten by a fish.

Rational coping statements. Rational coping statements are self-talk statements students can say to themselves to counter a fear. For example, if a student was afraid he would drown in a lake while swimming, a rational coping statement might be, "If I don't go past the rope, I should be safe; I can always yell for help." The purpose of rational coping statements is to help students identify less anxious self-talk and more effective coping strategies.

INDIVIDUAL INTERVENTIONS FOR ADOLESCENTS

To help adolescents learn the principles of cognitive behavior therapy, the following interventions have proven effective.

Thoughts and feelings (Vernon, 2006a). To help adolescents learn that emotional problems are caused by their thoughts, invite them to write responses to stimulus questions. The following are examples.

- The principal announces there will be no junior–senior prom this year. How do you feel, and what are your thoughts about this?
- The person you are going with starts dating someone else. How do you feel, and what are your thoughts about this?
- Your mother announces you will be moving to a different town, and next week is the last time you will attend your present school. How do you feel, and what are your thoughts about this?

After they have written their responses, give them a blank copy of the situations and have them ask a friend to complete it (without seeing how your student responded). After your student has both sets of responses, have the student compare them to see if they are similar, and if not, describe what the differences are. Help the student understand that the reason there might be differences is that people think differently, and how they think affects how they feel. For example, if your student felt angry about the prom being canceled, she would have been thinking things such as, "This isn't fair; this will ruin my whole year." In contrast, if she had felt mildly irritated, the thoughts would be something like, "It's not that big of a deal; I can find something else to do." Continue to help the student see how thoughts cause feelings.

Cognitive therapies embrace a variety of methods and strategies to help young clients deal with their concerns. The following intervention illustrates how to help adolescents deal with depression.

When you need a helping hand (Vernon, 2002). This intervention helps adolescents remember that they can control thoughts that contribute to depression and sadness. To implement this intervention, first invite the student to identify a specific depressing situation and help him or her identify the thoughts that contribute to the depression. For example, if a student broke up with a significant other, he might think that it was the end of the world, that he would never be in another relationship, or that there is something wrong with him. Ask the student to trace the outline of his hand on a piece of paper, and then help him identify how to dispute the irrational beliefs and cognitive distortions, such as by thinking that "This isn't the end of the world"; "There will probably be other relationships"; and "This doesn't mean there is something wrong with me." Have the student write the successfully identified disputes on the fingers of his hand tracing as a visual reminder of how to overcome the negative thoughts.

There are numerous other cognitive behavioral techniques that can be used to help young people learn to change their maladaptive thinking and, consequently, cope more effectively with problems they encounter. Role-playing, rational emotive imagery, rational role reversal, assertiveness training, bibliotherapy, self-help materials, and homework assignments can all be employed and readily adapted, depending on the developmental level of the child (Bernard, 2001; Vernon, 2002).

SMALL-GROUP COUNSELING

Cognitive behavioral techniques are also very effective in group counseling situations. There are two formats that are generally employed: a homogeneous group, in which all group members have a similar problem, and an open-ended group, in which group members take turns presenting problems with which they would like help (DiGiuseppe, 1999).

Homogeneous groups can focus on typical developmental problems, such as getting along with friends or dealing with the emotional ups and downs of adolescence. They might also emphasize skill development, such as anger management or study skills groups. They could also address specific situational stressors, such as divorce or living in an alcoholic family. Regardless of the focus, this type of group would have more structure than the open-ended group in that various activities would be introduced to help participants learn more about the topic and develop effective coping skills. The emphasis would be on introducing cognitive behavioral principles such as the connection between what they think and how they feel; the connection between how they think and feel to how they behave; and, ultimately, helping them apply these principles to the specific issue so that they have less intense negative emotions and more adaptive behavior. An advantage of the group approach is that participants can help each other develop the cognitive behavioral skills and apply them to their individual situation.

To illustrate, the leader of a divorce group for children would elicit feelings from participants about how their family situation is affecting them. In turn, the leader would probe for children's beliefs about this situation that could pertain to overgeneralzing, awfulizing, demanding, catastrophizing, and low frustration tolerance, such as, "This is the worst thing that could ever happen; it is unfair"; "Nothing will ever be the same again"; "They will never get over it"; "It is too painful to deal with"; and so forth. Using a variety of techniques such as bibliotherapy, journaling, rational role reversal, and feeling games, the leader would help children see that divorce can be a very upsetting circumstance, but, for example, wouldn't it be worse if one of their parents died? And even though it is painful, is it possible that in time they will adjust and feel somewhat better at least? The ultimate goal would be to help children deal with this unfortunate circumstance by recognizing that they can reduce the intensity of their negative emotions by changing their thinking about this event. Through the group format, children help each other challenge their irrational beliefs and identify effective coping strategies.

In an open-ended group, individuals bring present-day problems to the table, and the leader integrates cognitive behavioral principles into the discussion to help them think more clearly about the situation, experience more moderate as opposed to intensely negative emotions, and develop an array of coping strategies. For example, an adolescent might introduce the problem of feeling anxious about calling someone for a date. With the assistance of other group members, the leader would help this student identify his or her disturbing thoughts, such as "What if I get rejected?" "What if I stumble over my words?" "What if they laugh at me or hang up?" They would then help the client learn to dispute them. Different techniques such as role playing, writing rational limericks or stories, or identifying rational coping statements could be used with group members.

CLASSROOM APPLICATIONS

Given that almost 70% of children and adolescents who receive mental health services do so only at school, coupled with the fact that the number of students needing mental health services is increasing (Farmer, Burns, Phillips, Angold, & Costello, 2003), it is important to identify effective emotional education programs to implement in the school setting.

Of the cognitive therapies, REBT in particular has been psychoeducational in nature from its inception. From 1971 to 1975, The Institute for Advanced Study in Rational Psychotherapy (now called the Albert Ellis Institute) ran an elementary school in the building. The focus was on teaching rational thinking as a preventive mental health program in addition to the regular subjects (DiGiuseppe, 1999). The staff developed activities to help teach children effective thinking, feeling, and behaving strategies, and from these activities, Knaus (1974) developed a curriculum that would educate children in the ABCs of REBT. Since that time, other curricula (Vernon, 1989a, 1989b, 2006a, 2006b) have been developed that teach children to develop critical thinking skills, differentiate between facts and assumptions, distinguish between thoughts and feelings, link thoughts and feelings, identify what leads to emotional upset, distinguish between rational and irrational beliefs, and learn to challenge irrational beliefs. Vernon (1998a, 1998b, 1998c) also developed curricula to help children apply rational thinking concepts to typical developmental problems, and Bernard (2001) developed a comprehensive program that applies rational thinking concepts to improving school achievement.

The purpose of introducing these concepts in the classroom is to teach children principles they can apply to problems of daily living as well as to give them tools to use in solving future problems. A wide variety of cognitive behavioral methods are employed in delivering these lessons, including rational role reversal, self-help materials, worksheets, rational emotive imagery, thinking, feeling and behaving games, music and art activities, experiential activities, and didactic approaches. The primary focus is on prevention.

APPLICATIONS WITH PARENTS AND TEACHERS

Parents and teachers can also benefit from cognitive behavioral therapy in several ways. First, they can learn to apply the principles to their own issues, irrespective of their parenting or teaching. Second, they can recognize how cognitive distortions affect their parenting and teaching and learn to function more effectively by challenging these distorted thoughts. Finally, they can serve as rational role models for their children and the students they teach. Christner, Stewart, and Lennon (2006) discussed how CBT techniques can be incorporated into the consultative process, whereby the consultant and parent can "collaboratively explore how the parent's thoughts, behaviors, feelings, and physiological reactions influence the problematic situations" (p. 352). In addition to parent (or teacher) consultation, parent education is also a viable way to introduce CBT principles. Parents and teachers unwittingly fall victim to a number of dysfunctional beliefs, including uncertainty, self-condemnation, demands, and low frustration tolerance (Vernon, 2002).

- *Uncertainty* (anxiety). It is not uncommon for parents and teachers to be uncertain about what to do in certain situations involving children. Adults often think they should know exactly what to do and what the outcome will be.
- *Self-condemnation*. When children have problems at home or in the classroom, adults often blame themselves. For example, if Juan did poorly on his basic skills tests, his teacher might put herself down, thinking that this reflects on her poor teaching. Parents of children who turn to drugs condemn themselves for their poor parenting. In reality, parents and teachers cannot be totally responsible for a child's behavior or performance.
- *Demanding*. Parents and teachers often demand that children must behave a certain way, and if they don't, it is awful. These adults are often very authoritarian and have little tolerance for children who don't always put forth their very best effort. Needless to say, this has a negative effect on their relationships with children.
- *Low frustration tolerance*. Low frustration tolerance is related to the idea that children, as well as adults, should not have to experience any frustration or discomfort. These adults consequently try to make life easy for children, which means rescuing them and failing to follow through with reasonable consequences for misbehavior.

Professional school counselors can assist parents and teachers by helping them identify these cognitive distortions as well as others such as overgeneralizing or awfulizing, tunnel vision (e.g., only seeing the negative), and the like. Concepts can be presented through parent group meetings and teacher in-services.

SUMMARY/CONCLUSION

I presented a brief overview of cognitive behavioral therapy, which has successfully been employed with children and adolescents in school settings. Perhaps the most compelling reason for using a cognitive behavioral approach is that it can be used both for remediation and prevention and because it teaches children to identify and challenge the thoughts that create and perpetuate problems. Long-lasting change is more likely than with many other theoretical approaches.

(Note: See the CD-ROM for a list of references.)

CHAPTER 35

DEVELOPMENT AND IMPLEMENTATION OF BEHAVIORAL INTERVENTIONS IN SCHOOLS: A FUNCTION-BASED APPROACH

R. Anthony Doggett, Carl J. Sheperis, and Daniel J. Krenzer

Preview

School personnel are increasingly faced with the responsibility of teaching students important social and behavioral skills in addition to providing instruction in traditional academic material. In fact, government agencies have mandated that proactive interventions be developed and implemented for students with disabilities who display problematic behavior. Such suggestions have also been strongly recommended for individuals without documented disabilities who have long histories of displaying problem behavior. We review the motivating factors for engaging in problem behavior, methods for identifying the purpose of problem behavior, and intervention development, implementation, and monitoring guidelines for teaching proactive, replacement behaviors.

Professional school counselors often interact with teachers, administrators, parents, and other applied personnel in designing interventions for students who display problem behaviors in the school setting. Traditionally, professional school counselors have been encouraged to generate interventions based on the topography of the behavior (i.e., how the behavior looks) rather than the function of the behavior (i.e., the purpose that the behavior serves for the individual). Because the interventions developed to teach important behavioral skills need to be as idiosyncratic as the students displaying the problem behaviors, we will take a functional approach to intervention development. Readers interested in more traditional approaches to the implementation of behavioral techniques (e.g., group contingencies, token economies, Premack principle, overcorrection, response cost, time-out) should refer to Chapter 24, "Setting Up and Managing a Classroom." Specifically, we will discuss the motivating factors associated with problem behaviors, best practices in functional behavioral assessment, and proper methods for intervention development, implementation, and monitoring. Such knowledge will enable the professional school counselor to serve as a vital resource to schools and families and assist in improving the behavioral and academic skills of the children they serve.

Currently, school professionals are faced with the increasing responsibility of providing safe school environments in addition to providing academic instruction. As a result, schools have developed zero-tolerance policies, implemented target hardening procedures (e.g., controlled access entrances, metal detectors, body searches), and used segregation procedures (e.g., suspension, expulsion, alternative placements, self-contained classrooms) as methods for trying to control the display of disruptive behavior on school grounds (Quinn et al., 2001). Unfortunately, such restrictive or get-tough responses have proven ineffective, and the continued display of problematic behavior has served to threaten the process of schooling for all children (National Association of School Psychologists, 2002). As such, representatives of government agencies (e.g., Department of Education, National Institutes of Health) have advocated for more emphasis on the development of proactive procedures that are designed to provide social and academic skill acquisition (Drasgow & Yell, 2001; Kern, Choutka, & Sokol, 2002). In addition, these representatives have opposed methods solely designed to reduce or eliminate the display of disruptive behavior without an alternative or replacement skill development component. In an effort to promote best practice among professional school counselors related to behavioral problems in children, we discuss potential reasons for the display of problem behavior, assessment strategies for discovering the purpose of problem behavior, and intervention strategies for both reducing the display of disruptive behavior and promoting the occurrence of more adaptive behaviors.

REASONS FOR THE DISPLAY OF PROBLEM BEHAVIOR

Understanding the assessment of disruptive behavior and the implementation of proactive interventions requires a discussion about potential functions of problem behavior. *Function* refers to the purpose that the behavior serves for the student (Gresham, Watson, & Skinner, 2001). A student can choose to engage in any given behavior in a classroom setting (Quinn et al., 2001). However, the particular behaviors that the student chooses to engage in are greatly affected by learning history or the previous interactions that one has had with significant others or events in their environment (Martens, Witt, Daly, & Vollmer, 1999). For example, one student may immediately begin working on a new math assignment once it has been passed out by the teacher because completing similar academic assignments in the past has led to social praise from teachers. However, another student may look out the window, flip through pages of a book, or walk around the classroom before beginning the math assignment. Eventually, the teacher redirects this student to his or her seat and provides assistance in completing the worksheet. As such, this student conceivably avoids working on the worksheet until social attention is provided in the forms of redirection and assistance. Both students obtained and were reinforced by social attention from the teacher. In addition, both students were faced with the same set of choices when given the worksheet. However, their responses to the worksheet were greatly influenced by their prior history with similar academic demands.

Potential functions of behavior have previously been divided into five general categories:

- Positive social reinforcement (e.g., social attention from teachers or peers)
- Material or activity reinforcement (e.g., access to preferred items or activities)
- Negative reinforcement (e.g., escape or avoidance of aversive instructional tasks or activities)
- Negative social reinforcement (e.g., escape or avoidance of nonpreferred individuals)
- Automatic or sensory reinforcement (e.g., internal stimulation) (Carr, 1994)

Of these potential functions, obtaining social attention from teachers or peers and avoiding or escaping instructional demands appear to be the most common motivators for engaging in disruptive behavior in classroom settings (Kern et al., 2002). In addition, previous researchers have revealed that a particular problem behavior could serve only one function or could serve multiple functions (Iwata et al., 1994). Furthermore, several behaviors may serve the same function or each could serve a different function (Doggett, Edwards, Moore, Tingstrom, & Wilczynski, 2001). The task of the professional school counselor is not only to obtain detailed information about the problem behavior but, more important, to obtain information about the motivation for performing the problem behavior.

REASONS FOR FAILED BEHAVIORAL INTERVENTIONS

Teachers and other school personnel often report that they spend a significant amount of time and effort trying to reduce the occurrence of problem behavior that is exhibited by students in their classrooms. Traditionally, treatment efforts aimed at reducing the problem behavior have focused more on the topography of the problem behavior rather than on the function or purpose of the behavior (Hoff, Ervin, & Friman, 2005). In other words, textbook interventions have been universally applied to individuals who have demonstrated similar behaviors or been diagnosed with the same or similar disorders. However, reported research results have indicated that many universally applied school-based interventions have proven ineffective (Elliott, Witt, & Kratochwill, 1991; Newcomer & Lewis, 2004; Ysseldyke & Mirkin, 1982). Although several reasons for ineffective intervention results could be identified for a student, treatment selection without reference to the behavioral function of the problem behavior has been identified as a significant limitation. According to Vollmer and Northup (1996), at least four problems may arise when behavioral interventions are selected without reference to behavioral function. First, the problem behavior may inadvertently be strengthened through positive reinforcement. An example includes the use of reprimands delivered by a classroom teacher in an effort to reduce disruptive behavior. In fact, research has demonstrated that the increased use of reprimands by teachers often leads to a direct escalation in problem behavior by students whose behavior is maintained by obtaining teacher attention (Doggett et al., 2001; Kehle, Bray, Theodore, Jenson & Clark, 2000; Moore, Doggett, Edwards, & Olmi, 1999; Musser, Bray, Kehle & Jenson, 2001; Umbreit, 1995).

Second, the behavior may inadvertently be strengthened through negative reinforcement (e.g., avoidance or escape). A commonly used classroom management strategy that may strengthen problem behavior through negative reinforcement is the use of time-out. Studies have shown that time-out, or the removal of demands or attention, may negatively reinforce problem behaviors by allowing students to escape tasks or other individuals viewed as aversive or nonpreferred (Miltenberger, 2004; Moore, Edwards, Olmi, & Wilczynski, 2001). Third, the intervention may be functionally irrelevant to the problem behavior. For example, an intervention aimed at reducing teacher attention for problem behavior would be functionally irrelevant for a student whose behavior is primarily maintained by escape from academic demands. Finally, an intervention may not provide alternative sources of reinforcement for more proactive replacement behaviors. For example, in-school suspension, out-of-school suspension, and detention are commonly used punitive procedures designed to reduce problem behavior. However, such procedures do not teach alternative behaviors, nor do they provide reinforcement for the display of proactive behaviors.

Because approaches based solely on topography or diagnosis have proven ineffective in leading to positive outcomes, recent literature has been proliferated with assessment strategies that focus on identifying the function of problem behavior (Newcomer & Lewis, 2004). One such procedure is functional behavioral assessment (FBA). FBA has been defined as a collection of methods for gathering information about target behaviors, events in the environment that precede the target behaviors (antecedents), and events in the environments that follow the target behaviors (consequences). This information is then used to determine the reason for the performance of problem behavior (Gresham et al., 2001). Federal law requires FBA for students who are verified with disabilities and who display problem behaviors at school (Individuals with Disabilities Education Act Amendments of 1997). Furthermore, FBA is strongly recommended for individuals without disabilities who have a history of displaying disruptive behavior that impedes learning in the school environment (Drasgow & Yell, 2001). Finally, the primary goal of FBA is to identify the specific environmental events associated with the performance of problem behavior to enhance the probability of treatment effectiveness and to prevent a series of ineffective interventions based on best guesses and unconfirmed hypotheses (McComas, Hoch, & Mace, 2000).

Best Practices in Functional Behavioral Assessment

Best practice in FBA occurs in a 4-phase process: (a) description; (b) interpretation; (c) verification; and (d) intervention development, implementation, and monitoring (Ervin et al., 2001; Sterling-Turner, Robinson, & Wilczynski, 2001).

PHASE I: DESCRIPTION

The descriptive phase involves both indirect and direct procedures and is used to generate hypotheses about the environmental events that may be triggering or maintaining problem behavior. Indirect methods are used to obtain information from archival data or important others (e.g., teachers, administrators, parents) about the display of problem behavior and the potential functions of problem behavior. Traditionally, indirect methods have included record reviews, rating scales, and interviews. When evaluating student records, professional school counselors should review grade reports, group and individual standardized test results, discipline records, attendance records, medical history, Individualized Education Programs, and previous interventions. Appropriate use of rating scales requires individuals familiar with the student to rate the perceived impact of specific environmental events (i.e., antecedents and consequences) on the performance of problem behavior. Some of the more commonly used rating scales include the *Motivation Assessment Scale* (Durand & Crimmins, 1988), the *Problem Behavior Questionnaire* (Lewis, Scott, & Sugai, 1994), and the *Functional Analysis Screening Tool* (Goh, Iwata, & DeLeon, 1996). Other indirect methods for gathering information about the functional relationship between problem behaviors and environmental events are teacher and student interviews. Examples of structured or semistructured interviews include the *Functional Assessment Interview* (O'Neill et al., 1997), the *Preliminary Functional Assessment Survey* (Dunlap et al., 1993), the *Functional Assessment Information Record for Teachers* (Edwards, 2002; Doggett, Mueller, & Moore, 2002), and the *Student Assisted Functional Assessment Interview* (Kern et al., 1994).

The second aspect of the descriptive phase in FBA involves the use of direct methods. Direct descriptive assessment involves the collection of data on the performance of target behaviors and environmental events via direct observation. The most common type of direct observation technique used to obtain data about behaviors and functional relationships is an A-B-C assessment or contingency analysis (Bijou, Peterson, & Ault, 1968; Cooper, Heron, & Heward, 1987). A-B-C observations require that the observer record data on the occurrence of antecedent events (e.g., potential triggers), target behaviors, and consequent events (e.g., potential reinforcers). Direct descriptive data can be collected through narrative recording, event recording, or time-sampling procedures. Review of these procedures is beyond the scope of this chapter, and professional school counselors are encouraged to consult Alberto and Troutman (2002) or Miltenberger (2004) for additional information about these observation methods.

PHASE II: INTERPRETATION

Data obtained from the indirect and direct methods are used during the second phase, or interpretive phase, to develop hypotheses about functional relationships between the problem behaviors and the events that precede or follow the behaviors. In fact, McComas et al. (2000) recommended that summary statements be developed for each hypothesis. To illustrate, consider the student who had difficulty attending to the math assignment. One potential summary statement could be, "When the student is given a math worksheet (antecedent event), he or she will look out the window, flip through pages of a book, and walk around the room (observable behaviors) in order to obtain attention from the teacher or briefly escape the task (consequent events)." It is important to remember that information collected during the descriptive assessment phase is only correlational in nature. In other words, the school-based professional can only make informed suggestions about potential relationships between environmental events and problem behaviors. However, definitive statements about the specific events that occasion or maintain the occurrence of problem behavior cannot be made at this stage. To make statements about causal relationships, progression to the third phase must occur.

PHASE III: VERIFICATION

Verification of hypotheses developed during the interpretation phase occurs via experimental or functional analysis or through implementation of a function-based intervention. A functional or experimental analysis is a brief experiment designed to confirm or disconfirm prior suggestions made about potential functional relationships between environmental events and problem behaviors. In other words, predictable changes are purposely made in the student's environment to see how those changes affect the performance of problem behavior. As in the case described earlier, the teacher may be instructed to attend to the student every time he or she engages in problem behavior (usually through reprimands or redirections) during a 10-minute functional or experimental analysis condition to evaluate the effect of teacher attention on problem behavior. In another condition, the teacher may be instructed to only attend to appropriate behavior (usually through praise statements) during a 10-minute condition to see if teacher praise, in fact, does increase the display of appropriate behavior.

Most functional analysis research has been based on the work of Iwata et al. (1994) or Carr and Durand (1985) and has been expanded for proper use in classroom settings (Radford, Aldrich, & Ervin, 2000). Functional or experimental analysis conditions can be conducted in analogue settings (i.e., contrived settings designed to approximate the typical classroom setting) or in naturalistic settings (i.e., the child's actual classroom during regular academic instruction). Furthermore, functional or experimental analysis conditions have included manipulation of both antecedent conditions (e.g., level of task demand, amount of attention, presence or absence of peers) and consequent conditions (e.g., social attention for disruptive behavior, removal of task contingent upon the display of problem behavior). For a complete review of school-based experimental analysis conditions, professional school counselors are referred to Radford et al. (2000).

A primary advantage of experimental analysis is that it is the only method for demonstrating a causal relationship between target behaviors and antecedent and consequent events. Major disadvantages include the effort, time, and professional expertise required to implement such procedures (Miltenberger, 2004). In fact, researchers have suggested that many school-based professionals proceed to intervention after completing record reviews, rating scales, interviews, and direct observations if a clear relationship can be hypothesized from the descriptive methods (Doggett et al., 2001). Furthermore, recent researchers have demonstrated that function-based interventions can be used to validate the hypotheses generated from descriptive methods making functional or experimental analyses unnecessary (Doggett et al., 2002).

PHASE IV: TREATMENT DEVELOPMENT, IMPLEMENTATION, AND MONITORING

The last phase of FBA involves treatment development, implementation, and monitoring. Treatment should not consist of a single technique that is designed to simply eliminate the problem behavior. Instead, the behavioral intervention should be composed of a set of antecedent- and consequent-based strategies designed to reduce the problem behavior and, more important, increase the performance of alternative replacement behaviors (McComas et al., 2000). Such interventions have been referred to as *positive behavioral supports* and are mandated by federal law for students with disabilities and strongly encouraged for nondisabled students with histories of problem behavior (Drasgow & Yell, 2001). McComas et al. (2000) posited that interventions should match the values, resources, and skills of those persons who would be required to implement the procedures. They also emphasized that positive behavior supports should make the display of problem behaviors irrelevant, inefficient, and ineffective if the student is highly motivated to engage in the alternative behaviors that serve the same function or purpose as the problem behaviors.

Treatment development: Linking assessment to intervention. As was mentioned previously, positive behavior supports or proactive interventions will be composed of intervention elements designed to increase the display of appropriate behavior. These elements will include both antecedent- and consequent-based strategies. More attention has been given to antecedent strategies that could serve to prevent the problem behavior from occurring (Dunlap, Kern, & Worcester, 2001). Typically, variables that often trigger the display of inappropriate behavior are broadly defined as the curriculum (Dunlap & Kern, 1996). Once the curricular variables that occasion the occurrence of problem behavior have been identified through FBA methods, changes can be made to increase the probability that appropriate behavior will be displayed. While not exhaustive, modifications to the curriculum have included changing task difficulty, modifying task size or duration, changing the instructional media, incorporating the student's personal interests in the task, allowing the individual to choose the order of the tasks, changing the pacing of the instruction, and interspersing different tasks (e.g., short vs. long, varied vs. repetitive, long vs. short) over the academic period.

In contrast to antecedent strategies, consequent-based interventions have typically focused on contingencies of reinforcement (i.e., positive and negative reinforcement) in order to increase the display of appropriate behavior. Reinforcement, by definition, increases the probability that a certain behavior will be performed in the future (Skinner, 1953). Positive reinforcement refers to the presentation of a stimulus or event that increases the likelihood that a target behavior will be performed at a later time. Negative reinforcement refers to the removal of a stimulus or event that increases the likelihood that a target behavior will be performed in the future. Thus, both positive and negative reinforcement increase the probability that some target behavior will be displayed over time. Furthermore, it is important to note that negative reinforcement is not punishment (which decreases the probability that a behavior will be displayed in the future).

The most common classroom applications of positive reinforcement include differential reinforcement of alternative behavior (DRA) or differential reinforcement of other behavior (DRO; Mildon, Moore, & Dixon, 2004). DRA involves reinforcing the alternative behavior and ignoring or extinguishing the inappropriate behavior. Using the same example of the student engaging in the math assignment, a teacher using DRA would increase her social praise for working on the math assignment and systematically ignore the off-task behaviors. Conversely, DRO is used to provide reinforcement for a set interval of time that the problem behavior has not been displayed. In this case, the teacher using DRO would calculate the time between distributing the math assignment and initial off-task behavior. If the student gets out of his desk within approximately 5 minutes after being given the assignment, then the teacher would set the interval at 5 minutes. Positive social attention (e.g., verbal and physical praise) would be provided to the student after the 5-minute interval only if he or she worked on the assignment for the entire interval.

Thus far, the discussion of differential reinforcement has focused on providing attention contingent upon the display of appropriate behavior. However, differential reinforcement can be used to reduce the occurrence of escape-maintained behavior and increase the occurrence of working on a task or interacting with a nonpreferred individual. When negative reinforcement is applied, the terms *differential negative reinforcement of alternative behavior* (DNRA) and *differential negative reinforcement of other behavior* (DNRO) are used (Miltenberger, 2004). DNRA or DNRO could be used so that the problem behavior no longer produces escape from or avoidance of task demands or nonpreferred individuals. In other words, the contingencies could be arranged such that longer periods of on-task behavior, work completion, or social interactions lead to escape from the demand. For example, the student who avoided the math assignment could be taught to request a break after working on the worksheet for an appropriate period of time.

Another form of differential reinforcement that is gaining attention in the literature is noncontingent reinforcement (NCR), which refers to the delivery of reinforcers on a fixed schedule, independent of the display of problem behavior. For attention-maintained behavior, the teacher could provide social attention at set periods throughout the day, regardless of the display of problem behavior. For escape-maintained behavior, the teacher could provide scheduled breaks throughout the day that are noncontingent on the display of problem behavior. Mildon and colleagues suggested that NCR could serve as a viable intervention alternative for two reasons (Mildon et al., 2004). First, NCR reduces the student's motivation to engage in the problem behavior because he or she is obtaining the desired reinforcer (e.g., attention or escape) on a predictable schedule. Second, NCR disrupts the contingency between the problem behavior and the maintaining consequence, because the reinforcer is delivered independent of the display of problem behavior. One caution is that NCR procedures have not been researched as thoroughly as other differential reinforcement procedures, and the effectiveness of such a procedure is not as well established.

Finally, the implementation of traditional behavioral techniques can be very useful in managing student behavior as long as the interventions are related to the function of the problem behavior. For example, group-oriented contingencies can be very effective procedures for reducing peer attention for problem behavior and increasing peer attention for appropriate behavior, especially if the students earn free time together for following classroom rules. Furthermore, behavioral charts and school–home notes can often serve to provide social attention or other desired activities to students for engaging in appropriate behavior. Additionally, response-cost and time-out procedures can be useful additions to differential reinforcement for managing problem behavior maintained by social attention. Finally, other punishment-based procedures, such as overcorrection, can be a useful addition to curricular changes in the environment for reducing escape-maintained behaviors. For more guidance on implementing these traditional behavioral techniques, see Chapter 67, "Helping Students With Severe Behavioral Problems."

Treatment implementation and monitoring: Increasing treatment integrity. After the target behaviors and alternative behaviors have been clearly defined, the functions of the problem behavior have been verified, and the treatment protocol has been developed, the professional school counselor will have to work closely with other school personnel to ensure that the intervention procedures are implemented properly (Sterling-Turner et al., 2001). The amount of time devoted to ensuring that the intervention is implemented properly will vary with each student and teacher. However, proper training is crucial for proper intervention implementation (Sterling-Turner, Watson, & Moore, 2000). When interventions are not implemented properly, the true impact of the intervention remains unknown. In other words, it will be difficult to determine if the FBA results were incorrect and led to inappropriate intervention design or if improper treatment implementation led to the failed efforts. If the results of FBA were incorrect, then the professional school personnel need to review the FBA data in order to generate and test other hypotheses. If the treatment was implemented with poor integrity, then the professional school counselor needs to determine if the teacher lacked the skills to implement the intervention or the motivation to implement the procedures (Watson & Robinson, 1996).

In order to ensure proper treatment implementation, direct behavioral consultation (DBC) has been suggested (Sterling-Turner et al., 2001). Although Watson and colleagues discuss the procedures involved in DBC elsewhere in this edition, the procedures will be briefly reviewed here. First, the teacher should be provided with a rationale for implementing the treatment that is linked directly to the results of the FBA. Second, the intervention should be modeled for the teacher, and the teacher should be allowed to practice implementation of the intervention while receiving reinforcing and corrective feedback. Once the teacher becomes more proficient in implementing the intervention, then assistance can be faded. However, it would still be important to have the teacher monitor his or her own integrity in implementing the intervention over time.

SUMMARY/CONCLUSION

Functional behavioral assessment seeks to answer the questions, *What is triggering the problem behavior?* and *What is maintaining the problem behavior?* Once these questions are answered, function-based interventions can be developed to increase the display of appropriate, replacement behaviors and decrease the display of problem behaviors by making them ineffective, inefficient, and irrelevant. Interventions or positive behavior supports are not composed of one technique but include both antecedent- and consequent-based strategies for increasing the display of appropriate behavior. Finally, intervention implementation and monitoring are also crucial components for ensuring treatment success. Table 35.1 reviews the steps in conducting FBAs and implementing function-based interventions.

(Note: See the CD-ROM for a list of references.)

TABLE 35.1

STEPS IN CONDUCTING A FUNCTIONAL BEHAVIORAL ANALYSIS (FBA)

Phase I: Description

Step I:	Conduct record reviews, interviews, and complete rating scales.
Step II:	Identify and clearly define problem behaviors.
Step III:	Conduct A-B-C observations or other direct observations.

Phase II: Interpretation

Step I:	Review all data obtained from the FBA.
Step II:	Develop hypothesis statements about antecedent events that could be setting off or triggering the problem behavior.
Step III:	Develop hypothesis statements about consequent events that could be maintaining the problem behavior.

Phase III: Verification

Step I:	Conduct experimental or functional analysis conditions, if necessary.
Step II:	Implement function-based interventions, if satisfied with results from the preceding phases.
	Identify and clearly define replacement behaviors.
	Identify antecedent strategies.
	Identify consequent strategies.
	Provide training and feedback to teacher.

Phase IV: Treatment Development, Implementation, and Monitoring

Step I:	If you did not implement treatment in the verification phase, then implement it here, following the abovementioned steps.
Step II:	Monitor the treatment for proper implementation through direct observations and treatment integrity checklists.

CHAPTER 36

ADLERIAN COUNSELING TECHNIQUES

Mardi Kay Fallon

Preview

Adlerian theory has been used for decades to help counselors and educators under-stand the inner world of the student. By exploring how a student understands and experiences the world, the professional school counselor can develop effective inter-ventions that teach the child how to adapt to and cope with life's difficulties in a co-operative and socially responsible manner. Misbehavior is seen as a learning issue, and all students are seen as desiring to belong and interact in a healthy and benefi-cial manner with others. Adlerian interventions seek to help the student understand his misbehavior and to learn how to develop greater self-control. Professional school counselors can use a variety of interesting and creative techniques to help the stu-dent to achieve this level of self-awareness. Adlerian counseling is very appropriate in today's multicultural schools and can be adapted to work with special needs populations.

Proponents of Adlerian counseling have developed several principles regarding stu-dents and student behavior that are of practical use to the professional school coun-selor. These principles are also applicable to students with special needs and from diverse backgrounds, making Adlerian theory a viable option for today's school populations.

A basic tenet of Adlerian theory is that all behavior is purposeful. A student is a social being, someone who observes her environment, forms opinions about how things work, and acts upon those (often faulty) assumptions. Therefore, every behavior, no matter how unusual or dysfunctional, has a goal and a purpose. If one can understand the goal and purpose of a student's behavior, then one is able to understand the motives of that student. Understanding a student's motives helps the professional school coun-selor to understand how best to help the child change her problem behavior (Pryor & Tollerud, 1999).

Because children are social beings, they have a need to belong and live coopera-tively with others. Indeed, Adlerians consider the ability of a child to have a positive social interest (e.g., sharing, showing concern for others, and developing empathy) as a measure of that child's mental health. However, because of the natural conditions of childhood, all students experience a sense of inferiority and of being weak and vulner-able. Thus, they strive to achieve superiority, which is seen as working to obtain a sense of mastery and self-control (Carlson & Sperry, 2001).

Children live within a subjective world and tend to distort what they see and ex-perience in order to fit that worldview. They develop a form of private logic, which helps them to make sense of themselves and their world (Sapp, 1997). Students begin by ob-serving their families and developing a set of beliefs and expectations based upon those experiences. This sets up a paradigm through which the student seeks to find meaning as well as ways to belong and achieve superiority (Ehly & Dustin, 1989).

In essence, these tenets set up a belief that students choose their behaviors as a means to obtain goals. However, the assumptions upon which the student's decisions were made may be faulty, leading to misbehavior that is problematic. Misbehavior, then, is viewed more as a learning difficulty than a character flaw. Indeed, misbehavior is believed to arise from discouragement, from a student not being able to find a way to meet his needs and goals in a cooperative and beneficial manner (Dreikurs & Soltz, 1964).

UNDERSTANDING MISBEHAVIOR

There are essentially four main goals of misbehavior, each of which has specific qualities and attributes that can alert the professional school counselor to the particular intervention that may be most beneficial to the student in question. The four goals of misbehavior are attention, power, revenge, and inadequacy.

The goal of *attention* is very common with students in a school setting. Here, students feel that they are only of value if they can get others to notice or serve them (Sweeney, 1981). When a student is seeking attention, an adult's tendency is to feel annoyed. This is, in fact, one way to assess what a student's motives may be, to determine from the beleaguered adult just what feelings the student's behavior has elicited. The student seeking attention will initially tend to stop misbehaving when first corrected, and then begin repeating the attention-seeking behavior soon after (Dinkmeyer, Pew, & Dinkmeyer, 1979). Corrective action for attention-seeking would be to withhold attention until the student behaves appropriately (Pryor & Tollerud, 1999). Eventually, the student should learn that the best way to obtain positive attention is to act appropriately and cooperatively.

The goal of *power* is the most likely misbehavior to result in a student being referred to the professional school counselor for intervention. With a power motive, students feel that they only count if they can force others to do what they want (Sweeney, 1981). Students acting on a desire for power elicit in the adult a sense of being challenged and wanting to engage in a power struggle with that student. The adult will want to show the student that he cannot get away with that kind of behavior. If the motive is indeed power, the student's behavior will tend to worsen as corrective action is taken (Dinkmeyer et al., 1979).

The way to correct power misbehavior is to avoid engaging in a power struggle. The professional school counselor will need to set clear limits (e.g., not hurting self, others, or acting destructively). No limits should be set upon the student's speech, however, since the goal of therapy is to help the child express his thoughts and feelings. When limits are set, the professional school counselor must be careful not to convey a sense of being punitive or judgmental. If a student continues to misbehave, the professional school counselor can give the child choices regarding which appropriate behavior the child can engage in. Otherwise, the professional school counselor could decide to use logical or natural consequences (Kottman & Johnson, 1993).

Logical consequences are statements of an expected outcome for a student's misbehavior that is fair and consistent. These consequences must be related to what a student actually has done and be geared to help the child understand her misbehavior and to see the benefits of behaving properly. The student needs to feel that she is respected and approved of despite the student's misbehavior. Punishment and rewards are to be avoided, as the student needs to learn to behave properly for the intrinsic value of co-operating with others. This will teach the student to learn responsibility and cooperate with others without seeking to be rewarded for good behavior (Pryor & Tollerud, 1999). Examples of logical consequences include the following:

> A student who throws a tantrum over a candy bar will not get that candy bar.
>
> If someone other than the child picks up the child's clothes, that person may put the clothes where the child cannot easily find them.
>
> A student who does not cooperate with other students will have to leave the game until she can agree to play cooperatively.

Natural consequences are events that can be expected to happen if the adult does not intervene. These are the things from which the adult seeks to protect the student; but allowing a student to experience a natural consequence allows that student to learn how to grow and prepares the student for the realities of life. If adults try to protect a student from these natural consequences, the student might get the message that he is inferior and unable to cope on his own (Dreikurs & Soltz, 1964). Examples of natural consequences would be that a student who goes outside in the rain without raingear gets wet, or a student who forgets his lunch money misses lunch, or a student who does not put his bike away has a rusty or stolen bike.

The final two goals of misbehavior are revenge and inadequacy. Both of these misbehaviors may indicate significant problems or issues, and the professional school counselor may wish to refer these students to community counseling where more time and attention can be spent on the students (Kottman & Johnson, 1993).

With the goal of *revenge*, the student believes that she must hurt others, because the student does not feel likeable (Sweeney, 1981). The goal of revenge is common among students who are the victims of physical or sexual abuse (Kottman & Johnson, 1993). When a student is acting out of a goal for revenge, the adult will feel hurt and outraged. Initially, any attempt to correct this student will result in violent behavior (Dinkmeyer et al., 1979). Corrective action would involve setting fair and clear rules and imposing natural consequences. The adult needs to take care not to give the student a sense of being disliked. This student will tend to respond better to encouragement, persuasion, and a sense that she is liked by others (Pryor & Tollerud, 1999).

Finally, the student who misbehaves due to a goal of *inadequacy* has learned to feel that he does not matter to others due to being stupid or hopeless. This student feels too discouraged to try, believing that he would fail, and then everyone would know just how inadequate he really is (Sweeney, 1981). Often, this type of student has experienced some history of abuse (Kottman & Johnson, 1993). Adults working with this kind of student often feel like giving up on the child. Any attempt to correct this student's behavior is likely to be met with futile, insincere attempts to change or try things (Dinkmeyer et al., 1979). A way to correct the misbehavior of inadequacy is to use a lot of encouragement and to help the student to see that he is valued (Pryor & Tollerud, 1999).

Encouragement is a specific technique geared to help a student understand that she is likable and helps a student change her motivation to misbehave. Adlerians believe that a student will learn better in an accepting, democratic environment, where the setting optimizes that particular student's ability to grow and develop. In such a nurturing setting, students tend to automatically change misbehavior into something more acceptable and constructive (Pryor & Tollerud, 1999). Encouragement does not refer to simple praise or reward but rather to statements that convey to the student a sense of respect and recognition that she is a competent, acceptable person. Encouragement can be used to build rapport with a student by showing the student that the professional school counselor has faith in the student's ability to do things. An Adlerian-style counselor will allow a student to do things on her own that the student is capable of doing. If the professional school counselor believes the student cannot do a task, the counselor can suggest that the student agree to do it together with the counselor. This is an opportunity to show the student how to problem solve. As the student works on a task, the professional school counselor can acknowledge the effort and improvements she is making and encourage the student to continue to try (Kottman & Johnson, 1993).

Through encouragement, a student who misbehaves learns to put forth effort to change and is motivated to remain on task. Providing praise before the student has learned these steps may not help the student to learn these necessary skills (Ehly & Dustin, 1989). Allowing a student to do things on his own and encouraging the student to accept the problems inherent in doing difficult things help him to grow and develop in a healthy manner. Since students often have trouble separating what they do from who they are, they tend to judge their value by how competent they are. If a student is allowed to develop competence and to learn to deal with life consequences, that student develops a positive sense of self. Students cannot be effectively shielded from life consequences; they need to be taught how to cope with them rather than be kept from them (Dreikurs & Soltz, 1964).

GOALS OF COUNSELING

The goals of Alderian counseling involve helping the student to develop a healthier way of being involved with others, to develop greater self-awareness, and helping the student to challenge and change her faulty goals and assumptions about life. Counseling involves a form of reeducation in which the student learns new ways to act, to feel self-esteem, and to decrease a sense of being inadequate or inferior. As the student learns to identify her own mistakes in thinking and behaving, she will be able to self-correct and start behaving more appropriately (Carlson & Sperry, 2001).

These goals involve developing an empathic relationship in which the student feels understood and accepted by the professional school counselor. This provides an environment in which the student can be led to explore and understand his beliefs, feelings, motives and goals regarding life. This exploration helps the student to develop insight into his own mistaken attitudes regarding goals, as well as how he has been acting in a self-defeating manner. Finally, the student learns to identify and consider new, viable ways to change problem behaviors and commit to actually changing misbehavior (Dinkmeyer et al. 1979).

THERAPEUTIC TECHNIQUES

Adlerian therapy uses a multitude of techniques to aid the student in exploring his behavior. Some of these techniques are appropriate to therapy in general, and others are more appropriate for individual or group settings. Some explanations of general techniques follow.

TRACKING

As a student moves about the room, the professional school counselor tells the student what she is doing, such as, "You are picking up the truck and taking it over there." This can be used to develop a relationship with the student and to convey to the student that what she does is of importance. This technique works well in play therapy (Kottman & Johnson, 1993).

RESTATEMENT

Restate the content of what the student says. If the student says, "The doll wants to hug you." The professional school counselor can respond with "The doll wants to hug me." Restatement would be most appropriate in play therapy and is a way to convey interest, develop rapport, and help the student to develop self-awareness (Kottman & Johnson, 1993).

REFLECTION

Reflect the emotion of the student to help him become more aware and understand his own feelings. The professional school counselor should seek to reflect both the surface level of the emotion as well as underlying feelings. An example might be a student throwing down a broken toy, kicking it, and saying, "That always happens to me!" The professional school counselor might say "Sometimes you feel angry because things don't work, and you feel like that often happens to you" (Kottman & Johnson, 1993).

EARLY RECOLLECTIONS

This technique requires the student to recall several early life events (which usually come from the time the student was 4 to 6 years old). These recollections help the professional school counselor to identify what the student has come to believe about the world, herself, and others. These recollections can reflect themes as well as specific emotions that are important to understanding the student. The professional school counselor can identify if the student conveys a sense of being safe, cared for, able to control things, and so forth (Kottman & Johnson, 1993).

THERAPEUTIC METAPHORS

Students will often use metaphor and symbolism in play, and the professional school counselor can use the student's metaphor to understand the child and help the child understand herself. This can be used in play therapy, in which a student will spontaneously use a metaphor such as, "Here's the daddy doll. He comes home and turns into a monster and eats up the whole family" (Kottman & Johnson, 1993). Obviously, this example provides the professional school counselor with a great deal of information about how the student feels and perceives the world.

MUTUAL STORYTELLING

The student's metaphors can also be used to help a student understand his beliefs and views of life. The professional school counselor can have a child tell a story with a beginning, middle, and end. The student's story may contain some mistaken beliefs or perceptions, and the professional school counselor can take the opportunity to retell the story in a more positive and adaptive light to help the student develop a new perspective (Kottman & Johnson, 1993). *The Mutual Storytelling Game* (Erford, 2000a), a Windows-based CD-ROM program, helps facilitate student storytelling by providing backgrounds and diverse characters.

THERAPEUTIC GAMES

Older students often do not wish to attend counseling or are unwilling to either discuss their emotions or to change their behaviors. Games that are bought in the stores and special games designed for counseling, such as the series developed by Erford (2000b, 2000c, 2000d, 2000e, 2001a, 2001b, 2001c, 2002a, 2002b, 2002c), can be used to engage the reluctant student. Playing games can afford the professional school counselor an opportunity to observe the student's behavior and to identify some of the student's attitudes about herself and others. Game-playing in groups, particularly, can provide information regarding social skills, ability to wait, taking turns, coping with disappointment, and so forth. The professional school counselor can use these opportunities to help the student explore her thoughts, feelings, and behaviors, develop a sense of competence, and build her self-esteem. Sometimes a student may talk while playing the game and provide more information than she would in a formal face-to-face session (Kottman, 1990).

ROLE-PLAY AND SIMULATION

Using creative dramatics can work to motivate older students in a group setting. Group members can use role-play to explore different behaviors and to observe how these behaviors affect others. Role-play and simulation can also help group members develop empathy for others, develop social skills, explore their inner world with others, develop listening and attending skills, cooperate with others, learn decision-making skills, and develop the ability to observe and evaluate both self and others (Kottman, 1990).

"COULD IT BE" QUESTIONS

"Could it be" questions involve the professional school counselor being aware of the feelings a student's misbehavior is eliciting and help the student to identify his misbehavior. So, if a professional school counselor is feeling annoyed by a student's obvious attempts to get the counselor to watch him, the counselor could say, "Could it be you are keeping me busy with you because you want me to pay attention to you?" This would help the student become more aware of the goals of his misbehavior (Poppen & Thompson, 1974).

PARADOXICAL INTENT

As an experiment, the professional school counselor can have the student do the opposite of what the student would expect, to emphasize the symptoms or misbehavior. This could help the student develop a greater awareness of the consequences of her misbehavior if she does not *resist* doing it but instead *deliberately* does it. For example, if a therapist tells a student, as an experiment, to deliberately not do her homework for one night, this might help the student become aware of the fact that she chooses her own behavior, that not doing homework is less attractive when it is permitted, and help the student see how silly or ridiculous that misbehavior may be (Dinkmeyer et al., 1979). This technique must be used carefully, for a limited time, with the appropriate student (and with the approval and support of the student's teacher) to work effectively.

SPITTING IN THE CLIENT'S SOUP

This technique refers to an old boarding-school activity wherein a student would spit in another child's soup in order to get that child to give up the soup. Here, the professional school counselor identifies the purpose of, and payoff for, a certain misbehavior and spoils the fun for the student by decreasing the pleasure he may derive from misbehaving. For example, the professional school counselor may reflect to an older student that his drinking problem may be a way for the student to keep connected to the father he claims to hate, because the father is an alcoholic and that is something they can share (Carlson & Sperry, 2001).

ACTING "AS IF"

The professional school counselor can have the student, as an exercise or assignment, act the way she would like to act. The student may initially resist, saying that it's just pretending and not real. However, the professional school counselor could relate it to trying on a new outfit or suit of clothes. The student could try it on and see if it works. If the student does try and feels better, she may decide to behave differently. This can be done for a certain period of time, and then the student can return to the counselor to discuss the results (Dinkmeyer et al., 1979). An example would be that a shy student could act as if she was friendly and say "hi" to everyone she meets.

CATCHING ONESELF

As the student becomes more aware, the professional school counselor can suggest that the student catch himself doing something the student wants to change. At first, the student will tend to catch himself too late to do anything. As the student practices, he learns to anticipate and avoid certain situations or to change his behavior. This can be done with a sense of humor and works well if the student can laugh at himself (Dinkmeyer et al., 1979).

CREATING MOVEMENT

Sometimes a student needs to be motivated to change. This tactic must be used carefully and in light of a sense of trust and the relationship the professional school counselor has developed with the student. To create movement, the counselor can use surprise to jar a student out of inaction. For example, if a student decided she wanted to give up, the professional school counselor may agree with her (Dinkmeyer et al., 1979). If used properly, not saying the expected thing could result in a moment of deeper self-awareness.

AVOIDING POWER STRUGGLES

Often, a child will try to fit the professional school counselor into a role based upon that student's expectations and beliefs about the world. Thus, a student may try to provoke the counselor into validating that the student is unlovable. The professional school counselor must avoid falling into this trap or risk confirming to the child that he is, indeed, unlovable. The counselor must keep aware of the feelings the child is attempting to elicit and avoid giving in to feelings of being hurt or discouraged. In particular, the professional school counselor needs to avoid any power struggles with the child (Dinkmeyer et al., 1979).

TASK SETTING AND COMMITMENT

The professional school counselor helps a student to identify what she can do about a problem and commit to doing it for a specific time. If the student is successful, she may feel encouraged and continue to change. If not, new behaviors could be explored, and the student could try again (Dinkmeyer et al., 1979).

PUSH-BUTTON TECHNIQUE

Students need to understand that they are responsible for both the good and bad feelings they experience. Humans create their own moods. In this technique, the student could be directed to mentally reexperience something that gave him a very good feeling. Then, the student could visualize an experience that made him feel very bad. As the child does this, the professional school counselor could help the student to learn to connect how one's thoughts about an experience lead to one's feelings about that experience (Carlson & Sperry, 2001).

GROUP-SPECIFIC TECHNIQUES

In groups, the group member gets to interact with peers in such a way as to be able to work on specific ideas and issues. To do this in a safe environment, group members must develop acceptance for each other (have respect and empathy). Acceptance could be modeled by the group leader who could also help specific group members develop their own ability to accept others.

- *Altruism* is the natural tendency in humans to seek to help each other. Group counseling could provide an opportunity for group members to extend help to each other. This can be modeled by the group leader, who can also encourage altruism and provide the group opportunities to use and develop this skill.

- *Spectator therapy* refers to the observation that some group members may interact little with the group, but may still be listening and developing a greater understanding of themselves. Just listening to others in a group situation can help a group member see himself in others and develop self-awareness.

- *Universalization* involves helping group members to understand that their problems are not unique, that they are not as alone as they thought. To understand that they share problems with others can help group members feel less alienated and lonely and thus able to look at various solutions. This sharing can be used to encourage exploration and discussion.

- *Feedback* helps group members understand how others experience them. This can help develop insight and greater self-awareness. It also helps the group member challenge her faulty beliefs and perceptions. Honest, authentic feedback can also convey to a group member that she is important to others and that others care and are concerned about the student.

- *Ventilation* provides group members the opportunity to express normally inhibited emotions. It also provides an outlet for internal pressures, promotes the expression and exploration of feelings, and helps the group member develop greater insight.

- *Reality testing* helps a group member test a faulty perception or belief within the group setting. For example, if a boy has developed a belief that girls are enemies and that he could never come to understand them, he could test this theory in the group by learning to talk to girls in the group. As he develops an ability to accept that his first assumptions were wrong, the boy may learn to look at other misperceptions or faulty assumptions and develop an ability to be self-aware (Dinkmeyer et al., 1979).

CONSULTATION

Adlerian principles also apply to consultation with teachers and parents. Parents need to understand their child's behavior and can benefit from learning about the four goals of misbehavior and ways to intervene with difficult behaviors. Weekly face-to-face consultations are optimal, but they are not usually practical. Therefore, the professional school counselor may have to seek some other way to consult with the parents, such as by phone. Contact with parents is an important way for the counselor to gather more information regarding the student and to suggest to the parents ways to deal with the student's misbehavior (Kottman & Johnson, 1993). Teachers, also, often can benefit from learning about the goals of misbehavior and identify new, creative ways to intervene with problem behaviors.

Adlerians also avoid assigning blame for a student's problems (as so often happens when parents blame schools, schools blame parents, and the student escapes responsibility for her behavior). Sometimes, a meeting with all parties (student, parents, and teachers) is advisable in order to improve communication and cooperation to deal more effectively with the student's misbehavior. Adlerian counselors also avoid using labels or overestimating evaluations and test scores. Each student is seen as an individual and not compared with others (Dinkmeyer et al., 1979).

SPECIAL TOPICS

Adlerian theory seeks to understand the individual within a social context; it is therefore conducive to ethnic and multicultural issues. A student with a diverse background may develop a sense of inferiority and become pessimistic about being able to meet his life goals. Adlerian techniques could be used to help that student understand his own innate worth and status and to raise that student's self-esteem (Herring & Runion, 1994).

Adlerians focus on understanding a student's subjective view of the world, respecting the individual student, believing that each student can learn and grow, and developing a student's ability to be cooperative and socially responsible. All of these tenets work well with multicultural and special needs issues. Many cultures value community and social cooperation, but the professional school counselor must operate from a sound understanding of the student's background as well as a sensitivity and respect for that student's culture in order to be responsible and effective in helping that student (Sapp, 1997). Children with special needs may also suffer from feelings of inferiority or faulty beliefs about how the world works and can also benefit from the Adlerian focus on self-worth of the individual student.

SUMMARY/CONCLUSION

The professional school counselor will find that Adlerian theory and therapeutic techniques are applicable to the work they do. I have provided a brief review of some of the basic tenets of Adlerian theory and how they apply to counseling children within a school setting. The professional school counselor can use the ideas presented in this chapter to identify the goal of a student's misbehavior and to develop an intervention that is specific and appropriate to the needs of that individual student. I also provided some guidelines for consultation, with a special emphasis to avoid placing blame and keeping the child responsible for his or her own behavior. The scope of this chapter was such that a more comprehensive review was not possible. Therefore, this chapter can provide only a brief overview of Adlerian theory and techniques, and the interested reader is advised to consult the reference section for further readings.

(Note: See the CD-ROM for a list of references.)

CHAPTER 37

USING GESTALT COUNSELING
IN A SCHOOL SETTING

J. Kelly Coker

Preview

Professional school counselors are faced with the challenges of large caseloads, large workloads, and not enough hours in the day to address those challenges. Identifying theoretically based approaches that are conducive to school settings is one way to make professional school counselors more effective and efficient. Gestalt counseling, while not traditionally viewed as a school-based approach to counseling, has some developmentally appropriate techniques that work well with children and adolescents in brief counseling environments.

As professional school counselors in training, it is not unusual to be grilled about the importance of learning about and adhering to theories of counseling and psychology during one's professional practice, even though the integration of theory into practice was not something always at the forefront of reconciling schedules or wading through sophomore credit checks.

Theoretical approaches and techniques in general, and Gestalt approaches and techniques specifically, play a significant and potentially useful role in the professional practice of school counseling (Ryder, 2003). Working from a theoretical framework can help the professional school counselor establish a frame of reference, keep the counseling process on track, and create a blueprint of proven techniques to lead to positive outcomes. Many of the original concepts of Gestalt therapy and counseling continue to be used in therapeutic settings, and some have been modified to work more effectively with children. In addition to sharing these original ideas as they relate to work with children, I will also present a brief history of Gestalt therapy and its founder, Fritz Perls; the major tenets of the theory; considerations for adaptation with younger populations; and specific Gestaltian techniques that are appropriate for a school setting.

HISTORICAL PERSPECTIVE

In his book *Gestalt Therapy Verbatim*, Fritz Perls (1969) wrote,

> One of the objections I have against anyone calling himself a Gestalt Therapist is that he uses technique. A technique is a gimmick. A gimmick should be used only in the extreme case. We've got enough people running around collecting gimmicks, more gimmicks and abusing them. (p. 1)

To do an empty-chair technique without first grasping Gestaltian principles, such as the importance of the development of a sense of self; the significance of the interaction between client, environment, and relationships; and the relevance of the here-and-now experience to meaningful growth would be, in Perls's view, irresponsible.

Frederick (Fritz) Perls spent 12 years in South Africa, where he formulated all of the basic ideas of what would become Gestalt therapy. Once he moved to New York in 1946, Perls began traveling throughout the United States, presenting on his new theory. It was not until the mid- to late 1960s, however, shortly before Perls's death, that Gestalt therapy became a significant force in the field of psychology. Perls developed the Gestalt Institute of Canada in 1969 and died of pancreatic cancer in March 1970. Gestalt therapy was still considered in progress at the time of Perls's death, and many of Perls's writings were published posthumously (Maples, 1999).

Perls has always been a controversial figure in modern psychotherapy. Current researchers and practitioners of Gestalt therapy have suggested that the approach has suffered due, in part, to Perls's approach to and interpretation of Gestalt therapy (Wagner-Moore, 2004). Many are familiar with Perls's famous participation in the *Three Approaches to Psychotherapy* (Shostrom, 1965) videos and his counseling interview with the client, Gloria. In 1965, three psychotherapists—Perls, Rogers, and Ellis—conducted counseling interviews with Gloria, a 30 year old female, to demonstrate their counseling theories. Throughout the interview, Perls drew attention to Gloria's nonverbal behavior (e.g., "What are you doing with your feet now?" "Are you aware that your eyes are moist?"). He also would have Gloria repeat or exaggerate her responses (e.g., "Can you develop this movement . . . now exaggerate this"; Dolliver, 1991). Perls sometimes directly challenged Gloria's verbal and nonverbal responses as being incongruent in an attempt to bring her experience into the here and now. When I have shown the Gloria series to counselors in training, the strongest reactions are often to Perls. Many have expressed how rude, crass, removed, and uncaring he appears with Gloria. Others have commented that he seems to be trying to upset her. Even scholars who have studied the films have commented on the uneasiness they experienced when watching Perls interact with Gloria (Dolliver, 1991). It is important, therefore, to separate the man from the theory and to realize that Gestalt theory and techniques have evolved over the years, and some techniques have been empirically validated. According to Wagner-Moore, "modern gestalt has retained many of Perls' original ideas but has also softened in many respects" (2004, p. 183).

MAJOR TENETS OF GESTALT THERAPY

While some contemporaries of Perls have specifically looked at the application of Gestalt counseling with younger populations, many of the original ideas of Gestalt theory may resonate with professional school counselors. In his work, *The Gestalt Approach & Eye Witness to Therapy*, Perls (1973) described some key concepts (see Table 37.1) that shape both Gestaltian theory and practice. Professional school counselors might consider how the examples in Table 37.1 fit in their work with children and adolescents.

The theoretical tenets can be examined in the context of the school setting with the following example. An 8-year-old boy is referred to the professional school counselor by his teacher for sucking his thumb during class. The teacher reports that the student will suck his thumb three or four times a day, and seems to "zone out" or lose

TABLE 37.1

KEY CONCEPTS OF GESTALTIAN THEORY AND PRACTICE

1. No person is totally self-sufficient; the person can only exist in an environmental field.

2. In relationship to this field, people will engage in either *contact* or *withdrawal.*

3. *Contact* refers to a person's attempts to reach out towards those people and things in the environmental field that are desirable or reinforcing.

4. *Withdrawal* refers to a person's attempts to remove or separate from people or things in the environmental field that are perceived as harmful, threatening, or otherwise negative.

5. Not every contact is healthy, and not every withdrawal is unhealthy.

6. The contact with and withdrawal from the environmental field are the most important functions of the total personality. They are the positive and negative aspects of the psychological processes by which people live.

7. Therefor, people are both an individual and a function of the environmental field.

8. The focus of Gestalt counseling is not on *why* behavior problems or neuroses exist or came to be, but on *how* the individual experiences her issues in the here and now.

9. The goal of Gestalt counseling is to give the client the means with which he can solve his present problems or issues and any that might arise in the future.

10. Gestalt counseling is largely experiential vs. verbal, with the goal of helping the client experience herself as much as she can in the here and now.

11. Increased awareness of here and now attempts at contact and withdrawal as well as interpreting success and failure of these attempts leads to new insight into more effective ways of interacting with the environmental feld.

focus when he does so. The professional school counselor first observes the student and notices the same behavior. During thumb sucking, the boy's eyes seem to glaze over, and he seems unaware of what's happening around him.

From a Gestalt perspective, the student is engaging in attempts to *withdraw* from his *environmental field* through thumb sucking. Since the Gestalt perspective does not assume all withdrawal behavior is unhealthy, the professional school counselor's first order of business would be to explore with the student how he feels when sucking his thumb, and how sucking his thumb in class is serving him in the here and now. Note that this technique would be a departure from a traditional behaviorist approach which would focus primarily on stopping the thumb-sucking through behavior modification. A Gestalt approach might include the counselor first trying to gather some key information about the student's perspective of his environmental field. For example, through experiential approaches such as drawing his family or drawing himself at school, the professional school counselor can gain insight into the student's reality. Then the professional school counselor might bring the thumb sucking behavior into awareness when it is occurring. So instead of talking about the behavior ("Why do you suck your thumb in class?"), the counselor might "catch" the child in the act of sucking his thumb and say, "I notice you are sucking your thumb right now, can you tell me how that feels? Does it make talking to me easier to suck your thumb? Do you notice that it makes being in class easier when you suck your thumb?" This line of questioning serves two purposes: (1) to bring the problem behavior into awareness in the here-and-now, and (2) to begin to link the here-and-now behavior to other contexts.

The professional school counselor then might work with the student to link the thumb-sucking behavior to other events or contexts. For example, does the thumb sucking occur only at school, or at home as well? Is the thumb sucking tied to particular feelings such as being anxious, or to particular events, such as being called on in class? The professional school counselor might also explore with the student his attempt to make contact with his environmental field. "When does it feel comfortable in class and with your teacher? What kinds of things do you do or say when you feel comfortable?" Ultimately, the goals might not be to stop the problem behavior (thumb sucking), but instead to increase positive interactions between the student and his environment, also increasing healthy contact attempts, which should naturally decrease the unhealthy withdrawal attempts.

WORKING WITH CHILDREN

Violet Oaklander, a Gestalt therapist who works primarily with children, suggested that using the Gestaltian approach with children provides a process-oriented experience that focuses attention on the healthy, integrated functioning of the total child (Oaklander, 2000). Oaklander defined healthy *contact* as a child's ability to be fully present in a particular situation. Students who are anxious, worried, grieving, scared, or angry pull themselves inward (withdrawal) and block healthy contact with their environment and the people in it. Resistant behavior in students, however, is not always negative. Children, like adults, will engage in self-protecting behavior which is sometimes a healthy response, particularly when the environment the student is withdrawing from is unhealthy.

PROCESS OF COUNSELING

Gestalt counseling can be ideal for short-term work because it is both focusing and directive (Oaklander, 2000). The therapeutic process involves several steps that can be accomplished in brief counseling sessions. These steps with accompanying examples will be outlined below.

1. *Establishing the therapeutic relationship.* The Gestaltian counselor sees this process as key. Establishing trust, boundaries, limits, and an independent "I/Thou" relationship sets the stage for further change. Since a key function in Gestalt counseling is to use the here-and-now experience, the student's willingness to view the professional school counselor as a person worthy of trust is paramount.
   Example: "Why don't we take a few minutes to get to know each other a bit. I want you to feel like I am someone you can trust and talk to. Is there anything you would like to know about me?"

2. *Contact functions.* As indicated above, contact involves the student's ability to be fully present in the interactions. Resistance, or breaking contact, is viewed as a way of coping with pain or stress, and is respected and valued during the interaction.

Example: "I noticed when I starting talking about your mother, you looked away and got quiet. Would you like to talk about something else for a few minutes before we go back to that topic?"

3. *Building self-support.* This process involves helping students strengthen their sense-of-self through personal expression. The use of a variety of experiential and creative techniques (i.e., clay, imagery, drawing, sandplay) is suggested to facilitate building self-support. Gestalt counselors often refer to this process as establishing a sense of self instead of building self-esteem. From a Gestalt perspective, it is the awareness of the total self—good and bad—that is important; not just making the student "feel better." Interventions that encourage the student to make choices, allow her to experience mastery, and allow her to experience a sense of power are all useful in building self-support.

Example: "I'd like for you to draw a self-portrait. This picture should represent how you see yourself; not how you think others see you. Now I'd like you to tell me three things you like about the person you drew, and three things you wish were different."

4. *Emotional expression.* Once the student experiences self-support, helping the student to experience blocked emotions is a key step in the process. Often students get the message from adults in their lives that particular feelings are "bad." "You shouldn't be angry!" is a phrase many students might hear. The Gestalt approach honors the feelings as neither good nor bad, just real; and then allows for safe expression of those feelings. In the counseling process, first talking about feelings to help students understand what different feelings are, and then expressing feelings through creative expression are strategies in dealing with emotions. Finally, learning skills for dealing with feelings when they occur is a part of the process.

Example: "Why don't you use this clay to make an image of your brother. Now tell your brother how you feel when he locks you out of his room. Is there anything you would like to do to this piece of clay to show how you feel?" (Smash it, roll it, cut it, etc.).

5. *Self-nurturing work.* In this stage of counseling, the professional school counselor works to reinforce the student's ability to reframe negative, external and internal messages about the self. The student is encouraged to actively nurture the self through ongoing creative expression (journal writing, drawing, self-talk, imagery).

Example: "You've done a great job in describing the ways in which you are a good friend to others. The next time you feel embarrassed to talk to someone during recess, remember to tell yourself what you've told me; that you are fun and a good friend to others."

6. *Dealing with process.* It is not unusual for students to continue to use ineffective coping mechanisms in an effort to get their needs met. Dealing with process helps to build the bridge between the counseling process and strategies for coping with the outside environment. This includes taking responsibility, experimenting with new behaviors, obtaining environmental support, and confronting self-defeating behaviors.

Example: "This coming week, I want you to experiment with sharing your feelings with your sister at least three times and then writing in your journal about that experience."

In addition, family work and parent education are key components to the therapeutic process. For professional school counselors, teacher education might be equally important. Parents and teachers can be asked to experiment with new behaviors and to allow for student experimentation with new behaviors. If a student periodically throws things at other students in a teacher's class, the teacher might agree to allow the student to retreat to a corner of the room with some paper and crayons if the student is feeling particularly angry. This honors the child's feeling of anger while providing a safer outlet for an expression of that anger.

THE USE OF LANGUAGE

An important step in using the Gestalt approach with a student is to examine the language used in counseling interactions. Some language methods in working with students include:

Using "I" language. "I" language is used to help the student take responsibility for his own behaviors, feelings, and thoughts. It is not unusual for students to engage in blaming and to use "you" or "they" language (e.g., "They just don't listen to me!" or "You just don't understand!"). Using "I" language, the student would be encouraged to say, "I feel frustrated when I don't think I'm being heard or understood." The professional school counselor can certainly model the use of this language as well. Instead of saying, "You got in trouble again with your teacher which is why you are back in the principal's office," the professional school counselor might say, "I'm aware of the situation with your teacher, and I'm sorry it resulted in more time spent with the principal."

Using "what" and "how" instead of "why." As discussed above, the "why" question is generally one to be avoided in the Gestalt approach. "Why" questions can put students on the defensive, and do not generally open the door to further communication. Instead of asking, "Why won't you listen to your teacher?" you might ask, "What are you usually doing when your teacher is talking? How do you feel when your teacher is talking?"

Using "won't" instead of "can't." In order to increase personal responsibility, students can be encouraged to substitute the word "won't," which implies more responsibility, for the word "can't," which relinquishes responsibility. So the statement, "I can't do my homework!" would be re-stated as, "I won't do my homework" (Thompson & Rudolph, 2000).

Sentence completion exercise. Sentence completion exercises are one way to help students use language differently to gain a different perspective on their problem (Tucker-Ladd, 1996). One such exercise has been used by the author when working with students (see Figure 37.1). This exercise encourages students to first visualize the issue or problem, and then to finish the sentences as written. The second step of the exercise is to make word substitutions for the existing leads. For example, the lead, "I had to . . ." becomes "I chose to . . ." and "I can't . . ." becomes "I won't . . . ." The other substitutions are listed in Figure 37.1. The use of this exercise encourages both personal responsibility

1. I had to _____ . (I chose to)

2. I can't _____ . (I won't)

3. I need _____ . (I want)

4. I'm afraid to _____ . (I'd like to)

5. I'm unable to _____ . (I'm willing
    to try to)

FIGURE 37.1. Sentence completion exercise.

and the concept of choice. It is suggested that the exercise be presented as a possible view of the problem, not an absolute. After all, there might be some problems or issues that the student has no real control over or choice about. For example, if the problem is that the student's parents have gotten a divorce, it may not be realistic to have the student change a sentence from, "I had to live with my Dad" to "I chose to live with my Dad."

THE USE OF GESTALT COUNSELING IN A SCHOOL SETTING

Not much has been written about the use of Gestalt counseling in a school setting, but one example was described by Alexander and Harman (1988). According to Marchi (1990), Gestalt therapy can be effective in helping others deal with death and loss. Alexander and Harman (1988) discussed the application of Gestalt counseling as a means of dealing with the aftermath of a student suicide at school. From a Gestalt perspective, the professional school counselor at a middle school where the suicide had occurred worked with students both in classroom and small-group settings. Starting in the classroom, the professional school counselor worked with the 150 students with whom the suicide victim, Jason, had daily contact. She went into each classroom informing the students she was there to help them say goodbye to Jason. She then asked where he had sat in the room, and using the empty chair technique, invited students to tell Jason anything about how they felt, what they would have done for him if they had known he was in trouble, and what they would like him to know. They all ended their statements with, "and goodbye, Jason" (Alexander & Harmon, 1988). Out of the large class experiences, the professional school counselor began some small groups for those students most directly affected by Jason's death. Again using a Gestaltian approach, the professional school counselor encouraged participating members to reflect on Jason and his death, and then express their feelings on large sheets of paper using whatever colors, symbols, shapes, and lines they wished. In describing their drawings to the rest of the group, feelings of emptiness, loneliness, confusion, and students' own suicidal fears emerged (Alexander & Harman, 1988). This one example illustrates the potential power of this approach for dealing with other crisis situations.

Another example of using Gestalt counseling with vocational clients was described by Ryder (2003). While Ryder focused primarily on use of counseling theory with adult vocational counseling clients, one can see applications with high school students on the path of making career decisions. According to Ryder, the essence of vocational counseling from a Gestalt perspective is to empower the student to take responsibility for his or her own decision making and to use techniques such as the empty chair, role playing, and psychodrama to encourage vocational decisions that are most compatible with the client's needs, life goals, and interests.

One of the techniques listed in both previous examples, the Gestalt empty chair, also has utility for other issues not as severe as suicide, including communication issues, relationship issues, and unresolved issues with others.

GESTALT EMPTY CHAIR TECHNIQUE

Perls (1969) referred to the empty chair as the place to implement the client's personality and other interpersonal encounters. Perls would use the empty chair technique both for dialogue with significant others, either living or dead, and for dialogue with other sides of the self. Empirical studies have compared use of the empty chair technique with use of client-centered, cognitive-behavioral, and experiential methods on a variety of issues (Wagner-Moore, 2004). In research on the use of the empty chair technique conducted by Greenberg in 1980s, at least three studies consistently found this technique was superior to empathic responding for increased depth of experience as well as superior to cognitive-behavioral approaches for greater conflict resolution immediately after treatment (Wagner-Moore, 2004). This author has used the empty chair technique with both children and adolescents, and has found that, while both age groups can benefit from dialogues with others, adolescents are more developmentally able to engage in dialogue with several sides of the self. Both approaches will be described in the following sections and demonstrated in Figure 37.2.

Dialogue with others. The professional school counselor arranges two chairs facing each other. The student is invited to sit in one chair and describe to the professional school counselor the person she is having a conflict or issue with. The professional school counselor helps to develop the picture of the person by repeating back key descriptors (e.g., "So your dad is a tall man with dark hair, very skinny, with big, strong hands. Is that right?").

The student is then invited to imagine the person (Dad) is in the other chair. The professional school counselor then says, "I'd like you to tell your dad anything you would like. You might talk to him about how you feel about being grounded this weekend, or anything else you'd like to say. Remember that you can say anything you want to dad right now without having to worry about what he might say or do in return." The professional school counselor intentionally "pulls back" from the experience at this point, not engaging in eye contact with the student so the student can have an uninterrupted discussion with dad. Further prompting is appropriate if the student does not know how to start, but efforts should be made to keep the client from turning back to the professional school counselor. For example, "Okay, that's very good, but now turn around and say that to your dad, not to me."

DIALOGUE WITH OTHERS

- Have the student sit in one chair facing another empty chair.
- Say to student, "I'd like for you to describe to me the person you are having a conflict with."
  - What does he/she look like?
  - What was the most recent conflict about?
- Say to the student, "I'd now like you to imagine (name person) is sitting across from you right now. You are able to say anything to him/her that you would like. Take a minute and think about the conflict, think about your feelings and your thoughts. When you are ready, I want you to talk to (name person) who is sitting right here in front of you.
- During the experience, the professional school counselor should sit out of the way and not make eye contact with the student. If the student turns to the professional school counselor or tries to address the counselor, the counselor should steer the client back to addressing the person in the empty chair. (Example: "Now tell that to [name person] instead of me.")
- Once the person has said all they want to say to the person they are having a conflict with, process the experience.
  - Is there anything else you would like to say?
  - How did it feel to say that to (name person)?
  - Is there anything you think he/she would want to say back to you? (If so, the student can sit in the other seat and talk as the other person).
  - What would it take for you to articulate those feelings in person?
  - Would you say anything differently?

DIALOGUE WITH SELF

- Have student sit in one chair facing another empty chair.
- Say to the student, "You've described an internal conflict you are having where your "heart" is telling you one thing but your "head" is telling you something else. I'd like you to imagine you are sitting in this chair as your heart, or emotional side, and in the other chair is your head, or logical side."
- Have the student start the dialogue from the emotional side with, "What I feel about this situation is. . . "
- Have the student move to the other chair when he/she is finished talking from the emotional side, and talk from the logical side. Start the dialogue with, "What I think about this situation is . . ."
- The client can respond to each side by moving from chair to chair until he/she feels the dialogue is complete.
- Process the experience.
  - Which side do you feel you are more in agreement with?
  - Which side do you think has the better argument?
  - Is there anyway to resolve these two sides to come to one resolution?
  - How will you know when this problem is solved? What will your heart tell you? What will your head tell you?

FIGURE 37.2. Gestalt empty chair technique.

Once the student has spoken her piece, the counselor can focus processing on here-and-now experiences, such as, "How did it feel to say those things to your dad?" "I noticed you raised your voice when you were talking about being grounded. What were you feeling then?" "You balled your fist up several times. Do this again now. Do it again. Now release your fist and relax your hand. Now say what you said again to dad, but with a relaxed hand instead of a fist." "How was that different?" Notice the questions are geared toward bringing into awareness all of the elements of the student's process during the exercise.

Variations of the activity could include having the student address the empty chair and then move to the empty chair and speak back as the person identified, or discussing with the student the pros and cons of actually having this discussion with the "real" person, if that person is still living or available. This technique can be particularly powerful when there are things left unsaid between the student and someone no longer available to them, either through death or absence. The empty chair technique can allow for true expression of feelings of loss, anger, sadness, and remorse.

Dialogue with self. Another way to use this technique (with adolescents, in particular) is to encourage the student to have a dialogue between two sides of the self. For example, female adolescents who are troubled by the recent end of a relationship often have conflicts between their "head" (I knew it was right to end it) and their "heart" (but I still love him so much). This variation on the empty chair would have the "heart" in one chair talk to the "head" in the other. The student would first talk from the heart. The heart would have lead sentences like, "What I feel about the breakup is . . . ." Then, physically moving to the other chair, the student would talk from the head. The head might start with something like, "What I think about the breakup is . . . ." The student can then explore the two sides and see which is stronger. She can also examine pros and cons of listening to the heart over the head and vice versa.

Summary/Conclusion

For other useful Gestalt techniques tailored for use with children, a recommended reading is *Windows to Our Children,* by Oaklander (1988). Building on Gestalt underpinnings, Oaklander described experiential games and interventions designed to help children experience their true feelings, their relationship with their environment and the people in it, their sense of responsibility for their actions and behaviors, and their sense of power and ownership in their world. While professional school counselors are responsible for a myriad of duties, none would argue that helping students cope with painful situations and solve difficult problems is a significant part of the role. Gestalt counseling provides professional school counselors with a theoretically based approach that is conducive to brief interactions and both insight and behavior change.

(Note: See the CD-ROM for a list of references.)

CHAPTER 38

USING ROGERIAN THEORY AND TECHNIQUES

Grafton T. Eliason and Jo Ellen Smith

Preview

Person-centered counseling offers professional school counselors a humanistic philosophy that incorporates the basic helping skills that are essential for all counseling relationships. Roger's therapeutic skills and counseling attributes are particularly applicable to the school setting (Eliason, Hanley, & Leventis, 2001; Rogers, 1951, 1969; Schmidt, 1999).

As the director of the Rochester Guidance Center at the Society for the Prevention of Cruelty to Children, Rogers (1980) experienced situations that significantly affected his theoretical understanding of the importance of following the client's lead. Rogers began to counsel a child who displayed serious behavior problems. Both Rogers and another colleague determined that the primary issue was the mother's rejection of her son. After many sessions with the mother and child with no change, Rogers decided to terminate therapy. The mother then asked if he provided adult counseling, wherein she shared with Rogers her personal story and her authentic desire for help. At this point, Rogers's role was primarily that of an active listener. As a result of this experience and the influence of Otto Rank, Rogers determined that by trusting the client's potential for self-awareness, by believing in the positive potential for growth through therapy, and by providing the right conditions, the individual would move naturally toward actualization. Rogers eventually began teaching classes in the Department of Sociology at the University of Rochester and wrote *The Clinical Treatment of the Problem Child* in 1939. In 1942, he accepted a full-time position at Ohio State University and wrote the unique and controversial book, *Counseling and Psychotherapy* (Rogers, 1980; Thompson & Rudolph, 1992).

NON-DIRECTIVE THERAPY AND CLIENT-CENTERED THERAPY

Rogers's theory, developed in the 1940s, was initially a reaction to the psychoanalysis used by his contemporaries. Rogers believed that the medical model was biased and prejudicial, so he eliminated diagnosis, interpretation, and advice-giving. Instead, Rogers emphasized the feelings that the client expressed through reflection, summarization, and clarification, with the aim of facilitating greater insight and self-awareness. This theory of counseling was called *non-directive therapy* (Rogers, 1980).

Rogers's approach continued to evolve as he began to develop a rigorous theory of therapy and compile personal attributes that a counselor should possess in order to foster a healthy therapeutic relationship with the client. He also began to understand that his philosophical underpinnings were actually a homegrown variety of existentialism. When providing a climate comprised of the specific counselor attributes of congruency (genuineness), unconditional positive regard (acceptance), and accurate empathic understanding, people become more flexible, autonomous, self-accepting, and self-actualized. As a result, they begin to experience more positive relationships and personal mental health. In 1951, Rogers wrote *Client-Centered Therapy*, which shifted the focus from non-directive methods to the phenomenological world of the client and one's personal frame of reference. The actualizing tendency becomes the primary motivation for change, and by providing the appropriate environment, positive change will occur (Rogers, 1951).

PERSON-CENTERED THERAPY

Person-centered therapy is a theoretical orientation that expands upon aspects of existential philosophy and phenomenological humanism. The etymology of phenomenology originates in the Greek word *phainomenon*, referring to a "phenomenon," or "that which appears or shows itself." Rogers held the view that the counselor–client relationship was the basis of his theory. He believed that establishing an atmosphere in which the relationship can grow facilitates the individual's move toward greater self-direction, self-awareness, and positive change. The optimal situation focuses on a combination of the counselor's attitude and the client's perception. There needs to be trust, confidence, acceptance, and a democratic style of equality. Goals are oriented to the personality rather than to symptoms, diagnoses, and the curing of a disease. The client must feel that he or she is being heard in a nonjudgmental manner. It is not enough for the conditions to exist—they must be successfully communicated as well.

THERAPEUTIC ATTRIBUTES

As a professional school counselor builds a relationship with the student based on Rogers's therapeutic attributes, change is facilitated by the student's growing trust and the feeling that he or she is accepted and understood. As the student's awareness grows, it enhances his or her ability to learn, adapt to the present environment, better cope with life stressors, and choose more socially appropriate behavior. Congruence, also known as genuineness or "realness," is the therapeutic stance in which the professional school counselor presents his or her real self rather than taking the position of an expert. The professional school counselor has the ability to maintain his or her own self-identity and convey this to the student (Thompson & Rudolph, 1992).

> The term "congruent" is one that I have used to describe the way I would like to be. By this I mean that whatever feeling or attitude I am experiencing would be matched by my awareness of that attitude. When this is true, then I am a unified or integrated person in that moment, and hence I can *be* whatever I deeply *am*. This is a reality which I find others experience as dependable. (Rogers, 1961, p. 51)

A professional school counselor who is perceived as "real" provides the student with the conditions to experience, tolerate, and accept feelings and emotions that cause difficulty in interpersonal interactions in the school, family, and community. It is often very rare for a student—or any individual, for that matter—to experience such a genuine response. The student then reacts positively when she perceives congruence, which enhances trust in the relationship and promotes change.

The second attribute, unconditional positive regard, or acceptance, implies that the professional school counselor believes in the student's innate possibility for positive growth. It includes the willingness to accept whatever feelings or emotions are present, resulting in a decrease in defenses and resistances, while promoting constructive change (Thompson & Rudolph, 1992).

> As a second condition, I find that the more acceptance and liking I feel toward this individual, the more I will be creating a relationship which he can use. By acceptance I mean a warm regard for him as a person of unconditional self-worth—of value no matter what his condition, his behavior, or his feelings. It means a respect and liking for him as a separate person, a willingness for him to possess his own feelings in his own way. (Rogers, 1961, p. 34)

Cochran and Cochran (1999) found that the counseling relationship, which includes the Rogerian attribute of acceptance, facilitates change in students with conduct disorders. In the most difficult situations, students with conduct disorders display negative behaviors resulting from the student's maladaptive beliefs concerning self and how she fits into her phenomenological world. Ongoing experiences of rejection or nonacceptance by others lead to feelings of emptiness, depression, and existential nonbeing. Behavioral responses result in a disruption of learning, inappropriate social interactions, or aggressiveness. This behavior not only impacts individuals but other students and teachers as well, further alienating the student from the love and acceptance she needs. This may result in the creation of labels such as "trouble maker" and a cycle that perpetuates the growing gap between the student and peers. Placed in a counseling environment that emphasizes unconditional positive regard and acceptance, the student's assumptions that she is unloved or uncared for are challenged. New awareness and acceptance are accompanied by a motivation for positive change.

Finally, accurate empathic understanding is the characteristic that a professional school counselor displays when accurately communicating the feelings and personal meaning that the student is phenomenologically experiencing. The result of these factors enables the student to increase self-awareness, congruence, and a more caring attitude toward self. Positive growth and greater freedom to become oneself is the outcome. Experiencing empathy in a counseling relationship not only facilitates students' acceptance of self, but can also enhance understanding of people different from themselves, thus decreasing tension and conflict in the school setting.

THE MOTIVATION FOR CHANGE

Change is inherent in individuals, yet positive and lasting change may be more difficult if there are barriers that the individual is unable to overcome without a supportive environment and a helping relationship. Rogers believed that a counseling relationship possessing appropriate attributes can facilitate renewed movement and growth. Each student possesses his or her own specific personal motivations for change. Being able to correctly identify the student's phenomenological motivation, genuinely engage the student in dialogue, accept the student's feelings and subjective reality unconditionally, and communicate accurate empathic understanding reinforces the initial motivation and provides an atmosphere necessary for further personal awareness and growth.

REAL SELF AND IDEAL SELF

Rogers (1959) believed that individuals are motivated to realize their innate possibilities, leading to the actualizing tendency, or self-actualization. An integral part of actualization is the process of differentiation, which generates a concept of the self (i.e., a symbolic representation of who one is) and an ideal self (i.e., a representation of who one wishes to be). If there is a large discrepancy between the real self and the ideal self, incongruency results and the student experiences anxiety. Individuals need warmth, support, and positive regard from others. When a student begins to experience positive regard independently of others, he or she develops a need for self-regard. In imagining the ideal self, conditions of worth are interpreted in relation to self-regard. Experiences are avoided or sought after based on their possible contributions to self-regard. Theoretically, a fully functioning individual has no need for conditions of worth or defenses. He or she is open to experiences, and there is congruency between the real self and the ideal self (Engler, 1984; Tomer & Eliason, 2003).

Students struggling with incongruency between the real self and the ideal self may hold distorted perceptions of their phenomenological self, their subjective reality, or who they think they "should" be. They may use defenses to protect themselves against experiences not fitting their conditions of worth. Defenses may also include selective perception, distortion of an experience, or denial. Person-centered counseling helps to lower these defenses and draw attention to the student's subjective reality. As the student gains self-awareness, distorted perceptions of self are reevaluated and goals related to the ideal self are reassessed. Eventually, the real self and the ideal self will benefit from a healthy subjective reality and move closer to congruency, lowering anxiety and raising the level of personal functioning (Tomer & Eliason, 2003).

THE CONTINUUM OF CHANGE

Movement and growth can be seen along a continuum identified by three characteristics: fixity, movement, and fluidity (see Table 38.1). The continuum of change begins with a fixed state resulting in distress, anxiety, and an inability to function at one's optimal level. The student experiences incongruity in his or her encounter of the world and his or her perception of self. Interpretations of events are viewed in a rigid manner and perceived as external facts. There is an unwillingness to communicate "self-to-self," resulting in conflict between the real self and the ideal self. Although there is significant distress, there is little desire for movement, and the individual is not aware of his or her personal issues; this results in alienation and withdrawal from others, particularly from relationships that are perceived as risky or dangerous (Rogers, 1961).

Indicators of movement along the continuum can be described as a process of becoming. Each new and individual experience has unique meaning as a result of the

TABLE 38.1

THE CONTINUUM OF CHANGE

Fixity	Movement	Fluidity
Experience of incongruity and distress	Becoming	Experience of congruence, peace, and self-actualization
Understanding experience in a rigid manner, perceived as external facts	Loosening of the cognitive maps established from past experience Meaning is modified with each new experience	Being; focusing on the present
Conflict between real self and ideal self Unwillingness to communicate self to the self, or gain personal awareness	Decrease in defensiveness Increased awareness of the previous inaccuracies of the real self and ideal self Openness to discovery and change	Reorganization of self-concept, with little discrepancy between the real self and the ideal self
Problems are unrecognizable and there is no desire for change	Recognition that problems exist, not entirely the result of external forces	Increased self-responsibility; lives with problems subjectively
Avoids close relationships that are perceived as being risky or dangerous	Increase in appropriate risk taking in interpersonal relationships An increased tolerance for personal vulnerability	Living openly with others; behaviors are in relationship to the immediate experience

loosening of cognitive maps established from past experiences. The student's responses are no longer dictated by distorted perceptions of events based on previous history. Current perceptions of reality are interpreted more accurately and based more fully in the present. Previous conceptions are modified with each new experience. Through the counseling relationship, personal defensiveness is decreased and an awareness of previous inaccuracies between the real self and ideal self is increased. This allows the student to open him- or herself to discovery and change and to focus in the present. Through the process of change, the student recognizes that issues negatively affecting optimal health do exist and are not entirely the result of external forces. With this awareness, the student discovers personal freedom and, in turn, a stronger sense of responsibility. Through the safety and modeling of the counseling relationship, the student develops a tolerance for personal vulnerability. This willingness to take personal risks is generalized to daily life experiences and interpersonal relationships outside of the counseling environment (Rogers, 1961).

The third characteristic on the continuum of change is fluidity. This is not a static stage but rather an ongoing process in which self-awareness, self-actualization, congruity, and a sense of peace continue to evolve. Fluidity is recognized by the experience of "being" and an ability to live more fully and genuinely in the present. Through the reorganization of self-concept, there is a narrowing discrepancy between the real and ideal self. The student addresses current issues and problems with flexibility and personal responsibility. Behaviors and interactions are based on immediate experiences and are appropriate to the social environment. Relationships are approached honestly, resulting in a more gratifying outcome (Rogers, 1961).

COUNSELING METHODS (TECHNIQUES)

Rogers was opposed to the general concept of techniques, feeling that they detracted from the genuiness of the counseling experience. However, there are basic methods of interactive communication, including active listening, reflection of thoughts and feelings, clarification, summarization, confrontation of contradictions, and open-ended statements that facilitate self-exploration. These basic methods have become an integral component of Rogers's person-centered theory (and many others) and are briefly described as follows (Thompson & Rudolph, 1992):

1. *Active listening*, or "being there," refers to the full attention of the counselor and the use of appropriate responses.
2. The counselor uses *reflection* to convey the essence of what the student has communicated so that he or she can see what has been expressed.
3. *Clarifying* is used by the counselor to focus on key underlying issues and to sort out confusing or conflicting feelings. It can also be used to make sure that the counselor is "on the right track." *Summarizing* points out themes for the student. The student can also summarize his or her own experience.
4. In order to *empathize*, the counselor must have an accurate understanding of the student's subjective world. It is the ability to grasp another's experience while maintaining one's separateness.
5. *Gentle confrontation* of the student's personal contradictions can be used to facilitate awareness.
6. *Open-ended statements* are used by the counselor to facilitate dialogue and thought. The student cannot respond to these with a simple yes or no answer. He or she must respond in more detail, or in a narrative style (Corey & Corey, 2002).

GROUP COUNSELING AND COLLABORATION CONTEXTS

Person-centered counseling is conducive to both group work with students and collaboration with other professionals. The counseling attributes are a good starting point for the establishment of group trust and cohesion. Rogers's methods (techniques), such as active listening, models appropriate group interaction and communication. Professional school counselors will also find using these attributes beneficial in any professional relationship or dialogue, including consultations and collaborations with parents, teachers, administrators, or individuals in the community (M. S. Corey & Corey, 2002).

MULTICULTURAL COUNSELING

Diversity in our schools and communities is now measured in broader terms than race and ethnicity (Paisley & McMahon, 2001). Socioeconomic status, disabilities, sexual orientation, and differences in lifestyle impact students' attitudes, values, and behavior. As schools become more culturally diverse, professional school counselors must attend to the unique needs of students, addressing both their personal characteristics as well as the context in which they live. Rogers has made considerable contributions to the field of multicultural counseling. His work has reached more than 30 countries and his writings have been translated into 12 languages. Rogers's approach has been used to develop mutual understanding and reduce tension among antagonistic groups (G. Corey, 2001).

One of the primary benefits of person-centered theory is increased self-awareness, which promotes students' ability to adapt to the multiple contexts in which they find themselves. Multidimensional factors influence students' self-views, which are sometimes congruent and sometimes incongruent. These influences include culture, family, media, peers, teachers, gangs, and others. In addition, it is important for the counselor to be aware of his or her own personal values and biases so that they do not interfere with the counseling relationship. There is a parallel between Rogers's attributes for positive counseling relationships and the basic components recommended for counseling culturally diverse students. Genuineness, acceptance, and empathy become the foundation for building any trusting therapeutic relationship (Sue & Sue, 1990). Constantine (2001) found a correlation between feelings of concern, warmth, empathy, and the counselor's ability to work effectively with culturally diverse students.

Though it may be difficult for professional school counselors to always communicate in such a direct way due to cultural differences, this limitation can be overcome through respect and sensitivity to the rich diversity that exists in our world. Some professional school counselors may also find it helpful to provide more structure to the counseling session than is usually needed in a person-centered framework. In addition, some cultures may view counseling, or asking for help, in a negative light. One way of reducing this stigma is to provide a supportive and open counseling environment. Both the professional school counselor and the student will grow from the cultural dialogue and counseling experience (G. Corey, 2001; Sue & Sue, 1990).

PERSON-CENTERED EXPRESSIVE ARTS THERAPY

Carl Rogers's daughter, Natalie Rogers, has continued to expand the scope of person-centered therapy with the integration of expressive arts. "Part of the psychotherapeutic process is to awaken the creative life-force energy. Thus, creativity and therapy overlap. . . . We express inner feelings by creating outer forms" (Rogers, 1993, pp. 1–2). Art, music, dance, and writing can each facilitate the healing process by providing an additional mode of personal expression, sharing, and personal awareness. The individual can also see tangible growth and progress as artistic expression changes throughout the counseling process. In schools, it may be difficult to incorporate a full range of expressive arts into counseling; however, we must endeavor to address the students' needs through a variety of methods. Students often respond positively to even basic means of creative expression, from drawing to the sharing of music.

CASE EXAMPLE

Jim was a junior high school student who presented for counseling resulting from anxiety, dropping grades, and feelings of depression. The professional school counselor, Ms. Gomez, provided a safe environment and used active listening skills. She listened closely to Jim's subjective reality and self-report. He described anxiety due to a perception that he was not living up to his parents' expectations. He experienced feelings verbalized as "letting them down," as well as loneliness and isolation from his peers.

The professional school counselor was empathic and accepted Jim with unconditional positive regard. Jim felt that this could be a trusting therapeutic relationship. Through the use of reflection, clarification, summarization, confrontation, and open-ended statements, Ms. Gomez was able to help Jim become aware of conflicting aspects about himself. By establishing a relationship based on Rogers's theory, the professional school counselor provided Jim with the conditions for movement toward growth and self-actualization.

Jim came from a family of doctors and grew up with the belief that he was obligated to follow the family path. During the counseling session, Jim came to discover that medical school was not his true interest or goal. Although he displayed a strong aptitude for science, his real interest was in environmental science and the politics involved in protecting the environment. He told the professional school counselor of his experiences of community service and volunteerism with a focus on ecology. He reflected a sense of belonging and worth. Within the successful counseling relationship, Jim became increasingly aware of the discrepancy between his real self and his ideal self. He became less influenced and motivated by external factors and focused more clearly on his personal experiences and needs. He was able to accept himself and his feelings and to reorganize his self-concept. He was also able to express his true feelings to his parents. This allowed him to follow his personal and educational goals, lowering his anxiety and depression. With increased self-awareness and feelings of congruence, Jim gained confidence in his decision-making ability, which facilitated movement, or "becoming."

SUMMARY/CONCLUSION

Rogers's counseling attributes and therapeutic methods are particularly applicable to the school setting. Person-centered theory offers professional school counselors a humanistic theory that incorporates basic helping skills that become the foundation for most counseling relationships. Facilitation of movement, self-awareness, and growth occur through a positive relationship between the professional school counselor and the student. Positive change is a result of congruence and self-actualization (Eliason et al., 2001; Rogers, 1951; 1969; Schmidt, 1999).

(Note: See the CD-ROM for a list of references.)

CHAPTER 39

SOLUTION-FOCUSED BRIEF COUNSELING: AN APPROACH FOR PROFESSIONAL SCHOOL COUNSELORS

John R. Charlesworth and C. Marie Jackson

Preview

Solution-focused brief counseling is presented as an efficient and effective model that professional school counselors can use to meet the needs of students in light of current school counseling program limitations. A general overview, the structure of the model, its basic steps, and techniques are presented.

In recent years, more and more emphasis has been placed on the professional school counselor's role in ensuring high student achievement (Hart & Jacobi, 1992; House & Hayes, 2002). This change of focus has reduced the amount of time counselors have available to provide traditional individual counseling services, although the need and demand for these services remains high. To continue meeting the individual counseling needs of students, professional school counselors have had to seek more efficient and effective counseling approaches. Solution-focused brief counseling (SFBC) is one approach that has shown great promise and that allows counselors to provide effective counseling to more students in less time.

SO WHAT IS SOLUTION-FOCUSED BRIEF COUNSELING?

SFBC is a counseling approach based on a newly evolving resource-oriented constructivist theory. It is an outgrowth of a wellness system to counseling rather than an approach based on mental health disorders or dysfunctional behaviors. This method builds upon existing "positives"—the strengths of the individual, the present resources, and the solutions already occurring for these individuals. It is solution focused rather than problem oriented and brief in terms of the number of sessions required, from the initial meetings to termination.

This counseling model has been deemed appropriate for schools for several reasons:

- SFBC is conceptually simple and easy to learn.
- It is perceived as more effective and more practical since the focus is on *what works* rather than *why* something is a problem.
- Its emphasis on strengths, successes, resources, and hope is an element useful for schools.
- The model spotlights small changes and reasonable coconstructed goals.

- SFBC encourages the acceptance and accommodation of diverse opinions and beliefs, which is appropriate for today's professional school counselors who operate in complex arenas with diverse student bodies.
- According to Murphy (1997), drawing upon past successes, existing positive attitudes, and effective working behaviors is more practical and less time-consuming than attempting to teach new behaviors. As such, Kahn (2000) believes solution-focused intervention is especially useful for the school counseling setting.
- A brief approach is crucial for the professional school counselor who has little time to give to individual counseling and must make a difference quickly out of necessity or refer a student to an outside resource who will have more time available for individual counseling.

DEVELOPMENT OF THE SFBC MODEL

The development of the SFBC model has been attributed to many counseling and psychology practitioners. Among them are Berg and Miller (1992), deShazer (1985), O'Hanlon and Weiner-Davis (1989), and Walter and Peller (1992). Applying the model in schools has been the subject of numerous writers in professional journals (see Bonnington, 1993; Bruce, 1995; Cook & Kaffenberger, 2003; Downing & Harrison, 1992; La Fountain, Garner, & Eliason, 1996; Littrell et al., 1992; Murphy, 1994). Books specifically written for the professional school counselor are also available. Murphy (1997) has written for middle and high school counselors, while Sklare (2005) has provided an easy and readable short text explaining a solution-focused approach for professional school counselors. He provided a step-by-step model based on the work of deShazer (1985).

According to Sklare (2005), it was deShazer who first developed the SFBC approach. Sklare pointed out that the SFBC model encompasses techniques learned in other counseling approaches, thereby making it easier to master than the more traditional approaches. Techniques used in SFBC that are common to many other counseling theories are listening, responding with empathy, asking open-ended questions, supporting, reinforcing, identifying goals, and applying scaling methods. These techniques are not new with SFBC. For example, scaling has been attributed to Wolpe and Lazarus (1966).

Professional school counselors have reported that, often, the counseling models learned in their university training programs require longer term counseling than is possible to provide in today's busy schools. Learning SFBC and using previously learned counseling skills makes the model more amenable for adoption by professional school counselors.

CENTRAL PHILOSOPHY AND BASIC ASSUMPTIONS

Understanding the basic rules and the assumptions on which SFBC is based is crucial for professional school counselors to "own the model" and accept it as clearly effective.

CENTRAL GUIDING PHILOSOPHY

As cited in Sklare (2005), deShazer and Berg and Miller proposed three basic SFBC rules as the central guiding philosophy for the model. These rules are

"If it ain't broke, don't fix it" (p. 9).

"Once you know what works, do more of it." (p. 9).

"If it doesn't work, don't do it again. Do something different" (p. 10).

ASSUMPTIONS

The number of assumptions purportedly underlying SFBC varies by author. Walter and Peller (1992) presented 12 assumptions of SFBC, and Murphy (1997) presented six assumptions. Sklare (2005) presented five assumptions, but added four guiding concepts. After reviewing all of the foregoing, the most obvious commonalties among them are as follows:

1. Counseling should focus on solutions rather than problems for beneficial change to occur.
2. An effective counseling strategy is to find and transform "exceptions" (i.e., those times when the problem is not present) into solutions.
3. Small changes lead to bigger changes.
4. Counselees have all the necessary resources to resolve concerns.
5. The counselor should focus on developing meaningful counselor–student coconstructed goals with emphasis upon what the counselee wants rather than on the counselor's ideas or opinions.

GUIDING CONCEPTS

Sklare's (2005) addition of guiding concepts is useful to the SFBC beginner; one might refer to them as rules for the professional school counselor to follow. The first one reminds the counselor to avoid exploration of the problem. A second reminder, to be efficient with interventions, suggests that the professional school counselor should accomplish as much as possible with the fewest number of interventions. Another concept is that insight does not provide solutions. Sklare reminded the counselor that it is more important to take action than to discuss how counselees became the way they are. The final guiding concept presented by Sklare is to focus on the present and the future. Having students think about what will be different in the future when the solutions are in place builds a belief that things will be better. Acknowledging the times in the present when solutions already exist increases the student's self-efficacy.

SFBC Is Working for Professional School Counselors

Professional school counselors are being trained in SFBC and responding to its use in training programs and in the schools quite favorably (Charlesworth & Jackson, 2002). Research supporting successful SFBC outcomes is increasing. Gingerich and Wabeke (2001) focused on the issue of the need for more empirical validation of solution-focused approaches while reporting empirical studies that lend support to its efficacy. Much of the school-based research was reported in anecdotal and case-study format and indicated successful outcomes. Gingerich and Wabeke listed a number of writers who have provided detailed discussions and case examples of the successful use of solution-focused models in schools. Two case studies in a public school setting were presented by Williams (2000). McKeel (1996) reported various research studies (see LaFountain, Garner, & Eliason, 1996; Littrell, Malia, & Vanderwood, 1995) as indicative of SFBC's effectiveness in schools.

An SFBC Counseling Model

There are several approaches to brief counseling found in the literature. These various models generally contain the same elements, although there may be slight differences in the terminology and sequencing of steps. The general organization of Sklare's (2005) approach has been selected to acquaint the reader with implementing SFBC.

Initiating the First Session

Since SFBC counselors assume that rapport with the student exists from the moment they meet, little time is spent attempting to develop it, unless it does not appear to be present. In those instances, additional time is spent developing rapport before proceeding.

Once good rapport has been established, counselors provide their students with an overview of how the sessions will proceed. Sklare (2005) included the following information:

- The student will be asked a lot of questions, some a little strange and others challenging.
- The counselor will be taking notes during the session.
- Near the end of the session, the counselor will move to another part of the room to write the student a message.
- The counselor will return and read the message to the student, then provide the student with a copy of the message while keeping one for the records.
- The counselor will ensure the student's understanding of the purpose of the message and its contents and provide the student an opportunity to ask questions and make comments.

Identifying Student Goals

One of the most significant predictors of success in any counseling approach, including SFBC, is the ability to help the student formulate clear goals. According to Sklare (2005), well-established goals add to the efficiency and effectiveness of SFBC. The goals established in this approach must, of necessity, be stated in small steps of obtainable, observable, measurable, behaviorally specific actions that the students are to "begin doing." Because of SFBC's focus on goals, when students present with problems, rather than pursuing the how and why of the problems, SFBC counselors help reframe the problems as goals.

The emphasis in SFBC is on helping students develop positive goals rather than negative "stop doing" goals. SFBC counselors initiate goal-oriented thinking by asking questions such as, "What is your goal in coming for counseling?" or "What would need to happen for you to consider your counseling sessions with me a success?" Questions such as these frequently lead to student goal statements that Sklare (2005) has classified as (a) positive, (b) negative, (c) harmful, or (d) "I don't know" goals.

Positive goals. These goals are stated as what the student wants to achieve in an observable, behaviorally specific, measurable, and attainable manner. When a student presents with a vague, general positive goal such as *I want to behave better in class,* the counselor must use appropriate questions to define the goal in more specific, concrete terms. Questions such as *What would you be doing that would indicate you are behaving better?* or *What would your teacher say you are doing when you are behaving better in class?* help produce concrete, explicit descriptions of what the student will be doing when making progress toward goals. The student will create clear images of the desired solutions. By continuing to emphasize what the student will be doing when he or she is moving toward goals, the counselor is implicitly suggesting to the student that success is possible. For additional detail for the goal picture, follow-up questions can be asked related to what the achieved goals will look like to the student or significant others.

Negative goals. Sklare (2005) defined negative goals as those stated as the absence of something. They typically refer to the student wanting self or others to stop doing something. Examples of these two types of negative goals are, *I want to stop making bad grades* and *I want my teacher to quit making me stay in during recess.* Such goals are very difficult to accomplish and, in most instances, are unattainable. To reframe negative goals into positive ones, the student must replace the "stop doing" behaviors (negative goals) with the presence of desired behaviors. Questions that assist students in reframing what they do not want into what they do want include, *If you stopped getting bad grades, what would you be doing?* and *What would you rather be doing instead of staying in at recess?* When the student has responded with a positive goal statement, professional school counselors will frequently need to use additional *What else would you be doing?* questions to elicit more specific details of the positive goal.

When a student presents with a negative goal that expresses the desire for others to change or stop doing something, the student is placing the responsibility for achieving the goal on someone other than him- or herself. Frequently the student is either requiring the other person to initiate change or expecting the counselor to "fix things." When presented with a negative (others) goal, such as the one previously stated (*I want my teacher to quit making me stay in during recess*), the professional school counselor must assist the student to reframe the goals into positive ones in which the student assumes responsibility for change. Questions that can help professional school counselors understand the student's motivation for wanting others to change include, *If they did change, what would that do for you?* and *How can I help you with this?* Such questions may lead a student, like the one with the negative goal, to respond that he would like to be able to go to recess to play with friends. With that as the student's positive goal, the professional school counselor could begin to obtain specific details of what the student would be doing to achieve that goal.

Harmful goals. Sometimes, students respond with harmful goal statements involving behavior that would be illegal, harmful, or not in their best interest. Such behaviors as becoming a prostitute, stealing, quitting school, taking, selling drugs, hurting others, damaging property and the like would not be supported by ethical professional school counselors. When helping students to modify destructive goals into productive positive goals, counselors need to uncover how these destructive goals are symptoms of students' unmet needs. Once the need is identified, professional school counselors help students establish healthy, attainable, positive goals to better meet their needs. As an example, if a student presents with a goal of *wanting to sell some drugs,* the professional school counselor could attempt to identify the student's unmet need by using a question such as, What will selling drugs do for you?" If the student responds with the explanation, "I want to get money so I can go to the prom," the counselor could then use this information to help the student identify more appropriate behaviors to attain the positive goal. When students present with impossible goals, such as wanting their separated parents to reunite, professional school counselors address these goals in a similar fashion as when working with negative goals.

"I don't know" goals. Quite frequently, students come to counseling not because they made the choice but because parents, administrators, teachers, or others have referred them. Sklare (2005) insisted that for change to occur, the student must be the customer. When the student is referred by another, the real customers are the ones who made the referral. Other-referred students are often difficult and resistant, acting as if they are merely visitors to the counselor's office. When these students are asked for their goal in coming to counseling, they commonly respond with the phrase, "I don't know." Other-referred students will typically identify the reason for their referral when the professional school counselor uses hypothetical "if" questions, such as "If you did know (or, *If you could guess*), why do you think you've been referred?" In some instances, obtaining from the student an underlying reason for being sent for counseling may require the use of repeated "if" questions. Using the "if" questions allows the student to "not know" and, in essence, to appear to guess the answer.

Some students have little, if any, motivation for counseling even when they have been able to identify why others have referred them for help. To convert such students from being reluctant to being more cooperative generally requires that the professional school counselor sell them on the benefits they will receive from counseling. For example, a student may have little motivation to get along better with a teacher, even though the consequence of undesirable behaviors is repeated stays in in-school suspension. A question to the student such as, *If we could help you get along better with your teacher so that you wouldn't have to spend so much time in in-school suspension, would that be something you would like to work on?* can be effective in increasing motivation for counseling. The success of this intervention depends upon the counselor's ability to recognize what students want and to help them to understand how counseling can help them get what they want.

Sklare (2005) described another approach for dealing with a reluctant student who believes the reason for being referred was due to an inaccurate assessment by the person making the referral. He identified this approach as the they're wrong, you're right technique. When a student strongly stresses that the referring person has made a mistake and that no problem for which the student needs help exists, the professional school counselor should respond, "So, you're convinced that you don't need help with getting along with your classmates. If we could find a way to prove that your teacher was wrong about you needing help in getting along with other children and that you were right about not having a problem all along, would that be something you would like to work on?" When a student indicates that he or she would like to correct the teacher's wrong impression, the professional school counselor can then help the student establish positive goals. By having the student elaborate on the question, *What would the teacher need to see you doing that would convince her that she was wrong and you were right?* positive goals are likely to evolve.

Even though the focus of the early phases of goal identification is to clearly outline measurable goals, it is not always accomplished at this phase. Other techniques such as the "miracle question" are used to build a picture of how the solution or solutions might look and thereby aid the development of concrete behavioral goals.

USING THE MIRACLE QUESTION

During the student goal identification process, the emphasis is on helping the student identify positive goals and the "doing" behaviors needed to accomplish the desired solutions. Frequently, hypothetical questions are needed to help students fully develop specific, observable, concrete behavioral goals and to gain a clear vision of what life will be like when they have attained these positive goals. According to Sklare (2005), because of its success, the miracle question, developed by deShazer, is one of the more frequently used hypothetical questions. Following is an example of a miracle question:

> Suppose you go to sleep tonight and while you are sleeping a miracle happens without you knowing about it. When you awaken the problem that brought you here has been solved. What's the first thing you would notice that would tell you the problem has been solved, what would be different?

Sklare (2005) suggested using an alternative hypothetical question with younger children who may not understand the concept of miracles. One example is as follows: *Suppose I had a magic wand and waved it over your head and your problem was solved; what would be different? What would you see yourself doing differently?* Another alternative hypothetical question is, *Imagine that it is 6 months from now and you have solved the problem that brought you for counseling. What would you notice that was different, and what would tell you that you no longer needed help with that problem?*

Whichever hypothetical question the professional school counselor uses, the student's responses need persistent clarification, using the student's own words or language to ultimately form detailed, specific, well-developed goals. Often students respond to one of the hypothetical miracle questions with a vague response, such as "I'd wake up and I'd be nicer to my brother." A question using the student's own words, such as "And when you are being nicer to your brother, what would you see yourself doing?" is likely to lead to a more specific goal. Further questioning about how others might react to these changes helps students to see how making little changes may produce favorable changes in others. For example, asking the question "If you started being nicer to your brother by helping him with his chores, how do you think he would respond?" might help the student to recognize the benefit of a simple change in his own behavior and also might help increase the student's motivation for change.

Sometimes students answer miracle-type questions by stating impossible goals, or goals that have little chance of being attained. They may want their parent's chronic illness to be cured, to have their lost pet returned, or to have a favorite relative move to their city. Frequently, students realize the professional school counselor cannot produce these results, but if a miracle could happen, that is what they would want. By responding to the student's impossible wishes with questions such as "How would things be different for you if your miracle happened?" professional school counselors can discover the student's real desires and help identify realistic goals.

IDENTIFYING INSTANCES AND EXCEPTIONS

After using the miracle question and constructing a clear vision of a successful resolution of a problem, the professional school counselor's next task is to help the student identify instances when he or she has been successful or partially successful at solving the problem. SFBC counselors believe that, regardless of the presenting problem, there are always times when the problem is either absent or less severe. These times are referred to as *exceptions*. Because students are often unaware of these occurrences, the professional school counselor must help them recall these exceptions and identify what they were doing that led to them.

Students' language often provides cues as to when these instances or exceptions have occurred. For example, when students use words or phrases such as *generally*, *sometimes*, *almost always*, and *most of the time*, it suggests there are times when the solution is already occurring to some degree. For example, if a student remarks that he almost always has trouble getting along with Mrs. Jones, it suggests that there are times when he does get along with her. The professional school counselor can help the student become more aware of these unrecognized successes through responses such as "Tell me about the times you were getting along better with Mrs. Jones" or by using questions that imply some degree of success.

MINDMAPPING

After professional school counselors have helped students to identify their unrecognized successes, the next step is to help students identify what they were doing that contributed to those successes. Students' responses to professional school counselors' questions about what they did to accomplish a goal provide the counselor with specific behaviors the student has used successfully. By continuing this process, professional school counselors help students develop mindmaps, which are like roadmaps, that guide students' approaches to solving their problems. Mindmapping is one of several techniques useful to the SFBC counselor.

CHEERLEADING

Another technique characteristic of SFBC is cheerleading as a way to acknowledge students' success and encourage more of it. Professional school counselors sincerely praise or cheerlead any success students demonstrate, no matter how small. The cheerleading helps educate students about what they did to make things better. It also provides encouragement and support for continued success, and increases a sense of personal control and self-esteem. Professional school counselors are cheerleading when they praise students, using genuine enthusiasm shown in their voice inflections, facial expressions, and bodily movements. For example, a student might report an instance in which she went to bed without her mother having to make her. The professional school counselor could cheerlead by responding with comments such as, "You mean you went to bed without your mother even having to tell you?" or "How did you manage to do that?"

SCALING

Professional school counselors use scaling questions with students for a number of reasons, including establishing a baseline to determine students' progress towards their goals. Students are asked to imagine or are shown a scale from zero (lowest) to 10 (highest) and asked to rate their perceived level of goal attainment at that time. Students generally provide a rating greater than zero, which indicates that things have been worse. Questioning the student about what they did to progress from zero to their current position helps students realize unrecognized personal resources and builds their confidence that they can make progress towards their goals.

Even when students report their current position on the scale as a zero or a 1, professional school counselors can provide complimentary feedback that highlights students' strengths and bolsters their hope. For example, if a student initially responds that his position on the scale is a zero, the professional school counselor could comment, "Considering what you have been facing, how have you managed to avoid being at a minus 10?" Such a response highlights the student's ability to cope with a difficult situation. For a student providing a low initial rating of 1 or 2, the professional school counselor might respond with "That's great! What did you do to move from a zero to a 2?"

Once an initial baseline is determined, professional school counselors can encourage a student's further progress by asking, "What would you need to do to move up one number?" Through follow-up questions, professional school counselors can help students clarify what behavior or behaviors are needed to make various degrees (i.e., 10%, or a 7 to an 8) of improvement toward their goals. The scale ratings also provide the student and counselor with feedback about progress and reinforce both the student and counselor for their continued efforts for improvement.

IDENTIFYING AND OVERCOMING OBSTACLES TO STUDENT SUCCESS

To prevent students from becoming discouraged as they pursue their goals, professional school counselors help them identify possible obstacles they might experience. Once obstacles are identified, possible courses of action to avoid or overcome them are explored. Questions such as, *What have you used successfully in the past to keep from getting off track?* are useful in initiating solution-focused discussions.

CONCLUDING THE INITIAL SESSION

The initial SFBC session is concluded by informing the student that the professional school counselor is going to move to another part of the room for a few minutes in order to reflect on and review the session notes before writing the student a brief message. The message is an extremely important step in SFBC, and is comprised of three parts: compliments, bridging statements, and task assignments.

Compliments. Effective messages include a minimum of three compliments that recognize and reinforce the student's strengths, resources, and accomplishments that were identified during the initial session. Using the student's own words that were used during the session makes the message powerful and meaningful. These compliments frequently address a student's desired behaviors, efforts, commitments, attitudes, thoughts, decisions, and attributes. The following is an example of the compliments part of a message: *Your decision to seek counseling demonstrates your maturity and genuine desire to learn how to express your anger in appropriate ways. I'm really impressed with your effort and ability to identify ways you have effectively expressed your anger appropriately in the past. Your insights, intelligence, and flexible thinking all reflect your desire and commitment for positive change.*

Bridging statements. The second part of the message is composed of bridging statements, which connect the compliments to the task part. Bridging statements provide students with a rationale for engaging in tasks that relate to the accomplishment of their goals. The following is a bridging statement that connects what the student wants (goals and solutions) to homework tasks: *Because of your strong desire to express your anger more appropriately, I would encourage you to engage in identified, assigned tasks.*

Tasks. The final part of the message contains task statements. Sklare (2005) recommended that the student's assigned homework tasks be intentionally vague, thereby, indicating confidence and trust in the student's ability to make responsible decisions about what tasks need to be completed to attain the goals. If concerns exist about a student's ability to benefit from vague tasks, the professional school counselor assigns tasks that make reference to the student's successful behaviors that were previously mentioned in the compliments portion of the message. Referring back to the compliments portion of the message written for the student with the anger management problem, the appropriate task portion of this message might include the following: *Because of your strong desire to express your anger more appropriately, I would encourage you to use more of the strategies that you identified that have worked for you in the past, and notice and continue to do what has been working for you.*

Before the initial SFBC session ends, the professional school counselor asks the student if there is any additional information he would like the counselor to know. Professional school counselors conclude the session by having the student assess the need for any additional sessions to accomplish the identified goals.

SUBSEQUENT SFBC SESSIONS

Sklare used EARS, an acronym for a sequence of steps attributed to Berg (as cited by Sklare, 2005), to guide the second and succeeding sessions: **E**licit, **A**mplify, **R**einforce, and **S**tart. Professional school counselors begin these sessions by *eliciting* or asking "What's better or different since the last session?" When students respond by identifying what is better, the professional school counselor *amplifies* these improvements by asking questions that help students recognize how changes in their behavior have favorably affected the behaviors of others. The letter *R* in EARS reminds the professional school counselor to *reinforce* or cheerlead the student for the changes in their behaviors that "made things better." The last step in the EARS sequence is *starting* over again by attempting to elicit, amplify, and reinforce additional student changes that have enabled the student to make progress toward their counseling goals.

Following the EARS sequence, *scaling* is once again used to assess progress toward a goal that was achieved since the last session. Students should not be reminded of their previous session scaling responses in order to obtain the most objective assessment of current position.

The additional session's assessment is once again used to determine the need for other meetings. The professional school counselor should begin to spread the sessions and plan for ending sessions completely. The message format continues to be the method for concluding sessions and, if follow-up sessions are necessary, the professional school counselor will continue to use the SFBC approach as outlined in this chapter. Figure 39.1 provides a helpful SFBC template that professional school counselors can use in sessions to keep the counseling process on track.

Summary/Conclusion

We have provided an overview of solution-focused brief counseling concepts for the professional school counselor. A quick look at the steps in SFBC has been presented to encourage professional school counselors to try this approach with students. It is efficient, effective, and versatile. According to Sklare (2005), SFBC acknowledges the power of focusing on the solution rather than the problem.

Additional Resources Related to Brief Counseling

Metcalf, L. (1995). *Counseling toward solutions: A practical solution-focused program for working with students, teachers, and parents.* West Nyack, NY: Center for Applied Research.

Presbury, J. H., Echterling, D. G., & McKee, J. E. (2002). *Ideas and tools for brief counseling.* Upper Saddle River, NJ: Prentice Hall.

Sklare, G. B. (2005). *Solution-focused brief counseling:Two actual interviews with a child* [Video recording]. Framingham, MA: Microtraining Associates.

(Note: See the CD-ROM for a list of references.)

Student's Initials _____   Age _____   Gender _____

Session # _____   Date of Session _____   Counselor _____

THE CENTRAL PHILOSOPHY OF THE SFBC APPROACH

1. If it's not broken, don't fix it.
2. If it works, do more of it.
3. If it doesn't work, stop doing it. Do something different.

First Session Format: Explain the process including use of questions, note taking, message, and provide student opportunity for asking questions.

I. **Obtain presenting goal(s):** (If more than one goal, have student identify the highest priority goal and mark it #1)

   a. "What is/are your goal(s) in coming here?"; "What's the reason you've come to see me?"

   b. *Validate* student's problem/goal and compliment them for wanting to make things better.

Restate Presenting Goal as a Positive Goal (if needed).

If Negative (Self): "What would you be doing instead," "if you weren't . . . then what would you . . .," "be doing differently," "in place of," "rather than," "start doing."

If Negative (Others): *Change to goals that give the student responsibility.* "If they did change, what would that do for you?" "How can I help you with this?" "How is this a problem for you?" "What difference does this make for you?" "What's the reason for that?"

If Harmful: *Determine student's reason for wanting harmful goal, reframe as identify healthy goals which meet their needs.* "What's the reason you don't want to . . .?" "What's the reason you want to . . . ?"

If Involuntary Student: *Help recognize what they will gain by changing.* "If you were to make this change, what effect would it have on you?" "Would it be in your best interest to want these changes?" "Is what they want for you something that you want as well—especially if it will help solve the problem of ...?"

Detail Goal Solution Steps/Cheerlead/Determine Others Responses

Use questions to help student describe detailed solutions for goals. "What would you be thinking/doing that show you were working toward or accomplishing . . . ?';" "First thing you would notice you were doing differently/that others would notice?" "If you did that/if that happened how do you think your teacher/etc. would respond to you?"

II. **Ask Solution Question:** "Suppose that during the night, while you were sleeping, *you* solved the problem. What is the first thing you would notice that was different once your awoke?" "What would you be doing differently?"

FIGURE 39.1. Solution-focused brief counseling template.

III. **Instances–Exceptions/How Brought About/Cheerlead:** (When are some of these things happening already or have happened even just a little bit then how brought about "How did you DO that?" followed by Cheerleading student's successes.

IV. **Student's Scaling:** (Identify student's current position on a 10-point scale: 0 = *problem worst*; 10 = *problem solved*). **Cheerlead behaviors that lead to current position.**

(*problem worst*) 0   1   2   3   4   5   6   7   8   9   10 (*problem solved*)

Student's ideas for improving one number on the 10-point scale (What are you going to DO to get from a ____ to a ____?)

Flagging the Minefield (Student's identification of and methods for overcoming obstacles to progress)

V. **Student's Questions About Session/Process, and Counselor's Responses**

VI. **Message:** (Compliments/Bridging Statement/Task) (Provide copy of actual message)

Risk Assessment:

Checked for ABUSE?   Yes/No   If signs or claims of ABUSE report IMMEDIATELY to appropriate authority.

Checked for suicidal/homicidal risk?   Yes/No   Depression Inventory Score _____

If risk, action taken: _____
_____

Additional Assessments:

Troubling Emotion: _____
_____

Behaviors: Needing to be Increased/Taught and/or Decreased: _____
_____
_____
_____

Faulty/Inaccurate or Flawed Cognitions: _____
_____
_____
_____

How would you rate the overall benefit of this counseling session for the student on a scale of 1 to 10? _____

Counselor Notes/Comments:_____
_____

FIGURE 39.1. *Continued.*

Using Family Systems Interventions
in Schools

Bradley T. Erford

Preview

In this chapter I describe family systems concepts and strategies that are useful to the professional school counselor. Strategies are illustrated by actual school cases. A 4-step initial family systems interview model is presented that is specifically designed to allow for an integrated use of strategies drawn from diverse family systems models.

When families come to me for help, I assume they have problems not because there is something inherently wrong with them but because they've gotten stuck—stuck with a structure whose time has passed and stuck with a story that doesn't work. To discover what's bogging them down, I look for patterns that connect. (Minuchin & Nichols, 1998, p. 43)

Professional school counselors understand that students bring the problems of life outside the school into the school, where problems can negatively influence the educational process (Keys, Bemak & Lockhart, 1998; Lockhart & Keys, 1998). Professional school counselors can employ brief family interventions with students and their families to address educational issues that are linked to the home (Hinkle, 1992; Kraus, 1998). Conceptualizing a school problem by its connections to the family system and using family systems techniques to address the problem offers a practical set of strategies for helping students.

Four Categories of Family Adjustment

Family systems interventions are helpful when the student's behavior is a response to stresses and changes with which the family is attempting to cope. When this is the case, it does not necessarily mean there is anything wrong with the family. Rather, it means that the family finds itself in a tough patch on its journey through life. Pittman (1987), in a book on treating families in crisis and transition, described four categories for thinking about the ways families get stuck in tough patches.

First, a family can get stuck trying to cope with a normal task of family development. For example, maybe the family was doing well before the first child had to go to school, but the transition to school for the child is proving a difficult challenge for the family.

The first edition version of this chapter was written by Dr. Estes J. Lockhart. May he rest in peace.

Second, a family can become stuck trying to use a structure with rules that are outdated for the challenges they face. For example, when children enter adolescence, the family faces the task of having to reorganize their rules.

Third, a family may be hit with one or more "bolts from the blue"—unexpected stresses, traumas, or discontinuities. For example, a family member may be lost through death, divorce may occur, or the family may be overwhelmed through job loss or illness, causing the family to have trouble coping. A family may find itself in trouble through the stress of having to be a caretaker for another family member with a disability or illness.

Whenever stress affects a family system and requires a change to the system's usual repertoire, a crisis can result. Such a crisis can cause nonspecific changes in the family, such as the loosening of boundaries, changing of rules, relaxation of expectations and prohibitions, loss of goals and values, revival of unresolved conflicts, and heightened tension between family members (Pittman, 1987). A student may carry the stress and tension from any of these nonspecific changes resulting from a family crisis into the classroom, where a crisis for the student may result.

Example 1: An Eating Disorder and Decreased Academic Performance

A young girl in elementary school began exhibiting eating problems and decreased academic performance. Her classroom problem was directly related to living alternating weeks in the homes of the two blended families of her divorced, and subsequently remarried, biological parents. The systems intervention was to bring in both biological parents with their new mates, who were now step-parents for the girl, and help the two sets of parents to align their discipline systems. The student was experiencing high anxiety by switching each week from a set of very loose family rules to a set of very rigid family rules. Also, the student was attempting to relate to new step-parents and new step-siblings. To intervene, the student was informed of the new procedures by both sets of parents in front of the professional school counselor. The professional school counselor then followed up with the girl and checked in by telephone with the two families.

Example 2: A Divorce and Anticipation of Decreased School Performance

The family may inform the professional school counselor of a crisis that is either anticipated or ongoing in the home, and the counselor can then work proactively and collaboratively with the family to prevent the crisis from seriously affecting the student at school. For example, consider a case in which a parent contacted the school counselor seeking help and worried that her child in middle school might be experiencing academic or social problems at school because the student's mother had divorced the student's father. The professional school counselor met with the student using a family systems perspective to address the issue. Together, the father and mother assured the student that he didn't cause the problem and couldn't cure the problem, but he could cope with it. Coping is a standard message that is helpful for students to hear from divorcing parents. Both the father and mother reassured their son they would be there to support him. The professional school counselor also obtained agreement from both parents that they would not use the student in any way as a pawn, message carrier, or person upon whom to vent on issues related to the failed marriage and divorce. The father arranged his schedule to meet regularly with the son. The purpose of this intervention was to make the changing complexity of the family crisis into a more specific, manageable reality, thus allowing the student to focus on schoolwork.

Example 3: Loss of a Father Through the Catastrophic Illness of AIDS

Sometimes the professional school counselor can help the student by simply conceptualizing that a student's dysfunction at school does not reside solely with the student and by providing resources, including referral information, to the family. For example, consider the case of a bright, very talented student who began to shut down and even become verbally aggressive when given negative feedback in school. The student had lost his father first to marital separation and then to death from AIDS. Prior to the parents' separation, the student felt they blamed him for much of their anger. During the final days of helping his mother take care of his father, the student experienced renewed fights between the three of them, along with negative interactions with his dying, bedridden father (e.g., statements of his failure as a son). The student viewed his situation as one in which he was constantly on edge, feeling rejected by a parent whom he mourned and also felt he had failed at the worst possible moment. The student was helped by having his mother seek his assistance in the grieving process and by her helping him to see that much of the rejection and failure he felt resulted from the failed marriage and his father's depression and pain as he approached death. Feeling blame in the home led to the student acting out at school. There was caretaker stress, bolt-from-the-blue stress, and the structural stress of a family that produced conflict by *triangulation*—in this case, forming an *alliance* between two members to blame a third. It was helpful to have the mother clarify that the son did not cause the divorce. Further, it was helpful for mother and son to understand that classic psychiatric syndromes such as dementia, anxiety, and depressive and psychotic disorders are commonly associated with HIV-related disorders (Kaplan & Sadock, 1998). This made some of the father's behaviors understandable and helped explain the mother and son's stressful relationships with him near the end of his life. In this complex case, it was important for the counselor to refer the mother to a family therapist in the community. The professional school counselor then became a case manager, serving as a liaison between school staff, mental health counselor, student, and family. It is important to note that the professional school counselor's initial family session led to the referral to an outside counselor. At home, in therapy, and at school the same message was reinforced: "Don't play the blame game with self or others."

Example 4: The Power of Context in Racial Victimization at School

The unique *context* in connection with *family beliefs*, in this case forces operating within the school, can lead to problems in school. For example, consider the case of a young African American male high school student who was being racially victimized by a group of White students in a school that had only a few minority students. The African American student refused to report verbal assaults against him by the White students and instead let verbal insults continue until they reached the level of physical confrontation. When the student's family was contacted, it was learned that the parents had told the son that racial victimization was simply a fact of life in the United States. They instructed him that in their family the way to handle racial victimization is to pay no attention to it and walk away. The student had been trying to follow his family beliefs. Unfortunately, the White students continued to name-call. The African American student, unable to take it any longer, stood his ground and prepared to fight. Luckily, the principal intervened.

A single-session intervention with the African American student's family helped them to see that their response of putting up with racial victimization would not work in the context of their son's school. Unlike the context in their youth, their son had little to no support from peers and was assaulted by students who did not respect the boundaries of others. The intervention was to *challenge family assumptions* in an appropriate and respectful way. The family changed their belief. The son was encouraged to contact administrators and professional school counselors, who then intervened.

THE FAMILY SYSTEMS PROCESS

The family system is a *self-organizing system,* which adapts to the stresses the family faces by sometimes having to reorganize its rules significantly. An example would be the death of a grandmother who had parented the kids while both parents worked long hours. It is a system in which various members are connected more or less closely in *subgroups,* for example the parental subgroup or the sibling subgroup. It is a system that draws *boundaries* to control the degree to which those outside any subgroup will communicate or interact with those inside the subgroup. For example, parents might tell their children not to go to a certain place or not to talk with certain people. It is a system in which family members set emotional boundaries to protect individual autonomy, which if too open or too closed, can lead to problems. Where boundaries are too open or loose, relationships can be dysfunctionally cohesive (*enmeshed*). For example, parents of a child with a serious mental health disorder or disability, in an effort to protect the child, may become enmeshed, fearing to set more open boundaries that allow for the child to be independent. The family is a system in which the leadership *hierarchy,* whether weak or strong, rigid or flexible, structured or chaotic, affects all members. Since *family rules* are not always explicit and may be very complex, professional school counselors can not assume anything about the family.

Also, the family is a system that the student cannot ever really leave completely in the sense that we can leave a job. We may attempt to disengage, separate or *cut off* from the family in some way, but we will never completely escape all of its influences. In fact one of the major challenges that adolescent students in America face is learning how to begin to leave the family appropriately. The families of adolescents may have difficulty helping their children to leave, and this can lead to struggles for power, with ramifications in the schoolhouse. Also, *cultural issues* must be taken into account. For example, a family from South America or Turkey may be sad that their child would even want to think about leaving the family prior to marriage.

The family organizes itself to adapt to environmental challenges and, subsequently, transcends the separate characteristics of individual family members. In one family this might mean individuals would engage in *complementary relationships*, strengthening each other and the family as a whole by providing that which each of the individual members attempting to adjust alone would have trouble providing for themselves. In another family, the attempt to adapt might lead to them getting stuck in a power struggle or some other dilemma.

Example 5: Preparing to Leave Home Influencing Student Achievement

Consider the case of a student whose family complained that their daughter wanted to be on her own and was no longer committed to the educational goals she once shared with her family, nor did she want to follow family rules. In this case, there was another issue combined with the normal developmental task of preparing to leave home. The girl served as a *parental child*, spending much time after school taking care of her younger siblings. This girl felt undervalued by her parents because she felt they continued to treat her as a child, making rules for her as though she was just another one of their children when she was on the verge of adulthood and parenting the other children. She wanted the freedom of an adult both at home and at school since she took on a parental role at home. Not getting what she expected led to a loss of commitment to the expectations of her parents and a desire to find a way out of the home so that she could be her own person. The student showed lack of motivation in school and began having conflicts with authority figures. The family reorganized positively in several ways. The family changed communication styles with the girl to more resemble those with their adult friends. The family *renegotiated family rules*. The parents remained in charge of the family *hierarchy*, leadership and decision making but adjusted the rules to recognize their daughter's developmental needs. They also took her out of the role of a parental child so that she was able to enjoy a normal life as an adolescent without the stress of intense parenting responsibilities.

Example 6: Student Violence Ignited by an Extended Family Member

Increasingly, those who take the family systems view address other contexts in the student's life besides the nuclear family. These may include, but are not limited to, in-laws; peer networks; and welfare, health, cultural, racial, ethnic, political, social, legal, sports, and school systems. Consider the following rare and unusual example of the power of an in-law to affect the student's behavior at school. The student would violently attack other students at the drop of a hat. The student had been referred to the county neurological clinic where the examining physician determined that he appeared to have a seizure disorder that would need to be evaluated in a residential center. While waiting for a bed in the residential program, the student was enrolled in an alternative school for troubled youth for part of the day and his regular school part of the day. The widowed mother of the student, who allowed an uncle to live with them, was never able to attend meetings at the school. One day, a social worker at the school dropped by the mother's home, explaining that she just happened to be in the neighborhood. During the visit, she learned that the uncle was a psychopath whom the mother had taken in as a deathbed request from her husband. This student went to school everyday wondering if his mother would be alive when he returned home and wondering what stress the evening would hold for both of them. Once the mother was helped to report the psychopathic uncle's behavior to the police, he was removed from the home, and the student ceased the violent attacks on other students. The student returned to his regular school full time, without ever needing to attend a residential program. While this example is a rare case, it is not rare for the professional school counselor to intervene with students who act out who live in stressful homes where alcohol, substance abuse, physical abuse, and severe mental health issues of family members produce high anxiety and affect student school performance.

Example 7: Parental Substance Abuse Affecting School Performance

An elementary student was refusing to do classwork and reacting in a hostile way when anyone attempted to make him work. This young elementary student lived with his mother and father in public housing where the parents were doing illegal hard drugs and the young boy was being intimidated daily. He was not able to do well at school because he sat wondering if he would return home to find his parents arrested and removed from the home and his favorite possessions removed from the house. Poverty and illegal drug activity are but two powerful influences in *the larger system*—outside home and school—that the school counselor had to deal with in order to help the student address educational issues. In this case, the counselor first *joined* with the family so that the family respected the professional school counselor as a trusted family member. Joining was a major family systems intervention in that it represented the first time this family, in serious violation of the law, had trusted anyone in the school system. Communication with the family and the school administration had resulted in angry conflicts. The professional school counselor helped the family to agree to *shelve their issues* temporarily with the school administration in order to do what was needed for their child. Next the professional school counselor suggested local resources the family could trust in helping them address their substance abuse issues, realizing that any progress in this area would likely take much time. Collaboration between family and counselor led to the student moving in with a nearby relative for a short time.

Example 8: Student Refusal to Attend School

There can be many possible forces driving a student's dysfunctional behavior. For example, a student may be refusing to attend school because he wants to avoid the stress of work. On the other hand, the student might be experiencing anxiety about separation from a major attachment figure, or worrying about harm befalling a major attachment figure while the student is at school. The student might even fear attack from a gang, or simply find the long day or interactions with classmates produce anxiety. There are many and varied reasons that might influence a student's refusal to attend school, and they might work in combination. The father of the student may have recently been diagnosed with cancer or there may be an impending parental divorce or loss of income. Any of these family systems dynamics might cause a reorganization of the family that results in anxiety for the student and can be inseparable from other forces working against the student attending school.

For example, consider a case in which a high school student's deceased grandfather had lived in the student's home. The student's father had a heart attack a few months prior to the student complaining of intense fear upon trying to enter the high school. This was a student who wanted to be in school. He was a high school senior with a high grade point average, a girlfriend at school, and a position on the varsity basketball team. He complained of desperately wanting to be at school, but being terrified by a feeling that all the energy in his body was leaving him as he tried to walk from his car into the school. He said that this had been coming on slowly in other settings like restaurants, and he had been coping by ceasing to visit settings that made him anxious. Now the problem had generalized to his school. The professional school counselor carried out individual desensitization and relaxation training with the student, combined with strengthening the family hierarchy and setting boundaries with his mother, who was enmeshed emotionally with the student. In this case school refusal was driven by separation anxiety. The student feared that if he left home and became locked into a full day of school, something might happen to someone he loved away from school that would be catastrophic (i.e., his father might suffer another heart attack or his mother with whom he was enmeshed might become ill). He could say that he knew these were irrational fears, but that didn't stop him from having them. His fears led to panic, resulting in a catastrophic feeling of a loss of all the energy in his body. It was important that he be given permission to leave class at any time and check in with parents and that he be allowed to go to the counselor's office as needed to listen to a relaxation tape.

FAMILY MEMBERS IN ATTENDANCE DURING A FAMILY SYSTEMS INTERVENTION

Although it is often helpful to bring in other family members when carrying out a family systems intervention, it is not always necessary. One reason that it can be helpful to bring in other family members is that people have difficulty reporting accurately on their own social situations (Haley, 1976). Another reason is to engage significant others directly in the support of the student. However, family systems interventions do not require the attendance of a family member. Also, taking a family systems perspective does not mean that the professional school counselor stops thinking about the individual student as an individual, with an individual's own heart, mind, temperament, will, and dreams. One can work individually while using a systems perspective.

For example, if the professional counselor wishes to encourage the student to respond more appropriately in an individual session, the counselor may use the family system intervention of asking the student how his deceased grandmother would advise the student if she were here. In this family systems intervention without any family members present, the influence of a deceased family member can hold great power. This type of family intervention could be referred to as an *invocation of significant others*, and is powerful with students who might otherwise resist or detour challenging issues. Obviously, the counselor could ask, "If your mother and father or sister or brother were here, would they agree with you?" These are the kinds of questions that allow for the family systems perspective to influence the intervention without any family member present.

Three Models of Family Systems Interventions

There are a wide variety of family systems intervention models. However, today there are few purists, meaning those who rigidly stick to one family system model (Nichols & Schwartz, 2001). The following three models can be useful for the professional school counselor. However, the brief descriptions that follow give only a general sense of each model. The reference section on the CD-ROM for this chapter includes works that treat the models in more depth.

STRATEGIC FAMILY SYSTEM INTERVENTIONS

Strategic family therapy describes family problems as being maintained by some combination of unsuccessful problem solving, weak leadership or hierarchy, inability to adjust to transitions in the family life cycle, interactive communication patterns that support dysfunctional interactions, or triangular relationships that result in coalitions of family members against each other. Problems are resolved by altering the above factors through techniques strategically applied, which often takes the form of a directive to be practiced outside of the counseling session. For example, the father and mother might be advised when feeling stress while parenting to avoid any anger at the moment. Instead, the two could meet for 14 minutes in the evening away from the child and each spend 7 minutes explaining his or her thoughts and feelings to the other while the other writes them down and gives no nonverbal or verbal responses. When someone is writing down what is said, it lends support to the feeling of being heard.

When developing strategic family systems, Haley was heavily influenced by a medical doctor and brilliantly creative psychotherapist named Milton Erickson with whom Haley collaborated and about whom Haley wrote (Haley, 1973). Milton Erickson, a hypnotherapist, had an uncanny ability to use language creatively to enlist a client's support in the process of change. One of Erickson's most powerful skills was to use metaphors and stories to engage the client and make indirect suggestions, often below the level of consciousness during an intervention. Haley suggested becoming a "metaphor enthusiast." Using metaphors, or recalling an interesting story analogous to the student's own situation, encourages increased engagement of the student in the intervention. The following application of the strategic model demonstrates the application of major strategic techniques in a school setting, including the use of therapeutic metaphor.

Example 9: Adolescent Who Fights With Peers

This case involves the family of an adolescent son who had begun to engage in serious fights with peers. A conversation with the family led to the conclusion that since the student had not had this anger problem prior to adolescence, it was possible that something could be happening with the family's adaptation to adolescence. This helped to *normalize* the situation by helping the family move from thinking of the adolescent as being abnormal and their family as dysfunctional to thinking of the family as needing to make a perfectly normal adjustment to a common life-cycle event, adolescence. The family set more appropriate limits and response costs and the parents were encouraged to continue to reach out to the son by telling him they were there to help him. The family needed to learn how to avoid getting into *triangular relationships* in which one parent would side with the son against the other when discipline issues at school were reported to the family. They needed support to believe that they still had influence on this young man.

Example 10: Strategic Use of Metaphor to Support Parents

The parents in the above example stated that they were worried about making decisions for their son. They said he was always accusing them of disrespecting him by setting all the rules rather than letting him take care of himself. But they said they felt caught in a bind because while they wanted to give him more freedom, they feared the outcome if they did, and they lost power through inaction. The metaphor of a ship at sea in a threatening storm was used to drive home the importance of the parents taking charge in the family. They were told to imagine they were out at sea on an ocean liner and a big storm threatens. They were asked which of the following statements from the captain would make them feel more secure: "Relax, stay inside. We have been through many of these storms before, and we know what to do," or "Look, I'd like to get your opinion on what would be the best course of action." And just imagine one's anxiety if the captain actually offered one control of the ship in such a situation (Lockhart, 1990). The family said they came back to this metaphor over and over again when feeling under duress from their son.

Also, this family had a *repetitive sequence of behavior* which they continued to try even though it failed them. The mother and father, unable to decide what to do about the son's anger at home and school, would sometimes begin to argue with each other over how to respond to their son's behavior. The mother would call for the father's help in disciplining the son. As the father, a rather quiet and analytical man, attempted to reason with his son, the mother would tell the father that he was not being tough enough in supporting her. Soon the parents would be fighting with each other as the son with the anger problem looked on and criticized them. The parents were challenged to communicate in a way that would break this repetitive cycle and be a better model for their son. A metaphor of a real experiment was used in which two rats in a cage receiving electric shock first tried to avoid the shocks by running around, and then, when the shocks continued, turned on each other. The parents said that was exactly how they felt. It was suggested that, when feeling at their wit's end, unlike the rats they could take a break and, when feeling a bit less stressed, return to problem-solving in a better state of mind.

STRUCTURAL FAMILY SYSTEMS INTERVENTION

The professional school counselor using structural family systems interventions looks for maladaptive boundaries, maladaptive hierarchy, or maladaptive reactions to changing developmental or social conditions as factors that can maintain problems. Problems are resolved by creating clear, flexible boundaries and more adaptive and flexible hierarchy responses to changing developmental or social conditions. The sequence of change in the structural model is to (a) join and accommodate to the family and (b) help the family change its structure.

Example 11: A Gender Issue in a Step-Family and at School

A young man from a blended family was disrespectful to female classmates. The professional school counselor helped the family to focus on the need for the student to learn more appropriate *boundaries*. For example, boundaries between the mother and student were nonexistent, leaving them emotionally fused or *enmeshed*.

The student and mother would talk to each other as friends or equals, and the student would speak to her not as a respected woman, but as a buddy. This made it difficult for the mother to separate herself as the parent. Meanwhile, the boundaries between student and step-father were closed, resulting in disengagement with little communication. In this situation, the professional school counselor invited the parents in and set an initial goal of *joining* with them. Once joined with the family, the professional school counselor was able to *reframe* the mother's enmeshment in a positive light. This parent behavior of being overly protective of her child, was reframed as, *You just seem to love your child too much*. The mother accepted this.

The professional school counselor *highlighted strengths and weaknesses*, such as the need for a discussion and reinforcement of appropriate boundaries for their son with regard to interactions with females. After joining sufficiently to be able to give negative feedback without loss of family respect, the counselor suggested that the step-father and son spend more time together having fun and discussing, among other things, how to act appropriately with females. This helped by *shifting the family members' relative positions* to interrupt the pattern in which the step-father and son interacted only for discipline reasons.

CONSTRUCTIVIST FAMILY SYSTEMS INTERVENTIONS

In a constructivist approach, the intervention is conceived as a collaboration in which the professional school counselor and student together construct a more desirable reality. Two examples of constructivist theory are solution-focused interventions and narrative-focused interventions (Hoyt, 1996). The professional school counselor's role in the constructivist approach is to acknowledge, praise and in other ways highlight and punctuate strengths of the family and collaborate with the family to arrive at resources and solutions for facing the family's challenging situation. The constructivist tends to ask questions more about what has gone right rather than what has gone wrong. They tend to collaborate rather than direct or coach. Virginia Satir anticipated the constructivist way of viewing the problem when she would refer to a problem as an accident in the interest of the self (Hoffman, 2002). The attempt by Satir was to normalize a situation by making it an accident that happened for the best of reasons, the needs of the self.

Constructivist interventions make much use of *looking for exceptions*, in which the student and/or family acts competently. The family is then encouraged to do more of their competent-type behavior. Both solution-focused and narrative-focused constructivist approaches make use of the *miracle question* in which the family imagines awaking one morning and finding everything is as it should be. This allows the family to begin building a vision more consistent with their ideal of how they would like to live. Solution-focused interventions are one the most popular of our day because they are cognitive in emphasis, easy to teach, and promise quick solutions (Nichols & Schwartz, 2001). DeShazer has stated that the basic rules of solution-focused interventions are (a) *If it ain't broke, don't fix it;* (b) *Once you know what works, do more of it;* and (c) *If it doesn't work, don't do it again, do something different* (Hoyt, 1996).

In constructivist approaches, the attempt is to help the family construct a sense of hope for the future out of the current situation based on successes in other situations. Both solution-focused and narrative-focused interventions give much attention to the language used to communicate about the situation that is presented. This involves the way in which a family conceives their situation and the language they use will either empower them to find the resources they need to succeed or disempower them. Haley anticipated this concern of the constructivists when he said, "The way one labels a human dilemma can crystallize a problem and make it chronic" (Haley, 1976, p. 3).

Example 12: A Middle School Student With ADHD

A middle school student was not staying on task in class. The family said that the main problem was ADHD. The student indicated in the session that either she was being unfairly picked on by the teacher or the work was boring and she got fidgety. The parents said that she had told them the main problems were the teacher doesn't like the student, the student can't get any help from the teacher, and the work is either too easy or too difficult. The professional school counselor, using a narrative intervention, asked the whole family for a meeting to discuss the way they would like to see their story proceed. In the narrative approach, the counselor *stayed one down,* on an equal footing or below the power level of the family. The counselor's goal was simply to carry on a conversation to help the family determine how they would like to rewrite their family story so that it fit with their view of how they would like to be a family.

The family preferred a story in which the student would heroically begin to complete homework, stay on task in school doing what she was directed to do, and actively seek help from the teacher when needed. The professional school counselor, using the narrative approach, helped the family to *externalize* the off-task behavior as a monster that would require the family working together to defeat. This *externalization of the problem* is a powerful technique for placing the problem outside the family and removing debilitating blame.

The professional school counselor used *language that suggested a successful ending* by saying to the student and family, "Well, when you are no longer having conflicts with the teacher and you are performing regularly, what kinds of relationships will you then have with your family or teacher?" The parents were also asked how they would feel when all of them had succeeded in defeating the monster. They talked of happiness, relief, joy, and a desire to do more interesting and fun things together. The professional school counselor *celebrated small changes* and approximations toward the desired behavior so that successes could begin to be experienced by the student and family. The counselor also worked with the psychiatrist to give feedback on the effects of the medication.

To clarify differing opinions, family members used a scaling intervention. Scaling is a technique regularly used in solution-focused interventions to encourage clearer more concrete understandings of how each situation is viewed by family members. Scaling can also be used as a baseline against which to measure change as student, teacher, and family report improvement or lack of progress. The student was also helped to *deconstruct a myth* the student had been using to cope with feelings of incompetence. The myth was that it is better to act out than to fail, look foolish, and take another blow to her self-esteem. This myth made its appearance in statements by the student, such as "What's the use anyway?" The teacher also indicated the student's lack of self-esteem by saying, "When she gets a little help at the start of a new lesson, she does well, but when she doesn't, she will just give up after hardly trying." The professional school counselor suggested that learning patience and delaying gratification is a sign of increasing maturity. The parents agreed. The goal of the constructivist approach is that the family will have renewed hope.

Initial Family Systems Interview for Professional School Counselors

The *initial family interview* is important because it is the first point of meeting the family and attempting to intervene. Following is a four-step initial interview model for professional school counselors using strategic, structural, and constructivist techniques and interventions.

FOUR-STEP INITIAL FAMILY INTERVENTION MODEL

- *Step one: Welcoming, joining, and reassuring.* Begin the interview by making sure everyone feels as comfortable as possible, connect with all individuals in a way that helps to establish rapport, and communicate reassurance that the professional school counselor cares about the pain in the family and is here to help all of them. A good reassuring statement to the family by the counselor is, "I am sorry this is happening to you, and I am going to work hard to help you." *Stay one down* and *listen empathetically.*
- *Step two: Interacting, normalizing, and collaborating.* Encourage family interaction and discussion around what has been attempted in the family effort to get unstuck and how the family is succeeding in difficult situations. Often it can help to view the situation as a normal part of the family life cycle or individual development or a bolt from the blue no one could predict which precipitated a crisis. *Highlight family strengths and encourage more of what works.* Discourage continuing what has failed. Treat the family with respect and parents as experts on their child.
- *Step three: Searching for patterns that connect and planning a new vision.* Listen to the family story of their situation. Whether through directives, coaching, or col-

laboration, help them to *frame, reframe, dream* or in some way *construct a more useful family story* along with concrete goals to make their vision a reality. Metaphors can help make a vision clear. For example, where blame has been a problem, the metaphor "Sounds like you are hoping future sights along the way won't be colored by earlier accidents" could be used. Or one might say, "It is hard to drive a car forward when looking through the rearview mirror."

- *Step four: Agreeing on a plan of positive action.* This step involves the family planning the necessary action for getting back on the road to a hopeful future. It can be helpful to provide a way to monitor the intervention, perhaps through brief phone calls.

SUMMARY/CONCLUSION

"Families don't walk in and hand you the underlying structural patterns that are keeping them stuck. What they bring is the noise—their own confusion and pain" (Minuchin & Nichols, 1998, p. 46). The task of the professional school counselor is to join with the family and look for the patterns that connect. Family members often reveal these patterns in stories that are memories connected to the situation at hand. These stories provide a map of the implicit rules of the family as they attempt to cope with their child's difficulties at school. Many times, the family presents the story of their child's school problem as a crisis in their family. Often this crisis of the family involves worrying how to respond to a current demand for changes to their rules and roles. In responding to the family crisis, the professional school counselor must integrate family systems techniques and interventions wisely in a way that empowers the family to help the student cope in school. This is a difficult task. It requires an appreciation of the complexity of family systems. It requires skill to encourage families to alter repetitive patterns of interaction that keep them stuck. Helping families requires the professional school counselor to respect the family's dreams and beliefs while helping them access their own resources to achieve positive change.

(Note: See the CD-ROM for a list of references.)

CHAPTER 41

Integrating Knowledge of Learning Styles and Multiple Intelligences in Counseling Diverse Students

Bradley T. Erford

Preview

Implementing the concepts of learning styles and multiple intelligences theory into counseling practice provides professional school counselors with additional tools for working with diverse students by encouraging students to view themselves broadly and develop their abilities in wide-ranging areas. Resultant techniques can provide a practical means to enrich the counseling process and empower individual students by approaching them in readily understandable ways as well as encourage less competitive, more productive, team-oriented approaches to life and work.

USING MULTIPLE INTELLIGENCES PERSPECTIVES IN COUNSELING DIVERSE YOUTH

Much of the effectiveness in counseling and teaching comes from the ability to see human beings from different perspectives and to interact in ways that are appropriate to each person's individuality. Much of the harm that results from stereotyping and prejudice springs from viewing people from narrow perspectives and losing sight of that individuality. Theories of multiple intelligences have become more widely used in educational classrooms and offer school personnel important considerations for effective practice. The central theme of these theories is that intelligence is more than a single, unitary factor, such as the intelligence quotient (IQ). Several researchers (Cattell, 1987; Guilford, 1982; Thurstone, 1938) have attempted to identify different kinds of intelligences. However, the most specific theoretical frameworks have come from the work of Howard Gardner and Robert Sternberg.

GARDNER'S DEVELOPMENTAL FRAMEWORK

Gardner (1993) suggested that the definition of intelligence using traditional quantitative measures, such as the IQ test, was far too narrow in scope. Gardner defined intelligence as "the ability to solve problems, or to fashion products, that are valued in one or more culture or community settings" (Oliver, 1997, p. 1). This definition expanded intelligence to include cultural and motivational factors. Gardner rejected the notion

---

This revised chapter was originally authored by David J. Lundberg and Brenda S. Hall in the first edition of this handbook.

that there is only one form of intelligence, arguing that all individuals possess several intelligences with specific types of intelligence stronger in different persons. He maintained the importance of hereditary factors but insisted that societal values, cultural resources, and individual opportunities are paramount in understanding and recognizing intelligences.

Gardner's perspective is multifaceted and pluralistic. Within his developmental framework are eight independent abilities, summarized in Table 41.1. Gardner believed individuals are born with the capacity to develop all eight intelligences, although cultural, social, and personal contexts determine how each intelligence is manifested. Thus, because each student's experience in the world is different, each will display a unique range of intellectual strengths and weaknesses. As such, students should not be categorized as being high or low in an intelligence area, but rather appreciated for the full range of their various intellectual abilities, each of which can be strengthened and expanded.

TABLE 41.1

GARDNER'S MULTIPLE INTELLIGENCES

Linguistic/Verbal intelligence focuses on the production and use of words and language. Linguistic/verbal intelligence is used in listening, speaking, reading, and writing. Example occupations: writers, poets, journalists, politicians, orators.

Logical/Mathematical intelligence pertains to higher order thinking, inductive and deductive reasoning, manipulation of numbers, the capacity to recognize patterns, and the ability to connect logical mathematical operations. Example occupations: mathematicians, engineers, microbiologists

Visual/Spatial intelligence uses skills involving spatial configurations, such as visualizing an object and creating mental images such as pictures, paintings, diagrams, or maps. Example occupations: artists, navigators, designers, topologists

Bodily/Kinesthetic intelligence addresses skills using the entire body or parts of the body through physical movement. It involves knowledge of the body, how it moves, and how it can be used to express emotion, solve motor problems, or construct products or displays. Example occupations: dancers, athletes, actors, builders

Musical/Rhythmical intelligence relates to music such as tonal patterns, rhythm, and beat. It involves recognizing, manipulating, and repeating musical sounds and rhythms. Example occupations: musicians, singers, musical performers.

Interpersonal intelligence addresses skills in interactions with others and involves the ability to get along with others, communication, and sensitivity to the concerns of other people. Example occupations: counselors, teachers, salespeople.

Intrapersonal intelligence centers around knowledge of oneself and involves awareness of one's internal aspects. It includes access to one's own feelings and emotions as well as an understanding of metacognition (how one thinks about thinking). Individuals who share themselves through literature, art, and speech display this intelligence.

Naturalist intelligence addresses the ability to recognize and classify living things and features of the natural world (e.g., animals, minerals, plants). Example occupations: farmers, biologists, chefs

STERNBERG'S TRIARCHIC FRAMEWORK

Robert Sternberg's early work on intelligence supported the view that traditional intelligence testing was too narrow. He sought to understand the information processing components related to the standard intelligence trait (Spearman's *g*). Sternberg (1985) outlined a theory of intelligence emphasizing three distinct, yet interrelated patterns that can be measured and developed. These facets are summarized in Table 41.2. ilities used to achieve one's goals in life, given a sociocultural context, through adaptation to, selection of, and shaping of environments" (Sternberg, 1998, p.1). Like Gardner, Sternberg emphasized the cultural, social, and personal influences on intelligence. Sternberg's theory of successful intelligence incorporated universal aspects of cognition as well as sources of group and individual differences.

GARDNER AND STERNBERG: COMMON GROUND

Gardner and Sternberg arrived at their conclusions about intelligence in very different ways. Sternberg worked from a more traditional scientific base and emphasized the empirical foundation for his theory of intelligence. Gardner emphasized the use of data but suggested that his findings were "less a set of hypotheses and predictions than . . . an organized framework for configuring an ensemble of data about human cognition in different cultures" (Gardner, 1994, p. 2).

Gardner and Sternberg shared the idea that this broader view of intelligences can be translated into educational practice. Sternberg has formulated specific principles of teaching for developing successful intelligences and reforming education (Sternberg, 1998). Many educators have discussed the applications of Gardner's work to instructional practices in schools and the implementation of multiple intelligences principles has occurred in schools across the country. Commonalities from the work of Sternberg (1997) and Gardner (1993) include the following:

1. All individuals have different minds with unique strengths and weaknesses.
2. People use aspects or types of intelligences based on a multitude of factors (e.g., cultural, social, personal) and experiences.
3. Intelligences can be developed and strengthened.

TABLE 41.2

STERNBERG'S TRIARCHIC MODEL

Analytical Intelligence is similar to traditionally valued analytic ability and involves problem solving, monitoring solutions, and evaluating results. It refers to how individuals process information and relate to the external world.

Creative Intelligence uses insight and original thought. It reflects how individuals use what they already know and develop new and different ways to complete tasks. Creative intelligence involves using imagination, innovation, and creativity to see the world in different ways.

Practical Intelligence can be referred to as "street smarts"—the ability to take what is learned and apply it to everyday living. This involves the ability to assess a situation and decide how to respond.

4. Intelligences can be assessed (although a widely accepted single instrument has not been developed).

5. It is important for educators and counselors to recognize and pay attention to different intellectual abilities.

6. Educators should develop educational strategies and use multiple approaches that encourage the use and development of various aspects of intelligences.

RECOMMENDED COUNSELING ACTIONS AND STRATEGIES USING MULTIPLE INTELLIGENCES

Several researchers (Mantzaris, 1999; O'Brian & Burnett, 2000; Shearer, 1997) have discussed the integration of multiple intelligences into counseling practice. Table 41.3 provides suggestions for using multiple intelligences to enhance the counseling process in three major areas: self-knowledge, possible courses of action, and self-esteem.

USING LEARNING STYLES IN COUNSELING

Understanding the concept of learning styles opens another avenue for interacting with diverse clients in a way that values each as unique individuals and allows a fresh and different way to expand counseling approaches to the helping process. Trying to understand cultural differences with clients can be an exasperating task, primarily because the factors involved seem almost endless (Lundberg & Kirk, 2003). The concept of learning styles, like that of multiple intelligences, offers a specific framework to interact with diverse students in ways that are harmonious and natural for those clients. These approaches promise not only increased effectiveness for professional school counselors but also refreshing and stimulating methods to invigorate the counseling process.

LEARNING STYLES: HOW THEY DIFFER FROM MULTIPLE INTELLIGENCES

Learning styles theory is concerned with differences in the process of learning, emphasizing the ways individuals think and feel as they absorb, process, and internalize information. An individual learning style is a unique collection of skills and preferences that affect how a person perceives, gathers, and processes information. Learning-styles models seek to identify affinities for specific instructional environments, strategies, and resources.

While learning styles and multiple intelligences are well documented, hold widespread interest in the educational community, and provide important implications for student development, they are very different concepts. Multiple intelligences theory is an effort to understand how culture and experiences shape human potential. Multiple intelligences focus on the content and products of education but do not address the individualized process of learning. Gardner (1993) explained that

> in MI theory, I begin with a human organism that responds (or fails to respond) to different kinds of contents in the world such as language, number, and other human beings. . . . Those who speak of learning styles are searching for approaches that ought to characterize all contents: a person who is deliberate with respect to

TABLE 41.3

COUNSELING APPLICATIONS OF MULTIPLE INTELLIGENCE THEORIES

Self-Knowledge

Find out about the student's culture, including values, resources, and opportunities.

Pay attention to the specific needs and talents of each child.

Help students examine their own assumptions about their potential, achievement, environment, thoughts, feelings, behaviors, needs, and concerns.

Create an environment that exposes individuals to the various intelligences through a variety of activities and a multitude of resources.

Provide opportunities for students to express themselves through diverse interventions and strategies such as talking, writing, drawing, puppets, role play, music, poetry, and small-group interaction.

Promote the awareness of individual strengths and weaknesses and the development of hidden talents.

Involve students in both individual and group interaction so that interpersonal and intrapersonal talents are discovered.

Possible Courses of Action

Encourage students to use self-knowledge and provide opportunities for them to practice new knowledge of self.

Help students reframe a problem using multiple intelligences to achieve a positive outcome. Once students realize that there is more than one way to resolve an issue or complete a task, they can use their self-knowledge, various talents, and resources to successfully address the concern.

Show students how to synthesize self-knowledge, possible courses of action, and evaluate which talents are most appropriate in specific situations. Synthesizing this information opens eyes to new and different possibilities and allows for new perspectives.

Self-Esteem

Plan activities that allow students to express and apply various types of intelligences that lead students to understand the relationship between their intelligences and their work in school.

Through interaction in small groups and other intrapersonal activities, individuals build social skills, learn to control their behavior, and enhance their self-esteem with peers. As students gain self-awareness they can appreciate and feel good about themselves as unique individuals. Students, especially low achievers, can build on successes and set goals that allow them to accomplish something meaningful in school.

music as well as to mathematics, a person who sees the "big picture" whether he is doing physics or painting. (pp. 44–45)

While both constructs promote a multifaceted approach to learning, their differences can be summarized as follows:

- Multiple intelligences theory focuses on the unique talents and strengths of students. Learning styles theories focus on individual preferences in the learning process.
- Multiple intelligences theory is an outgrowth of cognitive theory, related to intelligence testing; learning styles theories have roots in personality theory.

- Multiple intelligences theory addresses what is taught (content); learning styles theories emphasize how it is taught (process).
- Empirical studies relating multiple intelligences and student achievement are limited, while the impact of learning styles on student achievement is well documented statistically.
- Specific instruments for measures of multiple intelligences are being developed and tested. Learning styles assessments yielding valid and reliable scores already exist.

MODELS OF LEARNING STYLES

Learning style is broadly defined as the individual differences in the way a learner approaches the task of learning. More specifically, a learning style is the way each person begins to concentrate on, process, internalize, and retain difficult and new information (Dunn, Denig, & Lovelace, 2001). One's learning style preferences affect how a person learns, solves problems, and relates to others. Styles of learning tend to change and develop as people grow. Learning styles models recognize the role of cognitive and affective processes, and they bring attention to issues related to motivation and student achievement.

Understanding learning styles can be useful to students and professionals in several ways. Knowing their preferences helps students to plan for learning and to develop personal study strategies. Professionals can use individual learning preferences to design and implement effective instructional environments, strategies, and resources. Research supports the idea that when students are taught new and different information through instructional approaches that respond to their learning style preference, they score statistically higher on achievement tests (Dunn et al., 2001).

Kolb (1984) emphasized experiential aspects of learning such as concrete experience (feeling), reflective observation (watching), abstract conceptualization (thinking), and active experimentation (doing). Silver and Strong (1997) outlined four basic styles:

- *Mastery.* The mastery learner approaches learning in a concrete, step-by-step manner. Clarity and practicality are important values.
- *Understanding.* Students who prefer the understanding style enjoy questioning, reasoning, and evaluating using logic and evidence.
- *Self-expressive.* Self-expressive learners use feelings and emotions to handle new ideas and create outcomes. They respond to learning practices that require originality and creativity.
- *Interpersonal.* Individuals who fit the interpersonal learning style see learning as a social activity and a tool to help others.

One of the most widely recognized and researched learning styles models for elementary and secondary school students is the Dunn and Dunn (1992, 1993) framework. It focuses on 21 unique elements that can be classified into five distinct categories:

- *Classroom environment* elements include light (bright/soft), sound (sounds/silence), room temperature (cool/warm), and seating (formal/casual).

- *Emotionality* elements include levels of motivation, persistence, responsibility, conformity, and preferences for structure. Some students are persistent in terms of high levels of motivation or focus, and they provide their own structure. Others need direction for task initiation, focus, and structure.
- *Sociological* elements include learning alone, with peers, with collegial or authoritative adults, and the need for variety versus routine.
- *Physiological* elements include perceptual elements (auditory, visual, tactile, kinesthetic), time-of-day energy highs and lows, preference for snacks or fluids while learning, and the need for mobility versus passivity.
- *Psychological* elements include several methods of processing information. Individuals with strongly analytic preferences approach facts in a step-by-step sequence by first examining specific facts and then gradually integrating them into a whole concept. Global learners first address the overall concept before mastering the specific facts.

LEARNING STYLES ASSESSMENT

School professionals can assess a few characteristics of learning style preferences through observation, but there are specific instruments designed to examine the multidimensional characteristics of learning. Each learning styles model has its own assessment tool. Dunn, Dunn, and Price (1979) developed the *Learning Style Inventory* (LSI) to correspond with the 21 elements in their model. This questionnaire is the predominant learning preference assessment for school-age children. It was developed using content and factor analysis, and it consists of 104 self-reported questions. The LSI uses a 3-point scale for Grades 3 through 4 and a 5-point scale for Grades 5 through 12. Completion time is 30 to 40 minutes. Research supported the LSI as an instrument yielding reliable and valid scores (Dunn & DeBello, 1999). Adaptations of the LSI are *Our Wonderful Learning Styles* (OWLS) for Grades 2 through 5 and *Learning Style: The Clue To You* (LS:CY) for Grades 6 through 8. These tools identify elements associated with processing information from a broad perspective prior to examining the specific facts (global learning). Both assessments use various methods such as imagery, humor, fantasy, and imagination (Dunn, 1999).

LEARNING STYLES AND SCHOOL COUNSELING

Current school counseling practices require that professional school counselors actively engage in the ongoing development of students. By understanding, assessing, and using learning styles, counselors are better equipped to design and facilitate developmental strategies and interventions that meet the needs of diverse students. Inclusion of learning styles into counseling practice requires an understanding of learning styles models. Conceptualization of specific learning characteristics and preferences provides a framework for addressing individual student differences. With this knowledge, professional school counselors can assess individual learning styles and choose appropriate strategies and interventions.

In consultation with teachers and administrators, professional school counselors can use learning styles to develop optimal instructional practices for individual students and assist parents and caregivers in the understanding and accommodation of the child's educational and personal needs. Research in the area of counseling interventions and learning style preferences was limited (Griggs, 1983; Griggs, Price, Kopel, & Swaine, 1984), and studies tended to focus on learning styles of ethnic and cultural groups (Dunn & Griggs, 1993; Griggs & Dunn, 1995, 1996; Herring & Meggert, 1994). Griggs (1991) provided a system for matching specific counseling interventions with individual students' learning style preferences. Learning styles models provide professional school counselors with the opportunity to try a multitude of techniques.

RECOMMENDED COUNSELING ACTIONS AND STRATEGIES USING LEARNING STYLE MODELS

Griggs (1985) suggested that the learning styles elements of structure, perceptual strength, motivation, the sociological preferences, and the psychological factors are particularly relevant to counseling. The corresponding categories for these characteristics as outlined in the Dunn and Dunn model are emotionality, sociological, physiological, and psychological. The following are examples of possible counseling interventions to accommodate different modes within these areas.

EMOTIONALITY

With students who exhibit a need for more structure and motivation, professional school counselors may find that behavioral approaches are more suitable. The counselor and student may meet to set specific goals, using structured resources and techniques such as behavioral contracts.

This type of learner tends to expect the professional school counselor to initiate tasks and provide concrete solutions to issues. For students who are not likely to seek additional assistance, it is beneficial for the counselor to actively follow up on pending issues. Counselors should provide structured exercises as well as expectations for listening and talking for those students engaged in group work. Students preferring less structure may benefit from person-centered approaches, which allow feelings and desires to be expressed freely. Opportunities can be provided by the counselor for the student to initiate new behaviors and solutions.

SOCIOLOGICAL

Students who prefer learning alone may reject group methods and not respond well to group counseling. Others may respond well in a group setting but have more difficulty with individual modalities. For the group-oriented student, peer groups can be effectively used to promote participation and growth. Group counseling techniques for peer-oriented preferences may include dramatization of past experiences and present situations. Through role-playing and mime, students can safely express emotions, portray various aspects of their personhood, and practice how to handle confrontations.

For the student with a preference for learning on an individual basis, bibliotherapy is an effective strategy. The professional school counselor may choose several types of reading materials through which the counseling theme will be centered, basing the choices on the age, specific concerns, and needs of the individual students. It is important that the counselor be able to discern whether the student is one who prefers the rhythm and routine of regular, predetermined group and individual sessions, or one who is more comfortable "dropping-in" to see the counselor without a scheduled appointment.

PHYSIOLOGICAL

The auditory, visual, tactile, and kinesthetic senses have a great impact on learning. Auditorily perceptive students filter information using their listening skills, preferring to accept data by hearing it. Auditory learners find it easier to repeat words, recall conversations, and recite lines from reading materials. Traditional "talking through" counseling approaches often work best with these individuals.

Visual learners most often think by using images and pictures. They translate what is heard into images in their minds. Counseling strategies centered on observation, written materials, and imaging fit the visual preference. It is important for counselors to serve as role models and provide opportunities for observing the behaviors of others, such as peers and family members. Use of videotapes, films, books, and other written texts help individuals in the imagery of desired behaviors and solutions to problems. Once visualized, the behavior is often easily carried out.

Tactile and kinesthetic perceptual styles overlap. Having a tactile learning style means that the person learns best by touching. The kinesthetic style requires that the learner becomes physically involved in the experience for best results. These types of students often prefer to learn through movements that involve gross motor skills. Active learners thrive with "hands on" counseling approaches. The use of puppetry, drawing, painting, dance, and other creative art interventions provide alternative ways for emotional release and communication. Movement and manipulation of objects throughout the counseling session may assist kinesthetic learners to share their feelings and thoughts.

PSYCHOLOGICAL

Analytic processors think in a step-by-step sequential pattern. They examine the facts, absorb them, and formulate a conceptual framework. Global learners must understand the concept or idea first; then they attend to specifics.

When working with analytic thinkers it is important to be concrete and focus on details. Professional school counselors should be direct and ask pointed questions. Strongly analytic individuals prefer a more formal interaction.

Students who process globally need to gain an understanding of a situation before giving attention to its particular components. Professional school counselors can help these individuals by allowing them to talk in general terms about their concerns before identifying specific aspects they wish to address. The use of illustrations and the sharing of anecdotes are methods counselors can use to help clients determine the focus of their counseling experience. Global thinkers feel comfortable in a more casual environment; nondirective strategies work best.

SUMMARY/CONCLUSION

Continual assessment of multiple intelligences in counseling enhances the interaction between student and counselor, creating an environment that allows comfort, expression of the whole person, and maximum growth. Through the counseling process, individuals can become aware of the types of intelligences, identify their stronger talents, and develop strategies to effectively use those skills. Equally important is the opportunity for students to build on prominent intelligences and try new ways of expression, thus using one intelligence area to strengthen another. Professional school counselors who continually evaluate client development within the multiple intelligences framework can promote a fuller spectrum of personal, social, and intellectual capabilities in students. Beyond the school setting, this can lead to less competitive, more productive, team-oriented approaches to life and work. Combining learning styles and multiple intelligences can provide holistic models that reflect diversity and individual uniqueness. Attention to these models provides professional school counselors with multidimensional strategies to fulfill their mission of fostering learning and growth in all children. Multiple intelligences represent individual talents reflected by cultural, social and personal influences. Learning styles define how students acquire, store, and present information. Integration of these theories allows professional school counselors to understand both the broader context of each student's unique personal environment as well as the individualized processes of learning.

(Note: See the CD-ROM for a list of references.)

CHAPTER 42

GROUP COUNSELING IN SCHOOLS

Gary E. Goodnough and Vivian V. Lee

Preview

In this chapter, we discuss the different kinds of group counseling experiences offered in schools and examine strategies professional school counselors use to form groups and collaborate with other leaders in the school. We also provides a rationale for why professional school counselors need to offer a full menu of groups and information that will help implement group counseling as a central component of a systemic school counseling program.

To understand the role of group counseling in schools, professional school counselors must first understand systemic data-driven school counseling programs. The purpose of these programs is to promote academic success by supporting and enhancing the academic, career, and personal–social development needs of all students. These needs are identified through the examination of data, based on a systemic assessment of all constituencies within the school community (Lee & Goodnough, 2007). Goals are formulated and competencies are developed from the identified needs. These competencies identify what students should learn as a result of participating in a systemic data-driven school counseling program. Competencies are delivered to students via levels of programmatic intervention. Group counseling is one level of intervention or service delivery within the structure of school counseling programs (Lee & Goodnough, 2007).

Within a systemic data-driven school counseling program, group counseling is a means of delivering direct, targeted, and more intensive services to K–12 students. In this way, group counseling, like other aspects of the school counseling program, is data driven and linked to the mission of schools.

The professional literature suggests that group counseling is helpful to students (Whiston & Sexton, 1998). Increasingly, such group counseling interventions have solid empirical research to back claims of promoting social, career, and academic development (e.g., Muris, Meesters, Vincken, & Eijkelenboom, 2005; Webb, Brigman, & Campbell, 2005; Webb & Myrick, 2003). First, group counseling is an efficient intervention when compared to individual counseling, as the counselor can see multiple students simultaneously. Second, from a developmental and pedagogical perspective, students often learn best from each other. Group counseling provides an excellent forum to promote such student-to-student learning. Related to this, the power of the peer group can be garnered for positive growth and development under the skillful leadership of the professional school counselor. Finally, groups are a microcosm of society and as such provide real-life settings in which students can work out issues and problems (Brigman & Earley, 2001; Gladding, 2003). Group counseling is a major function endorsed by the American School Counselor Association (ASCA), and research suggested that 90% of professional school counselors spend time providing it to students (ASCA; 2005; Burnham & Jackson, 2000). Partin (1993) reported that professional school counselors on average spent 8% to12% of their time providing group counseling interventions.

Group counseling is one of the professional school counselor's most highly specialized skills. As such, it is important for counselors to have a thorough grounding in group counseling theory and practice. In addition, professional school counselors need to know how to take a leadership role and successfully implement group counseling into school counseling programs. Therefore, we will examine the different kinds of groups offered in schools, types of group interventions, strategies to use in forming groups, and how to collaborate with other school leaders to offer a full menu of group topics that have the potential to benefit all in the school system.

GROUP COUNSELING: DEVELOPMENTAL, REMEDIAL, AND SCHOOL CLIMATE GROUPS

What is group counseling in schools? Group counseling initiatives within a larger systemic data-driven school counseling program address developmental milestones, provide remediation, and promote a healthy climate within the school. By "developmental milestones" we mean that professional school counselors can reasonably expect that most or all students would benefit from participating in groups designed to promote academic, career, or personal–social development. For example, developmental groups that address academic development include study skills, test-taking strategies, and transition to middle or high school. Career development groups include goal setting and decision making, transitions to postsecondary options, career exploration, and college planning. Personal–social groups include peer relationships, friendship, self-esteem, forming safe–healthy romantic relationships, personal empowerment, and accepting a newborn sibling.

Group counseling is remedial in nature when it addresses topics or issues that impair the learning and development of specific groups of students. Remedial groups help students develop coping skills to assist them in coming to terms with difficult personal and social issues. These groups seek to empower students to regain control over their lives and engage (or reengage) in the learning process. Groups that address remedial issues may include divorce and family separation, sexual identity, substance use (self, family member, or friend), grief and loss, coping with HIV/AIDS in the family, anger management, conflict resolution, and learning to live in a blended family. Some groups are offered around issues that affect a large group of students. For instance, in regions where the military has bases, parents and family members frequently must leave home to serve in the military. Such deployments cause upheaval and uncertainty in a large number of homes and impede the learning process of many students.

Finally, remedial group topics may include issues that affect all students. These issues might be a natural disaster such as a hurricane; a tragic event such as the terror attacks of September 11, 2001; a specific incident of school violence; or a student death. Remedial group counseling can help students debrief the trauma they experience in the immediate aftermath of these and other tragedies. The issues that arise from these events, when unresolved, impair personal growth and impede the learning process. By responding to the remedial needs of students through group counseling, professional school counselors deliver an important and highly specialized service.

A third category of groups that professional school counselors offer address the culture and climate of the school. Some of these groups include issues related to diversity awareness, bias and prejudice reduction, conflict resolution, and respect of self and others. These groups may also address the cultural and institutional barriers to learning of certain groups of students (e.g., students of color; gay, lesbian, bisexual and transgendered youth; lower socioeconomic status students). Professional school counselors provide the needed support to these and other student groups, to help remove individual and systemic barriers and provide for equitable learning conditions and access to the best that school and society offer. (See Table 42.1 for an overview of different types of groups presented in the professional literature.)

To form groups in all three categories, professional school counselors need to assess students' needs broadly. The institutional culture and overall climate of the school can limit the access to and equity of group counseling to all student groups. Professional school counselors need to reach out to underserved populations in ways that are relevant and consistent with their needs. In this way, counselors can encourage students to consider group counseling as a safe and viable means of assistance in making decisions and solving problems.

Previous experiences with societal and institutionalized barriers and biases can diminish trust and cause students to doubt that the school and its representatives have their best interests at heart. In forming relationships with students, it is essential for professional school counselors to validate concerns, earn trust, and advocate for needs. This builds the professional school counselor's credibility and assists in creating a sense of inclusion for all students.

PSYCHOEDUCATION AND COUNSELING: GROUP INTERVENTIONS

Groups in schools led by professional school counselors exist on a continuum from being primarily didactic and psychoeducational in nature to being primarily therapeutic counseling experiences. Most groups have some elements of each, and some vary from session to session. Many developmental groups are primarily psychoeducational and focus on providing topic-specific information to small groups of students. The presentation of the information is carefully designed to directly apply to students' lives, to enhance age-appropriate development and academic success. For example, transitioning students can be taught about the environment they are transitioning into—whether it is middle school, high school, or a 4-year college.

Psychoeducation also has a place in remedial groups. Students coping with the loss of a loved one need to be taught about the stages of grieving, because such knowledge is helpful to the healing process. In groups dealing with the school climate, information is frequently taught to students (e.g., in a group on conflict resolution, students need to be taught about the characteristics of conflict and the different types of conflict; Ripley, 2003). Thus, the provision of psychoeducation to students in all types of counseling groups is common in schools and fits in well with the culture of K–12 education, as students learn new information.

TABLE 42.1

GROUP COUNSELING PLANS: INFORMATION FROM THE LITERATURE AND RECENT PUBLICATIONS

Author(s)	Topic
Hines and Fields (2004)	Task management skills, asking for help, and developing academic persistence for ninth grade students
Campbell & Bowman (1993)	Academically retained children
Nelson, Dykeman, Powell, and Petty (1996)	Disruptive and maladjusted students
Stewart & McKay (1995)	Aggressive elementary school students
Ripley (2003)	Conflict management
LaFountain, Garner, & Eliason (1996)	Heterogeneously-grouped solution-focused group counseling
Erford, Moore-Thomas, & Mazzuca (2004)	Understanding learning styles
Struder & Allton (1996)	Teenagers from divorced families
Riddle, Bergin, and Douzenis (1997)	Lowering the anxiety levels and improving the self-concepts of elementary school children of alcoholics
Arman and McNair (2000)	Elementary school-aged children of alcoholics
Akos (2000)	A psychoeducational group that helps develop empathy in children
Akos (2000)	Transition to middle school
Kizner & Kizner (1999)	Adopted children
Bradley (2001)	African American males
Bailey & Bradford-Bailey (2004)	African American males
Smith & Chen-Hayes (2004)	Gay, lesbian, bisexual, transgendered, and questioning youth
Reeder, Douzenis, and Bergin (1997)	Improving the racial attitudes of primary-age children.
Zinck & Littrell (2000)	Adolescent at-risk girls
Becky & Farren (1997)	Helping high school girls understand and avoid abusive relationships
Rosen & Bezold (1996)	High school girls: Preventing dating violence
Goodnough & Ripley (1997)	High school seniors transitioning to postsecondary schools and the military
Coker (2004)	Substance abuse prevention
Brooks (2004)	Stress management
Stone (2004)	Perpetrators of sexual harassment
Jackson & Grant (2004)	The influence of culture, gender, race and ability on the career development of high school students
Sears (2004)	Career development activities for middle and high school students
Niles, Trusty, & Mitchell (2004)	Career planning, equity, and access for high schools students

As we stated, psychoeducation can be presented in all three group categories. Typically, the provision of psychoeducation leads students to apply information to themselves. They often need assistance to do this. Such processing leads into the second aspect of group work in schools: counseling. It is in the processing that the professional school counselor's unique skill set is used. When students process information, they often reveal confidential information about themselves, thus opening themselves up to psychological risk. Professional school counselors are trained to manage this risk in culturally sensitive ways, thereby helping to promote growth and development through risk taking and sharing.

As students share and process together, the professional school counselor uses counseling skills to promote mutual trust and to help members develop a sense of inclusion within the group. Effective group counselors help to create an environment in which members become known to each other in meaningful ways. In a remedial group for children dealing with family situations in which alcohol or other drugs are being abused, a professional school counselor will not only use psychoeducation (i.e., the professional school counselor might teach about the roles taken in alcoholic families) but will also help promote healing by helping all students share their particular situations. By working with all members in this way, the professional school counselor helps students know they are not alone. In sum, professional school counselors provide psychoeducation to students and help them process that information in personally meaningful ways. Further, they harness the power of the group to provide an avenue for growth, remediation, and the improvement of the school climate.

Two Ways to Form Groups: Homogeneous and Heterogeneous

The aforementioned groups are homogeneous groups, in which all students are dealing with similar issues. For several reasons, it is appropriate that membership in some groups be restricted. First, students who share a common concern are able to identify with each other and help one another in ways that others might not. While group counseling is not about giving others advice, group members do provide their own unique perspectives; within these perspectives may be information and coping strategies that members find helpful. Related to providing support is the concept of *universality*; the knowledge that others share certain experiences and feelings reduces the sense of isolation that many students feel so they know that they are not alone. This process of universality is one of the key group process factors that promote growth and healing (Yalom, 2005). Finally, when groups are homogeneously formed, topic-specific psychoeducation can be provided in a manner that is beneficial to all.

While the benefits of homogeneously formed groups are evident, there are several reasons why groups might have a heterogeneous composition. In these groups, similarity of presenting concern is not necessary because students learn a method (e.g., solution focused, problem solving, cognitive-behavioral) whereby a variety of problems can be addressed. They also learn that the chosen method can be transferred to other situations with which they might be faced. These types of groups help to decompartmentalize learning and help empower students as they gain confidence to draw on their new skills to solve problems in a variety of challenging situations.

Another way heterogeneous groups are used is by having one or more group members serve as models for targeted students. For instance, an elementary school social-skills group might be less effective if all members have poor social skills. One of the reasons that group counseling works is that students learn from each other. If all students in a group are deficient in social skills, they cannot learn from each other. Because of this, elementary school counselors frequently have behavioral models in social skills groups. These model students are children who have good social skills; the target students can learn from them. As a result, this group is made up of a heterogeneous group of students, not all of whom need remediation in social skills.

GROUP COUNSELING SKILLS

To effectively lead groups in schools, professional school counselors need to have skills in the following four dimensions of group counseling: (a) be knowledgeable about the interrelationship between developmental theory and counseling theory, (b) have knowledge about the topic or content of the group, (c) understand group dynamics, and (d) understand the contextual factors that influence what their students' behavior means. First, professional school counselors must understand students from multiple developmental perspectives (e.g., cognitive, psychosocial, and racial or ethnic identity). From these related perspectives, professional school counselors select group counseling strategies and interventions that are appropriate to the developmental sophistication of students. For example, elementary school counselors may choose to use Adlerian strategies, because many Adlerian concepts are applicable to the developmental needs of young children.

Professional school counselors need to understand theoretical applications well enough to feel confident that selected strategies and techniques are within accepted methods of practice and are robust enough to achieve the objectives of the group. Second, competence in the content or topic to be addressed is essential. While it is not necessary for professional school counselors to be experts in every area of group they offer, they do need specific knowledge (e.g., they need to know how the topic tends to manifest in the population with which they are working). For example, to lead a group on bereavement, professional school counselors need not be experts on issues of loss and grieving, but they do need to be quite knowledgeable about it and, in particular, how processing grief and loss is mediated by factors such as the child's cognitive development and cultural and religious beliefs. This relates to the third group counseling skill: understanding the multiple contexts of children's lives.

The multiple contextual factors that impact the lives of students shape the ways in which students process the content and dynamic interactions in groups. For example, factors such as socioeconomic status, race or ethnicity, gender, religious or spiritual beliefs and practices, sexual orientation, institutional barriers to learning, and family composition all become screens through which students filter the content of the group and the process dynamics that exist within the group. These interdependent and inter-related factors challenge professional school counselors to continually engage in professional development to competently and ethically meet the group counseling needs of students.

Finally, professional school counselors need to keep all of this in mind as they hypothesize about group members' behaviors and facilitate the growth of the group. In doing so, professional school counselors are able to encourage group members to participate fully in the group and respect students' varied and diverse styles of meaningful participation. By attending to these dimensions of group counseling, professional school counselors build cohesion and keep the group focused on the task or topic at hand.

THE CONTEXT OF PUBLIC SCHOOL

Much has been written about the barriers that prevent effective group work in schools. Some of the obstructive forces described are scheduling problems, teacher resistance, school policies and practices that limit student access, and the overall culture of schools (Dansby, 1996; Greenburg, 2003; Ripley & Goodnough, 2001). To overcome these barriers, professional school counselors need to honor and understand the context in which they work. They need to understand that administrators and teachers are held accountable for students' academic performance—often as measured by standardized test scores. Additionally, the work of the professional school counselor when conducting groups is not traditionally seen as enhancing the academic achievement of students or presenting skills such as higher order thinking skills or learning styles that can be effectively used across academic disciplines by students. Additionally, teacher and administrator preservice training does not focus heavily on the role and function of systemic data-driven school counseling programs, methods of service delivery, and the appropriate duties of the professional school counselor (Fitch, Newby, Ballestero, & Marshall, 2001; Pérusse & Goodnough, 2002). As a result, many administrators' perceptions of school counseling reflect their own experiences with school counseling, many of which are older, traditional notions of school counseling. When administrators assume leadership positions in schools, they often perpetuate these past practices.

There are three main ways professional school counselors can attend to the legitimate concerns of administrators and help them envision and facilitate the counselor's implementation of group counseling in a contemporary and appropriate manner. The first concerns professional preparation. Prior to initiating a series of group offerings, professional school counselors need to commit themselves and their time to preparing and scheduling group counseling. This requires counselors to include group counseling in the strategic plan of the school counseling program. Additionally, as one of the programmatic levels of intervention (Lee & Goodnough, 2007), group counseling is an established part of the school counseling program calendar and therefore requires professional school counselors to allot significant time for group counseling. When a programmatic calendar is shared with stakeholders, it sends a message that group counseling is a priority. Additionally, professional school counselors plan for their groups in the same way teachers plan for an academic unit. For example, math teachers do not create their plans in secret, and neither should professional school counselors.

Professional school counselors make their group goals, objectives, and supporting materials available to the public as part of their school counseling program. In accordance with the ASCA (2004) ethical standards, counselors honor parental–guardian knowledge of their children and seek to team and collaborate with them to assist in student development. As part of the collaborative effort, professional school counselors seek out parent–guardian permission for their child's participation in group counseling. By preparing well for group counseling, they bring professionalism and rigor to this important method of service delivery.

The second way professional school counselors facilitate the implementation of group counseling is by collaborating and teaming with administrators to address, reinterpret, or revise salient school policies. School counseling interventions perceived by administrators to be outside the academic mission, such as group counseling, are often denied class time to meet so that students' focus remains on academic tasks. As a result of policies such as this, group counseling is oftentimes only offered during lunch, study hall, or before and after school. A school policy that posits *unconditionally* that instructional time cannot be compromised derails effective group counseling initiatives, unless counselors can demonstrate how group counseling can enhance academic achievement. For example, through leadership and advocacy, professional school counselors need to help teachers and administrators see that exceptions to such an important policy are already granted through other school-sponsored activities (e.g., in high schools, athletes in a variety of sports typically miss their last class of the day to travel to away games). This is permitted because participation in interscholastic sports is deemed beneficial for student growth and development—so much so that it supersedes academic time for certain students. It is an accepted belief that athletics offers students benefits that enhance academic achievement by fostering positive peer interactions, learning new skills that foster self-control, and developing a sense of empowerment by accomplishing challenging endeavors.

The task for professional school counselors is to influence and inform policy revisions or reinterpretations that allow all students to have the opportunity to gain similar benefits through group counseling, if they so desire. To do this, professional school counselors have to remind teachers and administrators that group counseling is part of the larger systemic data-driven school counseling program and, as such, shares the school's mission for academic success. More specifically, helping students effectively cope with grief and loss so that they can refocus on academic pursuits is as important for some students' personal–social and academic development as wrestling or volleyball is for others.

Thus, when school policy is reviewed, reinterpreted, or revised, professional school counselors collaborate with administrators and teachers to help shift the questions from "When can groups be run?" and "Do they take away from academic time?" to "How can we implement group counseling as a means of improving the quality of students' 'time on task' in math?" Additionally, once policies are reinterpreted or revised, they need to be adhered to by all teachers. This means that teachers' ability to deny students the right to attend groups must be prohibited, and they must not be permitted to count students as absent if they are attending a group meeting. Moreover, students should be given the same amount of time to do makeup work as they would for any other school-sponsored activity (Ripley & Goodnough, 2001).

Finally, professional school counselors and students must honor the privilege that comes with policy revision or reinterpretation. Care must be taken so that neither students nor professional school counselors abuse the system. When applied to attending group counseling during class time, this means that group members must arrive to the group session on time, the same as they would for class. It also means that students who abuse or ignore the rules of the school or the group forfeit their participation in group counseling.

Attending carefully to rules such as these and publicizing them broadly creates consistent behavioral expectations for students and reduces the ambiguity of the consequences of failure to follow school policy. Professional school counselors need to navigate dual role issues involved here. In all ways, they must enforce school policies while also being the group leader and embodying the characteristics and skills necessary for effective group leadership. When group counseling is implemented as described in this section, this powerful intervention becomes a valued part of the systemic data-driven school counseling program.

SUMMARY/CONCLUSION

Professional school counselors at all levels who do not lead groups are not adequately performing their jobs. This is because group counseling in schools is a central means of delivering a systemic data-driven school counseling program. Providing effective group counseling experiences to students requires leadership, specialized knowledge and skills, and the ability to advocate effectively for the inclusion of a program of group counseling within schools.

(Note: See the CD-ROM for a list of references.)

CHAPTER 43

VISUAL ARTS AND THE PROFESSIONAL
SCHOOL COUNSELOR

Joe R. Underwood and Nancy B. Underwood

Preview

*In this chapter, we show professional school counselors how to use visual arts as a ve-
hicle to assist students in self-expression. This chapter was not written as an attempt
to encourage the professional school counselor to become an art therapist; rather, it
was written by a licensed professional counselor and a teacher who use visual art as
a creative aid in the counseling and educational process. The examples of visual art
activities are practical, original, and field tested in the schools. The professional
school counselor will find these visual art activities to be effective in both individual
and group counseling settings.*

Art as a means of self-expression has been evident in societies since the advent of
the cave art of primitive peoples. Using art to record events, recall events, and
elaborate upon events has become an integral part of our communication system as
human beings. Visual art not only is appealing to view, it also can be a means of expressing ideas and of relating factual information in a pictorial format. Internationally
recognized symbols guide us to destinations and give us a sense of security in an ever-
changing world. While visual symbols provide generality in art, there is also individuality in art, which is evidenced by how people express themselves with art forms. Individual human beings may tell about themselves through artistic expression that is as
unique as handwriting. Artistic self-expression is as important as oral communication
and written words and can provide a means for professional school counselors, teachers,
and parents to learn more about those students with whom they interact.

People of all ages and abilities, especially K–12 students, can benefit from visual
art experiences. Visual art is a "here and now" experience that provides an immediate
result, a picture, that is straightforward and evokes feelings and emotions (Honore &
Edward-Allen, 1997). Visual art can be spontaneous or planned. Whenever it occurs,
visual art represents us and serves as a biographical record and as a means of expressing
personal information.

Carl Jung introduced the use of creative art practices to psychotherapy through
active imagination. His work focused on ideas derived from concentration on particular
images (McNiff, 1992). Art therapy began as an outgrowth of the clinical application
of creative psychologists, such as Jung, Naumburg, and Kramer (Kahn, 1999). McNiff
(1992) affirmed that art images produced in a counseling situation "expand communication and offer insight outside the scope of the reasoning mind" (p. 3). However, it is the
use and explanation of the visual artwork that affirms the uniqueness of individuals
and of visual art as a means of self-expression (Keys, 1983).

Campbell (1993) asserted that almost any student could be naturally visually creative. She maintained that visual art can enrich and lead to change in a student's life. Hence, visual art is a valuable tool of self-expression that the professional school counselor may use with clients. Artistic expression can become a neutral outlet for ideas and abstract concepts. It also can become a means of communicating and expressing feelings with people of all ages and can provide a visual record that may be kept as confidentially as would a journal (Kahn, 1999).

VISUAL ARTS IN COUNSELING

Henderson (1999) has successfully used images of animals as personal metaphors through a guided imagery experience in which participants select an animal as a symbol of self and then define qualities of that animal that relate to themselves. The use of the animal symbols affords the participants a creative means of self-expression.

Many professional counselors and therapists already use visual art in the practice of counseling (France & Edward, 1997; Jordan, 2001; Liebmann, 1986). Jacobs (1994) frequently used graphs, mirrors, charts, and visual demonstrations as he worked with clients to clarify and explore client concerns. Ziff (2004) offered a rationale, structure, and method for teaching art experientially as an adjunct to counseling. Magnusson (as cited in Whitmer, Thompson, & Loesch, 2000) used a spider web as a visual context to discuss friendship and personal support networks. Kottman, Ashby, and DeGraaf (2001) used the image of a large map in an activity to chart and map diversity.

Newsome (2003) exploited the image of a volcano when facilitating anger management training with teens who "blow their top" instead of controlling the release of their emotions. Newsome compared the image of a volcano exploding with "blowing your top" when you get angry. Then she assisted her clients in using the same image to develop ways to control their emotions. Newsome (2005) expanded the use of expressive arts to group supervision of counselor trainees. She successfully used select expressive arts activities as a means of increasing group understanding and personal awareness of the counselor trainees.

Whether visual art is used to explore personal problems or merely to explore personal creativity, it is a valuable tool for building observable products that represent the personality of the individual. Gladding (1998) addressed the usefulness of visual art activities for the professional school counselor, indicating that counselors should be mindful that the use of visual arts is an evolving process that increases in effectiveness as students become more aware and more comfortable with artistic expression: "Clients who can envision through paints, drawings, and sculpture what they have accomplished over a period of time or what they could be are more likely than not to stay with the process of change until they are satisfied with the process" (Gladding, 1998, p. 65).

Furthermore, visual art experiences enable students to use both visual and verbal skills in learning and communicating what they learn. Students also can be trained to develop left- and right-brain methods of learning in a creative and comfortable way through art (Edwards, 1989). Therefore, professional school counselors who incorporate the use of visual arts in their interactions with students promote student learning, foster alternative ways of student self-expression, encourage new and exciting ways of viewing student concerns, and affirm the uniqueness of students as individuals (Weiser, 2001).

Although teachers recognize that students have numerous learning styles, teachers typically teach to the visual learner (Harr, Hall, Schoepp, & Smith, 2002). If the visual learning style is the most common student learning style (Griggs, 1985; Silverman & Freed, 1991), the professional school counselor's use of visual arts as a counseling tool should be welcomed and appreciated by the majority of K–12 students.

VISUAL ART ACTIVITIES TO USE WITH K–12 STUDENTS

The following sections contain descriptions and examples of visual arts activities that the professional school counselor may use with students in Grades K–12. To protect the privacy of students (Hammond & Gantt, 1998), the authors created the examples that are included in this chapter. These examples are illustrations of concepts. The products produced by the students with whom the professional counselor uses these activities will vary with the age and talent of the students.

When professional school counselors use these activities with students, the process is much more important than the product. Talent and skill levels vary among students. The end product is a means to self-expression. The activities are neither Jungian based nor art-therapy based. They are designed only to enhance and motivate students to design visual products that will enhance self-understanding and make students and professional school counselors more comfortable with artistic expression and allow all students to create a visual product that may be used to foster dialogue and communication. The final product is not to be judged by artistic merit but rather by the quality of self-expression experienced by the students.

The National Art Education Association affirms that the arts teach students many valuable life lessons. Eisner (2002) wrote that the arts teach (a) students to make good judgments, (b) that problems can have more than one solution, (c) that there are many ways to see and interpret the world, (d) that small differences can have large effects, and (e) that what students do and think is important. All of these lessons are compatible with the goals of the ASCA national standards for school counseling programs (Dahir, Sheldon, & Valiga, 2002). These standards are incorporated into the ASCA national model (American School Counselor Association [ASCA], 2005).

Professional school counselors may align all visual arts activities in this chapter with the ASCA national model (ASCA; 2005) that promote students' academic success, career development, and personal–social development. Readers may refer to the ASCA national model for a thorough presentation of specific student competencies and indicators. Each visual arts activity contains an example of a student competency and an indicator(s) of the competency. Since some of the visual arts activities may be associated with more than one competency, the authors encourage professional school counselors to adapt the activities to relate to competencies appropriate for their school settings.

Activity 1: I Can

Competency: Academic Development Standard—Acquire Skills for Improving Leaning. The "I Can" activity allows students to demonstrate how effort and persistence affect learning positively.

Academic Development Standard—Achieve School Success. The "I Can" activity encourages students to take responsibility for their actions and learning.

Materials: Soda cans, colored pencils, unlined paper, clothesline or rope

Activity:

1. The professional school counselor leads an activity to help each student identify a goal that he or she *can* accomplish, identify ways he or she *can* achieve the goal, and to serve as a creative reminder of commitment to the goal.

2. On a piece of paper (see Figure 43.1, "I Can" worksheet, on the next page), have the student write a major goal he or she has for this year. It can be a personal goal, a school goal, or a spiritual goal—just be sure it is something realistic. For example, the student might write a goal such as the following:

> Improve my computer skills
>
> Have a positive attitude in science class
>
> Complete homework assignments

3. Emphasizing the positive concept of "I can," ask students to discuss ways they can reach their goals. Allow students to brainstorm ideas with each other. Then ask students to list at least four "I cans" that will lead them on their way to reaching their goal.

4. Instruct students to use colored pencils, draw pictures or symbols to represent their goals and "I cans," and attach them to a soda can so they can see a reminder of their goal.

5. The professional school counselor can tie a string to the soda cans and attach cans to a rope or clothes line. The soda cans will serve as a visual reminder of students' goals and "I cans" (see Figure 43.2).

Activity 2: Block-Letter Autobiography

Competency: Personal–Social Standard—Acquire Self-Knowledge. Through creating the Block-Letter Autobiography, students develop positive attitudes toward self as a unique and worthy person. Students also identify values, attitudes, and beliefs.

FIGURE 43.2. Examples of "I Can" activity.

"I Can" Worksheet

AN ACTIVITY TO HELP YOU IDENTIFY A GOAL
THAT YOU *CAN* ACCOMPLISH,
WAYS YOU *CAN* ACHIEVE THE GOAL,
AND A CREATIVE REMINDER OF YOUR COMMITMENT.

1. On a piece of paper, write a major goal you have for this year. It can be a personal goal, a school goal, an emotional goal—just be sure it is something realistic.

   Example: I want to improve my computer skills.

   I will have a positive attitude in science class.

   I will complete all homework assignments.

2. List at least four "I cans" that will lead you on your way to reaching your goal.

   I can   _____

   I can   _____

   I can   _____

   I can   _____

   I can   _____

   Example: I **can** practice word processing for 30 minutes daily.

   I **can** take a self-paced course about computer application.

   I **can** enlist the help of a friend who knows about computers.

   I **can** purchase software programs that will assist me with computers.

   I **can** use the computer in my lessons (PowerPoint presentations, word processed papers, etc.).

3. Draw pictures or symbols to represent your goal and "I cans," and attach them to a beverage can so that you can see a reminder of your goal.

FIGURE 43.1. "I Can" worksheet.

Materials: Writing paper, block letters (for tracing), poster board, colored pencils

Activity:

1. During an individual or group counseling session, the professional school counselor leads a brainstorming session about personal traits and characteristics.

2. Each student generates a list of traits and characteristics that describe him or her (adjectives or nouns) and writes a 20-word list of personal traits and characteristics.

3. Students develop pictures and symbols to represent the personal traits and characteristics on their 20-word list.

4. Using letters that are the student's initials, each student traces large block letter patterns on one side of a folded poster board.

5. Students fill the large letters with pictures and words that represent the 20 descriptive traits listed.

6. Students can share meanings of their letter pictures with the counselor or with other students in the group.

7. The professional school counselor can lead a group discussion about the combination of common and unique qualities of the students and may affirm the value of each student. Talk about ways to achieve balance among the aspects of students' lives that are depicted in the drawings (see Figure 43.3.)

Activity 3: Past, Present, Future Cover Story

Competency: Same as Activity 2

Materials: Scratch paper, poster board, pencils, rulers, stencils (lettering and picture), sharpies, colored pencils, markers, dictionaries, thesauruses, rope or ribbon

Activity:

1. Using scratch paper, students generate a list of important events in their lives from the past and the present. Students also list future hopes and dreams, such as career plans, travel, family, or education. The list should consist of at least six or seven meaningful events or ideas under each of the three time periods.

2. Students draw pictures and symbols to represent the meaningful events or ideas for each of the three time periods of their cover story on one side of a folded poster board. (They may wish to divide the poster board into three equal areas.)

FIGURE 43.3. Examples of Block-Letter Autobiography activity.

3. Students connect the areas representing the three time periods with a rope, ribbon, road design, or some other connecting graphic.

4. Information about each student's cover story may be discussed with the professional school counselor. The professional school counselor may encourage students to explore career implications of the cover story, to share common themes, and to affirm individual and group self-expression. Discuss alternative ways of achieving goals and consequences of choices (see Figure 43.4).

Activity 4: Career Mascots

Competency: Career Development Standard—Develop Career Awareness. By creating a career mascot, the student demonstrates skills to locate, evaluate, and interpret career information.

FIGURE 43.4. Examples of Past, Present, Future Cover Story activity.

FIGURE 43.5. Examples of career mascot (a yellow jacket was the school mascot).

Materials: Mascot stencil, paper, markers, and colored pencils. Your school newspaper or local newspaper should have a stencil of the school mascot.

Activity:

1. Students use the school mascot to represent a future work career and to explore occupations of their choice. Students are encouraged to select jobs that they might want to do in the future.

2. Students select three jobs in which they are interested and about which they would like to learn more. Students may interview a worker who currently has that job, look in magazines, or ask their parents for assistance in seeking information.

3. The professional school counselor encourages students to think of the job setting, what to wear on the job, typical duties, and symbols of the job.

4. Students trace a stencil of the school mascot. They portray the mascot doing one of the jobs they identified.

5. This activity lends itself well to a Career Day theme and a large group mural of different occupations. The mural could be displayed in the school library. Note: The work-related paintings and murals of Jacob Lawrence are good starting points for examples of career pictures. Also, the works of Norman Rockwell are useful as examples of people at work (see Figure 43.5).

Activity 5: Different Strokes for Different Folks

Competency: Personal–Social Standard—Acquire Interpersonal Skills. Through the process of participating in Different Strokes, students (a) recognize that everyone has rights and responsibilities; (b) respect alternative points of view; and (c) recognize, accept, respect, and appreciate individual differences and cultural differences.

Materials: Still-life display, paper, pencils, and dictionaries to define perspective in art and in life in general

Activity:

1. Students sit in a circle around a table with a simple still-life display set upon it (e.g., vase of flowers, hat and ball, teddy bear).

Figure 43.6. Example of Different Strokes for Different Folks activity.

2. Students are instructed to draw what they see.

3. After 15 minutes, students share their work with the group. Each picture will be different, because they each viewed the display from a different angle.

4. The professional school counselor leads a group discussion about how everyone can see the same situation, and see it differently, because they view it from different perspectives.

5. Students often react to a situation depending on their perspective. Discuss common problems and how different students coped with the problem as a result on a different perspective.

6. How students manage stress is a function of their perspective on the stress-producing situation. Discuss how students could change their perspective (e.g., reframing, cognitive restructuring) as a means of coping with stress (see Figure 43.6).

Activity 6: Symbol of Self

Competency: Personal–Social Standard—Acquire Self-knowledge. Through the creation of "symbol of self" the student (a) identifies values, attitudes, and beliefs, (b) identifies and expresses feelings, and (c) and identifies personal strengths and assets.

Materials: Paper and pencil for lists, graphic arts books with symbols for items, modeling clay (i.e., Crayola Modelmagic), toothpicks (for shaping), white glue, acrylic paint, and inexpensive small art brushes (if students are allowed to paint their symbols of self).

Activity:

1. Students brainstorm a list of 20 words, nouns or adjectives, that describe them.
2. Students draw pictures and symbols that represent the words.
3. Students pick 12 pictures or words to use to create a clay sculpture.
4. Encourage students to select things that they feel they can create with clay.

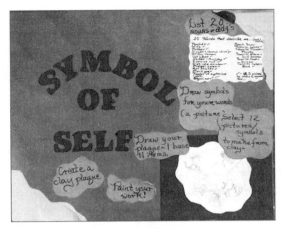

FIGURE 43.7A. Example of a poster describing a Symbol of Self activity.

FIGURE 43.7B. Examples of a Symbol of Self activity.

5. One item will become the base and the other 11 items will be made and glued onto the base. Make the base first and then the items to be mounted on it. You may use colored clay, or paint the items with acrylic paint and then glue them on the base.

6. Let the students' symbol-of-self become the basis for individual/group counseling sessions about student accomplishments. Discuss how to attain balance among those things that are important in the students' lives.

7. Allow students to use the symbol-of-self as paperweights or decorations (see Figure 43.7).

Activity 7: Success Medallions

Competency: Personal–Social Standard—Self-Knowledge Application. This activity is an excellent opportunity for students to identify short and long-term goals.

Materials: Medallion drawing sheet, pencils, clay, paint, yarn or rawhide

Activity:

1. Students create a circular medallion from clay, which represents recent positive experiences and future aspirations.

2. During a small or large-group counseling session, the professional school counselor talks with students about and gives examples of successful experiences to illustrate the concept of successful experience (e.g., learning to swim, playing a sport, performing in from of a group, getting good grades, receiving an award, making friends, raising a puppy).

3. The professional school counselor invites students to think of personal examples of successful experiences. The counselor asks students to list past positive successful experiences on a piece of paper (see Figure 43.8). Each student identifies a major success from 3, 2, and 1 years ago. Ask students to think of a symbol for each success and draw a picture of the symbols for each successful experience. Next, ask students to decide on a future goal for success and create a symbol to represent it.

4. Using clay, have each student create a medallion of success. Punch a hole in the medallion so students can attach yarn or rawhide and wear it around the neck.

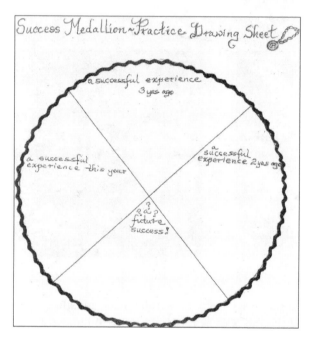

5. Students may also paint their medallion. When the medallion is completed, each student may attach it to yarn or rawhide and wear the medallion around his or her neck.

FIGURE 43.8. Examples of a Success Medallion activity.

Activity 8: Acrostic Self-Poem

Competency: Personal–Social Standard—Acquire Interpersonal Skills. The professional school counselor may use this activity to demonstrate effective communication skills and to allow students to demonstrate their personal understanding of positive self-statements.

Materials: Dictionaries, thesauruses, pens, pencils, art paper or calligraphy paper, calligraphy italic alphabet sheets, lettering stencils

Activity:

1. Students write an acrostic poem about themselves. They may use calligraphy skills or simply write the words in print or script.

2. The professional school counselor provides a brief explanation of an acrostic before students begin work on the activity:

"An acrostic is a word poem in which the student's name is written down the left side of a page. Using each of the letters in the student's name, each student writes a word or phrase for each of the letters in their name."

3. The professional school counselor should create an example of an acrostic about him- or herself to read as an example for the students. The students should brainstorm words and phrases that represent them. Using a dictionary and thesaurus, students refine the content of their acrostic. Each student reads his or her acrostic to the group or to the professional school counselor. Be sensitive to negative and degrading content, and discuss ways to reframe such comments into positive statements of self (see Figure 43.9).

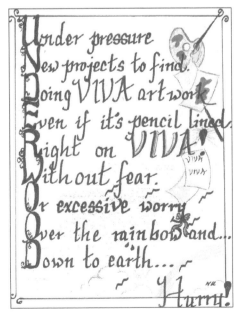

FIGURE 43.9. Examples of Acrostic Poem activity.

FIGURE 43.10A. Example of instructions for a color wheel.

Activity 9: Color Wheel

Competency: Career Development Standard—Develop Career Awareness. Students develop an awareness of personal abilities, skills, interests, and motivation as well as develop hobbies and vocational interests.

Materials: Art paper, dictionaries, pencils, wheel planner (example provided in Figure 43.10A), markers, watercolor pencils

Activity: Students select their favorite color and create a personal color wheel, explaining why that is their favorite color (see Figure 43.10B). The professional school counselor gives the following directions:

1. Write your favorite color in the circle in the middle of your paper.

2. Describe the 12 words with an adjective or phrase (e.g., blueberries—blueberry pancakes, sweet and mild in flavor).

3. Students color their color wheels with watercolor pencils or markers.

4. The professional school counselor may relate the color-wheel activity to one of the "color" personality models. Discussions about personal values represented by the color wheel promote the expression of feeling.

FIGURE 43.10B. Example of a completed color wheel.

Activity 10: The Feet of Clay

Competency: Personal–Social Standard—Goal Setting. Students will make decisions, set goals and take necessary action to achieve goals.

Materials: Drawing paper, pencils, inspirational reading, Model Magic Clay, plastic knives, paint

Purpose: Students ponder their past, present, future and the "steps" they have taken to lead them to their destination.

Activity:

1. Students talk about "where they are" in their lives. The professional school counselor may assist students to discuss (a) life assessment, (b) future goals, and (c) what has made you "what your are today."

2. For students in Grades 7 through 12, read an inspirational reading, such as Robert Frost's poem *The Road Not Taken* (cited in Lathem, 1969). For students in Grades 1 through 6, read a passage that is though provoking, such as Shel Silverstein's (1996) *Foot Repair*.

3. The counselor asks, "What sort of path are you following with your life?" and "If you could make a shoe to represent the path of your life, what would it look like?" The shoe may be a real shoe or a fantasy shoe.

4. Sketch the shoe. Think about how you use your feet to follow your life's path.

5. Give students a small amount of clay, and ask them to make a small replica of the shoe they would like to wear to lead them along life's path.

6. Encourage students to share their replicas with each other and to discuss the purpose of the shoe (see Figure 43.11).

SUMMARY/CONCLUSION

Visual arts can be used as a vehicle to assist students in self-expression as a creative aid in the counseling and educational process. The examples of visual art provided within this chapter are practical, original, and field tested in the schools, and professional school counselors will find the activities to be effective in both individual and group-counseling settings.

(Note: See the CD-ROM for a list of references.)

FIGURE 43.11. Examples of shoes for the Feet of Clay activity.

CHAPTER 44

MOZART TO MTV:
THE ART OF COUNSELING WITH MUSIC

James R. Cheek

Preview

Music of all genres and formats can be easily integrated into students' daily environ-ment as a fundamental part of academic, personal–social, and career development. The activities include music listening, performing, composing, and improvising. No previous musical training, skills, or talent are necessary—just enthusiasm, a passion for student achievement, and a willingness to allow the creativity and art of music to express itself for the ultimate benefit of all students.

Since ancient times, music has been universally recognized as a therapeutic means of communicating and expressing a wide range of emotional, mental, physical, and spiritual responses (Gladding, 2004; Kemper & Danhauer, 2005; Robarts, 2006). Cur-rently, music as a therapeutic intervention can be based on the assertion that an orienta-tion to music is innate and deeply seated in the brain itself; we all respond biologically in one manner or another (Darnley-Smith & Patey, 2003; Jensen, 2003; Robarts, 2006). Music may ultimately contribute to the health, wellness, and overall quality of life of both individuals and society through several major factors:

- Music can increase not only the awareness of our feelings but also the intensity and value of those feelings (Laiho, 2005; Robarts, 2006; Ruud, 1997).
- Music provides opportunities for increased achievement, mastery, and growth in cognition, motor skills, social–emotional communication, and emotional engage-ment (Gladding, 2004; Jensen, 2003; Laiho, 2005; Ruud, 1997).
- Participating in music-making can provide a sense of belonging and community identity (Laiho, 2005; Robarts, 2006; Ruud, 1997).
- Experiences with music can create a sense of meaning and consistency in life through identity development, a sense of agency, and individuation in a pluralistic society (Gladding, 2004; Laiho, 2005; Ruud, 1997).

Music in therapeutic interventions is being widely used and researched, especially in the specialized profession of music therapy. Although many professional school counselors consistently and effectively integrate music into their counseling repertoire, many others are still hesitant, if not somewhat fearful, of using music as part of their developmental counseling programs. Using music in counseling requires no previous musical training or talent on the part of the professional school counselor. All that is required of the counselor is the willingness to allow the creativity and art of music to express itself, whether it is Mozart or MTV.

According to the American School Counselor Association's (ASCA) national model (2005), school counselors should be partners in student achievement and, as such, should be integrated into all areas of the students' daily environment as a fundamental part of academic, personal–social, and career development. Music can be integrated into each of these developmental areas through the guidance curriculum (large-group/classroom guidance activities) and responsive services (individual/small-group counseling). Using music in counseling is not as intense or as prescribed as direct music therapy; rather, it is the use of components of music such as listening, performing, composing, and improvising that can prove beneficial for the students served by the professional school counselor (Gladding, 2004). The following interventions are not meant to be a comprehensive representation of music activities used in professional school counseling; they will hopefully serve as a creative springboard for professional school counselors to create their own unique musical interventions as part of their individual school counseling programs.

EMPIRICAL SUPPORT FOR THE POSITIVE EFFECTS OF MUSIC ON STUDENT DEVELOPMENT AND PERFORMANCE

Empirical studies involving the use of music in therapeutic interventions with children, adolescents, and adults are being conducted internationally through almost all of the helping professional fields. Recent meta-analyses of the effects of music for children and adolescents found that music had a considerable relevant effect in a variety of therapeutic and educational settings (Gold, Voracek, & Wigram, 2004; Standley, 1996). Music can actually *prime* the neurons of the brain for learning. Students will often remember the words to their favorite songs, even if they have cognitive difficulties in other areas. A common example is that many students and adults sing or hum the "Alphabet Song" when alphabetizing materials. As part of ongoing research regarding the educational impact of music on the development of the human brain, Jensen (1998, 2003) highlighted two important observations. First, the human brain seems to be designed for music and arts. Second, using music and arts in educational activities has measurable, positive, and long-lasting academic and social benefits. Jensen (1998, 2003) further suggested that music is an effective tool towards overall developmental purposes, including (a) a means of stimulation, (b) a carrier of words, and (c) a primer for the brain. Thus, according to Jensen, music is effective in increasing and decreasing the neurotransmitters responsible for attention and emotional engagement. In fact, music can be a teaching partner for creating and maintaining a wide variety of emotional states to maximize students' potential and overall achievement in less time with less work.

In general, music can empower, support, and enhance all areas of student development and achievement. It is one of the easiest and most effective tools that professional school counselors have at their disposal. Ruud (1997) has stated that

> music empowers us; it gives us a psychological and cultural platform from which
> to make our own decisions on matters concerning our own life. When we are

successfully engaged in music, we feel we are "somebody"; we gain the right to raise our voice. (p. 94)

RECOMMENDED STRATEGIES AND INTERVENTIONS

Following are recommended strategies and interventions to aid in the personal–social, academic, and career development of school-age youth.

PERSONAL–SOCIAL DEVELOPMENT

One of the most straightforward uses of music is to maximize and support student growth in the area of personal–social development. Using music-listening activities in counseling is especially effective for this developmental area and can be easily adjusted for many different issues and age groups (Newsome, 2003). Further, the combination of music with visual images can provide a stimulus for discussing how music represents feelings. Movies such as *Fantasia* (Walt Disney, 1941) and *Fantasia 2000* (Walt Disney, 1999) can be used with younger students as a catalyst for discussing how feelings can be expressed. The film's use of color and storytelling through music is highly motivational and provides a medium for students to identify and explore the range of human emotions and how they are communicated. An extension for the activity can involve the students creating their own art projects that represent emotions while listening to different types of music. Jensen (2003) suggested another method to encourage the emotional activation of the nondominant side of the brain. He recommended that students hold their art materials in the nondominant hands in order to remove any sense of artistic pressure and to further allow students to freely engage the emotions stirred by the music.

The use of music can be effective with groups addressing any issues or concerns relevant to their current situations. Hendricks, Robinson, Bradley, and Davis (1999) developed a school-based group intervention program using music techniques with depressed adolescents. The intervention involved individual members of the group choosing music that was relevant to them and their current experiences. The music therapy group used the individual selections to process the emotions and experiences that each piece of music evoked. Group members not only discussed the lyrics and their relevance but also discussed the tone (happy, sad, etc.), the tempo (fast, slow, etc.), and the key (major, minor) as indications of how the music made them feel. Each member of the group had the opportunity to share and process their musical selection. The intervention was shown to be effective in reducing depression.

Stephens, Braithwaite, and Taylor (1998) described another inventive and effective group technique. The small-group model consisted of four sessions that integrated HIV/AIDS prevention information with hip-hop music. Each session's music was preselected with a theme that included a HIV high-risk behavior. Participants discussed their general perceptions of each song and artist, which then led to the discussion of the risk behavior rather than the lyrics or song content. The intervention's effectiveness was a direct result of the use of culturally and environmentally appropriate topics and music that addressed the needs and interests of the target audience.

A variation on this technique is using music videos. Often the visual images combined with the music are expressions that the student feels he or she cannot communicate verbally. The images are often powerful representations of what many adolescents are experiencing, as evidenced by massive popularity of music television networks such as MTV or VH1 (Gladding, 2004). Additionally, this activity can be effective when working with individual students through many of the same techniques.

Since the students are bringing their music and music video recordings to school, limits need to be established regarding explicit lyrics and images that may be presented. Additionally, parents and guardians need to receive communication delineating the professional school counselor's permission and the limitations regarding bringing the music to school. In order to avoid potential problems, it may be helpful to let the students bring their compact discs (CDs), iPods, and tapes to the counselor's office before the school-day starts.

Conflict resolution is another major component of an effective school counseling program. Music can be used as an important part of conflict resolution activities. Using musical instruments, students can create musical representations of feelings that are involved in conflict through the use of small rhythm instruments such as wood blocks, drums, or tambourines. This activity can also be done with improvisational instruments made from various available materials. Using techniques adapted from the film *Stomp Out Loud* (Yes/No Productions, 1997), based on the stage show "Stomp," students can use any available materials (e.g., cards, boxes, pencils) to create musical instruments. Students can then create a Feelings Symphony or Music Collage to demonstrate various emotions (Bowman, 1987; Newsome, 2003), especially the feelings involved in the conflict. As part of the conflict resolution activity, the students must communicate with musical instruments before communicating with words. This activity can also be used with two or more individual students who are experiencing a conflict.

A cooperative nonverbal learning activity involving Vivaldi's "Four Seasons" is another method of reinforcing communication skills. While listening to the music, the students cooperatively create a drawing without speaking. The activity focuses on nonverbal communication and collaboration between the students (Newcomb, 1994). This activity could be expanded and integrated into a wide variety of counseling situations using a variety of musical selections.

Character/civility education programs are a vital part of creating safe and effective school climates. The professional school counselor can direct these efforts through classroom guidance activities using music. Educating students about various character traits is part of these activities. For example, the character trait of *respect* can be discussed and supported through Aretha Franklin's song, "Respect" (2003). Using a recorded background track of the song, the students can create new lyrics to demonstrate the basic concepts of the character trait of respect. As part of the culmination of the activity, students can create a line dance or ribbon movement dance to the song. Most likely, some students will want to assist with the movement activity. Table 44.1 outlines simple steps that can be integrated with the song "Respect" by Aretha Franklin. Adding movement to the composed words further strengthens the cognitive mapping and integration and adds an element of fun, cooperation, and team building to the activity.

TABLE 44.1

SIMPLE DANCE STEPS TO BE USED WITH THE SONG "RESPECT"

1. All students line up, shoulder to shoulder.
2. Starting with the right foot, do a "grapevine" step (step right, step behind with the left foot, step right again, and then touch the left foot beside the right foot).
3. Repeat the "grapevine" on the left foot (step left, step behind with the right foot, step left again, and touch the right foot beside the left foot).
4. Three-step turn to the right (take three steps while turning to the right).
5. Three step turn to the left (take three steps while turning to the left).
6. Do a humorous pose to the right ("Cleopatra" pose or "Strong Man" pose).
7. Repeat the pose to the left.
8. "Funky chicken move" (move the legs in and out while flapping the elbows with the hands tucked under the arms).
9. With the right foot, touch heel, then toe, heel, toe, heel, toe.
10. Then turn to the right one-quarter turn so that the lines are now facing the next direction.
11. Repeat the steps.

Although it sounds complicated, writing a song is a fairly simple and effective counseling technique. Newcomb (1994) suggested rewriting lyrics to traditional songs such as "Simple Gifts" and "Happy Birthday" in order to create awareness of personal strengths as well as how to give and receive compliments. One does not have to play a musical instrument to implement song writing. Prerecorded *karaoke* or background accompaniment tracks are readily available in many stores and provide a fun, orchestrated background for new lyrics. Lyrics to popular tunes can be created for a wide variety of counseling uses. Social-skills training and other proactive social activities can be supported and rehearsed by creating new lyrics to highly motivational music.

With regard to multiculturalism, the appreciation of ethnic and cultural diversity can be strengthened through classroom guidance where the music and dances of various cultures can be explored. Students of other cultures can present these musical aspects of their cultures for a more diversified view of individual differences. This can also be expanded to a school-wide activity culminating in a "World Party" celebrating the culture, food, history, and musical diversity of various cultures from around the world.

ACADEMIC DEVELOPMENT

The school counseling program should implement activities that support all students' ability to achieve academic success and become active contributing members of their communities and society as a whole (ASCA; 2005). Because musical experiences are naturally modifying to students' appropriate developmental levels, music can play a vital and effective part in activities that support academic development.

Stress in academic situations can directly impact the success and achievement of students. Besides reducing stress, music can also be used to impact specific stress problems, such as test anxiety. As high-stakes testing and standardized examinations become more pervasive, teaching students stress-reducing strategies is an important part of the professional school counselor's responsibilities.

Cheek, Bradley, Reynolds, and Coy (2002) suggested a technique called Stop, Drop, and Roll. Students participating in a group addressing test anxiety were instructed that, when they physically felt the "fire" of anxiety and stress, they should "stop" (actually put down their pencils and place their hands on the table while concentrating on the coolness of the surface), "drop" their heads forward, and "roll" them around gently while taking three deep breaths. Group members practiced the relaxation technique as classical music composed by Mozart was played. Students who had participated in the groups then taught their classmates the Stop, Drop, and Roll technique with the recorded music, allowing them to demonstrate their new skills in a supportive classroom setting. Also, during the days leading up to the test administration, a school-wide assembly was held to motivate all students to practice the Stop, Drop, and Roll technique to high-energy dance music.

Wilson (1986) suggested another musical intervention to assist students with standardized testing. She created a musical theater production using well-known tunes to promote appropriate test-taking skills. This program could be used with a variety of age ranges and could be adapted to a variety of testing situations. Following is an example from "Meeting the Challenge of Standardized Tests" (Wilson, 1986).

Verse 1

[to the tune of "On Top of Old Smoky"]

For standardized testing

Here's what you must do.

Bring number 2 pencils (hold up pencils)

And scratch paper, too.

(hold up paper)

Verse 2

You'll read from a booklet

And mark on the sheet (demonstrate sheet)

Fill in the best answer

And make your marks neat.

Verse 3

On a difficult question

You may be in doubt,

But it's better to guess than

To just leave it out.

Verse 4

If you finish early

And have time to spare

Check over your answers

Please take special care.

Academically, music can be used for a variety of learning experiences. Through collaboration and cooperation with classroom teachers, the professional school counselor can reinforce academic concepts through promoting optimal emotional states and learning atmospheres with music (Jensen, 2003). The *Schoolhouse Rock* video cartoon series (Newall & Yohe, 1995) addresses content in arithmetic, grammar, social studies, and science. As a professional school counselor, these can be used with certain individuals or prescribed as tutoring for a student who is struggling academically.

Likewise, students with musical intelligence (Gardner, 1999) can use and find success in their abilities that may not be adequately addressed in regular classroom settings. Recent intelligence theories suggest that intelligence is much more than verbal and quantitative abilities. Gardner's (1983) multiple intelligence theory proposed eight competencies—one discrete intelligence being identified as musical intelligence. Another related competency is bodily–kinesthetic intelligence associated with dance, acting, and athletics. Like other theories, some students are better at certain competencies than others. By allowing these students to use their talents and interests, professional school counselors can increase academic and personal self-esteem. Further significant research in cognition has suggested the more stimuli used to encode information, the greater the likelihood of subsequent recall as neural networks are strengthened (Jensen, 1998). Using music in counseling exponentially expands this effect.

CAREER DEVELOPMENT

The professional school counselor's role in career development is to assist students in their transition from school to work, including the development of a positive attitude toward work (ASCA, 2005). Although musical interventions for this developmental area are not as apparent as other areas, music can still be effective.

One of the important competencies for career development is awareness of career opportunities. After using the Internet and various other resources to explore career options, groups of students can create music-video commercials of various career opportunities to share with their classmates. As part of these videos, students should also demonstrate awareness of the training and educational requirements needed to achieve those career opportunities. For example, using music of the students' choice, a group of students can create a commercial for nurses. In the video presentation, both male and female students dress in nursing uniforms and role-play various aspects of nursing care. They include video footage of students studying science and math. When the video projects are presented as part of classroom guidance, then each group can discuss their findings. In addition, this activity is an excellent opportunity for the classroom teacher and the professional school counselor to collaborate in the content areas.

Besides creating video presentations, recorded music and music videos can be used to explore effective job communications. Videos showing both positive and negative representations of communication with supervisors and fellow employees can be shown and discussed. Gender stereotyping can also be addressed by the job roles represented in the selections.

As students get more comfortable with using music as part of their career exploration, they likely will suggest other possible interventions or projects. Once students have been given permission to be creative using music, the possibilities are limitless.

Summary/Conclusion

In summary, music can be incorporated into the many components of the school counseling program. Integrating musical experiences does not require extensive musical training or an unlimited financial budget. As stated by Newcomb (1994), using music in counseling "requires minimal musical skill and maximum enthusiasm" (p. 150). By sharing in the experiencing of music, a culture of acceptance and respect for the students' life experiences is created and maintained; the entire environment and atmosphere of the educational setting is fertile for maximum student success and achievement. The school is a better place because the professional school counselor made the difference as a partner and leader for success. The possibilities are limited only by creativity and the will to let the art of counseling with music enhance and transform the school counseling program for the ultimate benefit of all stakeholders.

(Note: See the CD-ROM for a list of references.)

CHAPTER 45

LITERACY-BASED STRATEGIES
FOR THE PROFESSIONAL SCHOOL COUNSELOR

Barbara Thompson Book and Teesue H. Fields

Preview

There are a number of literacy-based strategies that can support comprehensive school counseling services in classroom settings, small groups, and with individuals. These strategies include all of the six language arts: speaking, listening, reading, writing, viewing, and visually representing. While viewing and visually representing are important in a student's development, we will focus on the four traditional language arts—speaking, listening, reading, and writing—and, specifically, on the counseling strategies of journal writing, bibliotherapy, and storytelling.

Literacy-based strategies have a long history in individual and group counseling with K–12 students (Borders & Paisley, 1992). The professional school counselor can ask students to use various writing exercises to illuminate problems and their possible solutions (Riordan, 1996) or can give books to read to provide information or alternate solutions for problems (Gladding & Gladding, 1991). Storytelling has also been used to help students express feelings and handle problems through a neutral vehicle; instead of talking about him- or herself, the student can talk about the story character and let that fictitious person deal with the problem (Gardner, 1986).

For the professional school counselor, the use of literacy strategies is a natural fit, because the students are already engaged in many literacy activities in the classroom. In fact, when a professional school counselor joins with the already-existing academic activities or builds on those activities, the counseling program gains additional leverage and the comprehensive developmental guidance program complements the academic program of the school. As professional school counselors move to align their programs with the academic goals of the school (Fields & Hines, 2000), the use of literacy activities maximizes the professional school counselor's efforts and increases the chance that the school counseling program will be integrated into the school rather than being viewed as an adjunct service. We will highlight some of the literacy activities that might already exist in schools that the professional school counselor can use in classroom guidance and then discuss how some of those same types of activities might be used in individual and small-group counseling.

WRITING ACTIVITIES

Following are a number of writing activities that can be used in a literacy-based approach to counseling, including journaling, personal-response logs, and a writing notebook.

JOURNALING

Keeping a daily journal is a cornerstone of many classroom writing programs. Researchers of the writing process have established that professional writers use journals as a place to explore topics prior to their actual writing (Calkins, 1994). Based on this finding, the use of journal writing was introduced into the K–12 writing curriculum.

If the professional school counselor decides to tap into the classroom writing program, it is important to be aware of the way journaling is used in a particular classroom. Many teachers, in a belief that students do not have their own things about which to write, assign students a daily topic. Other teachers, in an effort to hold students accountable, correct and grade journals. Both of these practices tend to be counterproductive to self-expression.

By giving students a daily topic, teachers unintentionally send a message to students that their own ideas, feelings, or personal events are not important enough to write about in a journal. While it is true that sometimes students may not think they have anything important enough to record in their journals, teachers assume control of the student's writing when they supply a daily topic. As teachers assume control of the journal, students become increasingly less likely to want to write. This begins a cycle in which teachers (believing students do not have anything to write about) assign a topic, and students (not wanting to write about the teacher's topic) won't write or write poorly or uncertainly.

When using writing activities in conjunction with guidance activities, the professional school counselor could alternate open topic days with some assigned topics. However, when assigning topics, it is important to keep the topic broad enough for all students to be able to use. For instance, using the topic "write about your best friend," is constricting, while "write about a friend" is less so. It is important to also honor the wishes of students who choose not to write or who want to write about something else.

While it is unlikely that a professional school counselor would correct a child's journal, it is important to understand that many teachers do grade or correct journal entries, and this can affect the responses students have to the guidance journal. By demanding that students write editorially correct prose, a teacher restricts the topics students use in their journals. If a student knows that the teacher is going to correct spelling in a journal, he or she is unlikely to take risks in topic choice and language. For example, if a second grader has been to his favorite restaurant and wants to write about that experience, he is likely to change the topic because *restaurant* is a difficult word to spell. Knowing that the risk of spelling *restaurant* incorrectly may result in a red mark in his journal, he may abandon the topic in favor of something easier to spell such as "My Cat" or an "I like" entry. It is important for the professional school counselor to stress that guidance journals will not be corrected and that taking risks in spelling is acceptable.

PERSONAL RESPONSE LOGS

Another classroom writing activity that professional school counselors might try is the *personal response log,* used for reactions to reading assignments. These logs provide students a forum to write about their understandings, questions, and comments regarding their readings. These logs also provide students material from which to begin literature discussions with other students (Short, Harste, & Burke, 1996). If the professional school counselor is using reading materials with students or is reading aloud to students, he or she could make use of the personal response logs that are used for other literature activities.

WRITING NOTEBOOK

The writing notebook provides a place for students to collect pieces of their lives (e.g., snippets of writing, scraps of paper, photographs) as a platform from which to launch their own writing (Calkins, 1994). These notebooks could be used by the professional school counselor to launch classroom discussions about life problems or celebrations. For instance, if the counselor is conducting a classroom guidance unit on loss, students could put a variety of things in their writing notebook (e.g., pictures of people who have died, friends who have moved away, reactions to losses, newspaper articles about deaths or disasters, poems). This gives students a way to process different types of loss and share with others in the class some of the losses they have encountered.

While any of these writing activities might be valuable tools for the counseling program, it is also important to be aware of the various writing activities being used by all of the student's teachers. If a student is asked to keep too many journals or response logs, the student who is already a reluctant writer may resent having to do yet another writing activity. Rather than seeing this reluctance as resistance to the counseling strategy, the professional school counselor could give the reluctant writer an alternate activity.

Journaling, response logs, or writing notebooks can also be used in individual and group counseling in ways that are similar to their use in classroom guidance. The primary difference is that the professional school counselor knows the student better and there is more privacy, so more personal topics can be incorporated (Kandt, 1994). Once trust has been established with the individual or within the small group, the professional school counselor can ask the student to select a passage he or she is willing to share, and that passage can be the basis for a group or individual discussion. Of course the student must be allowed a "pass" if he or she does not want to share a passage. To protect the relationship of trust with the professional school counselor, it is important not to force student sharing.

When using various writing activities in counseling, sometimes a specific topic is assigned, and students are free to write about anything they wish within that topic. An example of a specific topic may be an anger journal, in which students record their thoughts, feelings, and behavior each time they get angry. The professional school counselor and student then analyze some of those situations to better understand what happened and to problem-solve possible solutions. If the intervention is nontopical journaling, the counselor and student may analyze the entries and notice patterns of depression or anxiety that were previously unrecognized in the counseling sessions.

BIBLIOTHERAPY

Pardeck and Pardeck (1993) defined bibliotherapy as the use of literature to help children cope with changes in their lives. Although most professional school counselors use the term *counseling* rather than *therapy* to describe their services, a search of the literature indicates that the term *bibliotherapy* is still used more often than the alternate term, *bibliocounseling.*

The classroom guidance program can easily integrate bibliotherapy into the many reading-related activities that are already part of the school curriculum. By joining with the classroom teacher to use techniques common to the school reading program, the professional school counselor can gain more time for the guidance curriculum. There are a number of classroom activities that can broaden the professional school counselor's approach to bibliotherapy.

TEXT SETS

Text sets (Short et al., 1996) are a collection of books, magazines, videotapes, music, posters, artwork, and so forth that are collected around a particular topic. The materials should be chosen to represent a variety of reading difficulties and should depict a range of cultural markers (e.g., race, class, gender, religion). Thus, a professional school counselor might assemble a text set on "getting along." This set would include a variety of printed materials depicting various ethnic, class, and religious groups, videos, artwork, posters, and music.

After assembling the materials, the professional school counselor would introduce the topic of the set and offer the students an opportunity to choose materials they would be interested in exploring. During the exploration time, which might be one class session or several, the professional school counselor serves as a facilitator, helping students choose materials, engaging students in spontaneous discussion, and monitoring the students' responses to the materials. In an ideal setting, the counselor would leave the materials with the classroom teacher, and the teacher would also facilitate the exploration. This would allow students extensive opportunities to use the materials prior to a discussion. Allowing students to choose among a variety of materials instead of having a book assigned to read can enhance the chance of success. Rudman (1995) stated, "When a book is assigned as medicine, the chances of its being accepted are slim. Rather if informal strategies are used . . . the likelihood of success is enhanced" (p. 3).

When students have had ample time to explore a variety of materials, the professional school counselor can let students choose from a variety of ways to respond to the materials, including sharing their favorite piece of the set, creating a word web using the topic as the center focus, brainstorming words the materials evoke, drawing a picture representing their feelings about the materials, and writing in their guidance journal about a particular piece. Creating a tangible response to the materials allows students to think through their thoughts and feelings prior to an oral discussion on the topic. Once students have made a tangible response, they can discuss their reaction with partners, in small groups, or with the whole class. Knoth (2006) stated in an article on bibliotheraphy that "sharing emotionally complex books before a difficult experience occurs may give children the ability to practice their own personal bibliotheraphy" (p. 275). Using texts sets provides children an occasion to explore these books.

LITERATURE DISCUSSION GROUPS

Literature discussion groups, literature circles (Short, 1997), or grand conversations (Peterson & Eeds, 1990) provide students with opportunities to express their understandings and personal responses to a text. If these already exist in the teacher's curriculum, the professional school counselor can join with the teacher to explore guidance topics. If the classroom teacher does not currently use literature discussion groups, the professional school counselor can introduce the strategy.

It is important to remember that literature discussion groups are not focused on the ability to read material but rather on the personal response to the material at hand. Therefore, it is possible for students to discuss books read to them. This makes discussion groups accessible to students from kindergarten through college. It also makes it possible for less proficient readers to participate in the same group with more proficient readers and for students who are just learning English to participate with their more proficient language users.

To establish literature discussion groups, the professional school counselor should consider the needs of the students regarding reading ability and, in the case of guidance topics, the students' experience with the topic. For example, if students have been reading books about family relationships, it is a good idea to arrange groups so that a variety of family configurations are represented in each group. Putting students from single parent families in the same group will not produce as rich an experience as having a mixture of family configurations in the same group. The same is true for reading ability. A mixture of abilities provides a mixture of responses and actually strengthens the reading abilities of less proficient readers.

Literature discussion groups can focus on materials students have read from a text set, a book they are reading during personal reading time, a book the teacher or professional school counselor has read to the entire group, or a book assigned specifically for the discussion experience. If the professional school counselor uses a book assigned specifically for the discussion, he or she should make sure that each student has a copy of the book and has had time to read the it prior to discussion time. When using this technique with an entire class, one strategy is to collect five or six titles about the topic and provide four or five copies of each title. The professional school counselor can then assign a book to each student or allow students to choose which book they would like to read, based on a book talk the counselor conducted for the entire class.

Once students have had an opportunity to read their book, they form a discussion group and talk about the book. There are many ways to facilitate the discussion. In her book *Literature As a Way of Knowing*, Short (1997) outlined several strategies for engaging children in discussion. One such strategy is called "Save the Last Word for Me." To begin this strategy, the professional school counselor asks students to write on a note card a sentence or two from the book they liked or they thought was important. When the groups meet, students put the cards in the middle of the group and shuffle them around. One student chooses a card and reads it. Each student then comments on the content of the card, with the writer of the card going last—thus having the last word.

The role of the professional school counselor during the discussion groups can vary. Depending on the students' history with literature discussion, the professional school counselor may actively participate by joining each group for a period of time, or the counselor may just oversee the groups, intervening when he or she sees that a group needs help moving forward.

It is also important for the teacher and the professional school counselor to remember that the group discussion will not always be about the book. Using the book as a platform from which to launch more personal discussions is part of the technique for the guidance program and, indeed, for the reading program as well. Often teachers will feel that if students are not talking about the book, they are off task. However, part of responding to literature is the opportunity for the students to relate the literature to their lives.

READING ALOUD

In conjunction with a text set, or at the beginning of a guidance session, reading aloud to students from a book that contains the topic at hand is a powerful manner in which to engage students in reading (Krashen, 1993). In choosing a book to read aloud, it is important to take into consideration the time frame, developmental level of the students, and quality of the literature.

The first consideration is the timeframe for the read-aloud. If classroom guidance time only allows a brief (20 minute) experience, a picture book might be the best choice. High-quality picture books are available for all ages and reading levels. If the guidance session meets daily or several times a week, or if the classroom teacher is willing to continue the read-aloud daily when the professional school counselor is not in the classroom, then a chapter book, Hi-Lo reader, or short novel might be an appropriate choice. Suggestions for read-aloud books can be found in *The Read-Aloud Handbook* (Trelease, 2001).

Another factor to consider in choosing a book is the developmental level of the students. Picture books as a genre are appropriate for all students; however, one needs to consider the students with whom the book is being used. For example, *Smoky Night*, by Eve Bunting (1994), is a book about friendship and tolerance that takes place during a riot. Clearly, this is a picture book that is inappropriate for use with preschool and kindergarten students, but it is appropriate for late primary or older students. The same caution applies to chapter books. While some second and third graders can read a book such as *The Giver* by Lois Lowry (1993), it does not mean that the content of the book is appropriate for them developmentally. In a similar way, adolescents are very sensitive to anything that might appear to be too babyish, so they might reject a novel such as *Charlotte's Web*, by E. B. White (1952), based on the age of the protagonist and the focus on talking animals, even though it is a wonderful book about friendship and loss.

Regardless of time or age level, the key to choosing a good read-aloud is that the book be good literature in its own right. In today's children's literature market, there are many books published that are issue books, which are written to "teach" students a lesson. While some are popular with students and well illustrated, there are an increasingly large number of books that are poorly illustrated and heavily didactic. These books do all the thinking for the student, allowing for no inference or true response on the part of the student. Some books may be so directive that they ask students questions in the context of telling the story. With the plethora of high-quality books for students published each year, these didactic books should be avoided. In addition to having dubious value for helping students think about issues, such books do not provide models of good literature that would enhance the academic program.

SUSTAINED SILENT READING

The professional school counselor can collaborate with classroom teachers regarding the books students have available for personal reading time (often called Sustained Silent Reading, or SSR). Many schools have adopted SSR on a school-wide basis. The professional school counselor can help ensure that materials placed in the individual class libraries contain topics that are congruent with the school's counseling program. For example, if the school is focusing in a particular year on maintaining productive friendships, then the professional school counselor can help teachers highlight books in which productive friendships are evident. By having the materials in the classroom and readily available for personal reading, the topic is introduced to students in an unobtrusive manner. Students can then take their personal reading and apply it to the guidance session.

BOOK LISTS

Along with helping teachers establish classroom libraries that feature books aligned with the school counseling program, the professional school counselor can maintain a list of materials appropriate for guidance in particular areas. These lists may be generated from the counselor's own personal reading or complied from a search of available materials. One technique involves searching Web sites (e.g., www.amazon.com or www.bn.com) for a particular topic. By typing "juvenile fiction" or "juvenile nonfiction" and the topic in the search field, a list of books is generated. Then, based on the reviews provided on the same Web site, the professional school counselor can add the book to the list. Not all reviews are equal, but well respected reviewers such as *Hornbook*, *School Library Journal*, and *Kirkus* are cited on these Web sites. If those reviewers have favorably reviewed the book, the professional school counselor can safely add that book to the list. However, best practice is still for the counselor to read a book before recommending it to students.

There are other sources of booklists to use with students. Perhaps the most used booklist is the one maintained by the American Library Association, which can be found on its Web site (www.ala.org). The American Library Association also publishes *Booklinks*, which contains materials thematically organized for teachers and librarians.

The National Council of Teachers of English (NCTE) and International Reading Association (IRA) also have publications that provide booklists. NCTE publishes a volume entitled *Adventuring With Books*, which is thematically arranged. IRA publishes *The Reading Teacher* and *The Journal of Adolescent and Adult Literacy*, which provide thematically based reviews of current literature for students and young adults.

STORYTELLING

While reading aloud is one way of sharing stories, many classroom teachers also use storytelling as a way to share a myth, book, or personal story. Storytelling can allow the teacher or professional school counselor to be creative and involve students in a more dramatic telling of the story. Also, the book is not between the teller and the listener. Although storytelling takes practice and not every professional school counselor may be comfortable telling stories, Mason (1996) reassured the novice storyteller that if the storyteller likes the story and concentrates on the story instead of the performance, then the storyteller's enjoyment will communicate itself to the audience, even if the telling is not perfect. To enhance the story, Mason recommended using different character voices, minimal props, and allowing students to participate in the story by making sound effects or saying a recurring line.

When selecting a story to tell, the professional school counselor must be sure it is age appropriate and can be adapted to an oral telling. Usually, there is also a time issue, so the story must be short enough to allow for reaction and discussion. There are a number of sources that included suggestions for stories that are appropriate for oral sharing (Gallard, 1996; Mason, 1996; Yolen, 1986).

Another approach is to allow students to tell their own stories. Although most writing classes encourage students to compose their own stories to encourage self-expression and help students understand the writing process, it is less common for students to make up oral stories within the classroom. This may be due in part to the time involved for each student to tell an oral story and in part to fears of inappropriate stories or revelations that are too personal for the classroom. Gallard (1996) strongly advocated teaching students to tell their own stories in the classroom. She believed that when students tell their personal stories, whether they are about triumphs or tragedies, they "strengthen the voices that will allow them to speak their personal truths all through their lives" (p. 18). Telling stories empowers students and allows them some control in situations in which they have very little input. Gallard (1996) also addressed the issue of privacy and suggested the teacher and students talk about privacy before teaching students to tell their stories.

If the classroom teacher has taught students to tell their stories, the professional school counselor can join the classroom storytelling with a guidance topic such as dealing with fear, making friends, or experiencing loss. If the students do not know how to tell stories, the professional school counselor can model storytelling on the chosen topic by telling about a personal incident from his or her childhood and then encouraging students to do the same, either in pairs, small groups, or for the whole classroom.

The professional school counselor is probably more familiar with storytelling in the context of individual counseling sessions. Gardner's (1986) mutual storytelling technique directs the counselor to ask the student for a story with a beginning, middle, and ending. The counselor then tells his or her own story using the same characters and situation but might provide some alternative resolutions or frame the feelings of the characters in different ways.

An alternative mutual storytelling approach (Scorzelli & Gold, 1999) has the professional school counselor and student alternate lines in the story. The counselor starts with "Once upon a time . . ." and the student gives the next line, and so forth. The counselor (or student) writes down each line so that both can see the story as it unfolds. As the story is being told, the counselor or student can emphasize feelings or actions or take the story in a new direction.

Storytelling in individual counseling can be enhanced by a number of props, including dolls, puppets, or a storytelling board that has a background scene with props and pictures of people that the student can insert as he or she tells the story. The professional school counselor can also make use of new technology and take advantage of computer programs that allow the student to select backgrounds, props and characters on the computer screen to aid in telling the story (Erford, 2001).

SUMMARY/CONCLUSION

Literacy-based strategies can be an effective way to support the objectives of a comprehensive developmental school counseling program. By joining with the classroom teacher to adapt activities already in use in the school's literacy program, the professional school counselor can expand opportunities to cover guidance-related goals while enhancing the academic mission of the school. Journaling, bibliotherapy, and storytelling can be used in classroom guidance, small-group, and individual sessions as effective counseling interventions.

(Note: See the CD-ROM for a list of references.)

Assessment in School Counseling

CHAPTER 46

WHAT ASSESSMENT COMPETENCIES ARE NEEDED BY PROFESSIONAL SCHOOL COUNSELORS?

Ruth B. Ekstrom and Patricia B. Elmore

Preview

The assessment competencies used and needed by today's professional school counselors were identified through research conducted by a joint committee of the American School Counselor Association (ASCA) and the Association for Assessment in Counseling and Education (AACE).

Assessment and evaluation skills are important parts of counseling. They are covered in school counselor training programs and in counselor certification requirements. The role of assessment in the work of professional school counselors can be found in models of school counseling work and in studies of school counselors. Work behaviors related to assessment are fundamental to the general practice of counseling (Sampson, Vacc, & Loesch, 1998).

ASCA/AAC JOINT COMMITTEE

What are the assessment competencies needed by today's professional school counselors? This was the question put to a joint committee of the American School Counselor Association (ASCA) and the Association for Assessment in Counseling (AAC; now known as the Association for Assessment in Counseling and Education [AACE]). These two professional organizations appointed a joint committee to develop a statement, in collaboration with practicing school counselors, about the assessment competencies needed to work as a professional school counselor.

The committee began discovering what others have said about the role of the professional school counselor and the assessment competencies needed in this role. Organizations and groups concerned with the preparation and certification of professional school counselors have given considerable attention to the assessment competencies needed by counselors. The following paragraphs summarize the committee found and also include more recent information about professional school counselors and assessment.

The committee began by looking at the Standards of the Council for Accreditation of Counseling and Related Educational Programs (CACREP). The 2008 version of these Standards lists *assessment* as one of the eight common core areas in which all counseling students are expected to have curricular experiences and demonstrated knowledge. According to these Standards, counseling students should have an understanding of individual and group approaches to assessment and evaluation, including the following:

- Historical perspectives about assessment
- Basic concepts of standardized and nonstandardized testing and other assessment techniques
- Statistical concepts
- Reliability
- Validity
- How age, gender, sexual orientation, ethnicity, language, disability, culture, spirituality, and other factors are related to the assessment and evaluation
- Strategies for selecting, administering, and interpreting assessment and evaluation instrument
- Ethical and legal considerations in assessment

In addition, CACREP expects that all professional school counselors know about program evaluation and research—two areas that are closely related to assessment. The CACREP Standards include a section about what professional school counselors are expected to know regarding the development, implementation, and evaluation of school counseling programs; counseling and guidance; and consultation. The development and evaluation of counseling programs often require that professional school counselors use data from standardized testing and needs assessments so as to improve student outcomes. The complete CACREP statement about the skills expected of all counselors, and specifically professional school counselors, can be found at the CACREP Web site (http://www.cacrep.org).

The ASCA/AAC joint committee also reviewed the National Association of State Directors of Teacher Education and Certification (NASDTEC) standards for the approval of school counseling programs (NASDTEC; 1991) and each state's requirements for the certification of professional school counselors. The state requirements are available on ASCA's Web site (http://www.schoolcounselor.org), in the section on Careers/Roles under the section for School Counselors and Members. Most public school systems require that counselors take advanced degree courses in testing/assessment and in program evaluation and research. Trevisan (2000) reviewed program evaluation expectations in state school counselor certification requirements. He found that 19 states and the District of Columbia required some form of program evaluation knowledge and skills, but only Colorado and Washington specifically required the CACREP program evaluation standards.

The National Board for Professional Teaching Standards (NBPTS) has also developed standards for the certification of professional school counselors, whose work they described as being "designed to advance student learning in the areas of academics, social/emotional and career development" (NBPTS; 2002). The section on student assessment reads, "Accomplished school counselors understand the principles and purposes of assessment, and the collection and use of data. They regularly monitor student progress and communicate the purpose, design, and results of assessments to various audiences." (The complete section on school counselor standards can be viewed at http://www.nbpts.org/pdf/schoolcounseling.pdf.) As you read the CACREP Standards, the certification requirements for your state, and the NBPTS Standards, think about your own counseling skills. Are there areas in which you might benefit from additional training?

CURRENT ASSESSMENT ACTIVITIES

Several surveys have demonstrated the assessment and evaluation activities of professional school counselors. Elmore, Ekstrom, Diamond, and Whittaker (1993) found that 67% of a group of ASCA members considered assessment and testing to be an important or very important part of their work. Assessment is one of five major activities of professional school counselors according to Burnham and Jackson (2000), who found that 90% of the professional school counselors in their sample interpreted tests individually for students, parents and teachers and that 81% conducted in-service training with school faculty about assessment instruments and procedures. A survey of professional school counselors in California (Blacher, Murray-Ward, & Uellendahl, 2005) found that they used a variety of standardized and nonstandardized assessment techniques including observing students individually or in groups and conducting structured student interviews four or more times a week; teacher- or counselor-completed student behavior rating scales about twice a week; and standardized achievement tests, student-completed ratings, and career inventories about once a week. The professional school counselors felt their training for carrying out observations and structured interviews had been good. They rated their training in using standardized tests and in the use of teacher- or student-completed rating scales as adequate. The counselors spent a good deal of time using assessment information. They interpreted assessments to students and parents about three times a week; they also used assessment information to identify students' academic achievement levels, career aptitudes and interests, and levels of social skills, each, about twice a week.

A national survey of high school guidance counseling in 2001–2002 (Parsad, Alexander, Farris, & Hudson, 2003) found that academic testing took between 10% and19% of the time for 30% of the professional school counselors, and more than 20% of the time for 19% of the counselors. Testing and interpretation of tests for career planning purposes was available in 93% of the high schools; this service was used by 56% of the students in Grades 11 and 12. Helping students with their academic achievement was the most emphasized goal of high school guidance programs. On the survey, public high school counselors were asked if their state or school district provided in-service training or professional development training on how to interpret test scores and assess student achievement. Overall, 52% of the counselors said they had received such training in the preceding 12 months. Training was most likely to be found in small schools (enrollment of less than 500); rural schools; schools in which 75% or more of the students were college bound; the southeast (62%; lowest in the northeast, 31%); schools that offered more than six vocational courses; and schools that did not have access to an area/regional vocational school. There was very little variation across the percentage of minority students enrolled (51% in schools with less than 6% minority enrollment; 52% in schools with 6% to 20% minority enrollment; 49% in schools with 21% to 40% minority enrollment and 54% in schools with 50% or more minority enrollment).

ASCA NATIONAL MODEL

In 1997, ASCA developed the *National Standards for School Counseling Programs* (Campbell & Dahir, 1997). The Standards addressed students' academic development, career development, and personal–social development, specifying competencies in each area that are defined by knowledge, attitudes, or skills that the student should acquire and be able to demonstrate. These ASCA Standards are the foundation of the ASCA national model (ASCA; 2005); information about this model is available online (http://www.schoolcounselor.org), under the section for School Counselors and Members. The national model also includes a delivery system that describes the activities and methods used to deliver the school counseling program. The management system involves the organizational processes and tools used to ensure that the program meets the school's needs. The use of data is an important part of this management system. The ASCA national model states that a comprehensive school counseling program is data driven. Data are used to affect change within the school and to ensure that every student receives the benefits of the counseling program. This is done through an analysis of students' needs, achievement and other data. The executive summary of the ASCA national model emphasized the importance of monitoring students' progress through the use of achievement-related data and standards and competency-related data. "Collection, analysis and interpretation of student data may be systemic by district or specific to school site, grade, class or individual."

The final component of the ASCA national model is accountability. This requires that professional school counselors collect and use data to evaluate the counseling program and to link it to student achievement. The ASCA standards and the national model make it clear that assessment and evaluation are important parts of the role of the professional school counselor, citing activities such as collecting data from a student needs assessment or disseminating information to help students interpret standardized tests. Professional school counselors are often asked to serve in these roles because they have a better understanding of assessment information than do teachers or secondary school principals, especially when assessment involves test selection, validity, communication of test results, and ethical practices (Impara & Plake, 1995).

As the executive summary of the ASCA national model (ASCA; 2005) points out, "in a world of increased high stakes testing, more and more school counselors are called upon to assist in the preparation for the testing." ASCA takes the position that the appropriate role of professional school counselors is to interpret test results and to analyze them in relation to other measures of student achievement, not to carry out the administrative and clerical tasks of a testing supervisor.

QUESTIONNAIRE RESULTS

After having reviewed the research about professional school counselors and assessment, the ASCA/AAC joint committee developed a list of 39 assessment-related activities that professional school counselors are often expected to do. This list was based primarily on the CACREP Standards and state certification requirements. All of the 39 activities appear in one or more state descriptions of professional school counselor work, although they may not always be *typical* of the work of professional school counselors. These assessment-related activities became the basis of a questionnaire that was administered to a random sample of counselor educators and professional school counselors selected from the ASCA membership list. Both the counselor educators and the professional school counselors were asked to indicate how important it is for professional school counselors to be able to carry out each activity (using the scale 3 = *essential,* 2 = *desirable,* and 1 = *not necessary*). Responses were received from 179 professional school counselors and from 63 counselor educators (Ekstrom, Elmore, Schafer, Trotter, & Webster, 2004).

Ten skills and abilities to carry out certain activities were rated as *essential* by 65% or more of both the counselor educators and professional school counselors. These essential skills and abilities are as follows:

- Referring students to other professionals, when appropriate, for additional assessment/appraisal
- Communicating and interpreting test/assessment information to students and helping them use it for educational and career planning
- Making decisions about the type(s) of assessments to use in counseling groups or for individual students
- Interpreting scores from tests/assessments, and using the information in counseling
- Reading about and being aware of ethical issues in assessment
- Communicating and interpreting test/assessment information to parents
- Communicating and interpreting test/assessment information to teachers, school administrators, and other professionals
- Making decisions about the type(s) of assessments to use in planning and evaluating counseling programs
- Reading about and being aware of current issues involving multicultural assessment, the assessment of students with disabilities and other special needs, and the assessment of language minorities
- Synthesizing and integrating test and nontest data to make decisions about individuals

In addition, the counselor educators rated eight other skills and abilities as *essential,* including several related to counseling program planning and evaluation:

- Selecting, administering, and interpreting instruments for use in career counseling
- Reading or referring to test use standards such as *Responsibilities of Users of Standardized Tests* or the *Code of Fair Testing Practices in Education*
- Selecting assessment instruments to use with counseling groups and individual students
- Interpreting data from needs assessments and other counseling program planning assessments
- Selecting assessment instruments to use in planning and evaluating counseling programs
- Adapting or designing surveys or other instruments to use in needs assessment for counseling program planning and/or in counseling program evaluation
- Designing and implementing plans to collect data for use in counseling program planning and evaluation

Many of the skills rated as essential by both professional school counselors and counselor educators are similar in content to parts of the ASCA (2004) ethical standards. You can read these ethical standards at the ASCA Web site (http://www.school-counselor.org) in the Legal and Ethical section under School Counselors and Members.

Survey results show that the counselor educators felt it was essential for professional school counselors to have the skills needed to develop and evaluate school counseling programs. They also felt it was essential for professional school counselors to be familiar with test standards such as the *Code of Fair Testing Practices in Education* (Joint Committee on Testing Practices, 2004), *Responsibilities of Users of Standardized Tests* (3rd ed.; AACE; 2004), and other key testing documents. You can find these documents at the AACE Web site (http://aac.ncat.edu/resources.html) under Key Documents in Assessment and Testing.

The results of this survey were used by the ASCA/AAC Joint Committee to develop a statement of Competencies in Assessment and Evaluation for School Counselors published in *Assessment Issues and Challenges for the Millennium* (Joint Committee of ASCA and AAC, 2001). This statement of competencies was approved by both ASCA and AAC in 1998 and can be found in Figure 46.1 and on the AACE Web site (http://aace.ncat.edu/documents/atsc_cmptncy.htm).

This statement is intended to help professional school counselors review and evaluate their own skills in the areas of assessment and evaluation. By reviewing these competencies, professional school counselors will be able to determine their own professional development and continuing education needs in the area of assessment and evaluation. After you have read the competencies, ask yourself how your assessment skills measure up to these standards. Then decide what steps to take to improve your own assessment skills.

IMPROVING ASSESSMENT SKILLS

Here are some suggestions to improve assessment competencies. First, check with ASCA at both the state and national levels to see what in-service training programs are available. Check also with colleges to see if courses in assessment skills for professional school counselors are offered. Second, explore the AACE Web site (http:// aace.ncat.edu). Look for links to helpful topics.

SUMMARY/CONCLUSION

We have identified the assessment competencies needed by professional school counselors. Professional school counselors are encouraged to engage in self-evaluation to determine if they have these competencies and to use the identified resources to improve their assessment skills.

(Note: See the CD-ROM for a list of references.)

COMPETENCIES IN ASSESSMENT AND EVALUATION FOR SCHOOL COUNSELORS

APPROVED BY THE AMERICAN SCHOOL COUNSELOR ASSOCIATION ON SEPTEMBER 21, 1998, AND BY THE ASSOCIATION FOR ASSESSMENT IN COUNSELING ON SEPTEMBER 10, 1998[1]

The purpose of these competencies is to provide a description of the knowledge and skills that school counselors need in the areas of assessment and evaluation. Because effectiveness in assessment and evaluation is critical to effective counseling, these competencies are important for school counselor education and practice. Although consistent with existing Council for Accreditation of Counseling and Related Educational Programs (CACREP) and National Association of State Directors of Teacher Education and Certification (NASDTEC) standards for preparing counselors, they focus on competencies of individual counselors rather than content of counselor education programs.

The competencies can be used by counselor and assessment educators as a guide in the development and evaluation of school counselor preparation programs, workshops, inservice, and other continuing education opportunities. They may also be used by school counselors to evaluate their own professional development and continuing education needs.

School counselors should meet each of the nine numbered competencies and have the specific skills listed under each competency.

COMPETENCY 1. SCHOOL COUNSELORS ARE SKILLED IN CHOOSING ASSESSMENT STRATEGIES.

a. They can describe the nature and use of different types of formal and informal assessments, including questionnaires, checklists, interviews, inventories, tests, observations, surveys, and performance assessments, and work with individuals skilled in clinical assessment.

b. They can specify the types of information most readily obtained from different assessment approaches.

c. They are familiar with resources for critically evaluating each type of assessment and can use them in choosing appropriate assessment strategies.

d. They are able to advise and assist others (e.g., a school district) in choosing appropriate assessment strategies.

---

[1] A joint committee of the American School Counselor Association (ASCA) and the Association for Assessment in Counseling (AAC) was appointed by the respective presidents in 1993 with the charge to draft a statement about school counselor preparation in assessment and evaluation. Committee members were Ruth Ekstrom (AAC), Patricia Elmore (AAC, Chair, 1997-1999), Daren Hutchinson (ASCA), Marjorie Mastie (AAC), Kathy O'Rourke (ASCA), William Schafer (AAC, Chair, 1993-1997), Thomas Trotter (ASCA), and Barbara Webster (ASCA).

FIGURE 46.1. Statement of Competencies in Assessment and Evaluation for School Counselors.

COMPETENCY 2. SCHOOL COUNSELORS CAN IDENTIFY, ACCESS, AND EVALUATE THE MOST COMMONLY USED ASSESSMENT INSTRUMENTS.

   a. They know which assessment instruments are most commonly used in school settings to assess intelligence, aptitude, achievement, personality, work values, and interests, including computer-assisted versions and other alternate formats.

   b. They know the dimensions along which assessment instruments should be evaluated, including purpose, validity, utility, norms, reliability and measurement error, score reporting method, and consequences of use.

   c. They can obtain and evaluate information about the quality of those assessment instruments.

COMPETENCY 3. SCHOOL COUNSELORS ARE SKILLED IN THE TECHNIQUES OF ADMINISTRATION AND METHODS OF SCORING ASSESSMENT INSTRUMENTS.

   a. They can implement appropriate administration procedures, including administration using computers.

   b. They can standardize administration of assessments when interpretation is in relation to external norms.

   c. They can modify administration of assessments to accommodate individual differences consistent with publisher recommendations and current statements of professional practice.

   d. They can provide consultation, information, and training to others who assist with administration and scoring.

   e. They know when it is necessary to obtain informed consent from parents or guardians before administering an assessment.

COMPETENCY 4. SCHOOL COUNSELORS ARE SKILLED IN INTERPRETING AND REPORTING ASSESSMENT RESULTS.

   a. They can explain scores that are commonly reported, such as percentile ranks, standard scores, and grade equivalents. They can interpret a confidence interval for an individual score based on a standard error of measurement.

   b. They can evaluate the appropriateness of a norm group when interpreting the scores of an individual or a group.

   c. They are skilled in communicating assessment information to others, including teachers, administrators, students, parents, and the community. They are aware of the rights students and parents have to know assessment results and decisions made as a consequence of any assessment.

   d. They can evaluate their own strengths and limitations in the use of assessment instruments and in assessing students with disabilities or linguistic or cultural differences. They know how to identify professionals with appropriate training and experience for consultation.

   e. They know the legal and ethical principles about confidentiality and disclosure of assessment information and recognize the need to abide by district policy on retention and use of assessment information.

(continues)

FIGURE 46.1. *Continued.*

COMPETENCY 5. SCHOOL COUNSELORS ARE SKILLED IN USING ASSESSMENT RESULTS IN DECISION-MAKING.

a. They recognize the limitations of using a single score in making an educational decision and know how to obtain multiple sources of information to improve such decisions.

b. They can evaluate their own expertise for making decisions based on assessment results. They also can evaluate the limitations of conclusions provided by others, including the reliability and validity of computer-assisted assessment interpretations.

c. They can evaluate whether the available evidence is adequate to support the intended use of an assessment result for decision-making, particularly when that use has not been recommended by the developer of the assessment instrument.

d. They can evaluate the rationale underlying the use of qualifying scores for placement in educational programs or courses of study.

e. They can evaluate the consequences of assessment-related decisions and avoid actions that would have unintended negative consequences.

COMPETENCY 6. SCHOOL COUNSELORS ARE SKILLED IN PRODUCING, INTERPRETING, AND PRESENTING STATISTICAL INFORMATION ABOUT ASSESSMENT RESULTS.

a. They can describe data (e.g., test scores, grades, demographic information) by forming frequency distributions, preparing tables, drawing graphs, and calculating descriptive indices of central tendency, variability, and relationship.

b. They can compare a score from an assessment instrument with an existing distribution, describe the placement of a score within a normal distribution, and draw appropriate inferences.

c. They can interpret statistics used to describe characteristics of assessment instruments, including difficulty and discrimination indices, reliability and validity coefficients, and standard errors of measurement.

d. They can identify and interpret inferential statistics when comparing groups, making predictions, and drawing conclusions needed for educational planning and decisions.

e. They can use computers for data management, statistical analysis, and production of tables and graphs for reporting and interpreting results.

COMPETENCY 7. SCHOOL COUNSELORS ARE SKILLED IN CONDUCTING AND INTERPRETING EVALUATIONS OF SCHOOL COUNSELING PROGRAMS AND COUNSELING-RELATED INTERVENTIONS.

a. They understand and appreciate the role that evaluation plays in the program development process throughout the life of a program.

b. They can describe the purposes of an evaluation and the types of decisions to be based on evaluation information.

FIGURE 46.1. *Continued.*

c. They can evaluate the degree to which information can justify conclusions and decisions about a program.

d. They can evaluate the extent to which student outcome measures match program goals.

e. They can identify and evaluate possibilities for unintended outcomes and possible impacts of one program on other programs.

f. They can recognize potential conflicts of interest and other factors that may bias the results of evaluations.

COMPETENCY 8. SCHOOL COUNSELORS ARE SKILLED IN ADAPTING AND USING QUESTIONNAIRES, SURVEYS, AND OTHER ASSESSMENTS TO MEET LOCAL NEEDS.

a. They can write specifications and questions for local assessments.

b. They can assemble an assessment into a usable format and provide directions for its use.

c. They can design and implement scoring processes and procedures for information feedback.

COMPETENCY 9. SCHOOL COUNSELORS KNOW HOW TO ENGAGE IN PROFESSIONALLY RESPONSIBLE ASSESSMENT AND EVALUATION PRACTICES.

a. They understand how to act in accordance with ACA's *Code of Ethics and Standards of Practice* and ASCA's *Ethical Standards for School Counselors*.

b. They can use professional codes and standards, including the *Code of Fair Testing Practices in Education, Code of Professional Responsibilities in Educational Measurement, Responsibilities of Users of Standardized Tests,* and *Standards for Educational and Psychological Testing,* to evaluate counseling practices using assessments.

c. They understand test fairness and can avoid the selection of biased assessment instruments and biased uses of assessment instruments. They can evaluate the potential for unfairness when tests are used incorrectly and for possible bias in the interpretation of assessment results.

d. They understand the legal and ethical principles and practices regarding test security, copying copyrighted materials, and unsupervised use of assessment instruments that are not intended for self-administration.

e. They can obtain and maintain available credentialing that demonstrates their skills in assessment and evaluation.

f. They know how to identify and participate in educational and training opportunities to maintain competence and acquire new skills in assessment and evaluation.

(continues)

FIGURE 46.1. *Continued.*

Competencies describe skills or understandings that a school counselor should possess to perform assessment and evaluation activities effectively.

Assessment is the gathering of information for decision making about individuals, groups, programs, or processes. Assessment targets include abilities, achievements, personality variables, aptitudes, attitudes, preferences, interests, values, demographics, and other characteristics. Assessment procedures include but are not limited to standardized and unstandardized tests, questionnaires, inventories, checklists, observations, portfolios, performance assessments, rating scales, surveys, interviews, and other clinical measures.

Evaluation is the collection and interpretation of information to make judgments about individuals, programs, or processes that lead to decisions and future actions.

FIGURE 46.1. *Continued.*

Note. From *Competencies in Assessment and Evaluation for School Counselors.* Available online from the Association for Assessment in Counseling and Education Web site (http://www.theaaceonline.com/competency.pdf). Reprinted with permission.

CHAPTER 47

HIGH-STAKES TESTING:

WHAT COUNSELORS NEED TO KNOW

Patricia Jo McDivitt

Preview

The scores of many of the tests currently administered in classrooms are tied to accountability systems whose results might have an impact upon the life chances of students. This chapter serves to inform professional school counselors of what they need to know about high-stakes testing, including understanding the purpose and the link to the standards-based educational reform movement.

A heavy focus is placed on the use of high-stakes testing to determine what students should know and be able to do. The scores of these tests are now tied to accountability systems on which the results might impact teaching and learning. The changing purpose and use of tests over the past few years serve to underscore how important it is for professional school counselors and all assessment professionals to understand the role that high-stakes testing plays in the classroom, including its link to curriculum standards, teaching, and learning.

As a result of high-stakes testing, professional school counselors and other assessment professionals are challenged not only to be actively engaged in understanding the use of high-stakes tests and the interpretation of the results but also to learn more about what these tests actually measure and whether students have had the opportunity to learn what the test questions are asking. I will summarize what professional school counselors need to know about high-stakes testing, including understanding the purpose and the link to the standards-based educational reform movement.

DEFINING THE PURPOSE OF ACCOUNTABILITY

It is important for professional school counselors and assessment professionals to understand the definition of high-stakes testing and its purpose in current educational settings. In the broadest sense, the purpose of any test is to gather data to facilitate decision making. However, there are many kinds of decisions as well as many kinds of information that help make such decisions (Mehrens, 2000). In the past, students' test results were often used to determine their academic strengths and weaknesses so that teachers could plan instruction. Other test results might help students understand their aptitudes and interests in order to explore possible career options or future educational plans. However, in the current educational setting, a great deal of the testing involves the use of tests that are directly tied to school accountability systems, where the results are used to make major decisions about an individual—decisions that might have a direct impact on the individual's future life opportunities.

A test is defined as "high stakes" if it carries with it serious consequences for students or others in the educational community, including teachers and administrators. For example, the results of high-stakes tests are sometimes used, along with other requirements, to determine whether a student is promoted to the next grade or graduates from high school. In addition, school-wide average student scores on a high-stakes test may also be used to judge an entire school's academic performance. For example, high scores on a given high-stakes test might receive praise and financial awards from the community at large; low scores on the same test might bring heavy sanctions.

High-stakes testing applications, such as those previously outlined, often put pressure on students, parents, teachers, and others in the educational community. For example, professional school counselors are now becoming more aware of the added pressure and impact that high-stakes tests are having on opportunities for students. In fact, while many students are becoming desensitized to the entire testing process, once they become aware of what is really at stake, the pressure to pass the test can be overwhelming.

Parents and guardians are also experiencing new pressures. The results of school-wide high-stakes tests may provide them with the opportunity to make important decisions concerning the best educational opportunities for their children. For example, parents and guardians of students in low-performing schools might have to decide whether to enroll their children in a different school or a charter school, or they might be given the opportunity to use federal or state funds to provide their children with additional special training. These decisions may well have a direct impact on a student's future opportunity.

Teachers also face significant added pressure because they are more challenged to help all students achieve the level of performance expected by administrators, parents, and the community at large: "There is a tremendous push to expand national and state testing—including testing students with disabilities and those with limited English proficiency—many of whom have not been included in those assessment systems in the past" (National Center on Educational Outcomes, 2002, p. 2).

As a result, according to Herr (2001), today's tests have

> become a high-stakes mechanism affecting the life chances of many young people and substantially defining the curriculum to which teachers will teach in order to have their students perform as well as possible in state assessments to which they are exposed. (p. 7)

HIGH-STAKES TESTING: RAISING ACADEMIC ACHIEVEMENT FOR ALL STUDENTS

High-stakes testing is also the key component of the educational reform movement. In 2001, President George W. Bush signed into law the No Child Left Behind Act of 2001 (NCLB). NCLB significantly strengthens the federal government's role in both elementary and secondary education and includes a plan for educational reform that focuses on accountability and the use of high-stakes test results to help raise the academic achievement for all students. NCLB outlines the requirements that all states were to implement reading and mathematics tests in Grades 3 through 8 and once again during Grades 10 through 12 by 2006. Science tests are also to be administered to all students at least once in the elementary, middle, and high school years by 2008. In addition, NCLB requires that high-stakes tests be aligned with state content curriculum standards and designed to provide results concerning each student's progression toward mastery of the defined standards. Schools are also to be held accountable for making sure that all students are making adequate yearly progress in learning. Because schools today are being asked to prove that their students are attaining the desired knowledge and skills that will enable them to be contributing members of society, professional school counselors and everyone involved in the process of educating students are now more than ever being asked to assume some responsibility for the outcome (Ardovino, Hollingsworth, & Ybarra, 2000).

CURRICULUM CONTENT STANDARDS: WHAT STUDENTS SHOULD KNOW AND BE ABLE TO DO

The use of high-stakes tests in the educational setting has its roots within the larger movement of the educational standards-based reform. The reform movement that emerged in the 1990s called for high standards for all students, centering around challenging subject matter, acquisition of higher order thinking skills, and the application of abstract knowledge when solving real-world problems (Swanson & Stevenson, 2002). Basically, the reform movement is based upon the following premise:

> All students must learn at high levels, regardless of such factors as race, ethnicity, socioeconomic status, native language or gender. Too often, disparities in achievement among urban, rural, and suburban schools, or between schools in rich and poor neighborhoods, or even between schools from seemingly similar communities are accepted as inevitable. Expectations from some students are often lower than for others, frequently leading to a narrowly defined curriculum for those students. Defining what students need to know and be able to do is intended to facilitate holding all students accountable for the same high learning, no matter what their background or particular school. (Woodward, 1999, p. 19)

In 1993 a Technical Planning Group for the National Education Goals Panel published *Promises to Keep: Creating High Standards for American Students*. The publication served to outline the establishment of curriculum content standards. Curriculum content standards specify what students should know and be able to do (McMillan, 1997). In most educational settings, the term *standard*, much like the term *objective*, entails a process of coming to an agreement about what should be taught. Traditionally, the content curriculum standards or learning targets would parallel educational goals, teaching objectives, and outcomes. However, the term *standard* in the current educational setting has an implication of higher levels of expectation and monitoring that were not commonly connected to the widely used educational objectives in the past (Solomon, 2002). Therefore, the goal of the educational reform movement in the 1990s has been to encourage the development of new and rigorous academic expectations that all students should meet as the United States enters the increasingly complex information age of the 21st century (Woodward, 1999).

In response to the national standards-based reform movement that took place in the early 1990s, many states adopted their own state-specific curriculum content standards. "What is common to standards initiatives is the aim to 'raise the bar' of learning for all students and to replace the minimum competency model sometimes relied on in the past" (Woodward, 1999, p. 20).

Many states also developed their own high-stakes tests, designed specifically to measure students' mastery of these state-specific content curriculum standards. These high-stakes tests are called *criterion-referenced tests*, or *standards-based assessments*. Traditional norm-referenced tests are used to compare performance and to determine students' relative strengths and weaknesses, based on the generalized set of objectives that are common across the country for a given content area. Standards-based assessments are used to determine what students can do and what they know, not how they are compared to other students who took the same test at a given grade level. "Standards-based assessments are the tools used to measure whether or not students have met a particular set of standards and to what level of proficiency" (Woodward, 1999, p. 23). In other words, standards-based assessments report how well students are doing relative to a predetermined performance level on the specified set of educational goals, skills, or outcomes included in the specific school, district, or state curriculum.

To understand high-stakes testing and its impact on teaching and learning, professional school counselors and all assessment professionals need to become familiar with the content curriculum standards upon which the high-stakes test questions are based. The analysis of the content curriculum standards will provide the professional school counselor with the opportunity to gain a full understanding of the fundamental principles underlying what is to be taught. When examining a state's content curriculum standards, professional school counselors might want to follow the guidelines outlined in the report on the review of education standards from the Goals 3 and 4 of the Technical Planning Group to the National Education Goals Panel (1993). A summary of the guidelines follows.

Are the content standards

- challenging, or do they simply hold students accountable to minimum acceptance levels of competency?
- useful for helping students to attain career or educational goals, including becoming productive citizens and lifelong learners?
- accurate and do they reflect sound instructional practices?
- clear and usable so that students, teachers, and parents can easily understand what the standards mean and what they require?
- assessable for all students and specific so that the attainment of the standards can be measured?
- adaptable and able to be implemented in a number of ways depending upon the needs of the students?
- developmentally appropriate?

PERFORMANCE STANDARDS: UNDERSTANDING LEVELS OF PERFORMANCE

The National Education Goals Panel's (1993) publication, *Promises to Keep: Creating High Standards for American Students*, also served to outline the establishment of performance standards, also known as academic proficiency levels. A *performance standard* is a statement that articulates the expectation about what standard all students are expected to meet for a given criterion. It describes an action of the student or a quality of his or her final product (Zmuda & Tomaino, 2001). Performance standards serve to indicate the degree to which the student has mastered the curriculum content standards. In other words, "performance criteria help define the standards by specifying what one would look for as evidence that the standards have been achieved" (Arter & McTighe, 2001, p. 41).

In terms of high-stakes testing, performance standards are also translated into scoring guidelines or performance-level descriptors. Performance-level descriptors are typically written to provide clear guidelines for what should constitute the different levels of performance (i.e., Advanced, Proficient, and Below Proficient) on the high-stakes test. They form the foundation for determining what and how much students are expected to know and be able to do in a given content domain for a particular subject area.

Performance standards can be defined in a number of ways. For example, in a physical education class, a performance-level descriptor or standard might be defined by whether a student can perform a set of physical activities to perfection (e.g., running in place for several minutes, walking on a balance beam without falling, jumping rope for a specified number of minutes). If the student is able to perform all of these physical activities to perfection, he or she would be deemed as having mastery of the standard. In this example, even if every student does not successfully complete each activity, the standard is obvious and easy to understand.

Developing good performance level descriptors involves a careful analysis of the curriculum content standards in order to summarize dimensions of performance. McMillan (1997, p. 36) outlined six steps to follow when summarizing the dimensions of performance that are used to assign a student work to a given level:

1. Identify dimensions of excellence.
2. Categorize and prioritize dimensions.
3. Clearly define each dimension.
4. Identify examples.
5. Describe performance continuums.
6. Try out and refine the continuums.

It is important to know that both curriculum content standards and performance standards have been articulated at a national level in documents published by national organizations, including the National Council of Teachers of Mathematics (NCTM), the National Council of Teachers of English, the National Council of Teachers of Social Studies, the American Association for the Advancement of Science, and the National

Science Teachers Association. For example, the *Curriculum and Evaluation Standards for School Mathematics* (NCTM; 1989) outlines a set of content standards for a reformed mathematics curriculum. The content standards are designed to build students' mathematical power, which involves higher order thinking skills such as problem solving, mathematical reasoning, communicating ideas, and the understanding of mathematics as it relates to real-life situations.

In addition to understanding the performance standards or what is to be expected, professional school counselors also need to have some knowledge of how the standards for performance or the "cut scores" for those who pass or fail are established. Establishing cut scores is directly tied to the purpose of the test. According to a recent American Educational & Research Association (AERA; 2002, p. 5) policy statement:

> There is often confusion among minimum competency levels (traditionally required for grade-to-grade promotion), grade level (traditionally defined as a range of scores around the national average on standardized tests), and "world-class" standards (set at the top of the distribution, anywhere from the 70th to the 99th percentile). Once the purpose is clearly established, sound and appropriate procedures must be followed in setting passing scores or proficiency levels.

With high-stakes testing, standards are typically set by a group of educators or panelists during a standard-setting process. The performance-level descriptors are used by the panelists during this activity to guide where the cut scores should be placed from an academic content standard perspective. The panelists are first asked to carefully review each description of performance and consider the following questions:

> How does each performance level descriptor (i.e., Advanced, Proficient, and Below Proficient) generally address the academic content standards or what students should know and be able to do?

> What are the general skills implied by each descriptor?

> What are the major differences involving what students should know and be expected to do for each level of performance?

Professional school counselors need to verify that the process by which the cut scores are determined is clearly documented and defensible. The purpose and meaning of the scores or performance standards needs to be clearly stated, and validity evidence must be gathered and reported, consistent with the test's stated purpose.

RECOMMENDED ACTIONS AND STRATEGIES: TECHNICAL QUALITY AND WHAT COUNSELORS NEED TO KNOW

High-stakes tests need to be fair and all students should be given the opportunity to learn the material covered in the test. In other words, a fair test is one that provides all students with an equal opportunity to demonstrate achievement. Fair tests are not biased against particular groups. In high-stakes testing, fairness also refers to students having the right to an opportunity to learn the material that will be on the test. For example, students must be told in advance what they need to do to show mastery of the standards, earn a diploma, or what behaviors are expected in school. The notice will give them the opportunity to prepare to meet the requirements (Freedman, 2001).

In addition to the need for high-stakes tests to be fair, they must also be valid: "Test validity means that the test measures what its producer intends it to measure—that is, what it purports to measure" (Freedman, 2001, p. 12). It is important for professional school counselors to know that whether a high-stakes test does in fact measure what it is intended to measure depends upon its clearly defined purpose and the domains of content that serve as the foundation for guiding the entire test development process. McMillan (1997) provided the following questions to help professional school counselors and other assessment professionals determine whether or not a test is valid: (a) What is the extent to which the test matches what is taught and what is assessed? (b) How closely does the test correspond to what has been covered in class and in assignments? and (c) Have students had the opportunity to learn what has been assessed?

In the development of any high-stakes test, professional school counselors need to understand that the development process must begin with a clear vision of what it means to succeed within a given context. At various times during the schooling process, students are expected to know and understand specific subject content, some of which they must know outright and some of which they must be able to retrieve using references when needed (Stiggins, 1999). Knowing what is to be asked of students and what students will be taught is important, because different achievement targets require the application of different assessment methods. The nature of learning is also qualitatively and quantitatively different for certain disciplines. For example, teaching and learning in the subject area of mathematics is often tied to a specified instructional sequence. Therefore, what students should know and be able to do is usually tied directly to the level and quality of the instruction in the classroom. However, when developing a high-stakes test to assess third-grade English/language arts standards, the learning targets might be more generalized and not tied to a specified instructional sequence.

In addition to being fair and valid, high-stakes tests must follow all relevant professional standards as outlined in *The Standards for Educational and Psychological Testing* (AERA/ APA/NCME; 1999). The Standards covers major aspects of assessment including validity, reliability, standard setting, item development, bias, and fairness review.

The AERA (2002) has also issued guidelines on high-stakes testing. The following is a summary of these guidelines, with a special focus on those most applicable to the work of the professional school counselor.

1. *Protection against high-stakes decisions based on a single test.* Decisions that affect individual student's life chances or educational opportunities should not be made on the basis of a single test score or test scores alone.
2. *Adequate resources and opportunity to learn.* When curriculum content standards are introduced as a component of educational reform and to improve teaching and learning in the educational setting, students must have adequate resources and the opportunity to learn.
3. *Alignment between the test and the curriculum.* If a high-stakes test is going to be used to measure students' mastery of curriculum content standards, the test questions must validly measure the content standard as required by the test blueprint.

4. *Validity of passing scores and achievement levels.* When high-stakes tests use specific scores to determine whether or not a student passes, the purpose and meaning of the passing scores must be clearly stated. The validity of the scores must also be established.

5. *Opportunities for meaningful remediation for examinees who fail high-stakes tests.* Students who do not pass a high-stakes test should be given opportunities for remediation. Remediation should focus upon the knowledge and skills the high-stakes test is intended to measure, not just the performance itself.

6. *Sufficient reliability for each intended use.* Scores must be reliable. "Reliability is concerned with the consistency, stability, and dependability of the results. In other words, a reliable result is one that shows similar performance at different times or under different conditions" (McMillan, 1997, p. 60).

7. *Ongoing evaluation of intended and unintended effects of high-stakes testing.* Ongoing evaluation is necessary. Professional school counselors need to be aware of both the positive and negative effects of high-stakes tests.

Additional information that serves to describe how a given guideline might apply to the professional school counselor as a test user and assessment leader in the educational and counseling setting is also provided. Finally, the American Counseling Association (2004) presented a Position Statement on High Stakes Testing (see Figure 47.1), similar in many regards to the area guidelines.

Summary/Conclusion

The standards-based educational reform movement and the more recent No Child Left Behind Act of 200, with its major focus on high-stakes testing and accountability, have had and will continue to have a major impact on professional school counselors and assessment professionals. In summary, professional school counselors need to make sure that the high-stakes test is fair and students have the opportunity to learn the material covered by the test questions; is valid and measures what it is intended to measure; includes the purpose and meaning of the scores or the performance standards are clearly stated; and follows all relevant professional standards as outlined in the Standards (AERA/APA/NCME; 1999).

(Note: See the CD-ROM for a list of references.)

The American Counseling Association's Position Statement on High-Stakes Testing

Continuing national concern over the effectiveness of the American educational system and some related legislation, especially the No Child Left Behind (NCLB) Act of 2001, has contributed to an increased use of "high stakes" assessment of academic achievement. High-stakes testing carries with it serious consequences for students or others in the educational community (e.g., whether a student receives a high school diploma or is promoted to the next grade, whether a school or school district receives rewards or sanctions based upon student performance). An important goal of high-stakes testing is to improve academic achievement and opportunities for all students. Schools are also held accountable for effective learning and instruction by making sure that all students are making progress toward mastery of the curriculum standards. The American Counseling Association (ACA) supports the use of testing and accountability in education. This position statement pertains to high-stakes testing as defined by NCLB and applied in public school education. It is intended to promote principles that ensure accuracy, equity, and fairness in how high-stakes tests are developed, administered, interpreted, and used in decision-making.

Rigorous testing is a necessary and welcomed process for strengthening learning and instruction. It is an important part of assessing how well students, educators, schools, and school systems are performing. The appropriate consequences of high-stakes testing include presentation of high standards and attainment of higher achievement by all students, improved teaching and instruction, and increased access to a quality educational experience for all students. High-stakes testing should increase, not decrease, opportunities for students, be designed to reflect the complexity of learning, and be used to improve instruction.

High Stakes testing can be of significant assistance to educators and policy makers at district and state levels, identifying which schools and school districts most need increased financial, material, and professional resources to achieve parity in the educational opportunities provided to diverse communities. Such test results can also indicate whether the educational system is providing a fair opportunity to learn regardless of students' socioeconomic status, racial or ethnic heritage, gender, or English language fluency. Essentially, high-stakes testing should contribute to motivation and implementation of student learning, instructional effectiveness, and effective policy decisions about distribution of resources.

Recommended Principles

Several basic principles derived from sound testing theory, ethics, and educational practice underlie the following recommended guidelines.

1. *Alignment.* High-stakes testing, along with other pertinent information, can be used to assess and improve the educational system in a state or district. Alignment of assessment with agreed-upon academic standards, curriculum and instruction is

(continues)

FIGURE 47.1. The American Counseling Association's position statement on high-stakes testing.

critical. Standards, objectives, instructional strategies and procedures, and assessment techniques should be continuously reviewed to improve both testing and instruction. Properly implemented high-stakes testing can be viewed as an indicator of program progress and collective student achievement.

2. *Multiple Measures.* No decision about student educational status or future opportunities or any teacher, school, or school system should be based on a single high-stakes test score. Decision makers should use multiple assessment measures from multiple respondent sources to inform educational decisions. For individual students, these could include teacher-made exams, portfolios of student work, grades, formative and summative assessments, classroom-based assessments, and other performance measures.

3. *Impact.* The impact of test decisions based on high-stakes testing results must be closely monitored to identify and minimize detrimental consequences on individuals or groups of students.

4. *Opportunity to Learn.* All students must have an equitable opportunity to learn the material to be assessed using high-stakes testing. This is especially important for racial and ethnic minorities, students with disabilities, students with limited English proficiency, and students from economically disadvantaged environments. High-stakes tests should measure student achievement, and every effort should be made to help all students reach the desired level of achievement by improving influences on student academic success, such as the quality of instruction, availability of school resources, and level of parental involvement.

5. *Availability of Remediation.* High-stakes tests should allow educators to understand a student's strengths and weaknesses to better deliver effective instruction to that student to enhance learning. Students should be given the opportunity to demonstrate mastery of content measured by high-stakes tests several times and students who fall below required levels of performance on high-stakes tests should be identified and provided remedial assistance (i.e., after school programs, summer school, tutoring).

6. 6. *Resources.* High-stakes testing procedures that demand individual and systemic accountability must be coupled with the necessary resources. When high-stakes tests identify consistent deficiencies, educational institutions need to make sufficient resources available to ameliorate problems.

7. *Development of Tests.* High-stakes tests must be of very high quality. Such tests must be technically sound; free of gender, racial, and cultural bias; and produce reliable, valid scores. High-stakes tests should be constructed using a variety of formats and facilitate demonstration of a range of cognition, including depth of knowledge.

8. *Usefulness.* A useful high-stakes test can be interpreted with ease by educators and the results can be readily understood by parents and students. Parents and students should also be well aware of the purposes and consequences of high-stakes testing.

9. *Validity of Scores for Diverse Populations.* A high-stakes test should adhere to the principles of universal design, including having questions that are concise and readable. The questions should measure what they are intended to measure, be sensitive of the diverse nature of student populations, and have a clear, easily understandable format and stimuli. If possible, high-stakes tests should be administered

FIGURE 47.1. Continued.

in a language the student readily understands. If not, reasonable accommodations, modifications, and alternative assessments must be provided across all testing situations for students with limited English proficiency. Test developers must provide guidance on approved accommodations and study the efficacy of those accommodations through field tests.

10. *Policies and Applications.* Policy makers at the state and federal levels are responsible for creating a fair, just, and accurate high-stakes testing process. Ongoing research should include, but not be limited to, studying the consequences of such testing, both intended and unintended; methods for improvement of the testing process and actual improvement to assessment models; the effects on graduation rates, dropout rates, student anxiety and mental health; the impact on referral for special education services; and the effect of high-stakes testing on instructional practices and course content.

Policy makers should further ensure that high-stakes testing is an open process, so that all persons affected understand what will be expected of them, what is to be measured, the implications of test results, and what future steps are required for academic improvement where needed. All technical information concerning the development, uses, criteria, and results of the test should be available for public inspection. State departments of education should develop, publish, and distribute information on the purposes of high-stakes testing, including cautions and limitations regarding its use.

Teachers, school administrators, and students should be involved in all phases of assessment program development. Teachers should be involved in external evaluation procedures, including review of questions for various considerations, such as whether oa question measures what it is intended to measure. Parents, school administrators, and the community at large should be given opportunities to review technical information and test interpretation information.

For the results of high-stakes tests to be accurate and meaningful, all those involved must adhere scrupulously to program policies and procedures. In addition, due process procedures for contesting decisions based upon high-stakes testing, such as appeals, waivers, and integrating other sources of information about the student's academic achievement, must be formalized, specific, and disseminated. Finally, student identities must be protected, with scores revealed only to those with a clear right to know as determined by the academic needs of the student.

CONCLUSION

High-stakes testing can be used to support accountability in education and to identify segments of an educational system that need assistance. The focus of high-stakes testing should be to improve the nation's educational system, and thus improve educational achievement and opportunities for all. In order to provide adequate safeguards, ACA encourages its members, educators and policy makers to become knowledgeable of and use the guidelines outlined in this position statement, the American School Counselor Association position statement (ASCA; 2004), the *Standards for Educational and Psychological Tests* (AERA, APA, & NCME; 1999), *Code of Fair*

(continues)

FIGURE 47.1. *Continued.*

Testing Practices in Education (JCTP; 2004), *Responsibilities of Users of Standardized Tests* (AACE; 2003), and *Rights and Responsibilities of Test Takers* (JCTP; 2000).

Adherence to these principles will lead to more accurate decisions about individual students, teachers and schools through the proper use of high-stakes testing. The American Counseling Association advocates the appropriate use of high-quality and fair high-stakes tests used to improve the education services delivered to children and youth. In the end, the goal of high-stakes testing should be to assure that students are able to benefit from rigorous educational programs delivered by highly qualified teachers, and graduate from high school with the educational foundation to access all of the opportunities offered by society.

REFERENCES

American School Counselor Association. (2004). *Position statement: High-stakes testing.* Retrieved May 1, 2005, from http://www.schoolcounselor.org/content.asp?contentid=211

Association for Assessment in Counseling and Education. (2003). *Responsibilities of users of standardized tests.* Alexandria, VA: Author.

American Educational Research Association, American Psychological Association, & National Council on Measurement in Education. (1999). *Standards for educational and psychological testing.* Washington, DC: American Educational Research Association.

Joint Committee on Testing Practices. (2000). *Rights and responsibilities of test takers: Guidelines and expectations.* Washington, DC: Author.

Joint Committee on Testing Practices. (2004). *Code of fair testing practices in education.* Washington, DC: Author.

Note. The American Counseling Association Position Statement on High-Stakes Testing was developed by an ad hoc task force of the American Counseling Association. The following counseling and education assessment professionals contributed to the drafting of this document: Dr. Bradley T. Erford (Chair), Alan Basham, Dr. Carol Dahir, Dr. John Fremer, Dr. Darrell Luzzo, Patricia Jo McDivitt, and Dr. Janet Wall. ACA–Governing Council liaisons were Dr. Michael Hutchins and Dr. Lynn Linde. From American Counseling Association, 2004, Alexandria, VA: Author. Reprinted with permission.

FIGURE 47.1. *Continued.*

CHAPTER 48

PARENTS' QUESTIONS ABOUT TESTING IN SCHOOLS, AND SOME ANSWERS

Mary Ann Clark and Larry C. Loesch

Preview

Testing in schools is both extensive and complex and, consequently, parents have many questions about testing and their child's part in it. We present some of the questions most frequently asked by parents about testing and some effective responses to those questions that can be used by professional school counselors.

Testing, or assessment, plays a vital role in education and is used for a variety of purposes. For example, assessment results may be used to monitor student performance, assess student potential, improve teaching and learning activities, evaluate programs and schools, and serve as the basis upon which to make school policy decisions. Test results also are often a major criterion upon which public perception about the quality of schools is based. Thus, testing is a fundamental activity in every school and a vital component for setting educational standards and monitoring progress toward them (CTB-McGraw Hill, 2006).

WHY DO WE HAVE TESTING IN THE SCHOOLS?

Tests yield individual and group student data that can be helpful in educational decision making and planning. Of course, each student is unique and varies in characteristics and range of abilities, talents, and achievements. For example, some are good at reading while others excel in math, and some achieve at their current grade level while others function above or below their current grade level. Because of the individuality and associated range of possibilities, school teachers, professional school counselors, administrators, and parents need as much information as possible about students in order to provide the best teaching and learning environments and activities for each student and classroom group. Testing is an effective and efficient way to obtain useful information about students. Some more specific reasons for testing include the following.

TO INCREASE LEARNING FOR EACH STUDENT

Education is most effective when it is tailored to the greatest extent possible to the specific needs and abilities of each student. Test data can help to pinpoint each student's strengths and areas in need of improvement and to identify the best ways for each student to be taught and to learn.

TO COMPARE STUDENTS WITH OTHERS AND WITH THEMSELVES

Educators and others responsible for making decisions that affect a child's education need comparative information—that is, it is important to know how each student is performing in specific learning and skill areas relative to other students in his or her grade as well as how the student is performing over time. Such educational decisions include which principles and competencies are to be taught, which activities and materials are to be used, which curriculum is to be followed, and how students should be organized in a classroom or school. Assessment data can provide decision makers with such comparative information. Of course, the information also is helpful as feedback for students, parents, and teachers.

TO FACILITATE APPROPRIATE EDUCATIONAL PLACEMENT

Test scores are one type of information (among others, such as grades and teacher and parent observations and information) that helps to place each student in the most appropriate educational situation. For example, although standardized test data may not be used as the sole criterion to enroll a student in a specific educational placement, they may be used for initial screening for further, more comprehensive evaluations as well, as subsequently to determine the effectiveness of the placement.

TO IMPROVE INSTRUCTION

Test results are perhaps the most common way to determine if learning objectives are being met, including learning objectives developed at the local, state, or national levels. Examination of total test and individual item results can help educators adjust teaching methods to achieve the highest possible learning benefits for each student. Also, grade- and school-wide test results may be used to assist in planning school improvements and curriculum modifications.

TO INFORM PARENTS

Parents have both a right and a desire to know how their child is performing in school, particularly in regard to the child's level of mastery of specific learning and performance objectives in relation to the student's grade level or to the student's peers, either locally, statewide, or nationally. Standardized test results are an objective way to provide such information to parents.

TO INFORM COMMUNITY MEMBERS

Test data help all members of a school community be informed about the performance of students in the community's schools in both absolute (i.e., how much knowledge and how many skills are actually being learned) and relative (i.e., compared to similar students at the state or national level) contexts. With this information, areas of both strength and concern at a classroom, school, and district levels can be readily identified.

WHAT KINDS OF TESTS ARE GIVEN, AT WHAT GRADE LEVELS, AND WHEN?

A wide variety of tests are administered in schools and for an equally wide variety of reasons. In general, tests may be administered in schools to assess a student's general cognitive ability (i.e., intelligence), academic and other aptitudes, achievement in various academic areas, career and leisure interests, and personal characteristics. All but one of these types of tests usually are administered only by student-services specialists, such as professional school counselors or school psychologists, in response to the unique needs and circumstances of individual students (e.g., for identification of learning problems or placement in specialized instructional circumstances, assistance with career planning, or application for postsecondary education). The notable exception is achievement testing, which is by far the most common type of testing done in schools. Achievement tests typically are either nationally standardized tests, which are purchased by the local school system or statewide from commercial testing companies and mandated tests, which are created and distributed by the state educational agency and administered in all public schools in the state.

Frequently, representatives of the local school system determine whether, which, and at what grade levels nationally standardized tests will be administered in the local schools. The tests selected usually have been chosen because they closely reflect the learning objectives of the school system at the various grade levels in which the tests are administered. Most school systems administer nationally standardized achievement tests because local-area learning objectives are usually more numerous (i.e., comprehensive) than those stipulated at the state level, and, therefore, national standardized tests usually give more specific information than statewide tests. For example, nationally standardized tests are used frequently to measure learning in areas such as reading comprehension and mathematics, social studies, science, and language arts skills.

All states have their own state-specific testing programs, but there are many commonalities among statewide testing programs. For example, most states administer their own (i.e., developed by the state's education agency) statewide tests to measure the mastery of student competencies deemed by the state education agency to be necessary at particular grade levels. In the vast majority of states, mastery at minimum criterion levels also is required for high school graduation. Frequently, students are given multiple opportunities to pass the tests.

Nationally standardized tests are administered at various times throughout the school year at the discretion of the local school district. However, statewide achievement tests typically are administered in the spring of the academic year. Some states now combine the two types of tests (i.e., national and state) under the umbrella of the statewide achievement testing program.

WHAT ARE ALL THE DIFFERENT TYPES OF TEST SCORES?

In general, there are two major types of achievement tests. The most common type is known as *norm-referenced* tests, which yield scores that compare a child's performance to that of a much larger group of other children at the same grade or ability level who took the same test at approximately the same time in the school year. This larger group is called the *norm group*. A student's test scores are often reported in percentile ranks, which tell where the student's score is in relation to the larger group. Percentile ranks range from a low of 1 to a high of 99, with 50 representing the middle (and average) score. For example, if a student has a percentile rank of 75, it means that 75% of the norm group students achieved a score lower than the student's score, and 25% of the norm group students achieved a score higher than the student's score. Of course, the greater the similarity between the student and the norm group members, the more valid the comparison.

Students do not pass or fail a norm-referenced test. Scores from norm-referenced tests are intended to give educators and parents an objective picture of how a particular student at a specific grade level is progressing in a specific subject or in school in general. Typically, norm-referenced scores can show whether a student is doing better in some academic areas rather than others or if the student is improving his or her relative standing in specific subject matter or skill areas over time.

Sometimes percentiles are reported for several norm groups, allowing a student's score(s) to be compared simultaneously to, for example, national, state, or local-area norm groups. Although a student's actual (or *raw*) score is the same on a particular test, the percentile corresponding to that score may vary, depending on the norm group to which it is compared.

The results of a norm-referenced test are sometimes reported as stanines instead of as percentile ranks. *Stanine* is an abbreviation for "standard nine," because the range of percentiles is divided into nine groups of percentile ranks. Thus, a stanine is actually a grouping of percentiles. Stanines vary from a low of 1 to a high of 9. The *approximate* percentile-rank bands represented by stanines 1 through 9 are 4, 8, 12, 16, 20, 16, 12, 8, and 4, respectively. For example, a student performing in the first stanine may have a percentile rank of 1, 2, 3, or 4. A student in the ninth stanine may have a percentile rank of 97, 98, 99 or higher. A student whose score is reported as the fifth stanine has achieved a score that is between the 40th and 60th percentile. Stanines provide much less specific information than percentiles, because each student's score lies within a band of percentiles.

Another frequently reported type of score is the *grade equivalent*, which shows the grade level of students for whom a score is considered average or typical. For example, a grade equivalent of 4.5 means that the student's score is the same as what the average score of students in the fifth month of the fourth grade would have been if those students had taken the same test. Grade equivalent scores should not be compared across test takers, because the same grade-equivalent score may not always stand for the same amount of learning for the students compared. In general, grade-equivalent scores are quite frequently misrepresented or misinterpreted and therefore should be used only with persons who have full understanding of what they mean.

The other major type of achievement tests is known as *criterion-referenced tests*. The "criteria" to which the title refers are statements of *very* specific skills or competencies for particular curricular areas, such as mathematics, science, or language arts. Although the scores from criterion-referenced tests may be reported in different ways, all of them basically reflect the numbers of skills or competencies the student has mastered in a particular educational area (i.e., subject). These scores are most often reported as percentage of correct answers achieved on a particular criterion-referenced test. In addition, the number of specific criteria met for each curricular area also usually is reported. Each score thus represents an individual level of achievement rather than a comparison to a norm group.

Many statewide testing programs use criterion-referenced tests and have a specific score that must be equaled or exceeded (often called a "cut" score) for the student to pass the test. A student's score for these tests also may be reported as percentile ranks to show how the student scored compared to a statewide norm group.

Both norm-referenced and criterion-referenced tests provide information about each individual student's level of performance and that of the student's peer group. Although one type is not necessarily better than the other, it is important to know which type of test is used to be able to interpret the resulting scores correctly.

HOW ARE ACHIEVEMENT TESTS DIFFERENT FROM COLLEGE ADMISSIONS TESTS?

Achievement tests are used for a variety of educational purposes in schools and are administered at various grade levels. In contrast, college admissions tests are intended to predict success in college and therefore often have the very specific purpose to assist in determining who is to be admitted to a college or university and who is not. They are administered to high school students, usually juniors or seniors, seeking admission to an institution of higher education. The students' test results are usually submitted with their college or university applications.

The *Scholastic Assessment Test* (SAT) Reasoning Test, administered by the College Board (2006), a commercial testing company, yields three main scores. The Critical Reading section assesses ability to use vocabulary and to comprehend written text effectively. The Math section assesses understandings of and ability to apply principles of mathematics. The Writing section assesses ability to develop and communicate ideas effectively. The College Board also administers the SAT Subject Tests, a set of achievement tests in subject areas such as history, mathematics, foreign languages, and science. Students usually have a choice of which SAT Subject Tests they take, although the tests taken may be specified or required by the college or university to which admission or advanced placement is sought. Scores on each form of the SAT are reported using a scale of 200 to 800, with an intended mean of 500. A percentile rank also is given on the student's score report, with the norm group being college applicants. More information about the SAT and issues related to it can be found on the College Board Web site (http://www.collegeboard.com).

The *American College Test* (ACT) is produced and administered by the American College Testing Program (2006), another commercial testing company. The ACT's *Tests of Educational Development* are curriculum-based achievement tests covering four subject areas: mathematics, reading, English, and science. Each test yields a score on a scale between 1 and 36. A composite score, which is the average of the four sections, also is reported. Corresponding percentile ranks are reported for college-bound seniors. For 2005 college-bound high school seniors, the average ACT Composite score was 21.9 for students who had completed a "college-bound core curriculum" and 19.5 for those who had not completed the core courses. More information about the ACT can be found at the American College Test Web site (http://www.act.org).

Colleges and universities often give applicants the choice of taking either the SAT or the ACT. However, some colleges do not require either for admission, and some require it only for placement purposes once the student has been admitted and enrolled. SAT or ACT scores also are often used for academic advising and scholarship or loan applications prior to or soon after admission to a college or university.

The *Preliminary Scholastic Aptitude Test* (PSAT)/*National Merit Scholarship Qualifying Test* (NMSQT) is administered each October to high school sophomores and/or juniors. It is designed to give students practice for the SAT Reasoning Test. However, the scores also are frequently used as criteria for students to qualify for scholarship and recognition programs.

WHAT OTHER TYPES OF ASSESSMENT ARE USED IN THE SCHOOLS?

One type of assessment becoming more widely used in schools is writing samples, and in fact, many statewide testing programs now require students to write narrative answers to questions. Another approach to assessment used more frequently is a portfolio of student work. With a focus on the outcomes of educational experiences, students use portfolios to display samples of their work in various subject-matter areas and are evaluated in regard to the final products of their efforts. Many educators believe it important to look at the whole student, and work samples provide for such an approach to evaluation of student performance. Unfortunately, portfolio assessment is notoriously unreliable (i.e., yields inconsistent evaluations), and therefore the results of portfolio assessment techniques should be considered cautiously.

ARE TESTING ACCOMMODATIONS MADE FOR CHILDREN WHO HAVE A DISABILITY?

In accord with the Americans with Disabilities Act of 1990 and Section 504 of the Rehabilitation Act of 1973 (as well as other applicable laws), any student who has a documented physical, emotional, or cognitive (e.g., learning) disability *may* be given special accommodations during testing. To receive accommodation, evidence of the disability must be presented to the school system or other agency administering the test *before* a test is administered. Typically, a student who has a disability that would qualify for a testing accommodation also will have either an Individualized Education Program (IEP) or be on a Section 504 plan at the school. Therefore, the planning team that worked with the parents, teachers, and child to develop the IEP or 504 plan will have given consideration to accommodations for the student's involvement in any testing situation. The college testing programs described previously also provide accommodations for students with documented disabilities. Such documentation of disability and needed test accommodation must be updated at a minimum of every 3 years for the college testing programs.

The testing accommodations provided to a student are determined on an individual basis and depend on the nature of the individual student's disability. Typical accommodations for students with disabilities include extending testing time, administering the test in an isolated (i.e., distraction free) environment, using a large print version of the test, having a reader present the items to the student orally,or allowing responding on a computer instead of paper-and-pencil form of the test. Testing companies or agencies are aware of when a student is given a testing accommodation in order to score the test properly. However, test accommodation information may or may not be disclosed to test score recipients.

WHAT CAN PARENTS DO TO HELP THEIR CHILD DO WELL ON TESTS?

One of the best things parents can do to help their student do well on tests is to become informed about the testing done in their child's school. Parents should talk with professional school counselors, teachers, and administrators to learn which tests will be administered to their child, when, and most importantly, for what purposes. Parents who are knowledgeable about the testing done in schools are the best possible test preparation and performance resources for their child.

Another important thing parents can do is to help their child adopt an appropriate attitude about participation in the testing process. Children do best on tests when they have a clear sense of why it is important to perform well (i.e., have motivation to do well). Parents can help their child achieve this perspective by talking with students about the testing process, its purposes, and how the results will and will not be used. In the ideal situation, the child will have a *little* anxiety about participating in the test(s) (because a *little* anxiety represents motivation to do well) but not be so anxious so as to inhibit performance on the test(s).

Children will do best on national or statewide tests when they are well prepared in regard to the material or skills being assessed. Therefore, parents can help children perform well on these tests by helping them to regularly keep up with their schoolwork. There is a strong, positive relationship between how well children do in school and how they perform on tests. In general, good students are good test-takers.

Parents also can help children do well on tests by helping them review what is to be covered on the tests. For example, parents can help their children review what they have learned in their classes at school, organize class notes and study aids, and develop a schedule for preparation. In other words, parents can help children develop good study habits, which are similar in many ways to good test-preparation habits. Many schools currently send home a booklet prior to test taking for parents to review with their child that contains sample test instructions and questions. Going over such materials can help familiarize a child with the format and sample content of tests they will be taking. It also can help parents become more familiar with what to expect with regard to the testing program.

Human performance of any kind has the greatest chance for success when the human body is well prepared to function. Test taking is no exception. Therefore, parents can help children do better on tests by ensuring that they are well rested and well fed prior to the testing period. Sufficient sleep and appropriate nourishment are essential for maximized mental performance, and parents can have a direct influence on these conditions for their child as the testing time approaches. For example, eating fresh fruits and vegetables and drinking natural fruit juices can help to reduce stress and enhance mental functioning, while eating processed junk foods such as burgers and fries and drinking carbonated drinks may increase stress and inhibit mental functioning.

Parents also can advise their child about good test-taking practices. For example, they can advise their child to arrive at an appropriate time before the test, have the appropriate test-taking materials ready, and listen to or read the test directions carefully. They can help their child with a time-management plan for taking the test, such as helping the child determine the average time for response to each item while allowing some time at the end for review of responses. Parents also can advise their child to find a sitting position of good posture and to shift sitting positions as necessary during the testing. They can discuss with their child whether guessing at answer choices is appropriate for the test, based on information that can be obtained from the test administrator before the testing. And finally, parents can talk to their child about reading each item and response choice carefully before making or selecting an answer.

WHAT ARE SOME OTHER GOOD SOURCES OF HELP ABOUT TESTS AND TEST PREPARATION FOR PARENTS?

Get on the Net! The Internet provides a wealth of information that is current and useful. A good tactic is to do a keyword search using any of the major Internet search engines and using phrases such as *educational testing, test taking, test preparation, study skills,* or *learning skills.* Also, investigate Web sites of the testing companies that produce and provide the tests to be taken. In addition, most states have a Web site for their department/division of education that usually contain information about state testing programs. Finally, many local school systems have their own Web sites that describe information and test dates concerning local testing programs. One note of caution about the use of the Internet for information: There are no quality controls on what is placed on the Internet, so exercise care in interpreting what is found.

(Note: See the CD-ROM for a list of references.)

CHAPTER 49

WHAT PROFESSIONAL SCHOOL COUNSELORS NEED TO KNOW ABOUT INTELLIGENCE TESTS

Jose Arley Villalba and Peggy S. Byrer

Preview

Professional school counselors need to understand the basic concepts of intelligence testing. We present general information, types and characteristics, ethical guidelines, multicultural aspects, and the responsibilities of professional school counselors with regard to intelligence tests.

Cognitive and general ability instruments, or intelligence tests (IQ tests), form the basis for most psychoeducational reports (Esters, Ittenbach, & Han, 1997). Psychological reports for individual students present data and recommendations related to special education services and Section 504 accommodations for which students may be eligible (Villalba & Sheperis, 2004). Current trends in school reform are calling for all educators, and especially professional school counselors, to establish a more active and defined role in special education placement procedures and services (Frye, 2005). Although most educators have received some type of basic instruction regarding assessment, instrument development, and working with individuals with special needs, professional school counselors who have a master's degree tend to have advanced coursework in assessment (Esters & Ittenbach, 1999). For these reasons, professional school counselors must be able to demonstrate their awareness and understanding of intelligence tests (i.e., IQ tests, cognitive ability measures), and how they affect school students.

School psychologists receive specific training and are typically responsible for administering and interpreting most intelligence tests in school settings (Casby, 1992; DeThorne & Schaefer, 2004; Villalba & Sheperis, 2004). However, most school psychologists are assigned to several schools within a district and may only visit one particular school once or twice per week. Professional school counselors also receive training in assessment and are often the most knowledgeable on-site staff member when it comes to intelligence tests. A professional school counselor's advanced training in assessment may lead some to become coordinators or co-coordinators of special education identification programs in their schools (Monteiro-Leitner, Asner-Self, Milde, Leitner, & Skelton, 2006). In addition, some professional school counselors who serve on school-based student assistance teams also are given the responsibility for administering brief intelligence tests for screening purposes. Consequently, professional school counselors become the person many colleagues and parents turn to when a concern arises on the subject of intelligence tests, psychological reports, or special education services.

Since most professional school counselors already have had one or more college-level course in assessment, this chapter will focus on basic characteristics of the more widely used intelligence instruments, how to understand test results, and how to use test results to develop an appropriate educational plan for students. In addition, an outline for presenting intelligence test information to parents and colleagues is provided. Ethical and multicultural considerations also are discussed, specifically with regard to what professional school counselors are and are not responsible for when dealing with intelligence tests.

Basic Characteristics of Intelligence Tests

Before the subject of common characteristics can be addressed, the types of intelligence tests must be explained. Basically, there are two types of intelligence tests: (a) brief tests, which are frequently used for screening purposes; and (b) comprehensive tests, which are commonly used for diagnosis, educational placement, and which form the cornerstone of most psychological evaluations and psychoeducational reports. Many professional school counselors, who have completed a master's degree and have taken a course in assessment, may administer a brief test, such as a *Slosson Intelligence Test–Revised* (SIT-R; Nicholson & Hibpshman, 1998) or *Kaufman-Brief Intelligence Test* (K-BIT; Erford, 2007). Comprehensive tests such as the *Stanford-Binet V* (SB-5; Roid, 2003), *Wechsler Intelligence Scale for Children–Fourth Edition* (WISC-IV; Wechsler, 2003), *Wechsler Adult Intelligence Scale–Third Edition* (WAIS-III), *Kaufman Assessment Battery for Children–Second Edition* (K-ABC-II; Kaufman & Kaufman, 2004a), and *Woodcock-Johnson Tests of Cognitive Ability–Third Edition* (WJ-III COG; Woodcock, McGrew, & Mather, 2001) must be administered and interpreted by certified or licensed school psychologists or other licensed professionals, including licensed professional counselors (LPCs). These comprehensive intelligence assessments are mentioned here because they are the most frequently used intelligence tests for assessing children and adolescents (Erford, 2007).

Whether an IQ test falls under the category of brief or comprehensive, the instrument is used to assess the cognitive ability of individuals (Cohen & Swerdlik, 2004). Perhaps a better way of interpreting the previous statement is that intelligence tests are used to gauge someone's *current ability*, the combined effect of potential and past experiences. Most of the instruments used to assess intelligence are indirectly or directly based on theories of intelligence. However, regardless of the particular theory an instrument is based on, most tests of cognitive ability share a few common characteristics.

Intelligence tests, whether they are administered to an individual or a group, rely on normative data and statistical analysis to determine their usefulness and appropriateness for measuring intelligence. From this data, test administrators are able to determine if test scores are valid and reliable and therefore applicable for administration to children, adolescents, and adults. For example, SIT-R normative data were collected from a sample of 1,800 individuals in preschool through adulthood (Nicholson & Hibpshman, 1998). The WISC-IV was normed using 2,200 children before it was published and made available for use by professionals (Wechsler, 2003). The SIT-R primarily measures verbal ability through a combination of items that assess vocabulary, word similarities and differences, memory for sentences, memory for digits, comprehension, quantitative reasoning, and general information. The K-BIT-2 (Kaufman & Kaufman, 2004b) uses a nonverbal scale (comprising of the Matrices subtest) and verbal scale (comprising the Verbal Knowledge and Riddles subtests) to determine an individual's full scale intelligence score. Used in conjunction with information from teachers, academic performance, observations, and achievement test scores, results from a brief intelligence test can be used by professional school counselors and other educators to determine appropriate educational options for students.

Most comprehensive intelligence tests provide a global, overall IQ score, in addition to scores for specific dimensions or categorical components of intelligence through the use of subtests. The subtests combine to provide the overall IQ score and factors (e.g., areas of specific cognitive ability, such as verbal reasoning, short-term memory, processing speed, organizational skills). For example, the K-ABC-II derives an IQ score from how a person performs on two factors: sequential processing facets and simultaneous processing facets (Kaufman & Kaufman, 2004a). For the WISC-IV, the overall IQ score is based on how a person performs on the verbal comprehension, perceptual reasoning, working memory, and processing speed indexes (Wechsler, 2003). In another example, the SB-V derives an overall IQ score from up to five different areas, if all five areas are assessed (Roid, 2003): fluid reasoning, knowledge, quantitative reasoning, visual–spatial processing, and working memory.

Regardless of the comprehensive intelligence test used to determine a student's ability, professional school counselors should recognize that IQ scores are not derived from only one area or type of intelligence, but rather efforts are made to test a child's full range of abilities (e.g., verbal reasoning, short-term memory, auditory processing, mathematical ability). Even more important, professional school counselors need to understand how these test results can be used in establishing a child's educational plan.

UNDERSTANDING INTELLIGENCE TEST RESULTS

Professional school counselors are responsible for familiarizing themselves with the more frequently used intelligence tests, even though they may not ever administer them (Erford, 2007). The more comfortable a professional school counselor becomes with the different components of intelligence tests, background information on how tests were developed, what population the tests are intended for, and the significance of the results, the more effective they will become at understanding intelligence tests as well as helping others (e.g., students, parents, teachers) understand the results on a particular test. Familiarity with intelligence tests starts with the understanding of how IQ scores are calculated and what the scores mean.

The calculation of IQ scores depends on two factors: (a) the chronological age of the person taking the test, and (b) the raw score received on the instrument administered. These two parts are used to determine the person's IQ score, or standard score (Cohen & Swerdlik, 2004). A person's chronological age is how old one is in years and months. A person's raw score is simply how many questions (or points) correctly answered. Using these two pieces of information, the test administrator compares a test-taker's raw score to other people in the same age range, as established by the test's developer and reported in the test manual. Age ranges and corresponding standard scores are determined by test developers based on how the normative sample performed on each part (subtest, subscale, index, factor, or total scale) of the intelligence test. This information, usually presented as a series of norm tables, is provided in the administrator's manual as part of the instrument kit. Once standard scores have been established, it is possible for professionals familiar with the test and general assessment procedures to interpret the scores. In essence, it becomes fundamental that professional school counselors understand what these standard scores mean before they can interpret them or help others (e.g., colleagues, parents) understand the significance of the scores.

To understand the significance of a student's standard score (IQ score), a professional school counselor must comprehend three things: the mean of the test in use, the standard deviation of the test in use, and the bell-shaped normal curve (see Figure 49.1). For an IQ score to signify something, it must be compared to the mean score on that test. The mean standard score for the WISC-IV, WAIS-III, K-ABC-II, SB-V, SIT-R, WJ-III COG, and K-BIT is 100. In addition, one must also know the standard deviation of these tests. With the case of the aforementioned instruments, the standard deviation is 15 points, with the exception of the SIT-R, which has a standard deviation of 16 points. Without getting too mired in statistical jargon, these two components, the mean and standard deviation of a particular intelligence test, allow the test administrator to determine if a test-taker's score is above or below the average score and by how much.

An individual's results on a comprehensive intelligence test administered by a school psychologist are used as one of the principle determinants for special education program qualification (Erford, 2007). Eligibility for special education services also is dependent on teacher observations, academic achievement/performance, adaptive behavior, and social and emotional functioning (Villalba & Sheperis, 2004). The location

FIGURE 49.1. Normal distribution of a bell-shaped curve ($M = 100$, $SD = 15$).

that a student's IQ score falls on the normal distribution curve can help determine if a child is of average, above-average, or below-average ability. For the purpose of special education, it may also help determine if the test taker is functioning in the Gifted range (typically an IQ score of 130 and above), Mentally Handicapped range (typically an IQ score of about 70 or lower), or if there is a significant difference between their cognitive ability (e.g., IQ score) and achievement—as represented by a standardized achievement test score—thereby suggesting the presence of a specific learning disability.

Results on IQ tests and other psychoeducational tests also can assist professional school counselors and other educators in determining the most effective way to teach a particular student, even if he or she does not qualify for specific special education services. The information gained from tests provide a wide array of information for how a student learns best, for a student's strengths and weaknesses, and perhaps for how proficient students are at grasping, retaining, and retrieving new information. Intelligence test scores also can assist in determining what types of classroom accommodations and curriculum modifications may be warranted for the student to be successful in the school setting. All of these data may be used by the professional school counselor to advocate for students and their families (Bowen & Glenn, 1998).

HELPING OTHERS UNDERSTAND INTELLIGENCE TESTS

The mere fact that intelligence tests are based on statistical principles and use professional jargon is enough to confuse most teachers and parents. Professional school counselors must be attuned to the confusion, frustration, fear, or indifference that is related to a student's intelligence test results. Also, professional school counselors may need to help teachers, parents, and students make sense of test scores and how the information will be used to alter a student's educational options.

Although it typically is not the responsibility of a professional school counselor to interpret the results of a comprehensive intelligence test to parents and colleagues, one should be aware of and ready to discuss what the results of the assessment mean for a specific student. Most parents want to know if their children are fine, how intelligence test results may affect their children's future, or even if they are possibly genetically or environmentally responsible for their children's IQ scores (Bowen & Glenn, 1998).

With regard to teachers, professional school counselors should make themselves available to answer questions about intelligence tests. Professional school counselors must be supportive and nonthreatening when responding to questions about intelligence. Not only can professional school counselors be instrumental in explaining what the scores mean and test administration issues, professional school counselors can also help teachers understand how to best use the test results to augment their teaching strategy towards a particular student (Bowen & Glenn, 1998).

Examples of how professional school counselors can communicate with parents and teachers to help them better understand intelligence tests include the following:

- Explaining the idea of *intellectual ability* (standard IQ scores) as *potential*, perhaps by comparing it to how many ounces of liquid a container can potentially hold (capacity), or how fast a car is capable of driving (velocity).

- Oftentimes, parents or teachers may be confused by the phrase, "Your child's IQ is in the 75th percentile" and left wondering, "Is that good or bad?" When explaining percentile ranks, it is helpful to look at the *unmentioned number* by subtracting the percentile from 100 and stating that new number along with the percentile rank. In the case of an IQ standard score in the 75th percentile, saying "In other words, your child's score is in the top 25%, when compared to other children his age" may be easier to comprehend.

- Using common, interpretative labels to categorize IQ standard scores—such as *average* for scores approximating 100, *above average* for scores between 115 and 129, *very superior* for scores above 130, or *below average* for scores below 85—is helpful when discussing a student's IQ.

- Although individual achievement tests are not discussed in this chapter, it may be necessary for parents and teachers to understand more clearly how achievement tests and ability tests are related. If a child has an IQ standard score of 109 and a reading achievement standard score of 79, then the professional school counselor may help the parent and teacher understand the discrepancy by saying, "The closer your child's reading score is to his potential, the IQ score, the more certain we can be that he is working to his potential. The 30-point difference between these two scores tells us we need to help your child read closer to his potential."

- Finally, parents and teachers should understand that IQ scores are neither *good* nor *bad*. In other words, it is not fair to attach a letter grade of "A" to a score above a 130 of a grade of "F" to a score below 70. Professional school counselors can help parents and teachers attain more realistic expectations by using what the percentage of the population actually scores in certain ranges (i.e., only 2% of the population is in the *very superior* intellectual range; most children [68%] score in the *average* range of intelligence) instead of referring to a particular score as *really good* or *not so great*.

Professional school counselors who administer brief intelligence tests as screening tools for further evaluation also must effectively explain the results of screening tests to parents. In addition, students taking the test may also want to know what the scores mean. Figures 49.2 and 49.3 include examples of English and Spanish versions of forms professional school counselors can share with parents and students to help them understand intelligence test results. Professional school counselors may also want to share this form with the school psychologist to get additional feedback or suggestions for sharing results with parents and students.

PROFESSIONAL SCHOOL COUNSELORS AND ETHICAL ISSUES REGARDING INTELLIGENCE TESTS

Professional school counselors are responsible for proper use and interpretation of assessment instruments (Erford, 2007); furthermore, it is up to the professional school counselor to gauge his or her own limits (ACA; 2005). For these reasons, professional school counselors must determine for themselves what tests they are comfortable using and have the ethical right to use. In addition, professional school counselors must be knowledgeable of when they cannot administer or interpret a particular instrument.

MAKING SENSE OF BRIEF INTELLIGENCE TEST RESULTS

Recently (*student's name*) took the (*name of brief intelligence tests*), which was administered by (school counselor's name) after parent/guardian permission was granted. This form includes the results of the test, what the score means, and how these results will be used. Test results are used as a screening tool to see if additional testing from (*insert title of educator, such as school psychologist*) is needed, in order to develop the best educational program for (*student's name*).

A person's score on an intelligence test is typically called an "IQ score." An IQ score is used to measure a person's cognitive ability, or rather, their potential and capacity to learn new ideas. Typically, tests that measure a person's intelligence use puzzles, memory tasks, math problems, logic and reasoning games, and pictures to come up with an IQ score. Because these tests measure potential, and not exactly how good someone is at school work, there are no such things as "perfect" scores or "100%." The *average* score on this test is 100, and most children (about 68%) score between 85 and 115. Scores between 116 and 130 are considered *above average* and scores between 84 and 70 are considered *below average*.

(*Student's name*) received a total score of (*score*) on the (*name of brief intelligence test*).

Due to (*student's name*) results on this intelligence test, the school counselor (*school counselor's name*) would like to recommend _____

_____

_____

_____

As you are sure to have questions about this recommendation, please contact me at (*school counseling office phone number*). You can also contact me if you have additional questions or would like further information about the test. Thank you for carefully reading over this form. I look forward to answering your questions and being as helpful as possible.

(*Name of School Counselor, Name of School, Phone number*)

FIGURE 49.2. Making sense of brief intelligence test results.

Most professional school counselors have the knowledge and training necessary to administer B-level brief intelligence tests (Erford, 2007), such as the K-BIT and SIT-R. A Level B test can be administered and interpreted by individuals with a master's degree in education or psychology who have also had graduate-level coursework in psychological appraisal. However, C-level tests (comprehensive intelligence tests such as the WISC-IV or SB-V) require specific coursework related to particular instruments, as well as advanced knowledge in psychometrics and should only be administered and interpreted by appropriately trained professionals, such as licensed counselors or psychologists and certified school psychologists. Usually, professional school counselors

HACIENDO SENTIDO DE LOS RESULTADOS DE UN EXAMEN DE INTELIGENCIA BREVE

Recientemente (*student's name*) tomo un examen llamado (*name of brief intelligence test*), cual fue administrado por (*name of school counselor*) después de recibir permiso de el padre/la madre/el guardián. Esta forma incluye los resultados de este examen, lo que significan los resultados, y como usaremos los resultados. Los resultados de este examen se usan de una manera preeliminaría para determinar si es necesario administrar exámenes y pruebas más compresivas. (*Insert title of educator, such as school psychologist*) es en individuo que administrara estas pruebas adicionales, si son necesarias.

Los resultados de un examen de inteligencia típicamente se llaman "IQ score." Un "IQ score" es usado para medir la habilidad cognitiva de una persona, o de otra manera, el potencial y la capacidad para aprender nuevas ideas. Típicamente, exámenes que miden la inteligencia de una persona están compuestos de varias partes como rompecabezas, ejercicios de memoria, matemática, juegos de lógica, y fotos, para determinar un "IQ score." Como estos exámenes miden potencial en vez de determinar el nivel de progreso académico de su hijo/hija, no hay semejante cosa como un valor de 100% o una evaluación perfecta. Es mas, el valor "average" en esta examen que su hijo/hija tomo es 100, y la mayoría de los niños (68%) obtienen valores entre 85 puntos y 115 puntos. Valores entre 116 y 130 puntos se consideran "sobre average" y valores entre 84 y 70 se consideran "bajo average."

(*Student's name*) recibió un valor total de (*score*) como su "IQ score" en el examen (*name of brief intelligence test*).

Debido a los resultados de (*student's name*) en este examen de inteligencia, en consejero escolar (*school counselor's name*) quisiera recomendar: _____

_____

_____

_____

Como es seguro que usted tendrá preguntas sobre esta recomendación, por favor llámeme a este teléfono (*school counseling office phone number*). Usted también me puede contactar si tiene otro tipo de pregunta o quisiera información adicional sobre este examen. Muchas gracias por prestarle atención a esta forma. Anticipo la oportunidad para contestar sus preguntas y para ayudarlo lo mejor posible.

(*Name of School Counselor, Name of Schoo, Phone Number*)

FIGURE 49.3. Making sense of brief intelligence test results (Spanish version).

should know their limits when it comes to Level C tests and should let colleagues and parents know about these ethical limits. Letting others know the ethical guidelines of the professional school counselor with regard to cognitive ability instruments should assist in clarifying to others what professional school counselors are and are not responsible for.

INTELLIGENCE TESTS AND MULTICULTURAL POPULATIONS

Developers of current editions of the more commonly used intelligence tests have accounted for increased numbers of minority children in the schools. Test developers of the Wechsler, Stanford-Binet, and Kaufman tests have made strides to include significant numbers of African American, Hispanic American, and Asian American children in the normative samples for these tests (Erford, 2007). However, that does not signify that these intelligence tests are completely applicable for use with minority populations.

Although most current editions of intelligence tests contain statistical information specific to most major ethnic groups, Cohen and Swerdlik (2004) believed these tests still show bias against some ethnic groups, such as African American and Hispanic American children and children from families with lower socioeconomic status. These are some of the reasons intelligence tests are multidimensional (contain various subtests) and contribute to the rationale and legal precedent that placement in special education programs cannot be based on IQ scores alone (Villalba & Sheperis, 2004).

Even though most of the items on intelligence tests have been designed to be culture-fair (i.e., without showing a positive or negative slant to a particular culture), none are culture-free (Erford, 2007). Tests that are culture-free (i.e., not impacted by the culture of the person completing the test) are very difficult to find. For this reason, professional school counselors must try to find those brief tests that are as culture-fair as possible.

In addition, when possible, professional school counselors must make sure that a child's ethnicity or race does not negatively impact his or her scores on a comprehensive intelligence test. Again, it is the responsibility of professional school counselors to familiarize themselves with the more popular IQ tests, even if they are not responsible for administering them, in order to best advocate for children—particularly for children from diverse backgrounds and their families.

SUMMARY/CONCLUSION

Professional school counselors are responsible for many aspects of a child's educational development. Being knowledgeable of intelligence tests is part of this responsibility. Professional school counselors must be familiar with IQ tests and how they impact children and families. They also must be aware of the expectations their colleagues may have with regard to cognitive testing.

A key step toward meeting this responsibility is to understand how best to present intelligence and other test information to children, parents, and teachers. Professional school counselors have the skills to advocate for fair testing practices and ensure that all educators use intelligence test results to help and benefit all students. Together with the appropriate school personnel, professional school counselors can ensure that intelligence test data are used to help students, parents, and teachers in providing the very best educational plan.

(Note: See the CD-ROM for a list of references.)

CHAPTER 50

A PRACTICAL APPROACH TO CAREER ASSESSMENT IN SCHOOLS

Jerry Trusty, Spencer G. Niles, and Terry L. Pertuit

Preview

In this chapter, we present a practical framework for career assessment in schools and take a comprehensive, developmental perspective on career assessment. We discuss various areas of career assessment and present priority areas for assessment at various developmental levels. Formal and informal career assessments are included, and the use of career development portfolios is described. We take a particular focus on using existing student data and employing assessment methods that are inexpensive and practical in terms of a professional school counselor's budgetary and time constraints.

According to the American School Counselor Association (ASCA; 2006), the average ratio of professional school counselors to students in U.S. schools in 2003–2004 was 1 to 488. Traditional, individual-based career assessment for every student is not practical for most counselors. Professional school counselors' time and budgets are likely limited, and assessment materials can be expensive. Thus, we offer effective methods of career assessment that are inexpensive in terms of time and money, and we offer a practical and flexible framework for assessment.

Assessment can be defined as the use of any formal or informal technique or instrument to collect data about a student (Niles & Harris-Bowlsbey, 2005). There are five basic reasons for using assessment to help students advance in their career development:

- Counselors can learn more about the needs of students.
- Counselors can learn more about the characteristics of students (e.g., interests, abilities, skills, values).
- Counselors can address environmental pressures that affect career development.
- Counselors can measure students' progress in their career development.
- Students can learn more about themselves and increase their understanding of the career-development process.

Career assessment is something that professional school counselors definitely need to do. The *National Standards for School Counseling Programs* (Campbell & Dahir, 1997) and the related student competencies and indicators (ASCA; 2005) speak directly to career assessment. If school counselors are to have comprehensive school counseling programs, as described in the ASCA (2005) national model, systematic career assessment is necessary. Career assessment data are a major component in *data-driven* school counseling program development. When general needs assessments are administered to students in schools, students generally indicate a high degree of need in career development areas. In fact, in our experiences, career-related needs are consistently the highest priority indicated by students overall. Career assessment data, therefore, are *accountability data.*

Career assessments can be formal or informal. Formal assessments have psychometric evidence such as reliability and validity data and normative data appropriate for the group with which the measure will be used. Because formal assessments often have a standard way for interpreting scores, the results can be reviewed, at least initially, with a large group of students. Examples of formal career assessments include the *Strong Interest Inventory* (CPP, 2008); the *Differential Aptitude Test Battery* (PsychCorp, 2007), and the *Career Maturity Inventory* (Crites & Savickas, 1996).

Although data from informal assessments are more subjective, they can be informative—but in ways different from formal assessments. The results of informal assessments should not be used for comparisons of students, and informal assessments often have no standard way for interpreting the results. The results of informal assessments are often reviewed in a collaborative way between the counselor and an individual student or a group of students (e.g., in small groups, in classroom guidance) and, thus, informal assessments are flexible. Examples of informal assessments include checklists, games, career fantasies, interviews, projects and products, and card sorts (Niles & Harris-Bowlsbey, 2005). Both informal and formal career assessments provide important and useful information to the counselor and student, and informal and formal assessments often complement one another.

Our career assessment framework stresses the use of career development portfolios for students. These portfolios—including collections of formal and informal assessment results, products resulting from guidance activities, samples of academic performance, and so forth—would follow students through elementary, middle, and high schools. At first thought, this might seem burdensome for professional school counselors. But these data are easy to collect; they are valuable data for students, parents, teachers, and counselors; they provide information across transitions from school to school; and these data can help professional school counselors develop and evaluate their programs across students' early childhood through 12th-grade (EC–12) development.

Although career development and career assessment become more focused as students progress to middle and high school, an EC–12 approach to career development and assessment is needed (Starr, 1996). That is, professional school counselors need to take a longitudinal view on career development and career assessment. Experiences and assessments of elementary school students should articulate well with their middle and high school experiences and assessments. In reality, all career assessments are formative evaluations, and none of the assessment data we use should be conceptualized as static outcomes, including assessments in the 12th grade.

Career development and career assessment should also be comprehensive. Although professional school counselors use the categories of students' (a) academic development, (b) career development, and (c) personal–social development, all areas are conceptualized as career development, because all are naturally related. To illustrate, Stone and Bradley (1994), in their school counseling text, noted that practically everything that elementary counselors do for students is for students' career development. For example, when elementary counselors deliver classroom guidance targeting study strategies or group counseling focused on social competency, they provide students with activities that promote skills needed for their career development. Other authors and practitioners (e.g., Gysbers & Henderson, 2006; McDaniels & Gysbers, 1992) take a similar holistic and comprehensive view on career development across the life span. Additionally, research (e.g., Trusty, 2004; Trusty & Niles, 2003, 2004) has demonstrated the importance of students' middle- and high-school achievement and experiences on later completion of the bachelor's degree.

In this chapter, a practical, flexible, developmental, and comprehensive approach to career assessment for elementary-school, middle-school, and high-school students is presented. Readers who are counselors may be tempted to only devote attention to sections that pertain to the students they serve directly. We assume and encourage an EC–12 perspective. (Actually, the perspective is more of an EC–16 and life-span perspective.) In the last section of this chapter, we present a qualitative, flexible method for career assessment at the middle-school and high-school levels.

CAREER ASSESSMENT AREAS

The Career Assessment Priority Matrix is presented in Table 50.1. This matrix does not include all possible areas of career assessment. However, it is fairly comprehensive, covering skills and abilities, self-perceptions, perceptions of the world of work, self-awareness, decision making, goal setting, and environments and perceptions of environments. In the columns on the right, the priority of the assessment area at the particular grade level is indicated (*low, moderate, high*). If the assessment area is not appropriate at the particular grade level, NA (not a priority) is indicated.

ACADEMIC SACHIEVEMENT

Of the areas in the matrix in Table 50.1, the first, *academic achievement*, is very important from the elementary level onward. Researchers have found that early academic achievement has long-lasting effects on students' career development. For example, school grades, even in the early elementary school years, are strongly related to whether students complete high school (Barrington & Hendricks, 1989); and achievement test scores in middle school strongly predict what postsecondary majors students choose (Trusty, Robinson, Plata, & Ng, 2000) and how much postsecondary education they pursue (Trusty, 2002). Achievement in middle school is clearly the result of what students learned in elementary school. The courses that students complete in high school—particularly intensive science and math courses—heavily influence students' success or lack of success in college (Trusty, 2004; Trusty & Niles, 2003, 2004).

Professional school counselors generally have access to achievement data at the elementary, middle, and secondary levels. The criterion-referenced, basic-skills mastery tests now required in several states supply limited information because of their nature. Information from these instruments will be less useful for students who are achieving at moderate or high levels. Group-administered formal ability assessments are used in many schools to determine which students should be tested further for gifted or enrichment programs (e.g., *Otis-Lennon School Abilities Test* [Harcourt Assessment, 2006]; *Cognitive Abilities Test* [Riverside, 2006]), and these supply some information. However, the best sources of achievement information are generally (a) scores on some

TABLE 50.1

CAREER ASSESSMENT PRIORITY MATRIX

Assessment areas	Priority/appropriateness at grade levels		
	Elementary	Middle school	High school
Academic achievement	high	high	high
Career exploration behavior	high	moderate	moderate
Perceptions of careers	high	high	moderate
Self-perceptions	moderate	high	high
Interpersonal skills	high	high	high
Environments (e.g., families)	high	moderate	moderate
Perceptions of environments (e.g., barriers, opportunities)	low	high	high
Self-awareness:			
strengths and obstacles	low	high	high
interests	NA	high	high
values	NA	moderate	high
Career awareness	NA	moderate	high
Decision making	NA	moderate	high
Goal setting	NA	moderate	high
Ability self-estimates	NA	moderate	high

Note. NA = not a priority.

national, standardized, norm-referenced comprehensive achievement instrument (e.g., *Iowa Test of Basic Skills* [Riverside, 2006]; *Stanford Achievement Test* [Pearson Education, 2008]); (b) school grades and other in-school performance criteria; and (c) the intensity of students' curricula. Score reports on standardized achievement instruments generally identify degrees of competence and obstacles in several specific academic areas. School grades are often inconsistent across schools and across teachers, but they may hold valuable information for identifying students' strengths and obstacles. Local performance criteria and students' performance products might become part of the career development portfolio that follows students through schools. Students' curricular experiences should always be a component of the career development portfolio. When professional school counselors, teachers, parents, and students have access to comprehensive data regarding students' achievement, all people involved in students' education are better prepared to make decisions (e.g., special programs, appropriate courses).

In high school, the most important gauge of achievement is the academic rigor of courses completed by students. In large national studies, researchers (Adelman, 1999; Trusty 2004; Trusty & Niles, 2003, 2004) reported that U.S. college students who completed more academically intensive coursework in high school were much more likely to graduate from college. The positive effects of rigorous high-school coursework on degree completion were evident for all major U.S. racial–ethnic groups. With regard to particular courses, completing advanced high-school math courses had a particularly strong influence on college success. Students' grades in these rigorous courses mattered little. Academic achievement is also related to most other aspects of career development and career assessment. For example, environments, and especially parents, have a strong influence on achievement.

CAREER EXPLORATION BEHAVIOR

The elementary school years should be a time of open exploration of careers. Career-related fantasy should be encouraged. As Herr, Cramer, and Niles (2004) maintained, the elementary school years are not a time in which children are encouraged to narrow their career options but a time when they are encouraged to broaden their perspectives. Across the elementary grades, the range of careers familiar to students should grow exponentially. Assessment of exploratory behavior might be reflected in students' knowledge of various careers and career areas, their fantasy or enthusiasm reflected in products they create, or in the career-related stories they tell or understand. At the middle- and high-school levels, career exploration may be needed for some students, but as students develop they generally become more focused on particular careers or career areas. Professional school counselors, however, should be cautious, because adolescents are often overly restrictive in their perceived range of desirable or possible careers.

PERCEPTIONS OF CAREERS

Students' exploratory behavior and perceptions of careers are closely related. Students often form perceptions of careers early. For example, students often form ideas about occupational prestige and gender roles when they are in elementary school. At the elementary level, students should begin learning various educational opportunities and, in a general way, begin connecting educational tasks to careers. Students should also begin connecting occupations and educational and training requirements. In middle and high school, and even into college, students are susceptible to overgeneralized or otherwise faulty perceptions of careers. At the more advanced educational levels, perceptions of careers are generally conceptualized as *career awareness*, an area discussed later in this chapter.

One critical area is students' perceptions based on gender roles. Students very early on develop ideas about the association between genders and careers (Helwig, 1998). Additionally, gender seems to be a primal basis for eliminating and choosing careers (Gottfredson, 1981), and students may limit their ranges of desired occupations very early in their lives. Therefore, assessments and activities that are focused on gender stereotyping of careers are appropriate at the elementary level and onward. And efforts should focus on both girls and boys. Over the last several years, girls and women have become less gender-stereotypical in their career aspirations and postsecondary educational choices, whereas boys and men have remained relatively gender-traditional in their aspirations and choices (Helwig, 1998; Trusty et al., 2000). The issue of traditional versus nontraditional gender roles is often political and controversial, and likely cultural. However, a system that functions best for individuals and society as a whole is one that uses all its talent and potential effectively. It seems that if this perspective is taken by professional school counselors, their work with students on gender roles would be less controversial for parents, teachers, school administrators, and communities. Professional school counselors should always consider the caveat that in traditional cultures, gender roles may be highly delineated.

Students' perceptions of careers and occupations can be assessed readily simply by having them indicate if they perceive particular careers or occupations positively, negatively, or neutrally. Also, having students relate the positive, negative, and neutral-specific aspects of careers would provide more data on their perceptions. Students' ability to connect occupations, tasks, and education/training requirements is also easily assessed in classroom guidance format.

SELF-PERCEPTIONS

A fairly high level of cognitive development is required for young people to reflect on themselves, reflect on the world of work, and match self and work. This requires abstract, second-order thinking, which is associated with the *formal operations* level of cognitive development, a level that is generally reached in adolescence (Muuss, 1996). However, children do develop self-perceptions and self-awareness, albeit at a more concrete level, through the elementary years (Herr et al., 2004). In the elementary grades, students begin to make concrete connections between their performance and their self-perceptions, and these early self-perceptions are the foundation for later, more complex and specific self-perceptions, career-related values, and ability self-estimates, which in turn are the bases for choices.

In recent years, professional counselors and researchers have come to focus on students' self-competence and self-confidence in their academic skills and other career-related areas of performance. Social self-perceptions are also important to young people's learning and functioning. There are various instruments that measure either general self-perceptions (e.g., self-concept, self-esteem) or specific self-perceptions (e.g., self-efficacy for specific tasks, domain-specific self-esteem or self-competence). Self-perceptions could also be assessed in a less formal manner. For example, a professional school counselor might ask an eighth-grader, "On a scale of 1 to 10, with 10 being the best, how are you at making things with your hands?" Special types of self-perceptions (e.g., career self-awareness, interests, values, ability self-estimates) become more important in middle and high school, and are discussed later in this chapter.

INTERPERSONAL SKILLS

Children learn and refine cooperation and teamwork skills in elementary school, and according to the ASCA standards, competencies, and indicators (ASCA; 2005; Campbell & Dahir, 1997), these are career-development skills. In fact, it is usually advantageous for professional school counselors to categorize interpersonal skills as career-development skills. In the first authors' experience as a professional school counselor in a middle school, a teacher once stated, "These kids don't need interpersonal skills, they need academic skills." Obviously, the teacher was not making the connections between interpersonal skills and education and work, and perhaps the teacher would have been more cooperative himself if he had. The message of this interchange was that interpersonal skills and social skills activities should be labeled as *career skills activities*.

Cooperative skills and teamwork skills can be assessed best through observations by teachers and counselors. A brief rating of students' strengths and obstacles would provide important data in students' career-development portfolios. Often, teamwork and interpersonal skills receive more attention in elementary and middle schools. The authors' contention is that interpersonal skills for high school students are often ignored, and that interpersonal skills are necessary for advanced levels of career development. For example, interpersonal skills are actually the major part of job-interviewing or college-interviewing, and interpersonal skills are often a major contributor to occupational advancement.

ENVIRONMENTS

Students' environments have powerful influences on their career development. Students in communities of lower socioeconomic status are likely limited in career-related resources. For example, youth clubs and organizations may not be available in particular communities; rural or otherwise isolated areas may be limited in career options; parents may not have access to professionals or extended family with knowledge of particular careers; mentors may not be available for children; or schools may not have budgets sufficient for extracurricular activities.

The most influential environmental force is the students' parents. The educational goal transmission process in families is very strong (Trusty & Pirtle, 1998). That is, the educational goals that parents hold for their children correspond highly to the goals that children hold for themselves. Parents want to help their children, and children rely on parents for career development help. In addition to parents' expectations for their children, parents' involvement in their children's education also carries strong influence. Parents' school-based involvement (e.g., involvement in parent–teacher organizations) carries some positive influence, but the major influence is from parents' home-based involvement. Home-based involvement includes (a) parents' regular communication with children regarding school and career, and (b) parents' support of their children's educational and career development. The influences of parental involvement carry into adulthood (Trusty, 1998, 2004).

First-generation college students, or students whose parents did not attend college, present some unique challenges. These students are likely to enter college with limited access to information about the college experience (Thayer, 2000), and they are likely to experience low levels of social integration in college (Nunez & Cuccaro-Alamin, 1998). First-generation college students are likely to have conflicting obligations, such as significant work and family responsibilities, that might interfere with career development. First-generation college freshmen are two times more likely than their non–first-generation counterparts to leave college before their second year, even when factors such as delayed enrollment and working full time are considered (Choy, 2001). Thus, these students and families will need to develop high levels of resilience if students are to be successful.

Data on environments can be assessed relatively easily. Teachers and professional school counselors, after working with students for a few months, will have a good idea of the resources, supports, situations, characteristics, and difficulties in students' environments. Some environmental characteristics are obvious, whereas others are not. For example, if a student is not receiving adequate physical care, problems are easily recognized. However, the emotional climate in families is not often readily recognized. Data on students' environments would identify opportunities and barriers to learning and to career development and should provide professional school counselors with important contextual information.

PERCEPTIONS OF ENVIRONMENTS

At the middle-school level and beyond, young people begin to have some comparative gauge of the positive and negative influences from their environments. In fact, middle school students' perceptions of parents' home-based involvement are more reliable than parents' reports of their involvement. Parents tend to positively bias reports of their own involvement (Trusty, 1996). Perceptions of environments have often been conceptualized as barriers and opportunities. Barriers are frequently described as *real barriers* and *perceived barriers*. If barriers to career development are perceived by a student as real, then barriers are real for that student; and barriers function to block the student's development, although other people may not perceive the barrier to be an actual barrier. Students' perceived barriers and opportunities can easily be assessed. Needs assessments administered to high school students often reveal perceived barriers. Also, the classroom guidance session is an appropriate format for assessing barriers and opportunities, although students may want to keep private their perceptions of some environmental barriers. Counselors should be aware that lack of information (e.g., financial aid information for postsecondary education or training) causes students to perceive barriers.

SELF-AWARENESS: STRENGTHS AND OBSTACLES, INTERESTS, VALUES

In middle school, students are forced to make decisions about the high school program they will pursue. These decisions are coming earlier and earlier in middle schools. High schools are requiring more and more credits for graduation; more students are taking high-school credit courses in middle school; and decisions are pushed deeper into the middle school years. For example, in many school systems, students and parents must decide during the sixth grade if students will take pre-algebra in the seventh grade, so they can take high-school Algebra I in the eighth grade, so they can take Calculus in the 12th-grade. In the context of increased credits for graduation and an increasingly prescriptive high-school curriculum required by colleges and universities, there is little flexibility once students have begun a particular high-school program track. Add to this mixture the cognitive developmental level of middle school students (concrete operations) and the psychosocial developmental crisis of students (identity vs. role confusion—if prior development was optimal), and it is clear that students are not ready for these decisions. However, this is the current reality in most schools.

Students' awareness of their own strengths and obstacles, interests and preferences, and values is necessary for effective decision making and goal setting. The correspondence of skills and abilities, interests, and values is salient for decision making and goals. It is important to remember that students and assessments of students are not static. For example, a student may lack skill and interest in mechanics because the student has not had learning experiences associated with mechanics. The interest inventory score and mechanical aptitude score are low because of lack of learning opportunity. Therefore, scores should be a starting point for new learning experiences, and not a static judgment of the young person's characteristics.

Aptitudes, interests, and values can be measured fairly quickly with a battery like the *COPS System* (i.e., COPS-Interests, CAPS-Abilities, and COPES-Values; EdITS, 2008), *CDM System* (Pearson Education, 2006), or with other instruments. Many commercial vendors of instruments are offering aptitude, interests, and values assessments in an online format, and sometimes the online versions are less expensive than the printed versions. Computer Assisted Career Guidance Systems (e.g., DISCOVER [ACT, 2008]; SIGI 3 [Valpar, 2008]; CHOICES [Bridges Transitions, 2008]) also include assessments of interests and values and may incorporate aptitude scores from other instruments. Some commercial instruments and computer programs have versions specific to middle school students. With regard to interest inventories, the *Self-Directed Search* (Hollandcodes, 2007) and the *Vocational Preference Inventory* (Psychological Assessment Resources, 2005) are relatively inexpensive.

However, the school or counseling program may not have budgets to cover commercial instruments or computer programs. There are alternatives. For example, *card sorts* are inexpensive and can be used in a group format for prioritizing career-related interests and values. The *Guide for Occupational Exploration* (GOE; JIST, 2008) is fairly inexpensive. Work-values exercises, along with other activities, are included in the book, and these may be copied and used in a classroom guidance format with middle school or high school students. There are additional resources that are free on the Internet, through U.S. government Web sites, state sites, and university sites (see, e.g., http://stats.bls.gov/oco/home.htm; http://online.onetcenter.org). Professional school counselors are encouraged to search the Internet for usable resources. Some instruments available through the Internet may not have the psychometric strength of some published, commercially available instruments; but several noncommercial instruments would likely be very useful for professional school counselors and their students (see, e.g., http://www.freeteachingaids.com). The *Educators Guide to Free Guidance Materials* (Educators Progress Service, 2008), among several other guides to free resources, may be accessed at this site.

CAREER AWARENESS

If students have access to the Internet, there are many resources that can be used for occupational, educational, and leisure information. For example, the *Occupational Outlook Handbook* (U.S. Bureau of Labor Statistics, 2008) is accessible through the Internet, along with many other government materials. Various national associations and societies representing numerous fields also have useful Web sites. Commercial materials (e.g., occupational card files, books) are available from vendors. However, printed materials on occupations often become quickly outdated and are a substantial investment.

Professional school counselors' assessments of students' career awareness might be connected to guidance activities aimed at career awareness, or degrees of awareness might be evidenced through products students produce. Assessments might be as simple as recording students' frequencies of accessing materials. Assessment may also include assignments connected to regular classes. For example, students in mathematics classes could be required to research surveyors' use of global positioning satellite (GPS) system technology.

DECISION MAKING

It is fortunate that most decisions required of middle school students are not highly specific (an exception might be decisions on what foreign language to take). However, several general educational decisions do come in middle school, and more specific decisions (e.g., part-time work, postsecondary education or work) are rapidly approaching. What is important for students in middle school and high school is that they learn decision-making models and apply models to the decision-making process (McDaniels & Gysbers, 1992). Students then have a template for decision making throughout their career development. It is difficult for professional school counselors to assess the wisdom of students' decisions. However, counselors can and should assess if students have learned and applied decision-making models. These data might simply be represented by a check on a checklist (e.g., student applied the decision-making model to the decision process). Similar to other data, these data are included in students' career development portfolios.

GOAL SETTING

Decision making and goal setting are closely related. When students make decisions, they are often deciding on goals. Setting goals comes easily for some students, but is difficult for others. Some students experience high levels of ambiguity and discomfort when engaging in goal-setting tasks. For some, there is a real fear to decide. Assessing if students have goals is relatively easy. An assessment of the clarity, consistency, and detail in long-term, intermediate, and short-term goals is straightforward. Assessing how realistic and appropriate those goals are is more difficult and requires professional school counselors to make judgments regarding the consistency among students' goals, potential, previous behavior, personality, and so forth.

ABILITY SELF-ESTIMATES

Ability self-estimates are a special type of self-perception. They relate strongly to students' learning experiences, achievement, and choices. In fact, ability self-estimates are generally a better predictor of career choices than scores on aptitude instruments (Prediger, 1999). This is good news for professional school counselors, because ability self-estimates are easy to assess quickly. Also, ability self-estimates can target work-relevant abilities that are not generally assessed in aptitude or achievement tests. The typical format for ability self-estimates is having students rate, on a scale of 5 or 10 degrees, their abilities in 10 or 15 areas. For example, professional school counselors could easily construct assessments for students to estimate their abilities in the following areas:

Mathematics	Writing	Reading
Organization	Teamwork	Selling things
Cooking	Carpentry	Growing things
Mechanics	Sewing	Electronics

Generally, each listed area is accompanied by a two- or three-sentence description of the tasks associated with the area. This list is by no means exhaustive, and students could supply ability self-estimates not included in a list but deemed important to them. Professional school counselors could easily tailor assessments to students in their schools. Ability self-estimates will be most accurate for students at more advanced levels (e.g., later high-school grades and beyond) and should be relied upon more at these higher levels. ACT has an *Inventory of Work-Relevant Abilities* (ACT, 2008), which is available commercially, and several Internet-based assessment sites include ability self-assessment instruments.

Another format for ability self-estimates is to have students do comparisons of their abilities. For example, students are asked their level of agreement with statements such as, "Math is one of my best subjects." Using a national sample of high school students, Trusty and Ng (2000) found that 10th-graders' comparative perceptions of math and English as best subjects were highly predictive of types of college majors chosen after high school. These intra-individual, comparative self-perceptions seem to guide young people's choices, and they are included in the qualitative career assessment structure presented below.

QUALITATIVE, GROUP-FORMAT CAREER ASSESSMENT

The *Life Career Assessment* (LCA; McDaniels & Gysbers, 1992) is a qualitative form of career assessment based on Adlerian theory. It is generally used in an individual counseling setting. Because of high student-to-counselor ratios in schools, we adapted the LCA to a classroom guidance format. We have found adaptations of the LCA to be very effective, providing rich data on adolescents' career development. It is effective for middle school students, but more useful for high school students. The data provide professional school counselors with a deeper understanding of students and provide students with a deeper understanding of themselves. The LCA is a sequence of items for assessing students' experiences and perceptions. In individual counseling, these questions are intermixed with counselors' reflections and empathy responses. In a classroom guidance format, these questions are presented to students on paper, and students write their responses. Students' responses then go into their career development portfolios. When professional school counselors meet with students for individual counseling or individual planning, professional school counselors use the data to facilitate students in self-awareness and career awareness, career planning, decision making, goal setting, and so forth. An outline for the Group-Format LCA is presented in Table 50.2.

(Note: See the CD-ROM for a list of references.)

TABLE 50.2
OUTLINE FOR GROUP-FORMAT LIFE CAREER ASSESSMENT

I.   Educational Experiences
    A.   General appraisal of your educational experiences
        1.   dislikes
        2.   likes
    B.   Particular subjects/classes
        1.   dislikes
        2.   likes
        3.   your best subject(s)
    C.   Teacher characteristics
        1.   dislikes
        2.   likes
        3.   your favorite teacher
    D.   Learning setting preferences
        1.   independent versus collaborative learning
        2.   experiential versus didactic learning
        3.   study style
        4.   memorable learning experiences within and outside school

II. Work Experiences
    A.   Last job
        1.   dislikes
        2.   likes
    B.   Job supervisor/supervision style
        1.   likes
        2.   dislikes
    C.   Repeat for previous jobs

III. Leisure
    A.   Describe weekend, weekday, evening activities
    B.   Fun and relaxation
    C.   Friends and social life

IV. Strengths and Obstacles
    A.   Three main obstacles
    B.   Three main personal (intrinsic) strengths
    C.   People who are resources for you

CHAPTER 51

A SELECTIVE OVERVIEW OF PERSONALITY
AND ITS ASSESSMENT

Ralph L. Piedmont

Preview

In this chapter I present an overview of what personality is and summarize this concept from the perspective of the psychoanalytic and trait schools. Strengths and weaknesses of the two schools are outlined and relevant measurement issues are discussed. The practical value of personality theory for counselors is highlighted.

Perhaps one of the most important concepts we have for understanding people is that of *personality*. However, as a term with widespread colloquial use, it has lost some of its professional precision. The purpose of this chapter is to provide some clarity as to how this term is used in the social sciences, including a basic definition of what personality is as well as providing a synopsis of two major schools of thought in the area. Also, I will discuss some of the measurement issues that coincide with these different theoretical schools. I hope that this chapter will give readers a general sense of the term's value as well as a framework for thinking critically about people: who they are, how they got here, and where they seem to be going.

PERSONALITY: A DEFINITION

The term *personality* is certainly applied often. Pets are frequently said to have personality. Some people seem to lack this important characteristic, while others just seem to "ooze" personality. Personality is often thought of as the ultimate definition of who each of us is as a person, but many believe that it is always changing. Such varied connotations underscore just how diffuse our understanding of the term really is. We all know personality when we see it, but it may be hard to put our fingers on what exactly we mean by "it." As such, a basic definition is in order.

Personality can be defined as the intrinsic, adaptive organization of the individual that is stable over time and consistent across situations (Piedmont, 1998). There are four important points to this definition. First, personality represents some structured system by which individuals organize themselves and orient to the world around them. This system is clearly located *within* the person and is not imposed by the environment.

Second, personality is an adaptive structure, which means that it enables us to manage effectively the many competing, often conflicting, demands we encounter from both within ourselves and from the environment. As such, we should not think about personality as being *good* or *bad*. It is what it is—a systematic way of optimizing our ability to survive and thrive in the world in which we live. Rather, the question we need to ask occurs when people wish to change their environments: Will their personalities work as well in the new context as they did in the original?

Third, personality is stable over time. This means that there is something about who we are and what we are that remains consistent throughout our lives. There is more to say about personality change, but for now we can say that despite all the "change" we may have experienced over our lifetimes, there is some thread that seems to tie together all our developmental experiences around consistent themes. There is something about who we were as children or adolescents that lingers with us today. Finally, personality is consistent from one situation to another. Although specific behaviors may change from one context to another, our view of the world and the personal goals we are pursuing remain essentially unchanged.

This definition should not be interpreted as saying that the environment does not have anything to do with how our personality develops. Culture, context, and situation all have an influence on our development and how we may express our personality. But there does lie within us some kind of psychological "stuff" that provides our basic needs, shapes how we perceive and interpret our external world, and selects the goals we ultimately pursue in our lives. Nor should this definition be construed as arguing that personality is a static quality. To the contrary, personality is a dynamic structure. It is always responding to the demands that develop from both within us and from the world around us. Adaptation is an active process in which we continually contour ourselves to the changing features of our environment. Further, there is a developmental aspect to personality. Just as humans are not born physically mature, so, too, personality is something that begins in a simple form and becomes progressively more sophisticated as it ages. These changes follow an orderly and lawful path, so that when one looks back over life, there can be seen patterns in behavior that lend a sense of continuity to one's life.

With this basic definition in mind, it should be evident that personality is a scientific construct that helps to organize the many diverse, and sometimes conflicting, behaviors and feelings of people into a more organized system that both promotes understanding and increases predictiveness. We now turn to a brief overview of two major schools of thought concerning how personality is defined and understood. These major schools are the Psychoanalytic and Trait perspectives. Of course, there are many other theoretical orientations, but these two were selected for three reasons: (a) these two approaches represent popular perspectives on personality and assessment; (b) they are perhaps maximally different from each other; and (c) they are particularly relevant to counseling professionals, who are most likely to encounter both of these perspectives in their own work. For those interested in learning more about personality theories from other perspectives as well as to learn more details about the theories presented here, the reader is referred to more specific texts on the topic (e.g., Cloninger, 2000; Monte, 1998).

THE PSYCHOANALYTIC PERSPECTIVE

The first person to provide a comprehensive, scientific description of personality was Sigmund Freud (1916, 1923, 1924). Freud is perhaps the best known of all the personality theorists. Although originally formulated over a century ago, Freud's ideas continue to have an impact on how we think about people today. Freud's theory was revolutionary for his time and made three great contributions to our understanding of people. First was his notion of the *unconscious*. The unconscious represents a region of our psychological world that is outside of our immediate sense of awareness and control. Despite its absence from our daily sense of experiencing, the unconscious has a direct and powerful impact on our behavior. For Freud, all of our motivations for life come from the unconscious regions of our mind. Freud likened the human personality to an iceberg. Just as most of the ice in the berg is located under water, most of the important aspects of who we are reside in the unconscious. Thus, for Freud, it is not what our conscious minds say that is important, rather it is what emerges from the dark recesses of our unconscious that is valuable.

The second great insight that Freud provided was the notion of *childhood sexuality*. For centuries, children were seen as just miniature adults, but without the same passions and motivations that characterize adult life. There was very little recognition that children had their own psychological needs. Freud pointed out that children are very sensual creatures. Having a limited cognitive capacity, children rely more on their feelings and emotions to guide them through their interactions with the world. The most important instinct is the one defined by the pleasure–pain continuum. Children always seek to find gratification for their pleasure needs (e.g., to be fed, held, relieved, comforted) and to reduce the tensions associated with unfulfilled desires. Whether or not these needs to avoid pain and to obtain pleasure are gratified has important implications for how the child's personality will develop.

The third contribution that Freud made was the idea of *psychic determinism*. This is the belief that there is a reason for every action a person performs. Just as in nature there is a reason for everything, so, too, in our inner minds there is a logic and consistency to what we do. That logic, especially of the unconscious mind, may not always appear as rational, but there are essential patterns and meanings to things in the inner world that, once known, can unlock our understanding of the person. These three ideas were revolutionary for their time and helped to significantly stretch our understandings of how the mind works. These concepts also define how Freud looked at people, as organic machines following an innate set of commands in an effort to find security and comfort. To understand psychoanalysis, there are two basic ideas to grasp: the structure of the mind and the processes by which it operates.

THE STRUCTURE AND PROCESS OF PSYCHOANALYSIS

Psychoanalytic model of the mind. Every personality theory posits an underlying structure to personality. For psychoanalysis, there is a tripartite structure that describes our inner world. The first structure is called the *id*. This is the basic element of personality and is the source of all our psychic energies and motivations (which Freud referred to as *instincts*). The id contains the basic impulses that drive our behavior. There is no logic or sense of order to the id. It runs on what Freud termed *primary process energy*. This is our basic, instinctual need to attain pleasure and to avoid pain.

The second structure is the *ego*. The ego represents our more conscious processes; it embodies the logic and order of conscious thought and operates on what is termed *secondary process energy*. The function of the ego is to gratify the needs of our psychic system in ways that are appropriate and respectful of environmental realities. Two qualities of a healthy ego are its abilities to tolerate tension (e.g., go without meeting or satisfying our needs) and synthesize diverse needs into a more unified set of goal strivings.

The third structure is termed the *superego*. The superego contains our moral values or conscience. The superego, like the id, is very demanding and requires an individual to provide immediate gratification of its needs. In the case of the superego, it demands that the person live up to very high levels of virtuous behavior.

The process of personality. What is of central interest to psychoanalysts is the dynamic way each of these three structures relates to one another. Each part of the mind has its own needs and drives. Both the id and the superego are very demanding and require instant gratification. The ego has the arduous task of working hard to gratify those needs, along with its own, in the context of specific environmental demands. There is no doubt that this system generates much conflict and tension. However, it is in the process of successfully resolving these tensions/conflicts that one's personality develops and creatively engages the external world. For example, the id always wants to have immediate sensual satisfaction; in this case, let us say that it wants to eat. You are shopping at the supermarket and the id is demanding food *NOW*. The ego must provide it because not satisfying an instinctual need only makes it grow stronger. To satisfy the id, the ego could just reach out and take that bag of potato chips sitting on the supermarket shelf and start eating. However, the superego realizes that stealing is morally wrong—someone has to pay for those potato chips first. The superego chastises severely, creating more demands on the ego. The environment poses its own challenges: The security guard will arrest you if you do not pay for the chips. So, the id has to wait (which it does not like to do), and the longer it has to wait, the more demanding it becomes. The ego has to devise clever and effective strategies for managing all these conflicting desires. This is where *defense mechanisms* come in.

Defense mechanisms are ego-based methods individuals use to help gratify the basic instinctual desires of the id. Defense mechanisms allow the ego to gratify needs, either directly (through consuming some object that provides satisfaction) or indirectly (through the use of imagery, ideas, or other substitutes to "fool" the id or superego into thinking the need has been gratified). For example, say we are back walking through the supermarket and the hunger demands begin. You know this is not the time or place for eating. What does the ego do? Well, it reaches into the pocket and pulls out a piece of gum to chew on. It is not food that fills the belly, but it could help the id believe that it is eating something, thus partially gratifying the instinct. This takes some pressure off the ego. Also, it is not morally wrong to eat gum, so the superego remains contented, and more tension is reduced (keep in mind that reducing tension is very pleasurable). If there is no gum, perhaps putting a pencil in the mouth, or maybe drinking a glass of water will work. All of these behaviors are substitute actions that help defend the ego against the ranting id's need for food. Then, once we have bought the chips and are outside in the car, we reach in and take a big handful of those salty, tasty taters; ultimate satisfaction is attained! In each instance, the ego has worked to reduce the conflicting needs of the psychic world in ways that are appropriate and effective.

In understanding a person, a psychoanalyst wishes to know how the individual copes with the stresses and conflicts associated with instinct gratification. What types of defense mechanisms are used? There are all different kinds, ranging from very simple or childish—*repression*, where you just unconsciously deny the existence of something—to more sophisticated techniques, like *sublimation*. With sublimation, a basic primitive impulse is transformed into a more mature, sophisticated impulse that is socially accepted and valued. For example, a sadistic need to cut and destroy animals gets turned into a desire to become a surgeon. The former, something scorned and infantile, gets changed into a noble urge to want to help others in pain. For Freud there is not much difference between the little boy who likes to pull the wings off of flies and the surgeon who operates on people in order to manipulate various body parts. Sublimation helps us to live effectively in social groupings by transforming baser instincts into urges that promote a greater social interest. Other defense mechanisms include displacement, projection, reaction formation, isolation, and rationalization.

MEASURING THE PSYCHOANALYTIC PERSONALITY

How does one go about measuring these levels of conflict and types of defense mechanisms? How does one gain access to a person's unconscious? To accomplish this, psychoanalysts use *projective testing*. A projective test is based on the principle of psychic determinism; that everything we do bears our characteristic stamp. If we put a person in an unstructured situation and ask that she make sense of this chaos, anything that the person creates will be an expression of her own internal, unconscious view of the world.

Perhaps the most well-known projective test is the *Rorschach Inkblot Test* (1921/1998). Here, individuals are presented with essentially meaningless inkblots. The designs are basically random, but respondents are asked to create a meaningful picture. The only way for them to make sense of this nonsense stimulus is to project some of their own inner organization onto it; respondents provide their own frame of reference for the interpretation. Therefore, when we look at the response, it tells us something about how the respondents structure their psychological worlds. People are not aware that they are projecting something of themselves onto the inkblot, but to the skilled interpreter, the Rorshach is like an X-ray of the personality, revealing the details of the unconscious domain. However, to interpret those responses requires an extensive amount of training and experience. The language of the mind, from the psychoanalytic perspective, is quite sophisticated and complex. It is a world of symbols and disguised meanings that do not always conform to the rules of logic adhered to in our conscious reality.

There are a number of different projective tests, and what characterizes most of them is their unstructured, fluid format. Most of these tests allow individuals to make as many or as few responses as they wish. Also, there are no right or wrong answers, and respondents are free to give any response they choose. The goal of this class of measures is to make plain the many hidden wishes residing in the unconscious. Another popular projective test is the *Thematic Apperception Test* (TAT; Murray & Bellak, 1973). Individuals are shown a picture and asked to relate what led up to the situation pictured, what is happening now, and what the outcome will be. Again, responses are evaluated for emotional conflicts and how they are handled by the person. *The House-Tree-Person Test* (HTP; Buck, 1964) is another commonly used projective technique. Here, a person (usually a child) is asked to draw a picture of a person, a house, and a tree. The drawing is evaluated for the size of the respective elements, their location on the page, and the details that are present or absent (e.g., the person has no hands, the house has no door). These details are sometimes referred to as emotional indicators. Whether or not they are present says much about the emotional world of the artist (e.g., figures that do not have hands may indicate the presence of depression). Again, it requires much training and experience to interpret this test. Nonetheless, any situation that is unstructured and allows a person to create something can be considered a projective test. Interpreting what is created is believed to reveal important aspects of a person's unconscious world.

STRENGTHS AND WEAKNESSES OF PSYCHOANALYTIC PERSONALITY THEORY

Psychoanalysis is valuable because it is a quite comprehensive theory that explains virtually everything about people. It offers insights that link together in meaningful ways behaviors and actions that on the surface may appear contradictory and counter-productive. The theory can highlight the clever and creative ways individuals find to cope with the worlds they live in. However, the theory is quite complex and requires much study to master.

That the psychoanalytic orientation is mostly clinically oriented is both a strength and a weakness. Its focus on conflict and primitive instincts provides rich material for weaving an understanding of a person's adaptive struggles with reality. This provides a clear point of departure for developing and implementing interventions. However, these interpretations usually stress personal weaknesses and inadequacies of the individual. Truly mature and healthy functioning is experienced by only a lucky few. Thus, the theory is lacking in its ability to document true strengths.

It also makes some assumptions about men and women that may be considered objectionable today. In fact, some see the theory as being a product of late Victorian Age thinking, but the entire theory developed out of the observations of one man, usually in response to experiences with only a single patient. Although important and insightful, it is not clear whether all of these insights are valid and generalizable to today. Few aspects of psychoanalysis are amenable to true scientific testing, and, therefore, there are few data available to speak about the ultimate utility of the theory. Yet, despite very little supporting empirical data, psychoanalysis is still one of the dominant scientific theories in the field today.

THE TRAIT APPROACH

The Trait Approach to personality takes a very different perspective to understanding the individual. Unlike psychoanalytic constructs, traits are empirically developed variables. Using sophisticated statistical analyses, trait researchers identify behaviors, attitudes, and beliefs that appear to covary with one another. In other words, seemingly diverse behaviors are identified that are observed to occur together frequently. A trait is then developed to explain or define why these various behaviors and attitudes cluster together. For example, we may notice that people who are very talkative also tend to be outgoing and sociable and like going to parties and being the center of attention. They also seem to be very perky and energetic, and they can also be very welcoming and approachable.To understand why these different behaviors go together, we may develop the trait of *extraversion*. Extraversion is a psychological construct that refers to an innate tendency of people to orient themselves to the actions and activities of the outer world of people and events. Behaviors such as time spent talking on the telephone, enjoying the presence of other people, and feeling upbeat and positive can all be linked together because they all reflect this underlying characteristic of extraversion.

McCrae and Costa (1990, p. 23) have defined traits as "dimensions of individual differences in tendencies to show consistent patterns of thoughts, feelings, and actions." There are two points of interest in this definition. First, traits are dimensions, empirically constructed labels that help us organize human behavior along meaningful lines. Second, traits are referred to as individual differences, qualities that describe people and upon which people vary in terms of how much they possess. Thus, when people talk about extraversion, it is recognized that not everyone has the same desire to talk on the phone and spend time in the company of others. Some people may, in fact, avoid doing those types of activities. These individuals would be considered *low* on extraversion (i.e., they are introverted). Traits are frequently bipolar in nature—that is, the two ends of the dimension represent opposite qualities (e.g., organized vs. sloppy).

One major characteristic of trait psychology is its emphasis on measuring people on specific traits and then determining how much of the trait the person has by comparing his or her score to the scores of some group (known as a *normative sample*). Individuals are considered *high* on the trait if they score higher than many of the people in the normative sample *low* if they do not. Most people usually fall in the middle of this distribution and are said to be *ambiverts* (this term refers to someone who can exhibit both aspects of the trait, depending upon the context). For example, an ambivert on the extraversion trait would be someone may who, at times, like going out and meeting others but can also, at times, have a desire for privacy and solitude.

But traits are more than just descriptive labels for organizing clusters of behaviors. They provide information about people that enables us to predict accurately outcomes in other aspects of the psychosocial world. In short, traits have been shown to carry impressive *surplus meaning*. Given the scientific basis of traits, much research has been done examining their predictive utility. We know that one's tendency to talk on the phone and desire to be with other people (i.e., one's level of extraversion) is linked to levels of happiness a person will experience in mid to later adulthood; it will predict levels of job success in certain types of jobs as well as predict specific types of occupational aspirations. Other traits (e.g., neuroticism and conscientiousness) have been shown to be powerful predictors of competitive performance outcomes in the academic, athletic, and occupational areas.

Traits have been linked to one's genetic makeup. It appears that about one half of the variance observed in traits is inherited genetically from our parents. Traits also have been shown to generalize cross culturally, so the same patterns in behaviors, attitudes, and actions we see in Western culture are also found to occur in other cultural contexts, such as in Asia and Africa. Thus, traits seem to be human universals for understanding human behavior. Perhaps the most intriguing aspect of research on traits has been the discovery that one's trait profile does *not* change in adulthood. After age 30, all things being equal (e.g., no psychotherapy or religious conversions), personality seems to be pretty much set; our trait dispositions will remain stable over our adult lives. The value of this finding is that it tells us that once we know someone's trait standing, we can make accurate predictions about behavior well into the future. Until age 30, our personality is still in flux and capable of modification. But after 30, we have created for ourselves an adaptive orientation to the world that will lead us in very specific directions to pursue personal goals that are the most satisfying to our needs (e.g., the achievement-oriented person will seek out competitive situations; the extravert will seek out the company of others).

There are thousands of personality trait variables available today in hundreds of different inventories and scales. Such a cornucopia of constructs can easily lead to confusion when deciding which traits to use. Fortunately, recent research has discovered that the majority of these traits cluster themselves around five broader dimensions know as the *Big Five personality domains*:

Neuroticism—The tendency to experience negative affect

Extraversion—Reflects the quantity and intensity of one's interpersonal interactions

Openness to experience—The proactive seeking and appreciation of new experiences

Agreeableness—The quality of one's interpersonal interactions along a continuum from compassion to antagonism

Conscientiousness—The persistence, organization, and motivation exhibited in goal-directed behaviors (Costa & McCrae, 1992)

Research has shown that these five dimensions do provide a useful language for talking about trait variables and that these factors do predict a wide range of important psychosocial outcomes, including mental and physical health and occupational, academic, and intrapersonal criteria (see Piedmont, 1998, for an overview).

MEASURING TRAITS

Trait-based measures are perhaps the most common type of tests used today. They are frequently referred to as *objective tests*. Unlike the projective tests discussed previously, objective instruments provide the test taker with very specific questions and a provided response format (e.g., from *strongly agree* to *strongly disagree*). There is no room for individualized responses on these types of tests. Scores are presented numerically, usually in the form of a *T* score. A *T* score is a standardized score that has a mean of 50 and a standard deviation of 10. Scores between 45 and 55 are considered normative (these are people who are in the middle of the distribution and are considered ambiverts). Scores above 55 are considered *high* (the individual scores higher than most in the normative sample), while scores below 45 are *low*. Only scores in the high or low ranges are seen as interpretable and defining of the person.

Perhaps one of the most widely used objective-type measures is the *Minnesota Multiphasic Personality Inventory–Second Edition* (MMPI-2; Butcher et al., 1989). This scale is widely used to assess *pathological functioning*, although scores on the instrument are also used to assess normal levels of functioning. When looking at a trait scale, it is important to determine what level of functioning is being assessed, normal or clinical. Normal traits refer to characteristics that define everyday traits in people not suffering from a mental disorder. Clinical traits represent aspects of psychological functioning that characterize more dysfunctional patterns of behaving. Although the two types of traits are related to one another (pathological traits are usually just more extreme versions of nonclinical traits), they do capture very different dynamics of the person. One should generally not use a clinical index to make hypotheses about non-clinical qualities. The MMPI-2 is most adept at capturing these more dysfunctional elements of personality. There are 10 clinical scales that capture broad aspects of psychopathology (e.g., depression, psychosis) as well as hundreds of smaller scales aimed at more specific traits (e.g., masculinity, somatic complaints). The instrument is used routinely by psychologists and psychiatrists in making psychological diagnoses. It also provides insights into one's psychological capacities and soundness.

The *Revised NEO Personality Inventory* (NEO PI-R; Costa & McCrae, 1992) is the only commercially available instrument designed to capture the Big Five personality domains. This instrument contains 240 items that measure each of the broad personality domains as well as more specific traits that underlie each of these five broad domains. Each domain has six subfacet scales. For example, the Conscientiousness domain is broken down into the facet scales of Competence, Order, Dutifulness, Achievement Striving, Self-Discipline, and Deliberation. These subscales can provide specific information on traits that may be directly relevant to specific counseling outcomes (e.g., academic success, interpersonal skills, self-esteem). McCrae and Costa (1991) have outlined the value of the NEO PI-R for counselors in diverse contexts.

STRENGTHS AND WEAKNESSES OF THE TRAIT APPROACH

The relative omnipresence of self-report trait measures is testimony to the popularity and utility of this approach to understanding personality. The value of trait measures is that they are empirically derived constructs, so they do represent something that does exist in nature. Further, trait measures provide an efficient method for collecting systematic information about people. Easy to administer and score, these scales can provide a wide range of information that has significant implications for predicting future behavior. Scores from trait scales are readily interpreted by comparison to normative samples, and information obtained from one respondent can be readily compared to another respondent, thus facilitating comparative assessments.

However, trait theory does not have the same interpretive depth as psychoanalysis. The psychoanalytic perspective provides detailed insights into the inner world of the individual. Issues surrounding emotional conflicts and maturity are central to psychoanalytic interpretations. Trait theory is still in its infancy and needs to generate more insights into how traits are acquired, both from genetic and environmental sources. Many questions still remain to be answered, including how traits develop over time and identifying the factors that influence how and when they become expressed.

Because traits reflect self-reported regularities in people's perceptions of their own behaviors, attitudes, and actions, there is no consideration of the unconscious. From the psychoanalytic perspective, self-report measures only tell you about superficial aspects of functioning. The more important, latent aspects of personality are not touched upon. If the unconscious is important to your understanding of a client, then trait measures may have limited utility. However, trait measures do have empirically documented predictive validity. Even if traits only capture more superficial aspects of personality, research shows that these dimensions can explain significant amounts of the variance in a wide range of outcomes. Projective tests, on the other hand, are hard to quantify and do not show as high levels of predictiveness as traits. Trait advocates still need to see some empirical support for the notion of an unconscious as well as some empirical justification for the interpretations that are generated by projective tests.

Another value of traits is their focus on mostly nonclinical characteristics. Traits provide useful summary descriptions of normal functioning. Although traits do have implications for clinical issues (e.g., differential diagnosis, treatment selection, and response to treatment), they also help us to understand a student's strengths. Projective testing frequently results in interpretations that are problem-focused, highlighting the weaknesses and vulnerabilities of the student. Even "normal" individuals can appear pathological on a projective report. Trait measures allow for a more circumspect examination of both the liabilities and assets of a student. However, unlike the psychoanalytic approach, trait theory does not have built into it a methodology for making clinical interventions. Although traits can describe what a student is like and the types of treatments that may be helpful, there are no current techniques for changing actual trait levels.

IMPLICATIONS FOR THE PROFESSIONAL SCHOOL COUNSELOR

The value of personality theory and measurement for professional school counselors cannot be understated. A personality theory provides a framework for systematically integrating the multidimensional nature of an individual into a form that promotes a sophisticated understanding of the developmental/adaptive journey of the student and provides a platform for intervening purposefully and effectively in the student's life. There are three benefits to using personality theories. First, professional school counselors can develop an appreciation for both the emotional weaknesses of a student as well as the psychological resources the student has available to draw upon. All too often, difficult students are seen only in terms of what they lack or what limitations they have. Personality theories cast an eye toward the possibilities for growth and development and thus promote a more holistic, integrative understanding of the individual.

Second, personality theory provides an explanation for behavior that speaks to the fundamental motivations of the student. Understanding what needs a student is trying to have gratified in the school environment can enable the professional school counselor to anticipate the kinds of problems a student may encounter. Personality theory can outline the typical ways which a student will cope with stress or react to pressured situations. It can also outline the types of instructional climates that may be most conducive for optimizing a student's learning.

Finally, personality theories can enable a professional school counselor to identify strategies for engaging students in meaningful dialogues and for selecting appropriate intervention strategies that will be more readily accepted by the student. By understanding how personality develops and influences behavior, professional school counselors can develop a realistic appreciation for which aspects of personality are changeable and which are not. Using personality theories as a way to understand how and why students struggle to adapt to their worlds, professional school counselors can provide the "intra-psychic lubricant" needed to smooth out problems and to enable healthy adjustment and personal growth.

Summary/Conclusion

This necessarily brief overview of these two major schools of thought only scratches the surface of what each approach has to offer in terms of understanding our inner adaptive worlds. There is much more to know about each of them. These two theoretical models are only a limited sampling of the larger number of such theories that exist in the field of personality. The Humanistic, Psychosocial, Cognitive, Behavioral, and Biological approaches, to name a few, provide rich insights into who we are that do not overlap with those contained in the Psychoanalytic and Trait perspectives reviewed here. There is much to be learned from studying personality theories. Although no one theory may have all the answers, learning about personality teaches the right questions to ask.

Professional school counselors should be strongly encouraged to learn a variety of personality theories and models of the mind. Learning and applying personality theories can greatly enhance the quality of counseling services. A personality theory provides a framework for systematically integrating the multidimensional nature of an individual into a form that promotes a sophisticated understanding of the developmental/adaptive journey of the student, and provides a platform for intervening purposefully and effectively in the student's life. Further, many personality theories also have associated measurement models and scales that help one collect and collate relevant information about an individual. There are seven advantages to using personality measures in counseling practice.

1. Measures of personality help promote an understanding of the student in terms of both strengths and weaknesses. Personality assessment can provide a holistic evaluation of the student in terms that are clinically relevant.
2. Such an understanding can breed increased empathy and rapport with the student. A better understanding of the student's conflicts, struggles, and aspirations helps to present a more nuanced portrait of the issues that surround the student's seeking treatment. Such information highlights multiple ways of engaging a student.
3. The results of personality assessment can be used to provide the student with feedback and insight into his or her life patterns. Using a particular measurement model can provide both the student and the professional school counselor with a common language for describing and discussing the conflicts, problems, and issues that the student is experiencing. This language can be used by the professional school counselor for making interventions and providing insights.
4. Data from personality assessments can also aid in differential diagnosis. Test scores provide an independent source of information about a student's behaviors and attitudes that is relevant for nosological classification. The information contained in such scores can help clarify underlying issues that may not be evident upon initial examination.
5. Test information can be used to anticipate the course of treatment for a student. Knowing the personality styles of the student can help the professional school

counselor anticipate potential problems and conflicts that may emerge in the therapeutic relationship (e.g., a person low in Agreeableness may frequently challenge the professional school counselor because such a person tends to hold a skeptical and suspicious outlook towards others). Professional school counselors can then either move to head off such potential disruptions or at least prepare for their emergence.

6. The results of personality assessment can also be used to match students to treatments from which they are most likely to benefit. For example, individuals high on Extraversion, who are sociable and talkative, will find interventions that require interpersonal interactions more helpful than do introverts, who may prefer and benefit from individual-based approaches.

Perhaps the most important benefit of personality assessment is what it affords our field as a whole. Using personality assessments enables us as professional school counselors to obtain objective, scientifically based information on students that can allow us to empirically document the value of our services. Regardless of what type of professional context one is in, the pressure is always on for counselors to do more and more in shorter and shorter periods of time. Through it all, both the providers and the consumers of our services are continuously exhorting us to demonstrate the impact of our interventions. How effective are our counseling services? In what ways do we impact our students? How much do we impact them? These are important, empirical questions that need to be answered. Personality measurements are one way of addressing these concerns. Working from a conceptual model that is consistent with the professional philosophy of the professional school counselor, personality measures provide systematic, verifiable data that can document the extent of our impact and the practical value of our services.

(Note: See the CD-ROM for a list of references.)

CHAPTER 52

BEHAVIOR ASSESSMENT

Carlen Henington

Preview

School personnel in education have increasingly focused on behavior assessment because of behavioral problems in the educational environment and accountability in educational outcomes. Although personality characteristics have, in the past, been an important consideration of problematic behavior for many professional school counselors, current emphasis has been on directly and accurately assessing the behavior and associated characteristics (Ollendick & Hersen, 1984; Shapiro & Kratochwill, 2000) such that responsiveness to intervention can be more readily obtained (Brown-Chidsey, 2005). To increase the accuracy of behavior assessment, procedures must be systematic, objective, and multidimensional.

MODELS OF BEHAVIOR ASSESSMENT

Behavior assessment is used to determine the nature of behavior difficulties of a child and to provide information in the development and effectiveness of an intervention plan to address the behaviors. The selection of an assessment model and the assessment techniques is key to an accurate and informative behavior assessment. As such, it is important to consider the nature (e.g., ongoing vs. a one-time assessment) and the goal (e.g., screening, diagnosis, prognosis, treatment design, intervention evaluation) of the assessment. Although there is no perfect assessment system or method, the information (or data) provided by the assessment must be reliable, valid, and useful in a problem-solving approach to assessment. The goal of administering each assessment component is to compare and contrast the obtained information in a methodical examination of unfolding hypotheses, much like the informed decision making that one uses when completing a difficult jigsaw puzzle. The question might be, *Where does each piece of information fit, and what does it tell us about our next move?*

In part, assessment of behavior is difficult because there are broad ranges of behavior that may be considered for assessment and a variety of classification systems used to describe problematic behavior in the problem-solving approach. Furthermore, there is often no clear distinction between normal and abnormal behavior and whether the behavior is or is not maladaptive to the situation; neither is there always a clear agreement between respondents and interviewees. One person may label a behavior as *difficult* and another may indicate it as *acceptable*.

There are two broad models that can be used to evaluate a student's behavior. The first, the medical model, assumes sharp distinctions between normal and abnormal behavior with the cause of the difficult behavior to lie within the child. This model is best characterized through the *Diagnostic and Statistical Manual,* which is published and updated by the American Psychiatric Association (2000) and tied to the *International*

Classification of Diseases (World Health Organization, 2007). The other, the multivariate model, uses statistical or psychometric properties to compare behavior of an individual to the general population and with emphasis on quantitative differences between normal and abnormal behavior. Most experts in assessment of behavior use a combination of these two models to design the assessment process, or system, with the goal of interpreting the assessment results from a specific theoretical perspective.

Although there are a number of theoretical perspectives from which to choose, behavior theory is particularly useful for assessing behavior in children. The information obtained through behavioral techniques can be used in a variety of ways, a broad range of useful information can be gathered, and the techniques allow ongoing evaluation such that change over time can be monitored. Furthermore, multiple informants can be used to provide a broad picture of the behavior in question and the results lead directly to intervention and the same assessment techniques can be used to evaluate intervention effectiveness (e.g., responsiveness to intervention). This responsiveness has recently become a focus of educators and interventionists through new legislation and an increase in accountability expected by parents and other professionals.

One addition to behavior assessment is the concept of functional behavior assessment. Mandated by the 1997 reauthorization of the Individuals With Disabilities Education Act (IDEA), the assessment process is intended to examine behavior problems through a functional understanding of the behavior, whether it is related to academic or behavioral difficulties. The functional approach involves the generation of a hypothesized function for the problem: academic (e.g., performance vs. skill deficit) or behavioral (e.g., escape, avoidance, attention, automatic) for the engagement of a behavior. This hypothesis is then tested through a series of assessment activities to examine each of the potential functions (Merrell, Ervin, & Gimpel, 2006). From this information about the potential function of the behavior, a behavior intervention plan (BIP) can be developed that is believed to more directly address the underlying problem. For example, a child who is disruptive in the classroom may engage in the disruptive behavior for a number of reasons: (a) he or she cannot do the work (a skill deficit) and needs extra assistance from the teacher (in this case, the function may be to avoid or escape the class work) or (b) he or she may be able to do the work but does not (performance deficit), and instead engages in behavior to gain attention from his or her peers or the teacher or to avoid/escape the work. Using a functional approach to the evaluation of the behavior problem can assist the counselor in making recommendations to more directly address the issue that lies beneath the problem behavior.

METHODS OF ASSESSMENT

Each method of behavior assessment provides different and important information and, therefore, each of the methods described within this chapter offers information that will be useful in determining the behavior and is likely to be valuable in the design of an intervention to address the behavior. Generally, a preferred method is to directly assess the behavior as it occurs. An example of direct assessment would involve a classroom observation of the child with behavior difficulties, whereas an indirect assessment would involve asking the teacher to describe the child's problematic behavior. It is also preferable to assess the behavior in the natural environment. There are times, however, that this direct assessment in the natural environment is not possible (e.g., too difficult or too dangerous).

This chapter will briefly present four common direct and indirect behavior assessment methods: direct observation, self-monitoring, self-report, and informant report. These methods will be presented in sequence starting with the most direct and ending with the most indirect. When several variations of a particular method are presented, those that can be considered more direct will be presented first, followed by the indirect methods. For each method, a brief description will be provided, followed by an example typical to the school environment. Each example will build on information presented such that a comprehensive assessment may be illustrated at the end of the chapter. Although some instructions for the methods will be provided, it is beyond the scope of this chapter. Therefore, interested professional school counselors are directed to the annotated bibliography located in Table 52.1, which provides additional resources to assist in learning more about each method.

TABLE 52.1

ANNOTATED BIBLIOGRAPHY FOR DIRECT AND INDIRECT BEHAVIOR ASSESSMENT METHODS

Assessment, Ninth Edition (Salvia & Ysseldyke, 2004, Publisher: Houghton Mifflin)
  Provides a comprehensive examination of a variety of assessment techniques and procedures, including traditional standardized, norm-referenced measures and nontraditional measures.

Assessment of Children: Behavioral, Social, and Clinical Foundation–Fifth Edition (Sattler, 2006. Publisher: Author)
  This is the latest version of this classic in assessment of children. Provides useful descriptions of instruments, extensive lists of resources, and a wide array of tables and appendices to assist in the selection of assessment instruments and methods, understanding of key concepts of assessment and evaluation across a large number of disorders and disabilities, and translation of the assessment into a clear report.

Assessment for Intervention: A Problem-Solving Approach (Brown-Chidsey, 2005; Publisher: Guilford Press)
  An informative guide to conducting problem-solving–based assessments in school and clinical settings through examination of environmental factors that may contribute to a child's difficulties. Includes descriptions of application, tools, and methods with case example to assist in understanding the process.

Clinical and Forensic Interviewing of Children and Families: Guidelines for the Mental, Education, Pediatric, and Child Maltreatment Field (Sattler, 1998; Publisher: Author)
  Provides a detailed set of guidelines for a variety of interviewing tasks completed with children and their families.

Conducting School-Based Assessments of Child and Adolescent Behavior (Shapiro & Kratochwill, 2000; Publisher: Guilford Press)
  This edited book compiles useful, detailed information for the professional school counselor in the four areas briefly described in this chapter.

DIRECT OBSERVATION

Direct observation involves assessment of behavior at the time it occurs and is the most direct of the behavior assessment methods or procedures. There are two forms of direct observation: observation in the setting where it naturally occurs, and observation conducted in a contrived or analogue setting. Direct observation in a natural setting is typically a preferred component in all methods or procedures of assessment. In this method, the behavior is observed by a trained individual (e.g., a professional school counselor, teacher, teacher's aide) who observes the child in a natural environment (e.g., classroom, playground, lunchroom). This procedure is time intensive but allows the greatest flexibility in collection of valuable data related to problematic behaviors. Direct observation is particularly useful for determining the precise behavior with information regarding its pattern, level, and likelihood of occurrence. Observation is also useful to determine levels of the behavior prior to, during (i.e., the eliciting and maintaining events for the behavior; Skinner, Rhymer, & McDaniel, 2000), and following intervention to determine treatment effectiveness (Brown-Chidsey, 2005).

CASE EXAMPLE

Although there are a number of observation procedures that are commonly used in the schools, the following example uses a momentary time-sampling procedure to directly observe disruptive behavior in the classroom. The disruptive behavior is described as *calling out without permission during teacher lecture.* The professional school counselor, asked to conduct a behavior assessment, would observe the child on several occasions in the classroom at a time that the teacher has identified as a time the disruption is most likely to occur. At 1-minute intervals, the professional school counselor observes the child and determines whether the behavior is occurring at that precise time. The counselor probably would use a clipboard with an observation sheet in this situation; however, another simple method of tallying the behavior is to move a paperclip from one pocket to another if the behavior has occurred at the precise moment of the observation. At the end of the time allotted for the observation (e.g., 20 minutes), the number of tally marks, or paperclips in the "observed" pocket, is counted and noted. The same procedure is followed on at least 1 more day. This procedure provides a direct, empirical method for assessing the number of times disruptive behavior occurs. To determine the effectiveness of an intervention, the number of tally marks during initial assessment can be compared to the number count collected after intervention is implemented. This could then be used to determine the effectiveness of the intervention as to whether the disruptive behavior has decreased to an acceptable rate or is likely to with continued use of the intervention.

ALTERNATIVE OBSERVATION METHODS

Another assessment procedure is to observe the problem behavior using narrative recording. This is a less direct assessment method, potentially offering rich information, but requires further assessment of the behavior. This method requires the professional school counselor to use a clipboard to write down as much information about the disruptive behavior as possible using the previously presented case example. This information includes what happens before, during, and after the child yells. This information is also known as the *antecedent, behavior,* and *consequence(s)*. For example, if the child disrupts the class only when frustrated, the professional school counselor might suggest that the teacher monitor the student's understanding of the material prior to assigning individual seatwork. In directly observing the behavior, the professional school counselor may notice that when the student yells there are a number of behaviors that also occur. In another example, the professional school counselor may notice that, frequently, when the student yells across the room, the teacher has left the room and the teacher's aide is in charge. This is another example of an antecedent to the behavior. In a third example, when the student yells out in the classroom, he looks around at the other students to see if they are watching. This information provides a hint that the student is yelling to obtain peer attention, and an appropriate intervention may be to encourage other students to ignore this student when he yells in the classroom. It is important for the professional school counselor to note what happens after the student yells. For example, if the teacher sends the student out of the room and to the principal's office it may be that the student is allowed to avoid school work when he or she yells out and, therefore yelling serves the function to escape from the classroom and the required class work. Thus, from this information the professional school counselor can determine what might need to change in the environment to assist the student in changing the disruptive behavior.

Not all behaviors can be easily assessed using observation methods. For example, internal conditions such as fear cannot be observed. However, there are physical indicators of fear, and these can be directly observed (e.g., changes in breathing, heart-rate). Another behavior that cannot be readily observed is an individual's thought process or behaviors that occur outside the typical school environment (e.g., nighttime sleep-patterns of a student who falls asleep in the classroom). A possible alternative, less direct than observation in the natural environment, is assessment of the behavior in a contrived situation that is engineered to simulate the natural setting; however, any departure from direct observation of behavior in the natural environment requires inference about the behavior. In this situation, additional data about the behavior must be collected from multiple sources to reduce the likelihood of error and to support the inferences (Cone, 1988). For example, using the example of the student who yells out in the classroom to illustrate, it may not be possible to observe the student in the classroom, or, when the observer is in the classroom, the behavior may not occur. Then, a contrived situation may be constructed. For example, based on the information provided by the teacher, the professional school counselor suspects that the student is able to avoid or escape schoolwork when he or she is disruptive (i.e., the function of the behavior is to avoid class work). To test this hypothesis, the professional school counselor may be required to provide the student with an academic task to be completed. Because the situation does not directly reflect actual occurrences in the classroom, the professional school counselor may have to collect additional data. An example of such data might be to determine the amount, difficulty, and type of academic work that the student is likely to attempt to avoid.

SELF-MONITORING

Self-monitoring is a procedure that uses the individual to observe, record, and report behavior. Researchers have shown that a variety of populations can effectively use self-monitoring to assess behavior (e.g., individuals with developmental delays, learning disabilities, emotional–behavioral disorders; Henington & Skinner, 1998). Self-monitoring has also been shown to be effective in assessing academic and nonacademic behavior. Nearly any behavior that occurs in a school setting can be assessed using self-monitoring (Cole, Marder, & McCann, 2000). Unlike direct observation, self-monitoring requires very little of the professional school counselor's resources. This procedure can be used either as a behavior assessment tool or as an intervention. One key asset is that self-monitoring can be used when direct observation is not possible (e.g., an adult is not present; the behavior is nonobservable, such as anger).

When using self-monitoring to assess behavior, it is important to provide the student with instruction about the procedures. The first step in the instruction is to describe self-monitoring to the student and suggest when it might be useful. This allows the student to understand that he or she is going to be working on the problem *situation*. Next, be sure that the student understands what the behavior is that will be monitored. It is important to be specific in the description of the behavior and, perhaps, to provide examples and nonexamples to assist the student in discerning the exact behavior to be monitored. Then, explain that when it is time to monitor the behavior, the student, using an internal dialogue, will ask himself if the behavior was occurring; if so, he is to record the behavior. Generally, it is helpful to problem-solve with the student how the behavior will be recorded (e.g., an observation form, or the "paperclip" method previously described). Once the student understands the self-monitoring procedure, it will be necessary to practice. Initially, the professional school counselor may find it helpful to model self-monitoring using the already provided example and nonexample behaviors. Then, have the student practice the procedure in as natural a setting as possible, with the professional school counselor providing feedback. This step is important because it increases the likelihood of accurate monitoring. However, if the student understands and accuracy is still a concern (e.g., due to the student's noncompliance, truthfulness), then the professional school counselor may want to add a systematic check that another individual conducts. For example, every so often, when the time to monitor occurs, the professional school counselor also records his or her observation, and a comparison is made between the two observers. To increase the student's motivation to accurately self-monitor, the professional school counselor may wish to provide the student with a reward for matching the observation of the professional school counselor.

When a student uses self-monitoring, it may be helpful to implement a reminder (a cue or prompt) to alert the student when to observe the behavior. This can be done with a verbal or nonverbal signal from another individual or through self-prompting (the student checks his or her own behavior). The observation can be done using a schedule (e.g., momentary time sampling described in direct observation or a less formal system, such as when he or she finishes a page of problems).

CASE EXAMPLE

In the following example, a 6-year-old boy often forgets to turn off the water in the boys' bathroom after he washes his hands. The female professional school counselor cannot accompany him into the bathroom to observe his behavior. Therefore, self-monitoring is an appropriate assessment technique. The professional school counselor discusses the problem with the student early in the morning or after school when others are not present. She describes self-monitoring. Then, the counselor models self-monitoring by enacting a scenario were she uses the bathroom to wash her hands. The boy stands outside the bathroom. When the professional school counselor leaves the bathroom, she asks herself if she has remembered to turn off the water. If she has, she says "Good" and makes a note of it by marking on a card taped to her desk. Then, the student enacts the same scenario, following all the steps. If he forgets, the professional school counselor reminds him. If he does it correctly, the professional school counselor praises him and rewards him with a star on top of his tally mark.

ALTERNATIVES TO SELF-MONITORING

A common variation of self-monitoring is peer monitoring (Henington & Skinner, 1998). In peer monitoring, a peer observes and records the data, whereas in self-monitoring, the student implements the procedures. It is important to remember that the more complex or difficult the behavior being assessed, the more training time will be needed. In some cases, the behavior may not be appropriate for self-monitoring.

SELF-REPORT MEASURES OF BEHAVIOR

There are two broad methods of obtaining information from the individual with the problematic behavior: individual interviews and self-report rating scales. It is generally believed that the individual may be a better reporter of their nonobservable and nondisruptive (internalized) behaviors such as fears, anxiety, and depression. Conversely, it is also generally believed that individuals with observable and more disruptive (externalized) behaviors such as oppositional, attentional, overactivity, and conduct problems are less reliable in their reports of their behavior. Although at times self-report data may be questionable in its validity, when other methods of behavior assessment are also used, self-report can add information that will be helpful in the assessment process and in development of potential interventions.

INDIVIDUAL INTERVIEW

This method assesses the individual's perceptions of the behavior in question. Interviews can be viewed on a continuum, with structured interviews at one end and unstructured interviews at the other end. Structured interviews provide preset questions asked by the professional school counselor. The interview generally starts with collection of broad information about the individual and progresses to information about the problematic behavior. The information about the individual assists in building an understanding of events, characteristics, and other relevant issues that may assist in assessing the behavior. Information obtained about the behavior may include (a) a description of the setting and/or circumstances surrounding the behavior, including the response of the individual and others to the behavior; (b) the onset, duration, frequency, and severity of the behavior; and (c) the history of the behavior and presence of the behavior in other family members (Lane, Gresham, & O'Shaughnessy, 2002). Structured interviews can be completed by the professional school counselor during a meeting with the informant; it also can be completed independently with the individual using a written form or computer program.

In unstructured interviews, the professional school counselor might begin with broad questions and then follow the response with additional questions to provide detailed information. The same general information obtained in the structured interview can be collected, but the professional school counselor allows the individual to provide the information with less direction and in a more flexible manner. Most professional school counselors use a combination of the structured and unstructured interview. In this case, the interview might be considered semistructured. The professional school counselor follows a general outline for obtaining information, but pauses to ask follow-up questions as needed.

SELF-REPORT MEASURES

Self-report measures, also called self-report ratings, provide information regarding an individual's perceptions of his or her behavior. Self-report measures, similar to interviews, provide qualitative information; but, quantitative data is often also available. There are as many types of self-report measures because there are types of behavior disorders and concerns. Some measures assess only one aspect of behavior (e.g., depression, anxiety, self-esteem). These measures are considered narrow-band measures. Conversely, some self-report measures assess a broad spectrum of behaviors (i.e., broad-band) and are often referred to as omnibus measures. These broad measures are generally used as screening tools, and often followed by the more specific measures to closely assess for specific difficulties.

Self-report measures can be based on two models to evaluate the behavior: (a) a theoretical model (use of a specific theory about behavior), or (b) a psychometric model (use of a statistical analysis). When the measure is based on theory, often the questions or statements on which the individual self rates are taken directly from the diagnostic criteria for the disorder or problem. For example, a question related to depression would state *I am often sad*, a criterion characteristic from the *DSM*. The individual would rate how valid this response is for him or her. For young children, a forced choice is often used (e.g., true or false). For older individuals, the choices are more expansive and placed on a continuum. In both cases, a number value is assigned to the response (i.e., *very true* = 3, *somewhat true* = 2, *not usually true* = 1, *never true* = 0). The number of items within the measure often depends on the criteria and the desired amount of specificity, information, and reliability of the measure. Each item will have a number value that is dependent upon the individual's response, and the total of the number values is then calculated (i.e., simple sum of scores). The subsequent total is usually compared to a set of reference scores that indicate whether the reported behavior–perceptions are noteworthy.

The psychometric procedure often uses the same rating format and varies very little in appearance from the theoretically based measures. The questions are often constructed from a theoretical perspective; however, the set of reference scores is empirically derived. In general terms, during instrument development, the measure is administered to a large number of individuals considered to exhibit a broad range of possible behaviors and responses, typical and atypical (e.g., a norm sample). The data from all of these individuals could then be statistically examined in two ways. Without going into great detail, the purpose of these analyses will be described. The first analysis, a factor analysis, determines what questions are related to each other in some statistically systematic way. Using this information the questions are usually refined and those that are related are considered to assess a specific behavior or characteristic as determined by an examination of the items themselves. The second analysis determines a *typical score* and (what might be considered) an *atypical score*. Using the numbers assigned to specifically grouped items, a derived score, usually a *T* score (a mean of 50 and a standard deviation of 10) is expressed as a cut score (similar to the theoretically derived scales) to indicate noteworthy response patterns. A percentile score is also often provided within a table to indicate where the individual would be placed in the norm sample if he or she had been in the original norm sample. For example, a percentile score of 60 would place the individual's score as exceeding 60 out of 100 individuals' scores in the norm sample.

Because self-report measures usually compare an individual to a preselected group or norm sample, the norm sample should be as similar to the individual as possible. For example, a child from a rural southern state should not be compared to children from a large urban setting. Likewise, it would be inappropriate for a young child to be compared to adolescents.

CASE EXAMPLE

The following example illustrates a combination of an individual interview, an omnibus self-report assessment measure, and follow-up narrow-band measures. The professional school counselor has received a referral for a preadolescent girl for whom her teacher has concerns about a recent change in the student's demeanor, falling grades, and sudden social isolation.

Once proper consent and assent has been obtained, the professional school counselor meets with the student and conducts a semistructured interview. In the interview, the professional school counselor obtains information that leads him or her to believe that the student may be experiencing moderate to significant emotional distress. After collecting information about the child's perception of his or her behavior, the professional school counselor then asks the child to complete a broad-based screening measure used by the school district to evaluate children. The professional school counselor scores the broad measure and confirms that there are a number of concerns uncovered by the screener related to depression and anxiety. It is important to note that screening instruments often do not distinguish the fine differences between anxiety and depression. The professional school counselor then follows the screening measure with two separate measures for children—one that specifically assesses depression and another that assesses anxiety. The professional school counselor then scores the narrow-band measures. If the scores are consistent with those of children the same age in the norm sample who have been diagnosed with either disorder, the professional school counselor can be reasonably assured that the child is experiencing distress similar to that of children with either depression and/or anxiety (which ever is indicated by the scores). The professional school counselor can then determine an appropriate intervention to assist the student with reasonable certainty that the intervention will target the correct behavior. As a follow-up to the intervention, the professional school counselor can then reevaluate using the same instruments, a self-monitoring technique, or an observation of specific behavior to determine if the intervention has been effective.

OTHER-REPORT MEASURES OF BEHAVIOR

The other-report method of assessing behavior, especially children's behavior, is the most frequently used assessment method. One of the reasons for this popularity is that, by their nature, report measures are a relatively brief method of obtaining information across a broad range of behaviors from multiple informants. This method is flexible enough to be applied to nearly any type of behavior without losing the integrity of the assessment process.

Other-report measures, also known as an informant report, are similar to self-report measures. Interviews are conducted with an individual familiar with the child to determine his or her perceptions of the behavior. The informant can also complete rating forms. Those individuals most likely to provide appropriate information include parents, caretakers, and teachers. Generally, informant-report measures are conducted with adults only; however, peers can also be asked to evaluate behavior. When peers are used, special care must be taken to protect the relationship of the child and his or her peers. When such risk occurs, use of the other measures described in this chapter may provide suitable and sufficient information to avoid risk to peer relationships. Thus, only in rare circumstances is the information provided by peers of sufficient importance that risk to the child is outweighed by the need for the additional information. Similar to self-report measures, there are two broad types of informant-report measures: informant-report interviews and informant-report rating scales.

INFORMANT-REPORT INTERVIEWS

According to Sattler and Mash (1998), the goal of assessment is to "obtain relevant, reliable, and valid information about the interviewees and their problems" (p. 3). The focus of the interview is determined by the nature of the behavior. Great diversity exists within interview techniques and, frequently, the form and structure of the interview is based on the theoretical training of the professional school counselor. Similar to student interviews, informant interviews can be structured, semistructured, or unstructured. When the professional school counselor is unsure of the problem behavior or questions the proposed referral question, he or she is likely to use a structured interview to gather a broad range of information. This increases the possibility of determining alternative hypotheses about the behavior and allows a more flexible approach to problem solving in behavior assessment. A professional school counselor who uses an unstructured interview method is more likely to focus on obtaining information directly related to a specific behavior or problem.

Generally, key informants of a student's behavior are those who are most likely to be in a position to observe the behavior: parents and teachers. Information obtained in a parent interview should include the following: family and developmental history of the child and a history of the behavior (e.g., symptom description, onset, duration, intensity or severity, past interventions). Teacher interviews are more likely to be behavior-specific, narrow in scope, and focus on obtaining detailed information about the behavior (Busse & Beaver, 2000). Information obtained in a behavior-specific interview should include an exact definition of the behavior, a history of the problem behavior (e.g., setting(s), surrounding events—antecedents and consequences), past interventions and their effectiveness, the goal of the assessment/intervention, potential incentives to use during intervention, and other available resources.

When conducting an interview with the parents, it is desirable to have both parents present to obtain the perspectives of the mother and father. Some professional school counselors may also want the student present for a part of the interview to allow direct observation of the parent–child interaction. Another variation is to have the entire family present. This allows observation of family interaction. Another alternative is to conduct a conjoint interview with the parents and the teacher. Sheridan, Kratochwill, and Bergan (1996) described a procedure for conjoint meetings. In any case, when the student is present, care should be taken to protect the professional school counselor's relationship with the student; and when appropriate, the student should be excused so that the student does not perceive the adults to be talking about him or her with no regard to vulnerable feelings.

INFORMANT-REPORT RATING SCALES

Although informant-report rating scales are considered to be the least direct form of behavior assessment, they are one of the most used assessment methods because they have strong psychometric properties and are relatively objective. Merrell (2000) described these strengths, stating that rating forms have been shown to have same rater consistency across time, items, and situations (i.e., reliability). He also stated that rating scales provide consistent information across respondents (i.e., validity). Additionally, they can be used for comparison across individuals and behaviors (i.e., norm referenced) and can be applied in meaningful ways (i.e., used to develop treatment and interventions). Other researchers have also discussed the strengths of the rating scale method (Schaffer, Fisher, & Lucas, 1999). Relatively little training is required to administer and score rating measures. Additionally, informant-rating measures can provide information about behaviors that are difficult to assess more directly (e.g., low occurrence behaviors, behaviors that the child may not accurately report). Rating scales often provide information about behavior that has been observed across long periods of time. This allows the professional school counselor to determine the presence of the behavior at other times in the child's development.

Potential problems with rating scales are predominately related to the vulnerability to rater bias. These biases include the halo effect (e.g., a tendency to view a child in a more positive way than would typically occur) and leniency or severity effect (e.g., a tendency to be too easy or too difficult in evaluation of the behavior). It is important that the professional school counselor remembers that ratings are perceptions and therefore, as stated previously, must be compared for consistency with other data collected about the behavior and the child. Table 52.2 provides annotated bibliographies of commonly used behavior assessments.

CASE EXAMPLE

In this example, a third-grade teacher has approached the school's professional school counselor about classroom management. The professional school counselor uses a brief behavior-specific interview, obtaining the teacher's perceptions of the behavior of her students. He discovers that the teacher has concerns about only one student in her class and that she has spoken with the parents about the student's behavior. The teacher reports that the parents have similar concerns.

The teacher is concerned about a student's variable grades and motivation, disruptive behavior, and lack of friends. This behavior assessment potentially will require a formal assessment and intervention with the student. The professional school counselor then contacts the parents to obtain permission for a formal assessment. He sends some broad-based parent-report measures to the parents and asks them to complete and bring them in when they come for an interview. The professional school counselor then asks the teacher to complete similar broad-based report measures. During the parent interview, the professional school counselor asks that the teacher be present for part of the interview (a conjoint interview) so that more comprehensive information can be collected about the behavior. The parents and the teacher agree and the professional school counselor uses the rating scale responses of the parents and teacher to conduct a behavior-specific interview.

The professional school counselor has now built a team of problem solvers to address the behavior. The team determines that a comprehensive assessment should be conducted. The professional school counselor makes arrangements to observe the student in the classroom and to interview the student. When the team completes their conjoint meeting, they leave with a belief that the behavior will be properly assessed and will lead to an effective intervention that will improve the student's behavior. The professional school counselor then selects from a variety of assessment tools described within this chapter to collect information and inform him of potential interventions to address the teacher and parents' concerns.

SUMMARY/CONCLUSION

As can be seen from this last example, a comprehensive behavior assessment is likely to include most if not all four components of behavior assessment: direct observation, self-monitoring, self-report measures, and informant-report measures. The more comprehensive the behavior assessment, the more likely important information will be collected and used to correctly identify the problem; and based on this information, the more likely an appropriate intervention will be developed to address the problem behavior. That is the ultimate goal of a behavior assessment—to address the behavior and alleviate distress that may either be a symptom or a cause of the behavior.

TABLE 52.2

ANNOTATED BIBLIOGRAPHY FOR COMMONLY USED BEHAVIOR ASSESSMENTS

Self-Report Inventories

Beck Youth Behavior Assessment System for Children, Second Edition–Self-Report of Personality (BASC-2-SRP; Reynolds & Kamphaus, 2004; Publisher: American Guidance Service)

Available in English and Spanish, assesses student's perceptions and feelings about school, parents, peers, and one's own behavior problems. Two forms: Child—ages 8–11 (SRP-C); adolescent—ages 12–18 (SRP-A); and young adults—ages 18–25 (COL). The SRP-C and SRP-A have identical composites scores (School Problems, Internalizing Problems, Inattention/Hyperactivity, Personal Adjustment, and the Emotional Symptoms Index—ESI, a composite score that consists of positive (adaptive) and negative (clinical) scores. The COL, excluding School Problems, has the same composite scores with slightly different subscales (e.g., Alcohol Abuse, School Adjustment). Includes 14 to 16 subscales (dependent upon the age level) with two new subscales added (Attention Problems and Hyperactivity) beyond those offered by the first edition. For the SRP-A and COL, four content subscales have also been added (Anger Control, Ego Strength, Mania, and Test Anxiety) to broaden content. Yields *T* scores for the 139 to 185 items using norms for the general population, males, females, and a clinical population. Strength is the ability to assess response sets or validity indices (e.g., "fake good," "fake bad") and use as a multiinformant instrument when combined with other BASC-2 measures.

Children's Depression Inventory (CDI; Kovacs, 1991; Publisher: Multi-Health Systems)

A 27-item scale appropriate for individuals ages 6-17. Assesses a number of depressive symptoms. Strength is ease of administration and scoring and use as either a screener or diagnostic tool. Uses cut scores rather than derived scores.

Reynolds Adolescent Depression Scale–Second Edition (RADS; Reynolds, 2001; Publisher: Psychological Assessment Resources)

A 30-item instrument appropriate for ages 13 to 18 years. Uses a 4-point rating scale to assess depressive symptomology. Strength is ease of administration and scoring.

Revised Children's Manifest Anxiety Scale (RCMAS; Reynolds & Richmond, 1985).

Assesses state and trait symptoms of anxiety. Appropriate for ages 6–19 years using 37 items to yield *T* scores on four subscales including a validity scale and a total score. Strengths include broad number of anxiety symptoms assessed, ease of administration and scoring, and the validity scale.

Informant Inventories

Achenbach System of Empirically Based Assessment (ASEBA; Achenbach & Rescorla, 2000; 2001; Publisher: Western Psychological Services)

This revised system includes a variety of new tools for use in assessment including School-Age and Preschool forms. The Child Behavior Checklist/1½-5/LDS and the Caregiver-Teacher Report Form 1½–5 (C-TRF; Achenbach & Rescorla, 2000) are for very young children. The Child Behavior Checklist for Ages 6 to 18 (CBCL/6–18) and Teacher Report Form (TRF; Achenbach & Rescorla, 2001) are for school-age children. All versions provide cross-informant scores on syndromes (e.g., internalizing, externalizing problems), scales consistent with diagnostic categories consistent with the *Diagnostic and Statistical Manual* (DSM-IV-TR; American Psychiatric Association, 2000), as well as competencies. Strengths include large research base to support validity of the instrument, wide familiarity to a number of professions in the mental health fields, translation into numerous languages with input from professionals from 16 cultures to validate diagnostic categories. Useful tools (ASEBA Quick References Guides) are available to assist the practitioner in using the ASEBA forms.

TABLE 52.2. *(continued)*

Behavior Assessment System for Children, Second Edition–Parent Rating Scale (BASC-2-PRS) and *Behavior Assessment System for Children, Second Edition - Teacher Rating Scale* (BASC-2-TRS; Reynolds & Kamphaus, 2004; Publisher: American Guidance Service)

> Published concurrently with the BASC-2-SRF, these two versions of the BASC-2 are intended to assess a child's clinical and adaptive behavior in the home and community (Parent Rating Scale) and school environment (Teacher Rating Scale). Both measures have three forms: preschool (ages 2–5 years), child (ages 6–11 years), and adolescent (ages 12–21 years). Requires approximately 10–20 minutes to complete. These measures have been expanded beyond the original BASC with extension of ages at both ends of the spectrum; the subscales Adaptability (to the adolescent level), Activities of Daily Living (to BASC-2-PRS) and Functional Communication (to all levels); and the Content Scale (to all levels; i.e., Anger Control, Bullying, Developmental Social Disorders, Emotional Self-Control, Executive Functioning, Negative Emotionality, Resiliency). Yields *T* scores using norms for the general population, males, females, and a clinical population. Strength is the variety of scales for differential diagnosis, validity indices, strong psychometric properties, and use as a multi-informant instrument.

Devereux Scales of Mental Disorder (DSMD; Naglieri, LeBuffe, & Pfeiffer, 1994; Publisher: The Psychological Corporation)

> New version of the *Devereux Scales* (School Form) with two forms: 111-item scale for ages 5–12 years and 110-item scale for ages 13–18 years. Either parents or teachers can complete this new version that provides *T* scores on six clinical scales, Attention (ages 5–12 years, only) and Delinquency (ages 13–18 years, only). Strengths include ratings that can be compared across raters and good discrimination between emotionally disturbed and nondisturbed children.

Functional Assessment Informant Record for Teachers (FAIR-T; Doggett, Mueller, & Moore, 2002; Edwards, 2002; Publisher: Author)

> Uses teacher provided information to assist in developing hypotheses about the function of students' behavior in the school environment including additional information about the problem behavior, antecedent events (task information, preceding activity), maintaining functions (persons present/absent), consequences of behavior and other actions, and past interventions. Strengths include ease of administration, direct link to behavior that either will supplement direct observation or allow hypotheses generation when observation is not an option.

Specialty or Narrow-band Informant Rating Scales

Attention Deficit Disorders Evaluation Scale–School and Home Versions (ADDES-3; McCarney, 2004; Publisher: Hawthorne Educational Services)

> This rating scale has two versions: Home (46 items) and School (60 items); and yields two subscale scores: Inattentive, Hyperactive-Impulsive. Although lacking in construct validity for the three subscales, internal consistency tends to be high. Strengths include support materials for interventions, large nationwide normative base.

Social Skills Rating System (SSRS; Gresham & Elliot, 1990; Publisher: American Guidance Service)

> This instrument includes self-, parent-, and teacher-rating forms to assess children's social behaviors. Useful for screening purposes for social difficulties, but behavioral and emotional problem scales may be less useful and valid than other instruments. Strength: multi-informant measure.

Sutter-Eyberg Student Behavior Inventory (SESBI; Sutter & Eyberg, 1984; Publisher: Author)

> Designed to be the companion to the *Eyberg Child Behavior Inventory* (Eyberg & Robinson, 1982), the SESBI focuses specifically on 36 behavior problems using a 7-point rating scale and yes–no problem identification system. Strength of this measure is that its use facilitates identification of problematic behavior for direct intervention.

(continues)

TABLE 52.2. (*continued*)

Formal Behavior Observation Systems

Behavior Assessment System for Children, Second Edition– Student Observation System (BASC-2-BOS; Reynolds & Kamphaus, 2004; Publisher: American Guidance Services)

Also available in an electronic version (BASC Portable Observation Program–BASC POP) in which observations are entered into a computer or PDA, allowing storage of five observation sessions from which to generate reports. Brief observation system that allows for examination of 13 specific categories of behaviors target behaviors (4 categories of positive–adaptive behaviors and 9 categories of problematic behaviors). Uses a momentary time sampling procedure, narrative procedure, and a checklist of behaviors. Strengths include ease of use, time efficiency, and direct observation of children and adolescents.

Behavior Observation of Students in Schools (BOSS; Shapiro, 1996; Publisher: Guilford Press)

Assesses key components of a student's academic behavior including three types of off-task behavior (i.e., verbal, motor, passive) as well as active and passive on-task behavior. Uses a time-sampling procedure. Teacher's direct behavior toward the target students is also tracked. A comparison peer is also observed. Strengths include distinction between active and passive behavior, focus on academic behavior.

Direct Observation Form (DOF; Achenbach, 1986)

Intended to be integrated with information obtained with other ASEBA products, this observation system examines 96 problems, many of which have overlap with items on the ASEBA rating forms completed by parents, teachers, caregivers, and youth.

State-Event Classroom Observation System (SECOS; Saudargas, 1992; Publisher: Author)

Observational coding procedure with a long history that uses a brief observation using a time sampling procedure. Provides for assessment of instructional situations, categories of student behavior (states and events), and teacher behavior. Strengths include the ability to assess a wide range of classroom occurrences, including peer and teacher behavior.

(Note: See the CD-ROM for a list of references.)

CHAPTER 53

CONDUCTING A STRUCTURED OBSERVATION

Cyrus Marcellus Ellis

Preview

Effective structured observations begin with proper planning and the involvement of teachers, parents, and students. Professional school counselors, to increase the effectiveness of the learning environment for teachers and students, need to recognize important behavioral components to accurately recognize student behaviors that interrupt the learning environment.

The new millennium presents professional school counselors with myriad issues related to accurately determining and meeting the educational, career, and interpersonal needs of students (Paisley & McMahon, 2001). As students, teachers, and administrators interact, there will undoubtedly be misunderstandings and problems. Professional school counselors work together with all members of the school community to recognize, evaluate, and determine intervention strategies to improve interpersonal behavior and academic performance. Of the many job-related duties professional school counselors perform, conducting interviews and observations directly relates to the role of ensuring that all programs foster student success (American School Counselor Associations[ASCA], 2000). In this role, professional school counselors may be asked to conduct structured observations to critically determine all factors that maintain a productive and orderly environment (Moore, Anderson, & Rumar, 2005).

Conducting a structured observation allows professional school counselors to assess student behavior, classroom environment, school climate, instructor behavior, and the impact of physical and psychological disabilities of students in the school (Asmus, Vollmer, & Borrero, 2002; Drummond, 2000; Ellis & Magee, 1999; Freiberg, 1998; Hagborg, 1998; Webb, Baxter, & Thompson, 1997).

BEHAVIORAL ASSESSMENT

Barnhill's (2005) work described the use of Functional Behavioral Assessment (FBA) as an essential part of the American education system since 1997, following the amendment phase of the Individuals With Disabilities Act (Sheperis, Doggett, Ota, Erford, & Salisbury, 2006). Barnhill (2005) defined FBA as a manner of acquiring information about preceding events, behaviors, and the consequences of student behaviors and the possible reasons for that behavior. The goal of FBA, Barnhill contends, is to find out the purpose of the behavior in order for school personnel to apply appropriate interventions that will help extinguish undesirable behavior.

Sheperis et al. (2006) added that behavioral assessment is a function of interactions between the individual and the individual's environment. Traditional behaviorists recognize that the individual's response to the stimuli that surrounds them is of the utmost concern. Sheperis et al. reinforced this notion by recognizing that a student's behavior cannot be examined in isolation; rather, it must be considered in the light of environmental conditions interacting with the student.

Sheperis et al. (2006) cautioned professionals that, when conducting behavioral assessments, they should focus on the assessment of behaviors in control of the student rather than the student's pathology. Professionals often include behaviors they believe needs an intervention; however, behavioral assessment is more about determining behavior that is in the student's control (i.e., fighting) rather than attempting to intervene with a particular disorder (i.e., Conduct Disorder). Behavioral assessment is a comprehensive assessment of a child's behavior within his or her voluntary control and not as a function of any disorder.

PLANNING THE STRUCTURED OBSERVATION

There are two methods of conducting a structured observation while following the dimension of FBA: direct assessment and indirect assessment. Direct observation methods tend to offer the highest degree of credible data (Gordon, Meadows, & Dyal, 1995; Shapiro & Skinner, 1990). Direct observation provides the best possible chance for obtaining salient information, and the individuals being observed can become reactive during the observation: "If the client knows he is being observed, his behavior may be quite different from when he is unaware of it" (Drummond, 2000, p. 256). Indirect assessment involves using historical reports of past events, interviews concerning the student's behavior, self-reports from the student, and other behavioral instruments and rating scales (Sheperis et al., 2006).

A structured observation, then, requires a systematic approach that requires the observer to view a series of factors shown to provide the greatest opportunity for credible results. Table 53.1 shows the initial planning considerations for a structured observation.

Professional school counselors need to pay particular attention to whether their active participation will inhibit data collection. If the planning phase determines that the professional school counselor should be removed from the observation, the substitute observer (i.e., paraprofessionals or support personnel) needs to engage in every dimension of the planning process as well as receive training in observation methods, data collection, and construct identification.

Professional school counselors, as well as support personnel, need to be involved in gathering background information from teachers, teaching assistants, and students to ensure that the targeted issue they will observe is clearly stated and understood *before* the observation commences (ASCA; 2000). Drummond (2000) echoed these concerns by identifying four areas that must be addressed when conducting observations: (a) an observable behavior understood by the observer, (b) an easy method of recording observations, (c) eliminating observer distractions, and (d) treating the observed with respect. Figure 53.1 provides an example of a pre-observation checklist to address the concerns raised by Drummond.

Ellis and Magee's (1999) work in determining the impact of the school environment on unsettling student behavior in the classroom provided a systematic approach to critically observe behavior. In their examination of student's disruptive behavior,

TABLE 53.1

PRE-OBSERVATION CHECKLIST INSTRUCTIONS

Institution:	Write in host school's name.
Planned Observer:	Write in the name of the individual who is scheduled to conduct the observation.
Planned Location:	Write in the location where the observation is scheduled to be conducted.
Planned Observation:	Write in the information concerning the date of the observation, when it will begin, and when it will end.
Date, Start, & End Time of Student to Be Observed:	Identify the student to be observed (ensure the student's confidentiality by, for example, assigning a case number).
Identification of Behavior That Is Disruptive to the Learning Environment:	Teachers report on events that are occurring before the presence of the problematic behavior. Behavior is noticed as a result of preceding events. Consequences of behavior upon the student.
Acceptable Behavior Is:	Be clear, from interviews with the educational team, on what acceptable behaviors are permitted.
Unacceptable Behavior Is:	State clearly what behaviors are unacceptable to the learning environment.
Possible Distractions Occurring During Observation:	List the possible distractions to an observer's observation. Be sure to include social desirability issues as well as other school functions that may impede the observation.
Procedures for Addressing Social Desirability:	Provide a plan of action to consider the impact of the observer on the data collection.

Ellis and Magee reviewed the student's background information, clearly identified the student's negative behavior (e.g., daily emotional outbursts, impulsive yelling, aggression towards other members of the school community) and evaluated the response of the school community to the student's exhibited behavior. Social desirability on the part of the observed student and a lack of preparation of professionals are two factors that contributed to awkward observation approaches, which yielded inaccurate conclusions. Using Ellis and Magee's work can assist in providing professional school counselors insight into describing unacceptable behavior.

BEHAVIORAL OBSERVATIONS

Professional school counselors may be called upon to observe student behavior within or outside of the classroom (Ellis & Magee, 1999; Shapiro & Skinner, 1990; Webb et al., 1997). Through direct observation methods, observers document the unconcealed actions of students as well as the environmental forces acting upon a student or a group of students (Shapiro & Skinner, 1990). Observing student behavior requires professional school counselors to correctly identify and define the behaviors that are problematic for student and teacher. Identifying problematic behaviors that disrupt student learning is

PRE-OBSERVATION CHECKLIST

Institution: _____

Planned Observer: _____

Planned Location of Observation: _____

Planned Observation Date and Start Time: _____ End Time: _____

Student to be observed: _____

Description of Questionable Behavior

_____

_____

_____

Acceptable Behavior

_____

_____

_____

Unacceptable Behavior

_____

_____

_____

Possible Distractions to Observation

_____

_____

_____

Procedures for Addressing Social Desirability

_____

_____

_____

FIGURE 53.1. Example of a pre-observation checklist.

a combined effort between the professional school counselor, other school personnel, students, and parents. As stated in the previous section, conducting a structured observation is a systematic process.

Asmus et al.'s (2002) work in developing a functional behavioral assessment model mirrors the work of Ellis and Magee (1999) by incorporating a process for behavior identification as a part of their model. Asmus et al. described the basis for their functional

TABLE 53.2
DIRECT OBSERVATIONAL METHODS

Observational Method	Method of Collection	Benefits
Anecdotal Observation: ABC analysis	Counselor prepares an observation form, divided in three sections, to record antecedent events, observed behaviors, and consequent events.	• Easy organization. • Recognizes events supporting inappropriate behavior. • Recognizes environmental conditions that assist or inhibit positive behaviors.
Frequency of Behavior: Tallying/Frequency/Timed Observations/Period Observation	Checklists, rating scales, professional school counselor–generated forms.	• Can focus on occurrence of behavior as well as duration. • Can establish an overlapping observation cycle. • Provides flexibility in the planning phase of the observation.

behavioral analyses as including "both a descriptive assessment of natural conditions and a functional analysis using analog conditions" (p. 70). While their functional analysis approach involves the process of experimentation, descriptive assessment involves a clear statement of the environment, behaviors to observe, and the method of collecting information. Ellis and Magee (1999), as well as Asmus et al. (2002), recognized the importance of targeting observable behaviors. Additionally, each recognized the need for pre-observation interviews, direct-observation techniques, clear data-collection methods, multiple periods of observation, and observation congruence between all observers.

METHODS OF DATA COLLECTION

Zirpoli and Melloy (1997) underscored the necessity of employing a systematic approach to behavioral assessment by stating four points that reflect the benefits of such an approach. Zirpoli and Melloy stated that a systematic approach to behavioral measurement assists school personnel in classifying a range of behavior problems, evaluating criteria concerning the efficacy of programs, targeting program modifications, and communicating needs with parents and all members of the school community. Asmus et al. (2002) confirmed this latter point by promoting the use of the assessment devices for guiding conversations with parents and teachers.

Reviewing the work of Zirpoli and Melloy (1997) provides professional school counselors with a variety of systematic approaches for conducting a structured observation. Table 53.2 lists two methods of observation, data-collection practices and the benefits of their use. The techniques used in the methods section of Table 53.2 are consistent with Shapiro and Skinner (1990) and Drummond (2000) as the best approaches for conducting observations. Figures 53.2 and 53.3 provide examples of forms for anecdotal and frequency of behavior observations, respectively. As human beings are the individuals conducting the structured observation, professional school counselors need to pay strict attention to additional variables to ensure that the observation is free from confounding variables. In addition to the process of determining observation needs, professional school counselors involved in structured observation need to (a) ensure the objectivity of the observers, (b) remain inconspicuous, (c) address the behaviors specified in the planning phase, and (d) rehearse observations to ensure proper documentation. Proper planning and efficient design promote the best possible chances for an observation to yield credible results.

Summary/Conclusion

A structured observation can help educators understand the nature of the academic environment. Initiating a structured observation involves more than watching students—it encompasses the blending of teacher, parent, student, and administrator views toward the clear identification of problematic conditions that need modification. Properly planned observations provide credible results that work to isolate and remedy problem behaviors, ensuring the academic success of each student.

(Note: See the CD-ROM for a list of references.)

OBSERVATION RECORD

Institution: _____

Observer: _____

Observation participant: _____   Location of observation: _____

Observation period: Start Time: _____   End Time: _____

Antecedent Events

State time and briefly describe events

(Example: 1020hrs, student running in hallway)

_____

_____

_____

Observed Behavior

State time and briefly describe events

(Example: 1020hrs Student collides with teacher's aide)

_____

_____

_____

Consequent Behavior

State time and briefly describe events

(Example: 1021hrs Teacher's aide drops books, turns, and makes the student stand
    against the wall)

_____

_____

_____

FIGURE 53.2. Example of an anecdotal observation report using ABC analysis.

FREQUENCY OBSERVATION RECORD

Child's Name: _____   Date of Observation: _____

Observer: _____   Identified Behavior: _____

Date/Time	Frequency of behavior	X	Duration of observation	Duration of behavior
(Example: 2-22/1430hrs	10	X	25 Minutes	0.4 per min.

FIGURE 53.3. Frequency and duration observational record.

CHAPTER 54

ASSESSMENT TRENDS:
ISSUES AND RESOURCES FOR COUNSELORS

Janet E. Wall

Preview

In the future, technology and assessment as aids to professional school counselors will change dramatically. It is almost a certainty that testing will become more efficient; testing will take on more interesting, creative, and relevant forms; testing and instruction will be more closely aligned; many more tests will be given online; and students will expect and even demand greater use of computers and the Internet. I address these issues and provide resources that professional school counselors need to stay in tune with how their assessment responsibilities are evolving.

TESTING WILL BECOME MORE EFFICIENT

With the introduction of computers and the Internet into the educational systems, various measurement approaches have blossomed. The most popular is a set of procedures and processes that fall into the category of computer-adaptive testing. This approach to testing uses the rapid calculation capabilities of the computer to select items tailored to a person's particular level of achievement or ability. Sireci (2003) provided a good overview of the intricacies of computer-adaptive testing, but a somewhat simplistic description follows. Consider a student who is taking a mathematics test via computer. The computer selects an item of average difficulty and presents it to the student. The student answers the question correctly (or incorrectly). The computer then selects a more difficult (or easier) item to determine how the student answers the question. If the student still answers the question correctly (or incorrectly), the computer then selects an even more difficult (or easier) item. The process continues until the computer, programmed by rules created by testing specialists, hones in on the actual achievement level of the student in question, and, at that point, the administration of items ceases. Such a process would be enormously cumbersome, if not impossible, to use in a paper-and-pencil testing environment. However, the computer is able to determine a student's level of achievement faster, with fewer items, and more accurately. This obviously creates efficiency useful to school personnel, both in time and money.

TESTING WILL TAKE ON MORE INTERESTING, CREATIVE, AND RELEVANT FORMS

Bennett (2002) suggested going beyond the limitations of multiple-choice tests and the use available technology to develop assessments that support learning and instruction in ways that a paper-and-pencil assessment cannot. Consider how technology can make assessment more interesting, performance oriented, realistic, and authentic. The introduction of audio, video, interactivity, graphics, and the ability to access multiple resources has allowed test developers to create, and test users to access, assessment items that move well beyond familiar repeat and recall items.

Technology-based assessment in the area of science can pose a situation in which the student has to create a hypothesis, collect and analyze data, test the hypothesis, render conclusions, and predict further action. This can be accomplished through items that offer the student the opportunity to select the tools of the experiment, collect the data, create graphs that display the data, change the variables, and draw conclusions. The computer can then judge how well, efficiently, and accurately the student was able to handle the necessary problem-solving and experimental requirements.

A language teacher can provide the opportunity for students to link audio and video technology with native language speakers to assist students in perfecting their pronunciation, dialect, and general competence in the language they are trying to learn. Consider further how valuable it could be for a student to better understand the culture and politics of the country whose language she is trying to master through interaction with citizens of that country.

Think about performance tests in areas such as nursing, architecture, physician assistant, realty, driver's education, history, social studies, and so on that present the student with a scenario to analyze. The computer allows the student to select the tools to use in handling the posed problem, to seek and select the information that might be needed, to sort and categorize the information, and to propose the best solution to solve the problem through a written composition that is analyzed by computer, not human, scorers. Further, the technology can allow for a comprehensive evaluation of how well the scenario was analyzed—all in a matter of moments rather than days or months.

Ponder the possibility of the counselor educator who needs to monitor and evaluate his or her interns at a school or agency. Technology such as video teleconferencing and video cameras can be used to assess and critique students through real-time observations of how they interact and assist students and clients, or to observe the intern as he or she interprets assessment results with a student or client. The use of blogs can serve as a useful technique for journaling, an activity that is frequently required as part of counselor training programs.

Recognize the benefits associated with the possibilities of administering and scoring written essays and passages by computer, as opposed to waiting for a team of readers to make a determination of the quality of the writing. Further, appreciate the speed and consistency with which computers can operate in scoring these essays. More and more research is showing the possibilities of automated scoring of extended responses (Attali & Burstein, 2006).

Technologies such as instant messaging, electronic chats, audio–video, video teleconferencing, Web cams, and artificial intelligence can augment assessment of students, especially to probe a student's understanding of a particular topic or counselor situation.

Tests Will Be More Closely Aligned With Instruction

There are multiple pressure points forcing school personnel to provide testing that is more closely aligned with instruction, and instruction more closely aligned with agreed-upon standards. The first pressure point is the issue of fairness. If a student is judged by a test to be competent or not, pass a class, or be promoted to a higher grade, then the test questions that help make that judgment must relate to the instructional program provided to the student. There are many ethical and legal ramifications to situations in which important decisions are made from assessments that do not reflect the curriculum that is provided to the student.

The second major pressure point is the implementation of the No Child Left Behind Act of 2001, which mandates alignment of tests to state standards. The pressure comes from the expectation that all schools should be reaching certain minimal annual standards.

Finally, technology will facilitate the matching of assessments to instruction, and then standards. Items can be stored electronically and coded to instructional objectives and standards so that large-scale assessments can focus on the particular standards of interest to state policy makers and school personnel. Another benefit of this approach is that both teachers and professional school counselors would be able to access student information in near real time, so that interventions can be implemented just as soon as the test results are known. Most states now have this type of information available to analyze both student and institutional performance (*Education Week*, 2006).

Many More Tests Will Be Given Online

A number of states are implementing or planning to implement statewide assessments over the Internet (*Education Week*, 2003). Online testing and assessment offers the capability of obtaining achievement information from many students with rapid data retrieval in time for policy makers to identify the curricular strengths and weaknesses that require specific attention. It offers the chance for classroom teachers and professional school counselors to access achievement information on individual students at the level of instructional objectives at a time when instructional interventions can actually make a difference, not months later. Since most schools have the capability to make information available to parents directly through e-mail or Web sites (*Education Week*, 2006; Kleiner & Ferris, 2002), test results can be transmitted to parents for their edification and action.

Negative Aspects of Online Testing and Related Resources

The examples cited in the previous section are some positive ways that computers and the Internet can expedite testing. However, there is a negative side to the joining of technology and assessment. Easy access to tests over the Internet increases the availability of tests and assessments that are lacking in technical evidence and documentation or are developed by individuals without appropriate expertise. Pick your favorite search engine and enter the term *educational testing*. If you use Google, be ready to view more than 4 million Web sites or links that claim to have related information.

Many online tests, assessments, and inventories can be downloaded or taken online from these sites, but most sites provide no evidence of the quality and utility of the assessment. Wall (2003, 2004b) provided a summary of how a professional school counselor should think about the advantages and disadvantages of technology-delivered assessments. Professional school counselors will need to be able to discern the differences between credible and noncredible instruments that are available via a few clicks through an Internet browser. Some guidelines for sorting tests that are credible from those that are not have been identified. These guidelines include statements of best practice in test administration, test quality, credibility of the developer, test interpretation, and access to professionals (Wall, 2000, 2004a). Also, Figure 54.1 provides a simple checklist that will help professional school counselors review, critique, and select an appropriate assessment.

Despite the availability of both good and bad assessments over the Web, pertinent information on tests and testing in general can be found on the Internet. Clearly, it is impossible to keep track of those millions of Web sites related to educational testing. The Web sites listed in Table 54.1 are a few that offer excellent, credible, and updated information on assessment issues in counseling and education.

In addition to keeping in touch with the information provided on the Web sites listed in Table 54.1, professional school counselors need to keep in mind the various professional association testing standards in order to differentiate what is credible from what is not, on the Internet. These testing standards apply to tests in paper-and-pencil format, but also to those available online or via computer. Professional school counselors need to be familiar with professional codes, standards, and policies such as the *Standards of Educational and Psychological Testing* (AERA, APA & NCME; 1999), *Code of Fair Testing Standards in Education* (JCTP; 2002), the *Responsibilities of Users of Standardized Tests* (AAC; 2003), *Qualifications of Test Users* (ACA; 2003), *ACA Position Statement on High Stakes Testing* (ACA; 2004) and *Rights and Responsibilities of Test Takers: Guidelines and Expectations* (JCTP; 2000). The guidance provided in these standards go a long way in assisting professional school counselors to identify, select, administer, score, and interpret test information.

SUMMARY/CONCLUSION

Access to current and new technologies will only increase over time. As such, professional school counselors need to harness the power of the Internet in performing their job functions. In doing so, professional school counselors can expand their influence and assist students in dealing with academic, career, and personal–social needs and issues.

(Note: See the CD-ROM for a list of references.)

DECISION-MAKING CHECKLIST

For each instrument you are considering, conduct a review and complete the checklist. Add additional criteria that may be particularly pertinent and important. If a criterion is not applicable, leave it blank. When you are done, add up the number of Outstanding, Acceptable, and Not Acceptable ratings to see how the instrument matched up to the criteria.

Instrument Name: _____   Publisher: _____

Evaluation criteria	Rating		
	Outstanding	Acceptable	Not Acceptable
Assessment's purpose matches my purpose			
Instrument's target audience is similar to my students or clients			
Quality of technical information (such as reliability and validity) are strong			
Development sample and norms represents my students or clients			
Delivery format is suitable to my students or clients			
Vocabulary is appropriate to my target audience			
Scoring for my students or clients is easy, accurate, and appropriate			
Scoring process minimizes errors			
Feedback of results is timely and useful			
Results reported are clear and helpful			
Recommended interpretations are supported by research			
Amount and kind of interpretation is appropriate to the needs of my students/clients (not too much or too little)			
Mechanism for storing results matches my needs and organizational capabilities			
Match between the mechanism for retrieving results and my needs and organizational capabilities			
Supportive documentation is available and provided by the publisher (such as technical reports and research studies)			
Technical reviews by unbiased and credible persons provide supportive information			
Information from colleagues who have used the instrument support its use			
My personal review of the instrument supports its use			
Students or clients who have taken the instrument support its use			
Cost is in line with benefit			
Costs are within my budget			
Add other criteria!			
Total			

FIGURE 54.1. Decision-making checklist. *Note.* From *What Do I Like to Do?: 101 Activities to Identify Interests and Plan Careers* (p. 139), by J. E. Wall, 2005, Austin, TX: PRO-ED, Inc. Reprinted with permission.

TABLE 54.1

SUGGESTED ASSESSMENT-RELATED WEB SITES

American Educational Research Association (AERA)

This organization is concerned with the educational process through scholarly inquiry and information dissemination. Many publications, newsletters, and reports are available via its Web site (http://www.aera.net). AERA is a member of the Joint Committee on Testing Practices (JCTP).

American Psychological Association (APA)–Science Directorate

The Science Directorate of APA focuses its efforts on providing information for the American Psychological Association's scientific and academic members. APA is a member of the JCTP, and the Committee's Web site is housed on APA's Web site (http://www.apa.org/science/testing .html).

Association of Test Publishers (ATP)

ATP is a nonprofit organization representing providers of tests and assessment tools and services related to assessment, selection, screening, certification, licensing, and educational or clinical uses of tests. The organization has many publications and information on assessment available on its Web site (http://www.testpublishers.org).

Board on Testing and Assessment (BOTA)

BOTA advises the federal government on a wide range of issues concerning the science and policies of testing and assessment in education, employment, and the military. Issues addressed by BOTA include the role of assessment in standards-based reform of education, the effects of high-stakes testing, the development of professional testing standards and policies to ensure appropriate test use, and the uses of assessment as tools of program evaluation and accountability (http://www7.nationalacademies.org/bota).

Buros Institute of Mental Measurements

This Web site represents the well-known Buros products and services including test reviews and searches. The reviews of tests can be very useful to individuals searching for an instrument with a particular purpose and set of characteristics (http://www.unl.edu/buros).

Joint Committee on Testing Practices (JCTP)

This Web site provides information on the activities of the JCTP. Several of the products produced by this organization's working groups are available by download from this Web site (http://www.apa.org/science/jctpweb.html).

National Association of School Psychologists (NASP)

NASP's prime goal is to promote educationally and psychologically healthy environments for all children and youth. Many policy statements, position papers, and responses to frequently asked questions can be found on its Web site. NASP is a member of the JCTP (http://www.nasponline.org).

National Association of Test Directors (NATD)

NATD is an association of professionals with responsibilities for administering assessment programs in K–12 public educational settings. Various publications, legislative information, and useful links can be found on its Web site. NATD is a member of the JCTP (http://www.natd.org).

(continues)

TABLE 54.1. (*continued*)

National Center for Educational Statistics (NCES)

This government office oversees the creation and implementation of the nation's large-scale assessment program called the National Assessment of Education Progress (NAEP). It is responsible for implementing the assessment plan, analyzing the results, and reporting the results to the general public and policy makers. It is perhaps best known for its product *The Nation's Report Card.* NCES also collects, analyzes, and reports on various other data about schools and education (http:// nces.ed.gov).

National Council on Measurement in Education (NCME)

This organization is devoted to educational assessment issues. NCME is a member of the JCTP (http://www.ncme.org).

Office of Educational Research and Improvement (OERI)

OERI is part of the U.S. Department of Education (http://www.ed.gov/offices/OERI). It provides national leadership for educational research and statistics. Many of its efforts involve evaluation and assessment. This office supports many of the research labs that investigate and disseminate information on educational progress, including assessment.

CLINICAL ISSUES IN SCHOOL COUNSELING

HELPFUL HINTS FOR PARENTS AND PROFESSIONALS WORKING WITH STUDENTS WHO HAVE ATTENTION-DEFICIT/HYPERACTIVITY DISORDER

David J. Carter, Patricia L. Walburn, and Bradley T. Erford

Preview

We provide awareness, knowledge, and skills to address the specific needs of the student with attention-deficit/hyperactivity disorder (ADHD) through a team approach. In most cases, students affected by this complex disorder are disadvantaged in the school, home, and social settings. We provide facts and strategies to dispel myths, provide user-friendly strategies and support for addressing the needs of the student with ADHD, and increase the awareness, knowledge, and skills of parents, teachers, and the professional school counselor regarding ADHD.

Attention-deficit/hyperactivity disorder (ADHD) is a complex medical condition affecting about 3 million school-age children (about 3%–5% of the school-age population) and is so multifaceted that one student with ADHD may have very different symptoms than another student. Navigating the academic arena can be frustrating—so much so that 35% of students with ADHD fail to finish high school (Lawlis, 2005).

HISTORY OF ADHD

Over the years the terms used to describe ADHD have changed (Barkley, 1990). During the first half of the 20th century, children who had ADHD were described as brain injured or brain damaged. During the 1950s and 1960s, the terms *minimal brain dysfunction* (MBD), *hyperactive child syndrome*, and *hyperkinetic reaction of childhood* were introduced into the literature. In 1980, the third edition of the American Psychological Association's (APA) *Diagnostic and Statistical Manual of Mental Disorders (DSM-III)* introduced the term *attention deficit disorder* (ADD). *ADD with hyperactivity* was used to describe students with characteristic distractibility, impulsivity, and overactivity. ADD without hyperactivity described the distractible and impulsive children who lacked significant hyperactivity. In 1987, APA's *DSM-III-R* introduced the term *attention deficit hyperactivity disorder* (ADHD) and listed 14 criteria. This conceptualization did not distinguish subtypes based on activity levels and reflected the thinking of the time that distractibility in and of itself was not characteristic of a mental disorder. In 1994 with the release of the *DSM-IV*, the current term *attention-deficit/hyperactivity disorder* (ADHD) was introduced.

ADHD is currently divided into three subtypes. Certain students, referred to as Predominantly Inattentive Type, have little or no problem sitting still but may have difficulty with organizational skills or staying focused on a task or activity. Others, referred to as Predominately Hyperactive-Impulsive Type, may be able to pay attention to a task but have significant difficulty controlling their impulses and motor activity. The most commonly diagnosed form of ADHD is the Combined Type; these students have significant symptoms of both Inattentive and Hyperactive-Impulsive Types.

Not all professionals distinguish between types of ADHD in the same way; therefore, addressing the student's specific individual symptoms is most effective. This requires a team approach, in which all significant observers and participants in a student's treatment provide information on how to best support the student. Professional school counselors, school psychologists, teachers, school administrators and parents are all key members of the team who observe and report on the student's progress. Professional school counselors have the responsibility of selecting and monitoring the students' treatment, making referrals, and linking parents to community resources. Parents should be encouraged to learn about and advocate for their child's rights within the educational system, including rights to an appropriate education in the least restrictive environment, and any need accommodations or special services (Rief, 2003). When parents know their role on the team, they are empowered to seek the best support for the student.

COMMON MYTHS SURROUNDING ADHD

A number of myths continue to permeate society. Following are nine commonly regarded myths about ADHD.

1. *ADHD is an "imitation disorder" and is not a real or recognized condition.* ADHD has been recognized as a debilitating disorder and disability by all major professional medical, psychiatric, psychological, legal and educational associations (Booth et al., 2002).

2. *Stimulant medications cure ADHD.* Research has shown that children and adolescents diagnosed with ADHD benefit from therapeutic treatment with stimulant medications, which have been used safely and studied for more than 50 years. However, medication only reduces symptoms during treatment. "Skills, not pills" create lasting changes in the lives of students with ADHD.

3. *Individualized Education Programs (IEPs) will always be provided for students with ADHD.* In most school districts, unless a diagnosis of ADHD has been provided by a physician or by a mental health professional after a psychological assessment, an IEP will not be initiated. In these cases the professional school counselor can recommend intervention strategies to the teacher or advocate for appropriate referral and treatment. Students with ADHD are often given accommodations through Section 504 of the Rehabilitation Act of 1973 or, when eligible, special education services through the Individuals With Disabilities Education Improvement Act of 2004, usually with a handicapping condition of other health impaired or learning disability.

4. *Students with ADHD are learning to make excuses rather than take responsibility for their actions.* Counselors, educators, and physicians routinely teach students and parents that ADHD is a challenge, not an excuse. Medication may address an un-

derlying chemical imbalance, but coping skills give them a fair chance of facing the challenges of growing up to become productive adults.

5. *ADHD is the parent's fault and due to bad parenting and lack of discipline. All that students with ADHD need is old-fashioned discipline.* Faraone and Biederman (1998) demonstrated that while ADHD may be an inherited condition, not all children in a family will develop it. While each child has different experiences within the family framework, primary parental disciplinary styles do not change from child to child. Quite often, however, the parent of an ADHD child will shift toward an authoritative parenting style in an effort to control the child's behaviors. Simply providing more discipline without any other interventions generally worsens rather than improves the behavior of students with ADHD. This only serves to exasperate a child who is already experiencing frustration. Traditionally, parenting styles have been categorized as Permissive, Authoritative, and Authoritarian, with the Authoritative parent being the ideal. Lawlis (2005) suggested a more comprehensive classification: the *Teacher*, who focuses on teaching a specific culturally accepted philosophy and values; the *Supporter*, who provides only support, believing the child's fate is out of anyone's control; the *Molder*, who attempts to form the child to their specific expectations and hopes; the *Guide*, who is passive, allowing the child to have self-expression without control or interference; the *Monarch*, who places their own needs before the student's and views every behavior as a reflection on themselves; and the *Dependent*, who sees the child as a commodity for serving their needs. Lawlis believed the *Teacher* to be ideal.

6. *Teachers and professional school counselors around the country routinely advocate for medication for students who are even a little inattentive or overactive.* When teachers and professional school counselors see students who are struggling to pay attention, concentrate, or are fidgety and disruptive, it is their responsibility to bring this behavior to parents' attention so that parents can make an informed decision and take appropriate action. The majority of professional school counselors and teachers do not simply promote medication; they provide information so that parents can seek out appropriate diagnostic and treatment services. Professional school counselors do not ordinarily diagnose students with ADHD, however they are the professionals who have the most direct contract with the student, teachers, and the parents. This places them in a position to observe behaviors, collect information, raise the possibility of ADHD, and bring information to the attention of parents. The parents should then have psychological and medical evaluations conducted, either privately or in cooperation with school personnel.

7. *Children will eventually outgrow ADHD.* ADHD may not disappear as a student grows older. Seventy percent of students with ADHD continue to manifest the full clinical syndrome in adolescence. Anywhere from 15% and 50% will continue to manifest the full clinical syndrome in adulthood (Barkley, 1990). Generally, hyperactive symptoms are likely to decline in adulthood while symptoms of distractibility and disorganization remain.

8. *Sugar, food dyes, and additives will increase ADHD activity.* Sugar causes a burst of energy (in anyone, not just students with ADHD). Restricting sugar intake

will not reduce ADHD symptoms. Food dyes and additives should be eliminated from everyone's diet, but this is becoming more difficult because of current food processing methods. Studies (Barkley, 1990) have shown that some students (perhaps 20%) have allergic reactions to these substances. However, food dyes and additives do not cause hyperactive symptoms in the vast majority of students with ADHD.

9. *It is not possible to accurately diagnose ADHD in children.* Although scientists have not yet developed a single medical test for diagnosing ADHD, diagnostic criteria have been developed, researched, and refined over several decades. The current generally accepted diagnostic criteria for ADHD are listed in the *DSM-IV-TR* (APA; 2000). Using these criteria and multiple methods to collect comprehensive information from several informants, ADHD can be reliably and accurately diagnosed.

DIAGNOSIS

When diagnosing ADHD, professional school counselors can help uncover evidence of clinically significant impairment in a child's social or academic functioning as well as document that the symptoms were evident prior to 7 years of age and were present in more than one setting. Some common ADHD assessments used include, but are not limited to *Conners' Ratings Scales–Third Edition* (Conners, 2008). Intelligence tests, such as the Kaufman (Kaufman & Kaufman, 2004) and Wechsler Intelligence Test Series (Wechsler, 1997, 2001), along with achievement tests, such as the *Woodcock–Johnson III* (Woodcock, Mather, & McGrew, 2001) be administered to assess for possible cognitive discrepancies and learning disabilities. In order to differentiate between ADHD and other behavioral disorders, assessments such as the *Child Behavior Checklist* (Achenbach & Rescorla, 2001) should be administered. Symptoms of ADHD must persist for at least 6 months and to a degree that is maladaptive and inconsistent with the student's developmental level.

It is widely believed that many students are misdiagnosed with ADHD because they have medical or psychological conditions that mask or mimic the symptoms of ADHD. Comprehensive medical and psychological evaluations are essential in differentiating between conditions that mimic ADHD and comorbid conditions that coexist along with ADHD. This increases confidence in the student's ADHD diagnosis.

Following are medical and psychological conditions that often cause students to behave in a distractible or overactive manner: Oppositional Defiant Disorder, Conduct Disorder, Generalized Anxiety Disorder, Dysthymic Disorder, Bipolar Disorder, Post Traumatic Stress Disorder, Major Depressive Disorder, Manic Episode, Schizoid Personality Disorder (and Schizophrenia, Schizotypal, and Schizo-Affective Disorders), physical or sexual abuse, grand mal seizures, petite mal seizures, substance use or abuse, asthma (actually the use of the inhaler causes overactivity in some), lead poisoning, hyperactive thyroid, anemia, allergies, Pervasive Developmental Disorder, Auditory Processing Disorder, Visual Processing Disorder, Motor Coordination Disorder, and others. When diagnosing ADHD, each of these conditions should be considered during clinical interviewing.

How Educators and Parents Can Help Students with ADHD

Teachers, parents, administrators, and professional school counselors can enact numerous strategies to help students with ADHD experience academic and behavioral success at school and home. These strategies are typically aimed at reducing inappropriate symptoms of distractibility/disorganization and impulsiveness/hyperactivity. Table 55.1 presents strategies that may be used to help students with ADHD. Parents play a key role in the academic and personal success of their children. Professional school counselors can reassure parents that ADHD is not their fault and that it can be treated effectively through parent training, family education, regular monitoring, behavior management, and medication, when appropriate. Parents can compliment the team process and provide continuity between the school and home.

Medication and Sleep Patterns

Medication is effective for treating impulsivity, inattention, and hyperactivity. Approximately 75% of students with ADHD respond positively to psychostimulants or tricyclic antidepressants (Barkley, 1990; Kaplan & Sadock, 1996). According to Hartman (1997), medications are often prescribed by child psychiatrists for 3 to 12 months in order to develop new patterns of behavior, and then the dosage is reduced or discontinued depending on the needs of the student. Medication alone is not the long-term solution (Lawlis, 2005). The use of behavioral and specific academic strategies will aid in preparing the student with ADHD for continued academic success.

Whether or not children with ADHD are on medication, they often have difficulty sleeping at night. This may be partially due to the ADHD or to the medication wearing off, making it difficult to manage their behavior during bedtime. A few tips for parents follow:

- Establish daytime routines with regular activities and mealtimes.
- Avoid giving caffeinated drinks in the afternoon and evening.
- Pay special attention to all the variables associated with a relaxing sleep environment, such as noise, room temperature, bedding, toys, and lighting.
- Keep the bedroom a sleep-specific area—no television, radio, games, and other distractions. A good night's sleep for a child and adolescent is 9 or 10 hours, with the same bedtime and wake time, 7 days a week.
- Keep track of sleep patterns with a progress chart and reinforce your child each morning.

Case Vignettes

The following vignette is typical of the type of behavior students with ADHD will exhibit in the classroom. It is important to recognize that although these behaviors are typical of a student with ADHD, not all students who exhibit these behaviors have ADHD.

Mark has more energy than most boys his age, but, then again, he's always been overly active. Starting at age 3 years, he was a human tornado, dashing around and disrupting everything in his path. At home, he went from one activity to the next, leaving a trail of toys behind him. At meals, he upset dishes and chattered nonstop. He was reckless and impulsive, even running into the street with oncoming cars, no matter how many times his mother explained the danger or scolded him.

On the playground, he seemed no wilder than the other kids. But his tendency to overreact, like hitting playmates simply for bumping into him, had already gotten him into trouble several times. His parents didn't know what to do. Mark's caring grandparents reassured them that "Boys will be boys, he'll grow out of it"—but he didn't. In third grade, Mark's teacher threw up her hands and said, *"Enough!"* In one morning, Mark had jumped out of his seat to sharpen his pencil six times, each time accidentally knocking into other children's desks and toppling books and papers. He was finally sent to the principal's office when he began kicking a desk he had overturned. In sheer frustration, his teacher called a meeting with his parents and the professional school counselor. But even after they developed a plan for managing Mark's behavior in class, Mark showed little improvement. Finally, after an extensive assessment, they found that Mark had ADHD–Combined Type. He was given medication to control the hyperactivity during school hours. With the professional school counselor's help, Mark's parents learned to reward desirable behaviors and send Mark to time-out when he refused to follow parental directions (Erford, 1999). Soon, Mark was able to sit still and focus on learning. Today, at age 14, Mark is doing much better in school. He channels his energy into sports and is a star player on the football team. Although Mark still gets into scuffles now and then, the professional school counselor is helping him learn to control his tantrums and frustration, and he is able to make and keep friends.

Summary/Conclusion

ADHD is a chronic behavior disorder of uncertain etiology that always begins in childhood. ADHD is most commonly diagnosed in boys, and the disorder often continues into adulthood. The central aspects include inattention/disorganization and hyperactivity/impulsiveness, and the student can exhibit one or both of these difficulties. Three typically used interventions for ADHD include specifically designed school services such as a structured classroom for children with behavior disorders, behavior management techniques, and medications. Classroom and home techniques include securing attention before directions, checking for comprehension, reducing environmental distractions, shortening assignments, and assigning work that is interesting.

A collaborative team approach provides educators, family members, and the student with ADHD with a mechanism for new possibilities. Working together will enable each member to grow through the team process toward a common purpose—to enhance the life of the student affected by ADHD.

(Note: See the CD-ROM for a list of references.)

TABLE 55.1

STRATEGIES FOR HELPING STUDENTS WITH ADHD

General Suggestions to Help Parents

- Break down target skills into steps that can be taught and practiced.
- Provide student-centered rationales for desired behaviors.
- Be consistent in expectations and tolerances.
- Establish a nonverbal cue (touch or signal) to let the student know when he or she is inattentive or behaving improperly and to prompt attention to desired behaviors.
- Acknowledge appropriate behavior immediately, being specific and genuine in your praise.
- Initially establish lower accuracy expectations that increase over time with the students' success.
- Give positive attention through the use of verbal praise and tangible rewards for behaviors you want to see more often and for approximations of desired behaviors until new behaviors are formed.
- Allow access to rewards at multiple points during the day for achieving or reaching target goals.
- Catch problem behavior as soon as it begins. Give corrective feedback privately. Be brief, specific, and matter of fact.
- Use response-cost behavioral monitoring (e.g., remove a leaf or apple from a constructed tree for each infraction. Once the leaves or apples are gone, a privilege is lost).
- Recommend parent support group association meetings.
- Recommend parenting classes to aid parents in the skills needed for addressing inappropriate behaviors or acquisition of desire behaviors.

Distractibility and Difficulty Focusing

- Maintain a consistent and predictable schedule.
- Realize that the student will be more inattentive just before lunch and late in the afternoon. Plan instruction accordingly.
- Provide short breaks with plenty of performance feedback and encouragement between tasks.
- Encourage parents to set up a recognized routine for home activities, including study time.
- Encourage parents to set up home study spaces with minimum distractions, and parent monitoring and availability.
- Allow preferential seating to lower distractions
    - near the primary area of instruction.
    - with distracting visual stimuli placed behind the student.
    - in a study carrel for independent work or test taking.
    - away from doors, windows, and other distractions.
    - surrounded by focused role-models who will neither distract the student nor allow the student to distract them.
- Keep materials in cabinets when not in use to decrease visual distractions.
- Use earphones (white noise, soft instrumental music) to keep down auditory distractions.
- Teach self-monitoring. Use tape-recorded time prompts, digital watches, special watches made for students with ADHD, such as those available at www.watchminder.com (Sonna, 2005). When the tone beeps or vibrates have the students self-monitor and self-reward to determine if he or she is on task.

TABLE 55.1 (*continued*)

- Provide a timeframe for specific steps or instructions (e.g., "10 seconds to get your name on the paper").
- Match academic assignments to the student's level of ability and attention span.
- Cut back on repetitive homework assignments beyond the point of mastery.
- Visually divide worksheets into blocks and columns to prevent the student from becoming visually overwhelmed.
- Provide more spacing on paper to improve visual organization.
- Limit the number of problems on a page to provide a sense of accomplishment.
- Use a timer to break assignments into smaller, more focused units. For elementary students, timed units should generally not exceed 10 or 15 minutes; for middle and high school students, 15 to 30 minutes.
- Give only one task or instruction at a time.
- Have the student rephrase the directions in his or her own words to be sure he or she understands.
- Alternate between low- and high-interest activities to sustain attention.
- Provide visual–tactile and multisensory approaches to instruction, such as story boards for recording sequence of events in language arts (Hartman & Bowman, 1996).
- Use classification strategies to aid in recall of information, such as the use of word families for spelling and reading (Hartman & Bowman, 1996).
- Make learning fun by creating life-like play in which desired skills are incorporated (e.g., setting up a post office to provide an opportunity to write, send, mail, and receive letters; Hartman & Bowman, 1996).
- Teach students to repeat the question or problem before attempting to answer it (Hartman & Bowman, 1996).
- Increase novelty and stimulation through the use of color, shape, and texture enhancements (Honos-Webb, 2005). For example, use brightly colored instructional materials with a clear and specific instructional purpose to engage the student's attention.
- Hold a review session at the end of the day for homework assignments, key points, and so on prior to tests.
- Give extra time to complete standardized tests, subject tests, projects, and assignments to ensure that grades reflect mastery of content rather than time constraints.
- Due to visual distractions limiting focusing ability, the student may need to be tested orally rather than through traditional written techniques.
- Give multiple-choice tests as opposed to fill-in-the-blank or essay tests to benefit these contextual learners.
- Allow middle and high school students the use of tape recorders to provide a reference to materials at a later time (Alexander-Roberts, 1995).
- Provide older students with copies of notes or allow other students to share their notes (Alexander-Roberts, 1995).
- Incorporate different learning styles into note-taking; for example, have students draw a pictorial representation of the concept (Alexander-Roberts, 1995).
- Teach and model the SQ3R method for reading and comprehending instructional material from texts (Alexander-Roberts, 1995).

Poor Organization
- Create tools to help students improve organizational skills.
- Have student write descriptions of daily and long-term goals.

continues

TABLE 55.1 (*continued*)

- Color-code assignment folders and notebooks using a different color for each subject.
- Create checklists for daily chores and tasks.
- Provide a separate homework folder. Label one side *Homework to be Completed* and the other side *Completed Homework Ready to Turn In.*
- Have student regularly compose To Do lists.
- Have student use an assignment notebook to dictate daily and long-term assignments. Check the notebook at the end of each class period to ensure student has documented homework assignments and notes completely and thoroughly. This will aid students and the parents who may be monitoring and assisting them with assignments at home.
- Maintain and post a consistent and predictable routine and schedule to promote the student's mental organization.
- Set time limits for chores/tasks to help the student develop a sense of time management.
- Have a well-organized student help transition the student with ADHD from step to step.
- Set up appropriate home and school study schedules with set times and a recognized routine.
- Break down long-term assignments and projects into logical organized steps:
    - List the tasks needing completion.
    - List all needed resources and materials.
    - List tasks in order.
    - Break down difficult tasks into smaller tasks (Sonna, 2005).

Task Incompletion

- Match academic assignments to the student's level of ability and attention span.
- Stress comprehension and application rather than memorization (Sonna, 2005).
- Allow ample opportunity for students to pursue their own areas of interests when possible (Sonna, 2005).
- Allow students to learn at their own pace; comparable to Montessori learning (Sonna, 2005).
- Incorporate the student's preferred learning style into lesson plans and assignments (Sonna, 2005).
- Give only one task at a time.
- Give adequate "getting started" instructions.
- Give an example of what the student is to do.
- Make sure multistep directions are written down, whether on the paper, chalkboard, or an index card.
- Make sure the student is on the right track when starting an assignment.
- Check progress frequently.
    - Have the student do 2 or 3 examples under supervision of a teacher, parent, or student helper to be sure he or she understands the process before completing items independently.
    - Maintain close proximity to the child to provide assistance, feedback and redirection as needed.
    - Compliment the student when proceeding correctly and redirect his or her performance when off track.
    - Have the student check with you after completing the first item, at the half-way point, and upon conclusion.

TABLE 55.1 (*continued*)

- Allow the student to seek assistance from designated peer tutors if needed.
- Involve peers in the learning process. Designate study buddies for tests and long-term projects.
- Insist that the student follow through and finish each task correctly before moving onto a more desired activity. This is called the Premack principle—high frequency behaviors must follow low frequency behaviors. For example, have the student finish language homework BEFORE engaging in a play activity.
- Use the word processor to compose written work. This will help counterbalance the frustration that stems from slow writing speed and rewriting handwritten compositions for editing and final drafts.
- Have the student divide long-term assignments into sections, setting a due date for each section and complying with each due date.
- Have the student rework all errors on tests and assignments to reinforce mastery and stress careful initial work habits.
- Require a daily assignment notebook that allows daily or at least weekly communication between the parent and teachers. This notebook should be signed by teachers and parents.
- Cut back on repetitive homework assignments beyond the point of mastery.
- Set time limits for work completion.
- Have the student complete a shortened version of a class project.
- Avoid heavy doses of desk work.
- For young students, tape record the homework and schoolwork instructions for moderate to complex assignments so the student can go back to listen to them later in class or at home.

Restlessness and Excessive Movement
- Alternate between low and high movement activities.
- Incorporate movement into activities as much as possible.
  - Give the student specific times when it is appropriate to get up out of his or her seat.
  - Provide opportunities for purposeful movement.
  - Provide a free-movement area in the back of the room where children can stretch or complete jumping jacks when restless (Sonna, 2005).
- Role-play action scenes that emphasize patient, deliberate activities.
- Provide many opportunities for kinesthetic activity during instruction.
- Change activities and posture frequently.
- Alternate between desk, floor, standing, group, and movement activities.
- Give the student sanctioned times out of his or her seat to let off energy.
- Provide short breaks involving physical movement between tasks.
- Allow students to move around while keeping them in the general proximity of their work, by requiring students to have only one body part touching their desk or chair (Sonna, 2005).
- Give ample warning prior to transitions, and guide students throughout (Sonna, 2005).

Impulsiveness
- Establish consistent routines, rules, and procedures.

(continues)

TABLE 55.1 *(continued)*

- Facilitate rule internalization by
  - creating posters with rules for various work periods.
  - asking the student to occasionally restate rules.
  - teaching the student to use self-instruction during work.
  - having the student recite rules to another student before beginning an assignment.
  - using tape-recorded cues or reminders.
  - defining clear and reasonable limits.
- Increase supervision at transition times (e.g., lunch, recess, specials).
- Have the student redo a messy or incorrect assignment to understand that carefulness and accuracy are more important work habits than quickness.
- Teach and reinforce problem-solving strategies.

CHAPTER 56

HELPING STUDENTS WHO HAVE ALCOHOL AND OTHER DRUG PROBLEMS

Gerald A. Juhnke, Elias Zambrano, and Scott W. Peters

Preview

Alcohol and Other Drug (AOD) abuse continues to be a major problem for high school and middle school students, and is even becoming problematic at the elementary-school level. The more routinely correlated negative effects of such abuse by students are well documented within existing literature (e.g., poor academic performance, student retention); however, more severe and sensational negative effects often reported via the news media are also related to AOD abuse among this population (e.g., suicide, aggravated assault). The cognitive-behavioral and adjunctive interventions described herein provide professional school counselors with practical and effective treatment options that can be readily implemented with AOD-abusing students.

HELPING STUDENTS WITH AOD PROBLEMS

Existing literature clearly supports many professional school counselors' perceptions and beliefs that high school and middle school students are (a) abusing alcohol and other drugs more frequently than ever before, (b) beginning AOD abuse at earlier ages, and (c) ignoring the inherent dangers associated with AOD abuse (Hogan, 2000; Johnston, O'Malley, & Bachman, 2000). An example of research reflecting such student AOD abuse and attitudinal deterioration is a University of Michigan Institute for Social Research longitudinal study. The research began in 1975 and is funded by the National Institute on Drug Abuse (NIDA). This research surveys nationally representative samples of 8th-, 10th-, and 12th-grade classes and annually includes almost 50,000 students from more than 400 public and private secondary schools. Survey results indicate that (a) 51% of the participants had used an illicit drug by the time they reached their senior year in high school, (b) the annual use of any illicit drug among seniors increased from 48% in 1995 to 51% in 2004, and (c) the percentage of seniors who had used an illicit drug within 30 days prior to survey participation decreased slightly from 24% in 1995 to 23% in 2004 (NIDA; 2004).

Data provided by the Substance Abuse and Mental Health Services Administration (2005a) report that (a) 18% of youth between the ages of 12 and 17 years had used alcohol within the past month, (b) 29% of youth between the ages of 12 and 20 years reported alcohol use within the previous 30 days, (c) prevalence of current alcohol use increased with age and led to a greater likelihood of risky behavior, and (d) binge drinking increased with age from 1% at age 12 to 27% at age 17.

Alcohol is not the only substance abused by students. Inhalant use is fast becoming one of the first substances abused by preadolescent and younger students (Hogan, 2000). Inhalant use is also prominent among adolescent students (Johnston et al., 2000). Concomitantly, hallucinogens are also used with increased frequency among adolescent students. However, among adolescent students, marijuana still accounts for 75% of all illicit drug abuse (Hogan, 2000). This data clearly demonstrate the need for professional school counselors to be able to effectively intervene with AOD-abusing students.

COGNITIVE-BEHAVIORAL COUNSELING INTERVENTIONS

Cognitive-behavioral counseling interventions have significant utility for professional school counselors due to their emphasis upon brief, time-limited interventions directed toward immediate student concerns. Three primary cognitive-behavioral counseling goals exist for professional school counselors helping AOD-abusing students (Nystul, 1999). First, professional school counselors help students understand how the students' thoughts, feelings, and behaviors engender AOD abuse. In other words, professional school counselors help students better understand what students say to themselves (e.g., "If I do drugs, others will think I'm cool and like me"); how they feel (e.g., anxiety, depression, anger); or what they do (e.g., argue, fight, withdraw) immediately before they AOD abuse. Second, professional school counselors promote understanding of how the students' AOD abuse is connected to negative consequences (e.g., failing grades, arguments with peers) and positive consequences (e.g., interactions with peers, feelings of confidence). Finally, professional school counselors help students explore new, healthier ways of thinking and acting, which reduce the probability of continued AOD abuse.

UNDERSTANDING THE AOD ABUSE SEQUENCE

Professional school counselors need to understand the AOD abuse sequence in order to help students. This sequence includes recognizing triggers, establishing trigger baselines, nonuse lists, positive consequences, and negative consequences

Recognizing triggers. Professional school counselors who treat AOD-abusing students first need to help them recognize the triggers (e.g., thoughts, feelings, behaviors, situations) that occur immediately prior to the students' AOD abuse (see Table 56.1). Commonly, AOD-abusing students will be able to describe the internal dialogue they have with themselves or the physical or psychological signals that foretell their upcoming AOD abuse. For example, a student might indicate her internal dialogue just before abusing:

> "I'm stressed. There is no way I can get through the rest of this calculus class without taking a hit to calm myself down."

Additionally, she may describe physical feelings such as an inability to relax or concentrate, and physical behaviors such as involuntary muscle contractions or psychomotor agitation (e.g., tapping her fingers, bouncing her leg). Psychological signals might include remembering how calming it was when she smoked marijuana the previous day or describing the depressed symptomology experienced most days when she is AOD abstinent. Furthermore, she might be able to identify specific situations or circumstances

TABLE 56.1
ALCOHOL AND OTHER DRUG TRIGGERS AND NONUSE SEQUENCE-OUTCOME LIST

Thought triggers	Feeling triggers	Behavior triggers	Situation triggers	Positive outcome	Negative outcome
Nonuse thoughts	Nonuse feelings	Nonuse behaviors	Nonuse situations	Positive outcome	Negative outcome

that increase the probability of her AOD abuse (e.g., the class prior to each Friday's calculus quiz, the nights before her calculus tests, the days in which she receives her calculus quiz scores).

Once the student recognizes triggers, they make trigger lists. Students rank order the triggers on the lists, indicating which triggers are the most powerful and which are most frequently encountered; thus, students first rank the strength of the individual triggers from zero (*When I experience this, I will not use at all*) to 10 (*When I experience this, I am inevitably going to use*) and rank the trigger frequency from zero (*I never experienced this trigger*) to 10 (*This trigger occurs constantly throughout my awake hours*). Give priority to the most powerful triggers and those occurring most often. In other words, triggers that students identify as indicating both inevitable AOD use and that constantly occur are the triggers that warrant the most attention at the onset of the counseling process.

Establishing trigger baselines. Concomitantly, the self-described severity and frequency of triggers presented by students serve as baselines that can be used to measure progress. In other words, these baselines allow both students and counselors to track treatment efficacy. Should students report a decrease in severity and frequency of triggers, progress is likely occurring and the interventions being used should be continued. However, should the severity and frequency of triggers increase, treatment and interventions warrant revision.

Nonuse lists. In addition to the trigger list, professional school counselors may wish to help students construct a "nonuse list," which emphasized identifying thoughts, feelings, behaviors, and situations occurring when students don't AOD abuse. The purpose of this list is to help students identify different ways of positively experiencing life without the need to AOD abuse.

Many professional school counselors with whom we have spoken have noted that many of their frequently AOD-abusing students will be AOD abstinent when (a) they are interacting with respected and admired peers who don't use, (b) they are participating in activities they are invested in and find interesting (e.g., athletics, engine repair class, choir), and (c) they don't experience overwhelming anxiety related to future performance (e.g., upcoming examinations, athletic events in which the student is participating). Thus, a nonuse list provides students with ideas on how they might better cope with experiences that commonly lead to AOD abuse by describing how they think, feel, and behave when they are not driven by the urge to use.

Positive consequences. Unfortunately, helping professionals often ignore or inappropriately minimize positive consequences resulting from student AOD abuse. This is a significant treatment error that dilutes counseling efficacy and disinvests student participation.

Students frequently experience multiple positive consequences as a result of their AOD abuse. These positive consequences can vary greatly depending upon the individual. Perceived peer support provided by other AOD-abusing students, escape from pressing concerns, and pure enjoyment of being under the influence are key reasons students abuse AOD. Honest discussion regarding the potential loss of these perceived positive consequences is necessary before students can begin the abstinence process; therefore, statements such as, "Tell me about the positive things you experience when you use" or "Help me understand what it is like drinking with your peers" are helpful.

The intent of these questions is not to have students romantically portray AOD abuse. Instead, professional school counselors are learning *why* AOD abuse and AOD experiences are important to the individual. Once the *why* is answered, counselors can begin working to appropriately address the void that will inevitably be created should students eliminate their AOD-abusing behaviors.

For example, should a 13 year-old male indicate that drinking with other teens provides him friendships; the professional school counselor and the student may need to identify other ways that the student can secure friendships without AOD abuse. Given the importance students place upon their acceptance by peers and their desire to fit in, securing alternative friendships can be daunting. However, failing to address this student's need for new, non–AOD-abusing friends, at best, destines the counseling process to limited success.

Negative consequences. When reviewing negative consequences resulting from student AOD abuse, it is helpful to first ask about the presenting circumstances that brought students to counseling and then link these to other academic, family, peer, psychological, or legal problems resulting from or potentially linked to their AOD abuse:

COUNSELOR: Shondra, I know that Vice Principal Myers referred you to my office. As I understand the situation, you had consumed alcohol and then had gotten sick at last Saturday night's homecoming game. Help me understand what that was like for you.

SHONDRA: It was awful. I was trying to be cool and instead I got drunk. When I got to the game, everything started spinning, and I threw up in the stands. I was so embarrassed. Now my parents know I was drinking and I'm grounded, and the people I was trying to impress laugh at me.

COUNSELOR: That sounds rough.

SHONDRA: Yeah . . . it is.

COUNSELOR: What have you learned from all of this?

SHONDRA: Well, I've learned that I don't want to drink anymore before games.

COUNSELOR: Tell me about other times you had some bad things happen when you drank alcohol or used drugs.

SHONDRA: I can't think of any.

COUNSELOR: Sometimes people tell me that they perform badly on tests or get bad grades because they were under the influence of alcohol when they took their tests or because they missed a lot of school due to their drinking. Has anything like that ever happened to you?

SHONDRA: Naw, nothing like that.

COUNSELOR: At other times students tell me that when they drink they get into arguments with their parents or family members.

SHONDRA: Well, a couple weeks ago, when my friends and I had been out drinking, I ran my mom's car into a ditch. I had to call my dad to get the car out. He was really upset. He said I'd have to pay the $480 to get the car fixed.

COUNSELOR: So, your drinking got you into trouble with your dad and caused you to pay the expenses for repairing your mom's car?

SHONDRA: Yeah, I guess I'm learning that drinking costs me a lot.

Within this vignette, the professional school counselor first attempts to help Shondra begin understanding the link between her drinking behaviors and other potential negative consequences. The professional school counselor describes the primary reason Shondra came for counseling, the vice principal's referral. Shondra reports two specific problems resulting from this incident (e.g., embarrassment, parental punishment [grounding]). The counselor then investigates potential negative consequences of alcohol consumption related to Shondra's school experience. This is denied. Therefore, the professional school counselor continues asking about other potential negative consequences of alcohol consumption occurring within Shondra's relationship with her parents. Toward the end of this session, the professional school counselor would likely summarize the problems reported by the student as linked to her alcohol use and ask the student to clarify how continued alcohol consumption is helpful.

COUNSELOR: Shondra, help me understand. You say that you were terminated from Wal-Mart because you've been too drunk to work your scheduled shift. You've said that you've gotten in trouble with the police for drinking and driving and had to pay over $400 to get your mom's car repaired. And, you've told me that you get real anxious when you buy beer, because your mom and dad would kick you out of the house if they knew you were continuing to drink. How is it helpful to you to continue drinking alcohol?

SHONDRA: I guess it's not.

COUNSELOR: Based upon your trigger list, you've basically said you consume alcohol when you get bored. So, what will you do differently when you get bored in the future?

SHONDRA: Well, I guess I'm not going to drink.

COUNSELOR: Okay, what will you do instead when you find yourself becoming bored or thinking that you may become bored.

SHONDRA: I don't know.

COUNSELOR: Well, on your nonuse list, you said when you are with Stacey, you don't use alcohol, because she is fun and she doesn't like beer. I'm wondering if you would be willing to call Stacey if you begin to feel bored.

SHONDRA: Yeah, I could do that.

COUNSELOR: What else could you do?

SHONDRA: I guess I could do some of the other things I said in my nonuse list, like take my dog for a walk or practice my clarinet.

At the conclusion of this vignette, the professional school counselor gently confronts Shondra by asking how continued drinking is helpful. Instead of dropping the discussion when Shondra reports her alcohol consumption is not helpful, the counselor uses the client's trigger list to help Shondra recognize one of the primary reasons she reportedly consumes alcohol (e.g., to escape boredom). Therefore, the counselor is therapeutically using both the student's trigger list and nonuse lists to help provide appropriate interventions.

Sometimes students are either unaware of potential negative consequences of their AOD abuse or purposely deny any negative consequences. Under these circumstances, professional school counselors may wish to use circular questioning. The intent is to learn how students believe they are perceived, valued, and respected by significant others. Thus, professional school counselors might ask a question such as, "Shondra, who is the most important person in your life." Once students identify their most important significant others, counselors can ask, "Based upon what you've told me, your mother is very important to you. Tell me, what would she say were the negative consequences of your drinking and drug behaviors?"

ASSORTED ADJUNCTIVE INTERVENTIONS

Using cognitive-behavioral interventions to help students more thoroughly understand their AOD abuse sequence (i.e., triggers, nontriggers, positive consequences, and negative consequences) is helpful. Three other adjunctive interventions warrant discussion, however, when counseling AOD-abusing students.

Psychoeducational interventions. Professional school counselors can plan and implement psychoeducational interventions using a cognitive-behavioral approach. Through the use of cognitive-behavioral strategies, the counselor can assist students in understanding that their thinking influences how they feel, which in turn affects what they do, with substance abuse being one possible outcome of this chain of events. Such structured and concrete strategies can assist the professional school counselor in helping young people with interpersonal learning about themselves in regard to AOD issues. This is especially helpful when counselors are responding to pre- and early adolescent referrals, in which the young client may benefit from developmentally appropriate interventions that are presented in visual and concrete terms. Such activities can be used in individual and group counseling with some modification. Following are two examples of such cognitive behavioral activities.

Feeling cards. Construct feeling cards by placing words that label a breadth of emotions (e.g., joy, excitement, fear, sadness, anger) on index cards. As in a card game, have the student take a card from the stack without being able to see the word on the card. After asking the student to turn the card over to see the feeling word, ask the student to write a situation on the card that might engender the feeling expressed on the card. Then ask the student to identify an action (or reaction) that might be taken in response to the situation identified from the feeling word on the card. After an action has been identified, ask the student to identify what kind of thought or belief about the event might have engendered the emotional reaction (feeling) to the event. Once an opportunity has been provided to articulate a belief about the situation, ask the student to consider an alternative thought or belief about the situation. Following the identification of an alternative thought or belief, ask the student to consider how the feeling and action might have been different. Allow a second round if time allows.

My-beliefs-and-me wheel. This activity borrows from an illustration to demonstrate the role of cognition on self-perpetuating cycles (Freeman, Pretzer, Fleming, & Simon, 2004) that can be created in response to given situations:

1. Ask the student to identify a recent situation that might trigger the use of AOD. Using the handout titled My Beliefs and Me (see Figure 56.1), ask the student to write words that describe the situation in the space labeled Event.
2. Ask the student to consider the event and then to describe beliefs or thoughts about the situation (e.g., how it may affect personal worth or relationships or how it may illicit negative consequences). After discussion, assist the student in identifying the dominant (irrational) belief at play, and describe it on the handout in the space labeled Belief. (A list of irrational beliefs that can assist you in guiding this discussion can be found in Freeman et al., 2004.)
3. After discussion, ask the student to identify and describe feelings that might be experienced in response to the identified belief. Ask the student to write a word describing their selected feeling (e.g., sadness, anger, excitement) in the space labeled Feeling.
4. Ask the student to identify potential behaviors that may be outcomes of the selected emotion (e.g., separate self from friends, skip school, use AOD). Ask the student to write the selected behavior in the space labeled Behavior.
5. Finally, ask the student to consider consequences that might occur as a result of the selected behavior. Ask the student to describe a selected consequence in the space marked Consequence.

Repeat this process, using a newly identified event (generated from the Consequence box) as the precipitating event. After the second repetition of the process, you can assist the student in processing how this cycle stemming from irrational thoughts or beliefs can continue, with the possibility that negative events will also continue. This provides an opportunity to introduce the concept of faulty or irrational beliefs in developmentally appropriate terms. Vernon (1989) provides such a presentation in her book *Thinking, Feeling, Behaving: An Emotional Curriculum for Adolescents, Grades 7-12.* After discussing faulty beliefs, provide demonstrated examples. Ask the student to reconsider choices made in the first two cycles. Using a new handout with the same

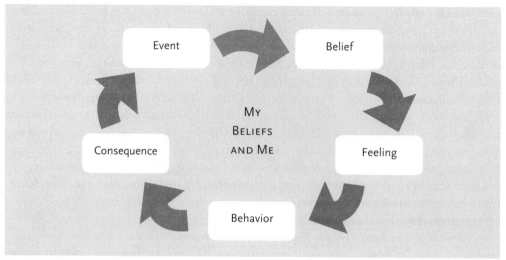

Figure 56.1. My-beliefs-and-me handout.

situation initially identified for the Event space, coach the student to consider other beliefs or thoughts that the he or she may choose regarding this event. A student-identified belief that demonstrates rational thinking is selected, discussed, and placed in the Belief section of the new handout. As before, the student then identifies emotions that the selected rational thought might engender, and selects one to place in the Feeling box. Now, the student identifies behaviors that may occur resulting from that feeling, and the selection of one (more positive than before) is selected and placed in the Behavior box. Once again, ask the student to consider consequences to this behavior, and then describe the selected consequence as a new entry in the Event box. Then, move through another cycle using the student's newly identified (and more positive) consequence as the precipitating event. To further empower the student with the concept of a measure of personal control, use additional practice cycles. Each cycle reinforces the student's power over an event through the interpretation (or belief) of that event.

 Contingency contracting. Many professional school counselors use contingency contracting when counseling AOD-abusing students. Contingency contracts are clearly worded contracts that describe acceptable and unacceptable student behaviors. Professional school counselors and their students jointly develop an outline indicating that AOD abuse will not be tolerated. Sanctions are stated (e.g., expulsion from school, specialized placement) as well as rewards for contract compliance (e.g., the student can attend shop class at no cost for materials, the student can participate in athletics).

 Sobriety contracts are one form of contingency contract. For example, a professional school counselor may have a student who is prescribed both Ritalin for attention-deficit/hyperactivity disorder and Topomax for AOD abuse. The professional school counselor and the student can identify a time at the beginning of each school day when they can meet for approximately 10 minutes or longer if necessary. During the scheduled meetings, the student verbally commits to remaining alcohol free and achieving academically so that he may graduate from school. Thus, the student may say something like, "Ms. Penn, I'm going to stay drug free today and promise to do my very best at learning so I will graduate and attend college." The professional school counselor then voices any specific concerns she might have about upcoming events that day which may trigger an alcohol use relapse. Here, Ms. Penn might say, "Charlie, I know you want to stay alcohol free and are committed to graduating, but I also know that midterm exams begin today. I am concerned you might feel overwhelmed or anxious and begin using alcohol to cope." The student then responds with how he anticipates handling the noted concern, "Oh, Ms. Penn, if I feel anxious or overwhelmed because of the midterms, I promise to speak with you first. I know I can handle it." Once the student indicates how he will respond the counselor is not allowed to ask further questions that day. The student then takes his medications in front of the professional school counselor (if appropriate) and places an "X" on the Sobriety Contract Calendar for that specific day. At the conclusion of each week, the professional school counselor and the student identify the progress made and discuss any changes warranted for the following week. The intent of this experience, then, is to ritualize this daily experience and encourage students to direct their own recovery.

12-step support groups. Another intervention that warrants discussion is the use of support groups. Incorporating a 12-step recovery program into a student's treatment for AOD abuse may enhance his or her chances of maintaining sobriety (Chatlos & Estroff, 2001; Elliott, Orr, Watson, & Jackson, 2005; Walfish, Massey, & Krone, 1990). Twelve-step groups such as Alcoholics Anonymous, Narcotics Anonymous, Al-Anon, and Alateen are all based on the premise that by sharing and challenging one another, sobriety among group members can be both achieved and maintained. Affiliation in a 12-step program along with other youth may meet several needs for the student, such as modeling, mutual support, shared experiences, sense of belonging, skill acquisition, and strategies to help maintain sobriety (Bristow-Braitman, 1995; Erlich, 1987; Robinson, 1996). Moreover, a central tenet of 12-step programs is living "one day at a time." This seems particularly relevant to a youth who tends to live in the moment. Rational recovery is founded upon rational emotive behavior therapy and encourages members to combat irrational thoughts related to their personal recovery.

Referrals. A final intervention that may be necessary when adolescent AOD abuse escalates and concerns arise about dependency is a referral for either outpatient and inpatient treatment. There are times when professional school counselors may be called upon to refer a student for further treatment. Referrals may require serious consideration when parents or school personnel raise concerns, or when the student self-refers. If a referral is necessary, it is important that professional school counselors have access to resources for both outpatient and impatient treatment programs. Additionally, it is important for the professional school counselor to be cognizant of how payments for services are to be made if required by those resources. For example, do the resources have established straight fees, or are sliding fee scales use? Also, are there resources within the community that offer pro bono services? The United Way (2005) provides such information through a community resource book that can direct the professional school counselor to treatment providers in their cities and counties. In addition, Substance Abuse and Mental Health Services Administration (2005b) published a list of more than 11,000 treatment programs across the country to assist the professional school counselor in locating an appropriate treatment program for the AOD student.

SUMMARY/CONCLUSION

We described literature indicating the prominence of AOD abuse among middle and high school students. Practical cognitive-behavioral interventions were described. Specifically, readers learned about the AOD abuse sequence and gained intervention ideas on how to help students (a) recognize AOD triggers, (b) recognize nonuse triggers, (c) discuss perceived positive AOD abuse consequences and cope with the potential loss of these positive consequences, and (d) link AOD abuse to negative consequences. Concomitantly, three adjunctive intervention techniques were described. These included contingency contracting, 12-step programming, and more intensive treatment. Although counseling AOD-abusing students is challenging, these interventions clearly provide a fundamental approach that can be helpful.

(Note: See the CD-ROM for a list of references.)

CHAPTER 57

HELPING STUDENTS WHO HAVE EATING DISORDERS

Dana Heller Levitt

Preview

Eating disorders and their less clinical forms of disordered eating and body image preoccupation continue to be on the rise. Professional school counselors are likely to see students presenting with such issues from elementary through high school. This chapter provides a brief overview of the symptoms and behaviors of eating disorders followed by a discussion of counseling and prevention strategies. Attention to developmental differences is provided, including manifestations and interventions. A final section provides resources for counselors as well as students, teachers, and parents.

Clinical eating disorders (e.g., anorexia nervosa, bulimia nervosa, binge eating disorders) can be found in about 5% of the general population. A greater number of people are included when the definition is expanded to include those with subclinical manifestations, such as disordered eating and disturbances in body image. Disorders that do not meet diagnostic criteria can affect 4% to 16% of the general population, with such cases being two to five times more common among adolescent girls (Mussell, Binford, & Fulkerson, 2000). Clinical eating disorders may be conceived as on one end of a continuum and healthy eating attitudes and body image on the other end, with differing values on each lying in between. Students who are dissatisfied with their bodies, dieting, or even at the healthiest point all have the potential to develop more serious problems.

The most common forms of clinical eating disorders are anorexia nervosa, bulimia nervosa, and binge eating disorder. Anorexia is marked by intense desires to lose weight, misperceptions about one's actual weight, refusal to gain weight, and a body weight that is at least 15% less than it should be (e.g., a student who should, according to height and body composition, weigh 100 pounds currently weighs no more than 85 pounds). Students with anorexia may intentionally fast and avoid food and may or may not engage in compensatory activities, such as excessive exercise or self-induced vomiting after periods of feeling that they have eaten too much.

Such acts of purging are a defining point of bulimia nervosa, a cycle of binge eating and purging. A *binge* is defined as eating an excessive amount of food in a discrete period of time, such as 2,000 calories in a 2-hour period. This should be differentiated from normative binges, such as snacking with friends or eating a lot of food at a social event. Purging, such as self-induced vomiting, use of laxatives or diuretics, or excessive exercise, is used as a means of compensating for the binge or may simply be a way to alleviate feelings of guilt, stress, anxiety, or another feeling that is released through this activity following a binge. Binge eating disorder is similarly characterized by binge episodes but does not include the purging cycle (American Psychiatric Association, 2000).

Almost every student is at risk. Disordered eating (i.e., dieting or in some other way modifying food intake to lose weight) affects students of all ages (Gabel & Kearney, 1998; Phelps, Sapia, Nathanson, & Nelson, 2000). Other factors must also be considered, including the evaluation of body size and negative attitudes toward the body (Pesa, Syre, & Jones, 2000). Body image dissatisfaction has been reported as the strongest predictor of eating disorders (Phelps et al., 2000). Eating disorders or their subclinical manifestations may have little or nothing to do with eating or body image. Sometimes, they are responses to traumatic events or feelings of losing control, and manipulation of eating may be one means of establishing a sense of identity or personal power. There is a direct link between self-esteem and body perceptions (Brook & Tepper, 1997; Franko & Omori, 1999; Israel & Ivanova, 2002; Loewy, 1998; Pesa et al., 2000; Phelps et al., 2000), and, as a result, little argument that eating disorders need attention in schools.

IDENTIFICATION OF AT-RISK STUDENTS

Eating disorders and related issues still predominantly affect females, with gender differences emerging at around the ages of 8 to 10 (Ricciardelli & McCabe, 2001). Male body image ideals and values have more recently spurred development of such concerns among boys and young men. The primary concern for boys is about being underdeveloped or not muscular enough, while girls are drawn toward thinness (Cohane & Pope, 2001). Poor coping strategies are related to eating-disorder risk in adolescent males and females alike (Garcia-Grau, Fuste, Miro, Saldana, & Bados, 2004). Eating pathology and appearance preoccupation are associated with depression and dysfunctional thinking, both of which affect students' overall self-esteem and well-being (Franko & Omori, 1999). There are numerous warning signs of eating disorders on any point along the continuum beyond dieting such as weight concerns, drives for thinness, feeling inadequate, and negative self-evaluation. Table 57.1 provides a brief overview of warning signs along the different dimensions of physical, behavioral, and psychological symptoms. If a student presents with any of these warning signs (particularly the physical and behavioral symptoms), it is important for the professional school counselor to ensure that the stu-

TABLE 57.1

PHYSICAL, BEHAVIORAL, AND PSYCHOLOGICAL WARNING SIGNS OF EATING DISORDERS

Physical	Behavioral	Psychological
weight loss	frequent trips to the bathroom	low self-esteem
hair loss	avoiding snack foods	external locus of control
edema (swelling)	frequent weighing	perfectionism
skin abnormalities	substance abuse	helplessness
discolored teeth	social avoidance	depression
scarring on the backs of hands self-injury signs	isolation	anxiety
	abnormal eating habits	anger

dent consults a health-care professional. In addition, important developmental issues arise at the elementary, middle, and high school levels.

ELEMENTARY SCHOOL

Although they are at an age when their focus should be on making friends and growth, boys and girls in elementary school worry about appearance and fitting in:

- Children as young as age 5 years express concerns about body image and becoming fat (Maine, 2000; Shapiro, Newcomb, & Loeb, 1997).
- By age 6 years, children use adult cultural criteria to judge physical attractiveness (Gabel & Kearney, 1998).
- Children tease, shame, and avoid friendships with peers who are fat or who are not conventionally attractive peers.
- Children imitate actions and attitudes of parents and adults; what messages are they sending about dieting and appearance?

MIDDLE SCHOOL

Dissatisfaction with body shape and size worsens as children age and enter middle school:

- Body image dissatisfaction increased from 40% in third graders to 79% in sixth graders (Ricciardelli & McCabe, 2001).
- Self-esteem is directly linked to body satisfaction; students with low self-esteem in other realms may be prime suspects.
- The top wish for 11- to 17-year-old girls is to lose weight (Maine, 2000).

HIGH SCHOOL

High school students have the increased burden of beginning to make adult decisions as well as the stress of trying to fit in both socially and physically:

- Discontent about their bodies and feeling fat has become normative, particularly for girls (Maine, 2000).
- Sixty-seven percent of females and 82% of males in high school believe appearance influences romantic appeal; 72% and 68%, respectively, attribute happiness to appearance (O'Dea & Abraham, 1999).
- High school students have lower physical self-esteem and more unhealthy weight control behaviors (Cohane & Pope, 2001; Israel & Ivanova, 2002; McCabe & Ricciardelli, 2001; Nylander, 1971).

COUNSELING AND PREVENTION STRATEGIES

The most widely used approaches to address eating disorders in the schools are individual and group counseling, involvement of family members, and classroom guidance programs. Professional school counselors can also implement school-based changes to create a more safe and accepting environment around the issues of eating disorders, weightism, and physical and overall self-esteem.

Prevention efforts that are generally centered on body satisfaction and education may be conceived at primary (e.g., curb dieting behaviors, concerns about weight/shape), secondary (e.g., reduce the duration of eating disorders), and tertiary (e.g., address and reduce impairment of established disorders) levels (Gabel & Kearney, 1998).

Activities should address all of the systems at play in the development of eating disturbances: family, sociocultural, self-deficits, body image concerns, self-esteem, and peer and parental involvement (O'Dea, 2000, 2004). Attempts should address the negative consequences of unhealthy weight control as well as encourage healthy eating and exercise (Mussell et al., 2000). Programs aimed at promoting body and self-acceptance and decreasing unhealthy weight loss have demonstrated success (Weiss & Wertheim, 2005).

Professional school counselors and other personnel must first examine their own beliefs and feelings about weight, shape, appearance, and self-esteem. Regardless of the form of intervention or age group to which it applies, professional school counselors' work should foremost focus on promoting body satisfaction. Counselors may then help students enhance self-esteem and personal efficacy by recognizing positive aspects of their physical appearance (O'Dea, 2004; Phelps et al., 2000; Weiss & Wertheim, 2005).

Some approaches, particularly peer-led approaches, can have negative effects. Programs that provide information about eating disorders led by recovered peers increase students' knowledge of eating disorders but also sometimes lead to an increase in their symptoms (O'Dea, 2000). Students introduced to beliefs, attitudes, and behaviors preceding eating disorders may hear suggestions of the desirability to lose weight and the means for doing so. For younger children, frequent coverage of eating disorders in this manner can normalize the problem and thereby create longer term difficulties.

A positive approach providing information on body image can be more beneficial. Addressing what makes them satisfied and dissatisfied with their bodies and introducing activities that desensitize them to the events eliciting body image dissatisfaction and eating disorders are useful tools (Gore, Vander Wal, & Thelen, 2001). Helpful activities may include guided imagery and relaxation, envisioning oneself as brave and strong, and encouraging pleasurable body-related activities (e.g., bike riding, getting a haircut, wearing favorite clothes).

INDIVIDUAL COUNSELING

The professional school counselor must be mindful of one's limits and be prepared to refer students who have severe impairments to counselors in the community who may offer more constant and intensive care. In addition to therapists, professional school counselors should become familiar with other helping professionals who can assist with eating disorders, such as nutritionists, dieticians, physicians, exercise physiologists, and psychiatrists.

Counseling the student with an eating disorder can be tricky. Education about nutrition, exercise, self-acceptance, and the physical dangers associated with eating disorders are essential. At the same time, the student's emotional distress and academic performance need to be addressed as well as development of identity and appropriate coping mechanisms (Gabel & Kearney, 1998; Garner, Garfinkel, & Irvine, 1986; Levine & Smolak, 2001). Many students with eating disorders may be defensive and resistant to help because they believe that their behavior has been effective in getting what they want (e.g., attention from peers, parental affection, a socially acceptable body size). Other times, students will refer themselves because their eating problems have gotten out of control. In these cases, the student's willingness to seek help to deal with the eating disorder and other problems in the student's life should be acknowledged and praised (Omizo & Omizo, 1992).

Garner et al. (1986), pioneers in eating disorder treatment, suggested that there are two tracks to consider: behavioral context and emotional context. The first track involves issues of weight, starvation, erratic eating, bingeing, vomiting, strenuous exercise, or whatever the student's physical manifestation of the eating disorder may be. Cognitive-behavioral approaches might include restructuring thoughts, assistance with meal planning, and challenging distorted attitudes about weight and shape. The second track is the emotional context that may involve underlying developmental issues, personality, and family and peer themes. A psychodynamic approach might include a developmental understanding of eating disorders as a type of fear, family separation issues, parental inattention to the student's needs, and a lack of self-regulation. Garner et al. suggested that eating disorders can be dealt with initially from either track, as each communicates to the student a desire to help and commitment to ensuring that both physical and emotional health is restored. Cognitive-behavioral and psychodynamic approaches are the most widely used with individuals with eating disorders; the affective level should be particularly attended to among preadult populations.

Counseling should match student development levels. The use of journals can be particularly helpful in tracking feelings and behaviors. For younger students with less cognitive capacity, simply keeping a "food-mood" diary may be enough. Professional school counselors working with older students in middle and high school may be successful in eliciting more complex processing by examining what was happening during periods of wanting to binge, purge, abstain from eating, and so forth. Engaging students in the process of analyzing, identifying, and transforming their environments is empowering at any developmental level (Levine & Smolak, 2001).

GROUP COUNSELING

Social influence and norms are critical for many school-age youth and are a significant correlate to unhealthy weight management (Eisenberg, Neumark-Sztainer, & Perry, 2005). Groups that focus on body image and the factors that lead to eating disorders are more likely to occur within the school setting. These groups provide students with opportunities to engage in activities and practice new behaviors with peers at a time when they are vulnerable to peer influences (Levine & Smolak, 2001). Students in body image awareness groups build support systems and facilitate connections with one another. It is important for counselors leading groups to ensure that they are being positive role models by addressing their own issues on the subject.

Structured group counseling gives students a focused means of talking about ways to promote positive body image. Several approaches incorporate education, insight, and action. Groups can focus on realistic goal setting, healthy body image, assertiveness, and perfectionism over 8 to 10 sessions (Rhyne-Winkler & Hubbard, 1994). Games, role-plays, and activities that encourage putting into perspective sociocultural and media messages about the importance of appearance empower students to feel good about themselves while contributing to the self-esteem of their peers. Activities may include identifying characteristics of admired people or collecting advertisements that teach students that fat is bad. Group sessions may include information on dieting and exercising, developing a food log, healthy exercise, eating behaviors, emotions associated with eating, self-esteem and autonomy, body image and goal setting, and develop coping skills. In all likelihood, this information will be most effective with students in elementary and middle school.

Students learn about advocacy and the forces that influence their feelings about their bodies while learning how to cope with everyday interactions with others and teasing about their bodies. These protective factors and the immediate feedback from peers in groups enable students to be more proactive in preventing their own and peers' eating-disorder risks.

There are dangers in counseling groups of this nature, however, as they can at times be explosive, heavily emotionally laden, or it may be difficult to get students to share openly about their private feelings. The professional school counselor should therefore exercise caution and patience and have appropriate supports in place for students in these groups.

INVOLVING FAMILY MEMBERS

Interventions for students with eating disorders are often ineffective without the support of parents and family members. Parents and other family members have a significant effect on students' self-image and self-esteem. Family members may contribute to unhealthy attitudes and behaviors about the body by modeling dieting and disordered eating as well as comments about students' and others' appearances and criticism of their students' changing bodies (Gore et al., 2001; Loewy, 1998; Maine, 2000; Mussell et al., 2000). Family dynamics have also been implicated in the development of eating disorders. Girls who report high levels of eating problems live in families marked by lower levels of cohesion, organization, and expressiveness. Families of students with eating disorders are more conflictual, lacking in secure attachments and warmth (Byely, Archibald, Graber, & Brooks-Gunn, 2000). Parents should always be involved in treatment. Consult the American Counseling Association and the American School Counselor Association's codes of ethics and local school policies for guidance on informed consent.

Because of the nature of eating disorders, family therapy is often highly recommended to explore the student's expression of anger, conflict, depression, anxiety, and any feelings that may be influenced by the home and family environment (Garner et al., 1986). This is further cause for professional school counselors to know community resources and make referrals for needed services. Professional school counselors must also work collaboratively with the students, therapists, and medical doctors when applicable. (Also, it is important that professional school counselors recognize their limits and make referrals as necessary.) Table 57.2 includes activities that professional school counselors can engage in to help families cope with eating issues. Within the school

TABLE 57.2

HOW TO HELP FAMILIES COPE WITH EATING DISORDERS

Educate families about eating disorders.

Send written correspondence home with students.

Facilitate family discussions about weight and health.

Alert families to how they might unintentionally send harmful messages.

Set limits, and openly discuss issues.

Ascertain eating habits, and foster family relationships by suggesting that they spend mealtimes together.

Facilitate an examination of family members' own feelings and prejudices about weight.

Make appropriate referrals to community medical and mental health professionals.

Emphasize that spending time with children can foster cohesive, warm relationships that protect students from eating disorders.

Discourage dieting.

Plan programs through parent–teacher association meetings.

Educate families about normal puberty and developmental changes.

setting, professional school counselors can take on a number of roles to prevent, identify, and provide services for students with eating disorders.

CLASSROOM GUIDANCE PROGRAMS

The topic of eating disorders can be covered within several elective courses as well as health and physical education curricula. Professional school counselors can encourage teachers to combine issues of nutrition, exercise, and self-acceptance into appropriate classes such that children learn about healthy, positive, and active lifestyles (Gabel & Kearney, 1998). Students can also be educated about the negative effects of starvation, erratic eating, and bingeing, including depression, anxiety, irritability, feelings of inadequacy, fatigue, preoccupation with food, poor concentration, and social withdrawal (Garner et al., 1986). Other content to address with students in classrooms includes body esteem and self-esteem, locus of control, approval-seeking behavior, body image and nutrition, excessive exercise, and perfectionism (Rhyne-Winkler & Hubbard, 1994).

Weiss and Wertheim (2005) proposed a four-session, large-group prevention program that may be likened to classroom guidance. The Making Choices program promotes self-acceptance through discussion of self-esteem, healthy dieting, and exercise. The unique aspect of this program that is most relevant to professional school counselors is its facilitation of full-class and small-group discussions. This may be a helpful means of encouraging dialogue in the classroom setting.

Classroom guidance programs addressing these topics create an environment in which students examine knowledge and attitudes about food and eating, develop positive and realistic attitudes toward their bodies, and gain accurate information (Rhyne-Winkler & Hubbard, 1994). Given the influence of peers, training students to provide peer-led programs might be a useful means of disseminating such information effectively. Students will be more likely to listen to each other on most issues. A select group of students to teach others about eating disorders and positive body image can be empowering for both leaders and recipients. Such opportunities serve as protective factors, much in the same way as peer mentoring programs on other issues, such as substance abuse, violence, and transition to new schools. In one such program, the Ophelia Project (www.opheliaproject.org), high school girls mentor middle school students to prevent and process relational aggression. Program coordinators found that increasing self-esteem in another realm creates more positive body image among participants. Students involved with the program also had significant influences on the school environment as a whole.

SCHOOL-BASED CHANGES

Professional school counselors should become knowledgeable about eating disorders and provide information and consultation to school personnel, parents, and students (Mussel et al., 2000). Discussions about biases and views can take place with teachers, coaches, and administrators who address weight reduction (Gabel & Kearney, 1998). Teachers may also be trained to infuse eating disorders into curricula and to listen actively, provide feedback nonjudgmentally, and to teach without lecturing so that they are more likely to identify students at risk and refer them for help. Given the developmental concerns of students at each level, professional school counselors must help to create a safe and nonjudgmental environment for students to feel healthy and grow (Akos & Levitt, 2002).

A safe school environment can begin with the professional school counselor, who is a resource to students, teachers, parents, and administrators and helps to ensure timely and appropriate interventions for at-risk students (Bardick et al., 2004). Table 57.3 addresses continuing initiatives that will prompt systemic changes and reduce prevalence of eating disorders (Rhyne-Winkler & Hubbard, 1994).

DEVELOPMENTAL CONSIDERATIONS

In order to best help students who are developing tendencies toward eating disorders, professional school counselors must consider developmental issues. Following is a review of differential considerations at the elementary, middle, and high school levels.

ELEMENTARY SCHOOL

Teaching students early about eating disorders, body-esteem, and self-esteem maximizes positive influences and decreases the likelihood of issues later in childhood and adolescence (Ohring, Graber, & Brooks-Gunn, 2002). Because young children respond well to action-oriented approaches, experiential components such as poetry, humor, and games in prevention curricula and interventions have proven successful (Mussell et al., 2000).

Young children have likely not experienced unsuccessful or chronic dieting and may not understand the concept of bingeing (Ricciardelli & McCabe, 2001). For those who show early signs of disordered eating, gradual exposure to feared foods with relax-

TABLE 57.3

INITIATIVES TO ENHANCE SYSTEMIC CHANGE

Provide training to become aware of the signs and symptoms of eating disorders.

Promote activities that foster healthy and realistic attitudes about weight, shape, growth, and nutrition.

Monitor how health and physical activity requirements are communicated to students and families.

Create an atmosphere in which students confront negative body talk.

Advocate for nutritional food and snack offerings.

Encourage the purchase of library and classroom materials with positive images about self-esteem and body image.

Encourage use of the term *fat* as neutral and nonderogatory.

Create a wellness program that will accomplish the following:

- Focus on prevention and early intervention.
- Involve teachers and administrators.
- Promote healthy attitudes and habits toward eating.
- Encourage self-control.
- Focus on improving self-esteem and autonomy.
- Make appropriate materials available in easily accessible areas.
- Foster discussions among the whole school community.
- Continually focus on the overall well-being of students.

ation training, role-playing to address social and familial problems, and development of alternative ways of thinking about problems are helpful elements (Gore et al., 2001).

MIDDLE SCHOOL

Perhaps the most important event at this level is the normalization of physical changes that take place in puberty (Ohring et al., 2002). Bodily changes, especially for students who mature earlier than others, are unfamiliar and create differences. Peer support is vital in middle school, particularly for students with eating disorders. Peer-led programs—whether they are groups, prevention workshops, or merely facilitated small-group discussions—allow students to promote sensitivity and positive body talk while learning that they may seek one another for support (Mussell et al., 2000). Because peers are so influential during middle school, encouraging students to talk sensitively and providing training for peer mentoring and facilitation to teach others about these issues can be an empowering and positive use of peer influence.

O'Dea (2004) described a 9-week program based solely on self-esteem that was effective in improving body image and offsetting dieting, weight loss, and eating-disordered behavior among female middle school participants. Based on the principle of student-centered learning, students worked in groups and incorporated teamwork, games, play, and drama in this content-free curriculum. The program was intended to foster a positive sense of self, positive and safe student environment, vicarious learning, feedback exchange, and a positive and supportive environment in which these girls felt infallible. The success of this program in modifying body image without directly addressing the topic demonstrates the benefits of self-esteem–based programming.

HIGH SCHOOL

It is important to target high school students with low self-esteem and other early signs of eating disorders, and small groups are particularly useful in facilitating intimate discussions among high school peers about these issues (Mussell et al., 2000). Peers help to debunk myths about appearance and offer alternative ways of handling difficult problems.

It is also useful to incorporate activities that have an activist twist, enabling students to work productively toward a solution to eating disorders, the pressures to be thin, and the negative attributions placed on overweight people by society. A program developed by the National Eating Disorders Association, GO GIRLS! (Giving Our Girls Inspiration and Resources for Lasting Self-esteem), teaches high school students about media awareness, activism, and advocacy while increasing self-esteem and preventing eating disorders (see www.nationaleatingdisorders.org). GO GIRLS! and other weekly groups discuss social pressures from media, peers, and parents before moving into subsequent sessions focusing on increasing physical self-esteem, building personal competence and developing an internal locus of control, reducing body dissatisfaction, and exploring appropriate weight-control measures.

Culminating sessions with young adults who have recovered from eating disorders might also be included (Phelps et al., 2000) but should be done cautiously and supervision because students are particularly vulnerable when they hear others' experiences with eating disorders. This is especially true as students have access to other attitudes about eating disorders. For example, proanorexic and probulimic Web sites are extremely dangerous places where people with active eating disorders attempt to convince others that these are positive and adaptive ways of coping and promote the ultra-thin, sickly, emaciated appearance of anorexia. Students have greater access to these sites with increased unsupervised time on the Internet, and the popularity of the chat sessions within them is high. Professional school counselors should be aware that such propaganda exists and that students are readily able to find, access, and be subject to the dangerous content therein.

Most counseling interventions for eating disorders are designed for work with adults. Adolescents who have the ability to think abstractly are likely to respond well to such approaches. The professional school counselor should be mindful of the developmental level and pressures that the student faces. Challenging students to think about the connection between their thoughts, problems, fears, or pressures and their eating disordered behaviors must be accompanied by the generation of alternatives that can be directly applied.

RESOURCES FOR STUDENTS, PARENTS, AND OTHER PERSONNEL

Professional school counselors have a tremendous effect on students and the school community by being intentional about helping students with eating disorders and related image concerns. Interventions at individual, group, familial, classroom, and school-wide levels can be challenging and require appropriate resources. "How to Help a Friend" (Table 57.4) is a useful tool to share with students who are concerned about friends and peers that will help them identify their own strategies for intervention. The following resources may also be shared with students, parents, and school personnel. Professional school counselors should consult these and other resources in their efforts to combat eating disorders.

- AboutFace: Combating Negative and Distorted Images of Women (www.about-face .org)
- Bodywise. 1-800-628-3812 (www.womenshealth.gov/pub/bodywise.cfm)
- Eating Disorders Coalition for Research, Policy and Action (www.eatingdisorder-scoalition.com)
- Maine, M. (2000). *Body Wars: Making Peace With Women's Bodies.* Carlsbad, CA: Gurze Books.
- National Eating Disorders Association. 206-382-3587 (www.nationaleatingdisor-ders.org)
- National Eating Disorders Association. (2005). *Eating Disorders Survival Guide.* Available online (www.nationaleatingdisorders.org)
- The Ophelia Project. (www.opheliaproject.org)
- Pipher, M. (1994). *Reviving Ophelia: Saving the Selves of Adolescent Girls.* New York: Ballantine Books.

Summary/Conclusion

Eating disorders and their subclinical manifestations do not appear to be diminishing in our society. Professional school counselors are on the front line to intervene in and prevent the development of eating disorders among students. At all developmental levels, students need attention and education about eating disorders, which can be addressed through classroom guidance, individual counseling, and group counseling. Parents can be educated about eating disorders, how to detect them in their students, and how home can either be a safe haven or contribute to these disorders.

As agents of change, professional school counselors are likewise encouraged to educate teachers and other administrative personnel about eating disorders—for example, how to detect and approach students about whom they have concerns and ways to make the school a safe environment, accepting of all body shapes. It is incumbent upon professional school counselors to attend to the reality of eating disorders in their schools, whether they are overt or more subtle manifestations among their students. Through prevention, education, and intervention, professional school counselors play an integral role for students, their families, the school, and the greater community to appropriately and effectively address this dangerous phenomenon.

(Note: See the CD-ROM for a list of references.)

TABLE 57.4

HOW TO HELP A FRIEND WITH BODY IMAGE AND EATING DIFFICULTIES

DO...

Create a safe environment to talk.

Encourage the person to seek help from a professional counselor, physician, or friend.

Expect anger or rejection at first; this may be an embarrassing or frightening first encounter.

Be patient—this is a long process and difficult issue.

Express your concern and desire to help.

Plan your approach carefully.

Speak with compassion and concern.

Model positive actions.

Provide specific information and resources.

Be willing to spend time listening and talking about related personal problems.

Take a look at your own attitudes towards weight, shape, and dieting.

Attempt to discuss feelings.

Explain your concerns with specific observations.

Offer support.

DON'T...

Nag, argue, plead, or bribe.

Criticize yourself or anyone else for being over- or underweight.

Blame yourself or anyone else for the person's difficulties.

Give simplistic suggestions about nutrition or self-control.

Comment positively or negatively about others' sizes and shapes.

Comment on the person's appearance.

Use scare tactics.

Become involved in a power struggle.

Spy or interfere.

Monitor eating.

Use food as a socializing agent.

Discuss weight, amount of calories or fat being consumed, or particular eating and
    exercise habits.

Expect 100% recovery immediately.

CHAPTER 58

HELPING STUDENTS WHO HAVE DEPRESSION

Debbie W. Newsome, Julia A. Southern, and Bradley T. Erford

Preview

Depression in youth has been the focus of increased concern during the past 3 decades. Whereas it used to be considered a disorder of adulthood, current researchers and mental health professionals are aware that many children and adolescents also deal with depression, a disorder that can be serious, complex, and, most important, treated (Merrell, 2001). Indeed, feeling depressed is one of the most common emotional responses experienced during adolescence (Yarcheski & Mahon, 2000). Young adolescents, in particular, are susceptible to depression because of the intense biological, social, and psychological changes that occur from late childhood to early adulthood. Professional school counselors are in a unique position to initiate activities and services designed to help prevent, identify, and coordinate the treatment of depression in youth (Rice & Leffert, 1997). In this chapter, facts about depression are presented, including information regarding types of depression, signs and symptoms of the disorder, factors influencing its onset, and associated risks. Suggestions for interventions that are based on outcome studies and research are described, including a list of resources to help professional school counselors to design preventive and remedial activities.

I'm normal, sort of. I take honors and advance placement courses. I was in the marching band, and I played varsity soccer for two years, but I have a distinct quality that separates me from the masses—I am sad most of the time. I don't sulk around or constantly plot ways to end my life; instead, I withdraw from regular activities a lot and spend a good deal of time thinking about my life and my purpose here. Somewhere down the line, amidst all the action and continuous responsibility, I lost track of myself. I felt trapped in all my relationships and virtually had no time to myself. I discontinued communication with my best friends, and my goal every week was to survive to the weekend, where I could relax and put everything on hold. I viewed myself as capable but also as always fallible. By November of my junior year, I was a wreck. Still, I refused to acknowledge my feelings as depression. I didn't think it could happen to me.

—*17-year-old high school student who was treated for depression*

DEPRESSION DEFINED

According to the National Institute of Mental Health (NIMH; 2001, 2002a), depression is a condition that can affect thoughts, feelings, behaviors, and overall health. It can affect sleeping and appetite, the way one feels about oneself, and the manner in which one thinks about things. In addition to affecting a student's current quality of life, depressive symptoms and disorders that begin during childhood or adolescence predict recurring or ongoing depression in adulthood. Unless it is treated, early onset of the disorder can predict more severe and negative symptoms later in life.

Depression is an internalizing disorder, as are anxiety disorders, social withdrawal, and somatic problems (Merrell, 2001). Internalizing disorders are characterized by overcontrol, which implies that individuals may overregulate or inappropriately control their emotions. In the case of internalizing disorders, the problems are maintained *within* the individual, in contrast to externalizing disorders, such as oppositional defiant disorder and attention-deficit/hyperactivity disorder (ADHD), which are characterized by acting out. The defining characteristic of the internalizing problem of depression is mood disturbance. Depressed youth experience difficulty regulating negative emotions effectively once they are experienced (Stark, Sander, Yancy, Bronik, & Hoke, 2000).

Whereas much of the research on depression refers to clinical depressive disorders, other manifestations of depression, while not severe enough to merit a clinical diagnosis, can cause distress in young people and call for the attention of professional school counselors. Petersen, Compas, and Brooks-Gunn (1992) described three types of depression: depressed mood, depressive syndrome, and clinical depression. Depressed mood is characterized by negative emotions, especially sadness and anxiety. Other emotions associated with depressed mood include guilt, disgust, anger, and fear. Students may experience depressed mood for a short or extended time. Depressed mood is one of the key symptoms of clinical depression; however, a child can experience depressed mood without being clinically depressed. Approximately one third of adolescents experience depressed mood (Petersen et al.) and may benefit from prevention or intervention activities initiated by professional school counselors.

Depressive syndrome refers to a collection of common symptoms associated with depression. The individual is experiencing some form of distress, but does not necessarily have a diagnosable problem (Merrell, 2001). Symptoms can include anxiety, sadness, loneliness, fearfulness, guilt, self-consciousness, and worry. The person may feel unloved and unlovable or a need to be perfect. Depressive syndrome, which is usually identified through the use of questionnaires, affects approximately 15% of adolescents (Petersen et al., 1992). Group counseling may be especially helpful for students struggling with depressive syndrome.

For depression to be considered a clinical disorder, a collection of symptoms must be evidenced that meet specific diagnostic criteria according to standardized classification systems, such as the *Diagnostic and Statistical Manual of Mental Disorders–Fourth Edition, Text Revision (DSM-IV-TR*; American Psychiatric Association [APA], 2000). Diagnosis is based on the intensity and duration of a set of symptoms that are serious enough to interfere with one's level of functioning. Examples of depressive disorders include Major Depressive Disorder and Dysthymic Disorder. Adjustment Disorder with depressed mood (or mixed anxiety and depressed mood) also is marked by depressive symptoms, as are Bipolar Disorders, Cyclothymic Disorder, and Mood Disorder due to medical condition or substance abuse. In this chapter, specific recommendations for helping students with bipolar, cyclothymic, or substance abuse–related disorders will *not* be addressed; instead, the focus is on helping students who struggle with depressive symptoms, Major Depressive Disorder, Dysthymic Disorder, or Adjustment Disorder with depressed mood.

It is likely that professional school counselors will encounter students dealing with depressed mood, depressive syndrome, and depressive disorders. Therefore, it is important to be knowledgeable of the diagnostic criteria for depression and other mood disorders so that appropriate interventions and/or referrals can be made (Kaffenberger & Seligman, 2007).

SIGNS AND SYMPTOMS OF DEPRESSION

Identifying depression in young people may be challenging because symptoms are often masked. Although the diagnostic criteria and key defining features of major depressive disorder are the same for youth as for adults, it may be difficult for them to identify or describe their feelings (NIMH; 2000). Instead, depressed students may appear irritable, act out, or withdraw from family and friends. Also, anxiety symptoms and somatic complaints are more common in depressed children and adolescents than in adults (Surgeon General, 2002). A list of common signs and symptoms of depression in young people is presented in Table 58.1 (NIMH; 2000; Rice & Leffert, 1997).

The diagnostic criteria for Major Depressive Episode and Dysthymic Disorder are outlined in the *DSM-IV-TR* (APA; 2000) as well as are Bipolar Disorder, Cyclothymic Disorder, and Adjustment Disorder with depressed mood. The primary features of each

TABLE 58.1

SIGNS AND SYMPTOMS OF DEPRESSION IN CHILDREN AND ADOLESCENTS

Feeling sad, empty, or hopeless

Increased emotional sensitivity

Lack of interest or ability to engage in pleasurable activities

Decreased energy level

Physical complaints (headaches, stomachaches, tiredness)

Frequent absences from school (or poor performance)

Outbursts (shouting, complaining, crying)

Boredom

Substance abuse

Fear of death

Suicidal ideation

Sleep/appetite disturbances

Reduced ability to think clearly and make decisions

Increased irritability, anger, or restlessness

Failure to make expected weight gains

Reckless behavior

Difficulty with relationships

disorder are summarized in Table 58.2; however, students may exhibit signs of depression without meeting the full diagnostic criteria for these disorders. These students, as well as students who are clinically depressed, are likely to benefit from early intervention by professional school counselors.

Depression in children and adolescents often is accompanied by other problems, some of which are clinically diagnosable. Examples of disorders that frequently co-occur

TABLE 58.2

DISORDERS THAT HAVE DEPRESSED MOOD AS A SYMPTOM

Type of Disorder	Characteristics
Major Depressive Disorder (MDD)	Uncommon in young children but increasing in prevalence after puberty, the life-time risk is 10% to 25% in women and 5% to 12% in men. MDD involves at least one Major Depressive Episode (extreme sadness and lack of interest in normal activities for 2 or more weeks at a time) without the occurrence of a manic episode or another disorder that better accounts for the depression.
Dysthymic Disorder	Common in children and adolescents (lifet-ime prevalence of 6%), but not diagnosed if a Major Depressive Disorder is evidenced. Depressed mood most days for at least 2 years (one year in children and adolescents). Symptoms may include poor appetite or overeating, poor sleeping or oversleeping, fatigue, poor concentration, and feelings of hopelessness.
Bipolar Disorder	Rare in young children but can appear in children and adolescents. Involves unusual shifts in mood, energy, and functioning. May begin with manic, depressive, or mixed manic and depressive symptoms. When the onset is before or soon after puberty, it may be characterized by a continuous, rapid-cycling, irritable, mixed symptom state and may co-occur with Attention-Deficit/Hyperactivity Disorder or Conduct Disorder (NIMH; 2000).
Cyclothymic Disorder	Onset typically is early adulthood, but the disorder can occur at younger ages. Characterized by chronic, fluctuating mood disturbance with many periods of hypomanic symptoms and many periods of depressive symptoms. During the initial 1-year period (for children and adolescents), any symptom-free periods do not last longer than 2 months (APA; 2000).
Adjustment Disorder with Depressed Mood	An Adjustment Disorder is a psychological response to an identified stressor that results in the development of emotional or psychological symptoms that are distressing to the individual. The symptoms must develop within 3 months after the stressor occurs and should resolve within 6 months after the stressor or its consequences have ended, unless the stressor is chronic. The predominant characteristics of Adjustment Disorder with Depressed Mood are tearfulness, feelings of hopelessness, and depressed mood (APA; 2000).

with depression in youth are Anxiety Disorders, Conduct Disorder, Eating Disorders, Personality Disorders, and Substance Abuse Disorders (Petersen et al., 1992; Rice & Leffert, 1997). Particularly high rates of comorbidity exist between depression and anxiety disorders. In studies of individuals ranging in age from 12 to 21 years, individuals with depression had rates of comorbidity with anxiety ranging from 33% to 75%. Variability in comorbidity rates across age groups can be partially attributed to the age dependent base rates of different disorders (Kovacs & Devlin, 1998). Also, depression may accompany medical conditions such as diabetes or other illnesses. Given the high rate of co-occurrence, professional school counselors will want to be sensitive to the possibility that the depressed student may also be struggling with one or more other conditions and plan interventions accordingly.

PREVALENCE

It is difficult to estimate rates of depression in children and adolescents with certainty (Merrell, 2001). A conservative estimate of 5% to 8% of adolescents struggle with either clinical depression or depressive syndrome (NIMH; 2001; Rice & Leffert, 1997). According to a NIMH (2001) report, approximately 2.5% of children and between 3% and 5% of adolescents experience clinical depression each year. Ten percent to 40% of youth report depressed or unhappy mood, with the rates increasing throughout adolescence (Rice & Leffert). The onset of depressive disorders appears to be occurring earlier in life than in previous decades. Early diagnosis and treatment can help offset difficulties that are associated with untreated depression when children reach adulthood (NIMH; 2001).

Prior to age 13 years, the rates of depression for boys and girls are similar. However, gender differences emerge between the ages of 13 and 14 years, with girls twice as likely to become depressed as boys (Merrell, 2001). One hypothesis for this difference is that girls tend to experience more challenges and stressors in early adolescence than boys, causing girls' depressive symptoms to increase more significantly during this time and throughout adulthood. Some theorists have suggested that these elevated levels of depression are rooted in girls' adherence to the female gender role, beginning during puberty and the concurrent transition from elementary to secondary school (Stice & Bearman, 2001). Additionally, physical changes during puberty often cause girls to develop body image concerns and dissatisfaction with their appearance. Deviance from the perceived "thin ideal" often sparks feelings of depressed mood and can in some cases result in the development of other harmful disorders. Regardless of the reasons for the differences, the increased rate of depression in girls may make it more likely that professional school counselors will work with girls struggling with depressive symptoms.

FACTORS ASSOCIATED WITH DEPRESSION

Several models of depression have been proposed, many of which have reciprocal components. Recognizing that interaction among causal factors is likely and that research on the etiology of depression is ongoing, current research on biological and psychosocial factors associated with depression in youth is presented next.

Biological factors. Much of the research about biological influences on depression has been conducted with adults rather than youth. Consequently, it is important to keep in mind when reading this section that generalizations about biological influences on depression may not be completely applicable to young people. Specific biological factors associated with the development of depression include abnormalities in the functioning of neurotransmitters and/or the endocrine system. In many cases, individuals may have a genetic predisposition to such abnormalities (Merrell, 2001).

Certain brain chemicals, including serotonin and norepinephrine, affect mood and have been linked with mood disorders (Merrell, 2001). When there are abnormalities in the level or function of these neurotransmitters, mood disorders can develop. Antidepressant medications such as fluoxetine (Prozac), fluvoxamine (Luvox), sertraline (Zoloft), and paroxetine (Paxil) block the reuptake of serotonin, thereby increasing its availability to brain cells. Other medications, such as venlafaxine (Effexor) and nefazodone (Serzone) affect the transmission of both serotonin and norepinephrine and can bring about relief from depressive symptoms (Stark et al., 2000).

Also associated with depression is abnormal functioning of the endocrine system, which releases hormones into the bloodstream. Various abnormalities in the functioning of the pituitary gland, thyroid gland, adrenal gland, and glands that release sex hormones have been linked with mood disturbances in youth and adults (Merrell, 2001; NIMH; 2001). In particular, hormonal changes during puberty may be associated with depressive symptoms (Stark et al., 2000).

Genetics play an important role in a person's vulnerability to depression and other mental disorders. It is theorized that multiple gene variants, rather than a single gene, act in conjunction with environmental factors and developmental events, thus making a person more likely to experience depressive symptoms (NIMH; 2001).

Cognitive and behavioral factors. Cognitive theory describes a strong link between an individual's cognitions, emotions, and behaviors. According to cognitive theory, people's interpretations of events, rather than the events themselves, trigger emotional upsets and mood disturbances (e.g., Beck, 1976). Such interpretations affect one's view of self, the world, and the future. Inaccurate interpretations or faulty information processing can lead to depressive symptoms in youth and adults (Asarnow, Jaycox, & Tompson, 2001; Beck, 1976; Kendall, 2000). Examples of faulty information processing include negative attributions and cognitive distortions.

Children with negative attribution styles may believe that they are helpless to influence events in their lives. They may also believe that they are responsible for any failures and problems that are experienced but not for successful, positive events (Merrell, 2001). For example, a student may believe that she is responsible for her parents' divorce and thus continually blame herself for the breakup of their marriage; or when something positive happens, like winning an award for achievement, the student attributes the event to luck.

Cognitive dysfunctions refer to negative, inaccurate biases that can result in unhealthy misperceptions of events. Studies have found that clinically depressed youth view themselves as less capable than their classmates, even though their IQ and academic performance does not differ significantly. Their negative perceptions often improve with the remittance of their depressive symptoms, indicating that these self-assessments may be dependent on the adolescent's state of mind during a given time (McGrath & Repetti, 2002). Cognitive theorists have identified several types of cognitive dysfunctions, including exaggerating the negative, minimizing the positive, overgeneralizing, catastrophizing, and personalizing. Cognitive distortions also are evidenced when young people engage in all-or-nothing thinking or selective abstraction, such as when taking a detail out of context and using it to negate an entire experience. Such distortions can result in negative automatic thoughts, which then affect emotions and mood states. Teaching students ways to correct faulty information processing is one way to effectively help young people who are depressed (Kendall, 2000).

Behaviors associated with negative cognitions and feelings can both contribute to and maintain depressive symptoms in children and adolescents. In particular, withdrawing from peers and family members can exacerbate feelings of depression and loneliness through the resulting lack of social reinforcement (Merrell, 2001). Related to social withdrawal is the tendency of depressed individuals to quit engaging in activities that formerly were pleasurable, such as athletics or hobbies, thereby creating a cycle that makes it difficult to alleviate depressive symptoms. To break the cycle, professional school counselors can help children identify activities they consider pleasurable and make commitments to participate in those activities between sessions (Stark & Kendall, 1996).

Challenges and stressors. Youth who experience numerous stressors may be more likely to experience depression than those who do not. Indeed, one model of adolescent depression developed by Petersen et al. (1992) and Peterson et al. (1993) proposed that the number and timing of changes and challenges in early adolescence affect mental health, with negative consequences being moderated by parental and peer support and coping skills. Challenges can be categorized as normative life events (expected changes, such as school entry and puberty), nonnormative events (e.g., divorce, abuse, moving away), and daily hassles (e.g., conflict with friends, excessive schoolwork). In a study of adolescents between the ages of 12 and 14 years, stress was found to have a strong causal effect on depression as well as a negative effect on self-esteem (Yarcheski & Mahon, 2000). The manner in which stress is experienced varies greatly from student to student. Recognizing the potential detrimental effects of stress, professional school counselors can conduct classroom guidance lessons and group sessions to teach students ways to manage stress effectively (see Chapter 89, "Helping Students Manage Stress," for specific examples).

Family and peer influences. A number of family-related factors are associated with depression, including extensive conflict, poor communication patterns, low family cohesion, and the emotional unavailability of parents (Merrell, 2001; Petersen et al., 1992). Having a parent with a mood disorder increases a young person's risk of experiencing depression, due in part to heredity and in part to the family interactions that occur if the parent's condition is not being treated successfully. In community settings, family counseling is often recommended when a member of the family is depressed; however, this option may not be available in the school setting. If not, professional school counselors can be instrumental in helping families become aware of opportunities for family counseling in the community.

Poor relationships with peers, not having a close friend, and being considered un-popular or different also can lead to depressive symptoms in students (Petersen et al., 1992). Certain populations, including gay, lesbian, and bisexual youth, may experience a greater degree of peer rejection and isolation, thus increasing their vulnerability to depression (Rice & Leffert, 1997). A critical role of the professional school counselor is to serve as an advocate for all students. Tolerance and acceptance can be demonstrated and taught in multiple ways, including parent and teacher training programs, classroom guidance lessons, and small-group sessions. See Table 58.3 for a list of risk factors for depression (NIMH; 2000).

CONSEQUENCES OF DEPRESSION

A wide range of intrapersonal and interpersonal problems can arise when depression goes undiagnosed and untreated in young people. A diminished sense of self-worth, a lack of confidence, and a general tendency to view oneself negatively often go hand in hand with depression (Merrell, 2001). For some students, the depression and ensuing fatigue can result in difficulties in concentration, motivation, and academic performance. Impaired relationships with peers and family members can both lead to and become a consequence of depression. The onset of depression is often correlated with inter-personal struggles, such as interpersonal deficits, role transitions, interpersonal role disputes, or grief (Mellin & Beamish, 2002). If left untreated, these underlying interper-sonal difficulties frequently persist into adulthood. In addition, youth with untreated depression are at an increased risk for physical illness, substance abuse, recurrent epi-sodes of depression, and suicidal behavior (NIMH; 2000, 2001). Consequently, there is a strong need to identify depressive symptoms early and make it possible for youth struggling with depression to get the help they need.

Suicide risk. The most severe problem associated with depression is the risk of sui-cide. Although most people who are depressed do not commit suicide, depressed youth, especially those dealing with what they perceive as a crisis, are at a greater risk for suicidal behaviors. The strongest risk factors for attempted suicide in young people are

TABLE 58.3
RISK FACTORS FOR DEPRESSION

Family history of mood disorders
Gender (adolescent girls twice as likely as boys to develop depression)
Stress
Loss of parent or loved one
Breakup of a romantic relationship
ADHD, conduct disorder, or learning disorder
Cigarette smoking
Chronic illness (e.g., diabetes)
Abuse or neglect
Other trauma, including natural disasters

depression, substance abuse, and aggressive or disruptive behaviors (NIMH; 2002a). The suicide rate among youth has increased dramatically during the past 3 decades, with suicide reported as the third leading cause of death among 15- to 24-year-olds (NIMH; 2002b). More girls attempt suicide than boys; however, boys are four times as likely to actually kill themselves and tend to use more lethal means (Surgeon General, 2002). In 1997, twenty-one percent of high school students nationwide reported that they had seriously considered attempting suicide within the past year, and 8% had actually attempted suicide (Centers for Disease Control, 2002).

Suicide attempts are often preceded by signals, warnings, or actual threats. Some of the signs to watch for include verbal messages (e.g., "I wish I were dead," "There's only one way out," "I won't be around much longer"), a preoccupation with death, changes in sleeping and eating patterns, decline in school performance, or giving away possessions. Suicidal behaviors and threats represent a cry for help and must be taken seriously. Professional school counselors typically have been trained in suicide assessment, and most schools have policies and procedures related to crisis intervention. When a professional school counselor has reason to believe that a student is contemplating suicide, the counselor will want to assess the nature and intensity of the student's thoughts and follow up with a response that will keep the student safe. Merrell (2001, p. 30) listed the following six basic steps that can be followed in responding to potentially suicidal youth (be sure these steps are consistent with your school system policy before implementing them):

1. *Thinking about suicide.* If there is plausible reason to believe that a student is considering suicide, ask the student about it directly. Keeping the wording developmentally appropriate, the counselor can ask, "Have you been thinking about hurting yourself?" or "Have you been thinking about wanting to be dead?"

2. *Suicide plan.* If there is any indication of suicidal ideation, the next step is to determine whether the student has made an actual plan. Ask questions such as, "Have you thought about how you might do it?" or "How would you do it?" Generally, more specific, thought-out plans indicate a greater risk of an attempt—although with impulsive youth, this is not necessarily the case.

3. *Method.* If the student has a plan, determine what has been already put in place to carry out the plan. What methods are being considered and how available are they? Determine the exact location of any lethal means (e.g., firearms, drugs).

4. *Intended place or setting.* Where does the student intend to commit the suicide act? Has he or she written a note, and, if so, what does it say?

5. *Immediate protective action.* If there is reason to believe that the student is seriously considering suicide, immediate protective action should be taken. If there is a risk of imminent danger, notify parents and whoever else needs to be notified, depending on the circumstances, school policy, and local laws. Do not leave a suicidal student alone, even briefly.

6. *Suicide contract and follow-up planning.* If there is no evidence of imminent danger but the professional school counselor is still concerned about the possibility of suicide, help the student complete a written contract in which he or she promises to (a) not engage in any self-destructive behavior, and (b) call an appropriate person or agency if he or she is considering self-harm. Make sure the student has names and

phone numbers of people to contact. Plan for ongoing counseling, be mindful of confidentiality issues, consult with others, and meet with the student's parents if the situation warrants doing so.

INTERVENTIONS

Professional school counselors have opportunities to intervene at multiple levels to help children and adolescents deal with depressive symptoms. Intervention can take the form of prevention, which is designed to reduce incidences of depression before problems begin, or direct counseling services for at-risk groups and individuals. Interventions at all levels need to be developmentally informed, with an overarching goal of enhancing or modifying students' internal and external resources that are amenable to change (Rice & Leffert, 1997).

A number of factors, including school policy and size, may dictate the nature and type of interventions the professional school counselor implements. Professional school counselors are responsible for a wide range of services and work with a large number of students, teachers, and parents. If too much time is spent with only a few students, the larger proportion of the student body may be shortchanged (Ripley, Erford, Dahir, & Eschbach, 2003). Recognizing the challenge of balancing multiple responsibilities, professional school counselors play crucial roles in assessing, coordinating referrals, and, when needed, providing direct treatment or follow-up services for students with depression (Rice & Leffert, 1997). They also are key leaders in planning and implementing prevention programs for students, parents, and teachers.

ASSESSMENT AND EVALUATION

Accurately assessing depression in children and adolescents can be challenging because the symptoms often cannot be observed directly and therefore may go unrecognized. By being aware of the signs, symptoms, and co-occurring conditions associated with child and adolescent depression, professional school counselors can help identify students who may be in need of services. The purpose of assessment is to inform treatment, which may involve direct counseling services at the school or elsewhere.

Typically, multiple sources of information are used to guide decision making and treatment planning. It helps to gather information from the child, parents, and teachers. Self-report instruments, structured or semistructured interviews, and behavior rating scales are some of the methods that can be used in assessment. Professional school counselors who have been trained in appraisal procedures may choose to use assessment instruments designed for depression screening, such as the *Children's Depression Inventory* (CDI), the *Beck Depression Inventory* (BDI-II), and the *Center for Epidemiologic Studies Depression Scale* (CES-D) (see NIMH; 2000). Professional school counselor who have not been trained to use a particular instrument should get supervision to ensure that the instrument is administered and interpreted properly. If the screening evaluation indicates the student has depressive symptoms and possibly a depressive disorder, the professional school counselor will want to provide referral information to parents so that a more comprehensive diagnostic evaluation can be conducted. In such cases, the professional school counselor can serve as a liaison between the referral agency and the family (Rice & Leffert, 1997).

DIRECT COUNSELING SERVICES

When helping students who have depression, direct counseling services are often warranted. These services may include individual counselling, referral, and group counseling.

Individual counseling. For some students, short-term individual counseling or group counseling may be warranted. Research has demonstrated the efficacy of certain types of counseling, especially cognitive-behavioral therapy (CBT), in alleviating depressive symptoms in young people (NIMH; 2001). The goal of CBT is to help children and adolescents develop cognitive structures that will positively influence their future experiences (Kendall, 2000). The cognitive component of CBT helps individuals identify and change negative, pessimistic thinking, biases, and attributions. The behavioral component, also important to the process, focuses on increasing positive behavior patterns and improving social skills (Asarnow et al., 2001).

Another type of counseling, interpersonal therapy for adolescents (IPT-A), was adapted from IPT for adults. Although it has not been researched as extensively as CBT with young people, studies have demonstrated that moderately to severely depressed adolescents who have undergone IPT-A treatment experienced a significant reduction in depressive symptoms and subsequent improvement in overall functioning (Mellin & Beamish, 2002). The two primary goals of IPT are to reduce depressive symptoms and to improve disturbed personal relationships that may contribute to depression. Both CBT and IPT were developed to treat depression but differ in theory and practice. Both approaches require training to be used effectively with students.

In conducting individual counseling with students who have depressive symptoms, Rice and Leffert (1997) recommended a cognitive-behavioral approach that focuses on developing internal and external resources that are amenable to change. The first step is to build a working alliance with the student, thereby fostering the development of an external resource. Other strategies can also be implemented:

> Coping or problem-solving strategies could be explored and improved. Students can learn how to match appropriate coping strategies to the type of problem situations they encounter. For example, active problem-solving in which an adolescent sets a goal, brainstorms possible solutions, anticipates consequences, and implements a plan of action, generally works for events or circumstances that are under an adolescent's control. Emotion-focused strategies (e.g., relaxation) may be used when circumstances are not under the adolescent's control but are nevertheless upsetting. Cognitive interventions could be implemented to challenge and revise inaccurate perceptions of self and others. Social skills (e.g., assertiveness training) could be addressed and practiced in order to increase the quantity and quality of relationships with peers and family members. (Rice & Leffert, 1997, p. 26)

Professional school counselors who work individually with depressed students should collaborate with family members and teachers so that they can support the work that is being done with the child. By consulting with parents and teachers, counselors can help significant others in the student's environment learn how to encourage the student's use of new skills (Stark et al., 2000).

Referral. At times, professional school counselors will work with students whose problems are severe and chronic. When this occurs, the appropriate response may be to make referrals to mental health professionals in the community. In particular, if the required interventions cannot be implemented in the school, if medication is a possibility, or if the student appears to be in danger of harming anyone, making a referral may be the preferred course of action. In such cases, the professional school counselor will want to meet with the parents of the student to discuss concerns and determine their willingness to pursue outside help. If they are willing to consider outside help, a letter written by the professional school counselor to the referral source can facilitate treatment and collaboration (Merrell, 2001).

Group counseling. Group counseling provides another mode by which students with depressive symptoms can be helped. Several outcome studies have demonstrated the efficacy of implementing comprehensive intervention programs that emphasize cognitive behavioral techniques (see Kaslow & Thompson, 1998, for a review of outcome studies of interventions with depressed children and adolescents). The intervention programs implemented in these studies followed a treatment-manual format, thereby providing a replicable scope and sequence of interventions. The following programs have been used successfully with young people:

- *Adolescent Coping With Depression Course* (CWD-A; Rohde, Lewinsohn, Clarke, Hops, & Seeley, 2005)
- *Taking ACTION Program* (ACTION; Stark & Kendall, 1996)
- *Interpersonal Psychotherapy for Adolescents With Depression* (IPT-A; Mufson, Dorta, Moreau, & Weissman, 2004)
- *Helping Students Overcome Depression and Anxiety: A Practical Guide* (Merrell, 2001)

Sources for these programs, including a brief description of each, are listed in Table 58.4.

The intervention programs described in Table 58.4 range from a minimum of 12 sessions to as many as 30 sessions; consequently, in some schools it will not be feasible to implement them as designed. Merrell (2001) suggested devising a modified comprehensive group program, incorporating key elements that the programs have in common, which include the following:

- Developing a therapeutic relationship based on trust and respect
- Education regarding depression
- Activity scheduling (monitoring, increasing participation in pleasant events)
- Emotional education (identifying and labeling emotions, identifying situations in which emotions are likely to occur, recognizing the link between thoughts and feelings)
- Cognitive change strategies (challenging negative or irrational thoughts, practicing appropriate attributions, increasing the focus on positive thoughts and events)
- Problem solving, negotiation, and conflict resolution
- Relaxation training

TABLE 58.4

RESOURCES AND INTERVENTION PROGRAMS FOR HELPING STUDENTS WITH DEPRESSION

Title	Description	Publishing information
Helping Students Overcome Depression and Anxiety: A Practical Guide (Merrell, 2001)	Provides comprehensive information about child and adolescent depression and other internalizing disorders. Offers practical guidelines for assessment and intervention. Describes more than 40 psychoeducational and psychosocial techniques that can be adapted for youth at different developmental levels. Provides reproducible worksheets for use with students.	Guilford Press 72 Spring Street New York, NY 10012 1-800-365-7006 www.guilford.com
Taking ACTION Program (Stark & Kendall, 1996)	A comprehensive intervention program designed for youth between ages 9 and 13 years, although activities can be adapted for younger or older students. Provides guidelines for 30 group counseling sessions that focus on affective education, problem-solving skills, social skills, coping skills, and cognitive interventions.	Workbook Publishing 298 Llanfair Road Ardmore, PA 19003 1-610-896-9797
Adolescent Coping With Depression Course (Rohde et. al., 2005)	A comprehensive cognitive-behavioral intervention program designed for small-group work with adolescents ages 14 to 18 years, although it may be adapted for younger students. Provides directions for 16 two-hour psychoeducational sessions. Activities are highly structured. Length of sessions may be problematic in a school setting.	Castalia Publishing Co. P.O. Box 1587 Eugene, OR 97440 1-541-343-4433
Interpersonal Therapy for Adolescents With Depression (Mufson et al., 2004)	Provides an overview of interpersonal therapy and depression, an in-depth description of applications of IPT for depressed adolescents, and a discussion of special issues related to working with youth. May be more appropriate for mature, insightful adolescents. Due to its clinical focus, it may be less applicable in a school setting.	Guilford Press 72 Spring Street New York, NY 10012 1-800-365-7006 www.guilford.com

- Social skills and communication skills
- Goal setting and relapse prevention (Merrell, 2001, p. 76)

When conducting groups for students who are depressed or who are at risk for depression, professional school counselors will want to adapt activities so that they are developmentally appropriate and so that students' real-life concerns are integrated into the format (Stark & Kendall, 1996). Including homework assignments between sessions, involving parents, and adding booster sessions that occur after the program has been completed are ways to increase the efficacy of the experience. Attention should be given to age range, gender composition, and group size, with 4 to 10 students in a group being ideal (Merrell, 2001). Whereas individual and/or group counseling may be beneficial and necessary for some students, a way to reach even more students is through school-based prevention programs.

SCHOOL-BASED PREVENTION PROGRAMS

School-based prevention programs can be effective in preventing depression in school-age youth. These programs may include student-oriented programs and parent and teacher training programs.

Student-oriented programs. Professional school counselors can be instrumental in coordinating and leading life-skills training programs to promote positive mental health in young people. Because all youth are exposed to sources of stress, and many youth are at risk for experiencing depressive symptoms of some type, it is important for professional school counselors to enhance students' ability to respond adaptively and cope well (Petersen et al., 1992). The goal of prevention programs is to help an entire population of students develop internal and external resources to help prevent the onset of depression or to lessen its intensity should it occur (Rice & Leffert, 1997). Prevention programs can be designed as classroom guidance, which is geared toward students, or as training programs, which are geared toward parents and/or school personnel. Topics for student-oriented prevention can include many of the elements that were described in the section on group counseling: emotional awareness, recognizing the link between thoughts and feelings, coping skills, problem-solving skills, interpersonal skills, conflict resolution, and relaxation training.

An example of a student-oriented prevention program—the Penn State Adolescent Study—was developed by Petersen et al. (1992) and Peterson et al. (1993) to promote mental health and increase coping skills among sixth-grade students. This 16-session psychoeducational program helped students develop positive emotional, cognitive, and behavioral responses to stressors and challenges. Each session emphasized a particular social skill, coping method, or challenge, and began with an activity that demonstrated the topic. Students were given opportunities to practice new problem-solving skills for issues such as peer pressure, making friends, and family conflict. Each session ended with a summary and discussion of major points that were then linked to upcoming sessions. Evaluation indicated that students' coping skills and problem-solving abilities improved after participating in the program, but the effects were not observable 1 year later, leading to the suggestion of following up with booster sessions throughout the school year would enhance the program's long-term effectiveness.

Parent and teacher training programs. In addition to planning student-oriented prevention programs, professional school counselors can initiate training programs for teachers and parents. Teachers and parents typically have more interaction with youth than any other adults. Training programs that facilitate the development of skills in communication, coping, and behavior management can be instrumental in promoting healthy interactions, thus helping prevent the development of depressive symptoms in young people. Also, programs designed to raise parent and teacher awareness about depression can help improve access to needed mental health care for children whose depression might otherwise go undetected. Many parents and teachers may feel reluctant or unprepared to relate children's academic or social difficulties with poor emotional health (Kirchner, Yoder, Kramer, Lindsey, & Thrush, 2000). Professional school counselors can collaborate with mental health providers in the community to lead workshops designed to disseminate information about depression, possible interventions, and community resources.

Kirchner et al. (2000) developed a pilot program, *Depression in the Classroom*, for K–12 teachers to educate participants about depression and suicide among children and adolescents. Program goals were to provide (a) information about the biological and psychosocial basis of depression; and (b) tools to increase educators' ability to detect depressive disorders, educate others about depression, and make referrals within the community. The program, led by mental health specialists from an academic medical center, combined didactic instruction with experiential activities (e.g., responding to video vignettes) and represented a collaborative effort between a medical academic center and school systems. Outcome results indicated that participants not only increased their own knowledge about depression but also shared their knowledge with colleagues and students. Also, a majority of the participants reportedly applied the skills learned in the course when interacting with depressed students in their classroom. This program represented a large collaborative effort between an academic medical center and several school systems. Similar programs, perhaps on a smaller scale, could be designed through the collaborative efforts of professional school counselors and community mental heath practitioners.

Summary/Conclusion

Child and adolescent depression is a serious but treatable condition that has received considerable attention. Many youth will experience depressed mood and other depressive symptoms, even though they may not be clinically depressed. Depression and depressive symptoms can interfere with learning, psychosocial development, and interpersonal relationships. If untreated, depressive symptoms can lead to mood disorders that continue into adulthood. On the other hand, early identification and treatment of symptoms can help put young people on a healthy developmental trajectory.

Professional school counselors have the knowledge and skills needed to enhance the psychological development and well-being of youth (Rice & Leffert, 1997). By understanding the signs, symptoms, and etiology of depression, professional school counselors can play crucial roles in identifying students who may be struggling with these disorders. They can intervene on multiple levels, both from a preventive and a remedial perspective. Prevention activities directed toward students can facilitate the development of positive coping and interaction skills. Programmatic efforts directed toward parents and teachers can increase their knowledge about depression and skill in adult–child interaction. Individual and group counseling can help students address dysfunctional cognitive processes, learn strategies for dealing with interpersonal concerns, and develop skills for coping with stress and negative emotions. Through such efforts, professional school counselors can be instrumental in helping students meet the challenges of development in ways that promote mental health.

(Note: See the CD-ROM for a list of references.)

CHAPTER 59

HELPING STUDENTS DEAL
WITH OBSESSIVE–COMPULSIVE DISORDER

Gail Mears

Preview

Obsessive–compulsive disorder (OCD), a neurobiological disorder once thought to be rare in children, affects 1 out of every 200 children (American Psychiatric Association [APA], 2000). Professional school counselors knowledgeable about the signs of OCD can help ensure early detection of OCD, referral for appropriate services, and effective in-school interventions.

Obsessive–compulsive disorder (OCD), previously thought to be uncommon in students, affects approximately 1 out of 200 students (APA; 2000). There are likely to be several students struggling with the debilitating effects of this disorder in most schools at any one time (March & Mulle, 1998). Children with OCD are consumed by intrusive, repetitive, distressing thoughts and accompanying repetitive rituals. These symptoms can significantly interfere with academic, psychological, and social functioning.

Unfortunately, OCD in school-age children often goes undetected or is misdiagnosed. Even when detected, the treatments that students receive are often inappropriate (Adams, 2004; Heyman et al., 2004; March & Mulle, 1998). This leaves students and their families confused and hopeless. With the right psychological, behavioral, medical, social, and academic interventions, however, students with OCD and their families can find relief from the debilitating effects of this condition.

Professional school counselors are in a key position to ensure that students with OCD are identified and effective resources are located. The purpose of this chapter is to aid professional school counselors in their efforts to help students with OCD, their families, and school personnel identify and better manage this condition.

What Is OCD?

OCD is a neurobiological disorder characterized by obsessions and compulsions, occurring either alone or in combination with each other. An obsession is a persistent irrational thought, image, or impulse that causes distress for the student. The student generally recognizes that these thoughts are irrational but is not able to stop them. Obsessions cause the student significant anxiety, which the student seeks to manage through the use of compulsions. Compulsions are behavioral or thinking rituals that reduce the anxiety caused by the obsession. The relief is temporary, however, and the student feels obliged to continue the use of rituals to manage the resulting anxiety (Adams & Torchia, 1998; American Psychiatric Association [APA], 2000; Chansky, 2000; March & Mulle, 1998).

OCD is a chronic disorder with symptoms that worsen over time if left untreated. This disorder has many ups and downs. During periods of stress, students with OCD may notice a significant increase in symptoms. Although the symptoms of OCD are similar for children, adolescents, and adults, unlike adults and adolescents, young children may not view their obsessions as irrational (Adams & Torchia, 1998).

Most young students engage in some form of ritualized behavior. These behaviors are not typically symptoms of OCD. Childhood rituals usually are in the service of helping children gain more mastery over their environment and they ultimately lead to a sense of competence. There is no excessive distress associated with these behaviors, and they do not interfere with social and academic functioning (Adams, 2004; Chansky, 2000; Merlo & Storch, 2006a; Thomsen, 1998). Children who insist on a particular bedtime ritual, carry a special object, or want favored stories read over and over again are not suffering from OCD—they are engaging in normal childhood behaviors. The adolescent who takes a long time to get ready for a date or who spends major blocks of time practicing a sport or instrument is also not suffering from OCD. These behaviors, while sometimes vexing to adults, do not interfere with the child's academic, social, and psychological development. The student who needs to touch every object in his bedroom 10 times before leaving for school, however, is showing definite symptoms of OCD. The symptoms of OCD cause distress to students, are time-consuming, and likely interfere with social, emotional, and academic functioning. The following are examples of students with OCD.

- Mary, age 13 years, finds school harder and harder to attend. For the past 2 years she has been increasingly plagued by sexual images she finds offensive, and she worries that she is crazy. She recites prayers to deal with the anxiety these images cause. It is becoming harder for Mary to pay attention to her classwork. She is often preoccupied by the need to pray. Additionally, the proximity of the males in her classes seems to trigger these sexual images. Her grades are dropping, and her school attendance is erratic. She no longer likes to spend time with her friends, is irritable at home, and is feeling more and more despondent.

- Sammy, age 10 years, is in fourth grade. He worries constantly about germs and getting sick. He is particularly worried about getting AIDS. He is careful not to touch anything that he considers dirty, such as doorknobs, faucets, trash, and toilets. He also does not like to touch things that other students have handled. He is often late for school, as he needs to wash and rewash his hands many times during the course of getting ready in the morning. During the school day, he repeatedly asks to go to the bathroom to wash his hands after touching objects handled by other students. His hands are red and raw, and Sammy seems to be anxious most of the time. He does not play with the other children anymore.

- Jimmy, age 9 years, feels the need for things to be "just right." He spends hours arranging objects in his room at home to feel comfortable. In school he is having increasing difficulty with his written work and with reading. His papers are full of erasure marks, and he generally is unable to finish assignments. When reading, Jimmy needs to reread each word, making sure that he pronounces each one correctly. Jimmy has frequent anger outbursts in the classroom.

What Types of Obsessions Do Children Have?

Obsessions may take many forms, and it is the intrusive, irrational, and distressing nature of these thoughts, images, or impulses that mark them as obsessions (APA; 2000). Obsessions that are commonly reported by children include fear of contamination (worry about germs, getting sick, dying), fear of hurting oneself or others, obscene imagery or thoughts of inappropriate sexual behavior, fear of sinning, need for symmetry or the need to have objects arranged in certain ways, doubting (e.g., Did I really lock the door?), or the need to repeat actions a certain number of times (Chansky, 2000; Thomsen, 1998; Merlo & Storch, 2006b; Waltz, 2000). Fear of dirt and germs is the most common obsession experienced by students and is reported by approximately 40% of students with OCD (Thomsen, 1998).

What Type of Compulsions Do Children Have?

Compulsions are behavioral or thinking rituals that the student feels compelled to perform to reduce the anxiety caused by the obsessions. To meet the criteria for a compulsion, the behavior or mental ritual must cause marked distress to the student, consume more than an hour a day, or interfere significantly with daily functioning (APA; 2000). Though rare, students can experience compulsions without accompanying obsessions. Common forms of compulsions include washing, checking, repeating behaviors, counting, hoarding, praying, and arranging things symmetrically. Washing rituals are the most frequent compulsions displayed by children, and boys are more likely than girls to engage in counting rituals (Adams & Torchia, 1998; Chansky, 2000; Thomsen, 1998).

What Causes OCD?

Historically, OCD was thought to be a disorder that resulted from poor parenting or some other form of environmental stress. Currently, OCD is understood to be a neurobiological disorder. OCD is associated with overactivity and structural abnormalities in multiple regions of the brain (Adams & Torchia, 1998; Osborn, 1998; Waltz, 2000). Students with OCD often have other neurological irregularities, such as tics and nonverbal learning problems (Adams & Torchia, 1998; March & Mulle, 1998). Serotonin, a neurotransmitter, is the brain chemical most likely involved in OCD (Adams & Torchia, 1998; Chansky, 2000). While it is not known if disregulation of serotonin is the main causative factor in OCD, all medications effective in relieving OCD symptoms affect serotonin pathways (Thomsen, 1998).

Stress can precipitate or exacerbate symptoms of OCD, but students with OCD are in the grip of a brain malfunction. Chansky (2000) referred to the symptoms of OCD as a brain hiccup. The obsessions and compulsions are involuntary and intrusive, and students with OCD do not feel as if they have the ability to stop the intrusive obsessions or to not engage the resulting compulsions. Students with OCD are literally stuck in their respective obsessions and resulting behavioral or mental rituals. This information is very important for parents who often feel responsible (and may have been actually blamed!) for producing this condition in their children.

Heredity is a likely factor in the development of OCD. Students may inherit a vulnerability to OCD, but heredity alone does not explain the actual expression of the disorder (Thomsen, 1998). Higher rates of OCD have been observed in students who have family members diagnosed with OCD, depression, anxiety disorders, or Tourette's syndrome (Adams & Torchia, 1998).

Research from the National Institute of Mental Health indicated that a group of students developed an acute and severe onset or exacerbation of OCD symptoms that is associated with a strep infection—Pediatric Autoimmune Neuropsychiatric Disorder Associated with Strep (PANDAS; Swedo, Leonard, et al. as cited in Chansky, 2000; Snider & Swedo, 2004). When a child presents with a sudden onset or increase in OCD symptoms, a referral should be made to a pediatrician to rule out PANDAS.

Who Gets OCD?

It is estimated that 1 in 200 students are diagnosed with OCD at any one time. This is likely an underestimate of the prevalence rate of OCD, because students are often secretive about their symptoms and family members and professionals often don't understand that the troubling behaviors displayed by the student may be a result of OCD (March & Mulle, 1998). The *DSM-IV-TR* (APA; 2000) sets a lifetime prevalence rate of OCD in children at 1.0% to 2.3% and notes that the prevalence rate of OCD in students is consistent across cultures. Students diagnosed with OCD may also have other diagnosed disorders including ADHD, Tourette's syndrome, developmental disabilities, nonverbal learning disabilities, anxiety disorders, and depressive disorders (Adams & Torchia, 1998). Ten percent to 30% of students diagnosed with ADHD and 40% o 60% of children diagnosed with Tourette's syndrome also qualify for a diagnosis of OCD (Comings, as cited in Dornbush & Pruitt, 1995).

Males and females are diagnosed with OCD in equal numbers. However, OCD tends to occur at an earlier age in boys than in girls. The average age of onset for males is between the ages of 6 and 15 years, and the average age of onset for females is between the ages of 20 and 29 years (APA; 2000). Clinically, OCD is similar for boys and girls. There is some indication that there is an increased likelihood that boys have family members with OCD, and boys seem to have higher rates of tic disorders than do girls (Thomsen, 1998).

What Are the Signs That a Student May Have OCD?

Children's obsessions and compulsions are not always apparent to an observer. Young children are more open about their compulsions, but older children and adolescents often hide these symptoms. Whether visible or not, the symptoms of OCD weigh heavily on students. The stress of dealing with their symptoms may lead to other behavioral problems. Sometimes students are able to control their compulsions in school but not at home. Parents' reports of OCD symptoms should be taken seriously, even if the student does not demonstrate the same behaviors in school (Chansky, 2000).

There are multiple signs that might indicate a student is struggling with the symptoms of OCD. According to specialists (Adams, 2004; Adams & Torchia, 1998;

Chansky, 2000; Chansky & Grayson, n.d.; Dornbush & Pruitt; 1995; Johnston & Frue-hling, 2002), school personnel should be attentive to a number of common signs (see Table 59.1).

How Is OCD Diagnosed?

A professional qualified to diagnose and assess mental disorders should always make the diagnosis of OCD. This professional will want to gather information from the student, parents, and relevant school professionals. Standardized questionnaires are often used to help in the diagnosis and evaluate the extent to which OCD is interfering with the child's social, emotional, and academic functioning. The diagnosis of OCD is often complicated by the presence of other comorbid conditions such as anxiety disorders,

TABLE 59.1

COMMON SIGNS OF OCD

Repeated requests to go to the bathroom. The child seeks to engage in washing rituals to manage the anxiety caused by contamination fears that get triggered in the normal course of the school day.

Repeated reassurance-seeking from teachers and other adult authorities. This goes well beyond the typical questioning that might be expected from any school child.

The appearance of daydreaming or disinterest in schoolwork. Students with OCD are preoccupied with their frightening obsessions and compensating ritual. When so much attention is focused internally, it is difficult to stay engaged with the classroom activity.

Bouts of anger or anxiety. This can be the result of being exposed to situations that trigger obsessions. A student with contamination fears may get quite upset when expected to share materials with another student. Anxiety and irritability may result when students are frustrated in their attempts to engage in compulsions. Therefore, the student whose request to go to the bathroom is denied may become quite agitated.

The need to do things in "just the right way." This can dramatically interfere with schoolwork. These types of obsessions can prevent students from finishing tasks in a timely manner. Students may suffer from reading or writing compulsions. OCD may prevent the students from finishing written or reading assignments as they struggle with the need to write or read perfectly, resulting in erasures and undone work. Students with OCD may resist writing or reading in an effort to avoid the associated obsessions and compulsions. As school becomes more and more burdensome, students may try and avoid school altogether.

Frequent tardiness for school or classes. Obsessions and resulting compulsions can make getting ready for school or the transition between classes very time-consuming. A student who needs to repeat behaviors over and over again, arrange and rearrange objects, or repetitively wash hands may be frequently tardy for school and classes.

Social isolation. The time students spend managing their OCD symptoms can greatly interfere with the time they have available for friends. Being with other students may reduce their ability to engage in compulsions or may risk triggering obsessions and compulsions (such as fear of hurting another). These students worry that their inability to control their compulsions will lead to being ridiculed by their peers. Social isolation is a way of managing these fears.

Depression and low self-esteem. The ongoing battle with obsessions and compulsions that students with OCD face is extremely discouraging, potentially leaving the student demoralized and hopeless.

oppositional defiant disorder, depression, eating disorders, ADHD, developmental disabilities, Tourette's syndrome, or nonverbal language disorders (Adams & Torchia, 1998; Adams, Wass, March, & Smith, 1994; March & Mulle, 1998; Thomsen, 1998). Acquaint yourself with experienced diagnosticians in your community who are equipped to evaluate students showing symptoms of OCD.

How Is OCD Treated?

Cognitive-behavior therapy (CBT) and behavior therapy (terms often used to indicate similar treatment formats) are considered the most effective treatment for students with OCD (Johnston & Fruehling, 2002; March & Mulle, 1998; Merlo & Storch, 2006a; Thomsen, 1998). Cognitive and behavioral strategies are designed to help students delay and reduce compulsive rituals when they are exposed to situations that trigger obsessions. They are also designed to empower students by providing information regarding the neurobiological roots of OCD and by helping students develop cognitive strategies that empower them to feel in control of, rather than controlled by, OCD symptoms (March & Mulle, 1998). Medication should be considered for students when symptoms are so severe that CBT is too anxiety provoking or when there is little or no response to CBT alone. Treatment in these cases should be a combination of CBT and medication. Medication alone does not help students develop the behavioral and cognitive strategies so useful in minimizing the impact of OCD symptoms (Johnston & Fruehling, 2002).

The medications most commonly prescribed for childhood OCD include clomipramine (Anafranil), fluoxetine (Prozac), fluvoxamine (Luvox), paroxetine (Paxil), and sertraline (Zoloft). Clomipramine, fluvoxamine, and sertraline have FDA approval for use with students diagnosed with OCD. All of these medications affect serotonin levels in the brain. All but clomipramine are in the family of drugs known as *selective serotonin reuptake inhibitors* (SSRIs) (Johnston & Fruehling, 2002).

Parents need to be involved in their child's treatment. Having a child with OCD is extremely stressful, and parents as well as children need support, information, and coping strategies. Sometimes, in an attempt to deal with their child's distress, parents become involved in their child's rituals. An example of this would be a parent that agrees to repeatedly wash the same article of clothing before the child agrees to wear it. Parents are important partners in their child's effort to learn strategies to better manage OCD (Chansky, 2000; March & Mulle, 1998).

How Can School Counselors Help?

Professional school counselors are key school resources for students struggling with the symptoms of OCD. According to experts (Adams, 2004; Adams & Torchia, 1998; Chansky, 2000), the following are actions that can help minimize the impact of OCD on students at school.

- Professional school counselors can educate school personnel about the signs of OCD. Statistics suggest that there are likely multiple children in any school with OCD. Educating teachers, principals, and parents about the signs of OCD will increase the likelihood that students will get the help that they need and avoid the academic, psychological, and social consequences of untreated OCD.

- Professional school counselors can consult with parents, teachers, the school psychologist, and outside mental health providers to ensure that students diagnosed with OCD receive appropriate in-school interventions. Some students with mild OCD will need no accommodations from the school. In fact, the school may not even be aware of the diagnosis. Students with moderate to severe OCD, however, may need professional school counselors and teachers to help manage programs designed to delay or reduce compulsive rituals.

- Professional school counselors can provide a place where students with OCD get a reprieve from the stress of the classroom and the stress of delaying rituals. The treatment of OCD involves helping students develop a plan to delay participating in compulsive rituals. The goal is a reduction in these rituals, not necessarily the elimination of these rituals. Part of that plan will likely include a "safe place" where students can go to recover from the stress of dealing with OCD.

- Professional school counselors can be alert to both the positive and negative changes that result from medication. Negative effects may include, but are not limited to, dry mouth, increased irritability, upset stomach, drowsiness, insomnia, and headaches.

- Professional school counselors can help parents find the educational, psychological, and medical resources that they will need to help their child manage OCD. Understanding that OCD is a neurobiological disorder and not the result of bad parenting can be an enormous source of support for parents.

- Professional school counselors can advocate that students with OCD get appropriate in-school accommodations. Students with OCD may be eligible for special educational services under Section 504 of the Rehabilitation Act of 1973 or, if educational functioning is severely compromised, under the Individuals With Disabilities Education Improvement Act of 2004.

- Professional school counselors can help create a positive classroom environment with peers. In more severe cases, it may be helpful to educate the student's classmates about OCD. In most cases, however, a more general classroom curriculum is recommended. Chansky (2000) suggested units on health issues that affect the body from head to toe. Most students will know someone struggling with a disabling condition and this identification may increase their ability to empathize with the student struggling with OCD in the classroom. Consent from the student and parents should always be secured before talking with classmates about an individual child's condition.

WHAT ARE SOME CLASSROOM STRATEGIES THAT WILL HELP CHILDREN WITH OCD?

Students should not be punished for symptoms of OCD over which they have no control. Taking away recess or giving detentions may only worsen the behaviors these punishments are designed to eliminate (Adams & Torchia, 1998). Some of the helpful classroom strategies identified by Adams and Torchia (1998) and Chansky and Grayson (n.d.) include the following:

- Find ways to accommodate the student's symptoms. Examples of supportive classroom accommodations include (a) allow students with writing compulsion to take tests orally; (b) grade students on the content, not the neatness, of their papers; (c) provide resources for a student with reading compulsions to listen to books on tape; (d) give extra time on tests; (e) develop signals and phrases with students to cue them when they appear stuck in OCD rituals that you are willing to help.
- Support students with OCD by identifying areas of strength. OCD is a demoralizing illness, and students need to be reminded of the things they do well.
- Help students with OCD manage social interactions. Set up opportunities for students to work collaboratively with peers. Avoid putting these students in situations in which they are likely to be ignored or left out.

For more specific ideas about classroom interventions, refer to Dornbush and Pruitt (1995).

Summary/Conclusion

Students can expect significant help with the debilitating symptoms of OCD. Though considered a chronic illness, with appropriate treatment and school and home support, students with OCD will likely experience a significant reduction in the distress and subsequent functional impairments associated with this condition. Unfortunately, educators and mental health practitioners are often misinformed about the cause of OCD and effective intervention strategies. Professional school counselors are in a key position to ensure that teachers and other school personnel are informed and alert to the signs and symptoms of OCD. Through partnerships with teachers, school nurses, school psychologists, and qualified mental health professionals in the community, professional school counselors can promote in-school strategies that will support students with OCD in their academic, social and emotional development. Professional school counselors play an important role in making school a satisfying experience that is not overshadowed by symptoms associated with OCD for students living with this disorder. (See Table 59.2 for additional resources for helping students with OCD.)

(Note: See the CD-ROM for a list of references.)

TABLE 59.2

ADDITIONAL RESOURCES

Organizations

Anxiety Disorders Association of America, P.O. Box 631409, Silver Spring, MD, 21263-1409 (www.adaa.org)

National Alliance for the Mentally Ill, Child and Adolescent Network, 200 North Glebe Road, Suite 1015, Arlington, VA 22203-3754

National Institute of Mental Health, Building 10, Room 4N 208, Bethesda, MD 20892-1255 (www.intramural.nimh.nih.gov/pds/web.htm)

Obsessive–Compulsive Foundation, 337 Notch Hill Road, North Branford, CT 0697 (http://www.ocfoundation.org)

Obsessive Compulsive Information Center, Madison Institute of Medicine, 7617 Mineral Point Road, Suite 300, Madison, WI 53717 (http://www.helathtechsys.com/mim.html)

Books

Adams, G. B., & Torchia, M. (1994). *School personnel: A critical link in the identification, treatment and management of OCD in children and adolescents* (3rd ed.). Milford, CT: OC Foundation.

Chanksy, T. E. (2000). *Freeing your child from obsessive-compulsive disorder: A powerful practical guide for parents of children and adolescents.* New York: Three Rivers Press.

Dornbush, M. P., & Pruitt, S. K. (1995). *Teaching the tiger: A handbook for individuals involved in the education of students with attention deficit disorders, Tourette Syndrome or obsessive-compulsive disorder.* Duarte, CA: Hope Press.

Johnston, H. F., & Fruehling, J. J. (2002). *Obsessive compulsive disorder in children & adolescents: A guide.* Madison: University of Wisconsin, Child Psychopharmacology Information Center.

March, S., & Mulle, K. (1998). *OCD in children and adolescents: A cognitive behavioral treatment manual.* New York: Guilford Press.

Rapoport, J. (1991). *The boy who couldn't stop washing.* New York: Penguin Books.

Thomsen, P. H. (1999). *From thoughts to obsessions: Obsessive compulsive disorder in children and adolescents.* Philadelphia: Jessica Kingsley.

Waltz, M. (2000). *Obsessive-compulsive disorder: Help for children and adolescents.* Cambridge, England: O'Reilly.

Multimedia Instructional Kit

How to respond to obsessive-compulsive disorder in the classroom. Available online through the Obsessive-Compulsive Foundation: http:/ /www.ocfoundation.org

CHAPTER 60

SEPARATION ANXIETY DISORDER
IN THE SCHOOLS

Henry L. Harris

Preview

Separation anxiety is a common emotional reaction that many students experience daily. It becomes problematic, however, when the emotional reactions negatively affect normal academic or social activities. For some students, separation anxiety is the cause of school avoidance, poor academic performance, and other disruptive behaviors. Without appropriate treatment, these individuals could possibly encounter additional emotional difficulties. I discuss characteristics of students with separation anxiety disorder (SAD) as well as interventions that could be helpful to parents, teachers, school administrators, and professional school counselors during the remediation process.

Anxiety is an emotional response that students experience daily. It is considered an important part of social development and a helpful reaction to a variety of situations. Even so, anxiety is often negatively perceived and misunderstood (Huberty, 1990). For example, some parents and teachers perceive students with anxiety disorders as readily recognizable and not having serious problems. When asked to actually identify students with anxiety, however, parents and teachers seem to have a difficult time doing so. When descriptions are provided about the behaviors of anxious students, their ability to identify those students significantly increases (Walkup & Ginsberg, 2002). Many students with anxiety exhibit the following:

- Trouble leaving the car and entering the school in the mornings
- Trouble learning and sharing in group or social activities
- Regular visits to the school nurse with physical complaints
- Difficulty demonstrating knowledge on tests or through classroom participation; considered underachievers
- High rates of absences (Walkup & Ginsberg, 2002, p. 85)
- Limited overall socialization experiences
- Greater risk of being teased by other students
- Tension within the family (Velting, Setzer, & Albano, 2004)

Given such negative consequences of anxiety disorder, it is imperative that professional school counselors be proactive when addressing this serious issue.

ANXIETY DISORDERS

The *Diagnostic and Statistical Manual of Mental Disorders–Fourth Edition, Text Revision* (DSM-IV-TR; American Psychiatric Association [APA], 2000) lists the following anxiety disorders that are sometimes diagnosed in children: Separation Anxiety Disorder, Simple Phobia, Social Phobia, and Generalized Anxiety Disorders. Much information is known about separation anxiety disorder (SAD) because it is one of the more frequent clinical anxiety disorders presenting in children (Berstein & Borchardt, 1991). According to Bell-Dolan (1995), SAD accounts for approximately 50% of all the anxiety disorders experienced by children; however, SAD is a clinical disorder that amplifies symptoms seen in normal childhood developmental processes. For example, separation anxiety is initially seen in small children when they are 9 to 18 months old. Some become apprehensive in the presence of strangers, when they are placed in unfamiliar surroundings, experience general distress, cry, become withdrawn, or cling to parents, especially when parents attempt to leave (Huberty & Eaken, 1994).

For most children, normal separation anxiety intensifies during early childhood and then gradually decreases between 3 and 5 years of age (Masi, Mucci, & Millepiedi, 2001). Separation anxiety becomes an issue of concern for professional school counselors when (a) the normal functioning of the student is hampered by the intensity, length, and frequency of behavior; (b) the demonstrated behavior is inappropriate for the current situation; (c) the student lacks the ability to make the behaviorally appropriate transition; and (d) the behavior significantly affects how the student functions in society (Huberty, 1990; Huberty & Eaken, 1994).

SEPARATION ANXIETY DISORDER

Separation anxiety disorder is a childhood condition that occurs in approximately 5% of young children in the United States who are ages 7 to 11 years and it is not as common in teenagers, affecting approximately 1.3% of American teens (APA; 2000); median age for onset is approximately 7.5 years of age (Last, Perrin, & Hersen, 1992). SAD is characterized by excessive anxiety and worry about being separated from home or from a major attachment figure, and students with this disorder often believe that something tragic will happen to them or their parents (APA; 2000). Sometimes when students are asked what they are afraid of they communicate a fear of being displaced and never finding their parents again (Sarason & Sarason, 1987). They may also be preoccupied with dreadful images of crooks, monsters, or other dangerous animals that could possibly harm them or their parents. Students with SAD have often been described in one extreme as individuals who are intrusive, demanding, and in need of constant attention, and in the other extreme as being very conscientious and constantly desiring to please others (APA; 2000). Furthermore, some young children with SAD may also "display disruptive, oppositional, and avoidance behaviors that cause significant family interference in child and family functioning" (Pincus, Eyberg, & Choate, 2005, p. 164).

Sleep could be another issue for some students with SAD because they are afraid to stay in a room by themselves and may insist someone stay with them until they fall asleep. They may have repeated nightmares and report occurrences of seeing people in their room or peering eyes staring at them. Sometimes during the night when they awake, they seek comfort in their parent's bedroom. When this is not possible, they will either sleep next to their parent's bedroom door or seek the companionship of a sibling or family pet (Tongue, 1994). Even during the daytime hours, some students may refuse to let the major attachment figure out of their sight and at times become hysterical when that figure is physically in another room (APA; 2000). Similar reactions may occur when separation is anticipated, as when students are getting dressed and ready in the morning. They will cry, become angry, and even try to physically strike the individual who is causing the separation (APA; 2000).

Some students with SAD experience excessive worry only when they are away from their home surroundings. If they participate in a camp, attend school, or visit relatives or friends, these students have a strong desire to return home. When this is not possible, they may make attempts to contact parents, feel sad, lose their ability to concentrate, fake illnesses, become contentious, or experience social withdrawal (Tongue, 1994).

Realize that older students with SAD have fewer symptoms than younger children and they may report feeling faint or dizzy (APA; 2000). More often, unrealistic worry about major attachment figures and school refusal are behaviors reported by students from 5 to 8 years of age. Extreme worry and distress at the time of separation is more common in students ranging from age 9 to 12 years. Adolescents most often report somatic complaints and school refusal (Masi et al., 2001).

SCHOOL REFUSAL

Approximately 75% of students with SAD present with school refusal (Masi et al., 2001). School refusal is not about the student's fear of school but rather the student's fear of the separation from his or her parent. Jongsma, Peterson, and McInnis (1996) offered the following behavioral observations related to school refusal:

- Constant hesitancy or refusal to attend school because of the desire to stay at home with the parent. Some are preoccupied with thoughts that, if separated, something terrifying will happen to them or their parents.
- Emotional strains and complaints such as crying, temper outbursts, or begging the parents not to take them to school (when expecting separation from home to attend school or following arrival at school).
- Commonly expressed complaints of headaches, stomach pains, or feeling nauseated prior to attending school or following arrival.
- When departing home or arriving at school, the student may stay excessively close to the parent.
- Fear of the separation from the parents is accompanied by low levels of self-esteem and self-confidence.
- Students communicate and express a fear of failure and anxiety along with the refusal to attend school.

When students with SAD refuse to attend school, it could lead to academic problems and social isolation. Even when attending school, their excessive demands "often become a source of teacher and peer frustration, resulting in resentment, ridicule, and conflict within the classroom" (Deluty & DeVitis, 1996, p. 108).

INTERVENTIONS

There are a number of interventions professional school counselors can use to help students, teachers, and families cope with SAD. The interventions designed and selected should ideally reflect a team effort involving the professional school counselor, parents, teachers, administrators, the school psychologist, and school nurse. Professional school counselors should first have adequate knowledge about separation anxiety and the behavioral characteristics associated with it. Professional school counselors must be aware of their personal feelings and biases toward students and parents who may be experiencing separation anxiety; for example, by exploring the following questions:

How do I honestly feel about students with SAD?

Am I able to accurately identify students with SAD?

Do I believe that the parents are solely responsible for their children's behavior?

Do I feel more discipline would solve the problem?

Is this child a "crybaby" and simply trying to gain attention?

Do I perceive this child's behavior as disruptive and caused by overprotective parents?

Am I displaying too much sympathy towards this child?

Do I have the time, skills, or available resources needed to help these students and their families?

The intervention team should also explore the same questions.

Once the questions have been thoroughly explored, the next phase should involve professional school counselors consulting with parents, teachers, and school administrators to provide information on students suspected of having anxiety-related issues, such as excessive worry, frequent absences, or somatic complaints (Scott, Culley, & Weissberg, 1995). During the consultation process, professional school counselors should make sure that parents, teachers, and school administrators are knowledgeable about various aspects of SAD and how it potentially affects the academic and social development of students. For teachers and administrators, in-service training focusing on separation anxiety issues would be helpful (Huberty, 1990). Professional school counselors could additionally help students with SAD by creating a safe environment where students could go to reduce their anxiety during anxious moments, check in with them at the beginning of school to access their anxiety levels, teach them age-appropriate relaxation techniques, and possibly alter their arrival times to school if the separation anxiety becomes too extreme at the beginning of the day.

The school psychologist is often a valuable resource for the professional school counselor. The role played by the school psychologist will depend on the severity of the problem, the level of parental involvement, and school policy (some school systems may require outside help). The school nurse may contribute by conducting a preliminary physical on students experiencing somatic complaints. They are also in a position to recommend to parents that the student undergo a thorough physical examination. Eliminating physical ailments as causes of the student's pain and discomfort (Scott et al., 1995) allows the association to be made between anxiety and somatic issues. The process of creating a mental health or developmental plan can begin to help the student develop more effective coping skills.

CONSULTING WITH PARENTS

When discussing SAD with parents, professional school counselors should gather as much information as possible about the child and the family. Eisen, Engler, and Geyer

(1998) contended that parents of children with SAD may unknowingly facilitate anxiety during their child's anxious moments by being overprotective, excessively reassuring, or having aversive parent–child interactions. It would therefore be helpful to genuinely explore with parents (a) their parenting style; (b) whether they have experienced any form of anxiety themselves; (c) any recent sudden or negative life events or stressors; (d) their perspective on the student's personality and behavior; (e) the length of time the student has been experiencing separation anxiety; (f) whether or not other family members have previously encountered this problem; (g) whether the student's siblings have been affected by the behavior; and (h) their role in helping design and implement selected interventions.

Professional school counselors can also assist parents during consultation by helping them recognize their own feelings about SAD, because some feelings could reveal personal, subconscious levels of anxiety and discomfort regarding the student. Professional school counselors should encourage parents to be aware of their child's personality and convey relevant information to school personnel. Furthermore, professional school counselors may assist parents in the following ways:

- Teaching parents appropriate ways to prepare the student before the separation occurs
- Making parents aware of appropriate transitional objects to use with the student, such as a picture or a small toy
- Encouraging parents to never make fun of their child or say things such as "Big boys and girls don't cry" or "Other kids are going to tease you if you cry" (Hewitt, 1995)
- Encouraging parents to leave school when it is time to leave, because sometimes the situation becomes more chaotic when the parents stay longer than normal
- Encouraging parents to never sneak away from their child, always say goodbye, and return at the expected time
- Encouraging parents to send their child a short e-mail message as a positive reinforcement for staying in school if access to computers is available in the school

SYSTEMATIC DESENSITIZATION

Systematic desensitization is a behavioral modification intervention designed by Wolpe (1958) to eliminate fear and anxiety by exposing the individual to the feared stimulus in a carefully graduated manner (Carson, Butcher, & Coleman, 1988). The first step in this process consists of relaxation training. Children with SAD could be taught simple relaxation techniques such as learning how to breathe or tightening and relaxing different muscles in the body (progressive muscle relaxation training). Some students may be too young to fully understand this concept, so the professional school counselor should modify this technique according to the student's developmental level. The student is then instructed to practice relaxation skills daily, ranging from 10 to 20 minutes while listening to a tape of relaxation instructions.

The next step includes developing a hierarchy of fears, with situations producing the highest level of anxiety placed at the top graduating down to situations causing little or no anxiety at the bottom (see Table 60.1 for a sample hierarchy).

The student should be in a relaxed mood when each session begins. The professional school counselor asks the student to imagine the lowest anxiety-provoking situation on the hierarchy and signal by raising a finger if he or she experience anxiety. If no anxiety is experienced, this format is followed until the student reaches the highest situation on the hierarchy without experiencing any anxiety (Huberty, 1990; Lee & Miltenberger, 1996). This approach may be more applicable for use with older children or adolescents.

PROBLEM SOLVING

Professional school counselors could also use problem solving as an intervention to help students with SAD. Problem solving is known as a step-by-step process in which the student generates and tests a number of different methods for coping with specific anxiety problem situations. The student should be initially taught to identify a specific anxiety situation. Next, emphasis is placed on the student generating as many alternative actions to reduce the anxiety. The professional school counselor then encourages the student to explore the costs and benefits of each alternative action and decide which is most effective or appropriate. Finally, the student evaluates the outcome and tries a different solution if the desired effect was not achieved (Velting et al., 2004). Throughout the problem-solving process it is important that professional school counselors help students remain as calm as possible if they hope to achieve the desired results.

IN VIVO DESENSITIZATION

In vivo desensitization is an alternate form of systematic desensitization and may be more practical for professional school counselors to use in the school setting, especially for students who refuse to attend school. This approach requires the student and parent to be active participants (Huberty & Eaken, 1994).

The professional school counselor, parents, teachers, school nurse, and the school psychologist cooperate in varying degrees to establish a hierarchy of tasks specifically designed to bring the student closer to the class or school environment where the most

TABLE 60.1

SAMPLE HIERARCHY (HUBERTY, 1990)

Step 11.	Child is in the classroom with activities occurring.
Step 10.	Child is alone in the classroom.
Step 09.	Child is alone in the classroom with the teacher.
Step 08.	Child enters the classroom alone.
Step 07.	Child enters the classroom with a parent.
Step 06.	Child walks to the classroom alone.
Step 05.	Child walks to the classroom with the parent.
Step 04.	Child enters the school building alone.
Step 03.	Child enters the school building with the parent.
Step 02.	Child gets into the car with the parent.
Step 01.	Child gets dressed and prepares to go to school.

anxiety occurs. The professional school counselor, along with the help of the parent, is responsible for gradually exposing the student to each step in the hierarchy. When anxiety is reported, that particular step is repeated until the anxiety no longer exists. The process requires patience and continues until the student has completed all steps in the hierarchy without experiencing anxiety (Huberty & Eaken, 1994). (See the sample hierarchy developed by Huberty, 1990, in Table 60.1.)

This technique can also be taught to parents to use with children outside of school. For example, the hierarchy could include items for the anxious child such as playing outside in the backyard with the parent inside, playing alone in a room for 5 minutes, sleeping in his or her own room 1 night a week, or staying at home with a sitter (Phelps, Cox, & Bajorek, 1992).

TOKEN ECONOMIES AND POSITIVE REINFORCEMENT

The token economy is a type of positive reinforcement system. This intervention rewards students with tokens or points only when a level of desired behavior is reached. Parents should be involved in designing the reward system, which could range from using actual tokens for use at the local arcade or exchanging points for prizes. In some situations, this intervention could be paired with in vivo desensitization and tokens/ points awarded when one of the steps in the hierarchy is completed.

PLAY THERAPY

Play therapy is another form of counseling that professional school counselors should consider using when helping students with SAD. During the play sessions students are provided the opportunity to express their emotions through what they do best, play. According to Landreth (1993) and Guerney (1979), play is the student's symbolic language of self-expression and during the process of play therapy students have the opportunity to fully experience all parts of the self because the play is self-directed and safe. Students with SAD's are ideal candidates for this form of counseling because one of the major goals of play therapy is to help reduce anxiety and stress levels in the emotional mind of a vulnerable child (Landreth, 1993).

ART THERAPY

Professional school counselors should also consider using art therapy as a form of counseling students with SAD. Art therapy includes various activities such as drawing, using a sand tray, sculpting, finger painting, storytelling, and using music. This process provides individuals the opportunity to confront their concerns and unresolved issues through artwork. The goal of art therapy is to help students with SAD manage their anxiety more effectively through artistic expression of what lies within their inner world. This approach may be particularly useful for nonverbal children and for students who have difficulties expressing internal conflicts (Thompson, 2003).

OTHER INTERVENTIONS

Professional school counselors should also consider conducting classroom guidance activities that focus on separation anxiety. Reading animated books about characters confronting this sensitive issue could prove beneficial (see Table 60.2 for resources for students in the pre-K to sixth-grade level and Table 60.3 resources for parents, teens, and teachers). Other appropriate cognitive behavioral interventions could include modeling, relaxation, cognitive restructuring, shaping, and flooding. Group counseling is another option professional school counselors should take into consideration for students, along with filial therapy training for parents (Guerney, 1997; Johnson, 1995). If a decision is made to use medication, such as antidepressants, along with traditional counseling to help students with SAD, parents should consult with a credible child psychiatrist and be thoroughly informed about the potential positive and negative effects of the medication. Ultimately, the type of counseling approach used will vary and depend on a number of different factors including the severity of the problem, available school resources, professional school counselor's training experience, and the level of parent involvement.

SUMMARY/CONCLUSION

Separation anxiety is an expected and healthy emotional reaction that is a part of normal development for many children and should only become a concern for professional

TABLE 60.2

BOOKS ON SEPARATION ANXIETY FOR THE PRE-K THROUGH SIXTH-GRADE LEVELS

Benjamin Comes Back/Benjamin Regresa, by A. Brandt, 2000, Publisher: HarperCollins.

Don't Forget to Write, by M. Selway, 1994, Publisher: Ideal Children's Books.

Freddie's First Night Away, by D. Steele, 1992, Publisher: Dell.

I Don't Want to Go to School: Helping Children Cope With Separation Anxiety, by N. Pando, 2005, Publisher: New Horizon Press.

I'm Scared (Dealing With Feelings), by E. Crarey, 1996, Publisher: Parenting Press.

Into the Great Forest: A Story for Children Away From Parents for the First Time, by P. Marcus, 2001, Publisher: American Psychological Association.

Lester's Overnight, by K. Chorao, 1997, Publisher: Dutton/Plume.

Maybe She Forgot, by E. Kandoian, 1990, Publisher: Cobblehill/Dutton.

Mommy Don't Go, by E. Crarey, 1996, Publisher: Parenting Press.

Mommy, Daddy, Come Back Soon, by D. Pappas, 2001, Publisher: American Psychological Association.

My First Day at Nursery School, by B. Edwards, 2002, Publisher: Bloomsbury-USA Publishers.

My Somebody Special, by S. Weeks, 2002, Publisher: Harcourt.

Pinky & Rex Go to Camp, by J. Howe, 1999, Publisher: Simon & Schuster.

The Good-Bye Book, by J. Viorst, 1992, Publisher: Simon & Schuster.

The Kissing Hand, by A. Penn, 1995, Publisher: Child Welfare League of America.

The Runaway Bunny, by M. W. Brown, 1991, Publisher: HarperCollins Children's Books.

Wemberly Worried, by K. Henkes, 2000, Publisher: HarperCollins.

When Mommy and Daddy Go to Work, by J. Cole, 2001, Publisher: HarperCollins.

You Go Away, by D. Corey, 1999, Publisher: Albert Whitman.

TABLE 60.3

BOOKS AND WEB SITES FOR PARENTS, TEENS, AND TEACHERS

Books

Artful Therapy, by J. A. Rubin, 2005, Publisher: Wiley.

Child Art Therapy, 25th Anniversary Edition, by J.A. Rubing, 2005, Publisher: Wiley.

Everyday Goodbyes: Starting School and Early Care: A Guide to the Separation Process, by N. Balaban, 2006, Publisher: Teacher College Press.

Freeing Your Child From Anxiety: Powerful, Practical Solutions to Overcome Your Child's Fears, Worries and Phobias, by T. Chansky, 2004, Publisher: Broadway Books.

Helping Your Child Overcome Separation Anxiety or School Refusal: A Step-By-Step Guide for Parents, by A. R. Eisen and L. B. Engler, 2006, Publisher: New Harbinger.

Separation Anxiety in Children and Adolescents: An Individualized Approach to Assessment and Treatment, by A. R. Eisen and C. E. Schaefer, 2005, Publisher: Guilford Press.

Your Anxious Child, by J. S. Darcey and L. B. Fiore, 2000, Publisher: Jossey-Bass.

Web Sites

Anxiety Disorders Association of America (www.adaa.org)

Childhood Anxiety Network (www.childhoodanxietynetwork.org)

The Child Anxiety Network (www.childanxiety.net)

National Mental Health Association (www.nmha.org)

National Alliance for the Mentally Ill (www.nami.org)

Separation Anxiety Disorder (www.worrywisekids.org)

school counselors when the anxiety begins to negatively affect the individual academically, emotionally, and socially. Professional school counselors must have accurate knowledge about the characteristics associated with SAD, including appropriate assessment tools and appropriate interventions. Professional school counselors should make the effort to work collaboratively with parents, teachers, administrators, school nurses, and school psychologists to formulate a plan to help families and students with SAD, always striving to convey patience, empathy, understanding, and a sense of hope.

(Note: See the CD-ROM for a list of references.)

CHAPTER 61

TEST ANXIETY

Vicki Brooks-McNamara

Preview

The importance of test scores continues to be a focal point for grade promotion, and anxiety can develop when a student feels pressure to perform. Professional school counselors who understand the physiological and psychological responses to anxiety can facilitate student development of positive coping strategies. Included in this chapter are suggestions for parents, teachers, and students to reduce test anxiety and increase test performance.

*S*tress, *fear,* and *anxiety* are terms that are often used interchangeably. An example of *eustress,* or good stress, is the anticipation of a happy upcoming event (e.g., a dance, an award; Seaward, 2004). Acute *distress* is instantaneous (e.g., being scared by a clap of thunder), while chronic stress or anxiety occurs slowly over time and results in a continued state of heightened anxiety. An example of chronic stress or anxiety would be the expectation of performing near-superior levels on tasks both at home and school.

Professional school counselors can often help to determine if the cause for concern is due to anxiety or a phobia. *Phobia* is defined as an irrational fear that is specific to an identified source and extends beyond the normal fears associated with child and adolescent development (e.g., fear of heights; Terry, 1998). Extreme measures are often used to avoid the source of fear (e.g., repeatedly ill on testing days, emotional outbursts when testing occurs). Certainly, students can develop test phobias and in such instances, professional school counselors could be helpful in ameliorating symptoms or suggesting outside resources for consultation, evaluation, and intervention.

In the current educational context, standardized tests continue to be a focal point for progress monitoring and grade promotion. When a student feels pressure to perform at exceptionally high levels, anxiety can develop. Basic human fears (Seaward, 2004) can be translated into test anxiety as follows:

- Fear of the unknown (What is the test about?)
- Fear of failure (What if I don't pass?)
- Fear of rejection (Will my family/friends still love me if I fail?)
- Fear of isolation (What if I am the only one who fails?)
- Fear of loss of self-control (What if I am so scared during the test that I can't think?"

A basic understanding of physiological responses to anxiety can assist professional school counselors in developing appropriate intervention strategies. Two categories of anxiety are evidenced in the literature: state (e.g., specific moment in time, result of an event) and trait (e.g., over time, personality characteristics; Landers & Arent, 2001). Anxiety affects all domains of the individual: spiritual, emotional, social, intellectual, and physical. Under stress/anxiety, the body responds physiologically by initiating the fight-or-flight syndrome (see Figure 61.1). When the stress is continued over time, the body's systems begin to weaken. Visible external symptoms (e.g. sleeplessness, irritability) can appear.

FIGURE 61.1 The body's response to stress. *Note.* From *Leadership, Advocacy, and Direct Service Strategies for Professional School Counselors* (p. 350), by R. Perusse and G. E. goodnough, 2004, Belmont, CA: Wadsworth/Cengage Learning. Copyright 2004 by Wadsworth. Reprinted with permission.

FIGURE 61.2. Inverted U arousal performance. *Note.* From *Managing Stress: Principles and Strategies for Health and Well Being* (p. 9), by B. L. Seaward, 2009, Sudbury, MA: Jones & Bartlett. Copyright 2009 by Jones & Bartlett. Reprinted with permission.

Sport performance research has identified the relationship between arousal and performance (see Figure 61.2) (Landers & Arent, 2001). Simply put, as arousal increases from a minimal state (waking up) to a fully conscious and alert state, performance increases. However, if arousal continues and creates a heightened anxious state, performance begins to decline.

The optimal state of performance is called *eustress* (Seaward, 2004). Continued and heightened anxiety creates distress, and a decline in performance occurs (Landers & Arent, 2001; Seaward, 2004). Anxiety can create psychological roadblocks to learning (Slavin, 2000). Among the major student stressors are peer acceptance and classroom performance, including test results (Brooks, 2004). Tables 61.1 through 61.4 provide numerous tips for various stakeholders to help reduce test anxiety.

RELAXATION TECHNIQUES

Relaxation techniques vary greatly, and they are subject to one's preferred style of learning, cognitive, and affective abilities. Students with acute visualization and imagery capabilities are essentially unlimited with regard to relaxation and visualization development.

Research has documented the positive effects of visualization, relaxation, and imagery in overall psychological and physiological function and performance. The study of psychoneuroimmunology (integration of mind, nerve, and immune systems) provides exciting data that support the interconnectedness of the body (Seaward, 2004).

Professional school counselors may want to inform or obtain consent from parents before sharing with the student visualization, imagery, and relaxation informa-

TABLE 61.1

SUGGESTIONS FOR PARENTS/GUARDIANS TO HELP STUDENTS REDUCE TEST ANXIETY

Keep reactions and personal feelings about the test to a minimum (whether positive or negative).

Focus on the range of scores rather than specific scores.

Reframe negative reactions (e.g., "I'm a failure") to one of hope (e.g., "*We* can work together to do better").

"Check-ins" can include discussion of feelings about the upcoming test.

Understand fears associated with testing. Allow time for discussion of "what-ifs."

Instill acceptance of the student *before* the test; regardless of the results, the student is *not* the test.

Keep *your* fears to yourself.

Avoid negative words (e.g., *scared*) when talking about the test.

Understand the test, ask questions about it, and become familiar with it.

Ask the student to create a practice test or together create a mini-version of the test.

Carefully regulate the addition of extra homework. It can be interpreted as overkill.

Know when to ask for professional outside help (e.g., Is this student exhibiting trait anxiety? Is this a phobia?).

Teach positive coping strategies (see Chapter 70, "Helping Students Acquire Time-Management Skills").

Help identify assets (e.g., learning style).

Note. Adapted from "Guiding Your Student Through Testing Mania," by S. Squires and K. Jacobs, November 2001, *Family Life*, 60–65.

TABLE 61.2

SUGGESTIONS FOR TEACHERS TO HELP STUDENTS REDUCE TEST ANXIETY

1. Create a classroom environment that is welcoming, encouraging, and accepts repeated trials to attain success.
2. Engage students in planning how and what will be learned. This team approach can help reduce subject-matter anxiety.
3. Make sure subject matter matches test content.
4. Give practice tests containing similar content and format as the standardized or final test.
5. In testing situations:
   - Give clear and simple instructions.
   - Break down directions and/or the test into segments.
   - Avoid time constraints (or if timed tests are necessary, conduct dress rehearsals with time factors).
   - Teach students to check their work.
   - Begin each test with the least difficult and work up to most difficult.
   - Provide an easy to follow format for selecting answers.

Note. Adapted from *Educational Psychology: Theory and Practice*, by R. E. Slavin, 2000, Needham Heights, MA: Allyn & Bacon.

TABLE 61.3

TIPS FOR STUDENTS

Study at a regular time and place. Identify a location for study.

Plan study sessions with a group of successful students.

Study as soon after the class as possible. Make study checklists for each class.

Use odd hours during the day to study (1-hour intervals are excellent).

Limit blocks of time for studying to no more than 30 to 45 minutes on one course. Take a 3- to 5-minute break before moving to another subject.

Eat complex carbohydrates or protein on breaks, not high sugar foods (e.g., candy, cola).

Keep organized notes from class. Match and file assignments with each chapter.

Review your notes daily and weekly.

Do not re-write notes. Use a highlighter for identifying important points. Write in extensional, ideas and descriptions. Review highlighted material for tests.

Write key words/phrases in margins; use these for last-minute review.

Study the most difficult or boring subjects first.

Identify the time of day when you learn the best (morning or evening).

Block this time for intensive study.

Sit in the front of the class.

If the teacher talks fast, learn to work with another student to share notes.

If the teacher is organized, take notes in outline form or use information from the board or overheads.

If the teacher is disorganized, take notes by leaving space between notes to fill in later.

If the class is mostly discussion, take bulleted notes and write key ideas or statements below the bullets.

If the class has a lab with it, make sure you have a lab notebook for recording all materials (e.g., drawings).

Try to incorporate all learning styles: auditory, visual and kinesthetic. Hear the lecture (auditory), write the notes (kinesthetic) and review the notes/materials by reading (visual) and sharing with a study group (auditory).

Study by self-testing with note cards; divide pages length-wise (e.g., left side for questions and right side for answers); use a cover sheet to cover answers when studying from the book or notes.

Learn relaxation and visualization skills (see Table 61.5).

Develop short- and long-term goals.

Vocabulary is important on all standardized tests; read recreationally as well as academically.

tion or materials. Familial religious and personal preferences might preclude the professional school counselor from using relaxation, visualization, or imagery as coping strategies for reducing test anxiety. Tables 61.5, 61.6, and 61.7 present sample relaxation exercises.

DECREASING TEST ANXIETY VIA SYSTEMATIC DESENSITIZATION

Systematic desensitization requires that the individual be relaxed while he or she is introduced to small doses of the anxiety producing event (e.g., test). During daily relaxation practice, additional test anxiety factors can be introduced (e.g., smells and noises in the room, the teacher's voice, pencil in hand, reading the directions, taking the test). A minimum of 4 weeks should be allowed for the practice of systematic desensitization. As an alternative to real-life implementation, the gestalt of the entire test day can be replicated visually in the mind (covert desensitization) while consciously practicing the mastered relaxation exercise (Seaward, 2004).

A practice test could be given while the student is in a relaxed state and continues reinforcement of the learned skills (e.g., deep breathing, cloud breathing; see Table 61.6). A support person may need to assist the student on the first several attempts to verbally encourage relaxation and deep breathing. The student may need verbal instructions (e.g., put the pencil down, close your eyes and complete 10 cycles of deep breathing before picking your pencil up and continuing with the test).

SUMMARY/CONCLUSION

The pressure for students to achieve academically can lead to increased anxiety and fear. By first understanding the physiology of the fight-or-flight response (see Figures 61.1 and 61.2) and then applying successful strategies and interventions (see Tables 61.1–61.8), all stakeholders can begin to feel a sense of control over the requirements and standards for academic success in school. Various Web sites (see Table 61.9) can also provide timely and updated information on testing tips, managing stress, and learning strategies.

(Note: See the CD-ROM for a list of references.)

TABLE 61.4

SUGGESTIONS FOR INCREASING ACADEMIC PERFORMANCE

1. Continually monitor academic progress in each class.
2. Meet with teachers (months ahead of time, if necessary) to identify material being taught and regularly covered.
3. Consult the school learning specialist for additional suggestions.
4. Hire a tutor to enhance skills.
5. Learn test-taking tips.
6. Know the test scoring criteria. If there are no penalties for guessing, always supply an answer. If there is a penalty for guessing, only guess when answers can be narrowed to two choices.
7. Read all answers before selecting a choice; sometimes when several choices are possibly correct, a best answer exists.
8. Use the entire allocated time (e.g., bring a watch to place on the desk to self-monitor time). Check work if finished early (e.g., mark on worksheet questions to review if time permits).
9. Answer the easiest and shortest questions first.
10. Answer questions in this order: multiple choice, true–false, fill-in-the-blank, and short answer–essay last.
11. Look for answers in other test questions. Make notes in the margin or on scratch paper.
12. When taking an essay test:
    • Quickly jot down information prior to writing your response.
    • Read all questions and develop a plan/outline before beginning.
    • Highlight words in the question that guide the answer (e.g., *compare* = similarities and differences; *describe* = details; *prove* = evidence).
    • Begin writing by rephrasing the question, stating the answer, providing details to support the answer and summarizing main points for the conclusion.
    • Essay questions often require a synthesis of class discussions.
13. When taking multiple choice tests:
    • Read the directions carefully.
    • The first time through the test, answer only the questions with known answers; mark others to come back to.
    • Watch for grammatically correct answers (e.g., matching the question).
14. Predict test questions from class and written notes.
15. Save all tests, lab handouts, and class materials. Keep materials organized by chapter/ lecture/lab.
16. The night before the test, get enough sleep, and eat well.
17. The day of the test, get up early, have a healthy breakfast, relax, and arrive at the test site early.
18. Take water to drink (if allowed). During breaks, eat a protein bar (not candy or high-sugar foods).

Note. Adapted from "Guiding Your Student Through Testing Mania," by S. Squires and K. Jacobs, November 2001, *Family Life*, 60–65; and *Educational Psychology: Theory and Practice*, by R. E. Slavin, 2000, Needham Heights, MA: Allyn & Bacon.

TABLE 61.5

PROGRESSIVE MUSCLE RELAXATION

Ideally, the individual should be lying on their back with the arms comfortably at the sides. After initial familiarity with the process, relaxation can be accomplished in a variety of positions, although not necessarily with the same results.

- Begin by contracting the toes (curling) and holding the contraction for a count of five, then relaxing the toes while taking one cycle of breathing (see breathing example below).
- Continue moving up the legs, torso, shoulders and head. Individual muscle-group contractions should be held for 5 seconds followed by relaxing the muscle(s) and completing a breathing cycle before moving to the next set of muscles. Suggested order of progression: feet, calves, thighs, buttocks, stomach, chest, back (press to floor), hands, arms (press to floor), neck (press back of head to floor), and face (wrinkle/scrunch).
- Practice contracting and relaxing individual muscle groups in a progressive order. Focus on identifying muscle groups potentially holding the tension or anxiety. This can be used for future identification of anxiety and early application of interventions.
- Upon initial mastery of individual muscle group relaxation, combining muscle groups (e.g., feet, legs and buttocks) can reduce time allocation.

Note. Adapted from *Managing Stress: Principles and Strategies for Health and Well-Being,* by B. L. Seaward, 2004, Sudbury MA: Jones & Bartlett.

TABLE 61.6

BREATHING

General Breathing
- Assume a comfortable position (preferably lying down)
- Close the eyes
- Inhale through the nose to the count of five
- Hold the air for a count of three
- Exhale slowly through the mouth to a count of five
- Before inhaling pause (1-2 count), then repeat

Breathing With Visualization
- Assume a comfortable position
- If the position is sitting up, rest the hands on the thighs
- Close the eyes
- Visualize a cloud, and inhale the cloud through the nose for a count of five
- Hold the cloud in the lungs, giving it a "hug" with the lungs
- Slowly exhale the cloud out through the mouth to a count of five
- Make sure all of the cloud is out of the lungs
- Pause before repeating

Note. Adapted from *Managing Stress: Principles and Strategies for Health and Well-Being,* by B. L. Seaward, 2004, Sudbury, MA: Jones & Bartlett.

TABLE 61.7

SAILING YOUR SHIP (ALSO CALLED *Your Special Room*)

This activity combines all five senses (i.e., olfactory, auditory, visual, affective, and kinesthetic). Beginning-level muscle relaxation and breathing exercises will need to be mastered prior to this exercise. Initially, an outside person may need to talk the student through the exercise. The voice should remain soft, slow, and calm. Elapsed time in early attempts will be 10 to 20 minutes. Upon visual mastery, the entire mental exercise can be completed with positive results in 3 to 5 minutes. Another option is to move directly to the special room without the pre–special-room activities.

Assume a comfortable position (preferably lying on the back) with the eyes closed. Take several slow, deep breaths (using the counting or cloud method). When ready, begin with the following thoughts or commands (allowing several seconds between each to inhale through the nose and exhale through the mouth):

- Picture a large, white, sandy ocean beach; feel the wind blowing gently through your hair.
- Smell the fragrance of the sea. Feel the warmth of the sand beneath your feet as you walk toward the dock.
- The sun's rays warm your skin. The smell of the sea is familiar and comforting.
- At the dock, observe the special boat, noting its colors, the magnificent woodwork and all the details that make it such a special boat.
- Slowly walk along the dock, feeling the sun, smelling the sea.
- Arriving at the boat, step onto the deck.
- Gently untie the boat and begin to slowly sail out to sea and feel the gentle rocking of the waves.
- The warmth of the sun feels relaxing, and the sea smells fresh.
- Walk down the steps in the middle of the boat to the cabin. Upon reaching the bottom of the stairs, the special door to the special room is visible.
- Reach into your pocket and pull the key out to open the door to the special room.
- Unlock the door and enter the room; look around and feel comfortable and relaxed with all the beauty in the special room.
- Lie down and enjoy this special place while feeling the gentle rocking of the boat and the fresh smell of the sea.

Continue by allowing time to lapse while in the special room. Then, reverse the order: sit up, walk to the door, open/shut the door, lock the door, walk up the stairs, stand on the deck, sail back to shore, tie up the boat, walk along the dock to the sand, and walk along the beach. All the while, continue to reinforce the warmth of the sun and sand and fresh smell of the ocean.

When learning relaxation skills, consideration should be given to several key components: a safe and peaceful space is essential, the mind must be quiet, and a comfortable position should be obtained before beginning the relaxation exercise.

Note. Adapted from *Managing Stress: Principles and Strategies for Health and Well-Being,* by B. L. Seaward, 2004, Sudbury MA: Jones & Bartlett.

TABLE 61.8

IDEAS FOR APPLYING SYSTEMATIC DESENSITIZATION

- Include the student when developing the practice test and brainstorming the scenarios.
- Allow the student to take a shortened test to explore the possibilities for incorporating relaxation and imagery during the test.
- Allow the student to verbalize "what ifs" and encourage dialogue of successful coping strategies (e.g., breathing).
- Mantras can also be successfully employed prior to or during the test (e.g., calm; "I know I'm good").

Note. Adapted from *Managing Stress: Principles and Strategies for Health and Well-Being,* by B. L. Seaward, 2004, Sudbury, MA: Jones & Bartlett.

TABLE 61.9

ADDITIONAL RESOURCES: TESTING INFORMATION WEB SITES

The Education Trust (www2.edtrust.org/edtrust). Gives individual state results.

FairTest (www.fairtest.org) Advocacy group working to reduce flaws in standardized tests and equity for all students.

GWired (http://gwired.gwu.edu/counsel/). Search box at bottom of page, type *test anxiety.* Item #7 has good tips/strategies and ways to reduce test anxiety.

KidsHealth (http://kidshealth.org). In search box, type *text anxiety.* Item #4 has great tips and strategies.

The Nation's Report Card (http://nces.ed.gov/nationsreportcard). Compares test results by state and includes exam questions.

Score! Educational Services (www.escore.com). Can help identify weak academic areas. Has fees/costs attached.

Students First (http://ub-counseling.buffalo.edu). In search box, type *test anxiety.* Provides good explanation of cause and effect, reduction, coping strategies, study habits, and test anxiety. Click on "Self Help Materials" for resources on study skills, stress management.

Study Guide and Services (www.studygs.net). A wealth of information and links to guides on test-taking strategies, preparing for tests, learning, studying, classroom participation, specific subject help.

Sylvan Learning Centers (www.educate.com). Can help pinpoint weak academic areas. Has fees/costs attached.

CHAPTER 62

HELPING STUDENTS WHO HAVE POSTTRAUMATIC STRESS DISORDER

Kelly M. Murray

Preview

Students are increasingly exposed to traumatic events and diagnosed with posttraumatic stress disorder (PTSD). PTSD is characterized by a reexperiencing of the trauma, avoiding the trauma, and persistent physiological arousal. Familiarity of symptoms, how to conduct an assessment, and common treatment modalities are of paramount importance to the professional school counselor.

Current research suggests that students are increasingly exposed to traumatic events and consequently diagnosed with posttraumatic stress disorder (PTSD). There is substantial research suggesting that students may suffer significant psychological, social, and biological distress in relation to exposure to a traumatic event (Perrin, Smith, & Yule, 2000; Stallard, Velleman, & Baldwin, 1999). Studies have investigated the sequelae of symptoms evident when students are exposed to major traumas, such as violence in the home or community, exposure to war, natural disasters, man-made disasters, serious medical illness, accidents, and sexual abuse (Horowitz, McKay & Marshall, 2005). These studies also indicated that symptoms of PTSD, although similar in many respects to those observed in adults, are sometimes manifested differently by students. Therefore, assessment and treatment modalities must be shifted accordingly. Professional school counselors may see students present with exposure to any number of traumatic events. Familiarity with the types of symptoms likely to be seen, how to conduct an assessment, and the most common types of treatment modalities is important in helping students work through trauma.

HISTORY

PTSD was formally recognized as a disorder in 1980. Prior to that, it was brought to public awareness during World War I, when it was named *combat neurosis*. In World War II, the symptoms of PTSD were defined as *traumatic neurosis* and manifested by consciously reliving and resolving traumatic memories associated with war experiences (Kardiner, 1941; Kardiner & Spiegel, 1947). The first large-scale study of PTSD occurred as a result of the Vietnam War (Egendorf, Kadushin, Laufer, Rothbart, & Sloan, 1981; Yager, 1976). It was also at this time that studies were conducted to document the prevalence of PTSD in the general population as a result of other traumatic stresses, such as rape, domestic violence, and childhood sexual abuse (Frank, Turner, & Steuwart, 1980; Kilpatrick, Veronen, & Best, 1985; Russell, 1983). *The Diagnostic and Statistical Manual of Mental Disorders–Third Edition* (*DSM-III*) (American Psychiatric Association [APA], 1980) first recognized the constellation of posttraumatic symptoms as a disorder in 1980. There was initial skepticism about the diagnosis of PTSD being used for children, however (American Academy of Child and Adolescent Psychiatry [AACAP], 1998). Since that time there has been considerable research on how trauma affects children, how symptoms of PTSD are manifested in children, and how assessment and treatment may differ for children compared to adults.

CLINICAL PRESENTATION

According to the *Diagnostic and Statistical Manual of Mental Disorders–Fourth Edition, Text Revision (DSM-IV-TR)* (APA; 2000), for a child, adolescent, or adult to meet the criteria for PTSD, symptoms must follow exposure to an extreme traumatic stressor. The person must have experienced, witnessed, or been confronted with an event that involved actual or threatened death or serious injury or a threat to the physical integrity of self or others. The person's response must have involved fear, helplessness or horror, and this may have been expressed by disorganized or agitated behavior. The way that a student reexperiences the trauma and manifests distress is likely to change with age and maturity, becoming more adult-like and closer to the *DSM-IV-TR* description of the disorder.

Students will often exhibit irritability, anger, and aggression, or they may be quite verbal about the trauma and their ensuing feelings, while others do not wish to discuss the incident or how they are feeling. Very young children who have experienced trauma may present with few symptoms listed in the *DSM-IV-TR*. This may be in part because they do not have the necessary verbal or cognitive skills to communicate their symptoms. Therefore, infants, toddlers, and preschoolers may present with anxiety symptoms such as fears of monsters, animals, separation anxiety, and fear of strangers. These children may avoid situations or circumstances that may or may not have a link with the trauma, have sleep disturbances, and have preoccupations with symbols or words that may or may not have a certain link with the traumatic event (Drell, Siegel, & Gaensbauer, 1993; Scheeringa, Zeanah, Drell, & Larrieu, 1995). The student (like an adult) must express his or her symptoms for longer than 1 month to meet the criteria for PTSD. The disturbance must also cause clinically significant distress or impairment in social or academic functioning.

EPIDEMIOLOGY

The student's subjective appraisal of the situation appears to be an important factor in explaining why some are significantly affected by a traumatic event while others are not (Joseph, Williams, & Yule, 1997; Massad & Hulsey, 2006). A review of 25 studies indicated that three factors have consistently been found in the development of PTSD in students: (a) the severity of the trauma exposure; (b) trauma-related parental distress; and (c) temporal proximity to the traumatic event (Foy, Madvig, Pynoos, & Camilleri, 1996).

Parental reaction to the traumatic event has been found to influence the student's PTSD symptomology. Numerous studies have reported the impact of familial support and parental emotional reaction to the trauma on the student's PTSD symptoms. These studies indicated that familial support across a broad range of traumas mitigated the development of PTSD in students. Parental distress about the trauma and/or the presence of parental psychiatric disorders also predicted higher levels of PTSD in the student. A study of Holocaust survivors and their offspring found that the offspring were more likely to respond to trauma with PTSD if their parents had PTSD (Yehuda, Schmeidler, Giller, Siever, & Binder-Brynes, 1998). Lyons (1987) postulated that the best predictor of outcome for students was the ability of parents and other significant adults to cope with the trauma. Another predictor for positive outcome was the student's intelligence quotient (IQ); higher IQ appears to protect people from developing PTSD (Saigh, Yasik, Oberfield, Halamandaris, & Bremmer, 2006) and is a strong predictor of resiliency (Silva et al., 2000).

The literature has differed on gender differences in the development of PTSD. Some researchers have found no gender differences; others have indicated that girls develop more severe and long-lasting PTSD symptoms when exposed to traumatic events, even though boys are more likely to be exposed to such events (Helzer, Robins, & McEvoy, 1987). Some studies have found the age of the student at the time of exposure to significantly mediate the development of PTSD symptoms. These findings have not been consistent and are more likely a reflection of developmental differences in clinical manifestations of PTSD than age mediated differences in prevalence (AACAP; 1998). Many studies have evaluated students of diverse ethnic backgrounds and have documented that PTSD occurs across numerous cultural and ethnic groups.

Traumatized students often exhibit symptoms of cooccurring disorders in addition to PTSD. It is not always easy to diagnose PTSD as both the students and parents may minimize symptoms. For young children who do not have the cognitive or verbal skills to accurately self-report their symptoms, it is often difficult to get a clear diagnostic picture. Relying on parental report can also be problematic as parents may be dealing with their own trauma as well as trying to support their child. Parents may also not be aware of the existence or severity of their child's symptoms.

Students who present with PTSD may also exhibit symptoms of depression. Brent et al. (1995) reported a large overlap in symptom criteria between PTSD and major depressive disorder (MDD). MDD sometimes precedes and predisposes students to the onset of PTSD. The comorbidity of students with PTSD and other anxiety disorders is also common. Given the many manifestations of traumatization, it is not surprising that rates of comorbidity with PTSD are high. Many students develop fears associated with specific aspects of the trauma, which can eventually become phobic. Others find themselves extremely anxious much of the time and have difficulty controlling their worries. Panic disorder is not uncommon as children react to their own internal state of anxiety with physical symptoms. Some children experience "survivor guilt" and ruminate over cognitions that they should have done more to help others. Increased alcohol use by adolescents exposed to a traumatic event has been documented as has comorbidity to a host of other psychiatric disorders.

ASSESSMENT

PTSD is often difficult diagnose. While the professional school counselor may not be directly involved in the diagnosis of PTSD, the following assessment procedures are helpful in understanding the diagnostic process. According to the *DSM-IV-TR* (APA; 2000), symptoms usually begin within 3 months after the trauma, although there may be a delay of months, or even years, before symptoms appear. The symptoms of the disorder and the relative predominance or reexperiencing, avoidance, and hyperarousal symptoms may vary with time. Duration of the symptoms varies, with complete recovery occurring within 3 months in approximately 50% of cases, with many others having persisting symptoms for longer than 12 months after the trauma. In some cases, the course is characterized by a waxing and waning of symptoms. Symptom reactivation may occur in response to reminders of the original trauma, life stressors, or new traumatic events.

A thorough and proper assessment requires a face-to-face interview with the student in which she is directly asked questions about the traumatic symptoms experienced. It is important to also interview the parents so as to gather as much information as possible. The use of empathy, establishment of rapport, and a safe environment where the student can discuss painful and angry feelings are very important to acquiring accurate information. Particular attention should be given to using developmentally appropriate language when assessing the student.

Both the parents and the student should be asked directly about the traumatic event and about PTSD symptoms in detail. Specific questions related to reexperiencing, avoidant, and hyperarousal symptoms as described in *DSM-IV-TR* should be asked. Other symptoms that often present comorbidly with PTSD should be assessed, such as symptoms of depression, anxiety, substance abuse, and acting-out behaviors. Obtain reports of any preceding, concurrent, or more recent stressors in the student's life as well. Some examples of stressors may be child abuse, significant conflict within the family, frequent moves, death in the family, and exposure to community violence (AACAP; 1998).

The professional school counselor should be aware of developmental variations in the presentation of PTSD symptoms, especially with young children. For an accurate assessment, ask about developmentally specific symptoms when interviewing young children. AACAP (1998) reported that there are a few published semistructured assessments available such as the *Structured Clinical Interview for DSM-III-R*, and the *Diagnostic Interview Schedule Clinician-Administered PTSD Scale for Children and Adolescents*. AACAP also reported that the following child–parent rating forms may be clinically useful for following the course of PTSD symptoms in children: (a) *Child PTSD Reaction Index*; (b) *Trauma Symptom Checklist for Children*; (c) *Checklist of Child Distress Symptoms–Child and Parent Report Versions*; (d) *Children's Impact of Traumatic Events Schedule*; (e) *Child PTSD Symptom Scale*; and (f) *Impact of Events Scale*. There are two newer assessment instruments that are currently being used to assess for *DSM-IV-TR* PTSD criteria and that also have a good record of validity and reliability. These instruments are (a) *Child PTSD Symptom Scale* and (b) *PTSD Index* (Foa, Johnson, Feeny, & Treadwell, 2001; Steinberg, Brymer, Decker, & Pynoos, 2004). Using a single instrument limits the type of information needed to make a PTSD diagnosis, however, as a student must have a certain number of symptoms from each of three different categories to meet *DSM-IV-TR* criteria. It is difficult for any single instrument to assess for all of these criteria. Therefore, there is no good substitute for a thorough and direct interview with both the student and parents. It is also sometimes useful to speak with the student's teacher or teachers to get a history of symptomology manifested at school with a particular emphasis on changes in school behavior, interaction with peers, concentration, activity level, and academic performance since the traumatic stressor.

In addition, it is a good idea to initially meet with the parents without the student. When interviewing parents, the goal is to gather as much information as possible so that an understanding of the parents' perspective on the trauma and relationship with the child can be determined. It is also important to assess information on the following:

- Family psychiatric and medical history
- Marital conflict, separation, divorce, abuse
- Developmental history, including the student's temperament and mood
- Academic history and performance in school prior to and after the trauma
- Student's current functioning
- Impact of the trauma on the family and parents
- Presence of parental PTSD symptoms
- The perception of how much support is available to the child from the family (Perrin et al., 2000)

In the interview, have the student recall as much of the trauma as possible. After the student has told his or her story, go back and clarify or prompt with additional questions. Tracking the timeline of the trauma and subsequent symptoms is useful in making a diagnosis of PTSD. If unsure about the sequence of events or a particular symptom, ask about it directly. As much as possible, try to obtain the student's report of trauma-related attributions and perceptions. Query beliefs about the event, how the student feels subsequent to being exposed to the stressor, level of responsibility, and perception of family support (AACAP; 1998). The student's feelings, thoughts, and behaviors related to the event should be queried as well as his or her thoughts and feelings about the future. With very young children who find it difficult to developmentally discuss the trauma and their thoughts, feelings, and behaviors related to it, it is often useful to use other methods of gathering information. According to Perrin et al. (2000), giving the student pencil and paper and encouraging the student to draw something about which he or she can tell a story is useful in gathering information and helps the student feel comfortable enough to disclose. Encourage the student to elaborate on his or her story, and then try to link the story with some part of the traumatic event to facilitate emotional release. After the student has become more comfortable, ask him or her to draw the traumatic event. Discuss the picture, and ask the student to describe the sensory components, feelings, thoughts, and coping strategies used during and since the trauma. It is also important to help normalize the student's reactions to the traumatic event as well as to positively reinforce the student for having courage to draw about and discuss the traumatic event.

While the professional school counselor is assessing the student for PTSD symptoms and the associated sequelae symptoms, he or she should also be asking the student about and noting other symptoms often associated with PTSD, such as depressive symptoms, suicidal ideations, anxiety symptoms, substance abuse, and conduct disorder behavior.

TREATMENT

To date there is limited empirical outcome research on the treatment of students with PTSD. Direct exploration of the event is likely to be more efficacious in older and more mature students. For younger children, more indirect methods of addressing traumatic issues, such as art and play therapy (use of drawings, puppets, dolls, etc.) may be indicated. The use of multiple informant assessment, especially with young children, is likely to elicit more information about the traumatic event and the manifestation of symptoms. For this reason, information collected from young children should be supplemented by parent reports.

A treatment plan should be based on the clinical presentation of the child and should address PTSD symptoms as well as other emotional–behavioral symptoms the student may be experiencing. Each student's course of PTSD and associated symptoms will be variable and may be extremely idiosyncratic in the nature, intensity and length of symptoms. Therefore, different treatment modalities may be needed, depending on the student and the nature of the presenting symptoms and problems. Some will require short-term, long-term, or intermittent treatment. Others may require different levels of care (e.g., outpatient care, partial hospitalization, inpatient hospitalization). The professional school counselor may also need to decide which treatment modality will be the most efficacious for the student—individual, family, or group therapy (AACAP; 1998).

There are quite a few authors who advocate for psychoeducation for parents, teachers, and family members in order to help normalize PTSD symptoms and enlist their help in treating the student who has PTSD (Galante & Foa, 1986; Molta, 1995). Education about the traumatic experience and subsequent symptoms may also be helpful to the student who has been exposed to a stressor. The student often has perceptions, feelings, and symptoms about the stressor that can be normalized to help increase self-efficacy and thereby decrease anxiety.

Individual therapy is another modality that can be extremely helpful to students who have been exposed to a stressor. There are many different theoretical orientations that are used by professional school counselors to help students with PTSD. Psychoanalytic or psychodynamic approaches are sometimes used and often help to expose defense mechanisms that are being used and also to redefine current significant relationships in the student's life. Play and art therapy are also often used to accommodate students who are developmentally incapable of benefiting from a direct verbal exchange with a professional school counselor. These indirect methods of addressing traumatic issues may be helpful to students so as not to retraumatize them as they think about and talk about the traumatic event.

There is also significant empirical support for cognitive-behavioral therapy (CBT) in the literature for the treatment of PTSD (Dalgleish, 2004; Feeny, Foa, Treadwell, & March, 2004). The goals of CBT treatment are the reduction of PTSD symptoms, the development of positive coping skills, and an increase in the individual's sense of well-being. It is helpful to provide both the parents and student with education and information on PTSD and its effects on all levels of functioning. Normalizing the student's, parents', and family's feelings and responses also may help to lessen anxiety and alleviate the severity of symptoms. This form of psychotherapy also focuses on the teaching of progressive muscle relaxation, thought-stopping, positive imagery, and deep breathing prior to having the student discuss the traumatic event. Mastering these skills gives the student a sense of control over thoughts and feelings rather than being overwhelmed by them, and will help the student approach the discussion of the traumatic event with confidence, thereby reducing uncontrollable reexperiencing of fears and symptoms. At the center of CBT is also the use of in vivo exposure to help the emotional processing of traumatic memories. This process is done in such a way as to help the student process his or her emotional reactions to the event in a safe and trusting way to master and lessen feelings about the traumatic event.

Pynoos and Nader (1988) described a "psychological first aid" approach for students exposed to community violence that may be offered in schools as well as traditional treatment settings. This model emphasized clarifying the facts about the traumatic event, normalizing student's PTSD reactions, encouraging expression of feelings, teaching problem-solving techniques, and referring the most symptomatic children for ongoing treatment.

Family therapy is a way to integrate the whole family into the student's treatment. Parental support and reaction to the student are likely to affect the student's symptomology. Most experts assert that inclusion of the parents and/or supportive others in treatment is important for resolution of students' PTSD symptoms. Including parents in treatment helps them to monitor their child's progress and symptomology and also helps them to resolve their emotional distress related to the trauma (AACAP; 1998; Cohen, Berliner, & March, 2000).

Trauma-focused groups for students and parents can lead to beneficial open discussions of perceptions, attributions, and feelings about the traumatic event. Group therapy is often used after major traumas and disasters as a way to help debrief and normalize the event for the student. School-based group crisis intervention may be particularly useful after trauma and disaster situations.

SUMMARY/CONCLUSION

As students are increasingly exposed to traumatic stressors and events, it is likely that the professional school counselor will be called upon to assess and intervene with a student with PTSD or PTSD-like symptoms. Familiarity and knowledge of *DSM-IV-TR* criteria for PTSD is essential for the professional school counselor to understand the complexity of this disorder. With a comprehensive assessment and proper treatment, most students will typically improve within 3 to 6 months, while others may need longer term treatment.

(Note: See the CD-ROM for a list of references.)

CHAPTER 63

HABITS, TICS, AND SELF-MUTILATION (CUTTING): A BEHAVIORAL APPROACH TO ASSESSMENT AND TREATMENT

T. Steuart Watson, Brad A. Dufrene, and Kristi Hofstadter

Preview

The purpose of this chapter is to provide an overview for identifying, assessing, and treating habits and tics. Information related to the etiology and epidemiology of habits and tics will also be provided.

TICS

Tics are sudden, brief, repetitive, rapid, stereotyped motor movements or vocalizations that are nonrhythmic and generally believed to be involuntary. Tics can be exacerbated by fatigue, stress, and medical conditions and may also be triggered by specific environmental events. Motor tics involve the singular or recurrent contraction of one or more of the body's muscle groups (e.g., eye blinking, head jerking, shoulder shrugging). Vocal tics involve singular or recurrent vocal sounds, words, and/or phrases (e.g., throat clearing).

Tics are categorized as either simple or complex. Simple tics are limited to individual muscle groups (e.g., eye blinking, facial grimacing) or utterances (e.g., sniffing, snorting). Complex motor tics involve recurrent coordinated patterns of motor movement such as retracing one's steps or twirling when walking. Complex vocal tics involve recurrent repetition of words, phrases, or complete sentences. Tics often emerge as simple and over time may develop into more complex patterns.

The average age of onset for tic disorders is approximately 7 years of age. However, the onset of tic disorders has been observed in individuals as young as one year of age and as old as 18 years of age (Burd & Kerbesian, 1987). Most often, motor tics appear before vocal tics. Typically, tics take a cephalo-caudal trajectory (head-downward) in that they begin in the face and gradually move downward to affect the neck, shoulders, and trunk.

DIAGNOSIS OF TIC DISORDER

An accurate diagnosis of tic disorders depends upon the length of time that tics have been present as well as the concurrent or independent presence of motor and/or vocal tics. Three classifications of tic disorders that occur across a continuum of severity are listed in the *Diagnostic and Statistical Manual of Mental Disorders–Fourth Edition, Text Revision) (DSM-IV-TR;* American Psychiatric Association, 2000). *Transient tics* are singular or recurrent episodes of motor or vocal tics that are present for at least 4 weeks but not longer than 12 months. *Chronic tics* are motor or vocal tics that are present for more than 1 year. *Tourette's syndrome* (TS) is characterized by the presence of multiple motor and one or more vocal tics that have been present for more than 1 year. However, a diagnosis of TS does not require that motor and vocal tics occur concurrently.

Although tic disorders have been studied since the early 20th century, their exact etiology is unknown. Currently, the areas that are receiving the greatest attention are genetic and neurobiological influences, although some researchers have approached the etiology of tic spectrum disorders from a learning perspective. Each of these areas is discussed.

GENETICS

Results of family and twin studies indicate that genetic factors may play an important role in the transmission and expression of tic disorders. Family genetic studies have found that the recurrence of tic disorders in affected families is higher than the expected rate (Pauls, Raymond, Leckman, & Stevenson, 1991). In studies of monozygotic twins, the concordance rate for TS and tic spectrum disorders has been found to range from 50% to 90% (Hyde, Aaronson, Randolph, Rickler, & Weinberger, 1992; Price, 1985; Price, Kidd, Cohen, Pauls, & Leckman, 1993; Walkup et al., 1988). Studies using dizygotic twins have found concordance rates for TS and tic disorders that range from 8% to 23% (Price, 1985). Although these studies suggest that genetics may be responsible for tic spectrum disorders, to date no genetic markers have been identified.

NEUROBIOLOGICAL

While evidence of genetic contributions to tic spectrum disorders is mounting, a body of research exists that implicates neurobiological factors. Neurochemical systems that have been implicated in tic disorders are the dopaminergic, serotonergic, noradrenergic, opiod, cholinergic, GABAergic, cAMP, arginine, vasopressin, and oxytocin systems (Haber, Kowall, Vonsattel, Bird, & Richardson, 1986; Leckman et al., 1988; Peterson, Leckman, & Cohen, 1995; Sallee, Stiller, & Perel, 1992). Neurochemical explanations of tic disorders are based on EEGs and other brain-imaging techniques as well as the effects of specific drugs for treating tics.

Although tic spectrum disorders may be more common in students than previously thought, prevalence data suggested that Tourette's syndrome remains a relatively rare disorder. TS affects between 3.1 and 105 out of 10,000 school-age children (Apter et al., 1993; Caine et al., 1988). Boys are five times more likely to be diagnosed with TS (Burd, Kerbesian, Wikenheiser, & Fisher, 1986) while Caucasians are more likely than African-Americans and Hispanics to develop TS. Additionally, children are more likely than adults to be affected by TS as evidenced by substantially lower prevalence rates for adults (e.g., 1–2 per 10,000; APA, 2000). Prevalence rates for transient tic disorder in children have been reported between 12% and 16% (LaPouse & Monk, 1964; Torup, 1972). According to Peterson, Campose, and Azrin (1994), the prevalence rate for chronic tic disorder may lie between the rates for transient tic disorder and TS.

LEARNING

Some researchers have approached the etiology of tic spectrum disorders from a learning perspective (Watson, Dufrene, Weaver, Butler, & Meeks, 2005; Watson & Sterling, 1998a). These researchers have argued that, in some instances, tic behaviors may be the result of an interaction between neurobiology and learning. For example, an individual predisposed to tics and tic behavior may, due to a variety of environmental consequences (e.g., reduction in muscle tension, access to social attention), increase his or her rate of tics over time, and the tics may assume varied and unusual forms as a result of shaping and response generalization (Houlihan, Hofschulte, & Patten, 1993; Pray, Kramer, & Lindskog, 1986). In addition to explaining the origin of tics, a body of literature is emerging in which specific environmental stimuli that alter the rate of tic behaviors are being identified (Malatesta, 1990; Watson et al., 2005; Watson & Sterling, 1998a; Woods, Watson, Wolfe, Twohig, & Friman, 2001). Identifying such variables may allow practitioners to quickly develop effective and individually tailored interventions.

HABITS

Habits are learned, benign, persistent, stereotyped behaviors that appear to serve no meaningful purpose for the individual. Habits may be maintained by positive reinforcement (attention), negative reinforcement (reduction of unpleasant physiological arousal), or automatic (sensory stimulation) reinforcement and elicited by many discriminative stimuli (e.g., transitional objects) (Watson & Sterling, 1998b). Most individuals will engage in some habit behavior (e.g., foot tapping, thumb sucking, hair twirling) over the course of their lives. Because most habits are benign and often transient, most go untreated. However, some habits may result in substantial negative physical, social, academic, occupational, or psychological discomfort for the individual who exhibits them. For instance, habits may result in negative interactions with parents, teachers, or peers. The student who sucks her thumb may be teased by peers, scolded by parents, and suffer physical damage (e.g., malocclusions). Because habits may result in substantial negative consequences, they are an important concern for parents, professionals (e.g., professional school counselors, physicians, psychologists), and the student who engages in the habit. The most common habits seen in clinical settings are trichotillomania (hair pulling), bruxism (teeth grinding or clenching), nail biting, and thumb sucking.

ETIOLOGY AND EPIDEMIOLOGY OF HABIT DISORDERS

Current research indicates that habits are learned behaviors that are not indicative of underlying psychopathology. Children who engage in habits do not significantly differ from children who do not on measures such as the *Achenbach System of Empirically Based Assessment* (ASEBA; Achenbach & Rescorla, 2001) or *Eyeberg Child Behavior Inventory* (Friman, Larzelere, & Finney, 1994). It has been suggested that habits are caused by states of anxiety or tension (Hadley, 1984), thus fostering the idea that individuals who exhibit habits are "nervous," and the anxiety or tension they feel causes them to exhibit these "nervous" habits. Support for the theory that individuals who exhibit habits experience significantly more anxiety and tension than others has been mixed (Glaros & Melamed, 1992; Klatte & Deardorff, 1981; Woods, Miltenberger, & Flach, 1996).

From a behavioral perspective, it is likely that some habits are directly reinforced while others become conditioned reinforcers (i.e., they are paired with either an unconditioned reinforcer like food or with another conditioned reinforcer like playing in the tub), and as a result, are maintained for long periods. For instance, a student who normally receives little social attention from parents may be reprimanded when he sucks his thumb. Social attention provided contingent upon thumb sucking might serve to increase the future likelihood of thumb sucking. Thumb sucking may also provide tactile and kinesthetic stimulation of the oral tissue during times of minimal stimulation which may also maintain the behavior (i.e., automatic reinforcement).

Because habit disorders cover such a wide range of topographically different behaviors, it is extremely difficult to obtain overall prevalence estimates. However, rough estimates for specific habits have been reported. Peterson et al. (1994) reported prevalence data for habits most commonly seen in clinics. Bruxism is estimated to occur in 7% to 88% of the population. The wide range in prevalence rates is due to the varied definitions used by researchers who study bruxism. Estimates for the prevalence of trichotillomania are only available for adults (0.6% to 1%) (American Psychiatric Association, 2000; Diefenbach, Reitman, & Williamson, 2000). Trichotillomania is more common in females, except for during the preschool years, when it is more common in males. Prevalence rates for nail biting increase from preschool to adolescence, where it peaks at roughly 45%, but then steadily declines to a rate of 4.5% in adults. Nail biting is most common in females. Thumb sucking occurs in 30% to 40% of preschool children and 10% to 20% of children 6 years and older.

IDENTIFICATION OF HABITS AND TICS

Identifying, assessing, and treating habits and tics focuses on operationally defined, observable behaviors and employs a multimethod and a multi-informant approach for collecting data (Haynes, 1998). Methods for accurately and operationally identifying habit and tic behaviors include interviews, direct observation, and permanent product measures (e.g., nails, hairs) where possible. Figure 63.1 presents a decision tree that may help the professional school counselor determine which method of data gathering is most appropriate in a given circumstance.

INTERVIEWS

Interviews should be conducted with parents, teachers, and the student (when appropriate). The purpose of the interview is to first gain general information related to the student's developmental, medical, social, and academic histories. During the medical portion of the interview (with parents), information related to current and past medications as well as physician evaluations should be gathered in order to determine if there are possible organic causes for the habit or tic.

After developmental, medical, social, and academic histories have been gathered, specific information regarding the habit or tic should be obtained. Questions related to

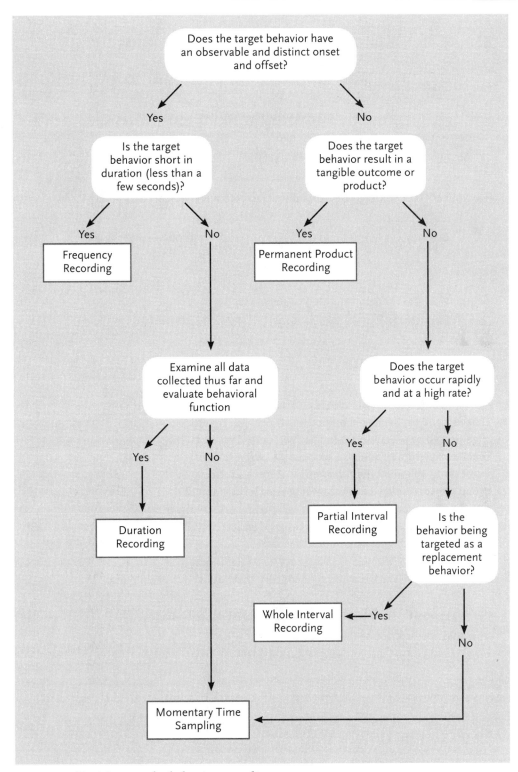

Figure 63.1. Decision tree for behavior recording.

Date: _____   Student Name: _____

Date of Birth: _____   Grade: _____

Parent/Guardian Name: _____

DEVELOPMENTAL, MEDICAL, AND SOCIAL INFORMATION

At approximately what age did your child:

    Sit up _____   Walk _____   Say first words _____

    Potty train _____   Use simple sentences _____

Has your child been diagnosed by a physician with any medical condition?

    ❏ Yes   ❏ No

Diagnosis	Date Diagnosed
_____	_____
_____	_____

Please list all past and current medications taken by your child.

Medication Name	Dates Taken
_____	From _____ to _____
_____	From _____ to _____

Does your child:

    have friends at school?   ❏ Yes   ❏ No

    have friends in the neighborhood?   ❏ Yes   ❏ No

    get teased by peers?   ❏ Yes   ❏ No

    get along well with adults?   ❏ Yes   ❏ No

    get along well with other children?   ❏ Yes   ❏ No

    use age-appropriate behavior when playing?   ❏ Yes   ❏ No

    play with age-appropriate toys/games?   ❏ Yes   ❏ No

Describe other health or social concerns: _____

BEHAVIOR

Describe in detail the behavior(s) of concern that your child is exhibiting.

_____

Please provide a demonstration of the behavior(s) described above.

When did you first notice this behavior? _____

What have you done to change this behavior? _____

How long has your child exhibited each behavior? _____

Has the behavior changed in any way over the course of occurrence?   ❏ Yes   ❏ No

How?	When?	In response to what (in your opinion)?

FIGURE 63.2. Abbreviated parent interview form.

FUNCTIONAL HYPOTHESIS DEVELOPMENT

In what situation or setting is your child most likely to perform the behavior(s)?

_____

During what time(s) of the day is your child most likely to exhibit the behavior(s)?

_____

In what situation(s) or setting(s) is your child least likely to perform the behavior(s)?

_____

During what time(s) of the day is your child least likely to exhibit the behavior(s)?

_____

What typically occurs before the behavior(s)? _____

_____

What typically follows the behavior(s)? _____

_____

How do others (for example, peers, teachers, and parents) respond to this behavior?

_____

HYPOTHESIZED FUNCTION (CIRCLE ONE):

tangible reinforcement   negative reinforcement   social attention
       automatic reinforcement

FIGURE 63.2. *Continued.*

when the behavior was first noticed, what the behavior looks like (having the student or parent perform the behavior may be appropriate), previous treatment attempts, and other areas of concern are important at this point. Following this, questions related to the times when the behavior is most frequently exhibited, events that precede the behavior (both physiological and environmental) and events that typically follow the behavior (e.g., social attention, reduction of unpleasant physiological stimulation) should be asked. Information gathered from such questions can facilitate the development of hypotheses regarding possible functions of the behavior (e.g., access to social attention, negative reinforcement). The function of behavior can generally be regarded as the "why" of behavior. See Figures 63.2, 63.3, and 63.4 for examples of abbreviated parent, student, and teacher interview forms, respectively.

Any student may exhibit a particular behavior for a number of reasons. Research indicates that there are four general classes of reasons (consequences) that account for the maintenance of problem behaviors: (a) tangible reinforcement, (b) social attention, (c) negative reinforcement, and (d) automatic reinforcement (Iwata, Dorsey, Slifer, Bauman, & Richman, 1994). However, social attention, negative reinforcement (escape or avoidance of an unpleasant activity or physiological state), and automatic reinforcement (sensory stimulation) appear to be the most common consequences that maintain habits or tics. In the function based treatments section of this chapter, it will become apparent that determining the "why" of behavior (identifying maintaining consequences) can be extremely useful for developing treatment.

Date: _____   Student Name: _____

Date of Birth: _____   Grade: _____

Parent/Guardian Name: _____

BEHAVIOR

Describe in detail each of your habits or tics. _____

_____

Please provide a demonstration of the behavior(s) described above.

When did you first start doing this behavior(s)? _____

_____

How long have you been doing this behavior(s)? _____

_____

Do you notice a sensation or feeling that occurs before the behavior(s)? ❑ Yes ❑ No

If yes, which behavior? _____

Describe the sensation. _____

How do you feel AFTER you have done the habit or tic? _____

How do others respond to you when you do the habit or tic? _____

FUNCTIONAL HYPOTHESIS DEVELOPMENT

In what school and home situation are you most likely to do the habit(s)/tic(s)?

_____

During what time(s) of the day do you do the habit(s)/tic(s)? _____

_____

In what school and home situation(s) or setting(s) do you hardly ever perform the habit(s)/tic(s)? _____

During what time(s) of the day do you hardly ever perform the habit(s)/tic(s)?

_____

What typically happens before your habit(s)/tic(s)? _____

_____

What typically happens after your habit(s)/tic(s)? _____

_____

HYPOTHESIZED FUNCTION (CIRCLE ONE):

tangible reinforcement   negative reinforcement   social attention
    automatic reinforcement

FIGURE 63.3. Abbreviated student interview form.

DIRECT OBSERVATION

Following interviews with parents, teachers, and the student, direct observations of the student should be conducted. Direct observations can be used to verify information gathered during interviews as well as to obtain additional information related to the presenting problem. Observation times may be selected based on information gathered during interviews that indicates when the habit or tic is most likely to occur. Ideally, direct observations should be conducted across a number of occasions and settings (again based upon information gathered during interviews). During direct observations, the practitioner should record the presenting problem on dimensions including frequency and duration. Such information can be useful in developing a baseline for which to evaluate treatment success and for developing and verifying hypotheses regarding the potential functions for a particular behavior. In addition, close attention should be paid to those events that precede (antecedents) and follow (consequences) the presenting problem. A number of published observation forms designed specifically for use in school settings are available to aid practitioners in recording antecedents, behaviors, and consequences (Watson & Steege, 2003).

PERMANENT PRODUCTS

In some cases it may not be possible to directly observe habits. For instance, if the student engages in hair pulling only in private, then it would be impossible to observe the behavior. Additionally, some students may react to observation (referred to as "reactivity") such that the behavior may not be exhibited during observation times. Permanent products can serve as one means to overcome such hurdles. Permanent products refer to those relatively enduring "remnants" of behavior. With trichotillomania, it may be possible to measure bald spots on the scalp to determine if hair is being pulled from a particular region. The student may also be instructed to save pulled hairs in order to obtain an accurate count of the number of hairs pulled during a day. In the case of nail biting, the length of the nails on each hand can be measured. Permanent product measures provide information that can be used to verify behaviors reported by parents, teachers, or the student. Not all habit behaviors (e.g., thumb sucking, hair twirling) and tics are amenable to collecting permanent product measures because they do not leave enduring, measurable remnants.

RATING SCALES

In addition to informant report, direct-observation, and permanent product measurement, rating scales may prove useful for evaluating symptom severity and client response to intervention. With regard to TS and tic disorders, the *Yale Global Tic Severity Scale* (YGTSS) is a semistructured, clinician-rated scale for measuring tic severity during the past week. Research indicates that the YGTSS yields reliable and valid scores and is sensitive to treatment gains (Leckman et al., 1989; Storch et al., 2005). The YGTSS may be a useful tool for evaluating student's level of tic severity prior to and following intervention.

Date: _____   Student Name: _____

Date of Birth: _____   Grade: _____

Teacher Name: _____

ACADEMIC PERFORMANCE

Please indicate how the student is performing in the area of reading as compared to same-grade peers.

❑ Significantly above peers   ❑ Above peers   ❑ Comparable to peers
❑ Below peers   ❑ Significantly below peers

Please indicate how the student is performing in the area of math as compared to same-grade peers.

❑ Significantly above peers   ❑ Above peers   ❑ Comparable to peers
❑ Below peers   ❑ Significantly below peers

Please list any academic areas that are particularly *difficult* for the student:
_____

Please list any academic areas that are particularly *easy* for the student:
_____

Please list any academic areas that are of particularly *low* interest for the student:
_____

Please list any academic areas that are of particularly *high* interest for the student:
_____

BEHAVIOR

Describe in detail the behavior(s) of concern that the student is exhibiting.
_____

Please provide a demonstration of the behavior(s) described above.

How often is the behavior exhibited (per day)? _____
_____

Please describe any previously implemented interventions: _____
_____

What do you do when the student does the habit or tic? _____
_____

How do the other students respond? _____
_____

FUNCTIONAL HYPOTHESIS DEVELOPMENT

In what situation or setting is the child most likely to perform the behavior(s)?
_____

During what time(s) of the day is the child most likely to exhibit the behavior(s)?
_____

FIGURE 63.4. Abbreviated teacher interview form.

In what situation(s) or setting(s) is the child least likely to perform the behavior(s)?

_____

During what time(s) of the day is the child least likely to exhibit the behavior(s)?

_____

What typically occurs before the behavior(s)?

_____

What typically follows the behavior(s)?

_____

Does the behavior occur more often during a particular academic subject or task?

_____

Do any of the following occur after the behavior?

- ❑ Teacher attention   ❑ Peer attention   ❑ Task termination
- ❑ Assistance with work   ❑ Access to rewards   ❑ Self-stimulation
- ❑ Removal from social situations

HYPOTHESIZED FUNCTION (CIRCLE ONE):

tangible reinforcement   negative reinforcement   social attention
   automatic reinforcement

FIGURE 63.4. *Continued.*

FUNCTION-BASED TREATMENTS

ANTECEDENT INTERVENTIONS

Information gathered during interviews and direct observation may identify specific antecedent events that reliably precede the habit or tic. If a reliable antecedent is identified, then the following procedure may be implemented. First, identify similar antecedents that have not elicited the habit or tic in the past. Next, arrange the environment such that there are numerous opportunities for the nonelicited antecedent to occur and heavily reinforce all appropriate behaviors other than the habit or tic (differential reinforcement of other behavior). Finally, the event that elicited the habit or tic may be gradually reintroduced. For example, if assessment data indicated that a vocal tic is most often exhibited when a student is assigned difficult multiplication problems (e.g., double-digit multiplication with regrouping), then the student can be provided with simpler math problems (e.g., single-digit multiplication problems) and then provided positive social attention contingent upon the absence of the vocal tic (e.g., "I really like the way you are quietly working on your math worksheet"). Difficult multiplication problems can be gradually reintroduced while continuing to provide positive social attention contingent upon the absence of the vocal tic.

SOCIAL ATTENTION

If interview and direct observation data indicate that social attention is maintaining the occurrence of a habit or tic, the primary intervention is to withhold attention when the habit or tic is exhibited (extinction) and to provide social attention when appropriate behaviors other than the habit or tic are exhibited (differential reinforcement). Watson and Sterling (1998a) identified social attention as the maintaining variable for a vocal tic exhibited by a 4-year-old girl during meal times. Treatment consisted of withholding social attention following the vocal tic (extinction) and providing verbal statements (social attention) contingent upon not exhibiting the vocal tic (differential reinforcement).

NEGATIVE REINFORCEMENT

If interview and direct observation data indicate that escape from an unpleasant activity (negative reinforcement) is maintaining a habit or tic, then the practitioner must develop an intervention in which the student cannot escape the unpleasant activity. In one case of a student who exhibited a vocal and motor tic primarily in the classroom setting, it was determined (from interview and observation data) that the student was able to escape academic demands following the exhibition of the vocal and motor tics by being directed by the teacher to go to the back of the class to "calm down." Thus, vocal and motor tics allowed the student to escape academic demands that were present in the classroom. After discovering why the student exhibited vocal and motor tics, it was rather easy to develop treatment based on this information. First, the student was no longer allowed to escape academic tasks following the vocal and motor tics (extinction). Next, the student was allowed to take breaks (escape academic tasks) following completion of gradually increasing work requirements (differential reinforcement and shaping).

AUTOMATIC REINFORCEMENT

Quite often, habit and tic behaviors are maintained by automatic reinforcement (sensory stimulation). In such cases, the practitioner must develop an intervention that either blocks sensory stimulation or punishes the behavior. For instance, Watson and Allen (1993) attached a post to a child's thumb, thus preventing her from receiving tactile–kinesthetic stimulation provided by thumb sucking (extinction). Sometimes, however, it may not be possible to simply prevent access to sensory stimulation gained by the habit or tic. In such cases, it may be necessary to punish the habit or tic. A very effective treatment for eliminating thumb sucking is to place an unpleasant tasting substance on the thumb (e.g., Stopzit, Thumbz, Ambisol) after the student is observed sucking his or her thumb (punishment) and rewarding behaviors other than thumb sucking (differential reinforcement). It is important to note that whenever punishment procedures are implemented, some sort of reinforcement should be provided for the nonoccurrence of the problem behavior (differential reinforcement).

GENERAL TREATMENT PROCEDURES

HABIT REVERSAL

Some treatment approaches are effective despite the fact that they are not based on the function of the behavior. Habit reversal (HR) procedures represent one such approach.

HR techniques are among the most effective nonpharmacological treatments for habits and tics (Watson, Howell, & Smith, 2001). The original habit reversal procedure (Azrin & Nunn, 1973) contained 13 steps. Follow-up research indicated that all 13 steps were not necessary for the procedure to be effective. Three of the original 13 components are now considered sufficient for effective treatment: (a) awareness training, (b) competing response training, and (c) social support training. This approach to habit reversal has been labeled simplified habit reversal (SHR) (see Figure 63.5).

The first step in SHR is *awareness training*. Awareness training involves the student becoming aware of her habit or tic and the sensations that precede it. Awareness is accomplished by having the student describe the habit or tic, describe the sensations that precede the habit or tic, acknowledge therapist demonstrations of the habit or tic,

AWARENESS TRAINING

❑ Student identified and described the habit or tic
❑ Student identified and described preceding sensations or urges to perform the behavior
❑ Student verbally acknowledged demonstrations of the habit or tic
❑ Student verbally acknowledged own performance of the habit or tic

CRITERION FOR ADVANCEMENT:

❑ Student demonstrated the ability to detect urges with at least 80% reliability

COMPETING RESPONSE TRAINING

❑ Student and practitioner selected a physically incompatible competing response
❑ Practitioner demonstrated the chosen competing response
❑ Student practiced the competing response

CRITERION FOR ADVANCEMENT:

❑ On request, the student correctly performed the competing response

SOCIAL SUPPORT TRAINING

❑ A support aid was assigned to the student
❑ Support aid was trained to praise competing response performance
❑ Support aid was trained to prompt student to perform the competing response
❑ Support aid consistently praised and prompted competing response performance
❑ Student demonstrated the ability to independently perform the competing response

FIGURE 63.5. Treatment integrity checklist–habit reversal.

and acknowledge her own habit or tic. Awareness training should include multiple opportunities for the student to acknowledge therapist demonstrations and identify self-produced habits or tics. Therapists should praise the student for displaying awareness of the habit or tic and provide corrective feedback to the student when she does not display awareness of the habit or tic. Successful awareness training may be completed in one to two sessions with additional student practice outside of the therapy session (e.g., at home). Successful completion of awareness training is necessary for teaching additional SHR components. Professional school counselors may be confident that a student has achieved awareness by observing the student acknowledge awareness for the habit or tic without prompting.

Competing response training follows awareness training and involves the student and therapist selecting a competing response, the therapist demonstrating the competing response, and finally the student practicing the competing response. Typically, the behavior chosen as the competing response is physically incompatible with the target response (e.g., hands in pockets or lap for trichotillomania). The student is trained to engage in the competing response for 1-minute contingent upon the occurrence of the habit or tic. Initially, the professional school counselor may prompt the student to engage in the competing response immediately following exhibition of the habit or tic. Eventually though, the student should be expected to engage in the competing response independent of prompts. Competing response training typically occurs across one to two sessions with additional practice at home and throughout the day. During training, the student should experience multiple practice opportunities with the competing response. Professional school counselors should praise the student for engaging in the competing response prior to exhibiting the habit or tic and prompt the student to engage in the competing response if he performs the habit or tic. Professional school counselors should pay careful attention to the level of independence that the student attains with regard to independently engaging in the competing response. Acquisition of the competing response is evidenced by student engagement in the competing response prior to exhibition of the habit or tic (e.g., student folds hands prior to raising forearm, placing finger in mouth, and biting fingernail).

The final component of SHR is *social support training*. The purpose of social support training is to provide the student with an aid who will help implement SHR. Social support training involves three components. First, an individual who has regular contact with the student throughout the day is recruited to assist the student. Second, the aid is trained to praise the student following accurate display of the competing response. Finally, the aid is trained to prompt the student to engage in the competing response in the event that the student engages in the habit or tic. For a more detailed account of SHR, readers should refer to *Tic Disorders, Trichotillomania, and Other Repetitive Behavior Disorders: Behavioral Approaches to Analysis and Treatment* (Woods & Miltenberger, 2001).

PHARMACOLOGICAL TREATMENTS

Pharmacological agents traditionally have been the treatment of choice for tic spectrum disorders. Neuroleptics are the most commonly used pharmacological agents and work by blocking the reuptake of the neurotransmitter dopamine. Neuroleptics are categorized into two types: typical and atypical. Typical neuroleptics include haloperidol (Haldol) and pimozide (Orap). Haloperidol and pimozide are equally effective in treating tic spectrum disorder, with each reducing the frequency of tics by roughly 70% to 80% (Kurlan, 1997; Leckman, Peterson, Pauls, & Cohen, 1997). Although typical neuroleptics are effective in significantly reducing tic frequency, they possess a long list of possible side effects including those that range from mild (e.g., dry mouth, constipation, weight gain) to severe (e.g., extra-pyramidal symptoms [EPS], tardive dyskinesia [TD], and seizures).

Atypical neuroleptics are becoming increasingly popular and include olanzapine (Zyprexa), clozapine (Clozaril), and risperidone (Risperdal). The atypical neuroleptics are often as effective as the typical neuroleptics but carry less of a risk for serious side effects such as EPS and TD. The atypical neuroleptics may, however, cause less serious side effects (e.g., dry mouth, constipation, weight gain, restlessness, and incontinence) (Blin, 1999).

SELF-MUTILATION

Self-mutilation (SM) is the deliberate, direct destruction or alteration of body tissue without the presence of suicidal intent (Favazza, 1998; Miller & DeZolt, 2004). The *DSM-IV-TR* (2000) does not classify SM as a specific disorder. The most widely accepted classification system for SM was developed by Favazza (1996). In this classification, SM is divided into three categories: (a) *major*, which refers to infrequent but highly destructive behaviors such as enucleation, castration, and limb amputation; (b) *stereotypic*, which refers to behaviors such as head banging and self-biting; and (c) *superficial/moderate*, which refers to behaviors such as cutting, pinching, scratching, and nail biting. Superficial/moderate SM is the most common form of SM and typically involves the arms, wrists, inner thigh, and stomach. Superficial/moderate SM behaviors overlap with behaviors that are often classified as habits (e.g., trichotillomania, nail biting) since they are repetitive, volitional, and appear to serve no adaptive role. The remainder of this discussion will focus on superficial/moderate SM because it continues to be an important topic for school personnel.

Skin cutting may be the most common form of episodic superficial/moderate self-mutilation (Favazza, 1998). Skin cutting is often a symptom, or an associated feature, of Borderline, histrionic and antisocial personality disorders, posttraumatic stress disorder, dissociative disorders, eating disorders, and depression. Research indicates that cutting behaviors appear most often during adolescence, may be more prevalent in girls, may sometimes, but not always, be precipitated by incidents of sexual and/or physical abuse, and have an underestimated prevalence (Favazza, 1998; Ross & Heath, 2002). Recent estimates suggest that almost 14% of adolescents have engaged in self-mutilation, including cutting at some point, with females nearly twice as likely to have engaged in self-mutilation (Ross & Heath, 2002).

Skin cutting is often strategically performed in that areas chosen for cutting are easily hidden by clothes. Because individuals who engage in skin cutting are often secretive and reluctant to contact mental health services, identification, assessment, and treatment are often difficult. Furthermore, the lack of standardized instruments for assessing SM is problematic. A comprehensive assessment of skin cutting should include direct observations and interviews with the student suspected of cutting, caregivers, and other adults who frequently observe the individual (e.g., school personnel). Direct observations should include checking for cuts and the presence of heavy clothing that may serve to hide damage. When the student is interviewed, she should be asked directly whether or not she is engaging in skin cutting. If the student is engaging in skin cutting, then a suicide risk assessment should be immediately conducted.

Functional assessment techniques may also be employed in the assessment of skin cutting. While few empirically based assessment instruments are available for skin cutting, functional assessment techniques may be appropriate because skin cutting is topographically similar to other superficial/moderate SM behaviors (e.g., trichotillomania, nail biting) which are amenable to functional assessment procedures. During the assessment stage, information related to antecedents (e.g., triggers), specific behaviors (e.g., jagged lacerations to the thigh), and consequences (e.g., social attention, reduction of unpleasant physiological and emotional arousal) of skin cutting should be gathered. Precise definitions and reliable antecedents and consequences of skin cutting may be useful during the treatment stage. For example, one individual may frequently engage in skin cutting in response to anxiety evoking events and may be maintained or negatively reinforced by anxiety reduction. Treatment for such an individual may involve teaching the individual to engage in diaphragmatic breathing and progressive muscle relaxation in the face of anxiety-evoking situations because such behaviors could produce similar consequences (i.e., anxiety reduction).

The empirical literature contains scant data regarding effective treatments for skin cutting for children and adolescents. Pharmacological treatment (e.g., SSRIs) may be effective for treating conditions (e.g., anxiety, depression) that are associated with skin cutting, thereby reducing the occurrence of cutting (Favazza, 1998). Additionally, behavioral techniques such as simplified habit reversal may be effective because skin cutting is topographically similar to other habit behaviors (e.g., trichotillomania, nail biting) that are effectively treated by simplified habit reversal. Finally, function-based treatments (e.g., modification of antecedent events, programming alternative responses, manipulating consequences) may prove effective for treating skin cutting. It is important to note that the discussion of SM provided here is cursory at best. Interested readers should refer to Favazza (1998, 1999) or Lieberman and Poland (2006) for a more detailed discussion of assessment and treatment for SM.

Summary/Conclusion

Although habits and tics appear to be benign disorders, there exists the possibility for significant social, educational–occupational, psychological, and physical damage. From a learning perspective, habits and tics represent learned behaviors that are affected by specific environmental events. The research literature supports the use of behavioral procedures for the assessment and treatment of habits, tics and self-mutilation. Those procedures appear to offer relatively quick and effective means for treating habit and tic disorders, and self-mutilation.

(Note: See the CD-ROM for a list of references.)

CHAPTER 64

REACTIVE ATTACHMENT DISORDER IN SCHOOLS: RECOMMENDATIONS FOR PROFESSIONAL SCHOOL COUNSELORS

Carl J. Sheperis, R. Anthony Doggett, Nicholas E. Hoda, Robika Modak, and Angela R. Cole

Preview

Children who experience pathogenic care prior to age 5 years can develop reactive attachment disorder (RAD). This disorder, which manifests in a host of behavioral problems, is of growing concern to professional school counselors. We discuss the characteristics of RAD, diagnostic criteria, issues related to the school system, and recommendations for professional school counselors.

When students transfer in and out of school systems, professional school counselors face a host of difficult administrative issues, including maintaining student records, gathering accurate evaluations of progress, and establishing relationships with families. No school population is more transitory than are students from foster care. Some students in foster care experience as many as 50 or 60 placements in several different school districts (Sheperis, Renfro-Michel, & Doggett, 2003). Many of these students also have mental health issues related to abuse or neglect that eventuated their foster-care placement, thus creating more concerns for professional school counselors. In fact, some evidence suggests that students in foster care are more likely to receive behavioral health-care services than any other group of Medicaid-eligible children. Often, these health-care services are related to a disruption of healthy attachment patterns resulting in reactive attachment disorder (RAD).

A commonly misunderstood and underdiagnosed disorder, RAD is a growing concern for professional school counselors (Parker & Forrest, 1993). This disorder begins in early childhood and affects academic, behavioral, cognitive, affective, social, physical, and spiritual–moral development (Doane & Diamond, 1994; Leick & Davidsen-Neilson, 1990; Levy & Orlans, 1998). RAD also can be positively treated through intervention (Hayes, 1997). Professional school counselors are in a unique position because of their prolonged interactions with these students to recognize symptoms of serious underlying problems and make appropriate referrals. We present professional school counselors with information about reactive attachment disorder, its development, some methods of treatment, and guidelines for intervention in a school system. However, before expounding upon the nature of RAD, it is important to explain the process of attachment and its function in a student's life.

ATTACHMENT

Attachment is a process common to humans and many animal species. Disruptions in the process affect humans throughout their entire lives and can negatively affect the ability to form healthy relationships. Bowlby (1969) saw attachment as an instinctual, evolutionary process that occurs in four stages. He believed that the process of attachment functioned as a survival drive of the species. The process begins with an infant's communication of needs for proximity and physical contact through vocal and behavioral cues (e.g., crying, latching on, grasping). Acknowledgement and fulfillment of these needs by a caregiver begin to positively shape the infant's behavior. Infants begin the second stage of attachment between 8 and 12 weeks of age by establishing indicators of caregiver preference through behavioral cues such as reaching and scooting. According to Bowlby, the third stage of attachment occurs from 12 weeks through 24 months of age. This is the stage that Ainsworth, Blehar, Walters, and Wall (1978) believed to be the true process of attachment. In this stage, infants and toddlers begin to anticipate caregiver actions and adjust their own behavior in accordance with these anticipated events. Thus, consistency of the primary caregiver's display of affection and attention to the needs of the child are critical components in the formation of healthy adjustments on the part of the child. An understanding of caregiver independence and the development of reciprocity in the infant–caregiver relationship characterized Bowlby's fourth stage of attachment development, thus moving into a more sophisticated aspect of the process. The key facet across all of these stages is consistency in the provision of behavioral reinforcement to infant and toddler basic emotional and physical needs. In essence, this reinforcement is a method of conditioning the child to use human relationships as a sense of security and comfort (Wilson, 2001).

When the provision of infant and toddler basic needs is not conducted in a consistent fashion, attachment becomes disrupted, resulting in insecure attachment patterns and adverse reactions toward human relationships. In research, disrupted attachment has been linked to psychiatric syndromes, criminal behavior, and drug use (Allen, Hauser & Borman-Spurrell, 1996; Rosenstein & Horowitz, 1996). Chronic inconsistency in meeting infant and toddler needs as well as the introduction of early childhood trauma (i.e., abuse or neglect) may result in the formation of RAD.

REACTIVE ATTACHMENT DISORDER

A personal difficulty that professional school counselors may face with regard to RAD is a lack of ability to prevent the development of the disorder. RAD develops from a lack of appropriate bonding between infant and primary caregiver, which ordinarily occurs well before a child comes of school age. Thus, the goal for professional school counselors is identification of problem behaviors and acquisition of appropriate resources (Hayes, 1997). The *Diagnostic and Statistical Manual of Mental Disorders–Fourth Edition, Text Revision* (*DSM-IV-TR*) (American Psychiatric Association [APA], 2000) criteria for RAD includes (a) "evidence of a clearly disturbed and developmentally inappropriate social relatedness in most contexts, beginning before age five" (p. 130); (b) evidence of pathogenic care; and (c) a presumption that the pathogenic care is responsible for the disturbed behavior. There are two types of RAD—inhibited and disinhibited—that relate to the presentation of behavioral problems. Inhibited RAD is described as a lack of response to social interactions, whereas in disinhibited RAD, the child attaches easily to strangers.

IDENTIFICATION OF RAD

Childhood psychological disorders often affect various areas of functioning (e.g., behavior, cognition, academic progress, and developmental processes; Achenbach, 1995). Many disorders also share similar symptoms. These commonalities make it difficult to differentiate RAD from disorders such as attention-deficit/hyperactivity disorder (ADHD), mental retardation (MR), depression disorder, oppositional defiant disorder (ODD), conduct disorder (CO), autistic disorder and other pervasive developmental disorders, learning disorders, and expressive and mixed receptive–expressive language disorders (Sheperis et al., 2003). To effectively coordinate academic services, it is necessary for professional school counselors to understand how to differentiate between a child with RAD and a child exhibiting behaviors characteristic of other disorders. Thus, an understanding of diagnostic criteria for the disorder is warranted.

The principle factor in accurate diagnosis is the presence of an abusive and neglectful environment (i.e., pathogenic care) prior to age five (APA; 2000). However, this factor is not solely indicative of RAD (Sheperis et al., 2003). Children with RAD often have poor interpersonal skills and have difficulty establishing appropriate relationships with peers and adults (Levy & Orlans, 1998). These boundary issues manifest in (a) an inability to interact with either familiar people (i.e., inhibited type) or (b) in an "indiscriminant sociability" (i.e., disinhibited type; APA; 2000). For example, children with an inhibited type may be very introverted and, similar to autistic disorder, may not respond to familiar people or caregivers (Sheperis et al., 2003). These children may also respond to cordial interactions in an aggressive manner. Other indicators of inhibited type RAD include poor hygiene, muscular rigidity, and/or lack of affection (Lake, 2005). On the opposite end of the spectrum, children with a disinhibited type of RAD may be charming, express feelings of love to strangers, and may even invite these strangers home (Wilson, 2001). Lake (2005) noted that these children may give hugs to people who approach them and will go with that person if asked. This behavior can establish a pattern of further victimization through interactions with predatory individuals. To accurately diagnose either type of RAD, the disturbed pattern of interaction must have begun prior to age 5 years (APA; 2000).

SIMILARITIES TO OTHER DISORDERS

When psychological disorders share similar characteristics, a process of differential diagnosis is necessary. Differential diagnosis requires attention to exclusionary criteria of disorders with similar characteristics. For example, a child with RAD may appear very similar to a child with attention-deficit/hyperactivity disorder (ADHD). Specifically, both may exhibit little connection between cause-and-effect thinking. For example, a child may behave impulsively and hyperactively. However, unlike children with RAD, children with ADHD will have formed relationships with caregivers and other supportive persons (APA; 2000). Also, the impulsive–hyperactive behavior of children with ADHD differs somewhat from disinhibited behavior exhibited by children with RAD. In particular, the child with RAD displays inappropriate boundaries and may act as if a relationship exists with a complete stranger rather than being reserved and curious (APA; 2000).

Children with RAD may also display behaviors and characteristics similar to mental retardation (MR). However, if criteria are met for MR, the child cannot be diagnosed with RAD. Accurate assessment of a child's behavior requires a working knowledge of human developmental levels (e.g., cognitive functioning and age-appropriate behaviors). An accurate diagnosis of RAD requires that disruptive behavior must be a result of pathogenic care rather than MR or other cognitive deficits (APA; 2000). RAD may, however, occur in conjunction with cognitive deficits and developmental delays. More specifically, although both RAD and MR may result in a child's inability to form meaningful, healthy relationships with significant persons such as caregivers, failed relationships for a child with RAD result from pathogenic care rather than developmental issues.

Some behaviors exhibited by children diagnosed with RAD can also be characteristic of childhood depression. With either disorder, a sense of depression can be manifested in isolation and a lack of pleasure from customary activities. The attitude of children with RAD is often pouty, sulky, and sullen (Sheperis et al., 2003). To further exacerbate depressive characteristics, children with RAD typically have a wide range of cognitive distortions and lack belief in fairness and good in the world. Considering the deprivation of basic needs that children diagnosed with RAD often suffer due to pathogenic care during infancy and early childhood, these distortions can be understood to some degree. However, they should not be accepted. This distorted belief system may result in a lack of belief about being able to influence the path their life will take (Sheperis et al., 2003). Such an extreme external locus of control in RAD children may increase inhibition and decrease self-modulation related to more serious behavior (e.g., suicide, reactive and predatory behaviors, juvenile delinquency). A child with RAD may often exhibit behaviors similar to children with either oppositional defiant disorder (ODD) or conduct disorder (CD) (APA; 2000).

Characteristic of either CD or ODD, a child with RAD may be both overtly and passively aggressive. Also characteristic of either disorder, children with RAD may be deceitful or lie to manipulate others (Sheperis et al., 2003). According to Levy and Orlans (1998), RAD also manifests in chronic lying and generalized delinquent behavior (e.g., stealing and fighting). Because the behaviors characteristic of RAD, CD, and ODD are so similar in nature, it is difficult to differentiate the disorders without an appropriate psycho–social history. The main differentiating criterion is the presence of pathogenic care prior to age 5 years.

Children with RAD may also share similarities with children who are diagnosed with autistic disorder or have other pervasive developmental disorders (APA; 2000). Both fail to make appropriate attachments to caregivers. The primary difference is that behaviors related to RAD must have developed within the framework of an abusive or detrimental environment while a child with autistic disorder or a pervasive developmental disorder may have been raised in a supportive and caring environment. The *DSM-IV-TR* stated that children with autistic disorder or a pervasive developmental disorder will present impairment in the quality of communication and will display patterned behavior consisting of restricted, repetitive, and stereotyped movements (e.g., overly preoccupied with a stereotyped and restricted pattern of abnormally intense or abnormally focused interest, need to perform a routine or ritual which has no apparent purpose, hand-flapping or wringing, and obsession with parts of objects).

ACADEMIC ISSUES RELATED TO RAD

Repeated changes in foster care and school settings often lead to academic skills or performance deficits for children with RAD (Zirkie & Peterson, 2001). Professional school counselors can help establish effective learning environments in which teachers can recognize individual learning preferences and realize when a student needs assistance in learning a particular skill. A skill deficit can occur when a student has not met the mastery criteria of a curriculum but advances to the next grade (e.g., social promotion). This promotion becomes a problem because the child is expected to complete tasks at a more advanced level than his or her ability may allow. An example of an academic performance deficit occurs when behavior problems affect academic performance (e.g., a child with RAD who is unwilling to complete assignments because of a general dislike and mistrust of adults). Unlike children with reading and math disorders or expressive and mixed receptive-expressive language disorders, the academic difficulties of children with RAD may stem from a lack of stability and continuity of care rather than from a cognitive or neurological deficit. Professional school counselors can affect positive outcomes for these children through the acquisition and coordination of quality services (Zirkie & Peterson, 2001). The primary step in this process for a child exhibiting symptoms of RAD, particularly a foster child or an adopted child, is to review the child's academic record and to examine the frequency of school transfers with the length of stability in each school. The professional school counselor should also examine academic records for patterns of problems, both in academic behavior (e.g., previous grade retentions or advancements) and in social behavior (e.g., numerous suspensions, refusal to complete tasks or assignments, lying, and/or impulsive or aggressive behavior). One potential method of achieving this task is to conduct regularly scheduled meetings with the student (Parker & Forrest, 1993).

RAD is most amenable to mental health intervention during early childhood (Zeanah, 1996). Thus, early identification of problem behaviors and appropriate referral are key tasks for professional school counselors (Pfaller & Kiselica, 1996). Although early intervention programs such as Head Start are often warranted, appropriate academic services may not be identified until the child is of school age. Once in the schools, these children are in need of structure and order in a caring, supportive environment to succeed academically (Parker & Forrest, 1993). By virtue of their knowledge of the school system, professional school counselors can identify and advocate assignment to appropriate teachers who could provide such an environment for these children.

Because of the multitude of school-related problems identified, children diagnosed with RAD are at-risk for academic failure. Professional school counselors may also establish dropout prevention services for these children. However, the efficacy of such programs with this population is yet to be tested. Early identification of academic difficulties is preferred to dropout prevention. If academic problems are identified early, professional school counselors can advocate for intervention in academic areas as needed. The school counselor may refer the student to be tested for special education services.

When Individualized Education Program (IEP) meetings are held for the student, the professional school counselor and special education coordinator should ensure that the appropriate personnel are present (e.g., legal guardian of the student, special education representative, administration representative, juvenile justice officer, an expert on RAD). The professional school counselor may also act as a liaison ensuring that appropriate services are provided for the student. This role would provide added success to IEP meetings, because the professional school counselor would have ongoing contact with mental health counseling agencies, other psychological service providers, juvenile justice officials, child welfare agencies, and other parties providing services to the student and family. The professional school counselor is in a good position to establish open communication with the student's guardian or guardians, ensuring that they are informed about the services being provided. Serving as a liaison also provides the family with a contact person for questions about the process.

LEGAL ISSUES

Children who are in foster care or who have been adopted often have complex custodial issues, and professional school counselors are in a unique position to ensure that the school is a safe and secure environment (Zirkie & Peterson, 2001). School officials must be aware of the custodial rights of each student and limit access to the disclosure of information to appropriate sources as dictated by the Family Educational Rights and Privacy Act of 1974 (FERPA) and the Individuals With Disabilities Education Act Amendments of 1997 (IDEA). For example, school officials must obtain appropriate consent for individualized assessment procedures, special education services, or any special treatment that is not provided to all students. Also, school officials must ensure that children are only released from school to those with custodial power. Custodial rights and the power to consent may be legally granted to a biological parent, adoptive parent, foster parent, guardian ad litem, or human services agency. Professional school counselors can ensure appropriate care in these matters through review of academic records and appropriate dissemination of information to school officials.

RECOMMENDATIONS FOR PROFESSIONAL SCHOOL COUNSELORS

Following are recommendations for best practice in working with students with RAD.

1. If a student is suspected of having reactive attachment disorder, he or she should be referred for appropriate assessment by a mental health professional.
2. Establish a supportive relationship with the student.
3. Obtain accurate academic records from all previous school districts.
4. Examine academic records for evidence of a pattern of a problem behavior.
5. Obtain behavioral observation data.

6. Consult the school psychologist.

7. Establish an IEP and include all key players in the formation of the plan (i.e., foster parents, guardians ad litem, human services professionals, mental health counselors).

8. Identify appropriate services for the student.

9. Coordinate efforts with teachers and IEP team members.

10. Maintain continued contact with classroom teachers.

11. Conduct regularly scheduled parent meetings.

12. Maintain phone contact with parents or caregivers.

Professional school counselors may also use a cognitive behavioral intervention to aid the child with RAD. This process occurs in three phases: (a) identification of cognitive errors (such as self blame), (b) assessment of cognitive distortions within the child's reasoning process, and (c) cognitive errors are replaced with accurate cognitions (Sheperis et al., 2003). More intervention may be used as the child becomes stable. The professional school counselor and teachers should develop reasonable goals and techniques as the intervention process takes place. For example, if the goal is to lessen anxiety, the technique should be as simple as stress management.

Summary/Conclusion

Attachment is an instinctual process that occurs between a child and his or her primary caregiver. When that process is disrupted, students have difficulty with self-regulation and forming healthy relationships. This disruption, under chronic abuse or neglect conditions (e.g., pathogenic care), can develop into reactive attachment disorder. RAD affects many areas of a student's life, including school. Professional school counselors are in a unique position to help stabilize several domains through advocacy and targeted interventions. Because disrupted attachment has been linked to psychiatric syndromes, criminal behavior, and drug use (Allen et al., 1996; Rosenstein & Horowitz, 1996), it is important to intervene early and to work toward stabilization. Professional school counselors can help students and their families to access appropriate resources and can ensure that appropriate academic interventions are in place.

(Note: See the CD-ROM for a list of references.)

CHAPTER 65

HELPING STUDENTS
WITH INTELLECTUAL DISABILITY

Amy J. Newmeyer and Mark D. Newmeyer

Preview

The professional school counselor can play an important role in advocating for students with intellectual disability. In the following chapter, we review the current definition of intellectual disability and educational implications from existing federal education laws. Issues surrounding sexuality, vocational training, and comorbidity are also addressed.

DEFINITION OF INTELLECTUAL DISABILITY

In 2002, The American Association of Intellectual and Developmental Disabilities (AAIDD) published a revision of the 1992 definition and classification system for intellectual disability. The AAIDD definition is generally considered the "gold standard" for the diagnosis of intellectual disability. However, it is important to keep in mind that individual state laws may have alternative definitions/cutoffs for determining eligibility for services, and it is therefore of great importance for professional school counselors to be aware of their local laws regarding eligibility. For further information, please refer to the AAIDD Web site (http://www.AAIDD.org). The AAIDD definition of intellectual disability is as follows: "Intellectual disability is a disability characterized by significant limitations both in intellectual functioning and in adaptive behavior, as expressed in conceptual, social, and practical adaptive skills. This disability originates before age 18" (AAIDD; 2008, ¶ 1).

In the 2002 revision, five dimensions for classification and diagnosis were defined (see Table 65.1). The goal of defining these dimensions for any individual is to determine needed supports that will improve the individual's overall functioning in the environment. Once descriptions of each dimension have been made, they should be incorporated into a profile of support needs. Support needs can change during different periods of an individual's life (childhood vs. adulthood). Supports are defined as "resources and strategies necessary to promote the development, education, interests, and personal well-being of a person with intellectual disability" (AAIDD; 2008, ¶ 15). Support functions are teaching, befriending, financial planning, employee assistance, behavioral support, in-home living assistance, community access and use, and health assistance. There should be an understanding that support needs and intensity of supports will change over the life span of an individual and should be reassessed on a regular basis (AAIDD; 2002).

TABLE 65.1

FIVE DIMENSIONS FOR CLASSIFICATION AND DIAGNOSIS OF INTELLECTUAL DISABILITY

I. Intellectual Abilities
   A. The person's intellectual functioning is approximately two standard deviations or more below the mean on standard psychometric tests (typically, the Stanford-Binet V or Wechsler intelligence test appropriate for the age of the student).
   B. Standard error of the mean should be considered when interpreting the results of any test.

II. Adaptive Behavior (conceptual, social, and practical skills)
   A. Three basic factor clusters exist: (a) cognitive, communication, and academic skills; (b) social competence skills; and (c) independent living skills.
   B. Adaptive skills should be interpreted based upon strengths and weaknesses and should be seen within the context of the individual's unique community and cultural environment.

III. Participation, Interactions, and Social Roles
   A. Participation in community activities seen within the environments typical of their chronological age peers and are consistent with the cultural diversity of the individual.

IV. Health (physical health, mental health, and etiologic factors)
   A. This dimension can be described by using International Classification of Diseases and Related Health Problems, 10th Revision (ICD-10) diagnostic codes for physical health, and the *Diagnostic and Statistical Manual of Mental Disorders–Fourth Edition, Text Revision* (DSM-IV-TR) criteria for mental health.
   B. It should be understood that health factors may affect outcomes of both intellectual and adaptive measures.

V. Context (environment and culture)
   A. The 2002 AAIDD definition uses an ecological approach, involving consideration of three levels: (a) immediate setting (person, family, and advocates); (b) neighborhood, community, and organizations providing support; and (c) patterns of culture, country, and sociopolitical influences.
   B. Positive factors should be identified for the individual with intellectual disabilities that provide opportunities and foster well-being.

EDUCATIONAL IMPLICATIONS

There are several current laws that affect student placement and special education services in the school setting. The Individuals With Disabilities Education Improvement Act of 2004 (IDEIA) indicates that individuals with intellectual disability may receive services through their local school district through age 21. Additionally, starting at 14 years of age, and updated annually, a statement of transition needs (Individualized Transition Plan; ITP) should be added to the Individualized Education Program (IEP). By 16 years of age, a statement of transition services for the individual must be in place, including a statement of interagency linkages as appropriate. Meanwhile, the student's school program must be in the Least Restrictive Environment (LRE) that allows optimal functioning.

The Rehabilitation Act of 1973 and amendments, commonly called Section 504, prevent discrimination against individuals with disabilities in any institution receiving federal financial assistance. This includes the local school district.

The professional school counselor has a vital role in both of these processes. The professional school counselor should be part of the team meeting to develop the IEP. Several types of assessment are routinely used in assisting with development of the IEP and the ITP, which have implications for counselors in the school setting.

Assessing student activity needs and skills in relevant domains for development of the IEP can involve an ecological inventory and observations in various community settings. This is relevant to students of all ages and should be completed every 3 years. Planning for school-to-work transition and development of the ITP involves a vocational and transitional assessment by interview and observation in various settings. The professional school counselor may also serve as a link to appropriate community agencies that can offer job assistance and community assistance following graduation from high school. This assessment should be updated annually from age 14 years through graduation.

Evaluation of behavioral problems that could affect school and community functioning may involve functional analysis, interview, observation, and referral to appropriate community resources. This may occur daily or weekly until the behavioral problems have stabilized. Evaluation of IEP objectives by observation in the school setting as well as by an interview with parents may occur more frequently as needed. Student and family satisfaction with services provided may be determined by interview, questionnaire, or observation. This should be performed annually, or more often if needed.

SUPPORT SERVICES FOR FAMILIES

The professional school counselor may also be involved in provision of other services to families of students with intellectual disability. Many families will adapt to having a child who has been diagnosed with intellectual disability. However, other families may require ongoing counseling and intervention in their adaptation to the special needs of their child. Various factors that have been found to be associated with adaptation include stability of the marriage, age of parents, parental self-esteem, number of siblings, socioeconomic status, degree of disability, parental expectations, support of extended family, availability of community programs, and respite services. Professional school counselors may play a vital role in identifying families at risk and assisting families with accessing available resources and respite services within the community setting (Shapiro & Batshaw, 1999).

When using the AAIDD definition, classification, and systems of supports, professionals and other team members must do the following:

- Evaluate limitations in present intellectual and adaptive behavior functioning within the context of the individual's age, peers, and culture;
- Take into account the individual's cultural and linguistic differences as well as communication, sensory, motor, and behavioral factors;
- Recognize that limitations often coexist with strengths within an individual;

- Describe limitations so that an individualized plan of needed supports can be developed; and
- Provide appropriate, personalized supports to improve the functioning of a person with intellectual disability. (AAIDD, 2008, ¶ 5)

The reader is referred to the AAIDD Web site for further examples of support services that are sometimes needed by families of students with intellectual disability (http://www.aamr.org/Policies/faq_mental_retardation.shtml).

SEXUALITY ISSUES

The professional school counselor can play an important role in assuring that sexuality issues are addressed for students with intellectual disability. Traditionally, communication over issues of sexuality has been largely avoided in this population; however, this lack of communication can lead to risk for exploitation and misunderstanding. In 1996, the American Academy of Pediatrics' (AAP) Committee on Children With Disabilities released a policy statement regarding sexuality education for children and adolescents with developmental disabilities. In this statement, summarized in Table 65.2, they emphasized major objectives to sexuality education for this group of students.

Families of children with intellectual disability may also raise questions regarding sterilization. Sterilization is greatly discouraged, unless there is a medical reason for doing the procedure. Alternative methods of birth control should be discussed with the student and the student's physician. Laws regarding sterilization vary locally, and the family should be referred to the physician for a detailed discussion of options (AAP; 1999).

SOCIAL-SKILLS TRAINING

Many students with intellectual disability may have difficulty with social skills in the school setting, often because their developmental level lags behind that of same-age peers. The professional school counselor may be able to assist these children with social skills by providing counseling and training regarding appropriate behavior in certain

TABLE 65.2

MAJOR OBJECTIVES OF SEXUALITY EDUCATION FOR STUDENTS WITH INTELLECTUAL DISABILITY

Providing information that is tailored to the level of understanding of the particular student.

Teaching students to express physical affection in an appropriate manner.

Discouraging inappropriate public displays of affection in the community (e.g., hugging strangers).

Expressing expectations that behavior conforms to family and community standards for privacy and modesty.

Teaching students about appropriate behaviors in a public and private settings.

Teaching students about their right to refuse to be touched at any time and about the importance of telling a parent or caregiver if they have been touched inappropriately.

Discussing pleasure and affection when teaching students about sex (AAP; 1996).

settings, such as how to have a conversation with another peer. Learning these skills may greatly enhance a student's ability to function in an inclusive setting.

COMORBID ISSUES

Students with intellectual disability often have comorbid behavioral and mental health conditions such as depression, anxiety, or aggressive behavior that will affect their functioning in a school or community environment. It is important that these issues be addressed appropriately to ensure maximum functioning of the individual. The professional school counselor can play a role in identifying these conditions, providing counseling services, and referring the student and his or her family for interventions including medication management or psychological services when appropriate.

SUMMARY/CONCLUSION

The professional school counselor can play an important role in advocating for students with intellectual disability. This role may include being part of the IEP team as an advocate for the student to receive appropriate services at school. The professional school counselor may be involved in obtaining information regarding the student's functioning in the school and home settings that will assist with forming appropriate IEP goals, as well as an effective ITP to maximize the student's community functioning upon graduating from high school. Issues of sexuality and social skills may be effectively addressed by interventions offered by the professional school counselor. Table 65.3 provides some resources for professionals helping students with intellectual disability.

(Note: See the CD-ROM for a list of references.)

TABLE 65.3

RESOURCES RELATED TO INTELLECTUAL DISABILITY

American Association on Intellectual and Developmental Disabilities (AAIDD)
444 North Capitol Street NW, Suite 846, Washington, DC 20001-1512;
    202/387-1968; 800/424-3688; www.aaidd.org

The Arc of the United States
1010 Wayne Avenue, Suite 650, Silver Spring, MD 20910; 301/565-3842;
    www.thearc.org; e-mail: Info@thearc.org; Web publications: www.TheArcPub.com

Division on Developmental Disabilities, The Council for Exceptional Children
1110 North Glebe Road, Suite 300, Arlington, VA 22201-5704; 888/232-7733; 703/620-3660;
    TTY: 866/915-5000; www.dddcec.org; e-mail: cec@cec.sped.org

National Dissemination Center for Children with Disabilities (NICHCY)
www.nichcy.org/pubs/factshe/fs8txt.htm

This source contains information regarding mental retardation, including an eight-page handout that can be used by teachers or families to help understand mental retardation. There is also a link with materials to help students understand the IEP process so they can participate in the development of their IEP (www.nichcy.org/stuguid.asp#st1).

CHAPTER 66

STUDENTS WITH LEARNING DISABILITIES:
COUNSELING ISSUES AND STRATEGIES

Adriana G. McEachern

Preview

Approximately 49% of students in exceptional education classes have been diagnosed with learning disabilities (LDs). Professional school counselors can help these students be successful academically and cope with personal and social issues imposed by their disability. I will discuss LD issues relevant to professional school counselors and counseling strategies that can be used to help these students.

Learning disabilities (LDs), intriguing and puzzling disorders, are of concern to educators, parents, researchers, professional school counselors, and students (Coplin & Morgan, 1988; Kirk, Gallagher, & Anastasiow, 2000). The intriguing aspects of LD are that there are multiple causes and multiple types, and even students with the same type of LD may have different sets of deficiencies. LDs are puzzling because these students may have normal or even gifted intelligence, yet they are not always successful in school. Researchers have been studying LD since the 1800s, and the term *learning disabilities* was first proposed by parents and Samuel Kirk in 1963 to describe the condition (Kirk et al., 2000). Although relatively young in terms of label, LD is the largest special education category of disability, comprising 49.2% of all children requiring school-based special education services (U.S. Department of Education, 2002). There are estimates of 1,000 newly diagnosed cases each day (Mercer, 1997), with twice as many males as females diagnosed with LDs (Oswald, Best, Coutinho, & Nagle 2003).

DEFINITIONS AND PREVALENCE

Learning disorder is an umbrella term that refers to disorders that affect the understanding or use of language, written or spoken, that manifest in difficulties with listening, thinking, reading, writing, and mathematical calculations (U.S. Office of Education, as cited in Blackbourn, Patton, & Trainor, 2004). These disorders affect students' ability to either interpret what they see and hear, or link information from different parts of the brain. In most states, students identified with LD must meet three criteria:

- Inclusionary criteria to establish a statistically significant discrepancy between academic achievement and the capacity to learn (Blackbourn et al., 2004; Brody & Mills, 1997; Marsh & Wolfe, 1999); that is, achievement test scores one or more standard deviations below ability estimates indicate LD (Mendaglio, 1993).
- Exclusionary criteria to establish the LD is not a result of a visual or hearing impairment, mental retardation, serious emotional disturbance, or cultural differences.

- Need criterion to establish students have a specific need for support services in special education to help them learn (Turnbull, Turnbull, Shank, & Smith, 2004).

To identify a need for services, the Individuals With Disabilities Education Improvement Act of 2004 (IDEIA) recommended that general education teachers use scientifically based teaching practices and curriculum-based assessment to regularly document student progress. Students who do not show adequate progress may be referred for determination of eligibility for more intensive interventions in a special education program (Wright & Wright, 2005).

CHARACTERISTICS AND IDENTIFICATION OF STUDENTS WITH LD

LD can manifest itself in several ways, such as specific difficulties with spoken and written language, coordination, self-control, or attention deficits. Students with LD may experience problems with learning tasks, memory, and paired-associate learning (Bender, 2001). Research indicates that these impairments are due to central nervous system dysfunction that causes the brain and the perceptual systems of the brain to work differently from the way they function in students without LD (Kirk et al., 2000; Obrzut & Hynd, 1983; Rourke, 1994). Nutritional factors, such as food allergies, have been suggested as another possible cause for LD, and recent evidence has linked prevalence of LD with heredity (Thompson & Rudolph, 2000).

Characteristics of students with LD will differ among individuals who may exhibit deficits in the cognitive, motor, or social domains (Cartwright, Cartwright, & Ward, 1995). Those with cognitive difficulties will experience problems in reading, arithmetic, or thinking. Some have problems with gross or perceptual-motor skills while others have social deficiencies. Reading deficiencies are the most common among students with LD, and the term *dyslexia* (now referred to as Developmental Reading Disorder in the *Diagnostic and Statistical Manual of Mental Disorders–Fourth Edition, Text Revision*, 2004) has become synonymous with a reading disability. Those with reading problems may not be able to decode the sounds of the letters in the alphabet that result in slow oral reading and poor reading comprehension. These students are not likely to read for pleasure (Fletcher et al., 2002). Many students with LD may have problems with written composition and exhibit poor spelling, handwriting, and difficulty with grammar and punctuation (Graham, 2004). A student with language deficits may have difficulty understanding what is said and expressing him- or herself verbally. Approximately two thirds of students with LD have mathematics difficulties, are unable to learn math concepts, and will have difficulty managing money (Geary, 2003).

Other characteristics of these students include disorganization, inattentiveness, lack of motivation, and poor problem-solving skills (Smith & Luckasson, 1995). Toro, Weissberg, Guare, and Liebenstein (1990) found that students with LD were not able to generate as many alternative solutions to problem-solving situations when compared to students without LD. Some children may also experience hyperactivity and impulsivity and are distracted easily (Ariel, 1992). Students with LD also tended to be more disruptive in class, had more classroom behavior problems, and showed less tolerance for frustration (Toro et al., 1990). In addition, they were more prone than their peers without LD to have family-related problems such as financial difficulties and lack of educational stimulation.

Studies have shown that LD students have lower academic self-concepts than their normal achieving peers (Hagborg, 1996). They often experience difficulty making and keeping friends and may demonstrate inappropriate social behavior (Cartwright et al., 1995; Thompson & Rudolph, 2000). One study that asked individuals with LD to rank order areas in which they felt deficient showed that they listed social relationships and skills, developing self-esteem and confidence, and overcoming dependence as the top three areas (Chelser, cited in Skinner & Schenck, 1992).

The federal government outlines specific procedures for identifying students with LD and a process that must be followed in evaluating these students under the Education for All Handicapped Children Act of 1975, the Individuals With Disabilities Education Act Amendments of 1997, and the Individuals With Disabilities Education Improvement Act of 2004 (Cartwright et al., 1995; Kirk et al., 2000; Turnbull, Turnbull, & Wehmeyer, 2007). Failure to follow this process can result in civil court actions, state and federal sanctions, and loss of funding for the school district. A multidisciplinary team (e.g., teachers, school psychologist, social worker, professional school counselor, behavioral specialist) must conduct the evaluation, and the child's parents must be involved and give consent. Professional school counselors often participate in the multidisciplinary team (Parette & Holder-Brown, 1992). Assessment instruments must be administered in the child's native language, and more than one criterion (e.g., verbal or written expression, listening comprehension, reading, mathematics reasoning and calculations) must be evident for the diagnosis. An Individualized Education Program (IEP) is developed based on the unique needs of the student (Ariel, 1992). The IEP specifies the educational and related services (e.g., counseling) that will be provided and acts as a monitoring device to assure the student is in fact receiving services as agreed to by the parents and school personnel. The IEP must include (a) an assessment (e.g., medical, personal–social, behavioral functioning, current educational performance, academic achievement, cognitive and motor functioning); (b) goals and short and long-term objectives; (c) educational services to be provided, names of individuals who will provide such services, and specific timelines; and (d) annual evaluation procedures.

PERSONAL, SOCIAL, AND EDUCATIONAL NEEDS

Students with LD often experience frustration in completing day-to-day tasks and assignments. They may display fear of failure, fear of learning, and approach tasks with reticence. They may say, "I can't do this," "I don't know how," or "I'll never learn this." In addition, they may demonstrate low frustration tolerance and be prone to exhibit temper tantrums and disruptive behavior when confronted with learning situations (Ariel, 1992; Turnbull et al., 2004). Feelings of failure, worthlessness, and low self-esteem can further compound learning problems; therefore, students with LD often need individualized counseling to help them cope with their feelings and adjust to their disability (Thompson & Rudolph, 2000; Vernon, 1993). They will need encouragement and support from parents, teachers, professional school counselors, and other significant adults in their lives. They will also need to develop academic strategies that will help them cope with the specific deficiencies of their LD.

Students who have difficulty forming interpersonal relationships, or who may act socially inappropriately, will benefit from group counseling and social skills training. Students with behavior problems can be helped with behavior modification and contingency contracting strategies implemented by the professional school counselor as well as teachers in the classroom. High school–age students will need help in developing career goals and plans (Skinner & Schenck, 1992). Students with LD also need professional school counselors to act as advocates for them to assure they receive the services identified in the IEP.

COUNSELING STRATEGIES

The use of brief, solution-focused counseling has been recommended and proven effective for use with middle and high school students with LD (Amatea, 1989; Littrell, Malia, & Vanderwood, 1995). This approach can be implemented in both individual and group counseling interventions. Thompson and Littrell (1998) used a four-step, brief counseling model with a small sample of high school students with LD who were experiencing personal problems. The four steps included (1) identifying and defining the problem; (2) discussing previous attempted solutions and outcomes; (3) using the Miracle Question (i.e., "Suppose that one night, while you were asleep, there was a miracle and this problem was solved. How would you know? What would be different? How will parents, friends, and teachers know without your saying a word about it?" [de Shazer, 1988, p. 4]); and (4) having students generate a task or activity to accomplish their desired goal or goals. The researchers reported that all students participating in the study made progress toward their goals, with all but one reaching their desired goals. Positive changes in cognition and affect were also reported.

Play techniques, art, music, and expressive writings can be used with elementary school students in individual counseling to elicit and express feelings toward the disability, school-related experiences, peer conflicts, and family difficulties (Lockhart, 2003; Newsome, 2003). These interventions provide a nonthreatening and creative outlet for students that can be adapted to their developmental levels, needs, and unique concerns (Newsome, 2003). When using play techniques with children with hyperactivity who may become overstimulated by the toys and the playroom, Carmichael (2006) recommended limit setting. For example, the child is instructed to select five or six toys initially. If the child shows symptoms of overstimulation, the toys are reduced by one. Expressive writing activities such as journaling and timed writing exercises can encourage self-exploration and reflection (Bradley & Gould, 1999; Gladding, 2005).

Some contend that group counseling activities may be more effective than individual counseling in helping students with LD address social, personal, and self-esteem problems because of the nature of the interaction with others (Elbaum & Vaughn, 2001; Lombana, 1992). For example, group counseling has been proven to be successful with students with LD to increase self-esteem, increase social skills and competence, and improve behavior (Omizo & Omizo, 1988). Small-group activities that include the use of role play and puppets with elementary-age children with LD have improved school attendance and reduced suspensions (Schmidt & Biles, 1985). Educational groups at all grade levels can help students with LD identify and use learning strategies and techniques to help them compensate for academic deficiencies (Baum, 1990). Some of these strategies include checking for spelling errors before submitting assignments, using a calculator to assure accuracy, writing down all homework assignments, and finding alternative ways of learning (e.g., films, visitations, hands-on activities, use of technology). Bibliotherapy and audiovisual resources with elementary-age children with LD can also be used to demonstrate appropriate behavior in certain situations (Vernon, 1993). Students who have difficulty remembering can be taught mnemonic strategies (memory devices and strategies); strategies created by the students themselves are most effective (Hunt Riegel, Mayle, & McCarthy-Henkel, 1988). Academic interventions with an emphasis on peer-collaborative work and feedback have proven successful with middle school students in enhancing academic abilities and self-esteem (Elbaum & Vaughn, 2001). One example is a group designed by Baumberger and Harper (1999) for male fifth and sixth graders titled, "Understanding and Coping With Learning Disabilities." This group model is designed to help students with LDs understand and value their specific learning styles, compensate for their learning problems, and learn ways to cope with feelings of low self-esteem and replace these with feelings of self-worth.

COGNITIVE-BEHAVIORAL APPROACHES

Cognitive-behavioral counseling techniques can be applied in individual and group counseling to teach skills and coping strategies. These techniques can be especially useful for students with LD who demonstrate inattentiveness, impulsivity, and hyperactivity (Williams & Mennuti, 1997); however, it can also be used with students who exhibit fear of learning and low self-concept. Designed for older elementary and adolescent students, cognitive-behavioral approaches can be most effective when combined with concurrent consultation and training for parents and teachers. The professional school counselor links the school and home components, thus providing an integrative, multimodal, holistic, collaborative approach to address the student's needs. Group sessions and parent and teacher training can occur simultaneously, and the professional school counselor may want to provide these opportunities. The objectives of this approach should include (a) increasing knowledge of, and adjustment to, LD; (b) teaching the cognitive-behavioral approach so that faulty beliefs and distorted thoughts can be disputed and new thoughts, feelings, and behavior can be generated; (c) changing self-defeating, self-deprecating, absolutist language; and (d) changing behaviors and feelings associated with negative thinking patterns. Behavioral self-management should be included along with contingency contracting and weekly cognitive–behavioral homework assignments to monitor students' motivation throughout the intervention process (Corey, 2006; Williams & Mennuti, 1997).

Omizo and Omizo (1987) successfully used a group counseling approach with students to eliminate self-defeating behavior and increase self-esteem and internal locus of control of middle school students with LD. The intervention consisted of seven weekly sessions, 1 ½ hours each, that focused on helping students identify self-defeating behaviors, the feelings and consequences associated with these behaviors, and the choices needed to eliminate them. A visual-imagery activity was used in which group members visualized barriers that prevented them from eliminating self-defeating behaviors and ways of surmounting these barriers.

STRESS REDUCTION, IMAGERY, AND RELAXATION TRAINING

In the same way Omizo and Omizo (1987) incorporated guided visual imagery into their group counseling intervention, professional school counselors can use visual imagery, relaxation, and stress reduction techniques in individual and group counseling sessions (Gladding, 2005; Romas & Sharma, 2000; Vernon, 1993). Visual imagery is a powerful technique that can be used to help students visualize beforehand situations that may be potentially threatening or stressful (e.g., speaking in front of the class, taking an exam, asking a peer to a social event). Regular practice of visual imagery has been shown to improve competitive performance (Romas & Sharma, 2000). Autosuggestion or talking with oneself can also help these students build self-confidence and self-esteem. Students can couple self-talk with other relaxation methods such as progressive muscle relaxation or meditation. Some examples of self-talk are, "I can behave calmly in stressful situations," "I can perform to the best of my abilities," and "I am a happy and competent person." Students can make up their own self-affirmations and repeat them periodically throughout the day.

CAREER COUNSELING

In comparison to their non-LD peers, students with LD tend to lack skills in identifying and attaining career choices and have been described as being less mature in work-related attitudes (Rojewski, 1992). Further, many students and their families are not aware of the contingencies of the school-to-work process and will need help from professional school counselors to understand how this process works (Baker, 2000; Battles, Dickens-Wright, & Murphy, 1998; Boone, 1992). An important factor for professional school counselors to understand when providing career services is the effect of the disability on specific job requirements of chosen careers; these need to be presented realistically to students (Lockhart, 2003). Students with LD also need knowledge and skill development on the job search, completing employment applications and résumés, conducting effective job interviews, and following up with prospective employers (Farley & Johnson, 1999).

Students with LD who are planning to attend postsecondary institutions following graduation need assistance with activities related to educational planning such as evaluating available training prospects and materials, completing applications for postsecondary training, taking entrance examinations such as the *Scholastic Aptitude Test* (SAT) and the *American College Testing Program* (ACT), setting personal goals, and accessing self-help resources. Professional school counselors can empower students with LD to take greater control of their lives by informing them about their legal rights related to discrimination in employment or educational settings. It is important for these students to know that services from the Division of Vocational Rehabilitation may help defray the cost of educational training and provide job evaluation and placement assistance (Dowdy & Evers, 1996). Students with disabilities may need special accommodations (e.g., tutors, academic support, readers, books on tape, psychoeducational assessment, disability services, and counseling) and considerations on the job sites or educational facilities (Wood & Beale, 1991). Having students engage in group experiences during their junior and senior years can help facilitate transitions based on their career choices. McEachern and Kenny (2007) recommend two psychoeducational group models that can be used with high school students with disabilities to help transition from school-to-work and school-to-postsecondary education. Group interventions should be documented in the students' IEPs and written into their Transition Plans (Dowdy & Evers, 1996).

Computer assisted career guidance systems such as DISCOVER (ACT; 2000; ACT; 1984), the *System of Interactive Guidance and Information* (SIGI and SIGI Plus; Katz, 1975), and Internet resources can help high school students become more involved in the career awareness and exploration process (Zunker, 2002). Students can work individually on computers and receive immediate feedback. Access to large databases at the local, state, and national levels can provide students with college admissions, financial aid, vocational–technical training, internships, and scholarship information. Professional school counselors can help students interpret and discuss the results of their searches along with helping them with résumé preparation, employment interviewing, conducting job searches, and learning other career-related skills by using computer-assisted guidance programs and the Internet. Professional school counselors may want to purchase the book *The Internet: A Tool for Career Planning* (Harris-Bowlsbey, Dikel, & Sampson, 2002), published by the National Career Development Association (telephone 866-367-6232).

PEER FACILITATION PROGRAMS

Peer helpers can be used to work with students with LD to help them adjust to school situations and to act as special friends (Myrick, 2002; Vernon, 1993). Professional school counselors can pair trained peer helpers with students with LD based on the student's special needs and interests. These helpers act as positive role models, conflict mediators, advisors to help students with LD navigate successfully in the school environment, and tutors to help them improve academically. One peer-assisted academic learning strategy, researched in kindergarten to secondary education classrooms, that has been shown to be efficacious in improving reading in LD students is the Peer-Assisted Learning Strategies program (PALS; Fuchs & Fuchs, 2005). LD students are paired with students with strong academic skills for about 30 minutes of instruction 3 to 5 days per week. Students helped by their PALS's peers improved in word recognition, reading fluency, and reading comprehension. The professional school counselor can facilitate and monitor peer helper interactions and provide supervisory feedback during peer-helper classes and meetings.

TEACHER AND PARENT CONSULTATION

Some have suggested that parents and teachers tend to have more negative feelings about students with LD than they do about non-LD students (Rothman & Cosden, 1995). Further, some teachers feel underprepared to work with students with disabilities in their classrooms (Smith & Luckasson, 1995) and may view the students' special needs as problematic (Wicks-Nelson & Israel, 2003). Professional school counselors can consult with teachers individually or in groups to assist in building skills and developing effective academic interventions. Professional school counselors can help teachers learn more about the effects of LD on students' learning and classroom behavior by conducting workshops and in-service trainings during faculty meetings. Some classroom strategies that have worked with students with LD include the following:

- Rearranging seats so students face away from distractions and are seated in areas accessible to school personnel who can help them focus their attention.
- Assigning smaller amounts of work (e.g., 8 math problems instead of 20).
- Providing demonstrations of expected tasks and giving explanations in brief, clear steps.
- Organizing materials in color-coded folders.
- Moving around the room to check on students' progress.
- Having students write down instructions.
- Using colored highlighters to emphasize important information.
- Repeating important points.
- Tape-recording directions.
- Using written checklists.
- Using individualized cues and prompts.
- Presenting material in a variety of ways (e.g., visually, orally, kinesthetically).
- Rewarding students for demonstrating appropriate behaviors.
- Using media and technology to enhance instruction (Hunt Riegel et al., 1988; Mastropieri & Scruggs, 2007).

Similarly, groups can be conducted for parents to help them strategize ways to help their children be successful. One study showed that students of parents who participated in a 9-week parent effectiveness workshop improved their self-concept in comparison to students whose parents did not participate (Elbaum & Vaughn, 2001). In addition to parent effectiveness workshops, professional school counselors can also help parents by teaching them (a) behavior management techniques; (b) how to help their children with school assignments; (c) how to structure the home and study environment; and (d) how to communicate more effectively with their children and teachers (Lombana, 1992). Many parents need help understanding their children's behavioral reactions to their disability and the challenges these reactions present. Parents will need assistance in learning how to focus on their child's strengths rather than the disability (Baumberger & Harper, 1999). Support groups can help parents share successful strategies and increase awareness that others share similar frustrations and challenges (Lombana, 1992; Thompson & Rudolph, 2000).

ADVOCACY AND COLLABORATION

Professional school counselors can advocate for LD students to ensure that their special needs are being met (Lockhart, 2003; Quigney, 2005). Advocacy begins by helping to ensure that students with LD are appropriately identified so that educational and counseling services can be provided to facilitate school success. Professional school counselors can facilitate the identification process by educating teachers, parents, and other school staff on the characteristics and needs of these students. Advocacy entails continuous, collaborative consultation with multidisciplinary team members to effectively pool resources, identify and resolve problems, and share decision-making and responsibilities for the implementation of educational strategies (VanTassel-Baska, 1991). It is also critical that professional school counselors serve as members of their school improvement and strategic planning committees as other venues for advocacy.

Professional school counselors can help parents become effective advocates for their children. Parents need information on the academic effects of LD, public policy and laws related to the disability and educational placement, the IEP process, and special educational programs that can help their children (Lockhart, 2003; Maker & Udall, 1985). Professional school counselors must work collaboratively with community agency personnel and appropriate specialists that can help students with LD and their families outside the school setting (Lockhart, 2003). In addition, professional school counselors need to demonstrate cultural sensitivity and understanding with parents who, because of their ethnicity or recent immigrant status, may not be fluent in English or knowledgeable about the expectations of the school or of their child's disability (Lockhart, 2003). Finally, students with LD need to be taught to be their own advocates. Self-advocacy skills can help these students become more involved in decision making that affects their academic and career goals. Advocacy skills can be taught and practiced by students in small-group and large-group guidance interventions (Bailey, Getch, & Chen-Hayes, 2007).

Summary/Conclusion

Learning disabilities affect the understanding or use of language and can manifest in different ways for various students. These may include cognitive deficiencies in writing, spelling, reading, arithmetic, and thinking; gross or perceptual-motor skills may also be affected. Problems with hyperactivity, impulsivity, distractibility, problem solving, and social skills may be evident. Students coping with LD may experience low self-esteem, feelings of failure, frustration, and difficulty making and keeping friends.

Counseling strategies implemented through individual and group counseling can help students with LD at all levels to develop effective problem-solving, social, and academic skills that will help them be successful in school. Some of these include brief-solution focused counseling, play techniques, expressive arts and writings, role-play, puppets (elementary age), bibliotherapy, cognitive-behavioral techniques, stress reduction, relaxation, guided visual imagery, and career exploration. To help these students compensate for academic difficulties, education-focused groups can be conducted to teach students specific techniques such as mnemonic strategies, organizing school materials, using calculators and computers to check for math and spelling errors, and the use of audiovisual and other instructional aids. Students with LD can be paired with their higher functioning peers for tutoring and social support.

The federal government has delineated specific procedures in the Education for All Handicapped Children Act of 1975 and IDEIA (2004) that involve a multidisciplinary approach to identify and place students with LD in appropriate learning environments. An Individualized Educational Program is developed for each student that outlines the educational, social, and counseling services that will be provided. Professional school counselors can also conduct workshops with teachers and parents to assist them in dealing more effectively with the needs of these students in the classroom and at home. Support groups can help parents connect with others who share similar concerns. Advocacy and collaboration with school staff and community personnel is critical to ensure that the needs and rights of students with LD are met. Teaching students with LD self-advocacy skills can also help them become more self-sufficient in making academic and career choices.

(Note: See the CD-ROM for a list of references.)

CHAPTER 67

HELPING STUDENTS WITH SEVERE BEHAVIORAL PROBLEMS

Gregory R. Janson

Preview

Professional school counselors are often called on to provide support, crisis resolution, and treatment and prevention strategies for students with severe behavioral problems at every grade level. The interventions that offer the most promising approach to helping students are systemic in nature, in which the professional school counselors serves as both counselor and facilitator, bringing together students, teachers, parents, administrators, and staff. In this chapter, I present strategies for working with all these groups within the context of the extended school community.

Teachers and administrators polled just 50 or 60 years ago reported their most significant behavioral challenges were gum chewing, cutting in line, running in hallways, talking out of turn or making noise, and violating the school's dress code. More recent studies show that these minor offenses have been replaced by robbery, assault, drug abuse, pregnancy, and sexually transmitted infections. Bullying, victimization, and the lingering terror created by school shootings are now a permanent part of the educational landscape. During this same time frame, experimentation with alcohol, drugs, smoking, and reckless behaviors have begun in early adolescence and even middle childhood. Against this overwhelming backdrop, the professional school counselor is the one individual who has the skills and the mandate to facilitate a systemic approach to managing severe behavior that includes all constituent groups: teachers, students, administrators, staff, and parents.

SCHOOL AND COMMUNITY CLIMATE

The first step to managing severe behavior in a school setting is to understand the broader systems in which it occurs. When students live in environments that are dangerous or chaotic—at home, in school, or in the community—they become physically and emotionally reactive. A community–school climate assessment, conducted together with your colleagues, puts student behaviors in context and helps to discriminate between violent reactions to difficult circumstances and more individual pathology. Is your community a safe one? Is your school a place where students *feel* safe, where they can learn without looking over their shoulder or worrying about being bullied in the restrooms or hallways? Do students look forward to coming to school? Are their lives at home safe? What looks like anger or depression in a classroom might well be an appropriate reaction to the stress of living in a dangerous environment. Some students cope by becoming the identified patient; others become the troublemaker.

UNDERSTANDING SEVERE BEHAVIOR

Behavior serves a purpose, even when it does not seem to make sense because it antagonizes others and isolates students or appears self-destructive (Dreikurs, 1972, 1990; Kottman, 1995; Sweeney, 1989). Severe behavior can be linked to power, control and significance, attention, self-protection, anger, hate, guilt, sadness, and resentment. In the absence of overt disruptive, aggressive behaviors, there may be symptoms of anxiety, dissociation, or depression related to disorders of attachment (James, 1989, 1994; Stosny, 1995). Severe behavior is often associated with a history of victimization, trauma, abuse, and neglect—which can make it challenging to separate issues that are developmental or environmental from more pathological issues. It is well known that trauma "freezes" or impairs emotional development, but when a 6-foot tall, 160-pound teenager is angrily looming, theory is not the first thing that comes to mind. The fact that a history of untreated trauma can lead a 16-year-old to act and respond with the emotional maturity of an 11-year-old is quickly forgotten.

Conceptually, severe behavior in all its forms is an expression of the limited cognitive, affective, and physical resources that students have available to them at any given developmental stage. The more distressed the individual, the more maladaptive the behavior and the greater its frequency, intensity, and duration. Severe behavioral problems are seldom limited to classrooms and are accompanied by a host of other problems that can include substance abuse, expressions of anger through vandalism or violence, depression, anxiety, suicidal thoughts or behaviors, self-mutilation, or inappropriate sexual activity.

Under many disciplinary codes, behaviors that are considered unacceptable are labeled *severe* and get lumped together. Smoking marijuana on school grounds and threatening another student with a knife both earn suspension or expulsion, but they are radically different acts. Dyeing one's hair black is not the same as bringing a pint of vodka to school. Fidgeting and refusing to follow instructions due to the anxiety of being homeless or because of familial stress may lead to the same behaviors in class as a student with attention-deficit/hyperactivity disorder, but the interventions will need to be radically different.

Good behavioral assessment is an ongoing process that should be broad based, longitudinal, and consider all the systems in which the student functions as well as the student's character and temperament. Careful assessment can place behaviors in context and help to structure consequences that contribute to the student's growth and learning. This is where the professional school counselor's input is crucial to formulating an effective educational disciplinary policy.

RELATIONSHIP AND GUIDANCE ARE CURATIVE

Even with all the dramatic changes that have altered schools over the past 50 years, one constant remains: A trusted teacher is still the person students turn to when life at home is unsafe and no one is there to help (Doyle, 2003). What changes student behavior positively and permanently is relationship and guidance (Janson & King, 2006). Successful interventions adhere to the basic principles of guidance and provide a corrective emotional experience. Harsh discipline, behaviorally based interventions, and behavior punishment–reward systems are seldom effective with difficult students, because they rely on authority and power. Once the environment changes or the source of authority is out of sight, the student's behavior often reverts to "same old, same old." Worse, these types of behavioral interventions can actually reinforce maladaptive behavior, creating a cycle of reciprocal negative interactions and constituting a form of emotional abuse (Garbarino, 1978, 1979, 1987; Shumba, 2002a, 2002b; see Chapter 84). In effect, teachers can become part of the problem (Janson & King, 2006; Krugman & Krugman, 1984).

CULTURE AND LANGUAGE

When families immigrate to the United States, students who learn English are seldom taught feeling words, making it sometimes challenging to correctly interpret affective reactions. For example, a teacher could easily misinterpret a student response as anger when the real emotion is frustration. Students who learn English faster than their parents may become mediators between the family and the outside world, a position of power and control that may create problems in relating to adults and authority figures at school. Part of your intervention might involve helping a student's parents access the resources they need to master a new language. This can do a great deal to reduce stress at home and stabilize the family.

THE PHYSIOLOGY OF ANGER AND STRESS-MANAGEMENT TECHNIQUES

Students who display aggressive and disruptive behaviors make it easy to forget that it takes two to fight: Every angry person needs another person to fight with (Sweeney, 1989). Anger can be overwhelming, and few of us are trained to deal with angry confrontation. Awareness of how these reactions affect us, and how they can be minimized with specific relaxation techniques, is a key component of dealing with any severe behavioral challenge. Educating others about anger, anger management, and relaxation techniques is a vital role for professional school counselors (Kassinove, 1995).

ATTEND TO THE PHYSIOLOGICAL ASPECTS OF SEVERE Bbehavior—YOURS AND THEIRS

When we are confronted by severe behavior, defensiveness, fear, anger, and the activation of our fight–flight reflex can leave us breathing faster, heart thumping in our chests, dry-mouthed and sweaty palmed. Our stomachs knot, our jaws clench—sometimes hard enough to make the muscles bulge so that little vein that runs up our foreheads suddenly stands out in stark relief. An angry reaction can be seen by anyone and can raise the level of potential danger. Exercise self-awareness of your bodily reactions as you evaluate a potential threat. If you can sit, sit. Sitting interrupts and decreases the force directed against you when the student suddenly has to look down at you instead of going toe to toe. Lower your voice so the other person must be silent to hear it. Breathe slowly, talk quietly and calmly, and offer choices. Acknowledge the student's emotion, communicate your understanding, and identify an acceptable alternative course of action (Landreth, 2002).

USE REGULATION AND MEDITATION

Most students have trouble with impulse control and with regulating their emotional thermostats. Group training does not have to single out students with behavioral problems. All students can benefit from identifying their emotional triggers and becoming aware of their bodily responses, which can be countered by deep breathing, disengagement, progressive muscle relaxation, and emotional self-regulation (Fink, 1979). When severe behavior occurs, make your office a safe haven. Keep a comfy chair in your office with a set of headphones and a quilt. Have older students put the headphones on and listen to an album like Enya's *Watermark* or any slow music with a soothing rhythm. The quilt provides warmth to counter the effects of stress and gives a sense of comfort and security. For most students, 10 to 15 minutes is all that is required for the crisis to pass and their bodies and minds to settle down. Secondary benefits accrue in the form of strengthened relationship; even with consequences, relationships grow stronger when boundaries are pushed to the limit and the relationship remains intact.

COUNSELING INTERVENTIONS

An effective systemic approach requires building relationships with and between everyone in the system: students, parents, teachers, staff, and administrators. When these groups communicate with each other in meaningful ways, everyone wins. This is a challenging task under the best of circumstances and not always compatible with the minutiae of your everyday professional responsibilities. It means leaving your office for the uncertainty of the hallways, cafeteria, and other areas of the school where you can interact with people in genuine, personal ways that build relationships outside the confines of the school counselor's office, where relationships are more formally and strictly defined (Hazler, 1998). It also means helping others to leave their comfort zone and consider ways to enhance their ability to form positive relationships with difficult students and their parents. Successful interventions will depend in large part on their involvement and support for your efforts.

COUNSELING INTERVENTIONS WITH STUDENTS: THEY NOTICE YOU NOTICE

A number of counseling interventions have been shown to help students with severe behavioral problems adjust to the academic environment. These include (a) accentuating the positive and personal; (b) not expecting gratitude or appreciation; (c) having faith in their ability to succeed; (d) providing encouragement; (e) using student interests; (f) self-disclosing; (g) experiencing real reactions; and (h) addressing hunger and homelessness.

ACCENTUATE THE POSITIVE AND PERSONAL

Notice positive points, and comment on them! Can't find a positive point? Search until you do. Make your enthusiasm and optimism contagious. An unexpected word of encouragement makes students feel acknowledged and valued, but is particularly effective with troubled students. They may seem unresponsive or indifferent, *but they will notice you noticed!*

BE PREPARED TO DRIVE ON ONE-WAY STREETS

Effective relationship building with difficult students means being without expectations for gratitude or appreciation. Counselors are trained to give clients unconditional positive regard and empathy, regardless of the client's attitude. This may be more difficult for other professionals. Helping them see opportunities to build relationships even as students push the limits can be as simple as acknowledging students' underlying feelings when their behavior earns unpleasant consequences: "It must be tough to have people telling you what to do all the time and have to deal with these consequences."

HAVE FAITH IN STUDENTS, AND COMMUNICATE THAT FAITH

No one can predict future behavior, and to do so with a troubled student only reinforces a negative expectation that can become a self-fulfilling prophecy. Faith and encouragement counter discouragement and disaffection; at least *one* affirmative, predicable relationship with an adult is necessary for positive growth and development (Hamburg, 1986). You may or may not see immediate positive results from your actions, but it is not unusual for many counselors (and teachers) to hear from students long after they leave school. And what they often hear is, "You were the only person who believed in me," not "You really knew a lot about physics."

PROVIDE ENCOURAGEMENT AND POSITIVE REINFORCEMENT

Separate students from behaviors. Make it a point to share how effective encouragement and personal warmth can be. Be the person who says, "I know that you have what you need to accomplish what you need to accomplish, and when you are ready, you will do it," or "I may not approve of the direction you are taking, but I will wait for you as long as it takes." There are a number of resources that provide the specific language and techniques of encouragement you can share with teachers and administrators (Dreikurs, 1972, 1990; Sweeney, 1989).

USE WHAT STUDENTS ARE INTERESTED IN TO BUILD RELATIONSHIPS

What do they care about? When you see them in the hall, are they wearing a university sweatshirt or team colors? In the cafeteria, do you see them in a shirt with the logo of a band that you or your own children like? Find small starting places to build your relationships.

RISK SHARING YOURSELF AND WHO YOU ARE

This makes you real to young persons who pay far more attention to how you act and who you are rather than what you say. Counselors receive extensive training in self-disclosure and are able to practice these skills under supervision, but teachers, staff, and administrators may feel awkward, uncomfortable, or vulnerable making self-disclosures. Even a brief training can help others gain a degree of comfort and practice talking about themselves with difficult students. Good topics include revealing what they like, what they succeeded at, what they are not good at. What teams do they root for? What foods do they like? How about music, bands, cars, movies? These tidbits need not be major disclosures, but each interaction forms another strand of potential relationship, another possible connection that starts the process of reducing a student's isolation, anger, and loneliness.

DISCOMFORT, FRUSTRATION, ANGER, AND EVEN FEAR ARE APPROPRIATE REACTIONS TO FEEL

Students with behavioral problems can be frustrating, aggravating, difficult to work with, and hard to like. Daunting to engage, they are often intimidating, menacing, or scary to peers and teachers alike. Accepting your own discomfort and validating teachers' discomfort is a solid starting point. Many of these students are unaware of the impact they have on people, or they revel in the negative attention. When their behavior alienates others, it contributes to more isolation, anger, sadness, and withdrawal. We are entitled to our anger, but only at a student's behavior, never the personhood of the student. Interactions with students who are depressed, despondent, or who might be suffering from a self-destructive eating disorder can leave anyone feeling inadequate, unsure, and concerned about the possibility of self-injury or suicide. Have we done the right thing? Helped enough in ways that were helpful? Uncertainty, guilt and worry are normal reactions. They are a part of working with at-risk students.

HUNGER AND HOMELESSNESS

These are chronic stressors for growing numbers of students and their families. Concentrating in math class may be impossible when you are hungry. Accepting a verbal reprimand from a teacher without lashing out may be hard if you are living in a car or have shuffled from couch to couch in the homes of friends and relatives. Like many school districts, does yours need to develop contingency plans to help manage the emotional trauma of being homeless while at the same time helping with shelter, food, clothing, and hygiene? Loss of school and attendance records is a major challenge for homeless families.

SPECIAL DEVELOPMENTAL EMPHASES WITH STUDENTS

Depending on your work setting, different types of interventions may be necessary, based on the developmental stage of your students. For elementary students, play therapy techniques are highly effective and can be adapted for use by teachers in the classroom and by parents at home. Every elementary school should have a playroom or special area where students can retreat to play through stressful experiences and difficult feelings. Time alone in a playroom or with a counselor teaches students the helpfulness of disengagement without the punitive aspects of a typical time-out. It teaches responsibility and pride in the ability to self-regulate emotions. The benefits of play therapy can be woven into and across an entire curriculum (Van Hoorn, Scales, Nourot, & Alward,

1999), and there are a number of books filled with techniques and ideas for working with students who seem unreachable (Axline, 1964, 1969; Kottman, 1995; Webb, 1991). If a time-out is the only option, 5 minutes is just as effective as 20 minutes for most students (McGuffin, 1991).

For students in middle school, transitioning from the relative safety of an elementary school to a middle school can be harrowing. Bullying is commonplace and is likely to be a major issue as students begin to experiment with their physical and psychological power. Victims and bystanders often share experiences that are characterized by a full range of traumatic psychological and physiological reactions that follow many of them into later life (Janson, Carney, Hazler, & Oh, in press; Janson & Hazler, 2004). Bullies, like their victims, are also more likely to experience future relationship problems and a past history of bullying is associated with later criminal behavior (Huesmann, 1994). Counseling interventions that address all three groups (i.e., bullies, victims, and bystanders) in a manner that stresses community and cooperation are those most likely to minimize the negative consequences of aggression and violence (Hazler, 1996).

The predictable struggles of adolescence can be magnified by traumatic experiences from childhood that may emerge symptomatically in high school. Students may self-medicate with drugs and alcohol as well as experiment with them. When social skills are poorly developed, compensatory isolation, loneliness, self-injurious behaviors, aggression, and other severe behaviors may emerge. Teachers can help to identify students who would benefit from some kind of training in communication, assertiveness, problem-solving, and anxiety or anger management. Group, peer mediation, and self-training can improve social and communication skills and go a long way toward reducing severe behavior (Hansen, Giacoletti, & Nangle, 1995).

COUNSELING INTERVENTIONS THAT HELP TEACHERS

Work closely with teachers to identify at-risk students for severe behaviors to lay the groundwork for preventive action. Again, rating scales and checklists can help identify patterns and symptoms and form a basis for discussion. When crises arise, you will already have in place the kind of relationships with teaching colleagues that are necessary for effective systemic interventions.

MAKE TIME TO BUILD RELATIONSHIPS

When teachers believe in a student, against the odds, the possibility of changing that student's behavior improves geometrically. When students lack positive relationships with teachers, they tend to respond to negative expectations instead. When a disruption occurs in class, returning to the lecture may be an effective way of calming down the rest of the students after an incident. However, when problems arise repeatedly, teachers must decide whether to ignore the issues, address a student privately, or devote class time to processing them. Severe behaviors affect the learning of everyone in the room. Although class time taken away from learning content material may be worrisome, we know that the most effective learning includes feelings as well as cognitive material (Palmer, 1998; Rogers, 1974; Rogers & Freiburg, 1994). These types of learning have a place in classroom life.

USE THE SAME HALLWAY TECHNIQUES AS COUNSELORS

Teachers who are popular with students, who seem to have the least trouble managing lunch period in the cafeteria, or who give the least number of detentions are often teachers who have taken the time to form relationships with students outside the bounds of the classroom. Teacher–student relationships in classroom settings can be limited, but in the hallways, there is freedom to interact more freely as people. The most effective way to enhance relationships with students may be to take full advantage of the dozens of spontaneous interactions in hallways, and chance encounters in cafeterias, the playground, playing fields, and other areas outside the classroom or office (Hazler, 1998).

SHARE TRICKS OF THE TRADE

Teachers may say, "I'm a teacher, not a counselor!" but teaching is the most ancient of helping professions. Counseling techniques and relationship building can be taught to anyone willing to learn and can be highly effective when used by teachers. There is a personal incentive involved as well: Many teachers who learn and apply these skills report that their own relationships, self-confidence, and self-image improve (Kottler & Kottler, 2000). That is a significant payoff for them and a good use of your time!

BE CONCRETE AND PREDICTABLE!

A predictable routine is essential for emotionally volatile students, and interventions as simple as using a calendar with events and requirements clearly written out can help provide structure. Straightforward, positive language may be the best way to communicate with students who have severe behavior issues. Humorous sarcasm is often lost on these students and is frequently misinterpreted. Here is an effective technique to suggest to teachers to improve communication. Have students repeat back to you what you have said to them, to make certain they understand. If you find yourself getting frustrated, stop and ask what the student is hearing. What they may be hearing may have little to do with what you were trying to say.

TOUCH CAREFULLY, AND THEN ONLY IN THE CONTEXT OF AFFIRMATION

Share your knowledge about appropriate touch with teachers. It is not prudent to touch students without first having built a solid relationship. An affirming pat on the back or light touch on the forearm may be rejected; grabbing a student's arm, as a teacher may do with a younger child or even with an adolescent, may earn them a punch. Students who have been traumatized; sexually, physically, and emotionally abused; or placed in foster care may react violently to physical contact. Within the context of their experiences, this reaction may be appropriate. Don't assume!

HELP TEACHERS TEACH AS THEY ARE

It takes courage for teachers to stand up in front of a classroom and be themselves. It takes genuineness, openness, and a willingness to be vulnerable as a person that many of us understandably fear (Palmer, 1998). Addressing our defensiveness, our inadequacies, and our avoidance can make it easier to form positive relationships with difficult students once they realize that we, too, are far from perfect. Developing a clear teaching philosophy that embraces imperfection as well as achievement can also help us achieve our own potential, personally and professionally. Help teachers support each other by setting time aside to develop these beliefs more formally. A clear teaching philosophy should also include beliefs and biases about severe behavior and how to respond to students.

SUPPORT BELEAGUERED TEACHERS

It is not uncommon for teachers to have more than one student in a class with severe behaviors of differing types. These teachers often feel overwhelmed and unsupported. Your encouragement, professional expertise, and helpful techniques can turn a hopeless morning into a day with possibilities. Sometimes, placing a college student interested in service learning in the classroom can provide needed extra support.

HELP TEACHERS SUPPORT EACH OTHER

Organize regular gatherings that connect teachers with you and with each other in ways that enhance professional growth and development. Informal gatherings can be facilitated by the participants taking turns and provide opportunities to debrief, brainstorm, and share ideas and techniques. It is also an opportunity to keep tabs on difficult students and their progress. An informal brown-bag lunch or short meeting can pay large dividends by building a sense of collegiality and decreasing feelings of isolation. These gatherings should be used for personal and professional support, not administrative tasks and agendas. Separate in-service trainings can give teachers opportunities to learn and practice crisis resolution skills, behavioral assessment, peer mediation, and alternative ways of resolving interpersonal differences. Some in-services may qualify for continuing education credits, making the time invested serve a dual purpose.

THE PAYOFF FOR FORMING CLOSER RELATIONSHIPS WITH DIFFICULT STUDENTS MAY NOT BE ACADEMIC

Teachers who build positive relationships with difficult students may not see advancement in academic classroom work, though behavior might improve. What the relationship can achieve is to improve quality of life, self-esteem, and sense of inclusion, all of which may have solid future payoffs. Students may not be able to form a positive school identity without some degree of academic success, but without the relationship connection that keeps difficult students engaged, academics are not likely to even appear on the radar.

BE CONTENT WITH LESS THAN PERFECTION

Behavioral change is a painstakingly slow process for most of us. This is particularly true for a student with behavioral problems who has had a long history of negative reinforcement and a failure identity or "bad guy" reputation (better than no identity!). Look for slight improvements in attitude, interactions with peers, and in the way he or she relates to you. Small decreases in intensity, frequency, and duration of behavior represent solid progress. Students who are able to sit in class, rather than disrupt it, or participate in some minor way instead of looking at their hands for an hour have achieved an enormous success.

AVOID REVIEWING PAST FAILURES

The memory of past failures burns in our hearts and minds; we do not forget failure. Reminding students of their past mistakes is a counter-productive strategy. When not reacting defensively, most troubled students focus on negatives and pronounce harsher judgments on themselves than do adults. Better to remind them of past successes: Even angry or disheartened students ready to give up and drop out in their junior year have successfully completed 10 grades. That is a lot more success than failure.

SPECIAL TREATMENT

Is a teacher willing to negotiate varying timelines, passing scores, or quiet places to take exams for students with behavioral problems? Where should students sit? Where can students go if they need to calm down? Will a student need a break before class ends? This can often be quietly accomplished by asking the student to run an errand. These likely challenges can be anticipated; however, teachers sometimes worry how others will view the appearance of special treatment for those students who "do not deserve it." These issues only apply if students are in competition with each other. In a school that encourages every student to do his or her personal best, providing extra consideration for those who need it is a community responsibility. Some students need little support from a teacher to work hard and excel. Others need more help and support to hang on. Providing the support that students need to thrive models caring, consideration, and kindness. It also helps develop students' skills in negotiating (vs. "lawyering") to obtain what they need.

IMPACT OF ASSIGNMENTS

Certain assignments that involve talking or writing about family and family experiences can be triggers for severe behavior. Students in foster care, or who have been abused or traumatized at home, often react by withdrawing or acting out. Assignments relating to personal experiences should be carefully considered for their impact on these students.

MEET THE STUDENT WHEREVER HE OR SHE IS

Reassure teachers that not liking a difficult student or being afraid of that student are normal reactions. These are often the hardest students to reach. They may be violent and aggressive, anxious and isolated, or indifferent, withdrawn and depressed. Help make a realistic appraisal of any threat: safety comes first. Help teachers understand a student's context and put the student's behavior in perspective. Coming back to school from a suspension can create major problems for both teacher and student; these events are seldom well planned or structured by the system. As a professional school counselor, you are trained to anticipate these bumps in the road, putting you in the unique position of being able to advocate for students and support teachers at the same time.

BECOME A "WINDTALKER"

During World War II, Native Americans who spoke Navajo played a key role in transmitting information by talking in their unique language. Help teachers become *Windtalkers* by developing their own special language or code to communicate with difficult students. "Codes" can be used to communicate to students when to get back on task and used by students to signal when a time out is needed. Signals can be discrete messages expressed in words or nonverbally that are unique and private to the two individuals. Just having such a code helps build a positive relationship.

IDENTIFY HOT BUTTONS

Many students have a marvelous ability to ferret out and push our hot buttons. Swearing or abusive language sends some teachers spiraling while others will have little or no reaction, leaving them freer to offer the student a choice: amend the behavior or deal with the consequences. Identifying and managing areas of a personal reactivity reduces vulnerability and adds a measure of control, increasing response options for teachers.

HELP TEACHERS UNDERSTAND THE IMPACT OF MEDICATIONS

Medications may cause students to fall asleep during class, suffer from reduced impulse control, or constantly feel irritated and angry. Ritalin is both addictive and overprescribed. Nearly all children improve focus and concentration with Ritalin since it stimulates that part of the brain that regulates impulse control. Prescription drugs used to treat asthma, allergies, epilepsy, depression, anxiety, and other common disorders of childhood and adolescence typically have side effects that include dry mouth, gastric complaints, headaches, stomachaches, bowel complaints, dizziness, sedation, irritability, and confusion (Willens, Spencer, Frazier, & Biederman, 1998). Sucking on a sugar-free lozenge can help alleviate the discomfort of dry mouth, though the school's rules may prohibit the use of candies. As a counselor, you can help negotiate these issues. The other side of the medication issue is what to look for if a student stops taking prescribed medication. Could that be a contributing factor to behavior?

COUNSELING INTERVENTIONS WITH ADMINISTRATORS AND STAFF

Many administrators find that their exercise of power is severely limited because they must answer to different groups with competing agendas. However, we also know that an involved and committed principal who is willing to lead by example can be the single most powerful and effective means of moving a school community from disaffection to involvement and connection. Building solid relationships with school administrators can gain you strong allies.

EXPLAIN AND PROMOTE A SYSTEMIC APPROACH

Solicit ideas and opinions from all constituents before making recommendations. Then develop a clear written plan that explains what you are proposing and why, supported by reasonable goals and objectives. Everyone's role should be detailed, as should some form of outcome measures. Demonstrate the clear advantages of what you propose, including economic advantages, if you can identify them. In practical terms, a school that students look forward to attending is a school with a high attendance rate, and that has real monetary benefits.

ADMINISTRATORS CAN CREATE A CULTURE OF RECOGNITION AND APPRECIATION

Schools characterized by cheerful cooperation, appreciation, and mutual respect are schools that students enjoy attending and places that teachers, staff, and administrators look forward to coming to work. They are the schools where principals know students by name and set policies that foster pride, inclusion, and cooperation. With little or no outlay of resources, administrators can develop programs that provide recognition and mutual appreciation (teacher of the week, most improved student or class, most friendly). There should be a number of awards that focus on relationship so that all students are included, not marginalized further. Time invested in creating a culture of appreciation pays off in better grades, enthusiastic students, better behavior, and fewer financial losses due to absenteeism, vandalism, detentions, and Saturday schools.

RECOGNIZE ADMINISTRATORS AS CONDUITS TO THE SCHOOL BOARD AND COMMUNITY AT LARGE

Community resources are not always well coordinated with school resources. Administrators are ideally positioned to identify opportunities and make outside connections. These links can support your efforts and help students to learn new skills and competencies, develop their creativity, and enhance their physical well-being, particularly after school, when many students are on their own until their parents get home at 7 p.m. or 8 p.m.

INCLUDE STAFF

Secretaries, office managers, support staff, cafeteria workers, and custodial staff can play important supportive roles in helping students and parents feel welcome and included. Involving these essential members of the school community in your trainings and activities to help them react to severe behaviors in positive ways that provide understanding and avoid negative reinforcement. Inclusion and increased job satisfaction helps make their school day more productive and enjoyable as well.

DISCIPLINARY CODES

Educational discipline should focus on how to help students learn, negotiate, and have consequences that are logically connected to the offense (Dreikurs, 1972, 1990; Sweeney,

1989). Harsh penalties and excessive rules actually reduce students' level of responsibility. Suspension and expulsion often serve as negative reenforcements for students. Sometimes, a suspension can help break a student's cycle of behaviors. More often than not, however, suspension serves to separate students from the school community and further isolate them. Suspensions also may be welcomed by students as legalized truancy. In-school consequences are always preferable to out-of-school consequences. Reviewing your school's discipline plan to ensure that it is educational rather than punitive and relies on consequences rather than punishment should top your agenda.

DEALING WITH RESISTANCE

Like students with severe behaviors, other individuals in the system may have little hope that the future will be better. A teacher may say, "Don't waste your breath. Things around here never change." An administrator may tell you, "Sorry, there's nothing I can do." Students will look at you skeptically: "Yeah, riiiiiiiiiight." When faced with resistance, model qualities you want others to model for students: optimism, patience, understanding, openness, affirmation, a group ethic, and willingness to cooperate and negotiate. When students with severe behavioral problems cannot see a positive future for themselves, there is little motivation to listen to you or follow rules. Help them create a positive vision of the future by forging relationships in noncrisis times.

CORPORAL PUNISHMENT

Corporal punishment and harsh discipline are not effective in managing severe behaviors, though a number of school districts in the United States still use paddling (Wenning, 1996). You may have to address beliefs about discipline and corporal punishment with administrators and teachers and offer creative alternatives to parents, countering myths about spanking and corporal punishment.

DO NOT REINVENT THE WHEEL!

Make connections with professionals in the community who can support your efforts. Invite educators from local colleges or universities to talk about suicide, sexuality, and violence. Make use of undergraduates in the fields of family studies, sociology, social work, and psychology who are looking for service learning opportunities. See if graduate programs may be willing to place practicum and internship students with you.

COUNSELING INTERVENTIONS WITH PARENTS AND CAREGIVERS

Get parents on board! Behavioral change starts at home, so let parents do their share. Show them how to get the job done. Contact with parents prior to a behavioral crisis helps to prevent the relationship from turning adversarial when severe behavior erupts. They are a vital link in the process of managing severe behavior, and it is unlikely that interventions will succeed without them. Make sure parents hear from you when things go right, not just during a crisis!

STRESS CALM, ASSERTIVE, CONSISTENT RESPONSES TO DIFFICULT BEHAVIOR

Clarity is important. Help parents avoid sarcasm and learn to state what they expect directly and calmly. If there are rules to be followed and chores to be done, the list should be posted in writing in a prominent place. Make sure that parents are prepared for the realities of slow change (their own as well as their child's). It is hard for exhausted parents to ignore negative behaviors and push themselves to develop creative learning consequences rather than punishment. Likewise, good behavior is often ignored, or not rewarded, and consistency seems elusive when parents are overwhelmed with work and dealing with their children and/or each other. Sometimes it is just easier to ignore behaviors that are inappropriate, dangerous, or aggressive. Punishment then tends to become arbitrary and dependent on the parents' mood, not on the child's behavior. Inconsistent parenting styles, or parenting styles that are overindulgent or extremely authoritarian, can create chaos in the lives of children. Communication patterns based on screaming, yelling, nagging, and threats foster oppositional and defiant behaviors. Corporal punishment often simply aggravates the severity and frequency of negative behaviors. The primary cause of treatment failure is because parents abandon the treatment plan too soon and do not stay the course of treatment (Wenning, 1996).

HELP PARENTS AND CAREGIVERS MODEL THE BEHAVIORS THEY WANT TO SEE

Help parents understand the eventual payoff for ignoring bad behavior and modeling kindness, cooperation, and patience in the face of rudeness, defiance, and disobedience. With younger children who are having problems regulating their aggressive behavior, only nonviolent videos, games and television programs should be permitted. Strive to be nonviolent, praise-oriented, and nonpunitive (Wenning, 1996). If the adults in the household are separated or divorced or have ended a relationship, advise them to not criticize their ex-partner in front of the children. They should avoid fighting in front of their children, and practice offering choices with well-thought-out consequences for negative behaviors that you can brainstorm with them.

WHO'S IN CHARGE HERE?

Parents often forget that they are the adults in a household. Students' behaviors at home often lead to fights between parents or between parents and teachers and the school. The child who is "out of control" at home is all too often the one who is really running the show. Tip parents off that if they find themselves fighting over a child's behavior, stop and consider what is really happening. Once parents and teachers start arguing, the focus shifts off the student, who is often then "in the clear."

LET THE PAST STAY IN THE PAST

Keep the focus in the present and future. Children are all too well aware of their failures and shortcomings, especially children with behavioral problems. When parents focus on failure, children become discouraged. Are parents optimistic about their child's future? When they are not, that child is more than likely to meet their negative expectation.

CREATE CONSEQUENCES THAT ARE LOGICAL, REASONABLE, RESPECTFUL AND CONNECTED TO BEHAVIOR, NOT GRADES

With many students, a poor grade is a motivator to do better. Parental supports, such as assigned study times and mild restrictions can be effective in improving behavior and school performance. However, with children who suffer from severe behaviors, grades are an expected source of failure, and multiple consequences can create a cycle of increasing opposition or withdrawal and isolation. Consequences should be well understood by students in advance and should not be piggybacked. An "F" in English should not be compounded by adding social restrictions, grounding, removal of privileges, and other, harsher punishments. When too many consequences pile up, they lead to discouragement, and children simply give up. Most parents underestimate the tremendous emotional and social pressure on any child with multiple academic deficits. The consequences of a failure identity at school extend well beyond a poor grade.

CREATE OPPORTUNITIES FOR SUCCESS

Work with parents to create situations in which their children can experience success at least two or three times a day. A simple task, properly executed—such as getting home on time, knowing the difference between one tool and another when helping with a project—each tiny success contributes to building self-esteem and reducing severe behavior. Do family members know how to express appreciation for each other? Do parents reward good behavior? Checklists and specific instructions about how to express appreciation and give encouragement are easily found in most counseling texts.

CREATE IMMEDIATE SYMPTOM RELIEF AT HOME

Suggest to adults to do the unexpected (Dreikurs, 1990). When a student comes home with a failing grade and an attitude to go with it, take that child out for a favored excursion and provide empathy and support. Do not argue with an angry adolescent! Disengage from them, hard as that might be. Let them go to their rooms and stew over their predicament (which is theirs, not yours!). Give choices, and avoid ultimatums that only serve to escalate the level of tension. Whatever the parent's pattern of behavior might be, suggest a change and things will most likely improve (Sweeney, 1989). When parents break their pattern of interaction by acting positively and unexpectedly, children are often astonished and must change their own behavior to compensate.

SUMMARY/CONCLUSION

A systemic process may be slow and often frustrating to implement, considering the logistics involved, but the changes accomplished will be more permanent and accepted by more people than changes established by harsh disciplinary policies or the frequent use of suspensions and expulsions. Finally, even as you care for others and struggle to create systemic change for students, families, the school, and your community, make sure that you do not leave yourself out of the equation. Make certain your needs are met, that you have adequate peer supervision and support, and good nutrition, exercise, and adequate rest. The best example you can set for students with severe behavioral problems is the example of a satisfying and productive life, lived in close connection with others who care for you as you care for them.

(Note: See the CD-ROM for a list of references.)

CHAPTER 68

UNDERSTANDING ELIMINATION DISORDERS: WHAT SCHOOL COUNSELORS NEED TO KNOW ABOUT ENURESIS AND ENCOPRESIS

Gregory R. Janson

Preview

Elimination disorders are common in school-age students, carrying a severe social stigma that can negatively affect relationships with peers and adults, academic achievement, and personality development. Emotional, social, cognitive, and physical growth and well-being may also be threatened. Rarely associated with psychopathology, these disorders are highly treatable using simple behavioral methods that are well within the professional school counselor's scope of practice. I provide an overview of key issues, counseling strategies, and treatment options for professional school counselors seeking to understand elimination disorders and work with students who are challenged by enuresis and encopresis.

WHAT SCHOOL COUNSELORS NEED TO KNOW ABOUT ENURESIS AND ENCOPRESIS

A significant number of children and adolescents afflicted with enuresis (i.e., urination in clothing, bedding, or other inappropriate places) and, to a lesser extent, encopresis (i.e., fecal soiling in clothes or other inappropriate places) will be found in every professional school counselor's setting. The vast majority of these children do not suffer from psychopathology, yet the overwhelming prospect of dealing with an elimination disorder and the social taboos against discussing bowel and bladder functions often leaves these students isolated and hopeless (Murphy & Carr, 2000). They are often blamed by their own parents at home, and if their problem becomes publicly known, they are ostracized and humiliated—shamed by adults and ridiculed by peers.

The tendency of helping professionals is to ignore elimination disorders or to "medicalize" them. A quick referral is often the first response to a parent's request for help. Those few parents who seek the help of a physician are usually told that the issue is one of immaturity that the child will outgrow (Vogel, Young, & Primack, 1996). This lack of support puts students doubly at risk. Since their parents are poorly informed and ill-equipped to deal with elimination disorders, the net result is secrecy and silence, or punishment and folk remedies (Schaefer, 1996). The risks are not just psychological: Elimination disorders have been identified as the second leading cause of child abuse, after crying (Kempe & Helfer, 1980).

The good news is that these disorders are easily and safely treatable, with little training or expense (Houts, 2000; Houts & Abramson, 1990; Ondersma, Ondersma, &

Walker, 2001; Ondersma & Walker, 1998). Simple behavioral methods are highly effective, in timeframes that vary from a few days to several months.

How Can Professional School Counselors Help?

You may have little or no training in the treatment of elimination disorders, making referral a logical response to anything beyond the occasional playground "accident"; however, 95% of the cases involving these disorders are developmental in nature. This suggests that involvement in treating students with enuresis or encopresis is appropriate and within a professional school counselor's scope of practice. Whether you as a professional school counselor feel confident or overwhelmed by the thought of working with these disorders, you already possess the interpersonal skills, assessment training, and counseling experience needed to treat elimination disorders. The investment of time and energy needed to acquire the additional skills and knowledge necessary to help most students achieve continence is relatively minimal. Most can be obtained through continuing education credit that is already needed to maintain licensure and certification. The purpose of this chapter is to provide all the basic information needed to make a start.

Enuresis

Little is known about the causes of enuresis, and although genetics seem to play a role, no specific genetic links have yet been identified (Mikkelsen, 2001). Only 15% of children with enuresis come from families in which the biological parents reported no history of enuresis. About 75% of enuretic children have a first-degree biological relative with a history of enuresis. Sex is a factor as well: Females tend to achieve dryness more quickly than males, in whom enuresis is so much more prevalent and enduring that some researchers suggest that boys should have different criteria for diagnosis, raising the age of continence from 5 to 8 (Verhulst & Al, 1985).

To qualify for a diagnosis, enuresis can be intentional or involuntary and must occur at least twice a week for 3 months. Enuresis can occur just at night (nocturnal), just during the day (diurnal), or both. Males with nocturnal enuresis outnumber females by 2 to 1. Diurnal enuresis is more common in females but is seldom seen in children over the age of 9 years (de Jonge, 1973). Children with diurnal enuresis are the most likely to have an underlying medical condition, but whether they do or not, daytime wetting is so stressful that drug treatment is almost always recommended, requiring a physician referral (Reiner, 1995). Enuresis can be due to a sudden urge to urinate and loss of control, the intentional delay of urination due to anxiety or overinvolvement in activities, or, more rarely, in conjunction with behavioral disorders. Professional school counselors are likely to receive a referral for daytime wetting because these events tend to take place on school days early in the afternoon and are extremely distressing to the child. Understandably, these children report lower levels of self-esteem than children with nocturnal enuresis (Wagner, Smith, & Norris, 1988). Even when a student's enuretic behaviors do not reach a diagnostic threshold, nighttime bedwetting can be a serious problem.

ENCOPRESIS

In 85% to 98% of cases of encopresis, there is no underlying medical condition, yet some research has shown that these children may have had far fewer bowel movements as infants (Pettei & Davidson, 1991). Identical twins are six times more likely to develop constipation problems than are fraternal twins (Bakwin & Davidson, 1971), suggesting the possibility of a genetic factor in encopresis—but this factor has not been identified.

Encopresis can be intentional or unintentional and must occur at least once a month for 3 months. Most common is Encopresis With Constipation and Overflow Incontinence (retentive encopresis with seepage due to constipation). Encopresis Without Constipation and Overflow Incontinence is intentional soiling. It is rare and usually associated with trauma and behavioral disorders. Encopresis can be retentive (caused by constipation and resulting overflow incontinence); stress-related (diarrhetic in nature and caused by trauma, stress, or anxiety); or manipulative (intentional soiling in clothes or other places, without constipation). The male-to-female ratio for encopresis is nearly 5 to 1 at every age level. Implementing an effective treatment plan means careful charting and observation over time to discriminate between these subtypes (American Psychiatric Association, 2000).

The stigma and social disgrace attached to encopresis is extremely damaging. Serious deficits in self-esteem and self-image, isolation, and withdrawal are common developmental risks for these children. Not the least of their complaints relates to the physical pain that can accompany chronic constipation, from which most encopretic children suffer (Ondersma & Walker, 1998).

LOSING CONTINENCE

Some children lose urinary or fecal continence after having successfully achieved it. The distinction between primary and secondary enuresis does not bear heavily on treatment strategies (Mikkelsen, 2001). Secondary enuresis usually occurs between ages 5 and 8 years and is associated with disturbing or traumatic events. These may include divorce, separation, a sibling's birth, having a new partner move in, or a family life in which chaos, abuse, neglect, punishment, or overprotection are the norm. Secondary encopresis can also develop after stressful or traumatic life events (Ondersma & Walker, 1998). It is not uncommon for children to suffer intermittent episodes of encopresis over a time span of years.

PARENTS AND FAMILY

Parental attitudes and the degree of family difficulties are the most significant factors in predicting the length of time needed to achieve continence, deal with relapse, and maintain long-term continence. Most parents do not seek help for a child who is suffering from an elimination disorder, believing that their child has control over wetting or soiling but will not exercise it, or is lazy, careless, or defiant (Schaefer, 1996). Accordingly, parents blame and punish their children, creating a threat to the emotional, psychological, and physical safety of the child (Walker, Kenning, & Faust-Capanille,

1989). Enuretic children from dysfunctional families may be at the greatest emotional and physical risk (Warzak, 1993).

Bedwetting can create tremendous strain on a family, and professional school counselors can anticipate the need for stress-management strategies. Broken sleep, cleanup and remaking the bed in the middle of the night, the seemingly endless piles of laundry to be washed the next day, and the social stigma of being a "bed-wetter" or the parent of one, all contribute to a shared sense of hopelessness, shame, and failure in both children and parents (Foxman, Valdez, & Brook, 1986).

Children with encopresis are at great risk since most encopretic events occur when the child is fully awake, suggesting that soiling is intentional. Parents, teachers and other students do not realize that soiling is most often caused by constipation, when liquid seeps around a bowel blockage. It is hard to imagine how these students deal with the anger, disgust, frustration and abuse heaped on them by their own families as well as by peers and teachers.

Some parents may choose to ignore or tolerate an elimination disorder while supporting the child or adolescent emotionally, in the hope that their child will simply outgrow the behavior (Mikkelsen, 2001). There is some truth to this belief. Encopresis after age 16 years is unusual, and the rate of spontaneous remission for enuresis after age 5 years ranges from 5% to 10% per year. This means, however, that a child who is enuretic and not treated at age 5 years only has a 50% chance of achieving dryness by age 10 years. Ignoring an elimination disorder means needlessly subjecting a child to potentially severe social, emotional, and relational consequences, which are only likely to become more problematic as a child grows older. Although some positive links have been made between moderate sibling teasing and good treatment response (Butler, Brewin, & Forsythe, 1988), children faced with multiple negatives from parents, siblings, and peers fearfully avoid normal social events such as sleepovers, attending camp, or overnight trips (Ondersma & Walker, 1998).

COUNSELING STRATEGIES

The same basic counseling strategies apply to enuresis and encopresis, starting with preventive education for students, teachers, and parents. Appropriate referrals and broad-based behavioral treatment strategies that are holistic in approach produce success rates in the 80% to 85% range for both disorders (Mikkelsen, 1991, 2001; Murphy & Carr, 2000; Ondersma & Walker, 1998). Professional school counselors can play a crucial role by supporting and observing a student from initial assessment through the treatment period, providing fine-tuning and encouragement. This is critical to success, especially during the 3 months after treatment starts, yet this role is nearly always omitted for logistical reasons (Ciminero & Doleys, 1976; Dittman & Wolter, 1996).

TAKE POSITIVE ACTION!

The most important first step is crisis resolution if an enuretic or encopretic event occurs at school. Provide reassurance to the child and other students and make certain that teachers are aware of how to react and are ready to follow established procedures that ensure good hygiene. This might involve having a parent pick the child up from school to wash and change, then return. However, this approach could become a form of negative reinforcement and increase the level of anger and frustration experienced by parents. If possible, a more effective process might call for a gentle reprimand, and instructions to the child to wash out his or her clothing, followed by a shower or wash. Afterwards, the child would change into fresh clothing kept at the school for just this purpose (Schaefer, 1996). Important questions might include *Who will supervise the child during this process?* and *How will the teacher address the incident with the rest of the class?*

MEET WITH PARENTS AND MAKE THEM COCOUNSELORS

Parents need information, reassurance, and a sound treatment strategy that conveys hope and optimism. If possible, involve them as cocounselors and a source of positive reinforcement. This is a critical success element. A good relationship with the child's mother, in particular, can improve a home environment and help maintain parental commitment to treatment long enough to achieve continence (Van Londen, Van Londen-Barentsen, Van Son, & Mulder, 1993). Maintain a library with resources and pamphlets you can obtain online or from a counseling center. Even simple fact sheets can convey essential information and normalize the prevalence of elimination disorders. Remember that information alone is almost never enough to achieve continence; ongoing contact is essential (Houts & Liebert, 1984; Houts, Peterson, & Whelan, 1986).

MAKE REFERRALS WHEN NECESSARY

Develop a referral list of clinicians, physicians, and family counselors who are skilled in the treatment of elimination disorders and who will help you first rule out medical or organic causes. Following the referral process and physician's report, parents may then decide to ask you to remain involved and help design a treatment plan. Make certain you have the proper releases from all the parties before starting.

CHECK ACCESS TO SERVICES AND MEDICATIONS

Does the family have insurance? Can they pay for counseling services and medications? Can they afford to consult a pediatrician or purchase a bell and pad urine alarm system? Desmopressin, the treatment drug of choice for enuresis, is expensive. Many parents, when they discover the cost, choose to live with an elimination disorder rather than treat it. Are alternative medications available if cost is an issue? Is immigration status or homelessness a barrier to receiving aid?

ASSESS

Make broad-based, systemic assessments. Standard assessment formats are appropriate, and should include questions regarding traumatic events. Specific attention should be given to the attitudes of both child and caregivers to episodes of enuresis or encopresis, feelings about past failed attempts to achieve continence, and beliefs about achieving future success. There are excellent scales available to measure these attitudes (Butler, Redfern, & Forsythe, 1993; Morgan & Young, 1975).

CONSIDER COMORBIDITY

Here is where your daily contact with the student can pay significant dividends, ensuring that nothing is overlooked. There is a 30% higher comorbidity rate of attention-deficit/hyperactivity disorder and enuresis than expected by chance alone, requiring simultaneous treatment of both disorders (Biederman, Santangelo, Faraone, Kiely, & Al, 1995; Boon, 1992). Most students with enuresis do not suffer from psychiatric disorders, but there is a strong chance that enuresis is only one of several hurdles faced by these students (Swadi, 1996). Levels of depression, anxiety, and loneliness that may not meet diagnostic thresholds are common, as are higher rates of behavioral and emotional problems, night terrors, sleep disturbances, and delays in speech, learning, and the development of motor skills (more so with older children).

INCLUDE THE CHILD OR ADOLESCENT ON THE TREATMENT TEAM

Active participation means lower relapse rates and improvements in self-esteem. With younger children, play therapy may be the best method of communicating with, involving, and supporting the child (Landreth, 2002). Children with encopresis tend to have personalities characterized by shyness, passivity, obedience, and stubbornness. Stoic and depressive, they can seem irritatingly indifferent and oblivious to peers and adults (Schaefer, 1996). Outside the professional school counselor, few professionals may have the patience or communication skills necessary to effectively gain the trust and cooperation of these children.

CREATE PERSPECTIVE, REASONABLE EXPECTATIONS, AND A SAFE ENVIRONMENT

The sense of hopelessness and discouragement that accompanies a history of failed attempts at continence means that parents are less likely to help their child follow through with a treatment plan and more likely to prematurely terminate treatment once it starts (Kelleher, 1997). The most significant barriers to success are pessimistic parental attitudes, failure to follow a treatment plan long enough, familial distress, and psychiatric disturbance in the child. Other barriers include lack of motivation on the child's part and unrealistic expectations. Prepare the family for the time commitment needed to attain continence; bedwetting does not cease overnight. Teach parents to remain calm and nonpunitive; corporal punishment is not effective with elimination disorders (Schaefer, 1996). With encopresis, the treatment plan must be followed without deviation to succeed and ongoing incidents of soiling should be expected during treatment. Make prior provisions for following a process that everyone, including the student, has agreed is reasonable. Adults and students should be taught to respond to soiling incidents quietly and calmly, avoiding recriminations, ridicule, or shaming. Reframe failures and setbacks as steps to success!

CONSIDER CULTURAL FACTORS

There is ample evidence in the literature that African Americans tend to distrust White medical personnel, a finding that resonates with more specific research suggesting that African Caribbean families are less likely than Whites to seek the help of a physician in dealing with enuresis (Rona, Li, & Chinn, 1997). Degree of acculturation, ethnicity, immigration status, and access to services should be a vital part of your assessment.

COUNSELING IS NOT EFFECTIVE WITH ELIMINATION DISORDERS!

Individual and family counseling are not effective treatments for enuresis or encopresis, except for those situations in which issues arise that are related to traumatic events, stress, anxiety, or difficulties in family communication (Protinsky & Dillard, 1983; Protinsky & Kersey, 1983; Stein, 1998). Psychological factors tend to be more significant issues for older children (Rutter, 1989). In complicated family situations, where there may be domestic violence, chemical dependency, and abuse, referral to a community mental health agency or a family counselor may be the most helpful course of action.

TREATING ENURESIS

Behavioral treatments using a urine alarm in combination with other behavioral approaches are the most effective therapy for enuresis, achieving improvement in 85% of cases (Ondersma & Walker, 1998). A urine alarm system alone is not as successful in treating enuresis as combining an alarm with psychological interventions, especially those that involve parents as cocounselors (Houts, Berman, & Abramson, 1994). Initial interventions can be as simple as creating a chart with stickers that reward dry nights. The use of medications can be helpful, but potential side effects and high relapse rates make behavioral treatments the first choice in most instances (Friman & Vollmer, 1995; Friman & Warzak, 1990). When a motivated child is not able to achieve dryness using the previously described methods, a combination of desmopressin (DDAVP; a synthetic anti-diuretic hormone), a urine alarm, and a mix of other behavioral interventions combined with supportive family counseling has produced 100% success rates (Mellon & McGrath, 2000).

BELL AND PAD/URINE ALARMS

Urine alarms work on a simple principle: When urination begins, it completes an electrical circuit, setting off loud buzzer or bell. Children either wake up or contract their pelvic floor muscles to refrain from urination. Modern versions offer sealed pads, strips worn inside pajamas or clothing, body-worn alarms, and miniature ultrasound monitors worn around the waist that measure bladder capacity and ring at a preset point. All yield results similar to the traditional bell and pad (Pretlow, 1999). A urine alarm alone is an effective means to achieve complete dryness for nearly two thirds of children with enuresis over a 5- to 12-week period (Houts et al., 1994). Relapse is common, particularly in children and adolescents with secondary enuresis. However, reconditioning using the bell and pad is successful with more than two thirds of those who relapse (Doleys, 1979).

AROUSAL TRAINING

If cost is an issue (bell and pad kits range from $60 or $70 to $130), similar success can be achieved by anticipating when bladder capacity might be reached (2–3 hours after falling asleep) and using a simple alarm clock to wake the child (El-Anany, Mahraby, Shaker, & Abdel-Moneim, 1999). Although effective, this approach can be very disruptive to parents' sleep patterns.

DRY-BED TRAINING

Dry-bed training (DBT) is the single most effective treatment for enuresis, combining a urine alarm with other behavioral and psychological interventions (Azrin, Sneed, & Foxx, 1974; Azrin, Thienes Hontos, & Besalel-Azrin, 1979; Scott, Barclay, & Houts, 1992). These include retention control, overlearning, rapid awakening, hygiene, hourly awakening of the child by the parents, positive rewards for staying dry and urinating in the bathroom, and gentle reprimands for wetness. Rehearsal is also a component of the DBT program, in which the child practices getting out of bed and physically going to the bathroom. DBT is one of the least used approaches, employed by just 5% of families and seldom recommended by physicians, possibly due to the time and effort required to achieve dryness. For professional school counselors, developing the competence to teach this method to children and parents is relatively simple because the techniques are clearly and simply described in the literature.

OVERLEARNING

Overlearning involves having children increase liquid intake by small amounts each evening until they can drink a large volume before bed. Dryness takes longer to achieve using this method, but it adds effectiveness to a urine alarm and lowers relapse rates (Houts et al., 1986).

RETENTION CONTROL TRAINING

Retention control training involves giving positive rewards to children who can drink and retain large fluid amounts (Butler, 1998). Practicing stream interruption can help to improve functional bladder control (Friman & Warzak, 1990). These methods alone can help some children achieve dryness, but are far more effective when used in conjunction with a urine alarm (Walker, 1995).

FULL SPECTRUM HOME TRAINING

Full spectrum home training combines retention control, overlearning, bed-changing, hygiene, and charting dry and wet nights with a basic urine alarm. Children are also rewarded for retention control (holding urine) during the day. This approach is of particular interest to professional school counselors because it has a success rate of about 80% with only one session with a counselor (Houts & Liebert, 1984; Houts, Liebert, & Padre, 1983).

DRUG TREATMENT

Although drugs can produce dramatic results within 2 weeks, relapse rates of 95% are common when they are discontinued (Monda & Husmann, 1995). The two most commonly used drugs are imipramine (Tofranil) and desmopressin (DDAVP). Imipramine is an inexpensive tricyclic antidepressant that seems to act on renal systems rather than as an antidepressant (Vogel et al., 1996). Common side effects include exhaustion, disturbed sleep, and gastric discomfort. Higher doses can affect cardiac function; overdoses can be fatal. DDAVP is a synthetic antidiuretic hormone that comes as a nasal spray and concentrates urine, reducing urinary output. It is the present drug of choice for treating enuresis and reported to be most successful where a family history of enuresis exists (Butler et al., 1998; Hogg & Hussman, 1993). Headaches and stomachaches are common side effects of DDAVP, which is considered a safe drug with few negative effects.

TREATING ENCOPRESIS

The vast majority of encopretic children and adolescents (85% or more) suffer from retentive encopresis, a condition characterized by chronic constipation with overflow incontinence that occurs when liquid seeps around bowel impactions. The average course of untreated encopresis tends to be 2 to 3 years with a spontaneous annual remission rate of approximately 28%. Encopresis is extremely rare after age 16 years, but it does exist. With treatment, improvement can occur in a matter of weeks and continence achieved within 2 or 3 months. As a group, these children tend to be first born, male, and exhibit symptoms and a course that suggest that the disorder may be psychological in origins but physiologically self-perpetuating once constipation is established and becomes chronic (Schaefer, 1996).

Short-term behavioral interventions combined with medical management have produced 85% success rates with children suffering from encopresis within a 6-month time frame (Fireman & Koplewicz, 1992). Step one is always a medical examination to rule out physiological pathology, which is rare. The next step is to evaluate for constipation and the presence of bowel distention (psychogenic megacolon) caused by chronic constipation. The physician will then outline a medical management strategy for the parents to follow, including the use of laxatives and a dietary plan high in fiber and liquids. This forms the foundation for behavioral interventions, including toileting routines, mild consequences for soiling (e.g., washing one's own clothing), biofeedback for anal sphincter training, positive rewards and avoidance of negative reinforcement, and a plan for dealing with encopretic events that occur in school.

Education is a critical part of the professional school counselor's role, because teachers and parents are seldom aware that overflow incontinence can take place without a child's awareness or that soiling can be associated with severe constipation. Providing facts about encopresis can help ensure that a child with a potentially dangerous condition is quickly identified and receives the appropriate medical referral.

UNDERSTANDING THE PHYSIOLOGY OF ENCOPRESIS AND EFFECTS OF CONSTIPATION

Nearly all encopretic episodes are associated with constipation and overflow incontinence, not with oppositional and defiant or conduct disordered behavior (Murphy & Carr, 2000). Constipation in children is common and can be due to dehydration, a diet low in fiber, or hereditary factors. Other factors include the intentional avoidance of defecation due to anxiety, stress, fear of an unfamiliar environment, unwillingness to stop an activity, or intentional manipulation. Constipation easily becomes chronic, stretching the bowel walls and weakening colon muscles. This causes a decrease in the physiological cues that indicate the need to defecate and leaves the child in a state of lethargy and pain (Christophersen & Edwards, 1992). A condition known as *psychogenic megacolon* can then arise, where stools become hard and dry, forming an impaction. These stools block and distend the colon, enlarging and thinning out walls of the bowels. Overflow incontinence occurs when liquid collects above the impaction (which has become rock-like and impervious to liquid) and drains around it, leaking from the anal sphincter, which loses tone and sensitivity. Soiling then occurs without the child's awareness; odor is the first cue that something is wrong. The seepage is often yellow in color, may have a pasty consistency, and has an extremely noxious odor. This condition is common and dangerous in children with encopresis, requiring immediate medical attention (Walker, 1978). Sometimes, the damaged section of thinned bowel must be removed surgically. As easier, more regular bowel movements occur, avoidance of defecation due to the fear of painful movements is reduced (Walker, 1995). Once constipation is resolved and normal toileting established, colon and bowels will regain tone and sensitivity (Murray, 1994). Teachers can help make certain that daily liquid intake meets therapeutic levels and that a toilet routine is followed without singling out a child for ridicule.

SOILING EVENTS

Most soiling occurs during the daytime, at a frequency that can vary from once a month to multiple episodes in a single day, creating one of the most severe psychosocial stressors a child can experience. Episodes tend to take place later in the afternoon or immediately following the end of the school day during play. Elementary school teachers, professional school counselors, or the school nurse are most frequently the people outside the family who must deal with an encopretic event. These professionals should have procedures in place that ensure good hygiene, minimize the impact of the event on the child, and help teachers manage the reactions of other students.

ATTITUDES OF PARENTS AND CHILDREN

Most parents blame their children for soiling and are too embarrassed to seek help, often concealing the behaviors unless directly questioned (Walker, 1995). Children with encopresis may seem indifferent to their episodes of soiling, which reduces anxiety and is perhaps their most effective psychological defense against scorn and ridicule. However, most children suffering from encopresis also report that they are eager to become continent (Landman, Rappaport, Fenton, & Levine, 1986). These children suffer deficits in self-esteem, present with emotional and behavioral problems, and, like their parents, report feelings of shame, frustration, hopelessness, and distress.

FORMING THE TREATMENT TEAM

Forming a treatment team is an invaluable role for the professional school counselor. Successful treatment requires a multidisciplinary, cooperative approach that includes coordinating the efforts of parents, teachers, physicians, dieticians, and the school nurse. Families may need a broad range of support services, starting with a thorough education on the importance of diet and nutrition. Emotional support, the encouragement to weather predictable setbacks, and understanding that less than 100% compliance can sabotage the program are all critical elements. Physiological factors involved in restoring lost bowel control caused by chronic constipation dictate that failure to follow the strategy scrupulously will set the program back to the beginning.

ASSESSMENT

As with enuresis, standard assessment formats are appropriate for professional school counselors to use, as long as there is a focus on encopresis. Questions asked of both parents and children should be direct and explicit (Schaefer, 1996):

- Was continence ever achieved?
- How often does soiling occur?
- Do you know when you need to go to the bathroom?
- How often do you have a bowel movement?
- Is moving your bowels painful for you?
- Were coercive methods used in toilet training or was training commenced prior to age 15 months?
- Are there specific patterns related to soiling events?
- Is there a family history of bowel difficulties?
- Have there been other gastric complaints, psychological problems other than encopresis, or traumatic experiences or events?
- Are you afraid to use the bathrooms here at school?

Bullying often takes place in school bathrooms, and many children avoid restrooms for fear of being victimized (Hazler, 1996). The most effective ways to elicit information from younger children is through interviews with parent or with play therapy, dolls, puppets, or sand-tray play or drawings, which all have the dual benefit of building a relationship while providing affirmation and empathy. When possible, information should be shared by physicians and professional school counselors.

MONITORING

Charting progress, encopretic events, and diet and fluid intake is an essential task for parents, children, and teachers. Most children soil themselves without realizing it; others hide their feces or dispose of their underwear out of shame. Some may intentionally deposit feces in bureau drawers, under furniture, or in other more obvious places. Careful diaries of toileting behaviors and soiling episodes can help determine if encopresis is retentive, related to trauma or anxiety, or manipulative in nature. Establishing these patterns has a central bearing on treatment and referral decisions (APA; 2000). Diaries also provide a record that can be reviewed, enabling professional school counselors to assess progress (and demonstrate progress to the student!), reframe soiling events and beliefs about continence, and re-tailor the plan to accommodate each individual child and family (Goldstein & Book, 1983).

LOOK FOR A DECREASE IN FREQUENCY AND SIGNS OF HOPE THAT CONTINENCE CAN BE ACHIEVED

As the bowel trauma caused by chronic constipation heals and more sensitivity and stable bowel control is gained, fewer incidents of soiling will occur. This fosters hope, but also look for and encourage small changes in the child's attitude and movement from isolation to one of greater connection with others.

MEDICAL MANAGEMENT AND DIET

The treatment of retentive encopresis begins with the treatment of chronic constipation. While professional school counselors and teachers may not be directly involved in medical management, a working knowledge of what a child's morning is like prior to school is important to understanding and supporting the healing process. Medical management almost always includes the use of laxatives to establish a predictable toileting schedule. With children suffering from retentive encopresis, laxative treatment success rates average 70% (Nolan, Debelle, Oberklaid, & Coffey, 1991). It can take a year for an enlarged bowel to heal, yet children do not seem to develop dependence on laxatives after treatment (Houts & Abramson, 1990; Murray, 1994). A well-planned diet high in bulk, fiber, and liquid intake, if followed, can be as effective as laxative treatments (Houts & Peterson, 1986). Parents administer laxatives under medical supervision and on a rigid schedule, usually daily. To establish a predictable toileting routine and restore normal colon shape and tone, parents encourage children to defecate when they get up every morning. If they cannot, parents then administer a glycerin suppository. Following breakfast, if the child is still unable to defecate, a Fleet enema is given, insuring a bowel movement at a regular time each day. When soiling ceases and bowel movements occur regularly, the use of suppositories can be slowly discontinued. One suppository-free day is chosen by the child for the first week following cessation of soiling, then one suppository-free day is added to each successive week as long as soiling does not occur, until suppositories are completely discontinued. If soiling occurs, the process begins anew until 2 weeks without suppositories or soiling is achieved. Continence is generally achieved within 4 or 5 months using this method (Wright, 1973).

BEHAVIORAL AND BIOFEEDBACK THERAPY

Behavior therapy consists of a system of positive rewards and reinforcement for proper toileting routines, checking clothing for soiling, gentle reprimands for soiling incidents, and good hygiene (cleanliness and having the child wash out his or her own laundry). Combining behavioral techniques can increase effectiveness. Adding biofeedback training can be helpful since encopretic children tend to tighten their anal sphincters rather than relax them when attempting to defecate, anticipating that the bowel movement will be painful (Loening-Baucke & Cruikshank, 1986).

RESPONDING TO INCIDENTS OF SOILING

Most adults are at a total loss on how to respond to soiling incidents. Professional school counselors can help parents develop an effective repertory of creative responses and rewards to help reduce soiling and attain continence. A review of the literature showed that the single most important factor in treating all types of encopresis or enuresis is positive reinforcement (Houts & Abramson, 1990). The use of desired rewards provides powerful incentives for children and adolescents and should be given for each bowel movement made on the toilet and for each day of continence. The reward most prized by children is one-on-one time with parents engaged in an activity of the child's choice (Wright, 1973).

Secondary positive reinforcements consist of typical token rewards for toys, candy, movies, games, or a trip to a water park or video arcade. Negative reinforcement, administered after each soiling incident, should be limited to a mild reprimand, having the child wash soiled clothing, 5- to 15-minute time-outs, extended periods of time in the tub or shower (15 to 30 minutes), and loss of play (Nintendo or Play Station) or television time. Some researchers suggested simply using only mild reprimands; all recommend having the child wash his or her own clothing. You can help others understand that encopretic children suffer enough consequences. Encouragement, hope, and affirmation are most needed.

INTENTIONAL OR MANIPULATIVE SOILING

Intentional or manipulative soiling as part of a pattern of oppositional and defiant behavior or conduct disorder is uncommon. However, coping with this type of behavior is a challenge most adults find impossibly difficult. Trauma, neglect, abuse and abandonment are almost always a part of the clinical picture with these disturbed children and adolescents. Treating them and their families may well require referral to a specialty clinician. What you can do is educate teachers, administrators, and students; help students recognize secondary behavioral gains; and identify better ways to communicate or gain significance (Walker, Milling, & Bonner, 1988). Of all students, these are perhaps the ones most in need of unconditional positive regard if change is possible.

Summary/Conclusion

Despite the common occurrence of elimination disorders, these students have few advocates and often simply suffer in silence. Where is the best place to begin the helping process? The most logical place may be with a self-inventory of your feelings and experiences with elimination disorders as a child or with a child you know. Are you comfortable talking to students, parents, and teachers about bodily functions? Are you revolted by the prospect of dealing with encopresis? As with all counseling, knowing yourself is always the best starting point.

The next step should be to begin a process of self-education. Get the training and supervision you need to develop competency and self-confidence. Learn the step-by-step treatment plans and interventions described in the literature. Then educate others through brief in-service trainings for teachers, administrators, and staff. Be prepared to deal with the biases of others, even as you validate their discomfort of others. These are not easy topics to discuss. Send literature to all parents and/or invite them to a training and discussion group. A significant part of these efforts should include dispelling myths that elimination disorders are difficult to treat, shameful, should be ignored, and the child's fault. Help others understand the prevalence and "invisibility" of elimination disorders, particularly nocturnal enuresis. Teachers need to be aware of secondary symptoms: academic deficits, lethargy, depression, anxiety, and somatic complaints.

Finally, decide what services you are willing to offer. Are you willing to be the point person on the treatment team? Provide general education for teachers, students, and parents? Provide direct services, treatment planning, charting, trainings? Perhaps provide a single session of full spectrum home training for individuals or groups, or instructions on how to use a urine alarm? Once you have made these decisions, incorporate them into your overall psychoeducational curriculum and publish a formal standard of care for your school that anticipates the needs of students with elimination disorders.

Helping a student with an elimination disorder may be one of the most challenging undertakings you accept as a professional school counselor, yet with a very reasonable commitment of time and energy, you can provide effective interventions, a much needed continuity of care, and hope for the future. No helping professional is better positioned to affirm and encourage these students than a professional school counselor.

(Note: See the CD-ROM for a list of references.)

CHAPTER 69

COUNSELING HIGH-FUNCTIONING
STUDENTS WHO HAVE AUTISM

Henry L. Harris

Preview

Autism is the fastest growing category of developmental disorder and involves mild to severe deficits in a person's ability to communicate and socially interact with others. It is also much more common in boys than in girls, may show signs of development before age 3 years, and affects all racial and ethnic groups regardless of socio-economic level. Individuals that have been diagnosed with autism but who do not have intellectual disabilities are often referred to as having high-functioning autism (HFA; Klin, Pauls, Schultz, & Volkmar, 2005). Currently there is no known specific cause of autism nor is there a cure. In this chapter I provide an overview of autism, characteristics of students with high-functioning autism, assessment and diagnostic information, suggestions for professional school counselors, and a list of resources.

Autistic Disorder, Asperger's Disorder, Childhood Disintegrative Disorder (CDD), Rett's Disorder, and Pervasive Development Disorder–Not Otherwise Specified (PDD-NOS) are the five conditions in a group of developmental disorders typically known as autism spectrum disorders (ASDs). While each condition has a specific diagnostic criteria outlined in the *Diagnostic and Statistical Manual of Mental Disorders–Fourth Edition, Text Revision* (DSM-IV-TR; American Psychiatric Association [APA], 2000), autism is by far the most common of the disorders. Since the 1990s, the rate of diagnosis of autism has increased 10% to 17% annually. Currently, for every 166 births, one child is born with autism. During the 1990s, the U.S. population increased 13%, disabilities increased 16%, and the rate of diagnosed autism increased 172% (Autism Society of America, 2006b).

The vast majority of children born with autism require long-term care and services. Special education costs are more than $8,000 per year and some specially structured programs cost more than $30,000 annually. If care is needed in a residential school, the cost significantly increases and ranges anywhere from $80,000 and $100,000 per year. While there is not cure for autism, genetics and early prenatal exposures have been suggested as possible causes. With early detection and intensive therapeutic interventions and education, these individuals will have the opportunity to develop skills that will help them reach their potential (Centers for Disease Control, 2006).

GENERAL CHARACTERISTICS OF AUTISM

Autism is a complex disorder characterized by the development of unusual behaviors in the areas of socialization, communication, and interest and activities before 3 years of age (Heflin & Alaimo, 2007). According to Bregman (2005) "the defining feature of autism is presence of a distinctive impairment in the nature and quality of social and communicative development (influenced by specific biological and environmental circumstances of the individual)" (p. 3). Parents are typically the first to notice autistic symptoms in their child, as they may observe their children not reaching appropriate developmental milestones (see Table 69.1). Howlin and Moore (1997) discovered in their study of over 1,200 parents, that more than 50% reported they recognized something was different about their child within the first year of life, 25% were told by their doctor not to worry, 10% were told to come back later because their child would probably grow out it, and less than 10% were given a diagnosis when they discussed their concerns with the doctor.

Children diagnosed with autism may have difficulty socially interacting with others. From a very early age they may appear aloof and most comfortable when left alone, having little need for interaction with other people. In social settings, autistic children may respond solely to adults or engage other children in one-sided scripted play in which they direct the action. As they grow older, rather than playing creatively with other children, they may spend their time gathering factual information on narrow topics or ask unusual, personal, and rhetorical questions to attain factual knowledge on a topic of interest (Bregman, 2005).

Some autistic individuals have abnormal communication skills, particularly delayed echolalia, whereby they repeat language phrases previously heard months, sometimes years before. They may also improperly use pronouns in a reverse manner using *you* when referring to themselves and *I* when referring to someone else (Hart, 1993). Autistic individuals may fail to orient to another person's voice or use other forms of communication such as gesturing. For example, an autistic individual who wants some-

TABLE 69.1

COUNSELING RESOURCES

Autism Research Institute (ARI), 4182 Adams Avenue, San Diego, CA 92116 (www.autismresearchinstitute.com)

Autism Society of America, 7910 Woodmont Ave, Suite 300, Bethesda, MD 20814-3067 (www.autism-society.org)

Center for Autism and Related Disorders (CARD), Corporate Headquarters, 19019 Ventura Blvd. Suite 300, Tarzana, CA 91356 (www.centerforautism.com)

Future Horizons, Inc, Resource Center for Autism & Asperger's Syndrome, 721 West Abram Street, Arlington, TX 76013 (www.futurehorizons-autism.com)

National Alliance for Autism Research (NAAR), 99 Wall Street, Research Park, Princeton, NJ 08540 (www.naar.org)

National Institute of Neurological Disorders and Stroke (NINDS), 6001 Executive Blvd, Bethesda, MD 20892-9663 (www.ninds.nih.gov)

Treatment and Education of Autistic & Related Communication Handicapped Children (TEACCH)—A Division of the UNC Department of Psychiatry; University of North Carolina at Chapel Hill, Chapel Hill, NC 27599 (www.teacch.com)

Wrightslaw—A legal resource for parents, educators, advocates, and attorneys providing accurate, reliable information about special education law, education law, and advocacy for children with disabilities (www.wrightslaw.com)

thing unattainable may take another person by the hand and lead the individual to the desired object. This is a nonverbal method used to accomplish an end goal and is also referred to as using another person as a tool because normal communication skills may be lacking (Wetherby & Prizant, 2005).

Individuals with autism may demonstrate a very narrow range of interest and activities, which limits their ability to reason and use their imagination. They may have unusual attachment to parts of an object rather than the complete object itself. Rather than roll a toy car around the floor, some autistic individuals may spend their time spinning the wheels on the car (Heflin & Alaimo, 2007). Some individuals with autism also have an obsessive desire for the preservation of sameness and might became abnormally upset when a change is made in an established routine. If a routine change occurs in their schedule, such as taking a different route to school, sometimes these individuals may have temper tantrums until familiar order is restored (APA; 2000). Individuals with autism also may have uncoordinated gross motor or fine motor skill development, be physically overactive or extremely underactive, display signs of distress for reasons others may not understand, and experience sensory integration problems related to certain sounds, noises, or textures that others may not be aware of (APA; 2000; Hart, 1993; Heflin & Alaimo, 2007; National Education Association [NEA], 2006).

Although autism is defined by a specific group of behaviors, it is important for professional school counselors to recognize that individuals diagnosed with autism can act very differently from one another. They may display a combination of the behaviors ranging from mild to very severe. Two students with the same diagnosis may act very differently from one another because of the differences in their development (National Institutes of Child Health & Human Development [NICHD], 2006).

HIGH-FUNCTIONING AUTISM

High-functioning autism (HFA) is a label used to describe children that meet the diagnostic criteria for Autistic Disorder (AD) but who are able to speak and have an average or above-average IQ. They are also able to function close to or above a normal level in society. Some individuals with HFA may be perceived as "oddballs," who at times lack common sense because of basic social mistakes they make. For example, they may forget to knock on the door before entering a room, have poor table manners, step directly in front of someone without consideration for space; when they are greeted by others, they may not always respond (Wikipedia, 2006). Because of their inability to maintain socially appropriate interactions, they may also become isolated, manipulated, and possibly victimized by their peers (Little, 2001).

The ability to accurately perceive social events and predict social behaviors in others is required for HFA individuals to actively participate and become engaged in social situations. When such social communication skills are absent, these individuals may experience abnormal levels of anxiety and stress, which contributes to them experiencing frequent tantrums, and in some circumstances, withdrawal or anger (Myles 2003). Such behaviors are sometimes misinterpreted as defiant and willful rather than resulting from challenges to self-regulation (Laurent & Rubin, 2004).

Individuals with HFA are extremely literal in their interpretations and often adhere rigidly to routine and order. When routine and order is changed, they may experience abnormal levels of discomfort that others may fail to understand. They also may become distracted before completing tasks and have difficulties transitioning between activities. Students with HFA may be performing academically at or above their grade level in some or all of their subjects, yet their unusual behavioral mannerisms often interfere with their progress (Zager & Shamow, 2005). During situations of sensory overload, which could result from being in a class with too many students, walking down a crowded hallway, eating lunch in a noisy cafeteria, or having too many objects in a classroom setting (e.g., pictures on the wall), students with HFA may not be able to self-regulate their sensory experiences. As a result, they may have a strong emotional reaction, appearing stressed or withdrawn (Laurent & Rubin, 2004). As Gutstein (2000) succinctly phrased it,

> the high functioning child with autism specializes in studying social relationships in a universe where the sheer amount of noise invading his brain constantly threatens to overwhelm him. He learns to specialize in avoiding chaos, by shutting out and avoiding most elements of variability and novelty. Instead he focuses on the non-changing aspects of his environment. Elements that remain the same provide him with the greatest experience of meaning and relation. He is obsessed by his search for stable patterns and unchanging relationship in his social universe like the immutable laws of mathematics, the unvarying progression of video games and other predictable sequences that occurs the same way over and over. He focuses on an interaction style which for him, is a matter of survival. The only means he has for enjoying social encounters is to discover ways to predict and or control social events. Each time he participates in an interaction that progresses in a predictable manner is a victory for science. (pp. 37–38)

ASSESSMENT AND DIAGNOSIS

An accurate assessment of autism is imperative and should be completed as early as possible because this is the first step in developing an intervention plan (Van Bourgondien, 1996). Physicians play a critical role in this process because from birth to age 3 years they are primarily the only professionals that have routine contact with children before they enter school. While most physicians recognize the value of early assessment and intervention, for a variety of reasons many have a difficult time identifying children with developmental delays and disorders (Gabovitch & Wiseman, 2005; Howlin & Moore, 1997). During office visits, both physicians and parents have the opportunity to monitor the child's physical, social, emotional, and cognitive development through developmental screening. This developmental screening identifies important milestones that children should accomplish at specific ages. Given the variation in how each child develops, some observed differences may indicate only a mild delay while other differences may indicate more serious concerns that should be addressed (Gabovitch & Wiseman, 2005).

When significant developmental delays are observed, a more formalized assessment is needed. The *Autism Diagnostic Observation Schedule* (ADOS; Lord, Rutter, DiLavore, & Risi, 2001), *Childhood Autism Rating Scale* (CARS; Schopler, Reichler, & Renner, 1988), and *TEACCH Transition Assessment Profile* (TTAP; Mesibov, Thomas, Chapman, & Schopler, 2007) are useful screening tools that require special training to administer and interpret. The *Autism Behavioral Checklist* (ABC; Krug, Arick, & Almond, 1980), the *Modified Checklist for Autism in Toddlers* (M-CHAT; Robins, Fein, Barton, & Green, 2001), the *Social Responsiveness Scale* (SRS; Constantino, 2005), and the *Social Communication Questionnaire* (SCQ; Rutter, Bailey, & Lord, 2003) are additional screening tools that could be completed by parents and/or teachers.

Once the assessment is complete and the diagnosis is made, the next phase of development is to create a treatment plan with a group of professionals knowledgeable about autism, as this could impact the overall process (Van Bourgondien & Mesibov, 1989). Because of the various services the child may need, professionals from multiple backgrounds could be helpful. This multidisciplinaryassessment team may include some or all of the following professionals:

- *Developmental pediatrician*—Has specific training in the evaluation and care of children with developmental delays including autism spectrum disorders. May also help to locate resources for families within each community to provide additional support.
- *Child psychiatrist*—A medical doctor may be initially involved in the diagnosis and if needed can prescribe medication and provide help in other areas concerning behavior emotions and social relationships.
- *Clinical psychologist*—Specializes in understanding the nature and impact of developmental disabilities including autism spectrum disorders. May perform psychological assessments and help with behavior modification planning and social skills training.
- *Occupational therapist*—Help clients improve coordination of basic motor functions and reasoning skills that will help them accomplish common daily-living tasks such as dressing and eating; may also work on sensory integration.
- *Physical therapist*—Helps to improve the use of bones, muscles, joints, and nerves to develop muscle strength, coordination, and motor skills.
- *Speech–language pathologist*—Involved in the improvement of communication skills including speech and language.
- *Social worker*—May provide counseling services or act as case manager helping to arrange services for the family as needed (Autism Society of America, 2006a).
- *Licensed professional counselor*—May provide social skills training to the individual or counseling to family members and also serve as a case manager.
- *Chiropractor*—Can provide series of chiropractic adjustments such as upper cervical adjustment and cranial sacral therapy.
- *Nutritionist*—Can monitor the child's nutritional concerns by evaluating feeding history, dietary intake, and suggest blood tests that reflect nutritional status to determine whether the child has nutritional deficiencies.
- *School teacher*— Responsible for helping develop and monitor the Individualized Education Program (IEP) for children in the school setting. Should have knowledge

of autism and training through Treatment & Education of Autistic and Related Communication Handicapped Children (TEACCH) organization.

- *Professional school counselor*—Can be an important voice of support for children with autism and their families. Should attend IEP meetings, provide social-skills training and counseling services to students with autism, and consult with other members of the team when necessary to help individual develop functioning social, emotional, and communication skills in the school setting.

Parents and other professionals must work collaboratively and serve the best interest of the child. Opening lines of communication is paramount to monitor the child's progress. Parents must keep themselves informed about their child's disability, be organized, and always prepared to consult with members of the assessment team (Autism Society of America, 2006b).

SUGGESTIONS FOR PROFESSIONAL SCHOOL COUNSELORS

Students with HFA bring unique needs to the school setting and there are a number of interventions that professional school counselors may provide to help them reach their maximum potential. First and foremost, professional school counselors should be aware of their personal feelings and attitudes toward high-functioning autistic students and their parents. Furthermore, professional school counselors should have sufficient knowledge about autism and the characteristics associated with this HFA. When knowledge about HFA is lacking, professional school counselors are advised to attend conferences, workshops, read literature, and consult more experienced professionals. If professional school counselors discover themselves harboring negative attitudes toward students with HFA and their families, they should explore reasons why the attitudes exist and attempt to resolve them.

COUNSELING HFA STUDENTS

There are a number of counseling interventions that professional school counselors may use when working with high-functioning autistic students, and for this to be effective they must take into consideration the unique characteristics of each HFA student. Even though many HFA students perform well academically, issues related to anxiety, isolation, and depression many need to be addressed (Zager & Shamow, 2005). To confront anxiety professional school counselors could use a variety of modified cognitive behavioral techniques such as guided imagery, relaxation, and modeling. For example, the anxiety experienced in some high-functioning autistic students may be decreased by helping them become aware of what causes their anxiety and then teaching them appropriate relaxation techniques such as deep breathing. A modified structured version of guided imagery focusing on positive things they enjoy rather than things they fear may also help. Music therapy may also be a useful avenue for professional school counselors to explore (Stahmer, Collings, & Palinkas, 2005).

If behavioral problems exist, professional school counselors should consider using an applied behavioral analysis (ABA) approach. The first step in ABA is to identify the behavior that needs to be changed. Once the behavior is identified, appropriate strategies should then be developed that will alter the behavior. During this time, the professional school counselor may provide reinforcements to elicit and maintain desired behavior. When an intervention is not successful, another technique is developed (Schoen, 2003).

Video modeling is another technique that has been effective in teaching appropriate social behaviors to children with autism. This approach involves videotaping another student performing the desired behaviors. The videotape is then shown repeatedly to the student that desires the skill (Carothers & Taylor, 2004). Professional school counselors are encouraged to have the student role-play the newly observed behavior as a method of strengthening the new observation. It may also be helpful for the professional school counselor to participate by modeling the observed videotaped behavior for the student and then guide the student in using the desired behavior. Professional school counselors may further assist students with HFA by (a) seeking a buddy with good social and communication skills who might accompany them to some less structured social situations; (b) helping them to join groups related to their interest and strengths; (c) helping them create a daily schedule for school that should be written in a way that helps the child anticipate changes and remain calm when those changes occur; and (d) providing individual counseling using a variety of approaches to help develop social skills and concrete problem solving (TEACCH, 2006).

INTEGRATED PLAY GROUP

Children who develop normally will typically engage in stimulating play that is imaginative, socially interactive, and pleasing. Unfortunately, many children with autism do not engage in this type of play. Therefore integrated play groups (IPGs) could be used with children aged 3 to 11 years to decrease social isolation and improve social and symbolic play skills (Wolfberg, 1999). IPG consists of guides, expert players, and novice players. The guides are competent group leaders, the expert members are peers with good social, communication, and imaginative skills, and the novice players are children with autism. The groups ordinarily consist of three to five members with a higher ratio of experts to novices, meet twice per week from 30 minutes to an hour, and are highly structured and follow consistent routines (Lantz, Nelson, & Loftin, 2004).

IPG has three levels of group leader support. Level one is modeled and directed play. During this time, the group leader directs the group interaction. Verbal guidance is the second level of support where the group interaction is developed from a distance. During the last level of support, the group leader does not interact with the children as they play, but is available for supervision (Lantz et al. 2004). According to Wolfberg (2003) children with autism who have experienced IPG have improved their social language skills, ability to sustain social interactions, the quality of their play, and developed friendships.

MEDICATION

Behavioral problems that keep individuals with autism from effectively functioning at home or school—such as aggression, severe tantrums, and self-injurious behavior—are often addressed using medications that have been developed to treat similar symptoms in other disorders. Unfortunately many of these medications have not been officially approved for use in children, yet they are prescribed by the doctor as needed. The doctor prescribing the medication should have experience working with individuals with autism, prescribe the lowest, most effective dose possible, and closely monitor the child while on the medication. Parents should also be aware of the possible side effects and realize that individuals with autism may respond to medications differently than normally developing children. If a child is taking prescription medication, parents must consider whether school officials should be made aware of this.

CONSULTING WITH PARENTS

Parental involvement has been identified as a key component in building a strong and effective educational experience for children with disabilities (Stoner et al., 2005). The Individual With Disabilities Education Improvement Act of 2004 (IDEIA) and No Child Left Behind Act of 2001 (NCLB) mandate that parents of children with disabilities have the legal right to be involved in aspects of their child's education. The interaction between parents and educational professionals, however, is often poorly organized and fragmented. The level of cooperation is also damaged sometimes because of the frustration, tension, and confusion created, and it ultimately affects the delivery of services and the well-being of students being served (Lake & Billingsley, 2000).

When consulting with parents of children with autism, professional school counselors should attempt to establish and build trust by genuinely listening to parental concerns, respecting their views, and following up on promises made. They should also strive to help parents understand the Individualized Education Program and prepare them for IEP meetings by discussing procedures, identifying members on the IEP team, and, if needed, attempting to make procedural changes that will equalize the role of all team members present at such meetings. Professional school counselors should also provide parents with information concerning other related services, make them aware of their legal rights, and develop a line of communication that recognizes and values their expertise as parents. Parents are empowered when educators value, recognize, and learn from parental expertise related to their child with autism (Stoner et al., 2005).

CONSULTING WITH TEACHERS

When consulting with teachers on issues concerning HFA students, professional school counselors may find it helpful to follow guidelines outlined by the organization Treatment & Education of Autistic and Related Communication Handicapped Children (TEACCH). TEACCH (2006) suggested placing high-functioning students with autism in regular classrooms in which their classes are interesting to them and relate to their strengths. Their desk area should also be neatly organized and without clutter, because this could be distracting. Also, when directions are written on a test, it might prove beneficial if the directions are highlighted or bolded (NEA; 2006; Swanson, 2005).

If students are assisted by an individual aide, the aide should be knowledgeable about autism and receive specific training regarding high-functioning autism. Knowledgeable professional school counselors may provide some of this training. The aide should not be considered a baby sitter and is most useful to the student when assistance is provided throughout the day in developing and implementing the student's structure such as through developing schedules, modifying assignments, and completing checklists (Swanson, 2005; TEACCH, 2006). Professional school counselors should also help teachers understand that because students with autism often have difficulty processing language, it is helpful to slow down the pace of instruction and keep the language clear. Teachers are encouraged to be clear, brief, and concise about their expectations and even rehearse behaviors for new situations (Zager & Shamow, 2005). Finally, to help other students understand students with HFA in their class or school, it might prove helpful if professional school counselors provide classroom guidance services explaining some general information about autism. If needed, professional school counselors should also consult with teachers and help them find ways to effectively discuss autism with their students.

Summary/Conclusion

The number of children diagnosed with autism has significantly increased over the years, and there is no sign this trend will ease. Many of these children are now students enrolled in public schools with the right to be included in regular classes whenever possible (IDEIA; 2004). Professional school counselors are encouraged to become advocates for students with autism and their families (Mulick & Butter, 2002). Effective advocacy requires accurate knowledge about autism and associated characteristics, counseling, and psychoeducational interventions. Despite the challenges that many students with autism encounter, they can be successful if school personnel are provided the appropriate support services. School administrators, professional school counselors, teachers, parents, and other support professionals must all work together to ensure that students with autism have the opportunity to lead more productive and satisfying lives.

(Note: See the CD-ROM for a list of references.)

SPECIAL ISSUES AND POPULATIONS IN SCHOOL COUNSELING

CHAPTER 70

HELPING STUDENTS ACQUIRE TIME-MANAGEMENT SKILLS

Vicki Brooks-McNamara

Preview

Developing and applying time-management strategies can help reduce frustration and missed deadlines. I provide examples of positive strategies, including goal setting, prioritization, development of timelines, and action plans as well as worksheets for accomplishing these strategies.

Time management falls under a larger construct called *social engineering*. Simply defined, social engineering is the ability to reduce obstacles (without avoiding them) to achieve the desired goal with minimal effort (Seaward, 2002, 2004). To reach this result efficiently and effectively is the essence of time management. We cannot manage time, but we certainly can manage ourselves within the construct of time. Thus, managing oneself with respect to time involves prioritizing and effectively carrying out the priorities for everyday work, play, and rest (Seaward, 2004).

Symptoms of poor time management can include rushing, vacillation, missed deadlines, and feeling overwhelmed. Over time, poor time management can lead to burnout. Burnout occurs when the individual cannot effectively maintain normal routines or behaviors (Henschen, 2001). Psychological symptoms include apathy, anxiousness, confusion, and incompletion of tasks. Increased heart rate, altered sleep patterns, and increased blood pressure are physiological symptoms of burnout (Henschen, 2001; Seaward, 2002, 2004).

Applying successful problem-solving strategies (e.g., goal setting) can help reduce time-management issues. For example, maintaining an overall 3.0 GPA can only be met by setting short- and long-term goals for each subject. For math, the short-term goal might be to obtain 80% or higher on tests. Short-term steps are needed to achieve the ultimate 80% goal and can include meeting with a study group three times per week or regularly reviewing homework with a checklist for completion. The time-management strategy of prioritization could assist in short-term goal achievement.

Professional school counselors' tasks include asking open-ended questions leading to the identification of both short- and long-term goals. After a goal is identified, the development of an action plan can begin. Progress checks and identifying available assets (e.g., parent or other adults) can increase the likelihood of goal achievement. Although the pace of everyday life has increased, the tested methods of time management remain the same (Roesch, 1998).

Time management can be a learned familial or cultural trait (e.g., acceptance of late arrivals), and some behavior characteristics get in the way of effective time management (e.g., perfectionism and procrastination; Seaward, 2002). As such, effective management of time is a learned skill, and the keys to overall success revolve around planning and organization. An excellent beginning for student organization would be the purchase of a daily/weekly/monthly planner and parents, and teachers should be included in the student's efforts to use the planner.

CONTROL OF TIME

Managing daily activities can be made easier by following simple guidelines that involve setting goals and getting organized. The guidelines have a built-in assumption: Success is the desired end result. Success, as referred to in this chapter, encompasses all aspects of life (e.g., school, home, friends).

SET GOALS

One must set goals specific to each task or desired accomplishment. Short-term goals are essential for reaching the stated long-term goal. Both short and long-term goals should be clearly defined with a plan of action and measurable outcomes including (a) *What do I want?* (goal); (b) *How I am going to get there?* (action plan); (c) *How will I know when I get there?* (measurable outcome).

The goal-setting worksheet in Appendix 70.A assists individuals in identifying the long-term goal (LTG) (e.g., 3.0 GPA) while establishing short-term goals (STG) with specified action plans (P). Each STG has a measurable outcome (MO), indicating what a successful result is for specific goals. Finally, the summation of each STG's MO leads to LTG successful completion (e.g., attaining a 3.0 GPA).

GETTING ORGANIZED

Attaining goals involves planning and organizing time. Organizational tips include the following:

1. *Keep a daily/weekly planner.* Write homework assignments and tasks down immediately upon receiving them, and transfer information to a monthly/semester calendar.
2. *Prioritize tasks using the prioritization worksheet* (see prioritization worksheet in Appendix 70.A). This worksheet can be used for daily, weekly, monthly, or semester prioritization. In the top section, no order or ranking should occur when listing tasks. Ranking occurs in the ABC Section. Using information from the ABC section, prioritize tasks as follows: *high urgency* with *high importance* (I); *low urgency* with *high importance* (II); *high urgency* with *low importance* (III); and *low urgency* with *low importance* (IV). The last section provides a list with (I) having the highest priority for immediate completion and (IV) the lowest priority for completion. Prioritization errors often occur when enjoyable tasks are ranked as urgent-important (e.g., calling my friend).
3. *Monitor one's use of time for 1 week.* The activities timesheet in Appendix 70.A provides a means for recording time spent on individual activities. The right-hand column summarizes the total hours per week for each activity, while the bottom row summarizes daily totals. Time should only be recorded in half-hour incre-

ments. After tallying time-use over a week, a schedule of time can be created to assist with urgent-important task completion.

4. *Schedule time for task completion* (see the Scheduling Time worksheet in Appendix 70.A). After completing the goal setting, prioritization, and time allocation worksheets found in Appendix 70.A, development of a schedule can begin. Several methods can be employed (e.g., boxing, time mapping). Table 70.1 provides additional time-management tips.

SUMMARY/ CONCLUSION

Effective use and management of time can create opportunities for engaging in pleasurable and fun activities. Through development of positive habits (e.g., using a daily planner), organization can become a reality. Once essential tasks are identified and goals established, the process for attainment becomes a roadmap for success. Clearly, success can occur as a result of careful thought, planning, organization, and effective time management. Table 70.2 provides a listing of Web sites and additional information for aid in time management.

(Note: See the CD-ROM for a list of references.)

TABLE 70.1

ADDITIONAL TIPS FOR MANAGING AND SCHEDULING TIME

Calculate time needed per assignment.

Record the time it takes to read five pages of the textbook. Use this time as a measure for blocking out time needs by class.

Identify the best time of day for learning (e.g., early morning or early evening).

During each study session, review previous lecture notes or materials. Reread the notes highlighting the important word(s) or ideas. Review the highlighted material for the test.

Take breaks during study time (e.g., every 30 minutes, take a 5-minute break).

Predetermine a stop time for studying. Hold to it. This will provide a short-term goal with a reward at the end.

Break large tasks down into smaller tasks.

Identify the time of day in which you are most productive. Use this time for completing urgent and important tasks.

Let go of attempting low-priority items. Do not stop a high-priority task for a less ranked task.

Each day, review the daily/weekly/monthly/semester planner. Reassess and redirect if necessary.

Learn to speak up. Share with others (especially family) urgent and important tasks and goals with assigned timelines. By knowing these, others can support you in achieving your goals.

Note. Adapted from study handout materials used in the Athletic Counseling Center, University of Wyoming.

TABLE 70.2

WEB SITES AND ADDITIONAL REFERENCES

http://teacher.scholastic.com/professional/futureteachers/time_management.htm
Tips for managing and creating effective teaching time

www.wannalearn.com/Academic_Subjects/Study_Skills
Links to study skills information, videos, books (by age groups) for helping students learn to study

http://dmoz.org/Reference/Education/How_To_Study
Links to study guides, creating good study habits, academic tips

www.ucc.vt.edu/stdysk/htimesch.html
Time scheduling suggestions from Virginia Tech

www.collegeboard.com/student/plan
Links for homework tips, life outside of the classroom; personal time management tools, time management tips for high school students

www.clt.cornell.edu/campus/learn/ssworkshops/skresources.html
Links to effective time management system; weekly and semester calendar

http://ub-counseling.buffalo.edu/stresstime.shtml
Time management with steps and other links for help

www.coun.uvic.ca/learn/program/hndouts
Links to self-management checklist, planning study time as well as other links for tips and suggestions

Davis, M., & Eshelman, E. R. (2000). *The relaxation and stress reduction workbook.* Oakland, CA: New Harbinger.

Gore, M. C., & Dowd, J. F. (1999). *Taming the timestealers: Tricks of the trade from organized teachers.* Thousand Oaks, CA: Corwin Press.

GOAL SETTING

LONG-TERM GOAL (LTG):

To get to the long-term goal (LTG), I must:

SHORT-TERM GOALS (STG):

1. _____   3. _____
   _____   _____

2. _____   4. _____
   _____   _____

My plan (P) for each short-term (STG) to be accomplished:

STG #1 (P)	STG #2 (P)	STG #3 (P)	STG #4 (P)
_____	_____	_____	_____
_____	_____	_____	_____
_____	_____	_____	_____
_____	_____	_____	_____
_____	_____	_____	_____
_____	_____	_____	_____
_____	_____	_____	_____

I will know when I have achieved each STG by this measurable outcome (MO):

STG # 1 _____
_____

STG # 2 _____
_____

STG # 3 _____
_____
_____

STG #4 _____
_____

STG #1MO + STG #2 MO + STG #3 MO + STG #4 MO = LTG = SUCCESS

PRIORITIZATION WORKSHEET

Write down all tasks needing to be completed. Do not worry about order or rank.

1.   6.

2.   7.

3.   8.

4.   9.

5.   10.

ABC RANK ORDER

Under **Column A,** write the items that **MUST** be done. Under **Column C,** write the items that you would **LIKE** to get done but that are not essential (can wait). Under **Column B,** write all others.

Column A	Column B	Column C
_____	_____	_____
_____	_____	_____
_____	_____	_____
_____	_____	_____
_____	_____	_____

Now organize the list in the *important* versus *urgent* matrix.

		IMPORTANT	
		High Importance	Low Importance
URGENT	**High Urgency**	A. B. I. C.	A. B. III. C.
	Low Urgency	A. B. II. C.	A. B. IV. C.

Then, begin to work on these tasks in the following order:

I. (A)   III. (A)
    (B)   (B)
    (C)   (C)

II. (A)   IV (A)
    (B)   (B)
    (C)   (C)

Note. Adapted from *Managing Stress: Principles and Strategies for Health and Well-Being,* by B. L. Seaward, 2002. Sudbury, MA: Jones & Bartlett.

TIME ALLOCATION WORKSHEET

My Time: Hours Per Day

	Mon	Tue	Wed	Thurs	Fri	Sat	Sun	Total
Sleep:								
School:								
Classes								
Lunch								
Clubs								
Sports								
Friends								
Free								
Dressing:								
School								
Date								
Other								
Study:								
Math								
English								
History								
Science								
Other								
Other:								
Total: 24 hours								

SCHEDULING TIME

Boxing Example (effective for weekends):

8:00–12:00	=	work on term paper (research)
12:00–1:00	=	lunch/exercise
1:00–5:00	=	2 hrs draft writing; other classes 2 hrs
5:00–7:00	=	time with family/dinner
7:00–9:00	=	movies
9:00–10:00	=	relax/bed

Time-Mapping Schedule (Saturday example):

9:00–9:30	=	eat breakfast; gather research materials
9:30–10:00	=	travel to library
10:00–10:30	=	determine how to locate needed reference using the librarian for assistance
10:30–11:00	=	gather first section of paper's research
11:00–11:30	=	take notes; write up outlines/narratives
11:30–12:00	=	organize for next section of research
12:00–12:30	=	gather second section references
12:30–1:00	=	take notes; write up outlines/narratives
1:00–1:30	=	travel home
1:30–2:00	=	lunch
2:00–2:30	=	reward for hard morning in library
2:30–3:00	=	review English
3:00–3:30	=	review science
3:30–4:00	=	math
4:00–	=	relax; dinner; fun with family or friends

Boxing & Time-Mapping Schedule (weekday example for study time):

7:30–3:00	=	classes (if free hour: library research)
3:00–6:00	=	sports/clubs
6:00–7:00	=	dinner
7:00–7:45	=	math homework (most difficult subject)
7:45–8:30	=	English homework
8:30–9:15	=	science homework
9:15–10:00	=	history homework (easiest)

Note. Adapted from *Managing Stress: Principles and Strategies for Health and Well-Being,* by B. L. Seaward, 2002. Sudbury, MA: Jones & Bartlett.

CHAPTER 71

Understanding Special Education Policies and Procedures

Tracy C. Leinbaugh

Preview

Professional school counselors are often members of multidisciplinary teams charged with determining student eligibility for special education and related services. In addition, students with disabilities are served within the framework of a comprehensive developmental counseling program. In this chapter I provide a summary of special education policies and procedures for the professional school counselor.

As the role of the professional school counselor has evolved and expanded over the past 50 years (Baker & Gerler, 2004), so have the challenges, including the challenge of providing services to students with disabilities. Results of a survey of professional school counselors indicated that although they provide many services to students with disabilities, they felt only somewhat prepared (Milson, 2002). It is reasonable to expect the number of students with disabilities to increase, because enrollments of these students have risen yearly since data began to be collected in 1976–1977 (Parrish, 1999). To effectively meet this challenge, it is the professional school counselor's responsibility to acquire a basic knowledge of the disabilities that qualify students for special education and related services under the Individuals With Disabilities Education Improvement Act of 2004 (IDEIA) and the policies and procedures followed by schools to ensure that students with disabilities receive a free and appropriate public education (Schmidt, 2004).

A Brief History and Description of Special Education Law

The Education for All Handicapped Children Act of 1975 (P.L. 94-142) was enacted by Congress in to meet the needs of students with disabilities. The federal regulations implementing the law were put in place in 1977. The 1990, the name of the act changed to the Individuals With Disabilities Education Act of 1990 (IDEA; P.L. 101-476) and "people first" language was added (e.g., student with a disability, child with a specific disability) throughout (Yell, 1998). The act was again amended in 1991 (P.L.102-119), reauthorizing Part H, the section providing funding for the planning and implementation of early intervention programs and naming the section The Early Intervention Program for Infants and Toddlers With Disabilities (Murdick, Gartin, & Crabtree, 2002). The 1997 IDEA Amendments (P.L. 105-17) included clarifications to the law and extended and restructured the original nine subchapters into four subchapters, or parts (Yell, 1998). The 2004 reauthorization of the act changed the name to the Individuals With Disabilities Education Improvement Act of 2004 (IDEIA).

The first subchapter of IDEIA is Part A, which provides the definitions, or general provisions, of the law. Part B provides detailed information regarding the grant program that requires every state receiving federal assistance under IDEIA to ensure that a free and appropriate public education (FAPE) is provided to all qualified children and youth with disabilities within the state. Procedural safeguards protecting the interests of students with disabilities are also included here.

Parts C and D are discretionary support programs. Part C, originally Part H of the Education of All Handicapped Children Act Amendments of 1986 (P.L. 99-457), extends the protections in Part B to infants and toddlers with disabilities (birth to age 3 years).

Part B has been permanently reauthorized, but Parts C and D are discretionary and support programs that are authorized on a limited basis and must be reauthorized approximately every 5 years. All 50 states are participants in federal funding and have developed policies and procedures to implement a free and appropriate education to all children and youth with disabilities.

PRINCIPLES AND PROVISIONS OF IDEIA

It is important for professional school counselors to know that not all students with disabilities are included in the categories served by IDEIA. Only those whose disability adversely affects their education and who require special education and related services to achieve are covered. IDEIA specifies the following categories of disabling conditions (Turnbull, Turnbull, Shank, Smith, & Leal, 2002; Yell, 1998): specific learning disabilities, speech or language impairments, mental retardation, emotional disturbance, other health impairments, multiple disabilities, deafness, hearing impairments, orthopedic impairments, autism, visual impairments (including blindness), traumatic brain injury, development delay, and deaf-blindness.

These categories are the minimum which states are required to serve. States do not have to adopt every category exactly as specified. They may combine categories, divide categories, use different terminology, or expand the definitions, but all students with disabilities who fall within the categories and meet the appropriate criteria as specified by the IDEIA must be served for states to receive the federal funding provided by the law.

In addition, states must identify and evaluate all children and youth with disabilities from birth through the age of 21 years. If a state does not require that students without disabilities receive an education between the ages of 3 and 5, and 18 and 22 years, they are not required to provide an education for those with disabilities.

IDEIA contains provisions to ensure that all students with disabilities who qualify for special education and related services receive a FAPE and that procedural protections are granted to the students and their parents or guardians (Yell, 1998) including the following:

- Zero reject
- Free and appropriate education (FAPE)
- Least restrictive environment (LRE)
- Identification and evaluation

- Confidentiality of information
- Procedural safeguards
- Technology-related assistance
- Personnel development
- Placement in private schools

Following is a closer examination of each of these provisions and what each means.

ZERO REJECT

The zero reject principle means that all students who are eligible for special education and related services under IDEIA are entitled to a FAPE. This entitlement is unconditional and without exception, and it extends to students attending private schools. The local public school district is responsible for identifying, assessing, evaluating, and providing services for all eligible students in private schools within the district's boundaries. Parents do not have to request that a school district do this. Each school district is legally responsible for locating all children and youth with disabilities. States generally meet this mandate through the establishment of Child Find programs.

FREE AND APPROPRIATE PUBLIC EDUCATION

IDEIA requires each state to have policies that ensure all students with disabilities a free and appropriate public education. Each state may establish its own special education standards to meet this mandate, but they must, at a minimum, meet those specified by IDEIA. State standards may exceed those set by IDEIA. Local school districts must meet their state's standards regardless of whether they meet or exceed IDEIA's. To ensure that a FAPE is provided to each student with a disability receiving special services, an Individualized Education Program (IEP) must be developed.

LEAST RESTRICTIVE ENVIRONMENT

The provision of least restrictive environment mandates that all students with disabilities are to be educated with their peers without disabilities to the maximum extent *appropriate* for each student. This is determined by the multidisciplinary team, which includes the parents, professionals, and the student, when possible, during the development of the IEP.

IDENTIFICATION AND EVALUATION

IDEIA mandates a nondiscriminatory (fair and unbiased) evaluation that serves two purposes: (a) to determine whether a student has a disability and (b) if it is determined that a disability exists and the student is eligible, to decide the nature of the special education and related services the student needs to ensure that a free and appropriate public education is provided. This evaluation must be full and formal, consisting of many different procedures that are specified by IDEIA. All procedures must conform to certain standards and are administered and interpreted by trained personnel. Protection is guaranteed in evaluation procedures by the following:

- Tests must be administered in the native language or mode of communication of the child.
- Standardized tests must be validated for the intended purpose and must be administered by trained personnel following the publisher's instructions.
- The evaluation must assess the child's specific areas of educational need. Useful information provided by the parents is included in the evaluation.
- Technically sound instruments must be used to assess multiple areas: cognitive, behavioral, physical, and developmental.
- No single test or procedure may serve as the sole criterion for determination of disability, programming, or placement.
- The evaluation team is multidisciplinary and includes at least one member who has knowledge in the suspected area of disability.
- All areas related to the suspected disability must be assessed.

CONFIDENTIALITY

The privacy rights specified by IDEIA are similar to those in the Family Educational Rights and Privacy Act of 1974 (FERPA), often referred to as the Buckley Amendment. IDEIA extends protection to four areas: (a) the right of parental access to records, (b) the right of the parent or guardian to amend their child's records, (c) the right of protection from disclosure of information to others without permission from the parent or guardian (or the student if at the age of majority), and (d) the destruction of records.

PROCEDURAL SAFEGUARDS

IDEIA includes procedural safeguards to protect the interests of students with disabilities. Included are general safeguards, the right to an independent educational evaluation, the right to the appointment of surrogate parents if needed, and dispute resolution.

General safeguards of particular importance to the professional school counselor are the requirement of notification and consent and the stay-put provision. Schools must notify parents of any change in placement or program and must obtain consent from the parents before the initial evaluation and placement in special education. All parties on the multidisciplinary team must agree to any change in program.

TECHNOLOGY-RELATED ASSISTANCE

IDEIA mandates that assistive technology devices and services must be provided and included in the IEP if necessary to provide a FAPE as special education or a related service or to maintain the student with a disability in the LRE.

PERSONNEL DEVELOPMENT

Personnel providing services to students with disabilities must be trained and licensed in their specific fields, and in-service training must be provided to all education personnel working with students with disabilities, including general education teachers. Professional school counselors should participate in opportunities to increase their knowledge and skills to effectively serve students with disabilities.

PRIVATE SCHOOL PLACEMENT

When the local education agency is unable to provide a FAPE and places a student with a disability in a nonpublic school, the local education agency retains responsibility for seeing that the IEP is implemented, a FAPE is provided, and that all education expenses are provided. The parents or guardians of the student are not financially responsible for the costs of the placement.

IMPLEMENTATION OF IDEIA

Although states develop their own procedures for implementing the IDEIA, the basic process of identification of students with disabilities and provision of special education and related services is similar for each. As a member of the school-based team, the professional school counselor should be familiar with the basic procedures. The specific policies and provisions for each state are outlined in a manual with sample forms that are available from the special education directors of each school district or from the state's department of education. Following are the steps generally followed when implementing the provisions of IDEIA.

SCREENING

Screening, although not required, is considered good practice. It helps identify which students might need further testing to determine whether they qualify for special education. Screening often is done through the administration of group tests.

PREREFERRAL

Schools are prohibited from placing into special education students who have experienced lack of instruction or who have limited English proficiency and who, because of those educational needs, do not perform well in general education. Many schools have teams of teachers and other education specialists, including professional school counselors, for the purpose of providing immediate and necessary help to teachers experiencing challenges with students and to guard against misidentifying students as having disabilities, as this practice can have serious consequences. Accurate records of all interventions and the results are kept, often by professional school counselors, to document the need for a full evaluation, should the team decide that the next step is needed.

REFERRAL

The prereferral intervention team may decide to submit to the child study team a formal, written request for a student to receive a full and formal nondiscriminatory evaluation. The form for this request usually asks for specific and comprehensive information regarding basic screening results, areas of education concerns that prompted the referral, the nature of prereferral interventions and results, and any concerns expressed by the student or the family.

NONDISCRIMINATORY EVALUATION

This requirement of IDEIA is for the purpose of finding the answers to two questions: (a) does the student have a disability and, if so, (b) what is the nature of the specifically designed instruction and related services that the student needs? Parental consent is required for the evaluation to proceed. The evaluation consists of many different procedures that measure the student's cognitive, behavioral, physical, and developmental functional levels and must conform to certain standards and involve specified individuals. All areas related to the suspected disability must be assessed, including health, vision, hearing, social–emotional functioning, intelligence, academic performance, communicative ability, and motor ability.

Procedures used in the evaluation must be nondiscriminatory on a racial or cultural basis, must be valid for the purpose used, and must accurately reflect the student's aptitude and achievement level. All existing data on the student are reviewed, including school records, observations, work products, and information from the parents. The whole child is evaluated and a broad view is taken of the student's needs and strengths.

EVALUATION TEAM

The multidisciplinary evaluation team includes, at a minimum, the student's parents; at least one of the student's general education teachers; at least one special education teacher; a representative of the school district who is qualified to provide or supervise instruction to meet the unique needs of students with disabilities and who has knowledge of the general education curricula and of the availability of local education resources; someone who can interpret the instructional implications of the evaluation results; related services personnel; and the student, when appropriate. The professional school counselor, who possesses many of the skills required by IDEIA, is an important member of this team.

Each professional who administers a test compiles a written report of the instrument used and the findings and presents it at a team meeting. If the student is found to not have a disability and is ineligible for special education, the parents must be given a notice on ineligibility, and the student remains in general education without special education and related services. If the student has a disability and qualifies, the team determines specifically what kind of specially designed instruction and related services the student needs, keeping in mind that the school has a duty to provide an appropriate education and access to the general education curricula to the maximum extent appropriate (Reddy, 1999). The school must provide a continuum of placements, from least to most restrictive, which can include regular class placement, special education resource services, a self-contained classroom, a special school, home instruction, or hospital or institution placement (Little & Little, 1999).

DEVELOPING THE IFSP AND IEP

Infants and toddlers with disabilities require an Individualized Family Services Plan (IFSP) which takes into consideration the strengths and needs of the family as well as the child. Schools that include preschool programs for children with disabilities may stipulate that the professional school counselor provide many of the services required by the family, including case management. Professional school counselors may also provide case management for elementary and secondary special education students (Dunn & Baker, 2002; Shepard-Tew & Creamer, 1998). Students with disabilities ages 3 through 21 years require an Individualized Education Program (IEP) based on the student's development and needs and specifying outcomes for the student.

The IEP assures that the student will benefit from special education and have the opportunity for an equal education, independent living, economic self-sufficiency, and full participation and is often developed by the same team that conducted the evaluation. In the development of the IEP, the team must consider the student's strengths, the parents' concerns, the results of the evaluation, and any special factors, including the following:

- Appropriate strategies to address behavior for students whose behavior impedes the learning of self or others.
- Language needs as related to the IEP for the student with English as a second language.
- The use of Braille or other appropriate reading and writing media for the student who is blind or who has a visual impairment.
- Language and communication needs and opportunities to communicate with peers and professionals in their language and mode for students who are deaf or have hearing impairments.
- Assistive technology devices and services as appropriate (Turnbull et al., 2002).

The IEP must contain the following:

- The student's level of performance.
- How the disability affects the student's involvement in the general education curriculum.
- Measurable annual goals (short-term objectives).
- Special education and related services provided to the student, modifications to the program, and supports provided.
- Amount of participation in both academic and nonacademic activities with nondisabled peers.
- Individual modifications in the administration of state- and/or district-wide assessments of achievement given to all students.
- Dates for beginning services and anticipated frequency, location, and duration of services.
- Transition plans, including (a) beginning at the age of 14, a statement of needs related to transition services; (b) beginning at the age of 16, a statement of needed transition services; and (c) 1 year before the student reaches the age of majority, a statement that the student has been informed of his or her rights under IDEIA.
- How progress toward annual goals will be measured and how the parents will be informed of the student's progress.

Movement in school must be promoted by the IEP related to seven adult outcomes: postsecondary education, vocational training, employment with others without disabilities, continuing and adult education, adult services, independent living, and community participation (Turnbull et al., 2002).

IEP team meetings must be scheduled at times that facilitate parental attendance. If the parents do not participate, the team must develop the IEP to serve the student. Parent consent is not required to implement the IEP, but the parents may challenge it at any point. The IEP must be in effect at the beginning of the school year. In cases where students are determined eligible for services at some time during the school year, the team may not wait until the beginning of the next school year to begin the development of the IEP.

The IEP must be reviewed at least annually, and the team must review and revise it to address five matters: (a) any lack of expected progress; (b) the result of a reevaluation (required every 3 years); (c) information about the student provided to or by the parents; (d) anticipated needs; and (e) other matters related to the student's education.

The professional school counselor may write annual goals for the student with a disability related to social–personal development. Goals may address helping the student and the parents understand the nature of the student's disability and the possible effects on learning, socialization, and personal development and helping the student adjust to school and socialize with peers. Methods of achieving these goals may include parent education, parent support groups, individual counseling with the parents, individual counseling, group counseling and support groups, and classroom guidance activities involving the student. Among others, such student services may address issues such as personal adjustment, loss and grieving, social skills, family and peer relationships, conflict resolution, decision making and problem solving, goal setting, study skills, career planning, and self-esteem (Allen & Latorre, 1998).

Summary/Conclusion

Students with disabilities are increasingly receiving special education in general education classrooms with their nondisabled peers. Professional school counselors are highly trained educational specialists who provide services to all students, including students with disabilities. These services may require serving as a member of a prereferral intervention team or a multidisciplinary team. The professional school counselor may write annual goals for the IEPs of students with disabilities and be responsible for the implementation of those goals. When implementing a developmental, comprehensive guidance, and counseling program, students with disabilities are recipients of responsive services, classroom guidance, and individual planning, just as students without disabilities are. A basic understanding of the federal laws, provisions, and procedures relating to special education are beneficial for the professional school counselor to understand and to ensure that each and every student may benefit from his or her education.

(Note: See the CD-ROM for a list of references.)

CHAPTER 72

UNDERSTANDING SECTION 504 POLICIES AND PROCEDURES

Amy J. Newmeyer & Mark D. Newmeyer

Preview

Section 504 of The Rehabilitation Act of 1973 can be used to provide school accommodations for a variety of disabilities not covered under the Individuals With Disabilities Education Improvement Act of 2004 (IDEIA) guidelines. It is important that professional school counselors have an understanding of this law and how it can be used to best serve students who need various accommodations in the school setting. We review Section 504 policies, discuss differences between policies and procedures for IDEIA and Section 504, and conclude with two case examples.

Section 504 of The Rehabilitation Act of 1973 is a law that prohibits discrimination on the basis of disability in any program or activity that receives federal financial assistance. Thus, all public school systems are covered under the scope of this law. The U.S. Department of Education's Office for Civil Rights is responsible for enforcing this law in different areas including employment practices; program accessibility; and preschool, elementary, secondary, and postsecondary education. In a school setting, this means that students with disabilities should be able to access the same services as students without disabilities. Section 504 defines eligible students as those who have a physical or mental impairment, have a record of such an impairment, or are perceived as having such an impairment (Schulzinger, 1999).

There are several important differences between IDEIA and Section 504:

- Section 504 applies to elementary, secondary, postsecondary, and work settings whereas IDEIA applies only to elementary and secondary school settings (Betz, 2001).
- Section 504 does not list specific groups of eligible students; rather, it defines eligible students as those who have a physical or mental impairment that substantially limits one or more major life activities, including caring for self, performing manual tasks, walking, seeing, hearing, speaking, breathing, learning, and working.
- Section 504 describes "appropriate education" as those services that meet the needs of the student with a disability as adequately as those students without a disability.
- Section 504 does not require that a diagnostic evaluation be performed to determine eligibility.
- Section 504 does not provide funds to the school system to provide services.
- Section 504 requires that the school district designate an employee that will ensure compliance with the law and handle any grievances.

- Section 504 requires the school district to ensure that tests and other evaluation measures are given in a way that reflects the student's skills and are not affected by impairment.
- Students eligible for Section 504 accommodations remain in a general education classroom because 504 guarantees access, not services or specialized instruction (Schulzinger, 1999).

Examples of students who may qualify for Section 504 accommodations include the following:

- Students who have a chronic medical condition that causes them to miss extended periods at school because of appointments for health care and therapies or symptoms of pain and fatigue.
- Students who have side effects from prescribed medications.
- Students who need an assistive communication device to participate in the classroom.
- Students who are evaluated for IDEIA but may be ineligible. These conditions may include mild learning disabilities or attention-deficit/hyperactivity disorder.
- Students who cannot take written or oral tests because of impaired writing or communication skills (Schulzinger, 1999).

Reasonable accommodations for eligible students may include physical rearrangement of the classroom, lesson presentation, assignments, test taking, organizational skills, behaviors, or medication administration. Some examples include the following:

- Changing the volume of homework while maintaining the same educational standards.
- Allowing rest periods for children who are easily fatigued, or rearranging the classroom schedule to allow for a shortened academic day.
- Providing an extra set of materials for the student to use at home.
- Providing access to health care during field-trip and off-campus activities.
- Seating the student near the teacher to minimize distractions.
- Asking the teacher to repeat instructions or write them down for the student.
- Breaking assignments into smaller segments (Schulzinger, 1999).

Section 504 states that a group of professionals rather than an individual should decide placement and services. The referral for a section 504 plan may come from a professional, parent, or the student. The school must have a designated 504 coordinator who is responsible for coordinating services and assembling the team (Betz, 2001). However, the law does not state which school personnel must be present as members of the team. The professional school counselor can play a vital role in assisting this team to determine appropriate services and to advocate for students with special needs. Other personnel who should be present include the student's teachers, parents, school nurse, and other related service providers. Although the law does not require a written document, it is generally encouraged to ensure that everyone involved is aware of the accommodations and plan for services. Many experts recommend the 504 plan follow the same format as an Individualized Education Program (IEP).

THE ROLE OF THE PROFESSIONAL SCHOOL COUNSELOR

The professional school counselor is in a position to advocate for a student who may benefit from a 504 plan and can initiate a referral for a 504 plan by contacting the school's 504 coordinator. Additionally, by providing a linkage between the family, classroom, school, 504 coordinator, and other support systems, the professional school counselor often greatly facilitates the collaborative process and also plays a vital role by informing and educating principle individuals regarding the benefits of utilizing 504 accommodations. That is to say, educators and families may not fully understand the importance that 504 accommodations may have in a student's educational development (Brady, 2004).

Huefner (2000) cited examples of situations that may require consideration of a 504 plan:

1. A student has recently been diagnosed with ADHD or a mild learning disability, but is not eligible for an IEP.
2. A student with a medical illness has recently returned to school and may have requested extra help.
3. A student who has a chronic health condition.
4. A family notifies school personnel of the presence of a physical or mental impairment for their child, of which the school was previously unaware.
5. When school personnel believe a child is at risk for falling behind in school because of a physical or mental condition.

CASE STUDY 1

A 9-year-old female student in a third-grade classroom has recently been diagnosed with attention-deficit/hyperactivity disorder, predominantly inattentive type. She has normal intelligence and does not have any evidence of learning disabilities or a language disorder. She does not have any significant behavioral problems in the classroom setting. However, she is inattentive and distractible, and frequently forgets to write down assignments or turn them in, significantly affecting the grades that she receives. This student may qualify for accommodations under Section 504. Possible accommodations include the following:

- Changing her classroom seat so that she is close to the teacher and distractions from other students are minimized.
- Establishing an assignment book that is checked by her teacher at the end of the day to ensure that she has written down all assignments. Her parents can be responsible for checking the assignment book to ensure that assignments are completed and returned to school.
- Repeating directions if necessary to ensure that she has heard them correctly.
- Giving extra test-taking time, if needed.
- If medications are administered, excusing her from the classroom at the appropriate time to receive the medication.

Case Study 2

A 13-year-old male student has recently been diagnosed with cancer. He has always been a good student and has no known behavioral or academic problems. However, he has missed several weeks of school because of hospitalization and is now on a medication regimen at home that also requires medications be administered during the day at school. Although he wants to attend school, his teachers are noticing that he seems exhausted by the end of the school day and often falls asleep in class. Possible accommodations for this child include the following:

- Rearranging his class schedule so that all academic courses are scheduled during the morning so that he can be excused for the afternoon, if fatigued.
- Providing an extra set of books for use at home or in the hospital so he can keep up with homework.
- Allowing for more than the maximum number of absentee days if he is able to complete the missed work on time.
- Allowing for a note-taking buddy in his classes to send him notes when he is absent.
- Excusing him from class when necessary to administer medications.
- Allowing for use of a wheelchair for off-campus field trips if his participation is limited because of exhaustion.

Summary/Conclusion

Section 504 of The Rehabilitation Act of 1973 is a law ensuring that students with medical or psychological conditions have equal access to services in facilities and programs receiving federal financial assistance. However, many school and medical professionals are not fully aware of the regulations set forth in Section 504. This often results in confusion regarding the use of a 504 plan, and thus available services and accommodation may be overlooked (American Academy of Pediatrics, 2000) (see Table 72.1 for some online resources related to Section 504). The professional school counselor should be aware of the presence of the 504 statute, as it can be used to provide certain accommodations to students with disabilities who do not qualify for services under the IDEIA regulations. Additionally, the professional school counselor is frequently called upon to be the 504 case manager for students and can also act as an advocate for the student with a disability by initiating the process of forming a 504 plan and serving as a member of the 504 team.

(Note: See the CD-ROM for a list of references.)

TABLE 72.1

ONLINE RESOURCES ABOUT SECTION 504

www.504IDEIA.org/504overview.html
> This site contains information regarding Section 504 plans and the differences between eligibility for Section 504 and IDEIA.

www.diabetes.org/advocacy-and-legalresources/discrimination/school/504plan.jsp
> This site contains information from the American Diabetes Association, including a sample 504 plan for a patient with diabetes, which could be modified to cover another chronic medical condition.

www.wrightslaw.com/info/sec504.accoms.mods.pdf
> This document contains a list of sample modifications and accommodations that can be written into a section 504 document for a child with behavioral or learning difficulties in the classroom.

www.bridges4kids.org/articles/4-04/SevierAcc.html#top
> This site contains information regarding possible accommodations for section 504 plans for children with a variety of different chronic health conditions. It is used by the Sevier County school system in Tennessee.

CHAPTER 73

HELPING STUDENTS WHO HAVE DISABILITIES BY USING MULTIDISCIPLINARY TEAMS

Amy Milsom

Preview

Multidisciplinary teams are widely used in school districts to assess the needs of students with disabilities and to develop interventions for those students. Bringing specialized skills and knowledge, professional school counselors are often integral members of those teams, which can include school and community agency personnel as well as parents and students. By identifying specific roles, I outline ways that professional school counselors can help students with disabilities via multidisciplinary teams through the various stages of the special education process (i.e., referral, assessment, IEP development, implementation, and evaluation). Advantages and disadvantages of three different team models (multidisciplinary, interdisciplinary, transdisciplinary) are also discussed.

Approximately 12% of school-age students (ages 6–21 years) have disabilities (U.S. Department of Education, 2002). The Individuals With Disabilities Education Improvement Act of 2004 (IDEIA; P.L. 108-446), defined students who are eligible for special education services as those who meet the criteria for one or more of the following disabilities: autism, hearing impairment, mental retardation, orthopedic impairment, other health impairment (including attention-deficit/hyperactivity disorder), emotional disturbance, specific learning disability, speech or language impairment, traumatic brain injury, and visual impairment.

Since 1975, federal disability legislation (i.e., P.L. 94-142, the Education for All Handicapped Children Act) has mandated that school districts identify and provide special education and related services to students with disabilities. As a result, these students are now being educated in public schools and, to the greatest extent possible, in general education classrooms. In addition, as part of their ethical responsibility to provide comprehensive counseling and guidance services to all students, professional school counselors perform a variety of activities for students with disabilities.

To receive federal funding, school districts must adhere to guidelines outlined in P.L. 94-142 (renamed the Individuals With Disabilities Education Act in 1990, then amended in 1997 and reauthorized in 2004). Although some guidelines have changed over time, the specific requirements for the assessment and ongoing evaluation of students with disabilities have remained fairly consistent, and IDEIA mandates that all educational decisions are made by a group of individuals. Many students with disabilities also receive special services under Section 504 of the Rehabilitation Act of 1973 (Section 504). Section 504 does not identify specific individuals who must be involved with the determination of necessary services for eligible students, but it is not uncommon for numerous school personnel to collaborate in the design and implementation of services for students with disabilities under this legislation.

MULTIDISCIPLINARY TEAMS

Multidisciplinary teams are known by many names, including child study teams, staffing teams, and assessment teams, to list but a few. MDT is the acronym commonly used in relation to the plethora of school-based teams that are composed of a variety of professionals. MDTs are used to provide an unbiased and comprehensive evaluation of a student. Input from individuals with different skills and expertise will likely be less biased than input from only one individual (Kaiser & Woodman, 1985).

MDTs can be used for numerous purposes in schools; however, they are probably most commonly associated with initial assessments of students to determine eligibility for special education services, for Individualized Education Program (IEP) development and implementation decisions, and for reviewing special education placement decisions on an informal basis (Pfeiffer & Heffernan, 1984).

The composition of MDTs will vary depending on the purpose of the team. IDEIA (2004) mandated that a team of professionals and the student's parent jointly review assessment data to determine the student's eligibility for special educational services. Overton (1996) indicated that these types of MDTs often include professionals such as a special education teacher, school psychologist, and school administrator. Other members might include a regular education teacher and a professional school counselor or other support staff member, such as a speech–language pathologist or rehabilitation counselor.

Yell, Rogers, and Rogers (1998) indicated that an MDT used for special education eligibility and an MDT formed for the purpose of generating an IEP do not necessarily consist of the same individuals, although they could. In addition, team composition will vary depending on the specific needs of the student. IDEIA stated that an IEP team must contain a special education teacher, regular education teacher, parent, local education agency (LEA) representative (typically a school administrator), the student (when appropriate), and other support personnel such as a professional school counselor or speech–language pathologist. Table 73.1 provides examples of how team composition might vary depending on the purpose of the team and the needs of the student.

PROFESSIONAL SCHOOL COUNSELORS AND MDTS

The American School Counselor Association (ASCA) supports professional school counselors' involvement with students with disabilities and created a position statement to guide practitioners in determining appropriate roles and responsibilities related to those students (ASCA; 2004). ASCA indicated that, although participating on and providing feedback to MDTs are important responsibilities, professional school counselors should not participate on MDTs as representatives of the administrative staff (i.e., replacing a school administrator as an LEA). In addition, ASCA encouraged professional school counselors to engage in collaborative efforts with MDT members to determine student eligibility for special educational services, generate necessary interventions, and imple-

TABLE 73.1

MDT VARIATION

Student	Purpose	Team members
15 years old with a learning disability	Initial assessment	School psychologist Special education teacher Parent Professional school counselor
	IEP development	Special education teacher Regular education teacher Administrator (LEA) Parent Student Professional school counselor
6 years old with severe mental retardation	Initial assessment	School psychologist Special education teacher Parent
	IEP development	School psychologist Special education teacher Regular education teacher Administrator (LEA) Parent Speech–language pathologist School nurse Professional school counselor

ment counseling and guidance interventions (individual, small group, and classroom) when relevant.

Although they are not required to participate on MDTs, professional school counselors are often integral members of those teams. In fact, in a national survey of professional school counselors, 100% indicated that they provide services to students with disabilities and 80% indicated that they participated on MDTs for those students (Milsom, 2002). Fairchild (1985) indicated that because MDT members often tend to focus mainly on the academic needs of students with disabilities, professional school counselors can help bring focus to students' holistic needs. They can help other team members become aware of and determine relevant interventions to address the career and personal–social needs of students (Milsom, Goodnough, & Akos, 2007).

Professional school counselors can become involved with MDTs in a variety of ways, and it is likely that their involvement will vary not only from school district to school district but also from building to building within the same district. Through MDT involvement, professional school counselors provide services to students with disabilities during the initial referral process, assessment, IEP development, IEP implementation, and evaluation.

REFERRAL STAGE

Professional school counselors are often the first individuals in a school to be contacted when a student is having academic difficulties or when some other educational need becomes apparent. Parents or teachers might contact the professional school counselor to find out what options are available to students with learning difficulties or other disabilities. In those instances, professional school counselors should follow school district protocol for formally requesting an initial assessment for special education eligibility. They also might be asked to maintain contact with family members throughout the initial referral process, but they should not be responsible for administrative tasks related to the referral (e.g., disseminating assessment paperwork, scheduling the initial team meeting).

ASSESSMENT STAGE

During the assessment stage, professional school counselors might be responsible for collecting data related to the student's academic history and current academic status, interpersonal functioning, or classroom behavior. In addition to summarizing academic records and looking for patterns, professional school counselors might use a variety of checklists to evaluate social skills or to monitor behavior in an attempt to identify strengths and weaknesses in those areas. They can formally observe students in their classrooms and in less structured settings (e.g., playground) to collect numerous types of behavioral data (e.g., time on task, interpersonal skills). To facilitate an unbiased assessment, school counselors are often more appropriate choices to conduct observations than are classroom teachers, whose perspectives might reflect negative or positive past experiences with students.

IEP OR 504 PLAN DEVELOPMENT STAGE

IEP and 504 plan teams determine annual goals for students, and this MDT's job is to identify areas of student needs as well as plans or interventions for addressing those needs. In addition to bringing attention to the general career and personal–social needs of students, professional school counselors also can help to identify critical upcoming school transitions such as those from grade to grade or high school to postsecondary settings (Milsom, 2007). They can identify skill or knowledge deficits as well as appropriate resources and interventions that could be used to help a student prepare for the transition.

In addition, if the team determines that a student would benefit from counseling services, the professional school counselor would be responsible for developing a counseling intervention plan, with input from the team when relevant. Many students with disabilities benefit from counseling interventions that target issues such as self-esteem, social skills, or anger management, and professional school counselors possess the knowledge and skills needed to develop interventions in these areas. In addition, professional school counselors are familiar with counseling approaches (e.g., behavioral techniques, play techniques, group work) that have been shown to be effective when used in interventions for students with disabilities.

In addition to developing transition programs and counseling interventions, professional school counselors might also be involved with the development of a behavior management plan. With knowledge of issues such as human development, motivation, and reinforcement, they can help teachers to develop behavior management plans that will be developmentally appropriate, manageable, and effective. They may also consult with family members to help establish consistent expectations between home and school.

Finally, professional school counselors often perform what some might describe to be *appropriate* administrative tasks during this stage. For example, if the MDT determines that a student needs a revised course schedule, the professional school counselor could be responsible for creating an appropriate course schedule. Also, if the most significant needs of the student fall into the expertise of the professional school counselor (e.g., while a student is receiving academic accommodations under Section 504 related to severe burns, his main difficulty is coping with and accepting his new appearance), it may be appropriate for the professional school counselor to chair the meeting and/ or coordinate the services provided to that student. In those types of situations, professional school counselors will have opportunities to practice group facilitation skills and model effective leadership characteristics (Lockhart, 2003; Milsom et al., 2007). Keep in mind, however, that in most instances a professional school counselor should simply participate as a collaborative team member who provides input and shares feedback rather then one who holds administrative authority.

IMPLEMENTATION STAGE

During the implementation stage, professional school counselors can carry out the programs and interventions designed during the IEP or 504 plan meeting that would fall under the descriptor of *related services.* Interventions might include one-on-one counseling, small-group work, or classroom guidance lessons related to academic, career, or personal–social areas. Target areas might include transition planning, career development, interpersonal needs, and behavior management.

Collaboration and consultation with team members is also important during this stage. Professional school counselors are frequently the liaisons between the school and community agencies that might be involved in providing services to a student. Professional school counselors might also be responsible for coordinating communication between the school and the family. Additionally, ongoing consultation and collaboration with teachers and other team members can help to ensure the successful implementation of services; professional school counselors can serve as consultants to teachers or other personnel who want feedback on their implementation of classroom-based or other types of interventions.

EVALUATION STAGE

Evaluation of student progress can involve independent as well as collaborative data collection. For example, professional school counselors can attempt to individually evaluate the effectiveness of the social skills interventions they have implemented, or they can also obtain feedback from other team members regarding student progress in relation to that goal area. In addition, professional school counselors might be responsible for collecting and summarizing data related to specific IEP goal areas (e.g., academics, social skills, behavior). Outcome data not only can help the team determine if or how goals should be modified over time but also the data can serve as an indicator of school counselor effectiveness.

TEAM FUNCTIONING

Professional school counselor involvement in MDTs also requires an understanding of team dynamics. Hardman, Drew, Egan, and Wolf (1993) indicated that MDTs help to facilitate collaboration among professionals; however, researchers argue that collaboration and communication among MDT members is often minimal (Carpenter, King-Sears, & Keys, 1998; Huebner & Gould, 1991; Ogletree, Bull, Drew, & Lunnen, 2001). A discussion of three MDT models (multidisciplinary, interdisciplinary, and transdisciplinary) will help to clarify this potential problem. All three of these models fit under the general descriptor multidisciplinary; they involved a variety of professionals. Since one of these models is also called *multidisciplinary*, the term *MDT Model* will be used in reference to the model to avoid confusion with the generic MDT.

MULTIDISCIPLINARY TEAM MODEL

The MDT Model involves team members functioning independently of one another—they collect assessment data and share findings with the team. For example, a special education teacher might collect data related to reading comprehension, and a professional school counselor might conduct an observation to assess interpersonal needs. This information would be brought to the team, but a team leader (perhaps an assistant principal) is then responsible for moving the team toward final decisions regarding educational placement and type of services to provide. Team members proceed to independently provide services specific to their areas of expertise. Although they might be aware of what services other team members are providing, they are not influenced by those activities (Carpenter et al., 1998). Ultimately, there is little teamwork involved in the MDT Model. In addition, families are typically excluded from the decision-making process, and team members independently initiate family involvement to monitor progress or provide feedback (Ogletree et al., 2001). The potential for overlap of services is great, given the limited amount of communication among team members.

Although professional school counselors have training in group process and dynamics, the MDT Model provides them little opportunity to use these skills, because the team does not engage in shared decision making or discussion. In addition, while professional school counselors could certainly initiate consultative or collaborative relationships with team members, the team philosophy might encourage team-member resistance to these types of relationships. As a result, professional school counselor involvement on teams adhering to the MDT Model likely would include independent assessment and implementation of services with minimal interaction with other members outside of the team meeting. Finally, with family contact being inconsistent across team members, professional school counselors might find contact with families to be awkward. Also, with minimal awareness of the services that other team members are providing, they may struggle to respond to family questions regarding non–counseling-related services.

INTERDISCIPLINARY TEAM MODEL

The interdisciplinary team model (IDT Model) is characterized by interdependence among members rather than independence (Ogletree et al., 2001). IDT Model team members assess students within the realm of their own disciplines, but assessment activities are coordinated with those of other team members (Carpenter et al., 1998). Decisions regarding types of services to provide are jointly determined and members occasionally work together to provide services (Ogletree et al., 2001). A case manager, rather than a team leader, helps to facilitate communication among team members and often acts as a family liaison (Carpenter et al., 1998).

The IDT Model allows professional school counselors to perform some of the roles ASCA (2004) recommended in relation to students with disabilities. First, the IDT Model supports and encourages professional school counselor collaboration with other team members, particularly during the IEP or 504 plan development stage. The IDT Model also provides more opportunities for professional school counselors to influence group process. Finally, consultation and collaboration with families is expected.

TRANSDISCIPLINARY TEAM MODEL

The third team model, transdisciplinary (TDT Model), involves a coordination of services, cooperation and collaboration among team members, and active parental involvement throughout the process (Carpenter et al., 1998). Using the TDT Model, a case coordinator works with the family to determine assessment needs. Then, with the consultation of other team members, only a few team members conduct the assessment. Service-delivery decisions are collaboratively determined. In addition, services are provided by a few team members with input from the rest of the team. The result is a well-coordinated effort (Ogletree et al., 2001).

Carpenter et al. (1998) indicated that professional school counselors perform many roles on a team operating from the TDT Model, with one of the main roles being that of a collaborative consultant working jointly with team members during the assessment, IEP development, implementation, and evaluation stages. Professional school counselors can also act as family and community liaisons, case managers, and providers of direct services. Also, the TDT Model provides professional school counselors ample opportunities to facilitate group process.

Although the TDT Model is often believed to be the most effective means of providing comprehensive, coordinated services to students with disabilities, each team model has advantages and disadvantages (see Table 73.2). These advantages and disadvantages must be weighed before deciding how to approach the provision of special educational services. Ogletree et al. (2001) believed that "teams must be satisfied and confident in their adopted model" (p. 142). In an attempt to create a model that matches the needs of the school district and the team members, it is not uncommon for teams

TABLE 73.2
ADVANTAGES AND DISADVANTAGES OF MULTIDISCIPLINARY TEAM MODELS

	MDT Model	IDT Model	TDT Model
Advantages	Convenient	Equality among team members	Collaboration
	Efficient	Complementary services	Empowers families
		Efficient	Holistic services
Disadvantages	Exclusion of family	Minimal family involvement	Team member resistance
	Lack of collaboration	Time-consuming	Time-consuming
	Fragmented services		

to combine various aspects of the three models. With their understanding of group processes and the importance of collaboration, professional school counselors can help school districts decide how they want to approach the formation of MDTs and determine which components of the three different models (MDT Model, IDT Model, or TDT Model) should be adopted.

Summary/Conclusion

MDT involvement supports the provision of comprehensive school counseling services to all students (e.g., ASCA; 2005). By sharing the responsibility for developing and implementing services for students with disabilities among team members, MDTs encourage professional school counselors to develop collaborative relationships with school personnel as they work to address the academic, career, and personal–social needs of students with disabilities. When related services are required, school counselors can design relevant responsive services interventions (e.g., classroom guidance, individual planning meetings) and implement those either independently or in collaboration with teachers or parents. MDTs also provide professional school counselors the opportunity to take on leadership and advocacy roles for students with disabilities. Finally, the inherent evaluation component of MDTs designed to address the special educational needs of students provides professional school counselors with opportunities to collect outcome data and demonstrate their effectiveness.

Although their services are not clearly mandated by disability legislation, it is apparent that professional school counselors can bring specialized skills and knowledge to MDTs. They should initiate and advocate their involvement on these teams. Having a basic understanding of disability legislation, MDT team models, and the various roles they can assume during different stages of the special education process is important if professional school counselors want to contribute effectively to the MDT team process.

(Note: See the CD-ROM for a list of references.)

CHAPTER 74

MEDICATION ISSUES IN SCHOOLS

Mark D. Newmeyer and Amy J. Newmeyer

Preview

The professional school counselor plays an important role in managing medication in the school by facilitating communication between the student, family, school, and physician, thereby maximizing therapeutic benefit. This type of multimodal approach best benefits the student. The professional school counselor can be actively involved in providing many of these ancillary services, including personal counseling, social-skills training, and management of behavior in the classroom. Although the focus of this chapter is on psychotropic medications, the principles discussed are generally applicable to medication management in other chronic conditions.

Many students are diagnosed with chronic conditions requiring complex and time-consuming treatment regimens and require ongoing management over their lifetime (Newacheck & Taylor, 1992). The quality of life for this population and their families is frequently influenced by their capacity to successfully manage the conditions and integrate treatments into daily functioning. Students and their families who do not adhere to treatment regimens for pediatric chronic illnesses create clinical problems that may contribute to unnecessary hospitalizations and increased risk for illness-related complications, psychosocial maladjustments, and increased medical costs (Riekert & Drotar, 2000).

Changes in health care and how services are delivered, such as briefer hospital stays, limited reimbursements, and limited practitioner time with patients have created a responsibility shift. Families are much more responsible for assuming treatment services that once were typically delivered in clinical settings (e.g., administration of medicines to childhood cancer patients; Tebbi, Richards, Cummings, Zevon, & Mallon, 1988). Riekert and Drotar (2000) observed that families may not be prepared for or capable of assuming such treatment-related duties. Additionally, trends in scientific investigation that have emphasized a biological base for mental health disorders have contributed to various new classes of pharmacological interventions (Ingersoll, 2000).

Since students spend a major portion of the day in a school setting, school personnel must be mindful of the students' medical management. Professional school counselors and school nurses are in a position to facilitate student adherence to medication management.

Laws, School Policies, and Recommendations

The professional school counselor should be aware of state laws and local school policies regarding medication administration in the school setting, because they vary regionally. In some schools, nonmedical personnel can administer medication. Some students may be required to self-report for medications each day without a reminder by school personnel. The following is a review of the American Academy of Pediatrics (AAP; 1993) committee on school health recommendations for the administration of medication in schools:

> Each school or school district should develop a defined policy regarding medication administration in the schools.
>
> The school should require a written statement from the physician that provides the name of medication, dose, time of administration, and physician's phone number. Diagnosis should be provided unless there is a reason that this information is confidential.
>
> The physician should alert the school of any serious side effects of medication.
>
> If there is a risk of severe reaction, the appropriate emergency response plan should be outlined by the physician.
>
> The physician should state whether the child is capable of self-administering the medication. (This may not be possible in some states.)
>
> The parent or guardian should provide written permission for medication administration at the school.
>
> The school should develop a policy regarding self-administration of over-the-counter medications. (This may not be possible in some states.)
>
> Secure storage should be available for all medications.

Many longer acting medications are now available that allow the student to take dosages only at home, eliminating the necessity of school administration. The professional school counselor and school nurse should be aware of what medications the student is taking at home and whether infrequent home administration may be contributing to nonresponse in the school setting, although *there is no legal basis for requiring parents to inform school personnel.* Monitoring the student for potential side effects such as drowsiness, stomachache, or headache is another role for the professional school counselor and school nurse. A student with these side effects may present to the professional school counselor because he or she is not doing well in class, falling asleep, and so forth. Being able to facilitate appropriate intervention with the student and family may prevent serious health issues associated with side effects or nonadministration of medications.

BASIC CLASSIFICATIONS OF DRUGS, NAMES, AND PROPERTIES

Rapid development of new medications in the last few years has resulted in a dramatic increase in the number of medications that are available to address behavioral and psychiatric issues in children and adolescents. Because students often receive these medications at school and spend a significant portion of their day at school, the professional school counselor must be familiar with these medications and their uses and side effects. Any noted side effects should be reported to the student's parent and the prescribing physician, if consent has been obtained from the parent. The following review will be limited to psychotropic medications, as these are the most common types of medications used in the school setting. However, this list is not exhaustive. Review the current edition of the *Physician's Desk Reference* (PDR; Medical Economics Company, 2006) for extensive information about any medication.

Note that since the time of the first edition of the PDR, changes in labeling on more than one class of antidepressant medications have been released by the Food and Drug Administration (FDA). This type of recommendation by the FDA is commonly referred to as a *black box* and indicates that the risk of the side effects is significant, although the medication has not been withdrawn from the market. The changes have been made based on the concern that the risk of suicidal ideation is higher on these medications. For further information, please refer to the FDA Web site (http://www .fda.gov/cder/drug/antidepressants/default.htm). School personnel, including the professional school counselor, should be aware of the potential side effects of these medications and provide monitoring and appropriate intervention as indicated.

ANTIDEPRESSANT MEDICATIONS

Selective serotonin reuptake inhibitors (SSRIs) are used to address symptoms of anxiety and depression. Commonly used medications in this class include the following:

Celexa (citalopram)

Lexapro (escitalopram)

Luvox (fluvoxamine)

Paxil (paroxetine)

Prozac (fluoxetine)

Zoloft (sertraline)

These medications are usually administered once daily, in the morning or evening. Common side effects include nausea, weight loss, insomnia, excessive sweating, and sedation.

Tricyclic antidepressants are also used to address anxiety, depression, or inattention and hyperactivity. Commonly used medications include the following:

Elavil (amitriptyline)

Pamelor (nortriptyline)

Tofranil (imipramine)

Side effects include fatigue, constipation, dry mouth, blurred vision, and drowsiness. These medications may have effects on the electrical pattern of the heart.

Wellbutrin (buproprion) may also be used for anxiety, depression, or inattention and hyperactivity. Side effects are similar to those of tricyclic antidepressants. Wellbutrin may increase a student's risk of seizures.

Eskalith (lithium) may also be used to address mania and/or depression. Common side effects include fine tremors, increased thirst, nausea, headache, weight gain, and increased urinary frequency (Kline, Silver, & Russell, 2001).

Effexor (venlafaxine) is a new, commonly used antidepressant.

Remeron (mirtazapine) is a newer antidepressant, not related to the other medications. Side effects include drowsiness and nausea (Medical Economics Company, 2006).

STIMULANT MEDICATIONS

Stimulant medications are commonly used to address inattention, hyperactivity, and impulsivity often associated with attention-deficit/hyperactivity disorder (ADHD). Commonly used medications include **Ritalin, Metadate, Methylin,** and **Concerta** (methylphenidate); **Dexedrine** (dextroamphetamine); and **Adderall** (dextro- and levo-amphetamine). These medications are available in short-acting formulations that last up to 4 hours per dose and long-acting formulations that last up to 12 hours per dose. Each child may metabolize the medications differently. For example, a long-acting medication that typically lasts through the school day may, for a particular child, lose its positive effects before the end of the school day. If a child on one of these medications is having problem behaviors primarily in the afternoon, this should be reported back to the family and prescribing physician to allow for appropriate adjustment of dosage and time of administration. This information may be relevant when determining medication effects in the classroom setting. Common side effects include loss of appetite, headaches, stomachaches, and motor tics (Kline et al, 2001; Medical Economics Company, 2006).

 Strattera (atomoxetine) is a newer nonstimulant medication that is also used to treat ADHD and/or associated anxiety or mood disorder symptoms. Strattera has also been the subject of an FDA warning for an increased risk of suicidal ideation and/or liver damage. For more information, see the FDA link (http://www.fda.gov/cder/drug/infopage/atomoxetine).

ANTIPSYCHOTIC MEDICATIONS

Antipsychotic medications are used to address aggression and psychosis. Traditional or "typical" antipsychotic medications include the following:

 Haldol (haloperidol)

 Thorazine (chlorpromazine)

 Mellaril (thioridazine)

 Common side effects include sedation, dystonia (i.e., increase in muscle tone and spasms of neck, mouth, and tongue), and tardive dyskinesia (i.e., involuntary movements of extremities, trunk, or facial muscles). New medications in this class are called "atypical" antipsychotics. These medications may be used to treat aggression, bipolar disorder, or psychosis and include the following:

 Risperdal (risperidone)

 Zyprexa (olanzapine)

 Seroquel (quetiapine)

 Geodon (ziprasidone)

 These medications have lower risk of muscular side effects but may cause hyperglycemia and weight gain. Any muscular side effects should be reported immediately to the prescribing physician (Kline et al., 2001; Medical Economics Company, 2006). A new and increasingly popular medication in this category is **Abilify** (aripiprazole).

ANTIEPILEPTICS

Although these medications are most commonly used to control seizures, they may also be used for symptoms of aggression. Commonly used medications include **Depakote** and **Depakene** (valproic acid) and **Tegretol** (carbamazepine). Side effects may include nausea, vomiting, sedation, and easy bruising. Individuals taking these medications should monitor liver and blood functioning (Kline et al., 2001). New antineuroleptics, including **Lamictal** (lamotrigine), **Topamax** (topiramate) and **Neurontin** (gabapentin), have fewer side effects and do not require extensive monitoring with blood tests (Medical Economics Company, 2006).

ANTIHYPERTENSIVE MEDICATIONS

Some medications used to treat high blood pressure are also used to treat behavioral problems such as aggression and ADHD in children and adolescents. Commonly used medications in this class are **Catapres** (clonidine) and **Tenex** (guanfacine). Potential side effects include low heart rate, drowsiness, dizziness, headache, constipation, and dry mouth (Medical Economics Company, 2006).

COMORBID FACTORS: LEARNING DISABILITIES, LANGUAGE DISORDER, AND OTHER PSYCHIATRIC ISSUES

Many students with psychiatric conditions have comorbid conditions that are often overlooked when focusing on the behavioral issues in the classroom. For instance, many children with ADHD may also have learning disabilities, language disorders, and other psychiatric conditions such as depression or anxiety (Blondis, 1996). These comorbid conditions should also be addressed to maximize the student's functioning at school. Comorbid factors that are not addressed may limit response to medical treatment of the target condition. For example, a student being treated for ADHD who has a reading disability may continue to demonstrate ADHD-like behavior despite medication management if the reading disability is not addressed.

LINKAGE BETWEEN THE FAMILY, SCHOOL, CLASSROOM, AND MEDICAL COMMUNITY

The professional school counselor is in a distinct and important position to advocate for a student requiring medication management. The professional school counselor and school nurse may serve as a link between the family, the classroom, the school, and even the medical community, not merely by providing support but also by providing valued information.

While some families may adapt well to having a student requiring medication, others do not. Various research studies examining effective parental roles in managing their child's asthma indicated an alarmingly high nonadherence rate in spite of potential adverse risks to the child (Milgrom et al., 1996). Results are not that dissimilar across other student conditions requiring medications. Professional school counselors can influence the families' adaptation by providing them with information on the student's functioning in the school setting, encouraging a collaborative relationship with the medical community, making referrals for additional family support, and serving as a link between the school, classroom, student, and family.

The professional school counselor should also be aware of factors within the school environment that may affect teachers' ratings of a child's behavior, which will also affect their responses on a checklist of the positive effect of medication as well as side effects. For example, the likelihood of a diagnosis of ADHD in elementary school has been noted to be influenced by a child's school and social environment, class size, and culture (Harvey, Olsen, McCormick & Cates, 2005; Schneider & Eisenberg, 2006). Studies have also shown that there is a high rate of attrition regarding the use of medication and school resources for ADHD, particularly in high-risk demographic areas (Bussing et al., 2005). Lack of medication compliance at home should therefore be considered if a child who has been prescribed medication has a sudden increase in problem behaviors in the classroom.

The child's age may also play a role in the teacher's ratings of classroom behavior and possible side effects. Data suggest that once children with ADHD reach middle school, rating scales completed by multiple teachers show less interrater reliability, particularly for inattentive symptoms (Evans, Allen, Moore, & Strauss, 2005). This may be due to the shorter amount of time each teacher has during the school day to observe the child's behavior as well as differences in medication effects throughout the school day.

A crucial component of medication management is feedback given to the physician regarding medication efficacy. Particularly in the area of psychotropics, school performance and behavior are often part of the target symptoms of medication use. Communication between the physician and the school is often substandard due to the lack of understanding of what information needs to be conveyed and in what manner. A study surveyed pediatricians regarding the type of information they would find crucial in helping to manage ADHD medications (Hailemariam, Bradley-Johnson, & Johnson, 2002). The results indicated that pediatricians found the following information most useful, listed in descending order of preference: rating scales, informal observation, summary of 1 to 3 paragraphs, school achievement, side effects checklist for medication, and classroom direct observation.

The professional school counselor can play a vital role in obtaining this information and conveying it to the physician in a timely manner. Some resources are provided in Table 74.1, which will facilitate the communication of this information from school personnel back to the physician.

Summary/Conclusion

The professional school counselor can serve an important role regarding medication management in the school setting by facilitating communication between the student, family, school, and physician, thereby maximizing therapeutic benefit. This multimodal approach results in the best benefit to the student (Pelham, 2000). The professional school counselor can be actively involved in providing many of these ancillary services, including personal counseling, social skills training, and management of behavior in the classroom setting. Although the focus of this chapter has been on psycho-

TABLE 74.1

ONLINE RESOURCES

National Initiatives for Children's Healthcare Quality (www.nichq.org/NICHQ/Topics/ ChronicConditions/AD/HD/Tools/)—This site has a copy of the Vanderbilt assessment scales to download free of charge as well as instructions for scoring. There are teacher and parent rating scales for initial diagnosis and for follow-up of children with ADHD. The initial scale also includes questions pertaining to comorbid conditions including conduct disorder, mood disorder, and learning difficulties. These scales are easy to administer and can be used to facilitate communication with the student's physician.

Massachusetts General Hospital (www.mgh.harvard.edu/madiresourcecenter/schoolpsychiatry/ index.asp)—This site contains information for educators, parents, and physicians regarding the diagnosis, management, and treatment of mental health conditions in the schools. It contains a link to rating scales, with descriptions and information on downloading or purchasing. It includes a free downloadable medication side effects form.

Center for Health and Health Care in Schools (www.healthinschools.org/sh/medmgmt .asp)—This site contains information regarding the management of medications in the schools, including a summary of state policies and a PowerPoint presentation regarding the role of schools in maintaining health-care quality.

tropic medications, these principles are generally applicable to medication management in other chronic conditions.

(Note: See the CD-ROM for a list of references.)

CHAPTER 75

HELPING STUDENTS WHO HAVE HIV AND OTHER HEALTH PROBLEMS

Cyrus Marcellus Ellis

Preview

Helping students with HIV and other health problems is an immense undertaking by professional school counselors. Counselors who develop programs to intervene in students' health concerns must be cognizant of their professional stance, personal values, and legal obligations while building a credible program that addresses the needs of the student and the community.

Students in U.S. schools are faced with multiple risk factors that have the potential to damage their emotional well-being, academic success, family interaction, and future development (Landgraf, Rich, & Rappaport, 2002; Zwieg, Lindberg, & McGinley, 2001). In addition to school violence, substance abuse, and poor academic performance, additional risk factors exist that involve students' health status concerning sexually transmitted diseases (STDs), poor physical health following illicit drug use, chronic illness, Human Immunodeficiency Virus (HIV), and Acquired Immunodeficiency Syndrome (AIDS) (Sweeny, Lindegren, Buehler, Onorato, & Janssen, 1995; Zwieg et al., 2001). Students affected by the aforementioned issues need qualified and competent professionals to attend to the physical and emotional needs that will develop across their life span. Professional school counselors possess the education and training and are poised to intervene at various points of student growth, especially for students who are in need of specific health-related services (American School Counselor Association [ASCA], 2001).

Professional school counselors who attempt to intervene with students' various health problems need to be aware of the etiology and course of various diseases as well as the co-occurring physical and environmental factors influencing the affected student. Regarding adolescent HIV status, the Centers for Disease Control and Prevention (CDC; 2004) reported that youth 13 to 19 years of age in 33 states that were diagnosed with HIV/AIDS ($n = 1,118$) were approximately 61% male and 39% female. An alarming finding, often overlooked, is that racial disparity of HIV/AIDS cases. The CDC (2004) report showed that 70% of the patients with HIV/AIDS were Black, 15% were non-Hispanic/White, and 13% were Hispanic.

The CDC (2004), in conjunction with the U.S. Department of Health and Human Services (DHHS), published a report that lists the major areas of health concerns that children and adolescents will face in the near future. The CDC and DHHS recognized the issues of mortality, unintentional injury, violence, substance abuse and mental health, reproductive health, and the prevention of chronic diseases. A comprehensive intervention for students affected by HIV/AIDS and other health problems requires professional school counselors to (a) establish a professional stance on HIV and other health problems; (b) address health concerns that do not have a biological basis; (c) recognize the physical and psychological factors associated with students who are affected by HIV and other health problems; (d) apply cross-cultural skills in identifying at-risk behaviors for all populations of students; and (e) develop a comprehensive counseling program encompassing psychosocial support, education, and coping strategies.

ESTABLISHING A PROFESSIONAL STANCE

Professional school counselors addressing HIV/AIDS and other health-related issues may experience a variety of thoughts and emotions concerning the disease, the affected individuals, and the manner in which individuals become infected. It is important that they are clear on their professional orientation towards HIV as well as on their conduct while working with infected persons. With regard to HIV/AIDS, the American School Counselors Association stated that HIV and AIDS are diseases and not issues of morality: "The professional school counselor promotes prevention, health and education, while providing a vital link to the well being of students, staff, parents and the community" (ASCA; 2001). Because it is the responsibility of professional school counselors to encourage a safe learning environment while safeguarding the rights of all persons, they should establish their professional stance by incorporating the laws and ethics governing their profession and local area and disseminating it to the entire educational team. Every counselor is a professional governed by codes of behavior (Pate, 2000). Central to a professional school counselor's ethical stance is the need to recognize the student's and parent's choice in disclosing HIV information. A student's HIV status is confidential, and the student and/or guardian are not required to disclose this information. Professional school counselors who are clear on their professional stance are able to communicate this view to the public, thereby ensuring professional accountability and establishing the basis for trust between parents, teachers, administrators, and students. Table 75.1 summarizes ASCA's (2001) position statement concerning HIV/AIDS and the role of the professional school counselor. This information is critical for the formation of a sound professional stance when beginning to address HIV/AIDS and other health problems.

Professional school counselors are encouraged to sit down with school personnel and communicate the importance of having a sound counseling program that addresses student health issues and HIV/AIDS. Professional school counselors, when communicating their professional stance to school administrators, must understand local school policy and eliminate potential conflicts to ensure the establishment of effective counseling interventions (Shoffner & Williamson, 2000).

HEALTH CONCERNS WITHOUT A BIOLOGICAL BASIS

Many people think of health issues as those that relate to genetics, infectious diseases, or other medical issues involving biology. While that is true, there are a number of health conditions that emerge in youth that are derived not from biology but from events that occur in communities, the world, and even the playground. Engaging in activities or being in the area of these events place students at risk for developing a variety of health concerns.

TABLE 75.1

PROFESSIONAL SCHOOL COUNSELOR STANCE RELATING TO HIV/AIDS

American School Counseling Association Position Statement on HIV/AIDS
- HIV and AIDS is a disease.
- Professional school counselors promote prevention, health, and education.
- Professional school counselors are the link to student well-being, school staff, parents, and the community.

The Professional School Counselor's Role
- Counseling
- Support
- Collaboration between school health personnel to facilitate education programs for all members of the school community
- Clear and accurate information
- Active involvement in professional associations supporting professional codes of conduct

Collecting Necessary Reference Material
- School policy concerning enrollment of students with HIV and AIDS
- Community resources that promote healthy living, education, subject-matter experts, and outreach programs
- Identification of medical facilities providing medication, medication education, and support groups

Health concerns that can develop for youth who have been involved in or injured by unintentional events (e.g., tornadoes, hurricanes, earthquakes, car accidents) as well as intentional events (e.g., gang violence, school violence, sporting events) involve acquired brain injuries, infections, and the like. Table 75.2 displays these two areas professional school counselors ought to recognize when discussing and designing intervention programs to assist student health concerns.

Students also encounter physiological problems, better known as *chronic medical conditions* (Thies, 1999): "More than 200 chronic physical conditions affect youth under age 18" (p. 392). Students frequently contend with asthma, diabetes, leukemia, and gastrointestinal illnesses. These illnesses hamper the educational attainment of students and create strain within the family. Thies's (1999) work details the impact chronic physical conditions have on the cognitive capacity of youth and can help in coordinating appropriate academic interventions and health services between school health officials and community health and human service professionals.

CROSS-CULTURAL DATA

Race-based/cultural differences are important to consider as student's health concerns are being discussed. While health issues as well as HIV affect everyone, there are some significant differences when it comes to recognizing the impact and resulting behaviors of some health concerns as it relates to race, class, and culture. The impact of poverty on the coping skills of youth when exposed to smoking, drinking, drug use, sexual iden-

TABLE 75.2

STUDENT HEALTH RISK BEHAVIORS

Actions causing unintended injuries	Actions causing intended injuries
Seatbelt use in cars	Carrying a weapon
Helmet use on bikes and motorcycles	Fighting
Injury during physical activity	Date violence
Riding with individuals under the influence	Forced sexual intercourse
Drinking and driving	School violence
	Suicide
	Tobacco/alcohol use
	Illicit drug use

tity development, and gang violence are an important dimension for professional school counselors to consider when working with students. Wingood et al. (2006) understood this dimension of working in and around such populations by recognizing that poor African American girls lack the knowledge about safe sexual practices, through a lack of social support resources, to make decisions that are in their best interest against the pressure of their peer group.

The CDC (2004) provided a framework for working across the board to address the health concerns of youth: "Because many societal factors contribute to adolescent health, safety, and well-being, health promotion and prevention strategies should not be implemented in isolation; a collaborative effort across multiple societal institutions is necessary" (CDC; 2004, p. 5). This statement underscores the role of the professional school counselor to be an active member of the community so that coordinated events addressing student health can have a greater chance for success.

THE IMPORTANCE OF CONFIDENTIALITY

The counseling profession is made up of people with special status (Pate, 2000). *Special status* means that we are given passage into the personal lives of the people we serve. Pate reminds professional counselors that our ability to enter into client's lives and protect their dignity is essential for the community to trust us and our efforts. Without protecting the profession's trust with the community, professional counselors lose their ability to effectively intervene in the lives of our clients.

Most professional counselors working in schools and in agencies would love to keep the vast majority of clients' statements and issues confidential. Unfortunately, that is not possible. Local, state, and federal regulations provide guidelines on what can be kept confidential and what can be or needs to be shared. The rules for limiting confidentiality are different between states and between work settings. Because this is a text for professional school counselors, the importance of confidentiality will be focused on the school setting.

TABLE 75.3

STATE OF ILLINOIS'S ACTS CONCERNING CONFIDENTIALITY OF STUDENTS WITH INFECTIOUS DISEASES

Confidentiality of students with infectious diseases in Illinois is covered by 77 Ill. Adm. Code 697.400.
The Communicable Disease Prevention Act [410 ILCS 315/2a] regulates who can legally be informed of the identity of a child with human immunodeficiency virus (HIV).

States vary in their position on who can know about a child's health status. The first step in determining a state's regulations concerning youth and any infectious diseases is to consult the state's board of education. For example, Table 75.3 displays two policies from the state of Illinois as they relate to confidentiality of children with infectious diseases and HIV status. Various school systems may also have somewhat different policies and procedures.

The Illinois code and Illinois act listed in Table 75.3 have roots in Section 504 of the Rehabilitation Act of 1973, which offers protection under the law for children if they have infectious diseases. As professional school counselors enter into this level of examination, be prepared to digest a lot of information. Although it may be difficult to acquire this information, it is worth it when attempting to build a sound intervention program for students with health-related issues.

While state laws may provide the legal groundwork for the importance of confidentiality, the professional school counselor needs to dig a little deeper to recognize the importance of maintaining and communicating the need for confidentiality with all members of the educational team. Again using Illinois as an example, the people (by law) who can be informed of a child's HIV status include (a) district superintendent, (b) principal, (c) classroom teacher(s), and (d) those required to make program decisions.

Professional school counselors ought to recognize the questionable nature of allowing so many people access to a student's health condition. While it is in all of our interests to protect the public and provide for a salient learning environment, it is potentially harmful to the student to have information in the custody of others who are not committed to the same ethical principles that professional counselors share. If student's personal information is misused or is not protected, it can add to the psychological–emotional pain of students attempting to cope with their medical condition as well as impede future students from coming forward to disclose health conditions. Consulting the state's policies on this matter will aid in developing a program that educates all the members of the educational team with access to a child's health status on the importance of confidentiality.

RECOGNIZING PHYSICAL AND PSYCHOLOGICAL FACTORS ASSOCIATED WITH HIV AND OTHER HEALTH PROBLEMS

Students suffering from HIV and other health problems possess a multitude of physical and psychological problems associated with their illnesses. Professional school counselors working with affected students need to be aware of student physical and psychological needs when developing an intervention program. The ability to concentrate, visually focus, and sustain energy may all be manifested as physical and psychological side effects of an infected student (Thies, 1999). Additionally, students suffering with HIV and other health problems often experience noncompliance with medication regimens and depression and anxiety resulting from a variety of negative life events that reduce the student's emotional well-being and the family's inability to function (Elliott, 2001).

Professional school counselors need to work closely with teachers, school health personnel, and families to gain information concerning a student's health status as it relates to the course of the illness and the impact of the medications treating the illness. Students experiencing constant illness are at risk for academic difficulty: "Forty-five percent (45%) of students with chronic illness report falling behind in their school work, leading them to dislike school. At the high school level, 35% of students identified as 'other health impaired' report failing grades" (Thies, 1999, p. 392). The next step for the professional school counselor in constructing a comprehensive intervention addressing health issues is to develop a list of behavioral and emotive symptoms that are associated with students affected by HIV and other health problems. This list of symptoms needs to be inclusive of identifying the illness, the medications treating the illness and their side effects, and the emotive responses of affected students.

DEVELOPING A COMPREHENSIVE SCHOOL COUNSELING INTERVENTION

At this point, professional school counselors are prepared to construct a comprehensive intervention addressing HIV and other health problems in students. By incorporating the previous sections involving establishing a professional stance concerning HIV and other health-related problems, understanding the prevalence of HIV and health problems in children and adolescents and the recognition of the physical and psychological factors associated by various illnesses and HIV, the professional school counselor can operate a program from a sound foundation.

It is important to understand that the core of a program addressing HIV and other health related illnesses revolves around the reduction of negative risk behaviors of the people receiving the intervention or assistance. Therefore, the successful intervention implemented in schools needs to be based on behavioral practices designed to reduce risky behaviors in students that can lead to exposure or exacerbation of HIV and other illnesses (Holtgrave et al., 1995).

Holtgrave et al. (1995) provided a classic review of literature detailing the characteristics of successful HIV prevention programs in the community and schools. According to Holtgrave et al., a successful intervention addressing HIV and other health problems requires the professional school counselor to incorporate at least three ideological positions: (a) community relevance, (b) cultural competence, and (c) sustaining effective practices guiding interventions. Additionally, successful interventions encompass counseling and support that address negative life events that are barriers for positive health practices. In order to conceptualize Holtgrave et al.'s work, brief descriptions of their concepts are illuminated.

COMMUNITY RELEVANCE

The prevalence of HIV and AIDS is growing and affecting students, and interventions need to be clear and aligned with the requirements of the community being served; otherwise, the program will be seen as inattentive, nonessential, and a burden on school personnel and district assets (Holtgrave et al., 1995). Professional school counselors need to understand the reality of the students they serve while incorporating the desires of the community. Working closely with health and human service professionals, community hospitals, and local social workers begins the process of determining the relevance for the community and individuals.

CULTURAL COMPETENCE

The demographics of school systems are changing rapidly, and interventions addressing HIV and other health problems need to address all students from various perspectives. Professional school counselors need to develop culturally responsive programs that involve all levels of culture, race, demographics, gender, ethnicity, social mores, and familial value sets. Professional school counselors who are responsible for various educational levels need to ensure that their program is reflective of the developmental nature of their audience. Professional school counselors need to develop the proper message for elementary, middle/junior high, and high school students. For schools in which language may present barriers to clear communication, working with community members who can provide insight into how the message of the program will be received by its respective audience is also important.

EFFECTIVE PRACTICES

Table 75.4 displays Holtgrave et al.'s (1995) six empirically validated dimensions for effective practices when designing school-based HIV programs. The following characteristics of effective school-based programs are determined effective in part due to the program's ability to provide educational information, self-empowerment of involved individuals, and the teaching of positive behavioral practices.

Lohrman, Blake, Collins, Windsor, and Parillo (2001) offer additional points of effective school-based HIV programs, finding that parents need to be involved in the review of the curricular materials to determine if their children will take part in the educational program. Indeed, most school systems require parental involvement in this process. It is important that all members of the educational team review local policies to ensure compliance with policies that govern health-related programs. In many cases, this information is located on the Web for districts, school boards, or state departments of education. Additionally, effective practices for school-based HIV programs include policy revision and development. Professional development training emerged as a necessary requirement for teachers in the following areas: HIV prevention, violence prevention, suicide, sexual behavior, the influence of drugs and alcohol, and sexually transmitted infections prevention activities. Lohrman et al. also indicated that significant amounts of time (four or more class periods) must be dedicated to the topics of HIV instruction and prevention. Professional school counselors who undertake this

TABLE 75.4

SIX EMPIRICALLY VALIDATED BEST PRACTICES FOR SCHOOL-BASED HIV PROGRAMS

1. The use of social learning theory in program development
2. Reducing sexual risk-taking in adolescents to prevent undesired health risks
3. Accurate dissemination of HIV, AIDS, and other health information
4. Addressing media influences on sexual behavior
5. Addressing personal and group mores regarding the use of protection when engaging in sexual behavior
6. The use of role-playing to demonstrate appropriate communication

endeavor need to be aware of all the building blocks of effective HIV intervention and prevention programs.

OTHER HEALTH PROBLEMS

Comprehensive interventions for other health problems follow the same process as for HIV programs. Referring to Thies's (1999) work with chronic illness in children, Thies addressed the need to identify the condition and become familiar with the affect that condition has on the affected student. One may refer to the CDC Web site (CDC; 2002a, 2002b) for additional information concerning a variety of health conditions and effects on students.

To gain insight into the concepts presented in this chapter, Figure 75.1 provides the conceptual framework for organizing, implementing, and evaluating a comprehensive intervention for HIV and other health problems. This cycle indicates the need to develop a firm professional stance while constantly reevaluating the merits of the intervention.

SUMMARY/CONCLUSION

Professional school counselors developing programs to assist students with HIV and other health problems face a variety of challenges. Effective in-school health programs require professional school counselors to be knowledgeable of their ethical and professional stance concerning HIV and other health issues. The development of a sound intervention requires the professional school counselor to establish a credible health education program, become knowledgeable about the prevalence of various illnesses in the student's community, and understand the impact that physical and psychological factors have on learning. An efficient and successful program is constantly reviewing its practices to ensure that students and parents are receiving credible information, learning appropriate decision-making skills, and developing the ability to recognize risky behaviors that are destructive to student health.

(Note: See the CD-ROM for a list of references.)

| The professional school counselor develops a professional stance |

Determine needs based on population
- Determine prevention education or intervention education
- Identification of the illness
- Identification of medications treating the illness and side effects
- Physiological and psychological stressors of affected students
- The impact of the illness, medication, and psychological factors on learning

Determine personnel support and logistics
- School resources
- Community resources
- Professional development for teachers and health-support personnel
- Parental involvement
- Meeting space
- Number of hours devoted to HIV and health education

Program Review
- Review program goals to determine success
- Review feedback from parents, community members, and school personnel and make improvements where necessary
- Evaluate curricular materials for efficiency and usefulness
- Evaluate professional development training
- Review school policy and include any revisions into the education plan

Program development
- Inclusion of social learning theory
- Culturally appropriate
- HIV and health policy inclusion
- Community and parent review of educational curriculum
- Age appropriate
- Developmentally appropriate
- Addressing explicit and implied community needs

FIGURE 75.1. The organizational cycle of a comprehensive intervention for HIV and other health problems.

CHAPTER 76

SCHOOL SUPPORT FOR STUDENTS
WHO HAVE CHRONIC ILLNESS

Carol J. Kaffenberger

Preview

I will present information concerning ways in which a professional school counselor can facilitate school support for children with chronic illnesses and review barriers faced by children with chronic illness. A model for supporting children with chronic illness will be presented and strategies and resources for supporting children with chronic illness will be offered.

It is estimated that 21% of all students have a chronic illness, and one third of this population experience severe enough consequences of their disease to interfere with school performance (Newacheck & Halfon, 1998; Thompson & Gustafson, 1996). A chronic illness is one that has no cure but is not necessarily terminal (Huegel, 1998). Chronic illnesses require medical interventions and often result in debilitating consequences (Thompson, & Gustafson, 1996). Cancer, asthma, congenital heart defects, lupus, bowel disorders, cystic fibrosis, diabetes, hemophilia, juvenile rheumatoid arthritis, mental illness, and HIV/AIDS are among the most common chronic illnesses affecting students (Phelps, 1998).

Many students with chronic illness are frequently absent from school; experience psychosocial consequences including depression, difficulties with social and peer interaction, and lower academic achievement; and have a higher incidence of cognitive disabilities as a result of their illness or its treatment (Fasciano, 1996; Geist, Grdisa, & Otley, 2003; Sexson & Madan-Swain, 1993; Shiu, 2001; Thies, 1999; Thompson & Gustafson, 1996). Students who are out of school for extended periods with chronic illness require support as they transition from the hospital or home back to school. This process is called *school reentry* or *school reintegration*.

For the child with a chronic illness, being in school represents a return to normalcy; school is what students "do." Being in school as much as possible or making a successful transition back to school is associated with more positive long-term outcomes for students (Boekaerts & Roder, 1999; Houlahan, 1991; Prevatt, Heffer, & Lowe, 2000; Sexson & Madan-Swain, 1993).

School reentry or support for students with chronic illness is a complex process because schools are not always able to accommodate the special needs of students with chronic illness. School support must be tailored to the individual needs of the student and the family as well as the specific characteristics of the student's illness. School attendance and grading policies and homebound instruction regulations are often inflexible and serve as a barrier to successful school support (Fasciano, 1996; Prevatt et al., 2000). School personnel often feel unprepared to meet the individual needs of these students and lack information and resources concerning the disease or an understanding of the individual needs of the students and their families (Prevatt et al., 2000).

MODELS FOR SUCCESSFUL SCHOOL SUPPORT

Model programs have been developed that describe strategies for supporting students with chronic illness and for helping them make the transition back to school when they have been out for extended periods (Fasciano, 1996; Houlahan, 1991; Katz, Varni, Rubenstein, Blew, & Hubert, 1992; Nabors & Lehmkuhl, 2004; Prevatt et al., 2000). Model comprehensive school support programs have the following features in common (Fasciano, 1996; Kaffenberger, 2006a; Prevatt et al., 2000): They identify a coordinator of services, provide direct services to the student, consult with the family, educate and sensitize school personnel, sensitize classmates, and involve the medical team.

COORDINATION OF SCHOOL SUPPORT PROGRAMS

The success of programs to support students with chronic illness depends on the identification of a liaison who takes responsibility for coordinating the school support or school reentry process (Kaffenberger, 2006b; Prevatt et al., 2000; Shields, Heron, Rubenstein, & Katz, 1995). The liaison oversees the first phases of the process by meeting with the family and the student and convening the support team. The liaison should have access to the family, the student, members of the medical team, and the school staff.

The liaison meets with the parents to determine the student's continuing needs: to discuss how they want information about the child's illness communicated to teachers and the student's peers, to assess resources and available family support, and to obtain necessary parental permission to communicate with others about the student. The liaison begins the process by providing information to the family about available school services and the importance of involving the school from the time of diagnosis. With written permission from the parents, the liaison communicates with the medical team, gaining information about the diagnosis and treatment and any handicapping conditions or constraints placed on the student.

Next, the liaison meets with the student to assess his or her understanding of the disease and treatment process and to talk about how the student wants peers to find out about the illness. The liaison determines student desires concerning involvement and communication with peers and the school.

The liaison works with the school to educate and inform school personnel. A workshop for teachers and administrators is recommended as the best vehicle for sensitizing school personnel to the unique needs of the student informing them how to handle the classroom responses to the sick student (Baskin, Saylor, Furey, Finch, & Carek, 1983). The liaison is also called in to work directly with classrooms and peers (Benner & Marlow, 1991). Finally, the liaison keeps the lines of communication open, passing along updated information, and planning for school reentry.

Challenges to implementing school support. While the benefits of a comprehensive school support program cannot be denied, the reality is that such programs are not available to serve most students with chronic illness (Prevatt et al., 2000). While there is agreement that a comprehensive school support program is ideal, staffing issues, funding, and lack of supporting research data about the effectiveness of existing programs limits the number of programs being implemented.

The critical factor determining the success of the comprehensive school support program is the identification of a liaison to coordinate services. As Prevatt et al. (2000) recognized in their review of school reintegration programs, how the liaison is staffed and funded is one of the most significant barriers to the successful implementation of programs. While the literature underscores the importance of the liaison role, guidance about who is best suited to play this role is not offered.

A ROLE FOR PROFESSIONAL SCHOOL COUNSELORS IN THE SCHOOL SUPPORT PROCESS

Typically, the transition process is put together in a piecemeal fashion. Families are unsure of what their child's future holds and what their child will need, and they struggle to understand the school regulations and how to access services. Frequently, the school's response is slow. Schools scramble to educate themselves about the diagnosis, the needs of the student and family, and available resources. Well-meaning school personnel, lacking clarity about their role, knowledge about the illness, and available resources feel unprepared to meet the needs of these children and their families. Professional school counselors, however, by virtue of their training, skills, and leadership role in the school, are ideally suited to facilitate the school support or reentry for children with chronic illnesses and support the chronically ill student's siblings and family.

STRATEGIES FOR WORKING WITH CHILDREN WITH CHRONIC ILLNESSES

The following are strategies professional school counselors can use to coordinate school support for students with chronic illnesses:

1. *Make early contact with the family* (see Figure 76.1). As soon as you learn of the diagnosis of an illness, contact the parents. Recognize that the family is struggling to respond to the medical needs of the student and may postpone contact with the school (Case-Smith, 2004). Contacting the family early on provides a sense of hope as well as additional resources. No matter how long the student is expected to be out of school, planning for school reentry should begin early.

2. *Form a school support team composed of stakeholders* (see Figure 76.2). The purpose of a school support team is to coordinate services and implement the school support plan. The school support team may include the professional school counselor, public health or school nurse, social worker, teacher, and administrator. The school support team should consist of three to four individuals who will assume responsibility for providing and coordinating services to the student and family. Members of this team should be determined by school district organization and staffing and by the unique situation of each student and family. The school support team should identify a liaison that will assume primary responsibility for contact with the family and the health-care professionals; the liaison may be the professional school counselor, school nurse, social worker, teacher, or other school staff

Questions for the Family

At the time of the crisis, school personnel often postpone contact with the family. By taking the initiative, and making early contact with the family, you give the parent and child a sense of hope. You provide a resource outside the family circle. You establish your role as an advocate for students with illnesses and their siblings, and you facilitate school support.

❑ Tell me more about your child's diagnosis, treatment process, and how you expect these to affect him or her.

❑ Would you be willing to come to school for a meeting to share information, to hear about available school resources to help your child, and to plan for school support?

❑ How might school performance/attendance be affected?

❑ How much does your child know/understand about the illness?

❑ What do you want school staff, your child's teacher, the school community, and other children to know about the illness? Who do you want to tell them about it?

❑ Is there someone on the medical team with whom you would like us to work?

❑ How can we communicate? Who can we contact? Who will contact us?

❑ What support would you like from the school when your child is out of school? Cards? Class work? Video of class? Calls? Visits? Web Cam?

❑ Are you aware of resources, information, or support groups that are dealing with this illness?

❑ Have you used the Internet to access information and materials regarding the illness? Are you willing to share what you learn with the school? Would you like me to help you find information?

❑ Who is helping *you* through this?

❑ What can we do to help you and your family?

❑ How are the sick child's siblings doing? How can we support the siblings?

FIGURE 76.1. Questions to consider in your early contact with the family.

members. Consider documenting roles, responsibilities, and activities of the school support team (see Figure 76.3).

3. *Hold a school support meeting with the parents as soon as possible.* Determine who should attend this meeting based on the needs of the student and family. Include the school support team members, the student's teacher, school nurse, a special education teacher (if appropriate), Section 504 coordinator, and an administrator. Alternatively, it could be a meeting between the parents and the professional school counselor. The purpose of this meeting is to coordinate the school reentry process and negotiate the way the school can support the student and family. Discuss the following with the parents:

• Learn all you can from the parents about the illness, the expected course of treatment, and the psychological impact the experience is having on the student with the chronic illness and the student's parents and siblings.

CHECKLIST FOR SCHOOL SUPPORT TEAMS

❏ Convene the school support team.

❏ Review the medical alert list for the school.

❏ Develop goals based on the review of the medical alert list and the particular needs of students.

❏ Share expertise, and set goals for needs and future response strategies.

❏ When a student is newly diagnosed:

- Communicate with other members of the school support team
- Identify the liaison with the family (professional school counselor, social worker, public health nurse, or teacher with strongest ties to the family)
- Contact parent(s) of identified student
- Gather information regarding the illness from the parent and other sources.
- Arrange for parent conference:
  - Educate parents about school resources
  - Refer student to Child Study Team
  - Consider a Section 504 plan
  - Negotiate a plan for school support.
- Conduct an information workshop for faculty
- Conduct classroom lesson with student's peers.
- Meet with the ill student when appropriate or necessary.
- Meet with student's sibling(s), and consult with their professional school counselor
- Consult with homebound teacher
- Consult with student's doctor, psychiatrist, or other medical personnel

FIGURE 76.2. Suggested checklist for school support teams.

Suggested Intervention	Team Member Date	Comments
Contact family		
Convene school support team		
Identify team leader		
Facilitate parent conferences		
Develop school reentry plan		
Conduct faculty workshop		
Conduct classroom guidance		
Consult medical personnel		
Support ill child		
Support siblings and peers		
Follow up		

FIGURE 76.3. School support team planning.

RECOMMENDED READING FOR PARENTS

Deasy-Spinetta, P., & Irwin, E. (1993). *Educating the child with cancer, a guide for parents and teachers.* Kensington, MD: The Candlelighters Foundation.

Heugel, K., & Verdick, E. (Eds.). (1998). *Young people and chronic illness: True stories, help and hope.* Minneapolis, MN: Free Spirit.

Keene, N., Hobbie, W., & Ruccione, K. (2000). *Childhood cancer survivors: A practical guide to your future.* Sebastopol, CA: O'Reilly & Assoc.

Meyer, D. J., Vadasy, P. F., & Pillo, C. (1994). *Sibshop: Workshops for brothers and sisters of children with special needs.* Baltimore: Brookes.

Singer, A. T. (1999). *Coping with your child's chronic illness.* San Francisco: Robert D. Reed.

RECOMMENDED READING FOR CHILDREN AND ADOLESCENTS

Carney, K. L. (1998). *What is cancer anyway? Explaining cancer to children of all ages.* (Barklay and Eve Series, Book 5). Wethersfield, CN: Dragonfly.

Meyer, D. (1997). *View from our shoes: Growing up with a brother or sister with special needs.* Bethesda, MD: Woodbine House.

Mills, J. C. (1992). *Little tree: A story for children with serious medical problems.* New York: Brunner/Maze.

Vadasy, P., & Meyer, D. J. (1996). *Living with a brother or sister with special needs: Book for siblings.* Seattle: University of Washington Press.

ONLINE RESOURCES FOR INFORMATION AND SUPPORT

"A Site for Kids by Kids" This site links to a bulletin board on which kids can share and discuss their feelings and experiences (www.asiblingssite.com)

Allergy and Asthma Network/Mothers of Asthmatics, Inc. 703-641-9595 (www.aanma.org)

American Brain Tumor Association (www.abta.org/kids/home.htm)

(continues)

FIGURE 76.4. Resources.

- Provide the parents with resources (see Figure 76.4) and information about the services the school can provide, such as special education and Section 504 modifications, homebound instruction, and ways in which the student's peers can continue to have contact with the student. Provide information about the affect the illness may have on the siblings.
- Help the parents understand the needs of the siblings and offer assistance.
- Gain the parents' permission to discuss the student's illness with staff, peers, and the medical team treating the student.
- Develop a school support or reentry plan.

4. *Components of a school support or reentry plan.* Recognize that each student and family will require individualized services. Consider the following issues:

- Identify a liaison who will be the point of contact between the school and family and the school and medical professionals.

American Juvenile Arthritis Organization 404-872-7100 (www.arthritis.org/ajao)

Association of Online Cancer Resources Listserves regarding childhood oncology provide access to 99 mailing lists, a variety of online support groups, and related Web sites (www.acor.org)

Band-Aids and Blackboards This child-friendly Web site was created by a nurse educator to help kids and teens cope with chronic illness and returning to school (www.lehman.cuny.edu/faculty/jfleitas/bandaides/)

Brave Kids Online resources for children with chronic and life-threatening illnesses (www.bravekids.org)

Candlelighters Childhood Cancer Foundation Provides support for children and families (www.candlelighters.org)

The Childhood Brain Tumor Foundation (www.childhoodbraintumor.org)

Children's Health Information Network Congenital heart disease information, resources and support for families and professionals (www.tchin.org)

Children With Diabetes For families of children affected (www.childrenwithdiabetes.com/index_cwd.htm)

Crohn's and Colitis Foundation of America 1-800-932-2423 (www.ccfa.org)

Cystic Fibrosis Foundation 301-951-4422 (http://www.cff.org)

Depression and Related Affective Disorders Association (DRADA) Provides resources for teenagers and opportunities to buy depression related material (www.hopkinsmedicine.org/drada)

Juvenile Diabetes Research Foundation 1-800-533-2873 (http://www.jdf.org)

Kids With Heart National Association for Children's Heart Disorders 1-800-538-5390 (http://kidswithheart.org)

Lymphoma & Leukemia Society 1-800-955-4572 (http://www.leukemia-lymphoma.org)

National Childhood Cancer Foundation The NCCF provides resources to infants, children and adolescents with cancer (http://nccf.org)

Starbright Support for seriously ill children and their families (www.starbright.org)

FIGURE 76.4. *Continued.*

- Obtain the parent's permission to allow the liaison to coordinate services and have access to medical information or to communicate with a member of the student's medical team.
- Decide how the staff will hear about the student's illness, who on the staff will be told, and how they will be told. Decide how school staff will receive updated information. Discuss how peers and classmates can stay in contact with the student.
- Decide how the student's class and peers will hear about the illness, who will tell them, and what will they be told. Decide how they will receive updated information.
- Decide what steps should be taken to continue the student's education. If the student will receive homebound services, provide the parents with the necessary information for gaining those services. If the student's attendance is ex-

pected to be irregular, decide how the student will receive schoolwork and who will supervise its completion.

- Decide whether the student should be referred to the Child Study committee for consideration of special education or Section 504 modifications.
- Discuss how the siblings will be supported.
- Prepare for the student's return to school. Determine what medical and educational modifications will be required.

5. *Coordinate support services.* While the professional school counselor is not responsible for providing all of the services the student with a chronic illness might require, the professional school counselor can coordinate and facilitate those services. Support services could include a workshop for faculty and staff and a classroom presentation to students (see Figure 76.5).

- The purpose of the workshop for faculty and staff is to help them understand the medical and psychological needs of the student. Helping the school staff understand the needs of the student will increase the chances of successful school support or school reentry (Peckham, 1993). A member of the student's medical team, the public health or school nurse assigned to the student's school, the parents of the student, or the professional school counselor could conduct the workshop.
- The purpose of the classroom presentation is to increase peers' understanding of the medical and social needs of the student (Benner & Marlow, 1991; Treiber, Schramm, & Mabe, 1986). At the high school level, a group session for peers who are close to the adolescent should be held. This session should help peers gain accurate information about the student's illness and sensitize them to his or her social needs. The information could also be provided in a science class that focuses on a scientific understanding of the illness. A teacher, a member of the student's medical team, the public health or school nurse assigned to the student's school, the parents of the student, or the professional school counselor could conduct the classroom presentation.

6. *Provide support for the siblings.* Siblings' needs are often overlooked (Barrera, Fleming, & Kahn, 2004; Johnson, 1997). Well-meaning teachers, not knowing how to address the issue of the chronically ill student with his or her healthy siblings, ignore the opportunity to provide direct support. The professional school counselor can provide both direct and indirect help to the siblings by helping the staff and the siblings' peers understand their needs. If the siblings attend a different school, contact their school's professional school counselor.

7. *Coordinate support to the student with a chronic illness.* Support for the sick student may include providing direct services, individual or small-group counseling concerning adjustment to illness, coping strategies, school reentry preparation, and peer or academic issues. The professional school counselor can maintain contact with the student while he or she is out of school and encourage peers and teachers to maintain contact as well. The professional school counselor could also facilitate communication between the homebound teacher and school. By making the school community aware of the ongoing needs of the student with chronic illness, the professional school counselor is providing necessary services.

Summary/Conclusion

The professional school counselor can play an important role by providing school support for students with chronic illnesses. By making early contact with the family, forming a school support team, negotiating a role for the school, providing information and resources, developing a school reentry plan, supporting the siblings of students with chronic illness, providing a classroom presentation to the student's peers, and helping the school community to understand the needs of these students and families, professional school counselors can support reentry for students with chronic illnesses.

(Note: See the CD-ROM for a list of references.)

Purpose: The purpose of a staff workshop or class presentation is to provide accurate information to the staff and the classmates of the student with the chronic illness and to allay their fears. School support will be more successful when staff, peers, and classmates are informed about the illness and have had a chance to voice their concerns.

Who should facilitate: The workshop or classroom presentation could be conducted by school personnel (public health nurse, professional school counselor, social worker, teacher, administrator), a member of the child or adolescent's medical team (social worker, psychologist, nurse practitioner, physician, child life specialist), or by the parent of the student. The facilitator should be knowledgeable about the specifics of the disease and able to provide age-appropriate information to the students.

Before conducting the session: Obtain permission from the family and student before conducting the workshop or presentation and plan with them what to share.

Who should participate in the staff workshop: At a small elementary school, the workshop could involve the entire faculty and staff. At a large elementary school or a middle school, the student's team, those faculty and staff members who have contact with the student, should participate. At the high school level, the workshop should be conducted with the members of the faculty and staff who have contact with the adolescent.

Who should participate in the classroom presentation: At the elementary school level, the lesson should involve the student's classroom and peers. At the middle school level, the student's team should participate. At the high school level, the lesson should be conducted in the science class to discuss the medical aspects of the disease and in the homeroom to discuss the social and personal effect of the disease.

What to expect from the faculty, staff, and students: A discussion of serious medical issues will prompt memories of people in their lives who have been sick or died. The facilitator should expect to hear personal stories and questions. Faculty and staff will want to hear about how to treat the student, the ongoing medical concerns and responsibilities of the school, and what will be expected of the school staff. Students will have many questions about what it is like to have disease and how they should treat the sick student. At the high school level, expect existential questions about life and death.

FIGURE 76.5. School support for children with chronic illness: Presentation guidelines.

Faculty/Staff Workshop Outline

Suggested Procedures (30 to 45 minutes):

Opening

1. Introduce the presenters, especially if they are unknown to the staff.

2. Begin with an explanation about the purpose of the presentation:

   To learn about the disease that _____ has.

   To understand why he/she is out of school.

   To learn what we can expect when he/she comes back to school.

   To talk about what we can do to help the student.

3. Ask the staff what they know about the disease.

Information About the Disease

1. Provide information about the disease.

   Define the disease; include types, prevalence among children/adolescents, general prognosis, medical treatment, and side effects.

2. Provide information about the particular medical needs of the student.

Describe the School Support Plan

1. Inform staff about when the student will return to school.

   Describe feelings and concerns of the students and parents.

   Present homebound instruction plan and/or Section 504 plan, if needed.

2. Discuss the responsibilities of faculty and staff for educational, medical, and psychological support of the student.

3. Identify a liaison, the point of contact, for updated information about the student and the student's medical/educational needs.

Discuss Faculty Responsibilities to Help the Sick Student

1. Brainstorm ideas about how to help the sick student. How will the school contact the student when he or she is at home or in the hospital (e.g., cards, e-mails, visits, phone calls)?

2. Discuss ways to keep the student involved in school activities.

3. Discuss ways to support the student's siblings.

4. Discuss faculty questions and concerns.

(*continues*)

Figure 76.5. *Continued.*

Presentation to Classmates Lesson Plan

Suggested Procedures (30 to 45 minutes):

Opening

1. Introduce the presenters.

2. Begin with an explanation about the purpose of the lesson:
   - To learn about (the disease) that (name of the student) has.
   - To understand why he/she is out of school.
   - To learn what we can expect when he/she returns to school.
   - To talk about what we can do to help the student.

3. Ask the children what they know about (name of the disease).

Information About the Disease

1. Provide age-appropriate information about the disease.

   > Define the disease; include types, prevalence among children/adolescents, general prognosis, medical treatment, and side effects.

   > Use visuals including videos, overheads, and worksheets to reinforce the goals of the lesson.

2. Address the following typical concerns of classmates:

   > Can I catch this disease?

   > How did ____ get this disease?

   > Will ____ get better?

   > Will ____ die?

   > How does ___ feel?

   > Is it painful?

Discuss What to Expect When the Student Returns to School

1. Inform the staff about when the student will return to school.

2. Describe the sick student's feelings and concerns about returning to school.

3. Allow time for questions.

Discuss What Classmates Can Do to Help the Sick Student

1. Brainstorm ideas about how classmates can help the sick student.

2. Talk about what is helpful and unhelpful.

3. Allow time for questions.

Figure 76.5. *Continued.*

CHAPTER 77

INTERVENTION STRATEGIES FOR PHYSICALLY OR SEXUALLY ABUSED TUDENTS

David J. Carter and Patricia L. Walburn

Preview

In this chapter we discuss causes, symptoms, and treatment strategies regarding the physical and/or sexual abuse of students. We briefly discuss the legal responsibility and consequences and explore the recognition, intervention, and reporting of student physical and sexual abuse. The information we present in this chapter is especially important for the professional school counselor who works closely with students and serves as an advocate and a first line of defense against abuse. To address the abuse cycle, the professional school counselor must understand the misperceptions about such experiences, including misperceptions about self, the abuser, and the behavior or act that was forced upon the student.

Professional school counselors who believe that a student's physical or mental health and welfare has been or may be affected by physical or sexual abuse have a professional and legal responsibility to report the case immediately to a law enforcement agency or to the state's department of child protection services. Every school should have a designated protocol for reporting abuse, and the following information should be given in the initial report to the local department of social services: "1) Child's name, age, gender and address, 2) Parent's name and address, 3) Nature and extent of the injury or condition observed, 4) Prior injuries and when observed, 5) Actions taken by the reporter (e.g., talking with the child), 6) When the act occurred, and 7) Reporter's name, location, and contact information, sometimes not required but extremely valuable" (Crosson-Tower, 2005, p. 31).

In the past decade, 16.2 % of cases referred to Child Protective Services have come from education personnel—the highest percentage from any profession. This indicates that educators are the primary line of defense against child abuse because of their frequent contact and relationship to children and adolescents. Educators are trained observers and have knowledge of the wide range of behaviors children exhibit at each developmental stage. They can quickly recognize outlying behaviors that might indicate abuse. Professional school counselors, in particular, are critical to identifying, reporting, and intervening in suspected abuse because they work closely with teachers and students, and are likely to be the child's primary support system, advocate, and designer of preventative programs (Crosson-Tower, 2005; Kagan, 1991).

In this chapter we address the recognition, intervention, and reporting of student physical and sexual abuse. Child abuse is defined as "any recent act or failure to act resulting in imminent risk of serious harm, death, serious physical or emotional harm, sexual abuse, or exploitation of a child (minor age as described by state statutes) by a parent or caretaker (including out-of-home care providers) who are responsible for the child's welfare" (Keeping Children and Families Safe Act, 2003).

The Keeping Children and Families Safe Act of 2003 defined sexual abuse as employment, use, persuasion, inducement, enticement, or coercion of any child to engage in, or assist any other person to engage in, any sexually explicit conduct or any simulation of such conduct for the purpose of producing any visual depiction of such conduct; or rape, and in cases of caretaker or interfamilial relationship, statutory rape, molestation, prostitution, or other form of sexual exploitation of children or incest with children.

Physical abuse is defined specifically as any nonaccidental injury to a child while the child is under the supervision of a caretaker. An accurate way to detect physical abuse is by direct observations of outward physical signs:

- Adult-size human bite marks. All bite marks should be assessed.
- Burns, especially from objects such as cigarettes, irons, and other objects.
- Marks that represent hard blows from whip-like objects that make a burn around the body, such as electrical cords.
- Bruises in specific shapes, such as hangers, handprints, and paddles.
- Bald spots from severe hair pulling (rule out trichotillomania)
- Frequent bruising around the neck, face, or head; the abdomen; or along the arms, especially around the wrist.
- Extreme sensitivity to pain or complaints of soreness and stiffness or awkward movements as if caused by pain.

Professional school counselors working with abused students must be familiar with the complex dynamics that arise when the student experiences abuse. One of the most critical components of rapport building with any child is the comprehension of his or her internal frame of reference. This is often difficult to do in cases of sexual abuse. An abused child is often confused about the issue that is apparent to others.

There are many characteristics that profile a victim of sexual abuse. Engel (2005) identified the following:

- Demonstrate fearful behavior (cringe, flinch) around adults.
- Low self-esteem and loss of self-respect.
- A strong need for closeness, affection, and love.
- Believing that he or she doesn't deserve better care.
- Difficulty in setting and enforcing social boundaries.
- Struggles with forming healthy peer relationships.
- Belief that he or she is not validated without a relationship.
- Strong desire to avoid confrontation.
- Tendency to suppress anger or act out in aggressive ways.
- Denying the seriousness of a stressful situation.
- Taking on the needs and responsibilities of others.
- Blaming others for relationship problems.
- Fear of being abandoned and alone.
- Belief that he or she should be treated poorly.

Because sexual abuse is shame based, it sends the message that the child is worthless, unacceptable, and bad. The child might feel defective, unwanted, and alienated from others. Abused children will often try to overcompensate for these feelings by striving for control or perfection. If the child is able to be successful in gaining power, especially over others, he or she becomes increasingly less vulnerable to further shame and more likely to blame others. Other children strive for superiority in an attempt to overcome shame. Like power seeking, this is a way to compensate for an underlying sense of defectiveness. The perception is that if the child strives for perfection he or she is no longer vulnerable and will therefore overcome shame. Both of these defense mechanisms are destined to fail, and the student will reinforce the belief that nothing he does is good enough (Engel, 2005).

An abused student will harbor many emotions arising from the abuse. Misperceptions about the experience, including those about self, the abuser, and the behavior or act that was forced upon the child linger and can be debilitating to the abused child. In many instances, total recovery from the emotional trauma never happens; rather, the abusee develops coping skills or defense mechanisms to help reduce the highly stressful recall of memories or ensuing flashbacks.

An abused student struggles to cope with abusive experiences while accomplishing common developmental tasks. After the abuse, the student may attempt to cope with the abuse rather than fulfill developmental tasks such as acquiring social skills, developing a sense of self, and learning to achieve. Although professionals have noted that a "loss of innocence" occurs when a student is abused, another loss may also occur—that of lost opportunities.

Rather than being free of mind to pursue playful, healthy, ego-strengthening activities, an abused student may struggle to survive emotionally and physically. In cases of long-standing, repeated familial abuse, an abused student must develop self-reliance and inner strength as a means of survival (Daro, 1988; Reyes, Kokotovic, & Cosden, 1996; Smith & Carlson, 1997). Not all children are able to achieve this, especially when sexual abuse is involved.

Students come to regard abuse and sexuality through their relationships with others. Fundamental sexual feelings and attitudes are based on early life experiences. There is nothing new in this concept; professional school counselors understand they may have to deal with students' physical and sexual abuse problems. Following are self-reflections professionals can ask themselves to explore their feelings and attitudes:

- How did your mother, father, and/or caretakers show affection and anger in the family?
- What kinds of punishment were used in your family or your ethnic group when you were a child?
- Remember and describe a time when you were punished physically as a child. What happened, and how did you feel at the time?
- Describe in your own words the relationship between corporal punishment and physical abuse?
- How do your personal experiences of corporal punishment affect your professional work on this issue? Do these experiences make it harder or easier to work with students who have been abused?

Childhood experiences that are based on trust and safe physical boundaries set the stage for the development of healthy coping skills. When trust is violated, students develop defenses against being hurt. Defenses (e.g., attitudes of excessive self-sufficiency, self-love, self-hate, blame taking, blame giving) come together to form an individual's personality. It is the professional school counselor's responsibility to differentiate between student-demonstrated defense mechanisms and coping strategies and act accordingly.

SIGNS AND SYMPTOMS

Professional school counselors have regular contact with students and should be able to recognize indicators of abuse. Interaction with the student will acquaint personnel to his or her normal behavior and will thus alert them to the student's mood swings, withdrawal, and atypical acting-out behavior. Feelings of helplessness related to abuse could be acted out through an eating disorder (Schwartz & Cohn, 1996). Physical signs include scratches, burns, welts, broken teeth, cuts, and bruises not associated with sports, skate boarding, and so forth. Pay attention to students who don't want to sit down or who sit carefully, as if injured. Young students may exhibit precocious sex play with classmates or objects, may ask more questions than normal, or know sexual terminology inappropriate for their age group. Others may refuse to undress for physical education, not be allowed to spend the night at a friend's house, or vice versa.

Abused students can habitually be late to school or exhibit prolonged absences because the abusing parent wants to keep an injured child at home until the evidence of abuse disappears. In some cases, students frequently arrive early at school and remain after classes rather than return home. They might be inappropriately dressed for the weather; students who wear long-sleeve shirts and sweaters on hot days may be covering up bruises, burns, or other marks of abuse. The student may be wary of physical contact from adults and peers. Students may also try desperately to get attention from adult figures such as teachers and the professional school counselor (Hampton, Gullotta, Adams, Potter, & Weissberg, 1993).

As a professional school counselor, keep in mind that abuse of students can be perpetuated by other students as well. For these reasons, become an expert at unmasking sexual con games that take place between students. The goal of any perpetrator is to successfully increase the trust and secrecy between him- or herself and the victim (Herron & Sorensen, 1997). Be on the lookout for students who violate boundaries, such as by wearing revealing clothing, standing too close to others, saying too much about themselves too soon, making sexual comments about other students' body parts, asking very personal questions, touching another students' legs or other parts of the body, or saying or doing things that are offensive or vulgar.

Also watch for victim boundaries that may be too closed, such as students who have few friends, rarely share feelings with others, rarely ask for help, seek isolation, or are cautious about letting trustworthy adults appropriately touch them (i.e., hand shakes, pats on the back). With the professional school counselor's help, students who have been abused can learn to set appropriate boundaries and identify and avoid students who look out only for their own interests. Table 77.1 provides a developmental

TABLE 77.1

SYMPTOMS OF ABUSED STUDENTS

Elementary School
Withdrawn, fearful
Depressed or flat affect, cries easily
Passive, avoids eye contact, sinks down in chair
Squirms in seat, painful to sit
Suspicious or frequent bruises, welts, cuts, burns, bite makes, choke marks, grab marks, scratches, pinch marks.
Somatic complaints (e.g., stomachaches, painful urination or bowel movements, headaches, dizziness)
Violent or sexual drawings or stories
Advanced sexual vocabulary
Imitating sexual or violent behavior alone or with other children during play, with toys
Hypersensitive to appropriate social touching (e.g., pats on the back, handshakes)
Restroom accidents (enuresis, encopresis)
Not allowed to spend the night at a friend's house
Behavioral problems (e.g., temper tantrums, regression, aggression, destructive behavior)
Verbal inhibition
Fear of adults
Arrives to school early and leaves late
Low achiever
Dressed inappropriately for the season
Poor hygiene
Difficulty staying awake
Extremely adaptable/flexible
Flashbacks   *(continues)*

listing of symptoms and strategies for helping students who have been abused (Francis, First, & Pincus, 1995).

HELPFUL STRATEGIES

Disclosure of abuse may be accidental or purposeful. Accidental disclosure occurs when others observe the abuse, when the student is injured, or when the student acts out sexually. Purposeful disclosure occurs when the student desires to end the abusive relationship. Whatever the circumstances of the disclosure, don't assume the student will be anxious to talk openly about the abuse. It is essential to evaluate the student's level of trust, emotional stability, memory skills, cognitive ability, social maturity, accuracy of recall of past events, and ability to verbalize accurately (Kagan, 1991).

The purpose of the initial meeting with the student is to determine the type of abuse that occurred and to ensure that the student is protected. The meeting should be conducted in a safe place, and the student should be comfortable in the setting. Remain

TABLE 77.1 *(continued)*

Middle School

In addition to symptoms displayed in elementary-age children, the residual affects of abuse create more complex symptoms in middle school.

Vandalism, destruction of property

Self-mutilation

Bullying, using force or intimidating smaller children

Angry or violent outbursts

Withdrawal from physical contact from teachers or other students

Physical complaints of headaches, dizziness, muscle cramps

Poor peer relationships; few, if any, friends

Severe drop in grades

Precocious sex play

Won't undress for gym

Low self-esteem

Vacillates between being ultra-adult and ultra-immature

Dishonesty (e.g., cheats, lies, steals)

Fear of failure

High School

Due to higher cognitive abilities, high school students develop even more complex behaviors as a result of dysfunctional coping abilities.

Self-destructive behavior (e.g., drugs, alcohol, cutting)

Extreme moodiness

Suicidal thoughts

Withdrawal from friends and family

School truancy, poor school performance

Sexually vulgar conversations and behavior with opposite sex

Obsessive cleanliness

Compulsive behaviors

flexible and follow the student's lead in regard to pace, breadth, and depth. Refrain from interrupting, and remain patient. Provide frequent praise for the student's bravery in disclosing (Saywitz, 2002). If the student gives any indication of experiencing high stress levels or retraumatization, make alternative strategies and arrangements to avoid revictimization of the student (Smith & Carlson, 1997):

- Set boundaries while giving the student a safe space for self-expression. Create an accepting environment by posing understandable questions sensitive to the developmental level of the student in terms of memory, language, reasoning, knowledge and emotional maturity (Saywitz, 2002). The primary goal is to help the student merge self-expression with self-discovery, leading to an emotional catharsis.

- Be objective, and maintain a neutral stance. Pay careful attention to your body language, tone of voice, and facial expression and avoid leading, suggestive, coercive or accusatory questions or content. Avoid close-ended questions; open-ended questions elicit the most accurate information (Saywitz, 2002).
- Empathy is of highest importance. It is permissible for you to self-disclose and show empathy in a warm and caring manner when appropriate and accurate to the situation. Express caring in a nonsexual manner. Remember that unconditional positive regard is a therapeutic process. Providing acceptance and understanding will help reduce the student's fears and anxiety (Frontes, 2005).
- Address the abusive issues in a straightforward manner, and explore with the student his or her feelings and thoughts in a firm but warm and fair manner. Examination involves helping the student get in touch with the irrational beliefs that affect his or her self-esteem and confidence. Explore the student's behavior therapeutically as a result of the abusive situation.
- Use techniques incorporating art, music, role-playing, and talk therapy for changing the attributes in abused children of all ages. For example, a student can create a "warm fuzzy friend list" to identify people and places to go to for safety and support (Celano, Hazzard, Campbell, & Long, 2002).
- Do not attempt to intervene by contacting parents regarding suspected abuse, because it could give the perpetrator an opportunity to cover his or her actions. It is not unusual for a parent who is suspected of abuse to withdraw the student and move out of state with very little warning.

In a majority of cases, the professional school counselor becomes the first person that the student talks to about the abuse, and so the counselor becomes the "outcry witness." Because the counseling relationship is addressing such sensitive issues with legal consequences, professional school counselors must be well apprised of the legal and policy protocols within their state and school district as well as the child protective services process (Hampton et al., 1993). Following is a list of strategies and techniques for addressing initial reports of abuse:

- Do not overreact.
- Sit facing the student, with no desk between the two of you.
- Stay calm, and use active listening.
- Remember, perpetrators rely on trust and secrecy to victimize, so be patient.
- Refrain from displaying anger, disapproval, or disgust toward the parents or perpetrator.
- Let the student know that you believe him or her.
- Refrain from asking leading questions or probing for information the student is unwilling to give.
- Help the student feel powerful by offering options.
- Place the blame on the offender and let students know it's not their fault.
- Ensure students' secrecy.
- Explain to the student, in age-appropriate language, mandated reporting and the steps that will be followed.
- Do not contact the student's parents.

- Ask the student if he or she feels safe returning home. If the student indicates feeling unsafe, contact CPS immediately for intervention.
- Report the abuse by contacting protective services or the police to come to the school for a written report.

CHILD PROTECTION SERVICES

Professional school counselors are required to contact the designated agency, including Child Protection Services (CPS), and/or law enforcement and provide information on suspected maltreatment when they recognize signs of child abuse or neglect. When the report is filed, CPS makes the following decisions:

1. CPS must decide if the report meets the statutory criteria for abuse or neglect, and then they must investigate to determine if the abuse or neglect can be substantiated.
2. CPS assesses the child's safety at home along with the need for emergency services or removal. CPS will also assess the risk factors involved for future abuse and neglect. If the investigation rules out abuse, the case is referred or the case is closed.
3. CPS assesses the family for strengths, needs, and factors contributing to the risk of child maltreatment.
4. During the planning phase(which includes strategies or services to achieve goals and outcomes along with specific time frames), CPS identifies outcomes and goals that will reduce or eliminate maltreatment.
5. Service provision includes both in- and out-of-house services such as family preservation, parenting education, foster care, and reunification services.
6. Evaluation, a critical step, involves assessing the safety of the child and the reduction of risks; the achievement of family outcomes, goals, and tasks; and reviewing progress and needs for continued services. If continued services are warranted, then CPS will return to the planning or service provision stages to reassess the needs of the case. If the evaluation is favorable, the case will be closed once it is determined that the family can protect their child without further CPS services.

COUNSELOR AND ORGANIZATIONAL LIABILITY

All states have laws requiring professional school counselors to report suspected abuse to the designated authorities, and they must follow rigid guidelines when they conduct counseling following disclosures or accusations of abuse from others. It is imperative for counselors to adhere to the ethical standards or the American Counseling Association and the American School Counselor Association and to follow the legal guidelines of their school system and respective district. If you are not sure what the protocol is in your school, immediately check with your building administrator. One professional school counselor had this to say: "I learned from a veteran counselor in my school that if I suspect abuse I am to immediately notify the principal, not the assistant principal, not the school psychologist, the principal." Other school districts require the professional school counselor to notify a law enforcement officer as the initial contact.

Consistent, effective reporting of abuse depends upon the professional school counselor's understanding the dynamics of abuse and reporting procedures. Cooperation among the professional school counselor, staff, administration, law enforcement, and child protective services is essential.

The following vignette is typical of the types of behavior students who have been physically abused will exhibit in the classroom.

Case Study

Kathy was 9 years old when her teacher became concerned about possible abuse. She was extremely shy and withdrawn and often took a great deal of time to comprehend information, although testing showed no significant physical or cognitive difficulties. Her mother, a professional nurse who had chosen to stay home with her four children, and her father, a store manager, found Kathy's slowness especially upsetting.

As Kathy's homework increased, she became more withdrawn and unhappy. The teacher suggested she seek help at home from her parents, especially with her English. At first Kathy began coming to school with peculiar marks on her hands and arms. On another day she arrived with burn marks covering a good part of her right hand. It had not been treated and had become infected. Using open-ended questions in a safe environment for self-expression the teacher asked Kathy about her injuries. The teacher learned that Kathy was being abused by her father. After drinking, he would "help her" with her homework, become agitated by her slowness, and burn her with his lit cigarette.

The school district's protocol for abuse involved meeting with the crisis team at the academic site to discuss intervention options. As head of the crisis team, the school principal was responsible for contacting Child Protection Services and inviting them to the school for a written report. In conjunction with information from Kathy and the crisis team, CPS was successful in assessing that Kathy's safety was in jeopardy at home, and emergency services were initiated. Kathy was placed with her grandparents and continued attending classes at her neighborhood school to promote continuity, stability, and to reduce additional stressors. Kathy's teacher was instrumental in communicating academic accomplishments and socialization concerns to the grandparents. After ongoing family counseling Kathy was returned to her home with periodic monitoring from her school and child protective services.

SUMMARY/CONCLUSION

Students who are physically and sexually abused are robbed of more than innocence—they are robbed of emotional stability, rational thinking, and interactions built on trust and well-being. The ability to form and maintain protective and appropriate boundaries is exhausted. Emotional desires that need to be explored and fulfilled are stunted and go unattended or are repressed and can lead to depression or anger.

A student's physical and mental welfare is a top priority in school, and the professional school counselor must serve as the student's safety advocate. With every interaction the professional school counselor can help the student take new steps toward an enhanced quality of life. In turn, through the student's taking control of the issues, both the professional school counselor and the student become empowered survivors.

(Note: See the CD-ROM for a list of references.)

CHAPTER 78

COUNSELING SEXUAL MINORITY STUDENTS
IN THE SCHOOLS

Mark Pope, Lela Kosteck Bunch, Dawn M. Szymanski, and Michael Rankins

Preview

We addresses the issues that are important for professional school counselors who counsel sexual minority students including gay, lesbian, bisexual, transgender, intersex, queer, and questioning (GLBTIQQ) youth. The issues include developing a context in which to discuss these issues; "coming out" or the developmental aspects of sexual identity development; the extent of the problems that sexual minority youth face in the schools and society; the effects of negative attitudes and violence toward these youth; and ethical and legal issues in dealing with sexual minority youth in the schools. In addition, we discuss school-based interventions that focus on the role of the parents and schools, separation (e.g., separate schools for sexual minority youth) or culture change, deliberate psycho-affective education, valuing differences, and the power of subtle symbols.

Fag. Dyke. Geek. Wuss. Dweeb. Queer. Lezzie. These are some of the words that sexual minority youth often hear as they progress through elementary and secondary schools in the United States. Whether these terms are directed at them because they look and act different or at others who look and act different, the point has been made: "You are different, and that is bad." "You're different and not a member of our group." These statements occur at a time when sexual minority youth so desperately want and need to belong.

This is the lexicon of adolescence in America. This verbal and physical harassment is designed to elicit conformity from those so targeted and security for the deliverer, "no matter how bad my life is, at least I'm not one of THEM. To be a boy or girl who is "different" from your peers' notions of what a male or female is supposed to do or be is to become the object of derisive comments challenging your sexual orientation. In the USA if you are a sensitive boy who cries at movies, or an athletic girl who wears jeans and no makeup, you are subject to whispers or catcalls from your peers. To be different during a time when conformity to your peer group is the norm is to be a target for verbal and physical harassment from that same group, especially about sexuality. (Pope, 2000, p. 285)

Professional school counselors are confronted regularly with elementary, middle, and secondary school students who are gay, lesbian, bisexual, transgender, intersex, queer, or simply questioning (GLBTIQQ) if they are different. Fontaine (1998) surveyed professional school counselors and found that more than half (51%) of both middle and high school counselors had worked with at least one student who was questioning their sexual orientation, and 42% had worked with at least one self-identified lesbian or gay student. Twenty-one percent of elementary school counselors also reported that they were aware of students in their schools who were identifying as gay or lesbian or who were questioning their sexual orientation. Professional school counselors need to know what to do when that young person walks into the school counseling office and says, "I think I might be a lesbian."

Unfortunately, there are no easy answers. This chapter, however, does provide some guidelines to aid the professional school counselor in helping these courageous young people. Young people who are different face physical and verbal harassment because they are different or just perceived as being different from peers. In this chapter, we will address the following issues: developing a context in which to discuss sexual minority student issues; "coming out," or the developmental aspects of sexual identity development; the extent of the problems that sexual minority youth face in the schools and society; the effects of negative attitudes and violence toward these youth; and ethical and legal issues in dealing with sexual minority youth in the schools. In addition, we discuss school-based interventions that focus on the roles of parents and schools, separation (e.g., separate schools for sexual minority youth) or culture change, deliberate psycho-affective education, valuing differences, and the power of subtle symbols.

DEVELOPING A CONTEXT IN WHICH TO DISCUSS THESE ISSUES

In this chapter we will discuss sex, sexuality, sexual orientation, and other related issues. Sex and sexuality in American society are taboo subjects. We know that we are supposed to know about it; we are excited about it; we talk about it in indirect ways; we sometimes even talk about it in direct ways, but that is generally considered unseemly. Perhaps our parents talked to us (rarely with us) about it. Our schools have had to fight hard to get an opportunity to teach about it. Socially, we are just not very comfortable with sex (LeVay & Valente, 2006).

Here, we will use the general term *sexual minority* to include a variety of young people who are in various stages of their psychosocial, gender, sexual, and cultural identity development processes, including gays (males who identify with a same-sex sexual or affectional orientation); lesbians (females who identify with a same-sex sexual or affectional orientation); bisexuals (males or females who identify with both a same-sex and opposite sex sexual or affectional orientation); transgender (individuals who are physiologically one gender but who are psychologically the opposite gender); intersex (individuals who have biological characteristics of both males and females); queer (individuals who identify as "different" sexually than the majority culture); and questioning (individuals who are unsure of their sexual or affectional orientation or gender identity). This sometimes will be abbreviated as either GLBTIQQ or GLBT in this chapter.

Further, there are a number of well-written articles and books on the etiology of sexual orientation (LeVay, 1991, 1999; LeVay & Valente, 2006). The topic of sexual orientation is complex, evocative, and confusing. To date, it remains unclear exactly how sexual orientation is determined. Moreover, because conservative religious and political groups tend to view homosexuality as a moral issue while others see it as a civil rights issue, it cannot be separated easily from either context: A person's sexual orientation has both political and religious implications. Finally, given the lack of definitive answers from scientific research, confusion and uncertainty tend to underlie the often-intense discussions about the sexual behavior and mental health needs of sexual minorities in our society (B. Barret & Logan, 2002; R. L. Barret & Robinson, 2000; Ciro et al., 2005; Pope & Barret, 2002a). Rarely does anyone agree on anything, yet it appears there is a growing research consensus about the roots of sexual orientation. It is imperative that this type of information be readily available to both parents and students. We make the assumption that the causes of sexual orientation are not known definitively but that sexual orientation is not mutable.

Social attitudes toward homosexuality have also undergone many changes: From the acceptance and integration of same-sex persons into the Native American tribes of North America (Roscoe, 1989); to the acceptance of same-sex unions by the Christian church in the middle ages (Boswell, 1980, 1995); to the persecution of homosexually oriented persons under the Victorians (Rowse, 1977); to the enlightened approaches of pre-Nazi Germany (Hirschfeld, 1935), pre-Stalinist Russia (Thorstad, 1974), and imperial China (Ruan, 1991); and finally to the removal of homosexuality from the psychiatric manual of mental disorders (Bayer, 1987), history has seen an ebb and flow in the social acceptance of same-sex orientations (Pope & Barret, 2002a).

In the past, sexual minority adults had to cope with active anger, religious hatred, psychiatric labels, and occupational discrimination. Pope and Barrett (2002b) described how aspects of this discrimination were reflected in the workplace:

> If they did not live in large cities such as New York, San Francisco, and Boston where vital lesbian and gay culture thrives, gay men and lesbians generally kept their sexual orientation a closely guarded secret. . . . Many of them fabricated social lives that included dates with persons of the opposite sex and rarely would share their vacation photographs with their co-workers. If there were a social event with co-workers, many would bring opposite sex "dates" that had been secured to help "cover" their secret. Some even chose careers on the basis of its "safety" in the event they did decide to come out. For example, it was not unusual to hear young gay men or lesbians speak of avoiding careers that involved working with children or commenting on "conservative" corporations that would not deal with their sexual orientation easily. Others carefully guarded their sexual orientation for fear that the promotions would be denied them if they were more "out." Fortunately today, for many lesbian and gay clients, much of this is changing, as it is not unusual to hear casual conversations about the social and relationship aspects of gay and lesbian co-workers in the workplace. (p. 215)

For today's sexual minority youth, there are many positive sexual minority role models available. GLBTIQQ individuals appear in virtually every aspect of daily life. They are more "out" to their families and coworkers, visible in their neighborhoods, assertive in demanding equal rights, and have moved beyond the fear and shame that used to keep most of them invisible. This change can be seen in all aspects of the media, gay-positive statements from national and local political candidates and in the debates within virtually all Christian denominations about the role of gay men and lesbians within the church (B. Barret & Logan, 2002).

"Coming out to self," or accepting one's own same-sex feelings, attraction, and orientation, is an important and necessary developmental task for anyone who is gay or lesbian, but it is especially important for the gay or lesbian adolescent (Pope, 1995). Males tend to define themselves as gay in the context of same-sex erotic contact, but females experience lesbian feelings in situations of romantic love and emotional attachment (Troiden, 1979). Coleman, Butcher, and Carson (1984) provided a good explanation of general developmental stages and the tasks associated with each stage:

> If developmental tasks are not mastered at the appropriate stage, the individual suffers from immaturities and incompetencies and is placed at a serious disadvantage in adjusting at later developmental levels—that is, the individual becomes increasingly vulnerable through accumulated failures to master psychosocial requirements. . . . Some developmental tasks are set by the individual's own needs, some by the physical and social environment. Members of different socioeconomic and sociocultural groups face somewhat different developmental tasks. (p. 111)

Pope (1995) stated that this developmental task of discovery and acceptance of whom one is and how one functions sexually plays an important role, especially in adolescence. This is, however, also the time for many gay males and lesbians when the greatest denial of differences exists from their peer group. Unfortunately, if the developmental tasks of sexual orientation identification are not accomplished during this critical time and are denied and delayed, then other tasks, such as relationship formation, are also delayed, causing a developmental chain reaction. It is very common to hear that gay men who came out when they were substantially past adolescence have all the problems associated with those of teenagers who have just begun dating. It is important to note that once the critical period has passed in the developmental task, it may be very difficult or impossible to correct the resulting psychological difficulties.

Adolescence is not an easy time in anyone's life because of the required psychosexual identity development. This tumultuous time is only made more difficult, however, when homophobic slurs and insults are hurled at young persons who may have already begun to realize that their sexual orientation is different from their heterosexual peers. Both verbal and physical harassment are designed to elicit conformity from those so targeted along with security for the deliverer ("No matter how bad my life is, at least I'm not one of THEM"). A large study of Minnesota junior and senior high school students found that approximately 11% were still unsure about their sexual orientation (Remafedi, Resnick, Blum, & Harris, 1992). Twenty percent of self-identified gay and bisexual men surveyed on college campuses knew about their sexual orientation in high school, and another 17% knew as far back as grade school that they were gay. The figures are 6% and 11%, respectively, for lesbians (Elliott & Brantley, 1997).

Coming to terms with one's sexual differences during the teen years make forming a sexual identity a greater challenge (D'Augelli, 1992). This is because youth are socialized in the home and school, in the media, and throughout most of their lives to appreciate falling in love with members of the other gender (Rotheram-Borus & Fernandez, 1995). Though there is wide variation in sexual identity formation in adolescence, some common themes emerge for many gay teens: feeling different, experiencing confusion, and, finally, expressing acceptance (Mannino, 1999; Ponterotto, Utsey, & Pedersen, 2006). Chung and Katayama (1998) reported that the formation of sexual identity is a developmental process composed of the stages of awareness of same-sex feelings, feeling confused because one's assumed sexual orientation differs from one's perceived orientation, tolerance and acceptance of a lesbian or gay identity, and integration of a sexual identity with other aspects of one's life.

Gay men and lesbians often report feeling different from others during childhood. Many of these differences are in gender nonconformity—that is, play and sport interests are more congruent with the other gender (Mondimore, 1996). Boys may find they are quieter, less active, and more sensitive than other boys, while girls may find that they are more physically active, assertive, and more "tom-boyish" than their peers. Marinoble (1998) described the difficulties experienced by many such sexual minority youth, including identity conflict, feelings of isolation and stigmatization, peer relationship problems, and family disruptions. Omizo, Omizo, and Okamoto (1998) found that common sentiments among young sexual minority persons include confusion, fear of not being understood, fear of negative or violent reactions from others, concerns about what kind of a future they might have, poor self-esteem, and internalized feelings of self-hatred. Within especially conservative cultures or families, such as those of some Asian American youth, there are few if any positive role models with whom sexual minority youth may identify (Chung & Katayama, 1998). For such youth, it is likely that feelings of isolation and confusion are magnified.

Some gay youth cope with their confusion by concretizing their gay identity very quickly. This is sometimes initiated by puberty, where feeling different takes on a clearer, more precise feeling of sexual attraction. Herdt and Boxer (1996), in a study of 200 ethnically diverse lesbian, gay, and bisexual youth, found that awareness of same-sex attraction occurred between ages 11 and 12, on average. Other gay teens try to deny their same-sex feelings and become super-heterosexual in an effort to retrain themselves, and still others become bewildered, guilt ridden, and lonely, escaping into substance abuse, depression, and suicidal ideation.

Not all gay and lesbian teenagers accept themselves, which is understandable given the constant battering they receive from some cultures and religions as well as from their peers, family, and society (Mannino, 1999). Eventually, however, the majority of gay youth who do accept their sexuality begin to feel a need to disclose their sexual orientation to others. There are many strategies to such disclosure, but close friends are usually told first, with parents being told later. The fear of rejection and isolation, along with parental sanctions, tend to be ever present; therefore, some sexual minority youth decide not to disclose at all, especially if they are still in high school or living with their parents or other family members (Newman & Muzzonigro, 1993). When young people do decide to reveal their sexual orientation to their parents, having some idea of a "format" for such a coming out process is often helpful. Savin-Williams (1990) reported in a study of gay and lesbian youth that most of those who had successfully come out to self could be described as (a) being politically and socially involved with other gays and lesbians, having numerous same-sex sexual encounters, regularly frequenting bars, and describing an early onset of same-sex sexual feelings that were beyond their control; (b) feeling accepted by family members and friends and feeling that they had even more friends than before they came out; (c) feeling they were accomplished and self-sufficient, but not feeling competitive and forceful or affectionate and compassionate; (d) being generally older and well-educated, coming from wealthy urban families; (e) measuring their self-esteem and sense of well-being by their relationships with friends and by their career and academic achievements rather than by their possessions and good looks; and (f) being politically liberal and supportive of the feminist movement.

Extent of the Problems That Sexual Minority Youth Face in the Schools and Society

Although we have already discussed a number of social and environmental difficulties that sexual minority youth may encounter, a more intensive focus on education and socialization issues is warranted because the schools are the workplace for young people. Owens (1998) captured the experience of sexual minority students in the schools:

> Schools are social molds where rigid expectations of conduct and behavior are reinforced. Conformity is tyrannical. The wrong clothes or the wrong comment can result in ostracism. Sexual conformity is enforced most rigidly. Those that do not conform are open to the physical, verbal, and mental bullying of the majority. Reports from lesbian and gay teens range from put-downs and "rude comments and jokes" through "profanities written on my locker" and threats to actual violence and physical abuse. The overall result is loneliness, fear, and self-loathing. (pp. 95–96)

Sexual minority youth face stigmatization and a significant number of stressors in the school environment, including ostracism, physical violence, and verbal harassment (Allport, 1958; Elze, 2003; Gustavsson & MacEachron, 1998; Horn & Nucci, 2006; Jordan, Vaughan, & Woodworth, 1997; Pope, 2000). The search for one's sexual identity (male or female) is an important part of adolescence (Sexuality Information and Education Council of the United States, 1995), but when that search is intertwined with minority status—that is, either race or sexual orientation—it is even more complex (Chung & Katayama, 1998).

In the United States, there is, in general, fear and loathing of gay and lesbian people. Ilnytzky (1999) reported that all antigay attacks in the entire United States dropped 4% in 1998, but the assaults that did occur were more violent and led to more hospitalizations than previous attacks. The number of attacks dropped from 2,665 in 1997 to 2,552 in 1998; however, the number of victims requiring inpatient hospitalization more than doubled, from 53 in 1997 to 110 in 1998. There also was a 71% rise in assaults and attempted assaults with guns. Incidents in which bats, clubs and other blunt objects were used increased by 47%. According to the 2004 FBI Hate Crime Statistics Report, the total number of reported antigay attacks dropped to 1,482. The majority of these reported offenses, 61%, were due to antimale homosexual bias (http://www.fbi.gov/ucr/hc2004/openpage.htm).

Gay and lesbian high school students face greater prejudice in school than African American teen students according to a CBS News poll that surveyed the attitudes of the high school senior class of the year 2000. The findings included the following: (a) one third of students know that gay or lesbian students were made fun of, verbally or physically abused, and threatened; (b) 28% of students polled have made antigay remarks themselves; (c) nearly a third of those polled have a family member or close friend who is gay or lesbian; (d) among those making antigay remarks, boys are more than twice as likely than girls to have done so; and (e) those who report their parents make antigay remarks are more than twice as likely to do so themselves (CBS News, 1999). A survey conducted in 14 American cities found more than 46% of gay youth who disclosed their same-sex sexual orientation ("came out") to friends lost at least one of them as a friend (Ryan & Futterman, 1997). Marsiglio (1993), in a national survey of young people who were 15 to 19 years of age, found only 12% would feel comfortable having a lesbian or gay male friend. Male youth in particular were more likely to hold negative stereotypes regarding lesbian and gay youth, as 89% of the male adolescents in this study reported that they felt sex between two men was "disgusting." Malinsky (1997), in a study of 27 self-identified lesbians and bisexual girls between the ages of 15 and 21, found that 25 (93%) of the study participants reported direct, firsthand knowledge of harassment based on actual or perceived sexual orientation. It is important to note that such harassment was sometimes directed at those who simply associated with these young lesbian or bisexual women.

The Gay, Lesbian and Straight Education Network (GLSEN) rated 42 of the nation's largest public school districts on their policies and programs designed to serve sexual minority students and school workers. Only four districts got an "A"—Los Angeles; San Diego; Philadelphia; and Dade County, Florida. Twenty major school districts received a grade of "D." According to spokesperson Kate Frankfurt, "that means nearly 2 million students go to school in districts that fail" in basic gay human rights (Herscher, 1998, p. A20).

These negative feelings toward sexual minority youth are being reinforced by school workers' indifference to these issues. Derogatory remarks by fellow students directed at sexual minority students often go unchallenged by teachers, administrators, or professional school counselors, whereas a similar racist statement would likely prompt a reprimand (Elze, 2003; Krivascka, Savin-Williams, & Slater, 1992; O'Conor, 1994; Pope, 2000). The dynamics are complicated when sexual minority school employees are trying to hide their sexual orientation and distance themselves from sexual minority youth (Jordan et al., 1997). Reluctant or unable to support sexual minority youth, these sexual minority teachers, professional school counselors, administrators, or other school staff fail to provide the role modeling or safety that other cultural minority school workers (e.g., African American, Asian American, Native American, or Hispanic American) provide for students from their own specific culture.

Fontaine (1998) found that those who were the perpetrators of harassment and intimidation of sexual minority students were aided by the indifference of school workers: "Homophobic and intolerant educational environments can only exist with the implicit and/or explicit cooperation of schools' officials and personnel. Evidence suggests that teachers, counselors, and administrators exhibit distressingly high levels of homophobic attitudes and feelings" (p. 8).

Rofes (1989) wrote eloquently about the violence against sexual minority youth and pointed out its effects:

> Many young people—especially those who were cross-dressers, or young men who were effeminate, or young women who were "too butch" (tough, indepen-

dent, and "masculine")—found their peers hostile, often to the point of violence. For gay youth who could "pass" and remain undetected in the school system, advocates found the hiding process robbed students of much of their energy and vitality. Whether lesbian and gay youth were open about their identities or were closeted, societal prejudice took its toll; young gay people were often anti-social, alcohol- and drug-abusing, and/or depressed to the point of suicide. (p. 449)

Anthony Gomez, a 14-year-old student at Hayward, California, described his own experience in the following manner:

A lot of people pick on me at school and pick fights with me. At school, I've had *fag* spray-painted on my locker, gay porn pinned to my locker, and death threats on my locker too. I had three boys suspended the other day for harassing me, saying they're trying to pick fights with me, calling me a faggot, a queer, and all that stuff. (Gray, 1999, p. 81)

Finally, The Associated Press ("Anti-Gay Slur Carved on Student," 1999) reported that two college preparatory school students in Greenwood, Massachussets, at the Northfield Mount Hermon School, were convicted of assault and battery for carving an antigay slur into another student's back because he liked to listen to the British rock band Queen. Jonathan Shapiro, 18, and Matthew Rogers, 20, used a pocket knife to cut "HOMO" into the back of a 17-year-old student at the school. "There was apparently a disagreement over the style of music he liked," said Police Chief David Hastings. "Rogers called it a gay band." Hastings described the wounds as "deep enough to draw blood. When I saw them, they were three days old and they were still very visible. The letters were 4- to 5-inches high and ran all the way across his back." The victim, a junior, did not require hospitalization, and initially kept quiet about the incident. He left school and returned to his family. Shapiro, of Keene, New Hampshire, and Rogers, of Franklin, Tennessee, were placed on probation for 3 years for this crime. Rogers had accepted an appointment to the U.S. Naval Academy, but his appointment was withdrawn because of the incident. Concerned Students of Des Moines reported that the average high school student hears approximately 25 antigay remarks in a typical school day ("Agenda," 1997).

EFFECTS OF NEGATIVE ATTITUDES AND VIOLENCE TOWARD THESE YOUTH

Adolescents who are different from their peers face a variety of barriers to healthy psychological development, most of which are created and delivered by their peers, family, culture, and society (Pope, 2000). Besner and Spungin (1995) reported a variety of consequences for the lesbian and gay adolescent such as a high incidence of acting out in school; rebelling against authority; abusing alcohol and other substances; feeling depressed, isolated, and confused; engaging in prostitution; and attempting suicide, many times, succeeding. Jordan et al. (1997), in a study of 34 lesbian and gay high school students, reported a clear relationship between derogatory language directed against sexual minority students by their peers and adults in the school setting and self-harmful behavior, such as suicidal ideation, attempted suicide, running away, poor academic performance, and truancy. Considering the stress of adolescence and the additional "cultural minority stress" of being a sexual minority youth, it is particularly disheartening to discover that a survey found that less than one in five lesbian and gay adolescent students could identify someone who was very supportive of them (Telljohann & Price, 1993).

Remafedi (1987) found, through a series of studies of self-identified gay male adolescents, that they were at high risk for physical and psychosocial dysfunction as a result of experiencing strong negative attitudes from parents and peers. In a follow-up to those studies, Remafedi, Farrow, and Deisher (1991), in a study of 137 gay and bisexual male youths, found that 30% had attempted suicide once and 13% had made multiple attempts. The mean age of those attempting suicide was 15.5 years. Three quarters (75%) of first attempts came after the teenagers had labeled themselves bisexual or gay. (Documentation of risk factors that increase the potential for suicide in sexual minority youth, titled "Factors Which Increase Risk of Suicide for Sexual Minority Youth," are posted at www.umsl.edu/~pope.)

According to Gibson (1989), suicide is the leading cause of death among gay youth. They are from three to five times more likely to attempt suicide than are their heterosexual peers (Bailey & Phariss, 1996; Brown, 1991; Gibson, 1989; Hafen & Frandsen, 1986; Mondimore, 1996; Russell & Joyner, 2001). Gibson (1989) also found that gay male adolescents are six times more likely to attempt suicide than are their heterosexual counterparts.

Currently, there is much discussion among researchers about these statistics, based on the skewed demographics of the populations sampled (Muerher, 1995; Saulnier, 1998). The results of many of these studies have been criticized for the retrospective nature of the reports, the involvement of many of the youths in social service systems, and the recruitment of study participants from bars, which might inflate the actual numbers. It is quite difficult to gather generalizable data on this population because of the difficulty of operationalizing sexual orientation and the previously cited issues.

ETHICAL AND LEGAL ISSUES IN DEALING WITH SEXUAL MINORITY YOUTH IN THE SCHOOLS

The question of what is the ethical and legal role of the professional school counselor when counseling sexual minority students is an important practical one. Ethically, the role is clear. Professional school counselors assist students in discovering who they truly and honestly are and to help them develop a strong and positive personal and cultural identity.

Research conducted by Nicolosi (1991) described an approach called *reparative therapy* (RT) that claims to change sexual orientation (always from gay to straight, rather than the opposite). RT parallels another "treatment," *conversion therapy* (CT), hailed by conservative Christian groups as proof that prayer and meditation can "drive the sin out" and bring the "sick homosexual" back to health. Both RT and CT have received abundant attention, and both have been soundly condemned by the American Counseling Association, the American Psychiatric Association, the American Psychological Association, the National Association of Social Workers, the National Association of School Psychologists, the American School Health Association, the American Federation of Teachers, the National Education Association, and the American Academy of Pediatrics. Mental health workers are warned that research indicates both of these "treatments" are more likely to be harmful than helpful. Many believe it is unethical for mental health professionals to practice CT or RT (B. Barret, 1999; Just the Facts Coalition, 2000).

As to queries regarding whether sexual orientation is open to change, Money (1990) stated the following:

> The concept of voluntary choice is as much in error (as applied to sexual orientation) as in its application to handedness or to native language. You do not choose your native language as a preference, even though you are born without it. You assimilate it into a brain prenatally made ready to receive a native language from those who constitute your primate troop and who speak that language to you and listen to you when you speak it. Once assimilated through the ears into the brain, a native language becomes securely locked in—as securely as if it has been phylogenetically preordained to be locked in prenatally by a process of genetic pre-determinism or by the determinism of fetal hormonal or other brain chemistries. So also with sexual status or orientation, which, whatever its genesis, also may become assimilated and locked into the brain as monosexually homosexual or heterosexual or as bisexually a mixture of both. (p. 4344)

Further, according to Coleman (1982),

> it is unethical and morally questionable to offer a "cure" to homosexuals who request a change in their sexual orientation. While there have been reports that changes in behavior have occurred for individuals seeking treatment, it is questionable whether it is beneficial to change their behavior to something that is incongruent with their sexual orientation. (p. 87)

Legally, the role of the professional school counselor is limited by school district policies as well as by state laws and regulations that govern the credentialing of professional school counselors in their state. Also, if the school counselor is licensed as a professional counselor or other mental health professional, the person must operate within the bounds of confidentiality as outlined in the state laws and judicial cases that govern the specialty. Some school districts may require parental disclosure and consent; others may not. Professional school counselors, therefore, must be knowledgeable of the specific policies, laws, and regulations that govern their conduct. It is, however, of the utmost importance to sexual minority students that professional school counselors be seen as their ally and their protector in the school.

Clearly, the shift toward the protection of sexual minority students in the schools is gaining momentum. In 1993, Massachusetts became the first state to ban antigay discrimination in its schools and create a statewide "safe schools" program. The U.S. Department of Education issued guidelines in March of 1997 stating that gay and lesbian students are covered by federal prohibitions against sexual harassment.

In 1996, a jury in a federal appellate court in Nabozny v. Podlensy, 92 F.3d 446 (Nabozny v. Podlensy, 1996) deliberated for only 2 days and found Ashland, Wisconsin, public school officials liable for not protecting Jamie Nabozny, a student who had suffered years of relentless physical, sexual, and verbal harassment for being gay. He had been beaten to the point of requiring surgery, urinated on, called antigay epithets, and made to suffer repeated assaults and indignities. In a landmark settlement reached after that verdict, he was awarded over $900,000 in damages. In its decision, the federal appellate court decision spelled out the constitutional obligation of public schools everywhere to treat abuse of lesbian and gay students as seriously as any other abuse.

In 1998 a jury in Louisville, Kentucky, awarded $220,000 to a 17-year-old girl because the school she attended acted with "deliberate indifference" by permitting other students to call her "lezzie," assault her, and attempt to rape her. Other lawsuits are working their ways through the courts, including a 12-year-old boy who is suing his Pacifica, California, school district for refusing to intervene in his years of harassment, and a gay teen brutally attacked by eight other students who secured the American Civil Liberties Union to aid his lawsuit against the Kent, Washington school district, as well as lawsuits filed by the American Civil Liberties Union in Kentucky and Texas on school board's prohibiting the gay and lesbian school clubs from meeting.

SCHOOL-BASED INTERVENTIONS

In order to protect sexual minority students, schools must take an active role in eliminating antigay harassment and creating a positive environment for these students. In this section, the role of parents and school workers will be explored along with specific issues dealing with separation (e.g., separate schools for sexual minority youth) or culture change, deliberate psycho-affective education, valuing differences, and the power of subtle signs.

ROLE OF PARENTS AND SCHOOL WORKERS

Parents and school workers often teach homophobic attitudes in quite subtle, and sometimes not so subtle, ways (Besner & Spungin, 1995; Fontaine, 1997). Some adults do this very consciously because they believe that this is the best way to eliminate such behavior in young people, that it will somehow persuade the student—through their disapproval—not to be gay or lesbian. For other adults, it is not a conscious process, only one that is ingrained and reinforced through others in their environment. Many never contemplate that they are, in fact, emotionally victimizing the sexual minority student.

Through persistent derogatory jokes, behavioral admonitions ("Don't be a sissy" or "Don't hold your hand that way; that's too gay" or "Girls don't sit like that"), and overheard homophobic conversations, gay and lesbian students absorb these negative attitudes regarding sexual minorities becoming victims of the adults they trust and who profess love for them. How do these gay and lesbian children deal with this incongruity?

Some respond by denying their sexual orientation and dating and engaging in sexual activities with members of the opposite sex, trying to pass as heterosexual. Others respond by developing a strong contempt for those gays and lesbians who are more open and obvious. They may take out their own sexual frustrations through varying degrees of aggression toward gay and lesbian members of the community. Other gay and lesbian teenagers respond by withdrawing from society and becoming shy and isolated. They are reluctant to join in social activities with friends and family and live in a world all their own. Some of these teenagers are so filled with self-hatred they cannot find anything acceptable or positive to say about themselves. Some seek out groups that believe their homosexual orientation can be changed. These individuals will go to great extremes and will be highly motivated to do whatever it takes to be straight (Besner & Spungin, 1995, p. 47).

In Savin-Williams's (1990) study predicting self-esteem among lesbian and gay youth, the teenagers with the highest levels of self-esteem felt accepted by their mothers, male and female friends, and their academic advisors. Lesbian youth who had positive parental relationships felt comfortable with their sexual orientation. Satisfying parental relationships, maternal knowledge of their homosexuality, and having relatively little contact with fathers predicted positive self-esteem for gay men. Mothers are important for self-esteem for both gay men and lesbians and are viewed as considerably more supportive, warm, and compassionate than fathers. Early parent–child interactions, physical affection, childhood rearing practices, and family religious teachings are considered good predictors of the state of comfort students have with their sexual orientation.

Pope (2000) and Pope and Englar-Carlson (2001) reported that messages that parents give to their children are important in the child's developing self-esteem. Phrases such as "Be who you are and never be afraid to express your feelings" or "I love you for you" or "It's okay to talk about anything with me, even if I do not like what you have to say, I will always love you" convey a message of unconditional, positive acceptance—no matter the situation. Unfortunately, parental words spoken in haste and anger can destroy years of positive communication. The best parents weigh the impact of their words before speaking them to their children, never saying negative phrases, even in jest, because such phrases are powerful and will rarely be forgotten by the child.

When a student discloses his or her sexual minority status ("comes out") to school personnel, it is a major life event and deserves to be treated in a sensitive and caring way by the school worker. (Some guidelines to help school personnel respond to students who disclose their sexual minority status are posted at http://www.umsl.edu/~pope/disclose.html.)

SEPARATION OR CULTURE CHANGE

During the 1980s and 1990s, between the political far-right's attempts to take control of school boards and the unionization of school workers, the schools became the battleground on which many of the tough political questions of the day were played. During this time, the issue of what to do with sexual minority students also came to the top of the school agenda.

Responses to these issues varied considerably among schools. In the New York City schools, the Harvey Milk School was established in 1985 for gay and lesbian students who were not succeeding. In Dallas, Texas, a private school for lesbian and gay youth opened in 1997 (Williams, 1997). In the Los Angeles Unified School District, Dr.

Virginia Uribe established Project 10, a dropout prevention program offering emotional support, information, and resources to young people who identify themselves as lesbian, gay, or bisexual or who wish to obtain information about sexual orientation (Uribe & Harbeck, 1992). Shortly thereafter, the San Francisco Unified School District, under the leadership of Kevin Gogin, began a similar program called Project 21 (Gustavsson & MacEachron, 1998). Most other school districts have established programs like Project 10 and have chosen not to go with the separate school that isolates sexual minority students from the mainstream.

Changing the school culture is imperative in this process of stopping school violence against sexual minority youth (Pope, 2000). Each stakeholder in the school system has a vital role in solving this problem, including school-board members; administrators; teachers; professional school counselors; school nurses; school social workers; school psychologists; and cafeteria, maintenance, and transportation workers. School stakeholders need tools to combat this violence that will enable them to at least promote an environment of tolerance and, ideally, to foster the creation of an environment in which sexual minority youth, like all other youth, are appreciated and valued. Merely being a sympathetic teacher is insufficient; teachers themselves need more training. Sears (1992), in a study of 258 teachers-in-training, found that fully 75% of the sample expressed interest in attending a school sponsored workshop on strategies in working with sexual minority students. Such a workshop would be expected to provide up-to-date information along with more knowledge and skills regarding sexual orientation, sexual identity, and gender identity.

Schremp (1999) reported the following in the *St. Louis Post-Dispatch*:

> A school newspaper survey in the Kirkwood Call last year showed 61% of the students who had answered said they insult people every day using such words as "gay." Kirkwood, Missouri High School Principal Franklin McCallie equated his student's use of "gay" or "fag" as a putdown to a racial or ethnic slur. . . . In November, his teachers took a "Teaching Respect for All" workshop (created by the Gay, Lesbian, Straight Educators Network and Parents and Friends of Lesbians and Gays). . . . "I just felt that it is so obvious that a principal and a staff of a high school ought to be on the side of safety for all students, that it really shouldn't be a monumental step whatsoever," he said. "I'm not telling you that everyone agrees on the subject of homosexuality. I think that we are in agreement that everyone be safe in the schools." (p. B4)

The "Teaching Respect for All" workshop was created by the Gay, Lesbian, Straight Educators Network (GLSEN) and Parents, Family, and Friends of Lesbians and Gays (PFLAG) and is an important resource in combating violence against sexual minority students and transforming the school culture that tolerates such violence. Bauman and Sachs-Kapp (1998) outlined a "Hate Hurts" campaign to raise awareness of sexual minority youth issues among school stakeholders. As Principal McCallie said in the newspaper article, "You do not have to accept homosexuality as equal to heterosexuality, but you do have to accept that everyone should be safe in the schools" (p. B4). Professional school counselors must be in the forefront of such programs.

DELIBERATE PSYCHO-AFFECTIVE EDUCATION

What connects the recent shootings in the schools with antigay violence is reported in the May 3, 1999 article and cover story in *U.S. News and World Report*:

> Surely it is a rare and complicated convergence of factors. Still, experts see some common threads in the spate of shootings: These adolescent boys can't manage their emotions. They feel rejected, enraged, jealous. They were boys who never learned how to identify, accept, and cope with their feelings. ("Why?," p. 19)

In American culture, boys are not taught how to handle feelings—not by their fathers nor by the schools (Pollack, 1998; Pope & Englar-Carlson, 2001). Pope (1998, 2000) stated that elementary and secondary schools in the UnitedStates do an acceptable job of cognitive education, excellent on information, and okay on critical thinking, but most schools fail when it comes to "affective" education. This is not what is being termed *moral education*, or *character education*; it is affective education, psychological education, or psycho-affective education. Teaching these important affective skills, such as interpersonal, social, and psychological skills, is rarely included in any school curriculum, even though such pioneers as Sprinthall (1984) have written about deliberate psychological education for many years.

The deliberate psycho-affective education of our children must become a priority or we will continue to see even more school killings by young people who feel they have no hope, no place to turn, no one to talk to, no one who listens, and who have no perspective on life (Paphazy, 2003; Pope, 1998, 2000; Pope & Englar-Carlson, 2001). These students feel that any personal rejection or emotional hurt they experience is a tragedy from which they can never recover. Because they only have feelings of hurt and emotional pain and have no other interpersonal skills to cope with these overwhelming feelings, they blast away, taking out people whom they believe have caused them that pain (and often innocent bystanders), but their rage is directed at the institution they know best: Their parents take their rage to their workplace because that is their primary institutional focus; their children take their rage to schools.

For example, in the Jonesboro, Arkansas, massacre of 10 students and a teacher by an 11-year-old boy and a 13-year-old boy with semiautomatic weapons, shooting their victims as they exited school during a fire alarm, many of their classmates now tell how the boys had talked about doing this for awhile. What caused this? According to news reports, one of the boys was "enraged" over having been "dumped by his girlfriend."

Pope (1998, 2000) reported that many people in U.S. society and school systems undervalue psycho-affective education. Although the schools cannot cure all the ills of society, education is more than information and even more than critical thinking. It is also about who we are and who we love during a time in our lives (school age) when we have many questions about those issues. Not enough attention to these issues is given in our schools. We must educate the whole child not just the cognitive part. What we are seeing is the effect of that omission.

Professional school counselors are important to the total care and education of students, from elementary school through high school (Pope, 1998, 2000). The following three types of professional school counselor activities are examples of deliberate psycho-affective education in the school: mental health counseling, career counseling, and providing a safe place to openly discuss sex (Morrow, 1997; Pope & Barret, 2002b; Pope, Prince, & Mitchell, 2000). The more that homosexuality and sexuality in general is treated as taboo and not discussed openly, the greater the risk of homophobia and misinformation, and the greater the risk of violence to sexual minority youth. Many of these issues are addressed in the personal–social domain of the American School Counselor Association's *National Standards for School Counseling Programs* (Campbell & Dahir, 1997).

VALUING DIFFERENCES

Respect, appreciation, and valuing differences are essential to stopping the violence against sexual minority students (Pope, 2000). Teachers, counselors, administrators, and parents need to be more outspoken in their desire to teach their children about developing positive self-esteem and greater acceptance of differences. Although most individuals would agree with this on a case-by-case basis, everyone seems to have his or her area of difficulty in the acceptance of diversity (Besner & Spungin, 1995, p. 36).

As a result of such difficulty, inclusive diversity training workshops have been developed. *Inclusive* is used here to mean that "diversity" is inclusive of ethnic and racial minorities as well as sexual minorities (Pope, 1995). An excellent tool in teaching individuals to appreciate and value human differences is the *Myers-Briggs Type Indicator* (MBTI), a Jungian-based personality inventory. One of the most important outcomes of using the MBTI is to teach the importance of the individual's opposite personality traits. For example, although your personality preference may be for extraversion and others for introversion, there is no inherent hierarchy in which one is better than the other; in fact, both are required for successful functioning in the world (Myers & McCaulley, 1985).

Other tools are available for teaching multicultural and diversity lessons, including GLSEN's "Teaching Respect for All" and Besner and Spungin's (1995) model workshop for educators on homophobia in their Appendix B. The National Coalition Building Institute, B'nai B'rith, and the American Friends Service Committee all offer excellent workshops on these topics and more (Owens, 1998; Pope, 2000).

In terms of the school curriculum, it is important to integrate and infuse gay and lesbian examples into all courses where appropriate (Pope, 1995, 2002). For example, when discussing U.S. history and the role of Native Americans, it would be appropriate to mention the revered position of *winktes* and *berdaches* (Native American terms for sexual minority persons) in the spiritual life of American Indians as the shaman or medicine person of the tribe as well as many examples of female warriors (Katz, 1976). After reading "The Picnic," a short story by James Baldwin, a world famous African American author, teachers can discuss Baldwin's gay orientation and the results of having a double oppression (being gay and African American).

Finally, school workers who are sexual minorities themselves should be encouraged to disclose their sexual orientation or gender identity and be offered support and employment protection. One openly gay or lesbian teacher can affect the atmosphere of the entire school in a positive way (Munoz-Plaza, Quinn, & Rounds, 2002). The importance of sexual minority role models cannot be overstressed and open sexual minority school workers challenge the myths and stereotypes for all students, not just the GLB-TIQQ ones (Owens, 1998).

THE POWER OF SUBTLE SIGNS

There are many ways of letting sexual minority students know that professional school counselors, teachers, administrators, and other school workers are supportive of their struggle. If, because of your school district, you are unable as a teacher or professional school counselor to be as overtly supportive as you would like to be, there remains a number of other ways in which you can still relay to sexual minority students a message of your support.

Following are a few of the more obvious ways to show your support:

- Have a "safe zone" or "safe space" sticker at the entrance to your office or classroom (available from the Bridges Project of the National Youth Advocacy Coalition or at www.glsen.org).
- Have available in your school guidance office and library literature on sexual minority youth concerns (see www.umsl.edu/~pope/bibliographies.html).
- Post online resources for sexual minority students:
  - International Lesbian and Gay Youth Association (www.ilgya.org)
  - Parents, Family, and Friends of Lesbians and Gays (www.pflag.org)
  - Gay, Lesbian, and Straight Educators Network (www.glsen.org)
  - Gay and Lesbian Teen Pen Pals (www.chanton.com/gayteens.html)
  - *Oasis* (teen magazine) (www.oasisjournals.com)
  - Outright (www.outright.com)
  - Out Proud, National Coalition for GLBT Youth (www.outproud.org)
  - The Cool Page for Queer Teens (www.bidstrup.com/cool.htm)
  - National Gay and Lesbian Task Force (www.ngltf.org)
- Offer free family counseling services on campus to deal with the issues of homosexuality.
- Use gay and lesbian positive examples in your teaching or counseling.
- Use inclusive, stigma-free language in the classroom and in all communication, such as using *partners* instead of *husbands and wives.*
- Post pictures of famous sexual minority people (see a list at www.umsl.edu/~pope/famous.html).

By demonstrating an accepting attitude, school workers can send a strong message to students and create a tolerant environment within the entire school. The issues of tolerance, acceptance, and value can all be explored under the umbrella of diversity.

SOME FINAL THOUGHTS

The role of the professional school counselor in working with sexual minority students is clear. Professional school counselors assist students in discovering who they truly and honestly are and then help them develop a strong and positive personal and cultural identity so that they can live happy, successful, and productive lives in society.

Further, the professional school counselor is expected to take a leadership role in protecting and advocating for sexual minority students as well as developing and implementing school policies that eliminate the verbal and physical harassment of all students, including sexual minority students. This is especially important because research indicates that sexual minority students are more likely to disclose their sexual minority status to their professional school counselors than to any other school worker (Harris & Bliss, 1997). Professional school counselors must therefore be prepared for when sexual minority students present themselves for counseling (Brown, 1991; Ciro et al., 2005; Pope, 2000).

Further, the relationship is clear between derogatory language/harassment directed against sexual minority students by their peers and adults in the school setting and self-harmful behavior, such as attempted suicide, suicidal ideation, running away, poor academic performance, and truancy (Bontempo & D'Augelli, 2002; Ciro et al., 2005; Jordan et al., 1997; Russell & Joyner, 2001). Professional school counselors must not allow such language or physical harassment for any student.

Clearly, the momentum is turning toward the protection of sexual minority students in the schools. In 1993, Massachusetts became the first state to ban antigay discrimination in its schools and create a statewide "safe schools" program. The U.S. Department of Education issued guidelines in March 1997 stating explicitly that lesbian and gay students are covered by federal prohibitions against sexual harassment.

Indeed, changes are occurring for sexual minority students. Sam Hanser, a 16-year-old high school student in Newtown, Massachusetts, has spoken on national television of assaults at the hands of his classmates: "A lot of people called me *faggot* and spat on me and did a lot of annoying things," said Hansen. Massachusetts, however, was the first state to pass a law making harassment of lesbian and gay students a crime. As a result, Sam has been empowered and taken on a role of leadership. He runs a hotline for lesbian, gay, bisexual, transgender, and questioning youth and speaks publicly about sexual minority youth issues. "I think that seeing diversity starts the whole process of being comfortable and acceptance of different people" (CBS News, January 21, 1999).

Attitudes on sexuality and sexual orientation are indeed changing, and this should bode well for sexual minority students. Although the message is not as strong as many of us would like, it is becoming clear that although people can have their own private hatreds, expressing those hatreds publically as physical or verbal harassment or writing them into policy will not be allowed. The harassment of sexual minority students and teachers should not be tolerated in America or in any society.

Heterosexism, which according to Lorde (1984) is defined as a "belief in the inherent superiority of one pattern of loving and thereby its right to dominance" (p. 45), and homophobia, which is the fear of being gay and hatred of gays and lesbians (Herr, 1997), must be exposed just as racism and sexism have been.

The Massachusetts Governor's Commission on Lesbian and Gay Youth issued a report in 1993 that summarized succinctly a blueprint for ending violence in the schools against gay and lesbian youth. The recommendations included the following:

1. Promulgating school policies that protect gay and lesbian students through

   - antidiscrimination policies that explicitly include sexual orientation for students and teachers, including teacher contracts;
   - policies that guarantee equal access to education and school activities;
   - antiharassment policies and guidelines that deal with handling incidents of antigay language, harassment, or violence; and
   - multicultural and diversity policies that are inclusive of lesbian and gay culture (Pope, 1995, 2002);

2. Training teachers in multicultural issues (which are inclusive of lesbian and gay culture) and suicide and violence prevention as well as changing teacher certification requirements and school accreditation to include this training (Pope, 1995, 2002);

3. School-based support groups for gay and straight students;

4. Curriculum that includes gay and lesbian issues; and

5. Information in school libraries for gay and lesbian adolescents.

As a consequence of this report, the Massachusetts Board of Education unanimously adopted the nation's first state educational policy prohibiting discrimination against lesbian and gay elementary and secondary students and teachers (Besner & Spungin, 1995). Many cities in the United States have adopted similar policies in their schools.

Summary/Conclusion

We have presented the issues that are important for professional school counselors who are counseling sexual minority students, including gay, lesbian, bisexual, transgender, intersex, queer, and questioning youth (GLBTIQQ). The issues included developing a context in which to discuss the issues; "coming out" or the developmental aspects of sexual identity development; the extent of the problems that sexual minority youth face in the schools and society; the effects of negative attitudes and violence toward these youth; and ethical and legal issues in dealing with sexual minority youth in the schools. In addition, we discussed school-based interventions that focus on the role of the parents and schools, separation (e.g., separate schools for sexual minority youth) or culture change, deliberate psycho-affective education, valuing differences, and the power of subtle symbols.

The lives of sexual minority students in the schools *are* getting better. It is important, however, not to minimize the detrimental effects of verbal and physical violence and harassment on sexual minority students' academic performance and social development. Professional school counselors must focus on the recommendations we have presented for improving the school environment and the quality of the life for sexual minority students. It just makes it better for all students.

(Note: See the CD-ROM for a list of references.)

CHAPTER 79

HELPING STUDENTS FROM
CHANGING FAMILIES

Bradley T. Erford

Preview

I provide practical interventions for professional school counselors who must address the needs of students from families with diverse living arrangements such as step-parents, single parents, and interracial parents, which in this chapter is referred to as the surface structure. I provide general guidelines, assessment procedures, and case histories with interventions.

To be a professional school counselor is to be sensitive to the changing nature of families. Day in and day out, professional school counselors witness the transformations of families in diverse forms of living arrangements, which will be referred to as the *surface structure* of families. Professional school counselors are called upon to provide interventions for the challenges that family transformations and stress present in an atmosphere of rising levels of poverty, substance abuse, homelessness, and violence (Erford, House, & Martin, 2007; Erford, Newsome, & Rock, 2007; Keys, Bemak, & Lockhart, 1998; Lockhart & Keys, 1998; Weist, 1997).

The task of helping students and their families in often-stressful transformations through a landscape filled with mountains of substance abuse, poverty, and violence can be seen as dismal. It can also be seen as a great opportunity to take part in the creation of a new chapter in the history of human resiliency. This chapter includes specific examples and guidelines for helping students from families in transition (e.g., single-parent, step-parent, nontraditional families such as gay lesbian, interracial, and homeless) in the interest of assisting professional school counselors determined to promote competency and resiliency in the face of these challenges.

SINGLE PARENTING, STEP-PARENTING, AND COHABITATING SURFACE STRUCTURES

How much are the surface structures of students and their families changing today? Demographic data from the Population Resource Center provides strong evidence that the American family is experiencing vast change (Sado & Bayer, 2001). For example, in terms of surface structure, in the year 2000, one quarter of U.S. households (23%) were made up of nuclear families (i.e., a married man and woman and their children), which significantly differed from the 1960s, when the nuclear family made up 45% of households.

In the first edition of this book this chapter was written by Dr. Estes J. Lockhart, may he rest in peace.

Cohabitation (i.e., unmarried individuals living together as couples) doubled in the 1990s, increasing from 3.2 million in 1990 to 5.5 million in 2000. Cohabitation is becoming a significant trend, with one third of cohabitants parenting children. In 1990, 9% of children under age 18 lived in single-parent families, but by 1999, twenty-seven percent of children younger than 18 years resided in single-parent homes. One of the reasons for many of the single-family homes was out-of-wedlock birth, which reached its highest rate in 1999, when 33% of all births in the United States were out of wedlock. However, one must not be quick to assume that single parenting or any other surface structure provides a simple cause-and-effect relationship with a student experiencing difficulty at school. For example, while children of divorce have a higher rate of emotional and substance-abuse problems, these effects are "caused not by divorce alone but by other frequently coexisting yet analytically separate factors" (Coontz, 1997, p. 29). Research from a Rand study, titled "Student Performance and the Changing American Family," implied no negative effects on academic performance based on changed family surface structure alone; however, the Rand study pointed out that predictions for youth in single-parent families show a negative effect academically, because these families tend to have increased poverty and lower educational attainment by mothers (Grissmer, Kirby, Berends, & Williamson, 1994).

While a professional school counselor can't directly alter the economic well-being or educational attainment of a single parent, they can provide resources for single parents, referring them to agencies and groups in the community that can provide economic support, educational opportunities, or mental health and physical health services. Professional school counselors can also assist single parents with parenting skills either through direct consultation or referral to parenting programs. Professional school counselors can also help students find the strength to rise above troubled backgrounds, in part by running loss groups in which students from families in transition can find needed support. Perhaps one of the most important things a professional school counselor can do is to be a person whom students know cares for them. In that role of trusted, caring significant other, the professional school counselor can help the student understand that the challenges facing his or her family were not caused by the student, nor are they the student's responsibility to correct. However, the student can learn to cope and have a successful, meaningful life.

TRAUMA IN CHANGING FAMILIES

As the trend toward diverse surface structures in families grows, some of the patterns that are currently thought of as nontraditional will become more commonplace. For example, families increasingly are living in metropolitan areas. In 1970, two out of three households were in metropolitan areas, whereas toward the end of the last century, four out of five households were in metropolitan areas (Bryson, 2001). In urban schools, 30% to 60% of students lived with caregivers other than their biological parents (Hampton, Rak, & Mumford, 1997). These caregivers may be foster parents, grandparents, step-parents, or adoptive parents. Many of the families in care-giving arrangements will require more services, because the students may present with the effects of traumatic early-life experiences (Schwartz, 1999).

Professional school counselors can support families who are experiencing trauma by helping them find social support and therapy in the community, by listening to the student and family in a caring way, and by helping the student and caregiver maintain a supportive relationship with each other. Professional school counselors can also inform teachers and administrators, with parental permission, of the situation and seek their support of the student, particularly in helping the student feel a sense of belonging and identification. Professional school counselors can help students who are experiencing trauma to use individual strengths and resources. Some crucial aspects of a recovery environment (resiliency) for students who are involved in traumatic family situations are parental distress, parental psychopathology, individual strengths and resources of the student, social and system resources and intelligence, communication skills, sense of self-efficacy, coping abilities, talents, and feelings of bonding (Meichenbaum, 2002).

HOMELESS, INTERRACIAL, AND GAY AND LESBIAN SURFACE STRUCTURES

Professional school counselors are increasingly helping students from homeless families, interracial marriages, and gay and lesbian couples. An increase in interracial marriages has led to a surge in interracial babies, increasing from less than 2% in 1960 to 5% by 2001 (Sado & Bayer, 2001). Families with children constitute 40% of people who become homeless in cities, and this percentage is higher in rural areas (Shin & Weitzman, 1996). Students from homeless, gay and lesbian, and interracial families will most often require help with acceptance and full inclusion.

HOMELESSNESS

Homeless students present with a specific set of difficulties, including frequent relocation, lack of a permanent address, lack of a place to study, lack of a place to store personal items including school items, difficulty attending or participating in school events, and the stress of living in shelters with strangers and no private space. Homeless students might carry in their backpacks everything that is important to them. Professional school counselors can help these students find a safe place to keep a few personal items. It is also helpful to assist these students find a place to study or arrange for them to have a study period at school for completing homework that would otherwise be very difficult to complete, thus leading to the students' falling behind. Embarrassment about living arrangements is prevalent, and helping homeless students know how to speak about it with other students is valuable. Students who are homeless often have difficulty accessing special education programs; professional school counselors can be advocates for special education services where needed.

The most significant problems are perhaps those that homeless families experience on the street and in the shelters which the student may need to discuss with the professional school counselor. It is important to know that the student may be hesitant to discuss his or her family situation. Joining with the student so that the student will risk sharing his or her secrets is a key to providing help. Additional information on homelessness may he found at the U.S. Department of Housing and Urban Development (www.hud.gov/homeless).

GAY OR LESBIAN FAMILIES

Students from gay or lesbian families most often need help coping with the issues of anger and embarrassment. They may be angry with one or both of their parents or because of society's perception and treatment of the family structure. It can be helpful for the student who is angry to take part in family therapy with a mental health counselor. The professional school counselor can deal with this anger at school as anger would be dealt with in counseling a student for loss. The embarrassment can be addressed through the cognitive technique of challenging assumptions. The student's belief that his or her peers will label the student on the basis of his or her gay or lesbian parents needs to be challenged. Existing data on students of lesbian mothers suggest that students may fare better when the mothers are in good psychological health and living with a lesbian partner with whom childcare is shared (Patterson, 2002). It is helpful for the student to normalize his or her situation as much as possible. It is supportive for children in lesbian and gay families to be able to interact with peers in similar situations. Additional information on gay and lesbian families can be found on the American Psychological Association Web site (www.apa.org/pi/parent.html).

INTERRACIAL FAMILIES

Many interracial families share close, caring relationships and strong parenting skills, which will be strengths to draw upon when intervening to help these students find acceptance and full inclusion. The professional school counselor is encouraged to search for strengths in the culture and race of students who present with a need for acceptance and inclusion. Professional school counselors need to be aware of different approaches families from diverse cultures and races may take in relation to issues such as parenting, spirituality, or the anger they may express toward outside agencies or even the practitioner (Boyd-Franklin & Bry, 2000). For example, a family member who has experienced racism or who feels alienated by outside agencies may go to school meetings with a "chip on her shoulder." The professional school counselor can join with this parent prior to the school meeting and gain that parent's respect—or, at least, the beginning of trust—and can therefore make the parent feel she has an advocate within the system and feel more secure in the meeting.

The remainder of this chapter provides basic information a professional school counselor must consider when helping students from families with diverse surface structures, particularly those in transition. It provides specific examples of the kind of issues presented to professional school counselors by changing families in a landscape of high stress and suggests helpful interventions for students and families. These interventions not only focus on assessing needs and surface structures but also strengths, resources, and resiliency. For example, studies have concluded that interventions in which a student feels that someone in or outside the family truly cares promote resiliency in the face of substantial risk factors (Boyd-Franklin & Bry, 2000).

Basic Considerations When Counseling Students from Changing Families

When counseling students from changing families, professional school counselors should consider several basic facets, including noting differences in families with similar surface structures, assessing comorbidity and premorbidity in the family, staying positive no matter how stressful the family challenge, being aware of general factors that are fostering family resilience, assessing family strengths and needs, and providing for the direct or indirect delivery of support.

NOTE DIFFERENCES IN FAMILIES WITH SIMILAR SURFACE STRUCTURE

There are nearly infinite ways to be a family. While the considerations offered in this chapter for intervening with families based on their surface structure can be helpful, professional school counselors must use interventions wisely in the context of the actual family receiving the help. For example, the popular image of a single parent might be the single mother on welfare, but in reality, one seventh of single-parent households are headed by fathers, and two thirds earn enough to be above the poverty line (Sugarman, 1998).

A family that has become a single-parent family because of the separation of supportive and caring yet incompatible parents has different needs than a single-parent family in which the parents are angry with each other, poorly educated, and, prior to the divorce, were attempting to cope with alcoholism. As a third possibility, single-parent families often result from the death of a beloved parent and spouse. In the first family, the focus will be on ensuring that the student understands that he or she was neither the cause nor cure for the troubles between two very loving and supportive parents. In the second family, the focus likely will be on the possible traumatic effects resulting from living in a family filled with anger and alcoholism and making sure that the angry parents do not put the student in the middle of their anger. In the third family situation, the focus will be on loss. Professional school counselors who help single-parent families will have to be able to flexibly shift from one set of intervention skills to another.

ASSESS COMORBIDITY AND PREMORBIDITY IN THE FAMILY

Attempting to cope with one stressor is very different from being forced to cope with a series of unexpected short-term traumas or a sustained series of traumatic events including a prolonged trauma (Meichenbaum, 2002). Clinicians refer to having more than one serious need as *comorbidity* and a significant need prior to the problem at hand as *premorbidity.*

Comorbidity and premorbidity must be considered when addressing the needs of a student from a family that is undergoing a challenging transition. For example, children who have witnessed domestic abuse exhibit more control problems and more hostile cognitions about women (Geffner, Jaffe, & Sugarman, 2002). Thus, a professional school counselor helping a student from a family that is transitioning through a difficult divorce in which there has been domestic abuse should be sensitive to the need for intervention or referral for additional clinical services to address a serious condition premorbid to the stress of the divorce. There may be a need to help the student through group work with social skills and control problems at school, but concurrently the family should seek clinical counseling to address the trauma of victimization and negative thoughts associated with women.

STAY POSITIVE, NO MATTER HOW STRESSFUL THE FAMILY CHALLENGE

It is essential to stay positive. Stressful life events can also have long-term positive effects (Updegraff & Taylor, 1999). Consider the case of a young man who, 20 years earlier, had been a student in an alternative school. The young man said he remembered a counseling session in which the counselor had asked him to think about something positive he could take from his current situation to carry with him in life. He said that prior to his mother's separation from his father, he had experienced physical abuse and watched his mother be physically abused. He said, looking back it was easy to see why he'd become aggressive enough to end up in the alternative school. He said that he had decided back then in response to the directive in the counseling session to always remind himself when tough situations faced him in life that he had already made it through worse than he would ever face. He told the counselor that when he was feeling upset about his recent employment situation, he said to himself, "I've been through much worse and handled it, so I know I'll make it through this fine." Thus, it is useful for professional school counselors helping families undergoing difficult transitions to remember the folk wisdom that says, "What doesn't kill me will make me stronger." It is important to communicate to students and families going through tough or even traumatic experiences that their ability to endure and continue to cope is impressive.

BE AWARE OF GENERAL FACTORS FOSTERING FAMILY RESILIENCE

Child-focused studies have pointed to the importance of 10 general factors in the family system in fostering resilience (McCubbin, McCubbin, Thompson, Han, & Allen, 1997). These include family problem-solving communication, equality, spirituality, flexibility, truthfulness, hope, family time and routine, social support, health, and family hardiness (in which the family steels itself and views itself as having a sense of control and influence over the outcome). Meichenbaum (2002) cited a list of studies that suggested protective factors characteristic of resilient children and adolescents, including close relationships to a caring parent figure, supportive extended kin, a sense of belonging and identification, warmth, structure and high expectations in parenting, cohesive families, socioeconomic advantages, and extended family networks. The effective professional school counselor helps students develop these resiliency characteristics through work with students and families.

ASSESS BASIC FAMILY STRENGTHS AND NEEDS

When you are assessing family strengths and needs, it is helpful to collapse the family resiliency factors mentioned by McCubbin et al. (1997) and the protective factors of resilient children and adolescents mentioned by Meichenbaum (2002) into the following five main categories:

Parenting

Legal–Economic

Structural–Social

Beliefs

Health

Parenting includes decisions regarding schooling, academics, and discipline as well as warmth, structure, and high expectations. *Legal–Economic* refers to the custody, school records and alimony issues as well as financial well-being of the family. *Structural–Social* refers to all the structural relationship issues in a family such as hierarchy, leadership, alliances, coalitions, cohesion, boundaries, differentiation, extended kinship, social network support, family time, family hardiness, sense of belonging and identification and communication style (see Chapter 40, "Using Family Systems Interventions in Schools"). *Beliefs* include values, sense of equality, spiritual issues, sense of hope, and truthfulness. *Health* refers to mental and physical health issues.

Often when intervening with high stress families in transition, the professional school counselor will have to assist the family in parenting issues around academics and will have to encourage teacher support for the student during times of crisis. After all, the bottom line for educators is academic performance.

PROVIDE FOR THE DIRECT OR INDIRECT DELIVERY OF SUPPORT

Most professional school counselor direct services will be in the parenting, academic support, and social support areas. The professional school counselor will often become a case manager or consultant for the family in the area of mental and physical health and economic support, providing referrals and liaison services to other professionals. The area of belief systems is a difficult one for the professional school counselor. Issues of truth, hope, trust and spirituality, when they are conceived as a search for meaning, are the stock and trade of a professional school counselor's work, and yet when applied to families in crisis, based on the family's view of these issues, the professional school counselor may choose to refer out for these services. However, even this decision is made complex by the work setting of the professional school counselor. A professional counselor working in a public school would generally stay away from spirituality, specifically in terms of religion, when it is approached by the family, while a professional counselor working in a parochial school might find the issue of religion appropriate and even central. The examples given throughout the remainder of this chapter come back to these general factors of resiliency and protection, giving specific guidelines in areas that are central to the surface structure of families.

INTERVENTION EXAMPLES BY SURFACE STRUCTURES

This section includes several examples of family interventions upon varying surface structures.

Single-Parent Family: Basic Guidelines

1. *Parenting.* Being a single parent can lead to work overload with accompanying high stress. While the health and safety of the children is the primary responsibility, the need to provide and maintain a home environment that encourages learning and good behavior in school is also critical. This educational dimension of parenting can be very demanding for single parents because of the required amount of time that quality collaboration and coordination between home and school.

2. *Legal-Economic.* Single parents frequently must raise children with fewer financial resources. Custody battles, child-support payments, and alimony payments may cause financial, social, and other stresses. Also, there may be issues between custodial and noncustodial parents over visits and access to school meetings and records. The law is that noncustodial parents have the same access to school records as do custodial parents, unless a judge has ruled otherwise and that ruling with the judge's signature is in the student's record.

3. *Structural-Social.* A parent and child may become enmeshed or emotionally fused, thereby feeding each other's emotional problems. A child may assume the role of a spousal child, taking the place emotionally of the absent parent. Either of these situations can lead to conditions of anxiety or depression. Hierarchy issues can result in fights over who is in control, and coalitions of the child and one parent against the other parent may occur. At the same time, close relationships between parent and child in times of crisis can be helpful, and a child taking on an appropriate supportive role such as helping the parent with monitoring siblings for a limited time can be a growth experience for the student. In cases of divorce, it is important to help parents avoid putting the child in the middle of spousal disagreements or emotional upset. Professional school counselors should not witness fighting between angry couples, whether the child is present or not. The message should always be that, no matter what your interactions in other places, in the professional school counselor's office, everyone can feel safe and emotionally protected. This can be particularly important in gaining the respect of the parents. It can be helpful for the parents to see that for a brief time they are able to interact appropriately, and when the child is present, the child can observe them interact in a way that is appropriate, not hurtful.

4. *Belief Systems.* A single parent who starts dating can bring new individuals into the home and cause a host of difficulties, including the children feeling that the parent cares more for the new friend than for them. Children may also worry that someone they don't know will be making decisions for them, which can lead to conflicts of trust and loyalty. In single-parent families that occur because of separation or divorce, parents may believe they are guilty for not preventing the divorce. Children may worry that they helped to cause a separation or should be responsible for fixing it. Children may even imagine that their parents will reunite. In such cases, the Three Cs Maxim can be helpful. Parents tell children they didn't *cause* the separation and can't *correct* the situation, but they can learn to *cope* with the situation.

5. *Mental–Emotional and Physical Health Issues.* Parents and children may experience feelings of loss. Financial weakness may result in family members lacking proper health care, such as dental, vision, and medical services, which can seriously affect education. Community health services, service clubs, and helpful medical providers can often address the most serious problems.

EXAMPLE 1: SINGLE PARENT WITH A MIDDLE SCHOOL STUDENT

Tom was a student who grew up in a home with an abusive father and found it hard to understand why his mother continued to live with his father. When he stated these feelings to his mother, she always responded that she loved his father and hoped he would change. Tom's father frequently informed his mother and the children that he would change because he cared too much for them to continue hurting them. He was an alcoholic, however, and became very angry when drunk. The final straw for Tom's mother came when Tom was a middle school student and his father sexually abused Tom's sister. Tom's mother reported her husband to social services, and criminal charges were filed.

At school, Tom evidenced much social anxiety. He missed school frequently, particularly on stressful occasions such as test days. He hung out with antisocial peers who verbally abused other students and teachers. One-on-one, Tom was very pleasant with adults but was frequently referred to the office for joining in verbal attacks on others.

Assessment. The professional school counselor began to work with Tom and witnessed the school avoidance, verbal threats and taunts, academic failure, and social anxiety. She decided to invite Tom's mother to the school for a brief family session. In the session she learned about the stressful family abuse Tom had witnessed. The mother said she barely could get by financially, because she was a clerk in a local department store and made just above minimum wage. Now with her husband in jail, the home was the most pleasant it had been in many years, but financially she was slipping and having to work an extra half job, which didn't give her the time to help Tom or his sister with their schoolwork. Parenting was stressful for Tom's mother, becaise she didn't have the time or energy to provide the high structure or academic help Tom needed. She and Tom had become close allies during his father's drunken rages.

The professional school counselor determined that Tom and his mother had an *enmeshed relationship*, meaning they were fused emotionally and were feeding into each other's anxiety. The professional school counselor figured that the enmeshment had much to do with Tom's social isolation and school avoidance. At the same time, the professional school counselor was aware that during the trauma suffered by the family it was normal for Tom and his mother to become extremely protective of each other as well as becoming the eyes and ears for each other's pain. The professional school counselor learned from Tom and his mother that Tom had very low self-esteem. He expected to be treated poorly and figured he got what he deserved. On the positive side, Tom felt that his mother and sister loved him. Even his father, while treating him horribly, nonetheless maintained that he cared for Tom. Tom had on-grade-level academic skills and loved to read. Also, in one-on-one interactions, he was very sociable and pleasant. Tom possessed some strengths, and it was essential for the professional school counselor to help him recognize and build on those strengths.

Intervention. To address parenting concerns about supervision, the professional school counselor suggested to Tom's mother that she ask social services to help arrange and pay for a slot in a YMCA afternoon program, where Tom would be supervised and would also get help with his homework. The professional school counselor, after receiving appropriate information releases, called social services and followed up with a short memo requesting the YMCA afternoon program for Tom. To address the possible trauma, enmeshment, and parenting skills, she also asked about the possibility of social services paying for mental health counseling. In the process, the professional school counselor learned that in criminal cases such as that of Tom's father, the court provided money for therapy for children through a state fund, and social services would recommend and pay for mental health counseling. The professional school counselor assured the social-services caseworker that she would encourage the mother to make an appointment for Tom and herself for mental health counseling. The professional school counselor, after receiving appropriate information releases from Tom's mother, was able to inform the family therapist of the need for boundaries in the enmeshed relationship between Tom and his mother.

To address issues of self-esteem and personal trauma, the professional school counselor also let Tom know that she understood the pain he had suffered and that she wanted him to drop in for short meetings to get things off his chest, as needed. During these meetings, the professional school counselor learned that Tom had been traumatized by his father's behavior and made to feel worthless. Following suggestions by Meichenbaum (2002) for child-focused intervention in cases of trauma, the professional school counselor provided Tom an opportunity to appropriately talk about his experiences. She nurtured Tom's coping skills and worked on stress-related symptom reduction. She helped Tom value himself and find meaning in his experiences that he could take with him in life. She helped him combat his sense of isolation and encouraged him to have hope. The professional school counselor gave Tom's mother a 10-minute telephone check-in every 2 weeks to see how things were going and to reassure her that she was available to the mother, when needed.

Step-Parent Surface Structure: Basic Guidelines

1. *Parenting.* Parenting issues are often the focus of difficulty in step-families. Both parents may have had different parenting experiences in previous marriages. Ex-spouses of the two remarried parents may have been more supportive or less supportive. Children often expect to continue in a comfortable and habitual pattern. This can be a set-up for the step-parent who then ends up in a battle with the child resulting in stress for the entire family. Being a member of two different households, the child may have difficulty handling the parenting differences when he goes from one biological parent's home to the other.

2. *Legal–Economic.* Resentment about payments to the ex-spouse can become an issue in some families. Finances can become an issue when parent and step-parent have differing opinions about how to manage money for a step-child, such as for buying clothes, automobiles, trips, and education. As with single parents, non-cus-

todial parents might have problems with access to children from another marriage or to school records.

3. *Structural–Support.* Remarriage may increase or decrease prior support networks. For example, if an older step-parent didn't expect to parent a young child that his or her spouse brings to the marriage, different expectations about duties with children can lead to stress. Where children feel they are members of two different households, stressful relationships can result. It is important for parents to realize that it is not necessarily easy for children to bond with a step-parent, and doing so will take time.

4. *Beliefs.* Beliefs about religion, discipline, academics, dress, curfews, dating, and extracurricular activities can lead to stress for the family and children.

5. *Mental and Physical Health.* The emergence of feelings of loss is often a major issue in step-families (e.g., the child may suffer the loss of a close relationship with a biological parent; the children may still be hoping that somehow their biological parents will get back together).

EXAMPLE 2: STEP-PARENT WITH HIGH SCHOOL STUDENT

Linda was a high school student who had lived with her father for 10 years after her parents' separation and divorce. Her father remarried a woman who felt very strongly that children should be parented using an authoritarian model. She had a daughter who was in college whom she pointed to as an example of high success with authoritarian parenting. The father, on the other hand, believed in a much looser, hands-off approach. He and his new wife were both intellectuals who constantly battled over authoritarian parenting versus what the father defined as humanitarian parenting. While the daughter in college and the one in high school didn't engage in sibling rivalry, the parents of the two fought over the differences in the two children. Linda, who had a good relationship with her step-mother when her father and her step-mother were dating, began to express extreme anger toward her step-mother when her step-mother began to discipline her.

Many of their battles were over issues such as 15- and 30-minute curfew violations, which her father felt should be ignored or merely mentioned and forgotten, while her step-mother demanded punishment. Other issues such as drunkenness after dates worried both parents. Even in this area, however, the father argued that these events happened only occasionally and should be punished mildly, while the step-mother felt the girl should be seriously monitored and sent for therapy. Additionally, Linda and her father both indicated a feeling of loss of the close relationship they had prior to the father's remarriage. The step-mother, on the other hand, felt that Linda and her father still had a close relationship, and that she, the new wife, was less important to her new husband than his daughter. The father stated that while he didn't want his new family to function this way, if he had to choose one over the other, it would have to be his child, "his blood."

Linda's decline in academic performance brought on additional battles between step-mother and father. The step-mother wanted the father to set tight limits and monitor his daughter's work. The father said that his work prevented rigorous monitoring because he frequently had business meetings at night. The step-mother said she could provide the necessary monitoring with the father's support. When the father agreed, Linda began a war with her step-mother and accused her father of abandoning her. Linda demanded to spend more time with her biological mother, who didn't have the where-withal or desire to take on additional parenting duties. The non-custodial biological parent refused to level with Linda and instead led her to believe that at some time in the future Linda would be able to live with her.

Assessment. Much of Linda's decline in academic performance was directly related to structural issues in the family that interfered with the parents' ability to parent her. A battle raged constantly over the hierarchy and leadership of the family. The step-mother wanted a very authoritarian leadership style and expected to be at the top of the hierarchy. She had grown up in a family in which her father was mentally troubled, and her mother took charge and provided what little order existed. She vowed to herself that, in her life, there would not be the frustrations, anxiety, and embarrassment born of the chaos brought on by her father. Her role model had been a strong woman who led and protected the family from a weak man. The father had grown up in a liberal family in which any behavior was acceptable, and he became highly responsible because he chose to do so. He believed that being a family was essentially a task in democracy in which all family members, parents and children, had equal votes and voices.

In this situation, the daughter constantly used her alliance (and almost spousal relationship) with her father prior to the arrival of her step-mother to build a coalition against her step-mother. The daughter constantly complained to the father that her evil step-mother was victimizing her. The wife complained that Linda was in charge of the family and would send both Linda and the family in a tailspin if she were not stopped. The father felt caught in the middle of powerful forces, between his own beliefs about being a family, his loyalty to his daughter, his desire to succeed in his marriage, and his hope for his daughter to succeed academically.

When school teachers or the professional school counselor attempted to intervene with the family, the educators would experience the frustration of a family that meant well but could not agree on a plan for getting the daughter back in line academically. Also, it was clear that the family was not going to carry out a plan consistently, even if it was agreed upon.

Intervention. The main issues were parenting and academics, beliefs, and family structure, which all were intricately wound together, keeping the family stuck and the child in trouble. The initial approach in this situation is to determine whether there are any serious family problems such as alcoholism or mental illness and to address struc-tural issues that keep the family from being able to make decisions or follow through on them. If there are serious problems (ruled out in this case), the professional school counselor should provide referral information. Clearly, in this family the structural issue is the daughter's coalition with the father that kept the step-mother feeling in a one-down position and that her husband was not supportive. This is a difficult situa-tion, usually requiring couples therapy, because it is usually accompanied by bitterness of a spouse who feels the expectations of the marriage are not being met. In this case, the step-mother also has differentiation issues from her family of origin, meaning she becomes very emotionally upset in the face of what she sees as the same loose, undependable, democratic leadership that wrecked her family. She is unable to stay in a cognitive problem-solving mode with her husband or anyone else who she feels represents this type of thinking—even a professional school counselor or family therapist.

The key for the professional school counselor is *not* to suggest couples therapy, because this will alienate the couple (although, if the couple mentions couples therapy, the professional school counselor should commend them on their wisdom and give them several good referrals). What *can* be done is to ask the parents if they would be willing to shelve their personal beliefs about parenting and academics in the interest of arriving at a compromise plan that everyone involved could carry out successfully. Getting that agreement, the professional school counselor would suggest that they simply list what is necessary for a young person to succeed in school, including proper study time in the evening, monitoring by a parent to ensure that homework and test reviews are being done appropriately, and communication between home and teachers to check on results and performance in class. The father and step-mother can agree to those things. The structured nature of the plan will appeal to the step-mother. The father can still have close discussions with his daughter, but ultimately he must require that the very simple plan be followed. He can talk with his daughter about her feelings but not about blaming anyone for anything.

The issue here is to get around the serious structural and belief issues that will require much commitment and therapy while going for a simple plan that will enable the daughter to perform in school. If the couple should ask how the professional school counselor feels about their beliefs, it is important to say that there are many ways to parent a child successfully, but all successful plans require consistency, commitment and support. Do not try to resolve the step-mother and daughter issues. Do use the father and daughter relationship as a way to reward the girl for success, and suggest that the parents make certain to find individual time to have fun for themselves while enduring the stress of parenting a young adolescent in a step-family arrangement. Commend the parents on coming for help and caring enough to do the right thing.

Interracial Parent Surface Structure: Basic Guidelines

1. *Parenting*. Different cultures frequently have different beliefs about parenting. For example, Latinos typically place a high value on respect for parents from children. Adolescent rebellion or disrespect to parents can be horrifying to a Latino parent while it is fully acceptable as a stage of development to Western Europeans (Boyd-Franklin & Bry, 2000).

2. *Legal–Economic*. Different cultures have differing beliefs about who should and should not work and under what conditions.

3. *Structural–Social*. The child with parents of different heritage may experience his or her identity as multiracial. Many of the positive or negative feelings that can be generated around this multiracial identity (especially as the young person enters adolescence) is influenced by parental attitudes about classifications of race and societal attitudes. When the child with a multiracial identity encounters strong racist attitudes toward her, the child's identity can be influenced in very negative ways. The child can become socially isolated in a community that lacks appreciation of

diversity. Extended family problems between the grandparents and parents regarding racial issues also can bring tension to the home of the multiracial child.

4. *Beliefs.* Issues with the school system about classification can arise. It is important for the school system to honor the family's belief about how their child is to be identified.

5. *Health.* Where racial victimization or bullying exists, the professional school counselor will want to intervene to prevent future trauma. Schools can affirm students' feelings, take their concerns seriously, and enforce regulations against hate-bullying toward students. There are also programs for sensitizing the student body, staff, and parents about the effects of bullying and how to address it.

Consider the case of a male high school student with a multiracial. He lived in a town where he encountered strong racism almost daily, both among school classmates and from townspeople while simply walking down the street. The essential intervention was to help him build a couple of close relationships with kids in the town. He was to ignore taunting on the streets from adults and discuss it at school with his professional school counselor and at home with his parents, but not to retaliate. Several important student body leaders were invited and responded positively to coming to his defense at school when any bullying started.

Foster Parent, Adoptive Parent, and Grandparent Surface Structure: Basic Guidelines

1. *Parenting.* Foster children may have seen many different parenting styles and need help adapting to yet another one. In the case of grandparents, they may be a little behind on the parenting issues of the day and need help in updating their parenting skills. Also, grandparents and others who adopt or serve as foster parents may be doing so in the interest of friends, relatives, or their own children who may be divorcing or have died. In this case, the foster parents, grandparents, or adoptive parents will themselves be grieving while attempting the new task of parenting. When a foster family takes on numerous children, their attention may be divided, and the neediest children tend to get the most attention. Where the child has moved from school to school, academic performance may be affected, students may lack good learning and study skills, or students may focus more on basic survival needs rather than education needs.

2. *Legal–Economic.* Legal issues are similar to single parenting and step-parenting.

3. *Structural–Social.* Finding afterschool programs for students so that guardians can rest may be helpful. The child may have trouble bonding with new parents, and this may result in conflict at home and worry on the part of the foster parent, grandpatent, or adoptive parent.

4. *Beliefs.* Children who have lived in foster homes might believe they will not be able to remain with their adoptive parents. Foster and adoptive children may not believe they will remain at the school they are attending and therefore will not have a strong commitment to the school or teachers. These children may have guilty beliefs about why they do not have a stable home life and parents.

5. *Health.* Other children may ridicule foster or adoptive children. Also, these children might have suffered trauma, neglect, or serious emotional stress in previous settings and might therefore require psychotherapy.

EXAMPLE 3: INTERRACIAL PARENT WITH ADOPTED ELEMENTARY STUDENT

Terrence was a second-grader who was adopted by an interracial couple. The woman was Caucasian and the father was African American. They were both professionals but decided that the woman would stay home with the child. The woman was happy with this decision because she thought her husband could better provide economically, and she felt more competent to parent a young child than her husband. He agreed. The wife also looked forward to taking some classes during the day at a local college.

At school, Terrence was very active. When the parents were informed of this, they questioned if they should have the child assessed for attention-deficit/hyperactivity disorder. Teachers reported that Terrence was difficult to keep on task and had trouble gaining acceptance from the other children because of his overactive behavior. Though he was very active, Terrence did not hurt anyone.

At home, the family reported having no trouble getting Terrence to bond with them, yet he spoke as though he would be leaving the home and that nothing in the house, including things in his room, belonged to him.

Assessment. Terrence had lived in many foster homes and was having trouble understanding that adoption meant he would stay forever with these parents. Also, Terrence had learned to bond quickly as a survival mechanism. He wanted the love and caring immediately and for as long as he could with the parents with whom he was placed. Terrence placed little value on the schoolwork or students because he believed that he would have to leave any friendships, school projects, or work fairly soon. He lost many relationships with friends, teachers, and parents and had developed a survival mechanism to protect himself. He never committed completely to friends and schoolwork. He was anxious because he never knew what would happen to him next, and he knew he could not perform in school as well as many of the other students.

Intervention. The main intervention was for the parents to convince Terrence that he would be with them forever. His adoptive father and mother informed him that the furniture in his room was his forever, and that he would never be leaving their home. At school the professional school counselor and teachers reinforced the stability of his placement. They said they expected him to stay with them, and they wanted to help him do well. Terrence's mother began helping him get on track academically. The professional school counselor suggested that the parents wait and see how Terrence did at the school before considering an evaluation for ADHD. The professional school counselor said it was natural for Terrence to be a little anxious, given his situation, and perhaps he was just a very active boy. The plan was to provide him with structure in the class to help him learn to follow class rules, and as he adjusted to parents and school, hopefully he would find friends and begin to replace his old survival skills with some new ones. The professional school counselor set up some times for the adoptive mother to visit the classroom and to become a parent volunteer to help Terrence make the adjustment. In addition, the professional school counselor made an appointment to meet with the family in a month and review how Terrence was adapting.

Summary/Conclusion

A key to helping changing families is to not get lost in their differences. It helps to be aware of issues that frequently arise with a particular type of family, and at the same time stay open and sensitive to the individual nature of the family. There are many ways to be a family, and a particular family, no matter the type in terms of surface structure, may not evidence the issues typically associated with that type of living arrangement. For example, there are gay and lesbian relationships in which children feel embarrassed and there are those in which they do not. Some interracial families receive tremendous support from their extended families and others do not. Some single, step, and cohabiting families have educational attainment, economic well-being, and social support which makes coping with family transitions much easier for them than for those families lacking in any of these three factors. Many individuals will experience traumatic events (about 61% of men and 51% of women), but posttraumatic stress disorder is quite low—in general, 5% among men and 10% among women (Meichenbaum, 2002). Individuals and the families in which they grow up may respond very differently to similar events and circumstances. It is important to keep an open mind when working with families in transition. Professional school counselors need to approach all changing families according to both their strengths and needs.

(Note: See the CD-ROM for a list of references.)

CHAPTER 80

HELPING AT-RISK STUDENTS

Jill Holmes-Robinson

Preview

In this chapter, I address the professional school counselor's role in assisting students deemed at risk. I provide cognitive-behavioral approaches in brief modified formats and an intrusive counseling model for use with secondary school–age students. These therapeutic techniques will assist the professional school counselor in need of quick interventions to provide effective counseling to help students identified as at risk.

In accordance with the American School Counselor Association (ASCA), the primary goal of the professional school counselor is to assist in the growth and development of each student. This includes contributing to the mental health as well as the "academic, career and personal/social success of 'at-risk' students" (ASCA; 2004a, p. 1). The following chapter addresses the needs of middle and high school–age students at risk by providing therapeutic interventions centered in brief cognitive-behavioral approaches that are modified for use with secondary students. These therapeutic techniques will assist the professional school counselor in providing efficient and effective counseling for helping students who are at risk.

THE STUDENT AT RISK

There are probably as many definitions of students at risk as there are school districts. Students may be considered at risk if they have a greater potential for performing below academic potential, dropping out of school, or engaging in behaviors that are harmful to self or others (e.g., substance abuse, violence; ASCA; 2004a). For the purpose of this chapter, students at risk are defined as students who exhibit one or more of these problems.

It is the charge of the professional school counselor to work with the student to develop integrated and effective counseling plans that are consistent with the abilities and circumstances of the student (ASCA; 2004b). With this charge in mind, it is imperative that professional school counselors view students at risk with an appreciation and clear perspective for the student's background, life circumstances, and likely reasons for at-risk behaviors. Often the student at risk is trying to deal with personal issues such as low self-esteem, family problems, unresolved grief, neglect, or abuse. These issues may be compounded with the use or abuse of drugs and alcohol. In addition to personal issues are socioeconomic and environmental issues.

The Research Network on Successful Adolescent Development among Youth in High-Risk Settings (as cited in Jessor, 1993) suggested that it is essential for individuals working with students at risk to know of the social contexts in which they are growing up that place them at risk. These include social and environmental issues such as (but not limited to) poverty, limited access to opportunity, or racial/ethnic marginality.

The majority of these youths were living and attending schools in urban and rural settings. A disproportionate number of low-income youth living in major metropolitan areas tend to be of African American and Hispanic ethnic backgrounds in addition to Asian immigrant populations. In contrast, many youth growing up in poor rural communities are White/Caucasian and ethnic minorities (e.g., African American, Native American) as well as increasing numbers of Hispanic immigrants living in poverty-stricken communities throughout the southern and western United States. Understandably, there are a number of issues that arise regarding the mental health and wellness of low income students growing up in these communities that place students at risk. Professional school counselors must provide comprehensive school counseling services to these growing populations.

The Goals and Professional Challenges of Helping At-Risk Students

When counseling students at risk, the primary goal of the professional school counselor is to identify characteristics and maladaptive behaviors and then intervene before these students establish a pattern of self-destructive behavior. When providing services to students at risk, the professional school counselor is responsible for providing responsive programming, including short-term individual counseling; programs to strengthen personal–interpersonal skills; staff development to school and district staff and consultation and support to parents or guardians of students demonstrating at-risk behaviors (ASCA; 2004a). Due to the increased amount of administrative responsibilities that saturate counselor's time—in addition to the high volume of student contact and counseling responsibilities—there is a need to identify quick, pragmatic interventions that can be used within context of the counselor's limited time frame.

Any student can be identified as at risk given particular circumstances. Thus, approaches also need to consider the student's static issues such as age, race/ethnicity, gender, and sexual orientation. For example, scholars in multicultural counseling tend to endorse the notion that various racial groups may require approaches or techniques that differ from White Anglo-Saxon middle-class clients (Sue, 1990). Beyond static issues, the at-risk student may be averse to counseling, may be oblivious to the need for counseling, or mandated to attend counseling, all of which cause additional factors for consideration. Given these diverse elements (e.g., student's at-risk status, static issues, counselor's workload, time constraints) there is a need to identify therapeutic approaches that are suited for addressing this population within the context of aforementioned factors.

The Effectiveness of Brief Counseling

Conceptually planned, brief therapy is typified by the intentional consideration of time limits throughout the change process (Steenbarger, 1992). Brief cognitive-behavioral approaches focus on the following: (a) coping skills to teach students ways of dealing with potential stressors, and (b) restructuring therapy emphasizing the learning of new beliefs and thought patterns. Perhaps a comprehensive explanation of brief counseling would be an intentional acceleration of those change ingredients found in all therapies. By actively bonding with students and, when appropriate, having an intrusive approach, brief therapists serve as developmental catalysts, initiating change that could otherwise take months or years. The brief counseling model views students' concerns as ongoing problems maintained within a particular context. The professional school counselor and student focus on attainable goals and successes to empower the student to take responsibility and control. There are four components emphasized for therapeutic change in planned, brief counseling: (a) strong working alliance; (b) acknowledgment and use of student's strengths and resources; (c) active involvement and connection between counselor and student; and (d) identification of clear, concrete goals (Steenbarger, 1992).

Students who benefit most from brief therapy are those who have a recent onset of problems and who primarily require focused symptom relief as opposed to a broad personality change. This certainly describes the at-risk secondary school-age student who is dealing with issues of peer pressure and a host of other developmental issues. Brief therapy also may be more conducive to at-risk minority students who, according to the literature, are often seeking direct, clear, and immediate coping skills for their problems and prefer active rather than passive approaches to counseling (Sue, 1990).

Students unsuitable for brief counseling include those who have underlying patterns of chronic maladaptive behavior that may require long-term counseling and referrals for outpatient treatment. Brief therapy has been effective in a variety of practice settings, including preference of use by professional school counselors and in college counseling centers. Studies incorporating long-term follow-up in their design reported that changes produced in brief counseling were positively sustained. This was particularly shown in individuals counseled for depression who maintained symptom relief for periods of a year or longer (Steenbarger, 1992). To address the needs of middle and high school at-risk students, brief intervention can be used with specific modified forms of cognitive-behavioral therapies to provide quick intervention and produce effective behavioral change.

HOLMES MODEL OF INTRUSIVE BRIEF COUNSELING: AN OPTION FOR PROFESSIONAL SCHOOL COUNSELORS FOR USE WITH STUDENTS AT RISK

Cognitive-behavioral approaches tend to be more successful as students mature in age and as their cognitive abilities become more concrete. For the at-risk middle and high school students, it is most productive to provide them with brief therapeutic forms of cognitive-behavioral therapy coupled with reality-based therapies that are conducive to their short teenage attention span. Brief therapeutic interventions are also beneficial for the professional school counselor who has numerous time constraints, a large student case load, and administrative duties.

Holmes (1999) developed an integrative approach to counseling that merges brief intervention and cognitive behavioral approaches with intrusive counseling. Intrusive counseling can be defined as probing and direct information-seeking counseling. The intrusive counseling style is displayed in the form of asking pertinent, factual questions in an assertive manner. This style of counseling can assist the counselor in expediting case conceptualization, thus helping the professional school counselor to develop a quick and clear understanding of the student's issues.

Holmes (1999) suggested an integrative model of brief therapy that incorporates four phases: (a) contact, (b) challenge, (c) conversion, and (d) empowerment (see Figure 80.1). This model was specifically designed for multicultural and majority students who are deemed at risk; however, many elements can be used for general student populations. Traditionally, in brief counseling, both the counselor and client take responsibility for the flow of work involved in the counseling process. In the Holmes model, however, the professional school counselor serves as a facilitator, allowing the student to think, process his or her actions, and actively work on establishing better goals and more effective appropriate behaviors.

Figure 80.1 should be read as an inverted triangle. The professional school counselor can quickly move though the model or use it progressively, depending on the amount of contact and time with the student. The model can be used to facilitate student thinking, behavior change, problem solving, and development.

The first phase, Contact, involves the active fostering of a positive alliance with the student, information gathering using intrusive counseling, assessing the student's patterns, and determining the student's appropriateness for brief work. The intrusive counseling style is displayed in the form of asking pertinent, factual questions in an assertive manner such as, "Tell me what happened?" or "Do you have . . . ?" or "Are you . . . (failing classes, pregnant, etc.), and what have you done to try to deal with the situation?" In the Contact phase, emphasis is placed on understanding the student's issue and worldview. An appreciation of the student's worldview incorporates the counselor's developing, as much as deemed necessary, a quick understanding of the student's environment/background, getting clarity on the student's family life, and cultural and/or religious beliefs that are all applicable to how he or she views the world and the circumstances encountered there.

The second phase, Challenge, uses the relationship of an established working alliance to challenge nonproductive, maladaptive patterns of behavior. This phase incorporates the use of various cognitive-behavioral techniques such as the philosophical views of William Glasser's choice theory and reality therapy and Albert Ellis' rational-emotive behavior therapy (REBT).

Choice theory maintains that behavior is internally motivated and chosen. The theory supports the belief that the only behavior we can control is our own (Glasser, 1998). Reality therapy is the intervention that helps students deal with personal problems by creating more realistic quality worlds (what they want) and/or figuring out better choices. Reality therapy differs from most psychotherapies because it focuses on the present and helps people understand that they can choose a better future. REBT maintains that beliefs contribute to or cause one's emotional reactions; how you think about a situation reflects how you will react and feel. REBT contends emotional problems are the result of one's beliefs, which need to be challenged (DiGiuseppe & Barnard, 1990; Zoints & Zoints, 1997).

During the challenge phase, questions can be asked such as, "How did you contribute to the situation?" or "Tell me how you are thinking about the situation, what thoughts are going through your mind?" This phase ends with helping the student es-

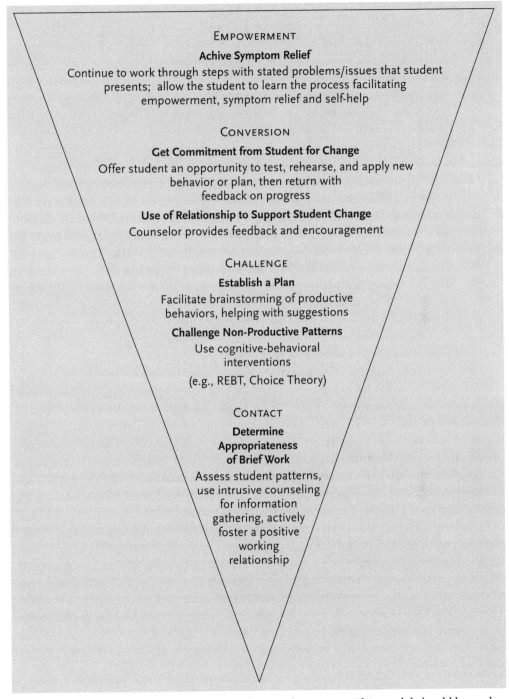

FIGURE 80.1. Holmes model of intrusive brief counseling. *Note.* This model should be read as an inverted triangle, starting first with Contact and proceeding upward to Empowerment. From *Counseling in Student Affairs: Utilizing Brief Therapy to Bridge That Gap Between Theory and Practice* (pp. 17–18) by J. Holmes, 1999, Charlottesville, VA: Unpublished manuscript. Copyright 1999 J. Holmes. Reprinted with permission.

tablish a plan for change via brainstorming and offering suggestions and reevaluation of the situation. The professional school counselor asks questions such as, "What could you have done differently?" and makes suggestions such as, "Perhaps you may want to try . . ."

During the challenge phase, the student must commit to the professional school counselor that her or she will try the newly agreed upon behavior. This allows the professional school counselor to make productive suggestions for behavior change without being responsible for getting the student to comply. It also allows the student to take responsibility for his or her own decisions and actions without placing blame on the counselor or on others.

In the third phase, conversion, the professional school counselor supports the student by encouraging his or her ability to change. The professional school counselor again assists the student in identifying more productive behaviors and/or actions and offers the student the opportunity to commit to a goal, plan of action or new behavior, and to test, apply, and rehearse newly developed insights and skills. The professional school counselor can get a commitment from the student by asking, "Are you willing to try . . . ? The counselor can then state, "When we meet again, I want you to tell me how things turned out." The professional school counselor does this while offering feedback on performance and reinforcement of goals. During this process, it is imperative that the counselor avoid pitying, enabling, or taking responsibility for the student's actions (or inaction that may produce negative outcomes).

This process of recognizing negative or ineffective behaviors or thought patterns and developing more productive behaviors (the process of rehearsing these steps each time the student encounters problems) leads to the final stage, empowerment. During the empowerment stage, the student, while working in conjunction with the professional school counselor, achieves symptom relief and learns an effective process of self-help. In this stage, the counselor validates the student's willingness to try new behaviors or approaches and elicits feedback from the student regarding his or her opinion of the process and achieved outcome. The counselor can state, "I applaud you for what you decided to do and it seemed to work well; what do you think?"

Termination can occur spontaneously or through more traditional transitional procedures. If the student indicates by actions (verbal or otherwise) that he or she has achieved "symptom relief" (e.g., a solution achieved or positive closure) this may produce a spontaneous termination without further need for follow up. The counselor and student can then decide to move on to another issue or problem, following the same format. Table 80.1 provides a helpful listing of the various phases of the model and associated questioning strategies.

SUMMARY/CONCLUSION

Given at-risk students' unique circumstances, it is imperative for the professional school counselor to have a comprehensive appreciation for their backgrounds and be able to use a variety of counseling techniques that are both effective and efficient. Modified versions of cognitive-behavioral therapies and integrative approaches such as the Holmes model of intrusive brief counseling can assist the professional school counselor in providing students at risk with behavior change in a pragmatic format that is beneficial for the student and easily applied by the professional school counselor.

(Note: See the CD-ROM for a list of references.)

TABLE 80.1
QUESTION REFERENCE SHEET FOR HOLMES MODEL OF INTRUSIVE BRIEF COUNSELING

Holmes' model of intrusive brief counseling incorporates four phases: (a) contact, (b) challenge, (c) conversion, and (d) empowerment to assist the at-risk student (see Figure 80.1). Following are suggestions of how to phrase questions through the various phases.

Contact: Involves the active fostering of a positive alliance with the student and information gathering using intrusive counseling. In the Contact phase, emphasis is placed on understanding the student's issue and "worldview". Questions may be phrased as:

- Tell me what happened?
- Do you have . . .?"
- Who is at home with you?
- What classes are you failing?
- Are you . . . (pregnant, taking drugs, etc)? What have you done to try to deal with the situation?"

Challenge: Uses the relationship of an established working alliance to challenge non-productive, maladaptive patterns of behavior. Questions may be phrased as:

- How did you contribute to the situation?
- Tell me how you were thinking about the situation, what thoughts were going through your mind?
- How do you know this is true?
- Say you do [fail the exam, have to speak with... or what if your mother doesn't stop drinking], what do you think will happen?

The challenge phase ends with helping the student establish a plan for change offering suggestions for reevaluation of the situation. Questions may be phrased as:

- What could you have done differently?
- Perhaps you may want to try . . .

Conversion: Counselor serves as a support to the student, encouraging his/her ability to change. Identify more productive behaviors and/or actions. Questions may be phrased as:

- Are you willing to try . . . ?
- When we meet again I want you to tell me how things turned out.

Empowerment: Student achieves symptom relief and learns an effective process of self-help. Statement may be phrased as:

- I applaud you for what you decided to do and it seemed to work well, what do you think?
- Now you know something you can do that will provide you with positive results, good job!

CHAPTER 81

THE PROFESSIONAL SCHOOL COUNSELOR
IN THE RURAL SETTING:
STRATEGIES FOR MEETING CHALLENGES
AND MAXIMIZING REWARDS

Deborah L. Drew and Dorothy Breen

Preview

The rural setting presents challenges and rewards to the professional school counselor. We offer strategies to assist professional school counselors in creating and delivering programs that meet the needs of rural students.

The practice of school counseling in a rural setting is both rewarding and uniquely challenging. There is a sense of close community, caring, and trust and appreciation of skills and services offered, but circumstances such as isolation, cultural issues, and limited resources present challenges to the professional living and working in those settings.

Sutton and Pearson (2002) provided statistics from the 1998 U.S. Department of Education's National Center for Education Statistics. They stated that "rural and small town schools comprise 37.8% of the total number of schools an . . . more than a quarter of U.S. public school students receive their education in rural and small town schools" (p. 226).

Professional school counselors play a critical role in students' lives (Kuranz, 2002), especially in rural settings. To be most effective, professional school counselors must recognize the challenges and thrive on the rewards of the rural setting. In this chapter we discuss four prominent challenges presented in the literature: rural isolation, rural culture, limited resources, and ethical dilemmas. We offer strategies for meeting these challenges and maximizing the counseling benefits to the rural school setting. Admittedly, the research was sparse regarding these strategies and is supplemented with findings from our ongoing research.

ISOLATION

In rural settings, the professional school counselor may be the only counselor in the school, school district, and community. There is often a lack of contact with other professional school counselors (Breen & Drew, 2001). Consequently, there may not be peer support and access to professional colleagues for collaboration, supervision, or consultation available nearby. There are few opportunities for professional development and, those that are available may require the professional school counselor to drive long distances. The need for socialization is important, especially for young, unmarried professional school counselors. As one counselor stated, "Isolation is difficult—it's very difficult being a single person in this community" (Sutton & Pearson, 2002, p. 272). According to Helge (as cited in Sutton & Pearson, 2002), the impact of isolation has been identified as a contributor to high turnover rates among education specialists in rural schools.

THE RURAL CULTURE

Unique is a term used in the literature when describing the rural culture and the rural school environment (Apostal & Bilden, 1991; Breen & Drew, 2005; McIntire, Marion, & Quaglia, 1990; Sutton & Southworth, 1990). The rural community offers close personal relationships, personal recognition, caring, involvement, traditional values, and independence. However, it takes time to get to know the people and become established. Other challenges include limited resources, distrust of the unfamiliar, and lack of privacy and anonymity (Breen & Drew, 2001).

Rural schools tend to be smaller, more personal centers of community identity (McIntire et al., 1990). By their very definition, rural schools are usually

> geographically isolated, [and] located in less densely populated areas. These conditions limit opportunities of rural youth for adequate health services, social and recreational activities, relevant educational experiences and exposure to vocational life styles which could be a means of changing their future. (Sweeney, 1971, p. 6)

In recent studies, researchers have found that rural students are more likely to use tobacco, drugs, and alcohol, while "rural areas are less equipped to deal with the consequences" (Hines, 2002, p. 197).

LIMITED RESOURCES

Lack of resources is one of the chief complaints that professional school counselors have about the rural setting. Financial resources are limited, and counseling resources may not be readily available (Hines, 2002). The professional school counselor may perceive that he or she is expected to "wear many hats" and "be all things to all people" (Breen & Drew, 2001). The professional school counselor might take on the role of generalist: "In the small, understaffed school, the realities of limited resources demand that the counselor, or few counselors, take responsibility for the total range of student needs" (Sutton & Pearson, 2002, p. 276).

The National Institute of Mental Health (2000) stated that "the nearly 60 million Americans living in rural and frontier areas have the same kinds of mental health problems and needs for services as individuals who live in urban and suburban areas. Yet, rural areas have unique characteristics that present barriers to mental health care" (p. 1). Furthermore, "for many students and families the school counselor is the first mental health provider they see" (Paisley & McMahon, as cited in Kuranz, 2002, p. 173) and "may be the only mental health provider they ever see" (Kuranz, 2002, p. 173).

The unique circumstances of the rural setting affect career development: "Reduced accessibility to higher education, narrow rural school curricula, limited exposure to the world of occupations and few role models have been major limitations" (Apostal & Bilden, 1991, p. 153).

ETHICAL DILEMMAS

The unique characteristics of the rural setting also present dilemmas to the professional school counselor trying to maintain good ethical standards. Maintaining boundaries is especially difficult for counselors who may face expectations to "be all things to all people" (Breen & Drew, 2001). Both the American Counseling Association's (ACA; 2005) code of ethics and the American School Counselor Association's (ASCA; 2004) ethical standards require counselors to practice within the bounds of individual professional competence. Though ethical standards require referral, resources for referral may be remote.

The professional school counselor keeps information confidential (ASCA; 2004). Small-school expectations of "knowing" about students may challenge adherence to this standard. Teachers, administrators, and parents in rural settings are accustomed to knowing, and knowing about, students. In fact, these people may know much more about the student than the professional school counselor does because of their involvement in the rural community. School policies may not adhere to this ethical standard, and professional school counselors may be caught between school policy and ethics.

Dual or multiple relationships provide both the professional school counselor and the client and families with a sense of closeness, familiarity, and community, but they also can present ethical dilemmas. Meeting clients in a variety of roles and settings—at school, the store, church, the gym, the doctor's office, the bank, and so on—challenge basic ethical principles of confidentiality. ASCA (2004) advises that professional school counselors avoid dual relationships that impair professional judgment and, if unavoidable, then "the counselor is responsible for taking action to eliminate or reduce the potential for harm" (Section A.4.a.). The rural setting makes avoiding multiple relationships virtually impossible. A professional school counselor who has worked or lived in the same community for several years may be familiar with siblings, cousins, aunts, uncles, parents, and grandparents of current students. It is possible that too much familiarity can compromise objectivity and challenge sound practice. High visibility, while at times a benefit, makes the analogy of "living in a fishbowl" quite applicable to the rural professional school counselor (Miller, 1994): "Particularly in small towns and rural communities it is difficult for school counselors to avoid overlap between their personal and professional lives" (Herlihy & Corey, 1997, p. 145).

The "counselor everywhere you go" (Breen & Drew, 2001) phenomenon can create an ethical dilemma by leading to stress and burnout, thus compromising good practice. The ACA code of ethics calls for counselors to be "alert to the signs of impairment from their own physical, mental, or emotional problems and refrain from offering or providing professional services when such impairment is likely to harm a client or others" (2005, C.2.g.). But, who takes over when the professional school counselor is impaired?

STRATEGIES FOR WORKING IN RURAL COMMUNITIES

There are many strategies available to address the needs of the rural professional school counselor. The following are designed to help deal with the isolation of working in a rural setting, understand the rural culture, enhance the limited available resources, and resolve ethical dilemmas.

COPING WITH ISOLATION

In order to cope with the professional isolation of working in rural communities, professional school counselors should take on a leadership role and develop support networks.

Lead the way. The rural professional school counselor may avoid working in isolation by becoming a leader and taking responsibility for meeting the needs created by the isolation of the rural community. Worzbyt and Zook (1992) suggested that professional school counselors take a leadership role rather than a service provider role. Build networks and partnerships in your community. The proverb "It takes a village to raise a child" resonates with truth (Bunch & Gibson, 2002, p. 16). Look for opportunities *within* the rural setting to meet the needs created by the setting. Invite professionals from the community, county, state, and university or college faculty and graduate students to provide training, consultation, and services. Request that your state department of education hire counselors to work as consultants, supervisors, and mentors for rural professional school counselors.

Develop support networks. Network with neighboring school districts. Engage in consultation and supervision. Use structured group and peer supervision models. Ask school administration to provide time and funding for supervision, mentoring and professional development. Become involved in state and regional professional counseling associations. Together, advocate for the needs of rural professional school counselors (Allen & James, 1990; Breen & Drew, 2001; McIntyre et al., 1990; Sutton & Southworth, 1990).

UNDERSTANDING THE RURAL CULTURE

The rural community is unique. Getting to know and appreciate the unique aspects of rural culture will contribute to the effectiveness of the professional school counselor (Allen & James, 1990; Braucht & Weime, 1990; Breen & Drew, 2001; Breen & Drew, 2005; McIntire, et al., 1990; Sutton & Pearson, 2002; Sutton & Southworth, 1990; Worzbyt & Zook, 1992). Become involved in the community in order to learn the cultural roles, norms, biases, and issues. Volunteer in the community. Spend time talking with individuals and families in an effort to respect rural lifestyle and values. Take time to carefully plan the school counseling program for the rural setting. Administer a needs assessment to determine specific areas to address. Think about the way in which the rural setting affects you and your work (Breen & Drew, 2005). Table 81.1 offers questions for rural counselors to contemplate.

TABLE 81.1

QUESTIONS FOR RURAL COUNSELORS

- In what ways does the rural setting help your counseling practice?
- In what ways does it challenge your practice?
- How does it change your work?
- How does it change your concept of the role of a professional school counselor?
- How does your rural professional role challenge your personal life?
- What can you draw upon from your training that focuses on rural counseling?
- What kind of training do you need to look for that focuses on rural counseling?
- What kind of support do you have that focuses on rural counseling?
- What kind of support do you need to look for that focuses on rural counseling?

Note. From "Professional Counseling in Rural Settings: Raising Awareness Through Discussion and Self-Study With Implications for Training and Support (p. 250), in R. K. Yep and G. R. Waltz (Eds.), *VISTAS: Compelling perspectives on counseling*, Alexandria, VA: American Counseling Association. Reprinted with permission.

ENHANCING LIMITED RESOURCES

Use resources that are available in the school, local community, surrounding communities, and nearest cities (Allen & James, 1990; Braucht & Weime, 1990; Breen & Drew, 2001; Sutton & Southworth, 1990).

Think of school counseling services as a program, not a person: "Look at your school in a new light. It's an employer filled with highly qualified professionals in teaching, health services, administration and support services, transportation, and food services" (Bunch & Gibson, 2002, p. 14).

Encourage these professionals, staff, and community members to collaborate in the school counseling program. For example, enlist the help of administrators, teachers, nurses, custodians, cooks, secretaries, bus drivers, parents, grandparents, and students as peer counselors, mentors and tutors. Work with teachers to integrate developmental counseling services into the classroom curriculum.

Use technology. Search Web sites for resources. In Table 81.2, we list several Web sites, some with links to other helpful programs and information.

Involve parents in the process. Help parents understand opportunities, deadlines, and expectations of career and college planning. Remember that people in rural areas are accustomed to solving their own problems—enlist their help.

Use regional programs. Help plan regional programs with other professional school counselors to offer greater exposure to information on health issues, careers, and colleges. Engage students in extracurricular activities that provide opportunities to interact with students from larger cities. Promote job shadowing.

Make appropriate referrals. Stay within your role as a professional school counselor and refer. Kuranz (2002) stated that "the context of the school mission . . . is to support academic achievement" (p. 173). Form relationships with community agencies and mental health agencies and health professionals.

TABLE 81.2

RESOURCES

American Counseling Association (**www.counseling.org**)

American School Counselor Association (**www.schoolcounselor.org**)

American Psychological Association (**www.apa.org**)

National Alliance for the Mentally Ill (**www.nami.org**)

National Association for Rural Mental Health (**www.narmh.org**)

National Rural Health Association (**www.nrharural.org**)

College Board, Inc. (**www.collegeboard.com**)

Princeton Review (**www.princetonreview.com**)

Student Financial Aid Form (**www.fafsa.ed.gov**)

In the rural community, professional school counselors need to think broadly when looking for mental health referrals and support services. See Table 81.3 for a list of ideas.

RESOLVING RURAL ETHICAL DILEMMAS

Keep ethical thinking in the forefront at all times. Be aware of ethical dilemmas presented by the rural setting. Provide school officials with a copy of codes of ethics (ACA; 2005; ASCA; 2004) and educate them about their implications (Dansby-Giles, 2002).

Clarify, define, publicize, and communicate the professional school counselor role (Herlihy & Corey, 1997). Develop and use a disclosure statement. Update job descriptions (Dansby-Giles, 2002). Educate administrators and school board members about the boundaries of competence, time, and the need for ongoing training and supervision. Follow, but also influence, school policies.

Discuss multiple relationships and confidentiality. Talk with students and their families about familiarity in the rural setting and how to handle dilemmas such as confidentiality and multiple relationships.

Set clear boundaries. Set limits on your work. Stay within the bounds of your competence, time, and job description. Refer! Keep the welfare of your students and their families in the forefront of your thinking, but recognize that you cannot and should not be all things to all people.

Follow an ethical decision-making model. A variety of practice-based models for ethical decision-making are available. Cottone and Claus (2000) summarized and compared nine models. Stone (2005) thoroughly discussed ethical issues faced by professional school counselors and offered a model for ethical decision making that encourages professional school counselors to consider the context of the school setting. The following are steps for ethical decision making offered by Remley and Herlihy (2005, p. 17) that incorporate a variety of ethical decision-making philosophies.

1. Identify and define the problem.
2. Consider the moral principles.

3. Tune in to your feelings.
4. Consult with colleagues or experts.
5. Involve your client in the decision-making process.
6. Identify desired outcomes.
7. Consider possible actions.
8. Choose and act on your own choice.

Consult and seek supervision. Engage in regular consultation with other professionals. Use the telephone to overcome distances. Discuss ethical issues in ongoing supervision.

Engage in professional development. Stretch the boundaries of your competence through regular professional development. Attend workshops on ethics and ethical decision making to stay current. Codes are revised approximately every 10 years. Use online resources for information and questions (e.g., www.counseling.org, www.schoolcounselor.org).

Practice Personal stress management. Take care of yourself, and implement relaxation strategies. Use your support system, and do not practice when impaired.

Purchase malpractice insurance. Even the best professional school counselors can be accused of ethical or legal violations. Help yourself by obtaining professional liability insurance. Your professional organization offers insurance for professional school counselors. Don't assume your school liability insurance will cover you (Remley & Herlihy, 2001).

TABLE 81.3

POTENTIAL REFERRAL AND SUPPORT SERVICES IN RURAL AREAS

- Physicians, physicians' assistants, nurse practitioners, community health nurses
- State and county agencies and local town offices
- Clergy and church programs
- Police and fire departments
- Funeral directors (for bereavement)
- United Way programs
- Regional and county assistance programs
- School to work programs
- State and national career resource centers
- Upward Bound and Talent Search programs
- Job service offices and offices for training and development
- State offices of substance abuse prevention and intervention
- State department of behavioral health services
- Vocational rehabilitation
- Local or regional domestic violence programs and child abuse prevention programs
- Local transportation services

Summary/Conclusion

Unique circumstances of the rural setting present both challenges and rewards to the professional school counselor. The rewards of close relationships, a sense of community, and appreciation of what the professional has to offer contrast with challenges that come from isolation, cultural issues, limited resources, and ethical dilemmas. More than one quarter of U.S. public school students attend rural and small-town schools. Professional school counselors play a critical role in the lives of these students. Employing effective strategies to maximize the benefits of the rural setting can help professional school counselors create school programs that truly meet the needs of rural students. Taking a leadership role, building networks, learning to value the rural culture, using the resources of the community, using technology, and practicing ethically are some of the ways that rural professional school counselors can meet the challenges and maximize the rewards.

(Note: See the CD-ROM for a list of references.)

CHAPTER 82

COUNSELING MULTIRACIAL STUDENTS

Henry L. Harris, Lyndon P. Abrams, and Edward A. Wierzalis

Preview

There is a growing number of interracial marriages and partnerships and, as a result, the number of multiracial children has increased. Although multiracial children's learning and developmental needs are similar to those of other children, they might encounter unique challenges because of their heritage. Gibbs and Moskowitz-Sweet (1991) defined a multiracial person as one who is a product of a union in which one parent is from one race and the other parent is from another race. The purpose of this chapter is to help professional school counselors understand some of the issues confronting multiracial students. We provide an overview of multiracial individuals, along with the brief history of interracial marriages followed by a review of research concerning multiracial persons and professional school counselors' perceptions of multiracial individuals. The final section concludes with implications for professional school counselors and a list of resources for parents and teachers.

Multiracial individuals—previously described as mixed, biracial, or interracial—represent a unique and growing segment of the school-age population. Furthermore, they represent a visible symbol of society's racial divisions and ambiguities (Chiong, 1998). According to Census 2000, multiracial individuals made up 2.4% (6.8 million) of the nation's overall population of 281 million people. Of the total multiracial population, 42% (2.8 million) were under the age of 18 (U.S. Bureau of Census, 2001). Forty percent of multiracial persons lived in the West, 27% lived in the South, 15% lived in the Midwest, and 18% lived in the northeastern region of the U.S. The percentage of individuals reported belonging to more than one race in Census 2000 also varied considerably depending upon race. For example, of 217 million Whites, only 2.5% (5.5 million) reported belonging to more than one race. There were 36 million African Americans reported in Census 2000, yet only 4.8% (1.8 million) indicated they belonged to more than one race, which is extremely low, as estimates suggest that between "75 percent and 95 percent of blacks could define themselves as something other than black because of their mixed heritage" (Valentine, 1995, p. 47). Furthermore, of the 4.1 million American Indian and Alaska Natives, 40% (1.6 million) reported belonging to more than one race; of the nearly 12 million Asians, 14% (1.6 million) reported belonging to more than one race; of the 874,000 Native Hawaiian and Other Pacific Islanders, 54% (476,000) reported belonging to more than one race; and of the 18.5 million Some Other Race category, 17% (3.2 million) reported belonging to more than one race (U.S. Bureau of Census, 2001).

Multiracial persons have traditionally been analyzed and judged from sociocultural and biological perspectives (Nakashima, 1992). The sociocultural perspective characterized them as social and cultural outcasts who were incapable of fitting in or gaining acceptance in any racial group. Park (1928) described multiracial individuals as strangers living in two different worlds. He envisioned their life experience as a period of crisis, resulting in restlessness, spiritual instability, and intensified self-consciousness. Stonequist (1937) asserted that multiracial persons were condemned to live in two different cultural societies that were hostile to each other and, as a result, they were destined to lead a life of loneliness and confusion because of the lower societal status they were assigned. Suggesting that multiracial children will automatically develop identity problems because of their heritage assumes they will be "rejected at face value by all ethnic groups and considered marginal but not actual members of these groups" (Kerwin & Ponterotto, 1995, p. 203).

The biological perspective characterized multiracial individuals as depressive, moody, unhappy, aggressive, impulsive, and mentally and physically weak race-conscious beings destined to have a variety of social, emotional, and psychological problems because of their unnatural genetic blend (Caste, 1926; Krause, 1941). Fueled by the eugenics movement during the early 1900s, multiracial people were also perceived to have a shorter life span, be less fertile, have larger than normal skulls and teeth too big for their jaws in addition to other complicated disabilities (Aikman, 1933). Some eugenicists believed that certain races were genetically superior to others, and the mixing of the races would dilute the superior White race, thus lowering the potential for future generations (Farber, 2003). The goal behind the sociocultural and biological perspective was to create a racially divisive climate by socially and legally discouraging Caucasians from marrying and/or having children with people of color (Nakashima, 1992).

History of Interracial Marriage

"I have nothing against interracial marriages, I just feel sorry for the children because they will not be accepted." "Marriage is difficult enough, why would you want to marry someone from a different race?" "The children will not know who to identify with and will grow up confused." "The children are going to suffer." This may be one of many responses given by people from different racial and ethnic groups when the topic of interracial marriage is addressed. Interracial marriages and unions have been a controversial part of U.S. history dating from the 1600s. According to Greenberg (1999), prior to the institution of slavery, interracial sex was quite common as well as some interracial unions; however, as race slavery began to replace servant labor in the south, the offspring of interracial unions began to blur the distinction between Black and White and free and slave. As a method to protect the economic interest of slave owners in the United States, Maryland, in 1664, became the first colony to create antimiscegenation laws designed purposely to discourage and prohibit interracial marriages and sexual relations between "freeborn English women" and "Negro Slaves" (Pascoe, 1991). Years later, in 1691, Virginia made it illegal for Caucasian women marry Native American and Blacks and also made it illegal for them to bear mixed-race children (Greenberg, 1999). In addition to the creation of antimiscegenation laws, the one-drop rule was also established (Zack, 1995). The one-drop rule stated that any person with one drop of Black blood in their body was considered Black, regardless of their physical appearance (Tatum, 1997). This rule was formally adopted by the U.S. Census in 1920 (Hickman, 1997).

Weinberger (1966) contended that 40 of the possible 50 states at some point had antimiscegenation laws, and the only racial minority group affected by all of the statutes was African Americans. Antimiscegenation laws were constitutionally upheld until 1967. In a landmark decision, the United States Supreme Court ruled in *Loving v. Virginia* (1967) that such laws banning interracial marriages were unconstitutional under the 14th Amendment. At that time, 16 other states had laws prohibiting interracial marriages (Taylor, Funk, & Craighill, 2006). Alabama was the last state to officially remove the language banning interracial marriages from the state's constitution, and close to half of the participants who voted did not want the language removed (Parker, 1999).

Following the 1967 Supreme Court decision, there was a significant rise in the number of interracial marriages. Consider the facts:

- Interracial marriages increased from less than 1% of the marriages in 1970 to more than 5% of marriages in 2000.
- The typical interracial couple consists of a White person with a non-White spouse, and the most common interracial couple is between White males and Asian females, as this pairing comprises 14% of all interracial couples (Lee, 2005).
- Asian women are far more likely to intermarry than are Asian males.
- Marriage between African American males and Caucasian females accounted for 8% of interracial couples in 2000 (Taylor et al., 2006).
- Compared to other minority groups, African Americans are least likely to marry someone from a different race (Lee, 2005).

The lower rates of interracial marriage among African Americans suggest that racial boundaries are more prominent, with racial prejudice being more noticeable for this group (Lee & Bean, 2004).

RESEARCH ASSOCIATED WITH MULTIRACIAL INDIVIDUALS

Multiracial individuals have constituted a segment of American society that has encountered various forms of prejudice and discrimination (Lee, 2005), and the research concerning this population has produced a variety of outcomes. Some studies have concluded that multiracial individuals were more likely to experience problems with depression, sexual conflicts, social marginality, interpersonal relationships, racial identity issues, substance abuse, delinquency, conduct problems, negative outcomes in schools such as being expelled or suspended, and social rejection (e.g., Bowles, 1993; Choi, Harachi, Gillmore, & Catalano, 2006; Collins, 2000; Cooney & Radina, 2000; Gibbs & Moskowitz-Sweet, 1991; Milan & Keiley, 2000; Teicher, 1968; Winn & Priest, 1993).

Other investigations of multiracial individuals have revealed more positive outcomes by discovering that multiracial individuals were (a) proud of their heritage; (b) emotionally secure with high levels of self-esteem; (c) comfortable dealing with issues relating to their identity; (d) independent, creative, and experienced good parental relationships similar to other single-race individuals; and (e) had less grade retention, higher GPA, and high test scores (e.g., Bracey, Bamaca, Umana-Taylor, 2004; Hall, 2002; Kerwin, Ponterotto, Jackson, & Harris,1993; Minville, Constantine, Baysden, & So-Lloyd, 2005; Radina & Cooney, 2000; Rockquemore & Brunsma, 2002; Suzuki-Crumly

& Hyers, 2004). In summary, Shin and Sanchez (2005) concluded in their review of multiracial research that investigations taken from clinical populations tended to find negative outcomes, while studies that sampled nonclinical multiracial populations found more positive results. Regardless of the population sampled, it is safe to assume that multiracial students may encounter certain forms of prejudicial behavior because of their heritage.

SCHOOL COUNSELORS AND MULTIRACIAL STUDENTS

The multiracial population has typically been an underserved group in schools and, because of their increasing numbers, writers in the counseling profession specifically encouraged professional school counselors to address their counseling needs more effectively in the school setting (Herring, 1992; Nishimura, 1995; Wardle, 1992). Nishimura and Bol (1997) collected data investigating the perceptions of the counseling needs of multiracial children from 120 professional school counselors. They did not report that multiracial children experienced any more or fewer problems compared to other children; however, middle school counselors were more likely to report that multiracial students experienced more behavioral problems. The professional school counselors also indicated that multiracial students presented both unique and general counseling issues, and the majority believed they were able to meet the counseling needs of multiracial students without changing their current counseling program.

Harris (2002) expanded the Nishimura and Bol (1997) study of professional school counselors' perceptions of multiracial students by increasing the sample size from a larger geographic region. The results indicated that (a) elementary school counselors perceived multiracial students to have more behavioral problems compared to other children, (b) secondary school counselors perceived minorities to be more accepting of multiracial children than nonminorities, (c) professional school counselors with 1 to 5 years of counseling experience were more likely to automatically categorize multiracial students specifically with the minority parent and also more likely to believe that presenting problems that multiracial students experienced were caused by identity conflicts, and (d) male school counselors perceived multiracial students to experience more academic problems compared to other students and were also more likely than female school counselors to perceive minorities as more accepting of multiracial students compared to nonminorities (Harris, 2002).

The Harris (2002) study also demonstrated how actively promoting cultural diversity and awareness programs in schools affected school counselors' perceptions of multiracial students. It is interesting to note that the majority of professional school counselors who indicated they were uncertain whether multiracial students exhibited more behavioral problems compared to other students were in schools that *somewhat* promoted cultural diversity and awareness programs. Professional school counselors that were employed in schools that *did not* actively promote cultural diversity and awareness programs believed that multiracial students were more likely to attribute problems to identity confusion and automatically categorized multiracial students with the minority parent. They also believed that multiracial students should identify most with the minority parent and perceived minorities to be more accepting of multiracial students compared to nonminorities (Harris, 2002).

Using additional analysis from Harris' (2002) data, Harris and Durodoye (2006) explored how the race of the professional school counselor affected their perceptions of multiracial students. Statistically significant relationships were found in the following areas:

- Caucasian school counselors were more likely than African American school counselors to believe that multiracial students would experience more difficulties adjusting to society when compared to students of other racial and ethnic backgrounds.
- Caucasian school counselors compared to African American school counselors were more likely to perceive multiracial children as displaying more negative social skills and attitudes toward adults compared to students of other racial and ethnic backgrounds.
- African American school counselors compared to Caucasian school counselors were more likely to believe it is socially and psychologically best for multiracial students to live in a neighborhood mirroring the minority parent.
- African American school counselors compared to Caucasian school counselors were more likely to perceive minorities as being more accepting of multiracial students.
- A larger number of African American school counselors compared to Caucasian school counselors believed that multiracial children should racially identify most with the minority parent.
- African American school counselors were more likely than Caucasian school counselors to believe that the presenting problems multiracial children experienced were the result of a racial identity conflict.
- While African American school counselors reported that they had taken a multicultural counseling course more frequently than Caucasian school counselors, African American school counselors were more likely to work in racially nondiverse schools and even less likely to promote cultural diversity and awareness programs compared to Caucasian school Counselors (Harris & Durodoye, 2006).

SUGGESTIONS FOR PROFESSIONAL SCHOOL COUNSELORS

The numbers of multiracial students enrolled in schools are likely to increase, so it is therefore imperative for professional school counselors to examine their own lives and explore how race, ethnicity, and culture have shaped their attitudes, values, and personal feelings about multiracial students and their families if they hope to create a culturally responsive school environment (McRoy & Freeman, 1986; Nishimura, 1995). Harris (2002) suggested professional school counselors begin this self-analysis by asking the following questions:

How do I feel about interracial marriages and partnerships?

Do I perceive some more favorably than others?

How do I feel about multiracial children?

How do I feel and or react when I see a member from my own racial group romantically involved or married to someone from another racial group?

What preconceived thoughts come to my mind when I see a multiracial student having academic or behavioral problems?

Does the gender or physical appearance of the multiracial student affect my perceptions?

Do I assume the problems multiracial students experience are a result of a confused identity?

How do teachers, students, and administrators treat multiracial students in my school?

How are multiracial students identified on school forms? Who makes that decision?

Do I believe multiracial students can be just as successful as other students?

What impact does my gender or socioeconomic status have on my perceptions?

If I have negative or inaccurate perceptions of multiracial individuals, what must I personally do to do overcome them? (Harris, 2002)

This self-analysis is helpful for professional school counselors seeking to become culturally competent professionals.

Research in the counseling profession has addressed identity formation concerning multiracial individuals (Bowles, 1993; Poston, 1990; Rockquemore & Brunsma, 2002; Teicher, 1968), and in a pluralistic society where race is such a determining factor, identity formation can be a challenging task for all children. When one is a member of a minority group, the identity formation challenge deepens, and the task is much greater (Chiong, 1998). It would therefore be helpful for professional school counselors to become aware of six important environmental factors needed to facilitate the development of a healthy identity for multiracial students (McRoy & Zurcher, 1983).

1. Parents should acknowledge and discuss their racial heritage with their children. If multiracial children inquire about skin color or hair texture, receive strange looks from people, or hear negative comments because they are multiracial, parents must be willing to openly address these matters in a caring manner.

2. Parents must be flexible in promoting the development of a positive racial identity. Ladner (1984) identified three methods used by parents of multiracial children to confront the issue of racial identity: (a) deny that race is important and implore "my child is human above all else" (p. 7); (b) promote one parent's racial identity over the other; and (c) teach their children to promote a multiracial identity. Parents should not encourage multiracial children to choose one parent's racial identity over the other. When they are forced to disown part of their heritage, their sense of self may not be firmly grounded, which impedes the healthy development of their identity. Failure to identify with one parent means that identification with the other parent cannot be truly integrated as part of the multiracial child's self-identity (Bowles, 1993). According to the American Academy of Child and Adolescent Psychiatry (1999), multiracial individuals who culturally identify with both parents tend to grow up much happier compared to multiracial children embracing a monoracial identity. Multiracial children may also experience massive feelings of guilt and shame if they are forced to choose one parent's racial identity over the other (Winn & Priest, 1993).

3. Multiracial families should live in a racially diverse neighborhood so their children will have the opportunity to develop relationships with a culturally diverse group of peers and attend a culturally diverse school (McRoy & Zurcher, 1983). When multiracial children live in a racially segregated neighborhood, they may be more inclined to adopt the racial identity of the neighborhood. Consider multiracial individuals from Black/White unions; regardless of their physical appearance, they were identified as Black and lived in the Black community because it was the most accepting. While this perception bears some truth, professional school counselors should not automatically assume that minorities are always more accepting of multiracial children or believe it is best socially or psychologically for them to live in a neighborhood reflecting the minority parent. According to Buttery (1987) and Dhooper (2003) this is sometimes a difficult issue for both the minority and majority communities.

4. McRoy and Zurcher (1983) encouraged multiracial families to have frequent contact and social interactions with racially diverse organizations and institutions. Frequent contact with diverse groups and organizations allows people from all racial backgrounds the opportunity to form more realistic perceptions of each other.

5. Multiracial children are encouraged to avoid forming stereotypical attitudes toward other racial, ethnic, and culturally diverse groups. Parents are role models for their children, and if they have prejudicial attitudes that they are unaware of, their children may be influenced as well. Just because two people are in an interracial relationship does not mean they have resolved all of their issues concerning race. Winn and Priest (1993) discovered in their study that multiracial children consistently expressed the belief that their parents had not sufficiently prepared them to deal with prejudice and racism. They also believed they were experienced negatively by White society and experienced prejudice from their parent's minority culture as well.

6. McRoy and Zurcher (1983) suggested that the family identify itself as a multiracial unit, based upon the integration of the five previous recommendations.

Professional school counselors must understand the role of one's physical appearance and its impact on multiracial students. Some multiracial students who are a combination of Native American and some other race may worry they do not look Native American enough to claim it. In addition, multiracial youth of African American and some other race display similar views. Many visibly wear their African American heritage, yet other parts of their background are not always seen in their appearance or formally acknowledged. Multiracial students, particularly in high school, are generally aware of their physical appearance and how others perceive them. In this way, their appearance can influences how they self-identify (Lopez, 2004). Root (1998) discovered multiracial females endured more ridicule and rejection because of their appearance than multiracial males for body size, hair texture, hairstyles, hair color, bust size, eye shape, and eye color. Such experiences potentially reinforce feelings of "not belonging." Because schools are one of the most important social environments for acceptance and rejection, professional school counselors must recognize the impact of physical appearance when working with multiracial students.

Teachers, administrators, and other support personnel may have more contact with multiracial students than some professional school counselors. Wehrly, Kenney, and Kenney (1999) encouraged professional school counselors to help educators become more culturally competent through training and in-service workshops. Some of this training should specifically include information on knowledge and skills needed to work with multiracial students and other children raised in multiracial families. Apparently, this type of training may still be needed, because in 1994, the principal of Randolph County High School, located in eastern Alabama, threatened to cancel the school prom when he discovered that some students had intentions of bringing a date of a different race to the event. One multiracial student felt the principal's views were biased against interracial dating and when she asked whom she was supposed to take to the prom, the principal indicated that her multiracial heritage was a problem. The principal further stated that her parents had made a mistake producing a multiracial child and he was trying to prevent other students from making the same mistake. The parents of the student filed a lawsuit, and the case was settled out of court. The remarks highlighted some of the difficulties that multiracial children experience, reflecting racial division in the schools (Steele, 1995) and the need for diversity training. Harris (2002) noted professional school counselors who worked in schools that actively promoted cultural diversity and awareness programs held more accurate perceptions about multiracial individuals and their families.

Professional schools counselors are also encouraged to increase their knowledge concerning identity development when assessing multiracial students. More recent models proposed by Kerwin and Ponterotto (1995), Poston (1990), and Rockquemore and Brunsma (2002) offer more accurate concepts of identity development for multiracial individuals than previous models. Regardless of which group multiracial students choose to identify with publicly, conflicts may exist over how they privately identify themselves (Chiong, 1998). Also, when consulting with parents of multiracial students it is helpful for professional school counselors to provide support and understanding. It might be beneficial to know the racial or ethnic background of each parent because certain combinations of multiracial offspring experience differential acceptance levels in different communities. Black/White multiracial persons are more racially polarized by society and likely to experience greater challenges in dealing with both communities (Chiong, 1998; Dhooper, 2003). Professional school counselors should also sensitively explore how the parents view their child's racial identity at home, how they would like to see their child's racial identity incorporated in the school, the level of involvement of the extended family, the racial make-up of the family neighborhood, socioeconomic status of the family, and the types of coping skills they provide to their multiracial children for dealing with issues concerning prejudice and racism (McRoy & Freeman, 1986).

In counseling situations, professional school counselors should be aware of themes which may arise for multiracial children, including uniqueness, physical appearance, acceptance and belonging, and self-esteem (Root, 1994). Furthermore, professional school counselors are encouraged to take into consideration the developmental age of multiracial children. While role playing, art therapy, and music therapy are appropriate therapeutic tools, multiracial students from pre-K through elementary age may be best suited for play therapy. Play therapy is a form of counseling that allows children to demonstrate what they are experiencing through play. When working with adolescents, counselors must be able to tell the difference between typical adolescent behaviors and behaviors resulting from their multiracial heritage (Gibbs & Moskowitz-Sweet, 1991). During counseling sessions, if multiracial clients display negative behaviors because of racial and ethnic factors, they must be allowed to act out or verbalize their feeling in a safe environment.

Professional school counselors should genuinely explore how multiracial students feel about their identity and realize that, for some multiracial adolescents, how others perceive them in society may influence how they identify themselves racially (Lopez, 2004). In addition, professional school counselors should (a) strive to build a trusting relationship with multiracial students who are sensitive to racial factors; (b) help multiracial students explore multiple sides of their heritage; (c) help multiracial students see the connection (if any) between the presenting issue and their multiracial heritage; (c) involve the family and community resources when necessary (Dhooper, 2003); and (d) share with parents of multiracial students and school teachers information on appropriate multiracial resources (see Table 82.1) and school activities, such as those included in the curriculum titled "Serving Children in Biracial/Biethnic Families" (Gerstenblatt, 2000).

SUMMARY/CONCLUSION

Multiracial students need and deserve broader support from schools and communities; however, before this support becomes a reality, the way society perceives and classifies multiracial students must also change. The possibility of this change occurring increases only after professional school counselors, teachers, administrators, and communities become more aware of some of the unique issues faced by multiracial students (Chiong, 1998). Professional school counselors are in a unique position to become advocates for multiracial students, and while they have developmental and learning needs similar to those of single-race children, they also encounter unique challenges because of their heritage, which represents a visible symbol of society's racial divisions. Professional school counselors must beware of the challenges encountered by multiracial students and their families and strive to become social change agents for this growing population.

(Note: See the CD-ROM for a list of references.)

Table 82.1

List of Resources Supporting Multiracial Population

Association of Multiethnic Americans (founded 1988)

www.ameasite.org

Represents America's multiracial, multiethnic community

Mavin Foundation (founded 1998)

www.mavinfoundation.org

A nonprofit organization that empowers multiracial, multiethnic, and transracially adopted youth, families, and communities

The Multiethnic Education Program

www.multiethniceducation.org/index.html

A project of the International Child Resource Institute

My People Are... Youth Pride in Mixed Heritage Film, Action Booklet & Peer to Peer Training.

www.multiethniceducation.org/publications.html

A powerful new resource for classrooms and families

Project RACE (founded 1991)

www.projectrace.com

Nonprofit organization responsible for advocating for multiracial children and adults

Serving Biracial and Multiethnic Children and Their Families (founded 2003)

www.multiethniceducation.org/publications.html

Teaching Tolerance

www.tolerance.org/about/index.html

Provides educators with free educational materials that promote respect for differences and appreciation of diversity in the classroom and beyond

CHAPTER 83

THE SPECIAL NEEDS OF BOYS

Margaret A. King and Gregory R. Janson

Preview

There are significant differences in the school experiences of boys and girls, particularly in primary school classrooms. Many boys lag behind girls in literacy and academic achievement and are often retained in grade. Boys are more frequently referred for behavioral issues and are more severely disciplined, often to the point of exclusion, humiliation, and ridicule. These differences are often due to boys' unique developmental differences, which need to be taken into account by teachers and counselors. Professional school counselors can advocate for the special needs of boys by raising awareness, understanding differences, and facilitating interventions that consider those differences.

Professional school counselors routinely help children maneuver through the challenges posed by the daily demands of schooling. As children negotiate the pressures of peer relationships, academic achievement, and self-regulation during the course of their school day, the professional school counselor is a caring, reliable voice that children can depend on for affirmation and support. Beyond supporting children one-to-one, professional school counselors are in a unique position to raise awareness and facilitate systemic change when a specific need is identified. Boys, especially young boys, need advocacy and support from the professional school counselor.

Boys as a group are not doing well in school, and for many young boys, the day-to-day challenges of schooling often lead to behavioral problems, low academic achievement, and failure (Kindlon & Thompson 1999; Pollack, 1998; Sax, 2005). Professional school counselors can improve the daily experiences of these boys by working with them one-on-one and in small groups as well as seeking the support of other professionals in the system to change the culture of the school so that teachers and administrators better understand and respond to the special needs of boys. In this chapter we focus on the issues that affect boys' behavior and strategies that school counselors can use to raise awareness of the issues and improve the experiences of boys in school.

BOYS' BEHAVIOR

There is a difference in the way girls and boys go through the school day and the academic year, with boys' behavior and achievement lagging behind on average. Boys receive the majority of disciplinary actions from teachers and administrators and are more likely than girls to be expelled or suspended from school. Boys receive the majority of *D*s and *F*s and are more likely than their female peers to repeat a grade or drop out of school. The factors underlying these statistics are complex and involve academic, socioemotional, and biological issues (Blum, 1997; Kindlon & Thompson 1999; Pollack, 1998; Sax, 2005).

ACADEMICS

The introduction of boys to formal schooling is often difficult because of the emphasis on oral and written language skills (Kindlon & Thompson, 1999; Pollack, 1998; Sax, 2005). Boys who are developing appropriately may still be 1 to 2 years behind girls, and, for some boys, this delay may continue throughout their schooling. The delay boys experience at the beginning of their academic experiences may subsequently turn into a crippling deficit because the approach used to teach literacy skills often is not consistent with the developmental needs of boys. This is particularly true if the curriculum materials reflect the view that many boys have of literacy—that reading and literacy are feminine activities—and they are far less likely to respond or participate (Blair & Sanford, 2004; Millard, 1997).

Many boys who are referred to the professional school counselor because of problems with behavioral or social–emotional issues and low academic achievement are subsequently screened for learning disabilities or disorders of childhood, such as attention-deficit/hyperactivity disorder (ADHD). These boys may be referred to counselors for their academic and behavioral problems yet may be experiencing these problems as a result of normal growth and development. Although counselors may not be curriculum experts, they may be able to help teachers and administrators better understand the nexus of academic instruction and boys' development. This is an important prerequisite to effective interventions.

When boys' performance and behavior appear in conjunction with a delay in early literacy skills, they are frequently labeled as having learning disabilities. Such a disability—or even just the label—can affect boys' ability to develop the most basic skills of reading, writing, arithmetic, or a combination of the three. The information processing systems of children with learning disabilities do not work well, impairing their ability to master the academic tasks set before them (Martino, 2003). However, if the delay is due to developmental factors, disability interventions may be both inappropriate and ineffective. An approach that takes the developmental progress of each child into account is needed so that appropriate accommodations can be made. Professional school counselors can help teachers learn about appropriate accommodations; without them, these children are left behind, whether the issue is disability or developmental.

Boys are also more likely than girls to have hearing and auditory processing problems. Boys do not hear as well as girls and often have difficulty processing what they hear (House of Representatives Standing Committee on Education and Training, 2002; Rowe, Pollard, & Rowe, 2005; Sax, 2005). Participation in the classroom culture is sometimes difficult for boys because they do not hear or understand what their teachers or peers are saying to them. Additionally, boys typically have slower processing times. Consider the following case involving Robert.

Robert, who is in fifth grade, never seems to complete his work. As is common practice, his teacher often gives multistep oral directions and believes that if Robert paid closer attention, he would be able to complete his work. In fact, Robert *is* paying attention but hears only the initial instructions the teacher made and is still processing that information after the teacher has completed all the instructions. Robert has learned not to ask the teacher to repeat the instructions because he will only be reprimanded for not listening. As the pattern repeats itself over time, Robert learns that he cannot meet the teacher's expectations and that he has no other recourse or source of help. He simply withdraws.

Boys routinely seem unable to follow directions or complete tasks because they are not listening. What appears to be inattention may actually be an inability to hear or efficiently and quickly process and understand the directions. When children cannot hear or see well, they rarely say so; therefore, it should also be noted that hearing and vision screenings are essential for young children.

These are some of the academic and biological differences that affect the success or failure of boys in school. In addition to academic differences, there are also differences in behavior that affect the schooling experiences of boys.

BEHAVIOR

Boys' behaviors are powerful predictors of whether they will be successful in school. Many boys are active, loud, and inattentive, a trio of behaviors which often elicit negative reactions from teachers. Over time, their behavior can lead to mental health diagnoses such as ADHD. Consider the case of Robert.

> Robert is in kindergarten. He spends most of his day sitting and completing worksheets, but he never seems to finish more than one or two a day. The other children complete four or five in the time it takes Robert to complete his name on the first sheet. He is constantly playing with things in his desk, getting out of his seat, sharpening his pencil, and tapping other students on the head. In the afternoon, he becomes more inattentive because he often misses recess to finish his work. Robert becomes a candidate for a referral.

Even though there are legitimate cases of ADHD, it is overdiagnosed in boys (Kindlon & Thompson 1999; Pollack, 1998). It may simply be that Robert needs an active and engaging learning environment rather than sitting at his desk completing worksheets all day. In addition, Robert needs an opportunity to participate in recess. Recess provides a physical break from the constraints of the classroom and stimulates creative and social interactions (Pellegrini & Bohn, 2005; National Association for Sport and Physical Education, 2001; National Association of Early Childhood Specialists in State Departments of Education, 2002).

Boys are also physically active and aggressive, often receiving social reinforcement for these behaviors since they conform to gender type and the perception that such children are just "all boy." However, this confirmation can put boys in a double bind, because these behaviors are not prized in classrooms. Boys also use physical movements to communicate play, affection, and anger, leaving many teachers confused about what boys are communicating when they use physical movements. Consider the following example.

> John and Sam, who are in first grade, are pushing and shoving in line as the group prepares to go outside. The teacher immediately reprimands the boys, and when the shoving and pushing does not stop, she takes away recess. Sam and John do not understand why the

teacher is upset, because they were just playing and showing how much they like each other. A similar situation occurred with David, a kindergartener, who came running out of the bathroom and ran into his teacher. His teacher became very upset and placed him in time-out. David is very confused because he was just showing the teacher that he liked her.

These are examples of developmentally appropriate and predictable rough and tumble play (Pellegrini, 1988; Pellegrini & Smith, 1998; Reed & Brown, 2002) as well as a demonstration of action love that is characteristic of boys' behavior (Pollack, 1998).

James, a third grader, has outbursts of anger. On one occasion, James did not finish his homework. The teacher started to tell him how he never completes his assignments and that he needs to take responsibility for his work or he will be held back a grade at the end of the school year. Other children stood by, watching. Suddenly, James appeared to "lose it" and started to yell at the teacher and kick the other children. The teacher immediately sent James to the principal's office. He was suspended from school for 3 days. James was embarrassed and hurt but had no way to say to the teacher, "Don't tell me I am bad in front of my classmates."

Teachers often confuse boys' behaviors with the real motivations underlying the behavior. Over the years, James developed this strategy as a way to protect himself from the feelings he experienced as a result of shame, embarrassment, and hurt. Suspending James serves no legitimate purpose and separates him from the environment within which he needs to learn self-regulation and manage negativity in relationships.

Like James, many boys often display oppositional behavior when they are at a loss as of how to deal with a challenging situation. They refuse to conform to group rules, complete assignments when they are due, or respond to teachers' request.

Kenny is in sixth grade. The class has decided to make cards for a special day to recognize their parents or caregivers. All children in the class are required to participate. Kenny refuses to make a card. The teacher reminds him. He continues to refuse to participate. The teacher knows that Kenny lives with his grandparents and that his mother is in jail and that his father seldom visits. The teacher acknowledged at the beginning of the assignment that children could do a card for the person who cares for them, a grandparent, aunt, uncle, or stepparent. Even though Kenny understood the assignment, he did not want to make a card. The teacher would not change the assignment for Kenny. He became very oppositional and was finally asked to leave the classroom.

For Kenny, thinking of his mother in jail and having to make a card for his grandparents was very painful, even though they were his primary caregivers. Many such children, and others in foster care, would find the act of making the card for their mother too painful. The alternative—to substitute someone else—would constitute an intolerable act of disloyalty. The way Kenny responded to his pain was to defy the teacher, a form of psychological displacement often used by adults as well as children. Most mental health professionals would find Kenny's behavior understandable and appropriate, given his age, developmental stage, and traumatic experiences with the loss of his mother. In situations such as this, planned peer consultation and discussion can help teachers to better understand boys' needs and brainstorm creative and effective responses.

COMMUNICATING WITH BOYS

Boys often have trouble communicating their needs and abilities to teachers and administrators. In part, this may be because the vast majority of teachers (over 90%) are female. Overstructured and understructured schooling environments may be a contributing factor; both are detrimental to boys. Sometimes the discipline of choice is to shame and embarrass children into compliance (Newberger, 1999; Pollack, 1998). Sometimes the emphasis of schooling is on the needs of the group rather than on the needs of the few, or the one. Regardless of why boys lag behind their female peers, we must change the way we communicate with boys and create learning environments that allow them to grow and develop into healthy adults and lifelong learners. Professional school counselors, with their strong background in human development and relationship building, have the training and professional endorsement needed to work with teachers and administrators to identify and implement appropriate strategies.

If boys are to do well in school, educators must begin to understand them and develop strategies for meeting their needs in a manner that communicates personal warmth, inclusion, and affirmation. How can teachers enable boys to use their strengths? What do we do with boys who are active and aggressive or who are slow at processing information? What do we do with boys who are oppositional or who have trouble following directions? How do we balance the needs of a traumatized child against the needs of the group? What strategies should professional school counselors use to respond to the issues boys face when interacting with the schooling environment?

FIVE WAYS PROFESSIONAL SCHOOL COUNSELORS CAN HELP

What can professional school counselors do to help boys succeed in school? Professional school counselors should work collaboratively with teachers and administrators using the following strategies.

ASSIST SCHOOL PERSONNEL IN ACKNOWLEDGING THAT THERE ARE SIGNIFICANT DEVELOPMENTAL DIFFERENCES BETWEEN YOUNG BOYS AND GIRLS

Awareness and recognition of the developmental differences between boys and girls is important to choosing how to handle boys' behavior. These are *differences*, not *deficits*. Boys are more likely to respond to the schooling environment if school personnel understand that long-established approaches to instruction may not be consistent with the way boys learn. Literacy is one example of those differences. Good literacy skills are crucial to school success, but boys tend to respond to literacy differently than girls. Boys need to have experiences with multiple forms of literacy, and literacy needs to be integrated throughout the curriculum. Otherwise, boys will not feel successful. They will be less engaged in the learning that occurs in school, and they will be less likely to develop a love of reading that will serve them well. Boys are more likely to engage in literacy experiences when provided with opportunities to do the following:

- Acquire and use materials for reading and writing that contain information that speaks to boys' interests
- Read nonfiction, including informational books, how-to books, instruction manuals, and newspapers
- Read nontraditional school materials such as comics and graphic novels
- Use technology for recording and writing
- Focus on the content of boys' writing rather than their handwriting
- See male role models reading and writing

Another example of how boys and girls differ is in the way they process information. Many boys have information or auditory processing problems. Processing problems often mean that boys may be slower at responding to requests, following directions, and completing assignments. Educators should take the following steps:

- State directions and requests slowly and loudly
- Repeat directions and requests often
- Allow extra time for boys to respond to directions and requests
- Provide extra time for boys (or all students) to complete assignments
- Assign fewer worksheets and less seatwork
- Provide direct assistance to individual boys who have the most difficulty following directions and completing assignments

CREATE A HUMANE APPROACH TO DISCIPLINE

The professional school counselor has an opportunity to model appropriate discipline techniques and should work with school personnel to create a caring, supportive, and helpful approach to educational discipline. All children, especially boys, need discipline that involves teaching appropriates way to behave while affirming the child (Landreth, 2002). Discipline should not shame, humiliate, scorn, denigrate or exclude; it should not be harsh in nature (Pollack, 1998). Boys tend to avoid and distrust adults who harshly or unfairly punish them (Newberger, 1999).

Boys also have difficulty describing their feelings. Their responses to shame and pain may be a display of anger, disrespect, and aggression that is then met with escalating hostility from the adult. As a result, many adults discipline boys more harshly than necessary (Newberger, 1999). Changing this cycle of negative responses from boys and harsh discipline from adults is essential. Strategies that support humane approaches to discipline suggest that adults engage in the following:

- Maintain self-control and a calm demeanor when interacting with boys
- Never attack or demean the child's sense of self or personality
- Focus on teaching rather than on punishment
- Respect the child's dignity by talking with boys about their behavior in private
- Use fair discipline practices
- Offer nurturing, caring, and personal warmth
- Support rather than shame or humiliate
- Negotiate rather than force compliance

- Follow through, and keep your word
- Set clear and age-appropriate limits rather than threaten

By using humane and reasonable approaches to discipline, boys are more likely to learn how to behave appropriately because they are more likely to develop respect for the adults who are implementing the discipline. Most important, it is when limits are pushed or exceeded that the greatest learning takes place within relationships. This is a place where professional school counselors can help teachers design interventions. The most effective response teachers can make to a student in distress who is acting out is to calmly acknowledge the needs expressed, communicate understanding of the child's emotions and the motivations beneath the behavior and target more acceptable choices and alternatives (Landreth, 2002).

WORK WITH THE SCHOOL LIBRARIAN TO ESTABLISH A RESOURCE AREA IN THE SCHOOL

The professional school counselor can work with the school librarian to develop resources that could be shared by school personnel and parents. Resources could include books, articles, Web sites, video and audiotapes, and other information that would be useful in helping adults understand boys better. A few resources to begin with include the following:

- David Booth (2002). *Even Hockey Players Read: Boys, Literacy, and Learning*
- Michael Gurian and Kathy Stevens (2005). *The Minds of Boys: Saving Our Sons From Falling Behind in School and Life*
- Dan Kindlon and Michael Thompson (1999). *Raising Cain: Protecting The Emotional Life of Boys*
- Lucinda Neall (2002). *Bringing the Best Out In Boys: Communication Strategies for Teachers*
- Eli Newberger (1999). *The Men They Will Become: The Nature and Nurture of Male Character*
- William Pollack (1998). *Real Boys: Rescuing Our Sons From the Myths of Boyhood*
- Leonard Sax (2005). *Why Gender Matters: What Parents and Teachers Need to Know About the Emerging Science of Sex Differences*

SHARING INFORMATION THROUGH MEETINGS AND WORKSHOPS

The professional school counselor is in a position to share information with colleagues through informal meetings, study groups, and scheduled workshops. Study groups have become a wonderful way for teachers to study a topic and to work collaboratively to improve and change practices. The professional school counselor may work with other school personnel to implement a school-wide plan for integrating boy-friendly practices throughout the school. Patience is required—systemic change of this nature does not happen overnight and needs time to take hold.

ADVOCATING FOR THE NEEDS OF BOYS AT THE LOCAL, STATE, AND NATIONAL LEVELS

Acquiring information about boys and sharing the information with local school personnel and parents as well as community, civic, and professional organizations is the first step toward changing the world of boys for the better. The professional school counselor can also work with professional organizations, community, and civic groups to create awareness of the needs of boys. Through local media, the professional school counselor can advocate for improving the lives of boys in the community. Creating awareness is the first step towards creating an environment of affirmation and advocacy.

SUMMARY/CONCLUSION

Many boys enter school at a distinct developmental disadvantage when compared to their female peers. Curriculum favors verbal expressions of intelligence rather than the visual–spatial abilities characteristic of many boys' intelligence (Miyake, Friedman, Rettinger, Shah, & Hegarty, 2001), and a large numbers of boys begin school developmentally a year or two behind their female peers. Teachers often perceive boys' behavior as oppositional, defiant or noncompliant when, in reality, boys' reactions may be due to differences in their approach to their environment. Boys are often loud and aggressive, fail to hear or understand instructions, and typically demonstrate a defiant, gender-socialized reaction to behavioral discipline approaches that rely on scorn, ridicule or humiliation. These characteristics often elicit a pattern of negative responses over time from school personnel. The long-term negative effects of this disparity include psychological and academic deficits, a failure identity in school, reduced self-esteem and lost potential. With minimal resources, professional school counselors can advocate for the special needs of boys by helping teachers and administrators understand the very real differences between boys and girls, and providing alternative approaches that ensure the inclusion, affirmation, and valuing of every student.

(Note: See the CD-ROM for a list of references.)

CHAPTER 84

EMOTIONAL SAFETY IN THE CLASSROOM: THE PROFESSIONAL SCHOOL COUNSELOR'S ROLE

Gregory R. Janson and Margaret A. King

Preview

Emotional security in the classroom is vital to students' positive growth and development, yet classrooms may become emotionally dangerous when sanctioned behavioral management practices lead to a repetitive pattern of negative interactions between teachers and students. Younger children in elementary school classrooms may be at the greatest risk for this type of emotional maltreatment, which is largely unrecognized by teachers. This chapter discusses the effects of emotional maltreatment in school settings and presents professional school counselors with preventive strategies to raise awareness of the issues and improve the emotional lives of students.

Research has established that an affirming relationship between teachers and students creates a safe environment that is conducive to academic achievement and students' positive growth and development (Hamre & Pianta, 2005). Conversely, that same relationship can interfere with learning and development when exchanges between teacher and student are characterized by negative interactions. The damage done by these negative relationships is often unintentional and almost invisible to the teacher, since the basis of the exchange is frequently embedded in sanctioned behavior management practices. These practices pose a serious threat to students' cognitive development and mental and emotional well-being when they become part of the culture of the classroom (Garbarino, 1987; Shumba, 2002a). For some students, the culture of the classroom becomes so negative that the interactions between the teacher and the student escalate to the level of emotional maltreatment and qualify as a form of child abuse (Garbarino, 1979; Janson & King, 2006; Krugman & Krugman, 1984; O'Hagan, 1993). In these situations, the student is seldom recognized as a victim, but instead becomes the "identified patient."

In practice, teachers believe that emotional maltreatment is harmful to children, but tend not to recognize it when they see it (Shumba, 2002b). Instead, most teachers believe that the perpetrators of emotional maltreatment are parents (O'Hagan, 1995) and are unaware of the role that they, as teachers, may play in creating schooling environments that are emotionally unsafe for children. Behavioral strategies that may constitute emotional maltreatment include singling out individual children to criticize or punish, threatening children with the loss of recess if they fail to complete all of their work, isolating children through the excessive use of timeouts or punitively seating them away from the group, modeling inappropriate behaviors and a lack of self-control (such as yelling or screaming at children who do not act appropriately), and failing to show unconditional positive regard for every student. These strategies are commonly employed in the name of classroom management or discipline, and when conceptualized as such, make it difficult for teachers to recognize the element of emotional maltreatment implicit in the interactions. Some researchers have described this dynamic as a form of hidden trauma or bullying (Olweus, 1996; Twemlow, Fonaby, Sacco, & Brethour, 2006). The picture is further complicated because victims are unlikely to complain. Younger children are doubly at risk because they are most likely to be maltreated by teachers and staff (Benbenishty, Zeira, Astor, & Khoury-Kassabri, 2002) as well as bullied by peers (Smith, Madsen, & Moody, 1999). They are also least likely to recognize emotional maltreatment because they so often see these strategies as appropriate discipline and believe that teachers have the absolute right to punish any child who is not complying with group rules. Many children may also believe that they deserve to receive this kind of discipline because it is the type of discipline that is used in their homes. Older children and adolescents may see teachers' discipline strategies as unfair and object to them, but they may still fail to recognize them as emotional maltreatment. Teachers of younger children may also be more isolated than teachers at the high school level, because adolescents interact with many different teachers while younger children tend to remain in a single classroom.

Emotional maltreatment has serious consequences for students' physical health as well as their psychological well-being. Students who experience emotional maltreatment by school personnel may display the same range of symptoms and behaviors as those who experience more overt and dramatic forms of interpersonal violence such as peer-on-peer bullying and community violence. These negative effects include problems with behavior (both acting out and inwardly directed anxiety and depression), emotional adjustment, school avoidance, self-esteem, personality development and academic accomplishment (Geiger & Fischer, 2006; Kairys, Johnson, & Committee on Child Abuse and Neglect, 2002). Somatic symptoms such as stomachaches, headaches, asthmatic attacks, bowel upsets, respiratory ailments and other stress-related illnesses are common. Equally important, when a student cannot rely on his or her teacher to be emotionally safe, that student loses the single-most important human resource outside the home: a trusted teacher (Doyle, 1997, 2003). Without that source of support, reassurance and validation, students living dangerous lives outside of school may have nowhere to turn.

Even though teachers and administrators are highly trained, licensed professionals, they may have difficulty understanding emotional maltreatment and how to prevent it. They may not have adequate training and experience in guidance strategies that rely on the relationship between teacher and student to effect change as opposed to behavioral strategies that rely on the teacher's superior size, power, and authority to enforce compliance. On the other hand, professional school counselors have the training, credibility, and professional mandate to consult regarding behavior management and to counter the negative effects of emotional maltreatment, not just through their one-on-one work with students but through education and prevention that ensures both the physical and emotional safety of students. Through a process of assessment, raised awareness, prevention, and intervention, professional school counselors can support educators and administrators and make schools safer, more affirming, student-centered environments that enhance the positive growth and development of every student.

IS YOUR SCHOOL A SAFE SCHOOL?

Safe schools are environments where children *feel* safe, both physically and psychologically. This makes the prime question: Is your school a safe school? Such a question can be threatening to school personnel, so it makes sense to begin with a low-key approach that perhaps addresses groups of teachers, administrators, and staff separately as part of a wider initiative on school climate. Sitting down with small groups of teachers may be the best place to begin any kind of assessment, and talking about the school as a whole may be a less threatening way to initiate a dialog than focusing on individuals' behavior or even self-reflection. Later, as comfort levels rise and defensiveness is less of an issue, a more self-reflective/self-evaluative approach can be considered. Once a sufficient degree of trust and safety is established, administrators and teachers can be invited to joint discussions. Being sensitive to the power dynamics of your school and how well teachers relate to each other and to administrators and staff is essential to a positive outcome.

Initial questions can be simple: Is our school a safe haven for the students who come here? Do you feel students look forward to coming to school? Are there students who regard school with dreadful anticipation? Why? Who are they and how might we help them? Do our students see us as reliable, predictable adults who can be counted on to provide support as well as instruction? How do we know? How might we do better?

PHYSICAL SAFETY

When most educators and parents sit down to talk about a "safe school," they generally talk about the physical safety of children, and it is likely that this is where your own discussions would begin. Physical safety is far easier to gauge than psychological safety because it is measured using observable, external factors: (a) making sure the physical environment of the school is safe and (b) implementing disciplinary policies and procedures to deal with attendance, drugs, alcohol, weapons, fighting and student conduct. Unfortunately, schools that pride themselves on safety often promote zero tolerance for prohibited behaviors; harsh suspension and expulsion policies; and security procedures that can include metal detectors, security officers, and identification cards. While adults may feel safer with metal detectors and harsh disciplinary policies, many of these procedures have the opposite effect on students. They create alarm, serving as constant, fearful reminders that danger is ever present. This reduces students' sense of responsibility and community, and creates a low-grade, persistent level of emotional turmoil and uncertainty. Harsh disciplinary procedures can also lead to alienation and disrupted relationships as well as a siege mentality (Hyman & Snook, 1999) as opposed to an educational discipline approach that stresses relationships, structures consequences that encourage responsibility, and provides opportunities for students to remain engaged with their peers, the school, and the teacher (King, 2004). The tone and timber of these policies and procedures have a significant influence on the degree of affirmation and emotional security that students feel.

The corporal punishment of children through paddling or other physical means is presently legal in 22 states and represents a major form of child assault that remains unrecognized by many parents and educators. The United Nations Convention on the

Rights of the Child (1989) requires educators and schools to respect the dignity and physical person of the child and specifically forbids corporal punishment in schools. This may be one of the reasons that only two of the 194 member nations have failed to ratify the Convention. One nation is Somalia, which lacks a recognized government. The other is the United States. If your school practices corporal punishment, it is a place to begin.

In settings where corporal punishment is illegal or is not used, school personnel may employ closely related disciplinary actions that are physical in nature and that have the same negative effects as corporal punishment. These actions include pushing, shoving, grabbing, "propelling" a student (grabbing an arm or an elbow and propelling the student from one place to another), throwing things, and intimidation through non-verbal gestures and expressions that are based on physicality and power. These are all forms of emotional maltreatment. Regardless of how free from physical harm a child may be, the relationship between physical safety and psychological safety is deeply intertwined. Environments that are both secure and stable depend on trust, warmth and affirmation, not just physical safety. Discussions should center not only on whether children feel safe *in their person* but *emotionally safe* as well. Do existing policies and procedures at your school foster a sense of safety, inclusion, and well-being?

EMOTIONAL SECURITY: STICKS AND STONES WILL BREAK MY BONES, BUT NAMES WILL NEVER HURT ME

Research on children's emotional and social development concludes that name-calling does hurt children and adolescents, often affecting them as powerfully as "sticks and stones" and playing a key role in rising levels of school violence (Astor, Benbenishty, Zeira, & Vinokur, 2002; Garbarino & Delara, 2002; Geiger & Fischer, 2006; Jenson & Howard, 1999; Olweus, 1993). School personnel might need to initially discuss their beliefs regarding corporal punishment, emotional maltreatment, discipline and the nature of children. Subsequent conversations should focus on (a) how to recognize emotional maltreatment and (b) how to create emotional security for children. Adolescents are often victims of emotional maltreatment in schools; however, the younger the student, the greater the risk, suggesting that professional school counselors focus their initial efforts on younger students.

EMOTIONAL MALTREATMENT: HOW DO WE RECOGNIZE IT?

Emotional maltreatment is a form of child abuse defined as a repeated pattern of damaging interactions between children and adults (Kairys et al., 2002; O'Hagan, 1995). The behaviors associated with emotional maltreatment include shaming, rejecting, isolating, ignoring, terrorizing, and corrupting (Griffith & Zigler, 2002; Shone & Parada, 2005). These interactions frequently occur in schools as well as in homes, with research suggesting that emotional and verbal abuse in schools occurs most frequently as a result of interactions between teachers and students (Hyman & Snook, 1999). This may be a surprise to many teachers who view themselves as mandated reporters of child abuse but assume that "accepted practice" means that disciplinary practices cannot be abusive. A quiet classroom that appears ordered and disciplined may well be a place where desperate children are too terrified to do anything but sit and comply with the teacher's instructions (Krugman & Krugman, 1984). Consider the following cases.

> John, age 5, is often isolated from his classmates because he frequently speaks out of turn. His teacher repeatedly states to the whole class that when John can control his tongue, he will be able to join the group. When John's behavior does not improve, he is moved farther and farther away from the group. John spends most of his kindergarten year in isolation, does not acquire the necessary skills to successfully complete kindergarten and is retained in grade.

> Sara, a third grader, is obese. The other children in her class will not play with her and call her names. When Sara complains to her teacher, she is told that if she didn't eat so much and wasn't so fat she would have friends. When Sara's parents attempt to intervene, the teacher uses information she has gathered on childhood obesity as the reason for her response and reminds the parents that they should not allow Sara to eat so much. The taunting continues with no intervention from the teacher.

> Robert, a second grader, likes math but does not like to take timed tests. He becomes scared and is unable to focus. He is never able to finish a math test in the designated time. On Tuesday and Thursday, Robert's teacher gives timed tests. Each Tuesday and Thursday, Robert complains of a stomachache before leaving home for school. When the teacher begins the test, Robert begins to cry. The teacher tells Robert to stop acting like a baby, and if he continues she will send him to the preschool classroom.

In each of the preceding situations, the teacher is using a strategy that is institutionalized in many classrooms. In the case of John, a child is isolated from the group because the child is demonstrating behaviors that are either annoying or difficult for the teacher to handle. The isolation may include moving the desk or work space to a corner of the classroom, making the child sit in the hall alone, sending the child to sit in the principal's office, or keeping the child in at recess. In Sara's case, the teacher used information about childhood obesity to justify not intervening when other children were verbally abusing and rejecting Sara. In addition, the teacher used scapegoating and blaming the victim as a technique for rationalizing Sara's situation. If Sara didn't eat so much, she wouldn't be obese and her peers would not reject and humiliate her. Sara's learns that it is her fault and that she deserves the treatment she is receiving. Robert's teacher has inappropriate academic expectations of Robert. She uses name-calling, verbal threats, and public humiliation as a means to gain control and force Robert to change his behavior. The impact of emotional maltreatment, the shaming and humiliation presented in these examples, is not limited to Robert, John and Sara. Bystanders to the abuse of others learn hard lessons that stay with them, negatively affecting their feelings and beliefs about life and relationships long after they have left the classroom (Janson, Carney, Hazler, & Oh, in press; Janson & Hazler, 2004).

Teachers are often insensitive to issues of emotional maltreatment because they are taught to believe that almost any measure is justified to maintain order and to control children. Many teachers, like many parents, may believe that the best way to ensure a child's compliance and obedience is not through guidance and relationship but through shaming, belittling, and humiliating, or with the implicit threat of physical force. They also believe that abuse occurs in the home and not in the school—teachers simply do not believe that they are capable of abuse. Professional school counselors, on the other hand, are familiar with the subtleties of abuse and the multiple facets of emotional maltreatment. As such, they are in a strong position to provide the appropriate guidance and support to teachers to help create emotionally safe classroom environments.

EMOTIONALLY SAFE CLASSROOMS

Research has established that the most successful classrooms are those in which children believe they are valued, included, and emotionally supported (Hamre & Pianta, 2005; Hyson, 2004; Sylwester, 1994). The quality of the student–teacher relationships has a direct bearing not only on the emotional security of the student but on that student's academic performance, sense of self-confidence, self-esteem, and positive growth and personality development (Klem & Connell, 2004). Classrooms should be a place where students can openly express their feelings. In such emotionally secure classroom environments, students learn and grow into socially competent individuals. Strategies used to create this inner security must be based on reflective practice and a personal and ethical commitment to teaching that is characterized by positive teacher–student interactions, personal warmth and affirmation, and unconditional positive regard for children. This does not suggest that negativity can be avoided, but rather that students need to learn how to deal with negativity in relationships and regulate their emotions in a safe environment where they *feel* securely attached to adults who respond to their needs in developmentally appropriate ways (Twemlow, Fonagy, & Sacco, 2002). When children feel as though they belong, and when they can depend on their teachers to be reliable and predictable, they have the best possible opportunity to learn and develop healthy personalities. Through consultation, in-service training, and the facilitation of discussion groups, professional school counselors can assist teachers in creating emotionally safe classrooms in a supportive, nonthreatening manner. The following seven-step process is offered as one model of this type of facilitation, training and discussion.

SEVEN STEPS TOWARD CREATING EMOTIONALLY SAFE CLASSROOMS

Systemic change is needed to create emotionally safe classrooms, and professional school counselors are well-situated to facilitate the necessary dialog and discussion that can lead to greater emotional security for children. The process of systemic change may be slow, and there needs to be buy-in and commitment by the participants. The payoff for patience and a commitment to the principles of affirmation is not just for students, however—emotionally safe classrooms are places where teachers thrive as well. The seven steps to creating emotionally safe classrooms are as follows:

1. *Study, prepare, present:* Examine your own beliefs. Study about safe schools and emotional maltreatment and abuse. As you educate yourself, you will be better able to educate others about the significance of emotional security to learning and the growth and development of healthy, well-adjusted children. Use your knowledge to engage teachers and administrators at your school about emotional maltreatment in schools. Become an expert!

2. *Prioritize:* Make students' emotional security your priority and help to make it a priority in your school. Develop a network of educators in your school who can share information with others at local, state and national meetings and conferences. Write about the issues related to emotional maltreatment in school publications, newspapers, and professional journals. Seek funding for projects to expand the work.

3. *Make time to network and collaborate:* You will need time to discuss these issues, to allow ideas to settle, and to give sufficient opportunity to try new strategies. Brainstorming with colleagues and offering your services for consultation makes managing a difficult student's behavior everyone's concern and helps take the pressure off of individual teachers to "have all the answers." Encourage your school and district to set aside time as a part of the professional development plan to talk about emotional maltreatment in schools and to develop strategies for change. Meet regularly.

4. *Create materials:* Develop handouts, research summaries, tip sheets, worksheets and other resources and materials to help teachers create and implement strategies to support emotionally safe classrooms. Assist teachers in using the materials in their in individual classrooms.

5. *Tap administrators:* Involve school and district administrators in the work. They are in a position to create policy and provide resources to make emotionally safe classrooms a priority. They can also help recruit participants and organize training activities.

6. *Involve parents:* Parents want what is best for their children, so encourage them to participate in the training. Encourage them to communicate with school personnel regarding their views on creating emotionally safe classrooms. Urge them to form parent groups to support the development of emotionally safe schools.

7. *Engage the community:* Raise awareness in the community. Hold meetings and forums where teachers, parents, and community members can interact and identify strategies that can be used in the larger community to promote emotionally safe schools. Seek support from local businesses, libraries, and mental health organizations.

Summary/Conclusion

Professional school counselors can help foster a culture of affirmation and inclusion in their schools by raising awareness of the negative impact of punitive behavioral practices and facilitating discussions that explore self-reflective practices and creative guidance alternatives, thus encouraging the implementation of emotionally safe classrooms. Emotionally safe classrooms are inclusive places where children are valued, affirmed, and accepted by their teachers, even when their behaviors are inappropriate. This secure environment helps children foster a healthy sense of self, learn to effectively self-regulate their behavior, and develop social and academic competence. By using the power of the relationship and the principles of guidance and inclusion, educators will better deal with difficult behaviors and situations without shaming, humiliating, ridiculing, or isolating.

(Note: See the CD-ROM for a list of references.)

CHAPTER 85

COUNSELING CHILDREN OF POVERTY

Donna S. Starkey

Preview

In this chapter, I address the implications of poverty on the lives of children, the measures professional school counselors take to mediate those effects, and the challenges faced when working with children of poverty. The concept of resiliency is discussed along with specific interventions used by professional school counselors working with this population.

Children live in an ever-changing combination of family, environmental, and social systems. As of 2003, estimates indicated that nearly one fifth of American children lived in poverty, and that number includes greater than one half of children living with single mothers (Federal Interagency Forum on Child and Family Statistics, 2006). Poverty has affected families and children as the economy has stagnated, the job climate has offered limited opportunities for lower skilled workers, and access to insurance or other benefits has decreased (Vernon, 2004). Numerous conditions affect children living below the poverty threshold, including inadequate housing, low educational attainment, and limited access to health care.

Poverty, or low socioeconomic status, carries a stigma in modern society. Higher class status in U.S. culture is associated with feelings of power, security and privilege. Families who remain in poverty are often viewed as lazy or inferior by those in higher socioeconomic brackets. In addition to judgments about behavioral or initiative differences, perceived intellect is also linked to class. The poor in our society are regularly stigmatized in school, employment, and other settings as being intellectually inferior.

From a developmental perspective, research has indicated a direct link between poverty and subsequent effects on the developing child. Mothers living in poverty receive fewer prenatal services, have children with higher levels of disability and morbidity, and find their ability to obtain services and opportunities limited by financial constraints (Feerick & Silverman, 2006; Pagani, Boulerice, Vitaro, & Tremblay, 1999). In addition, links existed between poverty and what are often termed *at risk* children, including those with low self-esteem, lower educational aims, and more frequent delinquent behaviors (Walsh, Howard, & Buckley, 1999; Pagani et al., 1999). In essence, counseling children who are poor has inherent implications that are not typical of the overall child and adolescent population.

COUNSELING ISSUES

Children of poverty are often lumped into a category known as at-risk children. But what does *at risk* really mean? The literature defines *at risk* children as those who come from a deprived background; that is, with high rates of poverty and unemployment as well as low rates of educational achievement (Bagley & Pritchard, 1998; Dupper &

Poertner, 1997). Additionally, these children are considered to be "'at-risk' of failing to succeed in life because of the adversities in their young lives" (Rak & Patterson, 1996, p. 368). Children of poverty experience higher rates of "substance abuse, juvenile delinquency, crime and violence, gangs, unsafe sexual practices, teenage pregnancy, single parenthood, limited health care, slum housing, and homelessness" (Dupper & Poertner, 1997, p. 415).

Research has linked the reality of children growing up in poverty with interpersonal, psychosocial, school, and community consequences. The Multicultural Counseling Competencies adopted by the American Counseling Association acknowledge that poverty, along with related socioeconomic status concerns, affect the client and influence the counseling process (Sue, Arrendondo, & McDavis, 1992). Children of poverty are more likely to suffer low self-esteem and self-image. Constant comparison to a middle- or upper class standard of living creates unique feelings of inferiority. Consider a child who lives in a transitional shelter with multiple families and attends school with children who live in single family homes in the surrounding community. Placement in a transitional shelter indicates an unstable housing history, which may not be true for the other children in the school setting. This community-based concern becomes a school concern as multiple moves from home to shelter to other housing affect a child's constancy and stability in a school setting.

Other school-based concerns exist for children who are poor. Children of poverty are more likely to underachieve according to middle-class standards, perform poorly in school, and/or drop out before graduation. They have greater incidences of tardiness and absenteeism. Tardiness and absenteeism are often linked to problems related to health-care access because children who are sick are less likely to go to school. Children who need but cannot afford essential services such as glasses, routine medication, or hearing aids find the simple act of participating in a school environment more frustrating, thus less desirable (Dupper & Poertner, 1997).

In addition, tardiness and absenteeism are linked to family values and beliefs surrounding the importance of education. Family values and behaviors affect the values and behaviors of children. Formal education is often valued less and is less accessible in families of poverty. Because adults in poverty are rarely well educated, they are less likely to value formal education, and their children are therefore less motivated to attend or complete school. Home environments of children living in poverty are not always conducive to the completion of homework, which subsequently affects a child's ability and willingness to attend school (Cross & Burney, 2005). As a result, children who drop out of school are more likely to be involved in the juvenile justice system, be unemployed, become young parents, and continue to live in poverty than are their counterparts who graduate from high school (Dupper & Poertner, 1997).

Delinquency is a prevailing community consequence of poverty. Children who live at or below the poverty level are more likely to become involved in the juvenile court system as they seek ways to achieve status that are in violation of social rules (Pagani et al., 1999). There are higher rates of theft, violence, and substance use in this population. Substandard housing and communities with high rates of crime and violence further contribute to a child's psychosocial and interpersonal concerns. Children who live in poor neighborhoods may not have access to healthy and safe outdoor play areas. Because of increased risk in the community, parents and caregivers may prohibit their children from playing outside or socializing with other neighborhood families; this, in turn, limits social opportunities, and the child's primary source of entertainment becomes a television or video game. Because the ability to communicate, get along with others, and learn social skills is a result of these types of childhood experiences, children of poverty may bring inferior or even maladaptive interpersonal skills to the school environment.

Does poverty cause delinquency or any of the other behaviors or consequences mentioned thus far? Not directly. Regardless, we know that children of poverty are at a greater risk for such problems and that counselors—especially those in a school setting—need to be aware of these possibilities.

INTERVENTIONS

While the impact of poverty on the lives of children is substantial and the consequences potentially severe, research has indicated that some children of poverty are able to avoid its devastating effects; indeed, many are able to thrive. The risk of poverty to children can be mediated or minimized through intervention (Chung, Hawkins, Gilchrist, Hill, & Nagin, 2002). A discussion of the resiliency of children is warranted to address the efficacy of interventions. Resiliency is a child's capacity to persist despite facing obstacles associated with identified risk factors such as poverty (Rak & Patterson, 1996). A number of factors contribute to a student's resiliency including a strong support network of primary and extended family, teachers, mentors, counselors and other competent, committed adults (Hause, 1999; Rak & Patterson, 1996). Professional school counselors are afforded a unique opportunity to promote resiliency in students by being one of these competent adults and by creating a committed support network for the students they serve.

It is clear that a focus on education is primary in addressing children of poverty: "Education, which increases a youth's skills and employment opportunities, is an important route" (Dupper & Poertner, 1997, p. 415) for children of poverty to take to counteract the potential consequences of these identified risks. Professional school counselors historically address the academic, personal, and career needs of the students they serve. They work as a "liaison between teachers, parents, support personnel, and *community* resources to facilitate successful student development" (Campbell & Dahir, 1997, p. 12). With an at-risk population such as children of poverty, the professional school counselor becomes an essential force in providing opportunities that facilitate resiliency and subsequent success.

To reach the students, professional school counselors must first reach the family (Dupper & Poertner, 1997). Families in poverty tend to focus on day-to-day issues to meet the basic survival needs of housing and nutrition. They are less likely to see the relevance in education that has no immediate impact on the families' well-being and lack the resources to connect education to long-term consequences and career potential (Cross & Burney, 2005). Because families of poverty may not value education the same as do families who are not poor,, the task of the professional school counselor is often to educate families about the role of education in advancing the lives of children. Families in poverty are not always aware that education can actually mediate negative outcomes such as delinquency and ongoing poverty.

In addition to educating families, the professional school counselor may be in a position to educate faculty and staff about the role and impact of poverty on students. Counselors can work with faculty to assist their understanding of a student's absences or a seeming lack of ambition in an otherwise academically competent student (Cross & Burney, 2005). Professional school counselors constantly serve as advocates for students and their families, and providing valuable information to the people involved in the lives of children of poverty is a form of that advocacy.

A third area for professional school counselors is to enlighten students to the role of education. Many children of poverty do not enter the educational domain with the middle-class values and aspirations espoused by a school system. By design, school systems expect students to complete a secondary education and then enter into a skilled workforce or postsecondary institution (Cross & Burney, 2005). A primary role of the professional school counselor is college and career preparatory activities. With children of poverty, this role is even more essential, as many of these children lack appropriate family role models related to completing a high school education, considering higher education, and exploring related career opportunities. Vocational choices are often linked to class status, suggesting that professional school counselors are in a position to link children of poverty to resources beyond the minimally skilled or trade occupations that might be expected by others. In fact, professional school counselors may find themselves serving as the only voice of high expectation related to postsecondary educational opportunities (Gillespie & Starkey, 2006).

Another area of influence afforded the professional school counselor is in the development and implementation of wrap-around services; that is, services that include community, family, health, social services, and educational perspectives. Such partnerships ensure greater involvement with at-risk children while distributing the burden for tending to these students' needs since the professional school counselor may not be able to address them all (Bryan, 2005). The involvement of committed networks of supportive and influential adults in the lives of children of poverty serves as a substantial force in mediating negative effects and providing children with the greatest potential for success.

In addition to individual and systemic intervention, professional school counselors are able to form and conduct group counseling opportunities for the students they serve. Children of poverty may feel out of place in a school setting comprised of higher socioeconomic status children. Bringing children together who have experienced similar circumstances, such as children whose families have moved recently or multiple times, can provide a safe opportunity for children of poverty to find their place in the school environment. Building on the concept of resiliency, group opportunities afford children the chance to try out new styles of interacting and shape the social and emotional skills needed for successfully navigating the academic community.

CHALLENGES FOR PROFESSIONAL SCHOOL COUNSELORS

Just as children of poverty face substantial challenges in achieving academic success, breaking the poverty cycle, and growing into well-adjusted, healthy adults, the professional school counselors who work with these students face their own set of challenges.

Counselor training programs are built on research containing inherent middle-class biases, which frequently results in counselors entering the workforce with their own set of biases (Sue et al. 1992). Professional counselors view clients as having greater likelihood for success when they are articulate, educated and interpersonally attractive. As such, some professional school counselors may view clients from low socioeconomic backgrounds as less desirable and less likely to benefit from or succeed in counseling due to differences in communication styles and behaviors.

As in all counseling settings, professional school counselors take care not to impose their own values and beliefs onto their clients. Master's level counselors have invested in substantial education and may carry similar expectations into their work with clients. Such expectations may not match the expectations or abilities of the clients they serve. For example, professional school counselors working in career preparatory activities could find that they link vocational choices to class status as the result of such expectations and biases. Similarly, children of poverty may find themselves uncomfortable working with professional school counselors they view as not being like themselves or of a noticeably different socioeconomic class. Professional school counselors must work to create an inviting presence for clients through an interpersonal and professional presentation that makes clients feel comfortable and is attentive to the diversity of the client population.

Without a doubt, one of the greatest challenges is working within an impoverished social and education system. Children of poverty live in school districts that may be likewise impoverished. This, in turn, affects the resources afforded professional school counselors as well as the number of school counseling positions available to serve the population, resulting in high student-to-counselor ratios (Cross & Burney, 2005). With the American School Counseling Association (2006) reporting the national student counselor ratio average at 488 to 1, professional school counselors in impoverished areas are likely to find themselves with an even higher assigned student population.

Counselors working in any school setting must be creative and flexible in order to provide services. Working with children of poverty is no exception. Because counseling occurs when and where it is needed, professional school counselors may find themselves setting up briefcase offices or rolling offices in order to most effectively bring services to their students. Professional school counselors must be sensitive to the diverse racial and ethnic backgrounds present in children of poverty and ensure that the tools they use to work with clients are reflective of that diversity. This may require multiracial toys and games that better fit the client populations. For example, multiple families of dolls from a variety of ethnic backgrounds allow children of step- and blended families to more closely approximate their own family system in play therapy (Kottman, 2003).

A subtle yet important distinction in working with children of poverty is the use of inclusive language. Professional school counselors attempting to understand a client's home life are better served asking students to draw or talk about where they sleep rather than assuming the children have their own bedrooms. Discussing adults in the home in terms of who takes care of the students is more inclusive than using traditional *mother* and *father* references. Because children of poverty often live in complex and sometimes chaotic family systems (Vernon, 2004), genograms may prove useful in discovering how the system affects the student. Additionally, the use of timelines may help professional school counselors understand the transient history of many children of poverty.

SUMMARY/CONCLUSION

Professional school counselors successfully working with children of poverty are aware of poverty's potentially lasting effects and consequences. Professional school counselors are in the unique position to provide interventions that will help mediate the negative consequences of poverty. Educating school personnel, families, and children is critical to the success of children of poverty. Professional school counselors link children and their families to critical resources through targeted career and postsecondary preparation as well as wrap-around services. An understanding of the biases against children of poverty allows the professional school counselor to act as an advocate for a population that, with intervention, has greater potential to break out of poverty. Professional school counselors are aware of the inherent challenges in this work and plan accordingly to foster the success of the students they serve.

(Note: See the CD-ROM for a list of references.)

CHAPTER 86

HELPING "UNFOCUSED STUDENTS": EDUCATIONAL AND CAREER PLANNING WITH ADOLESCENTS

Suzy Mygatt Wakefield

Preview

I offer insight into the magnitude of the issue of "unfocused kids." These are students who demonstrate an unwillingness or inability to focus on school and understand how their progress and choices while in school contribute to their options after high school. Many influences distract high school students from achieving their potential: distracting peer influence and excessive socializing, long working hours, and/or over-involvement in nonacademic activities. These "unfocused kids" seem to be an American phenomenon, and often, without adequate support, are allowed to follow the path of least resistance.

WHAT IS GOING ON BEHIND THE SCENES TO PRODUCE SO MANY UNFOCUSED KIDS? HIGH SCHOOL DROPOUT RATES: 1 OUT OF 3

The national high school dropout rate in the U.S. was reported to be 30%:

> In today's data-happy era of accountability, testing and No Child Left Behind, here is the most astonishing statistic in the whole field of education: an increasing number of researchers are saying that nearly 1 out of 3 public high school students won't graduate, not just in Shelbyville [near Indianapolis] but around the nation. For Latinos and African Americans, the rate approaches an alarming 50%. (Thornburgh, 2006, p. 32)

Virtually no community, small or large, rural or urban, has escaped the problem.

This has been a relatively unknown statistic until now, due largely to deceptive or flawed reporting practices. For example, the U.S. Census Bureau counts high school graduates as students who have a diploma *or* a General Education Degree (GED). That is deceptive. GED completers are not high school graduates, because to take the GED, a student must have left (i.e., dropped out of) high school.

> Graduation-rate estimates—usually between 85% and 90%—rely only on a couple of questions buried deep within the U.S. Census Bureau's Current Population Survey. The survey asks whether respondents have a diploma or GED. Critics say the census count severely underreports dropout numbers, in part because it doesn't include transients or prisoners—populations with a high proportion of dropouts. (Thornburgh, 2006, p. 33)

To be sure, not all unfocused kids are potential high school dropouts, but they tend to have done very little purposeful thinking about why they are in school or planning for what they want to do with the remainder of their lives. They tend to go through high school without a clear sense of educational focus or purpose. Many do the minimum to stay on track for graduation; although dropout statistics tell us that many students do not even do that (Bylsma & Ireland, 2002; Greene, 2002; Mortenson, 2001; Thornburgh, 2006). They do not appear to connect what they are learning in school with their lives outside of school. Many have apparently lost hope in the value of school (Snyder, Feldman, Shorey, & Rand, 2002). If they do not see value in what they are learning in terms of their personal goals, they appear to expend minimum effort, becoming academic underachievers.

> Two decades ago, a teacher in an average high school in this country could ex-
> pect to have three or four "difficult" students in a class of thirty. Today, teachers
> in these same schools are expected to teach to classrooms in which nearly half
> of the students are uninterested. (Steinberg, 1996, p. 184)

Brophy (1998) described student motivation as "the degree to which students invest attention and effort in various pursuits, which may or may not be the ones desired by their teachers" (p. 3). Not only do unfocused, unmotivated students appear to invest little effort in pursuits having to do with their formal schooling, but they may also show little interest or see little relevance in career guidance activities.

LACK OF ADULT SUPPORT

There might be other reasons why students do not focus on their plans after high school or make little connection to their future. They may come from homes where preoccupied parents or guardians spend little time helping them think through their future plans, let alone take an interest in their grades, friends, and activities. These teens may not feel that anyone really cares; the adults around them may appear to be so busy that they do not take time to sit down with their teens and help them think through their options. Adults often counter that it's the school's responsibility to provide career guidance. As Schneider and Stevenson (1999) pointed out, parents believe that "the major responsibility for helping adolescents select a career path and take the appropriate steps to get there rests with the school" (p. 165). In addition, some teens may be resistant or just indifferent to any efforts adults do offer to help them think about their futures. Teens may be so busy going to school, socializing with friends, participating in after-school activities, and working that they simply have little time to think about their plans and talk with someone else. They may not even think their thoughts about their future are worthy of someone else's time, so they are reluctant to discuss them. If there is no comprehensive career exploration and planning program at the school for all students, the problem is compounded.

CONDITIONS OF STUDENTS' LIVES OUTSIDE THE CLASSROOM

One wonders, when looking in on a typical American classroom, why some students appear focused and purposefully occupied with the teacher and classroom activities, while others seem so unfocused and preoccupied with other issues. They may pass notes to their friends, or stare into space, or simply sleep at their desks. In this country of remarkable opportunity, what is going on? How is it that we have so many adolescents in high school who appear so disengaged and unfocused? Even educators with many years of experience appear to be puzzled about this strange reality.

Steinberg (1996) provided considerable insight as to what is going on behind the scenes. His fundamental premise is that we cannot reform public school education in this country by simply analyzing and revitalizing how teachers teach and what curriculum is taught. Steinberg suggested that it is student motivation and attitude that has changed.

> The achievement problem we face in the country is due not to a drop in the intelligence or basic intellectual capability of our children, but to a widespread decline in children's interest in education and in their motivation to achieve in the classroom; it is a problem of attitude and effort, not ability. . . . Our findings suggest that the sorry state of American student achievement is due more to the conditions of students' lives outside of school than it is to what takes place within school walls. (p. 184)

Steinberg (1996) suggested that the forces on students *outside of school* must be considered, but they usually are not. Based on extensive research involving Temple University, Stanford, and the University of Wisconsin, with 2 years of planning and pilot testing, 4 years of data collection and another 4 years of data analysis, a team of researchers (including psychologists, sociologists, psychiatrists, and educational researchers), studied more than 20,000 teenagers and their families in nine diverse school districts (none were extreme or atypical) in two states (California and Wisconsin) during 1987–1990. The students were not necessarily high risk or exceptional in any way. They were typical of American teens everywhere.

The results of this comprehensive study of outside-of-school variables indicated that many forces may be at play simultaneously in the lives of teens: First, *parenting style* (e.g., authoritarian, permissive, authoritative, disengaged or "checked out") is a powerful force. Second, students' own healthy and unhealthy achievement attributional styles affect their achievement. That is, some students may see their achievements as a result of hard work and consistent effort, which is a healthy attributional style, because it incorporates variables under their control. But others may see their occasional good grades as a result of luck, a favorable teacher, an easy assignment, or their native intelligence. All of these contribute to an unhealthy attributional style based on variables not under the teen's control). The third issue involves the positive and negative impacts of peer cultures, while the fourth issue is that the adverse impact of teens working more than 20 hours per week can be devastating to achievement. Finally, the constant pressure on American adolescents to be involved in many activities at the same time is critical. In addition to keeping up with expectations or excelling in classes, this substantially cuts into many teens' outside-of-school time. In all, it was suggested that these variables combined to make our students far less competitive in the global marketplace than their Asian and European counterparts, who, in aggregate, must prioritize school, attend a much longer school day (including attending school on

Saturdays), take more difficult academic subjects, spend more time studying, work very few hours outside of school, and limit their socializing. Many American teens would undoubtedly find these expectations and limitations unpleasant, if not downright intolerable. To be sure, there are also many teens who work very hard in school, taking highly demanding courses, planning their curriculum pathways carefully, putting in long hours of homework night after night, limiting work hours to weekend down time, and achieving to their potential—but this chapter focuses on helping the other students, who are not so inclined.

Clearly, working long hours is a detriment to most students' ability to excel in their class work in school. Students in other industrialized nations seem to have more restricted work hours and put in considerably more time on their homework (4 hours a *day*, instead of 4 hours a week), which would contribute substantially to their being able to focus much more on academic achievement.

Steinberg (1996) defined the construct of *engagement* as follows:

> The degree to which students are psychologically "connected" to what is going on in their classes. . . . When highly engaged students are in class, they are there emotionally as well as physically. They concentrate on the task at hand, they strive to do their best when tested or called upon, and when they are given homework or other outside assignments, they do them on time and in good faith. They participate actively in class discussions, think about the material covered in their course, and genuinely care about the quality of their work. (p. 15)

Disengaged students present quite a different picture, as many public educators in America can tell you. Disengaged students do what they need to do to stay out of trouble and to get by, exerting minimum effort in class and doing little homework. Steinberg (1996) concluded that about 40% of students are just going through the motions of going to school.

OUTSIDE INFLUENCES ON STUDENT ACHIEVEMENT

A number of things outside of the school environment influence student achievement. These include parents and guardians, peer groups, work hours, and multiple influences.

THE IMPORTANCE OF PARENTS AND GUARDIANS

The contrast between engaged and disengaged students is stark. One wonders how we have spawned an entire population of disengaged students in many of our public high schools. What forces could be operating on these adolescents? To summarize Steinberg's (1996) major findings, (a) a high proportion of students do not take school seriously; (b) considerable time is spent on socializing with peers; (c) time is spent on out-of-school activities that do not reinforce what is being learned in school; (d) Black and Hispanic adolescent peer cultures tends to devalue achievement in school, as it is tantamount to selling out to White middle-class values; and (e) many American parents are just as disengaged from school as are their teens.

This last finding is particularly insightful, as Steinberg (1996) detailed four parenting styles: *authoritarian* (i.e., rigid, strict, and controlling); *permissive* (i.e., accepting, indulgent, and lenient); *authoritative* (i.e., accepting, firm, and supportive of developing a child's independence); and *disengaged* (i.e., emotionally aloof and uninvolved with their teen's progress in school, their spare time activities, or their friends). Steinberg speculated that 25% to 30% of parents are in this last category, which results in so many students being absent from school and eventually dropping out. To determine parenting attitudes, the researchers asked probing questions to assess how involved parents were in various aspects of their child's life—their spare time activities, their friends, and so forth. It is an interesting coincidence that some researchers suggested that the high school dropout rate is about 30% (Greene, 2002; Mortenson, 2001; Thornburgh, 2006), reflecting almost exactly the percentage of disengaged parents determined by Steinberg. For high school counselors, teachers, or administrators, it is easy to assume that *most* parents are involved with their teens because so many of them contact the school. In fact, some parents never do! Steinberg tells us that "only about one-fifth of parents consistently attend school programs. More than 40 percent *never* do" (p. 20). Steinberg also shares that research shows over and over, if parents are involved with their teens, their students do better in school. A key reason is that

> acceptance seems to matter most for children's overall adjustment and sense of self-worth; because they feel loved, they feel lovable. As a result, children who feel valued and supported by their parents have higher self-esteem, more positive self-conceptions, and a happier, more enthusiastic outlook on life. Not surprisingly, they are more sociable and more socially skilled. (p. 109)

When parents are involved, their teens feel accepted and valued. Quattrociocchi (2000) frequently emphasized this point in her writing and presentations to educators and parents by pointing out that "research shows that parental involvement is the single greatest factor in determining student success. Teens with highly involved families are three times more likely than their peers to earn a bachelor's degree or to complete other post-secondary programs" (p. 2).

THE IMPORTANCE OF PEER GROUPS

> Nearly 20 percent of all students say they do not try as hard as they can in high school because they are worried about what their friends might think. (Steinberg, 1996, p. 19)

As remarkable as this finding may appear, many educators and parents are aware of this negative peer influence on American students. Steinberg (1996) found that peer groups could have both a positive and a negative effect on student achievement, and that teens are particularly vulnerable to peer influence between the ages of 12 and 16 years. When looking at peer influence in all four predominant cultural peer groups (Asian, White, Black, and Hispanic), Steinberg found the following:

> Specifically, Asian students' friends have higher performance standards (that is, they hold tougher standards for what grades are acceptable), spend more time

on homework, are more committed to education, and earn considerably higher grades in school. Black and Hispanic students' friends earn lower grades, spend less time on their studies, and have substantially lower performance standards. White students' friends fall somewhere between these two extremes on these various indicators. (p. 157)

Steinberg (1996) has further found that in Asian peer groups, students frequently turn to each other for academic support and consultation in their classes whereas this is rarely done in White, Black, or Hispanic peer groups. In fact, the opposite appears to be true for Black and Latino students "who are far more likely than other students to find themselves in peer groups that actually devalue academic accomplishment" (p. 158). The reason is that scholastic success is sometimes equated with "selling out" one's ethnic and cultural identity to White, middle-class values.

THE INFLUENCE OF WORK HOURS

Working long hours may be detrimental to school achievement, particularly if students work more than 20 hours per week, according to Steinberg (1996). Students who work long hours often do not have the energy left to focus on their classes and class assignments. Most students do not, in fact, work to save for college but tend to spend the money on personal expenses. Worse, most students are not engaged in jobs that will help them explore a potential career interest. Steinberg made the distinction that working is not detrimental to academic achievement but the number of hours worked is harmful; specifically, fewer than 10 hours per week does not appear harmful whereas students sho work more than 20 hours per week are more likely to be harmed.

Further, very few jobs offer training that will transfer to adult jobs, as most teens work in restaurants, supermarkets, and retail stores. Steinberg (1996) gave a grim picture of employers' stranglehold on teenage workers, indicating that some major employers of teenagers lobby assiduously to keep child labor laws flexible; they also wage a public relations campaign "designed to convince American parents and students that adolescents somehow reap characterological, if not moral, benefits from spending their afternoons and evenings flipping hamburgers, stuffing burritos, and operating cash registers" (p. 167). American employers may or may not be sensitive to students' academic demands and limit their job responsibilities accordingly.

State laws might restrict students' working hours somewhat. Normally, a 16- or 17-year old cannot work more than 20 hours per week without a signed variance (by a parent, a school official, and the employer), but variances for working 40 or more hours a week are sometimes granted:

> For 16- and 17-year old students who want or need to work more than four hours a day and 20 hours per week, there is a special variance. The variance requires approval by the student's employer, parent, and school. The maximum is 28 hours a week, 6-hour shift lengths and limited to 16- and 17-year-olds during the school year in non-agriculture employment. . . . Additional variances may be granted by Labor and Industries. The request for a standard variance is originated by the employer. The variances can be granted up to and beyond 40 hours a week, 8-hour

shift lengths, and start and finish times during school and non-school weeks. (Department of Labor and Industries, n.d.)

THE INFLUENCE OF MULTIPLE ACTIVITIES

Another powerful force on teens is the pressure to participate in multiple activities. Some teens are involved in so many activities (particularly athletic activities) that their schoolwork suffers. Practice before and after school not only uses valuable study time but may leave a student exhausted and unable to concentrate on difficult academic material. Students and their coaches need to be honest about what makes up a reasonable amount of participation. Of course some coaches highly encourage and expect strong academic achievement, and students may be given team awards for their collective outstanding academic achievement by their local and state athletic associations. For example, in Washington State, the Washington Interscholastic Activities Association (WIAA) makes these team awards possible. Teams with the highest cumulative grade point averages are honored by the state association. Coaches are encouraged to send in their team members' grades, and the cumulative grade point averages of winning teams are made known to the public, thus encouraging academic achievement throughout the sports programs (WIAA; 2002).

U.S. high school students are known for spending a lot of time socializing with their friends while being involved in multiple activities and/or working long hours. It adds up. The national average for time spent on homework, according to Steinberg (1996), is less than 5 hours per week, hardly competitive with European and Asian adolescents. When school systems attempt new initiatives to alleviate and address these problems, the initiatives often meet resistance. For example, recently in Seattle, Nathan Hale High School administrators decided to move the start time for school 1 hour later, from 7:45 to 8:45, so that students could get an extra hour of sleep. However, the change ran into resistance, as many were concerned that "team sports, such as baseball and fast-pitch softball, will not have enough daylight to finish their games, or that they will conflict with classes" (Jensen, 2003).

Many students choose to play a sport each season. Many teams require a minimum grade-point average or a passing grade in four or more classes for students to qualify to stay on the team through the season; but sports, like other activities, may take away from needed study time. It's all a matter of priorities. Further, many students feel pressured to list multiple activities on their résumés to be competitive as candidates for selective college admission. Some U.S. high school students want to do it all (e.g., sports, other school activities, part-time work) at the expense of excelling in their academic classes.

LACK OF PLANNED, SEQUENTIAL CAREER-DEVELOPMENT PROGRAMS

Planned, comprehensive career development programs, integrated at each grade level, may no be available to help students think about, identify, and articulate their strengths, interests, and values and to explore the many occupational options in the world of work. Sometimes students may find that career guidance lessons are so few and far between that it is difficult to maintain a sense of continuity between one career presentation and the next. Students may be further discouraged because they have no mechanism, such as an education and career plan, or a career planning portfolio, in which to keep their assignments, papers, and notes. The career guidance program may appear disorganized in many high schools, with no clear guidelines or activities expected of all students. Gysbers (2001) addressed this concern as follows:

> My vision for guidance and counseling in the 21st century is fully implemented comprehensive guidance and counseling programs in every school district in the United States, serving all students and their parents, staffed by active, involved school counselors. When guidance and counseling is conceptualized, organized, and implemented as a program, it places school counselors conceptually and structurally in the center of education and makes it possible for them to be active and involved. As a result, guidance and counseling becomes an integral and transformative program, not a marginal and supplemental activity. It provides school counselors with the structure, time, and resources to fully use their expertise. (p. 103)

Kuranz (2002, p. 174) reported that, according to the American School Counselor Association (ASCA), "the average U.S. student-to-counselor ratio is 551:1." With ratios that high, it is virtually impossible for school counselors alone, without the help of other appropriate educators, to provide substantive, systematic, and sequential career guidance activities for all students. The high student–counselor ratios demonstrate the obvious need for sharing this responsibility with appropriate others. National leaders in the American School Counselor Association have developed the ASCA national standards (Campbell & Dahir, 1997; Dahir, Sheldon, & Valiga, 1998), student content standards for school counseling programs in the areas of academic, career, and personal–social development. The ASCA national standards in career development include the following:

A. Students will acquire the skills to investigate the world of work in relation to knowledge of self and to make informed career decisions.
B. Students will employ strategies to achieve future career success and satisfaction.
C. Students will understand the relationship among personal qualities, education and training, and the world of work. (Campbell & Dahir, 1997, p. 17)

ASCA has developed the *ASCA National Model: A Framework for School Counseling Programs* (ASCA; 2003), which incorporates a delivery system (for guidance curriculum) with integrated management and accountability systems. According to Bowers and Hatch (2002),

> historically, many school counselors spent much of their time responding to the needs of a small percentage of their students, typically the high achieving or high risk. The *National Model for School Counseling Programs* recommends the majority of the school counselor's time be spent in direct service to all students so that every student receives the program benefits.

These standards and model should be put into place in all school so that all students will receive age-appropriate, sequential, and meaningful career development activities. These carefully planned activities, based on the assessed needs of students, should help them with their career exploration, educational planning and goal-setting, and academic and technical preparation for their postsecondary education and workplace endeavors.

The "Academic Middle" and High School and College Dropout Rates

In high schools across the country, many students receive little in the way of career guidance and educational planning, let alone any sort of long-term financial planning for their education after high school. Sadly, a testimony to this lack of career guidance programming is our public high school dropout rate of nearly one in three students (Greene, 2002; Mortenson, 2001; Thornburgh, 2006). The national college dropout rate is about the same. In the aggregate, one in three freshmen does not return for their sophomore year (American College Testing, 2008). When disaggregated, the university-level student dropout rate is about one in four, while the dropout rate in public community and technical colleges after 1 year is almost one in two! These are disturbing figures, indicating that even many of our college-bound young people do not spend enough time thinking about and planning carefully for their futures, educationally or financially.

A further testimonial to this issue is that nearly 40% of students take remedial courses when they get to college. "In a district-sponsored follow-up study of the class of 2002, 35 percent of respondents said they had taken a remedial reading class in college and 38 percent said they took one in math" (Solomon, 2003).

Weak academic preparation for college is corroborated by Gray and Herr (1995), who suggested that many students from the "academic middle" are encouraged to enter college when they do not really have the strength of academic preparation needed, despite the fact that they have taken "honors" or college-preparatory classes. It seems that students in the academic middle are enrolled in honors classes that do not really prepare them for the rigors of college-level work. These researchers attribute our high college dropout rate to "the right to try/the right to fail" phenomenon that, in turn, creates a sort of massive social inefficiency.

In most countries, the idea of supporting the attendance of large numbers of youth in college who do not have the academic ability and/or preparation to be successful would be unimaginable, and dropout rates of 50% would be intolerable. But this belief is not shared in the United States, at least not yet. Why? First, until recently, the United States was perhaps the only nation that could afford these social inefficiencies. Second, this situation is tolerated because of a basic value that career development specialist Ken Hoyt (1994) calls "the right to try" and the "right to fail." That "1 in 100" individual who "battles the odds" and succeeds despite a poor high school record seems always to be in the back of the minds of Americans (Gray & Herr, 1995, p. 34).

Gray and Herr (1995) further shared that "because of open admissions, getting into college is relatively easy, whereas graduating is not. Only about half who matriculate ever graduate in 6 years" (p. 109). The other half leaves college, often in debt, to look for something else. Krumboltz and Worthington (1999) offered the notion that "floundering" is not necessarily bad. "Much valuable learning occurs in the trial-and-error work experiences that occur during this interval. However, the learning is haphazard and sometimes results in the learning of self-defeating attitudes and habits" (p. 314). Some students drop out of college when they run out of financial support (often with a loan obligation) or realize they have merely acquiesced to the wishes of others. Students may realize that they need to think for themselves and make their own way, which may be to work full time or go into the military. In short, students get a chance to mature and reevaluate their goals. These students, who have had time to align their ambitions, may return some years later with a much stronger sense of their own commitment and purpose.

Having Aligned, Misaligned, or No Clear Ambitions at All

At some level, however, all young people grapple with what they want to do with their lives. They give some thought about what they want to become—what skills they would like to develop, how they want to earn money, and what sort of lifestyle and friends they would like to have. Some put in a lot of time thinking about their futures and have well-defined goals and realistic plans involving the amount of education and training needed to reach their goals. Schneider and Stevenson (1999) coined the useful term *aligned ambitions*, describing these students as knowing what goals they want to pursue and realistically understanding the educational pathways required to attain them. Others have well-defined goals but unrealistic plans about how to achieve them. These students would be described as having misaligned ambitions. For example, a student who wants to become an attorney might assume that a master's degree is required and not understand the requirement of 3 years of law school, culminating with passing the state bar exam.

Still other young people have very unclear goals. Some teens appear to have almost no goals or ambitions they can articulate. From casual observation, it appears that, left unattended and without guidance, this last group of young people will tend to take the path of least resistance. They will do what makes the most sense to them in their perception of how the world works, from the way they see things. This, of course, may not be the way the world really works, but their unique (and possibly distorted) perceptions will dictate their behavior.

Limited Choice Repertoire

Capuzzi and Gross (1989) suggested that young people who make poor decisions about their lives make choices from their "limited choice repertoire," reporting that it is "their selected way of coping with the myriad challenges placed in their path that differentiates at-risk individuals from their peers" (p. 11). Capuzzi and Gross added that students' personal circumstances, over which they have little or no control, may impinge greatly on their ability to complete school. These circumstances might include a dysfunctional, destructive and/or abusive family environment, low family income that forces the student to work, or marginal academic ability. These young people at risk tend to choose what gives them an immediate solution instead of considering a range of alternatives or soliciting different advice from different people. That is, they demonstrate limited decision-making ability, a lack of significant persons they can go to for help and advice, and limited ability to model successful coping strategies demonstrated by others. Their limited choice repertoire is partly due to a lack of information because they are unaware of the range of choices they have and do not take adequate time to research their options.

Another term for a dysfunctional decision-making style is *foreclosure,* making choices too soon without considering enough appropriate alternatives. A purpose of career development in elementary and secondary grades is to help students avoid premature foreclosure of choices based on inaccurate, incomplete, or biased information and stereotypes. When disengaged, unfocused teens encounter the increasingly more academically difficult high school curriculum and find that there is really nothing there for them in terms of their own interests or goals, many choose to leave the public school system, as leaving is the path of least resistance. It is often reported that many students drop out in their senior year. For example, in the state of Washington, only 71.9% of seniors at the beginning of the school year in September 2000 graduated in the spring of 2001. Bylsma and Ireland (2002, p. 9) confirmed that "grade 12 experienced the largest annual dropout rate."

Reasons given for dropping out, reported in *Graduation and Dropout Statistics for Washington's Counties, Districts, and Schools Final Report, School Year 2001–2002,* included "expelled or suspended, poor grades, school not for me/stayed home, married and needed to support family, pregnant or had a baby, offered training, chose to work, or other" (Bylsma & Ireland, 2002, p. 9). By far, the greatest number of students who dropped out in their senior year attended 4 years but did not continue. One can speculate why this occurs. Many students realize that they have fallen too far behind in credits to graduate with their friends, and they opt to leave school before embarrassing themselves with this eventuality. At least, they can get a job, earn money, and do some of the things they want to do. Hoyt (2001) reported that approximately 22 million of the anticipated 50 million new jobs between the years 1996–2006 will require only 2 to 3 weeks of short-term, on-the-job training, so low-skilled, low-wage, dead-end jobs abound in the U.S. economy. The downside for young people leaving school to work in these jobs, if that is what they are leaving for, is that the jobs do not usually provide a living wage. Students must pursue further education and training if they wish to qualify for higher paying jobs. One's level of education is closely related to a lifetime salary. Dropouts earn substantially less than those with some college or further training.

THE PATH OF LEAST RESISTANCE

Fritz (1984) provided a conceptual framework for the path of least resistance. His insights are particularly helpful when working with young, unfocused students. Fritz used the metaphor of the river and suggested that, "You are like a river. You go through life taking the path of least resistance" (p. 7). He indicates that it is the layout of a riverbed across a terrain that determines the flow of the river:

If a riverbed remains unchanged, the water will continue to flow along the path it always has, since that is the most natural route for it to take. If the underlying structures of your life remain unchanged, the greatest tendency is for you to follow the same direction your life has always taken. (p. 5)

This metaphor applies to unfocused young people, who tend to follow the path of least resistance, unless there is some sort of intervention that changes the underlying structure of their lives. As engineers might excavate a new riverbed to redirect the flow of a river, so educators (and parents) need to support and redirect disengaged young people to help them take charge of the direction of their lives in more productive and positive ways.

THE RELATIONSHIP BETWEEN AN INADEQUATE EDUCATION AND POVERTY

School is academically challenging, and for many (given their state of readiness to learn), too challenging. Adelman and Taylor (2002) reported disturbing findings across the country when they surveyed teachers with the following question: "Most days, how many of your students come to class motivationally ready and able to learn?" Their results follow:

In urban and rural schools serving economically disadvantaged families, teachers tell us they are lucky if 10 percent to 15 percent of their students fall into this group. In surburbia, teachers usually say 75 percent fit that profile. It is not surprising, therefore, that teachers are continuously asking for help in dealing with problems. (p. 235)

These are disturbing findings, showing the possible basis of why so many students ultimately drop out of school if there are no safety nets (e.g., remedial courses, small classes, alternative programs, adult mentors, tutoring) in place to help keep them in school. Adelman and Taylor (2002) reported further:

The litany of barriers is all too familiar to anyone who lives or works in communities where families struggle with low income. In such neighborhoods, school and community resources often are insufficient for providing the basic opportunities (never mind enrichment activities) found in higher income communities. (p. 236)

Dropout rates are about the same for males and females but are higher for students from different ethnic groups and for students from disadvantaged backgrounds (U.S. Dept. of Education, 1996). According to the National Center for Educational Statistics (NCES; 2001),

in 1999, young adults living in families with incomes in the lowest 20 percent of all family incomes were five times as likely as their peers from families in the top 20 percent of the income distribution to drop out of high school.

From this information, one can infer that income is a greater predictor of high school completion than is ethnicity.

THE WORKING POOR

It is important to make the connection between the number of students who drop out of school who then become part of the working poor, thus contributing to the poverty rates in the United States.

> The attention comes against a backdrop of rising peril for dropouts. If their grandparents' generation could find a blue-collar niche and prosper, the latest group is immediately relegated to the most punishing sector of the economy, where whatever low-wage jobs haven't yet moved overseas are increasingly filled by even lower-wage immigrants. Dropping out of high school today is . . . an indicator of a host of poor outcomes to follow, from low lifetime earnings to high incarceration rates to a high likelihood that your children will drop out of high school and start the cycle anew. (Thornburgh, 2002, p. 30)

Herbert (2002), a New York Times writer, reflected on Barbara Ehrenreich's book *Nickel and Dimed: On (Not) Getting by In America*, which captures the frustration of adults who cannot earn above the minimum wage (or poverty) level.

> The poor are pretty well hidden from everyone except each other in the United States. You won't find them in the same neighborhoods or the same schools as the well-to-do. They're not on television, except for the local crime-casts. . . . Hiding the poor has been quite a trick, because there are still millions upon millions of them out here. (Herbert, 2002, p. 7)

As is widely recognized, adults and their children living at the poverty level often do not have enough food to eat, even if they use food stamps, or they will not be able to get needed medical care. They are often evicted from their housing, and their utilities are disconnected. Many adults, locked in at minimum wages due to their low skills, must work two or three jobs, on evenings and week-ends, to try to make ends meet. This is reality for millions of adult Americans.

BOOMERANG EFFECT—"ADULTOLESCENTS, OR TWIXTERS"

We have a relatively new phenomenon in this country—the phenomenon of *adultolescents*, or *twixters*. These are young people who choose (and are allowed) to remain with their parents or guardians, after most of their peers have chosen to be on their own. Many parents and guardians believe that if their graduating seniors go to college or a postsecondary training program that the students' futures will be somewhat secure. Some parents then experience a sort of "boomerang effect"—their youngsters leave home to attend college only to return after a year or so to live at home again, while they are sorting out their priorities. Adultolescents (i.e., young adults still living at home) were featured in *Newsweek* (Tyre, 2002), which reports that there are 4 million young adults, ages 25 to 34 years, living with their parents:

> Whether it's reconverting the guest room back into a bedroom, paying for graduate school, writing a blizzard of small checks to cover rent and health-insurance premiums or acting as career counselors, parents across the country are trying

to provide their twenty-somethings with the tools they'll need to be self-sufficient—someday. In the process, they have created a whole new breed of child—the "adultolescent" . . . Relying on your folks to light the shadowy path to the future has become so accepted that even the ultimate loser move—returning home to live with your parents—has lost its stigma. (Tyre, 2002, p. 39)

Grossman further discussed this phenomenon:

Social scientists are starting to realize that a permanent shift has taken place in the way we live our lives. In the past, people moved from childhood to adolescence and from adolescence to adulthood, but today there is a new, intermediate phase along the way. The years from 18 to 25 and even beyond have become distinct and separate life stage, a strange, transitional never-never land between adolescent and adulthood in which people stall for a few extra years, putting off the iron cage of adult responsibility that constantly threatens to crash down on them. They're betwixt and between. You could call them twixters. (Grossman, 2005, p. 44)

Where did the *twixters* come from? And what's taking them so long to get where they're going? Some of the sociologists, psychologists and demographers who study this new life stage see it as a good thing. The twixters aren't lazy, the argument goes; they're reaping the fruit of decades of American affluence and social liberation. This new period is a chance for young people to savor the pleasures of irresponsibility, search their souls and choose their life paths. But more historically and economically minded scholars see it differently. They are worried that twixters aren't growing up because they can't. Those researchers fear that whatever cultural machinery used to turn kids into grown-ups has broken down, that society no longer provides young people with the moral backbone and the financial wherewithal to take their right places in the adult world.

A Call for Action—What Needs to Be Done?

Many initiatives are necessary to help unfocused students get on track and stay on track. Professional school counselors can lead the way.

Acknowledge the Problem of Unfocused Students

Professional school counselors need to be aware of the *magnitude* of the problem of unfocused students. Usually, in any public school, many students are unfocused. They do not see the connection between what they are doing in school and how they are preparing a foundation for their lives after high school. Students who do not develop a plan for their education and goals tend to apply minimum effort and just get by. Many even drop out—as many as one out of three! The phenomenon of unfocused students is not isolated, but ubiquitous. Students who skipped school reported that "their number one reason why they skipped school was that they were discouraged about being behind"—in credits toward graduation (Houtz & Shaw, 2003). The highest dropout rate occurs in the senior year of high school (Bylsma & Ireland, 2002). Professional school counselors must understand the impact of this phenomenon because discouraged students leave school not only unprepared academically and vocationally, but also without a plan to continue their training and further develop their goals. For high school dropouts, this is a double loss. No diploma, no plan.

UNDERSTANDING THE CONTEXT OF CULTURE AND AMERICAN STUDENTS

Steinberg (1996) brought to light a number of factors contributing to low achievement: disengaged parents (e.g., as high as 30%); time spent on socializing; negative peer influence; long work hours; and involvement in multiple, nonacademic activities. Steinberg reported that "to European and Asian parents, school is the defining activity of both childhood and adolescence. Everything else comes second" (p. 182). And worse, Steinberg reported that "the average American high school student spends about four hours per week on homework outside of school. In other industrialized countries, the average is about four hours per *day*" (p. 19). This is an astonishing contrast! No wonder our students struggle so much in competing with their international counterparts. Zuckerman (2004) shared the following news about international competition for jobs:

> What's going on here? Well, clearly international competition and outsourcing have hit some sectors hard. In the past decade, China became the world's workshop. In this decade, India is becoming the world's back office. Cheap bandwidth and the Internet permit companies to tap into a huge supply of English-speaking workers, happy to take knowledge-based jobs for 10 to 20 percent of what American employees receive. "Offshoring" is moving up the food chain of services to include professions like engineering, design, accounting, legal work, actuarial and insurance work, medical services, and financial analysis. (p. 68)

So, where does this leave our students? It leaves them with a more competitive marketplace and a more urgent need than ever before to develop an education and career plan, take courses judiciously, do as well as they can, and prepare for the next step in their educational program. Otherwise, students will default to entry-level, unskilled work with low pay and little chance of advancement.

Unfocused, disengaged students *need extra support* in developing their future plans from professional school counselors, teachers, and their parents or guardians. As suggested, some may end up as young adults (*adultolescents*, or *twixters*), still living at home long after most of their peers have moved out on their own. Unfocused young people need adults who care about them and who will take the needed time to guide them, one-on-one, and who will push them to achieve. While they are in school, they may need help with placing limitations on their work hours and participation in nonacademic activities. They may need help with study skills and understanding that they are in control of their academic achievement. That is, their achievement level is not dependent on luck but is related to factors under their control, such as the amount of time they are willing to study and do their assignments, and the willingness to get help when they need it, instead of just ignoring the problem. Students also need to understand that they will have the opportunity to work for wages for many years. In contrast high school is fleeting. Students who do not see the value of high school need to be encouraged to see the connections between what they want to do and the training/education needed to do it.

INTERVENTIONS THAT CAN HELP STUDENTS TO BECOME MORE FOCUSED

Students need to be encouraged to consider technical training, as the world of work is filled with technical jobs, often requiring 2 years of technical training or less. Hoyt (2001) shared that there are 100,000 to 300,000 college graduates a year than there are jobs requiring a college degree! Gray and Herr (1995) reported that, "technical workers are the fastest-growing and economically most promising segment in the labor force," and "the largest number and fastest growing group of jobs among technical workers can be trained for at the 2-year associate degree level" (p. 109). Students can learn at home through online distance learning technical training programs, if they have the self-discipline to sit in front of a computer for long periods.

IDEAS FOR CAREER PLANNING

Many useful approaches are thoughtfully presented in Wakefield's (2004) book titled *Unfocused Kids: Helping Students to Focus on Their Education and Career Plans—A Resource for Educators* that can assist educators in helping young people with their educational and career planning. Topics include Societal Trends and Workplace Issues; Comprehensive School Counseling Programs; Project-Based Career Guidance Models; Innovative Approaches to Workplace Training; Involving Parents in their Teen's Career Planning; Innovative Career Development Activities/Games; Innovative Career Development Practices for Special Populations; and Internet Delivery Systems in Career Guidance.

The book (Wakefield, 2004) has something for everyone, including specific ideas in working with parents, how the ASCA national standards can be implemented using the template of the ASCA national model (ASCA; 2003), changes in the workplace from the old pyramid to the new diamond-shaped, newly developed O*NET and electronic portfolios, and the value of teaching employability skills. This book is virtually encyclopedic in its coverage, so readers are encouraged to look at chapters of their own particular interest.

SYSTEMIC CHANGE IS NEEDED IN OUR SCHOOL-WIDE CAREER GUIDANCE PROGRAMS

Many students leave our public education system without much career guidance training and support. Students need a *systemic* program coordinated by *all* appropriate educators (e.g., professional school counselors, administrators, teachers, career specialists) in order to graduate from high school. This systemic program should include the following:

- An education and career plan, including required and elective courses for grades 9 through 12, extracurricular activities, career areas to explore, volunteer/service learning, part-time jobs, field experiences (job shadows, internships, and mentorships), and tentative postsecondary plans.
- A career planning portfolio, including a student education and career plan, career search information, self-assessment results, postsecondary training and educational information, financial aid information, documentation of service learning and field experiences, copies of their best work, scholarships, honors and awards,

résumés, and so forth. In career planning portfolios, students are provided a systematic way of keeping track of and storing the information they gather through career guidance units, classroom presentations, field trips, shadow experiences, essays, interest tests, ability tests, and other portfolio items.

- A culminating project, required of all students in the senior year, focusing on a career interest. These projects usually have a prescribed time for completion and certain content requirements, often with an internship and a presentation to a panel.

If students could just complete these three items, they would be well equipped with skills and tools to navigate both their educational endeavors and work experiences after high school. The Franklin-Pierce School District in Tacoma, Washington, provides an excellent example of a program already in place that incorporates these three components (see http://www.fp.k12.wa.us).

WORKLOAD ISSUES IN PLANNING AND IMPLEMENTING CAREER GUIDANCE PROGRAMS

Monitoring student progress is an important issue in designing a program and how to share the workload must be carefully discussed with administrators, teachers, professional school counselors, career specialists, and district curriculum specialists. All appropriate personnel need to play a role, as it involves monitoring each student's completion of three different program components (i.e., career plan, career planning portfolio, and culminating project). With careful coordination and use of computer monitoring, the comprehensive career guidance program can run smoothly and be of great benefit to students.

MAKE OTHERS AWARE OF THE ISSUE OF "UNFOCUSED STUDENTS"

Professional school counselors must help other educators (e.g., administrators, teachers, career specialists, district curriculum coordinators, superintendents) understand that students need to quickly learn the value of back-up plans, financial-aid strategies, support groups for studying, and strategies for keeping their stress level under control as they move through their educational programs and workplace experiences. Otherwise, students may give up and drop out of high school or college. The monetary and psychological cost to young people who make poor or unsupported choices is staggering. Professional school counselors can do much to help parents and other educators understand the big picture. Solomon (2003) reported the following:

> One in four freshmen at four-year colleges don't [sic] return for their sophomore year, according to Education Trust, a nonprofit group that promotes high academic achievement. One in two freshmen at two-year colleges does not return. "I think people are catching on and beginning to recognize that this is one of the most serious issues confronting America," said Peter Negroni, senior vice president of K–12 education at the College Board, which develops the SAT, the PSAT and the AP program. "To me, it is the issue of our time." (Solomon, 2003)

(Note: See the CD-ROM for a list of references.)

CHAPTER 87

COMMUNITY OUTREACH INITIATIVES

Cheryl Holcomb-McCoy

Preview

In this chapter, I describe the professional school counselor's role in increasing community involvement in schools and list practical suggestions as to how professional school counselors can play a pivotal role in developing and maintaining school–community linkages. Also, a discussion of how community involvement in schools affects student success is provided.

Communities offer a wide range of resources that are valuable to schools and to the families they serve. These resources school volunteers, organizations that offer enrichment opportunities, businesses that offer career-related information and workplace experiences, and agencies that provide various social services for students and families. When schools and communities work together, they increase their capacity both to do more and to do it better (DeKanter, Ginsburg, Pederson, Peterson, & Rich, 1997; Gold, Simon, & Brown, 2003; Shirley, 1997).

A community-empowered school is one in which administrators, professional school counselors, teachers, staff, students, parents, and members of the community feel that they have a stake in the success of that school. By having a shared stake in a school's success, it is believed that the needs of students, families, and society will be addressed and ultimately met. Much of the impetus for community-empowered schools stems from educational reform initiatives that hope not only to improve the lives and futures of students but also to strengthen neighborhoods and communities. Despite common reservations about the involvement of community members in the day-to-day management of schools, the long-term advantages of sustained school–community partnerships and community-empowered schools have been well-documented. Many studies (e.g., Bryk & Schneider, 2002; Clark, 2002; Henderson & Mapp, 2002; Trusty, 1999) have found that schools with involved parents have students who

- earn higher grades and test scores, and enroll in higher-level programs.
- are promoted, pass their classes, and earn credits.
- attend school regularly.
- have better social skills, show improved behavior, and adapt well to school.
- graduate and go on to postsecondary education.

And better yet, research (e.g., Dryfoos, 2000; Sanders & Harvey, 2000) has indicated that community involvement and organizing contributed to the following changes in schools:

- Upgraded school facilities
- Improved school leadership and staffing
- Higher quality learning programs for students

- New resources and programs to improve teaching and curriculum
- New funding for after-school programs and family supports

The foundation of the work of successful community outreach initiatives, therefore, consists of building relationships among parents, educators, community leaders, and public officials. These relationships in turn foster increased involvement and shared norms among the people who are essential to school change.

In response to this movement toward community-empowered schools, many professional school counselors have accepted the challenge of playing a major role in developing school–community linkages or community outreach initiatives. The American School Counselor Association (ASCA) and the Council for the Accreditation of Counseling and Related Programs (CACREP) have even suggested that professional school counselors have the skills necessary to promote school–community partnerships. With that said, this chapter is designed to offer professional school counselors direction for promoting community outreach initiatives or partnerships. For the sake of clarity, community outreach initiatives will be used interchangeably with school–community partnerships.

COMPONENTS OF COMMUNITY OUTREACH INITIATIVES

According to Colbert (1996), successful school–community initiatives or partnerships are associated with four guiding principles:

1. Coordinate and integrate Epstein and Salinas's (1993) School and Family Partnership Types model.
2. Make community initiatives an integral part of the school's organizational and operating structure.
3. Identify and use effective parent and teacher models.
4. Maintain ongoing monitoring and evaluation of all community initiatives.

According to Colbert (1996), the first principle is important because it ensures that community outreach initiatives are relevant to various types of partnerships as delineated by Epstein and Salinas (1993). Epstein and Salinas purported that there are six types of partnership activities in schools:

1. Parenting skills, understanding of child development, home conditions for learning and the school's understanding of its families
2. Communications from school-to-home and from home-to-school about programs and student progress
3. The organization, schedules, and use of volunteers at and for the school, and the opportunities and schedules for audiences at school for student events
4. Family involvement in learning activities at home, including homework, class work, curriculum-related interactions, and decisions
5. Family involvement in school decisions, committees, school-based management, advocacy, and other practices of participation
6. Community collaborations and resources for students, the school, and families

Colbert believed that community initiatives should be varied across these types of partnerships and that one initiative may be relevant to more than one of the types.

The second principle suggests that community outreach initiatives should be an integral part of the school's organizational and operating structure. For instance, informing parents of new instructional strategies and engaging parents in activities that can enhance their student's learning are strategies that make outreach an ongoing component of a school's day-to-day existence. To do this, there should be planned and well-coordinated events where curriculum-related matters are relayed among parents, school operational groups, and a school's curriculum committee.

The third principle, identifying and using effective parent and teacher models, suggests that community outreach initiatives should strive to highlight parenting and teaching models or practices that foster healthy development of children. For instance, teachers and parents who exemplify exceptional skills and strategies would be enlisted as trainers or models for other teachers and parents. A means for identifying model parents and teachers must be determined by school personnel to achieve this principle.

Finally, it is critical that community outreach initiatives be closely monitored and evaluated. Ongoing feedback provides the information needed to continue or discontinue the initiative. Evaluation procedures and designs must be decided on before implementation.

In addition to the preceding four guiding principles, efforts to establish effective community outreach activities require new school policies and processes to meet the needs of all students, families, schools, and communities. According to Taylor and Adelman (2000), schools must make the following procedural changes to ensure effective school–community partnerships:

- Create shared decision making and appropriate degrees of local control and private-sector involvement. There must be guaranteed roles for the involvement of staff, families, students, and community members in the decision-making process of schools.
- Create change teams and agents to carry out daily activities associated with systemic change. Establishing a school-based, resource-oriented team, properly constituted with school, home, and community representatives is a first step. This team leads and steers efforts to maintain and improve a multifaceted and integrated approach to community outreach.
- Establish institutionalized mechanisms to manage and enhance resources for community outreach activities. These mechanisms should include ways to analyze, plan, coordinate, integrate, monitor, evaluate, and strengthen ongoing efforts.

According to Giles (1998), a critical component of successful community outreach is the perception or belief of the initiators. Giles suggested that the initiators of school–community partnerships must view the school and its surrounding community as a part of an interdependent social ecology that is only understood as a whole, rather than independent parts. In her observations, successful outreach initiatives address the strengths and difficulties in a school and community. Also, Giles suggested that successful initiatives involve the engagement of not only those parents who seek to get involved but of parents who are less likely to become involved in school-related activities (e.g., minority parents, low-income parents). As a means to get all parents involved, Giles suggested that outreach efforts begin with an activity in which parents can reflect critically upon the education of their children. This accomplishes more than activities such as parent education workshops, where educators and mental health professionals often view parents as patients in need of treatment. These "patient-like" activities, according to Giles, keep parents isolated from each other and dependent on the expertise of educators.

Heckman (1996) indicated that regular meetings with parents, students, teachers, counselors, administrators, and community leaders is a critical component of successful outreach initiatives. Parents, community members, and educators must meet together to identify common concerns, decide on which to focus, and then develop strategies for addressing them. By meeting regularly, parents learn more about their supportive role in their child's education, and teachers learn more about the lives of the students in their classrooms. Furthermore, community leaders, who are often left out of these dialogues, have an opportunity to offer their support and resources to resolve critical problems in the school.

COMMUNITY ORGANIZING

Community organizing for school reform refers to the actions of parents and other residents of marginalized communities to transform low-performing schools toward higher performance through an "intentional building of power" (Mediratta & Fruchter, 2001, p. 5). Its goals are both building community capacity and reforming schools. Ideally, in the participatory process of working for needed changes, people involved in community organizing groups learn how to take greater responsibility for the future of their schools and communities. Community organizers identify and attract the people to be involved in the organizations and develop the leadership within and relationships among the people that make the organizations effective.

Typically, careful data gathering, research, and participatory strategic planning precede the actions taken by community organizing groups. The actions are often in the form of negotiations with targeted institutions holding power around issues determined by and important to the organizers and communities they represent. The community organizing groups seek policy and other significant changes determined by and responsive to the people in a particular community.

Based on a survey of 200 groups engaged in community organizing for school change, the Cross City Campaign for Urban School Reform and its partner organizations identified the following characteristics of community organizing groups:

- "They work to change public schools to make them more equitable and effective for all students."
- "They build a large base of members who take collective action to further their agenda."
- "They build relationships and collective responsibility by identifying shared concerns among neighborhood residents and creating alliances and coalitions that cross neighborhood and institutional boundaries."
- "They develop leadership among community residents to carry out agendas that the membership determines through a democratic governance structure."

- "They use the strategies of adult education, civic participation, public action, and negotiation to build power for residents of low- to moderate-income communities that results in action to address their concerns." (Gold, Simon, & Brown, 2002, p. 12)

IMPLICATIONS FOR PROFESSIONAL SCHOOL COUNSELORS

As educational reform initiatives grow in popularity across the nation, it will become imperative for professional school counselors to play more of a visible role in community outreach. Whether it be coordinating community-based services, promoting community involvement in school decision-making, or acting as a liaison with community organizing groups, professional school counselors are, and will be, central to community outreach in all schools. The primary emphasis for professional school counselors in the realm of community outreach is to take on a leadership role in coordinating the efforts of diverse groups (e.g., parents, teachers, community members, staff, administration). Professional school counselors might use their expertise to facilitate discussions between these diverse school and community groups and restructure their method of communicating with each other. For instance, professional school counselors might revise the method used for teachers to communicate with parents and for parents to communicate with teachers. Such a restructuring of communication methods could enhance the information channels between parents and teachers and develop a sense of trust between the school and community.

Professional school counselors can do the following in addition to taking on a leadership role in the initiation of community outreach activities:

- Collaborate with other school personnel and community members to develop a working group or committee that will initiate and monitor community outreach initiatives.
- Coordinate monthly or weekly meetings or chats with groups of parents, community organizing groups, and community members. The chats should consist of parents of all groups and community institutions represented in the school and community.
- Acknowledge the role of power in school–community partnerships. Professional school counselors should become knowledgeable of how to conduct a power analysis that identifies the self-interests of different groups and individuals in a particular education bureaucracy. In other words, the purpose of implementing a power analysis is to uncover the influence of various groups in the decision-making process in a particular school. These analyses frequently reveal the absence of parents and community members in educational decision-making. Professional school counselors, if knowledgeable of this process, should enlighten educators regarding power's influence on the way students are educated and the involvement of families in the educational process.
- Assist with the monitoring and evaluating of community outreach initiatives. Professional school counselors should be able to use educational outcome data such as achievement scores, attendance, and drop-out rates to determine the effectiveness of community outreach initiatives. Also, professional school counselors should be

involved in evaluating less tangible outcomes of their outreach efforts such as students' attitudes toward learning and the school climate.

- Actively promote collaborative leadership in all community outreach activities. Successful community outreach is dependent upon trust between the community and school personnel. Therefore, by promoting collaborative leadership in which the responsibilities of leadership are shared among administrators, teachers, professional school counselors, parents, and community leaders, a sense of trust is fostered among the school community.
- Attend workshops and training sessions that focus on community outreach and school reform. Meeting with other professional school counselors, educators, and community leaders who are interested or involved in community outreach reinforces and encourages the maintenance of outreach programs.
- Conduct interviews or conversations periodically (at least 10 per year) with parents and community members to discuss community and school needs.
- Coordinate neighborhood walks for teachers and other school personnel each year. These walks, in which parents, community members, and educators gather at the school and then go out to visit families and businesses, provide an opportunity for community members and educators to discuss their concerns for the school and community.

Summary/Conclusion

Professional school counselors can play a pivotal role in enhancing the ways schools and communities connect. By focusing on linking communities and schools, school culture, quality of relationships among educators, parents, and students, and student educational outcomes will invariably change for the better. Further, since schools alone cannot solve all the problems they encounter, community outreach initiatives go beyond the school and draw upon the power of community institutions (e.g., families, churches, civic groups). Professional school counselors, like schools, are unable to address all of the problems on their student caseload. By accepting a leadership role in the development of a community-empowered school, they can improve the lives of students and aspects of life in the community that impact student education.

(Note: See the CD-ROM for a list of references.)

CHAPTER 88

IMPROVING STUDENT ACHIEVEMENT

Susan Jones Sears, Christopher Wood, and Lisa Hinkelman

Preview

We address what professional school counselors can do to help students acquire study and learning skills. Professional school counselors learn how to teach students a self-regulatory cycle of task analysis, strategy selection and use, and self-monitoring to help students develop responsibility for their own learning. A small-group counseling plan shows professional school counselors how they can help students apply the self-regulatory cycle to five basic study skills: (1) planning and using study time more effectively, (2) understanding and summarizing text material better, (3) improving methods of note-taking, (4) anticipating and preparing better for exams, and (5) writing more effectively.

With the national emphasis on standards-based educational reform, professional school counselors are encouraged to demonstrate how they can contribute to increased student achievement and remove barriers to student learning. In addition, they are urged to help close the achievement gap and advocate for rigorous preparation of all students including low-income and minority youth (The Education Trust, 1997). Reflecting the national interest in educational reform and closing the achievement gap, the American School Counselor Association (ASCA) developed the national standards for school counseling programs (Campbell & Dahir, 1997). The national standards address three domains: personal—social development, career development, and academic development. One of the student standards under the academic development domain reads that "students will acquire the attitudes, knowledge, and skills that contribute to effective learning in school and across the life span" (Dahir, Sheldon, & Valiga, 1998, p. 7).

The ASCA standards are designed to influence what professional school counselors do and what students learn as a result of participating in school counseling programs. The cited standard, as well as the other eight standards, attempt to connect professional school counselors and school counseling programs to current educational reform efforts and to the mission of schools—increasing student learning and achievement.

Some researchers have encouraged professional school counselors to help students acquire study and learning skills to improve achievement (Carns & Carns, 1991). Professional school counselors could either train teachers to add learning strategies to subject matter courses or assist in teaching study and learning strategies to students. For example, professional school counselors could assist the sixth- (middle school) or ninth-grade (high school) English teachers in delivering a 5- or 6-week classroom unit on study and learning strategies. Ideally, all teachers would be motivated to include learning strategies in their classes so these skills could be reinforced throughout the curriculum. However, that ideal may not be achievable in many schools for various reasons (e.g., teacher or principal resistance, lack of training).

Other researchers, in support of the same general goal of improved student achievement, have suggested that professional school counselors teach study skills courses focusing on when, where, how, and why to study (Anderson & Anderson, 1992). In Anderson and Anderson's view, a 5- or 6-week course for all sixth or ninth graders is a valuable use of student and professional school counselor time. Regardless of whether professional school counselors train teachers to teach study skills or teach study and learning strategies in small-group counseling or classroom guidance units, professional school counselors can help students acquire the skills needed to take more control of their own learning.

NEW DISCOVERIES ABOUT LEARNING

During the last 3 decades, exciting new discoveries about the nature of learning and how students regulate their own learning processes have emerged (Zimmerman & Schunk, 2001). Research on metacognition (i.e., awareness of and knowledge about one's own thinking) and social cognition has resulted in new perspectives about students' individual differences in learning. For example, some researchers attribute individual differences in learning to students' lack of self-regulation. They claim that students need to learn how to manage their limitations during their efforts to learn and thus learn to exert more control over their own learning processes (Zimmerman & Schunk, 2001). The remainder of this chapter draws upon new perspectives on how students learn to learn and concludes with an activity designed to help professional school counselors put these new perspectives into practice.

Developing Self-Regulated Learners

Tanya, a ninth-grade student, checks her academic planner (at her school all students receive a planner at the beginning of the ninth grade). She is upset to find that her science project is due on Friday and she hasn't even been to the library to begin her research. She also is reminded that her history report is due that afternoon. Since it is only half finished, Tanya has to try to think of an excuse that the teacher might accept and give her one more day to complete it. Oh no! She also sees that she has a poem due in English class tomorrow. The poem is supposed to use metaphors, but she can't even remember what a metaphor is. She begins to panic. She can't possibly get all of this work finished on time.

Tanya is not alone. Many students do not regulate their academic studying well (Butler, 2002). They do not set goals for themselves or use specific learning strategies for condensing and memorizing important material. Many do not plan their study time well and usually cannot evaluate the amount of time it takes to complete assignments accurately. Students often attribute their learning difficulties to vague generalities such as "I'm poor in math" or "I just don't test well." They may not ask for help from others because they don't want to "sound dumb" and have little confidence they can succeed. Educators and researchers need to become more interested in helping students develop the key processes of goal setting, time management, selection of appropriate learning strategies, ability to evaluate oneself accurately, help seeking, and use of self-motivational beliefs.

One reason many students simply are ineffective learners by the time they have reached middle or high school is that they have not been taught how to learn (Kiewra, 2002). Instruction in learning strategies was not incorporated into the schools' curricula. Educators almost always teach content but don't teach students how to learn, a precursor to acquiring the content students are being asked to master.

SELF-REGULATED LEARNERS

Students who take control of their own learning are often referred to as *self-regulated learners*. Academic self-regulation refers to self-generated thoughts, feelings, and actions intended to attain specific educational goals, such as analyzing a reading assignment, preparing to take a test, or writing a paper (Zimmerman, Bonner, & Kovach, 1996).

Self-regulated learners engage in a cycle of cognitive activities as they progress through a given task or assignment (Butler & Winne, 1995). First, they analyze task demands. For example, in our vignette, Tanya had a history report to do. To begin, she would review the teachers' written or verbal instructions regarding the assignment to make sure she understood the topic, the required products or outcomes, and the criteria upon which the teacher was going to evaluate the report. As she engaged in this first step, she also would draw upon her prior knowledge of what contributes to a good report (metacognitive knowledge about the task). Thus, she might remember that her history teacher wants the report to be clearly written, include appropriate references, and be at least five pages long. This first step of task analysis is very important because it sets the stage for further learning. Students' subsequent decisions about what learning strategies to use are based on their perception of the task demands (Butler, 2002). Based on their task analysis, self-regulated learners then select, adapt, and may even invent strategic approaches to achieve the objectives related to the task or assignment facing them. In other words, they draw upon their prior knowledge and experience to make decisions about what learning strategies to apply to the task at hand. For example, when trying to select learning strategies to apply to their current task, they try to remember approaches that worked for them in past situations with similar requirements or expectations.

When self-regulated learners have chosen and implemented specific learning strategies (examples of learning strategies are provided in the next section) they must monitor the outcomes associated with strategy use. Students need to know if the learning strategy or strategies they selected are helping them progress toward completing their tasks or assignments. Smart learners engage in self-evaluation by comparing their progress against criteria for successful completion of the task to generate judgments about how they are progressing. If students see gaps between their desired and actual performance, then they must adjust their learning strategies or activities. In addition, smart learners pay attention to external feedback such as scores and comments on tests and teacher or peer comments on written assignments so they can self-evaluate their performance. They use this feedback to diagnose their difficulties and find possible solutions. Thus, monitoring the outcomes of their learning activities is another very important step because students generate judgments about their progress and then make decisions about what to do next.

WHAT PROFESSIONAL SCHOOL COUNSELORS CAN DO

To promote or encourage self-regulation in students, professional school counselors, with the help of teachers, can assist students to engage flexibly and adaptively in a cycle of task analysis, strategy selection and use, and self-monitoring (Butler, 2002). Some researchers (Zimmerman et al., 1996) suggested applying cyclic self-regulatory methods to five basic study skills: (1) planning and using study time more effectively, (2) understanding and summarizing text material better, (3) improving methods of note-taking, (4) test anticipating and preparing better for exams, and (5) writing more effectively.

These researchers noted that most students have not developed these five skills, and yet each skill is essential for effective academic learning. All five essential academic skills, and selected strategies for implementing each, appear in Appendix 88.A.

These five essential academic skills can be taught successfully to upper elementary through high school students as long as the students understand the self-regulatory cycle: (a) the need to engage in task analysis before selecting the appropriate learning strategy or strategies, (b) self-monitor to determine the effectiveness of the chosen strategy, and (c) adapt whenever necessary.

PRACTICAL APPLICATIONS OF THE SELF-REGULATORY CYCLE AND ESSENTIAL ACADEMIC SKILLS

When students begin to learn unfamiliar material, they often cannot break down or analyze the task or assignment into components. They fail to set specific goals, develop effective learning strategies, or monitor progress. With instruction or training in the self-regulatory cycle, students can learn to analyze tasks, set effective goals, choose appropriate learning strategies, and monitor progress toward task completion. Learning the steps involved in a self-regulatory cycle not only enhances students' learning skills but also increases students' perceptions of control over their learning process.

To help professional school counselors apply the information in this chapter, Figure 88.1 contains a small-group counseling plan for either middle or high school. The outline used to describe the activity includes (a) the ASCA Standard illustrated; (b) student competencies identified in the activity; (c) background notes to professional school counselors to help them prepare for the group; (d) activities and procedures to be followed in each session; and (e) suggestions for student handouts.

SUMMARY/CONCLUSION

This chapter focused on what professional school counselors can do to help students acquire study and learning skills. Self-regulated learners were described and a self-regulatory cycle of task analysis, strategy selection and use, and self-monitoring was discussed. A small-group counseling plan was presented to encourage professional school counselors to apply the self-regulatory methods to five basic study skills: (1) planning and using study time more effectively, (2) understanding and summarizing text material better, (3) improving methods of note-taking, (4) anticipating and preparing better for exams, and (5) writing more effectively.

ASCA Standard A. Academic Development: Students will demonstrate the attitudes, knowledge, and skills that contribute to effective learning in school and across the life span (Campbell & Dahir, 1997, p. 7).

Student Competencies/Benchmarks:

1. Students can identify skills and behaviors that lead to successful learning; and
2. Students can demonstrate time management and task management skills to improve student learning.

Note to Professional School Counselor: Ask teachers to help you identify students who can benefit from instruction in learning strategies. Include students who are struggling and students who are *B* students but, with help, might become better students. This mix of group members provides balance for your group. Form small groups of four to six students. If possible, work with students who are taking the same subject that will allow you to use their subject matter to help them apply the skills you are introducing. Describe what you are doing to the students and teacher(s) so they can reinforce your efforts.

Suggestions for Student Handouts: Consider making a one-page handout of each of the five essential academic skills and selected strategies that are discussed in this chapter and distribute them to members of the group when discussed.

Activities/Procedures for Each Session
Session One: Follow these steps:

1. Conduct a warm-up activity to help the students get to know each other.
2. Explain the purpose of the group to the students and generate, with the members, a set of ground rules to guide the group process, (e.g., listen to others, don't interrupt, and respect the views of others).
3. Give students a copy of the handout on which you have reproduced the vignette of "Tanya" and ask them if they have ever been in a similar situation. Ask the students to describe the situations they experienced and the outcomes of those situations. Many will report negative rather than positive outcomes. Ask students if they would like to learn ways to avoid being in those situations again. This discussion should increase their interest in the group.
4. Using the information provided about self-regulated and "smart" learners in this chapter, describe how effective learners approach studying. In your discussion, stress that students must engage flexibly and adaptively in a cycle of task analysis, strategy selection and use, and self-monitoring.
5. Ask each student to choose one subject in which to improve his or her grade. Tell students you would like them to apply the self-regulatory cycle (task analysis, strategy selection and use, and self-monitoring) in that subject to see if they can improve their learning. Explain to students that you are going to teach them some learning strategies that they can select and use in their studying.
6. Ask each student to describe a current assignment. Use one of the student's assignments and show how to engage in task analysis. Ask the other students to listen carefully. After you have completed your demonstration, answer students' questions about the process of task analysis. Give students some examples of learning strategies described in this chapter.

FIGURE 88.1. Small-group counseling plan for high school or middle school students.

Session Two:

1. Briefly review the self-regulatory cycle explained in session one. Ask the students to describe how they have tried to apply what they learned in the previous session.

2. Distribute "Planning and Using Study Time More Effectively," and lead a discussion of each strategy. As a general rule for each of the sessions, ask students which of the strategies they now use and how effective the strategy is for them. Ask the students to choose a strategy to work on after each session. During the last 5 minutes of the session, give them homework (using one of the strategies or more).

Session Three:

1. Distribute "Better Understanding and Summarizing Text Material." Proceed in the same way as session two. Show students how to engage in self-questioning and summarizing. Use information from a text students are currently using so they can see you apply the skill.

Session Four:

1. Distribute "Improving Methods of Note-Taking." Review what has been learned so far. Introduce note taking and demonstrate some of the note-taking strategies such as mapping or linear outlining. Perhaps one of the students can help. Brief the student before the session so she can explain various strategies to the others.

Session Five:

1. Distribute "Better Anticipating and Preparing for Examinations." Show students how to use first letter mnemonics and mnemonic sentences to remember a series of words or facts. Using their own texts and assignments, help them see how they can use mnemonics to improve their recollection of facts for tests.

Session Six:

1. Distribute "Writing More Effectively." Show students how to set goals for their written work. If they have assignments due, use one to set written goals to help them think how they will approach the paper or assignment they are expected to complete.

Depending on how the sessions have gone, you may need to plan for a follow-up session to review all of the strategies and have students discuss which strategies have worked effectively for them.

Evaluation: Keep detailed records of the students' grades on tests and homework at the beginning, during, and 5 weeks after the group has terminated. You can use this information to determine if the students have made any improvement in their grades. Also, you may wish to interview the students to see if they feel more in control of their own learning.

FIGURE 88.1. *Continued.*

(Note: See the CD-ROM for a list of references.)

PLANNING AND USING STUDY TIME MORE EFFECTIVELY:
SELECTED STRATEGIES

1. **Set regular study periods each day.** By setting aside regular times each day, students discover that studying becomes more of a habit.

2. **Set realistic goals.** Many students tend to underestimate the amount of time needed to complete homework and assignments. They need to be encouraged to overestimate the time needed until their estimates are more realistic.

3. **Use a regular study area.** Students are more time efficient when they study in a study area that is well-lighted and free from distractions or noise. For some students, libraries may be effective places to study while others can create study areas at home.

4. **Prioritize tasks.** Students need to prioritize those activities that need to be completed first. Because one's attention is usually better at the outset, it is better to study difficult subjects before studying easy ones.

5. **Learn to say no to distractions.** Students must be willing to say no to their friends and others who want to talk or skip studying altogether.

6. **Self-reward success.** Students can improve their attention by making desirable activities contingent on completion of studying. This can include incentives such as food treats, watching television, or talking to friends on the phone.

Note. From *Self-Regulated Learning and Academic Achievement: Theoretical Perspectives* (2nd ed., p. 33), by B. J. Zimmerman and D. H. Schunk (Eds.), 2001, Mahwah, NJ: Erlbaum. Copyright 2001 by Erlbaum. Reprinted with permission.

BETTER UNDERSTANDING AND SUMMARIZING TEXT MATERIAL: SELECTED STRATEGIES

1. **Clarify and confront difficulties encountered.** For example, students can slow down to read more carefully and reread if the text meaning is unclear.

2. **Engage in self-questioning.** Students can ask themselves questions such as "Why is that true?" or "What does that mean?" to understand the material at a deeper level.

3. **Predicting what will come next.** Stopping to anticipate what the author will say before reading a text passage can help students develop greater understanding.

4. **Finding the main idea.** Analyzing passages in a paragraph and identifying the main idea that is being discussed increases understanding.

5. **Summarizing.** Students can summarize by paring down passages to their core meaning, focusing on the most important information, and substituting superordinate (e.g., a word whose meaning encompasses the meaning of another more specific word. For example, "animal" is the superordinate of "cat") terms for lists of items.

6. **Relating text to prior knowledge.** Students can relate new ideas in their text to previously stored information and can do so by developing analogies, examples, and comparisons.

Note. From *Self-Regulated Learning and Academic Achievement: Theoretical Perspectives* (2nd ed., pp. 54–55), by B. J. Zimmerman and D. H. Schunk (Eds.), 2001, Mahwah, NJ: Erlbaum. Copyright 2001 by Erlbaum. Reprinted with permission.

IMPROVING METHODS OF NOTE-TAKING: SELECTED STRATEGIES

1. **Use recording strategies.** Students need to be selective about what to include in their notes. Write down only main ideas and supporting facts. Listen for summary statements and write them down. Also, listen for signal words or phrases such as, "There are four main ideas in this article." Writing everything down burdens students and they often fall behind the teacher's comments.

2. **Use linear outlines.** Make a list of the topics and subtopics in traditional outline form and leave room in between for additional note-taking.

3. **Try mapping outlines.** Students can use a revision strategy involving the use of graphic representations to relate information visually using techniques such as tree diagrams, flow charts, concept webs and matrices. For example, a lecture comparing and contrasting religions might be depicted in a two dimensional matrix.

4. **Use the Cornell note-taking system.** In this system, a page is divided vertically with one column for recording and another for revising notes after the class is finished.

Note. From *Self-Regulated Learning and Academic Achievement: Theoretical Perspectives* (2nd ed., p. 76), by B. J. Zimmerman and D. H. Schunk (Eds.), 2001, Mahwah, NJ: Erlbaum. Copyright 2001 by Erlbaum. Reprinted with permission.

BETTER ANTICIPATING AND PREPARING FOR EXAMINATIONS: SELECTED STRATEGIES

1. **Revise lecture and text notes first.** Trying to memorize all oral and textual matter is not going to work for most students. Instead, students should concentrate on organizing only the most important information using one of the revision (note taking) strategies discussed above.

2. **Use elaborative interrogation.** Students should ask themselves questions intended to produce elaborations of the test material, for example, Why is this fact true? This strategy helps integrate new material with information already known.

3. **Use representational imagery.** By forming a vivid image of the word and its definition, students can remember lists of words or even concepts.

4. **Use first-letter mnemonics.** This entails remembering the first letter for each of a list of key words. For example, the names of the Great Lakes could be encoded in the form of the word HOMES (Huron, Ontario, Michigan, Erie, and Superior). Another example uses the word FACE to describe the spaces on the treble clef of the music staff. Students can learn to devise their own mnemonics.

5. **Use mnemonic sentences.** Students can remember a series of facts by constructing a sentence starting with the same letters: "my very eccentric mother just served us nine pizzas" for the planets in the solar system: Mercury, Venus, Earth, Mars, Jupiter, Saturn, Uranus, Neptune, and Pluto.

Note. From *Self-Regulated Learning and Academic Achievement: Theoretical Perspectives* (2nd ed., p. 99), by B. J. Zimmerman and D. H. Schunk (Eds.), 2001, Mahwah, NJ: Erlbaum. Copyright 2001 by Erlbaum. Reprinted with permission.

WRITING MORE EFFECTIVELY: SELECTED STRATEGIES

1. **Set goals.** Students should use a planning strategy for deciding the goals of the paper (e.g., to compare, to analyze, and to describe) and the sub-goals (e.g., what things to compare, analyze, and describe).

2. **Generate idea questions.** Students can ask questions to generate prose (e.g., what the object is, what the sequence of events is, what the facts on the object are, what the arguments or opinions are, and who the key players are).

3. **Use mapping or webbing.** Students can use strategies for establishing relations between ideas or events with visual concept maps or webs (e.g., linking generals to the wars they were in, the battles they fought, and the battles they won and lost).

4. **Vary sentence structure.** Students should make sure paragraphs vary in sentence structure from simple to compound and complex. Their writing is more interesting.

5. **Locate a peer editor.** Students can identify an appropriate classmate to read and give feedback about various aspects of the draft and do the same for the student helping them.

6. **Become a self-editor.** Students can learn to examine their draft by using a series of questions (e.g., Is there an introduction and conclusion? Did I achieve my main goal? Are any parts unclear or not supported? Did I give examples to illustrate the important points?).

Note. From *Self-Regulated Learning and Academic Achievement: Theoretical Perspectives* (2nd ed., pp. 113–114), by B. J. Zimmerman and D. H. Schunk (Eds.), 2001, Mahwah, NJ: Erlbaum. Copyright 2001 by Erlbaum. Reprinted with permission.

CHAPTER 89

HELPING STUDENTS MANAGE STRESS

Debbie W. Newsome, Nancy H. Whitlatch, Julia A. Southern, and Bradley T. Erford

Preview

Stress is a pervasive problem that affects students at all grade levels. Within recent decades, youth have exhibited more stress-related difficulties than in the past. The pressures of living in an increasingly complex society, accompanied by declining coping skills and social support, contribute to the increase in numbers of students facing stress-related health issues. We address sources of stress, outcomes associated with stress, and resources that help students cope more effectively with stressful events. We also provide prevention suggestions that professional school counselors can initiate in classrooms and intervention strategies for group and individual counseling.

"I don't know how I'm going to get it all done," lamented Abby, a 14-year-old high school freshman. "I have two big projects, three tests, and a ton of math homework. Mrs. Cook is going insane; I think she's mad at all of us. And soccer tryouts are tomorrow after school. Tiffany is acting all moody again and won't talk to me. Nobody understands—it's just too much."

Abby's concerns reflect what many young people experience on a regular basis. Time demands, relationships, and developmental transitions are just a few of the many stressors that are an ongoing part of students' lives. Do youth today feel more stressed than in previous generations? What exactly is stress, and how does it affect students' mental and physical well-being? Why is it that some individuals seemingly handle pressure and change with ease, while others suffer deleterious effects? What can professional school counselors do to help young people develop strategies to manage stress effectively? In this chapter, stress, its effects on young people, and examples of prevention and intervention activities that can be implemented by professional school counselors are described.

STRESS

The number of youth experiencing stress-related disorders, including depression, eating disorders, anxiety, social dysfunction, and substance abuse, has increased (McNamara, 2000). An estimated 35% of young people in the United States experience stress-related health problems (Lau, 2002). According to Heaven (1996), "teenagers and even children face stressful events that have the potential to severely disrupt their lives and negatively affect their psychological adjustment and health" (p. 44). Increased pressures faced by youth, coupled with declining coping skills and decreased social support, represent a challenge to professional school counselors and others who work with children and adolescents.

What Is Stress?

Stress can be defined in multiple ways. Lazarus and Folkman (1984) defined stress as "a particular relationship between the person and the environment that is appraised by the person as taxing or exceeding his or her resources and endangering his or her well-being" (p. 19). Stress can refer to an internal state, an external event, or the interaction between a person and the environment (McNamara, 2000). Perceptions of what is stressful vary widely among individuals. Indeed, something perceived as stressful by one person may be seen as trivial or even positive by another (Lau, 2002).

Stress can be viewed as a relationship between the events that happen to individuals and their physical, cognitive, emotional, and behavioral responses to them (McNamara, 2000). Several models describing the stress process have been proposed. Psychological models of stress focus on the reciprocal interactions between an individual and the environment. An example of such a model is presented in Figure 89.1. Adapted from

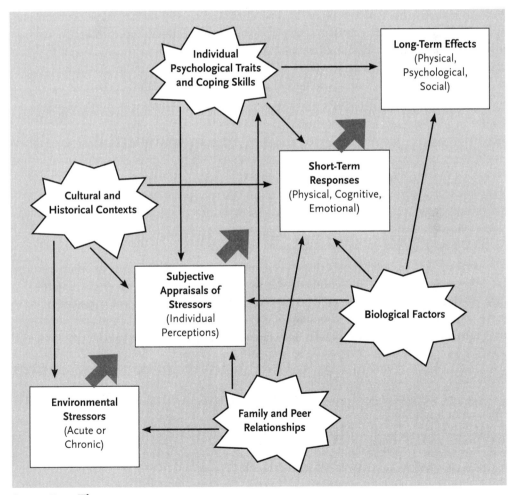

FIGURE 89.1. The stress process.

work conducted by Lazarus (1966), McNamara (2000), and others, the model is comprised of the following components: environmental stressors, an individual's subjective perceptions of the stressors, short-term responses, and long-term effects. Frequency, intensity, and timing of stressors can affect mental health, with outcomes being moderated by parental and peer support, individual psychological traits, and coping skills. Coping with stress is the process by which a person handles stressful situations and the emotions they generate.

TYPES OF STRESSORS

Childhood and adolescence may be marked by extremely stressful events and transitions as well as daily aggravations that require responses (Lau, 2002). Chronic demands or stressors are enduring aspects of the environment that involve deprivation or hardship and create ongoing challenges for an individual. Wadsworth, Raviv, Compas, and Connor-Smith (2005) found that chronic stress can cause an individual to become more susceptible to additional stressors and hinder their ability to employ effective coping mechanisms. Poverty, physical disability, and family dysfunction are examples of chronic stressors. In contrast, acute stressors, sometimes referred to as life events, involve changes or disruptions in existing conditions, such as those caused by accidents or illnesses. Chronic and acute stressors can be further classified as normative life events, non-normative events, and daily hassles (McNamara, 2000).

- *Normative life events:* Generic developmental challenges that everyone encounters. Normative events include physical changes, school transitions, emerging sexuality, changing peer and family relationships, and changes in cognitive levels.
- *Non-normative life events:* Unexpected, demanding events that may challenge the transitional experience. Examples include catastrophic phenomena (sudden, powerful events requiring major adaptive responses from the groups sharing the experience, including natural disasters, accidents, and terrorism) and unexpected changes such as parental divorce, injury, unemployment, or a family member's death or major illness.
- *Daily hassles:* Stable, repetitive stressors that tend to be irritating or annoying. Examples include parent–child conflict, academic demands, peer pressure, interpersonal concerns, and financial concerns. Ongoing hassles, in some ways, are more predictive of psychological symptoms than acute, episodic stressors and are associated with depression, anxiety, and conduct problems.

Normative, non-normative, and daily stressors can occur in multiple contexts, including school, home, and neighborhood.

School. Normative educational transitions, such as entering school for the first time, changing schools, or moving from one level to another (e.g., elementary school to middle school) can be significant sources of stress for young people. School-related factors that are unrelated to such transitions also can be stressful. Concerns about grades, teachers, homework, exams, extracurricular activities, and fitting in with peers are ongoing challenges that can be potentially taxing. Specific stressors in the school environment include impatient teachers, fear of failure, unclear assignments, work overload, expectations to achieve, and peer pressure, to name just a few. In an ongoing research study, middle school and high school students cited poor facilities, perceived unfair grading policies, uncommitted teachers, and negative school reputations as factors that impeded learning, thus serving as significant sources of stress.

One area that has particular relevance for students and school personnel is the emphasis placed on student and school performance, especially as it relates to high-stakes testing. Test anxiety has become more prevalent in young people, possibly due to the increasing frequency of testing and the importance placed on results (McDonald, 2001). Although low levels of stress can serve to motivate some students, high levels of stress can lead to test anxiety, which can be detrimental to performance. Being pressured to perform and then not meeting expectations can have upsetting, long-lasting effects (Lau, 2002). There are several things professional school counselors can do to help with test-related stress, including conducting workshops for parents and teachers, teaching psychoeducational lessons to classes about managing stressful feelings, and counseling small groups and individual students who struggle with test anxiety.

Family and peers. Relationships with parents, siblings, and other family members can be both a source of support and a source of stress for young people. Conflict and/or change in any of these relationships can be particularly stressful. Children and adolescents who are undergoing developmental transitions such as puberty may be especially vulnerable to strained family relationships or dysfunctional family systems. Parental divorce or remarriage, siblings leaving home, birth of a new family member, or parental unemployment are life events that can be quite stressful for children and adolescents. Distress arising from family relationships has been associated with several mental health problems, including depression, anxiety, and eating disorders (McNamara, 2000).

As in the case of family interactions, relationships with peers can be supportive, stressful, or both. As children grow older, peers become increasingly important and influential. Cliques, prejudice, and bullying can place difficult demands on young people, as can conflicts in values, increased intimacy, and issues related to sexuality. Professional school counselors are skilled at helping students with interpersonal issues, and preventive and remedial efforts targeted toward improving peer relationships can benefit all young people.

Other sources of stress. Anything perceived as a source of threat, harm, loss, or challenge has the potential to be stressful for children and adolescents. Personal health, the health of friends and family members, and planning for the future are among the many additional, yet common sources of stress. Dealing with poverty and ongoing financial issues can serve as a chronic stressor for children and parents (Wadsworth et al., 2005), as can minority group status and prejudice. The timing of puberty and its accompanying physiological changes can be quite stressful, especially for girls. When numerous stressors are experienced simultaneously, or when the timing of events departs significantly from the norm, youth are more likely to experience distress. Indeed, students who perceive combinations of school, family, peer group, and other life situations as stressful are likely to display symptoms of emotional and physical distress (McNamara, 2000).

People of all ages must deal with catastrophic events. Following the September 11th, 2001, terrorist attacks on New York City and Washington, DC, the American sense of safety and security was shaken to the core. Emotional distress associated with those attacks and other tragic events, including natural disasters and accidents, is expected. All youth should be watched for signs of emotional distress in the wake of exposure to any type of catastrophe. Helping young people cope with their distress is one of the most important challenges a mental health professional can face (National Institute of Mental Health, 2001).

STRESS-RELATED OUTCOMES

Exposure to stress triggers physical, emotional, and cognitive changes in the body. Immediate, short-term reactions to stress can motivate people to action; however, long-term exposure can lead to physical and psychosocial difficulties (Sharrer & Ryan-Wenger, 2002). Of critical interest to mental health professionals is the manner in which stress is appraised, because subjective appraisals affect the nature and intensity of stress-related responses.

Physiological responses. When someone perceives an event as acutely stressful (e.g., harmful, threatening, challenging), automatic physiological responses are activated. Blood pressure, heart rate, respiration rate, and perspiration increase, helping mobilize the body's resources for action (McNamara, 2000). The chemical messengers dopamine and norepinephrine are released in the sympathetic nervous system. The adrenal hormones cortisol and epinephrine, responding to signals passed from the hypothalamus, begin to circulate. Muscles tense and blood sugar increases as the body prepares for an anticipated emergency ("Disaster and Trauma," 2002).

As short-term responses, these physiological reactions to stress are not harmful and indeed may be helpful in cases of actual emergency. However, when exposure to stress is chronic and the stress response is overactivated, health-related problems occur. Gastrointestinal, circulatory, respiratory, and musculoskeletal disorders have been linked to stress, as have migraine, heartburn, diabetes, certain cancers, and rheumatoid arthritis (McNamara, 2000). Chronic stress can alter the immune system and hypothalamic-pituitary-adrenal (HPA) axis activity, leaving individuals more susceptible to physical illness and mental health disorders such as depression, alcoholism, and certain anxiety disorders.

Most of the research on physiological responses to stress has been conducted with adults, although children's responses are thought to be comparable. Children may not describe or interpret their physical symptoms in the same way as adults, however. In a study focusing on children's responses, second- through sixth-grade students were asked to describe the way their bodies felt during a past stressful event (Sharrer & Ryan-Wenger, 2002). The five most common physiological symptoms listed were headache, stomachache, getting sweaty, heart beating fast or feeling "funny," and feeling sick. Children also mentioned having tight muscles, being shaky, and tingling. Because people experience symptoms in different ways, professional school counselors will want to give students opportunities to describe the physiological responses they have to stressful situations. Physiological symptoms serve as signals that let youth know they are dealing with something stressful that may require action (e.g., active problem-solving, relaxation exercises).

Cognitive and emotional responses. Just as people respond physiologically to perceived stress, they also respond cognitively and emotionally. These responses, which are dependent on the individual's appraisal of the situation, are directly related to the process of coping, which is discussed in the next section. Immediate, short-term cognitive responses to stress include increased arousal and alertness and increased cognition and vigilance (McNamara, 2000). Initial emotional responses can include anger, fear, nervousness, and anxiety. Sharrer and Ryan-Wenger (2002) reported that children described feeling mad, worried, sad, nervous, and afraid when they were in stressful situations, with "mad" being the most common response. In instances of extreme stress (e.g., trauma), emotionally significant memories may be triggered ("Disaster and Trauma," 2002).

As in the case of physiological stress responses, short-term cognitive and emotional reactions to stress typically serve a purpose and are not, in and of themselves, harmful. However, exposure to long-term stress can have negative effects on psychological well-being. Some of the cognitive problems associated with too much stress include concentration difficulties, distractibility, and disorganization. For adolescents, the most common psychological outcome associated with stress overload is depression (Frydenberg, 1997). Other mental health conditions linked to stress include post-traumatic stress disorder (PTSD), obsessive–compulsive disorder, panic disorder, other anxiety disorders, substance abuse, and eating disorders (McNamara, 2000). Symptoms associated with these conditions can interfere severely with students' self-esteem, interpersonal relationships, and academic functioning.

COPING WITH STRESS

Lazarus and Folkman (1984) defined coping as cognitive and behavioral efforts directed toward managing any demands that are appraised as taxing or exceeding one's available resources. Personality and situational factors influence the ways in which people cope with these demands (McNamara, 2000). Conflict is commonly experienced in everyday life, and the degree to which young people are able to employ effective coping strategies can transform a conflict into a problem that can be solved productively, rather than result in negative outcomes (Frydenberg, 1997). A person's subjective appraisal of a situation affects the selection of coping strategies, which differ depending on the situation.

One way researchers categorized coping responses is based on whether the response is *problem-focused* or *emotion-focused* (see McNamara, 2000). Problem-focused coping strategies attempt to alter the source of stress whereas emotion-focused coping strategies attempt to reduce the emotional distress associated with a given situation. Generally, problem-focused strategies are associated with adaptive coping, reduced depression, and other positive outcomes, whereas relying exclusively on emotion-focused strategies can lead to maladaptive functioning. With problem-focused coping, individuals take active steps to deal with the situation, thus enhancing one's sense of control over the environment. Emotion-focused coping, in contrast, may involve avoidance, which provides temporary symptom relief but, over time, is less effective in reducing symptoms associated with stress. Professional school counselors can implement stress management interventions that are tailored toward helping students use active,

TABLE 89.1

COPING STRATEGIES USED BY YOUNG PEOPLE

Accessing Support—staying connected with family, friends, school personnel, church

Enhancing Self-Reliance—making decisions, problem solving, reframing

Ventilating Feelings—may be appropriate or inappropriate ventilation

Seeking Diversions—relaxing, engaging in activities or exercise

Avoidance—escaping, denying, or avoiding issues and/or people; substance use (Plunkett et al., 2000)

problem-focused coping strategies. Examples of stress management interventions are described later in this chapter.

Many types of coping strategies are used by children and adolescents. Typically, young people use a combination of problem-focused and emotion-focused strategies to cope with stressful situations. Coping strategies used by youth form the foundation for coping strategies used in adulthood (Plunkett, Radmacher, & Moll-Pharana, 2000).

Young people differ in their use of coping styles based on a number of factors (see Table 89.1), including age and gender (McNamara, 2000). Girls tend to use a wider range of coping styles and are more likely to seek social support. They also are more likely to vent feelings, seek spiritual support, positively reframe situations, and engage in wishful thinking. Boys, on the other hand, show a stronger preference for using humor, engaging in sports, and seeking other diversions, both positive and negative. Males may come across as more stable and difficult to irritate, whereas girls may ruminate and self-evaluate more. By being aware of these potential differences in coping style, professional school counselors can be better prepared to help all students develop and practice strategies that will facilitate adaptive adjustment.

PROTECTIVE RESOURCES

What factors help students cope effectively with stressful situations, thereby avoiding the negative psychological and physical effects of stress? Research on the resilience in young people indicates that protective resources, including social support and personal attributes or dispositions, seem to help people cope with stress more constructively, even in adverse circumstances (D'Imperio & Dubow, 2000; McNamara, 2000).

Social support. Supportive relationships with family members, peers, and other significant people play an important role in helping students cope with negative events. Supportive relationships can have a buffering effect on stress by preventing stressful events and hassles from occurring in the first place; making individuals feel less vulnerable when they do occur; reducing the impact and intensity of stress-related symptoms; and providing help, advice, and support to remove the stressor (McNamara, 2000).

Supportive families characterized by warmth, high levels of communication, involvement, and appropriate structure help promote positive adjustment and self-efficacy in children (Herman-Stahl & Petersen, 1996). Professional school counselors have the unique opportunity to help parents understand the connection between a child's life at home and life at school. Toward this end, professional school counselors can lead workshops designed to teach effective parenting practices and healthy family interaction patterns.

Similarly, positive relationships with peers can help buffer the negative effects of stress. Class guidance lessons and small-group sessions focusing on peer relationships can provide children with the skills needed to develop and maintain healthy friendships. Beyond this, professional school counselors can facilitate the development of a positive, supportive school climate by leading in-service workshops and providing consultation for teachers and other school personnel who work with students.

Personal attributes. Several personal characteristics can serve as protective factors against stressful events, including self-esteem, self-competence, optimism, and a sense of control (Herman-Stahl & Petersen, 1996; McNamara, 2000). Young people who view themselves as worthy and competent are less vulnerable to stress-related problems. Likewise, youth who approach life with expectations of favorable outcomes tend to cope more competently with stress (Herman-Stahl & Petersen, 1996). An internal locus of control, characterized by beliefs that outcomes are contingent upon personal effort, also appears to have a buffering effect against stressors (McNamara, 2000). Students who believe that their efforts can influence the outcome in a given situation are more likely to engage in proactive coping strategies when faced with difficulties. When internalized control is taken to the extreme, however, uncontrollable events may evoke maladaptive coping efforts rather than buffer against stress.

By overseeing the delivery of comprehensive developmental guidance programs, professional school counselors work to promote the personal attributes of self-esteem, positive outlook, and sense of control. By ensuring that all students receive systematic, developmentally appropriate instruction in these domains, professional school counselors facilitate the bolstering of student resiliency.

INTERVENTIONS IN SCHOOLS

If we are going to help young people cope in an increasingly demanding world, it is crucial to invest in primary prevention methods (McNamara, 2000), the goal of which is to help all children develop the psychosocial skills needed for meeting life's challenges. For those students who have been exposed to trauma or excessive stress, and for other students who may not be coping well, additional interventions in the form of group counseling, individual counseling, parent or teacher consultation, and/or referral to outside resources may be warranted. In this section, preventive measures that can be initiated by professional school counselors are described. Attention is also given to ways professional school counselors can help vulnerable students through group and individual counseling.

PSYCHOEDUCATIONAL INTERVENTIONS FOR STUDENTS

Initiating preventive measures *before* stress becomes a problem prepares students to deal with demanding situations more effectively. Professional school counselors can influence the largest number of students through classroom psychoeducational activities. Depending on school size, school policy, and the professional school counselor's role in the school may personally teach the lessons or may train classroom teachers to do so.

TABLE 89.2
RECOGNIZING STRESS

How does it feel when you are stressed?

How can you know that you are stressed?

What sorts of thoughts do you have?

How do you feel in your body?

How does stress affect your behavior?

How do you act toward other people when you are stressed? How do they act toward you?

How can you tell when other people are stressed?

Who do you know that is stressed?

Equipping students with generalizable coping strategies can help curtail many of the problems associated with stress overload (McNamara, 2000).

Stress management programs for children and adolescents, which can be a part of a comprehensive developmental guidance program, typically focus on (a) identifying sources of stress, (b) recognizing the physical and emotional consequences of stress, and (c) learning and implementing adaptive coping responses. Recommended components for preventive programs (McNamara, 2000) include education about the causes and consequences of stress; training in methods to reduce psychological and physical arousal; general problem-solving and decision-making skills; general cognitive skills (including cognitive restructuring); physical ways of coping with stress; study skills and time management; skills for increasing self-control and self-esteem; and social skills, including effective communication, conflict resolution, and assertiveness training. Numerous resources for professional school counselors describe developmentally appropriate activities for each of these topics, and several of the components (i.e., social skills, self-esteem, problem solving) are already part of the scope and sequence that comprise comprehensive guidance programs. In this section, general suggestions related to the components that have particular relevance to stress management are provided. These suggestions are broad, and professional school counselors will want to ensure that the related activities are developmentally appropriate for their student population.

Education about the stress process. It is important for students to be able to identify stressors and recognize their own personal physical and emotional responses to stress. McNamara (2000) offered some "starting questions" that can help students recognize their own responses to stress (see Table 89.2).

To help students develop self-awareness, ask them to keep a stress-awareness diary in which they record stress-triggering events as well as their symptoms and reactions. When the stress diaries are discussed, encourage students to describe their personal appraisals of the events. The discussion can provide an opportunity to teach ways to restructure negative thoughts (see Table 89.3).

Physical ways to manage stress. Nutrition, physical activity, and sleep quality all affect people's mental health (McNamara, 2000). Professional school counselors can share information about the relationship between good health and coping with stressors. Unfortunately, many students do not eat nutritionally balanced meals at home or at

TABLE 89.3

STINKIN' THINKIN'—4 STEPS FOR REDUCING NEGATIVE THOUGHTS

STOP: Stop before you react.

BREATHE: Belly breathe to keep from getting tense. It is impossible to be tense and relaxed at the same time.

REFLECT: Examine the situation. What is the concern? Am I threatened? What thoughts and feelings am I having? What's the worst that could happen? Can I handle it? Am I jumping to conclusions? Is there another way to look at the situation?

CHOOSE: What do I want to happen? What can I do? What coping behaviors will work? Do I have the time, skills, and desire to achieve a solution? Am I avoiding? DECIDE!

---

school. Also, insufficient sleep and exercise contribute to feelings of fatigue and irritability. Studies have shown that physical activity, in addition to strengthening muscles, bones, the cardiovascular system, and the respiratory system, helps decrease fatigue and moodiness (Lau, 2002). Regular physical exercise can boost self-confidence, increase resilience, and make students better able to handle frustration. Similarly, sleeping well "is central to coping with life, managing stress, and having positive feelings of well-being" (McNamara, 2000, p. 152). Children and adolescents, as well as adults, often spend far fewer hours than necessary getting quality sleep (Lau, 2002). Helping young people determine how much sleep they need and encouraging them to make commitments toward meeting that need can facilitate the stress-management process.

Learning how to relax is another important stress-management tool. Relaxation helps prevent some of the damaging physiological effects of stress and also helps prepare people to cope with stress more effectively. Being relaxed is both an outlook on life (i.e., calm, laid back) and a skill that can be learned. Developing relaxation techniques can help replace depleted energy resources and prevent the build-up of tension. Listening to music, taking a hot bath, drawing or painting, working in the yard, and participating in imagery exercises are all ways of relaxing. Help students explore ways of relaxing that are helpful to them, and encourage them to participate in at least one relaxation activity daily. Abdominal breathing (or "belly breathing"), progressive relaxation, and imagery are relaxation techniques that are easily taught and can be used by students in virtually any surrounding. It may be helpful to tell students that some people feel silly when trying out these relaxation skills, especially at the beginning. With time and practice, the techniques become more comfortable and can be employed easily to help reduce tension (see Figure 89.2).

Guided imagery or visualization can be used in conjunction with deep breathing to enhance relaxation. Imagery can be used with classes, small groups, or individuals. To normalize the process and ensure that students do not confuse it with hypnosis, explain that commercials use visualization to sell products and that athletes use visualization to improve performance. Begin with abdominal breathing. See Figure 89.3 for an example of an imagery exercise that can be read aloud after students have closed their eyes and started the breathing activity. After the students have completed the visualization exercise, tell them that when they feel stress in their bodies or have disturbing thoughts to imagine this safe place again and to practice breathing deeply. Depending on the age

Abdominal breathing can be done in a sitting or standing position. Speaking slowly and quietly, ask students to close their eyes and do the following:

Take a deep breath through your nose, very slowly. Pull the breath deeply into the bottom of your stomach (count 1-2-3-4). Then breathe out slowly through your mouth to the count of 8. (Repeat the breathing cycle) Place your hand on your stomach. You should be able to feel it move as you breathe. You will notice that as you continue breathing like this, you become very relaxed. (Repeat the breathing cycle) Now open your eyes. Notice the feelings you have in your body.

FIGURE 89.2. Abdominal breathing.

First, help the students move to a relaxed state through abdominal breathing. The counselor continues to speak slowly and quietly:

Your whole body feels more relaxed. I am going to ask you to picture something in your mind's eye. If at any time you feel uncomfortable, open your eyes. Now, picture a place where you feel safe and cared for. (Wait several seconds) Look around this safe, safe place. (Wait several seconds) What is around you? (Wait several seconds) Is this place inside or outside? (Wait several seconds) Are there people or pets around you? (Wait several seconds) What do you hear? (Wait) Do you smell anything? (Wait) Now, stay in this safe place for a few minutes. (Wait a few minutes) When you are ready, take a deep, deep breath and open your eyes.

FIGURE 89.3. Guided imagery.

of the students, you might encourage them to draw what they visualized, talk about their pictures, and/or discuss when they might imagine this safe place again.

Study skills and time management. Assignments, tests, and the pressure to succeed can all be sources of stress for students of all ages. Developing good study skills and time management skills are essential to academic success and stress reduction. Students can be taught to handle academic tasks in ways that are efficient and effective. Suggestions that promote effective use of study time follow:

- Practice active studying.
- Read the summary at the end of textbook chapters first. This will help you know what the author considers important.
- Read the questions at the end of the passage and all picture captions in advance. Try to answer the questions as you read.
- If you encounter a section that doesn't make sense, keep reading. Many times, questionable areas become clear with further reading.
- Review what you have read.

- Use mnemonics, a technique for improving the memory, to help remember important facts. (Adults will need to teach children how to use this tool.)
- Find an ideal study environment.
- Establish a regular place to study. This can help with structure and motivation. Keep it attractive and organized.
- Control internal and external distractions.
- Be aware of your own body clock. Choose times to study when your energy level is high.
- Take breaks.
- Use time management tools.
- Clarify your goals. What is most important and why?
- Avoid procrastination. Establish a routine and reward yourself for completing tasks on time (e.g., invite a friend over, participate in a favorite activity).
- Keep a calendar or day-timer. Write down assignments, due dates, and other scheduled events.
- Break down large tasks into manageable units, and plan for their completion.
- Keep a daily and weekly to-do list to help prioritize activities and assignments. Check off completed tasks.
- Recognize the need for balance and flexibility.
- Keep things in perspective. Worry saps time and energy and is nonproductive. If you find yourself getting anxious about schoolwork, take time to relax and practice deep breathing. By simply breathing deeply, anxiety decreases.

WORKING WITH PARENTS AND TEACHERS

Parent workshops. Parents or caregivers are experts on their children and interact with them daily. By offering parent-education workshops, which might be titled, "Helping Your Student Deal With Stress," parents can be given tools to help children manage stress more effectively and learn ways to reduce stress in the home. Any of the topics listed in the section titled *Psychoeducational Interventions for Students* can be included in a parent workshop. Professional school counselors may also want to share the following with parents:

- Teach parents deep breathing techniques to use when they feel stressed so that they can reinforce the practice with their children.
- Television, movies, and computer viewing of virtual violence can create stress.
- Sharing adult worries with children can contribute to children's stress.
- Overly high expectations can be stressful. Many times, parents are not aware of the expectations their children perceive. Although parents may not require straight As, children hear what is not said. A parent who expects perfection in him- or herself delivers a strong message that perfection is expected from each member of the family.
- Encourage parents to establish routines. Routines provide structure, eliminate uncertainty, and reduce chaos, which creates stress (Lau, 2002).

- Parents can be sensitive to overload on their families or their children and take steps to remove stressors. Parents have the responsibility of intervening on their children's behalf when necessary.
- Parents can be reminded of the importance of nutrition, exercise, and quality sleep to combat stress.
- Parents are essential in helping children at all levels with the study skills and time management skills described in the previous section.
- Parents can help children appraise stressful situations constructively and then implement appropriate coping strategies.

Many parents need to realize that *they* must be in control of the family. Parents, with the best of intentions, often allow children to make adult decisions. Children suffer stress if they are asked to make these decisions before they are developmentally able. The mantra "Our family is a benign and loving monarchy" allows children to know that they are being cared for, loved, and protected.

Working with teachers. In addition to working with parents, professional school counselors will want to consult with teachers and offer in-service training on topics related to stress management. Teachers need information that will help them identify students who are suffering from stress. Behaviors that may indicate problems with stress in students include nail biting, fidgeting, separation anxiety, school phobia, bullying, violent and/or disruptive behaviors, obsessive–compulsive behaviors, social problems, crying, and excessive worry. Helping teachers understand the links between thoughts, feelings, and behaviors promotes understanding, if not acceptance, of student behaviors and can pave the way for making necessary interventions. Teachers need to be reminded that the professional school counselor is available for individual and small-group counseling as well as whole-class guidance to help students cope with stress more effectively.

In-service workshops for teachers on stress management can focus on the same topics that are listed as psychoeducational topics for students. In particular, professional school counselors will want to provide information to school personnel about the stress process, stress symptoms, and associated consequences. It may be helpful to engage the group in deep breathing or progressive relaxation exercises as tools to use themselves and with their students.

Numerous stressors exist in schools—some are unavoidable and others are not. Professional school counselors can work with school personnel to identify stressors that are part of the school environment and find ways to eliminate or ameliorate those stressors that are amenable to change. For example, high-stakes testing has added stress to the school environment. Anxiety and stress surrounding educational evaluation is considerable (McDonald, 2001). Teachers sometimes unknowingly add to this pressure by reminding students throughout the year, "This will be on the final exam." During in-service workshops, it might be beneficial to have teachers brainstorm other wordings that might be less anxiety provoking. Most teachers want students to understand the importance of tests but unwittingly add to student anxiety and stress by focusing too strongly on that importance. Test anxiety can impair performance and negatively affect test results.

GROUP AND INDIVIDUAL COUNSELING

Group counseling. Children who experience traumatic life events can suffer fear-related problems that impede their normal functioning and cause them to become disengaged in learning. These students may benefit from interacting with peers and adults in a group setting to enhance their self-worth, security, and control (Robinson, Rotter, Robinson, Fey, & Vogel, 2003). Professional school counselors can help these students explore the self in relation to the life events that have affected them. Also, therapeutic stress reduction skills and coping strategies can be shared in counseling groups that deal with family changes, relationships, anger management, inappropriate behaviors, anxiety, and depression. When planning for group counseling, professional school counselors can use the following procedures:

- Ensure that proper, school-regulated procedures for obtaining parental permission for students to participate in a counseling group are followed.
- Explain the nature of the group to teachers, and request the names of students who might benefit.
- Interview selected students to identify appropriate candidates for group participation and assess their level of interest.
- Notify or seek permission from parents. If a note is sent home, state the type of group, length and number of sessions, and activities that will take place in the group. Include a phone number where the professional school counselor can be reached if there are questions.
- Plan for the group, including time, place, and number of sessions. Include the activities that will take place in each session. Consider students' developmental levels as activities are planned.
- Proceed with group sessions. During the first session, describe the purpose of the group and include an explanation of confidentiality and its limits in age-appropriate terms.
- Provide information about stress, its causes, and typical responses. Ask students to think of a situation that stresses them, then ask, "Where in your body do you feel that worry or stress?" and "What are your thoughts when you have those feelings?"
- Teach students relaxation techniques, including deep breathing, progressive relaxation, and visualization.
- In subsequent sessions, focus on learning and implementing coping strategies (mental strategies, physical ways of coping, interpersonal skills, problem solving, etc.). Provide students with opportunities to "rehearse" (through role play or other methods) their responses to anticipated stressful experiences.
- Encourage students to use their new skills and to teach them to family members.
- At the conclusion of the group, give students an opportunity to evaluate their experience.

Individual counseling. When stress is a significant problem for a particular student, individual counseling may be warranted. Students may self-refer or be referred by teachers or parents. In many schools, long-term individual counseling is discouraged, and it may be necessary to make an outside referral so that the student gets the necessary help.

When working with any student individually, professional school counselors will want to explain confidentiality and its limits. Take time to build a therapeutic relationship and give the student an opportunity to tell his or her story. This will aid in assessing the severity of the problem and making decisions about next steps. Is the stress fear-based, and, if so, is the fear specific or generalized? What is the students' sense of control, security, and self-worth? Recommended interventions to help individuals deal with stress while increasing his or her sense of self-worth and control. Include relaxation training, systematic desensitization, guided imagery, interpersonal communication skills training, decision-making and life-skills training, creating success experiences, bibliocounseling and encouragement (Robinson et al., 2003). In particular, professional school counselors should give students the opportunity to talk about what is stressful, identify their reactions to the stressful situation, explore effective coping strategies, and implement those strategies. If the student continues to manifest symptoms of distress or if the counselor suspects a more chronic condition (e.g., anxiety, PTSD, depression, abuse), it would be appropriate to suggest individual or family counseling in the community.

Summary/Conclusion

Stress is a pervasive problem that affects students at all grade levels. It seems that youth are experiencing more adverse reactions to stress than they have in the past. Stressors can come in many forms, including developmental transitions, life events, catastrophic events, and daily hassles. Indeed, change of any type can be stressful. When students experience stress, physical, cognitive, and emotional responses are likely. Chronic, long-term exposure to stress can be detrimental to physical and emotional health and well-being.

People cope with stress in numerous ways, with some coping strategies being more adaptive than others. Active, problem-focused coping tends to yield better outcomes than emotion-focused coping, particularly when the coping style is characterized by avoidance. In addition to individual coping styles, protective factors such as family and peer support, self-confidence, and an internal sense of control appear to affect the manner in which young people manage stress.

Professional school counselors can intervene on multiple levels to help students manage stress more effectively. Primary prevention methods include classroom guidance lessons, parent workshops, and teacher training sessions and consultation on topics related to stress management. In cases where students are at risk for stress-related problems or have evidenced poor coping skills, professional school counselors can offer group and individual counseling as well as coordinate services for those students who need outside professional help. Professional school counselors play instrumental roles in helping create safe, supportive schools and in teaching students and their caregivers life skills that will help them cope effectively with present and future stressors.

(Note: See the CD-ROM for a list of references.)

CHAPTER 90

HELPING STUDENTS MANAGE ANGER

John R. Charlesworth

Preview

The purpose of this chapter is to provide an introduction to anger management interventions, with specific focus on applications and techniques that professional school counselors can use in providing individual and group counseling to students with anger-related problems. Classroom guidance topics and activities for educating students about anger and effective anger management are also discussed.

The second edition of the *Dictionary of Psychology* (Chaplin, 1985) defined anger as "an acute emotional reaction elicited by any of a number of stimulating situations, including threat, overt aggression, restraint, verbal attack, disappointment, or frustration" (p. 27). Although mental health practitioners and researchers have discussed the lack of conceptual clarity of anger and its related processes (Smith, Larson, DeBaryshe, & Salzman, 2000), it is commonly accepted that anger is a normal human emotion that can be viewed at three levels: (1) *physical symptoms* of feelings of anger may include increased heart rate, muscular tension, and adrenaline flow; (2) *cognitive experiences* of anger frequently include distorted negative perceptions and interpretations of others' behaviors; and (3) *behavioral indications* of anger may include a variety of physical and verbal outbursts such as yelling, screaming, kicking, and fighting. These reactions to anger can be directed toward others or self.

Anger is generally perceived negatively because, unmanaged, it can lead to aggression and violence. But anger can also serve an adaptive, positive function. Anger can stimulate us to take action when we or loved ones are under the threat of attack and can serve as an impetus for us to take appropriate actions to bring about needed changes, such as better or more equitable rules or laws (Bowers, 1994).

Because anger is an emotion that can have adverse consequences for both self and others, it is important that the problem be addressed early on. Childre and Rozman (2003) noted that the problem is not anger itself but that individuals frequently do not know how to manage anger. Nowhere has the problem of anger management been more evident than with school-age students.

Professional school counselors are in a unique position to help individuals understand and effectively cope with feelings of anger, because they can provide students with needed classroom guidance and individual- and group-counseling anger-management programs and services, beginning with their entrance into elementary schools. The purpose of this chapter is to provide an introduction to anger management interventions, with specific emphasis on practical applications and techniques that professional school counselors can use while working with students in individual and small-group counseling. Instruction and activities that can be incorporated into guidance classroom lessons that educate students about anger and anger awareness will be introduced, and methods for reducing the development of anger-related problems will also be discussed.

COGNITIVE-BEHAVIORAL INTERVENTIONS

The most frequently used individual and group treatment approaches for anger (and those considered to be most effective) have a basis in cognitive-behavioral therapy (Beck & Fernandez, 1998; Childre & Rozman, 2003; Kassinove & Tafrate, 2002). Smith et al. (2000) conducted a comprehensive review of anger-management programs for students covering school-based programs and a variety of other treatment centers, including clinical and residential settings. The review provided professional school counselors with an understanding of the types and content of anger-management programs contained in the professional literature. Of the 37 articles included in the review, the vast majority (29 out of 37, or 78%) of the studies incorporated two or more treatment approaches, and the use of cognitive-behavioral interventions in these studies was almost universal.

The two most recognized theoretical cognitive-behavioral approaches to anger management are Beck's (1976, 2000) cognitive-behavioral therapy (CBT), and Ellis's (Ellis, 1977; Ellis & Harper, 1975) rational emotive behavior therapy (REBT). Although each of these approaches has distinctive features, both have much in common. Both approaches require students to identify the situations/events in which they experience anger. Emphasis is then placed on helping students to identify the thoughts/cognitions that precede anger. The major intervention common to both approaches is to help students determine whether these cognitions (thoughts) are rational or irrational (Ellis, 1977; Ellis & Harper, 1975), correct or false, distorted or inaccurate (Beck, 1976, 2000) and to replace irrational, inaccurate thoughts with more rational, accurate ones.

Ellis and Harper (1975) believed that students' unhealthy emotions are due to their adherence to 10 basic false philosophical beliefs or irrational thoughts. From his approach, Ellis attempts to change students' false assumptions by confronting their irrational thoughts, demonstrating how illogical the thoughts are, and teaching students how to replace the irrational thoughts with more rational ones that can result in students changing basic philosophical assumptions and values.

In contrast to Ellis's REBT, which is often highly directive, persuasive, confrontive and didactically oriented, Beck's CBT places emphasizes the importance of the student–counselor relationship, and primarily uses open-ended Socratic questioning to help students reflect upon and discover the inaccuracies of their own thinking. Both approaches value homework assignments, have students engage in behaviors designed to test the validity of cognitions, and frequently draw upon a wide range of behavioral techniques.

The following brief scenario illustrates some examples of the irrational, inaccurate thoughts that both Ellis and Beck believed frequently lead to inappropriate feelings of anger, and how a counselor might intervene:

> Tom asked his best friend and classmate, Jason, to wait for him so they could walk home together after school. When Tom discovered that Jason wasn't waiting for him after school, Tom had the following thoughts that created feelings of anger for him:
>
>> "Jason *should have* waited for me."
>> "It is *terrible* and *awful* that Jason didn't wait."
>> "You can *never* count on Jason for anything."

Given this scenario, both Ellis and Beck would help Tom see that his thoughts are irrational or inaccurate and help him to replace them with more rational, accurate thoughts. Ellis would be more likely to didactically teach Tom that his thoughts are irrational by confronting and telling him something like the following: "Although it would have been nice if Jason had waited for you, there is no law that says that he *must, has to, or should have* waited for you," "Although Jason didn't meet you, it isn't terrible or awful, your world isn't collapsing, but this is a minor annoyance because he didn't do what you wanted," and finally "Jason has done many things for you, and not doing that one thing doesn't mean you can't count on him for other things."

In contrast to Ellis's intervention in the scenario, Beck would be more likely to achieve the same ends by using Socratic questions, such as "Other than that you wanted Jason to wait for you, is there any reason why he *should have* waited for you? Was Jason's not waiting for you terrible or awful, or merely disappointing or annoying for you?" And, "Does Jason's not waiting for you in this one instance mean that you can never count on him, or does it just mean that he didn't wait this one time?"

Donald Meichenbaum's (1977) cognitive behavior modification (CBM) is another major cognitive-behavioral therapy that has been successfully used in treating anger. Like REBT and CBT, CBM shares the assumption that distressing emotions are typically due to maladaptive thoughts. CBM focuses on making students aware of and training them to develop more effective self-talk that will enable them to cope more effectively in problematic situations.

Stress inoculation training (SIT; Meichenbaum, 1985) is a particular coping-skills program developed by Meichenbaum to aid in stress reduction that has been demonstrated to be effective with a number of problems, including anger (Corey, 2000). SIT appears to be particularly beneficial when the student experiences anger in relatively specific situations. In addition to helping the student learn helpful behavioral techniques, the student is taught a number of relatively specific coping thoughts to assist them in working through the anger provoking situation.

BEHAVIORAL INTERVENTIONS

Cognitive-behavior approaches differentially incorporate a wide variety of behavioral techniques in treating anger problems, including the following:

- *Relaxation training.* Students can be taught to relax using a variety of modalities, including progressive relaxation (learning to systematically tighten and then relax the muscle groups of the body), yoga exercises, or meditation.
- *Homework assignments.* Students may be assigned to engage in self-monitoring of their thoughts and/or behaviors, keep an anger log, practice engaging in new behaviors, or participate in bibliotherapy.
- *Assertiveness training.* Before students are taught behavioral assertiveness skills, students are frequently taught the difference between nonassertive, assertive, and aggressive behavior. In addition, any cognitive distortions or irrational thoughts impeding assertive behavior are replaced (Lange & Jakubowski, 1976). Students can then learn assertiveness skills through modeling, role-playing, and graded task assignments in real-life situations.

- *Distraction techniques.* After learning to identify cognitive and/or bodily cues that are precursors of anger, students can be taught a variety of distraction techniques, including counting to 10, removing themselves from the environment, or using humor (e.g., picturing an aggressor in his or her underwear or wearing a clown's costume).
- *Imagery.* Students can use imagery to learn relaxation and as another distraction technique by envisioning themselves in calm, peaceful scenes. Professional school counselors can also use imagery to help students see themselves effectively using their learned cognitive and behavioral skills in what previously were anger-provoking situations.
- *Problem-solving skills.* Students can be taught a general problem-solving model to assist in identifying a wider repertoire of methods for coping with anger-provoking situations.
- *Social skills training.* Students can be taught a wide range of social skills, such as smiling and providing eye contact, to assist in developing interpersonal skills.
- *Communication skills.* Students can be taught how to actively listen and produce "I messages."

Phillips-Hershey and Kanagy (1996) provided practical suggestions on how to teach middle and high school students communication skills as a proactive way to deal with anger in a positive way. They specifically emphasized the need to teach students how to effectively use "I messages" and provided a number of methods they believed could be effectively used in classroom guidance or small-group counseling sessions. First, students are directed to identify all the things they feel angry about, what they do when they feel angry, the consequences of their actions, and whether the consequences experienced are what they wanted. The students are then informed that anger is okay, but that frequently the way people express anger makes a conflict situation worse. Second, a professional school counselor orally gives the students a "you message" and then asks that they discuss the impact of the message. The students are then given the same content in an "I message" format and again asked the impact of the message. After discussing the difference between their reactions to the "you messages" and the "I messages," students are directed to role-play two skits, each involving one of the messages and are then again asked to compare the different impact of the two messages. Next, students are given brief written scenarios and asked to write appropriate "I messages" for each. Finally, students are asked to role-play giving "I messages" to someone they feel anger towards. Phillip-Hershey and Kanagy (1996) also provided a method for evaluating the program for both the students and professional school counselor.

Professional school counselors who come from more of a pure behavioral counseling approach also use many of the behavioral techniques just described. As opposed to cognitive-behavioral-oriented counselors who see the main benefit of the behavioral techniques as producing changes in cognition, traditional behaviorists see the main benefit of these techniques as producing changes in behavior. Traditional behaviorists are also more likely to use positive reinforcement for students engaging in appropriate behavior and use extinction or punishment when needed to help eliminate aggressive behavior.

Play Therapy

Another viable method for reducing anger problems is individual play therapy (Fischetti, 2001). Rather than accepting that one standardized play-therapy approach is the most effective for all clients and situations, Fischetti (2001) preferred a prescriptive approach that enabled a professional school counselor to choose one they believe will be most effective. Fischetti (2001) identified three approaches useful for planning treatment for students with anger management problems. *Client-centered play therapy* is a nondirective approach that is a viable choice when the clinician can provide the student time to pursue their issues and personal growth. *Release play therapy* is a structured approach to assist clients in reenacting a stressful event and working through the pain and anger associated with it. Finally, *cognitive-behavioral play therapy* enables the clinician to use a wide range of behavioral techniques, such as antecedents, reinforcers, contingencies, modeling, relaxation training, systematic desensitization, and cognitive interventions such as learning to identify and replace dysfunctional thoughts, to best meet the treatment goals jointly developed with the student. A frequent component of cognitive-behavioral play therapy is student homework.

In addition to describing play-therapy approaches, Fischetti (2001) provided a number of case examples intended to demonstrate their treatment effectiveness. Kaduson and Shaefer (1997, 2001) and Jones (1998) provided a variety of individual and group play-therapy techniques and activities that can be incorporated into appropriate play-therapy approaches to assist students in working through anger-management issues. Examples of such techniques and activities follow:

- *The Mad Game* (Davidson, 1997, pp. 224–225) is used to help clients (ages 3–13 years) in individual or group play therapy learn how to express anger appropriately, both verbally and kinesthetically. Participants in the game are asked to take turns stacking cardboard bricks or plastic blocks, one on top of the other, as they make statements about what angers them. Once all bricks or blocks are stacked the identified student is asked to express something he really feels angry about and then knocks down the bricks.

- *Computer Storytelling* (Brewer, 1997, pp. 32–34) is used in individual play therapy to help students develop alternative feelings, thoughts, and methods for resolving a current struggle. The student is asked to develop an original story with a beginning, middle, and end. The student may choose to type the story, dictate and have the counselor type the story, or alternate typing paragraphs with the counselor. While the student is developing the story the counselor looks for the character representing the student and any themes or patterns that relate to problem-solving or relationship issues and may ask the student questions about them. Aggressive students enjoy a sense of mastery and control over the computer while learning to abide by the rules and procedures required to use it effectively.

- *Relaxation Training: Bubble Breaths* (Cabe, 2001, p. 346) is used in play therapy to help students learn relaxation training that can be used to reduce feelings of anxiety and anger, and the accompanying physical reactions. Students fill the room with bubbles and "pop" them as they fall. Students are then invited to pop the bubbles one at a time, which is more challenging but can be done with practice. Attention is then directed toward the deep breathing and controlled exhaling involved. The counselor follows this with instruction on how to breathe from the belly. Students are taught how they can use a series of three bubble breaths to relax when they begin to feel anxious or angry. This approach has been used successfully with all age ranges and with individuals as well as large groups.

- *Out of Control* (Jones, 1998) is a group play therapy activity for use with 4 to 15 students who experience anger and frustration when things don't go the way they want. Some small prize items (a few more than the number in the group) and a pair of dice are placed on a table in front of the group members. There are two rounds to the game. In the first round, each participant rolls the dice in turn. Those who roll doubles select a prize and open it; participants not rolling doubles cannot choose a prize. The dice is passed until all the prizes are gone. One participant may end of up with several prizes while others may end up with none. Before beginning the second round, students are told that this round is timed (5 minutes for smaller groups, 10 minutes for larger ones), and that double rolls are now used to select prizes from other members. The game continues until the allotted time elapses. Again, some participants may have several prizes while others may have none. At the end of the game the participants are given numerous questions to discuss, including, "What do you do when things don't go your way?" "How do you handle things when life doesn't seem fair or is out of control?" "What can you do when life seems out of control?" "Did anyone feel angry during the game, and, if so, how did you handle it?"

CLASSROOM GUIDANCE

There are many ways that professional school counselors can incorporate anger, anger prevention, and anger management into their classroom guidance and psychoeducational efforts. A combination of age-appropriate direct instruction, activities, and exercises (Golden, 2006) can be used to help students learn (a) what anger is; (b) the physiological cues associated with angry feelings; (c) the relationship between thoughts and feelings; (d) the difference between thoughts, feelings, and behavior; (e) cognitive and behavioral strategies for reducing arousal; (f) healthy versus unhealthy anger; (g) consequences of anger; and (h) general problem-solving and coping skills.

SUMMARY/CONCLUSION

Anger is a normal human emotion that can stimulate people to engage in constructive acts or lead to destructive behaviors. Frequently, anger problems first become apparent during a student's school years. Professional school counselors, particularly elementary counselors, are in a unique position to proactively help students better understand anger and learn effective anger management through classroom guidance classes. In addition, with knowledge and skill using cognitive-behavioral, behavioral, or play-therapy interventions, professional school counselors can provide students with anger problems effective, age-appropriate individual and group counseling services.

(Note: See the CD-ROM for a list of references.)

CHAPTER 91

BEREAVEMENT IN SCHOOLS: HOW TO RESPOND

Susan Norris Huss and Amanda Conklin

Preview

We will describe how the professional school counselor can take a leadership role in making a school "grief friendly." An overview of children's perceptions of death and typical grief reactions of different age groups is provided, followed by a brief description of the stages of grief and how these stages are experienced as age and individual specific. The major focus involves individual and group techniques, but brief attention will be given to preventive programs that can be included in a comprehensive developmental counseling program.

Bereavement is present in many forms in every school. Grief occurs any time a student experiences a loss. One out of every 20 American students under the age of 15 years loses at least one parent to death (Steen, 1998). The U.S. Census Bureau estimates more than 2 million children under the age of 18 years experience the death of a parent (Black, 2005). It is also estimated that in a secondary school of 800 students, 24 students will experience the death of a family member (Selekman, Busch, & Kimble, 2001). There are no estimates of how many children experience the death of a grandparent, sibling, close friend, or even a pet (Myers, 1999). Grief also occurs through non-death-related losses (e.g., not making the football team, losing a homework assignment, moving to a new building, or anytime there is a major change in one's life). This prevalence of bereavement dictates that professional school counselors must understand bereavement and its manifestations in students as well as be able to provide the security, continuity, and support that bereaved students need.

Students from preschool to late adolescence experience grief when a loss occurs. This is a relatively new belief. At one time it was believed that children did not have the capacity to grieve (Freud, 1957; Miller, 1971). Through the work of Piaget (Wadsworth, 1984) and Erickson (Bowlby, 1980; Eggan & Kauchak, 1992), this belief has changed. Bereavement and grief is very much a part of students' school experience and thus it becomes important for professional school counselors to be able to assist students and school personnel in the bereavement process.

The goal should be to create a "grief friendly" school environment. This environment is one that not only responds in a healthy way to a crisis but is also sensitive to the numerous and various losses students experience throughout a school year. Table 91.1 provides several characteristics of a grief-friendly school.

BELIEFS ABOUT DEATH

Age is a major contributing factor to how a student perceives death. Although past experience and cognitive ability also affect these beliefs for each individual, there are

TABLE 91.1

McGlauflin's (2002) Grief-Friendly School Characteristics

Supportive crisis action team

Knowledgeable about grief

Recognition of the uniqueness of every crisis, death, and loss in the school

Open and honest communication with students about any loss

Respect for all feelings

Acceptance of the consciousness of grief

Acknowledgment and respect of all the goodbyes in the school throughout the year

Remembering that education is the mission of the school

Maintenance of standards in a compassionate manner

Collective support for each other

some general perceptions about and general reactions to death for different age groups (see Table 91.2). It is important for professional school counselors to understand these differences in order to provide appropriate interventions for the student.

When working with bereaved students, it is essential to understand the developmental nature of the grieving process in children and adolescents. As students develop cognitively, their level of understanding of a death experience changes. With this new understanding comes a new set of questions related to the death as well as the possibility that they will grieve again for the death of a loved one. It is important not only to remember that anniversaries (death, birthdays) and significant events (graduation, prom, parents' night) may cause a reoccurrence of some grieving but also that simply a new level of understanding can bring about the same reoccurrence of grief.

The generally accepted concept of "stages of grief" takes on a new meaning when working with children. Those stages are generally shock and denial, anger, bargaining, depression, and acceptance (Kubler-Ross, 1969). Generally, one thinks of moving through one stage and into another; however, stages of grief can also be seen as a roller coaster, because they go up and down in intensity. Other students' experiences may be more like a coil—they grieve again and again in a spiral manner as their understanding increases. The major implications of this spiraling effect is to be aware that interventions such as loss support groups should not be limited only to recently bereaved students. The resolution of grief often requires cyclical processing as students grow up.

Although each person grieves in a unique way, there are some general reactions that could be considered normal grieving processes (Perry, 2001). These may include (but are not limited to) denial; emotional numbing; anger, irritability, episodic rage; fear and characteristic rushes of anxiety; confusion; difficulty sleeping; regressive behaviors; physical complaints such as stomachaches or headaches; and changes in appetite. All stakeholders need to acquire an understanding of common student bereavement characteristics.

TABLE 91.2
GENERAL AGE-RELATED PERCEPTIONS OF DEATH

Ages 3–5	Reversible; Temporary; Magical; Sense of security is threatened; May regress in behavior; May cry and become clingy
Ages 6–9	Permanence is understood; Universality belief begins; Personifies death; Wider social network; Model adult reactions; Curious about rituals; Very concrete questions
Ages 10–13	Overwhelmed; Wants facts; Believes may have caused the death; Begins to understand finality of death; Begins to realize they may die; May have psychosomatic symptoms; Grieves more like adults and "want to get on with life"
Ages 14–18	Accepts that death is universal; Intense feelings of adolescence carries over to grief; Turns to friends for support more so than adults; May be suicidal; May feel pressure to assume more adult roles

Note. Adapted from "Impact of Development on Children's Mourning," by G. H. Christ, 2000, *Cancer Practice, 8,* 72–81; "Grieving Children: Are We Meeting the Challenge?" by J. Selekman, T. Busch, and C. Kimble, 2001, *Pediatric Nursing, 27,* 414–419; and *Grief Counseling and Grief Therapy: A Handbook for the Mental Health Professional,* by J. W. Worden, 2001, New York: Springer.

PROACTIVE PROGRAMMING

A grief-friendly school provides opportunities (e.g., workshops, seminars, in-services) for all stakeholders in the school (e.g., teachers, staff, parents) to be informed about the common characteristics of grief in students as well as what is considered to be normal grief reactions. There should also be an updated, functioning crisis-response plan in place for those crisis situations that create losses in schools. There is not space in this chapter to detail these two preventive programs, but a professional school counselor can play an instrumental role in ensuring that these aspects are in place.

The comprehensive developmental school counseling program in a grief-friendly school should include classroom guidance activities related to bereavement and the grieving process. Since this form of "death education" may be questioned, it can be positively marketed as helping students to develop loss-coping skills to deal with the many losses commonly experienced in schools. The information students learn in these sessions provides the basis for student belief that the school is grief friendly. Learning loss-coping skills can provide a resource of learned behavior for major losses such as the death of a parent. It is important to remember that the mission of the school is to educate students and impart life skills. Loss-coping skills are an example of these life skills.

INTERVENTIONS

When a student has suffered a loss, interventions should provide opportunities to share feelings and memories; assist in identifying support systems; assist in the development of coping mechanisms to help them process as they go through the grieving experience; normalize their feelings; and provide a safe environment to do all the above (Huss, 1997).

GROUP COUNSELING

Group work is one way of providing interventions (Jacobs, Harvill, & Masson, 1994; Johnson-Schroetlin, 2000; Sharpnack, 2000; Yalom, 1991). Group work is efficient because it serves more than one student at a time, there are more resources and viewpoints within the group, and groups provide the needed sense of universality and commonality for the bereaved child. Detailed group program plans are available from Haasl (2000), Lehmann (2001a, 2001b), and Webb (2002).

Expressing, acknowledging, and owning one's feelings are extremely important when working with a bereaved student, who is often confused by conflicting feelings (e.g., relief and sadness if the death was after a prolonged illness). Having never experienced a feeling before may be frightening, and the student needs to understand that any feeling is okay and normal for someone experiencing grief. Most of the interventions discussed here can be used to assist in the understanding of feelings, expression of feelings, and understanding of the universality and commonality of feelings. This understanding of the universality and commonality allows bereaved students to move through the grieving process. In addition, the interventions described in the rest of this chapter can be used in group settings as well as when working with individuals.

Artistic activities. Art in many forms (e.g., music, drawing, sculpture) can be an effective means of expressing feelings about a loss. Students can draw pictures of how they feel or pictures of the loved one who has died (or of the loss), and share pictures and stories with the group. Students can express how they felt about the activity, whether or not it helped them to talk about the loss, what the picture means to them, or how it relates to the way they feel. They can also use modeling clay to create images that express feelings. Another good activity is to have students draw a picture of their family before and after the loss. This provides a basis for discussing family differences and similarities after the loss. It also provides an opportunity to discuss the student's remaining support system.

Bibliotherapy. Books provide a wide variety of opportunities for intervention with bereaved students. Books can be read to the student, with the student, or by the student and then discussed at a later session. A book about death can also be read to a class that is anxious about a classmate who has experienced death, and preparing a list of recommended books can provide support for families as they strive to assist in the bereavement process. The professional school counselor should develop a resource library, preferably in the media center. Reading or creating poetry that expresses feelings or grief concerning the loss can also help the student during the grieving process.

Playing. Toys and playing with young students may be helpful as a means of expressing feelings that are hard to express and hard to understand. Dolls, aggressive toys, animals (stuffed or plastic), and other toys and games can be used by the student in playing out anxieties and emotions involved with issues related to grief or loss. Puppets are especially helpful for reluctant participants.

Storytelling. Students from preschool through middle school may benefit from storytelling. Students can be given sentence starters that they can use to either tell or write a story. Examples of sentence starters are: Someday I would like to . . . ; I wish I would have . . . ; If I could . . . ; Whenever I see . . . ; and When I think about. . . . Sentence starters can be created to meet the specific circumstances of the student's loss.

Letter writing. Writing a letter to the person who died can be a powerful tool for saying good-bye or to share something that was left unsaid because of the death. A letter written to someone with whom the student desires to share feelings concerning the loss can be the beginning of communication. Families often send unintentional messages that it is not okay to talk about a loss. Writing a letter can begin the much-needed communication process.

Journaling. Encourage students to keep a journal of their feelings as well as questions they may have. Journal entries can be used to facilitate discussion with students to assist them during this transitional time. Keeping a journal allows students to express feelings and can be a record of their bereavement journey. They can reflect about feelings and see that feelings change during their journey in intensity, type, and duration.

Celebrating life through memory work. Memory work is a way of expressing feelings and normalizing what has happened. Group or individual collages can be made from pictures of the deceased loved one. Students can bring items belonging to the deceased person and share something about the relevance of the item or the memory of the person to whom the item belonged. Individual or group memory books can be made that include pictures, drawings, and letters. Memory books provide a way to keep the person who died in the student's life in an appropriate manner. By creating a memory book, the student is honoring the deceased without obsessing, thereby providing a mechanism for moving forward through the grieving process.

Closure. It is very important to plan events to provide closure when the grieving student is ready. This does not mean that the deceased is forgotten; it means the child is ready to move forward. Use balloons and bubbles in concluding activities by presenting them as methods of releasing or letting go. This could include letting go of someone, a feeling, an attitude, or other emotions connected to loss.

SPECIAL CIRCUMSTANCES

A great many students will experience the death of a close family member. The professional school counselor is often confused about the appropriate role to play. Some specific suggestions follow.

DEATH OF A FAMILY MEMBER

When a member of a student's family dies, the professional school counselor, if at all possible, should make contact with the family. Depending on the religion/culture of the family, the professional school counselor should participate in an appropriate manner. An example would be to visit the funeral home and talk with the student. That discussion could include the following

- An expression of sympathy.

- Informing the student that the professional school counselor will be visiting his or her classroom(s), asking for input into what he or she would like to be said, and telling the student exactly what will be shared. This eases the mind of the student and gives direction to the professional school counselor.
- What kind of support the professional school counselor will provide once the student returns to school (e.g., opportunities to talk, providing a quiet place when needed, talking with other students).

The professional school counselor should then visit the classroom(s) of the bereaved student and talk about how to be a good friend to a bereaved student. This visit should include the following:

- Setting the record straight. This is particularly needed if it is a violent death, since there may be many rumors.
- Helping the class decide how they will express their sympathy to the bereaved family (e.g., flowers, cards, visit to the funeral home or funeral).
- A discussion of how the student wishes to be treated when he or she returns to school. This often assures the other students that the bereaved student is doing okay because he or she has talked with the professional school counselor.
- A general discussion of grief and bereavement.
- A discussion about the feelings students are experiencing and why (e.g., fear that their parent may die, reoccurring feelings from a loss they have experienced in the past). It may be helpful to encourage students to tell their families that a friend has experienced this loss or, with younger students, to send a note home. This gives the families the opportunity to be alert to any needs that may arise from this experience.
- Awareness that this is a "teachable moment." It is an opportunity to either reinforce what was taught in a developmental guidance unit presented before the loss occurred or to teach those concepts now. It is much easier to work with grieving children if they have learned something previously that you can relate to.

Of concern for many professional school counselors when a family death occurs is the religious or spiritual questions that are often asked by the bereaved student (e.g., "Do you believe that when someone dies, they go to heaven?"). These questions should be redirected to what the student and student's family believes. The same is true of certain rituals associated with the funeral. These kinds of questions may also be asked during the classroom visit.

SUICIDE SITUATIONS

Educators may be unsure how to talk with students about suicide. Goodman (2002) suggested the following:

- Define suicide as when "someone chooses to make their body stop working."
- Give age-appropriate facts and explanations.
- Dispel myths about suicide.
- Retell good memories.

- Model feelings and thoughts for students.
- Emphasize suicide is a mistake, because there "is always another way out."

Get the message out to all students that suicide is not a good choice, and provide other choices to prevent a "copycat" suicide.

COMPLICATED GRIEF

Determining when a referral is needed is difficult because of the developmental nature of student bereavement. If the symptom persists for an extended period of time or does not lessen in intensity, it could be cause for alarm. The American Academy of Child and Adolescent Psychiatry (1998) recommended counseling for children who exhibit several of the following over and extended period: depressions so severe that a child shows little interest in daily activities; inability to sleep, eat normally, or be alone; regression in behavior to that of a less-mature child; imitation of the deceased parent; repeatedly wishing to join the deceased; loss of interest in friends or play and refusal to attend school; or a persistent and marked drop in school achievement. Cases involving complicated grief should be immediately referred to mental health professionals specializing in the treatment of such cases.

SUMMARY/CONCLUSION

This has been a brief description of some of the more important aspects of working with bereaved children in a grief-friendly school. The school may be and should be the most stable place in a student's life during the time immediately following the death of the loved one. This stability is supported by remembering the educational mission of the school and maintaining the usual discipline, expectations, and academic standards. At the same time, it is important to create an environment that respects the needs of the bereaved child, whether the loss involves a low grade, a lost friendship, or the death of a parent. It should also be the place that understands the developmental nature of childhood bereavement and thus provides ongoing support for the bereaved student. The professional school counselor needs to stay informed about available resources inside and outside of school to use not only for the bereaved students but also for those within the school.

The grief-friendly school has both proactive and reactive programming in place to assist all stakeholders in the bereavement process. Dealing with grief may be one of the most challenging aspects of the school counseling program, but because there is such a prevalence of grief in school, it is also one of the most important.

(Note: See the CD-ROM for a list of references.)

CHAPTER 92

ORGANIZING AND LEADING SCHOOL TRANSITION PROGRAMS

Patrick Akos

Preview

Research has demonstrated both risk and opportunity for students during normative school transitions. Professional school counselors, in collaboration with others, have an opportunity to provide programming that can influence the developmental paths and academic success of students. A brief commentary on transition research is presented, along with recommendations and resources for programming.

Transitions are crucial turning points in one's life. Regardless of the type of transition, most have inherent risk and opportunity. Starting something new usually causes most people stress and anxiety and taxes their coping abilities. At the same time, new opportunities can afford a fresh start, new relationships and the achievement of new potential (Akos, Queen, & Lineberry, 2005).

Professional school counselors are quite familiar with non-normative transitions. Non-normative transitions are unexpected changes that occur in one's life. Loss of a parent or guardian or the breakups of a family or a relationship are common examples of when professional school counselors intervene. These events create unexpected transitions for students and families, and often require school counseling services for grieving, managing emotions, facilitating closure, and/or developing coping skills. Most professional school counselors also prepare students and engage them in new ways to adjust and thrive in the new situation. As developmental specialists, professional school counselors understand the difficulty associated with an unexpected change, the impact events have on developmental tasks, and expend great energy to repair and foster students' adjustment and coping abilities.

While they receive much less attention, normative transitions can also be influential events in development and similarly carry extensive risk and opportunity. More importantly, normative transitions are both planned and predictable. Hence, these normative transitions are opportunities for proactive or preventative intervention by professional school counselors. Normative transitions include, but are not limited to, the transition into school, moving from elementary to middle to high school, and moving from high school to postsecondary education or work.

One example of an opportunity for such interventions is school entry. Several large-scale studies, such as the Head Start Transition Study (Ramey & Ramey, 1999), the National Education Longitudinal Study (Meisels, 1999), and the NICHD Study of Early Child Care (Kagan & Neuman, 1998) have investigated the importance of school entry to academic and social outcomes. In fact, most states have focused policy on preschool education, and more than 50% of elementary schools have programs targeted to pre-kindergarten children (Rimm-Kaufman & Pianta, 2000). While home environments play a large role in school readiness, professional school counselors may assist in developmental readiness assessment and conduct a variety of interventions to help with separation anxiety. The emerging research has demonstrated that several important child factors (e.g., temperament, language abilities, cognitive readiness), contextual factors (e.g., class size, peer relationships, the family processes), and the complex developing interactions between both are influential sources for later school success. Rosenkoetter (1995) recommended systemic (e.g., peer, family, school, community) collaboration with frequent contacts, agreed upon goals, and a focus on supporting the child's development of skills as a means to support the positive transition. Resources for professional school counselors to use in programming include *The Transition into Kindergarten* (Pianta & Cox, 1999), *Entering Kindergarten* (U.S. Department of Education, 2001), and *Even Start: Facilitating Transitions to Kindergarten* (Reidinger, 1997).

Another well-recognized and researched normative transition includes the transition from school to work or postsecondary school. Both the Carl D. Perkins Vocational and Technical Education Act in Title IIIE (Tech Prep) and the School to Work Opportunities Act of 1994 legislated career development activities for students (Ettinger & Perry, 1993). Career development is a traditional part of school counseling and outcome research in school counseling has established the effectiveness of some career interventions (Whiston, 2007). Additionally, the American School Counseling Association's National Standards recommend career development as a core outcome for school counseling programs (Campbell & Dahir, 1997). Many high schools have career development counselors and career centers preparing students for school to work and postsecondary education, and research demonstrates the importance of educational planning throughout the K–12 process (Akos, Shoffner, & Ellis, 2007).

In addition to general career development and college preparation, the Individuals With Disabilities Education Improvement Act of 2004 (IDEIA) legislated transition planning for special education students starting at age 14 years. IDEIA specified outcome-oriented practices to promote movement from school to postschool activities. Professional school counselors, due to career development training, are valuable collaborators with special education professionals in information dissemination, career assessment and planning, job exploration, and school or work placement (Milsom, Goodnough, & Akos, 2007). Wandry, Pruitt, Fox, and Anderson (1998) have called for "transition teams" including professional school counselors, special education professionals, and a variety of community agencies, to meet to effectively create transition plans that are appropriate for students with Individualized Educational Programs. Numerous programming resources exist, including *Transition Planning for Secondary Students With Disabilities* (Flexer, 2001), and *Enhancing Linkages to Postsecondary Education: Helping Youths Make a Successful Transition to College* (Bragg, 1999).

Less research has examined effective ways to promote student development and success between elementary, middle, and high school or between the various configurations that exist in school districts across the United States. The transition from elementary to middle school represents a noteworthy rite of passage. The distinctive aspects of the transition from elementary to middle school include both the vast contextual differences and the dual timing with personal development transitions. This difference between elementary school organization and procedures and those in the middle school are extensive. Multiple teachers, larger school buildings, block scheduling, lockers, and new and different peers characterize the move to middle school. Concurrent with this contextual change, significant personal change occurs with puberty. Dramatic physical, emotional, and cognitive change is more abrupt during early adolescence than any other time (other than infancy). Finally, when the two transitions happen concurrently, some detrimental consequences have been documented.

Research from developmental psychology, school counseling, educational leadership, and other fields have demonstrated the influence that the transition to middle school has on students. Research has demonstrated that students exhibit decreases in self-esteem, academic achievement, and motivation (Alspaugh, 1998; Harter, 1981; Simmons & Blyth, 1987; Wigfield, Eccles, Mac Iver, Reuman, & Midgley, 1991). Additionally, the transition to middle school has been associated with increases in behavior problems (Wigfield et al., 1991) and increases in psychological distress (Chung, Elias, & Schneider, 1998).

Although the contextual differences between middle and high school are less than those from elementary and middle school, seemingly more is at stake upon moving to high school. Mac Iver and Epstein (1991) suggested that most middle schools provide four to five bridge activities between the elementary and middle school, yet in the transition to high school, only two to three bridge activities were reported. One distinctive aspect of the transition from middle to high school is the intensity of the academic transition and educational or career planning. Students often choose academic tracks that impact not only the next 4 years of high school, but also their future postsecondary and work options.

Students' and parents' concerns about high school include academic themes such as homework and academically rigorous teachers (Akos & Galassi, 2004). Similar to the transition to middle school, reports have demonstrated declines in grades and attendance with the transition to high school (Alspaugh, 1998; Barone, Aguirre-Deandreis, & Trickett, 1991; Mizelle & Irvin, 2000; Reyes, Gillock, & Kobus, 1994). For both transitions, research reports have documented a variety of student, parent, and teacher concerns about moving between levels of schooling (Akos, 2002; Akos & Galassi, 2004; Maute, 1991; Mitman & Packer, 1982). For example, students have reported concerns about homework, bullies, and lockers (Akos, 2002; Akos & Galassi, 2004; Mitman & Packer, 1982) for the transition from elementary to middle school and keeping friends, getting good grades, and knowing how to study (Maute, 1991) for the transition to high school. Parents have also reported concerns about homework, peer pressure, and fitting in for both transitions (Akos & Galassi, 2004). Also, teachers have reported concerns about student peer pressure, fitting in, and getting along with others for both transitions (Akos & Galassi, 2004).

Theorists have proposed useful theories to understand transitional outcomes. Fenzel (1989) described role strain, or how individuals experience concepts like role ambiguity, role overload, lack of control, and conflict in the transition to a new environment. Koizumi (2000) conceptualized anchor points to describe information, knowledge, skills, or people in the environment that students use to evaluate and structure their experience. Most notable, Eccles et al. (1993) suggested that a poor person–environment fit explains many of the outcomes for the transition to middle school. Several of her published reports suggested early adolescent developmental needs (e.g., autonomy, peer support) are not met in most junior high environments (e.g., more controlling teachers, less decision making for students, more competition and ability grouping).

IMPLICATIONS FOR PROFESSIONAL SCHOOL COUNSELORS

Because transitions occur between levels of schooling, decisions about who should be responsible for transition programming are not always clear. Elementary school counselors play a large role in preparing students to move to middle school, and high school counselors are significant to high school entry. Usually, feeder schools offer proactive or preparatory interventions, while receiving schools provide both preventative, enrichment, and support services to help students cope and adjust to the new context. Middle school counselors have the dual responsibility of both a feeder and receiving school. In fact, because middle school is often viewed as a transition time from childhood to adolescence, middle school counselors and middle school personnel should invest significant time and energy into transition programming.

Another challenge in transition programming is the wide variety of tasks that are not all directly related to a traditional definition of school counseling. Administrative tasks may include preparing student schedules, securing medical records, determining student bus schedules, grouping students for teams, and tracking students for academic curriculum. A wide variety of educational or academic aspects (e.g., curriculum articulation, vertical teaming) also require administrator and teacher collaboration across school levels. This wide, cross-level, diverse set of tasks often results in a lack of communication, segmentation and/or duplication of services, or ambivalence about the responsibility of transition programming.

There are also few published reports that examine the effectiveness of transition programming, particularly for professional school counselors. The existing reports documented "shadow" programs for students (Ferguson & Bulach, 1994), education and peer support (Reyes et al., 1994), peer counseling and tutoring (Leland-Jones, 1998), group counseling in combination with parent and teacher support (Akos & Martin, 2003; Greene & Ollendick, 1993), social skills and drama curriculum (Walsh-Bowers, 1992), orientation program (Akos, Masina, & Creamer, 2004), and significant school restructuring, such as teams and teacher advisories in high school (Felner et al., 1993). Findings ranged from no effects (Reyes et al., 1994) to general student satisfaction, improved achievement, behavior and attendance, and more positive school environments. Further outcome research is needed, but the increasing accumulation of research on school transitions provides several recommendations for professional school counselors.

TRANSITION PROGRAMMING RECOMMENDATIONS

Following are several recommendations for conducting successful transition programming: create an extended, dynamic, and developmental transition program; collaborate with teachers, administrators, and school staff between levels of schooling; facilitate administrators and teachers engagement in the transition process; include and program specifically for parents and families; create intentional peer programming; use intentional extracurricular programs or activities to connect students to school; plan universal programming for all students and targeted programming for particular students; and evaluate transition programming and revise based on results.

CREATE AN EXTENDED, DYNAMIC, AND DEVELOPMENTAL TRANSITION PROGRAM

Results of the research on student perceptions suggest that students' needs during a transition are temporal and that a transition program needs to be responsive to developmental changes (Akos, 2002; Akos & Galassi, 2004; Maute, 1991; Mitman & Packer, 1982). For example, students in elementary school report that parents are more helpful than teachers, yet after they transition into middle school they report teachers are more helpful than parents (Akos, 2002). It may also be most useful to conceptualize a transition program from January to December (e.g., January to June for feeder schools and August to December in receiving schools) to help students prepare for and adjust to the new school. In doing so, students receive assistance for an extended period, and the responsibility for helping students during transition falls to both feeder and receiving schools. For example, elementary school counselors may provide transition groups (Akos & Martin, 2003) and deliver coping skills in fifth-grade classrooms to help prepare students for the move to middle school. Common articulation activities during the spring also include scheduling presentations, school tours, and ambassador or shadow programs. In the summer and fall, middle schools may prepare students through enrichment programs and fall orientation programs to induct students to the middle school. High schools have also begun to invest in smaller learning communities (SLCs), including distinct structures (e.g., advisory programs, physical separation of ninth-graders) to enhance the rigorous instruction, relevant curriculum, and meaningful relationships present in school to help students be successful in ninth grade. In fact, the American School Counselor Association (ASCA) has a recently published a position statement about the role of the professional school counselor in SLCs.

COLLABORATE WITH TEACHERS, ADMINISTRATORS, AND SCHOOL STAFF BETWEEN LEVELS OF SCHOOLING

Although professional school counselors in feeding and receiving schools may advocate and lead, other school staff is essential for successful and comprehensive transition programs. Professional school counselors between levels of schooling often meet to discuss students at risk, but it is equally fruitful that support staff (e.g., nurses, ESL coordinators, special education coordinators), administrators, and teachers communicate to facilitate a smooth transition. For example, Mizelle and Mullins (1997) recommended teacher shadowing between levels with processing meetings to discuss differences between the schools, classroom, and curriculum. In this way, transitional tasks not directly linked to professional school counselors, such as curriculum articulation or vertical teaming, can be initiated. Often, this complex task involves teachers from multiple feeder and receiving schools as well as central office personnel coming to consensus on curricular issues. This type of activity can be optimally led by professional school counselors using group leadership skills and aligns well with the new themes of leadership within the ASCA national model.

FACILITATE ADMINISTRATORS AND TEACHERS ENGAGEMENT IN THE TRANSITION PROCESS

Much of the transition research (Eccles et al., 1993) points to the classroom environment and teacher relationships as influential to transition outcomes. For example, Fenzel (1989) and Mizelle and Mullins (1997) speculated that the middle school concept (e.g., teaching teams, advisory) eliminates many of the negative outcomes attributed to the transition. Also, most of the published transition programs and SLCs significantly involve restructuring the environment (e.g., teaming, teacher advisory) of the receiving school. It is therefore crucial that professional school counselors collaborate with school personnel, especially teachers, on orientation programming and restructuring efforts.

INCLUDE AND PROGRAM SPECIFICALLY FOR PARENTS AND FAMILIES

Mac Iver and Epstein (1991) discovered that parents are more active participants in the education of their children when they are involved in transition programs. As research has shown, the benefits of parent participation in student achievement (Hess & Holloway, 1984), the transition to a new school seems to be an important opportunity to generate parental involvement. It is also significant that students, especially Latino students, mention parents as important sources of help during the transition between levels of schooling (Akos, 2002; Akos & Galassi, 2004). It may be useful to engage parents in the spring prior to the transition with school newsletters, parent meetings, and course scheduling. Later, receiving schools can use parent volunteers as part of orientation planning or conduct parent–teacher meetings or potluck dinners as part of early open houses to welcome and connect new parents to the school. It is important to discover contextually important, meaningful ways to involve parents, especially in the transition to middle school, as this is a particular vulnerable point (e.g., parental involvement typically drops in middle school considerably).

CREATE INTENTIONAL PEER PROGRAMMING

One developmental need common to students in both middle and high school transitions is the intense peer focus and desire for peer connection. Students report that peers are a positive aspect and the most influential source of help during transitions to middle and high schools (Akos, 2002; Akos & Galassi, 2004; Diemert, 1992). It is also common that misinformation or sensationalized negative information may be transmitted by peers. Research (Eccles et al., 1993) also speculated that the negative outcomes associated with transition are partly due to the upheaval of peer networks. Professional school counselors can use the developmental influence of peers to provide accurate information and easily accessible help for students through group counseling, peer mentoring or tutoring, or shadow or buddy–ambassador programs.

USE INTENTIONAL EXTRACURRICULAR PROGRAMS OR ACTIVITIES TO CONNECT STUDENTS TO SCHOOL

Connection or belongingness to school has been shown to be an important contribution to student adjustment and academic success (Akos, 2004; Osterman, 2000). Professional school counselors can facilitate these connections with activity fairs, information brochures, or student activity or club presentations to students new to the building. Often, sixth- and ninth-grade students have limited options for school-sponsored sports or clubs. Professional school counselors can advocate for inclusion of sixth- or ninth-grade students in extracurricular programs, no-cut policies, intramural programs, and school-sponsored activities specifically for new students. For example, schools could sponsor fifth- and sixth-grade or eighth- and ninth-grade school dances or intramural activities to help students bridge the transition and feel connected to school.

PLAN UNIVERSAL PROGRAMMING FOR ALL STUDENTS AND TARGETED PROGRAMMING FOR PARTICULAR STUDENTS

Transition programs are an excellent example of how professional school counselors can provide large-scale services for all students. For example, most schools provide an orientation program for new students. The counselor could conceive orientation as a process whereby schools work with students to accommodate different adjustment timetables. In fact, professional school counselors should direct services to students who may be having or who demonstrate more difficulty in transitioning. Specifically, students who struggle in the feeder schools (with grades, attendance, or behavior) will not magically be "fixed" in an optimal transition program. Rather, professional school counselors must examine school-level data to see who may struggle most in the transition. Although the research is not conclusive, many speculate that female students, urban minority students, and students with academic and/or behavioral struggles may be more at risk during the transition to middle school (Eccles et al., 1993; Seidman, Allen, Aber, Mitchell, & Feinman, 1994). Using cumulative folders and computerized records from the feeder schools, professional school counselors can check data in the first quarter at the receiving school to identify students who exhibit a pronounced drop in grades or increases in behavior problems or absences. Those with consistently low performance (e.g., low scores in both fifth grade and the start of sixth grade) obviously need intervention too, but transitional intervention may fill only part of those needs. For those with declines due specifically to transition, it may be useful to provide small-group sessions and/or individual counseling to help connect and engage these students to the new school.

EVALUATE TRANSITION PROGRAMMING AND REVISE BASED ON RESULTS

Although it seems obvious, any intervention or program that professional school counselors invest in should be evaluated to determine effectiveness. Transition program evaluation has a high level of complexity due to the multiple schools, varied outcome possibilities, and multiple stakeholders involved. It may be useful to examine school-level data on a large scale, by looking at grade, behavioral, attendance, and developmental outcome patterns across school transitions (fifth through ninth grade in some district configurations). It would also be important to conduct assessments or qualitative interviews with students and parents to see what specific aspects of transitions are challenging and what programming aspects are most useful.

Summary/Conclusion

As professional school counselors continue to help students with unexpected life changes, it is important that they capitalize on the influential and significant normative changes between levels of schooling. District configurations vary, and each transition represents a new opportunity to affect the developmental path for students. While most professional school counselors engage in some type of transition activity (e.g., registration), it is also necessary to provide leadership and advocacy for transition programs that are comprehensive and developmental, that include collaboration between levels and staff, inclusion of parent and peer programming, and evaluation of transition-related interventions.

(Note: See the CD-ROM for a list of references.)

CHAPTER 93

CRISIS INTERVENTION WITH INDIVIDUALS

IN THE SCHOOLS

Fran Steigerwald

Preview

Crisis work with individuals in the schools is becoming more common. Professional school counselors need to gain knowledge about the various physical, cognitive, emotional, and behavioral manifestations of crises in children so that they can recognize, assess, and intervene with students. Development of positive characteristics and skills along with an understanding and practice of some intervention and assessment models provide the needed resources for a crisis worker to plan the appropriate course of intervention with the individual student in crisis.

Some have called crises in children's lives not only a reality, but an epidemic. Pressures of violence and abuse, bullying, terrorism, family discord, economic depression, loss, disease, and addiction bombard children who are either victims or witnesses. Gratuitous violence in the media makes children regular bystanders to crisis. Situational crises often appear unexpectedly, and the effects of this exposure impact children's lives at school, where they are expected to learn and grow in a structured academic setting. In addition, children are developing and growing, and thus they often experience developmental crises as they work to master life tasks and progress through life transitions (Collins & Collins, 2005). In this fast-changing world, knowledge of support, intervention and coping strategies in crisis situations may not have kept pace with what is required to truly help students in crisis. This chapter is an overview of the work needed within the life of an individual student in crisis in a school setting. It deals with the systemic crisis work that is needed when the entire school ecology is affected by crisis.

First, I define crisis and then explore in general some pivotal crisis concepts, including the physical, mental, emotional, and behavioral components to crisis, and specific reactions of students. Next, I examine the training, characteristics, and qualities of effective crisis professionals. This is followed by appropriate intervention and assessment models that have been shown effective in the school setting. A special emphasis on understanding suicidal ideation, behavior, and intervention is stressed because of the destructive risks involved. The chapter ends with a summary of effective guidelines for working with school children in crisis.

A Look at Crisis

This section presents a definition of crisis and several essential concepts related to crisis.

DEFINITION OF CRISIS

There are many definitions of crisis. James and Gilliland (2001) worked these definitions into a consolidated, easy-to-understand idea that encompassed the major points: "Crisis is a perception or experiencing of an event or situation as an intolerable difficulty that exceeds the person's current resources and coping mechanisms" (p. 3). Key in this definition is the importance of the "perception" of the crisis, the response of the person exposed to it. This concept is emphasized in the Chinese word for crisis that is composed of two symbols, one representing *danger* and the other *opportunity*. How an individual is helped to perceive the crisis will provide much information as to whether he or she will cope well and grow from it, be overwhelmed and immobilized by it, or survive by protecting and blocking but have negative after-effects.

A crisis event is defined as "an event which produces a temporary state of psychological disequilibrium and a subsequent state of emotional turmoil" (Mitchell & Everly, 1993, p. 5). This disequilibrium or turmoil has been commonly referred to as *stress,* a phenomenon identified by Selye (1956) as a mind–body reaction that causes wear and tear upon the person. Stress has been defined as "a response characterized by physical and psychological arousal arising as a direct result of an exposure to any demand or pressure on a living organism" (Mitchell & Everly, 1993, p. 5).

CONCEPTS OF CRISIS

Crisis can be developmental, situational, or existential in nature (James & Gilliland, 2001). Whatever is the nature of the crisis, stress is always a major component. This stress is deeply personal, and its corresponding impairment is dependent upon the individual's perception of the crisis situation. Crisis stress is often observed as a combination of symptoms that are cognitive, emotional, physical, and behavioral. Researchers have worked to synthesize the many signs and symptoms of crises and stress. Tables 93.1, 93.2, 93.3, and 93.4 list general physical, mental or cognitive, emotional, and behavioral symptomology information gathered from the research of Girdano, Everly, and Dusek (1993), Mitchell and Everly (1993), and Myer (2001). Additional information from Greenstone and Leviton (2002) has been added pertaining to age-related and developmental reactions of students to stress and crises. The level of symptomology should be individually considered on a continuum ranging from *no impairment* to *severe impairment* in each area.

A crisis in an individual's life usually lasts for a maximum of 6 to 8 weeks (Hendricks & McKean, 1995; Janosik, 1984). After that, the symptoms usually diminish along with the obvious discomforts they caused. Helping the student during this time is of great importance in determining whether the he or she is able to resume the normalcy of life or whether there are resulting residual complications and long-term effects from the crisis: "Unless the person obtains relief, the crisis has the potential to cause severe affective, behavioral, and cognitive malfunctioning" (James & Gilliland, 2001, p. 3).

POSTTRAUMATIC STRESS DISORDER

Trauma can produce persistent symptoms that cause a diagnosable condition of stress and anxiety called *posttraumatic stress disorder* (PTSD). PTSD is a complex disorder

TABLE 93.1

PHYSICAL (AGE-RELATED) SYMPTOMS OF CRISIS AND STRESS

The body strongly reacts to crisis and stress. Repeated or prolonged stress can cause exhaustion, decreased immunity, and psychosomatic illness throughout an individual's life. Common symptoms include the following:
- secreted stress hormones (cortisol, aldosterone, epinephrine)
- increased neural excitability (rapid breathing, dizziness)
- increased cardiovascular activity (heart rate, blood pressure, stroke volume, cardiac output)
- increased metabolic activity (gluconeogenesis, protein mobilization, muscle wasting, decreased antibody production, fat mobilization)
- increased sodium retention and neurological sweating
- change in salivation and in gastrointestinal system tonus and motility

Symptoms common in preschool children (1–5 years)
- loss of bladder or bowel control, constipation
- speech difficulties, such as stammering
- loss of or increase in appetite

Symptoms common in school-age students (5–11 years)
- headaches or other physical complaints as stated above

Symptoms common in preadolescent students (11–14 years)
- appetite disturbances
- physical pain, such as headaches, vague pain, bowel problems, psychosomatic complaints
- skin eruptions

Symptoms common in adolescent students (14–18 years)
- physical complaints such as headaches, psychosomatic symptoms, bowel problems, rashes, asthma
- appetite and sleep disturbances
- hypochondriasis
- amenorrhea or dysmenorrhea
- loss of sexual interest
- agitation or decrease in energy levels

that is often comorbid and requires specialized help, and new crises can exacerbate and complicate PTSD. It is important for crisis workers to understand this disorder to make appropriate referrals. PTSD was added to the *Diagnostic and Statistical Manual of Mental Disorders–Third Edition* (DSM-III) in 1980. Refer to Chapter 62, "Helping Students Who Have Posttraumatic Stress Disorder," for further information on this topic.

UNDERSTANDING AND STRUCTURING CRISIS WORK

Corsini (1981) stated that counseling and crisis intervention are elementally different. Crisis intervention or management work requires quick and immediate action to provide the

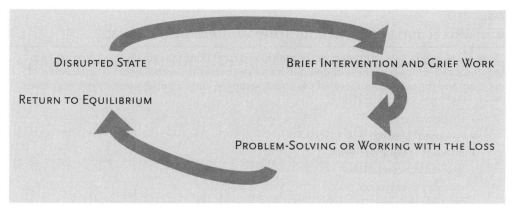

FIGURE 93.1. Lindemann's crisis intervention process.

support and direction that the student in crisis cannot provide for his- or herself. Crisis counseling may be appropriate once a person has been stabilized from the initial crisis.

Lindemann (1944, 1956) first offered a theory of crisis work, helping professionals and paraprofessionals to understand the needs of clients in crisis. He clearly provided a new framework for normalizing, not pathologizing, behaviors specific to people suffering from loss and trauma who felt unbalance or disequilibrium. Lindemann's proposed process took the clients through their disrupted state with brief intervention and grief work, to problem solving or working through the loss, and finally to a return to equilibrium. Lindemann's (1956) model is presented in Figure 93.1.

Today, brief solution-focused therapy follows much the same format. Crisis work focuses on facilitating an understanding of the crisis and its manifestations while not working on any ongoing problems as brief therapy would. Cournoyer (1996) stated that brief-treatment approaches are in the forefront of intervention models and that the research has shown effective outcomes. It is important to remember that crisis intervention is not a long-term counseling approach. It is short-term problem or solution-focused work to get the client back to a state of balance (Myer, 2001). Regardless of the approach, it is clear that crisis intervention involves an established procedure: "Every action and intervention must be thoughtful, measured, and purposeful" (Greenstone & Leviton, 2002, p. 7).

A Look at Crisis Professionals

Since crisis intervention and management is time limited, the ability to quickly establish rapport and an environment of trust and caring is essential. Rogers (1957) established the core conditions for successful counseling: empathic understanding, unconditional positive regard, and congruence. These basic conditions are necessary in crisis work to gain an understanding of the client's perception of the crisis; however, the crisis worker must be able to quickly exhibit these conditions with the student while being supportive and often directive and in control of the crisis event. In crisis intervention, the crisis worker is extremely active in working through the set phases, and it is this needed structure that helps the student in crisis proceed to balance (Cournoyer, 1996).

TABLE 93.2

MENTAL OR COGNITIVE (AGE-RELATED) SYMPTOMS OF CRISIS AND STRESS

There are always beliefs, attitudes, perceptions, and cognitions that go along with crisis. The negativity and intensity of these cognitions help determine the psychological interpretation of the crisis and the subsequent level of the stress response and/or impairment. These cognitive impairments reduce coping ability.

- thought overload
- confused thinking
- difficulty making decisions
- lowered concentration
- memory dysfunction
- intrusive thoughts
- nightmares
- reduced problem solving
- lowering of all higher cognitive functions

Symptoms common in preschoolers (1–5 years)
- night terrors
- confusion

Symptoms common in school-age students (5–11 years)
- night terrors, nightmares, fear of darkness
- poor concentration
- lost of interest in school

Symptoms common in preadolescent students (11–14 years)
- loss of interest in peer activity
- denial

Symptoms common in adolescent students (14–18 years)
- confusion
- poor concentration
- tendency to blame

Effective communication skills are essential, including listening, clarifying, understanding nonverbal cues, asking questions to obtain accurate information, legitimizing feelings, and responding well to the client's feelings and perceptions. These skills, along with withholding judgment, shame, and advice-giving, are skills that develop rapport and begin to help manage the student's crisis (Greenstone & Leviton, 2002).

Training in crisis theory, symptomology, intervention, and assessment are necessary for a competent crisis worker. It is also vital to understand the referral process, state and local law, legal implications of working with minors, parental notification, and commitment or hospitalization procedures. In addition to previously discussed qualities of crisis counselors, Myer and Hanna (1996) have included quick thinking, tolerance of medical trauma, sense of reconciliation with death, and sense of humor.

Awareness of multicultural perspectives, culturally biased assumptions of crisis, and the client's worldview of the events are necessary for correct assessment and in-

TABLE 93.3

EMOTIONAL (AGE-RELATED) SYMPTOMS OF CRISIS AND STRESS

"Emotion is an energy complex. . . . Our emotions form an immediate experience. When we are experiencing our emotions, we are in direct contact with our physical reality" (Girdano et al., 1993, p. 62). Emotions are immediate triggers in crisis. Expression of emotions in a crisis is healthy and should be encouraged. In crisis situations, it is normal for emotions to rise to uncomfortable levels as

- emotional shock
- fear
- anger
- grief or sadness
- depression
- feeling overwhelmed (helpless or hopeless)
- emotional flattening or denial
- moodiness and irritability
- decompensation
- depersonalizing

Symptoms common in preschoolers (1–5 years)
- fears of darkness, animals, strangers, or abandonment

Symptoms common in school-age students (5–11 years)
- generalized anxiety
- irritability
- withdrawal from peers
- fears about weather, safety, harm, loss or abandonment
- depression

Symptoms common in preadolescent students (11–14 years)
- depression
- loss of interest in peers and social activities
- anger
- fear of loss of family, friends, home, or personal harm

Symptoms common in adolescent students (14–18 years)
- depression
- indifference or apathy
- anger at perceived unfairness of crisis
- fear of loss
- guilt

tervention. Misinterpretation because of lack of sensitivity to cultural values, social or political backgrounds, and cultural behaviors in crisis can unfairly label clients and result in inappropriate interventions (Pederson, 1987).

Almost everyone can be taught the techniques . . . and with practice can employ them with some degree of skill. However, the crisis worker who can take intervention to the performance art level is more than the sum of techniques

TABLE 93.4

BEHAVIORAL (AGE-RELATED) SYMPTOMS OF CRISIS AND STRESS

Emotional energy prepares for action, and, in times of crisis, behaviors may be the first things seen and attended to. Behaviors are purposeful. They are often manifestations of the intent of working out the discomfort caused by the crisis, no matter how misdirected it may seem to the observer. Such behaviors include the following:

- changes in ordinary behavior patterns or regression
- inability to perform daily functions
- changes in eating, drinking, or sleeping habits
- self-harming behaviors
- changes in personal hygiene
- hyperarousal
- withdrawal, prolonged silences
- rebellion, fighting

Symptoms common in preschoolers (1–5 years)

- bed-wetting
- clinging to parents
- thumb-sucking
- cries or screams for help
- immobility with trembling and frightening expressions
- running either toward an adult or in aimless motion

Symptoms common in school-age students (5–11 years)

- thumb-sucking
- whining
- clinging
- aggressive behaviors
- competition with siblings for parental attention
- school avoidance
- regressive behaviors

Symptoms common in preadolescent students (11–14 years)

- sleeplessness or too much sleeping
- fighting
- attention-seeking behaviors
- withdrawing behaviors
- refusal to do chores

Symptoms common in adolescent students (14–18 years)

- poor or reduced performance
- aggressive behaviors
- withdrawing or isolating behaviors
- changes in peer group or friends
- irresponsibility
- delinquent behaviors
- rebellion
- refusal to do chores
- attention-seeking behaviors
- decline in struggling with parents

TABLE 93.5

ROBERTS'S SEVEN-STAGE CRISIS MODEL

Beginning with a thorough assessment.

Stage 1—ASSESS LETHALITY, examines how dangerous the student is to self and others and looks at the immediate psychosocial needs.

Stage 2—ESTABLISH RAPPORT, stresses the need to rapidly bond with the student using respect, acceptance, and reassurance.

Stage 3—IDENTIFY MAJOR PROBLEMS, allows for the student to vent about the precipitating event, and helps the student rank the problems by harm or potential threat.

Stage 4—DEAL WITH FEELINGS, uses active listening skills and communicates warmth, respect, reassurance, and nonjudgmental validation.

Stage 5—EXPLORE ALTERNATIVES, uses the calmness and rationality of the crisis worker, since the student is often distressed and unable to function clearly. Ideally the student and the crisis worker can join collaboratively; however, the crisis worker may often need to initiate discussion of adaptive coping mechanisms.

Stage 6—DEVELOP ACTION PLAN, develops and implements actions to help restore the student to balance and functionality. Reasonableness, encouragement, and supportiveness are essential ingredients in successful implementation.

Stage 7—FOLLOW-UP, completes the crisis resolution and sets times to meet (daily, weekly or monthly) to gauge the student's success in functioning.

read about and skills mastered. A master of this art is going to have some combination of the two and a good deal of . . . life experiences . . . professional skills . . . poise . . . creativity and flexibility . . . energy . . . quick mental reflexes . . . [and] attributes that crisis interventionists have found of utmost importance to themselves and their clients. These attributes are tenacity, the ability to delay gratification, courage, optimism, a reality orientation, calmness under duress, objectivity, a strong and positive self-concept, and abiding faith that human beings are strong, resilient, and capable of overcoming insurmountable odds. (James & Gilliland, 2001, pp. 17–20)

A Look at What Works

Successful crisis intervention requires that professional school counselors plan ahead, become familiar with effective models of intervention, and practice age-specific school interventions.

PLANNING AHEAD

For professional school counselors, it is important to realize that crisis work will be part of the routine. Planning ahead through knowledge of crisis and stress, training in handling these events, and ongoing self-preparation is essential. In the moment of the crisis, there is no time to contemplate, refer to a manual, or look up a step-by-step process in the files. Determine state law and school policy for parental notification, clients who are minors, and confidentiality. Make clear your ethical practice on involving family and guardians in crisis situations. Your plans need to be known, practiced, handy, and visible. Several models are clear, well-established, and proven effective. Two models of intervention and one model for assessment are outlined and discussed, with the emphasis on working with students. It is important to decide which model of intervention will be employed and make the necessary preparation. All three of these models offer practical interventions that can be implemented by a professional school counselor when an individual crisis erupts in a child's day.

MODELS

Roberts (1996; see Table 93.5) outlined a seven-stage crisis intervention model that "can facilitate early identification of crisis, problem-solving, and effective crisis resolution" (p. 26). It is important to maintain close contact and provide the student and family with resource information and community assistance as needed.

Greenstone and Leviton (2002; see Table 93.6) have a similar crisis intervention plan that calls for six major components along with some practical suggestions.

TABLE 93.6

GREENSTONE AND LEVITON'S CRISIS INTERVENTION MODEL

IMMEDIACY—Work "to relieve anxiety, prevent further disorientation [and] ensure that sufferers do not harm themselves or cause harm to others" (p. 8).

CONTROL—Work to "be clear about what and whom you are attempting to control, enter the crisis scene cautiously, [and] be clear in your introductory statements, do not promise things that might not happen. . . . direct and arrange the pattern of standing or sitting to gain the victim's attention, guide the sufferer with your eyes and voice rather than through physical force, use physical force only as a last resort and only if you are trained and authorized, [and] remove the victim from the crisis situation" (pp. 8–10).

ASSESSMENT—Work to "evaluate on the spot . . . make the evaluation quick, accurate, and comprehensive . . . focus your assessment on the present crisis and events. . . what are the precipitating events . . . ask short, direct questions . . . one at a time . . . allow enough time for the victim to answer . . . allow the crisis to be the victim's crisis . . . assess actual and symbolic meaning . . . listen for what is not being said . . . allow the victim to speak freely and to ventilate feelings . . . see the crisis as temporary . . . [and] return control to the victim as soon as possible" (pp. 10–13).

DISPOSITION—Work to "help the victim identify and mobilize personal resources . . . mobilize social resources . . . hold out hope that solutions are possible . . . develop options . . . [and] help the parties to the crisis make an agreement" (p. 13).

REFERRAL—Much preplanning is needed for this component. As a crisis worker, you need to have a comprehensive list of referral sources (agencies, community professionals, doctors, lawyers, clergy, hospitals, transporters, and law enforcement) with hours of operation, telephone numbers, and names, always accurate and available to you for immediate use. Provide the information (if a minor to the parent or guardian) clearly and in writing, asking for verification of information.

FOLLOW-UP—Work to determine whether follow up procedures have been done, providing further help or re-referrals, if necessary.

TABLE 93.7

AGE-APPROPRIATE INTERVENTIONS FOR STUDENTS RECOVERING FROM CRISIS

Interventions for preschoolers (1–5 years)
- play reenactment
- verbal and physical comforting and attention
- expression of feelings and concerns
- suggestions for comforting bedtime routines and support

Interventions for school-age students (5–11 years)
- patience and tolerance
- play reenactment; discussing emotions
- discussion about crisis experience with peers and adults with expectations that occur in crisis
- temporary relaxation of expectations in school and home
- opportunities for undemanding structure and routine

Interventions for preadolescent students (11–14 years)
- group activities geared toward resuming routine
- same-age activities
- undemanding but structured routine
- individual attention and consideration

Interventions for adolescent students (14–18 years)
- letter writing
- participation in the community
- discussion of feelings and concerns
- temporary reduction of expectations
- encourage discussion of crisis fears with family

Myer (2001) worked to expand the concept of assessment as paramount in effective intervention in his triage assessment model. This assessment begins by listening to the crisis story to determine the catalyst and the student's view. Next, assessment takes place within three domains: *affective* (identify and rank anger–hostility, or anxiety–fear, or sadness–melancholy); *cognitive* (identify and rank whether there is perceived physical, psychological, social–relationship, or moral–spiritual transgression); and *behavioral* (identify and rank behaviors as either approach, avoidance, or immobility). There are always reactions to crisis in these three domains, and it is vital to determine and rank severity of impairment in each area. Next, crisis workers are encouraged to begin to use appropriate interventions in the domains that appear with most impairment: affective (awareness, support, and catharsis); cognitive (clarifying, delimiting and ordering); or behavioral (guiding, protecting, and mobilizing).

AGE-SPECIFIC INTERVENTIONS IN THE SCHOOLS

Remember that crisis is in the eye of the person who perceives it. It is paramount that crisis workers suspend their judgment about the appropriateness of the student's reactions to the crisis. Working to understand the crisis and validating reactions from the student's perspective is essential. Students exhibit behaviors as a result of their emotional states. In school situations, these behaviors may be the first things noticed and attended to. School personnel must understand what the student really needs before they discipline the student's behaviors (Kohn, 1996). Table 93.7 provides age-appropriate interventions to help the student regain balance and reach precrisis levels of stress (Greenstone & Leviton, 2002, pp. 68–72).

A SPECIAL LOOK AT SUICIDE

One of the most devastating things that can happen in crisis is loss of life. When that loss of life is a student's, everyone involved asks what could have been done to prevent it, or why no signs were seen. For youth 15 to 19 years of age, suicide rates peaked in 1994 and have steadily declined since, comprising 12.3% of all teen deaths. But suicide is still the third leading cause of death among teens, after accidents and homicides. In this age group, the male to female ratio of completed suicides is 5 to 1. For children ages 10 to 14, suicide rates increased 99% from 1980 to 1997, with a small decline since that time. The largest increase in suicide rates was in Black children of this age group, where males still outnumber females (American Association of Suicidology, 2004). Professional school counselors must be able to assess the danger of suicide or homicide and know the steps to take in these emergency situations. If a professional school counselor reasonably suspects that a student may take his or her own life or the life of someone else, referral and/or commitment to a psychiatric facility is vitally necessary. While this topic certainly warrants more expanded coverage, Table 93.8 provides the basic steps in the assessment of suicide or homicide risk that is needed to determine the level of risk (compiled from Farberow, Heilig, & Litman, 1968; Glaitto & Rai, 1999; Gould & Kramer, 2001).

If there is any risk of suicide or homicide, always consult with supervisors or experienced clinicians before releasing a student from your office. Never leave such a student unattended. *Always* bring in another individual to assist and consult. If you detect a moderate or high risk of suicide or homicide, know the steps in your community that are necessary for referral for further assessment or to hospitalize if necessary. Have these emergency names, numbers, and modes of transport readily available.

Some short-term interventions follow:

- Write up a safety contract with the student, specifying actions when ideations occur.
- Make plans to remove the means.
- Make others aware, and get the support of family and significant others such as clergy or community resources.
- Contact mental health counselors for increased visitation or advise any counselor currently working with the student.
- Use further suicide assessment instruments to acquire more information, or refer for psychiatric evaluation.
- Call police if imminent (homicidal) danger is suspected.

Summary/Conclusion

The following list summarizes the ideas discussed in this chapter:

- Work to keep yourself grounded and healthy and your skills effective and developed.
- Understand the crisis through the perception of the person in the crisis. Actively listen to the story.
- Work to establish rapport and trust.
- Plan ahead with appropriate and adequate referral source information, allocated space for intervention, and an accessible model of intervention.
- Remember to be holistic. Observe and assess the physical, behavioral, emotional, and cognitive manifestations.
- Begin work where there is most impairment.

- Determine whether the effects are long-lasting and if referral for PTSD assessment is needed.
- Keep a multicultural awareness of the student's expressions of emotions, perspectives, and behaviors.
- Student misbehaviors are immediately noticeable. Ask yourself what the student needs rather than fall into the compliance/conformance trap.
- Make yourself an expert in suicidology. Know what to assess, how to do it, and how to refer in lethal cases.
- Never work in isolation. Involve the student's support system, and always involve your consultant/supervisor.
- Continue to develop and practice your art.

(Note: See the CD-ROM for a list of references.)

TABLE 93.8

BASIC STEPS IN ADDRESSING SUICIDAL OR HOMICIDAL INTENT

Step 1: Assess for predictors

- A. Sex and age
- B. Previous attempts
- C. Familiarity with someone who has attempted or completed suicide
- D. Use of drugs and/or alcohol
- E. Depression and/or medical conditions
- F. Warning signs, such as suicide talk, giving away personal items, sudden change in behavior and patterns, preoccupation with death (in music or reading)
- G. Sexual orientation issues (gay, lesbian, bisexual, and transsexual adolescents exhibit more self-harm and suicidal thoughts and behaviors)

Step 2: Determine the seriousness of the intent

- A. Solicit suicidal or homicidal thoughts
- B. Determine whether there is a plan, and solicit details to determine feasibility with the higher risk in specific details and actions. Regarding homicide, if specific individuals are named, there is a duty to protect and warn.
- C. Determine lethality, and check out the means and access. A gun is the most dangerous and lethal means, and if a loaded gun is kept available in the home, there is high risk

Step 3: Determine life stressors and life resources. If life is lately filled with many stressors and few supports, the likelihood of completed suicide is greater.

CHAPTER 94

SYSTEMIC CRISIS INTERVENTION IN THE SCHOOLS

Fran Steigerwald

Preview

Systemic crisis intervention in schools needs to be seriously addressed system wide, with the system being the school, the families, and the community. Many crises affect large numbers of people and must be addressed with a systemic developmental–ecological approach to facilitate optimal recovery for everyone, as well as to effectively solve problems and facilitate needed changes to prevent further incidents. Development of a comprehensive crisis plan is a large undertaking, but many of the elements are generic and can be universally incorporated, along with adaptations that need to be made for specific system needs. Understanding these components and having a plan in place to quickly activate can be the difference between extended problems and effective solutions. Professional school counselors play a pivotal role in systemic crisis intervention.

A junior high school student commits suicide. A kindergarten student disappears, and kidnapping is suspected. A family on vacation with their three elementary -age children is killed in an airplane crash. Gang slogans and activity spring up in the school hallways. A suspected gay student is beaten up behind the school. Two 15-year-olds overdose over the weekend. Four seniors are fatally injured on prom night in a car accident involving alcohol. A drive-by shooting kills the star basketball player. Five girls report being fondled and groped in the hallway by sixth-grade boys. In addition to these many possible school-life crises, 25 real incidents of school shootings occurred in the United States from 1996 to 2002, causing the media to call school violence a "deadly pattern" (Family Education Network, 2002).

While media make these incidents feel all too common, Collins and Collins (2005) defined these events further:

> Crises are rare and unexpected events, and it is daunting to anticipate and prepare for the circumstances and special challenges associated with various potential crisis events. This is true whether a crisis affects one individual or the entire school community. (p. 410)

Yet, schools have installed metal detectors, used armed police, enacted policies of zero tolerance, and insisted that students use transparent mesh book bags to help control the seemingly escalating violence. Still, crises seem an uncontrollable part of school life. What can be controlled is the school's professionals' knowledgeable and quick response to crises in order to prevent further exacerbation, trauma, and harm. All the above scenarios require a systemic crisis plan that is comprehensive, well planned, mobilizes many resources, and operates quickly.

WHAT IS SYSTEMIC CRISIS INTERVENTION?

Systemic crisis intervention is based in systems theory, which emerged in the 1940s. Goldenberg and Goldenberg (1998) summarized the development of systems theory as a new way to look at a problem, event, situation, or organization from the perspective of the interaction of all the components and of how the entire unit operates. Later, family therapy applied these concepts and elaborated the movement from looking at individual characteristics to interactions among individuals. The study became the system. Previously, scientific thinking was infused with "linear causality: A causes B, which acts upon C, causing D to occur" (Goldenberg & Goldenberg, 1998, p. 21). The circular causality of systems work stresses reciprocity. Forces do not move in a linear direction, but rather they are influenced by and are influencing other components in the system. Systems theory is more holistic, understanding that the whole is greater than the sum of its parts, and that each part continually impacts and is mutually affected by the others.

Systems theory offers distinct advantages to effectively solving problems and crises in schools. Carns and Carns (1997) stated the following:

> Initially, it is helpful to envision the school district as a supra or mega system, the individual schools as systems, the individual classrooms as subsystems, and even the small social or task groups within the classroom as smaller subsystems. Each child brings his or her interactional patterns and ways of relating to others in his or her own family system into the school subsystems. (p. 220)

Solutions are seen as the responsibility of everyone involved rather than one person's duty. The maintenance of positive change is more possible and effective with multiple input and change occurring at the interactional level. Keys and Lockhart (1999) proposed that professional school counselors take a multisystemic approach, expanding the systems to include school, home, peer group, and community: "To achieve such broad-based change, schools, families, and communities must engage in collaborative problem solving that engages the multiple expertise of members of each system" (Keys & Lockhart, 1999, p. 107).

Collins and Collins (2005) proposed a developmental–ecological model for crisis intervention. Students perceive and handle crises according to their age and evelopmental background: "Consideration of students' cognitive, social, and emotional development guides and directs developmentally appropriate crisis interventions" (p. 413). The many levels of systems that impact the students must also be considered for a comprehensive crisis intervention approach. Ecosystems theory examines interactions among students' various systems. Knoff (1986) provided the concept of ecology to graphically explain how all levels of systems interface and provide reciprocal influences.

Cavaiola and Colford (2006) examined crisis intervention as a process whereby the victim or affected persons need to be "restored to a level of functioning enjoyed before the onset of the crisis" (p. 209). The focus needs to be on preparedness, with emphasis on choosing a crisis team and developing a crisis plan.

The stated crises that began this chapter do not affect just one individual. Many people are affected, many need to be considered, and many resources need to be mobilized in crisis intervention. The National Education Association (2002) stated that in crises, communication is often the problem:

> The overall communication objective in a crisis is to quickly adjust . . . the school community position from one of response and reaction to one of relative control, and an ability to take proactive steps toward healing and a return to learning. (p. 4)

Caplan's (1964) crisis intervention model proposed the following three levels of response in times of crisis. These three components are used as a backbone for many crisis intervention plans.

1. Primary prevention (prevention) works to stimulate the environment and foster health so that crises are less likely to occur.
2. Secondary prevention (intervention) works to contain the crises and reduce negative impact once the crises have occurred.
3. Tertiary intervention (postvention) provides long-term care and support after the crises, also allowing feedback to improve future crisis response.

A Systemic Approach to Individual Crisis

In systemic intervention, the professional school counselor knows that the problem does not reside in the student alone but in the student's interactions with others in the system. It may be determined that this student was bullied and harassed on the playground, or that in the morning the student overheard his parents speaking of divorce. Resolution involves intervention with all the involved parties and resources.

Techniques to assess and intervene systematically, such as mapping, are important to know. Mapping can be conducted with the student, parents, or persons the professional school counselor determines to be close to the student. Minuchin (1974) and Minuchin and Fishman (1981) applied the concept of mapping in family work. It is this type of diagramming that examines through drawing the family structure and patterns of interaction, observing distances, connections, coalitions, repetitive sequences, and boundaries. Creative questioning by the professional school counselor elicits vital information regarding open and closed systems, negative or positive feedback loops, enmeshed or disengaged subsystems, boundaries, and power.

Mapping can be extended to include the classroom, teachers, school, and community. This more global approach has been referred to as *ecosystemic mapping*. In ecosystemic mapping, the diagrams include the larger social system and outer world of the child. Using community organizations and institutions—as well as the child, family, classroom, and school community—problematic symptoms and resiliency resources can be identified (Sherman & Fredman, 1986).

Cerio (1995) discussed other techniques that professional school counselors can use, such as worldview, hierarchy, and triangles. In *worldview*, the professional school counselor works to illicit the values that influence the interactions of the students with parents and others in their environment. A clash of values between home and school can create a problem. Examining the *hierarchical structure* often leads to an understanding of the power and influence dynamics as well as getting a clearer picture of the roles that are played out in the system. *Triangulation* refers to the process of involving a third party to take sides against another. Triangle work looks at the interaction of three members or parties as a way of resisting, sabotaging, or impeding change, since alliances influence the other member in the triangle and increase the degree of difficulty of arriving at and agreeing to solutions. Cerio summarized these techniques with five basic questions that a professional school counselor should ask to get a systems perspective:

1. What are the world views of the family and the school personnel?
2. What are the positions of the family members and school personnel in the family–school hierarchy?
3. What subsystems are involved with the problem?
4. What is the nature of the boundaries of the subsystems?
5. What triangles are in play related to the problem? (p. 43)

Individual crises can benefit from systems intervention by assessing the crisis and formulating the interventions from a more holistic perspective. A crisis that has gained public attention can be perpetuated by a member of the school community's mishandling of a situation. System-wide, school and community involvement in the plan outlining expected roles and duties can only help the crisis situation.

A SYSTEMIC APPROACH TO SCHOOL-WIDE CRISIS

Systemic counseling is needed when the school or school system is more visibly affected by the crisis, such as with a student suicide or homicide because many parts of the system will be affected. Best friends, neighbors, classmates, fellow students, and friends of friends all form concentric circles of closeness around the victim, and all experience some stress from the crisis. A general plan must be in place prior to the crisis to mobilize resources as needed and to involve the community for effective prevention–intervention action and the students' developmental–ecological needs and levels need to be considered.

The school needs a comprehensive guide to systemic crisis intervention that is available for immediate action. Professional school counselors should assist in the formulation and use of such a plan or be instrumental in beginning the dialogue to formulate such a plan.

A COMPREHENSIVE SCHOOL CRISIS PLAN

James and Gilliland (2001) explained that although comprehensive crisis plans take a great deal of time and resources to create, they are essential to effectively respond to crises. Plans all need to involve generic elements, so using an available outline as a template is helpful. But these plans also need to be specific to the school community's particular needs and demands. Beginning with a needs assessment is vital. James and Gilliland suggested a two-tiered team, the first involving the school–community resources for the larger planning picture, and a second tier composed of building response teams with information on the physical plant and its occupants. Some suggested roles for the crisis response team are the crisis response coordinator, the crisis intervention coordinator, the media liaison, the security liaison, the community–medical liaison, the parent liaison, crisis interveners, and the resource person. Poland and McCormick (1999) added an important additional team member called the *counseling liaison.*

James and Gilliland (2001) suggested the following elements be spelled out in a crisis response plan: (a) physical requirements set up for counseling, communications, operations, information, first-aid, and break centers; (b) logistics involving how communication will flow, procedural checklists, provisions, and building plans; and (c) the crisis response of getting and verifying the facts; assessing the impact of the crisis to determine the degree of mobilization; providing triage assessment to determine those who are most affected and in need of immediate intervention; providing psychological first-aid; having a model of intervention in place; providing crisis interviews; and the briefing, debriefing, and demobilizing phase.

In a school-wide crisis, the systemic crisis intervention plan is a very comprehensive project that involves the entire community. The National Education Association (NEA) (2002) provided information and guidance for developing and using a crisis plan. Their *Crisis Communications Guide and Toolkit* can lead the professional school counselor and crisis planning team through assessing the system's needs; developing a crisis response team and plan; and building local, state, and national crisis networks. The toolkit is organized into three main sections: being prepared before a crisis, being responsive during a crisis, and being diligent in moving beyond crisis.

In the first section, the NEA provides assistance by giving guiding principles for crisis response and prevention plans. These plans must be inclusive and collaborative among school community, staff, administrators, teachers, associations, law enforcement, fire department, mental health agencies, PTAs, and other community partners; have as a goal to be supportive of students and staff; provide strategies for information dissemination of the plan to all involved and know that members know what to do in case of an emergency; and be practiced and updated. This section also provides a checklist to assess how the system measures up to meeting crisis needs in terms of policy and procedure, operations, and aftermath.

In the second section, critical response actions are outlined and organized by the action to be taken each day and the media or communications challenges that may need to be addressed. Day one is focused on response. Day two is focused on information. Day three and beyond is focused on communication. Detailed responses are given in this useful resource, from reminders to mobilize resources to sending follow-up letters.

In the third section, attention is given to support for long-term healing, building partnerships, striving to achieve a "new normal," and dealing with the media. Information on handling donations and memorials and managing anniversaries and physical reminders is outlined:

> Victims of a crisis experience a real need to return to normal. It is a commonly expressed desire and although almost everyone articulates this need, they fail to achieve it. "Normal" as they once knew it is forever gone and changed. For many the recognition that such a "normal" is unattainable can be debilitating. As a result, counselors and crisis survivors find the concept of "a new normal" to be very reassuring and accurate. (NEA, 2002, p. 6)

As a response to school tragedies, President Bill Clinton directed the U.S. Department of Education (2000a) and the Department of Justice to produce a guide to help make schools safer. *The Early Warning, Timely Response: A Guide to Safe Schools* was published based on research and proven practical strategies. A follow-up publication (U.S. Department of Education, 2000b), *Safeguarding Our Children: An Action Guide*, was also developed to help schools implement safety plans. (A full text of these public domain publications can be accesses online; see U.S. Department of Education 2000a, 2000b). Professional school counselors should become familiar with these valuable resources.

CRITICAL INCIDENT STRESS DEBRIEFING (CISD) MODEL

"Critical Incident Stress Debriefing is a form of structured psychological debriefing conducted in small groups. It was originally developed . . . as a direct, action-oriented crisis intervention process designed to prevent or mitigate traumatic stress" (Mitchell & Everly, 1993, p. 3). CISD was first formulated and used with emergency and public service personnel, but its use has expanded and it is now used with most populations that have experienced a natural disaster, accident, trauma, or event critical enough to tax the coping skills of the people involved. It has been used successfully world-wide and with all ages, including school-aged children. Most areas of this country have trained CISD personnel available to assist commercial, industrial, and community groups.

When a crisis hits a school community, systematic crisis intervention assumes that all members of the community are affected to some degree and need attention. Students and their parents can be the beneficiaries of CISD work. However, often the professional staff, teachers, and crisis personnel are overlooked because all the focus is on the students. The caregivers also need care. Burn-out is especially severe if caregiver needs in a crisis are unattended. CISD is one way to provide staff, faculty, crisis workers, and witnesses an effective way to help them cope. Professional school counselors need to attend to the needs of the helpers (including themselves) following the immediate phases of a crisis.

CISD was the result of study and research by Mitchell and Everly (1993): "CISD is a crisis intervention process designed to stabilize cognitive and affective processes and to further mitigate the impact of a traumatic event" (p. 15). Some of the basic principles of CISD follow:

1. It is not therapy and should only be done by a team of people specifically trained in CISD.
2. It is a group process with the purpose of reducing stress and enhancing recovery.
3. Not all problems will be solved; referrals may be necessary.
4. A person can attend a meeting and not speak and still gain benefit.
5. It is best to have voluntary participation, but attendance is required for all to benefit.
6. CISD should take place after 24 hours and before 72 hours of the crisis (with variations depending upon the event).
7. CISD teams are "multiorganizational and multijurisdictional in structure" (p. 15).

8. CISD should be taken as one option of critical incident stress management.
9. Consult Chapter 93, "Crisis Intervention in the Schools," for a basic understanding of the symptomology and signs of stress in people during crises. It is important that people who have suffered from a crisis or trauma know that many physical, affective, cognitive, and behavioral manifestations are "normal" under the circumstances. There is a specific stage in the CISD intervention when this material needs to be shared with the participants.

The CISD response team for a regional response is usually made up of about 40 people, with about 12 mental health professionals and the rest being peer support personnel made up of community workers in emergency or stress-related fields, such as nursing, law enforcement, or first response teams. Once the need for CISD has been determined, team membership is formed from this community pool and is composed of three to five members, depending on the number and nature of the participants. A clergyman trained in CISD can also be present to act as a listener and a guide, although preaching or praying is not a part of CISD. The optimal number of participants is 4 to 20, but up to 30 participants can be handled if the time is lengthened to give everyone an opportunity to share. Detailed descriptions of each member's duties, preparation and set-up, and procedures for the debriefing are specific and prescribed. The normal time required for an intervention is from 1 to 4 hours. During each stage, participants as a whole are asked directed questions to help tell their story and usually take turns responding. People are allowed to pass if they choose not to say anything. Each stage has specific questions to move the process along. Leaders typically do not provide feedback after individuals share.

> The overall strategy for a CISD team during a debriefing is to start at the point which is easiest to discuss and then move gradually into more emotionally intense discussions. After handling the intense materials the group is gradually brought back out of the intense discussion to the less intense until the discussion finally concludes. (Mitchell & Everly, 1993, p. 86)

Table 94.1 presents a description of the seven stages of CISD (Mitchell & Everly, 1993, p. 144). Postdebriefing activities include one-on-one time with members who expressed or exhibited a need for extra attention during the CISD intervention. This connection can be a supportive word or a suggested referral for therapy. This one-on-one time can occur during refreshments following the CISD intervention. A postdebriefing meeting for the intervention team itself must occur to provide good mental health and prevent against stress overload for the team. Professional school counselors need to know how to access a CISD team or seek out specialized training or community support to start a CISD project. Knowledge and skill enhancement through CISD training and participation can greatly benefit a professional school counselor's sense of competency at times of crisis.

THE NOVA MODEL

The NOVA model (National Organization for Victim Assistance, 1997) has been used successfully with older students in group crisis intervention. It is similar to the CISD

TABLE 94.1
SEVEN STAGES OF CRITICAL INCIDENT STRESS DEBRIEFING (CISD)

Stage	Description/Purpose
1. Introduction	To introduce team members, explain process, set expectations.
2. Fact Phase	To describe the traumatic event from each participant's perspective on a cognitive level.
3. Thought Phase	To allow participants to describe cognitive reactions and to transition to emotional reactions.
4. Reaction Phase	To identify the most traumatic aspect of the event for the participants.
5. Symptom Phase	To identify personal symptoms of distress and transition back to the cognitive level.
6. Teaching Phase	To educate regarding what are normal reactions and adaptive coping mechanisms (i.e., stress management). Provide cognitive anchor.
7. Reentry Phase	To clarify ambiguities and prepare for termination.

model but requires less structure and allows for more interactions between the facilitator and the participants. A session generally lasts approximately 2 hours and should include enough students to provide good interaction but small enough to be able to identify for assessment the students who may need further help. The NOVA model session includes the following:

1. Introductions and safety and security statements; descriptions of physical, emotional, and cognitive reactions at the time of the event
2. Ventilation and validation of emotional upheaval
3. Descriptions of the aftermath and present reactions or feelings
4. Ongoing facilitation of validation, refraining from judgment, and drawing and bonding students together to normalize thoughts and feelings
5. Questions about the future with a discussion of coping strategies
6. Referral sources
7. Summarization to reaffirm experiences
8. Postgroup sessions (30 minutes) to distribute handouts, answer questions, or follow-up

This more informal group process is used to help all students affected by the crisis, and also should highlight those students who need further assessment and assistance.

STUDENT DEATH AND SUICIDE

When a student dies, the entire school community is affected because of the interpersonal nature of the ecosystem and because the death of a child is commonly considered unnatural. Developmentally, students are deeply connected with their peer group to master the tasks of industry and identity formation. They often see themselves as invincible. Death of a peer shakes students emotionally and cognitively. When schools are confronted with such a serious loss, sensitive, supportive, and prepared handling of the crisis is paramount. Proper handling of the crisis can influence the school community's emotional response as well as reduce harmful consequences. Collins and Collins (2005) discussed some of the tasks that are involved in this process:

1. Verifying the information and details
2. Dispensing of the information to the students
3. Stabilizing the situation, and providing student safety
4. Helping the school community cope with the loss (students, parents, teachers, staff)
5. Protecting the privacy of the family
6. Communicating with the media
7. Planning ongoing support and counseling

Preparing how information will be dispensed to the students involves knowing which students or groups of students may be most deeply affected. This can be accomplished by ecomapping the deceased student to determine interactions and levels of points of contact and relationships. Closest friends, associates, and teachers need to be told individually as quickly as possible to prevent speculation and rumors. Closer friends like those involved in clubs, homeroom, or activities need to be told in smaller groups, with two adult helpers present. Class-size groups for the remaining school community can similarly best handle the sharing of the information. Sharing details surrounding the death, allowing for questions, providing time to talk, providing available resources in the school or after school activities, and providing referral services for those students who request them are essential components. Memorials and follow-up can best be handled knowing the culture of the school community (Cavaiola & Colford, 2006; Collins & Collins, 2005; James & Gilliland, 2001).

A special note on student suicide needs to be clarified: "Student suicides differ from other school-based crises because of the self-initiated behavior, the complex underlying motivations, and the various cultural values and interpretations associated with the suicide" (Collins & Collins, 2005, p. 427). Information on suicide prevention, assessment, intervention, and postvention is vital to professional school counselors and personnel. There is serious evidence of contagion and cluster suicides occurring in school settings. The processing of a student suicide needs to be informed with this fact. Sensationalizing the suicide action and the student, encouraging media coverage, and memorializing or commemorating the suicide are inappropriate. Supportive groups for those who are deeply affected and for survivors are encouraged.

> A common, but inaccurate, myth is that talking about suicide in a classroom makes students more likely to try to kill themselves. In fact, when students are confronted with a peer's death by suicide, they need to talk about it and receive assistance in trying to make sense of a senseless act. The counselor can portray the student who committed suicide as an individual with problems who did not find an avenue to effectively deal with his or her problems. This should be done without abusing the victim's character. . . . The counselor can portray suicide as

a permanent solution to a temporary problem for which help is available. (Collins & Collins, 2005, p. 429)

Students' grief reactions are developmental and affect academics, emotions, and cognitions. Providing a safe supportive environment with understanding individuals where students can explore their reactions and reach some level of resolution or be referred for additional support are key functions of a crisis plan that involve the death of a student.

Summary/Conclusion

In summary, the following are 10 things to remember in systemic crisis intervention:

1. A systems approach to crisis is more holistic than individual work alone.
2. A systems approach to crisis broadens the scope of assessment and available resources.
3. Communication is essential in resolving systemic crises.
4. Systems intervention recognizes that problems reside in the interactions.
5. Being able to use systems techniques such as mapping, discovering subsystems and boundaries, hierarchy, worldview, and triangulation work enhance individual crisis intervention.
6. A comprehensive plan involving school and community needs to be in place before a crisis occurs, with all members of the team knowing their functions.
7. The professional school counselor plays a vital role in the formulation and implementation of such a plan.
8. Physical requirements, logistics, and crisis responses all need to be planned out.
9. Training in a systemic crisis intervention model (e.g., CISD, NOVA) is important for the professional school counselor.
10. Always remember to attend to the needs of the caregivers, professionals, and crisis workers.

(Note: See the CD-ROM for a list of references.)

CHAPTER 95

PARENTAL INVOLVEMENT IN SCHOOLS

Henry L. Harris, Edward A. Wierzalis, and Doris R. Coy

Preview

In this chapter, we focus on various aspects of parental involvement in schools. Different types of parental involvement will be examined, along with barriers that might prevent involvement and recommendations to increase parental involvement and partnerships. Brief descriptions of successful parental involvement programs and Internet resources are provided.

Parents and public schools play an important role in educating U.S. children. Parents are responsible for being involved in their children's lives by raising them in warm, nurturing, safe, and secure environments. According to Baker, Goesling, and Letendre (2002), the more parents are involved with their children, the more positive outcomes occur. Students that perform well academically often have parents who are interested and involved in their educational experiences from a very early age. Such parents engage in various supportive learning activities with their children, such as reading together and reviewing homework (Wade & Moore, 1998).

Public schools, in part, are responsible for providing children the opportunity to pursue a quality education. Pursuit of a quality education has proven to be more challenging for some students, particularly disadvantaged and minority students. As a result, public schools have been required by the No Child Left Behind Act of 2001 (NCLB) to close the achievement gap between disadvantaged and minority students and their peers (U.S. Department of Education, 2001). NCLB attempts to close the achievement gap by requiring schools to (a) help students meet challenging academic standards by testing them in math, science, and reading; (b) collect and report student achievement data by race, poverty level, children with disabilities, and English language learners; (c) make annual adequate yearly progress (AYP) reports that demonstrate how all students are meeting state goals in math and reading; and (d) by ensuring that all teachers are highly qualified.

NCLB (U.S. Department of Education, 2001) also recognizes the importance of parental involvement because parents are allowed to have access to schools, perhaps more now than ever before. For example, when schools are identified as "In Need of Improvement," schools must establish activities and programs to increase parental involvement and schedule regular meetings to discuss parents' concerns when they are requested by parents. Parents also have input in writing a parental involvement plan, and, once it is adopted, they must receive a copy of the plan. The ultimate goal is to increase the level of parental involvement and make parents full partners in the educational process of their children.

Parental Involvement

Parental involvement refers to the role that parents have in educating their children in school and at home (Christenson & Sheridan, 2001). According to Berger (1995), parental interest and support is the primary factor in their children's educational failure or success. Involved parents communicate to children that education is important to their families and also infuse the family's values into the school. Parental involvement also motivates students when they observe their parents taking an active interest in school (Gonzalez-DeHass, Willems, & Holbein, 2005; Scott-Jones, 1988). Helping students become more goal oriented has also been associated with parental involvement. Gonzalez, Doan Holbein, and Quilter (2002) revealed that when parents were involved, their children adopted an approach to learning in which they were more likely to seek challenging tasks, persist through academic difficulties, and experience satisfaction with their schoolwork. Marchant, Paulson, and Rothlisberg (2001) also discovered that when students perceived that parents valued the importance of effort and academic success, they had more confidence in their own academic competence and placed a higher priority on their academic ability, grades, and effort. While investigating parental involvement with kindergarten children, McWayne, Hampton, Fantuzzo, Cohen, and Sekino (2004) found that involved parents provided a rich learning environment at home with activities that included talking to their children about the value of school and helping them practice things they had learned in school. When compared to the children of less involved parents, these children displayed higher levels of social skills and greater achievement in mathematics and reading.

In summary, when parents demonstrate they value, show genuine interest, and actively participate in education, communication with their children improves, children get in less trouble and have better school attendance, resulting in higher grades and test scores. Because of expectations from parents, children are also more likely to develop better study habits, graduate from high school, and attend college. Parents develop a sense of pride because of their children's accomplishments and may even decide to further their own education (McNeil, 1999; Media Information Services, 1997).

TYPES OF PARENTAL INVOLVEMENT

Parental involvement entails a variety of parenting behaviors including discussing homework with children, attending Parent–Teacher Organization/Association (PTO/PTA) meetings, serving as assistants in the classroom, participating as school volunteers, participating in parental school advisory councils, or engaging in active communication with teachers and other school officials regarding the educational concerns of their children (Feurstein, 2000; Scott-Jones, 1988). Epstein's (2001) framework outlined six methods of parental involvement–partnerships:

1. *Parenting:* Helping all families establish home environments to support children as students. Activities include (a) family support programs to help families with nutrition, health, and other services; (b) suggestions for a home environment that supports learning at each grade level; (c) neighborhood meetings to help families and

schools understand each other; and (d) home visits during transitional phases to preschool, elementary, middle, and high school.

2. *Communication:* Design effective forms for school-to-home and home-to-school communications about school programs and children's progress. Activities include (a) annual conferences with every parent; (b) weekly or monthly folders of student work sent home for parental review and comments; (c) language translators to help families when needed; and (d) regularly scheduling useful notices, phone calls, newsletters, and other forms of communication.

3. *Volunteering:* Recognize and organize parental help and support. Activities include (a) parental patrols or other activities to help provide safety and operation of various school programs; (b) school and classroom volunteer program to assist teachers, students, administrators, other school personnel, or other parents; and (c) yearly postcard survey to identify all available talents, times, and location of volunteers.

4. *Learning at home:* Provide information and ideas to families about how to help students with homework and other curriculum-related activities, decisions, and planning. Activities include (a) information on homework policies; (b) how to monitor and discuss school-related work at home; (c) information for families on required skills for students at each grade level and in all subjects; and (d) summer learning packets.

5. *Decision making:* Include parents in school decisions; develop new parent leaders and representatives. Activities include (a) active PTA/PTO advisory councils, advocacy groups, school review boards, and various other committees for parental leadership and participation; (b) information on school or local elections for school representatives; (c) networking that will connect all families with parental representatives; and (d) advocacy groups to campaign and lobby for school reform and improvements.

6. *Collaboration with community:* Identify and integrate resources and services from the community to strengthen school programs, family practices, and student learning. Activities include (a) information for students and families on community health, cultural recreational, social support, and other programs or services; (b) service to the community by families, students, and the schools; (c) providing information that connects with learning skills and talents, including summer programs for students; and (e) participation in school programs for students.

There may be difficulties that parents, schools, and communities encounter when they work together to increase parental involvement. However, all groups must be willing to listen, understand, and diligently strive to overcome any potential barriers. Children are supported most effectively when families and schools have shared goals and work collaboratively to accomplish the goals (Epstein, 2001). Table 95.1 provides some suggested parental involvement activities, and Table 95.2 provides some Internet resources for more information on parental involvement.

BARRIERS TO PARENTAL INVOLVEMENT

Most parents care about their children's educational experience, but their level of involvement might be affected by a number of barriers. For example parents may be too

TABLE 95.1

EFFECTIVE PARENTAL INVOLVEMENT ACTIVITIES

1. *Parent Visitation/Observation Days.* Send personalized invitations for parents to sit with their child in the classroom (Benson & Martin, 2003).

2. *Parent/Student Switch Day.* A process in which students are excused one day from class only if a parent volunteer to take their place at school. The parent is responsible for following the student's daily schedule (with some exceptions) (Loucks, 1992).

3. *Newsletters.* Inform parents about various topics, including: homework strategies, reports about special school projects, teacher features, and parenting tips. The newsletters should be well designed and sent out to parents monthly or quarterly, depending on school needs (Loucks, 1992).

4. *Parent Classes.* Classes offered at school focus on topics such as how to help students with homework, tutoring strategies, parenting skills, drug education, and improving communications skills (Loucks, 1992).

5. *Lunch With Professional School Counselors.* Program designed by professional school counselors that involves going to the parents' places of employment (Evans & Hines, 1997).

6. *Parent Computer Day.* Invite parents to be instructed in the use of computers by their children (Benson & Martin, 2003).

7. *Coffee With the Principal.* Invite parents to participate in informal discussions with the principal on a regular basis (Benson & Martin, 2003).

busy; both may be employed; the student may come from a single-parent household; parents may have other children at home; they may feel inadequate and powerless about their abilities to influence the school; or they may believe school officials are the experts and do not need their assistance (Epstein & Dauber, 1991; Flood, Lapp, Tinajero, & Nagel, 1995). When perceived barriers that impact parental involvement are not confronted, students may not reach their academic, social, and emotional potential.

THE PARENT–TEACHER RELATIONSHIP

Parents and teachers sometimes have a difficult time working together because they do not trust each other. Teachers sometimes perceive parents as outsiders who lack the basic educational skills needed to help children learn. This perspective could cause some parents to develop negative feelings and attitudes toward school personnel (Anderson, 1999). Parents may also not fully understand the kind of role the school would like them to fill regarding their involvement at home and school. Furthermore, parents may question whether school officials are sincerely concerned about the educational welfare of their children (Eccles & Harold, 1993).

Some parents may have had negative experiences during their educational years and feel intimidated by school personnel, sometimes believing that teachers, professional school counselors, or administrators call them only to deliver negative news about their children or blame them personally for the problems their children are experiencing at school (Eccles & Harold, 1993; Miretzky, 2004). Some parents also fear

TABLE 95.2
INTERNET RESOURCES

Center for Parent Leadership (**www.centerforparentleadership.org**)

Family Involvement Partnership for Learning–Parents and Families (**www.ed.gov/Family/BTS/covpg.html**)

Kids Can Learn (**www.kidscanlearn.com**)

Institute for Responsive Education (**www.responsiveeducation.org**)

National Coalition for Parent Involvement in Education (NCPIE) (**www.ncpie.org**)

National Parent Information Network (NPIN) (**http://npin.org**)

Parent Educational Advocacy Training Center (**www.peatc.org**)

Technical Assistance ALLIANCE for Parents Centers (**www.taalliance.org**)

Wrightslaw (**www.wrightslaw.com**)

---

reprisals from teachers if they are perceived as too vocal when offering suggestions or expressing criticism (Levine & Trickett, 2000).

It is possible that the relationship between teachers and parents is strained because of their misperceptions of parental involvement. In a study conducted by Barge and Loges (2003), parents identified (a) monitoring student academic progress, (b) cultivating personal relationships with teachers, (c) using extracurricular school programs, and (d) developing community support systems as important aspects to positive parental involvement. On the other hand, teachers perceived helpful parental involvement as (a) communicating with the child and the school; (b) participation in the child's school and the child's life in general; (c) fundamental parenting duties including supervision of the child; and (d) discipline, particularly support for punishment administered by the school. Halsey's (2005) investigation of parental involvement in junior high schools revealed that a majority of teachers believed that many parents were not interested in participating in their children's education. Parents, on the other hand, believed that teachers only wanted a limited amount of involvement because they often did not receive personalized individual communication about how they could become involved.

Miretzky (2004) found that teachers and parents agreed that better communication was needed. Parents indicated they wanted to have their efforts, insights, and expertise valued more by teachers. The teachers stated that when parents unconditionally accepted their children's version of an event that happened in the classroom without clarifying the situation with the teacher, this hampered the development of a respectful and trusting relationship. Teachers believed their professionalism was being called into question and wondered if parents respected their training and experience. Both groups identified overcoming defensiveness as a significant element of creating more effective collaboration and communication. Teachers, specifically, believed that collaboration and communication would be become prioritized more if the school administration clearly endorsed their efforts (Miretzky, 2004).

THE ISSUE OF RACE

Race may be another factor contributing to mistrust because of the history of racial discrimination. Lareau and Horvat (1999) contended that some minority parents may approach the schools with challenges and criticism rather than deference and support. School officials must understand the sociopolitical history of parents who have children of color attending schools and recognize within racial group perspectives. Some may not completely trust school personnel for a number of valid reasons, including lack of a diverse understanding teaching staff. Parents of minority students frequently have personal experiences with schools related to controversial issues such as biased testing or racial tracking. Calabrese (1990) discovered that minority parents felt less welcome at school, were less likely to see their children's teacher as caring and supportive, and questioned the school's sincerity concerning any request for involvement. Minority parents, compared to White parents, were more likely to receive negative communication about their children and more likely to perceive school rules created without parental input as inconsistent and unusual. The parents did agree, however, that they must overcome their defensive habits in order to work with the schools more effectively (Calabrese, 1990).

Within traditional Latino culture, parents may not become involved with the school because of the high level of respect given to educators. Latino parents perceive educators as competent professionals and often believe it would be counterproductive to interfere with schools (Quezada, Diaz, & Sanchez, 2003). However, Latino parents in the Levine and Trickett (2000) study felt discrimination from school personnel. The perceived forms of discrimination they experienced caused them to feel resentful and distrusting of the school.

LANGUAGE AND POVERTY

School officials should be aware of how language could be a barrier limiting parental involvement. According to Sue and Sue (2002), European American culture places a strong emphasis on a person's ability to understand and speak English. As a result, individuals who are bilingual or from lower class backgrounds that do not use Standard English while communicating may be unfairly treated or perceived as inferior. In addition, their own sense of self-worth may be diminished because they may not be able to help their children complete their homework assignments or understand forms sent home (Quezada et al., 2003). Feurstein (2000) found that middle- and upper class teachers were able to communicate more effectively with middle- and upper class parents and least effectively with groups most different from themselves.

Many U.S. families are deeply affected by poverty, and economically disadvantaged students are at a greater risk for experiencing a variety of academic, socioemotional, behavioral, and health problems that can negatively affect their long-term development (McLoyd, 1998). Thus, it is crucial for schools to encourage parents from low-income families to become involved in their children's education. School officials should also be aware that some parents are living from paycheck to paycheck. In order to survive, these parents hold multiple jobs with rigid work schedules that prevent frequent participation in school-related events.

While numerous positive benefits of parental involvement have been demonstrated, the level of parental involvement can decrease as students progress from elementary through middle and high schools. Schools must maintain positive and open communication with parents to offset this decline in involvement. Parents, school officials, and communities must learn to build cooperative educational partnerships if students are to be provided with necessary educational skills.

RECOMMENDATIONS TO INCREASE PARENTAL INVOLVEMENT

School officials should seriously explore ways to overcome barriers and develop a school environment that facilitates parental involvement. Chavkin and Garza-Lubeck (1990) originally outlined six critical steps needed for successful parental involvement programs, and within this chapter, two additional steps are included. The steps consist of (1) motivation; (2) accurate assessment; (3) training of staff; (4) community outreach programs; (5) networking with community businesses and agencies; (6) parent–teacher partnerships; (7) role of school boards; and (8) role of the professional school counselor.

The first step required is *motivation*. School officials must be highly motivated and have a genuine desire to create a parental involvement initiative that welcomes parents from all racial, ethnic, and economic backgrounds to become valued partners in the education of students. School officials must have the desire, ability, and willingness to establish open lines of communication with parents to make them feel welcome.

Motivation also calls for flexibility, demonstrated by scheduling programs during times more convenient to parents, providing daycare to younger siblings for major school programs, conducting home visits to invite parents to school, offering to bring school-related functions to the site of parents' employers, and seek parental input regarding workshops or training sessions (Quezada et al., 2003; Stouffer, 1992). Schools should be especially committed to creating an open-school and open-classroom policy for low-income parents because, compared to middle-class parents, they are far less likely to run into their children's teachers in their neighborhood settings (Lott, 2003).

Step two calls for an *accurate assessment* of parental involvement. This helps establish accurate information reflecting the interest level and needs of the community. The assessment process could include methods such as informal observations; town-hall meetings with parents and school officials; examining preexisting data (e.g., number of parents attending PTA meetings, looking at the current number of parent volunteers, previous school history); reviewing current policies regarding parental involvement programs; organizing focus groups, mailed surveys, random telephone surveys, and local radio call-in programs (Pryor, 1996). When accurate knowledge is developed, specific programs can be designed to better address concerns.

Step three calls for continuous *training and staff development*, a vital component of successful parental involvement programs. In-service training could initially begin by exploring school officials' views of parental involvement and past experiences. School officials should be made aware that some parents (e.g., parents who lack education, have low incomes, are from culturally diverse backgrounds) may feel unwelcome in the educational environment and avoid schools. Workshops addressing these types of issues could prove beneficial in helping school officials become more aware of their own personal biases and also help them develop a better understanding of individuals from culturally different groups.

Step four involves school officials venturing out into the community to *establish a relationship* with its various members. Recreational facilities, churches, and cultural gatherings provide unique opportunities for educators to familiarize themselves with key community members who also may be able to further assist them in developing strong parent–school relationships (Chavkin & Garza-Lubeck, 1990). Employers should also be targeted during this step and encouraged to use family- and student-friendly business practices such as providing leave time for parents to volunteer in school or attend conferences, and, when possible, offer parental training and child care. Employers could potentially benefit by having better public and community relations, improved worker morale and loyalty, and a more qualified workforce for the future (U.S. Department of Education, 1996).

Step five involves schools *networking with social services agencies.* Chavkin and Garza-Lubeck (1990) suggested helping to arrange services for families in need is a significant part of the effort required to involve parents. Student achievement and attendance is based on more than just instruction, because factors such as health, housing, transportation, nutrition, and clothing play influential roles in determining student success.

Step six focuses on the quality of *parent–teacher partnerships.* Parents and teachers must, for the benefit of the children and the success of the school, work to create effective home–school partnerships. Parents and teachers must be willing to develop open lines of communication with one another and start perceiving each other as partners rather than adversaries.

Step seven focuses on the role of the *school board* in helping to encourage parental involvement. Devlin-Sherer and Devlin-Sherer (1994) suggested that school boards could be more proactive in promoting parental involvement by influencing administrators to establish meaningful parental involvement programs, requiring administrators to create realistic plans for parental involvement that would be reviewed periodically, and helping establish and promote guidelines for parental involvement initiatives.

Step eight involves the role of the professional school counselor in facilitating parental involvement. Brown (1999) suggested professional school counselors could become advocates for parents and students by regularly consulting with parents and offering a variety of parental education classes. Good communication skills (e.g., listening, paraphrasing, clarifying, interpreting, and reflecting feelings) are valued tools needed to work effectively with parents. Professional school counselors, because of their unique training, could offer workshops to bolster parental communication skills and help school personnel become more aware of diverse parental models

DIVERSE PARENTAL MODELS

School personnel must be respectful of the variety of nontraditional family structures that exist in today's culture. Children may not come from the model of a traditional family but may be from single-parent homes, or be children of same-sex couples, or be living with and raised by their grandparents. Schools need to be sensitive to nontraditional family needs and work diligently to provide them with support and create ways for them to be involved in their children's education. Grandparents raising grandchildren is a growing trend (Edwards & Daire, 2006) and it is imperative that their rights to be appropriately involved in their grandchildren's education is recognized by the school.

Same-sex parents are confronted with the prejudices and stereotypes that society subjects them to, thus making asserting their parental rights particularly challenging. Gay and lesbian parents operate without societal sanction or tradition (Hancock, 1995). School personnel may be uncomfortable and unsure as to how to incorporate same-sex parents into many of the activities that will foster parental involvement. However, same-sex parents have the right to be a part of their children's education and, as a result, schools must positively engage these parents in all school–parent partnerships. Same-sex parents share the same concerns for their children's emotional and physical safety and education as any other parental model.

Summary/Conclusion

Parents are stakeholders in educational reform and should have a role in the delivery of programs intended to enhance and improve the outcomes of their children's education. They must become more actively involved in their children's education and provide their children, regardless of circumstances, with a nurturing environment conducive to academic success. Professional school counselors, teachers, administrators, and other staff members must equally strive to do more to encourage parental involvement, especially from fathers and parents from low-income families. Schools must work to eliminate barriers that prevent parental involvement and realize that most parents would like to become full partners in the educational process. Finally, parents, schoolprofessionals, and members of the community should understand that it really does "take a village" to educate a child.

(Note: See the CD-ROM for a list of references.)

CHAPTER 96

PREVENTING PROFESSIONAL SCHOOL COUNSELOR BURNOUT

Kelly M. Murray

Preview

Burnout and attrition from the field of school counseling is quite high. It is a condition that emerges as a function of the complex interplay of environmental stressors and individual differences. Burnout is a slow and corrosive condition that causes fatigue, cynicism, lack of motivation, and, possibly, depression.

As a professional school counselor or school counselor in training, you may have wondered about burnout and even questioned whether you may be suffering some of the symptoms associated with it. *Burnout* is a term often read and learned during a training program. Because of professional training, it may be relatively easy to spot in other people. However, when it is the professional school counselor who is tired and feeling ineffective, it is often rationalized as being part of the job. In reality, burnout and attrition from the field of school counseling is quite high. A study of academicians and practitioners conducted by Wood, Klein, Cross, Lammers, and Elliott (1985) looked at symptoms of burnout and depression and discovered that 63% of participants reported knowing of colleagues whose work is affected by their impairment, while 32% of the participants admitted having feelings of burnout or depression that affected their own work. A 1994 study by Grosch and Olsen suggested that the average counselor has a productive life span of 10 years before burnout becomes a substantial factor. Some studies have described the prevalence of depression in psychiatrists to be at 60% to 90% (Swearingen, 1990; Wood et al., 1985).

Burnout is a slow, corrosive condition that tends to get progressively worse. This is especially true for the professional school counselor who will often overlook his or her own needs in order to be available to others. For school counselors, as with counselors in general, there are usually competing life demands. Not only must counselors be present daily for their clients and in their workplace, they are also attempting to balance multiple competing roles (e.g., spouse, parent, friendships, mentor relationships, community roles). This struggle for balance puts additional stress on mental and physical well-being, adding to the formula for burnout (Bryant & Constantine, 2006). As the professional school counselor continues to ignore or deny the extent of his or her burnout, symptoms get slowly worse and more pervasive.

In the past, definitions for burnout have been vague and all encompassing. Although there has been a good deal of research on burnout for human service workers, there has been relatively little research on burnout specifically for professional school counselors. The research that does exist for professional school counselors shows that the job is often stressful, intense, and unrelenting. The demands placed upon a professional school counselor are often plentiful and varied. They are called upon to work with students who present with a host of issues, the families and parents of these students, administrators, teachers, other mental health professionals, and other school officials. The professional school counselor may work in many different domains and wear many hats. Professional school counselors are relied upon to make critical decisions about students which may affect those students for the rest of their lives.

Wise (1985) reported that professional school counselors often experience a variety of on-the-job stressors. Such stressors are reported to be an overabundance of work, insufficient pleasure at work, inadequate structure and poor management, poor relationships with supervisory personnel, meager recognition for efforts, and the feeling of lacking control of one's situation. Other stressors that have been reported are a lack of time, excessive caseloads, being unable to catch up on backlogs of work, and a lack of support. Several other areas reported as unsatisfactory among professional school counselors were unavailability of adequate testing and interview facilities, lack of funding to attend conventions, lack of in-service training, lack of opportunity for advancement and promotion, and isolation from peers (Niebrugge, 1994). An important contributor to burnout is the absence of the opportunity to experience completion and follow through with students with whom professional school counselors work. Often the child or the counselor moves on, and, therefore, the counselor is unable to determine if the work he or she has done with the child has been truly effective. The lack of opportunity for the professional school counselor to conduct ongoing follow up with a particular student can cause the counselor to view his or her work as ineffective and unrewarding (Freudenberger, 1977). The stress and anxiety associated with these many demands may be intense and may take a toll on the professional school counselor.

Burnout has been defined as a reaction to chronic problems in coping with stress (Cherniss, 1980). Maslach and Jackson (1986) reported that burnout is a three-dimensional construct. The first component is described as *emotional exhaustion*. Frequently, professionals report feelings of being tired and overwhelmed with work demands. As emotional resources are expended, professionals feel they are no longer able to give of themselves at a psychological level. In this component the professional school counselor may feel overwhelmed by his or her job demands. The second component involves *depersonalization*. Professionals suffering from burnout develop impersonal attitudes and become indifferent in responding to students. They may have negative feelings and attitudes toward students. This distancing of others can lead professional school counselors to believe their student's deserve their afflictions. The last component of burnout is a *reduced sense of personal accomplishment* that is often manifested in feelings of incompetence and helplessness toward helping students.

Huberty and Huebner (1988) conducted a national survey of burnout among school psychologists. The major correlates of burnout identified in this study included clarity of role definitions, time pressures that result from excessive demands (e.g., heavy caseloads), external pressures beyond their control (e.g., teacher pressure), and internal pressure regarding how school psychologists perceived themselves (e.g., personality conflicts).

Huebner (1993) reported that results of several of his studies showed three sources of stress for school psychologists: (1) organizational factors such as role ambiguity, role conflict, and role overload; (2) interpersonal factors such as poor supervisors and lack of positive feedback as well as a low degree of peer support; and (3) intrapersonal factors including inadequate preparation for the job and personality characteristics such as workaholism and Type A behavior, lack of commitment to work, low self-esteem, empathy, external locus of control, job-related expectations, and attributional style.

SYMPTOMS OF BURNOUT

Burnout can have serious and pervasive consequences for professional school counselors and the students they serve. Individual differences in burnout reactions emerge as a function of the complex interplay of environmental stressors and individual differences. Kottler (1993) described burnout as the single most common personal consequence of practicing therapy. He believes that it is not a question of who will experience burnout, but how long the next episode will last. According to Kottler, symptoms of burnout include an unwillingness to discuss work in social and family circles, a reluctance to check messages or return calls, and an unseemly delight in canceled appointments. Daydreaming and escape fantasies occupy the professional counselor's thoughts. Cynicism, loss of enthusiasm and spontaneity, procrastination, physical fatigue, and lack of family and social involvement predominate. There is also a reluctance to admit that a problem exists. The use of alcohol and other drugs has also been linked with burnout among groups of helping professionals.

Kahill (1988) groups the symptoms of burnout into five major categories. The first reported category is *physical*. Burnout has been associated with general physical health and illness as well as with some somatic complaints such as sleep disturbance. The second category of symptoms is *emotional*. Some of the most commonly reported emotional symptoms are emotional depletion, irritability, anxiety, guilt, depression, and helplessness. Kahill found that burnout is most closely associated with depression. The third category of burnout symptoms is *behavioral*. A number of unproductive behaviors are associated with burnout. Such behaviors include job turnover, poor job performance, absenteeism, and substance abuse. The fourth category of symptoms is *interpersonal* and usually affects clients, friends, and family members. The final category of symptoms is *attitudinal*. Negative attitudes and cognitions may develop toward clients, work, family, oneself, and life.

The quality of support systems that are available to the helping professional has also been correlated to burnout. The supervisor can be a major source of stress or a significant figure in the prevention and management of burnout. Supervisors who respond effectively to professional school counselor needs increase feelings of confidence, competence, and control (Webber, 2006). Professional school counselors whose supervisors are not counselors may be at high risk of burnout, since such supervisors may possess neither the technical expertise nor the requisite emotional sensitivity to provide support related to some of the unique problems of professional school counselors (Lynch, 1999).

Inadequate preparation for the job is also a crucial intrapersonal variable in burnout. Perusse, Goodnough, and Noel (2001) report that only 30% of sampled school counselor programs required trainees to take a course in school counseling. Among professional school counselors, age has also been consistently associated with burnout. Modest inverse relationships have been reported, indicating that the likelihood of burnout decreases as age increases. This relationship suggests that professional school counselors eventually succeed in affecting the development of job satisfaction through changes in personal aspirations and needs, or in the job itself, or they leave the profession (Butler & Constantine, 2005; Huebner, 1993).

Burnout is described by Schaufeli, Maslach, and Marek (1993) as not an endpoint but a process. If the trend is not corrected, symptoms that began in a minor way may lead to serious depression, substance abuse, and other severe emotional distress that can be expected to lead to critical impairment.

STEPS TO MINIMIZE AND ELIMINATE BURNOUT

So, what are some steps that can be taken to minimize or, better yet, eliminate burnout? Corey (2009) offered advice to look within yourself to determine what choices you are making (and not making) to keep yourself alive. This can go a long way in preventing what some people consider to be an inevitable condition associated with the helping professions. It is crucial to recognize that you have considerable control over whether you become burned out. Although you cannot always control stressful events, you do have a great deal of control over how you interpret and react to these events. It is important to realize that you cannot continue to give and give while getting little in return. There is a price to pay for always being available and assuming that you are able to control the lives and destinies of others. Become attuned to the subtle signs of burnout, rather than waiting for a full-blown condition of emotional and physical exhaustion to set in. Develop your own strategy for keeping yourself alive personally and professionally. Table 96.1 lists a number of suggestions for preventing burnout (Corey, 2009), and Table 96.2 provides a list of resources to help professional school counselors deal with job stress burnout.

SUMMARY/CONCLUSION

Burnout and attrition from the field of school counseling are quite high, and the symptoms of burnout can be insidious. Burnout is often slow and tends to get worse over time. This is especially true if the professional school counselor ignores or overlooks his or her own needs. It can be relatively easy to rationalize the symptoms of burnout as being "just part of the job." With heavy caseloads, long hours, a population that presents with difficult and plentiful issues and potential lack of resources, a professional school counselor's job can be extremely stressful, intense, and unrelenting. Burnout symptoms can be serious and pervasive. It is imperative for the professional school counselor to be aware of what the definitions of burnout are and how to spot it in oneself and colleagues. Engaging in self-care and prevention is also essential to decrease the risk of burnout and minimize symptoms.

(Note: See the CD-ROM for a list of references.)

TABLE 96.1

SUGGESTIONS FOR PREVENTING BURNOUT

Evaluate your goals, priorities, and expectations to see if they are realistic and if they are getting you what you want and need.

Recognize that you can be an active agent in your life.

Find other interests besides work, especially if work is not meeting your important needs.

Think of ways to bring variety into your work.

Take the initiative and start new projects that have personal meaning, and do not wait for the system to sanction this initiative.

Learn to monitor the impact of stress on the job and at home.

Attend to your health through adequate sleep, an exercise program, proper diet, and meditation or relaxation.

Develop new friendships that are characterized by a mutuality of giving and receiving.

Learn how to ask for what you want, though don't always expect to get it.

Learn how to work for self-confirmation and for self-rewards, as opposed to looking externally for validation.

Find meaning through play, travel, or new experiences.

Take the time to evaluate the meaningfulness of your projects to determine where you should continue to invest time and energy.

Avoid assuming burdens that are properly the responsibility of others. If you worry more about your clients than they do themselves, it would be wise for you to reconsider this investment.

Take classes and workshops, attend conferences, and read to gain new perspectives on old issues.

Rearrange your schedule to reduce stress.

Learn your limits, and learn to set limits with others.

Learn to accept yourself with your imperfections, including being able to forgive yourself when you make a mistake or do not live up to your ideals.

Exchange jobs with a colleague for a short period, or ask a colleague to join forces in a common work project.

Form a support group with colleagues to share feelings of frustration and to find better ways of approaching the reality of a difficult job situation.

Cultivate some hobbies that bring pleasure.

Make time for your spiritual growth.

Become more active in your professional organization.

TABLE 96.2

RESOURCES TO HELP PROFESSIONAL SCHOOL COUNSELORS DEAL
WITH JOB STRESS AND BURNOUT

Burnout: Symptoms, Antecedents, and Assessments

Cherniss, C. (1980). *Professional burnout in human service organizations.* New York: Praeger.

Cordes, C. L., & Dougherty, T. W. (1993). A review and an integration of research on job burnout. *Academy of Management Review, 18,* 621–656.

Farber, B. A. (1991). *Crisis in education: Stress and burnout in the American teacher.* San Francisco: Jossey-Bass.

Golemiewski, R. T., & Munzenrider, R. F. (1988). *Phases of burnout: Development in concepts and applications.* New York: Praeger.

Grosch, W. N., & Oleson, D. C. (1994). *When helping starts to hurt: A new look at burnout among psychotherapists.* New York: Norton.

Grosch, W. N., & Oleson, D. C. (1995). Therapist burnout: A self psychology and system perspective. *Innovations in Clinical Practice, 14,* 439–454.

Heubner, E. S. (1993). Professionals under stress—A review of burnout among the helping professions with implications for school psychologists. *Psychology in the Schools, 30,* 40–49.

Schaufeli, W. B., Maslach, C., & Marek T. (Eds.). (1993). *Professional burnout: Recent developments in theory and research.* Washington, DC: Taylor & Francis.

Burnout: Interventions and Prevention

Cherniss, C. (1995). *Beyond burnout: Helping teachers, nurses, therapists, and lawyers recover from stress and disillusionment.* New York: Praeger.

Figley, C. R. (1995). *Compassion fatigue: Coping with secondary traumatic stress disorder in those who treat the traumatized.* New York: Brunner/Mazelm.

Gold, Y., & Roth, R. A. (1993). *Teachers managing stress and preventing burnout: The professional health solution.* Washington, DC: Falmer Press.

Grosch, W. N., & Oleson, D. C. (1995). Prevention: Avoiding burnout. In M. B. Sussman (Ed.), *A perilous calling: The hazards of psychotherapy practice.* New York: Wiley.

Jaffe, D. T., & Scott, C. D. (1988). *Take this job and love it: How to change your work without changing your job.* New York: Simon & Schuster.

Lambie, G. W. (2006). Burnout prevention: A humanistic perspective and structuredgroup supervision activity. *Journal of Humanistic Counseling, Education, andDevelopment, 45(1),* 32–45.

O'Halloran, T. M., & Linton, J. M. (2000). Stress on the job: Self-care resources forcounselors. *Journal of Mental Health Counseling, 22,* 354–364.

Osborn, C. (2004). Seven salutary suggestions for counselor stamina. *Journal of Counseling and development, 82,* 319–328.

Paine, W. S. (Ed.) (1982). *Job stress and burnout: Research, theory and intervention perspectives.* Beverly Hills, CA: Sage.

Pines, A., & Aronson, E. (1988). *Career burnout: Causes and cures.* New York: Free Press.

(continues)

TABLE 96.2 (*continued*)

Pines, A., Aronson, E., & Kefry, D. (1981) *Burnout: From tedium to personal growth.* New York: The Free Press.

Richardson, A. M., & Burke, R. J. (1995) Models of burnout: Implications for interventions. *International Journal of Stress Management, 2,* 31–43.

Spicuzza, F., & de Voe, M. W. (1982). Burnout in the helping professions: Mutual aid groups as self-help. *Personnel & Guidance Journal, 61,* 95–99.

Agencies, Organizations, and Advocacy Groups

American Institute of Stress (AIS): A nonprofit organization that serves as a resource and clearinghouse for information on stress-related matters. The Institute's services include newsletter reprints, monographs, and abstracts: 1-800-24-RELAX.

American Psychological Association (APA) Help Line: Call APA's help line at 1-800-964-2000 for information on resources and helping professionals in your area (choose the first option).

Internet Resources

Center for Anxiety and Stress Treatment (**www.stressrelease.com**); Phone: 619-542-0536. This site has a variety of resources that aid in stress reduction, including tips and techniques for reducing stress at work.

Pathways to School Improvement (**http://ncrel.org/ncrel/sdrs/pathways.htm**). This is an award-winning, multimedia homepage with an entire section devoted to professional development, complete with online videos and lectures on school reform and successful staff improvement and growth.

Teachers Helping Teachers (**www.pacificnet.net/~mandel**); Phone: 818-7801281. This is a networking site for teachers to ask and answer questions about the teaching field. They can also get information about special issues, such as burnout and job stress.

ABOUT THE EDITOR AND AUTHORS

About the Editor

Bradley T. Erford, PhD, is professor and director of in the School Counseling Program at Loyola College in Maryland. He is an American Counseling Association (ACA) Fellow and the recipient of ACA's Research Award, Hitchcock Distinguished Professional Service Award, Professional Development Award, and Carl Perkins Government Relations Award. He has received the Association for Counselor Education and Supervision's (ACES) Robert O. Stripling Award for Excellence in Standards and the Maryland Association for Counseling and Development's (MACD) Maryland Counselor of the Year, Professional Development, Counselor Visibility, and Counselor Advocacy Awards. His research specialization falls primarily in development and technical analysis of psychoeducational tests and has resulted in the publication of seven books, numerous journal articles, numerous book chapters, and eight psychoeducational tests. He is an ACA Governing Council Representative, past chair of the ACA–Southern (U.S.) Region, past president of the Association for Assessment in Counseling and Education (AACE), past president of the Maryland Association for Counseling and Development (MACD), past president of the Maryland Association for Counselor Education and Supervision (MACES), past president of the Maryland Association for Mental Health Counselors (MAMHC), and past president of the Maryland Association for Measurement and Evaluation (MAME). Dr. Erford is the past chair of ACA's Task Force on High Stakes Testing, past chair of ACA's Task Force on Standards for Test Users, past chair of ACA's Public Awareness and Support Committee, past chair of ACA's Interprofessional Committee, and member of the ACA 20/20 Vision Task Force. Dr. Erford is a Licensed Clinical Professional Counselor, Licensed Professional Counselor, Nationally Certified Counselor, Licensed Psychologist, and Licensed School Psychologist. He teaches courses primarily in the areas of assessment, human development, research and evaluation in counseling, school counseling, and stress management.

About the Authors

Lyndon P. Abrams earned a PhD in counseling from Texas A&M University–Commerce. He is a Nationally Certified Counselor and has professional counseling experience in the community settings. Dr. Abrams is currently an associate professor in the Department of Counseling at the University of North Carolina at Charlotte.

Patrick Akos, PhD, is an assistant professor of school counseling in the School of Education at the University of North Carolina at Chapel Hill. He is a former college, elementary, and middle school counselor and was recognized in 2004 as the American School Counselor Association's Counselor Educator of the Year. Dr. Akos's research focuses on the transition into and out of middle school and strengths-based school counseling. Currently, his research focuses on how school personnel can promote successful transitions and how school counselors can intervene and advocate for optimal development of early adolescents.

Stanley Baker, PhD, NCC, LPC, is a professor of counselor education at North Carolina State University. His professional K–12 teaching and school counseling experience was in rural and small-city locations in western and southern Wisconsin. He has been a counselor educator for 35 years at Penn State and North Carolina State universities and is a former editor of *The School Counselor* and *Professional School Counseling*. Research and writing interest areas include enhancement of the school counseling profession, evaluation of teaching methods in prepracticum courses and in supervision of counseling practicums, evaluation and accountability strategies in school counseling, research design and assessment strategies for counselor educators, the effectiveness of cognitive-behavioral primary and secondary prevention program strategies delivered by professional school counselors, and the enhancement of the research efforts of doctoral students in counselor education via faculty mentors.

Jan R. Bartlett, PhD, is an assistant professor in the School of Applied Health and Educational Psychology, in Counseling and Counseling Psychology at Oklahoma State University. Her K–12 professional school counseling experience was in a rural mountain school district in Arkansas. She has been a counselor educator, preparing professional school counselors in New York, Iowa, and Oklahoma. Research interests include the role of intergenerational connections in youth development, professional school counselor preparation and advocacy issues, and the impact of energy dissent on families and communities.

Patricia L. Barton, MS, LCPC, is a 1990 graduate of the Johns Hopkins University School of Continuing Studies. Currently, she is an Anne Arundel County Public Schools (AACPS), Maryland, principal and adjunct professor for Anne Arundel Community College. As a counselor specialist, Ms. Barton developed a family resource center for AACPS. She has written grants to increase parental involvement and is a trainer/coauthor for *Parenting for Success* and *Reaching All Parents.*

John B. Boshoven, MA, MSW, LPC, is a past president of the Michigan Association for College Admission Counseling (MACAC). He is an experienced counselor for the Ann Arbor, Michigan, public schools and serves as the counselor for continuing education at Community High School in Ann Arbor, the director of college counseling at the Jewish Academy of Metropolitan Detroit in West Bloomfield, a national trainer and content expert for the National Board for Professional Teaching Standards, and has a private college counseling practice.

Dorothy Breen, PhD, is associate professor of counselor education at the University of Maine. Dr. Breen is chair of the ACES Rural Counseling Interest Network. She is also a psychologist in private practice in rural Maine. She attained her master's degree in counselor education and doctorate in counseling psychology from the University of Wisconsin.

Vicki Brooks-McNamara, PhD, is a senior consultant with The Education Trust's National Center for Transforming School Counseling and a Fulbright Senior Specialist recipient. She retired as the department chair of school counseling in the Graduate School of Education, Lewis & Clark College, in Portland, Oregon. Prior to higher education, she was a public school educator (K–12) and a professional high school counselor in Colorado.

Lela Kosteck Bunch is the executive director of the Missouri School Counselor Association. Prior to taking her current position, she was an assistant professor in the Division of Counseling and Family Therapy at the University of Missouri–St. Louis. She also served as the director of guidance and placement for the Missouri Department of Elementary and Secondary Education. During her tenure in that position, she was instrumental in developing *The Guidelines for Performance-Based Professional School Counselor Evaluation* as well as in a major revision of the *Missouri Comprehensive Guidance Program Manual.* Her leadership also helped bring to fruition the Missouri Standards for Teacher Education Programs in School Counseling. In the past, she has worked as a professional school counselor, a supervisor of adult education, an outpatient therapist, and a psychoeducational consultant.

Peggy S. Byrer is a nationally certified psychologist and is employed as a psychologist in Indiana. She earned a bachelor's degree in sociology from Purdue University and holds graduate degrees in educational and school psychology, school counseling, and secondary education from Indiana State University. She is a member of several boards of directors for community agencies that address the needs of youngsters.

Barbara L. Carlozzi, PhD, is an assistant professor in the counseling and counseling psychology area at Oklahoma State University. Dr. Carlozzi coordinates the school counseling program and teaches in the counseling and counseling psychology programs. Her areas of interest are school counseling, counseling development, human development, and expressive writing.

Laurie A. Carlson is an associate professor in the counseling/career development program at Colorado State University. Dr. Carlson holds a PhD in counselor education from the University of Arkansas and is both a National Certified Counselor and National Certified School Counselor. Dr. Carlson's professional experience includes 10 years of experience in public schools, 4 of those years as a K–12 school counselor in Minnesota.

David J. Carter received his PhD from the University of Nebraska at Lincoln. He is an associate professor and clinical supervisor in counselor education at the University of Nebraska at Omaha. His private practice work is with children and adolescents. He is a past president of the Nebraska Counseling Association.

Tiffany D. Chandler is a graduate student at Mississippi State University.

John R. Charlesworth, PhD, is a counselor education and educational psychology faculty member at the State University of West Georgia. He received a master's and doctoral degrees in educational psychology with a minor in counseling from Mississippi State University. Dr. Charlesworth has experience as a professional school counselor and practicing licensed psychologist in variety of settings. He also has experience providing workshops and consulting services for schools and universities. His research interests are improving teacher and counselor effectiveness.

James R. Cheek, NCC, NCSC, LPC-S, earned his doctorate from Texas Tech University. Dr. Cheek's background as an educator includes experience as a school teacher, a professional school counselor, and director of counseling for a public school system as well as community practice working with children, adolescents, and HIV/AIDS populations. Previously, he has served as an assistant professor at St. John's University and Texas Woman's University. Currently, Dr. Cheek instructs and supervises graduate students at the University of Houston–Clear Lake and provides trauma and resiliency training and support for Hurricanes Katrina and Rita survivors in the Houston-area schools.

Gayle Cicero is a licensed clinical professional counselor and graduate of the Loyola College of Maryland with an MEd in guidance and counseling. She is currently employed as the coordinator of guidance and counseling for Anne Arundel County Public Schools. In that role, she combines experience as a teacher, professional school counselor, pupil personnel worker, school administrator, and developer of an interagency team to lead the school counselors of a large school system. Ms. Cicero is an active member of the Maryland Association of Counseling and Development and an adjunct professor at Anne Arundel Community College.

Mary Ann Clark, PhD, NCC, is an associate professor and school counseling program coordinator in the Department of Counselor Education at the University of Florida, Gainesville. She has been a professional school counselor and administrator in stateside and overseas schools prior to her university work. Dr. Clark has served as a consultant and speaker to school and community groups on topics including student assessment, school safety and violence prevention, and small-group counseling. Her areas of special interest include student success factors, character education, university/school partnerships, and career development.

J. Kelly Coker is a visiting associate professor in the school counseling program at the University of North Carolina at Chapel Hill as well as an adjunct faculty member in the mental health/marriage and family counseling programs at Capella University. Dr. Coker is a Licensed Professional Counselor in North Carolina and has worked as a counselor in school, agency, and college settings. Her primary areas of interest and expertise are creative arts in counseling, program evaluation in school counseling, the use of technology in counseling and supervision, and substance abuse counseling.

Angela R. Cole is a graduate student at Mississippi State University.

Amanda Conklin is a graduate student in the mental health and school counseling program at Bowling Green State University, Bowling Green, Ohio.

Doris R. Coy, PhD, is an associate professor at Northern Kentucky University, where her areas of expertise are school counseling and career development. She is past president of the American Counseling Association and the American School Counselor Association. She has published more than 100 articles and chapters and is the coeditor of three books. She is a former school counselor and teacher.

Carol A. Dahir, EdD, an assistant professor at the New York Institute of Technology, presents nationally on the areas of national standards-based school counseling programs, school counselor accountability, and career development. A former elementary school teacher, professional school counselor, coordinator of school counseling and guidance services, and director of pupil personnel services, Dr. Dahir has authored/coauthored three books, and her research agenda focuses on the impact of comprehensive school counseling programs, the national standards for school counseling programs, and school counselor accountability.

Joyce A. DeVoss, PhD, is an associate professor and coordinator of the MEd school counseling program at Northern Arizona University in Tucson. Her research and scholarly interests include school counselor leadership and advocacy training. She has worked as a professional school counselor, agency counselor, psychologist, and organizational consultant. She is primary author of *School Counselors as Educational Leaders*, published in 2006. She is the currently postsecondary vice president for the Arizona School Counselors Association.

R. Anthony Doggett, PhD, is the program coordinator and assistant professor in the school psychology program at Mississippi State University. Dr. Doggett received his PhD in school psychology from The University of Southern Mississippi. He completed a predoctoral internship and a 1-year postdoctoral fellowship in behavioral pediatrics at the Munroe-Meyer Institute for Genetics and Rehabilitation in Omaha, Nebraska. He has served as the president of the Mississippi Association for Psychology in the Schools and a professional consultant for the Mississippi Department of Education. His professional interests include applied behavior analysis, functional behavioral assessment, behavioral consultation, parent training, instructional interventions, and behavioral pediatrics.

Deborah L. Drew, EdD, is an associate professor and program coordinator of the school counseling program at Husson College in Bangor, Maine. In her private practice, she provides counseling, consultation, and supervision to rural Maine counselors and school systems. Formerly, she was a professional school counselor in rural areas of Maine. She attained her master's degree and doctorate in counselor education from the University of Maine.

Brad A. Dufrene is an assistant professor in the Department of Psychology at the University of Southern Mississippi. He received BS and MA degrees in psychology at Louisiana State University. He received his PhD in school psychology at Mississippi State University after completing an internship in pediatric psychology at the Munroe-Meyer Institute for Genetics and Rehabilitation at the University of Nebraska Medical Center. Current research interests include response to intervention systems for reading and mathematics and applied behavior analysis practices for children with high-incidence disabilities and behavioral issues.

Suzanne M. Dugger, EdD, is an associate professor in the Department of Leadership and Counseling at Eastern Michigan University, where she serves as the coordinator of the school counseling program. She holds credentials as a teacher, professional school counselor, Licensed Professional Counselor, national certified counselor, and doctoral limited licensed psychologist in the State of Michigan. Dr. Dugger was a founding member of the Association of Michigan School Counselors, is a past president of both the Michigan Association for Counselor Education and Supervision and the Michigan Counseling Association, and is currently the chair of the American Counseling Association's Midwest Region.

Ruth B. Ekstrom recently retired as a principle research scientist in the Higher Education Research Division of Education Testing Service (ETS). Her work at ETS included studies of test use, guidance and counseling, student achievement, and women's education and employment. Ekstrom holds a master's degree from Boston University and a doctorate from Rutgers University. She is the coeditor of *Assessing Individuals With Disabilities in Education, Employment, and Counseling Settings*, and coauthor of *Education and American Youth: The Impact of the High School Experience*. She serves on the editorial board of *Measurement and Evaluation in Counseling and Development*. In 1996, Ekstrom received the American Counseling Association's Extended Research Award for her career accomplishments.

Grafton T. Eliason, EdD, MDiv, is a Licensed Professional Counselor and coordinator of the school counseling program at California University of Pennsylvania. His research interests include existential personal meaning, death anxiety, grief, loss, and spirituality.

Cyrus Marcellus Ellis, PhD, is a professor of counselor education at Governors State University in University Park, Illinois. Dr. Ellis instructs graduate courses in the University's CACREP-approved counseling program, with special emphasis in the community counseling sequence. Dr. Ellis is an active member of the American Counseling Association, serving as co-chair of the Human Rights Committee. Dr. Ellis is the past president of the Illinois Association for Multicultural Counseling, a division of the Illinois Counseling Association. Dr. Ellis earned his PhD from The University of Virginia and received The William Van Hoose Memorial Award.

Patricia B. Elmore is interim dean of the College of Education and Human Services and professor in the Department of Educational Psychology and Special Education at Southern Illinois University–Carbondale (SIUC). She received her PhD in educational psychology with a specialization in educational measurement and statistics. She is a past president of the Association for Assessment in Counseling and Education (AACE), the 1994 recipient with Ruth B. Ekstrom and Esther E. Diamond of the American Counseling Association Research Award, and in 2003 recipient of the AACE Exemplary Practices Award. She was editor of *Measurement and Evaluation in Counseling and Development* and is editor of *Educational Researcher*. She coauthored *Basic Statistics* with Paula L. Woehlke and coedited the *Handbook of Complementary Methods in Education Research* with Judith L. Green and Gregory Camilli. Elmore is a Fellow of the American Counseling Association.

Mardi Kay Fallon is a doctoral candidate in counselor education at the University of Cincinnati. She currently works for Children's Home of Cincinnati as a diagnostic therapist.

Teesue H. Fields, EdD, NCC, is professor and program coordinator of Counselor Education at Indiana University Southeast. She has worked as a licensed psychologist in private practice and in a mental health center and as a psychologist and counselor in K–12 schools.

Nadine E. Garner, EdD, LPC, is the director of the School Counseling Graduate Program and an associate professor in the Psychology Department at Millersville University of Pennsylvania. She is coauthor of the book *A School With Solutions: Implementing a Solution-focused/Adlerian-based Comprehensive School Counseling Program* (ASCA, 1998). Dr. Garner created the workshop *A Multiple Intelligences Approach to Conflict Resolution,* which she presents internationally. As a former K–12 professional school counselor at Scotland School for Veterans' Children, Dr. Garner developed a comprehensive conflict resolution/peer mediation program.

Donna M. Gibson is an assistant professor of counselor education at the University of South Carolina in Columbia. She has worked in public schools, hospitals, private practice, and clinics as a counselor and psychologist, working with families and children.

Gary E. Goodnough is professor and chair of the Counselor Education Program at Plymouth State University. He has worked in public schools as a teacher, professional school counselor, and director of guidance. Gary consults regularly with school districts on comprehensive school counseling programs. He is the author of more than 20 articles and book chapters and is the coeditor of *Leadership, Advocacy and Direct Service Strategies for Professional School Counselors.*

Norman C. Gysbers is a professor with distinction in the Department of Educational, School, and Counseling Psychology at the University of Missouri–Columbia. He received his PhD from the University of Michigan, and his research and teaching interests are in career development, career counseling, and school guidance and counseling program development, management, and evaluation. He is author of numerous articles and book chapters, 15 monographs, and 17 books. He received the National Career Development Association's Eminent Career Award and the ASCA Mary Gehrke Lifetime Achievement Award. Gysbers has been the editor of the *Career Development Quarterly* and *Journal of Career Development,* president of the National Career Development Association, and president of the American Counseling Association.

Henry L. Harris is a former secondary school counselor and military veteran. He is a Licensed Professional Counselor and a licensed school counselor in the state of North Carolina. He is also an associate professor at UNC–Charlotte and coordinator of the MA program in counseling.

Trish Hatch, PhD, is the coauthor of *The ASCA National Model: A Framework for School Counseling Programs.* She is the director of the Center for Excellence in School Counseling and Leadership (CESCaL) and the director of the school counseling program at San Diego State University. Dr. Hatch is a former school counselor and site-level and central office administrator over school counseling programs. She served as vice president of ASCA from 2001 to 2003 and was awarded ASCA's administrator of the year in 2001. She is an appointed member of the National Panel for Evidenced-Based School Counseling Practices, has served as an assessment expert to the National Board for Professional Teaching Standards (NBPTS), and is a Trainer of Trainers for the Education Trust's Transforming School Counseling Initiative. Dr. Hatch is nationally recognized as a passionate and engaging keynote speaker, trainer, and consultant.

Patricia Henderson has been an active member of the counseling profession for the past 40 years. Her experience and research interests are in school counseling and administrative supervision. She had been an adjunct counselor educator for more than 20 of those years. Currently, she consults and writes about comprehensive school guidance and counseling programming, professionalism and supervision in school counseling, and conducting administrative supervision in counseling.

Carlen Henington, PhD, NCSP, is an associate professor in the school psychology program at Mississippi State University, where she directs the Summer Academic Clinic for elementary-school-age children who are referred for academic concerns. Her research and professional interests include evaluation and implementation of academic and behavioral interventions, and assessment and intervention in early childhood.

Edwin L. Herr, NCC, NCCC, is distinguished professor emeritus of education (counselor education and counseling psychology) and associate dean emeritus, the College of Education, the Pennsylvania State University. Dr. Herr served as a school counselor, a local director of guidance, and the first state director of guidance and testing and, subsequently, the first director of the Bureau of Pupil Personnel Services in the Pennsylvania Department of Education. Dr. Herr received a BS in business education from Shippensburg State Teachers College and an MA in psychological foundations, a professional diploma in coordination of guidance services, and an EdD in counseling and student personnel administration from Teachers College, Columbia University, where he was an alumni Fellow. Dr. Herr is past president of the American Association for Counseling and Development (now ACA); the National Vocational Guidance Association; the Association for Counselor Education and Supervision; and Chi Sigma Iota, the Counseling Academic and Professional Honor Society International. He is the author or coauthor of more than 300 articles and book chapters and 33 books and monographs, a former editor of the *Journal of Counseling and Supervision* (1993–1996) and *Counselor Education and Supervision* (1971–1974), and a member of several other editorial boards.

Peggy LaTurno Hines, EdD, is director for the National Center for Transforming School Counseling for The Education Trust. She is a Nationally Certified Counselor and a former program director for school counseling at Indiana State University. She is a former elementary and middle school counselor.

Lisa Hinkelman, PhD, is an assistant professor in the counselor education program at The Ohio State University, a Transforming School Counseling Initiative institution. She teaches school counseling courses with particular emphasis on the development of school counselor leadership, and her research examines the development and evolution of school counselor leadership from practicum to internship and into the practice of professional school counseling. Her work includes serving as project evaluator for Project Success, an Elementary School Counseling Demonstration Act project in the Columbus Public Schools.

Nicholas E. Hoda is a graduate student at Mississippi State University.

Kristi Hofstadter received her master's degree in school psychology from Miami University. Her research interests include functional assessment and analysis, behavioral and academic interventions, and behavioral treatment of habits and tics.

Cheryl Holcomb-McCoy, PhD, is associate professor in the Department of Counseling and Personnel Services at the University of Maryland at College Park. Her areas of research and scholarly interest include multicultural competence of professional school counselors, multicultural counseling training, and urban school counselor reform. Dr. Holcomb-McCoy is a former public school teacher and professional school counselor and is currently involved in the implementation of the first professional development school for professional school counselors in the Washington, DC, area.

Jill Holmes-Robinson, PhD, LCPC, NCC, is the director of the Georgetown University Women's Center. Dr. Holmes-Robinson is a licensed clinical professional counselor and a Nationally Certified Counselor who earned a doctorate in counselor education from the University of Virginia. She has served as an adjunct assistant professor of counseling and pastoral counseling at The Johns Hopkins University and Loyola College in Maryland. Dr. Holmes-Robinson is the former director of the Ithaca College Educational Opportunity Programs, which provided scholarships, academic support, and counseling to at-risk low-income students. Her areas of specialization are multicultural, career counseling, counseling at-risk students, and counseling issues specific to women.

Reese M. House works as a consultant for the National Center for Transforming School Counseling at The Education Trust in Washington, DC. He is professor emeritus at Oregon State University, where he focused on preparing school counselors to be proactive change agents and advocates for social, economic, and political justice. While at Oregon State University, he was instrumental in changing the school counselor preparation program to a mission-driven program. His background includes experience as a professional school counselor, community activist, and HIV/AIDS educator. Reese received his BS and MA from Ball State University and his EdD from Oregon State University. He has more than 40 publications on such issues as professional school counselors as advocates for change and HIV/AIDS prevention. He has delivered more than 200 presentations locally, regionally, nationally, and internationally on these same topics.

Susan Norris Huss, LPC, is an associate professor in the mental health and school counseling program at Bowling Green State University in Ohio. She received her PhD in counselor education from the University of Toledo after being a professional school counselor for 23 years. Dr. Huss has extensive experience in working with bereavement in schools. For 20 years, she led loss support groups for students who experienced a death. She has presented at local, state, and national levels in the area of bereavement and legal and ethical issues and has conducted research related to the efficacy of school-based loss support groups for parentally bereaved students. Dr. Huss is a past president of the Ohio Counseling Association and currently serves on the American School Counselor Association Ethics Committee.

Brian Hutchison, MEd, is a PhD candidate and University Fellow in the counselor education program at Penn State University.

C. Marie Jackson, EdD, LPC, NCC, is a former counselor education faculty member at the University of West Georgia. She has a master's degree in counseling from Jacksonville State University and a doctoral degree in counselor education from the University of Alabama. She has experience in public schools as a teacher, psychometrist, and a school counselor, K–12. She has been program leader for school counseling training programs in three university settings. In addition to her school counseling credentials and experience, she is a Licensed Professional Counselor and a Nationally Certified Counselor, and has worked in a psychiatric hospital outpatient setting as a therapist.

Gregory R. Janson is an associate professor of child and family studies at Ohio University, Athens. He is a Professional Clinical Counselor, a National Certified Counselor, and a certified family life educator. Dr. Janson has worked extensively both in community mental health and in private practice as a trauma specialist and family counselor with children and adolescents and their families. A former therapeutic foster parent, his current research interests focus on the impact of traumatic experiences and repetitive abuse such as bullying on victims and bystanders. Other research interests focus on issues affecting gay, lesbian, bisexual, and transgendered adolescents and their families.

Gerald A. Juhnke, EdD, LPC, NCC, MAC, CCAS, ACS, is professor and doctoral program director at The University of Texas at San Antonio. He is the past president of the International Association for Addictions and Offender Counseling (IAAOC) and the Association for Assessment in Counseling (AAC). Jerry is a former editor of the *Journal of Addictions and Offender Counseling* and a past co-chair of the American Counseling Association's Council of Journal Editors. He has authored or edited four books and has more than 30 refereed journal articles that have either been published or are currently in press. Jerry's direct clinical counseling and clinical supervision histories includes independent practice, community mental health, corrections, and schools. Jerry's most recent book is *Counseling Addicted Families: An Integrated Assessment and Treatment Model.*

Carol J. Kaffenberger is currently an associate professor at George Mason University in Fairfax, Virginia, and program coordinator of the counseling and development program. She teaches counselor preparation courses and supervises school counseling interns. Previously, she was a professional school counselor and special education teacher. She is a consultant for the Education Trust Transformation of School Counseling Initiative, and provides training for practicing school counselors nationally and locally. She has held a variety of leadership positions in Virginia School Counselor Association (VSCA). She developed a model for school reintegration for students with chronic illness and provides training to practicing school counselors, social workers, and public health nurses. Her research interests include supporting students with chronic illness and the transformation of professional school counselors. She has written professional articles and chapters on school reentry issues, coping with cancer, the diagnosis of mental disorders in children, and the transformation of school counseling.

Margaret A. King is a professor in early childhood teacher education at Ohio University. Dr. King served as secretary and governing board member of the National Association for the Education of Young Children. She is on the editorial board of *Early Childhood Research and Practice*. She has written and presented on boys and guidance, best teaching practices, and teacher development.

Daniel J. Krenzer earned a BS in psychology at Western Carolina University and is currently a PhD candidate in the school psychology program at Mississippi State University. His current research interests are cognitive abilities and processes, behavior assessment, and interventions for individuals with developmental delays.

Vivian V. Lee, PhD, NCC, is the higher education school counselor specialist at the National Office for School Counselor Advocacy of The College Board. Dr. Lee, a former teacher, secondary school counselor, site supervisor for school counseling interns, director of guidance and counseling, and full-time counselor educator continues to teach school counseling as an adjunct professor at University of Maryland at College Park. Dr. Lee has been involved with the Education Trust National Initiative for Transforming School Counseling, serving as a trainer, and has published articles and book chapters on developing school counseling programs, conflict resolution and violence, and group counseling. Dr. Lee worked in public education for 24 years before joining the College Board. She received her master's and doctoral degrees from the University of Virginia.

Tracy C. Leinbaugh, PhD, NCC, PCC, is an associate professor of counselor education at Ohio University. She received a PhD in counselor education, with a cognate area of psychology. Dr. Leinbaugh's clinical experience includes child/adolescent counseling, school psychology, school counseling, private practice, and work with incarcerated youth. She is a member of the American Red Cross Disaster Mental Health Team and clinical director of the Hocking Valley Regional Critical Incident Stress Management Team. She is currently licensed as a Professional Clinical Counselor, supervisor endorsement, school counselor, and school psychologist in Ohio and is a national certified counselor. Her research interests include child and adolescent issues and disorders, disability issues, school counseling, and families of children with disabilities.

Dana Heller Levitt is associate professor of counselor education at Ohio University. She received her master's and doctoral degrees from the University of Virginia. In addition to eating disorders and body image, Dr. Levitt also focuses on religiosity, ethics, and training and supervision for counselors across settings.

Lynn E. Linde is coordinator of clinical experiences at Loyola College in Maryland's School Counseling Program. She is a former branch chief for pupil services at the Maryland State Department of Education and representative to the ACA Governing Council. She is a past chair of ACA–Southern Region and past president of the Maryland Association for Counseling and Development (MACD).

Larry C. Loesch, PhD, NCC, is a professor in the Department of Counselor Education at the University of Florida, Gainesville. He is a former president of the Association for Measurement and Evaluation in Guidance (now AACE), Southern Association for Counselor Education and Supervision, Chi Sigma Iota, and the Florida Counseling Association. He was a corecipient of the American Counseling Association's Research Award and of its Hitchcock Distinguished Professional Service Award. He has served for more than 20 years as an evaluation and research consultant for the National Board for Certified Counselors. Dr. Loesch was selected as a Fellow of the American Counseling Association in 2004.

Kristi McCaskill, MEd, NCC, NCSC, is the counseling advocacy coordinator and FACT coordinator for the National Board for Certified Counselors (NBCC), Inc. and Affiliates. She is a graduate of the University of North Carolina at Chapel Hill.

Patricia Jo McDivitt began her career as an educator, serving as a classroom teacher and counselor for 12 years. In addition to her teaching experience, she recently served as president of the Association for Assessment in Counseling (AAC), a division of the American Counseling Association (ACA). Currently, she serves on the editorial board of Measurement and Evaluation in Counseling and Development. Patti also serves as a member of the Joint Committee on Standards for Educational Evaluation (JCSEE), where she has been instrumental in the development and launch of *The Student Evaluation Standards*. She has also authored numerous educational publications, including journal articles and book chapters on assessment.

Adriana G. McEachern, PhD, NCC, NCRC, LMHC, is an associate professor in counselor education and associate dean for academic affairs in the College of Education at Florida International University. She received her doctorate in counselor education from the University of Florida in 1989. She is past president of the Florida Counseling Association and chair of the American Counseling Association Southern Region. She has published numerous articles in the areas of child abuse, exceptional students and exceptional student education, and multicultural issues.

Gail Mears, PsyD, is a counselor educator at Plymouth State University, Plymouth, New Hampshire. She is a licensed clinical mental health counselor, teaches mental health counseling courses, and supervises internships. She has 27 years of experience as a psychotherapist, with a broad range of clients. In addition to her work as an associate professor of counselor education, she provides counseling services to college students through the Plymouth State College Counseling and Human Relations Center and the Plymouth State University Community Clinic, where she serves as the clinic director. She is the current president of the American Mental Health Counselors Association.

Amy Milsom, NCC, LPC, is an assistant professor at the University of North Carolina at Greensboro. She earned her doctorate from Penn State University and is a former middle and high school counselor. Her primary research interests are in the areas of students with disabilities, school counselor preparation and professionalism, and group work.

Robika Modak hails from Tupelo, Mississippi. He completed a BA in psychology at Millsaps College and is now pursuing a master's degree at Mississippi State University in school counseling.

Cheryl Moore-Thomas, PhD, NCC, is an associate professor of education in the school counseling program at Loyola College in Maryland, where she teaches courses in group and multicultural counseling. She has published and presented in the areas of multicultural counseling competence, racial identity development, spiritual identity development in African American children and adolescents, and accountability in school counseling programs. Additionally, Dr. Moore-Thomas consults with public school systems on issues of diversity and academic achievement.

Sally Murphy, PhD, was as an associate professor and clinical coordinator in the Counseling and Development Program, Graduate School of Education at George Mason University, Fairfax, Virginia. Sally worked in a variety of educational roles over the past 30+ years, including university professor, professional school counselor, and elementary school teacher. She has given numerous presentations at state and national professional conferences and has conducted workshops for school districts and local school communities on topical issues such as school counseling supervision, training school counselors on ASCA's national model, school counseling leadership, the transformation of school counseling, and ethical issues and legal implications for school counseling. She and her husband now live in Charlottesville, Virginia.

Kelly M. Murray, PhD, is assistant professor and director of PhD clinical education in the Pastoral Counseling Department at Loyola College in Maryland. Dr. Murray is a clinical psychologist whose treatment and research interests are in the area of women's health and trauma. She served as a Navy psychologist for 7 years and was on staff at both the National Naval Medical Center and the United States Naval Academy. Along with being on the full-time faculty at Loyola, she is visiting scientist at the Center for the Study of Traumatic Stress. Her research interests have been broad, and she has published empirical research on topics such as women and personality styles in relation to success, and health and psychological states during trauma and crisis.

Amy J. Newmeyer, MD, completed a postdoctoral fellowship at the Kennedy-Krieger Institute at the Johns Hopkins University School of Medicine upon completion of her medical degree from Ohio State University and residency from Akron Children's Hospital. She is double boarded in pediatrics and neuro-development disabilities and is currently on faculty at Cincinnati Children's Hospital.

Mark D. Newmeyer, EdD, is an assistant adjunct professor in the counseling program at the University of Cincinnati. He has an extensive background in a variety of school settings providing behavioral evaluation, testing, and assessment. His current research efforts include interventions that assist first-year college students to be successful.

Debbie W. Newsome, PhD, LPC, NCC, is an associate professor of counselor education at Wake Forest University, where she teaches courses in career counseling, appraisal procedures and statistics, and supervises master's students in their field experiences. She also serves as an adjunct clinician at a nonprofit mental health organization, where she counsels children, adolescents, and families.

Spencer G. Niles is a professor of education and the department head for counselor education, counseling psychology, and rehabilitation services at Penn State University. He served previously as professor and assistant dean in the Curry School of Education at the University of Virginia. He is currently the editor of the *Career Development Quarterly*. He has served on the board of directors of the National Career Development Association and was twice the president of the Virginia Career Development Association. He is past president of the National Career Development Association.

Terry L. Pertuit is a doctoral student in counselor education and supervision at Pennsylvania State University. She served previously as the assistant director of the gifted and talented program at Monclair State University in New Jersey. Terry also has extensive experience working with first-generation, low-income students through the Department of Education's TRIO Programs, Educational Talent Search and Upward Bound at Southeastern Louisiana University.

Scott W. Peters, PhD, LPC-S, has worked in the mental health field in Texas for the past 8 years. His areas of specialization are domestic violence, crisis intervention, and sexual abuse.

Ralph L. Piedmont is a professor of pastoral counseling at Loyola College in Maryland as well as the director of doctoral research for the Pastoral Counseling Department. His research interests include the five-factor model of personality and its relationship to spiritual phenomena. He has also developed a motivationally based measure of spirituality, Spiritual Transcendence, and is interested in documenting its predictive validity in a number of applied contexts.

Mark Pope, EdD, NCC, MCC, ACS, MAC, is professor and chair of the Division of Counseling & Family Therapy in the College of Education at the University of Missouri–Saint Louis, where his specialties include career counseling, addictions counseling, psychological testing, and multicultural counseling, including counseling with sexual minorities. He has written extensively on various aspects of counseling, including the career development of ethnic, racial, and sexual minorities; violence in the schools; teaching career counseling; psychological testing; international issues in counseling; and the history of and public policy issues in professional counseling. His works have appeared as books and chapters, as conference presentations, and in the *Journal of Counseling & Development, The Career Development Quarterly, The Counseling Psychologist,* the *Journal of Vocational Behavior, The Family Journal,* and the *Journal of Multicultural Counseling and Development.* He also served as the editor of *The Career Development Quarterly,* the premier journal in career counseling. Dr. Pope is the past president of the American Counseling Association; National Career Development Association; and Association for Gay, Lesbian, and Bisexual Issues in Counseling. He has been elected as a Fellow of the American Counseling Association, is a member of the American Psychological Association, National Career Development Association, Society for the Psychological Study of Lesbian and Gay Issues, Society for the Psychological Study of Ethnic Minority Issues, and Society of Counseling Psychology.

Michael Rankins, MEd, is a doctoral student in the Division of Counseling & Family Therapy at the University of Missouri–St. Louis. He has held positions at the Masters and Johnson Institute, St. Louis Effort for AIDS, Victim Service Council, and Hyland Behavioral Health. Formerly, he served as GLBT Diversity Coordinator with the University of Missouri–St. Louis Office of Student Life, where he established a GLBT & Allies Resource Center, a Women's Center, and a Men's Center. He also currently serves as advisor to PRIZM, the University of Missouri–St. Louis's GLBT Student Alliance. He has authored and coauthored a number of articles and chapters and has presented on numerous occasions at the annual conventions of ACA, APA, and ACES.

Susan Jones Sears, PhD, an emeritus faculty member, taught school counseling and clinical counseling classes at The Ohio State University for 25 years, after working as a practicing school counselor at both the elementary and secondary levels. Susan's publications include books, book chapters, and articles focusing on career development, the role of professional school counselors, and school counselor preparation. She has received national and state grants, including one of the six Transforming School Counseling Initiative grants from The Education Trust. Susan also has received numerous state and national awards for outstanding leadership and service to the counseling profession. She lives in New Albany, Ohio, and is president of the Ohio Counseling Association's Political Action Committee.

Carl J. Sheperis, PhD, NCC, LPC, is an associate professor in the Department of Counseling, Educational Psychology, and Special Education at Mississippi State University. His research interests include reactive attachment disorder, parent–child relationships, and peer conflict.

Jo Ellen Smith, MS, is a graduate of the counseling psychology program at Chatham College and has 20 years experience in the counseling field.

Brent M. Snow is a professor and chair of the Department of Counseling and Educational Psychology at the University of West Georgia. He was the principle investigator of one of the six national transforming school counseling grants funded by the Dewitt-Wallace Reader's Digest Fund, administered through The Education Trust. Previously, he was a faculty member at Oklahoma State University and the University of Idaho. He received his PhD from the University of Idaho, his MS degree from Oklahoma State University, and his BS degree from Brigham Young University.

Julia A. Southern is a school counseling graduate student at Loyola College in Maryland. She previously earned a bachelor's degree in communication arts and psychology from Salisbury University and has spent several years working as a public relations and events professional.

Donna S. Starkey, PhD, LCP, NCC, ACS, earned an MEd in community counseling from Delta State University and a PhD in counselor education from the University of Mississippi. She is an assistant professor of counselor education at Delta State University. Her experiences include counseling in a community mental health setting, serving as the counseling lab director in a university setting, private practice, teaching, and supervision of school and community counselors for licensure.

Fran Steigerwald, PhD, LPC, is assistant professor in counselor education at Radford University in Radford, Virginia. In 2000, she received her doctorate in counselor education from Ohio University in Athens. Her master's degree was from Cleveland State University in community mental health. She is a Licensed Professional Counselor in

Virginia and a Licensed Professional Clinical Counselor–Supervisor (LPCC-S) in Ohio. She has taught at Radford University in counselor education since 2002 and previously at Emporia State University in Kansas and at Ohio University. She has worked as an administrator and clinician in community agencies, private practice, and college counseling. Previous to her counseling work, she was an elementary school teacher and business professional. Her teaching and research areas of interest include ethics, counselor and student development, human development and sexuality, multicultural counseling, gender and women's issues, and crisis issues.

Carolyn B. Stone is an associate professor at the University of North Florida, where she teaches and researches the legal and ethical implications for working with minors in schools. Prior to becoming a counselor educator, Dr. Stone was a supervisor of guidance, an elementary and secondary teacher, and elementary and high school counselor.

Dawn M. Szymanski, PhD, is an assistant professor in the psychology department at the University of Tennessee–Knoxville. Her research interests are primarily in the areas of lesbian, gay, and bisexual issues; feminist therapy and supervision; multicultural counseling; psychology of men and masculinities; and counseling and research training.

Mei Tang, PhD, is an associate professor in the counseling program of University of Cincinnati. She graduated from University of Wisconsin–Milwaukee in 1996. She coordinates and teaches in the school counseling program at the University of Cincinnati. Her main research areas include multicultural issues in counseling, career development of minorities, and work with school-age populations. Dr. Tang has collaborated with local school and community agencies to provide services to diverse population in urban settings.

Barbara Thompson Book is associate professor of education at Indiana University Southeast, where she teaches classes in elementary literacy, children's literature, and ENL methods and is program coordinator of elementary education. Prior to joining IUS, she taught grades K–7 in Colorado, California, and Arizona.

Jerry Trusty is professor of education and coordinator of the Secondary School Counseling Program in the Department of Counselor Education, Counseling Psychology and Rehabilitation Services, Pennsylvania State University. Dr. Trusty has experience as a middle school and high school counselor. He has published numerous works on adolescents' educational and career development. Dr. Trusty is currently the associate editor of quantitative research for the *Journal of Counseling & Development.*

Lawrence E. Tyson, PhD, NCSC, is an associate professor in the Department of Human Studies, Counselor Education Program at the University of Alabama at Birmingham. He is the school counseling advisor and an American School Counselor Association Trainer for *National Standards for School Counseling Programs.* He is the primary author of *Critical Incidents in School Counseling* and *Critical Incidents in Group Counseling.* Prior to joining the faculty at UAB, he worked as a professional school counselor in central Florida. Dr. Tyson is also a contributing task force member for the development of the *Comprehensive Counseling and Guidance Model for Alabama Public Schools.* Dr.

Tyson continues to investigate the effect of Alabama's model on the implementation of school counseling programs in Alabama.

Joe R. Underwood, PhD, LPC, NCC, is coordinator of the school counseling program at Mississippi State University and director of MSU Summer Scholars, a summer residential program for gifted and talented junior and senior high school students. He is former state president of the Mississippi Association for Counselor Education and Supervision, Mississippi Counseling Association, and Mississippi Association for Gifted Students. Dr. Underwood often teaches staff development workshops for professional school counselors and classroom teachers.

Nancy B. Underwood, MS, teaches art for gifted and talented students at Armstrong Middle School in Starkville, Mississippi. She holds a Class AA license in gifted education and language arts. During the past 20 years, Ms. Underwood has taught university, high school, and middle school students. During summers, she is the creative writing instructor for a university residential theater camp for students in Grades 7–12. For the past 15 years, Ms. Underwood taught art and creative writing to 7th–9th grade students. She also coteaches a graduate course in counseling the gifted.

Ann Vernon, PhD, NCC, LMHC, is professor and coordinator of counseling at the University of Northern Iowa and a therapist in private practice, where she works extensively with children, adolescents, and their parents. Dr. Vernon is the director of the Midwest Center for REBT and vice president of the Albert Ellis Board of Trustees. She is the author of numerous books, chapters, and articles, including *Thinking, Feeling, Behaving* and *What Works When With Children and Adolescents.*

José Arley Villalba has a PhD in counselor education from the University of Florida. He is an assistant professor in the Department of Counseling and Educational Development at The University of North Carolina at Greensboro. He was a certified school counselor in Florida and has presented at several professional conferences, including ACA, AERA, and ASCA. His research interests include the development of school counseling interventions that are specifically designed for limited-English-proficient children, school counselor's knowledge regarding the needs of Latino and Latina students, and exploring the differences in mental and physical health disparities between rural and urban Latino and Latina youth. His teaching specialties include career counseling, multicultural counseling, introduction to school counseling, and supervision.

Suzy Mygatt Wakefield, PhD, GCDF, is a retired high school counselor and published author who presents her book, *Unfocused Kids—Helping Students to Focus on their Education and Career Plans—A Resource for Educators,* at professional conferences. She earned her master's degree in educational psychology at the University of Washington in Seattle and her PhD in school counselor education at the University of Michigan in Ann Arbor. Suzy has served as the president of the Washington School Counselor Association and president of the Washington Career Development Association. She was a high school counselor for 29 years, when she retired in 2001. She has also taught in the Career Development Certificate Program at the University of Washington, where she earned her Global Career Development Certification.

Patricia L. Walburn is an adjunct professor at the College of St. Mary's in Omaha, Nebraska, and works for the Omaha Psychiatric Associates specializing in children and adolescent maltreatment.

Janet E. Wall, EdD, has worked at the federal, state, and school-district levels in the areas of assessment, evaluation, and career development. Her work has spanned the public and private sectors. She is currently president of Sage Solutions, her consulting firm. She is past president of the Association for Assessment in Counseling and Education and is an officer for the Association for Counselors and Educators in Government (ACEG). As a member and former chair of the Joint Committee on Testing Practices (JCTP), she helped develop the *Code of Fair Testing Practices in Education*, the *ABC's of School Testing* video and leaders guide, *Rights and Responsibilities of Test Takers: Guidelines and Expectations*, and a book on assessment of individuals with disabilities. She chaired the group that revised the *Responsibilities of Users of Standardized Tests* (RUST) and was part of a task force that created the policy statement of the American Counseling Association on assessment competencies for counselors. She coedited a book titled *Measuring Up: Assessment Issues for Teachers, Counselors and Administrators* and is the author of five additional books, including three test-preparation books for the ASVAB, a book on interest activities, and one on interactive Web tools for career development. She serves on the national advisory board for Americorps*National Civilian Community Corps and Syracuse University's National Security Studies program.

Lacey L. Wallace, MEd, is a professional school counselor in the public schools of Maryland. She graduated with a BA in psychology from James Madison University in Virginia and an MEd in school counseling from Loyola College in Maryland.

T. Steuart Watson, PhD, is professor and chair of educational psychology at Miami University in Oxford, Ohio. He received his PhD from the University of Nebraska with a major in school psychology and a minor in applied behavior analysis. He has conducted extensive research on school-based consultation, strategies for improving treatment integrity, the treatment of habits and tics, the effects of extrinsic reinforcement on internal motivation, and the effects of olfactory stimuli on memory and learning. Dr. Watson is currently coeditor of the *Journal of Evidence-Based Practices for Schools*. Dr. Watson is involved in designing anticrime and anticorruption curricula for schools in the Republic of Georgia, El Salvador, Peru, Guatemala, Colombia, Mexico, and Nigeria.

Tonya S. Watson, PhD, is visiting assistant professor in the Department of Family Studies and Social Work at Miami University in Oxford. Ohio. She received her PhD from Mississippi State University with a major in school psychology, a minor in child clinical psychology, and a cognate in applied behavior analysis. Dr. Watson's research and clinical interests include studying the effects of olfactory stimuli on memory and learning, parent training, and behavioral interventions with young children.

Adam D. Weaver, PhD, is a school psychologist for Loess Hills AEA 13 in Southwest Iowa. He received his doctorate from Mississippi State University and completed his predoctoral internship at Munroe-Meyer Institute for Rehabilitation and Genetics at the University of Nebraska Medical Center. His research interests are behavioral consultation and the effects of rewards on academic performance and behavior.

Nancy H. Whitlatch, MAEd, NCC, is a former elementary school teacher and has worked as a professional school counselor at both the elementary and middle school levels.

Edward A. Wierzalis earned his PhD in counseling from the University of Virginia. He has professional counseling experience in both the school and community settings. He is presently a clinical assistant professor and also the coordinator of the School Counseling Track in the Department of Counseling at the University of North Carolina at Charlotte.

Christopher Wood, PhD, is an assistant professor in the Counselor Education Program at The Ohio State University. He was a high school counselor in Sumner, Washington, for 3 years and is a national certified school counselor. Chris taught Introduction to Counseling as well as practicum and internship classes at Oregon State University, the University of Arizona, and Ohio State University. His publications include articles on career development interventions, career and lifestyle planning, and school counselors' attitudes toward career and technical education.

Robert E. Wubbolding, EdD, is the director of the Center for Reality Therapy in Cincinnati, Ohio; director of training for the William Glasser Institute; and professor emeritus of Xavier University. A former elementary and high school counselor and adult basic education instructor, he is the author of 10 books on reality therapy, including *Reality Therapy for the 21st Century*. He has taught reality therapy in North America, Asia, Europe, and the Middle East and has received the Marvin Rammelsberg Award, the Herman Peters Award, the Mary Corre Foster Award, and outstanding alumnus of the University of Cincinnati, College of Education.

Teresa I. Yohon, PhD, instructor at Colorado State University, is a business and marketing education educator. Prior to this position, Dr. Yohon taught and managed a community college–level applied management program, where she counseled students and business people in career decision making. She has a master's degree in counseling, master's degree in management, and PhD in community resources.

Elias Zambrano, MA, is a retired certified school counselor, having worked as a professional school counselor for 28 years. During that time, he also served as the Safe and Drug Free Schools and Communities program coordinator and then director of guidance services for Northside Independent School District in San Antonio, Texas. He is currently a doctoral student at the University of Texas at San Antonio, in the counselor education and supervision program.